GARY DONELL

Byrd & Chen's Canadian Tax Principles

2021–2022 EDITION

Volume I

Please contact https://support.pearson.com/getsupport/s/contactsupport with any queries on this content.

Pearson Canada Inc., 26 Prince Andrew Place, North York, Ontario M3C 2H4.

ISBN 978-0-13-744765-7

ScoutAutomatedPrintCode

CONTENTS

The textbook is published in two Volumes:	**Volume I** = Chapters 1 to 10 **Volume II** = Chapters 11 to 21

Detailed contents of Volume I, Chapters 1 to 10 follows.

CHAPTER 1

Introduction to Federal Taxation in Canada

CHAPTER 2

Procedures and Administration

(Continued)

Chapter 2 - Continued

CHAPTER 3

Income or Loss from an Office or Employment

CHAPTER 4

Taxable Income and Tax Payable for Individuals

CHAPTER 5

Capital Cost Allowance

(Continued)

Chapter 5 - Continued

CHAPTER 6

Income or Loss from a Business

CHAPTER 7

Income or Loss from Property

(Continued)

Chapter 7 - Continued

CHAPTER 8

Capital Gains and Capital Losses

CHAPTER 9

Other Income and Deductions, and Other Issues

(Continued)

Chapter 9 - Continued

CHAPTER 10

Retirement Savings and Other Special Income Arrangements

(Continued)

Chapter 10 - Continued

Study Guide

Your two volume textbook is accompanied by a separate Study Guide that is available in print and online.

The chapters of this Study Guide correspond to the chapters of ***Byrd & Chen's Canadian Tax Principles.***

Each of these Study Guide chapters contains the following:

- Detailed guidance on how to work through the text and problems in the chapter.
- Detailed solutions to the Exercises and Self-Study Problems in the textbook for the chapter.
- A list of learning objectives for the material in the chapter.

In addition, the Study Guide contains:

- Two sample personal tax returns and two Self-Study Tax Software Problems in Chapters 4 and 11.
- A sample corporate tax return in Chapter 13.
- An extensive glossary.

PREFACE

Consistent with the title of this textbook, our objective is to instill a solid understanding of the basics of income tax and GST/HST through an appreciation of the tax principles, concepts, and unique vocabulary that make up the framework upon which the Canadian tax system has been built. This level of understanding is not solely directed at a theoretical or academic level; considerable emphasis is placed on practical everyday situations in preparation for careers where an understanding of tax in some form will be helpful at a minimum and essential at best.

The textbook will provide you with the elementary tools necessary to develop an awareness to help identify, analyze, and apply the tax law to a wide range of subjects ranging from determining the income tax liability or refund of individuals earning employment income, carrying on a business, earning investment income, identifying potential income tax benefits directed at students, investing in Tax-Free Savings Accounts (TFSAs), and understanding how the income tax law applies to corporations, trusts, and partnerships.

Our approach breaks down the necessary parts of the legislation, such as the *Income Tax Act* (ITA) and the *Excise Tax Act* (ETA), employs reference materials and interpretations of the Canada Revenue Agency (the "CRA") and longstanding legal and tax principles developed through the courts, all toward the goal of simplifying, to the extent possible, the tax learning environment to achieve success. We have provided numerous examples and step-by-step analysis together with an abundant supply of exercises and problem material to facilitate your journey through the world of Canadian tax.

For those pursuing CPA certification, we have ensured that the tax coverage is consistent with that required of CPA Canada as indicated for core level competencies in the most recent CPA competency map.

Study Guide

The major objective of the Study Guide is to provide students with convenient access to the solutions for the Exercises and Self-Study Problems. Having these solutions in a separate volume makes it easy for students to simultaneously view the problem while solving it and then consult its complete and detailed solution.

The Study Guide also provides a number of additional features to enhance the learning experience. These can be described as follows:

- Detailed instructions on "How To Work Through" each chapter in the text. This includes guidance on when to attempt Exercises and Self-Study Problems as the student reads through the text.
- A detailed list of "Learning Objectives" for each chapter. This allows the student to ensure that he/she has understood all of the relevant subjects covered in the chapter.

- Sample tax returns for both individuals and corporations. These are useful practice for students using the ProFile tax software that is available with this text.
- At the end of each chapter in the text there is a list of key terms that were used in that chapter. All of these terms are alphabetically listed in a glossary at the end of the Study Guide. This provides an easy way to find the meaning of a term introduced in one chapter, but is being referred to again in a subsequent chapter.

Features

The *Canadian Tax Principles* package contains a large number of problems, solutions, features, software, and examples to help guide you through your course in taxation.

Learning Objectives A detailed list of learning objectives is now available at the beginning of each chapter in addition to in the Study Guide. This allows you to check your understanding of the relevant subjects covered in the chapter.

Exercises These are short problems that are focused on a single issue. Exercises are presented throughout the chapters, directly following the relevant material. Solutions to the Exercises are in your Study Guide. This provides you with immediate feedback as to whether you have understood the material that you have just read.

Self-Study Problems (SSPs) These problems are more complex than the Exercises and include a number of comprehensive problems. We have marked the points within chapters where you should stop and complete each SSP. The SSPs are available on MyLab for download, in the "Chapter Resources" tab, and you'll find the solutions in your Study Guide.

Tax Software Self-Study Problems These SSPs are designed to be solved using the ProFile software that is available for users of *Canadian Tax Principles*. These problems are found in the Study Guide. The completed tax returns and solutions are available to download from MyLab. Look for updates on MyLab in the new year, as these will be updated to reflect the tax year.

Assignment Problems (APs) These problems vary in difficulty and include the most difficult non-comprehensive problems in the text. They are found at the end of each chapter. Solutions to these problems are available to instructors only.

Tax Software Assignment Problems Tax Software Assignment Problems dealing with personal tax returns are found at the end of Chapters 4 and 11. An additional Tax Software Assignment Problem, involving a corporate tax return, is located at the end of Chapter 14. Solutions to Tax Software Assignment Problems are available to instructors only. Look for updates on MyLab in the new year, as these will be updated to reflect the tax year.

Comprehensive Assignment Problems These are the most challenging type of problem material in the text. They are cumulative in that they incorporate issues from previous chapters. There are two comprehensive APs per chapter in Chapters 6 through 11, found at the end of the APs in the chapter. Solutions to these problems are available to instructors only.

Tax Returns The Study Guide contains tax return examples and self-study tax software problems, along with notes to their solutions. These provide useful practice for using the ProFile tax software. The tax returns are discussed in the book, and completed files are downloadable on MyLab, either in PDF or ProFile format.

Glossary At the end of the Study Guide is a comprehensive glossary that defines the key terms used throughout the text. Tied to this important resource, at the end of each chapter you will find a list of the Key Terms that are used in that chapter. This provides an additional resource for reviewing the text material in that, by reviewing this list, you can ensure that you are familiar with all of the concepts that are presented in the chapter.

What's New in this Edition

In this edition we have undertaken a significant revision of every chapter of the text to add and increase the emphasis on new concepts and principles together with an enhanced level of analysis, all from a practical perspective. As a result, some content coverage has been removed or reduced where the coverage was either of limited practical application, irrelevant to the core coverage, or considered above an introductory level. On the other hand, new content has been added (including a new introduction to most chapters) that either reinforces existing content or adds new analysis, topics, concepts, and principles that further support the main subject of each chapter. Additional explanations and references have also been added to clarify key concepts with a few "TIPS" added to provide additional assistance and an enhanced level of support. Finally, terminology, key and unique to income tax, has been revised to ensure consistency throughout each chapter. Throughout this process we have endeavoured to maintain the core subject matter, structure, and integrity of each chapter.

As the leading introductory income tax textbook in Canada, we recognize the importance and significant contributions of those many professors, instructors, and educators who have consistently used *Canadian Tax Principles* at colleges, universities, and other educational institutions for years. In revising and updating this edition we have prepared a list of changes to each chapter that highlight those significant changes and other specific changes that relate to previous content. These list of changes are titled "What's New" and are available for each chapter, providing a bridge between this and previous editions as well as a roadmap to the application of this edition.

The "What's New" documents for all of the chapters of this edition can be found on MyLab, in the "Instructor Resources" tab. Lastly, a new Introduction to Data Analytics has been written for this new edition, and can be found in this preface. This introduction describes how data analytics has come to be so important in our personal and professional lives, as well as how it relates to and integrates with *Canadian Tax Principles*.

MyLab

MyLab is the teaching and learning platform that empowers you to reach every student. By combining trusted author content with digital tools and a flexible platform, MyLab personalizes the learning experience and improves results for each student. Learn more about MyLab at https://mlm.pearson.com/northamerica/myaccountinglab/.

Pearson eText

This eText gives you access to the text whenever and wherever you have access to the Internet, through various devices. It contains the content of both volumes of the text and the Study Guide. The eText pages look exactly like the printed text and offer powerful functionality. You can create notes, highlight text in different colours, create bookmarks, zoom, and search.

Data Analytics Project

You will analyze a comprehensive data set and make a series of accounting decisions. This assignment is designed to prepare you for the data analytics competencies that have been included in the most recent CPA Competency Map. You will use Excel-based tools to assess data for accuracy, then organize and filter large quantities of information to make the data appropriate for income tax calculations. You will then incorporate income tax concepts, including the calculation of net income, taxable income, and tax payable using the outputs of your data analysis in Excel. This assignment also includes data visualization and incorporates tax planning concepts for a business. This is assignable from your instructor on MyLab. Also see page xvii in this Preface for an introduction to data analytics in taxation and how it applies to *Canadian Tax Principles*.

CPA Competency Alignment Map

This downloadable file ties the chapters to the 2020 CPA Competency Map. Students can use this mapping to understand the level of depth required for each broad topic area that is covered in taxation at the Entry, Core, or Elective course levels.

Practice Examinations

A 90-minute practice examination, along with a solution and suggested marking guide, is available for each of the chapters on MyLab. These examinations contain a variety of problems, including multiple choice, true/false, essay questions, and longer problems. The goal of Practice Examinations is to allow you to evaluate your ability to write the examinations in your tax course. To get the maximum benefit, you should write it under examination conditions, within a 90-minute time constraint. The materials that you use while writing this Practice Examination should be consistent with the materials that will be available during the examinations that you will be writing in your tax course. Download the Practice Examinations and solutions from MyLab.

PowerPoint Presentations

Revised by Sandra Pereversoff, Southern Alberta Institute of Technology, these PPTs provide the basis for a quick review of the material covered in the chapter. They are available on MyLab.

2021 Tax Rates, Credits, and Common CCA Classes

This is available as a PDF file, for reference. This tax information is also available at the front of Volumes 1 and 2, and CCA classes are available in the Chapter 5 Appendix.

Glossary Flashcards

To assist in this review, Glossary Flashcards are available on MyLab to further help test understanding of key terms in each chapter.

ProFile Tax Return Preparation Software

Access to Intuit Canada's professional tax preparation software, ProFile, is available free of charge to users of Byrd & Chen's *Canadian Tax Principles*. Visit https://www.intuit.com/ca/partners/education-program/registration/students/profile/ to register and for technical support.

Be sure to visit their ProFile Community pages to make use of the webinars, how-to videos, and tutorials they provide to help you learn to use the ProFile software, at https://quickbooks.intuit.com/learn-support/profile-community/misc/03/profile-en-ca.

For Instructors

Instructor's Solutions Manual (ISM) The ISM contains full solutions to all of the Assignment Problems, including Comprehensive Assignment Problems, in the chapters. These problems vary in difficulty and include the most difficult non-comprehensive problems in the text.

Solutions to Tax Software Assignment Problems Solutions to the Tax Software Assignment Problems in Chapters 4 and 11 (individual) and 14 (corporate) are available as an instructor download. This package includes both ProFile and PDF versions. Look for updates on MyLab in the new year—current calendar year updates take place in the first few months of the following calendar year.

PowerPoint Presentations Revised by Sandra Pereversoff, Southern Alberta Institute of Technology, these PPTs provide the basis for a quick review of the material covered in the chapter. They are available on MyLab.

TestGen Test Bank TestGen is a powerful assessment generation program that helps instructors easily create and print quizzes and exams. Download TestGen from MyLab. Also available are print-ready Word versions.

Problem Concordance This downloadable file provides concordance of problem material (now including Exercises as well) between the 2020–2021 and 2021–2022 editions.

Acknowledgements

In the normal course, *Canadian Tax Principles* requires regular annual updates that incorporate changes in tax credits, tax rates, and the numerous federal budget and other legislative changes made annually to both the income tax law and the GST/HST. Court cases and new or changed interpretations by the CRA add to the difficulty of ensuring that each and every edition reflects the current state of the law in all material aspects. While maintaining the technical accuracy and integrity of such a text is a considerable task by itself, it would be impossible without the support of a team of experienced and dedicated professionals who largely remain offstage and in the background but whose responsibilities take the text to new heights. I was very fortunate to have the support of the best team of professionals I have had the opportunity of working with. A very special thanks go out to Suzanne Simpson Millar (Queen Bee), an editorial guru who guided me through the publication world as the new lead author. I cannot recall a single question she was unable to answer, and I asked plenty. I would also like to thank the tireless work of copy editor and proofreader Leanne Rancourt and the efforts and dedication of Executive Portfolio Manager Keara Emmett in the Higher Education division of Pearson Canada.

I would also like to thank both Ruth Ann Strickland and Ann Bigelow, professors teaching income tax at Western University in London, Ontario. Ruth Ann and Ann have significant teaching experience and have been working with *Canadian Tax Principles* for many years. Their reputation precedes them, as is evidenced by rave online reviews from their many students. Ruth Ann and Ann reviewed each of the newly revised chapters, providing the benefits of their teaching experience and income tax expertise in making a number of suggestions and recommendations that went into the final product.

I would also like to thank the many teachers and thousands of students who have made valuable comments and suggestions over the years to help shape the text to where it stands today. I look forward to continued collaboration in the years ahead.

Finally I would like to posthumously recognize the amazing work of both Clarence Byrd and Ida Chen in creating and maintaining *Canadian Tax Principles* all these many years. They were a powerhouse couple with respect to their integrity and commitment to education and their unending professionalism. They were both colleagues and friends to my wife Michelle and I. In my last conversation with Clarence I vowed to continue the legacy of this text.

About the Authors

Gary Donell

I began working with the C.A. firm of Thorne Riddell in Montreal in the early 1980s. A few years later I made the move to Ottawa to begin my career with Revenue Canada, now the CRA. I spent 30 years at the CRA, retiring in 2015. In my early years with the CRA I was an auditor and was anxious to move on to other pursuits within the CRA, of which there were plenty. In preparation I read every income tax-related publication and textbook I could get my hands on, including legal books on statutory interpretation and the transcripts of every income tax court decision. While vacation and beach goers were reading the latest *New York Times* bestseller I was reading from the latest tax conference report and tax journals.

Eventually it all paid off when an opportunity arose to teach introductory income tax to CRA auditors in the late 1980s. I jumped on the opportunity and taught for a couple of years before applying for a job with the Income Tax Rulings Directorate of the CRA in Ottawa. The Rulings Directorate is responsible for income tax interpretations and, at the time, technically reviewing every form, publication, and tax guide published. I spent ten years at Rulings and learned a lot, but the teaching and education bug wouldn't let go of me after all those years. I returned to the training and education division of the CRA halfway through my career, where I spent the next 15 years teaching thousands of CRA auditors and writing a dozen or so courses on a wide range of income tax topics from an introductory to advanced level.

Shortly after retiring from the CRA I went to work as a consultant with Welch LLP in Ottawa where I spent the next five years dealing with practical everyday client issues, which was very rewarding thanks to tax manager/guru Don Scott and the many amazing people I had a chance to work with. I participated in in-house training and was involved in the writing of the annual CPA income tax update course, which Welch had been writing for many years. I also spent those same years teaching a dozen or so advanced tax courses for CPA Ontario every year.

To come full circle, my journey with Clarence Byrd and Ida Chen began in the early 1990s while working for CRA Rulings. I had just picked up the latest edition of the textbook (the 1991–1992 version, I believe) and had contacted them after finding a few errors. Clarence reached out, and the rest is history. I acted as the technical consultant for Clarence for the next 28 years.

Today I sit back thinking to myself that I have been indirectly preparing for this lead author role the better part of my life. I have amassed private sector experience working with accounting firms, CRA insider experience, course writing experience, and 20 years of teaching experience on top of it all. This wealth of different experience gives me a unique perspective that has allowed me to shape introductory income tax education. Income tax is ripe for the picking these days as opportunities abound both within the CRA and in the private sector. Unfortunately, many students choose to stay clear of income tax, believing it too difficult a subject. I can attest to the fact that the basic concepts and principles are not all that difficult to understand when properly and gradually presented. You will find that income tax it is not only interesting but enlightening in terms of just about every aspect of Canadian life. Armed with a solid understanding of income tax principles you may find yourself joining the ranks of tax specialists one day, but in the meantime this text will provide you with a solid foundation that you can build upon should you so choose.

Gary Donell, July 2021

Introduction to Data Analytics in Taxation

Over the last few years there has been an increasing trend toward enhanced computer capabilities, including AI or artificial intelligence platforms, that allow for greater analysis of data over a wider spectrum and for multiple purposes. The data analysis process can lead to the broad creation of unique algorithms targeted at increased efficiency in terms of resource allocation, an overall improvement in current business performance, together with tools to predict behaviour and trends that significantly impact future success and endeavours. The analysis process, however, can also be narrowed or streamlined to deal with day-to-day matters that may reveal errors and potential improvements, as well as service and compliance issues when it comes to ongoing client interactions and regulatory concerns with respect to tax and other matters. Globally we refer to these processes as "data analytics," which were recently included within the purview of CPA Canada's "CPA competencies" that stress the importance of a practical level of comprehension for those pursuing careers in fields such as business, accounting, and both income tax and GST/HST.

Many of us have already been exposed to the power of data analytics through the efforts of service providers such as Netflix and Amazon. These and other providers of goods and services use data provided through past transactions that is accumulated, measured, and analyzed to provide custom-made communications that inform us of goods and services that are likely to be of interest to us.

While there are at times privacy issues and concerns that cannot be ignored, the objective of data analytics is to use data at our disposal for the purposes of enhancing business performance, improving public relations, and in general identifying problems and their solutions as well as ensuring compliance in the applicable regulatory environments.

The Basics

Successful data analytics requires a reporting system that accumulates accurate and reliable information in a timely manner. The information should include multiple parameters that provide an opportunity for increased flexibility in handling information as required. For example, a business with significant credit sales may want to ensure that the accounts receivable data include information related to the credit-worthiness of clients to assist in identifying and reducing potential bad debt write-offs, including factors that cause a difference between accounting and income tax. Additional factors may include whether the time of year is influential, whether certain economic factors and trends should be considered, and stratification of data based on dollar amounts, number of days accounts are outstanding, and so on. The ultimate objective is that information be readily accessible within a system to be in a position to cherry-pick necessary information as warranted by specific circumstances. A system that has simply recorded only the basic essentials limits the capability to perform enhanced data analytics, which may in turn impede the profitability of the business.

Basic Data Analytics in the Private Sector

Data analytics in the private sector is in the early stages within many Canadian businesses other than those larger corporations, mostly public, that operate on a global basis in multiple countries. These larger Canadian companies face concerns as a result of operating in multiple tax jurisdictions with multiple variations in tax rates, including the value added tax (VAT), the Canadian equivalent of GST/HST, plus customs duties when products cross international borders.

In recent years the efforts of the Organisation for Economic Co-operation and Development (OECD), of which Canada is a member, has placed added emphasis on the "Base Erosion and Profit Sharing" (BEPS) initiative, which is designed to address what the OECD views as efforts by the world's largest companies to avoid home country taxation by engaging in a variety of cross-border transactions viewed by tax authorities as problematic. As a result, such companies today are subject to onerous reporting requirements that involve providing considerable data to tax authorities on an ongoing basis. These corporations use data analytics to determine the optimum efficiencies in each jurisdiction in which they operate, which includes the level of activity and income and other taxes and charges paid. The analysis allows them to realign operations, where necessary, in a timely manner.

Data Analytics and the CRA

Data analytics within the public sector, such as the Canada Revenue Agency (CRA), has been used extensively for years. The CRA is provided with millions of filed income tax and other returns each year. This wealth of information has historically been used by the CRA to assist in allocating audit resources where the need is greatest. While a random selection of Canadians are chosen for audit annually, the trend has been to use data analytics to develop algorithms that, often based on audit experience, has assisted in merging certain factors to identify files with a high probability of identifying taxpayers who have underpaid their income tax and GST/HST obligations.

The CRA employs data analytic techniques with data from multiple sources, including filed tax returns, published industry data, data provided by corporate law authorities within Canada, data from land registry and other property title registries, police and informants, and even other countries. These data when accumulated represents a treasure trove of information that when manipulated in the development of algorithms is quite successful at proving productive in terms of areas where compliance is an issue. An algorithmic initiative launched by the CRA in 2015 identified potential underreported tax obligations with respect to real estate transactions in both Vancouver and Toronto. For the period April 2015 to March 2020 the CRA audited 52,477 files, which yielded $1.554 billion in tax revenues, an average of almost $30,000 per file. This is a good example of the power of data analytics in terms of resource allocation. The CRA has been making increased expenditures both to hire new auditors and to purchase new technology to further enhance targeted efforts.

The recent results of the use of data analytics by the CRA is that they have identified rental property owners, farmers (particularly cattle ranchers), child day care providers, hardware stores, accommodation and ride sharing providers, music streaming, crowd funding, graphic design businesses, and mining and oil and gas extraction businesses as businesses with an increased likelihood of underpaid taxes. In addition, the CRA has identified issues with certain expenses, such as expenses for vehicles, home offices, office supplies, meals and entertainment, advertising, and incorporation expenses as worthy of increased audit attention.

Finally, the CRA is pursuing additional sources of information to enhance its data analytic capabilities. These sources include T4A reporting for professional fees, increased reporting for trusts (particularly family trusts), reporting on the sale of principal residences, and an increased effort to access accountant working papers and the issuance of information requirements (RFI). An RFI is a demand for information. Recently the CRA requested Rona Hardware to make its loyalty program information available. A court challenge by Rona proved unsuccessful. The RFI allowed the CRA to identify contractors participating in the loyalty program to be identified with respect to cash purchases that led to unreported income. Other businesses such as PayPal have also been issued RFIs.

Data Analytics in Introductory Taxation

Data analytics requires a reporting system that accumulates accurate, comprehensive, and reliable data that can be used to assess many important factors to taxpayers depending on the circumstances. Many of the important uses to which data analytics can be applied relate to compliance matters for businesses, property income such as rental properties, and employment expenses. These uses also predominate when it comes to identifying areas of interest to the CRA in terms of accurate income tax reporting. The ability to access the relevant information within the accounts of a taxpayer is critical to the analysis. The following represents a list of some of the more common identifiable items for data analytics:

- **Interest Expenses** Interest incurred by a taxpayer that is not deductible for income tax purposes leads to a conclusion that charges may relate to compliance matters such as late filing, tax audits, late filed election, and late payments of income tax including insufficient withholdings and instalments. In addition, if the taxpayer is a corporation there is greater flexibility provided for tax payments and instalments but only if the corporation is fully compliant in both income tax and GST/HST.

- **Penalties** The identification of non-deductible penalties can lead to many conclusions since there are numerous types of penalties for various infractions. Identifying the reasons behind the penalties may result in taking corrective action in future years. Penalty and interest identification may also result in action to recover the amounts through taxpayer relief applications.

- **Legal and Professional Fees** Determining the reasons behind these expenses, particularly larger than average changes, is important since they may relate to compliance matters relating to tax audits and notices of objection.

- **Contracts** Analyzing the existence of contracts to determine taxpayer risk where the work performed by the contractor is similar to work performed by employees. This would be particularly relevant for contractors who were ex-employees. Employer risks include CPP, EI, and other employee-related premiums together with interest and penalty charges.

- **Taxable Benefits** The reporting of taxable benefits should be scrutinized to ensure that the reporting is accurate and reflects appropriate GST/HST treatment. Where a taxpayer is a corporation, transactions between the corporation and related family members should be compared to transactions with other employees.

- **Stock Options (Emerging Trends)** Beginning in July 2021, new stock option rules come into effect. Determining whether the corporate taxpayer and its employees are subject to the new rules is important in understanding income tax obligations to both the corporate employer and employee recipients of such benefits.

- **Employee Expenses** Employee expenses are generally not deductible unless a valid T2200 form has been signed by the employer. The ITA sets a series of contractual conditions that relate to the nature of any contractual commitments by employees. Ensuring that these conditions have been met is key to an employee claiming expenses.

- **Travel Expenses** These expenses may lead the CRA to increased taxable benefits or an indication that there is a permanent establishment situated outside of Canada.

- **Advertising Expenses** There are many restrictions on the deduction of certain advertising expenses, particularly those incurred outside of Canada. Identifying the details of such expenditures will facilitate a determination of best advertising practices from an income tax perspective.

- **Capital Expenditures** The acquisition of certain depreciable property may entitle the purchaser to increased tax benefits such as accelerated depreciation (CCA) that may double the usual first-year tax deduction to allow all of the cost to be expensed. Ensure that the conditions for the tax deductions apply since the expenditure may have considered the after-tax cost as a condition of making the purchase.

- **Sales of Depreciable Property** Ensure that the disposition by sale or trade-in is accurately determined. This is particularly important where a business is sold along with all of the business properties.

- **Type of Income** Identifying and categorizing the type of income (business versus property) becomes critical in the case of a private corporation. Looking to cash account balances will help identify income that may be considered connected to a business even though it appears to be investment-type income. Tax savings are potentially quite high, avoiding cash flow issues in future years.
- **Capital Gain Transactions** Determining the details of such transactions, including the type of property sold, the period of ownership, the identification of the person from whom the property was acquired and sold, the reasons for the purchase, and the reasons for the sale, will help identify potential challenges by the CRA.

Data Analytics Conclusion

Data analytics provides businesses and others with a set of newly designed tools that utilize enhanced computer capabilities to analyze internal and external data in a manner that can greatly improve efficiencies by identifying areas of concern as well as areas of opportunity and improvement. The development of action plans to correct these inefficiencies and optimize short- and long-term goals is critical to the success of any entity. Data analytics employs a process where creativity can play an important role in using this valuable tool to the best advantage.

CPA Competencies in data analytics that are relevant to this title:

6.1.2 Assesses reporting systems, data requirements, and business processes to support reliable tax compliance

a) Explains the importance of reliable tax data obtained from transaction processing systems

6.1.3 Explains implications of current trends, emerging issues, and technologies in taxation

a) Identifies current trends, and recent updates, in taxation

b) Explains the implications of impending changes and their impact on an entity

c) Explains the potential impact of emerging issues and technologies in taxation

2021 Rates, Credits, and Other Data

A downloadable version of this document is available
as a PDF from MyLab.

Information Applicable to Individuals

Federal Tax Rates for Individuals

Taxable Income in Excess of	Federal Tax	Marginal Rate on Excess
$ -0-	$ -0-	15.0%
49,020	7,353	20.5%
98,040	17,402	26.0%
151,978	31,426	29.0%
216,511	50,141	33.0%

Federal Tax Credits for Individuals—Personal Tax Credits (ITA 118)

Reference

118(1.1) **Basic Personal Amount (BPA)** There are three alternatives dependent on net income. (1) For individuals with net income of $151,978 or less the BPA is $13,808, (2) for individuals with net income of $216,511 or higher the BPA is $12,421, and (3) for individuals with net income between $151,978 and $216,511 the BPA is calculated as $13,808 – [$1,387][(net income – $151,978) ÷ $64,533]

118(1)(a) **Married Persons** 15% the of **BPA** for the individual

118(1)(a) **Spousal** 15% of the **BPA** for the individual and:

if the spouse of the married individual is dependent because of a mental or physical infirmity, there is an additional amount of $2,295 added to the **BPA**. The total of these two amounts ($16,103) is reduced by the income of the individual's spouse.

118(1)(b) **Eligible Dependant** 15% of **BPA** for the individual and:

if the dependent person is dependent because of a mental or physical infirmity, there is an additional amount of $2,295 added to the **BPA**. The total of these two amounts ($16,103) is reduced by the income of the dependent person.

118(1)(b.1) **Canada Caregiver for Child under 18** 15% of $2,295 ($344).

118(1)(c) **Single Persons** 15% of the **BPA.**

118(1)(d) **Canada Caregiver** 15% of $7,348 ($1,102), reduced by 15% of the dependant's income in excess of $17,256.

118(2) **Age** The age credit base is $7,713. The base for this credit is reduced by 15% of the amount by which the individual's net income exceeds $38,893. Not available when income reaches $90,313. This credit is available to be transferred to a spouse or common-law partner.

118(3) **Pension** 15% of up to $2,000 of eligible pension income for a maximum credit of $300 [(15%)($2,000)]. This credit is available to be transferred to a spouse or common-law partner.

118(10) **Canada Employment Credit** 15% of up to $1,257. This produces a maximum credit of $189.

Other Common Federal Personal Credits (Various ITA)

118.01 **Adoption Expenses Credit** 15% of eligible expenses (reduced by any reimbursements) up to a maximum of $16,729 per adoption. This results in a maximum credit of $2,509.

118.02 **Digital News Subscriptions** 15% of the lesser of $500 and the cost of qualifying subscription expenses.

118.041 **Home Accessibility Credit** 15% of the lesser of $10,000 and the amount of qualifying expenditures for the year.

118.05 **First Time Home Buyers' Credit** 15% of $5,000 ($750) of the cost of an eligible home.

118.06 **Volunteer Firefighters Credit** 15% of $3,000 ($450) for qualifying volunteers.

118.07 **Volunteer Search and Rescue Workers Credit** 15% of $3,000 ($450) for qualifying volunteers.

118.1 **Charitable Donations—Regular** The general limit on amounts for this credit is 75% of net income. There is an addition to this general limit equal to 25% of any taxable capital gains and 25% of any recapture of CCA resulting from a gift of capital property. In addition, the income inclusion on capital gains arising from a gift of some publicly traded shares is reduced from one-half to nil. For individuals, the credit is equal to:

[(15%)(A)] + [(33%)(B)] + [(29%)(C)] where:

A = The first $200 of eligible gifts.
B = The lesser of:
- total gifts, less $200; and
- taxable income, less $216,511.

C = The excess, if any, by which the individual's total gifts exceed the sum of $200 plus the amount determined in B.

118.2 **Medical Expenses** The medical expense tax credit is determined by the following formula:

[15%] [(B - C) + D], where:

B is the total of an individual's medical expenses for him- or herself, his or her spouse or common-law partner, and any of his or her children who have not reached 18 years of age at the end of the year.
C is the lesser of 3% of the individual's net income and $2,421.
D is the total of all amounts each of which is, in respect of a dependant of the individual (other than a child of the individual who has not attained the age of 18 years before the end of the taxation year), an amount determined by the formula:

E - F, where:

E is the total of the dependant's medical expenses.
F is the lesser of 3% of the dependant's net income and $2,421.

118.3 **Disability—All Ages** 15% of $8,662 ($1,299). If not used by the disabled individual, it can be transferred to a person claiming that individual as a dependant.

118.3 **Disability Supplement—Under 18 and Qualifies for the Disability Tax Credit** 15% of $5,053 ($758), reduced by the total of amounts paid for attendant care or supervision in excess of $2,959 that are deducted as child care costs, deducted as a disability support amount, or claimed as a medical expense in calculating the medical expense tax credit.

Education-Related Credits

118.5
- **Tuition Fees, which Includes Examination and Ancillary Fees**
  - 15% of qualifying tuition fees
  - 15% of examination fees for both post-secondary examinations and examinations required in a professional program
  - 15% of ancillary fees that are imposed by a post-secondary educational institution on all of their full- or part-time students. Up to $250 in such ancillary fees can be claimed even if not required of all students.

118.62
- **Interest on Student Loans**
  15% of interest paid on qualifying student loans.

118.9
- **Transfer of Tuition Credit**
  If the individual cannot use the credit, is not claimed as a dependant by a spouse or common-law partner, and does not transfer the unused credit to a spouse or common-law partner, then a parent or grandparent of the individual can claim up to $750 [(15%)($5,000)] of any unused tuition credit. The amount that can be transferred is reduced by the amount of the credit required to reduce the student's federal tax payable to nil.

118.7 **Employment Insurance** 15% of amounts paid by employees up to the maximum Employment Insurance premium of $890 (1.58% of $56,300). This produces a maximum tax credit of $134 [(15%)($890)].

118.7 **Canada Pension Plan** The maximum credit base for all individuals is $2,876 [(4.95%) ($61,600 maximum pensionable earnings - $3,500 exemption)]. This produces a maximum tax credit of $431 [(15%)($2,876)]. The actual maximum CPP contributions for those individuals with pensionable earnings of $61,600 or more is $3,166 [(5.45%)($61,600 maximum pensionable earnings - $3,500 exemption)]. The difference of $290 [$3,166 - $2,876] is treated as a deduction under ITA 60(e.1) and reduces net income.

122.51 **Refundable Medical Expense Supplement** The individual claiming this amount must be over 17 and have earned income of at least $3,751. The amount is equal to the lesser of $1,285 and 25/15 of the medical expense tax credit. The refundable amount is then reduced by 5% of family net income in excess of $28,446. Not available when family income is more than $54,146.

122.9 **Refundable Teacher and Early Childhood Educator School Supply Tax Credit** A maximum of 15% of up to $1,000 ($150) of eligible expenditures that are made by eligible educators.

122.91 **Canada Training Credit** The lesser of training amount limit and 50% of eligible training costs incurred in the previous year. Minimum required working income must be $10,100 and maximum net income is $150,473.

127(3) **Political Donations** Three-quarters of the first $400, one-half of the next $350, one-third of the next $525, to a maximum credit of $650 on donations of $1,275.

127.4 **Labour Sponsored Venture Capital Corporations (LSVCC) Credit** The federal credit is equal to 15% of acquisitions of provincially registered LSVCCs.

ITA 82 and ITA 121

Dividend Tax Credit

- **Eligible Dividends** These dividends are grossed up by 38%. The federal dividend tax credit is equal to 6/11 of the gross up. The credit can also be calculated as 15.02% of the grossed up dividends, or 20.7272% of the actual dividends received.
- **Non-Eligible Dividends** These dividends are grossed up by 15%. The federal dividend tax credit is equal to 9/13 of the gross up. The credit can also be calculated as 9.0301% of the grossed up dividends, or 10.3846% of the actual dividends received.

Other Data for Individuals

ITA 82

Dividend Gross Up

Eligible Dividends For these dividends, the gross up is 38% of dividends received.

Non-Eligible Dividends For these dividends, the gross up is 15% of dividends received.

Chapter 4

OAS Clawback Limits The tax (clawback) on Old Age Security (OAS) benefits is based on the lesser of 100% of OAS benefits received and 15% of the amount by which "threshold income" (net income calculated without the OAS clawback) exceeds $79,845.

Chapter 4

EI Clawback Limits The tax (clawback) on Employment Insurance (EI) benefits under the *Employment Insurance Act* is based on the lesser of 30% of the EI benefits received and 30% of the amount by which "threshold income" exceeds $70,375 (1.25 times the maximum insurable earnings of $56,300). For this purpose, "threshold income" is net income calculated without the OAS or EI clawbacks.

Chapter 9

Child Care Expenses The least of three amounts:

1. The amount actually paid for child care services. If the child is at a camp or boarding school, this amount is limited to a weekly amount $275 (any age if eligible for disability tax credit), $200 (under 7 year of age), or $125 (age 7 through 16 or over 16 with a mental or physical impairment).
2. The sum of the **annual child care expense amounts** for the taxpayer's eligible children. The per child amounts are $11,000 (any age if eligible for disability tax credit), $8,000 (under 7 year of age), or $5,000 (age 7 through 16 or over 16 with a mental or physical impairment).
3. 2/3 of the taxpayer's **earned income** (for child care expenses purposes).

Chapter 10

RRSP Deduction Room For 2021, the addition to RRSP deduction room is equal to:

- the lesser of $27,830 and 18% of 2020 earned income,
- reduced by the 2020 pension adjustment and any 2021 past service pension adjustment, and
- increased by any 2021 pension adjustment reversal.

Chapter 11

Capital Gains Deduction For 2021, the deduction limit for dispositions of shares of qualified small business corporations is $892,218. There is an additional amount for farm or fishing properties of $107,782, providing a total of $1,000,000 for such properties.

Provincial Tax Rates and Provincial Credits for Individuals Provincial taxes are based on taxable income, with most provinces adopting multiple rates. The number of brackets range from three to five. Provincial tax credits are generally based on the minimum provincial rate applied to a credit base that is similar to that used for federal credits. In addition to regular rates, two provinces, Ontario and Prince Edward Island, use surtaxes.

Information Applicable to Individuals and Corporations

ITR 4301 **Prescribed Rate** The following figures show the base rate that would be used in calculations such as imputed interest on loans. It also shows the rates applicable on amounts owing to and from the CRA. For recent quarters, the interest rates were as follows:

Year	Quarter	Base Rate	Owing From*	Owing To
2018	I	1%	3%	5%
2018	II to IV	2%	4%	6%
2019	**All**	**2%**	**4%**	**6%**
2020	**I, II**	**2%**	**4%**	**6%**
2020	**III, IV**	**1%**	**3%**	**5%**
2021	**I**	**1%**	**3%**	**5%**

*The rate on refunds to corporations is limited to the base rate, without the additional 2%.

Automobile Deduction Limits

- CCA is limited to the first $30,000 of the automobile's cost, plus applicable GST/HST & PST (not including amounts that will be refunded through input tax credits).
- Interest on financing of automobiles is limited to $10 per day.
- Deductible leasing costs are limited to $800 per month (other constraints apply).
- Operating cost benefit = $0.27 per kilometre.
- Deductible rates = $0.59 for first 5,000 kilometres, $0.53 for additional kilometres.

CCA Rates See Appendix to Chapter 5.

Quick Method Rates (GST Only)

	Percentage on GST Included Sales	
	First $30,000	On Excess
Retailers and Wholesalers	0.8%	1.8%
Service Providers and Manufacturers	2.6%	3.6%

Note Different rates apply in the provinces that have adopted an HST system.

Information Applicable to Corporations

Federal Corporate Tax Rates are as follows (federal tax abatement removed):

General Business (Basic 38% - 10% Abatement)	28%
General Business (After General Rate Reduction of 13%)	15%
Income Eligible for M&P Deduction	15%
Income Eligible for Small Business Deduction (28% - 19%)	9%
Part IV Refundable Tax	38 1/3%
Part I Refundable Tax on Investment Income of CCPC (ART)	10 2/3%

Reference 89(1)

General Rate Income Pool A CCPC's general rate income pool (GRIP) is defined as follows:

- The GRIP balance at the end of the preceding year; plus
- 72% of the CCPC's taxable income after it has been reduced by amounts eligible for the small business deduction and aggregate investment income; plus
- 100% of eligible dividends received during the year; plus
- adjustments related to amalgamations and wind-ups; less
- eligible dividends paid during the preceding year.

125(1) **Small Business Deduction** is equal to 19% of the least of:

A. Net Canadian active business income.

B. Taxable income, less:

1. 100/28 times the ITA 126(1) credit for taxes paid on foreign non-business income, calculated without consideration of the additional refundable tax under ITA 123.3 or the general rate reduction under ITA 123.4; and
2. 4 times the ITA 126(2) credit for taxes paid on foreign business income, calculated without consideration of the general rate reduction under ITA 123.4.

C. The annual business limit of $500,000, less any portion allocated to associated corporations, less the grinds for large corporations and passive income.

123.3 **Additional Refundable Tax on Investment Income (ART)** is equal to 10 2/3% of the lesser of:

- the corporation's "aggregate investment income" for the year [as defined in ITA 129(4)]; and
- the amount, if any, by which the corporation's taxable income for the year exceeds the amount upon which the the small business deduction is determined.

123.4(2) **General Rate Reduction** is equal to 13% of full rate taxable income. This is taxable income reduced by the amount upon which the small business deduction is determined, income eligible for the M&P deduction, and the corporation's "aggregate investment income" for the year.

125.1 **Manufacturing and Processing Deduction** is equal to 13% of the lesser of:

A. manufacturing and processing profits, less the amount upon which the small business deduction is determined; and

B. taxable income, less the sum of:

1. the amount upon which the small business deduction is determined;
2. 4 times the foreign tax credit for business income calculated without consideration of the ITA 123.4 general rate reduction; and
3. "aggregate investment income" (of CCPCs) as defined in ITA 129(4).

126(1) **Foreign Tax Credits for Corporations** The foreign non-business income tax credit is the lesser of:

- the tax paid to the foreign government (for corporations, there is no 15% limit on the foreign non-business taxes paid); and
- an amount determined by the following formula:

$$\left[\frac{\text{Foreign Non-Business Income}}{\text{Adjusted Division B Income}}\right][\text{Tax Otherwise Payable}]$$

126(2) The foreign business income tax credit is equal to the least of:

- the tax paid to the foreign government;
- an amount determined by the following formula:

$$\left[\frac{\text{Foreign Business Income}}{\text{Adjusted Division B Income}}\right][\text{Tax Otherwise Payable}]; \text{ and}$$

- tax otherwise payable for the year, less any foreign tax credit taken on non-business income under ITA 126(1).

129(4) **Refundable Portion of Part I Tax Payable** is defined as the least of three items:

1. the amount determined by the formula

A - B, where

A is 30 2/3% of the corporation's aggregate investment income for the year, and

B is the amount, if any, by which the foreign non-business income tax credit exceeds 8% of its foreign investment income for the year.

2. 30 2/3% of the amount, if any, by which the corporation's taxable income for the year exceeds the total of:
   - the amount upon which the small business deduction is determined;
   - 100 ÷ 38 2/3 of the tax credit for foreign non-business income; and
   - 4 times the tax credit for foreign business income.
3. the corporation's tax for the year payable under Part I.

129(4) **Aggregate Investment Income** is the sum of:

- net taxable capital gains for the year, reduced by any net capital loss carry overs deducted during the year; and
- income from property including interest, rents, and royalties, but excluding dividends that are deductible in computing taxable income. Since foreign dividends are generally not deductible, they would be included in aggregate investment income.

129(4) **ELIGIBLE 2021 Refundable Dividend Tax on Hand** (RDTOH) is defined as follows:

Beginning Balance The balance in the eligible RDTOH at the end of the preceding taxation year.

Additions

- Part IV taxes paid on eligible dividends from non-connected taxable Canadian corporations. These are commonly referred to as portfolio dividends.
- Part IV taxes paid on eligible dividends from connected corporations to the extent that such dividends included a refund from the paying corporation's eligible RDTOH.

Deduction Dividend refund claimed from the eligible RDTOH account for the previous taxation year.

NON-ELIGIBLE 2019 Refundable Dividend Tax on Hand (RDTOH) is defined as follows:

Beginning Balance The balance in the non-eligible RDTOH at the end of the preceding taxation year.

Additions There are three items that are added to the non-eligible RDTOH beginning balance:

- The Part I refundable tax for the year.
- Part IV taxes paid on non-eligible dividends from connected corporations to the extent that such dividends included a refund from the paying corporation's non-eligible RDTOH.
- Part IV taxes paid on non-eligible dividends from non-connected taxable Canadian corporations.

Deduction Dividend refund claimed from the non-eligible RDTOH account for the previous taxation year.

186(1) **Part IV Tax** is assessed at a rate of 38 1/3% of portfolio dividends, plus dividends received from a connected company where that connected company was entitled to a dividend refund as a result of the dividend payment.

Tax Related Websites

GOVERNMENT

Canada Revenue Agency www.canada.ca/en/revenue-agency
Department of Finance Canada www.canada.ca/en/department-finance.html

CPA FIRMS

BDO www.bdo.ca/en-ca/services/tax/domestic-tax-services/overview/
Deloitte. www2.deloitte.com/ca/en/pages/tax/topics/tax.html
Ernst & Young www.ey.com/CA/en/Services/Tax
KPMG www.kpmg.com/ca/en/services/tax
PricewaterhouseCoopers www.pwc.com/ca/en/services/tax.html

OTHER

CPA Canada www.CPAcanada.ca
Canadian Tax Foundation www.ctf.ca
ProFile Tax Suite profile.intuit.ca

CHAPTER 1

Introduction to Federal Taxation in Canada

Learning Objectives

After completing Chapter 1, you should be able to:

1. Describe the purpose of the Canadian income tax system, the principal questions answered by the *Income Tax Act* (ITA) pertaining to Canadian resident individuals and corporations, and the four-step process used to determine one's income tax liability or refund (Paragraph [P hereafter] 1-1 to 1-9).
2. Explain the role that accounting plays in income tax (P 1-10 to 1-11).
3. List some of the different tax bases used by various levels of government to raise tax revenue (P 1-12 to 1-15)
4. List and describe the four principal entities referred to in the ITA (P 1-16 to 1-22).
5. Describe the three main ways that business is carried on and identify who is subject to income tax in each case (P 1-23 to 1-24).
6. Describe those entities that are exempt and those that are taxable (not exempt) (P 1-25 to 1-26).
7. Explain how the GST/HST differs from income tax in terms of how it is collected together with the entities that are accountable for GST/HST (P 1-27 to 1-28).
8. Explain the relationship between the assessment of taxes at the federal level and the assessment of taxes at the provincial level (P 1-29 to 1-40).
9. List some of the ways that taxation is used to achieve economic objectives (P 1-41).
10. Describe the differences between progressive, regressive, and flat tax systems, including some of the advantages and disadvantages of each (P 1-42 to 1-50).
11. Discuss the issue of who ultimately pays the cost of various types of taxes (P 1-51 and 1-52).
12. Explain the nature of tax expenditures (P 1-53 to 1-56).
13. Evaluate issues in tax policy on the basis of the qualitative characteristics of tax systems (P 1-57 to 1-59).
14. Describe the reference materials that are available on income tax databases (P 1-60 to 1-64).
15. Describe the general structure of the *Income Tax Act* (P 1-65 to 1-77).
16. List and explain the nature of other sources of income tax legislation (P 1-78 to 1-88).
17. Describe other sources of *income tax information* (P 1-89 to 1-93).

18. Describe the charging provisions of the ITA for residents and non-residents (P 1-94 to 1-110).
19. Identify the three types of residency and be able to determine the residence of an individual based on an evaluation of the facts (P 1-111 to 1-124).
20. Evaluate the residency status of an individual who is temporarily absent from Canada or is only resident for part of the year (P 1-125 to 1-143).
21. Explain how residency determinations are made for dual resident individuals and the impact of citizenship versus residency (P 1-144 to 1-150).
22. Explain and be able to apply the residency analysis for individuals (P 1-151).
23. Explain how residency is determined for corporations, deemed corporate residency, and how dual residency issues occur and how they are resolved (P 1-152 to 1-159).
24. Explain and be able to apply the residency analysis for corporations (P 1-160).
25. Explain how residency determinations are made for trusts (P 1-161 to 1-163).
26. Describe, in general terms, the various views of income that are held by economists and accountants (P 1-164 to 1-169).
27. Explain the source concept of income for income tax purposes and identify the specific types of other income that are subject to income tax in Canada (P 1-170 to 1-177).
28. Calculate net income by applying the rules found in ITA 3 (P 1-178 to 1-186).
29. Explain how net income is converted to taxable income (P 1-187 to 1-188).
30. Explain the principles of tax planning (P 1-189 to 1-192).
31. Explain and provide examples of tax avoidance or reduction and tax deferral (P 1-193 to 1-200).
32. Explain and provide examples of income splitting (P 1-201 to 1-207).

The Canadian Tax System

Introduction

1-1. Learning and understanding Canadian income tax begins with answers to some fairly basic questions, such as (1) Who is required to pay income tax? (2) How is income tax payable determined? (3) When and how does one go about paying income tax?

1-2. While those are clearly not the only relevant income tax questions, they are the most important in establishing a solid foundation upon which a more complex understanding can be built. The answers to those basic questions are the first step to successfully completing this introductory level course on federal income taxation, and they will give you an appreciation for the tax system you can carry with you into whatever endeavour you decide to pursue.

1-3. We won't sugar coat the fact that income tax as well as the GST/HST are complex, abstract concepts developed, with a surprising degree of logic, into legislation that covers thousands of pages. But rest assured that with appropriate study, this text will provide you with a good solid understanding. Completing the exercises and problem material as you work through each chapter will help solidify what you have learned and will prepare you for each successive chapter where additional building blocks are added.

A Word on Basic Concepts

1-4. In very general terms, Canadian income tax obliges residents of Canada (not necessarily Canadian citizens) who earn income in Canada and anywhere else around the world (referred to as worldwide income) to pay income tax on that income. The Canadian tax system also charges income tax to those not resident in Canada (non-residents) if they earn Canadian sources of income. We will clarify this point in this chapter.

1-5. If you are a resident of Canada or a non-resident earning Canadian source income you are required to communicate the results of your income to the Canada Revenue Agency (CRA). This federal government organization is mandated to administer and enforce both the *Income Tax Act* (ITA) for income tax and the *Excise Tax Act* (ETA) for GST or HST. Communication can take many forms depending on the circumstances, but the annual reporting of income is accomplished by completing and filing an annual income tax return. You can find the current versions of the individual income tax returns on the CRA website at https://www.canada.ca/en/revenue-agency/services/forms-publications/tax-packages-years/general-income-tax-benefit-package.html.

1-6. At this stage we have given you very broad answers to questions 1 and 3 above. The answer to question 2 requires the largest explanation and is the main subject of this text. Determining your tax payable, or your tax refund, depends on what income you have, what deductions are available to you to offset that income, and what personal tax credits are available. Taking a glance at the Income Tax and Benefit Return for the province in which you live will give you an idea of what is involved in completing a Canadian income tax return.

1-7. In terms of individual income tax there are four steps required for you to be able to answer question 2 and which form the basis for many exercises, assignment problems, and exam questions. The four steps are as follows:

- **Step 1: Net income:** Determine this amount by adding all income and deducting all available expenses and other deductions.
- **Step 2: Taxable income:** This is the actual tax base upon which an income tax liability or refund is based. This starts with net income and makes adjustments to subtract certain amounts.
- **Step 3: Gross tax:** Calculate gross taxes payable. This is generally determined by applying various tax rates to taxable income.
- **Step 4: Personal tax credits:** Determine the availability of personal tax credits, calculate the total amount available, and subtract it from gross tax.
- **The result = net tax payable or refund**

1-8. For those of you who decide to continue beyond individual income tax (Chapters 1 to 11) to learn about income tax for corporations, we can add that the four steps above also apply to the determination of corporate income tax with the exception of the personal tax credits in step 3. Instead corporations reduce their gross tax by a number of corporate tax reductions. The federal corporate tax return can be found on the CRA website at https://www.canada.ca/content/dam/cra-arc/formspubs/pbg/t2/t2-20e.pdf. The second volume of this text also includes coverage of trusts and partnerships as well as an understanding of international tax law and GST/HST (Chapters 12 to 21).

1-9. Before returning to answer the three questions raised above we will briefly look at the various taxes in Canada, how federal tax interacts with provincial and territorial income tax, qualitative characteristics of a good tax system, tax policy concerns, and a few other related topics to provide you with an understanding of some of the fundamentals of a tax system. In this text we will use the word "province" or variations of it to refer to both provinces and territories.

A Word on Accounting Principles and Income Tax

1-10. Many students undertake the study of introductory income tax as part of the educational requirements for obtaining a professional accounting designation, such as a Chartered Professional Accountant or CPA. Those educational requirements clearly include significant accounting education that looks to accounting practice, methods, and principles, such as the International Financial Reporting Standards (IFRS) and Accounting Standards for Private Enterprises (ASPE), which comprise Canadian generally accepted accounting principles (GAAP).

1-11. Income tax concepts, however, are not based on accounting concepts and rarely employ any mention of accounting whatsoever except in very restrictive circumstances. The ITA is legislation drafted by lawyers with the final arbitrators of disputes being judges, all of whom are lawyers and not accountants. This works well since the ITA is based on legal concepts. For example the determination of whether an individual is an employee versus a self-employed contractor is based on case law. The ITA operates on the basis of other laws, including property law, contract law, corporate law, the common law, law of trusts, and many others. This does not mean that one cannot learn the fundamentals of income tax at a practical level without obtaining a law degree, but it is important to recognize early on the significance of legal concepts in Canadian income tax and the lesser role of accounting. This appreciation becomes increasingly important in tax planning.

Alternative Tax Bases

1-12. Tax is generally defined as a compulsory contribution made by individuals, corporations, and other entities to federal, provincial, and municipal governments for many purposes but largely to finance public services. These contributions, which take many forms including fees, duties, royalties, and direct and indirect taxes, represent the revenues that governments at all levels rely on to meet annual budgetary expenditures.

1-13. Taxes come in all shapes and sizes, but learning the basics first requires an understanding of the tax base upon which the tax rates are applied. In income tax this tax base is referred to as "taxable income." The complexity of a tax base can vary considerably from a flat rate applied to a single transaction, such as a simple purchase, to a more complex system that includes multiple rates and offsetting credits applied to a comprehensive income base over a predetermined period of time (typically one calendar or fiscal year). Some of the more common taxes and their tax bases in Canada you are likely to see are the following:

Income Tax A tax on the income of individuals, corporations, and trusts. There are two levels of income tax in Canada—one applied by the federal government and a second by the province, which is generally based on where you reside on the last day of a calendar year.

Property Tax A tax typically imposed by a municipal government on the ownership of property situated in its jurisdiction, such as vacant land or a residential home.

Sales Tax A tax levied on the price paid for goods (e.g., clothes, cars, dishwashers) and services (e.g., haircuts, plumbing services). There are three types of sales tax in Canada: (1) the goods and services tax or GST (federal), (2) provincial sales taxes or PST (provinces), and (3) the harmonized sales tax or HST (combined federal and provincial). Provinces either have an HST system or a combined GST and PST system.

Payroll Tax A tax often imposed on employers only or on both employers and employees that includes contributions toward various government plans or programs such as the Canada or Quebec Pension Plans, the Employment Insurance plan, the Workers' Compensation Board, and, in some provinces, certain health care taxes.

Tariffs or Customs Duties A tax imposed on the importation or exportation of certain goods or services.

Transfer Tax A tax on the transfer of property from one owner to another, such as on the sale of vacant land or a residential home.

Excise and Other Similar Taxes Taxes, duties, fees, or other charges on items such as carbon emissions, tobacco, alcohol, insurance premiums, jewellery, gasoline, automobile air conditioners, vehicles that are not fuel efficient, and so on.

Capital Tax A tax on the capital of a large corporation, such as a bank or insurance company.

Wealth/Death Tax A potential tax imposed under the income tax laws when someone dies based on the value of property owned at the time of death. There are no inheritance taxes in Canada, meaning that the recipients of inherited property are not taxed simply as a result of having received inherited property.

Figure 1-1 Federal Government Revenues by Source

Personal income tax	50.1%
Corporate income tax	14.4%
GST	11.4%
Other sources	11.4%
Employment Insurance premiums	6.7%
Other excise taxes	1.8%
Non-resident income tax	2.8%
Custom and import duties	1.4%
Total	100.0

1-14. Figure 1-1 indicates the 2021/22 percentage distribution of federal revenues by source. As you can see there are three categories of income tax: 50.1% from individuals, 14.4% from corporations, and 2.8% from non-residents, for a total of 67.3%, which represents more than two-thirds of total revenue. If we add the GST, which contributes an additional 11.4%, the combined total is 78.7%, indicating the importance of both income and sales tax revenues to the federal government.

1-15. A few observations can be made from Figure 1-1. The first is that revenue from personal income tax is almost four times larger than revenue from corporate income tax and over four times larger than revenue from GST/HST. In addition personal income tax is almost double that of both corporate tax and GST/HST revenue. While the other revenue sources are important, it is clear that income tax imposed on individuals—one of the subjects of Volume 1 of this text—is, by far, the most important source.

Taxable Entities in Canada

Federal Income Tax

1-16. There are four specific types of entities mentioned in the ITA:

- Individuals (human beings)
- Corporations
- Trusts
- Partnerships

While there are other types of recognized quasi-entities, such as investment clubs and joint ventures, the entities themselves are not subject to tax. The income earned through these quasi-entities, however, is required to be included in the income of members, participants, or joint venturers, who are taxable entities. Discussion of other types of entities is beyond the scope of this text.

1-17. The principal objective of the income tax system is to raise revenues for government to provide services. Imposing tax liabilities upon an entity requires that the entity have a legal status. Legal status generally means being able to enter into contracts, incur debt, file lawsuits against other persons with legal status, and have lawsuits filed against the entity. Of the four entities mentioned only individuals (human beings) and corporations have the requisite legal status.

1-18. Corporations are given legal status by the federal or provincial law under which they are incorporated. Section 15 of the *Canada Business Corporations Act*, which creates and recognizes a federally incorporated company, reads as follows:

> *A corporation has the capacity and, subject to this Act, the rights, powers and privileges of a natural person.*

Almost all law in Canada uses the expression "natural person" to refer to a human being and as a result a corporation becomes a legal entity subject to the ITA and ETA in the same manner as a human being.

1-19. Trusts (other than trust corporations) and partnerships, however, are not legal entities but are better described as legal relationships. As a result they would not be "legal entities" subject to the ITA unless the legislation was written in such a way to specifically include them.

1-20. We mentioned that most legislation (including the ETA) uses the words "natural persons" to refer to human beings, but the ITA uses the word "individual" instead. The reason behind this is that, in the ITA, the word "individual" means both human beings and trusts. When the ITA wants to restrict law to human beings only, it uses language such as "individuals (other than trusts)." Check out the first sentence of ITA 110.6(2) for an example of this. In summary, the result is that there are three taxable entities—human beings, corporations, and trusts. In this text we will use the word "individuals" to refer to human beings and "trusts" to refer to trusts to avoid confusion.

1-21. A partnership is a legal relationship, not a legal entity. The policy of the ITA is to ensure that income earned through a partnership is taxed in the hands of the members/partners. The legislation does not create a taxable entity out of a partnership, but it does add rules to ensure that the calculation of income, deductions, and certain other things follows the same rules that would apply to corporations, trusts, and individuals. In summary, a partnership is not a taxable entity for purposes of the ITA. Partnerships are discussed in Chapter 18.

1-22. Taxable entities must file annual income tax returns to communicate the results of their income and losses to the CRA to assess their tax liability. Individuals file a T1 return, corporations file a T2 return, and trusts file a T3 return. Partnerships do not file an income tax return, but in many cases they are required to file an information return, which provides the CRA with information necessary to ensure that income is properly determined and reported in the hands of partners, who are taxable entities.

Forms of Business vs. Taxable Entities

1-23. There is sometimes confusion concerning the various ways in which business is conducted and whether certain business forms are considered entities. Business can generally be carried on in one of three ways: (1) by one individual in what is commonly referred to as a sole proprietorship, (2) by a number of persons together in a partnership, or (3) by a corporation in what many refer to as an incorporated business.

1-24. The ITA taxes all income, which includes income from a business. Income tax is imposed upon the taxable entity that is the owner of the business. Quoting the many courts that have considered this issue, the question comes down to "Whose business is it?" In terms of the three types of business forms, we have summarized the results below:

Sole Proprietorship The business owner is the individual proprietor, and that individual must report the business income on an income tax return (T1).

Partnership The business owners are all of the partners who are, in effect, part owners. Each of them is required to report the business income on his income tax return depending on whether he is an individual (T1), a corporation (T2), or a trust (T3). The ITA considers a partner's ownership interest in the partnership as a separate property that can be bought and sold, comparable in many ways to shares of a company.

Incorporated Business The corporation is the business owner and must report the business income on its annual T2 corporate tax return. Individual shareholders are not business owners. They are only considered to have an ownership interest in the company represented by the shares they own.

The takeaway from this discussion is that sole proprietorships are not an entity for income tax purposes, and therefore they cannot be a taxable entity.

Tax Exempt Entities

1-25. We have identified the three distinct entities as individuals, corporations, and trusts. In order to be in a position to label these entities as taxable entities they must meet the definition of a "taxpayer," which requires that the entity be liable or potentially liable for tax. ITA 149 is a rule that exempts certain entities from income tax (under Part I of the ITA), and as a result it cannot be ignored. Listed exempt entities include municipal governments (often incorporated), labour organizations (e.g., unions), registered charities, trusts that are registered retirement savings plans (RRSPs), registered education savings plans (RESPs), and Tax-Free Saving Accounts (TFSAs).

Taxable Entities

1-26. In summary individuals, corporations, and trusts that are not tax exempt are considered taxable entities that must file annual income tax returns that are either a T1, T2, or T3. Sole proprietorships are not taxable entities.

GST/HST

1-27. The ITA looks to the owners of income, such as a salary, business income, or investment income, to impose tax. The income tax is paid from income owned by taxable entities. The GST/HST is a different concept, however, since the tax collected on the sales of goods and service belongs to the government and is collected by a business owner on its behalf. In effect, GST/HST collected represents funds held in trust for the government.

1-28. Those persons who are registered (voluntarily or otherwise) for the GST/HST and carry on business, which the legislation refers to as a "commercial activity," are required to charge and collect the GST/HST as and when required on most goods and services, and then to remit it to the federal government and to periodically file GST/HST returns that report the results. Since the focus is on a business, the tax is imposed on a much broader group that includes individuals, partnerships, corporations, estates of deceased individuals, trusts, or any organization of any kind such as charities, societies, unions, clubs, and associations. You can see that partnerships, registered charities, and unions would not be taxable entities for ITA purposes but are for GST/HST.

Exercise 1-1

Subject: Taxable Entities for Income Tax Purposes

Which of the following are entities under the ITA that could be required to file an income tax return?

- Max Jordan (an individual)
- Jordan's Hardware Store (an unincorporated business)
- Jordan & Jordan (a partnership)
- The Jordan family trust (a trust)
- Jordan Enterprises Ltd. (a corporation)
- The Jordan Foundation (an incorporated registered charity)

Exercise 1-2

Subject: Taxable Entities for GST/HST Purposes

Which of the following are considered entities under the ETA that could be required to file a GST/HST return?

- Max Jordan (an individual)
- Jordan's Hardware Store (an unincorporated business)

- Jordan & Jordan (a partnership)
- The Jordan family trust (a trust)
- Jordan Enterprises Ltd. (a corporation)
- The Jordan Foundation (an incorporated registered charity)

Solutions to Exercises are available in the Study Guide.

Federal Taxation and the Provinces

Personal Income Taxes

1-29. Under the *Constitution Act,* the federal, provincial, and territorial governments have the power to impose taxes. The provinces and territories are limited to direct taxation as delegated in the Act, a constraint that leaves all residual taxation powers to the federal government. The provinces are further limited to the taxation of income earned in the particular province and the income of persons resident in that province. Within these limitations, all of the provinces and territories impose both personal and corporate income taxes.

1-30. Under the federal/provincial tax collection agreement, with the exception of Quebec, provincial taxes are calculated by applying a provincial tax rate to the federal income tax base of taxable income.

1-31. Despite the use of the federal taxable income figure, the provinces have retained considerable flexibility in their individual tax systems. This flexibility is achieved in two ways:

- Each province can apply different rates and surtaxes to as many tax brackets as it wishes.
- More importantly, each province is able to set different provincial tax credits to apply against provincial tax payable. While most provinces have provincial credits that are similar to credits that are established at the federal level, the value of these credits varies considerably at the provincial level. For example, the basic personal credit is over $11,000 higher in the province with the highest amount than it is in the province with the lowest figure.

1-32. The provincial differences complicate the preparation of tax returns. The level of complication varies from province to province, depending on the degree to which provincial tax brackets and provincial tax credits resemble those at the federal level.

1-33. Because of these complications, the problem material in this text will, in general, not require the calculation of provincial taxes for individuals, corporations, or trusts. However, because the combined federal/provincial rate is important in many tax-based decisions (e.g., selecting between alternative investments), we will continue to refer to overall combined rates, despite the fact that such figures are very specific to the province in which the income is taxed.

Exercise 1-3

Subject: Federal and Provincial Taxes Payable

John Forsyth has taxable income of $27,000. For the current year, his federal tax rate is 15 percent, while the corresponding provincial rate is 7.5 percent. Determine Mr. Forsyth's combined federal and provincial tax payable before consideration of any available credits against tax payable.

Solutions to Exercises are available in the Study Guide.

Corporate Income Taxes

1-34. The system used to calculate provincial corporate income tax payable is similar to the system that is applicable to individuals except as mentioned in the introduction to this chapter. Provincial corporate income tax is levied on taxable income. All of the provinces, with the exception of Alberta and Quebec, use the federal ITA to compute taxable income. As a result, two corporate income tax returns are required to be filed in Alberta and Quebec, whereas only one is required in the other provinces. All provinces have their own Corporate *Income Tax Acts*, which are much shorter than the ITA since they adopt most of the rules in the ITA.

1-35. With respect to the collection of corporate income taxes, only Alberta and Quebec collect their own corporate income taxes. In all other provinces corporate income taxes are collected by the federal government on behalf of the provinces.

GST, HST, and PST

1-36. Although detailed coverage of GST/HST can be found in Chapter 21, "GST/HST," we will provide a short overview here as part of our introduction to federal taxation. When the federal government proposed a joint federal/provincial goods and services tax (GST) in 1987, the lack of interest by provincial governments meant that the GST was introduced only at the federal level. Provincial sales taxes remained in place without significant change. As a result, two different sales taxes were charged, collected, accounted for, and remitted.

1-37. This situation was very costly and time consuming for businesses operating in more than one province, as they had to file multiple sales tax returns under different sets of rules. This was clearly an inefficient way to generate tax revenues and, not surprisingly, considerable pressure developed for combining both the federal GST and the provincial sales taxes into what is referred to as a harmonization, or HST.

1-38. Despite the obvious efficiencies that would result from harmonization, it has only been accepted in the four Maritime provinces of New Brunswick, Nova Scotia, Newfoundland, and Prince Edward Island and the province of Ontario. Quebec administers its own Quebec sales tax (QST), which is a somewhat harmonized system, and while its coverage is similar to that of the GST it is not identical.

1-39. The federal portion is 5%. The Maritime provinces add 10% for an HST rate of 15%. Ontario adds 8% for an HST rate of 13%.

1-40. The various provincial sales tax regimes have left Canada with a fragmented sales tax system. The effective rates range from 5% (GST only) to 15% (HST rate). Alberta and the three territories of Nunavut, Yukon, and Northwest Territories do not charge any PST and therefore they have only 5% GST.

Tax Policy Concepts

Taxation and Economic Policy

1-41. The traditional goal of tax legislation has been to generate revenues for the relevant taxing authority. However, it is clear that today's approach to tax legislation is multi-faceted. Tax legislation is used as a tool to facilitate a number of social and economic policy objectives:

> **Resource Allocation** Tax revenues are used to provide public goods and services. Pure public goods, such as the cost of our national defence system, are thought to benefit all taxpayers. As it is not possible to allocate costs to individuals on the basis of benefits received, such costs must be supported with general tax revenues. Similar allocations occur with such widely used public goods as education, health care, and pollution control. In some cases, the tax system also has an influence on the allocation of private goods. For example, excise taxes are used to discourage the consumption of alcohol and tobacco products.

Distribution Effects The federal tax system is used to redistribute income and wealth among taxpayers. Such provisions as the federal GST tax credit and provincial sales tax exemptions on food and low-priced clothing have the effect of taking taxes paid by higher income taxpayers and distributing them to lower income wage earners or taxpayers with higher basic living costs in proportion to their income.

Stabilization Effects Taxes may also be used to achieve macroeconomic objectives. At various times, tax policy has been used to encourage economic expansion, increase employment, and to assist in holding inflation in check. An example of this is the emphasis on stimulating the economy that is often found in annual federal budgets.

Fiscal Federalism This term refers to the various procedures that are used to allocate resources among different levels of government. These transfers currently exceed $80 billion per year. While this is less than transfers to persons and direct spending by the federal government, it is still a significant amount.

Taxation and Income Levels

General Approaches

1-42. Tax policy makers are concerned about the relationship between income levels and rates of taxation. Taxes can be proportional, in that a constant single rate is applied at all levels of income. In theory, this is our general approach to taxing the income of corporations. Canadian resident corporations are generally subject to a starting rate of 25% that represents a flat rate of 38% minus a rate reduction of 13%. The final effective rate, however, varies considerably depending on the type of corporation, the character of its income, and the location in which the income source is situated.

Exercise 1-4

Subject: Regressive Taxes

Margie Jones has taxable income for the current year of $895,000, of which $172,000 is spent on goods and services that are subject to harmonized sales tax (HST) at a rate of 13%. Her sister, Jane Jones, is a part-time student living in the same province and has taxable income of $18,000. During the current year, as a result of using some of her savings, she spends $27,500 on goods and services that are all subject to HST. Determine the effective sales tax rate as a percentage of income of the two sisters.

Solutions to Exercises are available in the Study Guide.

We suggest you complete SSP 1-1 at this point.

1-43. As an alternative, taxation can be regressive, resulting in lower effective rates of taxation as higher income levels are reached. Sales taxes generally fall into this regressive category, since lower income individuals spend a larger portion of their total income on these taxes and, as a consequence, pay a greater portion of their total income as sales taxes levied on their expenditures.

EXAMPLE Consider the Werner sisters:

Gertrude Werner has income of $200,000 and spends $40,000 of this amount. She lives in a province with a 15% harmonized sales tax on personal expenditures, resulting in the payment of $6,000 in HST. This represents a 3.0% effective tax rate on her $200,000 income ($6,000 ÷ $200,000).

Ingrid Werner has income of $40,000 and spends all of this amount. She lives in the same province as her sister, resulting in the payment of $6,000 in HST. This represents a 15% effective tax rate on her $40,000 income ($6,000 ÷ $40,000).

1-44. In contrast to the regressive nature of sales taxes, the present system of personal income taxation is designed to be progressive, applying a graduated series of tax rates to successively higher levels of income. An analogy can be drawn to a ladder with five rungs or steps. When you have taxable income you move to the first step. If your taxable income is below $49,020 you remain on that step. If your income exceeds $49,020 you move to the second step, where taxable income is taxed at 20.5%. You reach the top step, which applies a 33% tax rate, if your income exceeds $216,511.

Progressive vs. Regressive

1-45. As noted in the preceding paragraph, the federal income tax system taxes individuals using a progressive/graduated rate system. The major arguments in favour of this approach are as follows:

Equity Higher income individuals have a greater ability to pay taxes. As their income is above their basic consumption needs, the relative cost to the individual of having a portion of this income taxed away is less than the relative cost to lower income individuals, where additional taxation removes funds required for such essentials as food and housing. This is an essential feature of the taxation of individuals and is commonly referred to as the "ability to pay" principle.

Stability Progressive tax rates help maintain after-tax income stability by shifting people to lower tax brackets in times of economic downturn and to higher brackets when there is economic expansion. The resulting decreases or increases in income taxes serve to cushion the economic swings.

1-46. There are, however, a number of problems that can be associated with progressive rates. These can be briefly described as follows:

Complexity With progressive rates in place, efforts will be made to divide income among as many individuals (usually family members) as possible. These efforts to make maximum use of the lower tax brackets necessitate the use of complex anti-avoidance rules by taxation authorities. In 2018 the ITA underwent substantial changes the split income or "kiddy tax" rules in an attempt to stop efforts to reduce income taxes by sharing income with all family members. Previously the legislation only applied to children under 18 years of age. It now applies to all individuals.

Income Fluctuations In the absence of relieving provisions, progressive/graduated rates discriminate against individuals with highly variable income streams. That is, under a progressive system, an individual with $1,000,000 in income in one year and no income for the next three years will pay substantially more in taxes than an individual with the same $1,000,000 total earned over four years at a rate of $250,000 per year.

Family Unit Problems Progressive tax rates discriminate against single income family units. A family unit in which one spouse makes $250,000 and the other has no taxable income would pay significantly more in taxes than would be the case if each spouse earned $125,000. Based on 2021 tax rates and ignoring the impact of personal tax credits, federal income tax on $250,000 of taxable income would be $61,192. Federal income tax on $125,000 of taxable income would be $24,412. Therefore if both family members earned $125,000, rather than one family member earning $250,000, their total federal income tax would be reduced to $48,824, resulting in savings of $12,368 [$61,192 - $48,824]. In 2007 the federal government introduced pension income splitting, which allows those married/ common-law couples receiving certain pension income to split pension income received by only one of them. This reduced this particular problem to a certain extent. We discuss pension splitting in Chapter 9.

Economic Growth It is clear that the high tax brackets that can be associated with a progressive/graduated rate system can discourage both employment and investment efforts. This could serve to limit economic growth.

Tax Concessions The high brackets associated with progressive systems lead to pressure for various types of tax concessions to be made available. Because high-income individuals have a greater ability to take advantage of favourable provisions in the income tax legislation, they may actually wind up paying taxes at lower effective rates. In response to the possibility that, in extreme cases, some high-income individuals pay no income taxes at all, there is an alternative minimum income tax that is imposed on certain individual taxpayers (see Chapter 11).

Tax Avoidance and Evasion Progressive/graduated rates discourage income reporting and encourage the creation of various means to evade taxation. Evasion strategies range from simple bartering, to cash-only transactions, to offshore tax havens, and finally to criminal activities.

Reduced Tax Revenues There is evidence that, if tax rates are too high, the result may be reduced aggregate tax revenues. Some authorities believe that this begins to occur at tax rates between 40 and 50%. Prior to 1972 a major study of the tax system was undertaken, referred to as the Carter Commission Report. At the time the highest federal income tax rate was a staggering 80% that applied to taxable income in excess of $400,000. The report noted that few individuals actually paid tax at that rate, instead resorting to tax avoidance and evasion strategies. These excessive high rates were eliminated in the early 1970s.

We would note that, with the maximum federal rate at 33%, the maximum combined federal/provincial rate in most provinces exceeds 50%, going as high as 54% in some provinces for income approaching $250,000. While it is difficult to determine the degree to which this will encourage tax evasion, it is almost certain that maximum tax rates at this level will be a major factor in decisions involving significant amounts of income being moved out of Canada. Without resorting to tax evasion, high-income individuals have great flexibility in relocating their income. The Carter Commission report recommended that income taxes never exceed 50% on the basis that most Canadians considered it unfair for governments to take more than half of an individual's income in taxes.

Flat Tax Rate Systems

1-47. While progressive/graduated tax systems continue to be pervasive, there has been a worldwide trend toward flattening rate schedules. One of the reasons for this trend is the fact that effective tax rates are not as progressive as the rate schedules indicate. As mentioned in the preceding paragraph, high-bracket taxpayers tend to have better access to various types of tax concessions, which can significantly reduce the effective rates for these individuals.

1-48. The growing popularity of a flat tax rate system is premised on two flawed assumptions. The first is that everyone will somehow pay less tax and the second is that the income tax system will be simplified as a result.

1-49. Alberta, in 2001, is the only province that turned from a progressive/graduated rate system to a flat rate system. In 2015 they returned to the progressive/graduated system. Up until a few years ago the province considered a return to a flat rate system, noting that the only winners to that decision would be those individuals earning $128,000 or more a year. It is noteworthy that governments do not generally entertain a new tax system with the prospect of reducing tax revenues. A flat rate system frequently results in a broadening of the income base to ensure that tax revenues are maintained. This dispels the first premise that flat tax rate systems lower everyone's income taxes.

1-50. As to whether a flat rate system simplifies a tax system it is important to keep in mind that the application of tax rates to a tax base represents an insignificant part of the complexity within an income tax system. The complexity lies elsewhere, particularly in determining the tax base, which is constantly changing to keep up with ways in which business and business transaction are evolving. The conclusion is that flat tax rate systems have little to no impact whatsoever on complexity.

We suggest you complete SSP 1-2 at this point.

Tax Incidence

1-51. Tax incidence refers to the issue of who really pays a particular tax. While statutory incidence refers to the initial legal liability for tax payment, the actual economic burden may be passed on to a different group. For example, certain taxes on manufacturing might be the legal liability of the manufacturer. However, they may be partly or entirely shifted to consumers through price increases on the goods produced.

1-52. Policy makers must be concerned with this to ensure that the system is working as intended. It is generally assumed that the incidence of personal income tax falls on individuals. In addition, in their role as consumers, individuals assume the responsibility for a large portion of the various sales taxes that are levied in Canada. The incidence of corporate taxes is more open to speculation. Shareholders may bear the burden of corporate taxes in the short run. However, most authorities believe that, in the long run, this burden is shared by employees and consumers.

Tax Expenditures

1-53. In contrast to government funding programs that provide payments to various entities in the economy, tax expenditures reflect revenues that have been given up by the government through the use of tax preferences, concessions, and other tax breaks. These expenditures may favour select individuals or groups (senior citizens), certain kinds of income (capital gains), or certain characteristics of some taxpayers (those with disabilities).

1-54. In an effort to quantify the importance of these expenditures, the Department of Finance produces the publication, "Tax Expenditures and Projections" each year. Using this source, some examples of these costs are found in Figure 1-2.

Figure 1-2 Tax Expenditures

2013 Actual and 2022 Projections
Millions of Dollars

	Actual 2013	Projected 2022
Low rate for small corporations	2,950	6,035
Accelerated investment incentive for CCA	NA	1,740
Non-taxation of gains on principal residences	4,160	7,760
Registered retirement savings plans	13,435	16,145
Basic personal tax credit	31,055	45,965

1-55. It is clear that such tax expenditures are of considerable significance in the management of federal finances. It is equally clear that the provision of this type of government benefit has become entrenched in our tax system. This situation can be explained by a number of factors:

- It is less costly to administer tax expenditures than it is to administer separate government funding programs.
- More decisions are left to the private sector so that funds may be allocated more efficiently.
- Tax expenditures reduce the visibility of certain government actions. This is particularly beneficial if some social stigma is attached to the programs. For example, a child tax benefit system is more acceptable than increasing social assistance (welfare) payments.
- Tax expenditures reduce the progressivity of the tax system. As many of the tax expenditures, such as tax shelters, are more available to higher income taxpayers, they serve to reduce effective tax rates in higher tax brackets.

1-56. Tax expenditures are not only substantial, they are also difficult to control. This was expressed several years ago by a former auditor general, as follows:

> A cost conscious Parliament is in the position of a team of engineers trying to design a more fuel efficient automobile. They think they have succeeded, but the engine seems to go on consuming as much gas as it did before. They cannot understand the problem until they notice that, hidden from view, a myriad of small holes have been punched through the bottom of the gas tank. This is too often the way of tax expenditures. Revenue leaks away, and MPs do not know about it until it is too late.

Qualitative Characteristics of Tax Systems

General Concepts

1-57. Accounting standard-setting bodies have established such concepts as relevance and reliability as being desirable qualitative characteristics of accounting information. While not established with the same degree of formality, it is clear that there are similar concepts that can be used to evaluate tax systems. Some of these desirable qualitative characteristics can be described as follows:

Equity or Fairness Horizontal equity entails assessing similar levels of taxation for people in similar economic circumstances. If two individuals each have taxable income of $50,000, horizontal equity would require that they each pay the same amount of taxes. In contrast, vertical equity means dissimilar tax treatment of people in different circumstances, which is the basis for a progressive/graduated rate system. If an individual has taxable income of $100,000, then the individual should pay more taxes than an individual with taxable income of $50,000.

Neutrality The concept of neutrality calls for a tax system that interferes as little as possible with decision making. An overriding economic assumption is that decisions are always made to maximize the use of resources. This may not be achieved when tax factors affect how taxpayers save, invest, or consume. Taxes, by influencing economic decisions, may cause a less than optimal allocation of resources.

Adequacy A good tax system should meet the funding requirements of the taxing authority. It is also desirable that these revenues be produced in a fashion that is dependable and relatively predictable from year to year.

Flexibility This refers to the ease with which the tax system can be adjusted to meet changing economic or social conditions.

Simplicity and Ease of Compliance A good tax system is easy to comply with and does not present significant administrative problems for the people enforcing the system.

Certainty Individual taxpayers should know how much tax they have to pay, the basis for payments, and the due date. Such certainty also helps taxing authorities estimate tax revenues and facilitates forecasting of budgetary expenditures.

Balance between Sectors A good tax system should not be overly reliant on either corporate or individual taxation. Attention should also be given to balance within these sectors, ensuring that no type of business or type of individual is asked to assume a disproportionate share of the tax burden.

International Competitiveness If a country's tax system has rates that are out of line with those in comparable countries, the result will be an outflow of investment, business, and skilled individuals to those countries that have more favourable tax rates.

Conflicts among Characteristics

1-58. In designing a tax system, many compromises are required. Examples include the fact that flexibility is often in conflict with certainty, equity requires trade-offs in simplicity and neutrality, and some taxes with positive objectives are non-neutral in nature. An example of this last conflict is that the rates available to small businesses are favourable because the government believes that this attracts investment to this sector, thereby encouraging employment and the development of active business efforts. However, this may not result in the optimal allocation of resources to the business sector as a whole.

Evaluation of the Canadian System

1-59. Canadian tax policy makers often refer to the preceding qualitative characteristics in discussions involving taxation policies. This would make it appropriate to consider how the current system of federal taxation stacks up against these criteria. While any comprehensive evaluation of this question goes well beyond the objectives of this text, we offer the following brief comments:

- With respect to equity, Canada continues to encounter situations in which high-income individuals pay little or no tax and relatively low-income individuals are subjected to fairly high effective rates. While the alternative minimum tax was instituted to correct this problem, inequity is unlikely to be eliminated in a tax system that attempts to accomplish as many diverse objectives as does the current Canadian system.
- As noted previously, the Canadian system places a heavy reliance on the taxation of personal income and, in comparison, receives a low portion of its revenues from both corporate tax revenues and the GST/HST.
- The Canadian tax system can be complex, making compliance difficult at times for many taxpayers. In addition, administration of the legislation is made more difficult by the large number of provisions and the potential for conflicting interpretations.

  The inability to achieve a harmonized GST/HST system has made this situation much worse. As we have noted, different provinces have adopted different systems, thereby complicating interprovincial transactions. Further, in a given province, there are significant variations in the types of goods and services that are subject to taxation within a given system.
- With respect to international competitiveness, the situation is similar for corporations and individuals vis-a-vis the United States.
  - Over the last few years, tax rates on Canadian corporations have been reduced. These reductions leave Canada with corporate rates that compare favourably with most foreign jurisdictions. However, this situation changed dramatically in 2018 when the United States reduced its maximum corporate rate from 35% to 21%.

- Increasing the maximum federal tax rate on individuals to 33% in 2016 has made Canada less competitive with other countries, particularly the United States. With provincial taxes considered, several provinces tax individuals at a maximum rate of 54%. This compares to a maximum rate in some U.S. states of only 35%.

We suggest you complete SSP 1-3 at this point.

Income Tax Reference Materials

Introduction

1-60. To this point in our discussion of the Canadian tax system and related tax policy concepts, we have considered a variety of tax bases as they apply at both the federal and provincial level. However, with the exception of Chapter 21, which deals with the GST/HST, the focus of this book is on federal income tax on the income of individuals, corporations, and trusts.

1-61. Reference materials related to the federal income tax are extensive. In addition to the ITA, there are many other sources of information. These include other legislative materials, other publications of the CRA, court commentary and decisions, as well as interpretive materials from a wide variety of professional and academic sources.

1-62. If presented in paper format, a complete library of all of the relevant materials would run thousands of pages and would have to be included in a large number of separate volumes. Given this, almost all tax practitioners work with an electronic database that provides easy access to multiple sources of information through keyword searches.

1-63. These electronic databases are published by several Canadian organizations, including CCH, Carswell, and CPA Canada. You can also visit justice.gc.ca to access the Income Tax Act and Excise Tax Act.

1-64. A description of all of these materials is found in the sections that follow.

The Income Tax Act

Importance

1-65. This is the most important source of information for dealing with matters related to federal income tax. It is comparable to the operations manual for mechanics, the music score for an orchestra conductor, or the detailed topographical maps for geologists. The words of the legislation set the stage for the exercise of professional judgment for the CRA, tax practitioners, and the courts. The ITA includes the answers to the questions asked earlier of who is liable, what is the income tax base, and procedural issues such as filing requirements, payment obligations, and related penalties and interest.

1-66. The ITA is a lengthy document approaching 2,400 pages and is considered the most complex piece of federal legislation in Canada. It is written in a very legalistic style, which takes time to learn and become accustomed to. In many ways it is similar to the learning of a new language. The design of our text is such that it does not require the use of the ITA in order to understand and appreciate the content or complete the related exercises, assignment problems, or exams.

1-67. While the design of this text does not require the use of the ITA as a reference, it is still important to have some understanding of the structure of this document, which is surprisingly logical in its approach. One reason for this is that the organization of this book generally follows the structure of the ITA. In addition, you will find many references to the Act embedded as part of the text. There are two reasons for this:

- The most important reason for these references is to allow interested individuals to explore a particular issue to a depth that goes beyond the scope of this text. The presence of ITA references greatly facilitates this process.
- The use of references can sometimes be convenient. In dealing with a particular subject, it is often more efficient to refer to a subject with a specific reference to the ITA than to repeatedly use full textual descriptions of a subject.

1-68. Given these considerations, we will provide a description of the basic structure and content of this important legislation.

Structure of the ITA

1-69. Figure 1-3 shows the basic structure of the Act. As can be seen in this diagram, the major divisions of the ITA are referred to as parts. Some but not all of these parts contain two or more divisions (e.g., Part I of the Act contains Divisions A through J). Some divisions, but again not all of them, contain subdivisions. For example, Division B of Part I contains Subdivisions a through k. Note that while the parts are numbered I through XIX (1 to 19), there are actually 49 parts. This reflects the fact that when a new part is added, it has been more convenient to attach a decimal designation to the new part, as opposed to renumbering all of the parts that follow the new section. For example, Part I is followed by Part I.01, Part I.1, Part I.2, and Part I.3.

Figure 1-3 Basic Structure of the Income Tax Act

Part I - XIX (in **Divisions** and **Subdivisions**)	→	**Section** (1 - 281)	→	**Subsection** (Arabic numeral)	→	**Paragraph** (lower case letter)	→	**Subparagraph** (lower case Roman numeral)

1-70. Many years ago an attempt was made to renumber the ITA to make it easier to navigate with the intent of eliminating the numerous decimal point provisions. Tax practitioners were very vocal on insisting that it remain unchanged since they had learned where everything was located and were adverse to starting over again. The renumbering project was abandoned as a result.

1-71. All of the parts contain at least one section but this is where the similarity ends. There is considerable variance in the size of the parts. Part I.2, "Tax on Old Age Security Benefits," contains only one section and is little more than one page long. In contrast, Part I, the largest and most important part of the Act, contains Sections 2 to 180 and is over 1,200 pages in length.

1-72. The sections are labelled 1 through 281. However, as was the case with parts of the Act, decimals are used to label new sections, the result of which is that are over 600 sections of the ITA. For example, Section 12 is followed by Section 12.1, Section 12.2, Section 12.3 (repealed), Section 12.4, Section 12.5, and Section 12.6.

1-73. Sections may be further subdivided into subsections [designated with Arabic numerals, as in Subsection 84(1)]. This is followed by paragraphs [designated with lower case letters, as in Paragraph 84(1)(b)], and by subparagraphs [designated with lower case Roman numerals, as in Subparagraph 84(1)(b)(i)]. In some cases, the outlining process goes even further with clauses (designated with upper case letters) and sub-clauses (designated with upper case Roman numerals). Putting all of this together means that the reference:

ITA 13(7)(d)(i)(A)(I)

could be read as *Income Tax Act* Section 13, Subsection (7), Paragraph (d), Subparagraph (i), Clause A, Sub-clause I. However, the usual practice is to shorten it by only using the description for the last part of the reference. In the preceding example, the reference would be to Sub-clause 13(7)(d)(i)(A)(I). Also in practice, the relevant part of the Act (Part I in this case) is not indicated in such references. If we tried to get a sense of what the reference was about we would see that it is found in Part 1, Division B, Subdivision b. With that reference you would be able to determine that it has something to do with the computation of business or property income.

Parts of the ITA

1-74. The parts of the ITA are numbered I through XIX. As noted, because of the use of decimal designations there are actually 49 parts.

1-75. Approximately 62% of the sections of the ITA are found in Part I, which is simply titled "Income Tax." This part contains Sections 2 through 180 of the Act and, because of its importance, we will provide a more detailed description of this part in the following material.

1-76. Parts I.01 through XIX cover a variety of special taxes as well as rules related to matters of administration, enforcement, and interpretation. For example, Part IV is titled "Tax on Taxable Dividends Received by Private Corporations" and Part X.1 is titled "Tax in Respect of Over-Contributions to Deferred Income Plans." As the great bulk of our attention in this text will be focused on Part I of the ITA, there is little point in providing a list of these parts for you to read.

Part I of the ITA

1-77. Part I, the largest and most important part of the ITA, is divided into 11 divisions. Some of these divisions are further divided into subdivisions. The divisions and their more significant subdivisions are described in the following paragraphs:

Division A: "Liability for Tax" (ITA Section 2) This short division is concerned with the question of who is liable for payment of income tax in Canada. This division will be covered in this chapter.

Division B: "Computation of Income" (ITA Sections 3 through 108) This is the longest division in Part I and concerns itself with the determination of net income. Its first five subdivisions describe the major sources of income and deductions, which are as follows:

- **Subdivision a:** "Income or Loss from an Office or Employment" This subdivision deals with the ordinary wages and salaries that are earned by individuals as employees. As mentioned earlier, more than half of federal revenues are raised from individuals, much of which is attributed to employment income. Subdivision a, however, accounts for less than 40 pages of the almost 2,400 pages of the paper version of the ITA. The material in this subdivision is the subject of Chapter 3.
- **Subdivision b:** "Income or Loss from a Business or Property" This subdivision deals with two sources of income—business income and investment-type income referred to in the ITA as "income from property." Examples of income from property include rents, interest, dividends, and royalties. The material in this subdivision receives coverage in Chapters 5, 6, and 7.
- **Subdivision c:** "Taxable Capital Gains and Allowable Capital Losses" This subdivision deals with gains and losses resulting from the disposal of capital property. The material in this subdivision is covered in Chapter 11.

- **Subdivision d:** "Other Sources of Income" Covered here are miscellaneous receipts that technically do not qualify as income sources but which the federal government requires to be included in income and be subject to Part I tax. Miscellaneous receipts that are specifically mentioned are included in net income through this subdivision. Receipts that are not mentioned are not required to be included in income (e.g., inheritances, lottery winnings, etc.). Receipts required to be included in net income include spousal support received, various types of pension income, and certain annuities. This material is covered in Chapter 9.
- **Subdivision e:** "Deductions in Computing Income" This subdivision provides a list of miscellaneous deductions, such as RRSP contributions, moving expenses, child care costs, and spousal support paid. These deductions are located in this separate subdivision and referenced by ITA 4, which is a sourcing rule that requires that expenses be matched against the income to which they relate. As a result, business expenses must be expensed as part of Subdivision b, employment expenses as part of Subdivision a, and so on. ITA 4(2) clarifies that any of the Subdivision d deductions mentioned in ITA 60 to 64 are not considered to relate to a source of income and must be separately deducted in the calculation of net income through ITA 3, which will be discussed in Chapter 9. Expenses that do not relate to a source (e.g., employment, business, or property income) are only allowable if specifically mentioned in this subdivision and any listed conditions are met. These miscellaneous deductions are covered in Chapter 9.

These five subdivisions a through e are very important, as together they contain the necessary rules to determine the numbers that are used to calculate net income—the first step toward determining income tax liability or refund that we mentioned in the introduction to this chapter.

The remaining six subdivisions of Division B do not provide new sources of income but, rather, provide additional rules that may qualify, clarify, or restrict certain amounts and their impact on the calculation of net income. This means that in determining the components of net income in the first five subdivisions (a to e) you would be required to check to see whether any of the next six subdivisions (j to k) change anything. The remaining subdivisions are briefly described as follows:

- **Subdivision f:** "Rules Relating to Computation of Income" This subdivision contains a variety of additional rules related to the deductibility of expenses, income attribution, and the death of a taxpayer. These rules are covered in Chapters 6 and 9.
- **Subdivision g:** "Amounts Not Included in Computing Income" This is a very specialized subdivision, dealing with a limited list of specific types of receipts that are not subject to Part I tax and therefore are exempt. Examples would include personal injury awards, certain RCMP pensions, and select social assistance payments. It is given limited coverage in this text.
- **Subdivision h:** "Corporations Resident in Canada and Their Shareholders" Subdivision b contains a provision in ITA 12(1)(j) that requires taxpayers who receive dividends from a Canadian resident corporation, when calculating net income, to include the amount determined under Subdivision h. This subdivision contains the rules to determine how much to include and many other situations involving resident corporations. This material is covered in Chapters 12 through 17.
- **Subdivision i:** "Shareholders of Corporations Not Resident in Canada" This is a very specialized subdivision. But in a manner identical to that described for Subdivision h, Subdivision b contains a provision in ITA 12(1)(k) that obliges the taxpayer to include in net income any amount determined in Subdivision i for that taxpayer. Limited coverage is available in Chapter 20.

- **Subdivision j:** "Partnerships and Their Members" This subdivision deals exclusively with partnerships, specifically those taxpayers who are members/partners of a partnership. Allocations/entitlements to business or property income earned through a partnership are determined under the rules of Subdivision j and are required to be included in net income by ITA 12(1)(l) in Subdivision b. Partnerships are given detailed coverage in Chapter 18.
- **Subdivision k:** "Trusts and Their Beneficiaries" This subdivision covers trusts and estates and their beneficiaries. ITA 12(1)(m), also found in Subdivision b, requires most amounts determined by Subdivision k to be included in net income as income from property. The taxation of trusts is given detailed coverage in Chapter 19.

Division C: "Computation of Taxable Income" (ITA Sections 109 through 114.2) This division represents the rules necessary to go from net income to taxable income and is step 2 discussed in the introduction when determining whether there is an income tax liability or a refund. Taxable income for individuals is given initial coverage in Chapter 4, followed by more detailed coverage in Chapter 11. Taxable income for corporations is covered in Chapter 12.

Division D: "Taxable Income Earned in Canada by Non-Residents" (ITA Sections 115 through 116) Limited coverage of this material can be found in Chapter 20.

Division E: "Computation of Tax" (Sections 117 through 127.41) This division sets out the rules for both steps 3 and 4, providing the information necessary to determine ultimately whether there will be income tax to pay or a refund to receive for a given year. There are eight subdivisions within this division with the following headings:

- Subdivision a - Rules applicable to individuals
- Subdivision a.1 - Canada Child Benefit
- Subdivision a.2 - Canada Workers Benefit
- Subdivision a.3 - Climate Action Incentive
- Subdivision a.4 - School Supplies Tax Credit
- Subdivision a.5 - Canada Training Credit
- Subdivision b - Rules applicable to corporations
- Subdivision c - Rules applicable to all taxpayers

The computation of tax for individuals is largely covered in Chapter 4, with some additional coverage in Chapter 11. The corresponding material for corporations is found in Chapters 12 and 13.

You can see that the structure of the ITA to this point is logical, with one division building upon the next in a systematic manner. We can now provide a general summary linked to the four steps required to determine tax liability or a refund for individuals as follows:

Step 1 – Net Income = Division B (predominantly Subdivisions a to e)
Step 2 – Taxable Income = Division C
Step 3 – Gross Tax = Division E (Subdivision a)
Step 4 – Personal Tax Credits = Division E (Subdivision a)
Result = Net Tax Payable or Refund

Division E.1: "Minimum Tax" (ITA 127.5 through 127.55) This division contains the rules, including calculations, to determine whether this tax applies to specific individuals. Minimum tax is covered in Chapter 11.

Division F: "Special Rules Applicable in Certain Circumstances" (ITA 128 through 143.4) This division is devoted to very specialized situations (bankruptcies) and corporate entities (insurance companies, mutual fund corporations, mortgage investment corporations, and many more). Most of these rules are beyond the scope of this text, however there are two topics that are of general importance. These are immigration to Canada and emigration from Canada (ITA 128.1), which are covered in Chapter 20, and dividend refunds for private corporations (ITA 129), which is covered in Chapter 13.

Division G: "Deferred and Other Special Income Arrangements" (ITA 144 through 148.1) This division covers a long list of what are commonly referred to as deferred income plans. The more well-known plans include registered retirement savings plans (RRSPs), registered pension plans (RPPs), registered retirement income funds (RRIFs), and Tax-Free Savings Accounts (TFSAs). Detailed attention is given to this material in Chapter 10.

Division H: "Exemptions" (ITA 149, through 149.2) Covered here are a list of entities that are exempt from Part I tax. Listed exemptions include municipal governments (often incorporated), registered charities, non-profit organizations, RRSPs, and TFSAs (both of which are established as trusts). This division is not covered in this text.

Divisions I and J: "Returns, Assessments, Payment, and Appeals" (Division I, ITA 150 to 168) and "Appeals to the Tax Court of Canada and the Federal Court" (Division J, ITA 169 to 180) These divisions set out the rules and procedures when there is an income tax dispute with the CRA. Limited coverage of this material is found in Chapter 2.

Other Income Tax Legislation

1-78. While the ITA constitutes the major source of legislation relevant to the study of federal income tax, there are three other sources of legislative materials that are relevant. These are draft legislation, the *Income Tax Regulations* (ITR), and a group of international tax treaties and agreements between Canada and other countries. A general description of these legislative materials follows.

Draft Legislation

1-79. It is traditional for the federal government to issue a budget in the first quarter of each year. Budgets are presented as a Notice of Ways and Means Motion. While such proposals sometimes contain the relevant draft legislation, this is not always the case. In the absence of draft legislation, often the budget content is of a general nature only. Sometimes, however, examples are included to illustrate the mechanics of how the legislation will apply. Whether draft legislation is presented or not, it is common for the budgetary announcements to take effect on the date of the budget. This can present problems where, as is often the case, the legislation can take a considerable period of time until it is passed and becomes law, which occurs on the day of royal assent.

1-80. These time lags can create a somewhat difficult situation in which returns for a particular taxation year must sometimes be filed prior to the actual passage of the legislation relevant to that year. This creates an interesting dilemma, because the CRA cannot enforce the new law until it has received royal assent. Taxpayers, however, are encouraged to follow and apply the new law as if it had been passed. On January 1, 1990, the federal government introduced ITA 221.1, which is a rule that charges taxpayers interest on additional taxes that would have arisen from the date the legislation was announced. This measure is designed to encourage taxpayers to follow the new or revised law even though it is not yet in force.

Income Tax Regulations (ITR)

1-81. The ITA contains over 400 pages of regulations and supporting schedules that provide much of the detail necessary to support many of the provisions of the ITA. The legislative structure is identical to that discussed in Paragraph 1-69 under the heading "Structure of the ITA." Identifying whether an ITR is applicable is generally a straightforward effort. Simply look for either the word "prescribed" or "regulation" in a provision of the ITA.

1-82. Common examples of provisions of the ITR include the Part II rules on payroll deductions, information returns, and slips that must be issued (e.g., T4 employment slips); the Part XI details of capital cost allowance classes (CCA is the income tax equivalent to accounting depreciation and depletion); and the Part LVII (62) list of allowable medical devices and equipment for the medical expense tax credit.

1-83. ITA 221 allows the Governor in Council to make regulations concerning the administration and enforcement of the ITA. This is a much simpler and faster legislative process than what is required for the ITA. ITA 221 provides considerable flexibility, allowing the following to be included in the ITR:

- prescribing the evidence required to establish facts relevant to assessments under this Act;
- requiring any class of persons to make information returns respecting any class of information required in connection with assessments under this Act;
- prescribing anything that, by this Act, is to be prescribed or is to be determined or regulated by regulation; and
- defining the classes of persons who may be regarded as dependent for the purposes of this Act.

International Tax Treaties and Tax Information Exchange Agreements (TIEA)

1-84. Canada currently has over 100 tax treaties with countries that are either in force, signed but not yet in force, or undergoing negotiation or renegotiation. The most important of these are the treaty with the United States. While there is some variation between treaties, for the most part they are quite similar and are based on the model convention developed by the Organisation for Economic Co-operation and Development (OECD).

1-85. The purpose of tax treaties is twofold. First, they impose measures on countries to avoid double taxation where a person is liable for income tax on the same income in both of the countries that are party to the treaty. Second, they are used to create an exchange of information for the purposes of combating tax evasion. In situations where there is a conflict between the ITA and a tax treaty, the terms of the tax treaty override the ITA.

1-86. Tax treaties, as a rule, exist with respect to countries with which Canada regularly conducts business. In terms of tax avoidance and evasion, however, the concern is with countries in which Canada does not have a tax treaty, particularly where those countries are labelled as "tax havens." Tax haven countries are often defined as politically and economically stable countries, with flexible access, with little or no tax, and that do not share information with foreign tax authorities.

1-87. To address the difficulties of obtaining information in these tax haven countries, the federal government has entered into 30 TIEAs that are either in force, signed but not yet in force, or under negotiation. Examples include the Bahamas, the Cayman Islands, Panama, and the Isle of Man. In case you were wondering why these countries have agreed to share information with Canada concerning Canadian residents, it is because Canada has agreed to allow preferential tax treatment for investments by Canadians to those countries. This preferential treatment is normally restricted to countries with which Canada has negotiated a tax treaty. Chapter 20 will provide additional discussion of Canada's tax treaties, with special attention given to the Canada/U.S. tax treaty.

Income Tax Application Rules (ITAR)

1-88. Capital gains were not taxed prior to 1972. When the law changed in 1972 a large number of transitional rules were required, primarily to ensure that the effects of the new legislation were not retroactive. While their significance diminishes as time passes, they continue to have limited relevance today.

Other Sources of Income Tax Information

Electronic Library Resources

1-89. As noted in Paragraph 1-62, most tax practitioners rely on an electronic library for their tax reference materials.

CRA Website

1-90. The CRA has an extensive website at www.canada.ca/en/services/taxes. Almost all of the forms, guides, income tax folios, interpretation bulletins, and other documents provided by the CRA that are described in the following paragraphs are available on the website. The forms and publications can be viewed and printed online or downloaded in one or more formats. The website is constantly being expanded to provide more forms and publications, other informative content, and more personalized information on a taxpayer's various tax accounts.

CRA Publications

1-91. The CRA provides several publications to the public that, while they do not have the force of law, can be extremely helpful and influential in making decisions related to income taxes. These can be described as follows:

Income Tax Folios In 2013, the CRA introduced a new type of technical publication, called income tax folios. Their goal is to update the information contained in outdated interpretation bulletins. The income tax folios are organized into seven series, with each series divided into folios that contain chapters on specific topics. For example, under Series 1, Individuals, Folio 1 is titled "Health and Medical," and Chapter 1 covers the "Medical Expense Tax Credit." This chapter is designated S1-F1-C1, which stands for Series 1, Folio 1, Chapter 1. To date, progress has been very slow, with many important areas not yet covered.

Interpretation Bulletins As noted, over 500 interpretation bulletins were issued by the CRA prior to 2013 on a wide range of topics. The objective of these bulletins was to give the CRA's interpretative guidance on a range of commonly encountered situations of interest to tax practitioners. Currently, bulletins have either been canceled outright or are noted as having "archived content." Canceled bulletins are no longer valid, whereas archived bulletins continue to be of some limited use, depending on the circumstances.

Information Circulars While over 300 of these circulars have been issued, there are currently less than 60 in effect. The objective of these publications is to provide information regarding administrative and procedural matters.

Guides The CRA publishes a large number of technical and non-technical guides that provide information on particular topics of interest to taxpayers. Examples of guides are "Employed or Self-employed?" (RC4110) and "Students and Income Tax" (P105).

CRA News Releases, Tax Tips, and Fact Sheets The CRA publishes news releases on a variety of subjects, such as prescribed interest rates, program updates including EFILE, and maximum pensionable earnings. They also provide information on when monthly payments will be released under the Canada Child Benefit system and when quarterly payments will be released under the GST/HST tax credit program. Some of the news releases take the form of questions and answers, while others deal with the subject in some depth.

Advance Income Tax Rulings and Technical Interpretations In recognition of the considerable complexity involved in the interpretation of many provisions of the ITA, the Income Tax Rulings Directorate of the CRA will, for a fee, provide an Advance Income Tax Ruling on how it will interpret a proposed transaction, subject to certain limitations and qualifications. Advance Income Tax Rulings are available to the public, but only in severed format with much of the relevant information that may permit identification of the parties deleted. The result is that such publications are of questionable value for all taxpayers. The Income Tax Rulings Directorate of the CRA also provides both written and telephone technical interpretations to the public (other than for proposed transactions, where an Advance Income Tax Ruling is required) free of charge. Such interpretations, however, are not considered binding on the CRA. In general, such interpretations are often in the form of general advice and guidance.

Income Tax Technical News Prior to 2012, the CRA issued technical newsletters titled *Income Tax Technical News*, which provided up-to-date information on important, current tax issues. None have been issued since 2011 and existing newsletters are being canceled as new income tax folios are gradually incorporating their content.

Court Decisions

1-92. Despite the huge volume of information available for dealing with income tax matters, disputes between taxpayers and the CRA regularly find their way into the Canadian court system. Of the hundreds of tax cases that are reported each year, the great majority do not involve tax evasion or other criminal offences. Rather, they involve an honest difference of opinion between the taxpayer and the CRA, often based on a misunderstanding of the facts. Common areas of litigation include:

- the deductibility of both business and employment-related expenses;
- whether an individual is working as an employee or an independent contractor;
- establishing a property's fair market value;
- the question of whether a transaction took place at arm's length;
- the deductibility of legal fees and support payments; and
- distinguishing between profits that are capital in nature and those that are ordinary business income.

1-93. With the large number of court cases and the fact that they cover the great majority of issues that might arise in the application of income tax legislation, attention must be given to any precedential value established by the courts. While court decisions cannot be used to change the actual tax law, court decisions may call into question the interpretation of the ITA made by either the CRA or tax practitioners. Given the volume and complexity of court cases on income tax, we will cite only very important cases in our coverage of the various subjects in this text. However, a careful review of all relevant case material would be essential in researching any income tax issue.

We suggest you complete SSP 1-4 and 1-5 at this point.

Liability for Part I Income Tax

Residency Overview

1-94. The ITA contains 49 parts with many establishing a specific tax on a specific person determined using a base specific to that part. Examples of different parts of the ITA follow:

- Part IV imposes a tax on resident private corporations of 38-1/3% on taxable dividends received.
- Part XIII imposes a tax on non-resident persons for certain payments made by a Canadian resident.
- Part I.2 imposes a tax on individuals receiving Old Age Security (OAS) as a means of recovering some or all of the receipts where they have made too much income in a year.
- Part X.1 charges a tax as a form of penalty for those individuals who have overcontributed to their RRSPs.

  The common thread running through each of these and other parts of the ITA is that they stand alone and separate from other parts. In addition, they clarify who is subject to the tax, the tax base, and the tax rates.

1-95. The focus of this chapter and much of the text is on Part I tax. We have already established that the main taxable entities are individuals, corporations, and trusts that are not tax exempt. Those particular entities are only liable for tax under Part I, however, if they fall within the provisions of ITA 2. There are two mutually exclusive concepts and therefore two sets of general rules that apply in establishing liability:

ITA 2(1): Residents of Canada are subject to tax under Part I on all of their income regardless of where it is earned. This is referred to as "Worldwide Income."

ITA 2(3): Non-Residents of Canada are only subject to tax under Part I if they are (1) employed in Canada, (2) carry on business in Canada, or (3) have disposed of "taxable Canadian property."

It is notable that investment-type income earned in Canada by non-residents, while not subject to Part I tax, is taxable under Part XIII of the ITA. This is discussed further in Chapter 20.

The key to determining liability under Part I is the concept of "residency."

1-96. Before we begin our discussion, there are a few additional points to keep in mind in understanding residency. Residency is determined on either a factual basis, which looks to the facts to determine, in broad terms in the case of individuals, the place you call home. The underlying theory to both is that income tax should be payable by individuals who use both resources within a country and services offered by its government in the course of a given year. You can also be considered a deemed resident, but this requires legislation to that effect. ITA 250 contains the residency deeming rule that considers persons to be resident when certain conditions or tests are met.

1-97. While there are additional complexities we will examine in Chapter 20, the final point to keep in mind as you read through this material is that factual residency differs between individuals, corporations, and trusts. Individuals can live in a home in a specific country, which is a factor in determining factual residency. Corporations and trusts, however, do not have a home in that same sense. Corporations and trusts can be established and created in almost any country, therefore the place where the entity is created is largely ignored for factual residency purposes. Instead the courts will look to the decision-making authority and where decisions to guide that entity are made. This means that generally you would look to where board of director meetings are held for corporations and where trustee decisions are made with respect to trusts.

Part I Liability for Canadian Residents

1-98. We briefly mentioned the two provisions of ITA 2 and how one applies to establish liability under Part I for residents while the other applies to non-residents. We will now look at the ITA in a little more detail. ITA 2(1) reads as follows:

ITA 2(1) An income tax shall be paid, as required by this Act, on the taxable income for each taxation year of every person resident in Canada at any time in the year.

1-99. There are several terms used in this provision that require further explanation:

Person The word "person" is defined in ITA 248(1) and essentially means individuals, corporations, or trusts, whether or not exempt from tax. You can see that this is consistent with the description of "taxable entities." The word "taxpayer" would apply to individuals, corporations, or trusts as long as they are not tax exempt.

Resident ITA 2(1) also establishes that only residents of Canada are liable for Canadian income tax under Part I. Canada does not tax on the basis of citizenship, as does the United States. We would note that individuals with Canadian citizenship are not automatically factual or deemed residents of Canada. When completing exercises, problems, or exams we encourage you to avoid the use of the term "citizen" to refer to residents since they are not the same.

Taxation Year The term "taxation year" is defined in ITA 249(1). The general rule, which applies to all individuals and to trusts (except what are called "Graduated Rate Estates" (GRE)) is that the taxation year is the calendar year of January 1 to December 31. There are, however, two exceptions to this general rule:

Corporations ITA 249(1)(a) defines the taxation year of a resident corporation as its "fiscal period." ITA 249.1 defines a "fiscal period" as a period for which its accounts are made up, adding that the period cannot exceed 53 weeks. This means that the corporation can adopt the calendar year as its taxation year, but it is not obliged to do so. You may wonder why a fiscal period can be more than 52 weeks. The reason is that many corporations complete inventory counts at year end based on a certain day of the week. The law recognizes that, as a result, the length of a fiscal period may vary each year.

Graduated Rate Estates (GRE) A GRE is a trust that arises at the time of an individual's death. Such trusts can continue for up to 36 months after the date of death and, during that 36-month period, such trusts can use a non-calendar-based taxation year. A GRE is also eligible for the same graduated tax rates that apply to individuals, but only for the same 36-month period. GREs are discussed in Chapter 19, "Trusts and Estate Planning."

Taxable Income In our introduction to this chapter we provided a four-step methodology to determine the Part I tax liability or refund. The second step is determining taxable income. You can now see that it is ITA 2(2) that defines taxable income as follows:

ITA 2(2) The taxable income of a taxpayer for a taxation year is the taxpayer's income for the year plus the additions and minus the deductions permitted by Division C.

Net Income The reference to "income" means ITA 3. The income tax return uses the expression "net income" while many prefer to call it "net income for tax purposes." In this text we will use the expression "net income" when referring to ITA 3 but will use the expression "net income for tax purposes" when it is necessary to differentiate between net income for ITA purposes and accounting income. The determination of taxable income begins with net income and then certain amounts, specifically listed in Division C, are added or subtracted. The process of converting net income to taxable income will be given detailed attention in Chapter 11.

Part I Liability for Non-Residents

1-100. ITA 2(3) is the second provision in the ITA. It establishes Part I liability for non-residents of Canada and reads as follows:

ITA 2(3) Where a person who is not taxable under subsection (1) for a taxation year

(a) was **employed** in Canada,
(b) carried on a **business** in Canada, or
(c) disposed of a **taxable Canadian property**,

at any time in the year or a previous year, an income tax shall be paid, as required by this Act, on the person's taxable income earned in Canada for the year determined in accordance with Division D.

1-101. As noted, we will give very limited attention to the taxation of non-residents in this chapter. The comments in this chapter are very general and do not take into consideration the many complexities that exist in this area. In particular, the significant influence that tax treaties with other countries can have on the taxation of non-residents is given only limited consideration in this chapter. Detailed consideration of the issues associated with the taxation of non-residents, under Part I as well as other parts of the ITA, can be found in Chapter 20.

Employment Income Earned in Canada by Non-Residents

1-102. As the term is used in ITA 2(3)(a), Canadian employment income refers to income earned by a non-resident while working as an employee in Canada, generally without regard to the location of the employer. An example of this would be a U.S. citizen who is a resident of Detroit, Michigan, but is employed at an automobile plant in Windsor, Ontario. Such an individual would, in general, be subject to Canadian income tax on her Canadian employment income. However, as the individual is a non-resident, her other sources of income, such as interest earned in a U.S. bank account, would not be taxable in Canada.

Business Income Carried on in Canada by Non-Residents

1-103. The second situation in which non-residents are subject to Canadian taxes is specified in ITA 2(3)(b). This paragraph indicates that persons who carried on business in Canada during a taxation year are subject to Canadian taxes on the profits generated in that business. Some of the difficulties associated with applying this provision are related to determining what constitutes a business, the "carrying on of a business," and identifying where that business is being carried on. We will discuss this further in Chapter 6.

1-104. There are a few additional issues that must be resolved before concluding that a non-resident is carrying on a business in Canada. Some of the more significant concerns are whether the non-resident is operating his own business or acting for another's business as an employee or as a self-employed contractor. In addition, most income tax treaties only allow Canada to tax business profits under Part I if the business is carried on through a "permanent establishment," which is a defined term in tax treaties. Tax treaty concerns are discussed in Chapter 20.

Dispositions of Taxable Canadian Property by Non-Residents

1-105. ITA 2(3)(c) sets out the third situation in which non-residents are liable for Part I tax. This provision reads that non-residents are liable to Part I tax on gains resulting from the disposition of "taxable Canadian property."

1-106. Taxable Canadian property is defined in ITA 248(1) and discussed more completely in Chapter 20. However, you should note at this point that the major inclusions are:

- real property situated in Canada (e.g., land and buildings);
- certain capital property and inventories of a business carried on in Canada;
- a share of an unlisted corporation (e.g., generally private corporations), an interest in a partnership, or an interest in a trust if, at any time within the preceding 60 months, more than 50% of the fair market value of the share or interest was derived from certain properties, including Canadian real property, Canadian resource properties, and timber resource properties;
- a share of a listed corporation (e.g., generally public corporations) only if, at any time within the preceding 60 months, at least 25% of the issued shares of any class were owned by the non-resident taxpayer and/or non-arm's length persons, and more than 50% of the shares' fair market value was derived from certain properties, including Canadian real property, Canadian resource properties, and timber resource properties.

  The third and fourth items result in gains on investments in corporations, trusts, and partnerships owned by non-residents being subject to Part I tax where those entities hold significant amounts of Canadian real estate, resource properties (e.g., oil, gas, mineral rights), and timber resources.

1-107. This provision means that if a resident of the state of Washington sells a vacation property that she owns in Whistler, British Columbia, any gain on that sale will be subject to Canadian taxation.

1-108. To help solve the problems arising from difficulties associated with collecting taxes from non-residents, ITA 116(5) indicates that, if there is a gain from the sale of taxable Canadian property by a non-resident, the person purchasing the property is responsible for collecting an estimate of the required taxes (see Chapter 20 for a discussion of the requisite 25% withholding tax). Exceptions to this occur if:

- the purchaser had no reason to believe that the seller of the property was a non-resident;
- the minister (e.g., CRA) has issued a clearance certificate indicating that the non-resident has made arrangements for paying the taxes.

Property Income Earned by Non-Residents

1-109. As mentioned earlier, the liability provisions of ITA 2 do not apply to non-residents under Part I for investment-type income or what is called "income from property" earned in Canada (e.g., rents, interest, dividends, or royalties). This type of income is subject to Canadian income tax, but it is as a withholding tax under Part XIII rather than tax under Part I. Part XIII applies a flat rate of 25% based on the amount paid to the non-resident. Tax treaties frequently reduce this rate to below 25% and sometimes to zero. It is therefore prudent to determine whether the non-resident is a resident of a country with which Canada has a tax treaty.

1-110. ITA 215 of Part XIII requires the Canadian resident payor to withhold the standard 25% tax, which is based on the full amount of that payment. Failure to withhold may result in penalties being charged together with interest. These situations can sometimes present difficulties for those who were unaware that they were dealing with a non-resident. If, for example, you were renting a home in Canada owned by a non-resident and making payments directly to the non-resident owner, you would be required to withhold 25% of the rent and remit it to the CRA. Fortunately there are steps that can be taken to mitigate this risk, which are discussed in Chapter 20.

Exercise 1-5

Subject: Non-Resident Liability for Tax

Ms. Laurie Lacombe, a U.S. citizen, has Canadian employment income of $22,000. She lives in Blaine, Washington, and is a resident of the United States for the entire year. Ms. Lacombe does not believe that she is subject to taxation in Canada. Is she correct? Explain your conclusion, ignoring the Canada/U.S. tax treaty.

Solutions to Exercises are available in the Study Guide.

Residence

Importance and Overview

1-111. In our discussion of liability for Part I tax we learned that taxable entities (e.g., individuals, corporations, and trusts) are liable on their worldwide income if they are resident in Canada in the year. Alternatively, if the person is not resident in Canada (e.g., a non-resident), liability for Part I tax will only apply to Canadian employment income, Canadian business income, and gains on the disposition of taxable Canadian property. The key factor to being subject to Part I tax therefore rests with determining if a person is or is not a resident.

1-112. Residency is mentioned in the ITA 300 times, with another 100 occurrences in the regulations (ITR), but there is little in the way of legislative explanation to provide you with a sufficient and complete understanding of this important concept. Residency concepts originate with the courts, within the ITA to a limited degree specifically through ITA 250, and in Canada's income tax treaties. In addition, the CRA provides guidance in determining the residence of an individual in Folio S5-F1-C1. Understanding residency, however, begins with an awareness of the three general types of residency.

Figure 1-4
Residency Concepts

Type of Residency	Source
Factual	Jurisprudence
Deemed resident	ITA 250
Deemed non-resident	Tax treaties and ITA 250(5)

1-113. The three types of residency are (1) factual residence or what some call common-law residency, (2) deemed residency, and (3) deemed non-residency.

1-114. Factual residency was developed by the Supreme Court of Canada in a precedent-setting decision in 1946 called the Thomson case. The court said that residency was "a matter of degree to which a person in mind and fact settles into or maintains or centralizes his ordinary mode of living with its accessories in social relations, interest and conveniences at or in the place of question." This means effectively looking to the place where individuals call home. The factors considered in determining factual residency are discussed in the following paragraphs.

1-115. Deemed residency requires legislation such as ITA 250. Its purpose is to treat a person as a resident when they are not factually resident. The specific situations that deem a person to be a resident are discussed in the following paragraphs, but suffice it to say that one could be deemed to be a Canadian resident for income tax purposes if she has spent too many days in Canada, is employed outside of Canada by the Canadian government, or is a family member of Canadian government employees located outside of Canada.

1-116. Deemed non-residency is a tax treaty concept with a connection to the ITA where a person is a resident of both Canada and a country with which Canada has an income tax treaty (e.g., a dual resident). Tax treaties contain what are referred to as tie-breaker rules, the result of which is to treat the person as a resident of only one of the two countries. If, for example, the Canada/U.S. tax treaty considered a dual resident person to be a U.S. resident only, then he would be considered to be a non-resident of Canada even though he was a factual or deemed resident of Canada.

1-117. The three residency concepts are summarized in Figure 1-4.

Factual Residence of Individuals

General Concept

1-118. For the average Canadian individual whose job, family, dwelling, and other personal property are all located in Canada, the concept of residence is not at all ambiguous. Such individuals would clearly be Canadian residents and, as a result, they would be liable for Part I Canadian taxation on their worldwide income. Short departures from the country for holidays or business purposes would not generally have any effect on this conclusion.

1-119. However, for a growing number of individuals, the question of residence is more complex. It is also an important question. As tax rates and tax rules in different countries vary tremendously, the location of a person's residence can have a significant impact on the amount of taxes that will have to be paid.

1-120. As previously mentioned the concept of factual residency has been developed by the courts and not the ITA. The CRA has issued guidance in Income Tax Folio S5-F1-C1, "*Determining an Individual's Residence.*" The guidance applies the jurisprudence that has looked to the factors that one would expect to see if an individual calls Canada her home in the sense that she has centralized her mode of living, social relations, and so on. You will see that the most important factors are actually living in Canada or at least having a place to stay as well as raising a family.

From the CRA's perspective, residency becomes an issue when resident Canadian individuals want to sever their residential connection with Canada and establish residency in another country, particularly where that other country would charge less tax. The most generally applicable statement on this issue can be found in the folio as follows:

> **Paragraph 1.10** The most important factor to be considered in determining whether an individual leaving Canada remains resident in Canada for tax purposes is whether the individual maintains residential ties with Canada while abroad. While the residence status of an individual can only be determined on a case by case basis after taking into consideration all of the relevant facts, generally, unless an individual severs all significant residential ties with Canada upon leaving Canada, the individual will continue to be a factual resident of Canada and subject to Canadian tax on his or her worldwide income.

1-121. The CRA assesses the ongoing existence of connections to Canada and where those connections are significant, particularly residential ties, they are reluctant to concede that an individual has severed Canadian residency and become a non-resident. Residency analysis, however, is rarely that straightforward. In terms of severing residency intent plays a key role, but because of the difficulty of evaluating an individual's true intention, the CRA and the courts resort to objective verifiable evidence such as "residential ties," which are broken down into primary and secondary categories.

1-122. Paragraph 1.11 of Folio S5-F1-C1 goes on to point out that the ties that will almost always be considered significant are:

> **Dwelling** If an individual maintains a dwelling place in Canada, it will generally result in the individual being considered a resident. One possible exception to this rule would be when an individual who leaves Canada rents out a former dwelling place to an arm's-length party (e.g., a stranger) for an extended period of time. In this type of situation, owning a Canadian residence may not be considered a significant residential tie.
>
> **Spouse or Common-Law Partner** If an individual has a spouse or common-law partner who remains in Canada, it will generally result in the individual being considered a Canadian resident. An exception would be when the individual was living separate or apart from the spouse or common-law partner as a result of a breakdown in the relationship prior to the departure from Canada.
>
> **Dependants** If an individual has dependants, such as minor children, who remain in Canada, it will weigh in favour of the individual being considered a Canadian resident.

1-123. Folio S5-F1-C1 also refers to secondary residential ties. These are used by the courts in support of existing significant residential ties. Paragraph 1.14 lists the following examples of secondary residential ties:

- personal property in Canada (such as furniture, clothing, automobiles, and recreational vehicles);
- social ties with Canada (such as memberships in Canadian recreational or religious organizations);
- economic ties with Canada (such as employment with a Canadian employer and active involvement in a Canadian business, and Canadian bank accounts, retirement savings plans, credit cards, and securities accounts);
- landed immigrant status or appropriate work permits in Canada;
- hospitalization and medical insurance coverage from a province or territory of Canada;
- a driver's licence from a province or territory of Canada;
- a vehicle registered in a province or territory of Canada;
- a seasonal dwelling place in Canada or a leased dwelling place;
- a Canadian passport; or
- memberships in Canadian unions or professional organizations.

1-124. Secondary residential ties by themselves are never sufficient to establish residency. Such ties are often used in an analysis where the facts suggest that an individual may have strong residency ties to two countries and additional factors are necessary to arrive at a decision.

Exercise 1-6

Subject: Residential Ties

At the end of the current year, Simon Farr departed from Canada in order to take a permanent position in Ireland. He was accompanied by his wife and children, as well as all of his personal property. Due to depressed real estate prices in his region, he was unable to sell his residence at a satisfactory price. However, he was able to rent it *to a complete stranger* for a period of two years. He also retained his membership in CPA (Chartered Public Accountants) Ontario. After his departure, would he still be considered a Canadian resident for tax purposes? Explain your conclusion.

Solutions to Exercises are available in the Study Guide.

Temporary Absences

1-125. Many of the problems associated with establishing residency involve situations where an individual leaves Canada for a temporary period of time, typically one year or more. The issue here is, under what circumstances should an individual be viewed as having retained his Canadian residency status during the period of his absence from Canada?

1-126. It is important in that, if he is viewed as having retained his Canadian residency status, he will be subject to Canadian taxation on his worldwide income during the period of absence from Canada. While credits against Canadian income tax payable would usually be available for any income taxes paid on income earned in the foreign jurisdiction, the foreign taxes paid may be insufficient to cover the full Canadian tax liability where the Canadian income tax would have exceeded the foreign income tax.

1-127. Folio S5-F1-C1 makes it clear that the length of the period of time during which an individual is absent from Canada is not a determining factor with respect to residency. If an individual severs all primary and secondary residential ties, it appears that she will cease to be a Canadian resident, without regard to the length of the period of absence, unless there was some indication, based on the facts, that a return to Canada was foreseeable, An example would be a contract for a fixed period of time.

1-128. It is unusual to sever all residential ties if there is an intent to return that is foreseeable. Often only secondary ties remain, such as health cards, passports, professional memberships, and driver's licences. In these circumstances other factors are often considered. As described in Folio S5-F1-C1, these are as follows:

Intent The issue here is whether the individual intended to permanently sever residential ties with Canada. If, for example, the individual has a contract for employment, if and when he returns to Canada, this could be viewed as evidence that he did not intend to permanently depart. Another factor would be whether the individual complied with the rules related to permanent departures (i.e., as noted in Chapter 8, there is a deemed disposition of an individual's property at the time of departure from Canada, resulting in the need to pay taxes on certain gains).

Frequency of Visits If the individual continues to visit Canada on a regular and continuing basis, particularly if other secondary residential ties are present, this would suggest that she did not intend to sever Canadian residency.

Residential Ties Outside of Canada A further consideration is whether or not the individual does enough to establish residential ties with another country. The courts have stated that an individual can have more than one place of residence but, at a minimum, they must have at least one country of residence. If an individual leaves Canada and travels for an extensive period of time without settling in any one location, it will be considered as evidence that he had no intention of severing residential ties with Canada.

1-129. It is clear that there is considerable room for differences of opinion as to whether an individual has ceased to be a Canadian resident during a temporary absence from Canada. It is equally clear that the issue should be given careful attention by taxpayers who find themselves in this situation. The potential tax consequences of failing to deal properly with residency issues can be significant.

Exercise 1-7

Subject: Temporary Absences

Jane is a Canadian citizen who is employed by a multinational corporation. While she has worked for many years in the Canadian office of this organization, she agreed to transfer to the corporation's office in Florida. Before leaving, she disposed of her residence and other personal property that she did not wish to move. She canceled her Alberta driver's licence and health care card, and closed all of her Canadian banking and brokerage accounts.

Because her boyfriend remained in Edmonton, she flew back to Canada at least once a month. After 26 months, she decided that between the excessive heat and humidity in Florida and the travel required to maintain the relationship with her boyfriend, she would return to Canada. At this point, her boyfriend is not her common-law partner. Would Jane be considered a Canadian resident during the 26 months she was absent from Canada? Explain your conclusion.

Solutions to Exercises are available in the Study Guide.

Part-Year Residence

1-130. We have seen that individuals can be factually resident in Canada or can be deemed to be resident in Canada. We usually think of an individual as being resident throughout an entire year. The rules that deem individuals to be a resident deem them to be resident for the whole year. Factual residency is another matter, however, when it comes to timing. A non-resident individual can become a resident of Canada or a Canadian resident individual may sever her Canadian residency on any day within a year depending on the facts. When that happens we have what is called a "part-year" resident. Part-year resident rules apply to factual residency and not deemed residents. In addition, these rules only apply to individuals and not corporations or trusts.

1-131. The income tax consequences of part-year residency results in taking the taxation year of an individual, which as we have seen is the calendar year, and dividing it into two pieces based on the day that residency is established by a non-resident or severed by a resident. For example, if a resident Canadian individual severs residency May 27, 2021, then the part-year residency rules of ITA 114 will apply to consider the individual to be a resident from January 1, 2021, to May 26, 2021, and a non-resident from May 27, 2021, to December 31, 2021.

1-132. Determining the day when residency of an individual changes can at times be complex depending on all of the specific facts. The CRA, however, provides administrative guidance in Paragraph 1.22 of Folio S5-F1-C1 for resident Canadians severing residency and in Paragraph 1.25 of Folio S5-F1-C1 for non-resident individuals becoming resident in Canada.

1-133. Paragraph 1.22 of Folio S5-F1-C1 reads that the CRA is prepared to accept that the residency of an individual has been severed at the latest of the following:

- the date the individual leaves Canada,
- the date the spouse or common-law partner and/or other dependants of the individual leave Canada, or
- the date the individual becomes a resident of the country to which he is immigrating.

1-134. In Paragraph 1.25 of Folio S5-F1-C1 the CRA provides administrative guidance for non-resident individuals entering Canada. The CRA is willing to accept that the day that both landed immigrant status and provincial health coverage is obtained is the day that the individual becomes a Canadian resident.

1-135. Situations involving part-year residency require a fairly complex prorating of income, deductions, and personal tax credits. For example, an individual who is a resident of Canada for only part of the year will not be entitled to a full personal tax credit (see Chapter 4). The process for prorating such deductions and credits is specified in ITA 114 and ITA 118.91.

Exercise 1-8

Subject: Part-Year residence

Mark is a Canadian resident and, since graduating from university, has been employed in Vancouver. He has accepted a new position in the United States and, as of February 1 of the current year, flies to Los Angeles to assume his responsibilities. (He has been granted a green card to enable him to work in the U.S.) His wife remains behind with their children until June 15, the end of their school year. On that date, they fly to Los Angeles to join Mark. Their residence is sold on August 1 of the current year, at which time a moving company picks up their furniture and other personal possessions. The moving company delivers these possessions to their new house in Los Angeles on August 15. Explain how Mark will be taxed in Canada during the current year.

Exercise 1-9

Subject: Part-Year Residence

Mr. Jonathan Kirsh was born in Kansas and, until the current year, had lived in various parts of the United States. On September 1 of the current year he moves to Lethbridge, Alberta, to begin work at a new job. He brings his family and all of his personal property with him. However, he continues to have both a chequing and a savings account in a U.S. financial institution. Explain how Mr. Kirsh will be taxed in Canada during the current taxation year.

Solutions to Exercises are available in the Study Guide.

Sojourners and Other Deemed Residents

1-136. Individuals who are considered Canadian residents on the basis of the residential ties that we have discussed are generally referred to as factual residents. ITA 250(1) extends the meaning of resident to include certain other individuals who are considered deemed residents. It is the longstanding position of the CRA, however, that the deemed residency rules do not apply to a factual resident. We will explain the importance of this in the following paragraphs.

1-137. The deemed residency rules are important in that they broaden the scope of residents to include individuals who do not have sufficient residential ties to Canada to establish factual residency. As we shall see, an individual can be a deemed resident even if she does not set foot in Canada in the relevant taxation years.

1-138. There are two important tax consequences associated with deemed residents:

- Deemed residents are taxed on their worldwide income for the entire taxation year. This is in contrast to part-year factual residents, who are only subject to Canadian taxation for the portion of the taxation year that they are considered resident in Canada.
- Deemed residents are not factual residents of any province nor are they deemed to reside in a specific province and, as a consequence, they are not subject to provincial taxes. For purposes of horizontal equity and fairness with other Canadian taxpayers, ITA 120(1) requires deemed residents to pay an additional federal tax equal to 48% of the basic federal tax that is otherwise payable. This additional tax is designed to replace the provincial income tax.

1-139. Included on the list of deemed residents of Canada are the following:

1. Sojourners in Canada for more than half the year (183 days or more).
2. Members, at any time during the year, of the Canadian Armed Forces when stationed outside of Canada.
3. Ambassadors, ministers, high commissioners, officers, or servants of Canada, as well as agents general, officers, or servants of a province, provided they were Canadian residents immediately prior to their appointment.
4. An individual performing services, at any time in the year, in a country other than Canada under a prescribed international development assistance program of the Government of Canada, provided they were resident in Canada at any time in the three-month period preceding the day on which those services commenced.
5. A child of a deemed resident, provided they are also a dependant whose net income for the year was less than the base for the basic personal tax credit ($13,808 or less for 2021).
6. An individual who was, at any time in the year under an agreement or a convention with one or more other countries, entitled to an exemption from tax on substantially all of their income in any of those countries, because at that time the person was related to or a member of the family of an individual who was resident in Canada.

1-140. Of these items, numbers 1 and 6 require further explanation. With respect to item 1, a sojourner is an individual who is temporarily present in Canada for more than half of a regular 365-day calendar year, which is a period of 183 days or more during any one calendar year. The days do not have to be consecutive but are cumulative. If the 183-day limit is met, the individual will be deemed to be a Canadian resident for the entire year.

1-141. For the sojourner rule to apply, the individual must be a factual resident of another country during the 183 days in question. This means that an individual who severs his residence in another country and moves to Canada, becoming a factual resident, early in a taxation year will be considered a part-year resident, not a sojourner. Correspondingly, a Canadian resident who leaves Canada, severing Canadian factual residency, to take up residence in another country on September 1 will not be a sojourner, despite the fact that he was physically present in Canada for 183 days or more in the year. As noted, this is an important distinction because the sojourner is liable for Canadian tax on his worldwide income for the entire year, not just the portion of the year when he was in Canada.

1-142. Folio S5-F1-C1 indicates that sojourning means establishing a temporary residence and would include days spent in Canada on vacation trips. The CRA considers part days to count as one full day. The folio clarifies that individuals who, for employment purposes, commute to Canada on a daily basis are not considered to be sojourning.

1-143. Item 6 refers to situations where an individual is exempt from tax in a foreign country because she is related to an individual who is a Canadian resident. For example, the spouse of a Canadian diplomat working in the United States would be exempt from U.S. income taxes under the governing international tax treaty because she is the spouse of the diplomat. As the diplomat would be a deemed resident of Canada under item 3, the spouse would be a deemed a resident of Canada under item 6. This ensures that the spouse cannot avoid both tax in the United States and in Canada.

Exercise 1-10

Subject: Individual Residency

Ms. Suzanne Blakey was born 24 years ago in Paris, France. She is the daughter of a Canadian high commissioner serving in that country. Her father still holds this position. However, Ms. Blakey is now working in London. The only income that she earns in the year is from her London marketing job and is subject to taxes in England. She has never visited Canada. Determine the residency status of Suzanne Blakey.

Solutions to Exercises are available in the Study Guide.

Individuals with Dual Residency

1-144. There are situations in which the application of the normal Canadian residency rules would result in an individual being considered a resident (factual or deemed) of more than one country. For example, a member of the Canadian Armed Forces is deemed to be a resident of Canada because of ITA 250(1), but might also be considered a resident by the country in which she is stationed based on the residency rules of that country.

1-145. In the absence of some mechanism for dealing with the problem, such an individual could be subject to double taxation, with each country of residence assessing taxes on the same income. In such situations, the presence of a tax treaty becomes crucial. These bilateral treaties contain provisions, generally referred to as tie-breaker rules, which are designed to provide relief from the potential double taxation that is inherent in dual residence situations. The tax treaty provisions resolve the issue by applying rules that deem the individuals to be resident of one of the two countries only.

1-146. Each one of Canada's tax treaties includes legislation referred to as a "Conventions Act." One of the provisions of that Act includes a rule that states where there is an inconsistency between the ITA and the tax treaty, the tax treaty will prevail, thereby overriding the ITA. If the tie-breaker rules deem the individual not to be a resident of Canada, then ITA 250(5) will apply to deem that individual to be a non-resident of Canada. As a result the individual would only be liable to Part I tax under ITA 2(3), which limits Canada's ability to tax that individual to Canadian employment income, Canadian business income, and from dispositions of taxable Canadian property. Even though Canada has the right to tax non-residents on these types of income, it is important to be aware that the tax treaty may again override Canada's ability to actually tax these amounts.

1-147. As an example of a typical set of tie-breaker rules, the Canada/U.S. tax treaty resolves the dual residency problem for individuals by examining a list of factors. These factors are required to be applied in the following order:

Permanent Home If the individual has a permanent home available in only one country, the individual will be considered a resident of that country. A permanent home means a dwelling, rented or purchased, that is continuously available at all times. The dwelling could be part of a home, such as a furnished room. For this purpose, a home that would only be available occasionally for a temporary period would not be considered a permanent home. A home that is rented to third-party arm's-length persons (e.g., strangers) for an extended period of time would not be considered a permanent home since the home would not be available for occupation by the owner.

Centre of Vital Interests If the individual has permanent homes in both countries, or in neither, then the next step in the analysis is to look to the country in which the individual's personal and economic relations are greatest. Such relations are identical in many respects to the residential-type ties that are examined when determining factual residence.

Habitual Abode If the first two tests do not yield a determination, then the country where the individual spends more time will be considered the country of residence. The number of days spent in each country is often used in applying this test.

Citizenship If the above three tie-breaker rules still fail to resolve the issue, then the individual will be considered a resident of the country in which the individual is a citizen.

Competent Authority If none of the preceding tests resolve the question of residency then, as a last resort, the so-called "competent authority procedures" are used. Without describing them in detail, these procedures are aimed at opening a dialogue between the two countries for the purpose of resolving the conflict.

Residence vs. Citizenship

1-148. While Canada assesses taxes on the basis of residence, a small number of countries base the liability for tax on citizenship. Of particular importance in this regard is the United States. It is estimated that there are in excess of 1 million U.S. citizens residing in Canada. In the absence of mitigating legislation, such individuals would be taxed twice on most types of income.

1-149. Fortunately, the Canada/U.S. tax treaty provides for this situation. In simplified terms, such individuals are allowed to claim an exemption from U.S. tax on income that the tax treaty only allows Canada to tax. With respect to other income, the individuals are allowed to credit Canadian taxes paid against their U.S. income tax liability. Since Canadian taxes on individuals are generally higher than U.S. taxes, crediting Canadian income taxes on a given amount of income will often eliminate the U.S. income tax liability.

1-150. Despite the fact that the balance owing to the United States is usually nil, U.S. citizens who are Canadian residents must file a U.S. tax return each year. If this important requirement is overlooked, it can lead to significant difficulties with U.S. tax authorities. An option to avoid this result is to renounce U.S. citizenship, which must be carefully considered.

Residency of Individuals—The General Analysis

1-151. There is a five-step analysis that can be applied to determine residency for individuals:

1. Determine if the individual is either a factual or deemed resident of Canada.
2. Determine if the individual is a resident of another country (e.g., dual resident) and therefore liable for tax in that country.
3. If the individual is a resident of another country, then determine if it is a country with which Canada has an income tax treaty.
4. If Canada has a tax treaty with that other country, then apply the tie-breaker rules.
5. If the tie-breaker rules result in the individual being a resident of the other country, then the individual will be deemed a non-resident of Canada by ITA 250(5); otherwise, the individual will be a resident of Canada.

The complete analysis is only necessary if you are dealing with a dual resident of a treaty country. If, for example, the individual was a factual resident of Canada and not resident in another country, then only the first step would need to be completed.

Exercise 1-11

Subject: Dual Residency—Individuals

Using the tie-breaker rules of the Canada/U.S. treaty, determine the resident status of Dizzy and Donna for 2021 in the following two cases:

Case 1 Dizzy Jones is a saxophone player from Los Angeles who has always lived in the United States. He is not married or living common law with anyone. He decides to spend some time in Canada and arrives in Vancouver on May 5, 2021, looking for work in various nightclubs. A friend watches his home in Los Angeles while he is gone. He lives in boarding rooms and hotels throughout his time in Canada and returns to Los Angeles on February 14, 2022.

Case 2 Donna, a U.S. citizen, lives in the state of New York. In the fall of 2020, while attending a business convention in Toronto, she met Donald. They decided to get married the following year and live permanently in the United States as soon as Donald could arrange his business affairs in Canada. In December 2020, Donna took an eight-month leave of absence from her job and gave notice to her landlord. On January 1, 2021, Donna and Donald moved in together, sharing an apartment in Toronto, which was leased on a monthly basis while Donald finalized his business affairs. In August 2021, they terminated the lease and returned to New York where they were married and purchased a house.

Solutions to Exercises are available in the Study Guide.

We suggest you complete SSP 1-6, 1-7, and 1-8 at this point.

Residence of Corporations

Factual Residency

1-152. Corporations are taxable entities and are subject to Part I tax on the same basis as individuals, meaning that we need to establish liability based on the same residency concepts that apply to individuals. In the same manner as individuals, corporations can be factual residents, deemed residents, and deemed non-residents in the case of dual residency. The source for these three residency concepts is identical to that of individuals. The CRA has two folios dealing with residency—one for individuals and a second for trusts. Currently there are no folios dealing with corporate residency.

1-153. In determining factual residence of an individual we looked to many factors, such as a home, family, social relations, and so on. A corporation, however, does not reside anywhere in the same physical sense that the term applies to an individual. In determining factual residency for corporations we again must briefly turn our attention to the case law. The precedent-setting case used in Canada is the British case of DeBeers Consolidated Mines heard more than a hundred years ago in 1906. The relevant comment that answers the question of factual residence is as follows:

> A company cannot eat or sleep, but it can keep house and do business. We ought, therefore, to see where it really keeps house and does business... a company resides for purposes of income tax where its real business is carried on. I regard that as the true rule, and the real business is carried on where the central management and control actually abides.

1-154. The jurisprudence requires identifying the person or body of persons responsible for making the major decisions of a corporation related to things such as policy, strategy, and overall management. This would not include day-to-day management decisions. The determination of this factual residency for a corporation in Canada is referred to as "mind and management," the "directing mind," or "central management and control" (CMC). There are two steps in identifying who has CMC. It is important to remember that the actual place where a corporation is incorporated is not relevant when determining factual residence. In addition, the fact that a corporation carries on business in a country is also not relevant for determining residency.

1-155. The first step requires looking to who is responsible for the CMC. Corporate law provides that decision-making authority rests with a corporation's board of directors. The second step requires determining where the board of directors exercise their control. To illustrate, assume that a company incorporated in the Bahamas has a board of directors composed of three members, two of whom are resident in Canada and the third resident in the United States. If decisions are made at board of director meetings held in Canada every six months, then that would mean that the CMC is exercised in Canada. If instead the two Canadian directors fly to the U.S. to meet with the U.S. director in the U.S, then the CMC would be in the U.S. Attendance at a board of director meeting by telephone, video-conferencing, or any other means where the board members physically remain in their country would be the same as if the meeting were held partly in Canada and partly in the U.S. In this case, since two of the three directors (e.g., a majority) reside in Canada, CMC would be considered to be in Canada with the result that the Bahamas corporation would be a factual resident of Canada.

Deemed Residency

1-156. The rules of the ITA that deem a corporation to be a resident of Canada can be found at ITA 250(4). There are only two rules worth mentioning. The first and most important is that every company incorporated in Canada after April 26, 1965, is deemed to be a resident of Canada. Canada has ten provinces and three territories, each with their own corporate law. In addition, a company can be incorporated federally under the *Canada Business Corporations Act*. This means that, in Canada, there are 14 different corporate law statutes under which a corporation can be created or incorporated.

1-157. The second deeming rule refers to a company that is incorporated in Canada before April 27, 1965. Those companies are not automatically deemed to be residents of Canada unless one of two tests are met. The tests require that, at any time after April 26, 1965, the company either carried on business in Canada or was a factual resident of Canada because its CMC was in Canada. We would add that the date April 26 or 27, 1965, is only relevant for Canadian tax law and has no impact upon how other countries determine residency for purposes of their tax laws.

Dual Residency

1-158. As was the case with individuals, a corporation can be considered to be resident in more than one country. For example, a corporation that was incorporated in Canada after April 26, 1965, might have its CMC in the United States. This would make this company a dual resident—deemed resident of Canada and a factual resident of the U.S.

1-159. In the case of corporate dual residency we again must resort to the tax treaty to resolve the issue. The Canada/U.S. tax treaty provides the tie-breaker rule. The rule deems the company to only be a resident of the country in which the company was incorporated. If a company is incorporated in the United States and its CMC is in Canada, then the treaty would deem the company to be a resident of the U.S. only. ITA 250(5) would then apply for Canadian income tax purposes to deem the company (that was a factual resident of Canada) to be a non-resident. We would note that not all of Canada's tax treaties break the tie in favour of place of incorporation; some use the "effective place of management" as the test, which is similar to CMC. In this text we will continue to focus only on the tax treaty with the U.S.

Residency of Corporations—The General Analysis

1-160. As in the case with individuals there is also a five-step analysis that can be applied to determine residency for corporations as follows:

1. Determine if the corporation is either a factual or deemed resident of Canada.
2. Determine if the corporation is a resident of another country (e.g., dual resident) and therefore liable for tax in that country.
3. If the corporation is a resident of another country, then determine if it is a country with which Canada has an income tax treaty.
4. If Canada has a tax treaty with that other country, then apply the tie-breaker rules.
5. If the tie-breaker rules result in the corporation being a resident of the other country, then the company will be deemed a non-resident of Canada by ITA 250(5); otherwise, the corporation will be a resident of Canada.

The complete analysis is only necessary if you are dealing with a dual resident of a treaty country. If, for example, the company was incorporated in Canada and its CMC was also in Canada, then only the first step would need to be completed.

Exercise 1-12

Subject: Corporate Residency

Roswell Ltd. was incorporated in the state of New York in 2013. It carries on business in both the United States and Canada. However, all of the directors of the company live in Kemptville, Ontario, and, as a consequence, all of the directors' meetings are held in Kemptville. Determine the residency status of Roswell Ltd.

Exercise 1-13

Subject: Corporate Residency

Sateen Inc. was incorporated in Manitoba in 2012. However, since 2018, all of the company's business has been carried on outside of Canada. Determine the residency status of Sateen Inc.

Exercise 1-14

Subject: Dual Residency—Corporations

Using the tie-breaker rules, determine the resident status of the corporations in the following two cases:

Case 1 Taxco is a company incorporated in Nova Scotia in 2018 to hold investments in other Canadian companies. Taxco never carried on business in Canada. All the shareholders and members of the board of directors are residents of the United States. All board of directors' meetings are held in the U.S.

Case 2 Junkco is a company incorporated in Delaware in 2019. The majority of the members of the board of directors, however, reside in Montreal, where all board of directors' meetings take place. Junkco does not carry on any business in Canada.

Solutions to Exercises are available in the Study Guide.

We suggest you complete SSP 1-9 and 1-10 at this point.

Residence of Trusts

General Overview

1-161. To this point we have discussed factual, deemed, and treaty deemed non-residents for both corporations and individuals, but residency concepts are different for trusts. Aside from a few complex rules dealing with non-resident trusts there are no deemed residence rules in ITA 250 for trusts, and the likelihood of a dual residency issue is remote, which helps simplify things somewhat. This leaves us with factual residency as the one primary factor.

1-162. Prior to 2012 there was much confusion and uncertainty surrounding how to assess factual residency of a trust. In 2012 the Supreme Court of Canada, in the Fundy Settlement decision, ruled that the CMC concepts developed for corporations were to be used for trusts too. Factual residency therefore is determined on the basis of identifying who exercises the CMC of a trust.

We suggest you complete SSP 1-11 at this point.

1-163. Usually the CMC of a trust rests with and is exercised by the trustee, executor, liquidator, administrator, heir, or other legal representative of the trust. However, the residence of the trustee does not always determine the residence of a trust. For example, if trustees reside in different jurisdictions, the trust will reside where the more substantial CMC actually takes place. In addition, if a substantial portion of the CMC of the trust rests with someone other than the trustee, such as the settlor or the beneficiaries of the trust, the actions of these other persons must also be considered. It is where the CMC is factually exercised that will determine the residence of the trust.

Alternative Concepts of Income

The Economist's View

1-164. In the past, economists have viewed income as being limited to rents, profits, and wages. In general, capital gains, gratuitous receipts, and other such increases in net worth were not included. In this context, most economists perceived income to be a net concept. That is, income is equal to revenues less any related expenses.

1-165. In more recent times, the economist's concept of income has moved in the direction of including measures of net worth or capital maintenance. The oft-cited quotation "Income is the amount that can be spent during the period and still be as well off at the end of the period as at the beginning" is perhaps as good a description of the current concept as any available. This broader concept of income is based on the idea that income should include all increases in net economic power that occur during the relevant measurement period.

The Accountant's View

1-166. What we currently view as net income from an accounting point of view is the result of applying a fairly flexible group of rules that are referred to as generally accepted accounting principles (GAAP). In general, net income is determined by establishing the amount of revenue on the basis of point-of-sale revenue recognition. Then, by using a variety of cash flows, accruals, and allocations, the cost of assets used up in producing these revenues is matched against these revenues, with this total deducted to produce the accounting net income for the period.

1-167. If this same process is viewed from the perspective of the balance sheet, net income is measured as the increase in net assets for the period under consideration, plus any distributions that were made to the owners of the business during that period.

1-168. The current accounting model continues to value many assets at historical cost and records changes in value only when supported by an arm's-length transaction. This means that many of the increases in wealth that would be included in the economist's concept of income would not be included in accounting net income.

1-169. However, the gap between the two approaches is gradually being narrowed as accounting standard setters show an increased willingness to incorporate fair value measurement into their pronouncements, both with respect to balance sheet values and with respect to inclusions in net income.

The Income Tax Act—The Source Concept

1-170. The first point to keep in mind in learning income tax is that the income base upon which income tax is applied is significantly different than that of either economists or accountants. The reasons for the difference relate to the purpose. Economists apply a theoretical notion of income that examines the value of assets and services between two points in time, concluding that the increase would represent income in the broadest sense. While of academic interest, implementing such a system for income tax would not be possible. The accounting profession, on the other hand, establishes rules of presentation aimed at shareholders and other interested parties oftentimes with an emphasis on the bottom line. Income tax, however, is designed to raise tax revenues and meet certain policy objectives, such as a system of social payments and economic incentives. It is not surprising that with these different objectives the notion of "income" for income tax purposes would be quite different.

1-171. In this chapter we set out a four-step process to determine Part I tax liability or a tax refund. The first step in that process is to determine net income. Net income, or what the ITA refers to simply as "income," is effectively defined in ITA 3 by combining both income and deductions, determined in Subdivisions a to e of Division B of Part I of the ITA, in a specific manner. ITA 3 begins by referring to sources of income, which is our starting point.

1-172. Canadian income tax is based on what is referred to as a "source of income" concept that was adopted from tax law in the United Kingdom that goes back over 200 years. In everyday usage, the word "source" means the origin of a person, place, or thing, but this is not how it is used in the ITA. A source of income can be defined as a potential to generate a positive cash flow net of related expenses over a period of time from an activity produced by one's labour, capital, or property, either singly or in combination. Income that falls within this definition includes income from employment, business, and property or investment-type income.

1-173. An individual's labour is the source for employment income. Capital, labour, and property together are often the source for business income. Property such as shares, cash in a bank account, and rental properties are the source for property income such as dividends, interest, and rents. Income from a source would not include capital gains nor would it include any rights (contractual or otherwise) that a person would have to receive certain payments, such as spousal/common-law support payments or even payments from Employment Insurance, the Canada Pension Plan, or most other types of pension income.

1-174. As you can see, the source of income concept brings into net income employment, business, and property income but nothing else. When the government wishes to expand the tax base, specific legislation is required to do so. Capital gains, for example, would not be required to be included in income without the large number of rules that require capital gains and losses to be included. In addition, spousal support payments and other receipts are therefore only required to be included in income if the ITA includes provisions that specifically require them to be included in income.

1-175. There are three additional points about a "source of income" that are important to know:

> **(1) Continuity** The source concept looks to an activity over a period of time, implying that a single one-time transaction would not be a source. A single real estate flip transaction would be an example. Rules dealing with business income were specifically added to the ITA to counter this problem. We will discuss those further in Chapter 6 on business income.

(2) Capability to Generate a Positive Return The source concept requires that there is a profit motive with a capacity and potential to make money. The courts have looked to one's intention and whether the activity is undertaken in the same manner as would be expected of someone operating a successful business doing the same thing. In addition, the courts have added that the activity will not be scrutinized for lack of an actual profit as long as there is no personal interest or motivation. The fact that a profit is never realized does not mean that there is not a profit motive or a potential for a profit. "Income from a source" is an expression that looks to the underlying activity, and as a result a business loss would be considered income from a source. This issue is discussed further in Chapter 6 on business income.

(3) Income Is Determined on a Net Basis This final point ensures that any reference to income from a source means gross income minus related expenses. This concept is written into ITA 4.

1-176. In summary, net income comprises the following:

(1) Sources of income, including employment, business, and property income (Subdivisions a and b)

(2) Capital gains and losses from the disposition of capital property (Subdivision c)

(3) Other income specifically added by Subdivision d

(4) Other deductions specifically allowed by Subdivision e

If a receipt does not fall within any of categories one to three, then you are not required to include it in net income and you would not be liable for Part I tax on that amount.

Exercise 1-15

Subject: Source of Income

Indicate whether the following are "sources of income."

(1) A lottery ticket win of $10,000
(2) An inheritance of $25,000 from a family member
(3) You deposited the inheritance in a bank account and earned $600 in interest
(4) $800 in sales of surplus vegetables from your home-based garden; you and your family consume most of what you grow
(5) $48,000 in sales of vegetables from a 10-acre garden on property purchased alongside your home; you are a professional accountant; you and your family consume approximately 1.5 percent of what you grow
(6) A cash gift from friends

Solutions to Exercises are available in the Study Guide.

1-177. As you will see in the next section, ITA 3 will combine or aggregate the various components that make up what we will refer to as "net income." In this text we will use "net income" to refer to the income tax concept and "accounting income" to refer to the accounting equivalent.

Net Income

Structure and Components

1-178. Net income is effectively defined in ITA 3, which contains the basic rules for the determination of net income. There are a couple of ground rules to keep in mind about ITA 3 before we begin:

(1) The word "income" means income only and not a loss. When the ITA refers to a loss it will specifically say so. In other words, income is a positive concept. There is no such thing in income tax as a negative or even nil income unless the ITA specifically says so.

(2) Negative numbers are ignored. If there is a calculation such as $1,000 minus $4,200, the answer in income tax will be nil and not ($3,200). There is a general rule in ITA 257 that reads that negative numbers are ignored in all parts of the ITA unless the legislation says otherwise (a rare occurrence).

(3) A reference to employment, business, or property income is a net concept, meaning gross income minus allowable expenses specifically related to that source of income. As a result we will avoid referring to net employment, business, or property income or loss. The correct terminology is to simply say employment, business, or property income or loss.

(4) ITA 3 determines net income for one specific year only. This means adding 100% of all "current-year" components, whether income, losses, or deductions.

1-179. ITA 3 is made up of four main paragraphs, ITA 3(a) to 3(d). The four paragraphs are summarized as follows:

ITA 3(a) = Employment income determined in Subdivision a + business income as determined by Subdivision b + property income also determined under Subdivision b + other income specified in Subdivision d

ITA 3(b) = Taxable capital gains – allowable capital losses

ITA 3(c) = [(ITA 3(a) + ITA 3(b)) – deductions allowed under Subdivision e

ITA 3(d) = ITA 3(c) – any losses from employment, business, or property income – allowable business investment losses (ABIL). ABILs will be discussed in Chapter 8. The full amount of current-year losses must be deducted at ITA 3(d). You are not permitted to deduct a smaller amount.

ITA 3(e) and (f) conclude that if the ITA 3(d) amount is positive then that is your net income, and if the ITA 3(d) would otherwise be negative or nil then your net income is nil.

1-180. The component parts that make up net income are discussed in detail throughout most of Volume 1 of this text. To give you a basic understanding before we start to apply ITA 3 we have provided a general overview of the components as follows:

Employment Income (Loss) Employment income is made up of inclusions related to the activities of individuals who are serving as employees, such as salary, wages, stock options, and other benefits, less related deductions such as automobile and home office expenses. While it is possible to have an employment loss, this would be fairly unusual. Only individuals can earn employment income.

Business Income (Loss) Business income is made up of inclusions related to carrying on a business, such as sales and service fees, less deductions related to that activity. The business income rules are generally the same for individuals, corporations, and trusts.

Property Income (Loss) Property income is made up of inclusions related to the holding of property, less deductions related to holding such property. Examples of property income would include interest received on debt securities, dividends received on shares, and lease payments received on rental property. Note that property income does not include capital gains or capital losses, which are treated separately. While there are some differences in the rules for determining property income and those for determining business income, the calculations are sufficiently similar that they are included in a single subdivision. Like business income, property income can be earned by individuals, corporations, and trusts.

Capital Gains and Capital Losses Capital gains and losses arise when property (e.g., an asset) that has been used to earn business or property income is sold for an amount in excess of its cost. Capital gains and losses can arise on dispositions by individuals, corporations, and trusts. In Canada only one-half of capital gains are included in income and only one-half of capital losses are deductible. This has created the need for the use of special terminology. More specifically:

- The term "**taxable** capital gain" is used when referring to the taxable **one-half** of a capital gain. When the expression "capital gain" is used, it refers to 100% of the gain.
- The term "**allowable** capital loss" is used when referring to the deductible **one-half** of a capital loss. When the expression "capital loss" is used, it refers to 100% of the loss.

Unlike employment, business, and property losses, which can be deducted against any type of income, an allowable capital loss can only be deducted against taxable capital gains. Where allowable capital losses exceed taxable capital gains the excess becomes available to be claimed in other years and not the year in which those losses are realized. This will be explained in more detail in the next section.

Other Income There are some additional types of income that are largely applicable to individual taxpayers. Examples of these are receipts of pension income, spousal support, and social assistance payments.

Other Deductions These deductions do not relate to specific sources of income. As a rule they generally relate largely to individuals. Examples include spousal support paid, child care costs, moving expenses, and RRSP contributions.

Determining Net Income—Applying ITA 3

1-181. Figure 1-5 shows a graphical display of ITA 3. This rule is applied to individuals, corporations, and trusts. While some of the ideas involved in applying this formula will not be fully explained until later in the text, it is useful at this stage to provide the basic structure of this formula to enhance your understanding of how the material on the various components of net income is organized.

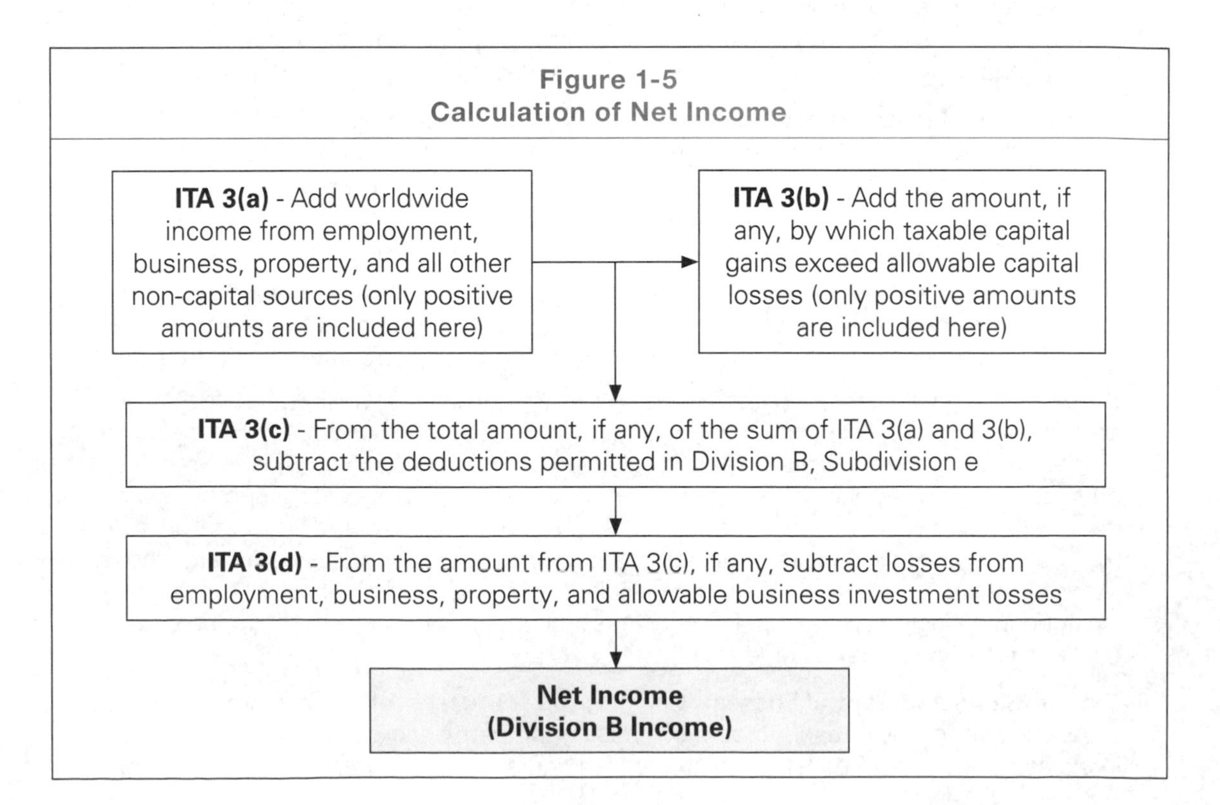

1-182. We will begin with a basic example to illustrate the concept.

> **EXAMPLE** During the current year, an individual has employment income of $25,000, taxable capital gains of $7,000, and allowable capital losses of $20,000.
>
> **ANALYSIS**
> ITA 3(a) = Employment income of $25,000
>
> ITA 3(b) = Taxable capital gains of $7,000 minus allowable capital losses of $20,000 = nil (remember that negative numbers are ignored and replaced with "nil")
>
> ITA 3(c) = ITA 3(a) $25,000 + ITA 3(b) nil – nil Subdivision e deduction = ITA 3(c) of $25,000
>
> ITA 3(d) = ITA 3(c) of $25,000 – no losses from business, employment, property and ABILs = $25,000
>
> Net income for ITA 3 = $25,000
>
> You will note that $13,000 of the allowable capital losses could not be used since there were only $7,000 of taxable capital gains. That $13,000 amount is not lost but instead becomes a "net capital loss," which can be applied against a positive ITA 3(b) amount in certain other years. This is discussed further in Chapter 11.

1-183. Let's modify the first example. We will keep employment income at $25,000 and consider that there is a new business that generated $7,000 in sales and $20,000 in expenses for a $13,000 business loss.

> **ANALYSIS**
> ITA 3(a) = Employment income of $25,000
>
> ITA 3(b) = N/A
>
> ITA 3(c) = ITA 3(a) $25,000 + ITA 3(b) nil – nil Subdivision e deduction = ITA 3(c) of $25,000
>
> ITA 3(d) = ITA 3(c) of $25,000 – business loss of $13,000 = $12,000
>
> Net income for ITA 3 = $12,000
>
> In this modified example you can see that the current-year business loss was able to be fully used against the employment income, whereas in the first example the excess allowable capital loss was restricted because it could only be deducted against taxable capital gains.

1-184. We will make one last modification to the first example to summarize issues with losses and to illustrate Subdivision e deductions such as an RRSP contribution. Assume that an individual had no employment income in 2021, but had $11,000 of allowable capital losses and $19,000 of business losses. In addition the individual had made an RRSP contribution of $5,000 that is deductible in 2021 but may be used instead in 2022 or later.

> **ANALYSIS**
> ITA 3(a) = Nil
>
> ITA 3(b) = Taxable capital gains of nil minus allowable capital losses of $11,000 = nil (remember that negative numbers are ignored and replaced with "nil")
>
> ITA 3(c) = ITA 3(a) nil + ITA 3(b) nil – $5,000 of Subdivision e deduction = ITA 3(c) of nil (again, this cannot be negative)
>
> ITA 3(d) = ITA 3(c) of nil – business loss of $19,000 = nil
>
> Net income for ITA 3 = Nil
>
> The unused allowable capital losses of $13,000 become "net capital losses" and the difference between the business loss of $19,000 and the ITA 3(c) amount of nil becomes another loss carryover of $19,000 called a "non-capital loss." Both of these loss carryovers can be deducted in other years, as will be explained in Chapter 11.

You may also have noticed that there was no benefit to deducting the RRSP contributions because this amount does not add to loss carryovers. In effect any Subdivision e deductions can only be used to the extent there is actual positive amounts of income under either or both of ITA 3(a) or (b). This can result in a loss of certain expenses such as child care expenses where one spouse has only business losses. Fortunately, in this case RRSP contributions are not required to be deducted in the year of contribution and can be carried to another future year. This is discussed in Chapter 10.

ITA 3 Net Income—Example

1-185. The following example provides an illustration of the application of ITA 3.

EXAMPLE Jonathan Morley has the following income and loss components for the year:

Employment income	$12,000
Employment Insurance (EI) benefits received	$ 6,000
Business loss (from restaurant)	(33,000)
Property loss (rental)	(7,000)
Property loss (interest expense of $5,000 accrued on funds borrowed to acquire shares.	(5,000)
No dividends were paid in the year	
Taxable capital gains	18,000
Allowable capital losses	(26,000)
Subdivision e deductions (deductible spousal support paid)	(10,000)

ANALYSIS Mr. Morley's net income would be calculated as follows:

Income under ITA 3(a):		
Net employment income	$12,000	
EI benefits received	$ 6,000	
Total ITA 3(a)		$18,000
Income under ITA 3(b):		
Taxable capital gains	$18,000	
Allowable capital losses	(26,000)	
Total ITA 3(b)		Nil
Balance from ITA 3(a) and (b)		$18,000
Subdivision e deductions		(10,000)
Balance under ITA 3(c)		$ 8,000
Business loss		(33,000)
Rental loss		(7,000)
Property loss (shares)		(5,000)
ITA 3(d) and net income (Division B income)		**Nil**

1-186. Mr. Morley's business, rental, and property loss on shares exceeds the amount calculated under ITA 3(c) by $37,000 [($33,000 + $7,000 + $5,000) – $8,000], resulting in a net income of nil. This $37,000 difference is his non-capital loss for the year, which can be applied and deducted in certain other years. In addition there is a net capital loss for the year in the amount of $8,000 ($26,000 - $18,000). Both of these loss categories will be discussed in detail along with other types of losses in Chapter 11.

1-187. The second step in determining Part I tax liability or a refund is to calculate taxable income. While this topic is discussed at length in Chapter 11, it is good to have a general awareness of it at this point. In the previous example we determined that Mr. Morley had a 2021 net capital loss of $8,000 and a 2021 non-capital loss of $37,000. Assume that, in 2022, Mr. Morley's net income was

$105,000, made up of business and employment income totaling $100,000, and $5,000 of taxable capital gains and no allowable capital losses. There were no Subdivision e deductions nor losses of any kind in 2022.

1-188. Taxable income starts with net income and deducts amounts under Division C. Loss carryovers are in Division C. Mr. Morley can deduct only $5,000 of the net capital loss since it is restricted to ITA 3(b) for the year in which the loss is applied. He can also deduct all of the non-capital loss of $37,000, which is not restricted in any manner. The result would be as follows:

2022 Net income		$105,000
Less: Division C deductions		
2021 Net capital loss	$ 5,000	
2021 Non-capital loss	37,000	42,000
2022 Taxable income		$ 63,000

Loss carryover balances available to apply to other years are:
2021 Non-capital loss balance = Nil [$37,000 – $37,000 applied to 2022]
2021 Net capital loss balance = $3,000 [$8,000 – $5,000 applied to 2022]

Exercise 1-16

Subject: Net Income

For the current year, Mr. Norris Blanton has net employment income of $42,000, a business loss of $15,000, taxable capital gains of $24,000, and Subdivision e deductions of $13,000. What is the amount of Mr. Blanton's net income for the current year?

Exercise 1-17

Subject: Net Income

For the current year, Ms. Cheryl Stodard has interest income of $33,240, taxable capital gains of $24,750, allowable capital losses of $19,500, and a net rental loss of $48,970. What is the amount of Ms. Stodard's net income for the current year? Indicate the amount and type of any loss carry overs that would be available at the end of the current year.

Exercise 1-18

Subject: Net Income

For the current year, Mrs. Marie Bergeron has net employment income of $42,680, taxable capital gains of $27,400, allowable capital losses of $33,280, Subdivision e deductions of $8,460, and a business loss of $26,326. What is the amount of Mrs. Bergeron's net income for the current year? Indicate the amount and type of any loss carry overs that would be available at the end of the current year.

Solutions to Exercises are available in the Study Guide.

We suggest you complete SSP 1-12, 1-13, 1-14, and 1-15 at this point.

Principles of Tax Planning

Introduction

1-189. Throughout this text, there will be a great deal of emphasis on tax planning and, while many of the specific techniques that are involved can only be fully explained after the more detailed provisions of tax legislation have been covered, there are some basic tax planning principles that can be described at this point.

1-190. Our objective here is simply to provide a general understanding of the results that can be achieved through tax planning so that you will be able to recognize the goal of more specific tax planning techniques when they are examined. In addition, this general understanding should enable you to identify other opportunities for tax planning as you become more familiar with this material.

1-191. The basic goals of tax planning can be summarized as follows:

- Tax avoidance or reduction
- Tax deferral
- Income splitting

1-192. While these classifications can be used to describe the goals of all tax planning arrangements, such arrangements seldom involve a clear-cut attempt to achieve only one of these goals. For example, the principal reason for making contributions to a registered retirement savings plan is to save for retirement, but in a way that defers income tax until later taxation years. However, such a deferral can result in an individual taxpayer reducing income tax today in favour of a lower tax rate in those later retirement years.

Tax Avoidance or Reduction

1-193. The most desirable result of tax planning is to permanently avoid the payment of some amount of tax. This very desirability is probably the most important explanation for the scarcity of such arrangements and, while the number of possibilities in this area is limited, they do exist.

1-194. An acceptable example of avoiding tax is the capital gains deduction that is available on the disposition of qualified farming or fishing property and qualified small business corporation shares. For 2021, the deduction limit for dispositions of shares of qualified small business corporations is $892,218. There is an additional amount for farm or fishing properties of $107,782, providing a total of $1,000,000 for all such qualified properties. These capital gains can be realized by an individual on a completely tax-free basis. The taxable capital gain would be included in net income through ITA 3(b), but the capital gains deduction would be part of the Division C deductions and therefore part of taxable income. For individuals in a position to enjoy the benefits of this provision, it is one of the best tax avoidance mechanisms available (see Chapter 11 for a detailed discussion of this provision).

1-195. Other forms of acceptable tax avoidance can be found in the taxable benefit rules of employment income, in that certain benefits can be provided to employees on a tax-free basis. These would include an employer's contributions to group sickness and accident insurance plans and private health services plans. In addition, the CRA has provided administrative concessions to allow some additional benefits to be made tax free to employees, such as employee discounts on products normally sold by the employer (see Chapter 3).

1-196. There remain numerous other planning opportunities that require more sophisticated and complex arrangements. Such arrangements often involve the use of trusts, partnerships, and private corporations and cannot be described in a meaningful manner at this stage of the material.

Tax Deferral

1-197. The basic concept behind tax planning arrangements involving the deferral of tax payments is the simple idea that it is better to pay taxes later rather than sooner. This is related to the time value of money and also involves the possibility that some permanent avoidance of taxes may result from the taxpayer being taxed at a lower marginal income tax rate at the time the deferred amounts are brought into income.

1-198. Such deferral arrangements may involve either the delayed recognition of certain types of income or, alternatively, accelerated recognition of deductions. As an example of delayed recognition of income, an employer can provide a benefit to an employee in the form of contributions to a registered pension plan. Such benefits will not be taxed in the year in which the contributions are made. Rather, they will be taxed at a later point in time when the employee begins to receive benefits from the registered pension plan, typically on retirement.

1-199. As an example of expense acceleration, the ownership of a rental property may allow the owner to deduct its capital cost at a rate that is usually in excess of any decline in the physical condition or economic value of the building. While this excess deduction will normally be added back to the taxpayer's income when the building is sold, the payment of taxes on some part of the rental income from the property has been deferred.

1-200. Deferral arrangements are available in a number of different situations and currently represent one of the more prevalent forms of tax planning.

Income Splitting

General Overview

1-201. Progressive income tax rates, as you will see in greater detail in Chapter 4, are built into the ITA. This means that, in general, the taxes payable on a given amount of taxable income will be greater if that amount accrues to one individual taxpayer than would be the case if that same total amount of taxable income is split between two or more individual taxpayers. The effect is even greater where one or more of the other individuals has no or little income and, as a result, is in the lowest tax bracket.

1-202. This does not mean that it would be advantageous to give part of your income away to perfect strangers. What it does mean is that, within a family, it is desirable to have a family's aggregate taxable income allocated as evenly as possible among the family members.

Example

1-203. The tax savings that can be achieved through income splitting are among the most dramatic examples of the effectiveness of tax planning. For example, if Ms. Jordan had taxable income of $866,044 (this is four times $216,511, the bottom threshold of the highest federal tax bracket in 2021 of 33%), her basic federal tax payable in 2021 would be $264,487 (this simplified calculation does not take into consideration the various tax credits that would be available to her).

1-204. Alternatively, if Ms. Jordan was married or living in a common-law relationship and the $866,044 could be split on the basis of $433,022 to her and $433,022 to her spouse/common-law partner, the federal taxes payable would total $243,180 [(2)($121,590)], a savings of $21,307 ($264,487 - $243,180).

1-205. If we carry this one step further and assume that Ms. Jordan has two adult children, and that the $866,044 in taxable income can be allocated on the basis of $216,511 to each individual, the total federal taxes payable will be reduced to $200,564 [(4)($50,141)]. This represents a savings at the federal level of $63,923 ($264,487 - $200,564) when compared to the amount of taxes that would have been paid if Ms. Jordan alone had been taxed on the entire $866,044.

1-206. When we add provincial effects, the potential savings would be around $100,000, a substantial reduction on income of $866,044. Making this savings even more impressive is the fact that it is not a one-shot phenomenon but, rather, a savings that could occur in each year that the income splitting plan is in effect.

Note to Students You will learn how to calculate the tax payable amounts shown in the preceding paragraphs in Chapter 4 of the text.

Problems with Income Splitting

1-207. While income splitting can be one of the most powerful planning tools available to taxpayers, there are several problems associated with implementing such arrangements:

- Splitting income with children often involves losing control over assets, a process that is emotionally difficult for some individuals.
- Splitting income involves decisions as to which family members are worthy of receiving benefits and how much those benefits should be.
- The CRA has an arsenal of anti-avoidance rules in the ITA that are specifically designed to defeat income splitting, including the recent 2018 broadening of the tax on split income (TOSI), a set of rules that tax split income at the top 33% federal income tax rate on certain types of income received by family members. This can make income splitting challenging in many situations. This tax is discussed in Chapter 11.

Exercise 1-19

Subject: Tax Planning

Mr. Stephen Chung, a successful flamenco dancer, has decided to make contributions to an RRSP in the name of his spouse, the mother of his 12 children, rather than making contributions to his own plan. What type of tax planning is involved in this decision? Explain your conclusion.

Exercise 1-20

Subject: Tax Planning

Mr. Green's employer pays all of the premiums on a dental plan that qualifies as a "private health services plan." The plan covers Mr. Green and his immediate family and benefits him since he does not have to pay the premiums. What type of tax planning is illustrated by this employee benefit? Explain your conclusion.

Solutions to Exercises are available in the Study Guide.

Abbreviations

We try to avoid using abbreviations as much as possible because we believe that not only is there is a tendency in income tax to overuse them, but there is also a risk that excessive use can interfere with the reading of the material. However, there are some expressions that are so commonly and frequently used that it wold be inefficient to discontinue their use entirely. As a result, in the remainder of this text, we will use the following abbreviations on a regular basis:

Abbreviation	Meaning
CRA	Canada Revenue Agency
CCA	Capital Cost Allowance (see Chapter 5)
CCPC	Canadian Controlled Private Corporation
FMV	Fair Market Value
GAAP	Generally Accepted Accounting Principles
GST	Goods and Services Tax
HST	Harmonized Sales Tax
IC	Information Circular

IT	Interpretation Bulletin
ITA	Federal *Income Tax Act*
Folio	A chapter in an income tax folio that is part of a series
RPP	Registered Pension Plan
RRSP	Registered Retirement Savings Plan
TFSA	Tax-Free Savings Account
TOSI	Tax on Split Income
UCC	Undepreciated Capital Cost (see Chapter 5)

Key Terms

A full glossary with definitions is provided at the end of the Study Guide.

Advance Tax Ruling
Allowable Capital Loss
Business Income
Capital Gain/Loss
Capital Property
Capital Tax
Consumption Tax
Customs Duties
Deemed Resident
Division B Income
Dual Resident
Employment Income
Fiscal Period
Flat Tax System
Goods and Services Tax (GST)
Harmonized Sales Tax (HST)
Income
Income Splitting
Income Tax
Income Tax Application Rules
Income Tax Folios
Income Tax Regulations
Income Tax Technical News
Individual
Information Circulars
Interpretation Bulletins
Net Income
Non-Resident
Part-Year Resident
Progressive Tax System
Person
Property Income
Property Tax
Qualitative Characteristics
Regressive Tax System
Resident
Residential Ties
Sojourner
Tariffs
Tax Base
Tax Deferral
Tax Expenditure
Tax Incidence
Tax Planning
Taxable Canadian Property
Taxable Capital Gain
Taxable Entity
Taxable Income
Taxation Year
Tie-Breaker Rules
Transfer Tax

References

For more detailed study of the material in this chapter, we would refer you to the following:

ITA 2(1)	Tax Payable by Persons Resident in Canada
ITA 2(3)	Tax Payable by Non-Resident Persons
ITA 3	Income for Taxation Year
ITA 114	Individual Resident in Canada for Only Part of Year

ITA 115	Non-Resident's Taxable Income in Canada
ITA 116	Disposition by Non-Resident Person of Certain Property
ITA 118.91	Part-Year Residents
ITA 118.94	Tax Payable by Non-Resident (Tax Credits)
ITA 248(1)	Definitions (Taxable Canadian Property)
ITA 249	Definition of "Taxation Year"
ITA 250(1)	Person Deemed Resident
ITA 250(4)	Corporation Deemed Resident
ITA 250(5)	Deemed Non-Resident
S5-F1-C1	Determining an Individual's Residency Status
S6-F1-C1	Residence of a Trust or Estate
IT-391R3	Status of Corporations

Self-Study Problems (SSPs)

Self-Study Problems (SSPs) provide practice in problem solving. Within the chapters, we have indicated where it would be appropriate to stop and work on each SSP. The problems can be downloaded by chapter from MyLab Accounting. Solutions are available in the Study Guide. Select problems can also be completed directly in MyLab and auto-graded.

Assignment Problems

Solutions to Assignment Problems (APs) are available to instructors only.

AP 1-1 Application of Qualitative Characteristics

In 2016, the federal government increased the maximum federal tax rate applicable to individuals from 29% to 33%.

Required: Evaluate the increase of the maximum federal tax rate on the basis of the qualitative characteristics of tax systems that are listed in your text. For your convenience, the list of qualitative characteristics presented in the text is as follows:

- Equity or fairness
- Neutrality
- Adequacy
- Flexibility
- Simplicity and ease of compliance
- Certainty
- Balance between sectors
- International competitiveness

AP 1-2 Conflicting Objectives

An objective of the Canadian tax system is to be competitive with the tax systems of our trading partners. This is particularly true with respect to the United States, where both individual and corporate tax rates are lower than those in Canada. However, this objective is often in conflict with other objectives of the tax system.

Required: Explain this statement. Reference should be made to other qualitative characteristics of tax systems.

AP 1-3 Qualitative Characteristics of Tax Systems

Discuss whether the following situations meet the objectives and match the characteristics of a good tax system. Identify any conflicts that exist and the probable economic incidence of the tax or tax expenditure.

A. Diamonds are South Africa's major export. Assume that a tax is levied on diamond production of Par Excellence Inc., which has a monopoly in the country. Movements of diamonds are closely monitored and accounted for.

B. Chimeree Inc. owns the largest diamond mine in Sierra Leone. A tax is levied on diamond production. Movements of diamonds are not closely controlled, and helicopters pick up shipments under the cover of darkness.

C. Gains on dispositions of principal residences are exempt from income tax in Canada.

D. A rule stipulates that only 50% of the cost of business meals can be deducted in calculating Canadian business income for personal and corporate taxable income.

E. A newly created country levies a head tax that requires every resident adult to pay the same amount.

AP 1-4 Application of Qualitative Characteristics

The city of Elysium is located on an island in the Nirvana River. Because of its desirable climate, it has attracted wealthy immigrants from all over the world. These immigrants have either built palatial new homes on the river waterfront or moved into luxurious residences, largely in high-rise buildings in the city's core.

In general, real estate values on the island are among the highest in the world. In order to protect their extremely orderly environment, the residents have prevented the development of any reasonably priced housing. To help maintain this environment the city has a large, well-trained security force.

The economic activity on the island consists of financial services, haute cuisine restaurants, and retail shops that feature high-end products from all over the world. Because of the high real estate cost, staff for these operations must live off island and commute in on a daily basis.

To accommodate residents of the island, the city operates a large heliport. This allows the residents of the island to quickly access a nearby airport where most maintain at least one private jet.

Until recently, the only other access to the island was via a city-operated ferry. This service was provided free of charge by the city. While it was rarely used by the residents of Elysium, the staff of the various businesses on the island relied on it for access to their jobs.

Last year, the city completed a four-lane bridge to access the island. In order to finance the tremendous cost of this project, there is a $10 toll for each trip across the bridge. To ensure that the bridge produces adequate revenues, the city has canceled the ferry service.

Required: Evaluate the $10 toll on the basis of the qualitative characteristics of tax systems that are listed in your text.

AP 1-5 Residency after Departure from Canada

Mr. Valmont has been employed on a full-time basis in Edmonton since 2010. He is employed by a Canadian subsidiary of a U.S. company that has its head office in Billings, Montana. While he has permanent resident status in Canada, he is a citizen of the U.S.

The U.S. parent company has offered Mr. Valmont a significant promotion that involves a large increase in remuneration. This promotion requires that he move to the company's head office in Billings no later than June 1, 2021. Mr. Valmont finds this to be an offer he cannot refuse.

As he is a U.S. citizen, moving to that country presents no problems. In preparation for the move, he gives up both his Canadian driver's licence and his provincial health card. He also cancels his Canadian permanent resident card. He is at his desk in Billings by May 27, 2021.

He and his spouse have three children, all of whom are attending school in Edmonton. They will remain in that city until the end of the school term. They depart Canada on June 30, 2021.

Mr. Valmont and his spouse have canceled all of their club memberships and closed their banking accounts. While they have listed their residence with an Edmonton real estate agent, it remains on the market at December 31, 2021. The real estate agent has indicated that, given the unique nature of the property, it could take up to a year to find a buyer.

Required: For purposes of assessing Canadian income taxes, determine when Mr. Valmont ceased to be a Canadian resident and the portion of his annual income that would be assessed for Canadian taxes. Explain your conclusions.

AP 1-6 Residency after Departure from Canada

Mr. David Hamilton was a long-time resident of Canada. On January 13, 2020, he departed from Canada to work in Qatar. The work was done under a contract of employment with an American company that was operating in Qatar.

1. Mr. Hamilton did not obtain resident status in Qatar or in any other country. He did not have a postal address in Qatar.
2. Mr. Hamilton obtained a work permit in Qatar that was valid until August 13, 2023.
3. After the work permit expired, Mr. Hamilton had to leave Qatar. He subsequently returned several times to meet with friends and business associates there.
4. Mr. Hamilton's Canadian driver's licence expired in August 2020 and was not renewed.
5. After taking intensive driving courses, Mr. Hamilton acquired a driver's licence in Qatar in December 2020 that was valid for five years.
6. Mr. Hamilton gave up his Canadian health card in 2021.
7. Mr. Hamilton has two adult sons who remained in Canada. One of the sons, Harold, has significant health issues.
8. Mr. Hamilton kept a credit card, bank account, RRSP, and investments in Canada when he began work in Qatar.
9. Mr. Hamilton continued to hold a Canadian passport.
10. He visited Canada four times in 2020 and three times during 2021. Each visit was for two weeks. His visits were largely to see his sons and his mother. The relationship with his wife was strained before he left for Qatar and deteriorated significantly afterwards. This led to their divorce in 2021. After his son Harold advised him to follow his dream of leaving Canada, he began the process of permanently leaving Canada. To this end, on July 1, 2021, he gave his share of the family home to his wife and closed all of his Canadian financial accounts. He paid regular support payments after the divorce occurred.
11. During his visits to Canada, he stayed in hotels and used rented vehicles.
12. In 2020, Mr. Hamilton's accountant filed a tax return for him as a resident of Canada.
13. Mr. Hamilton is well respected in his profession and considered to be a very responsible employee.

    Despite filing a tax return in 2020 as a resident of Canada, Mr. Hamilton believes that he gave up his Canadian residency on January 13, 2020, and wishes to revise his 2020 tax return to reflect this.

Required: Determine whether Mr. Hamilton is a resident of Canada. If you conclude he is not, provide the date that he ceased to be a Canadian resident. Provide reasons for your conclusion.

AP 1-7 Residency of Individuals—Five Cases

For each of the following individuals, determine their residency status for the year ending December 31, 2021. In addition, indicate what components of their income would be subject to Part I taxation in Canada, either as a resident or a non-resident. Provide the basis for your conclusions. Your answer should not take into consideration the influence of international tax treaties.

Case A Gary Short is a Canadian citizen who has lived and worked in Calgary, Alberta, all of his life. In January 2021, he is offered a significant promotion if he will accept a position in Australia. On accepting this position, he establishes residency in that country on February 1. However, because his children wish to finish the school year in Canada, his children and his wife do not join him until June 30, 2021. Because of the poor real estate market in his Calgary neighbourhood, his former residence is rented out under a long-term residential lease beginning July 1.

Case B Sarah Sloan is a U.S. citizen who lives in Detroit, Michigan. During 2021 she is employed five days per week in Windsor, Ontario. She commutes to Windsor on a daily basis. Her 2021 salary is $86,000 (Canadian). In addition, she has $900 (Canadian) of interest on a savings account with a Detroit bank.

Case C Byron Long is a citizen of France. However, having established landed immigrant status in Canada, he has worked in this country for over 15 years. On the unexpected death of his spouse, he receives an insurance payment of $2 million. He decides to use a large part of this payment for an extensive round-the-world cruise. He arranges a two-year leave of absence from his job and sails from Canada on July 1, 2021. He sells the family residence, but retains all of his Canadian banking and brokerage accounts.

Case D Hilda Stein is married to a member of the Canadian Armed Forces who is stationed in Germany during the year 2021. She is a German citizen and has never visited Canada. During 2021, because her husband is a member of the Canadian Armed Forces, she is not subject to taxation in Germany.

Case E Jessica Segal has always lived in Canada. She has been asked by her Canadian employer to spend part of 2021 (starting on August 1) and all of 2022 and 2023 working in the company's Frankfurt, Germany, office. Her employment contract requires her to return to Canada on January 5, 2024. Jessica sells her condo and furniture and reluctantly gives her beloved dog to her brother. She moves to Frankfurt in July 2021.

AP 1-8 Residency of Corporations—Four Cases

Each of the following cases provides information about an individual corporation. For each case, indicate whether the corporation would be considered a Canadian resident for the current year. Explain your conclusions.

Case A The Allor Company was incorporated in North Dakota in 2001. Currently, however, the head office of the corporation is in Regina, Saskatchewan. As all of the directors of the corporation are residents of this Canadian city, all of the meetings of the board of directors are held in Regina.

Case B Kodar Ltd. was incorporated in Canada in 2007. However, as its directors have come to hate Canadian winters, they have all moved permanently to the southern United States. Because of this, they hold all of their board of directors meetings in Phoenix, Arizona.

Case C The Karlos Company was incorporated in Minnesota in 2000. The two directors lived in Winnipeg, Manitoba, and for several years all of the board of directors' and shareholders' meetings were held in Winnipeg. In early 2005, the directors were replaced by residents of St. Paul, Minnesota. After this, all of the board of directors' and shareholders' meetings were held in St. Paul.

Case D Bradlee Inc. was incorporated in Canada in 1961. While it operated in Canada for a number of years, all of its operations, management, and directors relocated to the United States in 2008 where all board meetings have since been held.

AP 1-9 Residency of Individuals and Corporations

Pertinent facts are given for a different individual or corporation in each of the parts of this problem. For each part, indicate whether or not this individual or corporation would be considered a Canadian resident for income tax purposes during 2021. Explain your conclusion.

A. Brian Palm was born in Kanata, Ontario. In January 2021, after a record snowfall paralyzed the area, Brian concluded he was not prepared to continue dealing with Ontario winters. He wound up his Canadian affairs and, on July 31, 2021, he moved to Palm Beach, Florida. He has vowed to never set foot in Canada again.

B. Gunter is married to Rachel, who is a member of the Canadian Armed Forces serving in Germany. Except for a brief visit to Rachel's home town of Dartmouth, Nova Scotia, Gunter has never been to Canada. Gunter is exempt from taxation in Germany because he is the spouse of a deemed resident of Canada.

C. Sarah is a U.S. citizen living in Bloomfield Hills, Michigan. Most of her personal belongings are located in her parent's home in that city. However, throughout 2021, she has spent at least four days of every week living with her boyfriend in Windsor, Ontario. They plan to be married at some future date.

D. Martha is a U.S. citizen who, until 2021, had lived and worked in Canada as a landed immigrant for over 20 years. After winning $1.2 million playing black jack at the Montreal Casino on August 28, 2021, she left Canada on a two-year pleasure trip that will take her to virtually every country in the world. Her husband and children, all Canadian citizens, continue to live at the family home in Laval, Quebec.

E. Bronson Inc. was incorporated in Ontario in 1962. Until 1995, its only director resided in that province. In that year, the director was replaced by an individual resident in Corning, New York. All board meetings are held in the United States.

F. Ubex Ltd. was incorporated in Delaware in 1987. Until 2000, all of the directors of the corporation lived in Moncton, New Brunswick. During this period, the board of directors meetings were held in that city. Beginning in 2000, all of the directors have been residents of Green Bay, Wisconsin, and all of the board of directors meetings have been held in Wilmington, Delaware.

AP 1-10 Residency/Dual Residency—Individuals

Determine the residency status of the individuals in the following cases. Use the tie-breaker rules found in the Canada/U.S. tax treaty where appropriate.

Case A Ty Breaker is a citizen of the United States. He is a professional athlete, a successful entrepreneur, and single. During 2021, he plays for a Canadian soccer team and, as a consequence, he spends 194 days in Canada. Because of his extensive travel, he stores his few personal items in his mother's basement and lives in short-term rentals of hotel suites in both Canada and the U.S. His mother lives in Ontario. As he owns corporations in both countries, he has office space in both Canada and the U.S. In previous years, Ty has played for a U.S. soccer team and had spent less than 100 days per year in Canada.

Case B Jordan Marsh is a U.S. citizen who does construction work as an independent contractor. He has a home in Kalispell, Montana, which he has owned for many years. As work has been slow in that city in recent years, he decides to temporarily move to Lethbridge, Alberta, after hearing work is plentiful there. He moves on March 31, 2021. He does not sell his Kalispell residence because his brother needs a temporary home while he renovates. Jordan lives in a Lethbridge hotel until February 12, 2022. By this time he has realized that the work situation is worse in Lethbridge than it was in Kalispell. Given this, he returns to Kalispell.

AP 1-11 Alternative Views of Income

In your own words describe net income using ITA 3.

AP 1-12 Net Income—Two Cases

The following two cases make different assumptions with respect to the amounts of income and deductions for the current year for Christina Szabo, a Canadian resident.

Case A Christina had employment income of $46,200, as well as income from an unincorporated business of $13,500. A rental property owned by Christina experienced a net loss of $2,350. Dispositions of capital property during the current year had the following results:

Taxable capital gains	$14,320
Allowable capital losses	23,460

Christina paid deductible spousal support of $4,800 during the current year. While gambling was an unusual pastime for Christina, a recent trip to Las Vega resulted in roulette winnings of $123,000. The expenses of the trip were $8,450.

Case B Christina had employment income of $64,000, interest income of $2,600, and rental income of $4,560. Christina had a 50% interest in a partnership. During the current year the partnership had a business loss of $144,940. Dispositions of capital property during the current year had the following results:

Taxable capital gains	$32,420
Allowable capital losses	29,375

Deductible contributions of $12,480 were made to Christina's RRSP.

Required: For both cases, calculate Christina's net income (Division B income). Indicate the amount and type of any loss carry overs that would be available at the end of the current year.

AP 1-13 Net Income—Four Cases

The following four cases make different assumptions with respect to the amounts of income and deductions of Frank Denham for the current year:

	Case A	Case B	Case C	Case D
Employment income	$58,200	$82,600	$46,700	$33,400
Income (loss) from business	(12,300)	(8,400)	(62,300)	(46,200)
Rental income (loss)	5,400	12,200	2,600	(18,300)
Taxable capital gains	31,600	15,600	11,600	23,100
Allowable capital losses	(12,400)	(23,400)	(10,700)	(24,700)
Subdivision e deductions	(4,100)	(5,400)	(11,600)	(5,600)

Required: For each case, calculate Mr. Denham's net income (Division B income). Indicate the amount and type of any loss carry overs that would be available at the end of the current year, or state that no carry overs are available.

CHAPTER 2

Procedures and Administration

Learning Objectives

After completing Chapter 2, you should be able to:

1. Describe the role of the CRA and its basic organization (Paragraph [P hereafter] 2-1 to 2-9)
2. Explain the circumstances under which an individual is required to file an income tax return and the filing methods available (P 2-10 to 2-18).
3. Determine the dates on which income tax returns must be filed by living individuals who either carry on a business or not and the filing rules when individuals die (P 2-19 to 2-25).
4. Explain the basic withholding rules, including their purpose (P 2-26 to 2-33).
5. Explain the circumstances that result in an individual having to make income tax instalment payments (P 2-34 to 2-40).
6. Calculate the amount of any income tax instalment payments required of individuals and determine when they are due (P 2-41 to 2-50).
7. Explain the circumstances in which interest is charged under the ITA, particularly to amounts owing for a year, instalments, and penalties and the importance of the prescribed interest rate (P 2-51 to 2-58).
8. Calculate the penalties that will be assessed for the late filing of income tax returns and large late and deficient instalments (P 2-59 to 2-63).
9. Identify the dates on which the final balances owing for a year by living and deceased individuals are due (P 2-64 to 2-68).
10. Identify the dates on which income tax returns must be filed by corporations and the filing methods available (P 2-69 to 2-74).
11. Calculate the amount of income tax instalment payments required for corporations, including small CCPCs (P 2-75 to 2-80).
12. Identify the dates on which final balances owing for a year by corporations are due (P 2-81 to 2-82).
13. Calculate the interest and penalties that may be assessed on late income tax payments and for the late filing of corporate income tax returns (P 2-83 to 2-86).
14. Explain the general filing and payment requirements for trusts, including the new 2021 reporting rules, including what is required and how these rules change general filing requirements (P 2-87 to 2-97).
15. Explain the circumstances in which a taxpayer is required to file an information return (P 2-98).

16. Describe the record-keeping requirements for books and records and the CRA's role (P 2-99 to 2-104).
17. Briefly describe the My Account and My Business Account services available on the CRA website (P 2-105 to 2-106).
18. Describe the notice of assessment and notice of reassessment, and explain the normal reassessment period and the circumstances where it can be extended (P 2-107 to 2-111).
19. Explain when interest is paid on refunds and how it is calculated for both individuals and corporations (P 2-112 to 2-118).
20. Explain how to make adjustments to previously filed income tax returns (P 2-119 to 2-122).
21. Explain the initial procedures for disputing an assessment, including authorizing a representative, and the procedures for filing a notice of objection, including special rules that apply to large corporations (P 2-123 to 2-137).
22. Describe the procedures for continuing a dispute when a satisfactory settlement has not been reached with the CRA. Describe the steps in this process, particularly the difference between the informal and general procedures (P 2-138 to 2-147).
23. Explain the difference between tax evasion, tax avoidance, and tax planning, including the basic GAAR analysis (P 2-148 to 2-152).
24. Describe the collection and enforcement procedures available to the CRA, the restrictions imposed on collection action, and situations where the restrictions do not apply (P 2-153 to 2-155).
25. Describe some of the common penalties that can be assessed, including those applicable to tax advisors and tax return preparers (P 2-156 to 2-162).
26. Briefly describe the taxpayer relief provisions, particularly those relating to the waiving of interest and penalties. Describe the circumstances that would be required to consider a request for taxpayer relief (P 2-163 to 2-168).
27. Briefly describe the circumstances under which a voluntary disclosure would be permitted and the difference between the limited and general program (P 2-169 to 2-175).

Introduction

2-1. This chapter begins with a brief overview of the administration of the ITA and ETA by the Canada Revenue Agency (CRA). This is followed by a description of filing requirements and tax payment procedures applicable to individuals, corporations, and trusts.

2-2. This material on filing and tax payment procedures will be followed by a description of the assessment and reassessment process, including the various avenues that can be followed in appealing unfavourable assessments. Attention will also be given to issues related to tax avoidance and tax evasion, collection and enforcement procedures, and taxpayer relief provisions.

The CRA—Mandate, Structure, Administration, and Enforcement

2-3. The CRA is mandated to administer tax, benefits, and related programs, and to ensure compliance on behalf of governments across Canada. The CRA is responsible for the administration of the ITA, the ETA, as well as legislation relating to both the Canada Pension Plan and Employment Insurance.

2-4. In terms of the ITA and ETA, it is the Department of Finance that writes the legislation and develops the appropriate tax policies. The CRA is not involved in that process except, on occasion, to make suggestions based on factual situations encountered. The CRA interprets the ITA and ETA in a manner consistent with the tax policy objectives developed. Consultations between the CRA and the Department of Finance toward that end are not uncommon.

2-5. The CRA is established under the authority of the *Canada Revenue Agency Act,* which establishes a governance structure made up of a minister, a board of management, and a commissioner.

2-6. The minister of National Revenue is responsible for the CRA and is accountable to Parliament for all of its activities, including the administration and enforcement of program legislation such as the ITA and ETA. The minister has the authority to ensure that the CRA operates within the overall government framework and treats its clients (e.g., taxpayers) with fairness, integrity, and consistency.

2-7. The CRA has a board of management consisting of 15 members appointed by the governor in council, 11 of whom have been nominated by the provinces and territories. The board has the responsibility of overseeing the management of the CRA, including the development of the corporate business plan, and the management of policies related to resources, services, property, personnel, and contracts.

2-8. Unlike the boards of Crown corporations, the CRA board is not involved in all the activities of the CRA. In particular, the CRA board has no authority in the administration and enforcement of legislation, which includes the ITA and the ETA, for which the CRA remains fully accountable to the minister of National Revenue. In addition, the CRA board is denied access to confidential client information.

2-9. The chief executive officer of the CRA is the commissioner of revenue. In broad terms the general authority granted the minister of National Revenue, as well as those of the commissioner of revenue, are described in the ITA as follows:

> **ITA 220(1)** The Minister shall administer and enforce this Act and the Commissioner of Revenue may exercise all the powers and perform the duties of the Minister under this Act.
>
> The Commissioner of the CRA, who is a member of the CRA Board, is responsible for the CRA's day-to-day operations.

Returns and Payments—Individuals

Requirement to File—ITA 150

2-10. ITA 150(1) is a general provision that requires all taxpayers (individuals, corporations, and trusts) to file an income tax return referred to in the ITA as a "return of income." ITA 150(1) sets out the specifics, including the filing deadlines, which are based on the taxation year of the specific taxpayer.

2-11. While the main rules for filing income tax returns are contained in ITA 150(1), there are other important rules to be aware of that exempt a taxpayer from having to file an income tax return. The exemptions must be carefully considered, however, because of other situations such as benefits paid through the ITA that require the filing of an income tax return to qualify. For example, consider the case of an individual with young children whose income is low enough that no income tax is payable for that year. Technically ITA 150(1) sets out the filing date, but ITA 150(1.1)(b)(i) exempts the individual from having to file the income tax return for the year if there is no tax payable. The Canada Child Benefit (ITA 122.61), however, requires that an income tax return be filed annually to continue to qualify for the monthly benefits. The Canada Child Benefit is discussed in Chapter 9. Given the circumstances, the individual would need to file an income tax return to obtain the Canada Child Benefit.

2-12. There are many situations that require the filing of an income tax return. Some of the most common occur where a resident individual:

- has tax payable;
- is claiming a refund;
- has received a demand by the CRA to file a tax return (ITA 150(2));
- has disposed of a capital property (including their principal residence), whether or not at a gain or loss;

- has realized a taxable capital gain;
- has elected to split pension income with his spouse or common-law partner;
- has to contribute to the Canada Pension Plan or pay Employment Insurance premiums (including self-employed individuals who elect to make payments); or
- are eligible for the Canada Workers' Benefit, Canada Child Benefit, GST/HST credit, or other benefits, including the Climate Action Incentive payment.

2-13. The same rules apply to non-resident individuals who are liable for Part I tax because they have income from Canadian employment, are carrying on a business in Canada (Canadian business), or have disposed of taxable Canadian property. If a non-resident individual has no Part I tax payable they are still required to file an income tax return if they have a taxable capital gain or have disposed of taxable Canadian property at a gain or loss (unless it is not taxable in Canada as a result of a tax treaty with the non-resident's country). When non-residents earn income from Canadian employment or a Canadian business they may not be liable for Canadian income tax because withholding taxes have been taken and paid throughout the year. Such income taxes can only be recovered/refunded by filing a Canadian income tax return. The income tax return filed by non-residents is different than that filed for resident Canadians and is titled an "Income Tax and Benefit Return for Non-Residents and Deemed Residents of Canada."

2-14. Individuals can either file a paper form or, alternatively, use an electronic filing method. The advantage of electronic filing for the taxpayer, particularly if she is entitled to a refund, is that the return will be processed more quickly. CRA service standards for processing a paper return is eight weeks but only two weeks for electronically filed returns. For the CRA, electronic filing eliminates the possibility of errors in the process of transferring information from paper forms to their electronic records. While supporting documents (e.g., a charitable donation receipt) cannot be included with an electronic filing, the CRA has the right to request that such receipts be provided. Such requests are fairly common, particularly when large amounts are involved.

2-15. The CRA website has detailed coverage of the two alternatives for electronic filing. Both EFILE and NETFILE are automated transmission services that permit the filing of tax returns online. The main difference between them can be described as follows:

> **NETFILE** allows an individual to file his own personal income tax return directly to the CRA online through the use of a CRA certified tax software program. It is intended for use by those who prepare their own tax returns. This system can be used by almost all Canadian resident individuals.
>
> **EFILE** allows tax preparation service providers who are registered with the CRA to file tax returns for clients online. It is designed for those who prepare and file tax returns for clients. The NETFILE system cannot be used to file returns for clients.

2-16. CRA's filing statistics for the 2020 personal tax filing season covering the period from February 10, 2020, to December 20, 2020, show that there has been a significant decline in the percentage of taxpayers using paper filing over the six years. In years prior to 2020 the CRA statistics covered the period February to August, but because of the COVID-19 pandemic filing extensions were granted, resulting in the lengthier period to ensure that all income tax returns were accounted for.

2-17. Of the total 2019 returns electronically filed during 2020, 17,509,972 were filed under the EFILE program, while 10,024,675 were filed using NETFILE. An additional 69,641 returns were filed using the CRA's File My Return program. This is a service provided by the CRA for low-income individuals that have returns that change little from year to year. This program allows such individuals to complete their filing obligations using an automated phone service. Eligibility requires the receipt of an "invitation letter" from the CRA, which is sent by mail.

2-18. Almost 20 million of the 2019 income tax returns resulted in taxpayers receiving a refund. The average amount of the refund was $1,849, resulting in disbursements totaling over $36 billion. In contrast, 6.5 million returns showed a balance owing. The average amount was $6,401, for a total intake of almost $41.4 billion.

Due Date for Individual Returns

General Rule

2-19. As noted in Chapter 1, individuals must use the calendar year as their taxation year. This means that for every individual, the taxation year ends on December 31. Given this, ITA 150(1)(d)(i) indicates that, in general, individuals must file their tax return for a particular year on or before April 30 of the following year. Although the filing due date is extended to the next business day if the due date falls on a weekend, we will use April 30 (or June 15 if applicable, as explained in the following paragraph) as the due date in our examples and problems.

Individuals Who Carry on a Business

2-20. Individuals who carry on a business as a sole proprietor or as a member of a partnership in a year may need more time to determine their income. In recognition, the ITA provides an extended filing deadline. ITA 150(1)(d)(ii) extends the due date for filing to June 15 of the following calendar year.

2-21. The extended deadline would apply to the cohabiting spouse or common-law partner as well whether or not they participate in the carrying on of the business. The rationale for this is that the business income or loss of one spouse potentially affects the income tax return of the other. The individuals must be cohabiting, which generally means that they are living together in the year and have not been separated throughout the year.

2-22. An interesting feature is that, while the income tax return does not have to be filed until June 15, payment of all taxes owing is required by April 30. Any amounts that are not paid by April 30 will be assessed interest until the outstanding balance is paid. The relevant interest rate is described later in this chapter.

Exercise 2-1

Subject: Individual Tax Payment Date

Brandon Katarski's 2021 net income includes business income. When is his 2021 income tax return due? By what date must his 2021 income tax liability be paid in order to avoid the assessment of interest on amounts due?

Solutions to Exercises are available in the Study Guide.

Deceased Individuals

2-23. As will be discussed in Chapter 9, there are many tax-related complexities that arise when an individual dies. In order to provide the deceased individual's representatives with sufficient time to deal with these added complexities, the ITA offers the following extension of time to file the final income tax return:

> **ITA 150(1)(b)** ... in the case of an individual who dies after October of the year and on or before the day that would be the individual's filing due date for the year if the individual had not died, by the individual's legal representatives on or before the day that is the later of the day on or before which the return would otherwise be required to be filed and the day that is 6 months after the day of death.

2-24. For an individual whose filing due date is April 30, this provision means that if death occurs between November 1 of the previous year and April 30 of the current year, the return for the previous year does not have to be filed until six months after the date of death.

EXAMPLE A single individual who did not carry on a business dies on March 1, 2022, without having filed the 2021 income tax return.

ANALYSIS Since the individual died after October 2021 (from November 1) and on or before April 30, 2022, the normal filing due date of April 30, 2022, is extended to six months from the date of death, which would be September 1, 2022.

2-25. The provision works somewhat differently for an individual who has a June 15 filing due date as a result of carrying on a business or having a cohabiting spouse/common-law partner carrying on a business. The same rule applies, but the six-month extension only extends the filing date beyond June 15 if death occurs after December 15.

EXAMPLE An individual whose cohabiting spouse/common-law partner carries on a business dies on May 2, 2022, without having filed a 2021 income tax return.

ANALYSIS Since death occurred after October 2021 and before the filing due date of June 15, 2022, the filing date becomes the later of (i) June 15, 2022, or (ii) six months from the time of death, which would be November 2, 2022. The resulting extended filing date for the 2021 taxation year is therefore November 2, 2022. Given that the individual died partway through 2022, an income tax return will also have to be filed for 2022. The deceased filing extension does not apply to the 2022 year since the death would have had to have occurred between November 1, 2022, and June 15, 2023. The result is that the regular filing date of June 15, 2023, applies to the 2022 taxation year.

The 2021 income tax return for the cohabiting spouse/common-law partner is also extended by the same six-month period to November 1, 2022 (ITA 150(1)(d)(iii)).

Exercise 2-2

Subject: Deceased Taxpayer Filing Date

Sally Cheung dies on February 15, 2022. Sally's only income for 2021 and 2022 was from investments. Her cohabiting spouse carried on a business in both 2021 and 2022. Her representatives must file her 2021 and 2022 tax returns by what dates? Explain your answer.

Solutions to Exercises are available in the Study Guide.

Income Tax Withholdings—ITA 153

Salaries and Wages

2-26. A large portion of the income taxes and other withholdings (e.g., Canada Pension Plan and Employment Insurance) paid by individuals employed in Canada is collected through source deductions withheld by their employer. ITA 153 requires employers paying "salaries, wages or other remuneration" to withhold from these payments amounts determined by the ITR. The employers are then required to remit or pay the amounts withheld to the federal government within a certain timeframe. Income taxes withheld are credited to the account of the employees and form the basis for determining whether the employee will owe additional amounts on filing an income tax return or be entitled to an income tax refund.

2-27. The amount withheld by an employer is specified in Part 1 of the ITRs and is based upon the dollar amounts and frequency of payments. The CRA publishes annual payroll deduction tables by province each year to assist employers in determining the required withholdings (T4032). The base upon which source deductions are calculated can be reduced by certain tax credits based on the form TD1, "Personal Tax Credits Return" that is filled out by each employee.

2-28. The ITA allows taxpayers to either increase their withholdings or request a reduction in withholdings. Form TD1 can be used to increase withholdings beyond the required amount. An individual might choose to do this, for example, if their employment income withholding is based on rates in a low-tax-rate province, but the province where they reside is much higher (e.g., an individual who works in Alberta but lives in British Columbia). Another situation where this might be desirable would be where an individual began to receive large taxable spousal support payments, as these are not subject to withholding. In either of these cases, requesting additional withholding would allow the individual to pay extra taxes each employment pay period and avoid a large tax liability on filing his income tax return for the year or the requirement to pay instalments, which we discuss in the next section of this chapter.

2-29. A different type of problem can arise when an employed individual has significant deductions from income such as RRSP contributions, child care expenses, spousal support payments, losses, or non-refundable tax credits such as medical expenses and donations, which are not listed on the TD1 as credits that are allowed to reduce the base on which source deductions are calculated.

> **EXAMPLE** Monica Kinney has annual employment income that places her in the middle of the 29% tax bracket. Her employer would base her withholdings on her employment income for the year. However, if Monica is required to make recurring annual deductible spousal support payments of $20,000, her taxable income will be reduced by this amount, resulting in a reduction in federal tax payable of $5,800 [($20,000)(29%)]. If provincial income taxes are taken into consideration, a further reduction in income taxes payable would be available.

2-30. In this situation, Monica can request a reduction in the amount of tax withheld by her employer by using form T1213, "Request to Reduce Tax Deductions at Source." As long as the deductions, losses, or tax credits can be documented in a reasonable manner, the CRA will normally authorize the employer to reduce the tax withheld from the employee's remuneration. Technically the minister is only required to allow reduced withholdings if not doing so would cause "undue hardship" (ITA 153(1.1)).

Withholdings by Other Payers

2-31. In addition to requiring employers to withhold specified amounts from the salaries and wages of employees, ITA 153 contains a fairly long list of other types of payments from which the payer must withhold prescribed amounts. These include:

- retiring allowances;
- death benefits;
- payments from Registered Retirement Savings Plans; and
- payments from Registered Education Savings Plans.

2-32. ITA 153(1) applies when a person makes certain payments to others with respect to salary, wages, and even fees. The rules do not require that the payments be made to resident Canadians, and therefore non-residents offering their services in Canada as employees are subject to the same income tax withholdings as would apply to Canadian resident employees. In addition, non-residents providing non-employment-related services in Canada are also subject to a withholding of 15% of the gross amount of fees paid. In both instances the non-residents would have to file a Canadian income tax return to recover any overpayment of Canadian tax or if no tax is required as a result of an income tax treaty they could apply for a treaty-based waiver, which would exempt them from withholdings. This is discussed in Chapter 20.

ITA 153(1) and the Requirement to File Information Returns

2-33. ITR 200(1) requires that any person making a payment described in ITA 153(1) must file an information return to the CRA, typically in the form of a T4, T4A, or other information slip. A T4 slip details employment-related withholdings, whereas a T4A slip applies to "pension, retirement, annuity, and other income." ITA 153(1)(g) reads, in part, "fees, commissions or other amounts for services." The CRA is of the view that when payments are made for non-personal services such as a business paying for accounting, legal, plumbing, electrical, or other services, the business owner is required to file the information with the CRA even though there is no required withholding. Failure to do so will result in penalties. We discuss penalties in this chapter.

Instalment Payments for Individuals—ITA 156

Basis for Requiring Instalments

2-34. As discussed in the previous section, amounts to be applied to future tax liabilities must be withheld by the payer from certain types of income. Such income includes employment income as well as other less common sources.

2-35. For many individuals, particularly those earning employment income, the withholding of taxes constitutes the major form of tax payment in any taxation year. However, not all types of income are subject to withholdings. For resident individuals carrying on a business or earning investment income there are no required withholdings at source as there are with employment income. The ITA contemplates these situations and ensures a continuous flow of tax revenues through the use of what are referred to as instalment payments, which for individuals are required to be made on a quarterly basis toward one's current-year income tax liability. In summary, employers are responsible for the regular withholding and payment of taxes to the federal government on behalf of their employees, whereas for those earning other types of income the responsibility belongs to the person earning the income.

2-36. ITA 156(1) requires that every individual (except full-time farmers or fishers) make quarterly instalment payments. This requirement, however, is subject to ITA 156.1, which sets out the ground rules explaining that no instalments are required if:

> **ITA 156.1(2)(b)** The individual's net tax owing for the particular year, or for each of the two preceding taxation years, does not exceed the individual's instalment threshold for that year.

2-37. In provinces other than Quebec, "net tax owing" is generally defined as the amount, if any, by which the total federal and provincial tax owing for a particular year exceeds all income tax withheld for that year. This is generally equal to the amount of one's tax liability (e.g., the remaining amount you owe) as assessed by the CRA on filing the income tax return for that year. If taxes withheld and otherwise paid exceed the tax liability for that year, then you would be entitled to a refund. In that case the "net tax owing" would be nil since you would not owe anything. Remember that in the calculations there is sometimes a tendency to show net tax owing as a negative to reflect a refund, but the ITA does not allow negative numbers in these circumstances.

2-38. An "individual's instalment threshold" is defined in ITA 156.1(1) as $1,800 for residents of Quebec and $3,000 for residents of all other provinces. The amount in Quebec is smaller because the number only includes the federal tax, whereas the $3,000 amount in other provinces includes both a federal and provincial tax component.

2-39. In the beginning of this chapter we mentioned that the CRA is mandated to administer and enforce not only the ITA and ETA but also the *Canada Pension Plan (CPP)* and *Employment Insurance (EI) Acts*. Both of the CPP and EI Acts also include quarterly instalment payment rules that mirror the ITA. In practice the total instalment payments would reflect (outside of Quebec) federal and provincial income tax, CPP and EI premiums, and contributions on self-employed earnings (e.g., business income). Our coverage, however, is limited to income tax instalments only applying the $3,000 tax threshold.

2-40. While the legislation is based on when instalments are not required, it is usually more useful to give guidance in terms of when instalments are required. As a result, the requirement that obliges individuals to determine instalment payments can be restated as follows:

You are required to make instalment payments for 2021 if your estimated net tax owing for the current year (2021) or your actual net tax owing is more than $3,000:

- in 2021; and
- in either of 2019 or 2020.

Due Dates for Individuals

2-41. For individuals required to pay instalments, the quarterly payments are due on March 15, June 15, September 15, and December 15 of the year for which instalments are made.

Determining Amounts of Instalments

2-42. In simple terms, the required instalments will be based on an estimate of the net tax owing for the current year, or the actual net tax owing for the first preceding year (2020), or a combination of the first and second preceding years.

2-43. In determining the amount to be paid as instalments, individuals have a choice of three alternatives for calculating the required quarterly instalments as follows:

Alternative 1—Current Year One-quarter of the estimated net tax owing for the current taxation year [ITA 156(1)(a)(i)].

Alternative 2—First Preceding Year One-quarter of the net tax owing for the immediately preceding taxation year [ITA 156(1)(a)(ii)].

Alternative 3—Second and First Preceding Year The first two instalments (March 15 and June 15) are based on one-quarter of the net tax owing for the second preceding taxation year. The remaining two instalments (September 15 and December 15) are equal to the excess of the net tax owing for the preceding year over one-half of the net tax owing for the second preceding year [ITA 156(1)(b)], divided by two. Note that one-half of the net tax owing for the second preceding year is the amount that should have been paid in the first two instalments under this approach.

For those individuals whose income is increasing every year, alternative 2 and 3 result in the same total instalments, but the use of alternative 3 would mean that the first two instalment payments would be smaller than the third and fourth resulting in some deferral. Alternative 3 is consistent with the CRA instalment reminder, which is discussed in the next section.

Where income is declining every year, then the current-year method of alternative 1 would provide the lowest total instalment payments, although they would be based on estimates. A business with declining income due to COVID-19 illustrates in dramatic fashion a situation where instalments were likely based on alternatives 2 or 3 on the presumption that they would represent the least amount of instalment payments. Subsequent events reveal that the current-year estimates of alternative 1 are now the preferred course.

Where income has declined and instalments had already been made on the basis of current-year estimates that fail to materialize there is a flexibility built into the instalment methods that allow one to avoid future instalments for that year. If at some point in the year the estimates prove excessive, then subsequent instalments can be based on the revised estimates.

CRA Instalment Reminders

2-44. The CRA wants to ensure that individuals who are required to pay instalments have received an instalment reminder. If an individual is registered for the My Account service (see Paragraph 2-105), the CRA emails a notification that there is new online email; otherwise the instalment reminders are sent by actual mail. The instalment reminders are sent in February for the March and June payments and a second one in August for the September and December payments. Taxpayers are assured that, if they pay the amounts specified in these reminders by the due dates, no interest will be assessed for late or deficient instalments. There is no requirement, however, to follow the CRA reminder.

2-45. The amounts specified in these instalment reminders are based on alternative 3. The reason that the CRA has adopted this approach is based on information availability:

> **Alternative 1** The CRA would not know the current year's tax payable until April 30 or June 15 of the following year. This would be too late for advising an individual as to any of the current-year's instalments under this approach.
>
> **Alternative 2** The CRA would not know the previous year's tax payable until April 30 or June 15 of the current year. This would too late for advising a taxpayer as to the first required instalment for the current year and, in the case of June 15 filers, too late to provide information on the second required instalment for the current year.

2-46. Given this situation, alternative 3 is the only approach that could be used by the CRA to provide taxpayers with instalment information that would unequivocally avoid any assessment of interest.

2-47. While using the CRA instalment reminder may be considered risk free in terms of remitting instalments, it may not be the best solution for all individuals.

> **EXAMPLE** Ali Kern, a self-employed general contractor, had taxable income in both 2019 and 2020 that was in excess of $200,000. Unfortunately, in early 2021 he was in a serious accident and could not work all year. His business experienced significant losses in 2021, which ultimately resulted in a taxable income of nil.
>
> **ANALYSIS** The CRA's instalment reminders would base its calculations on the high levels of income for 2019 and 2020. Paying these amounts would be a very poor choice as it would, in essence, constitute an interest-free loan to the government. As Ali knew early in the year that he would have little or no income, his best choice would be to make no instalments based on his estimated current-year net tax owing of nil.

2-48. However, if an individual does not pay the amounts calculated in the CRA's instalment reminders, the taxpayer is basing some or all of the payments on estimates. If the estimates are too low, she could be assessed interest on any insufficient instalments.

Example of Instalments for Individuals

2-49. A simple example will serve to illustrate the alternative approaches to calculating instalments.

> **EXAMPLE** Mr. Hruba is not subject to any withholding on any of his income. He has the following amounts of net tax owing:

2019	$20,000
2020	32,000
2021 (Estimated)	24,000

> **ANALYSIS** The use of alternative 1 based on the 2021 estimate of $24,000 would result in quarterly instalments of $6,000 ($24,000/4), totaling $24,000 for the year.
>
> Alternative 2, based on the 2020 figure of $32,000, is the worst alternative. The quarterly instalments would be $8,000 ($32,000/4), totaling $32,000 for the year.
>
> Under alternative 3 (used in the CRA's instalment reminders), instalments 1 and 2 would each be $5,000 ($20,000/4). However, instalments 3 and 4 would each be $11,000 [($32,000 - $10,000)/2], resulting in a total of $32,000. This is preferable to alternative 2 in which all four payments would be $8,000 each.
>
> This analysis would suggest that alternative 1 provides the best solution. While the first two payments under alternative 3 are somewhat lower ($5,000 vs. $6,000), the total amount under alternative 1 is significantly lower ($24,000 vs. $32,000).

2-50. The CRA will charge interest based on instalments that should have been made using the alternative that results in the lowest total payments. The CRA will compare this against each actual instalment payment. Interest will be charged on any deficiency and will be reduced for any payment in excess of what was required. Interest will not be charged provided the amount calculated does not exceed $25.

Exercise 2-3

Subject: Individual Instalments

Marlene Carter, a resident of Ontario, had net tax owing for 2019 of $3,500, net tax owing for 2020 of $4,000, and expects to have net tax owing for 2021 of $1,500. Is she required to make instalment payments for 2021? If so, what would be the minimum quarterly payment and when would each instalment be due?

Exercise 2-4

Subject: Individual Instalments

John Lee, a resident of Newfoundland, had net tax owing for 2019 of $3,500, net tax owing for 2020 of $1,500, and expects to have net tax owing for 2021 of $4,500. Is he required to make instalment payments for 2021? If so, what would be the minimum quarterly payments and when would each instalment be due?

Exercise 2-5

Subject: Individual Instalments

At the beginning of 2020, the following information relates to Jesse Forbes:

Year	Tax Payable	Amounts Withheld
2019	$53,000	$52,000
2020	59,000	52,000
2021 (Estimated)	64,000	60,000

Is Jesse required to make instalment payments during 2021? If he is required to make instalment payments, indicate the amounts that would be required under each of the three alternative methods of calculating instalments. Indicate which alternative would be preferable.

Solutions to Exercises are available in the Study Guide.

We suggest you complete SSP 2-1 at this point.

Interest

When Interest Is Charged

2-51. Interest is assessed on any amounts that are not paid when they are due. For individuals, this would include:

- Any balance owing on April 30 of the current year for the taxes of the preceding year. The amount owing is due on April 30, without regard to whether the taxpayer's filing due date is April 30 or June 15.

- Any portion of a required instalment payment that is not remitted on the required instalment due date.
- On all penalties (ITA 161(11)). For example, interest is charged on penalties for late filing (see following discussion of this penalty).

2-52. Compound daily interest is charged on these amounts. In the case of amounts owing on April 30, the start date for interest is May 1, with the accrual continuing until the amounts are paid. For deficient instalment amounts, the interest clock starts ticking on the date the instalment is due. This accrual would continue until an offset occurs (see next paragraph) or the due date for the balance owing. At this latter date, further interest would be based on the amount owing at that date.

> **EXAMPLE** Marissa carries on a business in 2021 and is required to make quarterly instalment payments of $2,000. She misses her December 15, 2021, instalment. She files her 2021 tax return on April 30, 2022, reporting that she owes $5,000, which she pays in full on June 10, 2022.
>
> **ANALYSIS** Marissa will be charged interest on the instalment payment of $2,000 from December 15, 2021, to April 30, 2022. She will also be charged interest on the $5,000 tax owing from May 1, 2022, to June 9, 2022.

2-53. A further important point here is that interest accrued on late or deficient instalments can be offset by making instalment payments prior to their due date, or by paying an amount in excess of the amount required (creating contra interest). These excess amounts create a notional interest using the same high prescribed interest rates used to determine instalment interest. Interest on any excess amounts are only used to offset actual instalment interest. Any excess notional interest will not be refunded. If in the example in Paragraph 2-52 Marissa had made a $3,000 payment on January 31, 2022, no further interest would have been charged on the missed instalment payment. Notional interest on the $1,000 excess would continue to accrue until any interest charged was completely offset. No further interest would accrue. Marissa could either use the excess to offset the March 15, 2022, instalment payment (for the 2022 year) or the tax payable balance of $5,000 on filing her 2021 income tax return.

Prescribed Rates of Interest

2-54. There are a number of provisions in the ITA that require the use of a certain rate of interest. What we refer to as the prescribed base rate is an annual rate that is calculated each quarter, based on the average on three-month Government of Canada treasury bills during the first month of the preceding quarter. The CRA announces this prescribed base rate for each quarter a few weeks before the start of each quarter.

2-55. Many years ago there was a single prescribed rate. However, the government felt that this rate was sufficiently low that too many taxpayers chose not to make required tax payments. To address this problem, on amounts owing to the government, 4 percentage points were added to the prescribed base rate. At the same time, a third rate was established for amounts owed to taxpayers.

2-56. As a result, there are three general prescribed interest rates. ITR 4301 describes how these amounts are to be determined and to whom they apply. The rates that concern us here are as follows:

> **Base Rate** This rate, described in Paragraph 2-54, is applicable for all purposes except amounts owing to and from the CRA (e.g., the determination of certain taxable benefits, such as an employee who receives an interest-free loan from an employer. This is discussed in Chapter 3). For the first quarter of 2021, this rate was 1%, which is unchanged from the third and fourth quarter of 2020.
>
> **Base Rate Plus 2%** This rate is applicable when calculating interest on refunds to individuals and trusts, but not corporations. For the first quarter of 2021, this rate was 3%. Interest rates on short-term investments are much lower than the prescribed rate plus 2%.

To prevent corporations from overpaying instalments to take advantage of the higher offset interest rates paid by the CRA, the rate on amounts owed to corporations is only the base rate and does not include the extra 2%.

Base Rate Plus 4% This rate is applicable when calculating interest on late or deficient instalments, unpaid source deductions, and other amounts owing to the CRA by all taxpayers. For the first quarter of 2021, this rate was 5%.

2-57. It is important to be aware that ITA 18(1)(t) contains a general provision that prohibits any interest or penalties charged under the ITA and ETA from being claimed as a deduction. As a result, interest rates charged represent the full economic cost.

2-58. Many individuals are faced with the choice of either making their instalment payments or, alternatively, paying off other types of liabilities that they have accumulated. In many cases, the interest rate on other debts is higher than 6%.

EXAMPLE Jasmine Ho has determined that her March instalment for 2021 will be $7,500. She owes $7,500 on her Visa credit card for personal expenditures. Jasmine does not have the funds to pay both the credit card debt and her tax instalment.

ANALYSIS The annual interest rate that will be charged on her Visa balance is likely to be around 20%. This compares to a current rate on late tax instalments of 6%. Without regard to financial planning issues, Jasmine would clearly reduce her interest costs by paying off the credit card debt, as opposed to making her instalment payment.

Penalties

Late Filing Penalties

2-59. If the deadline for filing an income tax return is not met, the CRA assesses a penalty. For a first offence, this penalty amounts to 5% of the tax that was unpaid at the filing due date, plus 1% for each complete month (part months do not count) the unpaid tax is outstanding up to a maximum of 12 months. Interest is compounded and charged on both the taxes owing as well as the penalty amount charged at the highest interest rate. The maximum penalty would be 17% [(5%) + (1%)(12 months)]. Since the penalty only applies where there is unpaid tax the penalty will not apply if there are no taxes owed on the due date, or if the taxpayer is entitled to a refund.

2-60. If the taxpayer has not filed the current-year income tax return on time, has received a notice from the CRA demanding that the return be filed and has been assessed a late filing penalty in any of the three preceding taxation years, then the late filing penalty is increased to 10% of the tax owing, plus 2% per complete month up to a maximum of 20 months. The maximum penalty would be 50% [(10%) + (2%)(20 months)].

2-61. In terms of planning, the penalty for late filing is sufficiently severe that individuals should make every effort to file their income tax returns no later than the deadline (April 30 or June 15), even if all of the taxes owing cannot be paid at that time. This is of particular importance if they have been assessed a late filing penalty in any of the three preceding years.

2-62. This point is sometimes forgotten when the previous offence resulted in a negligible penalty that may have been overlooked. The penalty for a second offence will double, even if the amount involved in the first penalty was very small.

Late or Deficient Instalments Penalty

2-63. There is no penalty for late payment of income taxes as long as the income tax return is filed on time. In addition there are no penalties charged on moderate amounts of late or deficient instalments. However, there is a penalty when large amounts of late or deficient instalments are involved. This penalty is specified in ITA 163.1 and is equal to 50% of the amount by which the interest owing on the late or deficient instalments exceeds the greater of $1,000 or 25% of the interest that would be owing if no instalments had been made. As this penalty does not kick in unless the amount of interest exceeds $1,000, it would only apply to fairly large amounts of late or deficient instalments.

Exercise 2-6

Subject: Penalties and Interest for Individuals

Despite the fact that her net tax owing has been between $3,000 and $4,000 in the two previous years and is expected to be a similar amount during 2021, Mary Carlos has made no instalment payments for 2021. While her normal filing date would be April 30, 2022, she does not file her 2021 return or pay the balance owing until July 20, 2022. What penalties and interest will be assessed for the 2021 taxation year?

Solutions to Exercises are available in the Study Guide.

Due Date for Balance Owing—Living Individuals

2-64. If the combination of amounts withheld and instalments paid falls short of the total taxes payable for the taxation year, there will be a balance owing. For living individuals, ITA 248(1) defines the "balance due date" as April 30 of the following calendar year, without regard to whether the taxpayer qualifies for the June 15 filing due date because of the carrying on of a business.

Deceased Individuals—Balance Due Dates and Final Return

Balance Due Dates—Deceased Individual

2-65. The due date for the amount owing for the year of death is generally April 30 of the calendar year following death. In Paragraphs 2-23 to 2-25 we learned that there is a six-month filing extension where an individual dies after October of a year and before the applicable filing due date of either April 30 or June 15. The balance due date is slightly different and applies a six-month extension if death occurs after October of a year and before May of the following calendar year or between November 1 and April 30.

EXAMPLE Before filing her 2021 tax return, Joanne Rivers dies on March 31, 2022. For 2021 and 2022, she carried on a business. No instalments were required. There is a balance owing for both years. What are the due dates for these amounts?

ANALYSIS The filing of her 2021 return will be extended by six months to September 30, 2022, as the date of death occurred within the period November 1, 2021, and June 15, 2022. Since the date of death fell within the period November 1, 2021, and April 30, 2022, the same six-month extension to September 30, 2022, applies to the tax balance owing.

Her final 2022 income tax return will be due on June 15, 2023, with any balance owing for 2022 due by April 30, 2023.

Filing Returns—Special Rules Applicable on Death

2-66. Dealing with the death of an individual taxpayer can be a complex area of tax practice. In fact, for an individual with a substantial estate and/or a number of beneficiaries, it usually requires the services of tax practitioners who specialize in this area. Complete coverage of this subject goes well beyond the scope of this general text.

2-67. However, we will provide some coverage of a few of the more important issues that arise when an individual dies. For example, in Chapter 9 we discuss the deemed disposition of capital property at death, and in Chapter 11 we cover the special rules that apply to net capital losses in the year of death.

2-68. Additional filing issues related to deceased individuals, such as returns to be filed and available credits, are covered in an Appendix to Chapter 11.

Returns and Payments—Corporations

Due Date for Corporate Returns—ITA 150

2-69. Unlike the case with individuals, the taxation year of a corporation can end on any day of the calendar year. This makes it impossible to have a uniform filing date and, as a consequence, the filing deadline for corporations is specified as six months after its taxation year end (e.g., the fiscal year).

2-70. Under ITA 150(1)(a), corporations (other than corporations that are registered charities) that are either resident in Canada at any time in the year, carry on business in Canada, have a taxable capital gain, dispose of taxable Canadian property, or would be subject to Canadian tax if not for a tax treaty are required to file a T2 corporate income tax return within this six-month period. Information from the financial statements must accompany the T2 return along with other required schedules.

Filing Alternatives for Corporations

Paper vs. Electronic Filing

2-71. ITA 150.1(2.1) indicates that prescribed corporations must file their returns electronically. They do not have the option to paper file. For this purpose, prescribed corporations are those that have gross revenues in excess of $1 million. Corporations that are required to electronically file are subject to a penalty of $1,000 under ITA 162(7.2) if they paper file the return. Corporations with gross revenues of $1 million or less can choose to paper file or to file their return electronically.

Canadian Currency and Elective Use of Functional Currency

2-72. As a rule, transactions in foreign currency must be converted to Canadian currency (ITA 261(2)(a)) based on the day a transaction occurred. The ITA, however, permits corporations, on an elective basis (ITA 261(2)(b)), to file their corporate income tax return using a non-Canadian currency as long as the "functional currency" is that of the EU, the U.S., the UK, or Australia.

2-73. A "functional currency" is defined as one of the four currencies referred to in Paragraph 2-72 if that currency is, throughout the taxation year, the primary currency in which the taxpayer maintains its records and books of account for financial reporting purposes.

2-74. You should also note that the term "functional currency" has a different meaning in the ITA than it does in Canadian and International Financial Reporting Standards (IFRS). IFRS uses this term to refer to the currency of the primary economic environment in which the corporation operates, without regard to the currency in which the corporation keeps its books and records.

Instalment Payments for Corporations

Instalment Threshold

2-75. Corporations are generally required to make monthly instalment payments throughout their taxation year. However, this requirement is eliminated if either the estimated tax payable for the current year or the tax payable for the preceding taxation year does not exceed $3,000 (combined federal and provincial). In addition, special rules apply to certain Canadian controlled private corporations, or CCPCs. While CCPCs will be defined more precisely in Chapter 12, at this point we would note that, in general, a CCPC is a private corporation that is controlled by residents of Canada and does not have any of its shares listed on designated stock exchanges, which would include all major stock exchanges in North America. The special instalment rules applicable to these CCPCs will be discussed beginning at Paragraph 2-78.

Calculating the Amount—General Rules (Excluding Small CCPCs)

2-76. When instalments are required, they must be paid on or before the last day of each month in the corporate taxation year, with the amount being calculated on the basis of one of three alternatives. As laid out in ITA 157(1)(a), these alternatives are as follows:

1. **Current year**—12 instalments, each based on 1/12 of the estimated tax payable for the current year.
2. **First preceding year**—12 instalments, each based on 1/12 of the tax that was payable in the immediately preceding year.
3. **Second and first preceding year**—2 instalments, each based on 1/12 of the tax that was payable in the second preceding year, followed by 10 instalments based on 1/10 of the amount by which the taxes paid in the immediately preceding year exceeds the sum of the first two instalments.

You will note that unlike the case for individual instalments that use "net tax owing," corporate instalments are based on the full "tax payable" under Part I. This is because corporations are not subject to source deduction type withholdings on their income as are individuals who are employed.

2-77. Choosing between these alternatives is usually straightforward. The choice should be the instalment base that provides the minimum total cash outflow or, in those cases where alternative bases result in the same total cash outflow, the alternative that provides the greatest amount of deferral, which means smaller initial monthly payments with larger payments toward the end. For businesses that are experiencing year-to-year increases in their income and therefore their taxes payable, the third alternative based on earlier years will generally be the best choice. Note, however, the total cash outflow under the third alternative will usually be the same as the total cash outflow under the second alternative.

EXAMPLE The Marshall Company, a publicly listed corporation, estimates that its 2021 taxes payable will be $153,000. The company paid taxes of $126,000 for 2020 and $96,000 for 2019.

ANALYSIS The choices for instalment payments for Marshall Company would be:

1. 12 instalments of $12,750 each ($153,000/12) totaling $153,000
2. 12 instalments of $10,500 each ($126,000/12) totaling $126,000
3. 2 instalments of $8,000 each ($96,000/12) and 10 instalments of $11,000 each [($126,000 - $16,000)/10] totaling $126,000

While the total cash outflows under alternative 3 are the same amount as those under alternative 2, alternative 3 would be preferable because the first two payments are smaller and provide a deferral that is spread out over the last 10 payments. This would allow the company to increase cash flows by $5,000 for the first two months.

Calculating the Instalment Amount—Small CCPCs

2-78. CCPCs that meet the definition of a "small" CCPC are exempted from paying monthly instalments and are instead allowed to pay instalments on a quarterly basis as long as they maintain that status. ITA 157(1.2) defines a small CCPC as one for which:

- the taxable income of the corporation and associated corporations does not exceed $500,000 during the current or the previous taxation year;
- the taxable capital employed in Canada of the corporation and associated corporations does not exceed $10 million for the current or previous taxation year;
- an amount has been deducted under ITA 125 (the small business deduction) for the current or previous year; and
- a perfect compliance record has been maintained with respect to payments and filings (for GST, source deductions, and income taxes) during the preceding 12 months. Since

this status is connected to compliance, late payments of GST/HST and/or source deductions and related reporting requirements could result in a loss of status. In such cases the ITA requires the company to return to monthly payments.

2-79. For CCPCs that meet this definition, ITA 157(1.1) provides three alternatives for calculating instalments:

1. **Current year**—Four quarterly instalments, each based on 1/4 of the estimated tax payable for the current taxation year
2. **Preceding year**—Four quarterly instalments, each based on 1/4 of the tax that was payable in the immediately preceding taxation year
3. **Second and first preceding year**—The first quarterly instalment based on 1/4 of the tax that was payable in the second preceding taxation year, followed by three quarterly instalments based on 1/3 of the amount by which the taxes paid in the immediately preceding taxation year exceeds the first instalment

2-80. The payments are required on or before the last day of each of the fiscal quarters.

Exercise 2-7

Subject: Corporate Instalments

Madco Ltd. is not a small CCPC. It has a December 31 year end. For 2019, its tax payable was $32,000, while for 2020 the amount was $59,000. For 2021, its estimated tax payable is $74,000. What would be the minimum instalments for 2021, and when would they be due? How would your answer differ if Madco Ltd. was a small CCPC?

Exercise 2-8

Subject: Corporate Instalments

Fadco Inc. is not a small CCPC. It has a November 30 year end. For the taxation year ending November 30, 2019, its tax payable was $102,000, while for the 2020 taxation year the amount was $54,000. For the 2021 taxation year, its estimated tax payable is $17,000. What would be the minimum instalments for 2021 and when would they be due? How would your answer differ if Fadco Inc. was a small CCPC?

Solutions to Exercises are available in the Study Guide.

Due Date for Balance Owing—Corporations

2-81. Regardless of the instalment base selected, any remaining taxes are due within two months of the corporation's taxation year end. An exception is made in the case of CCPCs that have claimed the small business deduction in the current or preceding taxation year and where the taxable income of the CCPC and associated corporations in the preceding taxation year did not exceed $500,000. The balance due date for those CCPCs is three months after their taxation year end. The CCPC does not have to meet the "small" CCPC definition as described in Paragraph 2-78.

2-82. Note that the final due date for payment is earlier than the due date for filing returns. For example, a company with a March 31 year end that is not eligible for the small business deduction would not have to file its tax return until September 30. However, all of its taxes would be due on May 31. This means that this final payment will often have to be based on an estimate of the total amount of taxes payable for that year.

Exercise 2-9

Subject: Corporate Due Date

The taxation year end for Radco Inc. is January 31, 2021. Indicate the date on which the corporate income tax return must be filed, as well as the date on which any final payment of taxes is due.

Solutions to Exercises are available in the Study Guide.

We suggest you complete SSP 2-2, 2-3, and 2-4 at this point.

Interest and Penalties for Corporations

2-83. The basic rules for interest on corporate balances owing or receivable are generally the same as those applicable to individuals. However, as described in Paragraph 2-56, interest paid to corporations on overpayments is calculated at the prescribed rate, not at the higher rate applicable to individuals and trusts.

2-84. Note that it is especially important that corporations avoid interest on late tax or instalment payments. As pointed out in Paragraph 2-57, interest charged under the ITA is not deductible and therefore the payment of non-deductible interest on late tax payments represents a high cost of financing. For example, if a corporation is paying taxes at a rate of 25%, interest at a non-deductible rate of 6.0% is the equivalent of a deductible interest rate of 8.0% [6.0%/(1 - .25)]. Many corporations, particularly those that are publicly traded, are able to access financing at rates that are lower than this.

2-85. The previously covered penalties applicable to individuals for late filing of returns and for large amounts of late instalments (see Paragraphs 2-59 and 2-63) are equally applicable to corporations. In addition to the penalties applicable to individuals, ITA 235 contains a further late filing penalty applicable to large corporations. It calls for a penalty equal to .0005% per month of a corporation's taxable capital employed in Canada. This will be assessed for a maximum period of 40 months.

2-86. This is a fairly harsh penalty in that, unlike the usual penalties that are based on any additional tax payable at the time the return should have been filed, this penalty is based on the capital of the corporation, without regard to earnings or tax payable for the year. For example, CNR had December 31, 2018, shareholders' equity (roughly the equivalent of taxable capital employed in Canada) of $17.641 billion. If the .0005% penalty was applied to this balance for 40 months, the total penalty would be $3,528,200.

Returns and Payments—Trusts

Types of Trusts

2-87. There are a multitude of different types and categories of trusts with some of the more common being mutual fund trusts, charitable trusts, RRSP trusts, and personal or family-type trusts. Personal or family-type trusts can be broken down into testamentary and inter vivos trusts with the difference explained by when, and under what circumstances, the trust was created or established—a trust that is created when an individual dies would generally be considered a testamentary trust, whereas an inter vivos trust is one created between living persons. A final categorization relates to whether a trust is an express trust, which is one created with a person's express intent, as opposed to other less common situations where a trust may be created by law without any express intent.

2-88. Trusts are covered in Chapter 19, but at this stage a general awareness is important to understand some of the new and basic income tax administrative and procedural issues that arise given that trusts are taxable entities unless exempt, as discussed in Chapter 1. In tax planning the use of trusts is quite common, with inter vivos family-type trusts being created for multiple purposes, many of which are income tax related.

Filing Due Date and Payment of Taxes

2-89. The ITA uses the expressions "filing due date" to determine the filing deadline for an income tax return and "balance due date" to determine the date that any taxes owing for a taxation year must be paid before interest is charged. We saw that these two dates do not match for corporations that have a filing due date of six months after their year end and either two or three months (depending on the income tax status of the corporation) after the year end in which taxes have to be paid. Individuals eligible for the June 15 filing date still have to pay their taxes by April 30. Both the filing due date and balance due date for trusts, however, are the same, set at 90 days after their year end which, with few exceptions, is the calendar year. This means that, except in a leap year, the date is March 31 of the following calendar year.

General Requirement to File an Income Tax Return (T3)

2-90. In Paragraphs 2-10 and 2-11 we mentioned the general filing rules that first require taxable entities to file income tax returns by a set date and then a further rule that would override the filing requirement where, for instance, no taxes were payable for that year. The same rules technically apply to trusts, but the CRA had established its own set of rules and guidelines that essentially only required trust income tax returns to be filed if the trust had tax payable or had made distributions of its income or capital to its beneficiaries. Acquainting oneself with answering the question of whether a trust income tax return would be required to be filed would require reading the extended requirements listed by the CRA in the T3 Trust Guide (T4130).

2-91. Historically, requirements to file income tax returns and pay instalments by trusts were not as strictly applied as they were to individuals. For example, where individuals fail to make sufficient instalment payments on time, penalties and interest are automatically applied. Trusts, with the exception of graduated rate estates (GREs), are required to make instalment payments using the same rules of the ITA that apply to individuals, however the CRA has a longstanding administrative position that no penalties or interest will be charged where a trust does not make sufficient instalment payments. The effect of that position is that trusts are not required to make instalments.

2021 New Reporting Requirements

2-92. The federal government has been concerned with the expanding use of trusts in tax planning for many years. We saw in Chapter 1 in our discussion of residency for trusts that, in general, a trust is resident at the location where the major trust decisions are made, typically by trustees or executors. While this appears straightforward, there are many complexities in determining who is actually making those important decisions on behalf of a trust and who could benefit from trust income or capital. In other words, this information was unknown to the CRA, making it difficult for it to determine whether or not trusts were in compliance with the ITA.

2-93. In the 2017 federal budget the government announced their intention to enhance the information reporting requirements for both resident and non-resident trusts by requiring trusts to report a much broader range of information to the CRA. Details were provided in the 2018 federal budget, and in July 2018 draft legislation was introduced. The new rules are to become effective starting with the 2021 taxation year.

2-94. The new reporting will require most express resident trusts and all non-resident trusts that are required to file an annual income tax return to include the identity of all trustees, beneficiaries, settlors, and each person who has the ability to exert control or override trustee decisions over how income or capital will be distributed. For each person the information required will include their name, address, date of birth, country of residence, and a tax identification number such as a social insurance number.

2-95. The new reporting requirements do not apply to a long list of resident trusts that are express trusts, including a lawyers' general trust account, a GRE, a trust that has been in existence less than three months, and a trust in which the value of certain assets are $50,000 or less throughout the year. There are no exceptions for non-resident trusts, meaning that where they are required to file an annual T3 income tax return they will also be required to include the additional information referred to in Paragraph 2-94.

2-96. The new reporting requirement overrides the rule that exempts trusts from having to file an annual income tax return, meaning that many resident trusts that may not have been required to file an annual income tax return will now be required to do so along with providing the additional detailed information.

2-97. The additional information is required to be filed along with the T3 annual income tax return. Failure to file the information will result in a penalty of $25 per day with a minimum of $100 and a maximum of $2,500. If the failure is attributable to gross negligence (purposeful intent), then the penalty increases to a minimum of $2,500 and a maximum equal to 5% of the highest value of property held in the year.

Exercise 2-10

Subject: Income Tax Return of a Trust

The Sammira Trust is a Canadian resident express family trust established in 2019. The trust holds real estate and other investments valued at $840,000 in 2021. The trust has never had tax payable nor has it ever made any distributions of any kind to its beneficiaries. As a result, the trust has never filed a trust income tax return. Will the trust have to file an income tax return and the additional required information for the 2021 taxation year? If yes, what are the consequences of not filing?

Solutions to Exercises are available in the Study Guide.

We suggest you complete SSP 2-5 at this point.

Income Tax Information Returns

2-98. ITA 221(1)(d) gives the CRA the right to require certain taxpayers to file information returns in addition to the income tax returns in which they report the annual results of income for the purpose of determining whether they owe tax or are entitled to a refund. Information returns are described in Part II of the ITR and must be filed using a prescribed form containing prescribed information. Information returns differ from income tax returns in that their purpose is to both provide information to the CRA and the recipient of payments that are then used to complete the income tax returns. Common examples of these information returns and the related prescribed form are as follows:

- **T3** This form is used by trustees (which includes trustees of some mutual funds) and executors to report the allocation of the trust's income.
- **T4** This form is used by employers to report remuneration and taxable benefits paid to employees and the various amounts withheld for source deductions.
- **T5** This form is used by organizations to report interest, dividend, and royalty payments.
- **T4RSP** This form is used by trustees to report payments out of Registered Retirement Savings Plans.

Books and Records and the CRA

2-99. The importance and significance of keeping and maintaining adequate books and records is sometimes underappreciated. ITA 230 requires that every person carrying on a business keep books and records at the business location or the business owner's residence. The ITA requires that the books and records be sufficient to enable the CRA to determine the persons' tax liability.

2-100. The CRA does not dictate what books and records need to be kept but clarifies that ledgers and other books of account should also include all source documents in paper or electronic format, such as purchase and sales invoices, cash register receipts, credit card receipts, work orders, contracts, bank statements, and so on.

2-101. There are two categories of retention periods for these books and records. The first are prescribed by ITR 5800 and the second set out a standard six-year retention period measured from the taxation year to which the record relates (ITA 230(4)(b)).

2-102. A prescribed retention period applies to businesses being carried out by a corporation, such as its general ledger, share register, minutes of shareholder or directors' meetings, contracts, and agreements. The retention period is two years from the date the corporation was dissolved. A six-year retention period applies to the general ledger and contracts and agreements from the day that a business ceased where the business was carried on by someone other than a corporation.

2-103. The second retention period applies to any books and records other than those that are prescribed by ITR 5800 and is simply six years from the taxation year to which the records relate. This is often misunderstood as a simple six-year count. The six-year count, however, only starts with the year following the year in which the record is no longer relevant to the business.

> **EXAMPLE** Harinder has been carrying on a business as a sole proprietor since 2014. The business uses a calendar-based fiscal year. In 2014 she entered into a consulting contract with the federal government and purchased a car. She traded in the car in 2019. She continues to carry on the business in 2022.
>
> **ANALYSIS** The retention period for the contract is six years from the day the business ceases to be carried on; therefore, the contract must continue to be retained. The invoices and other documents relating to the car are subject to the six-year retention period measured from 2019, the last year it was used in the business. The car documentation must therefore be kept until the end of 2025.

2-104. ITA 231.1 contains the authority that allows the CRA to audit the books and records of the business. In addition, the CRA will also verify other information, including personal bank statements and credit cards, particularly where the business is operated as a sole proprietorship or partnership. Information and records can also be requested from third parties, such as suppliers and clients as well as from bookkeepers, accountants, and lawyers, although lawyers may be able to claim solicitor-client privilege, which is not generally available for accountants. If the books and records are considered inadequate. which includes not being complete, the CRA will issue what is referred to as an inadequate books and records letter where a specified period of time is given to correct the situation. Failure to do so is a serious matter that could result in a court order and penalties from $1,000 to $25,000 together with imprisonment up to 12 months.

Assessments and the CRA My Account Service

CRA Website—My Account Service

2-105. The CRA invests considerable resources on continual improvements to its website and electronic services. The goal is to reduce costs and provide faster, more efficient quality services to taxpayers. For example, the Auto-Fill My Return service allows individuals and authorized representatives to automatically fill in parts of a current-year income tax return. The CRA website contains the My Account service, which is a secure online portal that allows registered individuals to see many of their tax accounts online and manage their tax information. There is a similar My Business Account service available for businesses. The CRA website contains a list of its ever-expanding electronic services. For the My Account service, the available information includes access to notices of assessment, RRSP and TFSA contribution limits, instalments paid and payable, and many other past and present balances.

2-106. Recent additions and improvements to the My Account Service include the following:

- **Tax Schemes Overview** Provides alerts about current tax schemes and how to avoid them
- **Home Buyers' and Lifelong Learning Plans** Provides details, including payment information (these topics are discussed in Chapter 10)
- **Proceed to Pay Button** This new feature provides payment options for paying account balances including instalment payments
- **Request for Relief of Penalties and Interest** Provides a direct link to the forms necessary to file a taxpayer relief request (discussed at the end of this chapter)

Notice of Assessment

2-107. After a tax return has been filed, the CRA runs a number of tests on the filed return, such as verifying the eligibility for various deductions (e.g., RRSP deductions) and tax credits (e.g., age credit). After processing a return, the CRA completes a notice of assessment, which contains the amount, if any, of taxes to be paid or refunded, an explanation of any changes it has made to the return, and any interest and penalties that were assessed. For individuals, it also contains additional information such as the taxpayer's RRSP deduction limit. For individuals, the notice of assessment is available online in the My Account service, often within a few weeks of filing. A somewhat longer period is normally required for corporate income tax assessments and more complicated individual returns. The CRA will mail out the notice of assessment unless the taxpayer has opted instead to have email notification as soon as it is available to be viewed online.

Notice of Reassessment and Statutory Limitations

2-108. The notice of assessment does not free the taxpayer from additional scrutiny of the income tax return. The CRA is under pressure to issue notices of assessment quickly, so the initial assessment is not based on an in-depth review of the return. A more detailed review of many returns is done after the notice of assessment has been issued. The CRA has a matching program that compares information provided through information returns, such as by employers and financial institutions. The CRA has also developed unique and complex algorithms designed to help identify compliance issues that require investigation in the form of income tax audits. Once the CRA, on examination through an audit or otherwise, revises an income tax return they will then issue what is referred to as a notice of reassessment setting out the revisions, including explanations for the change(s). In a manner similar to that of a notice of assessment, the notice of reassessment can be viewed online if the taxpayer has registered for the My Account service.

2-109. In Canada there are a number of instances where the law imposes some form of liability upon certain persons. The liability is rarely intended to endure for all time, and as a result statute of limitation periods apply limiting the timeframe in which legal action can be taken. The period can vary considerably depending on the nature of a claim (e.g., traffic tickets, small claims court action). The ITA contains a statutory limitation period referred to as a "normal reassessment period." The normal reassessment period is defined at ITA 152(3.1) and begins on the date found on the notice of assessment and ends exactly three years from that date for individuals, most trusts, and CCPCs. The normal reassessment period is extended to four years for other corporations because of the greater complexity that may be involved in the review process. Finally, it is important to be aware that the ITA extends the normal reassessment period by a further three years in a number of very specific situations to ensure that the CRA has sufficient time to make the necessary adjustments to taxes payable. An example is the failure to file form T1135 when you own foreign property that costs more than $100,000 and you also fail to report any income earned on that foreign property.

2-110. The CRA can revise tax payable within this normal three- or four-year limitation period as many times as they wish. The CRA, however, is only allowed to reassess beyond that limitation period in the following two situations:

- If the taxpayer or person filing the return on the taxpayer's behalf has made any misrepresentation that is attributable to neglect, carelessness, or wilful default, or has committed any fraud in filing the return or in supplying information. If this threshold is met the CRA can only look beyond the limitation period to the specific item(s) that resulted in the misrepresentation.
- If the taxpayer has filed a waiver of the three-year time limit. The waiver is valid until revoked by the taxpayer, in which case it lasts for six months from that time. A waiver is generally restricted to a specific issue only and does not allow the CRA to look at other issues.

2-111. The final point to note is that the normal reassessment period begins with the date of the notice of assessment. If a taxpayer has not filed an income tax return for a specific year, then the three- or four-year limitation period clock has not begun.

> **EXAMPLE** Juan Fernando is a Canadian resident who did not file his 2015 income tax return until January 2021. He received a notice of assessment dated March 2, 2021. The normal reassessment period is three years from the date of the notice of assessment for that year, meaning that the CRA has until March 1, 2024, to reassess his 2015 income tax return.

Refunds

2-112. When tax has been withheld from income or instalments have been paid, the notice of assessment may show that there has been an overpayment of income tax and that the taxpayer is entitled to a refund. In the great majority of cases, such refunds are sent without any further action being taken. If, for some reason, the refund is not made, the taxpayer can apply for it in writing within the normal reassessment period. However, if there are other tax liabilities outstanding, such as amounts owing from prior years, GST/HST, or source deductions, the CRA has the right to offset the refund against these liabilities.

2-113. In addition there is a limitation period built into the ITA that requires that a refund for a specific taxation year will only be issued if the income tax return for that year is filed within three years from the end of that year. This would mean that if an individual was entitled to a refund for the 2018 year that the income tax return for that year would have had to be filed by December 31, 2021. If the return is filed January 1, 2022, or later, then the CRA will not refund the amount nor apply it against any other tax debt. This limitation rule applies to all taxpayers, including trusts and corporations.

2-114. Fortunately there is an option to recover such a refund, but the potential relief only applies to individuals and GREs, not corporations or other trusts. We discuss the "Taxpayer Relief" application at the end of this chapter.

Interest on Refunds

2-115. When a taxpayer is entitled to an income tax refund, interest may be included depending on the facts. The timing and calculation of interest is different for individuals and trusts than it is for corporations. Any interest received, however, is required to be included in the taxpayer's income, unlike the case where interest paid on income taxes owing is not deductible.

2-116. For individuals, interest is paid on refunds of income tax at the prescribed base rate plus 2 percentage points. Interest begins to accrue on the later of two dates:

- 30 days after the balance due date (generally April 30); or
- 30 days after the return is filed.

2-117. For an individual who carries on a business, the normal filing date would be June 15. If such an individual were entitled to a refund and waited until this date to file, interest would not begin to accrue until 30 days after June 15. If you filed the 2021 income tax return on April 30, 2022, and were entitled to a refund, no interest would accrue as long as the CRA pays any refund by May 30, 2022.

2-118. For corporations, interest on refunds at the prescribed base rate, without the additional 2 percentage points, begins to accrue at the later of the following two dates:

- 120 days after the corporate year end; or
- if the return is filed after the filing due date of six months from the year end, 30 days after the corporation's tax return is actually filed.

EXAMPLE The taxation year end of CTP Corporation is December 31. The filing due date for the 2021 income tax return is therefore June 30, 2022. If the company files its income tax return on June 30, 2022, and is entitled to a refund, interest will be calculated starting April 30, 2022, which is 120 days after the year end even though the income tax return is filed two months later. This is because the 30-day limitation only applies if the income tax return is filed after June 30, 2022. If, however, the income tax return was filed July 1, 2022, then interest would only be calculated from 30 days after that date, or July 31, 2022.

Adjustments to Income Tax Returns

2-119. There is no general provision in the ITA for filing an amended return. However, this does not mean that amounts included in the income tax returns of previous years cannot be altered. It simply means that the adjustment process normally takes place after the return has been processed and a notice of assessment has been issued.

2-120. There are many reasons why adjustments to a previously filed return could be necessary. Besides the obvious omissions or errors (i.e., omitting a charitable donation or medical expense receipt or making an error in recording the information on a T4), there are many other possible reasons. Information received after the return was filed (e.g., learning through a tax course that an elderly parent should have been claimed as a dependant) would make an adjustment of a prior return advantageous.

2-121. IC 75-7R3, "Reassessment of a Return of Income," sets out the following conditions under which the CRA will accept adjustments that reduce taxes payable for the year or increase or create a refund:

- The CRA is satisfied that the previous assessment was incorrect
- The reassessment can be made within the normal reassessment period or beyond if the taxpayer has filed a waiver with respect to that issue
- The requested decrease in taxable income does not solely depend on an increase in a permissive deduction such as capital cost allowance (CCA; discussed in Chapter 5)
- The change is not based solely on a successful appeal to the courts by another taxpayer
- The taxpayer's return has been filed within three years of the end of the year to which it relates where the adjustment would have created a refund

2-122. For individuals, changes can be requested online through the CRA website by using either the "Change My Return" or "Refile" feature of the My Account service or by mailing form T1-ADJ, "T1 Adjustment Request," to the tax centre responsible for processing their income tax return. When concluded the CRA will either send the taxpayer a notice of reassessment outlining the changes or a letter explaining why the requested changes were not made. Adjustment requests can also be made for both trusts and corporations, although the procedures are slightly different.

Disputes and Appeals

Representation by Others

2-123. At the initial stages of any dispute, an individual may wish to handle matters personally when the issues are relatively straightforward. The individual can communicate directly with the CRA and provide additional information where necessary when it is believed the issues can be satisfactorily resolved. However, if a dispute is not resolved after an individuals' best efforts, then reaching out to others well-versed in income tax, such as professional tax advisors, is the next step. Due to privacy and confidentiality concerns, anyone who acts on behalf of an individual must go through an authorization process. Once the process is complete the CRA will then communicate directly with the advisor/representative within the scope of the authority that was provided and any time limitations that were placed on that authority.

2-124. Authorizing a representative can be done in one of four ways (these are listed starting with the quickest to the slowest):

1. The individual taxpayer can authorize another individual directly through their "My Account" service.
2. The representative submits an EFILE authorization request. An EFILE request must be used with certified commercial tax software.
3. The representative submits a business authorization request to "Represent a Client."
4. The individual taxpayer can mail form AUT-01 to authorize a representative for access by phone or mail.

2-125. Finally, any individual can be authorized to interact with the CRA on behalf of a taxpayer, including an accountant, bookkeeper, spouse, common-law partner, or other family member or friend. Depending on the issue in dispute, the taxpayer can either set an expiry date on the authorization or can cancel the authorization at any time. The taxpayer's representative can also cancel the authorization at any time. The scope of the authorization is categorized into three levels: Level 1 allows only for information to be obtained, level 2 allows both information to be obtained and some changes to be made to an income tax return or transfer payments, and level 3 is full authorization.

Notice of Objection

General Rules

2-126. If communications with the CRA, including those of a representative, fail to resolve the dispute then the next course of action is a formal objection, which involves the timely filing of a a notice of objection. It is not uncommon to file a notice of objection during informal communications with the CRA rather than wait for an outcome, particularly if the deadline for filing an objection is close. This is often referred to as a protective objection.

2-127. The two general methods available for filing an objection are:

- by accessing My Account or My Business Account from the CRA website and selecting the option "Register my formal dispute" (also available through "Represent a Client" by your representative), or
- by mailing or faxing form T400A, "Objection—*Income Tax Act,*" or writing a letter to the chief of appeals at the relevant appeals intake centre explaining the reasons for your objection.

2-128. For corporations and trusts (other than GREs), a notice of objection must be filed within 90 days of the date on the notice of assessment or notice of reassessment. For individuals and GREs the deadline is much more generous, allowing an objection to be filed by the later of:

- 90 days from the date on the botice of assessment or reassessment; or
- one year from the filing due date for the year assessed or reassessed.

EXAMPLE An individual who is required to file his 2020 income tax return on April 30, 2021, files early on March 26, 2021. The notice of assessment for 2020 is dated May 14, 2021, and contains a change by the CRA to the individuals' detriment. A notice of reassessment is issued for the same 2020 year dated August 1, 2022, and contains another negative change.

ANALYSIS A notice of objection related to the May 14, 2021, notice of assessment must be filed before the later of August 12, 2021 (90 days after the date on the notice) or April 30, 2022 (one year after the filing due date of April 30, 2021). The deadline would be the later date of April 30, 2022, without regard for the fact that the return was actually filed before the filing due date on March 26, 2021. Since the August 1, 2022, notice of reassessment was dated after the one-year deadline of April 30, 2022, the notice of objection must be filed by October 30, 2022 (90 days after the date of the notice).

2-129. When an individual dies after October of the year and before their normal filing due date in the following year (April 30 or June 15), the filing date for the return is extended to six months after the date of death, thereby extending the date for filing a notice of objection by the same number of months.

2-130. If a taxpayer misses the deadline she can request an extension of the filing deadline for the notice of objection. Since many of the disputed issues result from a notice of reassessment mailed more than a year after the filing due date of the return, the relevant deadline is then 90 days from the date on the notice of reassessment. If the matter is complicated and requires professional help, 90 days may not be sufficient time to respond to the reassessment. The application for an extension must be made within one year of the deadline to file the notice of objection. A taxpayer must also show that she had intended to object during the limitation period but was unable to act or instruct another to act on her behalf and that she acted as soon as circumstances allowed. In other words, there has to be justification for failing to object on time.

2-131. After the notice of objection is received, the CRA is required to reply to the taxpayer with one of the following actions:

- vacating the assessment,
- confirming it (i.e., refusing to change it),
- varying the amount, or
- reassessing.

2-132. Unresolved objections are subject to review by the chief of appeals. These appeals sections are instructed to operate independently of the assessing divisions and should provide an unbiased second opinion. If the matter remains unresolved after this review, the taxpayer must either accept the CRA's assessment or, alternatively, continue to pursue the matter to a higher level of appeal.

2-133. The CRA has a guide covering the dispute process, "Resolving Your Dispute: Objections and Appeal Rights under the *Income Tax Act*" (P148 CRA brochure titled "Resolving Your Dispute: Objection and Appeal Rights under the *Income Tax Act*"). It contains coverage of the procedures needed to file a notice of objection, including a sample, as well as information on how to proceed with an appeal to the courts should the CRA not accept the objection as filed.

Rules for Large Corporations

2-134. In response to the practice of certain large corporations delaying the dispute process by filing vague objections, sometimes to give them additional time to consider new arguments or to await pending court decisions on similar matters of dispute, the federal government introduced restrictions on these corporations.

2-135. To prevent this perceived abuse, a corporation must specifically identify and address each issue to be decided, the dollar amount of relief sought for each issue, and the facts and reasons relied on by the corporation in respect of each issue when filing a notice of objection.

2-136. If the large corporation objects to a reassessment or additional reassessment made by the CRA, or appeals to the Tax Court of Canada, the objection or appeal is restricted to issues and dollar amounts addressed in the original notice of objection. There is an exception to this general rule for new issues that are raised by the CRA on assessment or reassessment. These limitations are only applicable to "large corporations," defined as a corporation with taxable capital employed in Canada that is in excess of $10 million at the end of the year to which the objection relates.

CRA Service Standards for Processing Objections

2-137. There has been no shortage of complaints concerning the length of time the CRA has taken to process objections. In 2016 the auditor general released a report that was highly critical of the delays, making a number of recommendations for improvement. Since then the CRA has taken steps to improve their service standards for handling objections. Currently the CRA categorizes objections into three levels of complexity: low, medium, and complex. Low complexity objectives are promised to be processed within six months; medium objections within one year; and complex objections generally within two years but could be longer.

Exercise 2-11

Subject: Notice of Objection

Jerry Fall filed his 2021 tax return as required on April 30, 2022. His notice of assessment dated May 20, 2022, indicated that his return was accepted as filed. On May 22, 2023, he receives a notice of reassessment dated May 15, 2023, indicating that he owes additional taxes as well as interest on the unpaid amounts. What is the latest date for filing a notice of objection for this reassessment? Explain your answer.

Solutions to Exercises are available in the Study Guide.

Tax Court of Canada

Deadline for Appeal

2-138. A taxpayer who does not find satisfaction through the notice of objection process may then proceed to the next level of appeal, the Tax Court of Canada. Appeals to the Tax Court of Canada must be made within 90 days of the date of the CRA's response to the notice of objection (referred to as a notice of appeal) or 90 days after the notice of objection has been filed if the CRA has not replied. It is not possible to bypass the Tax Court of Canada and appeal directly to the Federal Court level, except in very limited circumstances.

Informal Procedure

2-139. There are two levels of procedure in the Tax Court of Canada. On appeal, the general procedure will automatically apply unless the taxpayer elects to have his case heard under the informal procedure. The informal procedure applies where the total amount of federal tax and penalty involved for a given year is less than $25,000 or where a loss carryover in dispute is less than $50,000 or the appeal is limited to challenging the amount of interest charged. These limits apply on a year-by-year basis, meaning that if a business that has been audited for three years and reassessed for each year, the dollar limits are for each of the three years. If the dollar limits are exceeded a taxpayer may still appeal under the informal procedure but the claims must be limited to the maximum dollar limits. If, for example, the federal taxes and penalties total $32,000 for the 2019 year, electing the informal procedure means limiting the claim to $25,000 only. We would add that there are no dollar limits on the use of the informal procedure for GST/HST disputes.

2-140. Advantages of the informal procedure include the following:

- The rules of evidence remain fairly informal, allowing the taxpayer to represent herself or be represented by an agent such as an accountant.
- Under the informal procedure, even if the taxpayer is unsuccessful he cannot be asked to pay the court costs of the CRA.
- The informal procedure is designed as a fast-track procedure that is usually completed within six or seven months, whereas the general procedure may take many years.

2-141. Decisions of the Tax Court at the informal level are not permitted to be used as a precedent in other decisions. In addition, a decision of the Tax Court generally cannot be appealed under the informal procedure.

General Procedure

2-142. If the general procedure applies, formal rules of evidence must be used, resulting in a situation where an individual taxpayer has to be represented by either herself or legal counsel. Corporations are required to have legal counsel. In practical terms, this means that for cases involving substantial amounts, lawyers will usually be involved.

2-143. Under the general procedure, if the taxpayer is unsuccessful, the court may require the taxpayer to pay costs to the CRA. Under either procedure, if the taxpayer is more than 50% successful (e.g., if he is claiming $10,000 and is awarded more than $5,000), the judge can order the CRA to pay all or part of the taxpayer's costs. However, there is a tariff structure that can severely limit the costs that can be awarded by the court.

Appeals by the Minister

2-144. There are situations in which the CRA can intervene to have an appeal heard under the general procedure even though the taxpayer has applied for the informal procedure. Such circumstances are infrequent but recognize that an issue may impact a broader group of taxpayers, particularly those who have filed similar appeals. The taxpayer is given protection from the costs associated with this type of appeal by the requirement that the CRA be responsible for the taxpayer's reasonable legal fees when the amount of taxes payable in question does not exceed $25,000 or the loss in dispute does not exceed $50,000. This is without regard to whether the appeal is successful.

Resolution

2-145. Prior to the hearing by the Tax Court of Canada, discussions between the taxpayer and the Department of Justice (e.g., the CRA's legal counsel) are likely to arise. In many cases an out-of-court settlement is proposed with the prospect of limiting the number of cases that are actually heard by the court. However, if a hearing proceeds, the court may dispose of an appeal by:

- dismissing it; or
- allowing it and
  - vacating the assessment,
  - varying the assessment, or
  - referring the assessment back to the CRA for reconsideration and reassessment

Federal Court and Supreme Court of Canada

2-146. Either the CRA or the taxpayer can appeal a general procedure decision of the Tax Court of Canada to the Federal Court of Appeal. The appeal must be made within 30 days of the date on which the Tax Court of Canada makes its decision. The Supreme Court, however, had previously ruled that a decision of the Tax Court could not be overturned by an appeal court unless the claimant was able to show that the Tax Court judge made an overriding and palpable error in finding or in fact.

2-147. It is possible to pursue a matter beyond the Federal Court of Appeal to the Supreme Court of Canada. This can be done if the Federal Court of Appeal refers the issue to the higher court or if the Supreme Court authorizes the appeal. These actions will not usually happen unless there are new issues or legal precedents to be dealt with and, as a result, such appeals are not common. However, when tax cases do reach the Supreme Court, they often attract a great deal of public attention.

We suggest you complete SSP 2-6 at this point.

Tax Evasion, Avoidance, and Planning

Tax Evasion

2-148. The concept of tax evasion is not difficult to understand. It is described on the CRA website as follows:

> Tax evasion occurs when an individual or business intentionally ignores Canada's tax laws. This includes falsifying records and claims, purposefully not reporting income, or inflating expenses.

Tax evasion, unlike tax avoidance, has criminal consequences. Tax evaders face prosecution, a criminal record, and having to pay penalties equal to 200% of the taxes owed plus up to five years in jail. The CRA lists hiding assets in foreign jurisdictions, tax protesters (i.e., individuals who don't believe in paying income taxes at all), and tax scheme promoters as three of the most concerning forms of tax evasion, although there are many others. The CRA publishes a list of tax evasion prosecutions on its website to increase the integrity of the tax system, further compliance, and as a means of warning Canadians about tax fraud schemes.

Tax Avoidance and Planning

2-149. The concept of tax evasion is clear as it involves the deliberate and intentional breaking of the law. Arguably, tax planning arrangements that are within the letter of the law should be considered acceptable. The view of the CRA, however, is that tax planning arrangements that are within the law but that violate the "spirit" of the law are unacceptable. The CRA, consistent with this view, makes the following observations with respect to tax avoidance:

> Tax Avoidance results when actions are taken to minimize tax, while within the letter of the law, those actions contravene the object and spirit of the law. Tax avoidance would include all unacceptable and abusive tax planning whereas aggressive tax planning would be considered to "push the limits" of acceptable tax planning.

2-150. The CRA, prior to 1988, has a long history of unsuccessful challenges to what they believed to be tax avoidance. The courts were often reluctant to side with the CRA on the basis that a particular tax planning strategy failed to fall into the precise wording of dozens of anti-avoidance rules scattered throughout the ITA. In other words, the courts' view was that if Parliament (e.g., the federal government) took issue with certain tax planning arrangements, they had the power and were therefore free to add new anti-avoidance legislation to target the particular arrangement. In theory this may have been seen as an ideal approach, but in practice it was unworkable. It would mean that years would pass in which tax revenues were being siphoned out of the economy as the new targeted anti-avoidance rules worked their way through the slow legislative process. The General Anti-Avoidance Rule (GAAR) was introduced and became law in 1988 to provide the CRA with a general-purpose tool on which they could rely where the spirit of the law had been violated.

General Anti-Avoidance Rule (GAAR)

General Overview

2-151. There are three key concepts to understanding and applying the GAAR:

1. a tax benefit
2. a tax avoidance transaction, and
3. misuse or abuse.

2-152. In very general terms, a tax benefit is the actual tax savings as a result of the tax planning. A tax avoidance transaction is the transaction(s) that is part of the tax planning, the purpose of which is to obtain the tax benefit and which is primarily motivated by the tax benefit. Finally, the misuse or abuse refers to the intention of the specific law that has been circumvented, avoided, or abused. A simple example will demonstrate the concept:

EXAMPLE—The Facts Leanne Paquette owns a building in Calgary, Alberta. She has been approached by a representative of Linear Services Ltd. who has offered to purchase the building well in excess of its current value for cash. Leanne knows that if she sells the building in 2021 she will have a huge gain that will increase her income taxes by a substantial amount. Her advisor told her that if she sells the building for a small cash down payment to a purchaser with the remainder paid equally over five years that she will cut her income tax bill in half. The corporate purchaser, however, is not interested in a five-year payment plan but is willing to purchase the building from any owner.

Objective: The ITA allows a gain to be spread over five years through a reserve mechanism (discussed in Chapter 8). The policy rationale for the reserve is to recognize that a seller will receive only part of the cash and therefore may not be able to pay the income tax on the full amount.

EXAMPLE—The Tax Plan The following steps will be undertaken:

1. Leanne's advisor will create a new company.
2. Leanne will sell the building to the new company with a small down payment and repayment of the remainder over five years.
3. The new company will sell the building to Linear Services Ltd for cash.
4. The new company will pay the cash to Leanne over five years.

The sales price between Leanne and the new company and between the new company and Linear Services will be the same.

ANALYSIS

1. **The Tax Benefit:** Equals the tax savings.
2. **The Avoidance Transactions:** The creation of the new company (step 1) and the sale of the building by Leanne to that new company (step 2). Note that these transactions would not have been undertaken if it were not for the tax savings available.
3. **Misuse or Abuse:** The use of the intermediary new company was to enable Leanne to defer recognition of the gain, which is contrary to the purpose of the reserve mechanism.
4. **Result:** The reserve would be disallowed and the full amount of the gain would be included in Leanne's income in the year of sale (2021).

Collection and Enforcement

Collections

2-153. The CRA's collection powers are vast and include garnishment of employee wages, garnishment of a payment made to a taxpayer from others, offsets of amounts owing to a taxpayer, and the seizure of assets. Given this authority it is not surprising that there are some safeguards in place. In terms of income tax, collection action cannot be taken until a notice of assessment or reassessment has been issued since those notifications serve to establish an income tax liability.

2-154. We have also seen that a taxpayer can file a notice of objection to a notice of assessment or reassessment. In recognition of this, CRA Collections is prohibited from taking any immediate collection action when such notices are issued. The exercise of collection action is delayed as follows:

- 90 days after the assessment or reassessment date when no objection is filed;
- 90 days from the date of the notice from the CRA appeals division confirming or varying the assessment or reassessment where an objection has been filed and no further appeal has been made; or
- 90 days after a court decision has been made and there are no further appeals.

Note however that interest continues to accrue throughout these periods. Tax professionals will often advise taxpayers, depending on the circumstances, to pay the disputed amounts in full to avoid the accumulation of non-deductible interest.

2-155. Note that the collection of source deductions and GST/HST amounts are not subject to any collection restrictions. This reflects the fact that these amounts are collected on behalf of the government and are amounts held in trust that belong to the government.

Other Penalties

2-156. There are an abundance of penalties under the ITA and ETA. Penalties are either based on an automatic application for failing to do something (such as filing an income tax return on time or any form or duty imposed upon taxpayers or others) to penalties based on varying degrees of negligence and criminal penalties. At times what seems to be one infraction can turn into multiple penalties. For example, there is a penalty for failing to actually withhold an amount, another for failing to remit or send it to the CRA, and a third for failing to file an information return that tells the CRA everything about the required withholding. Penalty assessments also include interest charges.

2-157. Examples of some of the more commonly encountered penalties, aside from the late filing penalties discussed in this chapter, include the following:

Failure to File a Partnership Information Return—ITA 162(7.1) & (8) In Chapter 1 we mentioned that partnerships are not taxable entities and are therefore not required to file an income tax return, but they are required to file an information return (T5013) for each partner and a summary return. The penalty for not doing so is the greater of:

- $100, or
- $25 per day to a maximum of 100 days for a maximum penalty of $2,500.

The penalty is applied to each slip and summary separately, meaning that if there are four partners there would be four individual slips plus one summary for a total of five slips, each of which is subject to the penalty.

In addition, if the CRA has issued a demand for the partnership to file the information returns then a second penalty applies of $100 per month, or part of a month, for each partner for a maximum period of 24 months or $2,400.

Repeated Failure to Report Income—ITA 163(1) This penalty applies when there is a failure to report at least $500 in income in the current year and in any of the three preceding years. The penalty is the lesser of:

- 10% of the unreported income amount (not the taxes owing); or
- an amount equal to 50% of the difference between the understated tax and the amount of any tax paid in respect of the unreported amount (e.g., withholdings by an employer). For example, assume that an individual, with multiple short-term employment sessions in a year, forgot to include a T4 slip. Assume that the additional income would have resulted in $2,000 of additional income tax but the amount of income tax withheld was actually $2,200. In this case, the penalty would be nil.

False Statements or Omissions—ITA 163(2) This penalty applies in cases of gross negligence. Gross negligence has been defined by the courts to mean "A high degree of negligence tantamount to intentional acting, an indifference as to whether the law is complied with or not." This is the most commonly applied penalty by the CRA when conducting business audits and is equal to the greater of $100 or 50% of the understated tax.

The significance of this penalty cannot be overstated, but unlike many other penalties that place the onus on the taxpayer to prove that a penalty should not apply, the burden of proof is on the CRA in both gross negligence and criminal penalties. We would add that there are rules that have been added to the ITA that allow a taxpayer charged with very selective penalties to argue a due diligence defence in that they did everything in their power to comply with the ITA. Even when the ITA does not contain such a defence, the courts are often willing to vacate assessments of penalties as if a due diligence defence existed.

Tax Advisors and Tax Return Preparers

2-158. Tax preparers who prepare more than 10 returns for a fee are required to register with the CRA and file them electronically. Mandatory electronic filing applies to both the filing of T1 individual returns and T2 corporate returns. Individual taxpayers and volunteers who do not charge a fee to prepare tax returns for others are not required to register for an EFILE number. Tax preparers who do not EFILE may be charged a penalty of $25 for each paper-filed T1 and $100 for each paper-filed T2.

2-159. Civil penalties for tax advisors and tax return preparers who encourage or assist clients with tax evasive practices are found in ITA 163.2, "Misrepresentation of a Tax Matter by a Third Party." The penalty of most concern to accountants is the one for participating in a misrepresentation in the preparation of a return. The penalty is the greater of $1,000 and the penalty assessed on the tax return preparer's client for making the false statement or omission. The penalty on the client is equal to 50% of the amount of tax avoided as a result of the misrepresentation. The total amount of the tax preparer penalty is capped at $100,000, plus the gross compensation to which the tax return preparer is entitled to receive from the client.

2-160. IC 01-1, "Third-Party Civil Penalties," is an extensive information circular that contains 18 examples of the application of third-party penalties. While the examples cited in the IC illustrate clear-cut abuses, there are many situations in which it is to the taxpayer's advantage to pursue a more aggressive stance in claiming deductions. It is believed that these penalties discourage tax return preparers from suggesting or condoning this type of approach, out of fear that they may be liable for the third-party penalties if the returns are audited. In addition, it appears that an increasing number of tax return preparers are refusing to service certain types of high-risk clients.

We suggest you complete SSP 2-7 at this point.

Promoters of Abusive Tax Shelters and Tax Planning Arrangements

2-161. The CRA has a number of penalties applicable to tax advisors and promoters of what they consider to be abusive tax shelters and tax planning arrangements. For example, for many years the CRA has been actively pursuing taxpayers participating in "gifting tax shelter schemes" and promoters of these schemes.

2-162. The penalties in this complex area can arise from a number of misdeeds, such as participating in a misrepresentation, making or furnishing false or misleading statements, and being involved with the development of an "abusive" tax shelter. In addition to promoters, the penalties can apply to a tax advisor who, in the course of providing tax advice, is responsible for and contributes to the design of any of the tax avoidance elements of the arrangement.

Taxpayer Relief Provisions

Overview and Basic Rules

2-163. Many years ago the CRA frequently encountered situations in which taxpayers, most often individuals, were assessed penalties and interest on a wide range of matters that were thought to be unfair given the circumstances even though the ITA had not been complied with. Examples include individuals who failed to file tax returns as a result of health/medical reasons, those who followed incorrect advice given by the CRA, or those who were facing severe financial hardship and were unable to pay.

2-164. The CRA was unable to deal with these difficulties because they lacked the legal authority to do so and were therefore unable to forgive penalties and interest. In addition, many of the issues arose outside of the standard three-year normal reassessment period, adding another obstacle.

2-165. The only remedy at the time was an application for a remission order under the authority of the *Financial Administrations Act,* which required a lengthy political and administrative process that required two or more years before a decision could be rendered. Extensive administrative guidelines were in place to decide whether an application qualified.

2-166. In 1994 the federal government introduced ITA 220(3.1), which gave the CRA the authority to waive interest and penalties for a maximum of 10 calendar years. Other relief measures were also added that gave the CRA the ability to make refunds beyond three years (individuals and GREs only) and to accept certain elective provisions beyond their normal deadlines on the payment of a $100 per month penalty. This new legislation gave the CRA the authority to provide relief on a case-by-case basis.

2-167. These taxpayer relief measures represent a powerful tool to a tax advisor. All accountants, whether tax specialists or not, should be aware of their significance to clients and potential clients. An application (RC4288) for the waiver of interest and penalties must be completed setting out all the facts and circumstances. The CRA will not accept an application unless the facts fall into one of three categories of:

- extraordinary circumstance
- actions of the CRA, or
- inability to pay or financial hardship.

2-168. If an application is denied a second administrative review application can be made for reconsideration. If the second application is also denied the decision by the CRA on behalf of the minister can be challenged in the Federal Court, although the court does not have the authority to force the CRA to reverse its decision. The court can only suggest that the decision be reconsidered. The CRA publication IC07-1R1 titled "Taxpayer Relief Provisions" should be consulted for additional detail.

Voluntary Disclosure Program (VDP)

2-169. The voluntary disclosure program, or VDP, is another example of a different type of taxpayer relief. In this instance the VDP is designed to permit taxpayers to come forward and fully disclose their previous non-compliance. The enticement to come forward is that some penalties and interest could be waived. The VDP is another essential area of tax practice that is critical for all acountants to understand.

2-170. The VDP has been around for many years but underwent a major overhaul in 2018, which came into effect for applications submitted beginning March 1, 2018. Prior to that time there was one VDP program for all. Currently the VDP is split into two distinct parts referred to as a limited and a general program. The general program has the more generous advantages.

2-171. A valid VDP application (form RC199) requires meeting the following conditions:

1. **Be Voluntary** A taxpayer could not meet this condition if the CRA had made contact with the taxpayer concerning the issue of non-compliance with the likelihood that the non-compliance would be discovered.
2. **Be Complete** Information concerning all relevant years must be fully disclosed, or if information for some years is no longer available that fact must also be disclosed. Penalties and interest can only be waived for 10 years, and if the non-compliance exceeds 10 years all years must still be disclosed.
3. Involve a **potential penalty**.
4. Include **information that is at least one year past due**.
5. Include **full payment or must make a payment arrangement acceptable to CRA Collections**.

The Limited Program

2-172. The limited program applies to cases of intentional conduct to avoid detection including establishing offshore bank accounts. The materiality of the amounts involved, the number of years of non-compliance, and the sophistication of the taxpayer all play a role in determining whether the limited program applies. In addition, if a taxpayer has come forward shortly after a public announcement by the CRA to launch an audit program designed to detect the non-compliance, this fact will weigh in favour of acceptance under the limited program.

2-173. A successful application under the limited program will result in (1) waiving all gross negligence penalties for a maximum 10-year period and (2) avoiding criminal prosecution for tax matters. Any non-negligence penalties will be charged (such as late filing), and none of the interest is waived.

The General Program

2-174. Disclosures that do not fall within the limited program are considered under the general program. If the application is accepted, all penalties are waived for the 10-year period and criminal prosecution for tax matters will not be pursued. In addition, none of the interest is waived for the three most current years and only 50% of the interest is waived for the remaining years four to ten.

Other VDP Issues

2-175. There are a few additional points to be aware of when considering the benefits and advantages of a voluntary disclosure:

- As a rule a taxpayer is only allowed to make a disclosure under the VDP once.
- The CRA may require the disclosure of advisors who participated in the non-compliance.
- The CRA offers a pre-disclosure discussion without the necessity of divulging the names of the taxpayers, as a means by which representatives can get a sense of whether an application will be accepted and under which program.
- A second administrative review is available if the first application is declined.
- A judicial review by the Federal Court is available should the CRA decline the application.
- An application can be made under the taxpayer relief provisions discussed in Paragraph 2-166 to waive any interest not waived under the VDP.
- Additional information can be found in IC00-1R6, "Voluntary Disclosures Program."

Key Terms

A full glossary with definitions is provided at the end of the Study Guide.

Assessment	Net Tax Owing
GAAR	Notice of Assessment
Information Return	Notice of Objection
Instalment Threshold	Penalties
Instalments	Prescribed Rate

Reassessment	Tax Evasion
Small CCPC	Tax Planning
Source Deductions	Taxpayer Relief Provisions
Tax Avoidance	Taxpayer
Tax Court of Canada	

References

For more detailed study of the material in this chapter, we would refer you to the following:

ITA 150	Filing Returns of Income—General Rule
ITA 151	Estimate of Tax
ITA 152	Assessment
ITA 153(1)	Withholding
ITA 156	Other Individuals (Instalments)
ITA 156.1	Definitions (Instalments)
ITA 157	Payment by Corporation (Instalments)
ITA 161	Interest (General)
ITA 162-163.1	Penalties
ITA 163.2	Misrepresentation of a Tax Matter by a Third Party
ITA 164(1)	Refunds
ITA 165	Objections to Assessment
ITA 169-180	Appeals to the Tax Court of Canada and the Federal Court of Appeal
ITA 220	Minister's Duty
ITA 221	Regulations
ITA 222	Definitions (Collections)
ITA 223	Definitions (Seizure of Property)
ITA 224	Garnishment
ITA 227	Withholding Taxes
ITA 230	Records and Books
ITA 231.1	Inspections
ITA 261	Definitions (Functional Currency)
ITA 245-246	Tax Avoidance
ITR Part II	Information Returns
ITR 4301	Prescribed Rate of Interest
ITR 5300	Instalments (Individuals)
ITR 5301	Instalments (Corporations)
ITR 5800	Retention of Books and Records
IC00-1R6	Voluntary Disclosure Program
IC 01-1	Third-Party Civil Penalties
IC 07-1R1	Taxpayer Relief Provisions
IC 71-14R3	The Tax Audit
IC 75-6R2	Required Withholding from Amounts Paid to Non-Resident Persons Providing Services in Canada
IC 75-7R3	Reassessment of a Return of Income
IC 78-10R5	Books and Records Retention/Destruction
IC 84-1	Revision of CCA Claims and Other Permissive Deductions
IC 88-2	General Anti-Avoidance Rule: Section 245 of the *Income Tax Act*
IC 98-1R7	Collection Policies
S5-F4-C1	Income Tax Reporting Currency
P148	Resolving Your Dispute: Objection and Appeal Rights under the *Income Tax Act*

Self-Study Problems

Self-Study Problems (SSPs) provide practice in problem solving. Within the chapters, we have indicated where it would be appropriate to stop and work on each SSP. The problems can be downloaded by chapter from MyLab Accounting. Solutions are available in the Study Guide. Select problems can also be completed directly in MyLab and auto-graded.

Assignment Problems

Solutions to Assignment Problems (APs) are available to instructors only.

AP 2-1 Individual Tax Instalments

The following table contains information for Gladys Nite for the three years ending December 31, 2019, 2020, and 2021. The tax payable column is her combined federal and provincial tax payable. The amounts in the columns titled Case One, Two, and Three are the amounts withheld by her employer in three independent cases.

	Tax Payable	Case One	Case Two	Case Three
2019	$18,880	$14,480	$19,280	$15,280
2020	20,320	19,720	14,880	16,160
2021 (Estimated)	21,760	18,640	18,560	19,440

Required:

A. For each of the three cases:

- Indicate whether instalments are required for the 2021 taxation year. Show all of the calculations required to make this decision.
- In those cases where instalments are required, indicate the amount of the instalments that would be required under the approach used in the CRA's instalment reminder.
- In those cases where you have calculated the instalments required under the CRA's instalment reminder approach, indicate whether there is a better approach and, if so, calculate the required instalments under that approach.

B. For those cases where instalments are required, indicate the dates on which the payments will be due.

AP 2-2 Instalments, Interest, and Penalties for Corporations

Marcon Ltd. is Canadian company that is publicly traded on the Toronto Stock Exchange. For both tax purposes and accounting purposes, the company uses a June 30 year end. This choice reflects the seasonal nature of their business. The company's tax payable for 2019 and 2020, and the estimated tax payable for 2021, are as follows:

2019	$365,400
2020	472,600
2021 (Estimated)	407,900

Required:

A. Calculate the instalment payments that are required for the year ending June 30, 2021, under each of the alternative methods available. Indicate which of the alternatives would be preferable.

B. On what specific dates are the instalment payments toward Marcon's 2021 taxes payable due? In addition, specify when the 2021 corporate tax return is due and the date on which the balance owing is due.

C. If the company did not make any instalment payments toward its 2021 taxes payable, and did not file its corporate tax return or pay its taxes payable on time, indicate how the interest and penalty amounts assessed against it would be determined (a detailed calculation is not required).

AP 2-3 *Individual Tax Instalments*

For the three taxation years ending December 31, 2019, 2020, and 2021, assume that Bronson James had the following actual and estimated amounts of federal and provincial tax payable withheld by his employer:

2019	$ 8,946
2020	9,672
2021 (Estimated)	10,476

In order to illustrate the calculation of required instalments, consider the following three independent cases. In each case, Bronson's combined federal/provincial tax payable is provided.

Year	Case 1	Case 2	Case 3
2019	$ 7,843	$ 8,116	$13,146
2020	12,862	13,846	12,842
2021 (Estimated)	14,327	13,542	13,676

Required: For each of the three cases:

- Indicate whether instalments are required for the 2021 taxation year.
- In those cases where instalments are required, calculate the amount of the instalments that would be required under each of the three alternative methods.
- In those cases where instalments are required, indicate which of the three alternative methods would be the best.
- In those cases where instalments are required, indicate the dates on which the payments will be due.

AP 2-4 *Instalments, Interest, and Penalties for Corporations*

For both tax and accounting purposes, Lanterna Inc. has a July 31 year end. Lanterna is a publicly traded Canadian company. For the three years ending July 31, 2019, 2020, and 2021, it provides the following information with respect to its federal tax ayable:

2019	$132,650
2020	141,720
2021 (Estimated)	139,460

Required:

A. Calculate the instalment payments that are required for the year ending July 31, 2021, under each of the alternative methods available. Indicate which of the alternatives would be preferable.

B. If the company did not make any instalment payments toward its 2021 taxes payable and did not file its corporate tax return or pay its taxes payable on time, indicate how the interest and penalty amounts assessed against it would be determined (a detailed calculation is not required).

AP 2-5 *Essay Questions*

Provide answers to each of the following questions:

A. Individual taxpayers are advised to file their income tax returns even if they are not currently in a position to pay the tax that is owing. Explain this statement.

B. Depending on the circumstances, the filing date for an individual's income tax return may vary. What are the possible alternative dates?

AP 2-6 *Appeals*

Mr. Darcy O'Brien has just received a notice of reassessment requesting an additional payment of $72,500 for the 2018 taxation year. He is outraged in that he believes the CRA is harassing him because of his previous difficulties with the CRA. These previous difficulties resulted in his having to pay both penalties and interest.

He has asked for your services in dealing with the notice of reassessment and you agreed to meet with him on March 26, 2021. At this meeting, Mr. O'Brien assures you that his 2018 return was correctly prepared and filed on time and that there is no reasonable basis for the CRA claim. After he describes the issue, you decide it is likely that his analysis of the situation is correct.

Required: Indicate what additional information should be obtained during the interview with Mr. O'Brien and what steps should be taken if you decide to accept him as a client.

AP 2-7 Tax Preparer's Penalties

For each of the following independent cases, indicate whether you believe any penalty would be assessed under ITA 163.2 on any of the parties involved. Explain your conclusion.

Case 1

A company has established a limited partnership by acquiring a software application from a non-arm's length individual for $450,000. Units in the limited partnership are being sold by the company.

The prospectus for the offering states that the fair market value of the acquired application is $10 million, a value based on the work of an independent appraiser. The limited partnership is registered with the CRA as a tax shelter.

On audit, the CRA determines that the $450,000 paid for the software application is, in fact, its fair market value on the date of the transfer. In questioning the approach used by the appraiser, that individual indicated that his work was based largely on assumptions provided by the company sponsoring the limited partnership offering. The appraiser's fee for the work was $150,000.

Case 2

A very successful accountant lives next door to what appears to be a wealthy neighbour. Based on similar properties, his house appears to be worth more than $2 million and he has three cars, including a Ferrari and a Mercedes-Benz. In the last two years, the two neighbours have become friends.

As his accountant has retired, the neighbour asks the accountant to prepare his tax return. To this end, the neighbour provides a T5 that shows income of $90,000. As this appears to be on the low side, the accountant asks if he has any other source of income. The neighbour indicates that he does not, but also notes that, a few years ago, he won $20 million in the provincial lottery.

The accountant does not ask any further questions and prepares and files the return. When the friend is audited it is discovered that he has over $500,000 in unreported income.

Case 3

In preparing a tax return for one of his clients, an accountant uses the financial statements of another accountant to determine the client's business income inclusion. The accountant does not see anything in these statements that seems unreasonable.

When his client's return is audited, the CRA finds that the business income financial statements prepared by the other accountant contained material misrepresentations.

Case 4

In preparing a tax return for a new client, an accountant uses the client's accounting statements to calculate the client's net business income. As part of this engagement, the accountant reviews both the expense and revenue information that has been provided to him by the new client. The expenses seem to be related to the type of business of the client and the revenue and expense figures contained in the accounting statements seem reasonable. Given this, the accountant files the required tax return.

When the client is audited, the CRA finds a large proportion of the expenses claimed cannot be substantiated by adequate documentation and may not have been incurred. Furthermore, it appears that the client has a substantial amount of unreported revenues.

Case 5

In preparing a tax return for a new client, the accountant determines that his only income is $75,000 in business income. In preparing the tax payable figure, the accountant is advised by the client that he made a $110,000 charitable contribution during the current year. However, he has lost the receipt. He has requested a replacement but has not received it yet.

As it is now April 29, to avoid a late filing penalty the accountant files the tax return, claiming a tax credit for the contribution without seeing the receipt.

CRA Case—Chapter 2

Amber Brost is 35 years old and lives with her common-law partner, Tallulah, on the outskirts of Winnipeg, Manitoba. She has been carrying on an art supplies business since 2010. In 2009 Amber completed introductory accounting and income tax courses in preparation for establishing her own business with the goal that she would not have to rely on others except where necessary. When her business began she maintained books and records and made the regular ongoing entries to track every aspect of her business, including sales invoices, purchase receipts, and other source documents. At the end of every year she would meet with her accountant, providing the final amounts that were used to prepare basic financial statements and her income tax return, which were then electronically filed by the accountant. The accountant performed a review engagement only and did not conduct any audit of Amber's business.

Amber has always paid all income taxes, GST, and source deductions on time and even though she has until June 15 of each year to file she has almost always filed each year's income tax return by April 30. Her 2018 income tax return, however, was late filed on June 28, 2019. Amber explained that her accountant had to leave town to visit his father in Vancouver who had suffered a heart attack. Amber was uncomfortable dealing with anyone other than the accountant and decided to wait until his return, which did not occur until after her June 15 filing due date. Since she owed taxes she was assessed a late filing penalty of 5%. Amber has always paid quarterly instalments on time based on the CRA reminders, but because the business revenues were growing each year she always owed additional income taxes on filing.

Amber employs three individuals in the business, one of whom is Tallulah. The three employees provide sales service rotating at different times throughout each week. Tallulah's only additional role is to track the inventory, purchase additional items when necessary, and deposit daily cash at the local bank when Amber is not available. Source deductions, withholding, and information reporting are all handled by Amber as well as all GST returns.

In the summer of 2019 the business was audited by CRA for its 2017 and 2018 taxation years ending December 31. Reassessments were issued to Amber for both years. Inadvertently, Amber had claimed some personal expenses, resulting in some additional income tax together with interest. The amounts were not significant enough to cause the CRA to charge her with gross negligence penalties, but the CRA did issue her an inadequate books and records letter advising her that personal expenses should be excluded. The CRA auditor further advised that gross negligence penalties would be charged if, on a subsequent audit, it was found that the business continued to deduct personal expenses.

In late September 2019 while walking home, Amber was struck by a car at a crosswalk. She was rushed to the hospital and was in a coma for three weeks. Her recovery was slow but steady. Specialists advised Tallulah that Amber had suffered a brain injury that impaired her cognitive abilities, which included some memory loss. They believed she would fully recover but were cautious as to whether her full cognitive functioning would return. Amber began to show marked recovery after intensive therapy for two years, and by November 2021 she finally returned to her business on a full-time basis.

In the interim Tallulah had continued to watch over the business. Sales revenues had increased significantly following the accident as the public had been exceptionally supportive after local media outlets covered Amber's story. Tallulah learned how to account for the GST and source deductions, collecting and remitting them all on time, but Amber's 2019 and 2020 income tax returns had not been filed nor had any instalment payments been made. In addition, the financial statements for the business were still not prepared through the first six months of 2021. The CRA issued demands for Amber to file her 2019 and 2020 income tax returns. Given the circumstances, these demands were ignored.

Amber received a notice of assessment dated October 27, 2021, for her 2019 and 2020 taxation years on the basis of estimated revenue from her business. The notice mentions nothing about requiring her to file the two income tax returns. [**Note:** This is referred to as an arbitrary assessment and occurs when the CRA has issued demands to file that go unanswered. In effect, the CRA files the returns for the taxpayer. The purpose is to allow the CRA to assess income tax, interest, and penalties, including for deficient instalments].

The assessment notices for both years include the following:

- Estimated income taxes well in excess of the actual income taxes
- Late filing penalties for repeat offenders (10% plus 2% per month)
- Gross negligence penalties supported by the previous audit results
- Interest on deficient instalment payments
- Interest on all penalties
- Interest on the outstanding income taxes owed

Amber and Tallulah believed they would have some time to address the income tax returns and other tax matters, but they are now very concerned, particularly after recently receiving calls from CRA Collections, who while sympathetic, warned of the implications if Amber did not handle these matters quickly. Amber had planned to file her 2019 and 2020 income tax returns along with her 2021 return by April 30, 2022.

Amber's accountant recommended an individual well-versed in income tax matters of this kind, and on the December 8, 2021, Amber met with that individual.

Required: You are the individual meeting with Amber. You have been fully informed of the facts. Amber adds that while she is doing well financially she would not be able to pay the huge amounts shown as owing because of the substantial amounts of penalties and interest.

1. Explain to Amber what will happen if nothing is done.
2. Explain to Amber what actions are necessary to prevent collection action by the CRA.
3. How can Amber defend against the assessments?
4. When resolved, Amber will likely still be faced with large amounts of interest and penalties. Is there anything she can do about those amounts? If yes, explain what she needs to do and any supporting arguments that would have to be made.
5. What lessons can be learned from this case?

A suggested solution for this case is included in the Study Guide.

CHAPTER 3

Income or Loss from an Office or Employment

Learning Objectives

After completing Chapter 3, you should be able to:

1. Explain the basic rules and concepts of employment income (Paragraph [P hereafter] 3-1 to 3-4).
2. Explain the reasons for using, and the rules associated with, bonus arrangements for employees (P 3-5 to 3-9).
3. Describe the consequences of an employment loss on net income (P 3-10 to 3-11).
4. Distinguish between an employee and a self-employed individual earning business income and list the advantages and disadvantages of both classifications. In addition, explain the concept of a personal service business and the impact of such a classification (P 3-12 to 3-49).
5. Describe how non-salary benefits are taxed and the analysis to determine whether a benefit is required to be included in employment income (P 3-50 to 3-57).
6. List the different amounts that can be included in employment income under ITA 6(1) and the type of benefits that are legislatively excluded under ITA 6(1)(a) (P 3-58 to 3-61).
7. Apply the employee benefit analysis to common benefits, and determine how they are taxed and whether there are any administrative concessions made by the CRA (P 3-62 to 3-63).
8. Explain the basic elements of tax planning for employee benefits, including tax deferral opportunities and what the tax treatment to the employer is (P 3-64 to 3-76).
9. Describe the effects of the GST/HST/PST on taxable benefits (P 3-77 to 3-79).
10. Describe the three different ITA references to cars and trucks and the implications for income tax purposes (P 3-80 to 3-88).
11. Describe the three tax concerns to employees in terms of the use of an automobile in one's employment (P 3-89 to 3-90).
12. Explain the concept of personal travel, its importance, and how it is determined (P 3-91 to 3-94).
13. Calculate the standby charge and operating cost benefits that apply to employees who are provided with an automobile that is leased or owned by their employer (P 3-95 to 3-136).
14. Explain basic tax planning for company cars (P 3-137 to 3-138).
15. Explain the tax treatment of allowances that are provided by employers to their employees for travel costs (P 3-139 to 3-156).
16. Describe the taxation of various types of insurance benefits that are provided by employers to their employees (P 3-157 to 3-162).

17. Explain and calculate the income tax consequences when low-interest-rate or interest-free loans are made to employees as a result of their employment (P 3-163 to 3-172).
18. Calculate the income tax consequences that result from employees receiving and exercising stock options and from the subsequent sale of the acquired shares (P 3-173 to 3-194).
19. Describe the new stock option deduction rules, why they were introduced, the types of corporations to which they apply, and how the rules apply to both employees and employers (P 3-195 to 3-201).
20. List and describe other inclusions in employment income (P 3-202 to 3-211).
21. List and describe specific deductions against employment income that are listed in ITA 8 (P 3-212 to 3-235).
22. Explain how deductible work space in the home costs for employees are calculated and how the employment usage is determined (P 3-236 to 3-242).

Introduction

3-1. In this chapter we examine the income taxation of employees. Many of us at one time or another have been employed, receiving an hourly wage or salary (sometimes with tips, depending on the nature of one's employment) and other benefits, including medical prescription plans and dental plans, future pension plans on retirement, stock option benefits, and perhaps the use of an employer-provided car. Some employment requires that an employee pay union dues, make pension plan contributions, or pay certain travel expenses and other amounts while receiving regular allowances or reimbursements from the employer. These, along with other employment-related issues, will be discussed in this chapter to provide you with a practical understanding of how employees' income is taxed in Canada.

3-2. As discussed in Chapter 1, employment income is considered income from a source being one's labour. An individual can have multiple sources of employment income if the individual has two or more employers in a given year. The source concept applies on a net basis, meaning for each employment you need to determine which amounts are required to be included and which deductions you are entitled to. The difference between all inclusions and all deductions is your employment income from that source for the year. You are not permitted to deduct allowable employment expenses from one source of employment against another source of employment income.

Employment Income Defined

General Rules

3-3. Income or loss from an office or employment (employment income, hereafter) is covered in Part I, Division B, Subdivision a of the ITA. This relatively short subdivision is made up of Sections 5 through 8, the general contents of which can be described as follows:

> **Section 5** contains a description of the types of standard receipts that are considered part of a source of employment income.
>
> **Section 6** expands the list of what is required to be included in employment income by identifying specific other receipts and benefits and determining the dollar amount required to be included in employment income.
>
> **Section 7** sets out the rules used to determine income benefits from employer-provided stock option plans, their timing, and the dollar amounts to be included.
>
> **Section 8** lists very specific deductions that an employee may be entitled to, the effect of which is to reduce employment income from that employment source for the relevant year.

3-4. The standard types of receipts that are considered employment income are described in ITA 5 as follows:

ITA 5(1) Subject to this Part, a taxpayer's income for a taxation year from an office or employment is the salary, wages and other remuneration, including gratuities, received by the taxpayer in the year.

A few observations can be made from this ITA provision:

- The "taxpayer" is the individual employee.
- The reference to an "office" serves to extend the rules of employee taxation to others usually not considered employees, such as judges, members of Parliament, and members of the board of directors of a corporation. This is accomplished through the definition of an "office" found in ITA 248(1). Without this extension, individuals occupying those positions would not technically be considered individuals in an employment relationship.
- The reference to "employment," a defined term in ITA 248(1), refers to the position of an individual in the service of some other person. Determining whether certain individuals are actually employees as opposed to independent contractors is often a contentious issue. In Chapter 1 we mentioned that the ITA operates on the basis of legal rather than accounting concepts. These determinations therefore are often made applying legal principles that will be discussed later in this chapter. Remember that, aside from those in an "office," the rules of Subdivision a can only be applied to individuals in an employment relationship.
- Amounts received in the form of wages, salary, gratuities (i.e., tips), and any other types of compensation for services rendered (i.e., remuneration) is required to be included in employment income for the year. The frequency of the payments, whether hourly, weekly, monthly, etc., is not relevant. In addition, it is the gross amount of the remuneration that is required to be included in employment income (i.e., before withholdings of any kind).
- Only remuneration actually *received* in a given year is required to be included in income for that year. If, for example, your pay from employment for the period December 20 to December 31, 2021, is not payable until January 4, 2022, then that amount is included in your employment income for 2022 not 2021, even though it was earned and accrued by the employer in 2021. The employer, however, would be able to deduct the amount as an employment expense on an accrual basis in 2021.
- You will note that ITA 5(1) does not require that amounts received by an employee be received from the employer. The ITA only requires that the amounts received are as a result of that employment irrespective of who pays the amount. As a result, tips received from customers are considered received as a result of the employment and therefore required to be included in employment income. When analyzing these situations a good starting point is to ask whether the amount would have been received if not for the employment. If the answer is no, then the amount is likely employment income.

Cash Basis and Planning

Amounts Received—Timing

3-5. It is important to recognize that the ITA has been around for more than 100 years, and in those years the law has changed on a regular basis to ensure the integrity of the tax system and specifically to ensure, to the extent possible, that income tax cannot be avoided or deferred to an unreasonable degree. The fact that employment income is only taxed when received appears to imply that there may be some opportunities to defer tax at a minimum or perhaps to avoid it altogether given that the employer who is carrying on a business can deduct the remuneration as it accrues. Let's look at two examples:

EXAMPLE 1 An employee delays picking up their paycheque on December 30, 2021, and instead waits until January 2, 2022.

EXAMPLE 2 An employer mails employee paycheques December 31, 2021, that are all received in early January 2022.

ANALYSIS 1 In both examples it would appear that the employee only receives the amounts in 2022. In example 1 the employee was entitled to the paycheque and could have picked it up in 2021 but chose not to do so. In this case the pay is considered received, at law, in 2021.

ANALYSIS 2 In the second example there is a special timing rule in ITA 248(7) that deems the employee to have received the paycheque on the day it was mailed or sent by courier; therefore, the pay is again considered employment income for 2021.

Tax Planning Opportunity

3-6. The use of the term "received" serves to establish that employment income must be reported on a cash basis, not on an accrual basis. Business income, on the other hand and as we will see in Chapter 6, is determined on an accrual basis. This appears to present a deferral opportunity where an employer carrying on a business can accrue remuneration, claim it immediately as an expense, and only pay it in a subsequent year.

EXAMPLE A business with a December 31 year end declares an annual bonus to an employee in December 2020 based upon sales performance criteria, but stipulates that it will not be paid until January 2021.

ANALYSIS The business would be able to deduct the expense in 2020, the year that the liability to the employee arose, irrespective of when payment was made. The employee would not include the amount in income until the 2021 taxation year when the amount is received. If the bonus had been paid in December 2020, the employee would have had to include it in employment income in 2020. In effect, this arrangement defers the taxation applicable to the employee by one taxation year even though the payment has been deferred by only a few days.

You might ask at this point if the deferral can be extended even further to, say, six months, a year, or perhaps longer.

Limits on Deferral—Unpaid Remuneration

3-7. There are, as expected, limits to this type of deferral. ITA 78(4) was written specifically to address these situations and allows the deferral as long as the remuneration (i.e., the bonus) is paid before the 180th day of the employer's year end in which the expense was claimed. This means that the amount owing must be paid by the 179th day. If the bonus is not paid within this time limit, then the expense is disallowed for the year originally expensed but allowed in the year it is actually paid. In other words the employer is denied accrual treatment for the bonus and can only claim the bonus as an expense on the same cash basis that would apply to the employee, therefore eliminating the deferral advantage.

EXAMPLE An employer with a June 30 year end declares a bonus for an employee on May 31, 2020, that is payable March 1, 2021.

ANALYSIS The 179-day period is measured from the last day of the employer's taxation year, which in this case is June 30, 2020. The deadline therefore is December 26, 2020. Since the payment date of March 1, 2021, is not within that deadline, the employer will not be able to deduct the bonus for the 2020 year. It will instead be deducted in its year ending June 30, 2021, which is the year in which it was paid.

Limits on Deferral—Salary Deferral Arrangement

3-8. ITA 78(4) does not apply to a salary deferral arrangement (SDA). An SDA is an arrangement between an employer and an employee to defer the payments of remuneration for services rendered to a later year for the purpose of postponing/deferring the payment of income tax. In general the rule applies where the deferral exceeds three years. The effect is that the deferred amount is included in the income of the employee in the year the services are rendered (i.e., the year the income was earned), and the employer is allowed a deduction on the same basis. This type of arrangement is discussed in more detail in Chapter 10, "Retirement Savings and Other Special Income Arrangements." As a result the employee will be paying income tax on an amount that has not been received. This feature is designed to discourage this type of practice.

3-9. The tax consequences associated with the three types of bonus arrangements are summarized in Figure 3-1.

Figure 3-1 Bonus Arrangements

Type of Bonus Arrangement	Tax Consequences
Standard Bonus (Paid by 179th day of the employer's business year end)	Employer deducts when owed Employee includes when received
Other Bonus (Paid more than 179 days after the employer's business year end, but prior to three years after December 31 of the year in which the bonus was earned)	Employer deducts when paid Employee includes when received
Salary Deferral Arrangement (Paid more than three years after December 31 of the year in which services were rendered)	Employer deducts when owed Employee includes when services are rendered (see Chapter 10)

Exercise 3-1

Subject: Bonus

Neelson Inc. has a September 30 year end. On August 1, 2020, it declares a bonus of $100,000 payable to Mr. Sam Neelson, an executive of the company. The bonus is payable and paid on May 1, 2021. Describe the tax consequences of this bonus to both Neelson Inc. and Mr. Neelson. How would your answer change if the bonus was paid in October 2021?

Solutions to Exercises are available in the Study Guide.

We suggest you complete SSP 3-1 at this point.

Employment Losses—ITA 5(2)

3-10. In Chapter 1, in our discussion of net income under ITA 3, we mentioned that the word "income" means a positive or nil amount and that the word "loss" means that the deductions for a source of income exceeds the income amounts. Income from a source is included in ITA 3(a), whereas losses are included at ITA 3(d). ITA 5(2) continues this concept, recognizing that employment losses can occur and they are calculated using the same rules of Subdivision a that would apply where there is income. Without this rule, employment losses would be ignored.

3-11. If an employment loss were to occur, the excess employment deductions could not be directly applied against any other source of income. However, if there are other sources of income, including taxable capital gains, the same result can be achieved by deducting the employment loss under ITA 3(d) in the calculation of net income.

EXAMPLE An individual has employment income of $3,000 and employment expenses of $4,500, resulting in an employment loss of $1,500. The individual's only other source of income is $20,000 of income from property (e.g., interest). The employee has no Subdivision e deductions.

ANALYSIS The individual's net income would be calculated as follows:

Income from property ITA 3(a) & (c)	$20,000
Employment loss ITA 3(d)	(1,500)
Net income	$18,500

If the employee only had an employment loss of $1,500 and no other income, then net income would be nil and the individual would have a non-capital loss of $1,500 for that year. You will see in Chapter 11 that where the total current-year losses in ITA 3(d) exceed the ITA 3(c) amount, the excess becomes a "non-capital loss" for that year, which can be carried over to other years.

ITA 3(c) amount	$ Nil
Employment loss ITA 3(d)	(1,500)
Net income	$ Nil
Non-capital loss [$1,500 – Nil] =	$1,500

The ITA 3 structure is not only important in determining net income, but is also used to determine whether there are any loss carryovers as well as the amount and the type of loss carryover.

Employee versus Self-Employed

Introduction

3-12. In this chapter we are learning about the taxation of employees, which implies that the relationship between an individual and someone else is an employment relationship. If that is not the nature of the relationship, then there are two immediate implications. The first is that we cannot apply the rules of Subdivision a dealing with income from an office or employment, and the second is that we cannot determine the income tax consequences to this individual until we can establish if she has a source of income.

3-13. The question to answer first is whether the individual is in an employment relationship. Since the ITA operates on legal principles and concepts, we turn our attention to guidance provided by the courts in analyzing and answering that question. The vast majority of cases in this area involve determining whether an individual is an employee or is self-employed working for herself, which in the ITA means that she is carrying on a business of her own as either a sole proprietor or as a member of a partnership.

3-14. This distinction is of considerable importance, both to the individual worker and to the taxpayer using the services of that individual. If the individual is treated as self-employed when they are, in fact, an employee, there are implications to the employer using their services in terms of required withholdings for income tax, Employment Insurance premiums, Canada Pension Plan contributions, health care premiums, and other source deductions. We saw in Chapter 2 that there are penalties and interest charges for employers who fail to withhold, remit, and report these source deductions.

3-15. In terms of the individual providing the service, one of the most significant differences is the level of expenses the individual is entitled to deduct. Expense deductions for employees are much more limited than they are for individuals carrying on their own business. There are also differences as to the treatment of CPP contributions, which are discussed in Paragraphs 3-17 to 3-20. In addition, most businesses will be obligated to register for and collect GST/HST. We discuss these differences in the following paragraphs.

Employee Perspective

Deductions Available

3-16. As will be discussed later in this chapter, an individual's ability to deduct expenses from employment income is quite limited when compared to self-employed individuals carrying on a business. For example, a self-employed individual performing services at a specific work location can generally deduct the costs of driving to and from his home and that work location. The same deductions would not be available to an employee driving between her home and the location where she regularly reports to work.

CPP Contributions

3-17. If an individual is an employee, the employer will be required to withhold a portion of his pay for Canada Pension Plan (CPP) contributions and Employment Insurance (EI) premiums. With respect to CPP contributions, for 2021 both the employee and the employer are required to contribute 5.45% of up to $61,600 of gross wages reduced by a basic exemption of $3,500. This results in maximum contributions by both the employee and employer of $3,166.45, or a total of $6,332.90. We will round these numbers to $3,166 and $6,332 going forward.

3-18. In contrast, if an individual is carrying on a business (i.e., is self-employed), there will be no withholding of CPP from the amounts received as business income. However, this does not mean that the individual can escape these costs. A self-employed individual must make contributions on the same basis as an employee. Further, self-employed individuals are required to pay both the employee share and the employer share, resulting in a potential maximum payment of $6,332.

3-19. As noted in Chapter 2, CPP amounts for the self-employed are collected by the CRA. They are calculated on the T1 tax return where they become part of the amount owing for a year. Further, the amounts are included in the instalment base when instalments are required, which means that they may be a factor in determining the size of quarterly instalments. This could be viewed as a modest advantage of being self-employed as there is some deferral of the required CPP payments, as compared to their payment through payroll deductions.

3-20. However, any benefit resulting from deferral of the CPP payments is clearly offset by the fact that the self-employed individual has to pay double the CPP contributions (both the employee and the employer share) with no higher future pension benefit than employees. There is clearly an overall disadvantage to the self-employed individual.

EI Premiums

3-21. With respect to EI premiums, the amount that will be withheld from employee earnings amounts to 1.58% of the first $56,300 in gross wages, with a maximum annual contribution of $890. The employer is assessed 1.4 times this amount, a maximum of $1,245. This represents an effective rate for the employer of 2.21%.

3-22. Employees are generally required to participate in the EI program. One exception is for employees owning more than 40% of the voting shares of a corporate employer. In that case, any remuneration received by such an employee/shareholder is referred to as excluded employment and no EI premiums are payable. The EI rules are complex, which can make the determination of insurable employment difficult, especially in the case of an owner-manager employing family members. A non-arm's length employee (such as an adult child or a spouse) would only be eligible for participation in the EI program if it is reasonable to conclude that the employer would have hired an arm's length person under a similar contract of employment.

3-23. Self-employed individuals can choose to participate in the EI program on a voluntary basis for special (restricted) EI benefits, such as maternity benefits. They must opt in at least 12 months prior to making a claim, but once they opt in, they are committed for the taxation year. Further, if a claim is made under this program, the individual is committed for life or until they stop being self-employed. The good news is that self-employed individuals do not have to pay the employer's 1.4 share of EI premiums. This means the maximum cost for 2021 would be $890.

3-24. As is the case with CPP payments for self-employed individuals, EI premiums are collected by the CRA. This means that payments are either paid indirectly through instalments or on the balance due date for the return (i.e., April 30) , thereby providing a small amount of deferral. More importantly, with participation being voluntary, a self-employed individual can choose whether or not to participate in this program. Since the self-employed individual does not pay the employer's share of the EI (unlike the situation with the CPP), the EI rules appear to be advantageous to eligible self-employed individuals.

Employment Benefits

3-25. A significant disadvantage of being classified as a self-employed individual rather than an employee is the loss of employment benefits. An employee may receive a wide variety of benefits, such as dental and drug plans, membership in a registered pension plan, vacation pay, sick pay, or life insurance coverage. Such benefits have a significant value, in some cases adding as much as 20% to an employee's remuneration. Further, even if the self-employed individual were willing to pay for such benefits, some benefits may not be available to a single individual at a reasonable cost (e.g., extended medical coverage). In any case, a self-employed individual will have to receive significantly higher basic remuneration to be in the same economic position as an individual employee with generous benefits.

The Underground Economy

3-26. While we certainly do not condone this, as a practical matter, in some situations, being self-employed offers increased opportunities for tax evasion. There are stringent reporting requirements and many checks and balances with the CRA that make it difficult for employees to avoid detection if they fail to report their employment income.

3-27. In contrast, business income is sometimes received partially or wholly in cash, depending on the clients. When cash is received, the work is often performed for an individual who cannot benefit from the cost of the work for income tax purposes. In such cases receipts or invoices are not issued. A common example of this would be an individual who hires a self-employed contractor to renovate a principal residence paying a reduced amount by paying in cash to avoid paying the HST. The CRA cautions Canadians to avoid such transactions. Unless there is a written contract for the work there may be potential issues with warranties, building code violations, and liability issues for workers' compensation to name but a few of the non-income tax concerns.

Conclusion

3-28. As the preceding discussion indicates, the desirability of self-employed status is not clear cut. For an individual with limited deductible expenses, self-employment may not be advantageous from an economic point of view. Alternatively, if an individual's work is such that large amounts of expenses are generated, it may be desirable to be considered a self-employed individual. The ability to change employment to self-employment with the same employer, however, while tempting in certain cases, is exceedingly difficult to achieve if the nature of the relationship between the individual and the former employer is unchanged.

3-29. Non-tax advantages could include the ability to set work schedules and the freedom to choose the amount and type of work accepted. The added cost of accounting for the business and the implications of the GST/HST would also have to be considered. As noted in Chapter 21, in most cases a self-employed individual would have to register for GST/HST if she is not a small supplier.

Employer Perspective

3-30. There are several advantages to a business from using the services of self-employed individuals as opposed to employees. One of the major advantages associated with the hiring of these independent contractors (a.k.a. contracting out) is that the employer avoids payments for CPP, EI, workers' compensation, and provincial health care (where applicable). In addition the employer would not generally be liable for any negligence or other legal claims as would be the case with employees.

3-31. The amounts involved here are consequential. CPP and EI obligations add to the wage costs. Provincial payroll taxes further add to the total of wage costs. Further cost savings result from the fact that the employer will avoid the administrative costs associated with having to withhold and remit income taxes and the employee's share of CPP and EI payments.

3-32. In addition, using independent contractors avoids the costs of any employee benefits normally extended to employees. A less measurable benefit is that employers are freed from ongoing commitments to individuals because there is generally no long-term contract with self-employed workers.

3-33. Given all of these advantages, it is not surprising to find more businesses contracting services in order to control labour costs and limit liability.

Treating an Employee as an Independent Contractor

3-34. Where a taxpayer carries on a business, financial incentives may cause the taxpayer to want to treat existing employees and new hires as independent contractors for the reasons discussed. Individual employees may also favour that same categorization. But is this easily achievable?

3-35. Contracts can be drawn up referring to the individuals as independent contractors. Accounting statements and entries together with income tax returns can avoid referring to the individuals as employees and the individuals themselves can all be onside, but the law is clear that the description or categorization of an individual by lawyers, accountants, employers, or others is not determinative of their legal status as employees.

3-36. The analysis comes down to an examination of the facts and the application of established case law principles in determining whether a specific individual is or is not an employee. As a general rule attempting to change the status of an individual from an employee to that of a self-employed individual presents considerable challenges, particularly where the individual's only client is the employer and the duties of the individual have not changed in any meaningful way. In addition, a person may wish to treat all new hires as self-employed persons, yet the duties required of them are equivalent to employees of similar businesses. In these instances the likelihood of success is low.

A Brief Word on Personal Service Businesses

3-37. The benefit of successfully treating an employee as an independent contractor is reduced costs and liability to the employer largely without changing the deductible expense. The former employees would be considered as carrying on their own business with the result that the income received by them would be business income instead of employment income. Changing the nature of direct payments between the employer and employee without any material difference in the employee responsibilities would have a high probability of failure.

3-38. Many years ago (prior to the GAAR discussed in Chapter 2), in an attempt to resolve this concern, income tax practitioners came up with a solution. The plan called for the following general steps in no specific order:

Step 1: The individual employee would resign.

Step 2: The individual would then create a new corporation controlled by the individual.

Step 3: The individual would enter into an employment agreement with their own corporation to provide employment services.

Step 4: The individual's corporation and the former employer would enter into a contract to provide the services formerly provided by the individual employee.

3-39. The result was that the individual's corporation stood between the individual and the former employer in terms of providing employment services. Technically the individual was no longer an employee of the former employer but an employee of his own corporation. The result was that payments by the former employer to the individual that had previously been employment income were now business income to the individual's corporation. The individual would draw what he needed from his own corporation as salary and other amounts (which are discussed in greater detail in Volume 2 of the text, which deals with corporate taxation). The point is that this strategy achieved the results of economically converting employment income to business income.

3-40. The federal government response was a set of anti-avoidance rules that are commonly referred to as the "Personal Service Business" (PSB) rules. Our objective is not to go through all of the details of this legislation but to introduce one key element that will lead us to the next section in answering the question of how to determine whether or not a specific individual is an employee.

3-41. The key element of the PSB legislation first refers to the former employee as an incorporated employee since the employment services, rather than being provided directly by the former employee, are indirectly provided through his own corporation. The legislation then asks whether the former employee would be considered an employee of the former employer and therefore in an employment relationship if those services had been provided directly. If the answer is yes, then the PSB rules apply. In determining whether an employment relationship exists we turn to the same criteria used by the courts to answer the question. We discuss those criteria in the next section.

3-42. Before moving on to the next topic we would add that when the PSB rules do apply the results are extremely punitive. Special corporate tax credits that would normally reduce the federal corporate tax rate to 9% would no longer apply, with the result that the corporate tax rate would equal that of the highest tax brackets for individuals at 33%. In addition most expenses are severely restricted. The income tax outcome is, to say the least, severe.

Making the Distinction

Intent, Actions, and Behaviour

3-43. The general approach to distinguishing between an employee and an independent contractor is the question of whether an employer/employee relationship exists. The analysis is based on legal guidelines developed by the courts, with the leading case being the 2001 Supreme Court of Canada decision in *Sagaz Industries* [2 SCR 983]. The CRA has developed a guide titled "Employee or Self-Employed" (RC4110) to assist taxpayers in making that determination. The CRA guide is based on the precedential guidelines developed in the courts.

3-44. The CRA guide begins by recognizing a central principle of income tax law referred to as the Duke of Westminster principle established in 1936. That principle sets the groundwork for the acceptability of income tax planning subject to the GAAR discussed in Chapter 2. The principle is that taxpayers are generally free to arrange their affairs to reduce income taxes within the limitations of the ITA no matter how unappreciative the tax authorities are of their efforts. Structuring one's affairs, however, requires that the actions and behaviour of the parties are consistent with any agreements or understandings, whether in writing or not. What this means is that intent drafted into an agreement/contract does not automatically dictate a relationship unless the facts and circumstances are actually supportive of the agreement or understanding.

3-45. The parties must first each explain their intent and whether it was to create an employment relationship referred to as a "contract *of* service" or an independent contractor relationship referred to as a "contract *for* service." The intent may or may not be the same for both parties, but irrespective of that it is the starting point in the analysis. If there is a written agreement it is examined to determine whether the expressed intent is consistent with the words of the agreement. In the absence of an agreement it is the intent as verbally expressed by both parties that again serves as the beginning of the analysis.

3-46. The difficulty with parties expressing their intent is that there may a self-serving interest that is masking the true intent. As a result, the intent cannot be accepted at face value. Corroborative evidence is required to substantiate and support that intent. In other words, the analysis is directed at looking for factors that one would expect to see in a genuine employment relationship. The absence of these supporting factors then suggests that there is no employment relationship. The next section looks at the requisite factors indicated by the courts in assessing the existence of an employment relationship. No single factor by itself is determinative. The factors must be analyzed and professional judgment exercised to determine whether sufficient factors weigh in favour of an employment relationship or not.

Factors in Assessing the Existence of an Employment Relationship

3-47. Factors examined by the courts and the CRA in determining the existence of an employer relationship include the following:

> **Control** In an employer/employee relationship, the employer usually controls, directly or indirectly, the way the work is done and the work methods used. The employer assigns specific tasks that define the real framework within which the work is to be done. The nature of some specialty work, however, requires little if any oversight or control and in such cases the courts look to the right of the person paying any compensation to exercise control rather than the actual exercise of that control.
>
> **Ownership of Tools and Equipment** In an employer/employee relationship, the employer usually supplies the equipment and tools required by the employee. In addition, the employer covers the following costs related to their use: repairs, insurance, transport, rental, and operations (e.g., fuel).
>
> In some trades, however, it is customary for employees to supply their own tools. This is generally the case for garage mechanics, painters, and carpenters. Similarly, employed computer scientists, architects, and surveyors sometimes supply their own software and instruments. The courts have recognized this and as a result an individual is not automatically considered a self-employed person simply because she provides some or all of her own tools.
>
> **Ability to Subcontract or Hire Assistants** If an individual must personally perform the services, this is generally a factor in favour of an employment relationship. Alternatively, if the individual can hire assistants, with the payer having no control over the identity of the assistants, that fact would weigh against an employment relationship.
>
> **Financial Risk** In general, employees will not have any financial risks associated with their work. In contrast, self-employed individuals can have risk and can incur losses. Responsibility for fixed monthly costs is an indicator against the existence of an employment relationship.
>
> **Opportunity for Profit** In an employer/employee relationship, the employer alone normally assumes the risk of loss or reward of profit in the business. The employer also usually covers operating costs, which may include office expenses, employee wages and benefits, insurance premiums, and delivery and shipping costs. The employee does not assume any financial risk and is entitled to her full salary or wages regardless of the financial health of the business.
>
> Correspondingly, an employee will have little or no opportunity for profit. While there may be productivity bonuses for exceptional work, such amounts are not generally viewed as profit. The bigger question is whether the activity performed by the individual represents her own business or that of someone else. If it is her own business, you would expect to see investment and management decisions together with an opportunity for profit but also a risk for loss, as is the case for any business owner.

3-48. The determination of the existence of an employment relationship is a question answered by examining the facts, applying the various factors mentioned, and using one's professional judgment to assess the situation. Common facts supportive of an independent contractor relationship include:

- Having the individual register for the GST
- Having the individual work for other clients/businesses
- Having the individual advertise her services
- To the extent possible, having the individual cover her own overhead, including phone service, letterhead, equipment, and supplies
- Having the individual prepare periodic invoices, preferably on an irregular basis
- Having a lawyer prepare an independent contractor agreement

3-49. Much of the case law that examines the existence of an employment relationship relates to charges under the EI and CPP legislation. To avoid such difficulties taxpayers can request a CPP/EI ruling, the details of which can be found in guide RC4110. It is suggested that such a ruling only be obtained prior to hiring or engaging individuals for the first time or in resolving an audit assessment that has concluded that a relationship between the business and certain individuals is different than that reported by the business owner.

We suggest you complete SSP 3-2 at this point.

Inclusions—Employee Benefits

Basic Concepts—ITA 6(1)(a)

3-50. In the introduction we briefly summarized each of the four sections of Subdivision a. We saw that wages, salary, and tips were required to be included in employment income through ITA 5 and that ITA 6 covers other amounts that are required to be included as employment income. The first and most common item that we will briefly describe is "taxable employee benefits," which is covered in ITA 6(1)(a) and reads, in part, as follows:

> **ITA 6(1)(a)** There shall be included in computing the income of a taxpayer for a taxation year as income from an office or employment...the value of board, lodging and other benefits of any kind whatever received or enjoyed by the taxpayer, or by a person who does not deal at arm's length with the taxpayer, in the year in respect of, in the course of, or by virtue of the taxpayer's office or employment, except any benefit...

We have underlined a few of the more important words that require clarification:

- The "taxpayer" is the individual employee.
- A "benefit" has generally been defined by the courts as an economic advantage where the employee is the primary beneficiary, meaning that although the employer may benefit in some manner the employee is benefitting the most. An example would be an employee attending an all-expenses-paid conference in Hawaii in which he is allowed to bring his spouse whose attendance is not required. The free trip benefits both the employee and the employer, but it is only the part of the trip that covers the spouse's travel expenses that primarily benefits the employee, whereas the primary beneficiary of the employee's travel expenses would be the employer.
- The word "value" means the fair market value of the benefit, which is generally the amount that would be paid between two persons who do not know each other (i.e., arm's length). As a rule this would include a notional amount for GST, HST, or PST. In this course we have generally excluded these additional amounts in exercises and problems.
- The words "received or enjoyed" refer to when a benefit becomes taxable. The word "received" would apply to the receipt of property, such as cash or inventory.

The word "enjoyed" is meant to apply where an employee uses property of the employer such as automobiles, cottages, or aircraft, or the employer provides pay for accommodation for the employee through hotels, rental units such as apartments, or homes.

- The words "in respect of, in the course of, or by virtue of the taxpayer's office or employment" refer to what is commonly called a "capacity test." This means that the benefit must be because of the individual's employment. You will notice that, as in ITA 5, there is no requirement that the benefit be provided by the employer. If, for example, you receive a holiday gift worth $200 from a client of the employer it would be a taxable benefit required to be included in your employment income based on the day you received it. In addition, the benefit could have been provided to your spouse, in which case the benefit is still included in your income.
- Finally, the words "except any benefit" refer to a list of benefits we will discuss later in this chapter that are specifically excluded. One common example is access to a free dental plan. If the plan meets certain conditions, it will fall within one of the exceptions (e.g., a private health services plan). If, for example, the employer contributes $1,000 annually toward the plan for you, then that would have been a taxable benefit (an economic advantage) of the same amount, but since it is excluded no amount would be included in your income. The fact that you would not include the benefit in your employment income does not affect the employer, who would be entitled to expense the amount as a cost of doing business.

3-51. In summary, benefit taxation requires a five-step analysis:

Step 1 Is there a benefit? (an economic advantage)

Step 2 Has the benefit been received/enjoyed because of an individual's employment?

Step 3 Is the employee or someone related to the employee the primary beneficiary?

Step 4 What is the value of the benefit?

Step 5 Is the benefit excluded?

There may be a temptation to apply step 5 immediately after step 1, which is understandable if, for example, the benefit originated with premiums paid to private medical insurance plans by one's employer for which the private health services plan (PHSP) exception would apply to exclude the benefit from employment income. However, one cannot determine whether one of the exclusions could apply until first answering "yes" to steps 2 and 3. Step 4 is generally applied when the nature of a benefit makes it exceedingly difficult to value, in which case the CRA may administratively forgo any requirement to include an amount in employment income.

Exercise 3-2

Subject: Taxable Benefits

In each of the following cases, use the five-step taxable benefit analysis to indicate whether there is a taxable benefit to the employee and the amount of that benefit (excluding GST, HST, or PST). If there is no taxable benefit explain your reasons.

Case 1 An employee received the latest smartphone from her employer. The phone retails for $1,200. The employer advised the employee that the phone is to be used for employment purposes, but personal use is allowed. Any personal charges require the employee to repay the employer.

Case 2 An employer's office contains dozens of paintings. The employer wants to replace many with abstract art and decides to sell them to interested employees. One employee pays $500 for a painting valued at $2,500.

Case 3 One of an employee's friends works for the same employer and attends the employee's birthday party. The friend gives a cheque of $200 as a gift.

Case 4 An employee wants to purchase a home but has been turned down by three banks. The employer does business with one of the banks and calls them, agreeing to personally guarantee the mortgage as long as the employee is working for the employer. The employee receives the mortgage.

Solutions to Exercises are available in the Study Guide.

Inclusions—Non-Salary Benefits

Introduction

3-52. If salary and wages were the only employee compensation required to be included in employment income, this chapter would be both the shortest and least complex. However, this is not the case. Employers use a wide variety of other benefits, commonly referred to as fringe benefits.

3-53. There are three basic reasons for using these alternative forms of compensation:

Tax Considerations Different benefits have different tax consequences for employees depending on whether the employee benefit is or is not excluded. Through careful planning, an employee's taxes can be kept to a minimum, often at no tax cost to the employer. An example of this would be the provision of certain medical insurance plans, which are excluded and therefore can be received by employees on a tax-free basis.

Employee Motivation Employers believe that some forms of compensation motivate employees to apply greater effort to their employment duties, for example, the granting of stock options. These securities only have value if the fair market value of an employer's stock goes up. Given this, it is thought that employees will work harder toward increasing the value of the company's stock if they are granted such options.

Employee Retention Studies show that properly planned non-salary benefits play a major role in employee retention. For example, an employee who uses employer-provided day care would be more inclined to reject a job offer from a competitor who doesn't offer day care even though the monetary compensation would be higher.

3-54. While these are worthy objectives, they significantly complicate the determination of the appropriate values to be included in employment income. In addition to determining which benefits are taxable, there are often issues associated with the determination of the value that should be attached to these non-salary benefits.

3-55. In terms of learning, understanding, and being in a position to practically apply the legislation contained in ITA 6 there are a few points necessary to appreciate. Legislation is always the starting point to analyzing a situation to determine the income tax outcome. Legislation, however, is not always easy to understand given that it is written by lawyers in a language that often defies comprehension. Anyone who has looked at the fine print in any contract will immediately understand. As a result, the words of the legislation may be interpreted differently by different individuals, leading, of course, to tax disputes, which we discussed in Chapter 2.

3-56. While this course is not designed to focus on the legislation within the ITA or court decisions, it is our objective to provide you with a solid practical understanding of Canadian income tax principles and concepts. The practical application of income tax in Canada is based on the legislation, but what is more important at this point is to recognize that the interpretation of that legislation is based on (1) court decisions that have clarified in very specific instances how a situation is to resolved, (2) general interpretations by the CRA based on their view of how the legislation should apply that is consistent with their understanding of the purpose of the legislation, and

(3) administrative concessions by the CRA that are contrary to the legislation but favourable to taxpayers. Many administrative positions of the CRA are based on the cost of compliance of having to track the costs of relatively small-ticket items.

3-57. General interpretations by the CRA and administrative concessions are principally found in Folio S2-F3-C2, "Benefits and Allowances Received from Employment," and CRA guide T4130, "The Employer's Guide to Taxable Benefits and Allowances." As a rule the CRA has developed a number of administrative concessions over a wide range of income tax topics, but it is the area of employee benefits that tops the list. Therefore, a practical understanding of employee benefits requires a very general understanding of the ITA but an even greater understanding of the CRA interpretations, particularly their administrative concessions.

> **EXAMPLE** Jessica is employed as a manager in a large retail outlet in Calgary. She wants to go camping with friends but needs to purchase camping gear and supplies that would cost her $500. Her employer has a policy that allows employees to purchase at a discount the products it sells. Jessica takes advantage of the policy and purchases the supplies for $200. Her employer's cost of the supplies is $150.
>
> **ANALYSIS** Jessica has received a benefit (i.e., an economic advantage) of $300 because of her employment where she is the primary beneficiary. In addition, there are no legislative exclusions for this type of benefit. Technically she would be required to include an additional $300 in her employment income for the year. The CRA, however, has a longstanding position that allows employee discounts on the purchase of merchandise to be tax free as long as the price paid by the employee is not below the employer's cost. The policy does not apply to discounted services or to high-ticket items such as appliances, furniture, cars, and homes.
>
> **CONCLUSION** The benefit is not taxable to Jessica because of a CRA administrative concession.

Legislative Guidance

ITA 6(1)

3-58. ITA 6(1) is the largest subsection in ITA 6. As such it contains a number of paragraphs that list specific items that must be included in employment income. The more important paragraphs that are discussed in this text are the following:

ITA 6(1) Inclusions

- ITA 6(1)(b) — Amounts received as an allowance for personal or living expenses
- ITA 6(1)(c) — Director's or other fees
- ITA 6(1)(e) — Standby charge for automobiles
- ITA 6(1)(e.1) & (f) — Wage loss replacement plans, provided they are received on a periodic basis and are intended to replace employment income
- ITA 6(1)(i) — Salary deferral arrangement payments (to the extent they have not previously been included in income)
- ITA 6(1)(j) — Reimbursements and awards
- ITA 6(1)(k) — Automobile operating expense benefit

3-59. As further legislative guidance, we had mentioned in Paragraph 3-50 that certain employee benefits were legislatively excluded from ITA 6(1)(a). The more important of these exclusions are as follows:

ITA 6(1)(a) Exclusions

- Employer's contributions to:
  - registered pension plans;
  - group sickness or accident insurance plans, provided that any benefits received under the plan will be taxed under ITA 6(1)(f); and
  - private health services plans

- Counselling services in respect of the mental or physical health of the employee or a related individual, or related to re-employment or retirement of the employee
- Benefits resulting from reduced tuition provided to the children of teachers at private schools, provided the teacher is dealing at arm's length with the school and the reduction is not a substitute for salary or other remuneration from the school

Note If you were to read ITA 6(1)(a), you would find that the listed exclusions include both group term life insurance as well as benefits related to automobiles, which we have not included in the list above. The reason for this exclusion relates to the "value" of these benefits. ITA 6(1)(a) requires that the value or fair market value (FMV) of non-excluded benefits be included in employment income. The amount required to be included in an employee's employment income as a benefit for the use of an employer-owned car or employer contributions for a group term life insurance policy for the employee is not FMV but a completely different amount determined, by calculation, elsewhere in ITA 6. If, for example, you were provided the use of an employer-owned car that you used for both personal and employment purposes, then there would be a benefit. The determination of that benefit is not FMV and therefore is not determined through ITA 6(1)(a) but by a calculation through a combination of ITA 6(1)(e), (k), and 6(2), which will be discussed later in this chapter. The benefit attributable to contributions by an employer toward a group term life insurance policy for the employee is also not FMV; instead the amount of that particular benefit is determined separately at ITA 6(4), also discussed later in this chapter.

Tip Think of ITA 6(1)(a) as a default FMV rule that applies to most benefits except legislatively excluded and administratively excluded benefits. Where the income tax legislation requires that benefits be included in employment income but does not want to value the benefit using FMV, then separate rules are written in ITA 6 to both identify and value those specific types of benefits.

Other ITA 6 Provisions

3-60. ITA 6(1) identifies specific amounts that are required to be included in the employment income of an individual employee. Some of the paragraphs, such as ITA 6(1)(a), list exceptions or exclusions that must be considered to determine precisely what, when, and how much is required to be included. In contrast, the other subsections of ITA 6 are generally complementary to ITA 6(1), typically determining a dollar amount to be included or establishing additional rules and conditions that must be met. Some of the more important of these provisions are as follows:

- **ITA 6(2) and (2.1)** "Reasonable Standby Charges" establish the dollar amounts required to be included in income where an employer-provided vehicle is made available.
- **ITA 6(3) and (3.1)** "Payments by Employer to Employee" requires the inclusion of amounts paid either immediately before employment begins or subsequent to the period of employment.
- **ITA 6(4)** "Group Term Life Insurance" determines the dollar amount to be included in an employee's income where employer contributions are made to such insurance policies for employees.
- **ITA 6(6)** "Employment at Special Work Site or Remote Location" establishes an exception to ITA 6(1)(a) to exclude employee benefits in connection with board, lodging, and transportation in certain locations.
- **ITA 6(7)** "Cost of Property or Service" requires that the ITA 6(1)(a) benefit include the addition of applicable GST/HST/PST.
- **ITA 6(9)** "Amount in Respect of Interest on Employee Debt" determines the dollar amount of the benefit where an employee has benefitted from a low-interest or interest-free loan because of employment.
- **ITA 6(15) and (15.1)** "Forgiveness of Employee Debt and Forgiven Amount" establishes the dollar amount of the benefit where employee debt is forgiven.

- **ITA 6(16) through (18)** "Disability Related Employee Benefits" provides that certain disability-related employee benefits that would be taxable are not taxable if certain conditions are met.
- **ITA 6(19) through (23)** "Housing Loss and Eligible Housing Loss" determines the dollar amount of a benefit where an employer compensates an employee for a housing loss.

3-61. Most of these items will be covered in more detail later in this chapter or in other chapters of the text.

Common Employee Benefits

3-62. In the paragraph that follows we have listed and provided an overview of some of the more common employee benefits specifically addressed by CRA publications. We ask that as you read through the next few pages you consider the five-step analysis described in Paragraph 3-51, which we have reproduced below to assist you in understanding the logic of the various CRA interpretations.

Step 1 Is there a benefit? (an economic advantage)

Step 2 Has the benefit been received/enjoyed because of an individual's employment?

Step 3 Is the employee or someone related to the employee the primary beneficiary?

Step 4 What is the value of the benefit?

Step 5 Is the benefit excluded?

Specific Items

3-63. What follows is a description of the various benefits that are discussed in the CRA Employers' Guide T4130. The benefits are listed in alphabetical order. In some cases, the specific item will be discussed in more detail in a later section of this chapter. We have added alongside each item the words "Administrative Concession" to identify differences in income tax treatment due to specific concessions by the CRA.

Automobile Benefits When an employee is provided with an automobile owned or leased by the employer there will be a taxable benefit largely attributable to the extent it is used for personal purposes. The determination of the dollar amount of the benefit, however, can be complex and will be covered in a separate section of this chapter beginning at Paragraph 3-80.

Board and Lodging If an employer provides an employee with free board or lodging (e.g., meals and accommodation), we have seen that the economic advantage is the fair market value that establishes the dollar amount to be included in employment income as a result of ITA 6(1)(a). If the board or lodging is subsidized rather than free, the economic advantage is the fair market value reduced by any amounts paid by the employee.

The major exceptions to this general rule are contained in ITA 6(6) and are as follows:

- Board or lodging provided at a **special work site.** A special work site is defined as an area where temporary duties are performed by an employee who keeps a "self-contained domestic establishment" (e.g., a home, apartment, or similar place) at another location as their principal place of residence. Because of the distance between the two locations, the employee is not expected to return daily from the work site to their principal place of residence.
- Board or lodging provided at a **remote work site.** A work site is defined as remote when it is 80 kilometres or more from the nearest established community with a population of at least 1,000 people.

You may note that a special work site differs from a remote work site in that there is no mention of remoteness from other communities or its population. For example, if an employee is sent on a temporary assignment of one year from Toronto to Vancouver and the employer subsidizes housing costs, there would be no benefit because Vancouver in this case would qualify as a special work site. ITA 6(6) overrides ITA 6(1)(a) with the result that there is no taxable benefit to be included in employment income as a result of the subsidized housing costs.

Cell Phone and Internet Benefits If an employer provides an employee with a cell phone to carry out their employment duties there is no taxable benefit even if there is incidental personal use. This is consistent with the primary beneficiary concept of benefit taxation. If the employer pays for internet service for an employee in their home it is much more difficult to establish that the use is purely employment related, particularly where the individual and family members enjoy the benefits of the service for personal purposes. Technically if the reason for the employer paying for the service meets the primary beneficiary threshold, then none of the benefit would be taxable. The CRA, however, takes a view that a benefit should be established to the extent of personal use in both cell phones and internet service. This is inconsistent with the case law.

Employer-Provided Child Care (Administrative Concession) If an employer provides, at their place of business, child care that is not available to the general public, the services are managed by the employer, and the services are available to all employees, then the value of the benefit is not considered to be taxable. Note that this is an administrative concession by the CRA. If any of the conditions are not met the value of the benefit is taxable. If the benefit is taxable the CRA through another administrative concession will allow the benefit amount to qualify for the child care expense deduction (discussed in Chapter 9) even though child care expenses have to be "paid" to be claimed.

Discounts on Merchandise (Administrative Concession) In general, if an employer provides discounts on merchandise, it is not considered a taxable benefit. However, the discounts must be available to all employees and the discounted price cannot be below cost. In addition, discounts on services are not part of this administration concession. It has also been the CRA's longstanding position that "high-ticket" items are also not part of this concession.

Education-Related Benefits There are several types of benefits that relate to education:

- If an employer provides an allowance for an employee's children, the allowance will be included in the employee's income.
- If an employer pays the tuition for a course that is directly related to the recipient's employment, it is not considered a taxable benefit. This is due to the "primary beneficiary" test for benefit taxation.
- If an employer pays the tuition for a course that is related to the general business of the employer, it is not generally considered to be a taxable benefit. This is also due to the "primary beneficiary" test.
- If an employer pays the tuition for a course that is of personal interest to the employee, it is considered to be a taxable benefit.
- If an employer provides free or reduced tuition to a member of an employee's family the treatment will vary depending on the circumstances—it could be (1) an excluded benefit to the employee, (2) a taxable benefit to the employee, or (3) scholarship income to the family member.

Gifts, Awards, and Long-Service Awards (Administrative Concessions) Technically, all gifts and awards would be considered taxable employment benefits, and under ITA 6(1)(a) the FMV of that gift or reward would be required to be included in income when received. There is, however, a wealth of administrative concessions by the CRA in this regard.

Cash and near-cash gifts and rewards are always taxable benefits. Near-cash gifts would include gift cards, preloaded credit cards, and gift certificates.

Non-cash gifts and non-cash awards to an arm's-length employee, regardless of number, will not be taxable to the extent that the total FMV of all non-cash gifts and awards to that employee by the employer is less than $500 annually. Any amount in excess of $500 annually, however, will be taxable.

Gifts with an immaterial value, such as coffee mugs, T-shirts, and so on can be ignored.

A separate non-cash long-service/anniversary award, to the extent its total value is $500 or less, will not be considered a taxable benefit. If the FMV exceeds $500 then the amount in excess of $500 will be taxable. In order to qualify, the anniversary award cannot be for less than five years of service or for five years since the last long-service award had been provided to the employee.

In contrast, a performance-related award is considered to be a reward and a taxable benefit since it is equivalent to a bonus and other remuneration.

Insurance Because of the many issues involved with various types of insurance, coverage of insurance requires a separate section in this chapter, which begins at Paragraph 3-157.

Employee Loans An employee or family member who receives a low-interest or interest-free loan from their employer has received an economic advantage to the extent that the rate, terms, and conditions are more favourable to what the employee could have achieved on her own. Valuing this type of benefit, however, could prove problematic. The value to be placed on such loans is the subject of a special provision that sets out rules to determine the benefit amount. These rules are separately discussed in this chapter beginning at Paragraph 3-163.

Loyalty and Other Points Programs (Administrative Concessions) Technically, the costs savings from the use of loyalty points (e.g., frequent flyer points) earned while carrying out one's employment duties would be considered taxable (non-excluded). The CRA does not require the value of the points to be included as taxable employment benefits provided:

- the points are not converted to cash;
- the plan is not an alternative form of remuneration; or
- the plan is not for tax avoidance purposes.

Meals (Administrative Concession) In general, reimbursing employees for meals consumed when they are required to work overtime does not create a taxable benefit as long as the overtime is infrequent and the overtime is for a minimum of two hours. If an employer provides subsidized meals to employees, their value is not considered to be a taxable benefit provided the employee pays a reasonable amount that covers the employer's cost. The meals would not be taxable benefits by the legislation if the location was at a special or remote work site (ITA 6(6)).

Medical Expenses When an employer pays for an employee's medical expenses, it is considered to be a taxable employment benefit. The employee would be able to claim the medical expense tax credit for the medical expenses to the extent of the employment benefit (discussed in Chapter 4).

Moving Expenses Employer payments for most types of employee moving expenses does not create a taxable benefit. This subject surprisingly can be quite complex. It is discussed more completely in Chapter 9 of this text.

Parking (Limited Administrative Concessions) Parking has become one of the most contested and controversial topics in benefit taxation with mixed results in the courts depending on the facts and whether the employer or employee is the primary beneficiary. The CRA considers parking to represent an economic advantage and, therefore, subject to their administrative concessions, a benefit should be determined and included in employment income. Valuation can be an issue in some cases, however. For example if you drive to work and the employer provides you with free parking on their own premises the CRA expects a benefit to be added to your employment income based on what that parking spot would cost if it were made available on the open market. Administrative concessions by the CRA include:

- parking for employees with disabilities;
- parking for employees who regularly require a car to carry out their employment duties, meaning once at the office they will have to travel for employment during the week, coming and going to the same parking location; and
- scramble parking (e.g., parking at a site where there are significantly fewer spaces than the number of employees who use them).

Pooled Registered Pension Plans Employer contributions to these plans are not considered to be a taxable benefit. This is a legislative exception to ITA 6(1)(a).

Premiums for Provincial Health Care If an employer pays these premiums for an employee, the payments are considered to be a taxable benefit.

Premiums for Private Health Service Plans (PHSPs) PHSPs are insurance plans established for all employees or a group of employees to cover hospital and medical coverage including dental, vision, and prescription benefits. The payment of premiums by the employer is a legislation exception to ITA 6(1)(a) and no amount is required to be included in the employment income of benefitting employees.

Professional Membership Dues If the employer is the primary beneficiary of the dues, there is no taxable benefit (e.g., membership in the organization is a condition of employment). If the employee is the primary beneficiary, the payment of such dues creates a taxable benefit.

Note Professional membership dues are allowed to the employee as an employment expense if membership is a requirement of the employment and the dues are not reimbursed. Therefore, when an employer reimburses the dues and membership is a requirement of the employment, there is no taxable benefit since the employer is the primary beneficiary and no employment expense because the dues were reimbursed. If the employer reimburses dues where the membership is not required for the employment, then the reimbursement creates a taxable benefit since the employee is considered the primary beneficiary. In addition, no employment expense could be claimed since the professional membership is not a requirement of the employment. The employment expense (ITA 8(1)(i)) is discussed later in this chapter.

Recreational Facilities and Club Dues (Administrative Concessions) Employer payment of fees or dues for the use of these facilities or clubs would be an economic advantage to an employee subject to ITA 6(1)(a) as long as the employee is the primary beneficiary. The CRA extends concessions, however, in the following situations:

- Provision of an in-house facility that is available to all employees
- An arrangement where an employer contracts with a facility and then makes it available to all employees

At this point we have addressed only one side of the taxation of employment benefits, looking solely at employees. The flipside of the equation looks to the impact on the employer. An employer is carrying on a business (discussed in Chapter 6), and the question is whether the costs of providing benefits (whether taxable or not) to employees entitles the employer to a business expense. There are two relevant income tax principles that are applicable. The first is that symmetry is not a rule in income tax law. This means that income for one taxpayer does not automatically result in an expense for the other. The second is that any costs incurred on behalf of employees, irrespective of whether those costs relate to the employment duties or are strictly personal to the employee, remain deductible to the employer as a cost of doing business subject to any ITA legislation to the contrary. Dues for the use of recreational facilities and club dues are expressly disallowed to the employer by ITA 18(1)(l). This is discussed further beginning at Paragraph 3-70.

Stock Options Because of the complexity related to these benefits, this chapter contains a separate section dealing with employee stock options, beginning at Paragraph 3-173.

Social Events (Administrative Concessions) The cost of employer-provided social events create an economic advantage and therefore a benefit to participating employees. The CRA, however, will not assess a taxable benefit provided:

- they are made available to all employees; and
- they cost less than $150 per person.

If the cost is more than $150 person, the full cost, including the first $150, becomes a taxable benefit.

Spousal Travel Expenses Employer payment of these costs creates a taxable benefit unless:

- the spouse was along at the employer's request; and
- the spouse was mostly engaged in business activities during the trip.

The reference to "business activities" means on behalf of the employer's business.

Registered Retirement Savings Plans (RRSP) and Tax-Free Savings Accounts (TFSAs) If an employer makes a contribution to an employee's RRSP or TFSA, it is an economic advantage primarily for the benefit of the employee and therefore a taxable benefit. In the case of a contribution toward an employee's RRSP, the employee would be entitled to deduct the contribution within the limitations of the RRSP rules. This is discussed in Chapter 10.

Tickets to Events In general, the value of employer-provided tickets to events is considered a taxable benefit unless there is a business reason for the employee to attend the event (e.g., the employee's attendance is primarily for the benefit of the employer).

Note In general only 50% of entertainment-related expenses are allowed as a business expense. However, if the cost of the entertainment is a taxable benefit to an employee then 100% of the cost of the entertainment is allowed as an expense. This is discussed further in Chapter 6.

Tool Reimbursement If an employer reimburses an employee for tools used in their employment duties, it is considered a taxable benefit. You may be inclined to think that the primary beneficiary would be the employer, but since the tools are owned by the employee it is that employee who is considered to be the primary beneficiary.

Note The cost of certain tools may qualify an employee for an employment expense. This is discussed briefly in this chapter.

Transit Passes (Limited Administrative Concessions) In general, the provision of transit passes to employees creates a taxable benefit. An exception to this would be transit passes to current or retired employees of a transit company within their area of operation.

Note This concession is similar to the concession for merchandise discounts to employees.

Travel Allowances Because of the complexity related to allowances, this chapter contains a separate section dealing with these benefits. It begins at Paragraph 3-99.

Uniforms or Special Clothing The provision of uniforms or special clothing does not create a taxable benefit provided

- the employer supplies employees with a distinctive uniform that must be worn while carrying out employment duties; or
- the employer provides employees with special clothing to protect them from hazards associated with carrying out the employment duties.

Costs of cleaning these uniforms or special clothing is also considered a non-taxable benefit.

While the costs paid by the employer provide an economic advantage to the employee, the primary beneficiary is the employer.

Exercise 3-3

Subject: Gifts to Employees

During the current year, Jeffrey's employer provides him with a number of gifts and awards. Describe the tax consequences for Jeffrey that result from each of the following gifts and awards:

Gift	Fair Market Value
T-shirt with employer logo	$ 15
Birthday gift (gift certificate to Amazon)	75
Reward for exceeding sales targets	400
10-year anniversary award (Seiko watch)	275
Wedding gift (crystal vase)	300
Personal fitness award (tickets to sporting event)	250
Holiday season gift (gourmet food basket)	150

Exercise 3-4

Subject: Employee Benefits

John Nilson is an employee of a high-end furniture store. During the current year, John receives a number of benefits from his employer. Describe the tax consequences for John that result from receiving each of the following benefits. Ignore any GST/HST & PST considerations.

- A 35 percent discount on merchandise with a total value of $400.
- Reimbursement of $2,000 in tuition fees for a course in creative writing.
- Business clothing with a value of $1,500 to be worn during working hours. (John's employer requires all employees to dress very professionally for meeting with clients.)
- A set of china on the occasion of John's wedding anniversary costing $450.
- A private health care plan for John and his family. The employer pays an annual premium of $780 for this plan.

Solutions to Exercises are available in the Study Guide.

Tax Planning Considerations

Salary: The Benchmark

3-64. As previously discussed, some of the benefits provided to employees are fully taxable while other benefits can be extended without creating a taxable benefit. This has important implications in planning employee compensation.

3-65. As the bulk of compensation for most employees is in the form of wages or salaries, such payments provide the benchmark against which other types of compensation must be evaluated. From an income tax point of view, these benchmark payments are fully deductible to the employer in the year in which they are accrued and fully taxable to the employee in the year in which they are received. There is no valid tax reason for using a type of fringe benefit that has these same characteristics. Remember that symmetry is not a rule of law when it comes to income tax.

3-66. For example, if an employer rewards a valued employee with a holiday trip for achieving a sales goal, the cost of the trip will be fully deductible to the employer. Further, the trip's cost will be fully taxable to the employee on the same basis as if the amount had been paid in the form of additional salary. This means that, while there may be a motivational reason for using a holiday trip as a form of compensation, there is no significant income tax advantage in doing so. There may be a timing difference, however, if the holiday trip actually takes place in the following year since ITA 6(1)(a) only requires such amounts to be included in employment income when "enjoyed."

3-67. The most attractive form of non-salary compensation involves benefits that are deductible to the employer but are received tax free by the employee. This is where knowledge of both the legislative exceptions and the administrative concessions becomes important. For example, employer contributions to PHSPs do not create taxable benefits, therefore an employer can provide employees with a deductible dental plan without creating any additional tax liability for the employee.

3-68. From a tax point of view, this type of compensation should be used whenever practical, provided it is desirable from the point of view of the employee. For example, although providing a dental plan to an employee is a tax-free benefit, if the employee's spouse has already been provided with an identical family dental plan by an employer, this benefit may be of little or no value to the employee.

Tax Deferral

3-69. Also attractive are those benefits that allow the employer to deduct the cost immediately with taxation of the employee deferred until a later year. We have already considered an example of this involving the use of bonus arrangements. A further example of this would be contributions to a registered pension plan. The employer can deduct the contributions in the period in which they are made, while the employee will not be taxed until the benefits are received in the form of pension income on retirement. This will usually involve a significant deferral of taxation for the employee.

Recreational Facilities and Club Dues

3-70. In the preceding cases, the tax planning considerations are very clear. There are no tax advantages associated with benefits that are fully and currently taxable to the employee. In contrast, advantages clearly arise when there is no taxation of the benefit, or when the taxation of the employee is deferred until a later point in time.

3-71. There is, however, a complicating factor in the case of certain employer-provided recreational facilities or employer payment of club dues. While in some cases such benefits are not taxable to the employee, the employer is not allowed to deduct the cost of providing such benefits (see Chapter 6 for a more detailed description of these rules). This means that the advantage of no taxes on the employee benefit is offset by the employer's loss of deductibility.

3-72. Whether this type of benefit is tax advantageous has to be evaluated on the basis of whether the tax savings to the employee are sufficient to offset the extra tax cost to the employer of providing a non-deductible benefit. The decision will generally be based on the relative tax rates applicable to the employee and the employer. If the employee's marginal tax rate is higher than the employer's, this form of compensation may be advantageous from a tax point of view. There are also other non-tax factors that may be important, such as employee loyalty and employee health.

Two Problem Benefits—Automobiles and Loans

3-73. We previously pointed out that there are two general types of taxable employment benefits: those based on FMV through ITA 6(1)(a) and those that establish a dollar amount different from FMV. Two examples of non-FMV benefits are those relating to employer-provided automobiles and loans to employees.

3-74. The basic problem in both cases is that the employer cost will not match the employee benefit amount. In the case of the employee benefit associated with having the use of an employer-provided automobile, it is based on an arbitrary formula, under which the benefit amount can exceed the cost of the automobile. In the case of employee loans, the benefit amount is determined using the prescribed rate of interest, not the cost of the funds to the employer.

3-75. Because of this lack of symmetry in the measurement of the cost and benefit, a case-by-case analysis is required to evaluate the tax effectiveness of these types of benefits. In each situation, it must be determined whether the cost to the employer is greater than or less than the benefit to the employee. If the cost is greater, the employer may wish to consider some alternative and more tax effective form of compensation. This makes these benefits considerably more difficult to evaluate.

3-76. The taxable benefits associated with both employer-provided automobiles and employer-provided loans are discussed in detail at a later point in this chapter.

Exercise 3-5

Subject: Planning Employee Benefits

As part of her compensation package, Jill Tyler is offered the choice of a dental plan for her family, an annual vacation trip for her family, or an annual birthday gift of season's tickets to the ballet for her and her spouse. The alternative benefits are each worth about $4,000 per year. Indicate which benefit would be best for Jill from a tax point of view and explain your conclusion.

Solutions to Exercises are available in the Study Guide.

Inclusions—GST/HST & PST on Taxable Benefits

3-77. Many benefits included in employment income are goods and services on which an employee would have to pay GST, HST, or PST if they personally acquired the item or service. For example, if an employer provides a free domestic airline ticket to reward an Ontario employee for outstanding service, this is an item on which the employee would have to pay 13% HST if he purchased the ticket personally. This means that the taxable benefit should also include an HST component, as the employee has received a benefit with a real value that includes both the price of the ticket and the related HST.

3-78. Given this situation, ITA 6(7) requires the calculation of employee benefits on a basis that includes any GST/HST/PST that was paid by the employer on goods or services that are included in the benefit. In situations where the employer is exempt from these taxes, a notional amount is added to the benefit on the basis of the amounts that would have been paid had the employer not been exempt.

3-79. Throughout this course our principal focus is on income tax with the exception of Chapter 21, where we discuss the GST/HST. As a result we limit the addition of GST/HST throughout the examples, exercises, and problems. There are many complexities to the subject of taxable benefits and the GST/HST, including which benefits are subject to the tax, valuation, employee rebates, and employer responsibilities, including the possible claiming of input tax credits. The CRA guide T4130, referenced earlier, contains a two-page benefits chart at the end of the guide with a detailed list of different types of benefits and whether the GST/HST applies.

Exercise 3-6

Subject: GST on Taxable Benefits

Ms. Vicki Correli, as the result of an outstanding sales achievement within her organization, is awarded a two-week vacation in the Bahamas. Her Alberta employer pays a travel agent $4,500 plus GST of $225 for the trip. What is the amount of Ms. Correli's taxable benefit?

Solutions to Exercises are available in the Study Guide.

Inclusions—Automobile Benefits

Employees and Automobiles

Motor Vehicles, Automobiles, and Passenger Vehicles

3-80. The ITA, ignoring "zero-emission vehicles" and "zero-emission passenger vehicles," which are discussed in Chapter 5, uses three different terms to refer to cars, trucks, and vans. The three terms as defined in ITA 248(1), are "motor vehicle," "automobile," and "passenger vehicle."

3-81. A basic understanding is important in determining the income tax consequences of (1) employee benefit taxation where an employer provides the use of an *automobile* to an employee for employment purposes where there is some personal use, (2) allowances received by an employee from an employer to cover the costs of travel and motor vehicle use where the *motor vehicle* is owned by the employee, and (3) the amount of capital cost allowance (CCA, i.e., tax depreciation) that can be claimed by the employer-owner of a *passenger vehicle* used in the employer's business.

3-82. A motor vehicle is the broadest of the three terms and means an "automotive vehicle designed or adapted to be used on highways and streets." The word "automotive" generally means self-propelled, and therefore truck trailers, for example, would not qualify. Golf carts and boats would also not qualify since they are not designed for highway or street use. Almost all cars, vans, and trucks, however, would be motor vehicles.

3-83. A "passenger vehicle" is defined as an "automobile" generally acquired after June 17, 1987. This expression is one used in reference to the CCA system (which will be discussed in Chapter 5), but it relies on the definition of an "automobile." Many accountants and tax practitioners loosely refer to this concept as applying to "luxury vehicles" since the CCA restrictions apply to automobiles costing $30,000 or more before any GST/HST/PST and $55,000 for "zero-emission passenger vehicles."

3-84. An "automobile" is clearly the most important of the three definitions. If a car, truck, or van is not an automobile it cannot be a passenger vehicle, meaning that the CCA restrictions would not apply. In addition, employees are only required to include in their employment income benefits from *automobiles* provided to them by their employers. If the car, truck, or van is not an automobile, then the specific benefit provisions that we will discuss would not apply. This does not mean, however, that a benefit could not be calculated elsewhere. This will be discussed later in this chapter.

3-85. An automobile is defined as a motor vehicle that has a seating capacity of no more than nine people including the driver. Standard-sized buses would therefore not be considered automobiles or any other motor vehicle with a seating capacity of ten or more. The definition contains a lengthy list of exceptions, some of which are the following:

- Ambulances
- Fire trucks
- Police cars
- Motor vehicles acquired primarily to be used as a bus or taxi in transporting passengers in a transportation business
- A van, pick-up truck, or similar vehicle purchased or leased with a seating capacity of no more than three people (including the driver) used more than half the time to transport goods or equipment in the carrying on of a business
- A van, pick-up truck, or similar vehicle purchased or leased and used more than 90% of the time in the year it was acquired or leased to transport goods, passengers, or equipment in the carrying on of a business

The words "similar vehicle" are not considered to include cars but are considered to include SUVs (including cross-over utility vehicles) and extended cab pick-up trucks. Cars are only included where the term "motor vehicle" is used.

Exercise 3-7

Subject: The Definition of an "Automobile"

In each of the following situations, determine whether the car, van, pick-up truck, or similar vehicle is or is not an "automobile." Explain your reasons.

1. A business that offers shuttle service to hotel guests to and from airports purchased a shuttle bus that seats nine people including the driver. The shuttle bus is used a minimum of 95% of the time in transporting passengers in each year.
2. A local restaurant affected by COVID-19 expands its business to include delivery service. It purchased two small cars to be used as delivery vehicles, each of which seat a maximum of five people. The vehicles are used 80% of the time for business.
3. A local charity also affected by COVID-19 collects donations of food and clothing for local distribution and acquired two vans to pick up the donated items. The charity is tax exempt and does not carry on any business. The vans have a maximum seating capacity of two people.
4. A professional valuator purchased a Mercedes SUV for $125,000. The vehicle is used 75% of the time to travel to and from clients in the course of the business of providing valuation services.
5. A construction company acquires an extended cab heavy duty pick-up truck with a five-person seating capacity to transport both heavy equipment and workers to numerous construction sites. Assume it is used (a) 70% of the time or (b) 95% of the time in the year it was purchased.

Solutions to Exercises are available in the Study Guide.

Benefits When Motor Vehicles Are Not Automobiles

3-86. In our discussion of employee benefits we have seen that there are two general types of rules: one in which ITA 6(1)(a) applies to include the FMV of a benefit in employment income and the second that applies to other types of benefits that use something other than FMV. In the following pages we look at employee benefit taxation where an "automobile" is provided by an employer to an employee that is used in the employment duties. The rules of the ITA that establish the dollar amount of the benefit are specific to automobiles and are completely separate from ITA 6(1)(a). This leads to the question of what happens when the vehicle is not an "automobile" as defined in ITA 248.

3-87. The CRA is of the view that when a vehicle that is not an automobile is provided by an employer to an employee and there is personal use, such as travel to and from home and the work location, there is an economic advantage and therefore a taxable benefit. However, the rules we will discuss (e.g., the standby charge benefit and the operating expense benefit) only apply if the vehicle is an automobile. The result is that the specific automobile benefit rules cannot apply, but since the CRA considers there to be a benefit then the FMV rules of ITA 6(1)(a) must apply. The CRA administratively accepts that the value (FMV) of the benefit would be equal to the "reasonable allowance rates" based on the number of personal kilometres driven. The reasonable allowance rates for 2021 are $0.59 for the first 5,000 kilometres and $0.53 for any additional kilometres.

> **EXAMPLE** In 2021 an employee drives a delivery van owned by the employer. The van is not considered an "automobile." The employee personal use amounts to 8,000 kilometres.
>
> **ANALYSIS** The FMV of the employee benefit (ITA 6(1)(a)) acceptable to the CRA would be $4,540 [(5,000 km x $0.59) + (3,000 km x $0.53)]. The benefit amount is considered to represent a benefit for both the use of the van and the operating costs.

3-88. In our previous discussion we also noted that for a multitude of reasons the CRA provides administrative concessions in certain situations. The CRA is willing to provide such a concession to allow the total benefit to be reduced and calculated using $0.27 per personal use kilometre where an employee is driving an employer-provided vehicle that is not an automobile under certain conditions, such as needing the vehicle for on-call service. The CRA policy can be found at www.canada.ca/en/revenue-agency/services/tax/businesses/topics/payroll/benefits-allowances/automobile/automobile-motor-vehicle-benefits/benefit-motor-vehicles-defined-automobile.html. In the remaining pages of this chapter we will focus on benefits for employer-provided vehicles that are "automobiles."

Influence on Employment Income

3-89. Automobiles have an influence on the determination of an individual's employment income in three different situations. These situations can be described as follows:

> **Employer-Provided Automobiles** It is fairly common for a business to provide an automobile to an employee in order to assist the individual in carrying out her employment duties. The automobile could be owned or leased by the employer—both are considered employer-provided automobiles. In most cases, the employee will have some personal use of the vehicle that is provided. If this is the case, the employee will have a taxable benefit that must be added to her employment income.
>
> **Allowances** As an alternative to providing an employee with an automobile, some employers pay an allowance to employees for employment-related use of their own automobile, which again would include owned and leased vehicles. This allowance may be included in employment income and, when this is the case, the employee will be able to deduct some portion of the automobile's costs, including a depreciation component, as an employment expense.
>
> **Deductible Travel Costs** Under certain circumstances, employees can deduct various travel costs. If the employee uses a personally owned automobile for employment-related travel, a portion of the costs associated with this automobile can be deducted as an employment expense.

3-90. In this chapter we will give detailed attention to the benefit resulting from employer-provided automobiles, as well as to the appropriate treatment of allowances for automobile costs. With respect to automobile-related travel costs, the rules for these deductions are the same for both employees and businesses. Because of this, we will defer some of our coverage of this subject to Chapter 6, which deals with business income.

Personal Travel

3-91. The ability to determine the income tax consequences of using an automobile for employment purposes, whether provided by the employer or not, is based on identifying the number of kilometres driven for employment versus those driven for personal use. Throughout our coverage we will provide you with the personal and employment-related kilometres in advance; however, from a practical point of view it is important to understand some basic concepts as to how to go about differentiating between the two types of use.

3-92. Many individuals who use an employer-provided automobile believe it is used only for employment because it is only driven to and from work and to and from clients/customers/suppliers of the employer. The case law has consistently concluded that getting to and from one's work location from home is personal use, but that other driving is employment-related usage. In addition, the CRA has provided numerous interpretations of what is and what is not acceptable in terms of employment-related use. As a result, we can provide the following general guidelines:

Driving from home to one's work location and back = Personal Use (both trips)

Driving from home at the start of the day to a client/customer/supplier of the employer then to one's work location = Employment Use (both trips)

Driving to and from one's work location and a client/customer/supplier of the employer = Employment Use

Driving from one's work location at the end of the day to a client/customer/supplier of the employer and then back to one's home = Employment Use (both trips)

3-93. As you can see, it is only driving from one's home to one's work location and back that is considered personal use. Stopping at a client/customer/supplier before arriving at the work location at the start of the day and doing the same on the way home effectively results in all of the kilometres being considered employment-related use as long as the trips are required by the employment.

3-94. The CRA considers one's work location to be the place where an employee regularly reports for work. The CRA further considers that it is possible to have more than one work location, particularly if an individual employee spends considerable time on a regular and recurring basis at that location. In other words there is some element of uncertainty that is dependent on the facts. Regardless, it is important to be aware of the distinction between personal and employment-related use to be in a position to accurately determine one's personal kilometres. In addition, the CRA and the courts require that a log book or equivalent be maintained to provide the necessary details to support actual employment-related usage.

Tax Benefit—Employer-Provided Automobile

3-95. There are two types of costs that can be associated with ownership of an automobile. First, there is a fixed cost that arises from simply owning the vehicle over time. The value will decline, even if you do not drive it a single kilometre. For new cars the value can decline as much as 20% in the first year and at least 10% in the next four years.

3-96. In addition to this fixed cost or annual decline in value, there are recurring costs associated with operating the automobile. These costs will tend to have a direct relationship to the number of kilometres driven. However, the per-kilometre amount will vary significantly, depending on the type and age of the automobile that is being driven.

3-97. Income tax legislation reflects this economic analysis. The two main benefits that can be assessed to an employee who is provided with an employer-owned or-leased automobile can be described as follows:

Standby Charge This benefit is assessed under ITA 6(1)(e). This benefit reflects the fixed cost of owning an automobile. However, we will find that the dollar amount of the benefit will vary depending on the number of personal use kilometres.

Operating Cost Benefit This benefit is assessed under ITA 6(1)(k) and, as the name implies, it reflects the costs of operating the automobile. You should note, however, that it is not based on the employer's actual costs. It is assessed at a fixed rate for each kilometre that the employee drives for personal use.

3-98. As discussed in Paragraphs 3-77 to 3-79, a GST/HST/PST component must be included when taxable benefits provided to employees involve goods or services that would normally be subject to the GST, PST, or HST. Personal use of an automobile falls into this category. Both the standby charge benefit and the operating cost benefit that are discussed in the following material are calculated in a manner that includes a GST/HST/PST component.

Allowances and Deductible Travel Costs

3-99. Both allowances and deductible travel costs involve the determination of amounts that can be deducted by employees who own or lease their own automobile. Tax legislation places limits on the amounts that can be deducted for automobile costs. For 2021, lease payments in excess of $800 per month before taxes are not deductible where the vehicle is a "passenger vehicle." In addition, CCA cannot be deducted on luxury automobile costs in excess of $30,000 before taxes or $55,000 before taxes for zero-emission luxury vehicles. As these limits are the same for an employee who owns or leases a vehicle that is used in employment activities and for a business that owns or leases a vehicle that is used in business activities, they are given detailed coverage in Chapter 6 on business income, after we have covered CCA in Chapter 5.

3-100. However, it is important to note here that the limits that are placed on the deductibility of any automobile costs including CCA have no influence on the dollar amount of the taxable benefit that will be assessed to an employee who is provided with an automobile by an employer. This means that if an employer provides an employee with an automobile that costs $150,000, the employee's benefits will be based on the full $150,000 cost, despite the fact that the employer will be limited to deducting CCA on only $30,000 or $55,000.

Taxable Benefits—Standby Charge

Employer-Owned Automobiles

3-101. While ITA 6(1)(e) requires a standby charge benefit to be included in employment income, the actual calculations are found in ITA 6(2). If the employer owns the automobile, the basic standby charge is determined by the following formula:

[(2%)(Cost of Car)(Periods of Availability)]

3-102. The components of this formula require some additional explanation:

Cost of Automobile The cost of the automobile is the amount paid, without regard to its list price. It would include all related GST/PST/HST amounts.

Periods of Availability Periods of availability means months of availability. However, the number of months is determined by dividing the number of days the automobile is "made available" by 30 and rounding to the nearest whole number. Oddly, a "0.5" amount is rounded down rather than up.

Made Available Being *available for use* is considerably different than *actually used.* The language is intentional and means that an automobile sitting in one's garage without ever being used in a year would still be considered available for use as long as it could legally be driven (e.g., the licence plates are not expired). It used to be standard practice for employees with employer-provided automobiles to voluntarily return them to the employer when on extended leaves of absence such as vacations, but the CRA announced that such a practice would only make the automobiles unavailable if the employer required that the automobiles be returned during periods of absence. If the employer had a policy of requiring that automobiles be returned it would be difficult for the CRA to ignore that policy.

3-103. If we assume that an automobile was available throughout the year and cost $33,900, including $3,900 in HST at 13%, the standby charge would be $8,136 [(2%)($33,900)(12)]. If the automobile continues to be available to the employee throughout the year for subsequent years, the benefit would be the same each year, without regard to the age of the automobile.

3-104. You should note that the application of this formula can result in a situation where the cumulative standby charge will exceed the cost of the automobile.

EXAMPLE An employee has the use of an automobile that cost $56,500, including HST. This availability continues for five years (60 months).

ANALYSIS The taxable benefit resulting from the standby charge calculation would be $67,800 [(2%)($56,500)(60)]. This taxable benefit is 20% larger than the cost of the car to the employer.

Employer-Leased Automobiles

3-105. In those cases where the employer-provided automobile is leased by the employer the basic standby charge is determined by the following formula:

[(2/3)(Lease Payments for the Year Excluding Insurance)(Availability Factor)]

3-106. As was the case with the formula for employer-owned automobiles, the components of this formula require additional explanation:

Lease Payments The amount to be included here is the total lease payments for the year, including any relevant GST/PST/HST. This total would be reduced for any part of the lease payment that is for insuring the automobile. The insurance costs are included as part of the operating cost benefit.

Availability Factor This is a fraction in which the numerator is the number of days during the year the automobile is available to the employee and the denominator is the number of days during the year for which lease payments were made. If the employee had the use of the automobile throughout the lease period, the value of this fraction would be 1. The same 30-day rounding rule applies for both purchase and lease situations.

3-107. An example will illustrate these procedures:

EXAMPLE An automobile is leased for three months at a rate of $750 per month, including HST. The $750 includes a monthly insurance payment of $75 per month. An employee has use of the vehicle for 85 of the 92 days of the lease term.

ANALYSIS Since both (85 ÷ 30) and (92 ÷ 30) would round to 3, the standby charge would be $1,350 [(2/3)(3)($750- $75)(3 ÷ 3)].

3-108. Unlike the situation with an employer-owned automobile, it is unlikely that the taxable benefit associated with a leased automobile will exceed the cost of the automobile. In most normal leasing situations, the taxable benefit on a leased automobile will be significantly less than would be the case if the employer purchased the same automobile. This is attributable to the fact that lease payments are determined on the basis of the retail value less the expected residual value at the end of the lease.

EXAMPLE, A $55,000 (HST inclusive) vehicle could be leased for 48 months with a lease payment of $800 per month (HST inclusive).

ANALYSIS—Vehicle Purchased If the vehicle is purchased, the standby charge will be $13,200 per year [(2%)($55,000)(12)].

ANALYSIS—Vehicle Leased If the vehicle is leased, the standby charge will be $6,400 per year [(2/3)(12)($800)(12 ÷ 12)].

3-109. This example illustrates a fairly general result: For a given automobile, the taxable benefit for the employee will be lower in situations where the employer leases the vehicle rather than purchasing the vehicle. The only exceptions to this would occur when the lease has a very short term.

Reduced Standby Charge

3-110. When an employer provides an automobile to an employee, it is usually used by the employee for a combination of both personal and employment purposes. Among different employees, there are significant variations in the mix of use. Some employees may use the car almost exclusively in carrying out employment duties, while in other situations, particularly when the employer and the employee are not at arm's length (e.g., the employee is related to or is the owner of the business), the car may be used almost exclusively for personal travel. While we have not elaborated on this, the automobile standby charge benefit applies to an employee where the employer has made an automobile available to a family member of that employee. In such cases it would be likely that the use of the automobile is almost exclusively used for personal purposes.

3-111. This would suggest that there should be some modification of the basic standby charge in situations where the main or principal use of the automobile is for employment purposes. This, in fact, is the case. The ITA 6(2) standby charge formula provides for a reduction where the personal use of the automobile is not significant.

3-112. The reduction involves multiplying the regular standby charge for either an employer-owned or an employer-leased automobile by the following fraction:

$$\frac{\textbf{Non-Employment Kilometres (Cannot Exceed Denominator)}}{\textbf{1,667 Kilometres x Number of Months of Availability*}}$$

*The number of months of availability is calculated by dividing the number of days that the automobile is available by 30 and rounding to the nearest whole number.

3-113. In applying this formula, the numerator (i.e., the top number) is based on the number of kilometres driven for non-employment purposes (i.e., personal use). To prevent the fraction from having a value in excess of one, the numerator is limited to the value in the denominator. The denominator is based on the idea that, if the employee uses the automobile for as much as 1,667 kilometres of personal activities in a month (20,004 kilometres per year), the vehicle has fully replaced the need for a personally owned automobile and therefore there should be no reduction to the benefit.

3-114. This fraction can be used to reduce the basic standby charge provided two conditions are met:

- The employee is required by the employer to use the automobile in his employment duties; and
- The use of the automobile is "primarily" employment related. In general, "primarily" is interpreted by the CRA to mean more than half the time or 50%.

TIP: A standby charge reduction is available if (1) the number of employment-related kilometres is more than half of the total kilometres and (2) the average monthly personal use does not exceed 1,667 kilometres.

3-115. Technically the formula for the reduced standby charge must be determined when calculating the benefit. However, when either of the conditions is not met the formula will always equal 1 and, as a result, will not provide for any reduction in the basic standby charge.

Operating Cost Benefit—Employer-Provided Automobile

Basic Calculations

3-116. In those cases where the employer pays the operating costs for an automobile that is available to an employee, that employee is clearly receiving a benefit related to the portion of these costs that are associated with the personal use of the automobile. An obvious approach to assessing an operating cost benefit would be to simply pro rate operating costs paid by the employer between personal and employment-related usage. The problem with this, however, is that the employer would be required to keep detailed cost and mileage records for each employee. This approach is further complicated by the fact that some operating costs incur GST or HST (e.g., gas), while other operating costs are exempt from GST or HST (e.g., car insurance and car licences).

3-117. Given these problems, ITA 6(1)(k) has provided a legislative solution in the case of employer-provided automobiles. ITA 6(1)(k) applies to determine the operating cost benefit if the following conditions are met:

- A standby charge has applied to the individual as a result of being provided the use of an automobile by the employer.
- The employer has paid for the operating costs that would include personal use.
- The employee has not fully reimbursed the employer for the portion of the operating costs relating to the personal use within 45 days of the year end.

3-118. If the individual has not reimbursed the employer, then the operating cost benefit of ITA 6(1)(k) applies. The operating cost benefit is determined by multiplying a prescribed amount by the number of personal kilometres driven reduced by any repayment made by the employee to the employer for the operating costs within the same 45-day period. For 2021, this prescribed amount is $0.27. This amount includes a notional GST or HST component and, as a consequence, no further GST or HST benefit is added to this amount.

3-119. It is important to keep in mind that the actual operating costs are irrelevant to the calculation of the operating costs benefit under ITA 6(1)(k). The purpose of these rules is to apply a general formula to every employee who has the use of an employer-provided automobile.

Operating Cost Benefit—Alternative Calculation

3-120. There is an alternative calculation of the operating cost benefit. Employees who use an employer-provided automobile "primarily" (i.e., more than 50%) for employment purposes can elect to have the operating cost benefit calculated as one-half of the standby charge by notifying the employer before the end of the year. This alternative calculation is purely optional. In many situations, it will not be a desirable option as it will produce a higher figure for the operating cost benefit and as a result the decision will have to be carefully considered.

Operating Cost Benefit—Employee-Provided Automobile

3-121. When an employee is provided with an employer-provided automobile both a standby charge benefit and an operating cost benefit apply. When an employee provides her own automobile there is no standby charge and therefore the operating cost benefit of ITA 6(1)(k) cannot apply. ITA 6(1)(l) is designed to address this situation by requiring the value of an operating cost benefit to be added to employment income. Since there are no formulas provided, the FMV is to be used. The CRA calculates the benefit by multiplying the percentage of personal kilometres to total kilometres by the actual operating costs paid by the employer less any reimbursements made by the employee.

Parking

3-122. ITA 6(1.1) clarifies that any parking benefit is determined separately from both the standby and operating cost benefits. This means that the general benefit rule of ITA 6(1)(a) applies to parking. Parking as a benefit was discussed in Paragraph 3-63.

Payments by Employees for Automobile Use

3-123. Under ITA 6(1)(e), the standby charge benefit can be reduced by payments made by the employee to the employer specifically for the personal use of the automobile. In corresponding fashion under both ITA 6(1)(k) and (l), the operating cost benefit can also be reduced by such payments. Payments made to the employer for the use of the automobile must be made in the year of use, whereas payments to the employer for operating costs related to personal use can be made up to 45 days after the end of the year.

Example—Employer-Owned Automobile

3-124. The following information will be used to illustrate the calculation of the taxable benefit where an employee is provided with an automobile owned by an employer in 2021:

Cost of the automobile ($30,000 + $3,900 HST)	$33,900
Days available for use by employee	310
Months owned by the employer	12
Actual operating costs	8,500
Repayments made to the employer	Nil
Total kilometres driven	30,000
Personal kilometres driven	16,000

3-125. The 310 days of availability is rounded to 10 months (310 ÷ 30 rounded). The basic standby charge benefit to be included in employment income is calculated as follows:

Standby charge = [(2%)($33,900)(10)] = $6,780

3-126. A reduced standby charge is available where more than half of the kilometres driven were for employment purposes and the average monthly personal kilometres is less than 1,667. In this case employment use is less than 50% [(30,000 - 16,000) ÷ 30,000 = 46.7%] of the total kilometres and therefore the reduction is not available.

3-127. The operating cost benefit to be included in employment income is as follows:

Operating cost benefit = [($0.27)(16,000)] = $4,320

3-128. As the employment-related use of the car was less than 50%, there is no elective option to the calculation of the operating cost benefit.

3-129. As the employee does not make any payments to the employer for the personal use of the automobile or the operating costs, the total taxable employment benefit included in income is as follows:

Total taxable benefit = ($6,780 + $4,480) = $11,260

Example—Employee-Owned or -Leased Automobile

3-130. If we alter the information provided to assume that the automobile that was used in performing his employment duties was owned or leased by the employee, then the results would be as follows:

Standby charge = Not applicable (applies to employer-owned or-leased vehicles only)

Operating cost benefit = [($8,500)(16,000/30,000)] = $4,533

Exercise 3-8

Subject: Taxable Benefits—Employer-Owned Automobile

Mrs. Tanya Lee is provided with an automobile by her employer. The employer acquired the automobile in 2020 for $25,000, plus $1,250 GST and $2,000 PST. During 2021,

Ms. Lee drives the automobile a total of 28,000 kilometres. Employment use accounted for 16,000 kilometres, and 12,000 were for personal use. The automobile is available to Ms. Lee throughout the entire year. Calculate Ms. Lee's minimum 2021 taxable automobile employment benefit.

Solutions to Exercises are available in the Study Guide.

Example—Employer-Leased Automobile

3-131. To provide a direct comparison between the employer-owned and employer-leased cases, this example will be based on the same general facts that were used in the ownership example in Paragraph 3-124. If the employer were to lease a $30,000 car with a 36-month lease term, the lease payment, calculated using normal lease terms, would be approximately $822 per month, including HST (this $822 value cannot be calculated with the information given). With the exception of the fact that the car is leased rather than purchased by the employer, all of the other facts are the same. The standby charge benefit would be calculated as follows:

Standby charge = [(2/3)($822)(10*)] = $5,480

*The availability factor of 10 is calculated as (310 ÷ 30 rounded).

A Note on Calculations The ITA 6(2) formula (as described in Figure 3-2) requires the total lease payments made for the year to be multiplied by a ratio that has months available divided by the months leased. As lease payments are generally given on a monthly basis, the literal use of this formula would result in the following calculation:

Standby charge (ITA calculation) = [(2/3)(12)($822)(10/12*)] = $5,480

*The availability factor is calculated as [(310 ÷ 30 rounded)/(365 ÷ 30 rounded)].

Note that multiplying (12) by (10/12) is the same as multiplying by (10). Therefore, in our formulas we use the more simple presentation of [(2/3)($822)(10)].

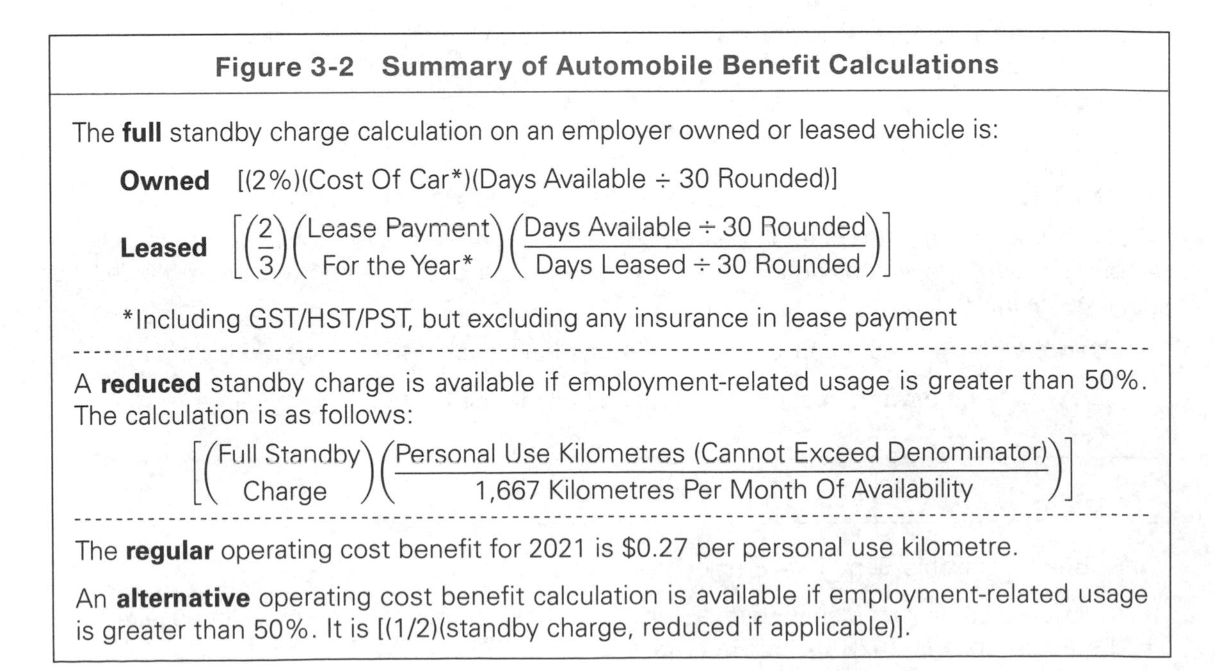

Figure 3-2 Summary of Automobile Benefit Calculations

The **full** standby charge calculation on an employer owned or leased vehicle is:

Owned [(2%)(Cost Of Car*)(Days Available ÷ 30 Rounded)]

Leased $\left[\left(\frac{2}{3}\right)\left(\begin{array}{c}\text{Lease Payment}\\ \text{For the Year*}\end{array}\right)\left(\frac{\text{Days Available} \div 30\text{ Rounded}}{\text{Days Leased} \div 30\text{ Rounded}}\right)\right]$

*Including GST/HST/PST, but excluding any insurance in lease payment

A **reduced** standby charge is available if employment-related usage is greater than 50%. The calculation is as follows:

$$\left[\left(\begin{array}{c}\text{Full Standby}\\ \text{Charge}\end{array}\right)\left(\frac{\text{Personal Use Kilometres (Cannot Exceed Denominator)}}{\text{1,667 Kilometres Per Month Of Availability}}\right)\right]$$

The **regular** operating cost benefit for 2021 is $0.27 per personal use kilometre.

An **alternative** operating cost benefit calculation is available if employment-related usage is greater than 50%. It is [(1/2)(standby charge, reduced if applicable)].

3-132. As was the case when the automobile was owned by the employer, there is no reduction for actual employment-related kilometres driven because the automobile was driven less than half the time for employment-related purposes. Also note that the benefit is based on the lease payment including HST.

3-133. The operating cost benefit has not changed from the employer-owned automobile case and is as follows:

Operating cost benefit = [($0.27)(16,000)] = $4,320

3-134. As in the case where the employer owned the automobile, with the employment-related use of the automobile at less than half there is no elective option for the operating cost benefit.

3-135. Since the employee does not make any payments to the employer for the personal use of the automobile, the total taxable benefit is as follows:

Total taxable benefit = ($5,480 + $4,320) = $9,800

3-136. Note that the total benefit is significantly less ($9,800 as compared with $11,260) when the employer leases the automobile as opposed to purchasing it. As indicated in our earlier discussion in Paragraphs 3-108 and 3-109, this would be the expected result in most cases.

Exercise 3-9

Subject: Taxable Benefits—Employer-Leased Automobile

Mr. Michael Forthwith is provided with an automobile that is leased by his employer. The monthly lease payments for 2021 are $525, plus $68 HST. During 2021, the automobile is driven a total of 40,000 kilometres, with 37,000 for employment use and 3,000 for personal use. The automobile is used for 325 days during the year. The employer paid a total of $11,250 in operating costs. When not using the automobile, company policy requires that it be returned to their premises. Calculate Mr. Forthwith's minimum 2021 taxable benefit for the use of the automobile.

Solutions to Exercises are available in the Study Guide.

Employer-Provided Automobiles and Tax Planning

3-137. Providing employees with automobiles is not a clearly desirable course of action. As is discussed in more detail in Chapter 6, there are limits on the ability of the employer to deduct the costs of owning or leasing an automobile. For example, leasing costs in excess of $800 per month before taxes are not deductible if the vehicle is a "passenger vehicle." Further, the taxable benefit calculations are such that they may produce a taxable benefit that exceeds the value to the employee of having the car.

3-138. This means that a decision by an employer to provide an employee with an automobile requires a careful analysis of all of the relevant factors. While a complete analysis of all of these issues goes beyond the scope of this chapter, some general tax planning observations can be made.

Require the Automobile to Be Returned In many situations, there will be periods of time when an employee does not use an employer-provided automobile. Examples would include vacation periods, extensive periods of travel for work, or absences as a result of illness. During such periods, the automobile will be considered available and increase the potential employment income benefits unless the employer requires the automobile to be returned to their premises, meaning that it would no longer be available for those days. Given this, the employer should have a policy of requiring vehicles to be returned during extended periods where the automobile is not used.

Record Keeping In the absence of detailed records, an employee could be assessed benefits as if all of the kilometres driven were for personal use. Avoiding this result requires the maintenance of log books where the information in support of benefits reported is kept current. The courts have historically not been sympathetic to individuals who are unable to explain their employment-related use because records were not kept.

Leasing vs. Buying As was previously noted, in many cases a lower taxable benefit will result when the employer leases the automobile rather than purchases it. One adverse aspect of leasing arrangements should be noted. Lease payments are made up of a combination of both interest and principal payments on the car. As the taxable benefit is based on the total lease payment, the interest portion becomes, in effect, a part of the taxable benefit. This is offset to some degree by the fact that the lease payments exclude the expected residual value when the lease period ends.

Minimizing the Standby Charge This can be accomplished in a variety of ways, including longer lease terms, lower trade-in values for older vehicles in purchase situations, larger deposits on leases, and the use of higher residual values in leasing arrangements. However, this minimization process is not without limits. As is explained in Chapter 6, refundable deposits in excess of $1,000 on leases can reduce the deductible portion of lease costs for "passenger vehicles."

Automobiles Costing More Than $30,000 With the taxable benefit to the employee based on the full cost of a passenger vehicle and any portion of the cost in excess of $30,000 not being deductible to the employer (this limit on the deductibility of passenger vehicle expenses is discussed in Chapter 6), it is difficult to imagine situations in which it would make economic sense for a profit-oriented employer to provide any employee with a passenger vehicle. The employee ends up paying taxes on an amount that can be significantly larger than the amount that is deductible to the employer. For example, the standby charge on a $150,000 Mercedes-Benz is $36,000 per year [(2%)($150,000)(12)], an amount that may be fully taxable to the employee depending on the number of personal-use kilometres. In contrast, the employer's deduction for capital cost allowance (tax depreciation) in the first year of ownership is limited to only $13,500 [($30,000)(30%) (1.5)].

Note It is unusual for an arm's-length employee to have the use of a passenger vehicle (e.g. a luxury automobile), but it is more common where the employer is incorporated and the employee, provided with a luxury automobile, is also a controlling shareholder or a major shareholder of the corporation controlled by family members. If it is determined that the automobile is only available to the individual because of her shares rather than her employment, then the automobile benefit rules are determined under ITA 15(5) instead of ITA 6(1)(e) and (k). The benefit calculations are generally the same, but the corporate employer would not be able to claim any expenses for the automobile, including any CCA. In other words, considerable care must be exercised when luxury automobiles are made available by corporate employers to employees who are also shareholders. This is discussed in Chapter 15.

Consider the Alternative The alternative to the employer-provided automobile is to have the employer compensate the employee by having him use his own automobile. In many cases this may be preferable to the employer providing an automobile. This is discussed in the next section on allowances paid by an employer to an employee for personal, travel, and automobile use.

We suggest you complete SSP 3-3, 3-4, and 3-5 at this point.

Inclusions—Allowances

Allowance vs. Reimbursement and Advances

3-139. A reimbursement is an amount paid to an employee to repay them for amounts personally expended on behalf of the employer's business while carrying out their employment duties. An example would be an employee who purchases an airline ticket for employment-related travel and who is later reimbursed for the cost of that ticket by the employer. The employee is not out of pocket as the cost is ultimately paid by the employer. Reimbursements of this type have no tax consequences for the employee. In addition, the travel expense is that of the employer rather than the employee. Reimbursements of personal and other items owned by an employee, such as tools used for employment purposes, however, are taxed as employee benefits under ITA 6(1)(a).

3-140. An employer can also pay an employee an advance to provide funds for an employment-related activity that would be subsequently accounted for once the activity has been completed. If, for example, an employee was required to travel to meet with current or potential clients/customers of the employer and the trip was expected to cost $3,000, the employee would request an advance of $3,000, which would then be used to pay for travel-related expenses including meals and accommodation. If on the conclusion of the travel it was determined that the trip actually cost $3,200, then the employer would pay the employee the additional $200. In this instance the result is economically equivalent to that of a reimbursement and there would be no tax consequences to the employee. The employer would be entitled to a business-related expense of $3,200 since it was the employer that incurred and paid for the travel costs.

3-141. The situation is more complex with allowances. Allowances would not include the reimbursements or accountable advances, which is consistent with the meaning given by the jurisprudence, which is described at Paragraph 2.56 of CRA Folio S2-F3-C2 titled "Benefits and Allowances Received from Employment" as follows:

> An allowance or an unaccountable advance is any periodic or lump-sum payment received by an employee who does not have to account for its use, An advance or unaccountable advance has the following characteristics...
>
> - A predetermined arbitrary amount that is not based on actual costs
> - Provided for a specific purpose
> - At the disposal of the employee without the need of providing receipts

General Rules

3-142. We will use the word "allowance" to refer to both allowances and unaccountable advances. An allowance is used to refer to amounts received by employees and is, of course, different than that of other types of employment income such as salary, wages, tips, and employment benefits. In practice, allowances generally involve payments to employees as compensation for travel costs, use of their own automobile, or other costs that have been incurred by employees as part of their efforts on behalf of the employer. A per-kilometre allowance for a travelling salesperson or a technician who does service calls would be typical examples of such an allowance.

3-143. ITA 6(1)(b) is the rule that requires allowances received by an employee as a result of their employment for personal or living expenses or for any other purpose to be included in the income of the employee as employment income subject to another list of exceptions. There is an important interplay between the receipt of allowances and the ability to claim certain employment expenses. If an employee has received an allowance that is not required to be included in employment income, this may prevent the employee from claiming the following employment expenses:

- ITA 8(1)(f) Salesperson's expenses
- ITA 8(1)(h) Travelling expenses other than motor vehicle expenses
- ITA 8(1)(h.1) Motor vehicle travelling expenses
- ITA 8(1)(j) Motor vehicle capital costs (interest and capital cost allowance)

Allowances—Exceptions

3-144. ITA 6(1)(b) provides a long list of exceptions to the rule that allowances must be included in income. The most important of these exceptions involve allowances received for the following:

- ITA 6(1)(b)(v) Reasonable allowances for travel expenses received during a period in which the employee was a salesperson (includes allowances for the use of a motor vehicle).
- ITA 6(1)(b)(vii) Reasonable allowances for travelling expenses for employees other than salespersons, not including allowances for the use of a motor vehicle.
- ITA 6(1)(b)(vii.1) Reasonable allowances for the use of a motor vehicle for employees other than salespersons

The three exceptions cover both motor vehicle expenses and other travel expenses for all employees including those who are salespersons.

Taxable vs. Non-taxable Allowances and Reasonableness

3-145. The preceding general rules mean that there are two possible outcomes when allowances are received by employees for travel and motor vehicle costs, both of which are dependent on whether an allowance is reasonable or not. Reasonable allowances are not included in employment income, but unreasonable allowances are included.

3-146. Legislators chose the word "reasonable" to allow objectivity to be used and applied to a set of facts. Courts have avoided attempts to define it and instead have typically made the following statement: "One draws the line between reasonable and unreasonable where one's good sense tells one to draw it" (Tax Court of Canada decision in 2831422 Canada Inc. v. The Queen, 2002 DTC 3930). The word "reasonable" does not therefore lend itself to establishing general principles and guidelines, but the word means that if the allowance is either unreasonably high or unreasonably low it would be required to be included in income, paving the way for the claiming of certain employment expenses that will be discussed later in this chapter.

3-147. In practical terms the reasonableness of an allowance is not determined by comparing the allowance with the actual costs. If that were the case two employees entitled to the same allowance for the exact same travel would be treated differently if one employee drove an $80,000 car while the other drove an old used car that only cost $1,000.

3-148. Instead, reasonableness is based on an amount that would be expected to cover the general costs from travel to and from a specific location at a specific time of year, including accommodation and meals where necessary. As a result, if someone asked you whether a daily travel allowance of $150 a day at a specific location, which would include hotel, meals, and daily transportation, was reasonable, you would be unable to answer without knowing more. If the allowance was for Toronto, Montreal, or Vancouver, one could argue that the allowance is unreasonably low; however, in outlying or less populated areas the allowance may be more than reasonable. In the alternative, a daily allowance of $500 or more could be reasonable if the travel was during the summer months in Vancouver where hotel occupancy was limited and hotel rates were particularly high.

Reasonable Allowances for Motor Vehicles

3-149. In Paragraph 3-144 we noted that ITA 6(1)(b)(v) and 6(1)(b)(vii.1) indicate that "reasonable allowances" for an employee's use of a motor vehicle do not have to be included in employment income. We discussed that reasonableness is a factual judgmental determination based on an element of common sense that is determined without regard to actual costs incurred by any one employee but rather the average expected costs, which is dependent on numerous factors.

3-150. In the case of reasonable motor vehicle allowances, the ITA adds two distinct rules that effectively deem reasonable allowances to be unreasonable. In such cases the allowance would then be included in employment income, again paving the way to deduct certain employment expenses. The two rules are as follows:

- The allowance is not based solely on the number of kilometres for which the vehicle is used in employment duties [ITA 6(1)(b)(x)].
- If the employee, in addition to the allowance, is reimbursed for all or part of the expenses of using the vehicle [ITA 6(1)(b)(xi)].

3-151. The first rule requires that the allowance be based solely on a kilometre rate applied to the number of kilometres driven for employment purposes. In practice such allowances are typically paid in advance with a monthly accounting for any difference once the employment-use kilometres are available. The payment of a fixed monthly kilometre-based allowance would cause a reasonable allowance to be deemed unreasonable and therefore included in employment income.

3-152. The CRA has an administrative position that if a per-kilometre allowance does not exceed the prescribed amount deductible to the employer as a business expense (discussed in Chapter 6), it will be considered reasonable, with the result that the allowance is not included in employment income. For 2021, the prescribed amounts are $0.59 per kilometre for the first 5,000 kilometres and $0.53 for each additional kilometre.

3-153. The second rule is designed to apply to deem a motor vehicle allowance to be unreasonable if an employee receives both an allowance for the use of the vehicle plus a reimbursement of expenses for the same use. This doubling up is considered unacceptable, with the result that the allowance is required to be included in employment income when received.

Exercise 3-10

Subject: Deductible Automobile Costs

Ms. Lauren Giacomo is required to use her own automobile in the performance of her employment duties. She receives an annual allowance of $3,600 for the use of her automobile. During the year, she drove a total of 24,000 kilometres, of which 6,500 kilometres were for employment use and 17,500 were for personal use. Her total automobile costs for the year, including lease costs, are $7,150. Determine the effect of these facts on Ms. Giacomo's employment income for the current year?

Exercise 3-11

Subject: Automobile Allowances

During the current year, Jacob Lorenz leases an automobile for $450 per month, a total for the year of $5,400. He drives a total of 60,000 kilometres, of which 35,000 are employment related and 25,000 are for personal use. His total operating costs for the year are $15,000. His employer pays him $0.10 for each employment-related kilometre driven, a total of $3,500. What amounts should Mr. Lorenz include and deduct in determining employment income for the current year?

Solutions to Exercises are available in the Study Guide.

Employer's Perspective of Allowances

3-154. From the point of view of the employer, paying allowances that are required to be included in employment income is the simplest solution from a compliance point of view.

All amounts paid will be included in the income of the employees and, as a consequence, there is no necessity for the employer to maintain detailed records of actual costs since those actual costs are those of the employees. It is up to the employee to keep the necessary details and to claim any deductible expenses.

Employee's Perspective of Allowances

3-155. From the employee's point of view, the receipt of a reasonable and therefore non-taxable allowance represents a simple solution to the problem. While records may have to be kept for the information needs of the employer, the employee has the advantage of simply ignoring the allowance and the related costs when it comes time to file a tax return.

Exercise 3-12

Subject: Travel Allowances

Sandra Ohm travels extensively for her employer. Her employer provides an allowance of $200 per day to cover hotel costs. Assume that the daily allowance is considered reasonable given the circumstances. In addition, she is paid $0.58 per kilometre when she is required to use her automobile for travel. This per-kilometre allowance is based on current published figures by the provincial automobile association for the average costs of an automobile.

For her work, during the current year, she travelled a total of 82 days and drove 9,400 kilometres. Her employer paid $16,400 for her lodging [(82)($200)], as well as $5,452 for kilometres driven [(9,400)($0.58)]. Her actual lodging costs were $18,300, while her total automobile costs were $7,200, including monthly lease payments. During the year she drove a total of 23,500 kilometres, of which 9,400 were for employment use and 14,100 were for personal use. What amounts should Ms. Ohm include and deduct in determining employment income for the current year?

Solutions to Exercises are available in the Study Guide.

Conclusion

3-156. At the end of the day, when an employer provides compensation to employees with respect to travel and other expenses, including the use of an employee vehicle for employment purposes, careful consideration will have to be made to determine the implications to both the employer and affected employees and the optimum structure to achieve the best tax consequences to all parties. Often little consideration is given until the CRA decides to question the methodology used and the income tax implications. Records will have to be maintained to support any income tax position taken that include whether allowances are or are not reasonable.

Inclusions—Employee Life & Disability Insurance Benefits

Life Insurance

3-157. The cost of providing life insurance benefits to employees is a taxable benefit under ITA 6(4). This means that any premiums paid on a life insurance policy by the employer must be included in employment income as a benefit. Lump-sum amounts paid out on the death of an employee pursuant to the terms of the insurance policy are not taxable.

Disability Insurance—Group Sickness or Accident Insurance Plans

3-158. The basic rules for group disability insurance plans are as follows:

Contributions by Employee Contributions made by an employee toward such plans are not deductible by the employee against employment income. However, they can be offset against disability benefits received that are required to be included in employment income.

Contributions by Employer Technically employer contributions to a group sickness or accident insurance plan are legislatively excluded from ITA 6(1)(a), however ITA 6(1)(e.1) modifies the exception, which will only apply as long as any plan benefits received would be required to be included in an employee's income (ITA 6(1)(f)). Benefits received are required to be included in the income of an employee provided they are (1) paid on a periodic basis (not up front in a lump-sum payment), and (2) paid to compensate the individual for the loss of employment income. If plan benefits do not meet both of these criteria (such as benefits for accidental death), then employer contributions will be considered a taxable benefit to the employee and required to be included in employment income.

Benefits Received (Employer Makes No Contributions) In the unusual situation where the employee makes all of the contributions to the plan, benefits will be received tax free. This is equivalent to the income tax treatment where individuals personally purchase their own life insurance policy, in which case no premiums paid are deductible for income tax purposes and any payouts on death are not income and therefore not taxable.

Benefits Received (Employer Makes Any Part of the Contributions) If the employer makes any part of the contributions, the benefits received by an employee will be required to be included in employment income. However, the employee can directly offset the income inclusion by the amount of any contributions that the employee has made to the plan in the year or in any preceding years prior to receiving the benefits. If plan benefits are not required to be included in employment income, then the employer's contributions are treated as a taxable benefit and included in employment income.

3-159. These rules give rise to three possible situations:

Employee Pay All Plans If the employee makes 100% of the contributions to the plan, the contributions will not be deductible, and any benefits received will not be included in employment income.

Employer Contributes—Benefits Not Taxed If the employer makes all or part of the contributions to the plan and benefits received are not taxed (because they are not periodic or do not replace employment income), the employer contributions to the plan will be treated as a taxable benefit to the employee and included in employment income. Any employee contributions to the plan would not be deductible.

Employer Contributes—Benefits Taxed If the employer makes all or part of the contributions to the plan and benefits received by the employee would be required to be included in employment income, then the employer's contributions do not create a taxable benefit. Any employee contributions to the plan are only deductible by the employee against amounts actually received from the plan in the year. The amounts can only offset the plan benefit amounts received. Any unused amounts of cumulative employee contributions can be used to offset benefit amounts received in subsequent years, providing an indefinite carryover.

3-160. The most common of these situations is the last one, in which the employer makes regular contributions that do not create a taxable benefit for the employee, with any benefits received being included in the employment income of the employee. Most of our examples and problems will be based on this type of situation.

3-161. You should note that these rules only apply to group plans. If the plan is not a group plan, any contributions made by an employer will be treated as a taxable benefit to the employee and required to be included in employment income.

EXAMPLE Jane Forthy's employer sponsors and makes regular contributions toward a group disability insurance plan that provides periodic benefits to replace employment income. During the period January 1 through April 1 of the current year, Jane's contributions to the plan totalled $1,200. On April 1 of the current year she was involved in a car accident that prevented her from working during the remainder of the year. During this period from April 1 through December 31, she received disability benefits of $16,000. In the previous year, the first year she participated in the plan, she contributed a total of $3,600 in premiums to this plan.

ANALYSIS Jane's income inclusion for the current year would be $11,200 [$16,000 - $1,200 - $3,600].

3-162. As noted in the previous section on life insurance, insurance services are exempt from GST/HST. Therefore there is no GST/HST amount added to taxable employment benefits as a result of premiums paid by employers for employee income maintenance and other insurance plans.

Exercise 3-13

Subject: Disability Insurance Benefits

Mr. Lance Bardwell is a member of a group disability benefit plan sponsored by his employer. The plan provides periodic benefits to replace employment income if an employee needs to make a claim under the plan. During 2020, Mr. Bardwell was required to contribute $300 to this plan. During 2021, his employer's share of the annual premium was $1,800. During the last six weeks of 2021, Mr. Bardwell became disabled and filed a claim that provided $5,250 in benefits from the disability plan. Because of this period of disability, his personal 2021 contribution to the plan was only $225. What amount will Mr. Bardwell include in his 2021 employment income?

Solutions to Exercises are available in the Study Guide.

Loans to Employees

General Rules

3-163. If an employer extends a loan to an employee that is either interest free or has a rate that is below the going market rate, the employee has received an economic advantage and therefore an employment benefit. The value of the benefit, however, is not FMV using the rules of ITA 6(1)(a), but rather a separate provision in ITA 6(9), the purpose of which is to determine the value of the benefit to be included in employment income. Paragraph 3-203 provides additional detail when an employer forgives an employee loan.

3-164. This provision is quite broad and applies whether the loan is made as a consequence of current, past, or future employment. The loan does not have to be made to the employee but can be made to a family member, and the loan does not have to be made by the employer. Regardless of who the loan is made to and who has made the loan, the related employment benefit is included in the employment income of the employee.

EXAMPLE Anita Gonzales began employment in January 2021. The employer is willing to secure the funds necessary for her to purchase a home. The employer offers to loan the funds directly to her or to her spouse, or to guarantee a low rate mortgage with a local bank, in which case the mortgage funds will come from the bank and not the employer.

RESULT Whether the mortgage funds are made directly to Anita or to her spouse by the employer or made to either of them by the bank the result is the same. Anita will be required to include any benefit in her employment income.

3-165. ITA 6(9) reads that the amount (e.g., value) of the employment benefit is to be determined by ITA 80.4(1). Under that provision the employment benefit begins with applying a prescribed interest rate (specified in ITR 4301 that was discussed in Chapter 2) to the amount owing for the period of time in which the loan was outstanding. The prescribed interest rate, which is established for each calendar quarter on the basis of Government of Canada Treasury Bills, is published and regularly updated by the CRA on their website. The amount of the employment benefit is reduced by any interest required to be paid on the loan by the employee during the year or within 30 days of the end of the year.

EXAMPLE On January 1 of the current year, Ms. Brooks Arden borrows $50,000 from her employer at an annual rate of 1%. Assume that during the year, the prescribed rate is 3% during the first two quarters and 4% during the last two quarters. Ms. Arden pays the required 1% interest on December 31.

ANALYSIS The taxable benefit to be included in Ms. Arden's employment income would be calculated as follows:

Imputed interest:	
Quarters 1 and 2 [(3%)($50,000)(2/4)]	$ 750
Quarters 3 and 4 [(4%)($50,000)(2/4)]	1,000
Total interest	$1,750
Less: Interest paid [(1%)($50,000)]	(500)
Employment benefit	$1,250

3-166. In general, interest calculations that are made for income tax purposes are based on the number of days the principal is outstanding, counting the day the loan is made but not the day that a loan payment is made. CRA publications demonstrate calculations using calendar quarters (IT-421R2). In situations where full calendar quarters are involved we will use this approach in our text and problem material.

3-167. Several additional points should be made with respect to these loans:

- If the rate negotiated with the employer is at least equal to (or greater than) the rate that the employee could have negotiated with a commercial lender, then under ITA 80.4(3)(a) there will be no benefit with respect to that loan regardless of subsequent changes to the prescribed rate. While not common, such situations could occur, for example, where an employer is willing to loan an employee funds interest free to purchase an automobile when automobile dealers are, at the same time, offering zero-interest financing as a promotion.

- Where the employer is a corporation and an employee is also a shareholder (minority or otherwise), then ITA 80.4(2) could apply to determine an interest benefit. The benefit would not be from employment but would be considered a shareholder benefit, which would be included in the income of the shareholder as income from property. The different rules that apply in this situation are described in Chapter 15, "Corporate Taxation and Management Decisions."

- Funds borrowed as a loan could be used to purchase investments (e.g., a source of income) or to purchase an automobile to be used in performing one's employment duties. The ITA permits interest on such loans to be claimed as an expense against the investment income earned on the purchased investments or as an employment expense in the case of an automobile purchased for employment purposes. The ITA, however, requires that there be a legal obligation to pay interest on the loan as a condition to claim an interest expense. The benefit determined under ITA 80.4(1) as an employment benefit is considered interest but not as a result of a legal obligation. To bridge the gap, ITA 80.5 deems any interest benefit determined under ITA 80.4 to be considered paid as a result of a legal obligation, meaning that the amount can be claimed as an interest expense if investments were purchased or an automobile acquired to be used in any manner for employment purposes. Referring to the example in Paragraph 3-165, if Ms. Arden had used the $50,000 loan to purchase investments she could have claimed an interest expense of $1,750, the $500 that she paid plus the $1,250 employment benefit. If Ms. Arden purchased investments, the benefit amount is employment income but the expense would be an investment expense.

- When a loan is to assist an employee to purchase a home, special rules in ITA 80.4(4) and (6) apply. The purpose of these rules is simply to cap the interest rate at the time of the loan and for each five years thereafter. This means that the rule is similar to a locked-in fixed-interest rate five-year mortgage but with an added benefit. If the prescribed rate decreases the employee benefit is calculated using the decreased lower rate, but if the prescribed rate increases the prescribed rate locked in at the beginning of the five-year period is used to determine the benefit. This guarantees that during the five years the benefit amount will never be based on a rate in excess of the locked-in rate.

Note This special treatment is only available where the benefit is employment related (ITA 80.4(1)), not shareholder related (ITA 80.4(2))

EXAMPLE On January 1 of the current year, an employee receives a $200,000 interest-free home purchase loan from the employer. Assume that the prescribed rate is 4% for the first quarter, 3% in the second and third quarters, and 7% in the fourth quarter. Annual payments begin in the following year.

ANALYSIS If interest is calculated on a quarterly basis, the benefit would be $8,500 [($200,000)(4%)(1/4) + ($200,000)(3%)(2/4) + ($200,000)(7%)(1/4)]. Alternatively, using the prescribed rate in effect at the time the loan was made, the amount is $8,000 [($200,000)(4%)]. As this is lower, the employment benefit would be $8,000.

Exercise 3-14

Subject: Housing Loan

On January 1, 2021, Mrs. Caldwell receives a $100,000 loan from her employer to assist her in purchasing a home. The loan requires annual interest at a rate of 1%, which she pays on December 31, 2021. Assume that the prescribed rate is 2% during the first quarter of 2021, 3% during the second quarter, and 1% during the remainder of the year. Calculate Mrs. Caldwell's employment benefit on this loan for the year 2021.

Solutions to Exercises are available in the Study Guide.

Tax Planning for Interest-Free Loans

General Approach

3-168. The income tax rules result in an employment benefit to the employee if the interest rate on the loan is lower than the prescribed rate in effect at the time. Given this, the question arises as to whether the use of employee loans is tax effective in providing employee benefits. As with other types of benefits, the question is whether it is better that the employer provides a loan or, alternatively, provides additional salary to allow the employee to pay the recurring interest on the loan through a commercial lender.

3-169. To determine whether a loan is an effective and preferable form of employee compensation, several factors have to be considered:

- The employer's rate of return on alternative uses for the funds
- The employer's tax rate
- The employee's tax rate
- The prescribed rate
- The rate available to the employee on a similar arm's-length loan

3-170. In analyzing the use of loans to employees, we begin with the assumption that we would like to provide a loan to one or more employees and we are looking for the most cost-effective way of providing the funds. As noted, the alternative to providing an employee with a loan is to provide that employee with sufficient after-tax income to carry an equivalent loan at commercial rates of interest.

3-171. It then becomes a question of comparing the cash flows associated with the employer providing the loan (this would have to include sufficient additional income to pay the income taxes on any employee loan benefit) with the cash flows required for the employer to provide the employee with sufficient income to carry an equivalent loan acquired from a commercial lender.

Example of Interest-Free Loan Benefit

3-172. The following example illustrates the calculations required to determine whether the use of a low- or no-interest loan is a tax effective form of employee compensation.

EXAMPLE A key executive asks for a $100,000 interest-free home purchase loan. At this time, the employer has an investment opportunity that is expected to provide a rate of return of 12% before taxes. Assume the prescribed rate for the period is 2%, while the rate for home mortgages is 5%. The employee is subject to a marginal tax rate, the tax rate applicable to additional income, of 45%, while the employer pays corporate taxes at a marginal rate of 28%.

Alternative 1—Provide Additional Salary In the absence of the interest-free loan, the employee would borrow $100,000 at 5%, requiring an annual interest payment of $5,000. In determining the amount of salary required to carry this loan, consideration has to be given to the fact that additional salary will be taxed at 45%. In terms of the algebra that is involved, we need to solve the following equation for X:

$$\$5,000 = [(X)(1 - 0.45)]$$

You will recall that this type of equation is solved by dividing both sides by (1 - 0.45), resulting in a required salary of $9,091:

$$X = [\$5,000 \div (1 - 0.45)] = \$9,091$$

Using this figure, the employer's after-tax cash flow required to provide sufficient additional salary for the employee to carry a conventional $100,000 mortgage would be calculated as follows:

Required salary [$5,000 ÷ (1 - 0.45)]	$9,091
Tax savings from deducting salary [($9,091)(28%)]	(2,545)
Employer's after-tax cash flow—Additional salary	$6,546

Alternative 2—Provide the Loan If the loan is provided, the employee will have a taxable benefit of $2,000 [(2% - Nil)($100,000)], resulting in additional taxes payable of $900 [(45%)($2,000)]. To make this situation comparable to the straight salary alternative, the employer will have to provide the executive with both the loan amount and sufficient

additional salary to pay the $900 in taxes on the benefit that will be assessed. The required amount would be $1,636 [$900 ÷ (1 - 0.45)].

The employer's cash flow associated with the after-tax cost of providing the additional salary as well as the after-tax lost earnings on the $100,000 loan amount would be calculated as follows:

Required salary [$900 ÷ (1 - 0.45)]	$1,636
Tax savings from deducting salary [($1,636)(28%)]	(458)
After-tax cost of salary to cover taxes on benefit	$1,178
Employer's lost earnings [(12%)(1 - 0.27)($100,000)]	8,760
Employer's after-tax cash flow—Loan	$9,938

Conclusion Given these results, payment of additional salary appears to be the better alternative. However, the preceding simple example is not a complete analysis of the situation. Other factors, such as the employee's ability to borrow at going rates and the employer's ability to grant this salary increase in the context of overall salary policies, would also have to be considered.

Exercise 3-15

Subject: Loans to Employees—Tax Planning

A key executive asks for a $125,000 interest-free home purchase loan. At this time, the employer has investment opportunities involving a rate of return of 7% before taxes. Assume that for the period, the relevant prescribed rate is 2%, while the market rate for home mortgages is 5%. The employee's tax rate on additional income (i.e., her marginal tax rate) is 42%, while the employer's marginal tax rate is 26%. Should the employer provide the loan or, alternatively, provide sufficient additional salary to carry an equivalent loan from a commercial lender? Explain your conclusion

Solutions to Exercises are available in the Study Guide.

We suggest you complete SSP 3-6 at this point.

Inclusions—Stock Option Benefits

Proposed Changes to the Stock Option Rules

3-173. In the 2019 federal budget the government announced that draft legislation would be released to address perceived unfairness in the taxation of employee stock options, particularly the 50% stock option deduction that results in only one-half of stock option employee benefits being included in income. The government identified that their primary concern was that employee stock options were being used to compensate wealthy executives of large mature companies when in their view such tax-deferred compensation should be limited to Canadian controlled private corporations (CCPCs) and non-CCPCs in the startup or emerging phase of their existence.

Draft legislation was released in June 2019 giving interested persons a six-month consultation period to provide feedback to the Department of Finance by December 2019. The government subsequently indicated that revised legislation would accompany the 2020 federal budget, which was postponed with no future date in sight as a result of the COVID-19 pandemic. As a result the taxation of employee stock options remained uncertain. On November 30, 2020, the federal government presented their 2020 Fall Economic Statement that included legislation to restrict access to the stock option deduction with respect to new stock options issued beginning July 1, 2021. These legislative measures do not change the basic rules of how stock options affect employment income, but they do have an impact on taxable income. Stock options issued before July 1, 2021, continue to follow the old rules where the stock option deduction was not affected.

The Taxation and Economics of Stock Option Arrangements

3-174. There are two separate sets of income tax rules that apply to employee stock options. The first rules are included in ITA 7, which is part of the employment income rules of Subdivision a of Division B of Part I. Division B contains all of the rules necessary to determine net income. The second set of rules are included in ITA 110, which is part of Division C, which takes one from net income to taxable income. The two sets of rules work together. We will refer to the ITA 7 result as the stock option benefit and the ITA 110 result as the stock option deduction. In this chapter we will provide information necessary to explain how the rules interact.

3-175. Employee stock options allow, but do not require, the employee holder to purchase a specified number of shares for a specified period of time at a specified acquisition price. Because of income tax considerations, at the time of granting, the option price is usually set at or above the market price of the shares. For example, options might be issued to acquire shares at a price of $10 when the shares are trading at that same $10 value. Setting an option price below the $10 trading price at the time the options are granted jeopardizes the ability to claim the stock option deduction, which is generally 50% of the stock option benefit.

3-176. At first glance, such an option would appear to have no value as it simply allows the holder to acquire a share for $10 at a time when that share is only worth that amount. In reality, however, this option could have significant value, in that it allows the holder to participate in any upward price movement in the shares without any obligation to exercise the option if the price stays at or falls below $10. Stated alternatively, the option provides full participation in gains on the option shares with no downside risk. Further, for an employee receiving such options, they provide this participation with no real investment cost until such time as the options are exercised.

EXAMPLE Because of his excellent work, Andrew Chang is given options to buy 1,000 shares of his employer's stock at a price of $10 per share. At this time, the shares are trading at $10 per share. One year later, Andrew exercises the options and acquires 1,000 shares at the option price of $10. He immediately sells the shares for $12 per share.

ANALYSIS Andrew has enjoyed a gain of $2,000 [(1,000)($12 - $10)] with no initial investment. This clearly illustrates why the options have a value, even when they are not issued "in-the-money." The expression "in-the-money" refers to situations where the option price ($10 in this example) is below current market value. In this example, the options are in-the-money when the market value is greater than $10.

3-177. Stock options are granted to employees in the belief that, by giving an employee an interest in the stock of the company, there is an incentive to make a greater effort on behalf of the company. In some companies, use of this form of compensation is restricted to senior executives. In contrast, other corporations make options available to larger groups of employees.

3-178. The issuance or granting of stock option rights to employees has no income tax consequences either for the corporate employer issuer or the recipient employee. The corporate employer issuer cannot deduct any amount as an expense to reflect the economic value of the issued options, and the recipient employee is not required to include any amount in employment income as a result of the granting of stock option rights.

Stock Option Benefits Rules (ITA 7)—Employees Only

3-179. We have seen in our discussion of employee benefits that ITA 6(1)(a) captures most types of benefits with the exception of those that are legislatively excluded (private health services plans, for example) and those where separate rules are established to determine the value to be included (e.g., loans and automobile benefits). When ITA 6(1)(a) applies it adds the FMV of the benefit to the employee's income. When an employer provides an employee with the ability to immediately acquire $5,000 of shares of the employer for $5,000, the employee owns a right to purchase those shares. That right has some value, and ITA 6(1)(a) would normally apply to add the FMV of that right to the employee's income. ITA 7(5), however, is a rule that overrides ITA 6(1)(a), stating that any economic advantage/benefit received by an employee can only be determined under ITA 7, which does not add any benefit when an employee is granted stock option rights.

3-180. If, however, an employee is also a shareholder of the employer and the stock option benefit is granted because of the fact that the individual is a shareholder (e.g., if options are only granted to shareholders), then the stock option rules in ITA 7 that follow would not apply. The result is that the employee/shareholder would be required to include a shareholder benefit in their income, which is treated as income from property and not employment income. The overall effect is that the stock option rules we will discuss are for individuals who receive stock option benefits because of their employment relationship with the employer.

Overview of the Income Tax Rules

3-181. This is a difficult subject to present in that it involves several different areas of tax legislation other than simply the employment benefit rules. Stock options influence the determination of taxable income and the calculation of taxable capital gains. While it would be possible to present this material on a piecemeal basis, we have found this to be confusing to our readers. An alternative would be to defer any discussion of this issue until Chapter 8 when all of the relevant material has been covered.

3-182. However, this fails to reflect the fact that stock option issues relate most directly to employment income. As a consequence, most of our material on stock options will be presented in this chapter. As this involves some material that will not be covered until later chapters, an overview of the stock option material that will be presented in this chapter is presented here:

Value at Issue As noted previously, the income tax rules give no recognition to the fact that stock options have a positive value at the time of issue (e.g., granting). The issuing employer can make no deduction and the recipient employee has no income inclusion.

Employment Income Inclusion—Measurement The amount to be added to employment income is determined on the date that the options are exercised (shares purchased under the terms of the stock option plan). The per-share benefit amount will be equal to the excess of the FMV on the exercise date over the option price, with the difference multiplied by the number of shares acquired. This amount will be nil or positive, as the employee would not normally exercise the options unless the FMV of the shares is equal to or exceeds the option price.

Employment Income Inclusion—Recognition While the benefit amount will be measured at the time the options are exercised, there are rules that do not require this amount to be actually included in employment income until the shares are sold. The determination of whether the benefit amount is to be included when the stock options are exercised or at a later date when the shares are sold will depend on the type of corporation that is issuing the stock options. Note that if the benefit amount is only required to be included in employment income when the shares are sold, the amount will be added to employment income in that later year even if the individual is no longer an employee of the corporation that issued the stock options.

Taxable Income Deduction Gains on the sale (e.g., disposition) of shares are generally considered to be capital gains, only one-half of which is included in net income. One-half of a capital gain is referred to as a "taxable capital gain." However, 100% of the stock option benefit amount is required to be included in employment income. As a rule, income tax policy is generally interested in taxing only one-half of the stock option benefit amount. To accomplish this the ITA requires that 100% of the benefit amount first be included in employment income, then a deduction is allowed that is equal to one-half of the benefit amount. The result is that only half of the benefit is actually subject to income tax. The one-half deduction is not an employment expense but rather a deduction taken after net income is calculated, which impacts taxable income. While general coverage of taxable income is found in Chapters 4 and 11, this deduction will be covered here as part of our discussion of stock options.

EXAMPLE An employee was granted rights to a stock option plan in November 2021. The right allows the employee to purchase 100 shares for $50 each, which is equal to the FMV of the shares at that time. In December 2021 the share value increases to $60. The employee exercises the option and purchases 100 shares for $50 each in early December 2021. The benefit amount is required to be included in employment income when exercised in 2021. Assume that the employee has no other income except $200 in interest.

ANALYSIS The granting of the stock option rights in November 2021 has no income tax consequences. The exercise of the option rights in December 2021 results in an employment benefit of $1,000 [($60 – $50)(100 shares)]. The employee's employment income, net income, and taxable income would be as follows:

Employment income	$1,000
Interest income	200
Net income	$1,200
Less: Stock option deduction (half of $1,000)	500
Taxable income	$ 700

Only half of the stock option benefit of $1,000, or $500, became part of taxable income.

Capital Gains Capital gains, which are discussed in Chapter 8, are generally determined as the difference between the sale price and cost of certain property such as investments. Therefore, if you purchase shares for $400 and sell them for $700 you would have a capital gain of $300. In the example above we looked at an employee who purchased shares for $50 each and then exercised the right to acquire them at a time when the share FMV was $60. The $10 per-share difference was included in employment income as a stock option benefit. If the employee were to subsequently sell the same shares for, say, $72 each there should be another $12 to tax as representing the additional increase in value. Technically, however, the capital gain would appear to be the difference between the sale price of $72 and the cost of $50 for a $22 capital gain. Clearly this doesn't make sense, since doing it that way results in taxing the increase in value from $50 to $60 twice—once as employment income and a second time as a capital gain. The ITA resolves this problem by increasing the original cost of $50 by the employee benefit amount of $10. As a result, the cost (referred to as the ACB or "adjusted cost base") is $60, so when the shares are sold the capital gain is only $12.

3-183. A simple example will serve to illustrate the calculations:

EXAMPLE An executive receives options to acquire 1,000 of the employer's common shares at an option price of $25 per share. At this time, the common shares are trading at $25 per share. The executive exercises the options when the shares are trading at $40 per share. In the following year, the shares are sold for $50 per share.

ANALYSIS The difference between $25 and $40 is employment income, while the difference between $40 and $50 would be a capital gain. This result is illustrated in the following calculations:

Employment income [(1,000)($40 - $25)]	
Included in net income	$15,000
Taxable income deduction (one-half)	(7,500)
Taxable income in year of exercise	$ 7,500

When the shares are sold, the additional tax consequences to the employee would be as follows:

Proceeds of disposition [(1,000)($50)]	$50,000
Adjusted cost base [(1,000)($40)]	(40,000)
Capital gain	$10,000
Inclusion rate	1/2
Taxable capital gain in year of sale included in net income	$ 5,000

3-184. Several points should be made with respect to this example:

- The employment income inclusion will always be measured at the time the options are exercised. However, it may not be required to be included in employment income until the year that the acquired shares are sold. This will be discussed in more detail in the material that follows.
- The one-half deduction of $7,500 is after net income has been determined in the calculation of taxable income. The employment income that will be included in the executive's current or future net income is $15,000.
- The availability of the $7,500 deduction requires that certain conditions be met. These conditions will be discussed in detail in the material that follows.
- As we have noted, when the $15 per-share employment income benefit is included in employment income, this amount will be added to the adjusted cost base of the shares, $40 per share ($25 + $15). This ensures that the $15 amount will not be taxed a second time as a capital gain. This cost adjustment is as a result of ITA 53(1)(j).

CCPCs vs. Public Corporations

3-185. As is discussed more fully in Chapter 12, "Taxable Income and Tax Payable for Corporations," a Canadian controlled private corporation (CCPC) is generally a corporation that is not controlled by non-residents, public corporations, or a combination of the two and does not have its shares traded on a prescribed stock exchange (e.g., a stock exchange in North America). Corporations incorporated in Canada by Canadian residents are almost always CCPCs. Our immediate concern here is with the difference between the tax treatment of stock options issued by public companies versus those issued by CCPCs.

3-186. In simplified terms, where an employee of a public company exercises stock options the benefit amount will be included in employment income in the year the option is exercised. In contrast, the benefit amount on the exercise of stock options issued to employees of CCPCs is not included in employment income until the year in which the stock option shares are sold.

3-187. This places employees of public companies who exercise stock options at a disadvantage, since they are required to pay income taxes on the benefit amount without having received any cash. This sometimes results in a need to dispose of some portion of the acquired shares to raise the needed cash to pay the tax obligation. The main reason for this different treatment is that, unlike public company shares, CCPC shares are usually difficult to convert to cash as there is no established market for the shares as there is with publicly listed corporations.

Rules for Public Companies

3-188. When options to acquire the shares of a publicly traded company are exercised, ITA 7(1)(a) describes the benefit amount as being equal to the excess of the FMV of the shares at the time of exercise minus the price paid to acquire the shares under the terms of the stock option plan. A deduction from taxable income, equal to one-half of the benefit amount, can be taken under ITA 110(1)(d) in the same year.

3-189. Note, however, that there are conditions attached to the ITA 110(1)(d) deduction. It is only available if, at the time the options were issued/granted, the option price was equal to or greater than the FMV of the shares at that same time. If the option price is less than the FMV of the shares at the time of issue/grant, no deduction can be claimed, with the result that the full amount of the benefit amount is then subject to tax.

EXAMPLE On December 31, 2019, John Due receives options to buy 10,000 shares of his employer's common stock at a price of $25 per share. The employer is a publicly traded company and the options are immediately exercisable. At this time, the shares are trading at $25 per share. On July 31, 2021, the shares are trading at $43 per share and Mr. Due exercises all of these options at that time. On September 30, 2022, Mr. Due sells all of his shares for $45 per share.

ANALYSIS The $18 difference between $43 and $25 represents the employee benefit amount, and the $2 difference between the sale price of $45 and $43 is a capital gain:

- **Issue Date** (December 31, 2019)
  Despite the fact that the options clearly have a positive value at this point in time, there are no tax consequences resulting from the granting of the stock option rights.

- **Exercise Date = Measurement and Recognition Date** (July 31, 2021)
  As the option price was equal to the FMV of the shares on the day that the options were granted, Mr. Due can claim the ITA 110(1)(d) deduction in calculating taxable income. The tax consequences resulting from the exercise of the options would be as follows:

Fair market value of shares acquired [(10,000)($43)]	$430,000
Cost of shares [(10,000)($25)]	(250,000)
ITA 7(1)(a) employment income inclusion **= Increase in net income**	**$180,000**
ITA 110(1)(d) deduction [(1/2)($180,000)]	(90,000)
Increase in taxable income for 2021	**$ 90,000**

- **Disposition Date** (September 30, 2022)
  The tax consequences resulting from the sale of the shares would be as follows:

Proceeds of disposition [(10,000)($45)]	$450,000
Adjusted cost base [(10,000)($43)]	(430,000)
Capital gain	$ 20,000
Inclusion rate	1/2
Taxable capital gain for 2022	$ 10,000

Note that, in the 2022 calculation, the adjusted cost base of the shares has been bumped up to the value of the shares at the time of exercise, reflecting the fact that the difference between the $43 per share value on that date and the $25 option price has already been included in net income. The ACB of each share would be the total of the initial cost of $25 plus the $18 employment benefit amount included in income.

Also note that, if the employee had sold the shares in 2022 for less than $43 the result would have been a capital loss. If this were the case, the taxpayer would not have been able to deduct the loss in 2022, unless he had taxable capital gains. This creates a situation that could be viewed as unfair in that the taxpayer has had to include gains up to the $43 value in 2021, but might not be able to deduct the loss resulting from a subsequent decline in value. Note that the taxpayer cannot carry back the capital loss against the 2021 gain because that amount was employment income and not a capital gain. Restrictions on the ability to deduct capital losses were discussed in Chapter 1 in the coverage of ITA 3 and will be expanded upon in Chapter 8.

Exercise 3-16

Subject: Stock Options—Public Company

During October 2019, Mr. Gordon Guise was granted options to buy 2,500 of his employer's shares at a price of $23.00 per share. At this time, the shares are trading at $20.00 per share. His employer is a large publicly traded company. During July 2021, he exercises all of the options when the shares are trading at $31.50 per share. In September 2021, the shares are sold for $28.00 per share. What is the effect of the exercise of the options and the sale of the shares on Mr. Guise's 2021 net income and on his taxable income? Identify these two amounts separately.

Solutions to Exercises are available in the Study Guide.

Rules for Canadian Controlled Private Corporations (CCPCs)

3-190. The basic public company rules that we have just described require the recognition of a benefit amount to be included in employment income in the year in which the options are exercised irrespective of when the options are sold. This may not be an insurmountable problem for employees of publicly traded companies, in that they can sell some of the shares or use them as loan collateral if they need to raise the cash to pay the income taxes on the benefit amount.

3-191. However, for employees of CCPCs, a requirement to include the benefit amount on the same basis exposing the additional employment income to income taxes at the time an option is exercised could create severe cash flow problems. As a consequence, a different treatment is permitted where stock options are granted by CCPCs. The benefit amount is still measured at the time the options are exercised, but no amount is required to be included in employment income until the shares are sold.

3-192. For CCPCs, the benefit amount is determined under ITA 7(1)(a) but modified by ITA 7(1.1), which changes the timing of the benefit amount to be added to employment income from the year the options are exercised to the year the shares are sold. The one-half ITA 110(1)(d) deduction from taxable income is also available to CCPCs provided the option price was equal to or more than the FMV of the shares at the time the option was granted. However, if this condition is not met, an additional provision under ITA 110(1)(d.1) allows the employee to deduct one-half of the benefit amount, provided the shares are held for at least two years after their acquisition. In other words, an employee of a CCPC has two opportunities to claim the 50% deduction but cannot claim them both. It is either one or none.

3-193. Using the same information from the example in Paragraph 3-189, altered to change the employer from a public corporations to a CCPC, the tax consequences would be as follows:

ANALYSIS FOR CCPC EXAMPLE

- **Issue Date** (December 31, 2019)
  Despite the fact that the options clearly have a positive value at this point in time, there are no tax consequences resulting from the granting of the stock option rights.
- **Exercise Date = Measurement Date Only** (July 31, 2021)
  While the benefit amount would be measured on this date, it would not be included in employment income at this point. Based on the increase in share value from $25 to $43 per share, the benefit would be measured as $180,000 [($43 - $25)(10,000 shares)]. The benefit amount, along with the related $90,000 taxable income deduction, would be deferred until the year in which the shares are sold.
- **Disposition Date = Recognition Date** (September 30, 2022)
- The tax consequences resulting from the sale of the shares would be as follows:

Deferred employment income [($43 - $25)(10,000)]		$180,000
Proceeds of disposition [(10,000)($45)]	$450,000	
Adjusted cost base [(10,000)($43)]	(430,000)	
Capital gain	$ 20,000	
Inclusion rate	1/2	10,000
Increase in net income		**$190,000**
ITA 110(1)(d) deduction [(1/2)($180,000)]		(90,000)
Increase in 2022 taxable income		**$100,000**

3-194. Note that this is the total increase in taxable income that would have resulted from simply purchasing the shares at $25 and later selling them for $45 [(10,000)(1/2)($45 - $25) = $100,000]. The structuring of this increase is different, and in some circumstances the difference could be significant. For example, there are additional rules that may reduce the amount of certain capital gains that may be taxed, but they only apply to capital gains and not employment income (see Chapter 11). On the other hand the greater the amount of employment income (not capital gains) the greater the likelihood of being able to contribute larger amounts to RRSPs (see Chapter 10). Although the timing is different, the $100,000 total increase in taxable income is the same as in the public company example in Paragraph 3-189.

Exercise 3-17

Subject: Stock Options—CCPC

In December 2019, Ms. Milli Van was granted options to buy 1,800 of her employer's shares at a price of $42.50 per share. At this time, the shares have a FMV of $45.00 per share. Her employer is a CCPC. In June 2020, when the shares have a FMV of $75.00 per share, she exercises all of her options. In September 2021, Ms. Van sells her shares for $88,200 ($49.00 per share). What is the effect of the exercise of the options and the sale of the shares on Ms. Van's 2020 and 2021 net income and her taxable income? Identify these two amounts separately.

Solutions to Exercises are available in the Study Guide.

We suggest you complete SSP 3-7, 3-8, and 3-9 at this point.

Employee Stock Option Deduction Restriction

3-195. A few years ago the federal government announced its intention to address fairness and efficiency in the income tax system and that it would be evaluating the fairness of the stock option deduction. Preliminary analysis indicated that almost 70% of the value of all stock option deductions claimed in 2018 were made by 2,400 individuals with total income of more than $1,000,000.

3-196. The government clarified that the purpose of the stock option deduction was to provide tax preferential income in order to attract the necessary talent and expertise needed by new startups and emerging companies with considerable growth potential. These type of companies lacked the necessary resources to afford competitive salaries. The initial analysis, however, revealed that the favourable income tax treatment afforded to stock options had resulted in their common use in executive compensation packages by large, mature public companies. In response, the stock option deduction, which represents the core of the preferential tax treatment, has been amended to restrict its availability effective for stock option plans granted beginning July 1, 2021.

3-197. Consistent with the intent to continue to provide support for new and emerging companies, the new restrictions will not apply to CCPCs and non-CCPCs with gross revenues of $500 million or less. Employees of non-CCPCs with gross revenues in excess of $500 million will continue to be able to claim the stock option deduction but only to the extent of an annual limit of $200,000 (per each employer an individual employee works for during a year), including persons non-arm's length with the employer.

3-198. The new rules operate on the basis of a "vesting year" and the categorization of stock option shares as either qualifying or non-qualifying based on the $200,000 annual limit. A vesting year is the calendar year in which shares can first be acquired under the terms of the specific stock option plan. The categorization between qualifying and non-qualifying stock option shares is then based on the FMV of the stock option shares at the time the stock option plan was granted.

> **EXAMPLE 1** Luyen is employed by a large Canadian public company. She is granted access to a stock option plan in November 2021 where she can acquire 20,000 shares of the company for $30 each beginning in 2022. The FMV of the shares at the time the stock option plan is granted is $25 each.
>
> **ANALYSIS 1** The vesting year is 2022, the calendar year in which she can first acquire shares under the terms of the plan. The value of the shares for the purposes of the $200,000 annual limit is based on the total value of all of the stock option shares on the date the plan was granted. At that time the shares were valued at $500,000 [(20,000 shares)($25 FMV)]. The rules only allow $200,000 of that $500,000 value, or 40%, to qualify for the stock option deduction. The remaining 60%, or $300,000, of value represent non-qualifying shares. Using these two percentages, 40% of the 20,000 shares, or 8,000 shares, qualify for the deduction, whereas the remaining 12,000 shares do not. The new legislation includes an ordering rule that considers the first stock option shares acquired to be qualifying shares.
>
> **EXAMPLE 2** Continuing with the same example, assume that Luyen purchases all 20,000 of the stock option shares for $30 each in March 2022 when the shares are trading for $40. Luyen then sells all of the shares for $47 in December 2022.
>
> **ANALYSIS 2** Luyen will have a stock option benefit in 2022 of $200,000 [(FMV $40 - $30 cost)(20,000 shares)]. The stock option deduction would be limited to $40,000 [(40%)(1/2)($200,000)]. The effect is that 60%, or $120,000, of the stock option benefit relates to non-qualifying shares for which no stock option deduction can be claimed, and

the remaining $80,000 represents qualifying shares for which the 50% stock option deduction of $40,000 can be claimed.

The ACB of the stock option shares prior to the sale in December 2022 are $40 each, which represents the $30 cost plus the $10 stock option benefit per share. The sale of the stock option shares for $47 results in a capital gain of $140,000 [(50%)($47 - $40)(20,000 shares)], one-half or $70,000 of which is a taxable capital gain required to be included in net income.

3-199. From an employer perspective, the new rules allow the employer to claim a taxable income deduction under new ITA 110(1)(e) equal to that part of the stock option benefit included in the income of an employee that relates to non-qualifying shares. Since the employee cannot claim a stock option deduction for non-qualifying shares, 100% of that stock option is taxable. The rules effectively treat that stock option benefit amount to the employer as if it were regular remuneration. In Example 2, the employer would be able to claim a deduction of $120,000.

3-200. An employer can also file a designation under ITA 110(1.4) to designate one or more shares under a stock option plan to be non-qualifying shares. The effect is that no stock option deduction could be claimed by the employee for those designated shares, but the employer would be entitled to a taxable income deduction under ITA 110(1)(e) for those shares. In Example 2, if the employer had filed a designation for all of the stock option shares, then Luyen would have included $200,000 in her employment income as a stock option benefit without the benefit of any stock option deduction, but the employer would be entitled to a taxable income deduction of $200,000.

3-201. The employer will be required to notify both the employees and the CRA whenever there are non-qualifying shares as a result of a stock option plan that exceeds the $200,000 annual limit or where the employer has filed a designation to treat stock option shares as non-qualifying. An employer that fails to make the necessary notifications will not be eligible to claim a taxable income deduction under ITA 110(1)(e).

Other Inclusions

Payments by Employer to Employee

3-202. Amounts received by an individual as an employee in an employment relationship will almost always be included in computing employment income. Payments made prior to or subsequent to an employment relationship would generally not be included in income in the absence of that employment relationship. ITA 6(3) was written to deal with these situations by deeming these pre- and post-employment relationship payments to be employment income. This includes payments for accepting employment (e.g., a signing bonus), non-compete payments for not accepting employment with the employers' competitors on the termination of employment, as well as contractually arranged payments for work to be completed subsequent to the termination of employment. ITA 6(3) requires that all such amounts be included in employment income.

Forgiveness of Employee Loans

3-203. There may be circumstances in which an employer decides to forgive a loan that has been extended to an employee. ITA 6(15) requires that the forgiven amount be included in the income of the employee in the year in which the forgiveness occurs. The forgiven amount is simply the amount due less any payments that have been made by the employee. ITA 80.4(3)(b) prevents the calculation of any interest benefit in the year the loan is forgiven.

Salary Advances

3-204. In this chapter we discussed salary, wages, tips, and other remuneration as being required to be included in employment income through ITA 5 when received. There is no requirement that the receipt of such amounts is only recognized as employment income if it is actually earned. This means that amounts received as salary advances are required to be included in employment income on the same basis as regular salary or wages. This would also require the employer to deduct all payroll withholdings.

3-205. When an employee receives an amount from an employer as a request for a salary advance it is important to determine the nature of the arrangement with the employer. If the amount received has specific repayment terms and other conditions consistent with a loan, then such amounts would not be required to be included in employment income as a salary advance. In that case the rules concerning low-interest or interest-free loans, as discussed beginning at Paragraph 3-163, would apply.

3-206. If an employee who has received a salary advance that is not a loan is required to repay part of the advance because the employment relationship has been terminated, the employee will be entitled to an employment expense for the repayment in the year the repayment is made (ITA 8(1)(n)).

> **EXAMPLE** Xenia began employment with an employer in October 2021. She will be compensated solely on the basis of sales commissions. Her employer provides her with a $20,000 salary advance in the first week of November 2021. Xenia earned $7,000 in commissions in December 2021, all of which was applied against her salary advance. Xenia earns an additional $8,000 in commissions in January 2022, which is also applied against her 2021 salary advance. She quits in February 2022 and repays the outstanding $5,000 to the employer in March 2022.
>
> **ANALYSIS** Xenia will include the $20,000 salary advance received in her employment income for the 2021 year. She will be entitled to a $5,000 employment expense for 2022. Technically she would have an employment loss of $5,000 from that specific employment.

Housing Loss Reimbursement

3-207. When an employee is required to move, employers often provide various types of financial assistance. As is discussed in detail in Chapter 9, an employer can pay for the usual costs of moving without income tax consequences to the employee given that the employer is the primary beneficiary of the move. In recent years, particularly when an employee is relocated from an area with a weak housing market to one with a strong housing market, it has become common for employers to reimburse employees for losses suffered on the sale of their homes (i.e., their principal residence).

3-208. Reimbursing an employee for housing losses would appear to be an economic advantage and therefore an employment benefit, which would be expected to be included in employment income, but many years ago the courts did not agree, claiming that there was no economic advantage to moving an employee from one home into another home. The government responded by adding legislation to require reimbursed housing losses to be specifically included in income as an employment benefit.

3-209. The main rule is found in ITA 6(19) and requires that the value of any employment benefit is equal to the reimbursed housing loss unless the loss qualifies as an "eligible housing loss."

3-210. ITA 6(22) defines an "eligible housing loss" as a loss that is related to an "eligible relocation." An eligible relocation is a move that would entitle the employee to claim moving expenses. While this issue is discussed in more detail in Chapter 9, we would note here that an employee is generally allowed to deduct moving expenses when they move at least 40 kilometres closer to a new work location (employment or business).

3-211. As a result of ITA 6(20) the first $15,000 of an eligible housing loss plus half of any amount greater than $15,000 is not required to be included in employment income and is therefore tax free. If, for example, an employee was relocated by the employer and the relocation entitles the employee to claim a deduction for moving expenses, and if the housing loss was $55,000, then only $20,000 [($55,000 – $15,000)(50%)] would be required to be included in employment income as a benefit.

Specific Deductions—ITA 8

Overview

3-212. Employment expenses are covered in ITA 8. Specifically, ITA 8(1) sets out the actual allowable expenses with additional modifying and complementary rules found in ITA 8(2) to (13). The most important of these additional rules is ITA 8(2), which sets out a general limitation that prevents the claiming of any employment-related expense unless it is specifically mentioned in ITA 8. If, for example, you were an employee and required a computer to use in your employment duties that you had to pay for personally, you could not claim a depreciation (CCA) component as an employment expense. You could, however, potentially claim the cost of leasing a computer. The reason for this difference is that there is an employment expense in ITA 8(1) that would recognize the lease cost as an expense but there is no ITA 8(1) expense with respect to purchasing your own computer, and as a result ITA 8(2) would deny the expense.

3-213. The ITA 8(1) list of employment expenses deductions is limited. In comparison, the ability to claim business expenses is much broader since there is no rule comparable to ITA 8(2) in that part of the ITA that deals with a business. Despite the limited list of employment expenses, the application of ITA 8 can be complex because the expenses are not available to all employees but only certain types of employees, often with numerous conditions added in order to qualify for a particular expense.

3-214. It is not uncommon in introductory income tax courses for many students to believe that payroll withholdings such as CPP, EI, and income taxes are employment expenses such that employment income essentially equals an employee's net paycheque. This could not be farther from the truth. Employment income begins with adding the gross salary and wages before any payroll withholdings, adding in taxable benefits and allowances, and only then deducting those employment expenses expressly allowed. The only payroll withholdings that qualify as employment expenses are union dues and employee contributions to a registered pension plan (RPP, not RRSP).

3-215. Our coverage begins with a brief description of the more significant deductions available and ends with a more detailed look at the most commonly claimed employment expenses. We will also look at the ability to claim part of the expenses of a home office, which is particularly important for the many employees who find themselves working from home.

> **ITA 8(1)(b) Legal Expenses** allows an employee to deduct legal expenses paid to collect or establish the right to salary or wages owed by an employer or former employer. Also deductible are legal costs incurred to recover benefits, such as health insurance, that are not paid by an employer or former employer, but that are required to be included in employment income when received. Any legal expenses reimbursed, or for which an award was received to compensate for the legal fees, reduce the amount that can be deducted. If the legal expenses are awarded or reimbursed in a year after the expenses were claimed, then the amounts reimbursed will be included in employment income under ITA 6(1)(j) in the year of receipt.
>
> **ITA 8(1)(f) Sales Expenses** covers the deductions available to individuals who earn commission income. It covers travel expenses, motor vehicle expenses, and other types of expenses associated with earning commissions (e.g., licences required by real estate salespersons). This expense is discussed in greater detail in this chapter.

ITA 8(1)(h) Travel Expenses covers expenses available to certain employees for travel expenses, other than motor vehicle expenses. An employee earning commissions can deduct travel costs under ITA 8(1)(f) or ITA 8(1)(h), but cannot use both provisions simultaneously.

ITA 8(1)(h.1) Motor Vehicle Travel Expenses covers expenses available to certain employees for motor vehicle expenses. An employee earning commissions can deduct motor vehicle costs under ITA 8(1)(f) or ITA 8(1)(h.1), but also cannot use both provisions simultaneously.

ITA 8(1)(i) Dues and Other Expenses of Performing Duties covers a variety of expenses, some of which are available to all employees and some of which are restricted to certain employees. Included here would be union dues, professional dues, office rent paid or costs of maintaining a work space in the home, salaries to an assistant, and the cost of supplies used in employment-related activities.

ITA 8(1)(j) Motor Vehicle and Aircraft Costs ITA 8(2) is very restrictive and only allows the deduction of certain employment expenses. Most capital expenditures such as the costs of purchasing capital property (e.g., computers, furniture) and interest paid on borrowings to acquire such property are not allowed as an employment expense. However, ITA 8(1)(j) provides an exception by allowing an employment expense for a depreciation component (CCA) together with interest expenses for motor vehicles and aircraft used for employment purposes.

ITA 8(1)(p) Musical Instruments This is a second exception to the general rule that employees cannot deduct capital expenditures. ITA 8(1)(p) allows an individual employed as a musician to deduct a depreciation component (CCA) for personally owned instruments or a fee paid to rent the instrument. Other deductible expenses include maintenance and insurance, but no deduction is allowed for any interest on borrowed money used to purchase the instrument.

ITA 8(1)(m) Employee's Registered Pension Plan (RPP) Contributions As was noted previously in our discussion of employee benefits, contributions by an employer to an RPP on behalf of an employee are legislatively excluded by ITA 6(1)(a) and are therefore not taxable employment benefits. On the other hand, employee contributions to an RPP are allowed as an employment expense. This deduction is given detailed attention in Chapter 10, which provides comprehensive coverage of the various retirement savings arrangements.

ITA 8(1)(r) Apprentice Mechanic's Tool Costs provides a second expense for tools required by an apprentice mechanic and purchased by the employee. The employment expense is a complex provision that allows for a deduction of the cost of eligible tools that are in excess of an annual threshold amount. The expense is restricted to employment income and cannot be used to create a loss. Unused expenses are carried forward to future years.

ITA 8(1)(s) Tradesperson's Tool Expenses provides for the deduction of up to $500 for tools that are required by a tradesperson. Only costs in excess of $1,257 can be deducted. As noted in Chapter 4, this amount is also the base for the Canada employment tax credit. This is one of two employment expenses allowed for tools.

ITA 8(4) Meals Both ITA 8(1)(f) and ITA 8(1)(h) refer to travel costs, which includes the cost of meals. ITA 8(4) provides a limitation as to when meals can be deducted as an employment expense. Meals must be consumed during a period of time in which the employee is required, by her employment duties, to be away from the municipality or metropolitan area where the employer's establishment is located for at least

12 consecutive hours. The restriction applies to the meal costs of the employee only. The employer's establishment is the workplace where the employee would normally report for work.

We would also note that ITA 67.1(1) further limits the deductibility of meal and entertainment costs to 50% of the amount paid. This limitation applies without regard to whether the individual is an employee or is carrying on a business and applies once the deductible amount has been determined. (ITA 67.1 is discussed further in Chapter 6.)

ITA 8(10) Certificate of Employer This provision adds an additional condition to the claiming of certain expenses, most notably those described in ITA 8(1)(f), (h), and (h.1), which will be discussed in greater detail on the following pages of this chapter. The condition requires that form T2200 "Declaration of Conditions of Employment" be signed and completed by the employer attesting to the fact that the conditions within those employment expense provisions have been met.

ITA 8(13) Work Space In Home provides rules to determine the conditions necessary for an employee to claim the expenses of an office space within one's home as an employment expense. This is also discussed in greater detail in this chapter.

The employee and partner GST rebate available on deductible expenses is covered separately in Chapter 21.

Employment Expense Essentials

3-216. The five principal employment expense provisions are as follows:

- ITA 8(1)(f) Salesperson expenses, the broadest category of expenses
- ITA 8(1)(h) Travel expenses except motor vehicle travel expenses
- ITA 8(1)(h.1) Motor vehicle travel expenses
- ITA 8(1)(i) Limited expenses, such as office supplies, office rent, and salary for an assistant
- ITA 8(1)(j) CCA and interest expenses of a personally owned motor vehicle

There are a few important observations to be aware of with respect to these five provisions:

1. ITA 8(1)(f) is a comprehensive rule that allows a broad range of employment expenses that would include the expenses referred to in ITA 8(1)(h), (h.1), and (i) but not (j). ITA 8(1)(f), unlike the other employment expense rules, contains an income limitation that restricts the expenses that can be claimed (e.g., deducted) to the commission type income received in the year.
2. ITA 8(1)(h), (h.1), (i), and (j) refer to separate and distinct types of employment expenses without any income limitation on how much can be claimed.
3. The expenses that can be deducted under ITA 8(1)(h) and (h.1) can only be claimed if no expenses are deducted under ITA 8(1)(f).
4. ITA 8(1)(f), (h), (h.1), and (i) require that the employee is responsible for paying the identified expenses as a result of a "contract of employment." The CRA prefers to see a written contract between the employer and the employee but will accept a verbal agreement where there is a clear understanding that the payment by the employee of expenses was implied.
5. ITA 8(1)(j) indirectly requires there to be a "contract of employment," since an employment expense under this provision is dependent on the ability to claim an expense under ITA 8(1)(f), (h), or (h.1).
6. With the exception of ITA 8(1)(j), an employer certification (T2200) is required for all of these employment expenses.

What this means is that salespersons who meet all the necessary conditions of ITA 8(1)(f) may choose to claim all expenses under ITA 8(1)(f) that cannot be claimed elsewhere (subject to the commission income limitation) or instead choose to limit the expense claim to travel expenses permitted under ITA 8(1)(h) and (h.1), which have no income limitation. We examine this in the paragraphs that follow.

Salesperson's Expenses—ITA 8(1)(f)

3-217. Employees who are involved with the selling of property or the negotiating of contracts are permitted to claim a deduction for expenses that are necessary to the performance of their duties as long as the following conditions are met:

1. The salesperson must be required to pay his own expenses under the terms of an employment contract. The employer must sign Form T2200 certifying that this is the case. While the form does not have to be submitted to the CRA, it must be retained and available if requested by the CRA.
2. The salesperson must be ordinarily required to carry on his duties away from the employer's place of business, which is typically the location where the employee ordinarily reports for work.
3. The salesperson must not be in receipt of a tax-free travel allowance (e.g., an allowance that was excluded from employment income).
4. The salesperson must receive at least part of their remuneration in the form of commissions or by reference to the volume of sales.

3-218. If all of the conditions have been met, ITA 8(1)(f) allows employment-related expenses to be deducted with the exception of (1) capital expenditures other than CCA for a personally owned motor vehicle, aircraft, and musical instruments and interest charges to finance their purchase; (2) expenses for the maintenance and use of club or recreational facilities; and (3) payments to an employer for the use of an employer-provided automobile.

3-219. Examples of expenses that can be deducted under ITA 8(1)(f) include:

- advertising and promotion
- accounting and legal fees
- cell phone, dedicated landline, and internet
- meals with clients (see note that follows)
- lodging/accommodation
- motor vehicle costs (other than CCA and interest, which are deducted elsewhere)
- parking (which is not considered a motor vehicle expense)
- office rent
- salaries to an assistant
- work space in the home costs (see the discussion in Paragraph 3-236)
- training costs
- transportation costs
- licences (e.g., for real estate sales)
- bonding and liability insurance premiums
- leasing expenses for computers and office equipment

Note on Meals The ITA 8(4) provision, which states that a taxpayer can only deduct meals when away from the municipality for at least 12 consecutive hours, does not apply to restrict the meal expense paid for clients. The restriction only applies to the employee's meal cost.

3-220. The amount of employment expenses that can be deducted under ITA 8(1)(f) is quite substantial, but it is limited to the commission income or other similar amounts received in the year.

This commission income limitation only applies to the types of expenses specifically allowed because of ITA 8(1)(f).

Travel Expenses and Motor Vehicle Costs

ITA 8(1)(h) and (h.1)

3-221. The conditions for deducting expenses under ITA 8(1)(h) and (h.1) are similar to those for deductions under ITA 8(1)(f), except that there is no commission income limitation. The conditions for these two provisions are as follows:

1. The person must be required to pay her own travel and motor vehicle costs under the terms of an employment contract. As was the case with commission salespersons, the employee must have Form T2200 completed and signed by the employer, certifying that this is the case.
2. The person must be ordinarily required to carry on her duties away from the employer's place of business.
3. The person must not be in receipt of a tax-free allowance for travel costs.
4. No deduction is claimed under ITA 8(1)(f).

3-222. ITA 8(1)(h) provides for the deduction of travel costs such as accommodation, airline or train tickets, taxi fares, and meals. As was the case with salespersons' expenses, once the employment expense is determined meal expenses are further reduced by 50%, and if the travel does not involve more than 12 consecutive hours away from the employer's place of business, no meal expense can be claimed by the employee.

3-223. ITA 8(1)(h.1) provides for the deduction of motor vehicle costs, other than CCA and financing costs. Such expenses include gasoline, oil, insurance, maintenance and repairs, licence and registration fees, and leasing costs. There are further restrictions on the amount that can be claimed as leasing costs when the vehicle is a passenger vehicle. This is discussed in Chapter 6.

The Salesperson's Dilemma

3-224. As we pointed out in Paragraph 3-219, all of the travel and motor vehicle costs that a salesperson could deduct under ITA 8(1)(h) and (h.1), as well as many of the expenses under ITA 8(1)(i), could also be deducted using ITA 8(1)(f). However, the use of ITA 8(1)(f) involves both good news and bad news:

- **Good News** The good news is that if the salesperson uses ITA 8(1)(f), they can deduct a broader range of expenses than those available in the other provisions (e.g., advertising and promotion).
- **Bad News** The bad news is that if a salesperson uses ITA 8(1)(f), the amount that can be deducted is limited by the amount of commission income received in the year

3-225. At first glance, the best course of action would to be to use ITA 8(1)(h) and (h.1) for the travel and motor vehicle expenses (this deduction would not be limited by commission income), and to then use ITA 8(1)(f) to deduct the maximum amount of other expenses that would not be deductible elsewhere. This alternative, however, is not available because the expenses available under ITA 8(1)(h) and (h.1) can only be deducted if no expense claim is made under ITA 8(1)(f).

3-226. As a result, in situations where the potential employment expenses that could be claimed under ITA 8(1)(f) exceed commission income received in the year, the salesperson must undertake an additional calculation to determine whether the total expenses that could be claimed under both ITA 8(1)(h) and (h.1) would be greater than the commission-limited amount of expenses under ITA 8(1)(f).

EXAMPLE Anastasia is an employee who, in 2021, received $12,000 in commissions and $60,000 in fixed salary. She qualifies for expense claims under ITA 8(1)(f). She paid the following deductible employment expenses in 2021;

Advertising & promotion	$ 7,400
Accounting fees	1,100
Travel for hotels and meals	8,700
Motor vehicle costs	5,300
Total expenses	$22,500

ANALYSIS All of the expenses could be deducted under ITA 8(1)(f), however the expense is restricted to the commissions received of $12,000. ITA 8(1)(h) would allow the expense of $8,700 and ITA 8(1)(h.1) would allow $5,300 for a total of $14,000. The best course of action is therefore to claim $14,000 of employment expenses through a combination of ITA 8(1)(h) and (h.1).

Exercise 3-18

Subject: Commission Salesperson Expenses

Mr. Morton McMaster is a commission salesperson. During 2021, his gross salary was $82,000 and he received $12,200 in commissions. During the year he had advertising costs of $8,000 and expenditures for entertainment of clients of $12,000. His travel costs for the year totalled $13,100. He is required to pay his own expenses and does not receive any allowance from his employer. What is Mr. McMaster's maximum expense deduction for 2021?

Solutions to Exercises are available in the Study Guide.

Other Employment Expenses—ITA 8(1)(i)

3-227. ITA 8(1)(i) contains a list of specific items that can be deducted in the determination of employment income. The available expenses apply to two different groups of employees. The first are employees who are required by the terms of an employment contract to pay for certain expenses, and the second group are all other employees.

3-228. Employees who are under a contract of employment can claim expenses for office rent, salary to an assistant, and supplies where the contract of employment requires the employee to pay for these amounts. If the contract did not mention the requirement to hire an assistant, then such an expense would not be allowed. These expenses must be certified by the employer with a T2200 form.

3-229. The word "supplies" is given a wide interpretation by the CRA following a surprising number of court cases dealing with this issue, many of which go back decades. Supplies are considered to include office supplies such as stationery, long distance telephone calls, and cell phone airtime, but not the basic monthly charge for a telephone or amounts paid to connect or license a cell phone and maintenance and operating costs associated with a work space in the home. It is important to be aware at this point that the justification for allowing expenses for a home office such as heating, electricity, light bulbs, cleaning materials, and minor repairs is that they are technically "supplies," which are specifically allowed under ITA 8(1)(i)(iii), which requires a contract of employment and employer certification (T2200). A wider range of home office expenses is allowed to commissioned employees through ITA 8(1)(f).

3-230. Other common listed employment expenses that can be claimed by any employee and that do not require a contract of employment include the following:

- Annual professional membership dues, if payment was necessary to maintain a professional status recognized by statute.
- Union dues that are paid pursuant to the provisions of a collective agreement.

3-231. As is the case with most employment expenses, any reimbursement of these expenses reduces the amount that can be claimed.

Automobile and Aircraft Expenses—ITA 8(1)(j)

3-232. An employee can deduct the operating costs of a motor vehicle that is used in one's employment through either ITA 8(1)(f) or (h.1). The allowable expense would be based on the proportion that the employment-related kilometres are of the total kilometres driven in a given year.

3-233. Income tax expenses are often divided on the basis of whether they are current or capital expenses. Motor vehicle operating expenses are generally recurring and are referred to as current expenses as opposed to capital expenses that typically are made to purchase property, including financing costs of acquiring such property. The ITA often permits the deduction of most current expenses but restricts the deduction of capital expenses. Capital expenses are not deductible unless a specific provision of the ITA permits some deduction. We saw in our discussion of ITA 8(1)(f) that capital expenditures cannot be made through that provision, restricting the claimable expenses to current expenses only.

3-234. ITA 8(1)(j) is a rule that applies to the cost of purchasing a motor vehicle and any interest charges for financing its purchase. An employee can deduct CCA and interest costs on a motor vehicle or aircraft used for employment purposes. The deductible amounts, however, are calculated in the same manner as they would be for a business, which is based on the proportionate use for employment purposes. CCA (discussed in detail in Chapter 5) is generally calculated on a 30% declining balance basis for automobiles and a 25% declining balance basis for aircraft.

3-235. When a motor vehicle is a passenger vehicle (see Paragraphs 3-80 to 3-85) there are three limitations to be aware of—one that relates to current expenses and two that relate to capital expenses. The restrictions are:

1. Leasing costs are limited to $800 per month (before GST/HST or PST).
2. Interest costs to purchase the vehicle are restricted to $300 per month.
3. The amount upon which CCA can be claimed is restricted to $30,000 for class 10.1 and $55,000 for zero-emission vehicles under class 54 (before GST/HST or PST).

These limitations are further restricted by the percentage of employment-related use. If the passenger vehicle is only used 20% of the time for employment purposes in a particular year, then the above limits would be restricted to 20% of each of those amounts (e.g., $160, $60, and $6,000, respectively).

Work Space in the Home—ITA 8(1)(i)(iii), 8(1)(f) & 8(13)

3-236. We have noted previously that any employee who is required by an employment contract to maintain a work space in the home can deduct a portion of the costs of maintaining or renting the home. Because of the obvious potential for abuse in this area (e.g., claiming personal home-related expenses to reduce one's income tax), ITA 8(13) establishes fairly restrictive conditions with respect to the availability of this deduction. Costs of a work space in the home for an employee are only deductible when the work space is either:

- the place where the individual principally (more than half the time) performs the duties of the office or employment, or

- used exclusively during the period in respect of which the amount relates for employment purposes and used on a regular and continuous basis for meeting customers or other persons in the ordinary course of performing the duties of the office or employment.

3-237. Once it is established that a work space in the home meets one of the two conditions it becomes a matter of determining which specific costs are deductible. We have seen that there are considerable restrictions on the ability of employees to deduct capital expenditures (CCA and interest). In terms of employees, the ITA only allows CCA claims on motor vehicles, aircraft, and musical instruments, and interest claims on motor vehicles and aircraft only. We also saw that ITA 8(2) does not allow any employment expense unless specifically listed in ITA 8. The result is that no employee can deduct CCA or mortgage interest on office space within one's home.

3-238. Employees who are not commissioned salespersons can only claim work space expenses that are considered either "supplies" as discussed in Paragraph 3-228 or a proportion of the rent based on the percentage of the floor space used for employment purposes if one's home is rented. Such expenses (other than rent) that relate to the home office space include maintenance costs such as heating, electricity, light bulbs, cleaning materials, and minor repairs.

3-239. Commissioned salespersons are entitled to the same home office expenses that non-commissioned salespersons can claim plus, because of ITA 8(1)(f), additional expenses that include an appropriate portion of property taxes and house insurance premiums. The insurance and property tax expenses would be subject to the commission income limitation.

3-240. **The ITA 8(13) Limitation** Once the home office expenses have been determined, there is a limitation within ITA 8(13) that prevents these expenses from either increasing or creating an employment loss. This limitation compares the deductible home office expenses with the employment income determined by adding all employment income such as wages, salary, tips, benefits, and allowances and subtracting all deductible employment expenses except the home office expenses. Any excess amount can be deducted in a subsequent year assuming that one can get past this same income limitation.

EXAMPLE Trent began employment in October 2021. He is required by an employment contract to perform most of his employment duties at an office in his rented home. He receives a base salary of $1,500 per month and generous commissions. Unfortunately, he was unable to earn any commissions in 2021 since he was slowly building up clientele. He expects large commissions in 2022. He received $4,500 in base salary in 2021 and has no employment expenses except for his home office, which are calculated as $6,100. His home office expenses to do not include home insurance, which is only deductible under ITA 8(1)(f).

ANALYSIS The home office expenses are not subject to the commission limitation in ITA 8(1)(f) but are subject to the limitation in ITA 8(13) that prevents Trent from increasing or creating an employment loss with home office expenses. As a result, Trent can only deduct $4,500 of his home office expenses. The remaining $1,600 [$6,100 – $4,500] can be claimed in 2022 and subsequent years. His 2021 employment income will be nil [$4,500 – $4,500].

Determining the Employment Use of a Home Office

3-241. The determination of deductible employment expenses and taxable automobile benefits are dependent on defining and then identifying personal use (see Paragraphs 3-91 to 3-94). In a similar fashion, one cannot determine the deductible home office expenses without being able to identify the proportion/percentage of space used for employment purposes. Many believe that it is a simple matter of measuring the square footage of devoted office space and then dividing by the total square footage of the home or apartment. A ten foot by ten foot office space in a 1,000 square foot home would represent 10% of the space in the home [(10)(10)/1,000]. This, however, is only the starting point.

3-242. The method acceptable to the CRA is to begin with the dedicated office divided by the finished livable space. This would not include an unfinished basement but would include parts of a basement that were finished. The next step is to determine the common areas of the home that are used throughout the work day. Common areas include hallways, corridors, bathrooms, kitchen, entrance ways, exits, and so on. You then determine how much time during the course of a working day that you are using these common areas against the total number of waking hours. To illustrate, assume that the dedicated work-related space accounts for 11% of the square footage of the living space of the home, and that the common areas account for another 8%. Further assume that the employment-related use of the common areas is half the number of waking hours for each of five days out of seven days. The percentage applied to the common areas would be [((0.5(5)/7)8%] = 2.9%. The business use would therefore be 13.9% [11% + 2.9%]. The lesson to be learned is to always include a component for the use of common areas and avoid short-changing yourself by only counting a devoted workspace.

We suggest you complete SSP 3-10 through 3-15 at this point.

Key Terms

A full glossary with definitions are provided at the end of the Study Guide.

Allowance	Operating Cost Benefit
Bonus Arrangement	Prescribed Rate
Canadian Controlled Private Corporation	Public Corporation
Employee	Salary
Employer/Employee Relationship	Self-Employed Individual
Employment Income	Standby Charge
Fringe Benefits	Stock Option
Imputed Interest	Taxable Allowance
In-the-Money	Taxable Benefit

References

For more detailed study of the material in this chapter, we would refer you to the following:

ITA 5	Income from Office or Employment
ITA 6	Amounts to Be Included as Income from Office or Employment
ITA 7	Agreement to Issue Securities to Employees
ITA 8	Deductions Allowed
ITA 80.4	Loans
ITA 80.5	Deemed Interest
ITR 4301	Interest Rates [Prescribed Rate of Interest]
S2-F1-C1	Health and Welfare Trusts for Employees
S2-F3-C1	Payments from Employer to Employee
S2-F3-C2	Benefits and Allowances Received from Employment (Under Review)
S4-F2-C2	Business Use of Home Expenses
IC 73-21R9	Claims for Meals and Lodging Expenses of Transport Employees

IT-63R5	Benefits, Including Standby Charge for an Automobile, from the Personal Use of a Motor Vehicle Supplied by an Employer—After 1992
IT-91R4	Employment at Special or Remote Work Locations
IT-99R5	Legal and Accounting Fees (Consolidated)
IT-103R	Dues Paid to a Union or to a Parity or Advisory Committee
IT-113R4	Benefits to Employees—Stock Options
IT-158R2	Employees' Professional Membership Dues
IT-202R2	Employees' or Workers' Compensation
IT-352R2	Employee's Expenses, Including Work Space in Home Expenses
IT-421R2	Benefits to Individuals, Corporations, and Shareholders from Loans or Debt
IT-428	Wage Loss Replacement Plans
IT-504R2	Visual Artists and Writers (Consolidated)
IT-518R	Food, Beverages, and Entertainment Expenses
IT-522R	Vehicle, Travel, and Sales Expenses of Employees
IT-525R	Performing Artists
RC4110	CRA Guide—Employee or Self-Employed?
T4044	Employment Expenses
T4130	Employers' Guide—Taxable Benefits and Allowances

Self-Study Problems

Self-Study Problems (SSPs) provide practice in problem solving. Within the chapters, we have indicated where it would be appropriate to stop and work on each SSP. The problems can be downloaded by chapter from MyLab Accounting. Solutions are available in the Study Guide. Select problems can also be completed directly in MyLab and auto-graded.

Assignment Problems

Solutions to Assignment Problems (APs) are available to instructors only.

AP 3-1 Bonus Arrangements

Marques Ltd. is a Canadian public company with a taxation year that ends on November 30. Its shares are widely held, and its senior management is made up of the four Marques brothers. As the year ending November 30, 2021, has been very successful for the company, it is declaring a bonus to each of the four senior executives. All of the bonuses are declared on November 29, 2021. The details of these arrangements are as follows:

Cheeco Marques Cheeco is the CEO of the company. Because of his conservative lifestyle, he does not have a current need for funds. Given this, his bonus will be paid on March 31, 2026, his expected retirement date.

Zeppo Marques Zeppo is the vice-president of finance of the company. He has plenty of current income and would like to defer the personal payment of tax until a later year. Given this, his bonus will be paid on January 1, 2022.

Groucho Marques Groucho is the vice-president of human resources of the company. Unfortunately, Groucho seems to have a constant need for cash. Based on this, his bonus will be paid on December 1, 2021.

Harpo Marques Harpo, who is in charge of information technology for the company, plans to leave the company in mid-2022. It has always been his dream to pursue a musical career and, to that end, he will need funds to carry him through the early stages of that endeavour. Given this, his bonus will be paid on September 1, 2022.

Required: For each of these brothers, indicate the taxation year in which the company can deduct the bonus, as well as the taxation year in which the recipient will include it in income.

AP 3-2 Employee vs. Self-Employed

The Alberta Motor Association (the payor) carried on a business of training and providing instruction to individuals who wanted to obtain vehicle operator's licences. Mr. Bourne (the appellant) had an arrangement with the payor to provide such instruction.

The payor had treated Mr. Bourne as an independent contractor from 2019 to 2021. Mr. Bourne was claiming that he was an employee of the Alberta Motor Association in 2021.

The facts in this case are as follows:

- The payor operated as a membership-based association (admitted)
- The payor had clients who wanted to obtain motor vehicle operator's licences (admitted)
- The appellant was hired as a driving instructor (admitted)
- The appellant entered into a written contract with the payor stating that the appellant was a contractor and not an employee
- The appellant had been under contract with the payor since 2019
- The appellant earned a set fee of $26 per hour
- The appellant also received fees for new bookings, student home pickups, and a fuel subsidy
- The appellant invoiced the payor
- The appellant did not receive any employee benefits such as health, dental, or vacation pay
- The payor did not guarantee the appellant a minimum amount of pay
- The payor's hours of operation were from 8:00 a.m. to 5:00 p.m. Monday to Saturday
- The appellant set his own schedule of hours and days of work
- The appellant could work anytime between 8:00 a.m. and 10:00 p.m. Monday to Sunday
- The appellant did not have a set minimum number of hours of work required
- The appellant kept a record of his hours worked
- The payor provided the appellant with the names of the students
- The appellant contacted the students and scheduled the road instruction
- The payor provided the appellant with an in-vehicle lesson guide
- The appellant chose the routes for the lessons
- The appellant was able to hire his own helper for administrative tasks
- The appellant provided the major tool, which was the vehicle
- The payor provided vehicle signage, mirrors, traffic cones, and an emergency brake
- The appellant paid for the installation and removal of the emergency brake provided by the payor
- The appellant incurred operating expenses, including vehicle expenses, liability insurance, and a driver training endorsement
- The appellant's vehicle expenses included insurance, maintenance, and fuel
- The payor's intention was that the appellant was a contractor and not an employee
- The appellant had a GST number
- The appellant charged the payor GST
- The appellant had operated his own taxi business since 2003
- The appellant maintained his own business books and records
- The appellant declared business income and business expenses on his 2019, 2020, and 2021 income tax returns

Required: Should Mr. Bourne be viewed as an employee of the Alberta Motor Association or, alternatively, an independent contractor? List all of the factors that should be considered in reaching a conclusion.

AP 3-3 Employer-Provided vs. Employee-Owned Car

Jordan Jones was hired by Barton Sales at the end of 2020 to fill an executive position in the company. He is scheduled to begin work on January 2, 2021. Barton Sales plans to transfer him to their Hong Kong office after two years.

As part of his compensation package, Jordan has considered having the company provide him with a car for his personal use. He does not require the vehicle for his employment duties and, as a consequence, it will be used for personal activities only.

Jordan anticipates that he will drive the car about 65,000 kilometres in both 2021 and 2022. He is considering two different cars and has collected the following information on them:

	Lexus ES	Audi S8
Purchase price	$60,000	$150,000
Estimated operating costs per kilometre	$0.32	$0.45
Estimated trade in at the end of two years	$30,000	$70,000

The company has agreed to provide an additional $150,000 in compensation, and they offer Jordan the following alternatives.

Option 1 They will purchase either car and allow Jordan to use it for the calendar years 2021 and 2022. If Jordan prefers the Lexus ES, the company will provide a signing bonus of $90,000, the difference in the cost of the two cars. The bonus will be paid when the car is delivered on January 2, 2021.

Option 2 They will provide Jordan with a $150,000 signing bonus. This bonus will be paid on January 2, 2021. He will use the funds to purchase one of the cars personally.

If the company buys either car, Jordan will pay his own operating costs and the company will take possession of the car after the two years.

Jordan's combined federal/provincial marginal tax rate is expected to be 51% in both 2021 and 2022.

Assume that the prescribed operating cost benefit will be $0.27 per kilometre for both 2021 and 2022.

Required: Advise Jordan as to which option he should choose if he decides that he wants:

A. the Lexus ES
B. the Audi S8

In both parts of this question your advice should be based on non-discounted cash outflows. Ignore GST and HST considerations in your solution.

AP 3-4 Taxable Automobile Benefits

The Jareau Manufacturing Company owns a car with an original cost of $30,000. The car has been owned by the company for two years. Jareau's company policy requires that cars be returned to the corporate premises when they are not being used by the employee.

During 2021, the car was used by the company's sales manager, Mr. Robert Stickler. During this year, Mr. Stickler drove the car 36,000 kilometres. Operating costs, all of which were paid by the company, totalled $3,920. In addition, the company deducted capital cost allowance of $5,610 related to this car for the current year.

Required: Ignore all GST/HST/PST implications. Indicate the minimum taxable benefit that would be allocated to Mr. Stickler in each of the following cases:

Case A Mr. Stickler has use of the car for the entire year. He drives it a total of 7,200 kilometres for personal purposes and 28,800 kilometres for employment purposes.

Case B Mr. Stickler has use of the car for 10 months of the year. He drives it a total of 15,000 kilometres for personal purposes and 21,000 kilometres for employment purposes.

Case C Mr. Stickler has use of the car for six months of the year. He drives it a total of 25,200 kilometres for personal purposes and 10,800 kilometres for employment purposes.

AP 3-5 Taxable Automobile Benefits

It is the policy of Caplan Ltd. to provide automobiles to four of its senior executives. The cars may be used for both employment purposes as well as personal travel. When it is not being used by the employee, company policy requires the cars to be returned to the company's premises.

For 2021, the details regarding the use of these cars is as follows:

> **Ms. Barbara Caplan** Barbara is provided with a BMW 300 Series, which the company leases for $650 per month. This amount includes $110 per month for insurance. She drives a total of 57,000 kilometres of which 21,000 are for employment purposes and 36,000 for personal use. Operating costs, all of which were paid by the company, totalled $11,300. Because of her extensive personal use of the vehicle, Barbara pays the company $200 per month. The vehicle is available to her for 12 months during the current year.
>
> **Mr. Sheldon Caplan** Sheldon is provided with a Lexus GS, which the company leases for $1,100 per month. No insurance is included in this payment. During the current year, Sheldon drives the car a total of 34,300 kilometres, of which 32,600 are for employment purposes and 1,700 for personal use. The operating costs average $0.27 per kilometre and are paid by the company. The car is available to Sheldon for eight months during the current year.
>
> **Ms. Melissa Caplan** Melissa is provided with a Mercedes S Class Sedan. The company paid $175,000 for this car two years ago. During the current year, the car was driven 62,000 kilometres, of which 23,000 are for employment purposes and 39,000 for personal use. Operating costs, all of which were paid by the company, totalled $27,500. The car is available to Melissa for 11 months during the current year.
>
> **Mr. Jerome Caplan** Jerome's car is an Audi A5 purchased by the company for $74,200. During the 10 months that the car was available to Jerome during the current year, he drove a total of 93,000 kilometres, of which 24,000 are for employment purposes and 69,000 for personal use. Operating costs, all of which were paid by the company, totalled $19,400.

Required: Calculate the minimum taxable benefit that will accrue to each of these executives as the result of having the cars supplied by the company. Ignore all GST/HST/PST implications.

AP 3-6 Loans to Employees

Trisha Frude has been employed for over 20 years with a large public company. It is the policy of this company to extend interest-free loans of up to $250,000 to facilitate employees with more than 10 years of service in purchasing a new home.

After living in a rental property all her working life, Trisha would like to purchase a residence. She has located an attractive property within biking distance of her office. In order to comfortably purchase this property, she needs a loan of $225,000.

Trisha has been approved for a five-year closed mortgage at a rate of 4.8% from her bank. She also applied for a loan of this amount on an interest-free basis from her employer. After receiving her application, her employer has agreed to extend a five-year, $225,000 loan on an interest-free basis in lieu of a (well-deserved) raise.

The company's accountant will calculate the after-tax cost of providing the loan. Her employer will offer Trisha the alternative of additional salary that has the same after-tax cost to the company of the loan.

The company is subject to tax at a combined federal and provincial rate of 27%. When funds are available, the company has alternative investment opportunities that earn a pre-tax rate of 11%. Because of Trisha's current high salary, any additional compensation will be taxed at a combined federal and provincial rate of 49%.

Assume that the prescribed rate for the current year is 2%.

Required:

A. Determine the tax consequences to Trisha and the cost to the company in terms of lost after-tax earnings of providing her with a $225,000 interest-free loan for the first year of the loan.

B. Determine the amount of additional salary that could be provided to Trisha for the same after-tax cost to the company that you calculated in Part A.

C. Which alternative would you recommend that Trisha accept? Explain your conclusion.

AP 3-7 Loans to Employees

Because of her outstanding performance, Tricia Fox is negotiating a significant increase in her annual compensation. After considering various alternatives, she has decided her preferable increase would be in the form of a $300,000 interest-free loan. She will use the proceeds of the loan to purchase income-producing investments. This means any interest on the loan, either amounts paid or amounts imputed as a taxable benefit, will be fully deductible.

Other information that is relevant to this decision is as follows:

- Her investments are expected to provide a pre-tax return of 11%.
- She can acquire a similar-term $300,000 loan at an annual rate of 4.6%.
- Her employer, a Canadian public company, is subject to tax at a combined federal and provincial rate of 28%. The company has alternative investment opportunities that earn a pre-tax rate of 5%.
- Her various sources of income are such that any additional income will be taxed at a rate of 49%.
- Assume that the relevant prescribed rate for all periods under consideration is 2%.

Required: Evaluate, from the point of view of the cost to the employer, Ms. Fox's suggestion of providing an interest-free loan in lieu of sufficient salary to carry a commercial loan at the rate of 4.6%.

AP 3-8 Employee Stock Options

Floretta Sutphin has worked for several years as an employee of a Canadian public company. In 2019, Floretta was granted options to acquire 2,000 of the company's shares at a price of $19 per share. At that time, the shares were trading at $17 per share.

In February 2020, with the shares trading at $27 per share, Floretta exercises 1,000 of the options. During the remainder of the year, the shares continue to increase in value, reaching a value of $32 per share in December 2020. At this time, Floretta exercises the remaining 1,000 options.

In the second quarter of 2021, reflecting poor earnings results during the first quarter of the year, the value of the shares declines to $30 per share. At this point, Floretta sells all 2,000 of her shares at this price.

Required:

A. Indicate the tax effect of the transactions that took place during each of the years 2019, 2020, and 2021. Your answer should include the effect on both net income and taxable income. Where relevant, identify these effects separately.

B. How would your answer change if the shares had been trading at $22 per share at the time the options were issued in 2019?

C. How would your answers to both Part A and Part B change if Floretta's employer was a Canadian controlled private corporation (CCPC)?

AP 3-9 Employee Stock Options

All of the long-term employees of Salter Inc. are allowed to participate in the company's stock option plan. In January 2019, Sharon Poulter was granted options to acquire 410 Salter Inc. shares at a price of $32.00 per share.

At the time of exercise, the Salter Inc. shares have a fair market value of $37.80 per share.

On November 15, 2021, the 410 Salter Inc. shares are sold.

Required: Indicate the tax effect for Sharon of the transactions that took place during 2019, 2020, and 2021 under each of the following independent cases. Your answer should include the effect on both net income and taxable income.

Case 1 Salter Inc. is a Canadian controlled private corporation. At the time the options were granted, the company's shares had a fair market value of $31.00 per share. The options are exercised on July 1, 2020. When the shares are sold, the proceeds of disposition are $45.80 per share.

Case 2 Salter Inc. is a Canadian controlled private corporation. At the time the options were granted, the company's shares had a fair market value of $34.00 per share. The options are exercised on February 28, 2019. When the shares are sold, the proceeds of disposition are $43.20 per share.

Case 3 Salter Inc. is a Canadian public company. At the time the options were granted, the company's shares were trading at $31.00 per share. The options are exercised on July 1, 2020. When the shares are sold, the proceeds of disposition are $42.10 per share.

Case 4 Salter Inc. is a Canadian public company. At the time the options were granted, the company's shares were trading at $34.00 per share. The options are exercised on February 28, 2020. When the shares are sold, the proceeds of disposition are $31.00 per share.

AP 3-10 Employment Income

Ms. Alexa Braxton has worked for AAAA Retailers for a number of years. AAAA is a Canadian controlled private corporation. It operates three children's clothing stores in the Edmonton area.

Her salary for the year 2021 was $120,000. AAAA withheld the following amounts from her earnings:

Federal and provincial income tax	$20,400
EI premiums	890
CPP contributions	3,166
Private health care plan—Employee portion	900
Union dues	100

Other Information:

1. AAAA provided Alexa with a car to be used in her employment duties. In addition, the company paid the 2021 operating costs of $10,250. The car was purchased, used, from a car dealer for $33,600, including GST of $1,600.

   The car was available to Alexa for all of 2021. During this period, she drove a total of 81,000 kilometres, 75,000 of which were used for employment purposes and 6,000 of which were for personal use.

2. Alexa earned the outstanding employee award for 2021. Besides a plaque, the award came with a cheque for $2,000 payable in January 2022.

3. In renegotiating her future compensation with AAAA, Alexa had asked for a $25,000 interest-free loan as one of her benefits. Because employee loans were not company policy, as an alternative she was granted options to buy 1,000 of the company's shares at $35 per share. This option price was higher than the estimated fair market value of the company's shares at the time the options were granted in January 2021.

   On July 15, 2021, Alexa exercised these options. At this time the fair market value of the shares was $48 per share. Alexa immediately sold all of the shares for $48 per share.

4. One of the reasons Alexa has stayed with AAAA is the employer-provided free day care in a facility located on AAAA's property. It is not open to the public. She has two sets of twins aged 2 and 4. She estimates that she would have to pay an annual minimum of $8,500 per child for day care without the facility.

5. AAAA offers all of its employees a 20% discount on full-price merchandise in all of its stores. Alexa purchased $2,800 worth of merchandise during 2020 and received discounts totalling $560. The discounted price of this merchandise was greater than its cost to the company.

6. AAAA provided Alexa with the following additional benefits:

Takeout meals eaten while working infrequently required overtime	$1,200
Private health services plan—Employer portion	1,800
Personal fitness trainer fees in the company wellness centre	700

7. Alexa was required by AAAA to use a large tablet to fulfill her employment duties. She was free to choose whatever tablet she wanted to use. AAAA would reimburse her for it and it would be considered the property of the employer. During 2021, she purchased:

   - an iPad Pro for $1,775 (GST inclusive)
   - a wireless printer for $450 (GST inclusive)
   - ink cartridges and paper totalling $550 (GST inclusive)

   The tablet and the printer were used exclusively for company business. Alexa is required by her contract of employment to acquire and pay for the cost of supplies she uses in the performance of her employment duties. The employer provides her with a T2200 attesting to this fact.

Required: Determine Alexa's employment income for the year ending December 31, 2021. Show all calculations.

AP 3-11 Commission Income and Work Space in Home

Jerald Gilreath is an employee of a Canadian publicly traded company. He works in their Calgary office and lives downtown in a high-rise condominium. In addition to his 2021 base salary of $175,000, he earned commissions of $21,460.

Other employment-related information is as follows:

1. Under the terms of an employment contract Jerald's employer requires him to pay all of his employment-related expenses, as well as provide his own office space. Jerald has the required Form T2200 from his employer.

2. Jerald's travel costs for 2021, largely airline tickets, food, and lodging, total $26,900. This includes $11,300 spent on meals while travelling for his employer. This meal total includes meals with clients of $4,300. All the meals are consumed while away for more than 12 consecutive hours from his employer's place of business.

3. Jerald is a member of his employer's registered pension plan. During 2021, $4,100 was withheld from his salary as a contribution to this plan. His employer made a matching contribution of $4,100.

4. During 2021, Jerald paid dues to his professional association of $422.

5. During 2021, Jerald was billed a total of $10,500 by his golf club in Calgary. Of this amount, $2,850 was the annual membership fee, with the remaining amount for meals and drinks with clients. He uses the club only when he is with clients. Assume that the meal expense is only the portion of the meals for clients.

6. For his employment-related travel, Jerald drives a car that he purchased on January 1, 2021, for $42,000, including GST. During 2021, he drove 52,000 kilometres, of which 43,000 were for employment purposes and 9,000 for personal use. Jerald had financed the car with a loan from a local bank and, during 2021, he had paid interest of $2,750.

   The costs of operating the car during 2020 were $10,920. Jerald has been advised by his accountant that, if the car were used 100% for employment purposes , the maximum CCA for 2021 would be $13,500 [(30%)(1.5)($30,000)].

7. Jerald uses 25% of his personal residence as an office. During 2021, the costs associated with his home were as follows:

Interest payments on mortgage	$ 9,100
Property taxes	3,750
Utilities	1,925
Insurance	1,060
Furnace, wiring, and foundation repairs	4,200
Total	$20,035

8. At the beginning of 2021, Jerald's employer granted him options to buy 500 of the company's shares at a price of $17.50 per share. This was the market price of the shares at the time the options were granted. During July 2021, when the shares were trading at $19.75 per share, he exercised all these options. In order to buy Christmas gifts for his family, he sold 100 of these shares in early December 2021 for $20.50 per share.

9. His employer has a policy of giving all employees gifts to promote employee loyalty and help local businesses. During 2021, Jerald received the following gifts:
   - A weekend for him and his wife at a local hotel. The value of this gift was $425
   - A $400 gift certificate at a local electronics store
   - A basket of fruit, nuts, and cheeses, with a value of $225

10. During 2021, Jerald purchased tickets to Calgary Flames games for $1,920. He used these tickets to attend games with key personnel from important clients. He also purchased tickets to a Montreal Canadians game in Montreal for $864. He used these tickets to attend the game with a prospective client located in Montreal.

Required: Calculate Jerald's minimum employment income for the 2021 taxation year. Ignore GST/HST/PST considerations.

AP 3-12 Employment Income—No Commissions

Mr. Jason Bond has been employed for many years as a graphic illustrator in Kamloops, British Columbia. His employer is a large publicly traded Canadian company. During 2021, his gross salary was $82,500. In addition, he was awarded a $20,000 bonus to reflect his outstanding performance during the year. As he was in no immediate need of additional income, he arranged with his employer that none of this bonus would be paid until 2026, the year of his expected retirement.

Other Information:
For the 2021 taxation year, the following items were relevant.

1. Mr. Bond's employer withheld the following amounts from his income:

Federal income tax	$16,000
Employment Insurance premiums	890
Canada Pension Plan contributions	3,166
United Way donations	2,000
Registered pension plan contributions	3,200
Payments for personal use of company car	3,600

2. During the year, Mr. Bond was provided with an automobile owned by his employer. The cost of the automobile was $47,500. Mr. Bond drove the car a total of 10,000 kilometres during the year, of which only 4,000 kilometres were driven for employer purposes and 6,000 for personal use. The automobile was used by Mr. Bond for 10 months of the year. During the other two months, he was out of the country, and company policy required the return of the automobile to the company.
3. During the year, the corporation paid Mega Financial Planners a total of $1,500 for providing counselling services to Mr. Bond with respect to his personal financial situation.
4. In order to assist Mr. Bond in purchasing a ski chalet, the employer provided him with a five-year loan of $150,000. The loan was granted on October 1 at an interest rate of 1%. Mr. Bond paid a total of $375 in interest for 2021 on January 20, 2022. Assume that, at the time the loan was granted and throughout the remainder of the year, the relevant prescribed rate was 2%.
5. Mr. Bond was required to pay professional dues of $1,800 during the year.
6. On June 6, 2021, when Mr. Bond exercised his stock options to buy 1,000 shares of his employer's common stock at a price of $15 per share, the shares were trading at $18 per share. When the options were granted, the shares were trading at $12 per share. During December 2021 the shares were sold for $20 per share.

Required: Calculate Mr. Bond's minimum employment income for the 2021 taxation year. Provide reasons for omitting items that you have not included in employment income. Ignore GST and PST considerations.

AP 3-13 Alternative Employment Offers

For several years, Alexandra Blanco has represented several companies as an independent sales representative. As she has been very effective for her clients, two of these companies, Mega Inc. and Tetra Ltd., are interested in hiring her as a full-time employee. Both of the employment offers would require Alexandra to begin service as of January 2021. However, the offers from the two corporations differ significantly in the form and content of their proposed compensation.

Mega Inc. Offer The offer from Mega Inc. contains the following provisions:

- She would be paid a salary of $280,000 per year. No commissions would be paid on her sales.
- Mega will provide an allowance of $35,000 per year to cover hotel, meals while travelling, and airline costs. The employer believes that the CRA will consider this allowance to be reasonable in the circumstances.
- No allowance or reimbursement will be provided for advertising and promotion expenses.
- Mega will provide her with an automobile for 12 months of the year, which they would purchase for $45,000. The employer will pay all of the operating costs for the automobile.
- Mega will provide Alexandra with a $250,000 interest-free loan for a period of five years. Alexandra will be investing all of these funds in publicly traded securities.
- Mega will provide Alexandra with a group disability insurance plan for which the company will pay all of the premiums. The plan provides periodic benefits that compensate for lost employment income. This will cost Mega $4,500 per year.
- Mega will provide Alexandra with an $800,000 face value life insurance policy. All of the premiums, which will total $2,900 per year, will be paid by Mega.

Tetra Ltd. Offer The offer from Tetra Ltd. contains the following provisions:

- Alexandra would be paid a salary of $190,000, plus a commission on all of her sales. Alexandra estimates that these commissions will total $90,000 during 2021.
- Tetra will reimburse all of her hotel, meals while travelling, and airline costs.
- No allowance or reimbursement will be provided for advertising and promotion expenses.

- While Tetra will not provide Alexandra with an automobile, it will provide an allowance of $1,800 per month to use her own automobile for employment purposes. Alexandra bought her car last year for $30,000. She estimates that the total cost of using her automobile for both personal and employment purposes during 2021 will be as follows:

Operating costs	$16,800
Capital cost allowance (tax depreciation) (100%)	4,500
Financing costs	2,200
Total	$23,500

- Tetra will provide Alexandra with a group disability insurance plan for which the company will pay all of the premiums. The plan provides periodic benefits that compensate for lost employment income. This will cost Tetra $5,000 per year.
- Tetra will provide Alexandra with a $1,500,000 face value life insurance policy. All of the premiums, which will total $4,200 per year, will be paid by Tetra.

Other Information

The following information is applicable to either of the alternative offers:

1. Alexandra estimates that her employment-related expenses during 2021 would be as follows:

Travel costs (hotel and airline costs)	$24,000
Travel costs (meals)	10,500
Advertising and promotion	26,000

2. Whether it is the employer's automobile or her own personal vehicle, she would use the car throughout 2021. She expects to drive this vehicle a total of 48,000 kilometres during 2021, with 32,000 of these kilometres representing employment use and the remaining 16,000 for personal use.

3. Assume that the prescribed rate is 2% throughout 2021.

Required:

A. Based on the estimates made by Alexandra, calculate Alexandra's minimum 2021 employment income for each of the two offers. Ignore GST and PST considerations.

B. Discuss the factors that Alexandra should consider in deciding between the two alternatives.

AP 3-14 Employment Income

For the past five years, Mr. Brooks has been employed as a financial analyst by a large Canadian public firm located in Winnipeg. During 2021, his basic gross salary amounts to $63,000. In addition, he was awarded an $11,000 bonus based on the performance of his division. Of the total bonus, $6,500 was paid in 2021 and the remainder is to be paid on January 15, 2022.

During 2021, Mr. Brooks' employer withheld the following amounts from his gross wages:

Federal income tax	$3,000
Employment Insurance premiums	890
Canada Pension Plan contributions	3,166
Registered pension plan contributions	2,800
Donations to the United Way	480
Union dues	240
Payments for personal use of company car	1,000

Other Information:

1. Due to an airplane accident while flying back from Thunder Bay on business, Mr. Brooks was seriously injured and confined to a hospital for two full months during 2021. As his employer

provides complete group disability insurance coverage, he received a total of $4,200 in payments during this period. All of the premiums for this insurance plan are paid by the employer. The plan provides periodic benefits that compensate for lost employment income.

2. Mr. Brooks is provided with a car that the company leases at a rate of $678 per month, including both GST and PST. The company pays for all of the operating costs of the car, and these amounted to $3,500 during 2021. Mr. Brooks drove the car a total of 35,000 kilometres during 2021, 30,000 kilometres were carefully documented as used for employment purposes with only 5,000 kilometres for personal use. While he was in the hospital (see Item 1), his employer's policy required that the car be returned to company premises.

3. On January 15, 2020, Mr. Brooks was granted options to buy 200 shares of his employer's common stock at a price of $23 per share. At this time, the shares were trading at $20 per share. Mr. Brooks exercised these options on July 6, 2021, when the shares were trading at $28 per share. He does not plan to sell the shares for at least a year.

4. In order to assist Mr. Brooks in acquiring a new home in Winnipeg, his employer granted him a five-year interest-free loan of $125,000. The loan qualifies as a home purchase loan. The loan was granted on October 1, 2021, and, at this point in time, the interest rate on open five-year mortgages was 5%. Assume the prescribed rate was 2% on this date. Mr. Brooks purchases a house for $235,000 on October 2, 2021. He has not owned a home during any of the preceding four years.

5. Other disbursements made by Mr. Brooks include the following:

Advanced financial accounting course tuition fees	$1,200
Music history course tuition fees (University of Manitoba one-week intensive course)	600
Fees paid to financial planner	300
Payment of premiums on life insurance	642

Mr. Brooks' employer reimbursed him for the tuition fees for the accounting course, but not the music course.

Required: Calculate Mr. Brooks' employment income for the 2021 taxation year.

CHAPTER 4

Taxable Income and Tax Payable for Individuals

Learning Objectives

Note Regarding Rates and Credits

A schedule of rates, brackets, credit amounts, and other data is available at the beginning of both volumes of this text (but not this Study Guide) and on MyLab. We expect you to refer to this information when calculating the credits covered in this chapter (i.e., you are not expected to memorize the rates, brackets, and credit bases).

After completing Chapter 4, you should be able to:

1. Calculate taxable income when an individual has basic deductions against net income (Paragraph [P hereafter] 4-1 to 4-9).
2. Calculate federal and provincial tax payable before the consideration of any tax credits (P 4-10 to 4-27).
3. Calculate the personal tax credits described in ITA 118(1), which include the:
   - spousal,
   - eligible dependant,
   - Canada caregiver for a child,
   - basic, and
   - Canada caregiver credits (P 4-28 to 4-73).
4. Calculate the age tax credit (P 4-74 to 4-75).
5. Calculate the pension income tax credit (P 4-76 to 4-80).
6. Calculate the Canada employment tax credit (P 4-81 to 4-83).
7. Calculate the adoption expenses tax credit (P 4-84 to 4-88).
8. Calculate the digital news subscriptions credit that is effective in 2020 (P 4-89 to 4-90).
9. Calculate the home accessibility tax credit (P 4-91 to 4-101).
10. Calculate the first-time home buyers' tax credit (P 4-102 to 4-104).
11. Calculate the volunteer firefighters and search and rescue workers tax credit (P 4-105 to 4-108).
12. Calculate the charitable donations tax credit when the donation is in the form of cash (P 4-109 to 4-120).
13. Calculate the medical expense tax credit (P 4-121 to 4-132).

14. Calculate the disability tax credit (P 4-133 to 4-142).
15. Calculate the tax credits related to tuition fees, examination fees, ancillary fees, and student loan interest (P 4-143 to 4-154).
16. Calculate the amount of education-related tax credits that can be carried forward or transferred to another individual (P 4-155 to 4-163).
17. Calculate the Employment Insurance and Canada Pension Plan credits (P 4-164 to 4-170).
18. List the types and amounts of tax credits that can be transferred to a spouse or common-law partner (P 4-171 to 4-173).
19. Calculate the political contributions tax credit (P 4-174 to 4-177).
20. Calculate the labour-sponsored venture capital corporation tax credit (P 4-178 to 4-182).
21. Explain the difference between refundable and non-refundable credits (P 4-183 to 4-185)
22. Explain the basic provisions of the refundable GST credit (P 4-186 to 4-190).
23. Calculate the refundable medical expense supplement (P 4-191 to 4-194).
24. Calculate the Canada Workers Benefit (P 4-195 to 4-200).
25. Calculate the refundable teacher and early childhood educator school supply tax credit (P 4-201 to 4-203).
26. Explain the Climate Action Incentive payments (refundable credit) (P 4-204 to 4-211).
27. Calculate the Canada training credit (P 4-212 to P 4-216).
28. Calculate the OAS and EI clawbacks (P 4-217 to 4-226).
29. Walk through the Comprehensive Example (P 4-227).
30. Complete a simple personal tax return using the ProFile T1 tax preparation software program.

Introduction

4-1. In Chapter 1 we had identified that there is a four-step process for determining whether individuals owe additional income tax or can expect an income tax refund in a specific year. The steps are (1) net income, (2) taxable income, (3) gross federal tax, and (4) income tax credits. In Chapter 1 we saw that net income is made up of several different components. These components are (1) income from employment, business, or property (e.g., investments), (2) taxable capital gains, (3) other income, and (4) other deductions.

4-2. At this stage we have, in terms of working our way through the four-step process, only provided coverage of employment income, which is simply one component of net income. However, with a good understanding of employment income we are ready to use what we have learned to take you through the four-step process for individuals whose only income is from employment. This means that, in this chapter, we will learn about components of taxable income, how to calculate gross tax payable for individuals, and how to apply the vast number of income tax credits available that are used to reduce income tax payable. By the end of this chapter you will have the knowledge necessary to prepare an income tax return for an individual whose only source of income is from employment. In subsequent chapters we will return to add other components of net income for individuals and will, at each successive stage, continue to apply this four-step process with the objective of gaining a practical understanding of how the income tax laws apply to individuals. This will provide the understanding needed to prepare income tax returns for individuals and, in many situations, members of their families.

4-3. In this chapter you will learn about some of the components of taxable income and most of the income tax credits, but there remain some additional items that are purposefully left out of this chapter and postponed to subsequent chapters. The reason for this is that you must first have a greater understanding of some of the other components of net income. For example, one of the income tax credits available to individuals involves dividends received from Canadian corporations. Dividends (e.g., property income) are not discussed until Chapter 7. Another example is a special deduction in determining taxable income that allows individuals to offset certain capital gains. The taxation of capital gains and capital losses is not discussed until Chapter 8. As a result, the final pieces of the puzzle must wait until Chapter 11, when we revisit taxable income and taxes payable for individuals.

Taxable Income of Individuals

Available Deductions

4-4. The deductions that are available in calculating taxable income of an individual can be found in Division C of Part I of the ITA. As indicated in the introduction to this chapter, some of these deductions will be dealt with in this chapter. However, coverage of some of the more complex deductions are deferred until Chapter 11. The available deductions, along with a description of their coverage in this text, are as follows:

ITA 110(1)(d), (d.01), and (d.1)—Employee Stock Options Our basic coverage of stock options and stock option deductions is included in Chapter 3. This coverage will not be repeated here.

ITA 110(1)(f)—Deductions for Payments This deduction, which is available for social assistance and workers' compensation received, is covered beginning in Paragraph 4-6.

ITA 110.2—Lump-Sum Payments ITA 110.2 provides a deduction for certain lump-sum payments (e.g., an amount received as a court-ordered termination benefit and included in employment income). It provides the basis for including this amount in income as though it were received over the taxation years to which it relates rather than the year in which it was received. Because of its limited applicability, no additional coverage is given to this provision.

ITA 110.6—Lifetime Capital Gains Deduction The provisions related to this deduction are very complex and require a fairly complete understanding of capital gains. As a consequence, this deduction is covered in Chapter 11.

ITA 110.7—Residing in a Prescribed Zone (Northern Residents Deductions) These deductions, which are available only to individuals living in prescribed regions of northern Canada, are given limited coverage in Paragraph 4-9.

ITA 111—Losses Deductible In Chapter 1 we discussed the mechanics of net income using ITA 3. We saw that any current-year losses that could not be deducted because of insufficient other income in that same year became either non-capital losses or net capital losses. These loss categorizations then become available to apply to other years. We generally refer to these as loss carryovers. Our initial coverage introduced you to the basic concepts, but there is much more involved that requires a fairly complete understanding of business income, property income, and capital gains. As a result we have deferred complete coverage of this common deduction until Chapter 11. Coverage of corporate loss carryovers can be found in Chapter 12.

Ordering of Deductions

4-5. ITA 111.1 specifies the order in which individuals must subtract the various deductions that may be available in the calculation of taxable income. As our coverage of these deductions is not complete in this chapter, we will defer coverage of this ordering provision until Chapter 11.

Deductions for Payments—ITA 110(1)(f)

4-6. ITA 110(1)(f) provides for the deduction of certain amounts that have been included in the calculation of net income. The items listed here are:

- amounts that are exempt from income tax in Canada as a result of an income tax treaty with another country;
- workers' compensation payments received as a result of injury or death;
- income from employment with a prescribed international organization; and
- social assistance payments made on the basis of a means, needs, or income test and included in an individual's income.

4-7. The effect of ITA 110(1)(f) is to remove from taxable income certain amounts that were included in net income. If, for example, an individual's only income in 2021 were $30,000 of workers' compensation payments, then that individual would include the $30,000 as "other income" and net income would be $30,000. ITA 110(1)(f) would allow a deduction of the same $30,000, with the result that taxable income would be nil. With no taxable income there can be no income tax owing. At first glance, this seems to be a fairly inefficient way of not taxing this type of income.

4-8. There is, however, a reason for this. There are a number of income tax incentives that are designed to apply to those individuals with low levels of income (e.g., the GST/HST credit). The incentives are often reduced when income rises above certain thresholds. The income thresholds use net income, and as a result it is imperative that in measuring access to these incentives all of an individual's income be considered, whether or not it is actually subject to income tax. In our previous example, if the individual in receipt of the workers' compensation was married or in a common-law relationship, the individual's spouse or partner would be unable to claim certain tax credits such as a spousal/common-law partner credit given that the income threshold for 2021 is $13,808. If taxable income were used, the individual would have had no income and the incentives would have been available.

Northern Residents Deductions—ITA 110.7

4-9. Residents of Labrador, the territories, as well as parts of some of the provinces are eligible for deductions under ITA 110.7. To qualify for these deductions, the taxpayer must be resident in these prescribed regions for a continuous period of six months beginning or ending in the taxation year. The amount of the deductions involves fairly complex calculations that go beyond the scope of this text. The purpose of these deductions is to compensate individuals for the high costs that are associated with living in such prescribed northern zones.

Calculation of Gross Tax Payable

Gross Federal Tax Payable

4-10. The calculation of gross federal income tax for individuals requires the application of up to five separate tax rates to an individual's taxable income. The rates are progressive, starting at a low rate of 15% and increasing to a high of 33% as the individual's taxable income increases. In order to maintain fairness, the income levels are indexed annually to reflect changes in the Consumer Price Index. Without such indexation, individuals could find themselves effectively subject to higher rates without having an increased level of real, inflation-adjusted income.

4-11. For 2021, the brackets to which these five rates apply are as follows:

Taxable Income in Excess of	Federal Tax	Marginal Rate on Excess
$ -0-	$ -0-	15.0%
49,020	7,353	20.5%
98,040	17,402	26.0%
151,978	31,426	29.0%
216,511	50,141	33.0%

4-12. Some explanation of the income tax brackets is required. The use of a marginal rate means that for the first $49,020 of taxable income the rate is 15.0%. Therefore, for an individual with exactly $49,020 of taxable income the federal income tax would equal $7,353 [(15%)($49,020)]. For an individual with exactly $98,040 in taxable income the first $49,020 is taxed at 15% and the next $49,020 [($98,040 - $49,020)] would be taxed at a rate of 20.5%, or an additional $10,049 [(20.5%)($49,020)]. Total gross federal income tax would be $17,402

[$7,353 + $10,049]. Because the income taxes are a combination of a 15% and a 20.5% rate in our example, the average rate would be 17.75% [($17,402/$98,040)].

4-13. It would be cumbersome to actually calculate gross federal income tax for each separate tax rate. The table is therefore designed to simplify the calculations. If, for example, an individual had taxable income of $300,000, rather than add the income taxes for each bracket we would simply look at the table and determine our starting point based on where the taxable income fits. Based on this, since taxable income exceeds $216,511 that would be our starting point. Income tax would be $50,141 on the first $216,511, as shown, and 33% on the excess amount of $83,489 [$300,000 - $216,511], which would equal $27,551. This is illustrated in the following paragraph.

4-14. As an example of the calculation of gross federal tax payable and the resulting average rate of taxation, consider an individual with taxable income of $300,000. The calculation would be as follows:

Tax on first $216,511	$ 50,141
Tax on next $83,489 ($300,000 - $216,511) at 33%	27,551
Gross federal tax payable (before credits)	$ 77,692
Average rate of tax ($77,692 ÷ $300,000)	25.90%

4-15. The preceding table assists in the calculation of gross federal income tax, meaning the income tax determined before any reductions as a result of available income tax credits. In 2021 there is a basic personal tax credit amount of $13,808, which will be discussed later in this chapter. This credit is available to all individual residents of Canada. A rate of 15% is applied to that credit amount, resulting in a reduction of gross income tax of $2,071 [(15%)($13,808)]. Economically this means that an individual with taxable income of $13,808 or less will not pay any federal income tax in that year since the federal income tax rate on that taxable income is also 15%. Therefore, while the 15% rate is, in fact, applied to all of the first $49,020 of taxable income, a portion of this amount is not really subject to federal income tax. The availability of other tax credits will further increase the amount of taxable income that could be effectively earned tax free.

4-16. A surtax is an additional tax calculated on the basis of the regular tax payable calculation. Ontario and Prince Edward Island are the only provinces that charge a surtax. In general there are no surtaxes at the federal level imposed on individuals except for the special surtax referred to in Paragraphs 4-26 and 4-27 that is a substitute for provincial income tax in situations where it would not apply.

Provincial Tax Payable before Credits

Provincial Rates

4-17. As is the case at the federal level, provincial tax payable is calculated by multiplying taxable income by a group of progressive rates. In general, the provinces (other than Quebec) use the same taxable income figure that is used at the federal level.

4-18. Between 2001 and 2015, Alberta was unique in that it used a single flat rate of 10% applied to all levels of income. In 2016, however, Alberta abandoned the flat-rate system and began to apply progressive rates. All provinces use anywhere from three to six different tax rates applied to various levels of income. In general, the income levels differ from those used at the federal level.

4-19. To give you some idea of the range of provincial rates, the 2021 minimum and maximum rates for provinces other than Quebec are found in the following table. The maximum rates include surtaxes where applicable. These rates are correct as of January 1, 2021. Rates may change after this time as provincial budgets are introduced.

As of January 1, 2021 Province	Minimum 2021 Tax Rate	Maximum 2021 Tax Rate
Alberta	10.00%	15.00%
British Columbia	5.06%	20.05%
Manitoba	10.80%	17.40%
New Brunswick	9.68%	20.30%
Newfoundland and Labrador	8.70%	18.30%
Nova Scotia	8.79%	21.00%
Ontario (maximum includes 56% surtax on tax payable)	5.05%	20.53%
Prince Edward Island (maximum includes 10% surtax on tax payable)	9.80%	18.37%
Saskatchewan	10.50%	14.50%

4-20. You should note the significant differences in rates between the provinces. The maximum rate ranges from 14.5% in Saskatchewan to 21% in Nova Scotia. This difference amounts to extra provincial taxes of $6,500 per year on each additional $100,000 of income above the top tax bracket. This can make provincial tax differences a major consideration when an individual decides where to establish residency in the country.

4-21. When these provincial rates are combined with the federal rate schedule, the minimum combined rate varies from a low of 20.05% in Ontario (15% federal plus 5.05% provincial) to a high of 25.8% in Manitoba (15% federal plus 10.8% provincial).

4-22. Maximum combined rates are lowest in Saskatchewan, where the rate is 47.5% (33% federal plus 14.5% provincial). They are highest in Nova Scotia, where the combined rate is 54% (33% federal plus 21% provincial). Because Quebec's calculations are completely different, that province has not been included in this list of rates. The overall rate in Quebec ranges from a low of 27.53% to a high of 53.31%.

Exercise 4-1

Subject: Calculation of Gross Federal Tax Payable (before Credits)

During 2021, Joan Matel is a resident of Ontario and has calculated her taxable income to be $56,700. Assume that Ontario's rates are 5.05% on taxable income up to $49,020 and 9.15% on the next $49,020. Calculate Ms. Matel's 2021 federal and provincial tax payable before the consideration of tax credits, as well as her average rate of tax.

Solutions to Exercises are available in the Study Guide.

Provincial Residence

4-23. Given the significant differences in provincial tax rates on individuals, it is somewhat surprising that the rules related to where an individual will pay provincial income taxes are fairly simple. With respect to an individual's income other than business income, it is subject to tax in the province in which the individual resides on December 31, the last day of the taxation year. This means that, if an individual moves to Ontario from Nova Scotia on December 30 of the current year, any income for the entire year, other than business income with a permanent establishment in another province, will be subject to income tax in Ontario. We would add, however, that if an individual would be considered to have established a residence in two or more provinces, ITR 2607 clarifies that the individual is only considered to be resident in the province that is their principal place of residence. If, for example, a resident of Newfoundland establishes a residence in Alberta for the purposes of employment but retains principal residential ties (discussed in Chapter 1) in Newfoundland where the individual regularly returns, then the residence would remain in Newfoundland.

Types of Income

4-24. In terms of the effective tax rates, the income earned by Canadian resident individuals can be divided into three basic categories based on how much of the income is actually subject to tax:

Ordinary Income This refers to income that is fully (100%) included in net income. It would include income from employment, business, property (other than dividends), and other miscellaneous types of income. In general, the effective tax rates on this category are those presented in the preceding tables. For example, the marginal rate for an individual living in Alberta and earning more than $350,000, would be 48% (33% federal plus 15% provincial).

Capital Gains As will be discussed in detail in Chapter 8, capital gains arise on the disposition of capital property. Only one-half of such gains are included in net income and taxable income. This means that the effective tax rate on this category of income is only one-half of the rates presented in the preceding tables. Returning to our Alberta resident who is earning more than $350,000, the marginal rate on capital gains would be 24% [(1/2)(33% + 15%)].

Dividends As will be explained in Chapter 7, when an individual receives dividends from taxable Canadian companies they are subject to a special set of rules designed to recognize that the income from which dividends have been paid has already been subject to income tax when earned by the corporation, and therefore the individual should receive some form of credit for the corporate income taxes paid. This results in a system that includes a dividend gross up. The gross up increases the amount of the dividend included in the individual's income, and a dividend tax credit attempts to approximate corporate income taxes paid.

There are two types of taxable dividends. The taxable dividends are either eligible or non-eligible dividends, depending on the type of corporation and the types of income earned by that corporation. The effective income tax rates for these two types of taxable dividends in Alberta applying the highest federal and provincial income tax brackets are as follows:

Eligible dividends	34.31%
Non-eligible dividends	42.31%

4-25. A more complete discussion of the different effective tax rates mentioned here is provided in Chapter 7 (dividends) and Chapter 8 (capital gains).

Taxes on Income Not Earned in a Province

4-26. As was discussed in Chapter 1, it is possible for an individual to be considered a resident of Canada for income tax purposes without being a resident of a particular province or territory. This would be the case, for example, for members of the Canadian Armed Forces who are stationed outside of Canada and are deemed residents.

4-27. Income that is not subject to provincial or territorial income tax is subject to an additional income tax at the federal level that substitutes for the fact that there is no provincial or territorial income tax. This additional tax is considered a surtax applied to non-residents of 48% on federal tax payable. This gives a maximum rate of 48.84% [(33%)(148%)]. This additional tax is paid to the federal government. Income from employment earned in a province or income from a business with a permanent establishment in a province are subject to provincial income tax even though the individual is not a resident of that province. In either of those cases, the federal surtax would not apply to that income.

Federal Income Tax Credits

General Comments

4-28. There are a number of income tax credits available to individuals and a few points to be aware of before we begin our detailed discussion.

Types of Income Tax Credits Tax credits generally fall into two categories: non-refundable or refundable. Most credits are non-refundable, meaning that if the amounts exceed gross federal taxes payable there will be no refund. On the other hand, refundable credits do result in a potential income tax refund (depending on gross federal tax payable) even if an individual has no income.

Tax Credit Base Most credits have a dollar base, such as the age credit, which begins with $7,713, and the pension credit, which is $2,000. Many tax credits are gradually reduced as certain thresholds are exceeded. The tax credit base for the age credit, for example, begins to be reduced when net income exceeds $38,893. The pension credit, on the other hand, has no income threshold, remaining at $2,000 each year.

Tax Credit Base Rates Most of the income tax credits apply a standard 15% rate to the tax credit base, but there are other credits, including the dividend tax credit, the political contributions credit, and the charitable donations tax credit, that use a different approach. In our examples, exercises, problems and examinations we will add the tax credit bases of all available credits to which the 15% rate applies, then apply that percentage to produce an amount that can be applied against gross federal taxes payable. Other credits will be handled separately. This approach is also used in the completion of individual income tax returns.

Indexation The impact of inflation can, over time, reduce the economic value of income tax credits. In recognition of this concern, almost all income tax credits, including any income thresholds, are indexed annually. New indexed rates are announced annually in December of each year.

Tax Credit Transfers Some non-refundable tax credits that cannot be used because of insufficient tax payable to apply them against may be transferrable to others, such as spouses, common-law partners, parents, or grandparents.

Provincial Amounts

4-29. In determining provincial income tax credits, the provinces use the same approach as that used at the federal level. That is, the minimum provincial rate is applied to a base that is indexed each year. In most cases, the base used is different from the base used at the federal level. For 2021, the basic personal tax credit at the federal level is $2,071 [(15%)($13,808)]. Comparative 2021 figures for selected provinces are as follows:

Province	Base	Rate	Credit
Alberta	$19,369	10.00%	$1,937
British Columbia	11,070	5.06%	560
Newfoundland and Labrador	9,536	8.70%	830
Ontario	10,880	5.05%	549

Personal Tax Credits—ITA 118(1)

Basic Personal Amount—ITA 118(1.1)

Background

4-30. As promised during the 2019 federal election, the Trudeau government provided a reduction in taxes by increasing the basic personal amount (BPA) for low- and middle-income

Canadians. As we shall see in the discussion that follows, the BPA reflects the amount of income that can be received by resident individuals on a tax-free basis given that this tax credit is available to all Canadian resident individuals. It does this by applying 15% to the BPA, which is then applied against gross federal taxes payable.

4-31. In the absence of this change, the indexed 2021 BPA would be $12,421. The government's proposal would see this amount eventually go to $15,000. However, this increase is to be phased in over four years, not reaching that level until 2023. The scheduled amounts for the BPA during this phase-in period are as follows:

2020	$13,229
2021	13,808
2022	14,398
2023	15,000

4-32. The basic personal tax credit amount of $12,421 is available to all resident Canadian individuals without any income threshold. The additional amount of $1,387 [$13,808 - $12,421], however, is subject to an income threshold. This is consistent with the government view that this enhanced BPA will not be available to wealthier Canadians. The extra amount of $1,387 will start to be eliminated when an individual's net income reaches the third tax bracket ($151,978 for 2021) and will be completely eliminated when net income exceeds the top tax bracket ($216,511 for 2021). The BPA of an individual claiming a spouse, common-law partner, or eligible dependant will apply to the claiming of that other individual. If, for example, the BPA of a supporting individual is $12,500 and the other supported individual is not infirm and has no net income, then the total credit to the supporting individual would be $25,000 [$12,500 for the individual + $12,500 for the other individual].

Calculation

4-33. The information in the previous paragraph means that:

- the BPA for individuals with net income equal to or less than $151,978 will be $13,808; and
- the BPA for individuals with net income equal to or greater than $216,511 will be $12,421.

4-34. The legislation for this provision is made somewhat complicated by the fact that there will be a pro rata reduction in the $1,387 BPA enhancement for individuals with net income between the third and fourth tax brackets.

4-35. For 2021, the difference between these two tax brackets is $64,533 ($216,511 - $151,978). Based on these numbers, the $1,387 enhancement is reduced by an amount determined by multiplying the $1,387 BPA enhancement by a fraction based on dividing the excess of the individual's net income over $151,978, by the $64,533 difference between the third and fourth tax brackets. Stated as a formula, the 2021 BPA is calculated as follows:

$12,421 + $1,387 - [$1,387] [(the lesser of the individual's net income and
$216,511 - $151,978) ÷ $64,533]

4-36. This formula reflects the legislative approach, which starts with the regular BPA, adds the enhancement, and subtracts any reduction in the enhancement. It can be simplified by starting with the enhanced BPA, as reflected in the following revised formula:

$13,808 - [$1,387] [(The lesser of the individual's net income and $216,511 - $151,978)
÷ $64,533]

4-37. This simplified formula will be used in both the text and the related problem materials.

4-38. A simple example will illustrate the application of this formula.

EXAMPLE John Basic has net income of $180,000 for the 2021 taxation year. What is the amount of his 2021 BPA?

ANALYSIS John's 2021 BPA would be calculated as follows:

$13,808 - [$1,387][($180,000 - $151,978) ÷ $64,533] = $13,206

TIP The formula is designed to reduce the additional $1,387 to the extent that net income is between $151,978 and $216,511. John's income of $180,000 is 43.4% of the way between these two numbers, so the $1,387 is reduced by $602 [(43.4%)($1,387)] resulting in a BPA of $13,206 [$13,808 - $602].

4-39. The BPA is the tax credit base for calculating the amount that is applied against gross federal taxes payable. The actual amount that reduces income tax is the BPA multiplied by 15%, which would equal $1,981 [(15%)($13,206)].

A Spouse or Common-Law Partner

General Overview

4-40. Throughout this chapter and many of the subsequent chapters there is discussion of spouses and common-law partners. It is important to have a basic understanding of what these words and expressions mean to determine the income tax consequences, particularly with respect to many income tax credits but also for many other income tax reasons. Some commonly used words and expressions have a popular understanding of their meaning, but the ITA frequently changes the rules by giving such words and expressions a completely different meaning.

4-41. The terms "spouses" or "married persons" are not defined in the ITA. This means that the common, everyday definitions apply, with the result that spouses and married persons are generally understood to mean individuals who are legally married, whether they are of the same sex or not.

4-42. Common-law relationships, on the other hand, are quite a different matter. Some would likely consider individuals to be in a common-law relationship as soon as they decide to live together under the same roof and share most things in a manner similar to married persons. Provinces and territories, however, each have their own rules as to when a commmon-law relationship is considered to be recognized at law. Some provinces and territories require that couples (same sex or not) live together in a "conjugal relationship" for a certain amount of time or a reduced amount of time where there is a child (which would include an adopted child) of the couple. Since the rules vary to some degree in each province and territory, the legislators of the ITA decided to define the expressions "common-law partner" and "common-law partnership" to clarify when a relationship becomes a common-law relationship for income tax purposes, regardless of which province or territory one resides in.

4-43. In general, you would be considered a common-law partner of another individual and therefore in a common-law partnership (i.e., a relationship) in the two following circumstances:

1. **The couple has cohabited for at least 12 months and do not have a child.** This requires living together with another individual in a manner similar to that of married persons in what is referred to as a conjugal relationship. The 12-month period must be continuous. If, for example, two individuals move in together in a conjugal relationship on January 1, 2021, and break-up on November 20, 2021, they would not be considered to have been in a common-law partnership in 2021. Once the 12-month period has been met it is deemed to continue until there is a period of separation that lasts more than 90 days.

EXAMPLE Two individuals begin living together on February 14, 2021. They separate on April 30, 2022. There is no child involved.

ANALYSIS They would not be considered to be in a common-law partnership for 2021 since at no time in that year were they living together for at least 12 consecutive months. They would be considered in a common-law partnership for 2022 since they had been living together for 12 consecutive months at some point in 2022 (e.g., from February 14, 2022). If they reconcile within 90 days of April 30, 2022, the common-law partnership will be deemed to continue as if there had been no separation. If, however, they reconciled more than 90 days later, then they would be considered to have started the relationship over, which could impact both their 2022 and 2023 tax years.

2. **The couple cohabits in a conjugal relationship and are the parents of a child.** In this case there is no required 12-consecutive-month time limit. The two individuals must generally have a child together (e.g., be the legal parents of a child, biological or adopted). If one of the individuals has their own child, this rule would generally not apply, meaning that the 12-month consecutive period of living together in a conjugal relationship would be required to be met to establish a common law partnership.

Individuals with a Spouse or Common-Law Partner—ITA 118(1)(a)

Two Credits

4-44. ITA 118(1)(a) is applicable to individuals who have a spouse or a common-law partner. It provides for two separate credits: one for the individual and one for that individual's spouse or common-law partner. We will refer to this latter credit as the "spousal credit," though you should recognize that it is equally applicable to common-law partners.

For the Individual—ITA 118(1)(a)((i)

4-45. This credit requires little explanation. It is simply 15% of the BPA as calculated using the formula presented in Paragraph 4-35.

For the Spouse—ITA 118(1)(a)(ii)

4-46. The situation here is more complicated. However, in situations where an individual has a healthy spouse who has no net income of their own, it is equal to 15% of the BPA.

4-47. There are two factors that can complicate this situation. The first involves situations where the spouse has net income. If this is the case, the BPA must be reduced by the spouse's net income.

> **EXAMPLE** Marjory Frank has net income of $100,000. Her spouse has net income of $5,200. Her spouse does not have a mental or physical infirmity.
>
> **ANALYSIS** Ms. Frank's spousal credit would be equal to $1,291 [(15%)($13,808 - $5,200)].

4-48. The second complication involves situations where the spouse or common-law partner is dependent on the individual by reason of a mental or physical infirmity. In this situation, ITA 118(1)(a)(ii) adds an additional amount of $2,273 to the tax credit base for the spousal credit, bringing the available tax credit base total to $16,103 ($13,808 + $2,295).

4-49. Using the example from Paragraph 4-47, if we assume that Ms. Frank's spouse was dependent because of a mental or physical infirmity, the spousal amount would be equal to $1,635 [15%][($13,808 + $2,295 - $5,200)]. The total credits available in to Ms. Frank under ITA 118(1)(a) can be summarized as follows:

Spouse	Not Infirm	Infirm
Basic personal amount (for individual)	$13,808	$13,808
Spousal amount ($13,808 - $5,200)	8,608	
Spousal amount ($13,808 + $2,295 - $5,200)		10,903
Credit base	$22,416	$24,711
Rate	15%	15%
Personal tax credits (individual and spouse)	$ 3,362	$ 3,707

4-50. There are several other points to be made with respect to the credits for an individual with a spouse or common-law partner:

> **Spouse or Common-Law Partner's Income** The income figure used for limiting the spousal amount is net income.

Applicability to Either Spouse or Common-Law Partner ITA 118(1)(a) technically applies to both spouses and, while each is eligible to claim the basic amount of $13,808 or less, IT Folio S1-F4-C2, :*Basic Personal and Dependant Tax Credits*," specifies that only one spouse or common-law partner may claim the spousal amount. S1-F4-C2 indicates that the spouse making the claim should be the one that supports the other. Support is generally described in S1-F4-C2 Paragraph 2.18 as providing the basic necessities of life, including food, shelter, and clothing. Where a spouse has no net income or a low level of net income such that a positive spousal amount would be available to the other spouse, it is generally considered that the requisite level of "support" has been met. For all practical purposes, the spousal credit (BPA) is available where one spouse has net income above $13,808 while the other does not.

Eligibility The spousal credit can be claimed where, at any time in the year, there is either a spouse or a common-law partner. If two individuals get married or meet the definition of common-law partners on December 31, 2021, then the eligibility requirement would have been met since they were married or living commonm-law at some time in 2021. The net income for the whole year, however, would have to be taken into consideration when claiming the spousal credit.

Multiple Relationships Based on these definitions, it would be possible for an individual to have both a spouse and a common-law partner. ITA 118(4)(a) makes it clear that, if this is the case, a credit can only be claimed for one of these individuals. In such cases, determining your tax credits may be the least of your problems.

Year of Separation or Divorce In general, ITA 118(5) does not allow a spousal tax credit in situations where the individual is making a deduction for the support of a spouse or common-law partner (spousal support is covered in Chapter 9). However, S1-F4-C2 indicates that, in the year of separation or divorce, an individual can choose to deduct amounts paid for spousal support or claim the tax credit for a spouse, but not both.

Exercise 4-2

Subject: Spousal Tax Credit

Johan Sprinkle is married and has 2021 net income of $35,450. His spouse has 2021 net income of $2,600. Johan has no tax credits other than the BPA for his spouse and himself. Assuming that Johan's spouse does not have a mental or physical infirmity, determine Johan's federal tax credit amounts for 2021. How would your answer differ if Johan's spouse were dependent because of a mental or physical infirmity?

Solutions to Exercises are available in the Study Guide.

We suggest you complete SSP 4-1 at this point.

Individuals Supporting a Dependent Person—ITA 118(1)(b)

Overview

4-51. This next tax credit applies if an individual is either (1) not married or living in a common-law partnership or (2) is separated and living apart from their spouse or common-law partner. If either situation applies and the person financially supports certain family members (e.g., related persons) that are wholly dependent on her, then she may be able to claim a tax credit for the support of one such person. If there are two or more dependents, the tax credit is restricted to the claimning of only one. If an individual is married or living in a common-law partnership and not separated from the other person, then she can only claim a tax credit under ITA 118(1)(a) and not an eligible dependent tax credit under ITA 118(1)(b).

EXAMPLE 1 George and Martha have one child, Franklin, who is eight years old. Both George and Martha have net income greater than $50,000.

ANALYSIS 1 Neither George or Martha can claim an eligible dependent credit for Franklin since they are married and not separated.

EXAMPLE 2 George and Martha have two children, Franklin who is eight years old and Thomas who is ten years old. Franklin has no net income but Thomas has $2,000 of net income earned from delivering newspapers. George and Martha are separated and Martha has full custody of both children.

ANALYSIS 2 George would be unable to claim the married/common-law partnership tax credit (ITA 118(1)(a)) or the eligible dependent tax credit (ITA 118(1)(b)) since he is separated from Martha and not supporting either of the children. Martha would be able to claim either Franklin or Thomas as an eligible dependent but not both. Since the dependent's net income would reduce the available credit, Martha should claim Franklin since he has no net income. This is her choice, since both children would otherwise be eligible. We would add that had George actually provided support in the way of support payments for the children, ITA 118(5) would disqualify him from claiming the eligible dependant credit for either of the children.

4-52. Like ITA 118(1)(a), ITA 118(1)(b) provides for two tax credits. The first is the BPA for the individual based on a 2021 base amount of $13,808 or less. The second credit, based on the same amount, is for a qualifying eligible dependant. With respect to this second credit, if the eligible dependant has a mental or physical infirmity an additional amount of $2,295 is added.

Eligibility and Eligible Dependant Defined

4-53. The claim for an eligible dependant is available to an individual who is not eligible to claim the spousal credit and who supports a person who is wholly dependent on him and actually lives with him in a self-contained domestic establishment (house, apartment, etc.). We will refer to this supported person as an eligible dependant.

4-54. To claim this credit, the eligible dependant must be "related" to the individual making the claim and "wholly dependent for support." ITA 251(2) defines related individuals as those who are related by blood, marriage, common-law partnership, or adoption. Related persons do not include aunts, uncles, nieces, nephews, and cousins, but would include parents, grandparents, brothers, sisters, and children of one's brothers and sisters.

4-55. The ITA refers to two levels of support. The first simply requires that one individual supports another, while the second is that an individual is "wholly dependent" for support on another. The second is much more comprehensive and involved. Support by itself generally means financial support to assist in providing the necessities of life such as food, shelter, and clothing. An individual may lack the financial means to provide these necessities and need to rely on others. Being wholly dependent for support means adding direction and guidance in day-to-day activities, including attending school, medical appointments, etc. This level of support is typically directed at minor children and incapacitated adult individuals.

4-56. In view of today's less stable family arrangements, the question of exactly who is considered a child for income tax purposes requires some elaboration. A child would include natural children, children who have been formally adopted, as well as the natural and adopted children of a spouse or common-law partner.

Application

4-57. As noted, this credit is most commonly claimed by individuals who are supporting a minor child. It is available to individual taxpayers who are single, widowed, divorced, or separated and supporting a dependant who is:

- related to the individual;
- wholly dependent on the individual (or the individual and others) for support;

- (a) under 18 at any time during the year, or (b) mentally or physically infirm, or (c) the individual's parent or grandparent;
- living with the individual in a home that the individual maintains (this would not disqualify a child who moves away during the school year to attend an educational institution as long as the home maintained by the individual remains the child's home); and
- resident in Canada (this requirement is not applicable to an individual's child as long as they are living with the individual).

4-58. The eligible dependant credit cannot be claimed by an individual:

- if the individual is claiming the spousal credit;
- if the individual is living with, supporting, or being supported by a spouse (the claim is only available for individuals who are either single or living separately from their spouse);
- for more than one person;
- if the dependant's net income exceeds $13,808, or $16,103 ($13,808 + $2,295) if they are mentally or physically infirm;
- if another supporting person is making this claim for the same individual; or
- for the individual's child if the individual is required to make child support payments to another individual for that child. As is noted in Chapter 9, when child support is being paid, only the recipient of such payments can claim this tax credit.

Calculation of Eligible Dependant Tax Credit

4-59. As we have noted, for 2021 the base for the eligible dependant credit is $13,808 or less, the same value that is used for the basic personal credit and the spousal credit. As was the case with the spousal credit, if the eligible dependant is dependent because of a mental or physical infirmity, an additional $2,295 is added to the 2021 base, bringing the total to $16,103. The amount of the base is reduced by the eligible dependant's net income for the year. As was the case with the spousal credit, the infirmity does not have to be severe enough to qualify for the disability tax credit. For 2021, the calculation of the eligible dependant credit is as follows:

Eligible Dependant Credit—Is Not Infirm
[(15%)(BPA - eligible dependant's net income)]

Eligible Dependant Credit—Is Infirm and Is Not under 18
[(15%)(BPA + $2,295 - eligible dependant's net income)]

In the second calculation we have shown that the additional amount of $2,295 is not available for a child under 18, but this is not entirely accurate and requires some clarification. The additional amount is available for a child under 18 but is handled through a separate provision of the ITA. This is discussed further at Paragraph 4-62.

4-60. As an example, consider an unmarried person with taxable income of $100,000 who supports a parent who has net income of $5,200. The total personal credits under ITA 118(1)(b) if the parent (1) was not mentally or physically infirm and (2) was dependent because of a mental or physical infirmity would be calculated as follows:

Eligible dependant	Not Infirm	Infirm
Basic personal amount (for individual)	$13,808	$13,808
Eligible dependant amount ($13,808 - $5,200)	8,608	
Eligible dependant amount ($13,808 + $2,295 - $5,200)		10,903
Credit base	$22,416	$24,711
Rate	15%	15%
Personal tax credits (individual and eligible dependant)	$ 3,362	$ 3,707

4-61. Note that this credit provides for the same total credits that would be available to an individual with a spouse who had net income of $5,200 (see Paragraph 4-49). For this reason, it is sometimes referred to as the equivalent to spouse tax credit.

Canada Caregiver Amount for Child—ITA 118(1)(b.1)

4-62. There is no general tax credit available for a child who is under 18 at the end of the taxation year. However, in those cases where such a child has a mental or physical infirmity, ITA 118(1)(b.1) provides a credit based on the 2021 base amount of $2,295 that is not reduced by any net income of the child. The credit applies where (1) an infirm child lives with both parents and (2) an infirm child lives with a single person who also claims the eligible dependant credit for the child or who could have claimed the eligible dependant credit if the child had no net income. The $2,295 is not added to the BPA for that credit. The $2,295 is treated as a separate credit without an income threshold. We will discuss in detail the meaning of mental or physical infirmity in our coverage of the Canada caregiver credit.

> **EXAMPLE 1** Mr. and Mrs. Barton have a 13-year-old child who has a physical infirmity. The child has net income of $1,000.
>
> **ANALYSIS 1** Either Mr. Barton or Mrs. Barton can claim a credit against tax payable of $344 [(15%)($2,295)].
>
> **EXAMPLE 2** Ms. Barton is divorced and has a 13-year-old child who has a physical infirmity. She had full custody and claims the child as an eligible dependant. The child has net income of $1,000.
>
> **ANALYSIS 2** Ms. Barton can claim this credit against tax payable of $344 [(15%)($2,295)] and can continue to claim the eligible dependant credit based on her BPA less the net income of the child.

Single Persons (Basic Personal Tax Credit)—ITA 118(1)(c)

4-63. Individuals living with a spouse, common-law partner, or eligible dependant receive a credit for themselves and their spouse or common-law partner under ITA 118(1)(a), or themselves and their eligible dependant under ITA 118(1)(b). For individuals who do not have a spouse, common-law partner, or eligible dependant, a basic personal tax credit is received under ITA 118(1)(c). This credit is equal to 15% of their BPA.

> **EXAMPLE** Jason Broad is 35 years old, single, has net income that is less than $151,978, is not in a common-law partnership, and has no dependants.
>
> **ANALYSIS** Jason can claim a tax credit against tax payable of $2,071 [(15%)($13,808)].

Canada Caregiver Tax Credit—ITA 118(1)(d)

Eligibility

4-64. This credit is available to an individual who supports a mentally or physically infirm individual who is either:

- a spouse or common-law partner of the individual; or
- a dependant who, in the year, is 18 years of age or older.

4-65. The term "dependant" for purposes of this credit is defined at ITA 118(6) and means the child or grandchild of the individual; the child or grandchild of the individual's spouse or common-law partner; or the parent, grandparent, brother, sister, uncle, aunt, niece, or nephew of the individual or of the individual's spouse or common-law partner.

Mental or Physical Infirmity

4-66. In our presentation on the spousal and eligible dependant credits, we noted that an extra base amount is available when the spouse or eligible dependant is mentally or physically infirm.

Mental or physical infirmity is also an eligibility requirement for the Canada caregiver credit. Given this, it is important to have some understanding of this concept.

4-67. The disability tax credit is discussed later in this chapter. This fairly substantial credit is available to an individual having one or more severe and prolonged impairments in physical or mental functions. For example, the disability tax credit would be available to an individual who could not dress or feed themselves.

4-68. It is clear that an individual who qualifies for the disability tax credit would also qualify for the Canada caregiver amount and for the extra base amount that can be added to the spousal and eligible dependant amounts. It is also clear that an individual with a less severe impairment could qualify for these amounts.

4-69. While there have been a number of court cases that have discussed the meaning of mental or physical infirmity, no consistent definition has emerged. For our purposes in this material, the following description will be used:

> The term mental or physical infirmity is not defined in the ITA and, therefore, it should be applied using its ordinary meaning. The standard dictionary meaning of an infirmity is a physical or mental weakness or ailment. The CRA is of the view that the degree of the infirmity must be such that it is expected to last for a considerable period of time. As a result, any temporary illness or injury would not be considered to meet the infirmity threshold.

Calculation of the Canada Caregiver Credit

4-70. The 2021 base amount for this credit is $7,348, reduced by the eligible individual's net income in excess of $17,256. This produces a maximum credit of $1,102 [(15%)($7,348)].

> **EXAMPLE** Jake Nicholsen's spouse has a mental infirmity. Her 2021 net income is $21,785.
>
> **ANALYSIS** Jake's caregiver credit would be equal to $423 {[15%][$7,348 - ($21,785 - $17,256)]}

4-71. Several other points are relevant here:

- Unlike the eligible dependant credit of ITA 118(1)(b) where a credit can be claimed for only one eligible dependant, the Canada caregiver credit can be claimed for each and every eligible individual. In addition, the Canada caregiver credit can be shared among supporting individuals as long as it is agreed upon between them.
- If an individual is entitled to claim a person for a spousal or eligible dependant credit, they would not be permitted to claim that person for the Canada caregiver credit (ITA 118(4)(c)).
- An individual will not be able to claim the Canada caregiver credit for a particular person if the individual is required to pay a support amount for that person to their current or former spouse or common-law partner.
- There is no requirement that the infirm dependant live in the caregiver's home in order to claim the Canada caregiver credit.
- Except in the case of children or grandchildren, to qualify for the Canada caregiver credit the infirm dependant must be a resident of Canada.

Exercise 4-3

Subject: Canada Caregiver Tax Credit

Joan Barton lives with her husband whose net income is $5,000. Two years ago her father and mother moved in with her. The father, who is 69 years old, is still very active. However, her 67-year-old mother is dependent because of a physical infirmity, but the infirmity is not severe enough to qualify for the disability tax credit. Her father's 2021 net income is $25,300. The corresponding amount for her mother is $21,400. Determine the amount of Joan's Canada caregiver tax credit, if any, for 2021.

Exercise 4-4

Subject: Infirm Spouse and Infirm Adult Child

Marcia Flood is married to Josh Flood. Josh has a mental infirmity. They have a 20-year-old son who has a physical infirmity. Neither infirmity is severe enough to qualify for the disability tax credit. Josh has 2021 net income of $5,600. Their son has no net income for 2021. Determine the amount of any 2021 tax credits that Marcia will have related to her spouse and son.

Exercise 4-5

Subject: Infirm Eligible Dependant Who Is a Child under 18

Darcy Gates is a single father who takes care of his nine-yearold daughter, Janice. Janice has a physical infirmity, but the infirmity is not severe enough to qualify for the disability tax credit. Janice has no net income for 2021. Determine the amount of any 2021 tax credits that Darcy will have related to his daughter.

Solutions to Exercises are available in the Study Guide.

Canada Caregiver Credit—Additional Amount [ITA 118(1)(e) & 118(4)(c)]

4-72. ITA 118(4)(c) provides a rule that prohibits an individual from claiming the Canada caregiver credit under ITA 118(1)(d) if the individual would be entitled to claim either the spousal or eligible dependant credit for that person. This means that it is the entitlement alone that prevents the ability to claim the Canada caregiver credit rather than an actual claim. This can create a problem, however, since the spousal tax credit and the eligible dependant tax credit are eroded on a dollar-for-dollar basis by the spouse or eligible dependant's net income. In the case of infirm spouses or eligible dependants, for 2021, these credits will be completely eliminated when their net income reaches $16,103 ($13,808 + $2,295).

4-73. In contrast, the Canada caregiver credit is only subject to reduction when the spouse or eligible dependant's income reaches $17,256 and eliminated altogether when net income reaches $24,604 [$7,348- ($24,604- $17,256)]. This means that if the net income of the infirm dependant is between $8,756 and $24,603, the tax credit base that would have been determined under the Canada caregiver credit of ITA 118(1)(d) will always exceed the tax credit base determined under ITA 118(1)(b). In this situation the income tax policy is that the individual making the claim should be allowed the larger amount determined under ITA 118(1)(d). To compensate for this loss of potential tax credit base attributable to different income thresholds in the two provisions, ITA 118(1)(e) provides an additional amount of credit base equal to the difference.

EXAMPLE Mark Stucky has an infirm spouse. Assume the spouse's 2021 net income is (1) $20,000 and (2) $10,000.

ANALYSIS—$20,000 The tax credit base for Mark's spousal credit would be nil ($13,808 + $2,295 - $20,000). The tax credit base for the Canada caregiver credit would be $4,604 [$7,348 - ($20,000 - $17,256)]. Given this, the additional amount would be $4,604 ($4,604 + nil).

ANALYSIS—$10,000 The base for Mark's spousal credit would $6,103 ($13,808 + $2,295 - $10,000). The base for the Canada caregiver credit would be $7,348. Given this, the additional amount would be $1,245 ($7,348 - $6,103). When this additional amount is added to the base for the spousal credit, the total is $7,348 ($6,103 + $1,245). The additional amount restores the Canada caregiver amount to what it would have been if not for the two different income thresholds.

Exercise 4-6

Subject: Canada Caregiver Tax Credit—Additional Amount

Sandy Hill is single and lives with her 63-year-old mother, Ariel. Ariel has a physical infirmity, but the infirmity is not severe enough to qualify for the disability tax credit. Ariel has 2021 net income of $18,000. Determine the amount of any 2021 tax credits that Sandy will have related to her mother.

Solutions to Exercises are available in the Study Guide.

Other Tax Credits for Individuals

Age Tax Credit—ITA 118(2)

4-74. Individuals are eligible for an additional tax credit each year beginning with the year of their 65th birthday. The credit is determined under ITA 118(2) and provides for a tax credit base of $7,713, which is reduced by an income threshold based on 15% of the individual's net income in excess of $38,893. This means that the tax credit base disappears altogether at an income level of $90,313 [($7,713 ÷ 15%) + $38,893].

EXAMPLE A 67-year-old individual has 2021 net income of $40,000.

ANALYSIS The tax credit base of the age credit would equal of $7,547 [$7,713 - (15%) ($40,000 - $38,893)]. The actual credit amount that would then reduce gross federal taxes payable would be $1,132 [(15%)($7,547)].

TIP There are two applications of 15% in this credit. The first occurs as part of determining the tax credit base and the second occurs when the resulting tax credit base is multiplied by 15% to calculate the amount that actually reduces gross federal taxes payable.

4-75. While the age credit is a non-refundable credit, as are most of the tax credits, any unused credit can be transferred to a spouse or common-law partner. Tax credit transfers between spouses and common-law partners will be discussed later in this chapter.

Exercise 4-7

Subject: Age Tax Credit

Joshua Smythe is 72 years old and has 2021 net income of $51,500. Determine the tax credit base for Mr. Smythe's age credit for 2021 and the amount that can be applied against his gross federal tax payable.

Solutions to Exercises are available in the Study Guide.

Pension Income Tax Credit—ITA 118(3)

General Rules

4-76. The pension income credit is equal to 15% of the first $2,000 of eligible pension income. This results in a maximum value of $300 [(15%)($2,000)]. The base for this credit is not indexed for inflation and has been $2,000 since 2006.

4-77. The credit is only available with respect to "eligible pension income." Eligible pension income is defined at ITA 118(7) as meaning (1) "pension income" for those individuals 65 and over and (2) "qualified pension income" for those individuals 64 and younger. Individuals are not allowed to claim the pension credit for the following types of payments:

- Payments under the *Old Age Security Act* or *Canada Pension Plan Act*
- Payments under certain provincial pension plans
- Payments under salary deferral arrangements
- Payments under retirement compensation arrangements
- Payments under an employee benefit plan
- Death benefits

4-78. Like the age credit, if an individual does not have sufficient tax payable to use this credit, it can be transferred to a spouse or common-law partner.

Individuals 65 or Over

4-79. For an individual who has reached age 65 before the end of the year, the pension credit is available on "pension income," which includes the following types of payments:

- Life annuity payments from a registered pension plan (RPP)
- An annuity payment out of a registered retirement savings plan (RRSP)
- A payment out of a registered retirement income fund (RRIF)
- An annuity payment from a deferred profit-sharing plan (DPSP)
- The interest component of other annuities

The ITA defines an "annuity" as amounts payable on a periodic basis at intervals that can be shorter or longer than one year.

Individuals under 65

4-80. For an individual who has not reached age 65 during the year, the pension credit is based on "qualified pension income." In general, this only includes life annuity payments from a registered pension plan. However, if the other types of pension income described in Paragraph 4-79 are received as a consequence of the death of a spouse or common-law partner, these amounts will also qualify for the pension credit, regardless of the age of the recipient.

Canada Employment Tax Credit—ITA 118(10)

4-81. This credit is available to all individuals who have employment income. From a conceptual point of view, it is designed to provide limited recognition of the fact that there are costs associated with earning employment income. As only limited deductions are available against employment income, as discussed in Chapter 3, this would appear to be an appropriate form of relief.

4-82. For 2021, the amount of the tax credit base is equal to 15% of the lesser of:

- $1,257, or
- all of an individual's income from employment (e.g., including taxable benefits, taxable allowances, stock option benefits, and salary and wages) without considering any employment expenses.

4-83. For most employed individuals, this will generate a reduction in gross federal taxes payable of $189 [(15%)($1,257)].

Adoption Expenses Tax Credit—ITA 118.01

4-84. The adoption expenses tax credit is available to an individual who adopts an "eligible child." As defined in ITA 118.01(1), an eligible child is a child who is under 18 years of age at the time that an adoption order is issued or recognized by a government in Canada in respect of the adoption of that child. For 2021, the indexed base for this credit is up to $16,729 of eligible adoption expenses. This provides a maximum credit of $2,509 [(15%)($16,729)].

4-85. The adoption expenses can only be claimed in the year in which the adoption is finalized. The total amount of eligible expenses is reduced by any reimbursement of adoption expenses or other types of financial assistance that is received unless the amounts are included in the individual's net income. Normally, if an employer reimburses any portion of an employee's adoption expenses, this amount will be treated as a taxable benefit. Given this, such amounts will not be deducted from the adoption expenses that form the basis for this credit as they will be included in the individual's employment income and therefore net income.

4-86. To qualify, eligible adoption expenses must be incurred during the "adoption period" (see next paragraph) and, as defined in ITA 118.01(1), include:

(a) fees paid to an adoption agency licensed by a provincial government;
(b) court costs and legal and administrative expenses related to an adoption order in respect of that child;
(c) reasonable and necessary travel and living expenses of the child and the adoptive parents;
(d) document translation fees;
(e) mandatory fees paid to a foreign institution;
(f) mandatory expenses paid in respect of the immigration of the child; and
(g) any other reasonable expenses related to the adoption required by a provincial government or an adoption agency licensed by a provincial government.

4-87. An "adoption period" is also defined in ITA 118.01(1) as follows:

It begins at the earlier of:

- the time that an application is made for registration with a provincial ministry responsible for adoption (or with an adoption agency licensed by a provincial government); or
- the time, if any, that an application related to the adoption is made to a Canadian court; and

It ends at the later of:

- the time an adoption order is issued by, or recognized by, a government in Canada in respect of that child; or
- the time that the child first begins to reside permanently with the individual.

4-88. In the usual situation, a child will be adopted by a couple, either legally married or cohabiting on a common-law basis. The rules recognize that more than one individual may be entitled to claim adoption expenses, allowing the adoption credit to be shared in any manner the individuals choose as long as the total amount claimed does not exceed the actual allowable amount. Accordingly, the claim can be made by either individual or split at their discretion.

Exercise 4-8

Subject: Adoption Expenses Tax Credit

Ary Kapit and his spouse have adopted an infant orphan. The adoption process began in June 2020 when they applied to an adoption agency licensed by the provincial government. Later that year they travelled to the foreign country to discuss an adoption. The cost of this trip was $4,250. Their provincial government opened the adoption file on February 13, 2021, and the adoption order was issued on August 27, 2021. In September, the couple returned to the country to pick up their new daughter. The happy family returns to Canada on September 18, 2021. The cost of this trip is $6,420.

Additional expenses paid during the first week of September 2021 were $1,600 paid to the foreign orphanage and $3,200 paid to a Canadian adoption agency. Legal fees incurred during the adoption period were $2,700. After arrival in Canada, an additional

$2,500 in medical expenses were incurred for the child prior to the end of 2021. Mr. Kapit's employer has a policy of providing reimbursement for up to $5,000 in adoption expenses eligible for the adoption expenses tax credit. This amount is received in September 2021 and will be considered a taxable employment benefit to Mr. Kapit. What is the maximum adoption expenses tax credit that can be claimed by the couple?

Solutions to Exercises are available in the Study Guide.

Digital News Subscriptions Credit—ITA 118.02

4-89. The 2019 budget provides for a temporary (2020 through 2024) credit for digital subscriptions with a qualifying Canadian journalism organization. The base for the credit is limited to $500 of the cost of such subscriptions. This provides for a maximum credit of $75 [(15%)($500)] starting in 2020. The $500 is not indexed nor is the credit refundable. The credit will typically apply to online news subscription services.

4-90. A qualifying Canadian journalism organization is defined as a corporation, partnership, or trust that is primarily engaged in the production of original news content. The news content must be of general interest or related to current events and must not be focused on a specific topic, such as sports or the arts. In addition, the organization must employ two or more arm's-length journalists in the production of its content.

Home Accessibility Tax Credit—ITA 118.041

Described

4-91. The government provides a non-refundable tax credit for renovations that will allow seniors and persons with disabilities to live more independently at home. The base for the credit is equal to the lesser of $10,000 and the amount of qualifying expenditures for the year. This means that the maximum credit amount that will reduce gross federal taxes payable is $1,500 [(15%)($10,000)]. The $10,000 limit is not indexed.

4-92. The credit is available to a qualifying individual or an eligible individual for qualifying expenditures on an eligible dwelling.

4-93. As is often the case with income tax legislation, this basic tax credit provision is supported by multiple defined terms that require further explanation. These explanations follow.

Qualifying and Eligible Individuals

4-94. A qualifying individual is an individual who is 65 years of age or older or who is eligible to claim the disability tax credit.

4-95. An eligible individual is a qualifying individual's spouse or common-law partner, or an individual who has claimed, or could have claimed under certain conditions, the eligible dependant or Canada caregiver credit for the qualifying individual. It would normally be a relative who ordinarily inhabits the same dwelling as the qualifying individual.

Eligible Dwelling

4-96. To begin, an eligible dwelling is a housing unit located in Canada. It must be owned by the qualifying individual or by an eligible individual. While it will usually be the principal residence of the individual, this is not a requirement. It can be a house, cottage, or condominium, but it cannot be a rented dwelling.

4-97. The credit can be shared where there is a qualifying individual and eligible individuals as long as the total claim does not exceed the $10,000 limit for that dwelling in the year. If there is more than one qualifying individual for an eligible dwelling, the total qualifying expenses remain at $10,000 for the dwelling. If the qualifying individual has more than one eligible dwelling in a year, the $10,000 limit applies irrespective of the number of such dwellings.

Qualifying Renovations and Expenditures

4-98. To be considered a qualifying expenditure in a qualifying renovation, the renovation or alteration must be made to allow the qualifying individual to gain access to, or to be more mobile or functional within the dwelling, or to reduce the risk of harm to the qualifying individual either when gaining access to the home or within the dwelling itself. The improvements must be of an enduring nature and be considered integral to the eligible dwelling. As a general rule, if the item purchased will not become a permanent part of the dwelling, it is not eligible.

4-99. Qualifying expenses can include materials, fixtures, labour, or professional services. Any work performed by professionals (e.g., electricians, plumbers) will qualify, however if the professional is related to a qualifying or eligible individual the work performed will only qualify if that professional is registered for the GST/HST. The credit will only apply to work performed in the year or goods acquired in that particular year. The expenses otherwise qualify if they are made or incurred in the year, meaning that it is not necessary that they be actually paid in the same year. Any expenses claimed for the home accessibility tax credit must be supported by receipts. This is expected to help the CRA battle the underground economy as receipts will be needed for qualifying labour in order to claim the credit.

4-100. Although the CRA website does not provide a list of qualifying expenditures, it does provide a list of some of the expenses that are not eligible for the credit, such as outdoor maintenance services and electronic home entertainment devices. Some renovations that would clearly qualify would be wheelchair ramps or lifts, walk-in bathtubs, and wheel-in showers.

4-101. Note that some expenditures would qualify for both this credit and the medical expense tax credit. For example, the cost of installing a ramp for a qualifying individual who is in a wheelchair would be a qualifying expenditure for both credits. Interestingly, the legislation is clear that, in cases such as this, the expenditures can be used in determining the base for both of these credits. This, in effect, results in a double credit for the same expenditure.

Exercise 4-9

Subject: Home Accessibility Tax Credit

Della and Marcus Jacobs are married and they are both aged 68. They jointly own the house they live in. Because a recent automobile accident damaged his back, Marcus has limited mobility and has great difficulty climbing stairs. During 2021, they spent $8,500 installing a ramp to replace the steps to the front door and $2,000 for a snow removal contract as Marcus was no longer able to shovel the snow. What is the maximum home accessibility credit that can be claimed for the 2021 taxation year, and who should claim it?

Solutions to Exercises are available in the Study Guide.

First-Time Home Buyers' Tax Credit—ITA 118.05

4-102. A tax credit is available for first-time home buyers who acquire a qualifying home in Canada. The credit is equal to 15% of the first $5,000 of the cost of a qualifying home, resulting in a maximum credit of $750 [(15%)($5,000)]. This amount is not indexed nor is it refundable. To be eligible for the credit, the buyer must intend to occupy the home no later than one year after its acquisition.

4-103. An individual will be considered a first-time home buyer if neither the individual nor the individual's spouse or common-law partner owned and lived in another home in the calendar year of the home purchase or in any of the four preceding calendar years.

4-104. The credit may be claimed by the individual who acquires the home or by that individual's spouse or common-law partner. For the purpose of this credit, a home is considered to be acquired by an individual only if the individual's interest in the home is registered in accordance with the applicable land registration system.

Volunteer Firefighters and Volunteer Search and Rescue Workers Tax Credits—ITA 118.06 and 118.07

4-105. A credit is made available for both volunteer firefighters and volunteer search and rescue workers. The required services are defined in the ITA as follows.

> **Volunteer Firefighters Services** In ITA 118.06 and ITA 118.07, "eligible volunteer firefighting services" means services provided by an individual in the individual's capacity as a volunteer firefighter to a fire department that consist primarily of responding to and being on call for firefighting and related emergency calls, attending meetings held by the fire department, and participating in required training related to the prevention or suppression of fires, but does not include services provided to a particular fire department if the individual provides firefighting services to the department otherwise than as a volunteer (e.g., as an employee).
>
> **Volunteer Search and Rescue Workers Services** This means services, other than eligible volunteer firefighting services, provided by an individual in the individual's capacity as a volunteer to an eligible search and rescue organization that consist primarily of responding to and being on call for search and rescue and related emergency calls, attending meetings held by the organization, and participating in required training related to search and rescue services, but does not include services provided to an organization if the individual provides search and rescue services to the organization otherwise than as a volunteer (e.g., as an employee).

4-106. Except for the type of services rendered, the conditions of service for the two types of credits are similar.

4-107. For either type of volunteer, at least 200 hours of volunteer service must be performed during the year to be eligible for the relevant credit. The required 200 hours can be solely one type of volunteer service or, alternatively, a combination of both types of services. The base for the non-refundable credit is $3,000, resulting in a credit of $450 [(15%)($3,000)]. This amount is not indexed.

4-108. Other relevant considerations are as follows:

- Individuals are required to take the credit that corresponds to the primary services they provide. For example, a firefighter who occasionally volunteers for search and rescue must take the volunteer firefighter credit. The legislation is written such that only one of the two credits can be claimed in any one year.
- Under ITA 81(4), there is an optional exemption from inclusion in net income for up to $1,000 in compensation per eligible employer received for these types of volunteer work. This exemption is only available to individuals who do not claim either of the two volunteer tax credits. Stated alternatively, an individual cannot have both the exemption and the tax credits.

Charitable Donations Tax Credit—ITA 118.1

Extent of Coverage in This Chapter

4-109. For income tax purposes, donations, even in the form of cash, are segregated into categories, each with a different set of rules. Additional complications arise when non-cash donations are made. To be able to deal with gifts of depreciable property, an understanding of capital gains and capital cost allowance (CCA, e.g., tax depreciation) is required. Given these complications, a comprehensive treatment of charitable gifts is deferred until we revisit taxable income and tax payable in Chapter 11. However, we do provide limited coverage of charitable donations in this chapter.

Eligible Gifts

4-110. In our coverage of donations in this chapter, we will deal only with cash gifts. Donations of other types of property are covered in Chapter 11.

4-111. In this chapter, our coverage will be limited to what is referred to in ITA 118.1 as total charitable gifts. These include amounts donated to entities such as:

- a registered charity;
- a registered Canadian amateur athletic association;
- registered news organizations;
- a Canadian municipality;
- the Canadian government;
- a university outside of Canada that normally enrolls Canadian students; and
- a charitable organization outside of Canada to which the Canadian government made a gift in the current or preceding year. In addition, a provision exists that allows the federal government to provide a limited 24-month registration for foreign charities that are involved in relief and humanitarian aid, provided the activities are in the national interest of Canada.

Limits on Amount Claimed

4-112. It is the policy of the government to limit the amount of charitable donations that are eligible for the charitable tax credit to a portion of a taxpayer's net income. Note that, while corporations deduct their donations from taxable income as opposed to receiving a income tax credit against gross federal taxes payable, the general limits on the amount of eligible donations are the same for corporations as they are for individuals.

4-113. The general limit on eligible amounts of charitable gifts is 75% of net income. For individuals, this limit is increased to 100% of net income in the year of death and the preceding year.

Calculating the Donation Credit

4-114. All of the credits that we have discussed to this point apply the lowest federal bracket of 15% to some defined base. In contrast, this credit's calculation uses a combination of three possible rates—15%, 29%, and 33%. This reflects the belief that if the credit was only at 15%, high-income individuals would not have an adequate incentive to make charitable donations.

4-115. The formula for calculating the credit for individuals is found in ITA 118.1(3). Stated in a somewhat more understandable fashion, it is as follows:

[(15%)(A)] + [(33%)(B)] + [(29%)(C)], where

A = The first $200 of eligible gifts.

B = The lesser of:

- the amount by which total eligible gifts exceed $200; or
- the amount, if any, by which the individual's taxable income for the year exceeds $216,511, which is indexed annually.

C = The amount, if any, by which the individual's total gifts exceed the sum of $200 plus the amount determined in B.

Note If the taxpayer's taxable income does not exceed $216,511, the lesser amount of component B will be nil. This means that none of the credit is based on the 33% rate, as none of the taxable income would be taxed at that rate. In these situations, the credit calculation is simply 15% of the first $200 of eligible gifts plus 29% of any eligible gifts in excess of $200.

4-116. The following example will serve to illustrate the application of this formula:

EXAMPLE For 2021, Doyle McLaughlin has net income of $620,000 and taxable income of $600,000. During the year, Doyle makes eligible gifts of $300,000.

ANALYSIS The maximum base for his charitable donations credit would be $465,000 [(75%)($620,000)]. Doyle's charitable donations tax credit would be calculated as follows (note that taxable income is used in the following calculation):

A = $200
B = The lesser of:
- $300,000 - $200 = $299,800
- $600,000 - $216,511 = $383,489 = the income taxed at 33%

C = Nil [$300,000 - ($200 + $299,800)]

The charitable donation credit would be equal to $98,964, calculated as [(15%)($200)] + [(33%)($299,800)] + [(29%)(Nil)]. As you would expect with Doyle's taxable income exceeding $216,511 by more than the amount of his eligible donations, none of his credit is based on 29%.

Exercise 4-10

Subject: Charitable Donations Tax Credit

For 2021, Travis Hoffman has net income of $350,000 and taxable income of $325,000. During the year, he makes eligible charitable donations of $225,000. Determine Mr. Hoffman's 2021 charitable donations tax credit.

Solutions to Exercises are available in the Study Guide.

4-117. Technically, individuals are only allowed to claim charitable donations they have personally made. The CRA, however, administratively allows either spouse or common-law partner to claim some or all of the donations made by the other individual. If neither individual has income taxed at 33%, combining the donations is advantageous given the 15% rate on the first $200 of donations. It would also be advantageous if one individual has sufficiently low income that not all of the couple's donations can be claimed, or if only one individual has income that is taxed at 33%. If both individuals have income that will be taxed at 33%, but neither can claim all the donations at that rate, the analysis is more complicated, as splitting the donations could result in a higher combined donations credit. The Intuit ProFile income tax software used in the Tax Software Problems will automatically determine the optimal split.

Carry Forward of Charitable Donations

4-118. With the limit set at 75% of net income, individuals will normally be able to claim all of the donations they make in a year. However, if donations exceed the 75% limit, a choice can be made not to claim all of the donations that year. Any unused amounts can be carried forward. The carry forward period is generally five years. However, for ecological gifts, the period is 10 years. Charitable donations may not be carried back to previous years.

4-119. A further point here is that this limit is based on net income. This means that an individual could have eligible donations in excess of taxable income. This could occur, for example, if an individual had Division C deductions that reduced taxable income such as the deduction of a large loss carry forward from a previous year. In situations such as this, it is important to recognize that the charitable donations tax credit is non-refundable. Given this, only the amount of donations required to reduce tax payable to nil should be claimed. Any additional amounts should be carried forward to future years. Any actual claim in excess of gross federal taxes payable would otherwise be lost.

EXAMPLE Barry Mann has net income of $80,000. This is further reduced to a taxable income of $20,000 because of the deduction of a non-capital loss carry forward from a previous year. Because of a fortuitous lottery win, he chooses to make a charitable donation of $100,000.

ANALYSIS The potential base for Barry's charitable donations tax credit is $60,000 [(75%)($80,000)]. However, if he were to claim this amount, the credit of $17,372 [(15%)($200) + (29%)($59,800)] would be far in excess of the tax payable on only $20,000 of taxable income. Claiming the maximum amount would result in simply losing the greater part of the available credit. The preferable alternative would be to claim only enough to reduce his tax payable to nil and carry the unused donations forward to another year.

4-120. Determining the amounts that will reduce taxable income to nil will be discussed in Chapter 11.

Exercise 4-11

Subject: Charitable Donations Tax Credit Carry Forward

For 2021, Terry Hoffman has net income of $350,000 and taxable income of $250,000. She has a charitable donation carry forward from 2020 of $225,000. Determine Ms. Hoffman's 2021 charitable donations tax credit. Until what year can she claim any unused portions of her 2020 donation?

Solutions to Exercises are available in the Study Guide.

Medical Expense Tax Credit—ITA 118.2

Qualifying Medical Expenses

4-121. There are many types of medical expenses that qualify for the credit under ITA 118.2. (For more detailed information, see Income Tax Folio S1-F1-C1, "*Medical Expense Tax Credit.*") The current list of qualifying medical expenses includes amounts paid for:

- the services of authorized medical practitioners, dentists, and registered nurses;
- prescribed drugs, medicaments, and other preparations or substances, including cannabis products used for medical purposes;
- prescription eyeglasses or contact lenses;
- preventive, diagnostic, and other laboratory work;
- dentures;
- premiums to private health services plans;
- the costs of home modifications for those with severe mobility restrictions and to allow individuals confined to a wheelchair to be mobile within their home (see also the related home accessibility credit coverage beginning in Paragraph 4-91);
- guide and hearing-ear dogs and other specially trained animals, such as service animals trained to help an individual manage severe diabetes;
- artificial limbs, aids, and other devices and equipment;
- products required because of incontinence;
- oxygen tents;
- the cost of rehabilitative therapy to adjust for speech or hearing loss;
- devices and equipment listed in ITR 5700 and prescribed by a medical practitioner;
- amounts paid for the design of an individualized therapy plan in situations where the cost of the therapy would be eligible for the medical expense tax credit.

4-122. The methodology for determining whether a specific medical expense qualifies for the medical expense tax credit is as follows: (1) identifying if the expense is described in ITA 118.2(2) and any conditions required to be met, and (2) if the expenditure is for a medical device or equipment if the device or equipment is specifically identified in ITR 5700 along with the purpose and reason for the purchase. If a medical expense does not meet either of these two tests, the expense will not qualify.

4-123. Although payments for attendants, nursing home care, and care in an institution are qualifying medical expenses, there are many complications with claiming these expenses since there may be alternative and preferable ways of claiming them. They will be briefly covered after the disability tax credit has been discussed.

4-124. Costs incurred for purely cosmetic reasons do not qualify for the medical expense tax credit because they do not meet either of the two tests discussed in Paragraph 4-122. Examples of non-qualifying procedures include liposuction, hair replacement procedures, Botox injections, and teeth whitening. Cosmetic procedures do qualify if they are required for medical or reconstructive purposes (e.g., facial surgery required due to a car accident).

4-125. Medical expenses may be specifically identified as meeting the conditions, including reason and purpose, but often the expenditure will fail to qualify unless it is prescribed by a medical practitioner. It is the provinces and territories who control the identification of authorized medical practitioners for the purposes of this credit. The CRA website contains a current list of these authorized medical practitioners by province. For example, acupuncturists are considered authorized in Alberta, British Columbia, Newfoundland and Labrador, Ontario, and Quebec, but not in other provinces. Homeopaths are currently authorized medical practitioners only in Ontario. This means that there is considerable variation between the provinces in the types of costs that qualify for the medical expense tax credit.

Determining the Credit

4-126. Qualifying medical expenses of an individual do not include any expense for which the individual has been or is entitled to be reimbursed unless the amount is required to be included in income. Any amount reimbursed under a public or private medical, dental, or hospitalization plan would not qualify for purposes of the medical expense tax credit, although the premiums paid for such plans would usually qualify.

4-127. The medical expense tax credit is determined by the following formula:

A [(B - C) + D], where

A is the appropriate percentage for the taxation year (15%)

B is the total of eligible medical expenses for an individual, their spouse or common-law partner, and any children who are under 18 years of age at the end of the year

C is the lesser of 3% of the individual's net income and $2,421 (2021 indexed amount). Note that the B - C total cannot be negative

D is the total of all amounts each of which is, in respect of a dependant of the individual (other than a child of the individual who is under 18 years of age before the end of the year), the amount determined by the formula

E - F, where

E is the total of the dependant's medical expenses

F is the lesser of 3% of the dependant's net income and $2,421 (2021 amount)

4-128. Dependants for this purpose has the same meaning described in Paragraph 4-65. If the individual has no dependants who are 18 years of age or older, components D, E, and F in the formula are not relevant and can be ignored. In this case, the B component is equal to the total of the qualifying medical expenses of the individual, their spouse or common-law partner, and minor children. This balance is reduced by the C component, the lesser of 3% of the individual's net income, and an indexed figure that for 2021 is equal to $2,421. This latter figure is the limiting factor if an individual's 2021 net income is $80,700 ($2,421 ÷ 3%) or higher.

4-129. If the individual has dependants who are 18 years of age or older, a separate credit base calculation is required for each of the dependants. The tax credit base is equal to the dependant's qualifying medical expenses, reduced by the lesser of 3% of the dependant's net income and $2,421 (E and F in the formula). The individual adds the total of these amounts to the tax credit base calculated for the individual, spouse, or common-law partner and any minor children.

4-130. Technically, only the individual who actually pays the expense is entitled to claim a medical expense tax credit. Administratively, however, the CRA allows either spouse to claim the medical expense credit, without regard to who actually paid for the expenses. The T1 guide even includes a tax tip, which suggests that since the credit can be claimed by either spouse or common-law partner, a comparison should be made to choose the best result.

Twelve-Month Period

4-131. Medical expenses can be claimed for any period of 12 months that ends in the year. This provision is extended to 24 months in the year of death. The ability to claim expenses for a 12-month period ending in the year is advantageous for individuals with large medical expenses for a 12-month period that overlaps two calendar years. Once a 12-month period has been chosen there is no requirement to use the same 12-month period each year thereafter. The rule is that the period must end in the year and one is only allowed to claim medical expenses in that period to the extent they have not been claimed in a previous year.

EXAMPLE Alex Lau has net income of $60,000 in both 2020 and 2021. In July 2020 he began a year-long corrective dental surgery program. During July to December 2020 he paid $10,000 in dental fees. During January to June 2021 he paid $12,000 in dental fees.

ANALYSIS The 2020 claim for $10,000 could be deferred and instead $22,000 could be claimed in 2021. The advantage of doing this is that the threshold amount reduction would be applied only once in 2021. If medical expenses had to be claimed in the year in which they were incurred, Mr. Lau would have to apply the threshold reduction of $1,800 [(3%)($60,000)] in both years. If the full amount is claimed in 2021, federal income tax savings would total $270 [(15%)($1,800)].

Example of Medical Expense Tax Credit Calculation

4-132. The following example will illustrate the medical expense tax credit formula:

EXAMPLE Sam Jonas and his dependent family members had the following net income and medical expenses for 2021. Sam paid for all of the medical expenses.

Individual	Net Income	Medical Expenses
Sam Jonas	$100,000	$ 5,000
Kelly (Sam's wife)	12,000	4,400
Sue (Sam's 16-year-old daughter)	8,500	4,100
Sharon (Sam's 69-year-old mother)	6,000	16,500
Martin (Sam's 70-year-old father)	12,000	200
Total medical expenses		$30,200

ANALYSIS Sam's 2020 medical expense tax credit, using the formula in Paragraph 4-127, would be calculated as follows:

Amount B Qualifying expenses ($5,000 + $4,400 + $4,100)		$13,500
Amount C Lesser of:		
• [(3%)($100,000)] = $3,000		
• 2021 threshold amount = $2,421		(2,421)
Subtotal		$11,079
Amount D		
Sharon's medical expenses	$16,500	
Reduced by the lesser of:		
• $2,421		
• [(3%)($6,000)] = $180	(180)	16,320
Martin's medical expenses	$ 200	
Reduced by the lesser of:		
• $2,421		
• [(3%)($12,000)] = $360	(360)	Nil*
Allowable amount of medical expenses		$27,399
Amount A The appropriate rate (minimum rate)		15%
Medical expense tax credit		$ 4,110

*Medical expenses can only be reduced to nil; the net result cannot be negative in this calculation.

Exercise 4-12

Subject: Medical Expense Tax Credit

Ms. Maxine Davies and her spouse, Lance Davies, have 2021 medical expenses totalling $4,330. While Ms. Davies has 2021 net income of $150,000, Lance's only income is $360 in savings account interest. They have three children. Mandy is 12, has 2021 medical expenses of $4,600, and no net income. Max is 21, has 2021 medical expenses of $8,425, and net income of $8,250. Matt is 23, has 2021 medical expenses of $120, and net income of $6,000. Ms. Davies pays all of the medical expenses. Determine Ms. Davies' medical expense tax credit for 2021.

Solutions to Exercises are available in the Study Guide.

Disability Tax Credit—ITA 118.3

Calculation

4-133. The disability tax credit is available under ITA 118.3 and, for 2021, the tax credit base is $8,662 and the amount that reduces gross federal taxes payable is equal to $1,299 [(15%)($8,662)]. In addition, there is a supplement to this amount for a disabled child who is under the age of 18 at the end of the year. For 2021, the base for the supplement is $5,053, providing a total maximum credit amount for a disabled minor of $2,057 [(15%)($8,662 + $5,053)]. Note, however, that the supplement amount of $5,053 is reduced by the total of amounts paid for attendant care or supervision in excess of $2,959 that are deducted as child care expenses (ITA 63), deducted as a disability support amount for attendant care expenses (ITA 64), or claimed as a medical expense in calculating the medical expense tax credit. This means that once such costs reach $8,012 ($5,053 + $2,959) for the year, the supplement for a child is completely eliminated. The child care expense and disability support deduction are "other deductions" that are part of the net income calculation specifically at ITA 3(c), discussed in Chapter 1. These two deductions are covered in Chapter 9.

4-134. To qualify for the disability credit the impairment must be prolonged, meaning that it has lasted or can reasonably be expected to last for a continuous period of at least 12 months. In addition, the effects of the impairment(s) are such that the individual's ability to perform more than one basic activity of daily living is significantly restricted and that the cumulative impact is to markedly restrict the individual's ability to perform such basic tasks that are normally taken for granted. The ITA defines "markedly restricted" in terms where almost all of the time (even with therapy, devices, or medications) the individual requires a disproportionate amount of time to perform basic activities of daily living.

4-135. In general, a medical doctor, nurse practitioner, or optometrist must certify on Form T2201 that a severe physical or mental impairment exists. In the case of restrictions on the ability to walk, a physiotherapist can make the required certification.

4-136. ITA 118.4(1) tries to make the conditions for qualifying for this credit as clear as possible. This provision points out that an individual clearly qualifies if they are blind. The following are listed as basic activities of daily living:

- Mental functions necessary for everyday life (memory, problem solving, goal setting, and judgment). The 2021 federal budget has expanded on these functions to include attention, concentration, perception of reality, regulation of behaviour and emotions, and verbal and non-verbal comprehension.
- Feeding oneself or dressing oneself
- Speaking such that the individual can be understood in a quiet setting by someone familiar with the individual
- Hearing such that the individual can, in a quiet setting, understand someone familiar with the individual
- Bowel or bladder functions
- Walking

Disability Credit Transfer to a Supporting Person

4-137. In many cases, an individual who is sufficiently infirm to qualify for the disability credit will not have sufficient tax payable to use it. In this situation, all or part of the credit may be transferred to a spouse/common-law partner or a supporting person who claimed:

- the disabled individual as an eligible dependant under the ITA 118(1)(b); or
- claimed the Canada caregiver credit under ITA 118(1)(d) for the disabled individual.

The legislation adds hypothetical situations to determine whether the above credits would have been available were it not for the fact that the individual wishing to take advantage of the transfer was married or living in a common-law relationship (which would have prevented an eligible dependant claim) or where the disabled individual was under 18 and had income above the threshold (which would have prevented a Canada caregiver credit claim).

4-138. The tax credit base that can be transferred is the same $8,662 that could be claimed by the disabled individual. Claims by supporting persons other than spouses and common-law partners are not permitted where the spouse or common-law partner of a disabled individual is claiming the disability credit as a transferred credit or has claimed any other non-refundable credit for the disabled spouse or common-law partner under ITA 118. In other words, spouses and common-law partners have preference. However, if the disabled individual has tax payable in excess of credits under ITA 118 (personal credits) to 118.07 (various credits including home accessibility), and 118.7 (CPP and EI credits), the credit must first be applied to reduce the disabled individual's tax payable to nil. If a balance remains after all tax payable has been eliminated, and a spouse or common-law partner has not made a claim, it can then be transferred to a supporting person.

4-139. Income Tax Folio S1-F1-C2, "*Disability Tax Credit,*" provides detailed guidance on the disability tax credit, including its transfer to a supporting person.

Exercise 4-13

Subject: Disability Tax Credit

John Leslie lives with his wife and 21-year-old blind son, Keith, who qualifies for the disability tax credit. Keith has no income of his own. During 2021, John paid medical expenses of $16,240 for Keith. None of these expenses involve attendant care. John's taxable income for 2021 was $100,000. Determine the total amount of tax credits related to Keith that will be available to John.

Solutions to Exercises are available in the Study Guide.

Other Credits and Deductions Related to Disabilities

4-140. Disabled individuals, or a supporting person, may have paid significant medical expenses involving attendant care and/or nursing home care. Both types of care are referred to as "attendant care." In general, the medical expense credit rules allow a claim for part-time attendant care (ITA 118.2(2)(b.1)) and full-time attendant care (ITA 118.2(2)(b)) for a disabled individual. There is, however, an important interaction between the medical expense credit and the disbaility tax credit that depends on whether the attendant care is part time or full time. The interaction can be described as follows:

- Neither the individual, nor a supporting person, can claim the disability credit if a medical expense credit is claimed for a full-time attendant. However, the individual or supporting person can claim the attendant care costs as medical expense tax credits (ITA 118.2(2)(b)). If one wished to claim the disability tax credit, they would have to forgo claiming the full-time attendant care as a medical expense.
- The disability credit can be claimed, however, if a medical expense credit is claimed for part-time attendant care (ITA 118.2(2)(b.1)). Part time is defined as expenses claimed of less than $10,000 for the year ($20,000 in the year of death). Note that part-time attendant care can only be claimed as a medical expense credit if no part of that care is claimed as child care costs or for attendant care required to produce income. This means that an individual can choose to claim a medical expense credit for part-time attendant care limiting the claim to $10,000, or claim the expenses as a deduction for child care expenses or the disability supports deduction assuming that the conditions of those deductions are met.

4-141. For disabled individuals who work, or who attend a designated educational institution or secondary school, the disability supports deduction (ITA 64) provides tax relief for a number of medical expenses, including attendant care, which would assist a disabled person to work or go to school. (See Chapter 9, "Other Income, Other Deductions, and Other Issues," for coverage of this deduction.)

4-142. There are complications and restrictions related to claiming these and many other types of medical expenses. Complete coverage of all the relevant rules goes beyond the scope of this text but is covered in detail in Income Tax Folio 1, "Health and Medical." There are three chapters that provide detailed guidance on the medical expense tax credit (S1-F1-C1), disability tax credit (S1-F1-C2), and disability supports deduction (S1-F1-C3).

Education-Related Tax Credits

Tuition Fees Tax Credit—ITA 118.5(1) to ITA 118.5(4)

4-143. Under ITA 118.5, individuals receive a credit against gross federal tax payable equal to 15% of qualifying tuition fees paid with respect to a specific calendar year, regardless of the year in which the tuition fees are actually paid (i.e., if $5,000 in tuition is owed for the current year and $1,000 of that was prepaid in the preceding calendar year, the tuition fee tax credit base for the current year is $5,000). Tuition fees must total at least $100, but there is no upper limit on this credit. The following tuition fees qualify:

- Tuition fees paid to a university, college, or other institution for post-secondary courses located in Canada.
- Tuition fees paid to an institution certified by the minister of Employment and Social Development for a course that developed or improved skills in an occupation. Fees paid for occupational skills that are not at the post-secondary level qualify for the credit, as long as the course provides the individual with skills in an occupation. An individual must be 16 years of age or older to qualify for the credit.
- Tuition fees paid to a university outside Canada for full-time attendance. To qualify the course must have a minimum duration of three weeks.
- For individuals who live near the U.S. border and commute, tuition fees paid to a U.S. college or university for part-time or full-time studies.

4-144. It is not uncommon for employers to reimburse employees for amounts of tuition paid, particularly if the relevant course is related to the employer's business. If the reimbursement is included in the employee's income, the employee can claim a credit for the tuition paid. However, if amounts reimbursed are not included in the employee's income, the tuition credit is not available.

Online and Correspondence Courses

4-145. The popularity of taking courses online and through correspondence as opposed to physical attendance leads us to question whether physical attendance is necessary and whether fees paid for such education would qualify for the tuition credit. In Paragraph 4-143 the first two bullets refer to universities, colleges,and other educational institutions in Canada without specifying the nature of how courses are attended, and as a result tuition fees would qualify whether they are for physical attendance, online attendance, or a correspondence courses.

4-146. The third and fourth bullets of Paragraph 4-143, however, refer to educational institutions outside Canada, which require full-time attendance or are attended by Canadians living near the border and who commute to those educational institutions in the U.S. In both cases there is a presumption of physical attendance. The CRA recognizes that Canadians can attend an educational institution in the U.S. through online courses as long as the courses are interactive and the educational institution recognizes that online attendance is full-time attendance. In effect, attending classes online would generally qualify. Where commuters attend educational institutions outside Canada, however, attending online would not qualify since one must commute for the tuition to qualify.

4-147. Taking courses through correspondence courses, however, would not be considered attendance since there is "little or no significant interactive, scheduled sessions with either the instructor or other students" (Paragraph 2.20 of Folio S1-F2-C2, "Tuition Tax Credit"). Therefore, the costs of correspondence courses taken from an educational institution outside Canada or for those attending U.S. educational institutions near the border with the U.S. where they live would not qualify for the tuition credit.

4-148. In summary, tuition paid for educational institutions in Canada described in Paragraph 4-143 include fees for actual physical attendance, online attendance, and correspondence courses. Qualifying tuition for attending U.S. educational institutions (other than commuting from Canada to the U.S.) would include physical attendance and online attendance but not correspondence courses. Finally, qualifying tuition for Canadians attending U.S. educational institutions near the border where they live would include physical attendance but not online attendance or correspondence courses.

Ancillary and Examination Fees Included in Tuition Fees Tax Credit

4-149. It has been noted that universities are relying more heavily on ancillary fees for such items as health services, athletics, and various other services, including examinations. To the extent that such fees are required for all full-time students (if the student is attending full time) or all part-time students (if the student is attending part time), these fees are eligible for inclusion in the base for the tuition fees tax credit.

4-150. The general provision of ancillary fees is found in ITA 118.5(3), while the provision for ancillary examination fees is found in ITA 118.5(4).

4-151. If such fees are not required of all full-time or part-time students, ITA 118.5(3) allows up to $250 in such ancillary fees to be added to the total, even if they do not meet the condition of being required for all full- or part-time students.

4-152. In addition, ITA 118.5(4) allows up to $250 in ancillary examination fees to be added to the total if they are not required to be paid by all students taking the examination.

4-153. Eligible fees include amounts for items such as the cost of examination materials or required identification cards. It does not, however, include fees for examinations required for entrance to professional programs. In addition, both of these ancillary fees are only eligible if the tuition fees were paid to a university, college, or other institution for post-secondary courses located in Canada.

Interest on Student Loans Tax Credit—ITA 118.62

4-154. There is a credit available under ITA 118.62 if a student or a related person has paid interest on student loans. The credit for the student is equal to 15% of interest paid in the year or in any of the five preceding years (to the extent that a tax credit was not already claimed). The interest paid must be on a loan under the *Canada Student Loans Act*, the *Canada Student Financial Assistance Act*, the *Apprentice Loans Act*, or a provincial statute governing the granting of financial assistance to students at the post-secondary school level. This credit is non-refundable and non-transferable.

Exercise 4-14

Subject: Education-Related Tax Credits

During 2021, Sarah Bright attends university in Canada for four months. Her total tuition for the year, including all ancillary fees, is $3,200, of which she prepaid $1,000 in 2020. The amount paid in 2021 includes $400 in fees that are only charged to students in her geology program. Interest paid for the year on her student loan was $325. Determine the total amount of education-related tax credits that would be available for Ms. Bright for 2021.

Solutions to Exercises are available in the Study Guide.

Carry Forward of Tuition Fees Tax Credit—ITA 118.61

4-155. There are situations in which a student does not have sufficient tax payable to use his tuition credit and, in addition, has not transferred it to a spouse, common-law partner, parent, or grandparent.

4-156. To deal with this type of situation, ITA 118.61 allows a carry forward of unused tuition credits. There is no time limit on this carry forward. In addition, ITA 118.62 provides for a five-year carry forward of unused interest credits on student loans.

4-157. Unfortunately, the calculation of the amount that is carried forward can be complex. Although the ITA uses tax payable and credit amounts to calculate carry forwards and transfers, Schedule 11 in the T1 individual income tax return uses taxable income and credit base amounts in its calculations. Both approaches will be illustrated in the example in Paragraph 4-163.

4-158. To carry amounts forward, the total available credits must be reduced by the student's tax payable, calculated using the following credits (note the medical expense tax credit is not included in the list):

- ITA 118 (personal)
- ITA 118.01 through ITA 118.07 (various credits)
- ITA 118.3 (disability)
- ITA 118.7 (CPP and EI)

4-159. The available amount is also reduced by transfers to other individuals. The resulting balance can be carried forward and is only available to the student in any subsequent year. However, once it is carried forward, it cannot be transferred to another individual. In other words, transfers are only available to other individuals for the year in which the tuition qualifies for a tax credit.

Transfer of Tuition Fees Tax Credit - ITA 118.9

4-160. ITA 118.9 provides for a transfer of the tuition tax credit to a parent or grandparent, however no transfer can be made if the spouse or common-law partner of the student has claimed a spousal credit for the student or the student has made a transfer of the tuition to the spouse or common-law partner. In effect, a spouse or common-law partner of the student takes priority over others. ITA 118.8 provides the rules for the transfer of tuition between spouses and common-law partners, and ITA 118.81 determines the amount of the tuition credit that can be transferred. The transfer is at the discretion of the student, and the legislation states that the student must designate in writing the amount that is to be transferred and the identity of the transferee.

4-161. The maximum transfer for an individual student in any year is the lesser of the available tuition credit and $5,000, multiplied by the tax rate for the minimum tax bracket (referred to as the "appropriate percentage"). This amount is $750 [(15%)($5,000)].

4-162. This $750 maximum amount must be reduced by the student's tax payable calculated after the same credits used to calculate the carry forward of tuition fee credits. As described in Paragraph 4-158, these are the credits available under ITA 118 through ITA 118.07, 118.3, and 118.7. If these credits reduce the student's tax payable to nil, the full $750 is available for transfer on a per-student basis. A parent or grandparent could have $750 transfers from any number of children or grandchildren.

4-163. An example will serve to illustrate both the ITA 118.9 transfer as well as the ITA 118.81 calculation limits on this transfer.

> **EXAMPLE** Megan Doxy has 2021 taxable income of $14,000, all of which is rental income. She attends university full time during 2021, paying a total amount for tuition of $8,000. Other than her tuition credit, her only other tax credit is her personal amount of $2,071 [(15%)($13,808)]. She would like to transfer the maximum credits to her father.
>
> **ANALYSIS—ITA Approach** Megan's tuition credit is $1,200 [(15%)($8,000)], well in excess of the maximum transfer of $750. However, this maximum of $750 would have to be reduced by Megan's tax payable after the deduction of her personal amount. This amount would be $29 [(15%)($14,000 - $13,808)], leaving a maximum transfer of $721 ($750 - $29). This would leave Megan with a remaining unused credit of $450 ($1,200 - $29 - $721), which can be carried forward to future years, but only for her own use. These calculations are the result of using the approach presented in the ITA. Technically Megan's net income and taxable income would both be $14,000. Gross federal tax payable would then be $2,100 [(15%)($14,000)] and her income tax credits before the tuition tax credit would be $2,071 [(15%)($13,808)]. Her net tax payable would be $29 [$2,100 - $2,071].

ANALYSIS—Tax Return Approach The alternative calculation approach that is used in the T1 income tax return begins with the total tuition amount of $8,000. The maximum transfer amount in this approach is $5,000. This would be reduced by $192 ($14,000 - $13,808), the excess of Megan's taxable income over her basic personal amount. This results in a maximum transfer of $4,808 ($5,000 - $192). Megan's carry forward amount is $3,000 ($8,000 - $192 - $4,808). Multiplying these amounts by 15% gives the same $721 [(15%)($4,808)] transfer and $450 [(15%)($3,000)] of unused credits as the preceding ITA approach.

Exercise 4-15

Subject: Transfer and Carry Forward of Tuition Tax Credits

Jerry Fall has 2021 taxable income of $15,000. He attends a U.S. university during 2021, paying a total amount for tuition of $23,500 (Canadian dollars). His only tax credits, other than the tuition credit, are his basic personal credit and a medical expense credit of $233 [(15%)($1,555)]. Determine Jerry's total tuition tax credit. Indicate how much of this total could be transferred to a parent and how much would be carried forward. Jerry is not married nor living in a common-law partnership.

Solutions to Exercises are available in the Study Guide.

Employment Insurance (EI) and Canada Pension Plan (CPP) Tax Credits—ITA 118.7

4-164. Until 2019, this credit was based on 15% of the amount of CPP contributions paid by employees or one-half of the CPP contributions paid by self-employed individuals. As of 2020, the amount paid is divided into two components, one of which is used to calculate the ITA 118.7 credit, and a second component that is treated as a deduction in the determination of net income.

4-165. For 2021, an employee's CPP contributions are based on maximum pensionable earnings of $61,600, less a basic exemption of $3,500. The maximum contribution for this year is $3,166 [(5.45%)($61,600 - $3,500)]. The base for the ITA 118.7 credit is calculated using a rate of 4.95%, and for 2021 it equals $2,876 [(4.95%)($61,600 - $3,500)], resulting in a credit of $431. The difference of $290 ($3,166 - $2,876) is used as a deduction in determining an individual's net income.

4-166. As self-employed individuals have no employer making a matching CPP contribution, they are required to make double contributions, a total maximum contribution of $6,332 [(2)($3,166)] for 2020. In terms of the ITA 118.7 credit, these individuals will have the same base as employees. Their maximum credit will be $410 [(15%)($2,732)]. The remaining $3,600 ($6,332 - $2,732) of their contribution will be a deduction in the determination of net income. This is equal to a deuction of $3,166 that is equal to the amount that an employer would have been able to deduct plus the $434 portion of what the employee would have been able to deduct if maxmum CPP contributions had been required.

4-167. For 2021, EI premiums are based on maximum insurable earnings of $56,300. The employee's rate is 1.58%, resulting in a maximum annual premium of $890 [($56,300)(0.0158 or 1.58%)]. This results in a maximum credit against federal tax payable of $134 [(15%)($890)].

4-168. Employers are also required to pay EI premiums, the amount being 1.4 times the premiums paid by the employee, which are fully deductible to the employer. However, these employer-paid premiums have no income tax consequences for the employee. While self-employed individuals can elect to participate in the EI program, unlike for the CPP they do not have to remit the employer's share. Their premiums will be limited to the same maximum of $890 that is applicable to employees.

Overpayment of EI Premiums and CPP Contributions

4-169. It is not uncommon for employers to withhold EI and CPP amounts that are in excess of the amounts required. This can happen through an error on the part of the employer's payroll system, especially for employees with variable hours. Even in the absence of errors, overpayments can arise when an individual changes employers or has multiple employers. The CRA's form T2204 is designed to assist taxpayers in calculating any overpayment of EI. Schedule 8 of the T1 individual income tax return provides similar assistance in calculating any CPP overpayment.

4-170. A refund of these excess amounts is available to individuals on filing an income tax return. While any CPP or EI overpayment is not part of the base for the tax credit, it will increase the refund available or decrease the tax liability that is calculated in the return.

> **EXAMPLE** Jerry Weist changed employers during 2021 and, as a consequence, the total amount of EI premiums withheld during the year was $990. In a similar fashion, the total amount of CPP contributions withheld by the two employers was $3,200. His employment income was well in excess of the maximum insurable and pensionable earnings.
>
> **ANALYSIS** In filing his 2021 income tax return, Jerry will claim a refund of $146, calculated as follows:

EI premiums withheld	$ 990	
2021 maximum	(890)	$100
CPP contributions withheld	$ 3,200	
2021 maximum	(3,166)	32
Refund		$132

Transfers to a Spouse or Common-Law Partner—ITA 118.8

4-171. In the preceding material, we have covered several tax credits that can be claimed by either spouse, such as the charitable donations credit. There are also four tax credits that can be transferred to a spouse or common-law partner under ITA 118.8:

- The age tax credit (see Paragraph 4-74)
- The pension income tax credit (see Paragraph 4-76)
- The disability tax credit (see Paragraph 4-133)
- The tuition fees tax credit to a maximum of $750 (see material beginning in Paragraph 4-160)

4-172. The maximum amount that can be transferred is based on the total tax bases of the preceding credits, reduced by a modified calculation of the spouse or common-law partner's tax payable. While the legislation is based on tax payable, the T1 individual income tax return uses a simplified approach based on taxable income, much like the alternative calculation for the tuition credit transfer. This approach starts with the total of the tax credit bases for all of the preceding credits. From this amount is subtracted the spouse's taxable income, reduced by the bases of:

- the basic personal credit,
- the Canada employment credit, CPP, and EI credits,
- the credits under ITA 118.01 through ITA 118.07 (various credits including the first-time home buyers' credit and the adoption expenses credit), and
- the tuition fees tax credit.

4-173. The resulting remainder, if any, is the amount that can be transferred to a spouse or common-law partner.

Exercise 4-16

Subject: Transfer of Credits from a Spouse

Mr. Martin Levee is 68 years old and has net income of $42,000. Of this total, $24,000 was from a life annuity that he purchased with funds in his RRSP. His spouse is 66 years old and blind. She has no income of her own (she is ineligible for Old Age Security) and was attending university on a full-time basis for four months of 2020. Her tuition fees for the year were $2,200 . Determine Mr. Levee's maximum tax credits for 2021. Ignore the possibility of splitting his pension income with his spouse.

Solutions to Exercises are available in the Study Guide.

We suggest you complete SSP 4-2 and 4-3 at this point.

Political Contributions Tax Credits—ITA 127(3)

Canada Elections Act

4-174. While no changes have been made in the ITA, the *Canada Elections Act* limits the ability to make political contributions to individuals only. More specifically, this Act contains the following provisions:

- There is a total ban on contributions by corporations, trade unions, and unincorporated associations.
- For 2020, the amount that can be contributed by an individual:
  - to each registered party,
  - in total to all the registered associations, nomination contestants, and candidates of each registered party,
  - in total to all leadership contestants in a particular contest, and
  - to each independent candidate

  is limited to $1,625 for the year. The limits increase by $25 on January 1 in each subsequent year.

Income Tax Rules

4-175. A federal tax credit is available on monetary political contributions made to a registered federal political party or to candidates at the time of a federal general election or by-election. The maximum value is $650 and it is available to both individuals and corporations.

4-176. However, as discussed in the preceding paragraph, the *Canada Elections Act* totally bans contributions by corporations. The credit is calculated as follows:

	Contributions	Credit Rate	Tax Credit
First	$ 400	3/4	$300
Next	350	1/2	175
Next	525	1/3	175
Maximum credit	$1,275		$650

4-177. The $650 credit is achieved when contributions total $1,275. Contributions in excess of this amount do not generate additional credits. Also note that most provinces have a similar credit against provincial tax payable. There is a difference, however, in that the eligible contributions must be made to a registered provincial political party.

Exercise 4-17

Subject: Political Contributions Tax Credit

Ms. Vivacia Unger contributes $785 to the Liberal New Conservative Democratic Party, a registered federal political party. Determine the amount of her federal political contributions tax credit.

Solutions to Exercises are available in the Study Guide.

Labour-Sponsored Venture Capital Corporations Credit—ITA 127.4

4-178. Labour-sponsored venture capital corporations (LSVCCs) are a form of mutual fund corporation, sponsored by an eligible labour organization, and mandated to provide venture capital to small and medium-sized businesses.

4-179. There is a 15% federal tax credit for provincially registered LSVCCs prescribed under the ITA. The maximum credit available is $750 [(15%)($5,000 net cost of shares)]. To be eligible for the federal credit, the provincially registered LSVCC would need to:

- be eligible for a provincial tax credit of at least 15% of the cost of an individual's shares;
- be sponsored by an eligible labour body; and
- mandate that at least 60% of the LSVCC's shareholders' equity be investments in small and medium-sized enterprises.

Dividend Tax Credit

4-180. The dividend tax credit is covered in Chapter 7 as part of our discussion of property income.

Foreign Tax Credits

4-181. The credits that are available for income taxes paid in foreign jurisdictions are covered in Chapters 7 and 11.

Investment Tax Credits

4-182. When taxpayers make certain types of expenditures, they become eligible for investment tax credits. These credits reduce federal tax payable. While these credits can be claimed by individuals as well as corporations, they are much more commonly used by corporations and, as a consequence, we cover investment tax credits in Chapter 14.

We suggest you complete SSP 4-4 and 4-5 at this point.

Refundable Credits

Introduction

4-183. The credits we have encountered to this point can be described as non-refundable. This means that, unless the taxpayer has tax payable for the current taxation year, there is no benefit from the credit. Further, with the exception of the charitable donations credit and education-related credits, there is no carry forward of these non-refundable credits to subsequent taxation years. This means that if the credits are not used in the current year they are permanently lost.

4-184. In contrast, refundable credits, to the extent not applied against gross federal taxes payable, are paid/refunded to individuals. In this section we will describe six of these refundable credits:

- The GST/HST tax credit
- The refundable medical expense supplement
- The Canada Workers Benefit
- The refundable teacher and early childhood educator school supply tax credit
- Climate Action Incentive payments (available in only some provinces and territories)
- The Canada Training Credit

4-185. With respect to the GST/HST credit, our coverage will be limited. This reflects the fact that, unlike the other five refundable credits, individuals do not calculate the GST/HST credit in their income tax returns. Rather, the CRA calculates the credit based on information included in prior-year income tax returns, which is then paid on a regular basis to eligible individuals. Given this, there is no need to provide coverage of the detailed calculation of this particular credit.

GST/HST Credit—ITA 122.5

4-186. One of the major problems with the goods and services tax (GST) is the fact that it is a regressive tax (see discussion in Chapter 1). In order to provide some relief from the impact of the GST on low-income families, there is a refundable GST credit available under ITA 122.5.

4-187. As mentioned in Paragraph 4-185, the GST/HST credit is determined by the CRA on the basis of eligibility information supplied in the individual's income tax returns filed for previous years. Because of this, it is only paid to individuals who actually file income tax returns.

4-188. The amount of the credit, as well as the relevant income threshold, is indexed on the same basis as other credits. The relevant amounts for 2021 are as follows:

- $299 for an "eligible individual." An eligible individual includes a Canadian resident who is 19 years of age or over during the current year, or is married or living common-law, or is a parent who resides with the child. In the case of a married couple, only one spouse can be an eligible individual.

- $299 for a "qualified relation." A qualified relation is defined as a cohabiting spouse or common-law partner. If the eligible individual does not have a qualified relation, they are entitled to an additional credit that is the lesser of $155 or 2% of the individual's net income in excess of $9,590.

- $299 for a dependant eligible for the eligible dependant tax credit.

- $157 for each "qualified dependant." A "qualified dependant" is defined as a person who is the individual's child or is dependent on the individual or the individual's cohabiting spouse or common-law partner for support. In addition, the child or dependent person must be under 19 years of age, reside with the individual, have never had a spouse or common-law partner, and have never been a parent of a child that they have resided with.

4-189. The total of these amounts must be reduced by 5% of the excess of the individual's 2019 "adjusted income" over an indexed threshold amount of $38,892. The system uses information provided on the 2019 tax return, since this return is normally filed by early 2020. "Adjusted income" is defined as total income of the individual and her qualified relation, if any.

4-190. The GST/HST credit is available to all eligible individuals, without regard to whether they have tax payable. The amount of the credit is calculated by the CRA on the basis of information included in the individual's income tax return for a particular year, and the amounts are automatically paid to the individual in subsequent years as long as annual income tax returns continue to be filed.

Refundable Medical Expense Supplement—ITA 122.51

4-191. The calculation of the GST/HST credit is not included in the income tax return. The five other refundable credits, including the refundable medical expense supplement, are included in the income tax return.

4-192. To be eligible for the 2021 medical expense supplement, the individual must be 18 years of age or over at the end of the year and must have either employment income or income from carrying on a business of at least $3,751. The credit is the lesser of $1,285 and 25/15 of the medical expense tax credit that can be claimed for the year.

4-193. The lesser amount is reduced by 5% of "family net income" in excess of an indexed threshold amount. Family net income is the sum of the income of the taxpayer and his spouse or common-law partner, but not that of an eligible dependant. For 2021, the income threshold is $28,164 and the credit is completely eliminated when family net income reaches $54,146 [($1,285 ÷ 5%) + $28,446]. A simple example will serve to illustrate this refundable credit.

EXAMPLE For 2021, Mr. Larry Futon and his spouse have medical expenses that total $5,000. His net income is $28,900, all of which is employment income. His spouse has net income of $500. Mr. Futon claims the Canada caregiver tax credit for his mother, who has net income of $8,000. Mr. Futon has no income tax credits other than personal and medical expense credits.

ANALYSIS Mr. Futon's allowable medical expenses for tax credit purposes would be $4,133 [$5,000 - (3%)($28,900)], resulting in a tax credit of $620 [(15%)($4,133)]. Given this, 25/15 of the credit would equal $1,033 [(25/15)($620)]. Since this is less than the maximum of $1,285, his refundable credit would be $1,033 less a reduction of $48 [(5%)($28,900 + $500 - $28,446)], leaving a balance of $985 ($1,033 - $48).

4-194. The receipt of this refundable credit does not affect an individual's ability to claim a tax credit for the same medical expenses that are used to calculate the refundable credit. In the preceding example, Mr. Futon's basic personal, spousal, Canada caregiver, and medical expense credit bases total $38,597 [$13,808 + ($13,808 - $500) + $7,348 + $4,133]. This is more than his taxable income of $28,900, which results in his net federal taxes payable being nil. This means that he will be entitled to the refund of $985.

Exercise 4-18

Subject: Refundable Medical Expense Supplement

During 2021, Ms. Lara Brunt and her common-law partner, Sara, have medical expenses that total $6,250. Her net income is $28,400, all of which qualifies as income for the refundable medical expense supplement. Sara has no income of her own. Determine Lara's minimum net tax payable for 2021. Ignore any credits other than the basic, spousal, and medical expense-related credits.

Solutions to Exercises are available in the Study Guide.

Canada Workers Benefit—ITA 122.7

4-195. When this refundable credit was first announced in 2007, the federal government stated that the purpose of the credit would be "to make work more rewarding and atractive for Canadians already in the workforce and to encourage other Canadians to enter the work-force." The simple fact is that, given the types of wages such individuals receive, they are often better off economically if they do not work. The types of wages that such individuals can earn are typically at the legal "minimum" (the minimum wage ranges from $11.45 per hour in Saskatchewan to $16.00 per hour in Nunavut). The amounts earned at this wage are typically offset by reductions in social assistance payments. Additional negative effects flow from loss of subsidized housing, prescription drug assistance, and other benefits that are available to individuals with little or no income.

4-196. It has been demonstrated that, if such individuals find employment, the result can be a reduction in their real income. Instead of rewarding their efforts, our current system can actually penalize individuals who make an effort to improve their economic status.

Calculation of the Canada Workers Benefit

4-197 To deal with this problem, the ITA provides a refundable credit for individuals over the age of 19 who have working income greater than $3,000. Working income is defined as employment income (i.e., no employment expenses deducted), business income, scholarships, and research grants. The amount of the benefit will depend on whether the individual is single or, alternatively, has a spouse or an eligible dependant. For this purpose, an eligible dependant is a child who lives with the individual and who is under the age of 19 at the end of the year.

4-198. The current Canada Workers Benefit (CWB) calculates a refundable credit of a maximum of $1,395 for single individuals and $2,403 for families with spouses, common-law partners, or eligible dependants. The income thresholds are not particularly high, with phase-outs for single individuals starting with net income of $13,064 and $17,348 for families. Where there are disabled individuals the threshold limits increase for singles to $24,569 and $37,176 for families.

4-199. The 2021 federal budget proposes to increase the CWB beginning in 2021, including the disability supplement. The phase-out limits will also be increased. This means that the overall benefits will increase and will be available to a wider range of both single and family income earners. A notable secondary earner exemption is also added (ITA 122.7(1.3)) that allows up to $14,000 of the income of a low-income eligible spouse to be excluded from the working income. The government refers to a couple with $50,000 of working income that would, prior to 2021, not be eligible for the CWB but because of the exemption would qualify and be entitled to receive $930. The new rates will apply beginning with the 2021 taxation year.

4-200. Eligibility for the credit has required the completion of an annual income tax return together with a completed schedule 6. Recent federal budgets, however, have obligated the CRA to process the credit without the necessity of completing schedule 6 as long as the necessary information is available to the CRA. Finally, the CRA is now offering advance pre-payments of this credit that will provide claimants with 50% of the amount they would have been entitled to on completion of form RC201. The federal government estimates that 2 million Canadians will benefit from this credit.

Refundable Teacher and Early Childhood Educator School Supply Tax Credit—ITA 122.9

4-201. The government has observed that early childhood educators often use their own funds to acquire supplies for the purpose of teaching or enhancing students' learning. In recognition of this situation, an eligible educator can claim a 15% tax credit for up to $1,000 of eligible expenditures. While it is unlikely that employed teachers will lack sufficient tax payable to claim the credit, the credit is refundable.

4-202. The definitions relevant to this credit are as follows:

Eligible Educator To be eligible for this credit, a teacher has to be employed in Canada and have a teacher's certificate that is valid in the province where they are employed. Early childhood educators qualify if they hold either a teacher's certificate or a diploma in early childhood education that is recognized by the province in which they are employed.

Eligible Supplies Eligible supplies will include the following durable goods:

- Games and puzzles
- Supplementary books for classrooms

- Educational support software
- Containers such as plastic boxes for themes and kits

Eligible supplies will also include consumable goods such as:

- Construction paper for activities, flashcards, or activity centres
- Items for science experiments, such as seeds, potting soil, vinegar, and stir sticks
- Art supplies, such as paper, glue, and paint
- Various stationery items, such as pens, pencils, posters, and charts

4-203. For the cost of supplies to qualify for this credit, employers will be required to certify that the supplies were purchased for the purpose of teaching or otherwise enhancing learning in a classroom or learning environment. Claimants will be required to retain their receipts for eligible purchases.

Climate Action Incentive Payments

Background

4-204. Carbon tax plans are recognized as an effective way of dealing with the crucial problem of global warming. Globally speaking, there is always some opposition to any plan that deals with the negative influence of carbon on the environment. All such plans involve penalizing some group, or economic sector, in order to reduce the influence of carbon on the environment and, not surprisingly, such groups or sectors create arguments to support their opposition to the applied penalties.

4-205. At the federal level, the Government of Canada has adopted a federal carbon tax. Several provinces have objected to this federal initiative and have refused to accept it in their jurisdictions. For these provinces, the federal government offered an alternative. If they adopted a robust plan of their own for dealing with climate change, there would be no consequences related to rejecting the federal carbon tax.

4-206. Four provinces have rejected the federal plan and have no effective plan of their own. These provinces are:

- Alberta
- Manitoba
- Ontario
- Saskatchewan

4-207. In order to ensure that there is a price on carbon pollution throughout Canada, the federal government has introduced the *Greenhouse Gas Pollution Pricing Act*. This is a federal fuel charge that applies only in those four provinces that neither accepted the federal carbon tax nor adopted a pollution control plan of their own.

The Refundable Credit

4-208. In applying this fuel tax, it was not the intent of the federal government to increase tax revenues. The macro effects of the fuel tax will be offset by a refundable credit, which the federal government has referred to as the Climate Action Incentive payment. It is expected that these payments, while making the use of polluting fossil fuels more expensive, will distribute to the residents of the provinces and territories where the fuel tax is applied an amount that is designed to offset the cost of the fuel tax for residents.

4-209. This payment is implemented through the federal income tax system in the form of a refundable tax credit. Individuals have to file an income tax return in order to receive this Climate Action Incentive payment, including completing schedule 14 even if they wouldn't otherwise be required to file an income tax return because they do not owe any income tax. This process is analogous to that applicable to the GST/HST credit.

4-210. The amount of the payments vary by province. The total paid is based on the number of dependants (family size) and is not income dependent. As an example of the amounts, the 2021 figures for Ontario are as follows:

Family Member	Payment
Single adult or first family member	$300
Second adult in a couple or for the first child of a single parent	150
Each child under 18	75

4-211. The anticipated 2021 payments for a single adult for the other three provinces are $490 (Alberta), $360 (Manitoba), and $500 (Saskatchewan).

Canada Training Credit—ITA 118.5(1.2) & 122.91

The Credit Base

4-212. The government is interested in encouraging working individuals to upgrade and maintain their skills through training and education. The Canada training credit was introduced to provide some financial assistance to achieve this goal. Beginning with the 2019 year, $250 will be added each year with a maximum lifetime accumulation of $5,000. The amount of the credit that can be accessed is based on the accumulation up to the end of the previous year. Any amount claimed reduces the eligible tuition credit on a dollar-for-dollar basis.

4-213. Eligibility for the tuition tax credit was discussed beginning in Paragraph 4-143. In general, the amount eligible for the Canada training credit will be the same as the amount that qualified for the tuition tax credit. The one exception to this is amounts paid to educational institutions outside of Canada. While these amounts will continue to be eligible for the tuition tax credit, they will not be eligible for the Canada training credit.

4-214. This credit is equal to the lesser of:

- one-half of the tuition costs incurred in the current year that are eligible for the tuition credit, or
- the individual's annual training limit.

4-215. The annual training limit is an amount that, beginning in 2019, accumulates at the rate of $250 each year for 20 years, to a maximum addition of $5,000. The first year in which a claim can be made, however, is 2020. To be eligible for this annual addition to the training account limit, an individual must:

- file a tax return for the year for the preceding taxation year;
- be between 26 and 65 years of age;
- be a resident of Canada throughout the preceding year;
- have earnings, subject to indexation, of $10,100 or more during the preceding year (including employment income, self-employed income, maternity EI benefits, parental EI benefits, and taxable scholarship income); and
- have net income in the preceding year that does not exceed the top of the third tax bracket ($151,978 for 2021).

Calculating the Refund

4-216. An example will serve to illustrate the required calculations.

EXAMPLE Michael is eligible to accumulate an amount in his Canada training account in each of the years 2019 through 2022. This means that the preceding-year balance for 2023 is $1,000 [(4)($250)]. During 2023, $2,500 in eligible tuition fees are paid.

ANALYSIS For 2023, Michael can claim a refundable tax credit equal to $1,000, which is the lesser of (1) 50% of eligible tuition of $2,500 or $1,250 and (2) the training limit from the preceding year, or $1,000. The Canada training credit claim of $1,000 reduces the eligible tuition to $1,500.

At the end of 2023, the balance in his Canada training account will be $250 ($1,000 opening balance + $250 for 2023 - $1,000 claimed in 2023). For 2024 and subsequent years, he can accumulate an additional $3,750 in his Canada training account. This is the accumulation limit of $5,000, less the $250 per year that was added during the five years 2019 through 2023.

WIthout the Canada training credit Michael would have been able to reduce income taxes in 2023 by a non-refundable tuition credit amount of $375 [(15%)($2,500)], but with the credit the reduction in income taxes is $1,225 [(15%)($1,500) + $1,000], representing $225 of a non-refundable tuition credit amount and a $1,000 fully refundable Canada training credit.

Social Benefits Repayment (OAS and EI)

Basic Concepts

Clawbacks

4-217. Many Canadian tax credits and benefits are available on a universal basis, without regard to the income level of the recipient. However, both Old Age Security (OAS) payments and Employment Insurance (EI) payments contain their own income thresholds.

4-218. With respect to OAS payments, the government assesses a Part I.2 tax on OAS benefits received by individuals with an adjusted net income above a threshold amount. In similar fashion, the *Employment Insurance Act* requires that individuals with an adjusted net income above a specified threshold amount repay a portion of any EI benefits received. These required repayments are commonly referred to as "clawbacks."

Treatment in Net and Taxable Income

4-219. Both OAS and EI receipts must be included in an individual's net income. However, in situations where part or all of these amounts must be repaid, it would not be equitable to have the full amounts received flow through to taxable income and be fully taxed.

4-220. This problem is dealt with by providing a deduction for amounts repaid. You may recall from Chapter 1 that one of the components of net income was other deductions (Subdivision e of the ITA). While we will not provide detailed coverage of this subdivision until Chapter 9, we need to note here that ITA 60(v.1) provides a deduction for repayments of EI, and ITA 60(w) provides a deduction for repayments of OAS amounts. This creates another interesting difference where the OAS and EI form part of net income but any repayments of these amounts only reduces taxable income.

4-221. As both the EI and OAS repayments are calculated on the basis of the individual's income in excess of a threshold amount, the question arises as to whether these tests should be applied using income figures that include the full amount received or, alternatively, income figures from which the repayments have been deducted. The solution to this problem will be discussed in the two sections that follow.

Employment Insurance (EI) Benefits Clawback

4-222. The *Employment Insurance Act* requires the partial repayment of benefits received if the recipient's threshold income is greater than $70,375 (1.25 times the 2021 maximum insurable earnings of $56,300). This $70,375 income figure includes all of the components of net income except the deductions for repayment of EI benefits [ITA 60(v.1)] and the deduction for the repayment of OAS benefits [ITA 60(w)]. As the EI clawback is deducted from the threshold income used for determining the OAS clawback, the EI clawback must be determined prior to calculating any amount of OAS clawback where both clawbacks could occur in the same year.

4-223. Once the amount of threshold income over $70,375 is determined, it must be compared to the EI benefits included in the current year's net income. The lesser of these two amounts is multiplied by 30%, and this becomes the amount that must be repaid for the year as what is referred to as a social benefits repayment. This amount can then be deducted under ITA 60(v.1) in the determination of net income for the year.

Old Age Security (OAS) Benefits Clawback

4-224. The OAS clawback is the lesser of the OAS payments included in income and 15% of the taxpayer's income in excess of the $79,845 income threshold. For this purpose, income is equal to net income computed after any EI clawback but before consideration of the deduction for the OAS clawback.

4-225. The current annual benefit from OAS is about $7,400. Assuming this to be the correct figure, all of the OAS benefit would be clawed back when the individual's net income reaches $129,178 [($7,400 ÷ 15%) + $79,845].

4-226. For higher-income seniors, OAS benefits are clawed back on a regular basis, with some individuals never receiving benefits during their lifetime. Given this, the government has an administrative procedure under which they withhold payments that they expect to be clawed back. Expectations are based on income tax returns filed in the two previous years. Currently, seniors who anticipate earning high levels of income that would clawback all of the OAS can simply decide not to apply for it until income levels are below the OAS threshold.

> **EXAMPLE** In her income tax returns for both 2019 and 2020, Sally Leung has reported taxable income in excess of $200,000 per year. Despite the fact that Sally is 70 years of age, she would receive no OAS payments in 2021.

Exercise 4-19

Subject: EI and OAS Clawbacks

For 2021, Ms. Marilyn Jacobi has employment income of $75,000, receives EI payments of $10,000, and receives $7,400 in OAS payments. No amount was withheld from the OAS payments because she had very low income in the previous two years due to large rental losses. Determine Ms. Jacobi's net income for 2021.

Solutions to Exercises are available in the Study Guide.

Comprehensive Example

4-227. While this chapter has provided a reasonably detailed description of the determination of tax payable for individuals, including small examples of some of the issues that arise in this process, a more comprehensive example is appropriate at this point. To focus on the federal tax calculations, we have ignored provincial income taxes and income tax withholdings on employment income.

Basic Data

Mr. Thomas Baxter is 66 years of age and his 2021 income is made up of employment income of $73,800 and Old Age Security benefits of $7,400. Because of large business losses during the previous two years, no amount was withheld from these payments. Mr. Baxter and his family live in Nanaimo, British Columbia.

For 2021, Mr. Baxter's employer withheld maximum CPP and EI contributions. Other information pertaining to 2021 is as follows:

1. Mr. Baxter's spouse is 49 years old and qualifies for the disability tax credit. Her income for the year totalled $5,000.
2. Mr. and Mrs. Baxter have two daughters, Kim, aged 14, and Lori, aged 17. Kim had net income of $2,700 for the year while Lori had net income of $2,000. In September 2021, Lori began full-time attendance at a Canadian university. Mr. Baxter paid her tuition fees of $5,000, of which $2,500 was for the fall 2021 semester and $2,500 for the 2022 semester. Lori is willing to transfer the maximum tuition credit to her father.

3. The family medical expenses for the year, all of which were paid by Mr. Baxter, totalled $2,843. Of this amount, $300 was paid for Kim and $900 for Lori.
4. During the year, Mr. Baxter made cash donations to registered Canadian charities in the amount of $3,000.
5. During the year, Mr. Baxter made contributions to federal political parties totalling $800.

Net and Taxable Income

Employment income	$73,800
OAS benefits	7,400
Less: CPP ITA 60(e.1)	(290)
Net income before clawback	$80,910
OAS clawback (Note 1)	(160)
Net income and taxable income	$80,750

Note 1 The required repayment of OAS is the lesser of:

- $7,400, the OAS payments included in income, and
- $160 [(15%)($80,910 - $79,845)].

Tax Payable/Federal Balance Owing

As Mr. Baxter is a resident of B.C. he is not eligible for the Climate Action Incentive payment. His federal tax payable and balance owing is calculated as follows:

Federal tax on first $49,020		$ 7,353
Federal tax on next $31,730 ($80,750 - $49,020) at 20.5%		6,505
Federal tax before credits		$13,858
Tax credits:		
Basic personal amount	($13,808)	
Spousal including infirm amount ($13,808 + $2,295 - $5,000)	(11,103)	
Additional caregiver amount (Note 2)	Nil	
EI premiums (maximum)	(890)	
CPP contributions (maximum)	(2,876)	
Canada employment	(1,257)	
Age [$7,713 - (15%)($80,750 - $38,893)]	(1,434)	
Medical expenses (Note 3)	(422)	
Mrs. Baxter's disability transferred	(8,662)	
Lori'stTuition for 2021 transferred ($5,000 - $2,500) (Note 4)	(2,500)	
Total	($42,952)	
Rate	15%	(6,443)
Charitable donations (Note 5) {[(15%)($200)] + [(33%)(nil)] + [(29%)($3,000 - $200)]}		(842)
Political contributions tax credit [($400)(3/4) + ($350)(1/2) + ($50)(1/3)]		(492)
Federal tax payable		$ 6,081
Social benefits repayment (Note 1)		160
Federal balance owing		$ 6,241

Note 2 As the spousal amount is larger than the Canada caregiver amount of $7,348, there is no additional Canada caregiver amount.

Note 3 Since both daughters are under 18 at the end of the year, their expenses can be aggregated with those of Mr. Baxter for the purposes of this calculation.

Total medical expenses	$2,843
Lesser of:	
• [(3%)($80,750)] = $2,423	
• 2021 threshold amount = $2,421	(2,421)
Allowable medical expenses	$ 422

Note 4 Since Lori has no tax payable before consideration of her tuition credit, it can be all be transferred to her supporting parent as it totals less than the $5,000 transfer limit. Alternatively, she could have chosen to carry forward these credits to apply against her own tax payable in a subsequent year.

Note 5 Since none of Mr. Baxter's income is taxed at 33%, this rate is not used to calculate the charitable donations credit.

We suggest you complete SSP 4-6 to 4-8 at this point.

Key Terms

A full glossary with definitions is provided at the end of the Study Guide.

Adoption Expenses Tax Credit
Age Tax Credit
Canada Caregiver Amount for Child
Canada Caregiver Tax Credit
Canada Employment Credit
Canada Pension Plan (CPP)
Canada Pension Plan Tax Credit
Canada Training Credit
Canada Workers Benefit
Charitable Donations Tax Credit
Charitable Gifts
Clawback
Climate Action Incentive Payment
Common-Law Partner
Dependant
Digital News Subscription Credit
Disability Tax Credit
Disability Tax Credit Supplement
Eligible Dependant Tax Credit
Employment Insurance (EI)
Employment Insurance Tax Credit
First-Time Home Buyers' Tax Credit
GST/HST Tax Credit
Home Accessibility Tax Credit
Indexation
Labour-Sponsored Funds Tax Credit
Medical Expense Tax Credit
Non-Refundable Tax Credit
Northern Residents Deductions
OAS Clawback
Old Age Security (OAS) Benefits
Pension Income Tax Credit
Personal Tax Credits
Political Contributions Tax Credit
Progressive Tax System
Refundable Medical Expense Supplement
Refundable Tax Credit
Regressive Tax System
Social Benefits Repayment
Spousal Tax Credit
Spouse
Student Loan Interest Credit
Tax Credit
Taxable Income
Teacher School Supply Tax Credit
Tuition Fees Tax Credit
Volunteer Firefighters Tax Credit
Volunteer Search and Rescue Tax Credit
Wholly Dependent Person

References

For more detailed study of the material in this chapter, we would refer you to the following:

ITA 110	Deductions Permitted
ITA 111.1	Order of Applying Provisions
ITA 117	Individual Taxes Payable
ITA 117.1	Annual Adjustment (Indexation)
ITA 118(1)	Personal Credits
ITA 118(2)	Age Credit
ITA 118(3)	Pension Credit
ITA 118(10)	Canada Employment Credit
ITA 118.01	Adoption Expense Credit
ITA 118.041	Home Accessibility Tax Credit
ITA 118.05	First-Time Home Buyers' Credit
ITA 118.06	Volunteer Firefighters Tax Credit
ITA 118.07	Volunteer Search and Rescue Workers Tax Credit
ITA 118.1	Charitable Donations
ITA 118.2	Medical Expense Credit
ITA 118.3	Disability Tax Credit
ITA 118.5	Tuition Credit
ITA 118.61	Carryforward of Unused Education Tax Credits
ITA 118.62	Credit for Interest on Student Loan
ITA 118.7	Credit for EI and QPIP Premiums and CPP Contributions
ITA 118.8	Transfer of Unused Credits to Spouse or Common-Law Partner
ITA 118.81	Tuition Tax Credit Transferred
ITA 118.9	Transfer to Parent or Grandparent
ITA 122.5	GST/HST Credit
ITA 122.51	Refundable Medical Expense Supplement
ITA 122.7	Canada Workers Benefit
ITA 127(3)	Federal Political Contributions Tax Credit
ITA 127.4	Labour-Sponsored Venture Capital Corporations Credit
ITA 180.2	OAS Clawback
ITR 5700	Prescribed Devices or Equipment for the Medical Expense Tax Credit.
IC 75-2R9	Contributions to a Registered Political Party or to a Candidate at a Federal Election
S1-F1-C1	Medical Expense Tax Credit
S1-F1-C2	Disability Tax Credit
S1-F1-C3	Disability Supports Deduction
S1-F2-C1	Qualifying Student and the Education and Textbook Tax Credits
S1-F2-C2	Tuition Tax Credit
S1-F2-C3	Scholarships, Research Grants, and Other Education Assistance
S1-F4-C2	Basic Personal and Dependant Tax Credits (for 2017 and Subsequent Years)
S1-F5-C1	Related Persons and Dealing at Arm's Length
IT-113R4	Benefits To Employees—Stock Options
IT-523	Order of Provisions Applicable in Computing an Individual's Taxable Income and Tax Payable

Sample Tax Return and Tax Software Self-Study Problem

The Chapter 4 Sample Tax Return and Tax Software SSP is available in the Study Guide.

Self-Study Problems (SSPs)

Self-Study Problems (SSPs) provide practice in problem solving. Within the chapters, we have indicated where it would be appropriate to stop and work on each SSP. The problems can be downloaded by chapter from MyLab Accounting. Solutions are available in the Study Guide. Select problems can also be completed directly in MyLab and auto-graded.

Assignment Problems

Solutions to Assignment Problems (APs) are available to instructors only.

AP 4-1 (Personal Tax Credits—Five Cases)

In each of the following independent cases, determine the maximum amount of 2021 personal tax credits, including transfers from a spouse or dependant, that can be applied against federal income tax payable by the individuals. In all cases, the individual's net income is equal to his or her taxable income. Ignore, where relevant, the possibility of pension income splitting. Unless otherwise stated, assume that each individual is less than 65 years old.

A calculation of tax payable is **NOT** required, only the applicable income tax credit base and the credit amount applied against federal income tax payable.

1. Cammy Tarbell has net income of $96,500, all of which is employment income. Her employer has withheld maximum EI and CPP contributions. She is married to Bob Tarbell, who has net income of $8,650. They have four children ages 3, 5, 7, and 9. All of the children are in good health and none of them have any income during the current year.

2. Scotty Severa has been divorced for a number of years. Because his former wife is an airline pilot who travels extensively, he has been awarded custody of their three children. The children are aged 7, 10, and 15 and they are all in good health. Scotty's net income is $71,400, all of which is spousal support payments. The two younger children have no income of their own. The 15 year old has income from part-time jobs of $8,640.

3. Donald Preble has net income of $126,325, all of which is rental income. His spouse, Donna, has net income of $6,340. Their daughter, Diane, is 26 years old and has a mental disability. While the disability is not severe enough to qualify for the disability tax credit, she has no income during the current year and continues to live with Donald and Donna.

4. Bibi Spillman is 68 years old. Her net income totals $65,420 and is made up of OAS payments of $7,400 and pension income of $58,020 from a former employer. Her spouse is 62 years old and has net income of $6,250.

5. Clarice McBryde has net income of $132,400, all of which is employment income with the exception of a deduction for CPP of $290. Her employer has withheld the maximum EI and CPP contributions. She and her husband, Moishe, have two children aged 11 and 13. Moishe and the children have no income of their own during the current year.

   The 13-year-old child was severely injured in a car accident two years ago and qualifies for the disability tax credit. No amount was paid for attendant care for this child during the current year.

   Clarice spent $12,500 installing wheelchair ramps to improve access to various parts of the family residence. She also spent the following on dental fees and fees for various medical practitioners:

Clarice	$ 4,420
Moishe	2,620
11-year-old child	1,875
13-year-old child	14,250
Total medical fees paid	$23,165
Reimbursement from company medical plan —Plan's annual maximum	(11,000)
Net medical fees paid	$12,165

AP 4-2 (Individual Tax Payable—Five Cases)

Mr. William Norris is 45 years old. The following five independent cases make varying assumptions for the 2021 taxation year with respect to Mr. Norris' marital status and number of dependants. In all cases, Mr. Norris had net income of $60,000, all of which is employment income with the exception of a CPP deduction of $290 (ITA 60(e.1)). Mr. Norris' employer withheld the required EI premiums and CPP contributions.

Case A Mr. Norris is married and his wife, Susan, has net income of $8,800. Susan's 73-year-old mother, Bernice, lives with them. Bernice has a mental infirmity that is not severe enough to qualify for the disability tax credit. However, it does make her dependent on William and Susan. Because of a large investment portfolio, Bernice had net income of $18,000 for 2021.

Case B Mr. Norris is married and his wife, Susan, has net income of $4,410. They have one child, Martha, who is 10 years of age. Martha had no income during the year. During the year, the family had medical expenses as follows:

William	$1,200
Susan	1,600
Martha	350
Total	$3,150

Case C Mr. Norris is married and his wife, Susan, has net income of $4,500. They have a son, Allen, who is 19 years old and lives at home. He attends university on a full-time basis during eight months of the year. Mr. Norris pays $9,000 for Allen's tuition. Allen had net income of $2,200, all of which is employment income during the summer months. He will transfer any unused credits to his father to the maximum extent possible.

Case D Mr. Norris is not married and has no dependants. On receipt of a $300,000 inheritance in December, he donates $50,000 to his local hospital, a registered charity. He chooses to claim $15,000 in 2021. He also makes contributions to a federal political party in the amount of $1,000.

Case E Mr. Norris is a single father. He has a daughter, Mary, who is 8 years old and lives with him. Two years ago, Mr. Norris graduated from a Canadian university. He currently has a Canada student loan outstanding. Mr. Norris pays back this loan in monthly instalments of $300. During the year, he paid $450 in interest on this loan.

Required: In each case, calculate Mr. Norris' minimum federal income tax payable for 2021. Indicate any carry forwards available to him and his dependants and the carry forward provisions. Ignore any tax amounts that Mr. Norris might have had withheld or paid as instalments.

AP 4-3 (Individual Tax Payable—Seven Cases)

The following seven independent cases make varying assumptions with respect to Roger Blaine and his 2021 tax status. In all cases where Roger earned employment income, his employer withheld the maximum EI premium and CPP contribution.

Case A Roger Blaine is 48 years of age and has net and taxable income of $65,000, all of which is from employment with the exception of a deduction for CPP in the amount of $290 (ITA 60(e.1)). During the year, Roger makes contributions to federal political parties in the amount of $1,000. Roger is not married and has no dependants.

Case B Roger Blaine is 48 years of age and has net and taxable income of $65,000, all of which is from employment with the exception of a deduction for CPP in the amount of $290 (ITA 60(e.1)). His wife, Martha, is 43 years of age and has net income of $4,650. They have one child, Eileen, who is 11 years of age and has net income of $3,000. During the year, the family had eligible medical expenses of $1,050 for Roger, $1,800 for Martha, and $300 for Eileen.

Case C Roger Blaine is 48 years old and his wife, Martha, is 43. Roger's only source of income is from rental properties. His net and taxable income is $65,000. Martha has net income of $9,400 all from investments. They have a 19-year-old disabled son, Albert, who lives with them. His disability qualifies him for the disability tax credit and he has no income of his own. During the year, Roger and Martha have medical expenses of $1,250. Medical expenses for Albert during the year total $8,350.

Case D Roger Blaine is 48 years of age and his wife, Martha, is 43. They have no children. Roger has net and taxable income of $65,000, all of which is from employment with the exception of a deduction for CPP in the amount of $290 (ITA 60(e.1)).Martha's net income is $14,000. Martha's 68-year-old father, Ahmed, and her 70-year-old aunt, Jaleh, live with them. Both are in good health. Ahmed's net income is $9,200 and Jaleh's net income is $11,000. Roger paid $375 in interest related to his student loan during the year.

Case E Roger Blaine is 48 years of age and his common-law partner, Bob, is 43. Roger has net and taxable income of $65,000, all of which is from employment with the exception of a deduction for CPP in the amount of $290 (ITA 60(e.1)).Bob has net income of $4,500. They have two adopted children, Barry aged 8 and Don aged 10. After living in rented premises for the last seven years, Roger and Bob decide to purchase a residence. They acquire a three-bedroom house in the suburbs at a cost of $245,000 and move into the house during the year.

Case F Roger Blaine is 48 years of age and his wife, Martha, is 43. Roger has net and taxable income of $65,000, all of which is from employment with the exception of a deduction for CPP in the amount of $290 (ITA 60(e.1)).Martha has net income of $5,050. They have a son, Albert, who is 19 years old and lives at home. He attends university on a full-time basis during eight months of the year. Roger pays $5,400 for Albert's tuition for two semesters during the 2020 calendar year and $525 for required textbooks. Albert's net income is $3,000 that he earned from summer employment. He agrees to transfer the maximum amount of eligible tuition credit to his father.

Case G Roger Blaine is 67 years of age and his wife, Martha, is 68. Martha has been completely disabled for a number of years and the extent of her disability qualifies her for the disability tax credit. Their son, Albert, is 38 years old, in good health, and lives with them to help care for Martha. Albert has $10,000 of income from spousal support. The components of Roger and Martha's income are as follows:

	Roger	Martha
Interest	$ 300	$ 50
Canada Pension Plan benefits	4,400	200
Old Age Security benefits	7,400	7,400
Income from registered pension plan	32,150	450
Net income	$44,250	$8,100

Required: In each case, calculate Roger Blaine's minimum federal income tax payable for 2021. Indicate any carry forwards available to him and his dependants and the carry forward provisions. Ignore any amounts Roger might have had withheld or paid in instalments and the possibility of pension income splitting.

AP 4-4 (Individual Tax Payable—Seven Cases)

There are seven independent cases which follow. Each case involves various assumptions as to the amount and type of income earned by Ms. Barbra Baines during 2021, as well as other information that is relevant to the determination of her 2021 income tax payable. Barbra's net income is equal to her taxable income in all cases.

In those cases where we have assumed that the income was from employment, the employer withheld the maximum EI premium and CPP contribution.

Case 1 Barbra and her husband, Billy, are both 67 years of age. Billy is sufficiently disabled that he qualifies for the disability tax credit. The components of the 2021 income earned by Barbra and Billy are as follows:

	Barbra	Billy
Interest	$ 2,600	$ 650
Canada Pension Plan benefits	12,600	Nil
Old Age Security benefits	7,400	7,400
Income from registered pension plan	22,300	1,230
Net income	$44,900	$9,280

Case 2 Barbra is 43 years old and has net and taxable income of $86,500, all of which is from rental income. Her husband died last year. She has two children. Mark is 15 and is physically infirm, but not sufficiently disabled to qualify for the disability tax credit. He has income from part-time work as a graphic artist of $3,450. The other child, Sandy, is 12 and is in good health and has no net income during the current year.

Case 3 Barbra is 58 years old and has net and taxable income of $102,000 from investments. She is divorced and has been awarded custody of her 21-year-old disabled son. The son qualifies for the disability tax credit. He has net income of $7,560 and is dependent on his mother for support.

Case 4 Barbra is 31 years old and has net income of $83,000 earned from employment. She makes contributions of $5,600 to registered charities. She is not married nor in a common-law partnership and has no dependants.

Case 5 Barbra is 58 years old and has net income of $93,500 earned from employment. Her common-law partner is 48 years old and has net income of $7,260. They have an adopted son who is 19 years old and lives at home. Medical expenses for Barbra and her partner total $3,200. Medical expenses for their son total $8,400. The son has net income of $5,600.

Case 6 Barbra is 45 years old and has net income of $84,600 earned from employment. Her husband, John, is 37 years old and has net income of $7,200. They have no children. However, they provide in-home care for John's father, who is 63 years old, dependent because of a physical infirmity, and has no net income of his own. His disability is not severe enough to qualify for the disability tax credit. Also living with them is Barbra's 67-year-old father. He is in good physical and mental health and has net income of $19,400.

Case 7 Barbra is 46 years old and has net income of $163,000 earned from employment. Her husband, Larry, is 41 years old and has net income of $7,240. They have a 20-year-old son who lives at home. He is dependent because of a physical infirmity, but it is not severe enough to qualify him for the disability tax credit. However, he was able to attend university on a full-time basis for eight months during 2020. Barbra pays his tuition fees of $8,300, as well as $640 for the textbooks he requires in his program. The son has agreed to transfer the maximum tuition amount allowable to Barbra. The son has net income of $9,600.

Required: In each case, calculate Barbra Baines' minimum federal income tax payable for 2021. Indicate any carry forwards available to her and her dependants and the carry forward provisions. Ignore any amounts Barbra might have had withheld or paid in instalments and the possibility of pension splitting.

AP 4-5 (Comprehensive Tax Payable)

Ms. Tanja Umstead is 46 years old and lives in Richmond, British Columbia. She is in good health and works in the sales department of a large publicly traded company.

Tanja's Personal Information

1. She is divorced from her husband and has custody of her 11-year-old daughter, Cynthia. The daughter is sufficiently disabled that she qualifies for the disability tax credit. The daughter has 2021 net income of $6,425, largely made up of interest on bonds purchased from an inheritance.

2. Tanja's 68-year-old mother lives with her and provides care for Cynthia on a full-time basis. She is active and healthy. As she receives no compensation for this work, Tanja has no child care costs during 2021. The mother's 2021 net income is $13,460.

3. Because of a 2021 decrease in Cynthia's mobility, Tanja has had to install access ramps in several locations in her home. The cost of these ramps was $14,600.

4. During 2021, Tanja worked nearly 300 hours as a volunteer search and rescue volunteer. She received $200 in compensation for this work.

5. Tanja's 2021 medical expenses are as follows:

Various prescription drugs (Tanja and Cynthia)	$ 3,465
Various medical specialist treatments for Cynthia	10,490
Prescription sunglasses for Tanja and Cynthia	875
Cosmetic surgery for Tanja	2,463
Dentist fees for Tanja's mother	3,300
Dentures for Tanja's mother	1,325

6. During 2021, Tanja contributes $3,500 to the Red Cross, a registered Canadian charity.

Employment Information

1. Tanja's salary compensation for 2021 is $93,500. In addition, she was awarded a year-end bonus of $12,000, all of which is payable in January 2022.

2. Tanja's employer sponsors a defined benefit registered pension plan (RPP). During 2021, Tanja and her employer each contribute $4,150 to the plan. In addition, her employer withheld maximum EI contributions of $890 and maximum CPP contributions of $3,166.

3. Her employer offers to pay the tuition for employees taking foreign language courses. Tanja is taking an intensive course in spoken Chinese at a British Columbia university. The tuition fee for the course is $3,600, all of which is paid for by her employer. The tuition payment is to be included in her employment income as a taxable benefit. The duration of the course is eight months, and Tanja must purchase her own textbooks for $150.

4. Tanja is provided with disability insurance by an employer-sponsored plan. During 2021, as a consequence of an automobile accident, she was unable to go to work for one month and receives benefits of $6,500. Starting in 2019, Tanja has been contributing $340 per year for the plan's coverage. Her employer makes a matching contribution each year.

5. Tanja's employer provides her with an automobile that was purchased several years ago at a cost of $39,500. During 2021, the car is driven 41,000 kilometres, 34,000 of which were for employment-related travel and 7,000 for personal use. Tanja is required to pay her own operating costs, which for 2021 totalled $7,240. Except for the one month that she was off from work, the car was available to Tanja throughout the year. During the one month that she was off, the car was left in her employer's garage as required by the employer's policy.
6. Tanja's employer provides all of its employees with financial counselling services. The cost to the company of the services provided to Tanja was $450.
7. As a result of winning a sales contest, Tanja received a one-week trip to Las Vegas. The value of this trip in Canadian dollars was $5,620.
8. Several years ago, Tanja received options to acquire 250 shares of her employer's common stock at a price of $25 per share. When the options were granted, the shares were trading at $25 per share. During 2021, Tanja exercises all of these options. On the exercise date, the shares are trading at $32 per share. Tanja is still holding the shares at the end of the year.

Required: Calculate Tanja's minimum taxable income and federal income tax payable for 2021. Ignore any GST/HST/PST considerations.

AP 4-6 (Tax Payable with Multiple Credits)

Ms. Eleanor Victoria's husband died two years ago. After her husband died, she moved from her house in Prince George, B.C., to a rented house in Victoria, B.C.

Ms. Victoria's widowed mother, Marjorie Vancouver, lives with Ms. Victoria and takes care of the house, Ms. Victoria's younger daughter, Amy, and all of the household cooking. She has 2021 net income of $8,000. She does not have a mental or physical disability.

Diane Victoria, Eleanor's older daughter, is studying psychology at McGill University in Montreal. Her field is addiction research with a special emphasis on gambling. She does volunteer work at a gambling addiction treatment centre in Montreal in the summers. As Eleanor has paid for her tuition and living costs, Diane has agreed that any credits available should be transferred to her mother.

Diane has decided not to file an income tax return this year as she is too busy with her studies and volunteer work. Her net income of $2,300 was earned from a part-time job on campus.

Other information concerning Ms. Victoria for 2021 is as follows:

1. Eleanor was born on May 15, 1969.
2. The birth dates and net income for the year of her dependants are as follows:

	Birth Date (Y/M/D)	Net Income
Diane	1997-05-14	$2,300
Amy	2005-10-11	Nil
Marjorie	1936-05-21	8,000

3. Eleanor's T4 for 2021 showed the following:

Salary	$62,202
Employee's EI premiums	890
Employee's CPP contributions	3,166
RPP contributions	2,406
Pension adjustment	7,829
Union dues	583
Charitable donations	175

4. Eleanor and her family had the following medical expenses for 2021, all of which Eleanor paid for:

Patient	Medical Expenses	Description	Amount
Eleanor	Grace Hospital	Ambulance charge	$ 392
Eleanor	Paramed Home Health	Nursing care	1,350
Marjorie	Dr. Zhang (Optometrist)	Contact lenses	110
Marjorie	Pharmacy	Prescription	75
Diane	Dr. Glassman	Physiotherapist	100
Amy	Walk Right Foot Clinic	Orthotics	450
Amy	Dr. Tamo	Dental fees	1,120
Total			$3,597

5. In addition to the $175 in charitable contributions withheld by Eleanor's employer, Eleanor and Diane had the following charitable donations for 2021:

Donor	Charitable Donation Receipts	Amount
Eleanor	Heart and Stroke Foundation	$ 375
Eleanor	Terry Fox Foundation	50
Diane	Addiction Research Council of Canada	100

Because of donations in previous years, neither Diane nor Eleanor qualify for the first-time donor's super credit.

6. During 2021, Diane attended university full time. Her tuition fees for the year were $7,000.

Required: Calculate Eleanor's minimum 2021 federal income tax payable (ignore the possibility of withholdings by her employer). List any assumptions you have made and any notes and tax planning issues you feel should be discussed with Eleanor.

AP 4-7 (Comprehensive Tax Payable)

Margarita Dalvi is a financial analyst employed by a large public company. Her 2021 salary is $143,000, none of which is commission income. Her employer does not require that she pay any travel or other expenses. In addition, she was awarded an incentive bonus of $34,500. Two-thirds of this bonus was paid during 2021, with the balance due in September 2022.

Ms. Dalvi's employer withheld the following amounts from her earnings:

EI premiums	$ 890
CPP contributions	3,166
RPP contributions	6,400
Federal income taxes	29,000
Contributions to United Way, a Canadian registered charity	4,000
Professional association dues	1,200

Ms. Dalvi is 55 years old and married to Jonathan Dalvi, who has been legally blind since an automobile accident that occurred several years ago. Jonathan turned 65 years old on December 25, 2021. He has 2021 income from investments of $7,200. The couple has three children:

Martha is 15 years old. She has 2021 net income from various part-time jobs of $11,000.

Mary is 19 years old and has mental health problems that prevent her from working on a full-time basis. She lives with her mother and father and has 2021 income from part-time jobs of $4,800.

Mark is 21 years old and attends university on a full-time basis for 10 months of the year. His tuition fees were $9,400 and paid for by Ms. Dalvi. As he has no income of his own, he has agreed to transfer the maximum tuition amount to his mother.

The family's 2021 medical expenses, all of which were paid by Ms. Dalvi, were as follows:

Ms. Dalvi and her husband	$ 6,200
Martha	1,800
Mary	11,300
Mark	2,500

Other Information:

1. Ms. Dalvi is provided with an automobile by her employer. The automobile is leased at a rate of $728 per month, including applicable HST. This payment also includes a payment of $50 per month for insurance coverage. During 2021, the automobile is driven 57,000 kilometres, of which 42,000 were employment related and 15,000 were for personal use. The automobile was used by Ms. Dalvi for 11 months during 2021. She was required to return the automobile to her employer's garage during the month she did not use it.

2. During 2021, Ms. Dalvi spent $14,800 on employment-related meals and entertainment with clients at local establishments. Her employer reimbursed $9,500 of these costs.

3. Throughout their marriage, the Dalvis have always lived in rented premises. Seeing the current level of mortgage rates as presenting an opportunity to acquire a residence, they purchase a four-bedroom bungalow in the same neighbourhood for $422,000 on July 1, 2021. On this date, her employer provides Ms. Dalvi with a $250,000 interest-free loan that will facilitate this acquisition. However, the balance must be paid on July 1, 2026. Assume that the prescribed rate is 1% throughout 2021.

4. During 2021, Ms. Dalvi receives several gifts from her employer:

   - As is the case for all of her employer's senior staff, she receives a $400 gift certificate that can be used for merchandise at a local clothing store.
   - In recognition of 10 years of continuous service, she receives an engraved wristwatch. The retail value of this watch is $1,200.
   - At Christmas all of the employees of her employer receive a gift basket containing gourmet food items. The retail value of this basket is $300.

5. Ms. Dalvi received options to purchase 1,200 shares of her employer's stock at a price of $37 per share two years ago. At the time the options were granted, the market price of the shares was $40 per share. During July 2021, when the shares are trading at $45 per share, Ms. Dalvi exercises all of these options. She is still holding these shares at the end of the year.

Required:

A. Determine Ms. Dalvi's minimum net income for 2021.

B. Determine Ms. Dalvi's minimum taxable income for 2021.

C. Based on your answer in Part B, determine Ms. Dalvi's federal income tax payable and amount owing (refund) for 2021.

AP 4-8 (Comprehensive Tax Payable)

Ezra Pinnock is 73 years old and is an engineering professor at a major Canadian university. He is in good health and lives in Toronto in a large house he inherited from his mother.

Employment Information

1. Ezra's salary received for 2021 is $163,000. As the result of negotiations by his union, he is entitled to receive an additional $8,000 in salary related to his work during 2021. However, this adjustment will not be received until January 2022.

2. During 2021, Ezra's employer deducts EI contributions of $890. Because of his age and the fact that he is collecting CPP benefits, Ezra no longer has to make CPP contributions.

3. Ezra's employer sponsors a defined benefit pension plan. Because Ezra no longer contributes to this plan, when he reached age 69 he was required to start withdrawing from his pension plan. During 2021, he received pension income from this plan of $26,000.

4. As much of Ezra's work involves distance education, he is required by his employer to maintain an office in his home. This home office occupies 18% of the space in his residence and is viewed as his principal place of business. The 2021 costs associated with this residence are as follows:

Electricity	$ 4,680
Property taxes	19,200
Interest on mortgage	12,000
Insurance	3,450
Repairs to roof	4,970
Lawn maintenance	863
Snow removal	647
Total	$45,810

5. Ezra is one of his university's more charismatic professors, and he does an extensive amount of travel promoting the university's programs. According to his employment contract, he is required to pay his own travel expenses. He receives an allowance of $1,000 per month ($12,000 in total) to cover his travel costs. The actual costs for 2021 are as follows:

Hotels	$4,200
Meals while travelling	1,650
Airline tickets	2,150

In addition to these costs, Ezra uses his personal automobile for some of the travel. During 2021, the mileage on the car totalled 32,000 kilometres, with 16,000 of these related to his travel for the university and the remaining 16,000 for personal use. Operating costs for the year totalled $3,200. His accountant has advised him that CCA on the automobile for the year (100% basis) would be $4,500. Ezra receives no allowance for the use of his automobile.

6. In 2021, having accumulated 10 years of service with his current employer, Ezra receives a cash award of $350 and a very fancy plaque. In addition, all of the university employees receive a basket of gourmet food at Christmas. The value of this basket is $325.

7. The university provides Ezra with $500,000 in life insurance coverage, as well as a supplemental accident and sickness insurance plan. The 2021 cost to the university for the life insurance coverage is $675, while the cost for the accident and sickness plan is $472. The accident and sickness plan would pay cash benefits due to injury or illness, but it would not pay periodic benefits to replace salary if Ezra were unable to work. Ezra does not contribute to the payments for the accident and sickness plan.

8. After he was injured in an accident, Ezra receives benefits under the accident and sickness plan of $1,245 during the year.

Other Income

Having worked for several other universities prior to joining his present employer, Ezra has 2021 receipts from the registered pension plans sponsored by these universities of $35,000. In addition, he receives Canada Pension Plan benefits of $13,000. Since he knows his income will remain quite high for the foreseeable future, Ezra has not applied for OAS.

Personal Information

1. Ezra has been married to Laurie Pinnock for over 40 years. Laurie is 64 years old and, because of a terrible skiing accident three years ago, she is sufficiently disabled that she qualifies for the disability tax credit. She has 2021 net income of $8,420, which includes $2,500 from a registered pension plan.
2. Ezra and Laurie have a 25-year-old son named Martin. He is currently unemployed and lives at home with this parents. His only income is $3,400 in Employment Insurance benefits.
3. Laurie's father, Ezekial, is 92 years old. He lives in Ezra and Laurie's basement granny suite, along with his 77-year-old common law partner, Brenda. Ezekial has a physical infirmity and has income from various sources of $17,300. Brenda is in good health, but she has no income in 2021. She moved to Canada five years ago, so she is not eligible for OAS.
4. During 2021, Ezra spent $11,400 for home modifications required to deal with the mobility restrictions caused by Laurie's disability. Since Ezekial has very poor night vision, Ezra also spent $1,200 on installing motion-activated external lights for Ezekial's safety.
5. During 2021, the family had medical expenses, all of which were paid for by Ezra, as follows:

Ezra	$2,850
Laurie	3,420
Martin	2,470
Ezekial	685
Brenda*	1,432

*All of Brenda's expenses were for elective cosmetic surgery.

6. During 2021, Laurie wins $200,000 in a lottery. She donates cash of $50,000 to the Safe Skiing Research Fund, a registered Canadian charity. Laurie has been a regular donor since her accident.

Required: For the 2021 taxation year, calculate Ezra's minimum:

1. net income,
2. taxable income,
3. federal income tax payable.

In determining these amounts, ignore GST/HST/PST considerations and the possibility of pension income splitting.

Tax Software Assignment Problems

Solutions to Tax Software Assignment Problems are available to instructors only.

Tax Software AP 4-1

This problem is continued in Chapter 11.

DISCLAIMER: All characters appearing in this problem are fictitious. Any resemblance to real persons, living or dead, is purely coincidental.

Mr. Buddy Musician (SIN 527-000-061) was born in Vancouver on August 28, 1953. He has spent most of his working life as a pianist and song writer. He and his family live at 111 WWW Street, Vancouver, B.C. V4H 3W4, phone (604) 111-1111.

Mr. Musician's wife, Natasha (SIN 527-000-129), was born on June 6, 1995. She and Mr. Musician have four children. Each child was born on April 1 of the following years: Linda, 2015; Larry, 2016; Donna, 2017; and Donald, 2018. None of the four children have any income of their own for 2020. Natasha's only income during 2020 is $3,200 from singing engagements.

Buddy and Natasha Musician have two adopted children. Richard (SIN 527-000-285) was born on March 15, 2003, and has income of $2,800 for the year. Due to his accelerated schooling, he started full-time attendance at university in September of 2020 at the age of 17. His first semester tuition fee is $3,000. These amounts are paid by Mr. Musician.

The other adopted child, Sarah, was born on September 2, 2000, and was in full-time attendance at university for all of 2020 (including a four-month summer session). Her tuition is $9,600. These amounts are also paid by Mr. Musician. Sarah has no income during the year.

Neither Richard nor Sarah will have any income in the next three years. They both have agreed that the maximum tuition amount should be transferred to their father.

Mr. Musician's mother, Eunice, was born on April 10, 1933, and his father, Earl, was born on November 16, 1931. They both live with Mr. Musician and his wife. While his father has some mobility issues, he is not infirm. His mother is legally blind. Eunice Musician had income of $9,500 for the year, while Earl Musician had income of $7,500.

Other information concerning Mr. Musician and his family for 2020 is as follows:

1. Mr. Musician earned $16,500 for work as the house pianist at the Loose Moose Pub. His T4 showed that his employer withheld $500 for income taxes and $280.70 for EI. No CPP was withheld as he had previously filed an election to stop contributing to the CPP on January 2, 2019.

2. During the year, Mr. Musician made his annual $3,000 donation to Planned Parenthood of Canada, a registered Canadian charity.

3. Mr. Musician has been married before to Lori Musician (SIN 527-000-319). Lori is 52 years old and lives in Fort Erie, Ontario.

4. Mr. Musician has two additional children who live with their mother, Ms. Dolly Nurse (SIN 527-000-582), in Burnaby, British Columbia. The children are Megan Nurse, aged 12, and Andrew Nurse, aged 14. Neither child has any income during 2020. While Ms. Nurse and Mr. Musician were never married, Mr. Musician acknowledges that he is the father of both children. Although Buddy has provided limited financial aid by paying their dental and medical expenses, the children are not dependent on Buddy for support.

5. Mr. Musician wishes to claim all his medical expenses on a calendar-year basis. On December 2, 2020, Mr. Musician paid dental expenses to Canada Wide Dental Clinics for the following individuals:

Himself	$1,200
Natasha (wife)	700
Richard (adopted son)	800
Sarah (adopted daughter)	300
Linda (daughter)	100
Earl (father)	1,050
Lori (ex-wife)	300
Dolly Nurse (mother of two of his children)	675
Megan Nurse (daughter of Dolly Nurse)	550
Total	$5,675

6. Mr. Musician signed a contract with Fred Nesbitt on January 13, 2020, to do permanent modifications to his house. The contract was for the installation of ramps with sturdy hand

railings outside his front and back doors to give his parents easier access to the house and modifications to their bathroom so they would be less likely to fall when using the shower. The contract price was $5,800. As neither of his parents has a severe and prolonged mobility impairment, these expenditures are not eligible medical expenses.

7. Mr. Musician paid four quarterly instalments of $1,000 each (total of $4,000) for 2020, as requested on his instalment reminders from the CRA. He paid each instalment on the due date.
8. Assume that Mr. Musician has not applied to receive either OAS or CPP benefits.

Required: With the objective of minimizing Mr. Musician's tax payable, prepare Mr. Musician's 2020 income tax return using the ProFile tax software program assuming Natasha does not file an income tax return. List any assumptions you have made and any notes and tax planning issues you feel should be placed in the file.

Tax Software AP 4-2

This problem is continued in Chapter 11.

DISCLAIMER: All characters appearing in this problem are fictitious. Any resemblance to real persons, living or dead, is purely coincidental.

George Pharmacy is a pharmaceutical sales rep who has been very successful at his job in the last few years. Unfortunately, his family life has not been very happy. Three years ago, his only child, Anna, was driving a car that was hit by a drunk driver. She and her husband were killed and their 14-year-old son, Kevin, was blinded in the accident. He also suffered extensive injuries to his jaw that have required major and prolonged dental work.

George and his wife, Valerie, adopted Kevin. Valerie quit her part-time job to care for him. She also cares for her mother, Joan Drugstore, who lives with them. Joan suffers from dementia, Parkinson's, and severe depression. The family doctor has signed a letter stating that she is dependent on George and Valerie because of her impairments. Joan does not meet the residency requirements necessary to qualify for Canadian OAS payments.

Valerie's parents separated two years ago in Scotland after her father, David Drugstore, suffered enormous losses in the stock market. They were forced to sell their home and David moved to Chile. David phones periodically to request that money be deposited in his online bank account.

George's brother, Martin, completed an alcohol rehabilitation program after being fired for drinking on the job. He is also living with George and Valerie while he is enrolled as a full-time student at Western University. George is paying his tuition, and Martin has agreed to transfer any available education-related amounts to George. Although Martin plans to file his 2020 income tax return, he has not done so yet.

Kevin is taking several undergraduate psychology courses at Western University. After hearing a talk given by an expert blind echolocator (a person who uses sound to locate objects), his goal is to become a researcher at the Brain and Mind Institute and study the use of echolocation. Kevin has agreed to transfer the maximum tuition credit to George.

Other information concerning George for 2020 is provided on the following pages.

Required: With the objective of minimizing George's tax payable, prepare the 2020 income tax return of George Pharmacy using the ProFile tax software program assuming Valerie does not file a tax return.

List any assumptions you have made and any notes and tax planning issues you feel should be placed in the file. Ignore HST implications in your solution by assuming that George does not qualify for the GST/HST rebate.

Personal Information	Taxpayer
Title	Mr.
First Name	George
Last Name	Pharmacy
SIN	527-000-509
Date of Birth (Y/M/D)	1956-07-02
Marital Status	Married
Canadian Citizen?	Yes
Provide Information to Elections Canada?	Yes
Own Foreign Property of More than $100,000 Canadian?	No

Taxpayer's Address
123 ZZZ Street, London, Ontario, N0Z 0Z0
Phone number (519) 111-1111

Family Members	Spouse	Child	Mother-in-Law
First Name	Valerie	Kevin	Joan
Last Name	Pharmacy	Pharmacy	Drugstore
SIN	527-000-483	527-000-517	None
Date of Birth (Y/M/D)	1955-12-30	2004-10-17	1935-02-24
Net income	$6,520 in CPP	Nil	$500

Family Members	Father-in-Law	Brother
First Name	David	Martin
Last Name	Drugstore	Pharmacy
SIN	None	527-000-533
Date of Birth (Y/M/D)	1936-01-12	1973-06-02
Net income	Nil	$8,300

During September, David was arrested in Chile. Valerie had to spend three weeks in Chile and pay $2,000 in bribes before she could get him released from jail. George had to pay Nannies On Call $3,500 for in-home help to take care of Kevin while she was gone.

T2202A (Martin)	Box	Amount
Tuition fees for Martin Pharmacy (brother)	A	8,000
Number of months in school—part time	B	0
Number of months in school—full time	C	8

T2202A (Kevin)	Box	Amount
Tuition fees for Kevin	A	3,600
Number of months in school—part time	B	8
Number of months in school—full time	C	0

Donor	Charitable Donation Receipts	Am't
Valerie	Mothers Against Drunk Drivers (MADD)	1,000
George	Canadian Institute for the Blind (CNIB)	3,000

T4	Box	Amount
Issuer—Mega Pharma Inc.		
Employment income	14	378,000.00
Employee's CPP contributions	16	2,898.00
Employee's EI premiums	18	856.36
Income tax deducted	22	114,000.00
Employment commissions	42	82,000.00
Charitable donations	46	400.00

During 2020, Mega reimbursed George $3,788 for meals and entertainment with clients, $2,268 for hotels, and $4,925 for airline tickets.

In addition to George's salary, he also earns commissions. His employer requires him to have an office in his home and has signed the form T2200 each year to this effect.

On October 1, 2020, George purchased a new computer and software that will be used solely in his home office for employment-related uses. The computer cost $3,600 and the various software programs cost $1,250.

House Costs	
Area of home used for home office (square feet)	650
Total area of home (square feet)	5,000
Telephone line including high speed internet connection	620
Hydro	3,200
Insurance—House	4,000
Maintenance and repairs	3,800
Mortgage interest	6,200
Mortgage life insurance premiums	400
Property taxes	6,700

(Y/M/D)	Patient	Medical Expenses	Description	Am't
2020-12-31	George	Johnson Inc.	Out of Canada insurance	731.00
2020-08-31	George	Dr. Smith	Dental fees	155.40
2020-09-19	George	Optician	Prescription glasses	109.00
2020-11-07	Valerie	Pharmacy	Prescription	66.84
2020-06-07	Joan	Dr. Wong	Psychiatric counselling	2,050.00
2020-03-22	David	Tropical Disease Centre	Prescription	390.00
2020-12-20	Martin	Dr. Walker	Group therapy	6,000.00
2019-10-01	Kevin	Dr. Takarabe	Orthodontics and dental	30,000.00

George paid $800 for the care and feeding of Kevin's seeing eye dog, Isis, during 2020.

George's 2020 RRSP deduction limit is $285,550.

Tax Software AP 4-3

This problem is continued in Chapter 11.

DISCLAIMER: All characters appearing in all versions of this problem are fictitious. Any resemblance to real persons, living or dead, is purely coincidental.

Seymour Career and Mary Career are your tax clients. They have been married for two years. Mary has progressed quickly in MoreCorp, the large publicly traded firm she is working for, due to her strong tax and accounting background. Her firm has an excellent health and dental plan that reimburses 100% of all medical and dental expenses.

Although Seymour has been working, his increasing ill health makes it likely that he will not be able to continue to work in 2020. He is contemplating a return to university as a student of music.

In order to estimate her possible financial position in 2021, Mary would like you to prepare her 2020 income tax return assuming that Seymour has no income for 2020.

Mary's 2020 RRSP deduction limit is $244,550.

Title	Ms.	Mr.
First Name	Mary	Seymour
Last Name	Career	Career
SIN	527-000-129	527-000-079
Date of birth (Y/M/D)	1982-12-08	1961-01-29
Marital Status	Married	Married
Canadian Citizen?	Yes	Yes
Provide Information to Elections Canada?	Yes	Yes
Own Foreign Property of More than $100,000 Canadian?	No	No

Taxpayer's Address
123 ABC Street, Saint John, N.B., E0E 0E0
Phone number (506) 111-1111
Spouse's address same as taxpayer? Yes

First Name	William
Last Name	Career
SIN	527-000-319
Date of Birth (Y/M/D)	2013-02-24
Net Income	Nil

T4 (Mary)	Box	Amount
Issuer—MoreCorp		
Employment income	14	152,866.08
Employee's CPP contributions	16	2,898.00
Employee's EI premiums	18	856.36
RPP contributions	20	Nil
Income tax deducted	22	48,665.11
Charitable Donations	46	1,000.00

Donor	Charitable Donation Receipts	Amount
Seymour	Canadian Cancer Foundation	500
Seymour	Salvation Army	250

Required: With the objective of minimizing Mary's tax payable, prepare her 2020 income tax return using the ProFile tax software program. Assume that Seymour has no income in 2020 and that he does not file an income tax return.

CHAPTER 5

Capital Cost Allowance

Learning Objectives

After completing Chapter 5, you should be able to:

1. Explain the general differences between a capital expenditure and an expenditure on income account (Paragraph [P hereafter] 5-1 to 5-2).
2. Describe the two types of capital property and how the ITA treats them as opposed to the treatment of expenditures on income account (P 5-3 to 5-8).
3. Describe the types of property specifically excluded from depreciable property (P 5-9 to 5-11).
4. Describe the general differences between the accounting for depreciable property and the income tax approach to depreciable property (P 5-12 to 5-24).
5. Determine the types of costs that are included in the amounts that are added to depreciable property classes (P 5-25 to 5-34).
6. Describe how income versus capital determinations are made in deciding whether one has a capital expenditure or not. Is there a checklist approach that can be used? What factors does the CRA usually look at? (P 5-35 to 5-41).
7. In general terms, describe the three types of rules that impact the CCA deduction that may be claimed (P 5-42 to 5-43).
8. Explain the purpose for the available-for-use rules and how these rules to different property (P 5-44 to 5-48).
9. Describe the general rules for including depreciable property in classes and the exceptions that allow separate classes (P 5-49 to 5-54).
10. Describe the basic CCA/UCC rules, including the calculations and interaction among specialty rules such as the AccII and the short fiscal period rule (P 5-55 to 5-58).
11. Be aware of the rates and methods that are applicable to common CCA classes to determine the maximum CCA for the period (P 5-59).
12. Describe the old half-year rule and its impact on the determination of maximum CCA for the period (P 5-60 to 5-63)
13. Explain what "net additions" are and the role they play in determining CCA (P 5-64).
14. Describe the Accelerated Investment Incentive (AccII), when it applies, and when it does not apply (P 5-65 to 5-76).
15. Describe the application of the AccII to classes 12, 13, 14, and 53. Explain how this differs from when the AccII is applied to other classes (P 5-77 to 5-82).

16. Describe the enhanced CCA provisions for zero-emission vehicles and zero-emission passenger vehicles in class 54 (P 5-83 to 5-91).
17. Explain the purpose of the short fiscal period rules and how they apply in the determination of maximum CCA (P 5-92 to 5-94).
18. Describe the additions to class 14.1, the general meaning of goodwill, and the special treatment it receives (P 5-95 to 5-101).
19. Describe situations in which tax planning considerations may be important in relation to depreciable property (P 5-102 to 5-106).
20. Describe the new depreciable property expensing rules for CCPCs, their exceptions, how the rules apply, and how tax planning advantages can be obtained (P 5-107 to 5-110).
21. Explain how dispositions effect the UCC of a class of depreciable property and the circumstances under which recapture, terminal losses, and capital gains can occur (P 5-111 to 5-125).
22. Explain the application of recapture and terminal losses to employees (P 5-126).
23. Explain the special disposition rule that applies to zero-emission passenger vehicles in class 54 (P 5-127 to 5-128).
24. Explain how the treatment of dispositions in class 14.1 differs from that for other CCA classes (P 5-129 to 5-134).
25. Explain Figure 5-2 in your own words (P 5-135).
26. Re-create the commonly used CCA schedule for a situation using your own numbers (P 5-136 to 5-137).
27. Describe the two separate class elections in your own words and explain why they may be useful (P 5-138 to 5-147).

Introduction

Understanding Depreciable Property

5-1. The income tax system draws a distinction between expenditures that are on account of income and those on account of capital, which are referred to as "capital expenditures." Expenditures on account of income generally refer to ordinary recurring expenses that arise as a result of carrying on a business or earning income from property or even employment income. Examples, with respect to a business, include office expenses, administrative expenses, and salary and other employee-related expenses. Expenses incurred on income from a source of property income, such as rental properties, include the same type of expenses including maintenance, advertising, and the payment of property taxes. These types of normal, everyday expenses are generally 100% deductible in the year to which they relate.

5-2. Capital expenditures, on the other hand, refer to costs and expenses incurred to purchase property, improve property, or create, enhance, preserve, or improve upon a business structure. Examples of property purchases include the purchase of machinery, equipment, office furniture, automobiles, buildings, and so on. Expenses of improvement would include an expenditure that preserves, enhances, or improves property but which is not simply ongoing routine maintenance. For example, a tune-up on an automobile would be routine maintenance and an expenditure on income, whereas replacing the engine of an automobile would be a capital expenditure since the automobile is, at a minimum, preserved or enhanced. Finally, legal expenses to negotiate a lease on a building that will be used to carry on a business would be considered a capital expenditure, although technically no property has been acquired. This is because the expenditure relates to the creation of a business structure.

5-3. You will notice that we have used the word "property" rather than the word "asset." While the word "asset" is used in the ITA, its use is often restricted as opposed to the word "property," which is used extensively. The difference often relates to the fact that the term "asset" is associated with accounting concepts whereas the word "property" has more of a legal connotation and is therefore used frequently in any legislation, including both the ITA and ETA.

5-4. The word "property" is broadly defined in the ITA to include both tangible and intangible property as well as capital expenditures that do not necessarily result in the acquisition of property as mentioned in Paragraph 5-2. An example of a difference between an "asset" and "property" would be prepaid expenses, which are typically shown on a balance sheet as an asset when materiality is not an issue. Prepaid expenses, however, would not be considered property for income tax purposes. Throughout this text we will continue to use the word "property" except where the ITA actually uses the word "asset" or where we discuss accounting concepts.

5-5. In terms of "capital expenditures," the ITA uses the general expression "capital property." Capital property is divided into two categories: (1) depreciable property and (2) capital property that is not depreciable, which is commonly referred to as "non-depreciable capital property." Examples of non-depreciable capital property include vacant land and various types of investments, including shares of corporations, mutual fund units, and interests in a partnership. We will examine non-depreciable capital property in Chapter 8 when we discuss capital gains and losses.

5-6. Our focus in this chapter is on depreciable property, which, as we have discussed, refers to a capital expenditure. In Chapter 3 on employment income we saw that employment expenses were restricted (ITA 8(2)) and that only very limited capital expenditures were allowed, specifically the cost of an automobile used for employment purposes or certain other capital expenditures including aircraft and musical instruments. The determination of how one goes about calculating the deductible amount of a capital expenditure for an employee-owned automobile is part of the capital cost allowance (CCA) system. The CCA rules are predomintaly found in Subdivision b of Division B of Part I of the ITA and will be discussed in detail in this chapter.

5-7. Subdivision b contains the rules for determining business and property income. In terms of capital expenditures, ITA 18(1)(b) takes front and centre and reads as follows:

> **18(1)(b)** In computing the income of a taxpayer from a business or property no deduction shall be made in respect of an outlay, loss, or replacement of capital, a payment on account of capital or an allowance in respect of depreciation, obsolescence or depletion except as expressly permitted by this Part.

5-8. ITA 18(1)(b) prohibits the deduction of a capital expenditure but goes on to add "except as expressly permitted." This is where ITA 20(1)(a) comes into the picture, which reads, in part, as follows:

> **20(1)(a)** Notwithstanding paragraph 18(1)(b) ... there may be deducted ... the following amounts: ... such part of the capital cost ... of property ... as is allowed by regulation.

5-9. The reference to "property" means depreciable property, and the reference to a regulation is to Part XI (i.e., Part 11) of the ITR. While there are plenty of rules, at this stage we will reference only two of the more important regulations that will assist in understanding the principal concepts of depreciable property and CCA.

5-10. The first is ITR 1102, together with general exclusions found in classes 8 and 14.1, which establishes what is not to be included as depreciable property. The more important exclusions are the following:

- Capital expenditures that are allowed to be deducted in full outside of the CCA system (e.g., landscaping capital expenditures are allowed as a deduction in certain circumstances [ITA 20(1)(aa)])
- Inventory (technically inventory would generally be considered a capital expenditure as property acquired)
- Property not acquired for the purpose of earning income (e.g., where a property is used in part to earn income and in part for personal purposes, there are rules that effectively treat the part of the property used to earn income as a separate property)
- Land even if there is a building on the land
- Non-depreciable capital property (i.e., investments)
- An animal
- A tree, shrub, herb, or similar growing thing

5-11. Once you have determined that you are dealing with a capital expenditure that is depreciable property, then the next step is to identify the class of depreciable property that applies to that expenditure. ITR 1100, together with a schedule, identifies classes by number from 1 to 55. Each class has a detailed description to help identify the specific class. Finally the rules then set out a method to calculate the annual deduction, which is frequently based on a specific percentage. We discuss the actual calculations plus a few more rules in this chapter.

Exercise 5-1

Subject: Capital Expenditures and Depreciable Property

For each of the following expenditures, identify whether the expenditure is on account of income (i.e., a regular expense) or is a capital expenditure. If the expenditure is a capital expenditure, determine whether it is depreciable property. Give reasons for your answer.

1. A pet store acquires six puppies to sell
2. A warehouse facility purchases two guard dogs
3. You purchase 100 shares of a public corporation for $5,000
4. You purchase an existing business and pay an additional amount for goodwill
5. You purchase a cottage that you rent out on a monthly basis
6. You replace all of the plumbing for the cottage at a cost of $15,000 while it is still being rented
7. At the beginning of 2021 you stop renting the cottage and use it exclusively for personal use
8. You pay $250,000 to purchase a franchise to operate a coffee shop

Solutions to Exercises are available in the Study Guide.

Tax and Accounting Procedures Compared

Introduction

5-12. Income tax operates largely on the basis of legal concepts and principles and not accounting concepts and principles. This means that accounting is largely irrelevant to income tax analysis and outcomes, which are based on the words of the legislation, jurisprudence, and administrative positions and concessions by the CRA. Nevertheless accountants prepare financial statements that include an income statement that sets out the profit or loss of a specific business. Different accounting principles are used to identify income and expenses and determine how they are to be treated. The end result is an accounting-based profit or loss. The income tax system, however, applies rules in determining net income or a net loss that are not always identical to those used by the accounting profession. This means that adjustments must be made to the accounting profit or loss to convert it to net income for income tax purposes. In this sense accounting concepts and principles are indirectly relevant in that they represent the starting point in determining net income.

5-13. In this next segment we will look at some of the differences and similarities between the ITA and accounting principles. Our objective is to assist you in understanding the necessary adjustments required to convert the accounting asset/depreciation concepts to the outcome required by the ITA.

5-14. There are many similarities between the CCA system that is used for income tax purposes and the depreciation concepts used in financial accounting. The objective of both is to allocate the cost of depreciable property over a number of years. Accounting, however, is much more concerned with matching the costs over the expected life of depreciable property.

The income tax system often has multiple objectives, including providing targeted incentives to encourage business growth by allowing accelerated write-offs that ignore the useful life. Some of the more significant differences between income tax and accounting are described in the material that follows.

Terminology

5-15. There are three central terms used in income tax that go by different terms in accounting. The three terms, described in Figure 5-1, are (1) the actual base upon which CCA/depreciation is calculated, (2) the actual CCA/depreciation amount, and (3) the account balance.

5-16. The base is the capital expenditure, which accountants simply refer to as the acquisition cost, whereas in income tax the expression "capital cost" is used. Capital cost includes the full cost of the property together with any other costs to put the property to the use it was intended. This would include any legal costs, delivery, and installation costs. The rule of thumb is that any expenses that relate to that expenditure are considered capital and added to the cost. A helpful test is if the expense would not have been incurred if it were not for the purchase of the depreciable property, then the expense is a capital expenditure by association.

5-17. The second point is the actual deduction. Accountants refer to this as amortization (see Figure 5-1), whereas in income tax the expression capital cost allowance or CCA is used.

5-18. The final point is the balance or account of undeducted costs. In income tax the account is called "undepreciated capital cost" or UCC, whereas the accounting profession uses "carrying value". The carrying value is determined on an asset-by-asset basis, whereas in income tax there is a separate UCC for each class of depreciable property. There is also a slight timing difference in the two concepts. In accounting, the carrying value at year end is equal to the acquisition costs minus amortization for the year. In income tax the UCC at year end is only reduced by CCA for the year at the beginning of the next year.

EXAMPLE A business with a calendar-based taxation year acquires depreciable property for $2,000 at the beginning of 2021. Amortization and CCA are both $400.

ANALYSIS The carrying value at December 31, 2021, is $1,600 [$2,000 - $400]. The UCC at December 31, 2021, is $2,000 but it is $1,600 at January 1, 2022 [$2,000 - $400]. The reason for this is because the CCA for a specific year is calculated using the UCC balance on the last day of that year.

Figure 5-1
Comparison of Accounting and Tax Terminology

Income Tax Term		Accounting Term
Capital Cost	←→	Acquisition Cost
Capital Cost Allowance (CCA)	←→	Amortization or Depreciation Expense*
Undepreciated Capital Cost (UCC)	←→	Carrying Value

*While these two terms are used interchangeably in most tax literature, for accounting purposes their use is more prescribed. Under Accounting Standards for Private Enterprises, the term "depreciation" is not used. The write-off of all types of business assets is consistently referred to as "amortization."

In contrast, under International Financial Reporting Standards, the term "depreciation" is used for tangible business assets, and the term "amortization" is reserved for intangible business assets.

Some Other Differences

5-19. In accounting, the cost of the assets are individually tracked for the purpose of determining annual amortization, the carrying value, and to determine whether there are any gains and losses when a particular asset is sold. The gains and losses are fully included or deducted in the determination of the accounting income or loss.

5-20. In income tax, individual capital cost is also required to be tracked as part of determining the amount added to the UCC of a particular class, to determine the annual CCA available, and to assess the income tax consequences if depreciable property is sold.

> **EXAMPLE—Accounting** Depreciable property is acquired for $8,000. Based on the estimated useful life of the property, accountants determine that the annual amortization should be $1,000. At the end of the 2020 taxation year the carrying value of the property is $5,000. The property is sold in 2021 for $9,000.
>
> **ANALYSIS—Accounting** In 2021, accounting income will include a $4,000 gain on the sale of the depreciable asset.
>
> **EXAMPLE—ITA** Depreciable property is acquired for $8,000. The property fell into class 8 (20% rate). Assume that the CCA claimed was limited to $1,000 for each of the first three years. UCC at the beginning of 2021 is $5,000. The property is sold in 2021 for $9,000,
>
> **ANALYSIS—ITA** The difference between the capital cost of $8,000 and the UCC at the time of sale of $5,000, or $3,000, is treated as recaptured depreciation, which is 100% included in income. The difference between the sale price of $9,000 and the capital cost of $8,000 is treated as a capital gain, only 50% of which is included in income. The result is a different treatment between income tax and accounting. In Chapter 6 we will discuss what are referred to as reconciliations, meaning adjusting amounts on accounting income statements so that the numbers are converted to what is required for income tax purposes. Some of these income tax consequences will be discussed in this chapter.
>
> **RECONCILIATION** Based on the example, accounting income would have included a $4,000 accounting gain on the sale of the depreciable asset and income tax would have required there to be added a recapture of $3,000 and a taxable capital gain of $500. As a result, if we assume that the accounting income were $100,000 and that there were no other adjustments required, we could determine net income as follows:

Accounting Income	$100,000
Add: Recapture	3,000
Add: Taxable capital gain	500
Less: Accounting gain	(4,000)
Net Income	$ 99,500

5-21. In determining amortization, accounting principles generally require the use of a straight-line method. Once determined, the method must be consistenly applied and the full amount of amortization is required to be claimed as an expense. An example would be an asset costing $10,000 with an estimated useful life of 10 years. Annual amortization would equal the same $1,000 accounting expense in each of the 10 years.

5-22. As mentioned in the introduction, the ITR set out the classes of depreciable property and the methods, rates, and other rules to be applied to determine the maximum available CCA in a given year. Once the maximum CCA has been determined the amount that is deducted for the year is at the complete discretion of the property owner(s).

5-23. Most businesses use straight-line amortization for accounting purposes. In contrast, the *ITR* require the use of the declining balance method in the majority of CCA classes. To illustrate the use of a declining balance method, assume there is a $10,000 capital cost that is included in a class with a 10% rate. The first-year CCA would be $1,000 [(10%)($10,000)], and the second-year CCA would be $900 [(10%)($9,000)], and so on. In each successive year the CCA would be based on the balance of undeducted amounts, or UCC.

5-24. In general the declining balance method often provides a faster write-off than the straight-line method because the percentage used is not reflective of the estimated useful life of depreciable property. In addition, most businesses deduct the maximum amount of CCA even though the CCA deduction is at the discretion of the business owner. The result is that the amount of CCA deducted is usually larger than the amount of the accounting amortization expense. Because of this, the amortization claimed for accounting purposes is usually significantly smaller than the CCA claimed. This fact alerts you to the realization that reconciliation adjustments will be required to convert accounting income or loss to the ITA's net income. To avoid making adjustments it is not uncommon for many small businesses to adopt the CCA system for accounting purposes.

Additions to Capital Cost

Determination of Amounts

General Rules

5-25. In general, property is depreciable property to the owner of the property regardless of whether the property was financed. Leased office furniture, automobiles, or other property would only be depreciable property to the owner lessor and not the lessee. As mentioned, capital property is only depreciable property and eligible for CCA if the property was used for the purpose of producing income from business, property, or in certain limited circumstances, employment.

5-26. Capital cost means the full cost to the taxpayer of acquiring the property and would include all freight, installation costs, duties, non-refundable provincial sales taxes, and legal, accounting, appraisal, engineering, or other fees incurred to acquire the property. Note that any refundable GST/ HST would not be added to the capital cost (see Paragraph 5-33).

5-27. In the case of property constructed by the taxpayer for use in producing income, the capital cost includes material, labour, and an appropriate allocation of overhead. In addition, it is the position of the CRA that property is being acquired to the extent of completed construction. If the property is paid for in a foreign currency, the Canadian dollar equivalent capital cost would be determined using the exchange rate in effect on the date of acquisition.

Capitalization of Interest

5-28. ITA 21 provides a taxpayer with an elective option to add the interest and other financing costs of money borrowed to acquire or finance the construction of depreciable property. This election has historically been used by major developers who are engaged in long-term construction projects and have no or little income throughout the construction period. The election provides them with an opportunity to avoid creating losses with large interest and other finnacing expenses every year and to instead add the financing costs to the capital cost of the depreciable property, which will increase future CCA claims.

Government Assistance

5-29. Another consideration in determining the capital cost of an addition to a CCA class is government assistance. Under ITA 13(7.1), any amounts received or receivable from any level of government for the purpose of acquiring depreciable property must be deducted from its capital cost. This includes grants, subsidies, forgivable loans, tax deductions, and investment tax credits. The purpose of this rule is to limit CCA to the actual out-of-pocket costs of a business.

5-30. This income tax requirement is consistent with the requirements of IAS 20, "Accounting for Government Grants and Disclosure of Government Assistance," which, in general, requires government assistance, including investment tax credits, to be deducted from the cost of assets for accounting purposes.

Non-Arm's-Length Acquisitions

5-31. The determination of the capital cost of depreciable property begins with the purchase price on the assumption that it is reflective of the fair market value (FMV) of that property. The FMV would typically represent the price that would be negotiated between informed persons acting in their own self-interest without regard to the outcome or impact on the other person. The ITA contains a number of rules that are designed to address situations and circumstances where this is not the case and there is some evidence of manipulation or coercion. These transactions are often referred to as non-arm's length, meaning that principles that support FMV are not present. Often there is some underlying income tax motivation for the deception. The income tax implications of these rules are quite punitive and will be discussed in more detail in Chapter 9.

5-32. At this point it is important to be aware that if the price paid for depreciable property appears too high or too low and the buyer and seller know each other or have some connection that may have influenced the price, the ITA can intervene to change the capital cost. This is a common theme that is applied to many provisions of the income tax law.

GST/HST and PST Considerations

5-33. GST/HST and PST is usually paid on the purchase of depreciable property and therefore is part of the capital cost. While we will not provide detailed coverage of GST/HST until Chapter 21, you should be aware of the following:

- GST paid by businesses on the acquisition of property will, in general, be refunded as input tax credits. Note that there are many complications related to this rule, and they will be discussed in Chapter 21.
- HST is the term used to refer to the combined GST and PST amounts that are collected in Ontario and all of the Atlantic provinces. In general, HST paid on the acquisition of depreciable property is refunded as input tax credits.
- QST (Quebec Sales Tax) is integrated with the GST system and, as a consequence, these amounts are refunded on much the same basis as GST.
- The PST that is paid in other provinces, such as Manitoba and British Columbia, is not refunded and, as a consequence, it is included in the capital cost of depreciable property.

5-34. From a technical point of view, all amounts of GST/HST and PST are, at least initially, included in the capital cost of depreciable property. However, to the extent that these amounts are refunded or there is an entitlement to an input tax credit, they are defined in ITA 248(16) as a form of government assistance and, as a consequence, the refunds are subtracted from the capital cost of depreciable property in the same manner as other government assistance, which generally means either including the assistance in income or, where the assistance relates to specific property, by reducing the cost of that property. In somewhat simplified terms, GST and HST amounts that are eligible to be refunded are not included in the capital cost of depreciable property in the year in which the property was acquired.

EXAMPLE Depreciable property is acquired for use in a business carried on in Manitoba at a cost of $11,200. The cost is determined as follows:

Initial cost	$10,000
Federal GST at 5%	500
Manitoba's 7% retail sales tax	700
Capital cost before adjustment for refundable GST	$11,200

ANALYSIS Provided that the business is registered for the GST and that the depreciable property is used in the provision of taxable supplies, the $500 federal GST will be refunded as an input tax credit. However, there will be no refund of the $700 paid to Manitoba. This means that the capital cost is $10,700 ($11,200 - $500).

Expenditures on Depreciable Property—Capital vs. Income

5-35. When a business owns depreciable property with extended useful lives (e.g., buildings or certain types of machinery), it is likely that, during their useful lives, the business will incur additional costs. When this occurs, a question arises as to whether the costs/expenditures are on income accountand therefore fully deductible business expenses or whether they are capital expenditures adding to the capital cost of the underlying property as discussed in the introduction to this chapter.

5-36. Determing whether a particular expenditure made to depreciable property is on income accountor is capital in nature is always a question of fact dependent on many factors. The determination, however, rests on whether the purpose of the expenditure is to enhance or improve the property beyond its original condition and is something other than regular, routine, or anticipated maintenance or repairs designed to keep the property operational.

5-37. The issue of capital versus income is one of the most widely contested issues in income tax. There is an abundance of case law in this area, some of which goes back 100 years. In the process of rendering their decisions the courts have developed their own judicial tests to determine how to decide whether a specific expenditure is income or capital. This has resulted in a number of judicial tests that tend to be applied in a checklist manner. While this approach is understandable to some degree, the result is the application of tests that were never intended to be applied to the type of expenditure being examined.

5-38. Some of the more important comments from the Supreme Court of Canada to keep in mind include the following:

- The solution to the problem is not to be found by any rigid test or description.
- It has to be dervied from many aspects of the whole set of circumstances, some of which may point in one direction, some in the other.
- It is a commonsense appreciation of all the guiding features that must provide the ultimate answer.
- It depends on what the expenditure is calculated to effect from a practical and business point of view.
- Where no capital property was acquired, nothing of an enduring benefit came into existence nor was any capital property preserved.

5-39. Each of the above precedent-setting statements by the courts related to a very specific type of expenditure that was anything but straightforward. In the last bullet the court was asked to decide whether a sizable expenditure ($1.2M) was fully deductible as on income account or was a capital expenditure. In the case (*International Colin Energy*), the company had used up most of its credit and capital and was on the verge of financial collapse. The company knew that its prospects were very good but they needed another large investor to be able to continue to survive and be profitable. The company paid a law firm a substantial fee for identifying investor candidates, one of which ended up merging with the company to form a new company that became quite profitable. The company deducted the fee paid, but the CRA disallowed it, claiming that it was capital and therefore non-deductible. The court ruled in favour of the company and allowed the expense. In its ruling the court stated that the expenditure was not capital because no capital property was acquired, nothing of an enduring benefit came into existence, nor was any capital property preserved as a result.

5-40. In deciding any capital versus income issue, large expenditures tend to be suspect and therefore investigated and challenged by the CRA. Avoiding and defending against such challenges requires understanding and applying the necessary tests together with a level of professional judgment. The CRA's website provides some general guidelines to be used in deciding whether an expenditure is on income account or is capital. We have summarized some of this commentary as follows:

1. Does the expense provide a lasting or enduring benefit?
    - The CRA notes that painting the exterior of a wooden building would not provide a lasting benefit and should be fully expensed.

- In contrast, putting vinyl or metal siding on a wooden building would be a lasting improvement and should be added to the capital cost of the building. Replacing damaged siding, however, would be a fully deductible expense on income account.

2. Does the expense maintain or improve the property beyond its original condition?
    - If a business repairs an existing set of wooden steps, the repair costs would be viewed as an expense on income account.
    - In contrast, if the wooden steps are replaced with concrete steps, this would improve the property and should be added to the capital cost of the property.

3. Is the expense for a part of the property or is it a separate property?
    - The CRA notes that the replacement of existing wiring in a building would normally be an expense on income account, provided it does not improve the property.
    - In contrast, buying a compressor for use in a business would be treated as a separate addition to the appropriate class (i.e., a capital expenditure).

5-41. The three preceding questions represent some of the tests frequently used by the CRA in determining whether an expenditure is on income or capital account. Remember, however, that these are guidelines that establish somewhat of a framework for determining the treatment of a specific expenditure and that no one test is decisive. Some courts have looked to intention to get a sense of whether the owner intended to improve the property or simply to maintain it at the same operational level. While the CRA will look at the dollar amount of the expenditure relative to the value of the property, this is simply a preliminary step to assess whether the expenditure is capital. The underlying assumption is that routine expenditures are small while capital expenditures are quite material. Such an assumption is always dependent on the facts.

CCA—General Restrictions

An Overview

5-42. Many years ago it was standard practice for businesses to purchase depreciable property at the end of their taxation year and claim CCA for the whole year even though the property may have been owned for only a few days of that year. At the time the ability to claim CCA for the year was simply based on whether the depreciable property was owned on the last day of the taxation year. This result did not change even if the property was delivered but not yet operational or was undelivered. The principal question was whether depreciable property was owned on that last day of the relevant taxation year. This remains the test to this day, but it is now qualified and affected by three main rules that limit, restrict, or delay the maximum CCA that may be claimed in the year that depreciable property is acquired.

5-43. The federal government believed that this result was unfair and that those purchasing depreciable property should not be entitled to a full year of CCA for property purchased on the last day of their taxation year. Over many years, three measures were added to the ITA to address this concern;

- **The half-year rule (ITR 1100(2)):** The purpose of this rule is to only allow 50% of the maximum CCA in the year that depreciable property is acquired. This was considered a reasonable approach that avoided the complexity of tracking the number of days that property was actually owned in the year. It is somewhat analogous to the 50% limitation on meals and entertainment expenses. In November 2018 the half-year rule was replaced for most depreciable property with a new temporary incentive that actually allows 150% of the maximum CCA rather than only 50%. We refer to this new incentive as the Accelerated Investment Incentive (AccII). Both the half-year rule and this new incentive are discussed in this chapter.

- **The short taxation-year rule (ITR 1100(3)):** This rule limits the CCA that can be claimed where the taxation year is less than 365 days. It generally applies to corporations that are carrying on a business. Corporate taxation years can be short (i.e., less than 365 days) in the first year, the last year, or can be deemed by the ITA to begin or end, therefore creating a short taxation year. This rule is also discussed in this chapter.
- **Available-for-use rules:** These rules were added to deny CCA for depreciable property that is not actually delivered at year end or that is delivered but is not ready for use because it is not yet in an operational state such that it cannot be used in the taxation year it was acquired. We will begin our discussion of these three rules with the available-for-use rules.

Available-for-Use Rules

5-44. For purchases of many types of depreciable property, the available-for-use rules do not present a problem. Most purchased depreciable property is put into use immediately and the owner is allowed to deduct CCA in the year of acquisition to the maximum extent allowed subject to other limitations such as those discussed in Paragraph 5-43.

5-45. ITA 13(26) is the main rule. It prevents the capital cost of depreciable property from being added to the UCC of the class of property to which the depreciable property belongs until the property has become available for use. CCA can only be claimed to the extent of the UCC balance on the last day of the taxation year, therefore if the available-for-use rules prohibit adding the capital cost until a later time then the effect is that no CCA can be claimed for that particular property in the year of purchase.

5-46. The available-for-use rules can be quite complex as they cover many different situations, but in general there are two separate sets of rules—one that applies to buildings and a second that applies to other types of depreciable property. The rules for buildings are much more complex as they contemplate the construction of buildings, including major additions and renovations, that can take years to complete.

5-47. For depreciable property other than buildings, the rules generally consider property to to be available for use, and thereby eligible for CCA, at the earliest of the following times:

- When the property is first used for the purpose of earning income
- The second taxation year after the year in which the property is acquired. This maximum two-year deferral rule is also referred to as the rolling start rule. If, for example, a purchaser carries on a business with a December 31 taxation year end, the purchase of depreciable property in December 2021 would be considered available for use at the beginning of 2023
- The day the property is delivered or made available and is capable of performing the function for which it was acquired
- In the case of motor vehicles and other transport equipment that require certificates or licences, when such certificates or licenses are obtained

5-48. Buildings are considered to have become available for use at the earlier of the following times:

- When substantially all (usually 90% or more) of the building is used for the purpose for which it was acquired. When a building is being constructed the owner is considered to have acquired it to the extent of the construction that has been completed. If, for example, 25% of a building costing $50 million is completed in each of four years the owner would be considered to have acquired $12.5M of a building in each year.
- The second taxation year after the year in which property is acquired. This maximum two-year deferral rule is also referred to as the rolling start rule. In the preceding example, $12.5M of the construction from year 1 would be considered available for at the beginning of year 3.
- The time that the construction, renovation, or alteration is completed.

Classes of Depreciable Property

General Rules

5-49. Part XI and Schedules II through VI of the *ITR* provide a detailed listing of classes and rates for the determination of CCA. There are over 60 classes that vary from extremely narrow (Class 33, which contains only one property that is a timber resource property) to extremely broad (Class 8 refers to property that is tangible capital property and not included in any other class). As the applicable rates vary from a low of 4% to a high of 100%, the appropriate classification can have a significant impact on the amount of CCA that can be claimed. This, in turn, has an impact on taxable income and therefore taxes payable.

5-50. In general, depreciable property does not belong in a class unless specifically included in the ITR description of that class. In addition, a particular class may change over time, meaning that the class of property acquired 10 years ago may not be the same class today for the same depreciable property. This means that knowing the actual date of purchase will also be important in determining the class that applies. Finally, when depreciable property is not specifically mentioned in a class then catch-all classes such as class 8 for "other tangible capital property not included in another class" will often apply.

> **EXAMPLE** A few years ago the CRA was asked which class movable skateboard ramps would apply to as opposed to fixed paved constructed surfaces for skateboards.
>
> **ANALYSIS** The CRA identified class 17(c) as applying to the fixed paved surfaces, which applies an 8% CCA rate. They went on to clarify that since movable ramps were not found in any class, the catch-all rule of class 8(i) would apply. The class 8 CCA rate is 20%.

5-51. For your convenience in working with CCA exercises and problems, the appendix to this chapter provides an alphabetical list of common depreciable property identifying the appropriate CCA class as well as the rate applicable to that class.

Separate Classes

5-52. The general rule is that all of the depreciable property that meet the descriptions for a particular class are all added to that same class. This of course means that each class may contain multiple properties. This is of considerable importance since the CCA that can be claimed is based on the UCC of a particular class on the last day of the taxation year. This means that a class with multiple properties that are being regularly replaced will always have a UCC balance upon which to claim CCA. The sale of individual properties within the class will not usually result in any income tax implications as long as the individual properties are not sold above their capital cost, which is usually the case for most depreciable property other than buildings.

5-53. A class with only one property that is not replaced, however, is much more problematic, since once that property is sold income tax consequences immediately arise. Depending on the circumstances, the tax consequences may or may not be favourable. In other words, there are benefits and disadvantages to having a class with only one property.

5-54. The ITA establishes a set of rules concerning classes of depreciable property, including whether a one-property class is possible, and some limited elective options to choose to separate each property that would have been lumped together with other property in a single class into a separate class. This type of elective option can at times provide some interesting and beneficial tax planning. The main class and separate class principles and concepts are as follows:

> **Separate Businesses** In Chapter 1 we discussed the importance of the "source" concept in identifying business, employment, and investment sources. We also mentioned that one could have multiple employment, multiple businesses, and different investments, all of which are separate and distinct sources. The ITA requires that profit and loss (i.e., income and expenses) be separately tracked for each source. ITR 1101 continues the source concept by clarifying that if a taxpayer owns depreciable property that would be

described in the same class, that the properties are to be placed in separate classes if they are used in separate businesses or to earn income from property. Assume, for example, that an individual operated the business of an accounting practice, a business of a coin laundry, and owned a rental property. Assume further that each of the two businesses and the rental property used property that would fit into class 8. The effect of ITR 1101 is that each source is considered to have its own separate class 8, and as a result there would be a class 8 for the accounting business, a second class 8 for the business of the laundry, and a third for the rental property. A complication sometimes arises in determining whether there are separate businesses as opposed to one single integrated business. The CRA and the courts look to the interconnection between the "businesses" to decide whether they represent two or more separate businesses or one integrated business.

Rental Properties Buildings acquired after 1971 at a cost of $50,000 or more are required to be placed in a separate CCA class where they are principally used for the purpose of earning rent. This separate class rule is also consistent with the source concept.

Class 10.1 Luxury Cars (i.e., passenger vehicles) The separate class rules apply to passenger vehicles that have a capital cost in excess $30,000. This means that if a business owns three luxury vehicles there will be three class 10.1 accounts. If there were three vehicles that were not luxury vehicles they would each fall into one class 10 account. We will discuss this further in this chapter.

Elections In the situations described in the preceding paragraphs, separate classes must be used. The taxpayer has no choice in the matter. There are other situations, however, where a taxpayer is allowed to elect separate class treatment. One of these situations involves "eligible non-residential buildings" (i.e., buildings acquired for something other than residential use) where the election to use a separate class can result in an additional amount of CCA (see Paragraph 5-59).

A second election involves property subject to high rates of technological obsolescence (e.g., photocopiers). In this case a separate class election can be made. This election is discussed later in this chapter.

A third election, popular when depreciable properties are being sold as part of the sale of a business without selling any buildings, allows depreciable properties in classes 1 to 12 (excluding class 10.1) to be included in a separate class 1. The elective strategy often results in saving income tax.

Elections are made by sending a letter by registered mail to the taxation centre where the taxpayer's income tax return is processed by the filing due date for the taxation year.

Capital Cost Allowance

General Overview

Basic Calculations

5-55. Once depreciable property has been allocated to the appropriate class there will be an increase in the UCC, which is the base for the calculation of CCA. The maximum CCA is typically determined by applying the rate that is specified in the ITR, on a declining balance basis, to the UCC for that class on the last day of the taxation year. On occasion CCA is based on a straight-line approach, but that is the exception and not the general rule. The following example will illustrate a basic CCA calculation using a declining balance based calculation.

EXAMPLE 1—Basic A business owns depreciable property included in class 10. Class 10 applies a 30% rate. The fiscal period of the business is January 1 to December 31. At the beginning of the 2021 taxation year the UCC balance was $100,000. No new depreciable property is acquired or sold. The taxation year is not a short year, the available-for-use rules are not a concern, and the business will claim the maximum CCA.

ANALYSIS 1—Basic The UCC balance on December 31, 2021 (the last day of the taxation year) is $100,000. Therefore the maximum CCA is 30% of the UCC, or $30,000. The UCC at January 1, 2022, would be $70,000 [$100,000 - $30,000]. If nothing changed in 2022 the maximum CCA would be $21,000 [(30%)($70,000)]. The UCC at January 1, 2023, would be $49,000 [$70,000 - $21,000].

5-56. In Paragraph 5-43 we discussed a few additional rules, such as the half-year rule, the AccII, and the short fiscal period rule. The following two examples will illustrate how the results change where both the half-year and short fiscal period rules apply using the same numbers as in the previous example.

EXAMPLE 2—First-year half-year rule applies: Using the same numbers, assume that the business purchased class 10 depreciable property in 2021 for $100,000. The UCC of class 10 at January 1, 2021, was nil. The property is available for use and the taxation year is not a short one.

ANALYSIS 2—First-year half-year rule applies: The UCC at December 31, 2021, is $100,000. The half-year rule (ITR 1100(2)) reduces the UCC by one-half of the capital cost of the first-year addition for the purpose of determining the CCA for that year. The result is that the maximum CCA would be $15,000 [adjusted UCC of $50,000)(30%)]. The UCC at January 1, 2022, would be $85,000 [$100,000 - $15,000]. If nothing changed in 2022, maximum CCA would be $25,500 [(30%)($85,500)] and the UCC at January 1, 2023, would be $59,500 [$85,000 - $25,500].

EXAMPLE 3—First-year half-year rule applies with short fiscal period: Using the same facts we will add that the business began April 1, 2021, but the taxation year end remains December 31. Therefore, the fiscal period of April 1, 2021, to December 31, 2021, is only 275 days [365 days in a year minus 90 days between January 1 and March 31].

ANALYSIS 3—First-year half-year rule applies with short fiscal period: Maximum CCA would be $11,301 [adjusted UCC of $50,000)(30%)(275/365)]. The UCC at January 1, 2022, would be $88,699 [$100,000 - $11,301]. If nothing changed in 2022 maximum CCA would be $26,610 [(30%)($88,699)] and the UCC at January 1, 2023, would be $62,089 [$88,699 - $26,610].

5-57. We will make one last revision, substituting the AccII for the half-year rule. The short fiscal period will remain the same. The following two examples will again illustrate how the results change where both the AccII and short fiscal period rules apply using the same numbers.

EXAMPLE 4—First-year AccII rule applies: Using the same numbers, assume that the business purchased class 10 depreciable property in 2021 for $100,000. The UCC of class 10 at January 1, 2021, was nil. The property is available for use and the taxation year is not a short one.

ANALYSIS 4—First-year AccII rule applies: The UCC at December 31, 2021, is $100,000. The AccII rule (ITR 1100(2)) adds one-half of the capital cost of the first-year addition for the purposes only of determining the CCA for that year. The result is that the maximum CCA would be $45,000 [adjusted UCC of $150,000)(30%)]. The UCC at January 1, 2022, would be $55,000 [$100,000 - $45,000]. If nothing changed in 2022 maximum CCA would be $16,500 [(30%)($55,000)] and the UCC at January 1, 2023, would be $38,500 [$55,000 - $16,500].

EXAMPLE 5—First-year AccII rule applies with short fiscal period: Using the same facts we will add that the business began April 1, 2021, but the taxation year end remains December 31. Therefore the fiscal period is only 275 days.

ANALYSIS 5—First-year AccII rule applies with short fiscal period: Maximum CCA would be $33,904 [adjusted UCC of $150,000)(30%)(275/365)]. The UCC at January 1, 2022, would be $66,096 [$100,000 - $33,904]. If nothing changed in 2022 maximum CCA would be $19,829 [(30%)($66,096)] and the UCC at January 1, 2023, would be $46,267 [$66,096 - $19,829].

5-58. While we have shown CCA and UCC calculations illustrating both the half-year and AccII rules, it is important to be aware that our focus will be on the AccII since it applies to purchases of depreciable property from November 21, 2018, to December 31, 2027. The half-year rules continue to apply but only in restrictive circumstances where the AccII does not apply. This will be discussed further in this chapter. We will next take a step back to take a closer look at the most common types of depreciable property you can expect to see and the classes where they can be found.

Commonly Used CCA Classes

5-59. The following is a brief description of the more commonly used classes of depreciable property, including the items to be added, the applicable rates, and the CCA method to be used. We would note that almost all of our examples and problem material will use the CCA classes that are described here.

Class 1—Buildings (4%, 6%, or 10%) In general, class 1 is a 4% declining balance class, applicable to buildings acquired after 1987. This class also includes bridges, canals, culverts, subways, tunnels, and certain railway roadbeds.

As previously mentioned, each rental building with a cost of $50,000 or more is placed in a separate class 1.

If an election is made to place new non-residential buildings acquired after March 18, 2007, in a separate class 1, the CCA rate will increase as follows:

- to 10% if the building is used 90% or more for manufacturing and processing,
- to 6% if it does not qualify for the 10% manufacturing and processing rate if used 90% or more for non-residential purposes, such as operating a non-manufacturing business or a manufacturing business where the 90% test has not been met. Generally the 90% test is based on the use of the square footage of the building.

Note that these enhanced rates apply only to new buildings that have not been used or acquired for use before March 19, 2007, and that have been allocated to a separate class 1 as a result of an election made by the owner. In addition, the building will qualify for the higher CCA rates where the owner leases the building to another person (lessee) who uses it to carry on a business in that building.

Class 3—Buildings Pre-1988 (5%) Class 3 is a 5% declining balance class. It contains most buildings acquired before 1988. As is the case for class 1 rental properties, separate classes were required for each rental building with a cost of $50,000 or more. As a result rental property owners may have rental properties in both class 1 or 3 depending on when they were acquired. Class 3 also includes breakwaters, docks, trestles, windmills, wharfs, jetties, and telephone poles.

Class 8—Various Machinery, Equipment, and Furniture (20%) Class 8 is a 20% declining balance class. It includes most machinery; equipment; structures such as kilns, tanks, and vats; electrical generating equipment; advertising posters; bulletin boards; and furniture not specifically included in another class. As will be discussed at a later point in this chapter, individual photocopiers, fax machines, and telephone equipment purchased for $1,000 or more can be allocated to a separate class 8 at the election of the owner.

Class 10—Vehicles (30%) Class 10 is a 30% declining balance class. It includes most vehicles (excluding certain passenger vehicles that are allocated to class 10.1, taxicabs allocated to class 16, and zero-emission vehicles allocated to classes 54 or 55), automotive equipment, trailers, wagons, contractors' movable equipment, mine railway equipment, various mining and logging equipment, and TV channel converters and decoders acquired by a cable distribution system.

Class 10.1—Passenger Vehicles (a.k.a. luxury cars) (30%) Class 10.1 is a class established for passenger vehicles with a cost in excess of a prescribed amount, which is currently $30,000. Class 10.1 is a 30% declining balance class. However, each vehicle must be allocated to a separate class 10.1. Identifying passenger vehicles that are class 10.1 requires a good understanding of the definition of an "automobile," which we discussed in detail in Chapter 3. We recommend you revisit and review Paragraphs 3-80 to 3-85.

There are five features of class 10.1 that set it apart from most other classes:

- Capital cost is capped at $30,000.
- Each passenger vehicle is required to be added to a separate class.
- In the year of sale/disposition, 50% of the normal CCA that would have been available had the vehicle been owned on the last day of that taxation year can be claimed as CCA.
- Terminal losses are not allowed in the year of sale/disposition.
- No recapture is required to be included in income in the year of sale/disposition.

Earlier we had mentioned that when depreciable property in a one-property class is sold that there could be income tax implications. Those implications are terminal losses (a deduction) and recapture (income). We can expand this somewhat to add that if depreciable properties are sold in classes with multiple properties these same income tax implications could occur. Class 10.1 avoids this possibility altogether. Terminal losses and recapture are discussed later in this chapter.

Class 12—Computer Software and Certain Low-Cost Property (100%) Class 12 includes computer software that is not systems software, books in a lending library, dishes, cutlery, jigs, dies, patterns, uniforms and costumes, linen, motion picture films, and videotapes. Dental and medical instruments, kitchen utensils, and tools are included, provided they cost less than $500. This class is subject to a 100% write-off in the year of acquisition.

Class 13—Leasehold Improvements (straight line) In general, only property owned (or deemed to be owned) by a taxpayer is eligible for a CCA claim. A leasehold interest is an interest that a tenant has in leased property. Any capital expenditure made by the tenant to the leased property represents what is called a leasehold improvement. Assume, for example, that you rent a house for three years and, with the permission of the lessor-owner, you renovate to add a home office. The home office construction costs $16,000. Technically the home office does not belong to you, which would mean that you are not the owner, and without legislation to the contrary you would not be able to claim any CCA with respect to the construction costs even though you use the home office to earn income.

ITR 1102(5) allows you to claim CCA on the renovation costs by recognizing a leasehold improvement as depreciable property. In such cases you do not have to identify a class since class 13 is established specifically to deal with this unusual situation.

Class 13 CCA is calculated on a straight-line basis, treating each leasehold improvement as if it were a separate property. The maximum CCA claim for a specific leasehold improvement will be the lesser of

- one-fifth of the capital cost of the leasehold improvement; or
- the capital cost of the leasehold improvement divided by the lease term remaining plus the first renewal option, if any.

The lease term is calculated by taking the number of full 12-month periods from the beginning of the taxation year in which the particular leasehold improvement is made until the termination of the lease. For purposes of this calculation, the legislation caps the lease term at 40 years. If the lease term expires or is cancelled, the leasehold improvement will be considered to have been disposed of at that time for nothing unless the owner agrees to some form of direct compensation.

If the three-year house rental mentioned in the previous example included a renewal option for an additional five years, and the leasehold improvement was completed in the first year of the three-year rental term, then the CCA for that first year would be equal to the lesser of

- one-fifth of the capital cost of $16,000 or $3,200; or
- the $16,000 capital cost of the leasehold improvement divided by the three-year lease term plus the five-year first renewal option. The result would be $2,000 [$16,000/(3 + 5 years)].

CCA for the first year would therefore be $2,000 and increased by the AccII of 150% to $3,000.

If a second leasehold improvement were made in the second year for $7,000, the maximum CCA would equal the lesser of

- one-fifth of the capital cost of $7,000 or $1,400; or
- the $7,000 capital cost of the leasehold improvement divided by the two years remaining in the current lease term plus the five-year first renewal option. The result would be $1,000 [$7,000/(2 + 5 years)].

In year 2 CCA would equal $2,000 for the first leasehold improvement plus $1,500 for the second leasehold improvement after applying the AccII of 150%. Total CCA for year 2 would therefore be $3,500.

Class 14—Limited Life Intangible Capital Property (straight line) Class 14 covers the cost of intangible capital property with a limited life. Specifically identified are patents, franchises, concessions, or licences. Such propereties are subject to a straight-line method based on the remaining legal life of the property. IT-477 (now archived) states that CCA should be calculated on a reasonable pro rata basis. A reasonable basis would include a determination using the number of days in the taxation year against the total days of the life of the property.

Class 14.1—Goodwill and Other Intangible Property (5%) Prior to 2017 property included in this class was referred to as "eligible capital property/expenditures" (ECP). It included intangible capital property and certain capital transactions that did not fit in any CCA class. In effect the ECP system was completely separate from the depreciable property rules even though there were some similarities with no shortage of extra complexity.

Beginning January 1, 2017, class 14.1 was introduced as a means of replacing the ECP rules and bringing them into the depreciable property system. There remains a number of transitional rules and some elective options to transition the pre-2017 system to later years, but they are well beyond the scope of this text and will not be discussed further. In our examples, exercises, and problems we will refer to additions that only occur after 2016 with no pre-2017 ECP balances.

The rate for any additions to this class is 5% applied on a declining balance basis. For those familiar with the ECP system, the CRA recently confirmed that any qualifying additions to the previous ECP system will fall into class 14.1. In general terms, the items that are added to class 14.1 include

- goodwill;
- incorporation costs;
- customer lists; and

- other intangible capital property that does not fit in any other class. In general this category will largely be intangible property with an unlimited life. Intangible capital property with limited lives are typically categorized as either class 14 or 44.

Class 14.1 will be discussed further in this chapter.

Class 44—Patents (25%) At one point in time, patents were categorized as class 14 where they were amortized over their limited legal life of 20 years on a straight-line basis. This CCA rate approach did not account for the fact that the economic life of most patents was usually a much shorter period. In response, class 44 was introduced to apply to patents whether or not they had a limited or unlimited life. The class 44 rate is 25% applied on a declining balance basis. Note, however, that a taxpayer can elect to categorize patents to class 14. This would be a useful alternative if a patent were acquired near the end of its legal life. For example, if a patent only had two years remaining in its legal life, allocating its acquisition to class 14 would result in the business being able to write off the property over two years at a 50% rate.

Class 50—Computer Hardware and Systems Software (55%) This class includes computer hardware and systems software acquired after January 31, 2011. CCA on this class is calculated on a declining balance basis, using a 55% rate. Depreciable property in this class would include computers, laptops, smartphones, tablets, and other devices and equipment that meets the general definition of "general purpose electronic data processing equipment" (ITR 1104)—that is, equipment that requires an internally stored computer program for its operation.

If an expenditure is not a capital expenditure (e.g., a disposable cell phone), it would not normally meet the definition of depreciable capital property and would be considered a current expense (on income account).

Classes 53—Manufacturing and Processing Property Machinery and equipment acquired after 2015 to be used in Canada more than half the time for the purpose of manufacturing or processing goods to be sold or leased is eligible for a 50% CCA rate applied on a declining balance basis.

Class 54—Zero-Emission Vehicles (30%) Qualifying zero-emission vehicles include new vehicles purchased after March 18, 2019, that operate with an electric battery, hydrogen fuel cell, or that are plug-in hybrids. Vehicles can include light, medium, or heavy duty vehicles used in a business. Zero-emission vehicles fall into two broad categories: "zero-emission passenger vehicles" or simply "zero-emission vehicles." Both types of vehicles fit into class 54 unless an elective option is chosen to be categorized as class 10 or 10.1. Zero-emission passenger vehicles share many similarities with ordinary passenger vehicles except that the cap on the capital cost is $55,000 instead of $30,000. The same "automobile" analysis discussed in Chapter 3 at Paragraphs 3-80 to 3-85 is equally applicable. We will discuss this class later in this chapter.

Exercise 5-2

Subject: Segregation into CCA Classes

For each of the following depreciable properties, indicate the appropriate CCA class. (The appendix to this chapter contains a listing of CCA classes.)

1. Taxicab (gas powered)
2. Reference books replaced every five to ten years
3. Periodicals and other books replaced every year
4. Manufacturing and processing equipment acquired in 2021

5. Franchise with a limited life
6. Automobile (i.e., passenger vehicle) with a cost of $120,000 (gas powered)
7. Government licence with an unlimited life acquired in 2021
8. Storage tank for water
9. Photocopy machine
10. Leasehold improvements
11. Residential rental property acquired for $200,000. The purchase price was allocated $150,000 to the building and $50,000 to the land

Exercise 5-3

Subject: CCA Error

During the taxation year ending December 31, 2021, your company acquired depreciable property for $326,000 and you incorrectly included it in class 1. Early in 2022 you discover that the property should have been included in class 10. What is the impact of this error on your company's 2021 CCA claim?

Solutions to Exercises are available in the Study Guide.

The Old Half-Year Rule (ITR 1100(2))

Pre-November 21, 2018

5-60. For many years, CCA calculations have been subject to what is referred to as the half-year rule, as briefly discussed at Paragraph 5-43 and illustrated with examples at Paragraph 5-55. Under this rule the UCC base at the end of the relevant taxation year to which the required CCA rate was applied was reduced by one-half of the net additions to the class made during the year. This served to reduce the amount of CCA that could be claimed in the first year.

5-61. This old half-year rule applied to most classes of depreciable property but there were a few exceptions, specifically

- class 14 (limited life intangible property), and
- certain depreciable property included in class 12, such as medical or dental instruments and tools costing less than $500, uniforms, and chinaware.

Revised ITR 1100(2)

5-62. The old half-year rule prevailed until the federal government presented its annual economic statement on November 21, 2018. This statement introduced a revised ITR 1100(2). This revised regulation contains a fairly complex formula that, in simple terms, does two things:

- Instead of reducing the UCC balance at year end for net additions to a class made in that year, the AccII increases the UCC allowing for an accelerated CCA claim for first-year additions.
- The revised rule retains the old half-year rule, restricting its use to first-year net additions to a class that generally would not qualify for the AccII.

5-63. The impact of the addition of the AccII leaves three possible alternatives with respect to first-year additions to a class of depreciable property. The first is to verify whether the AccII applies. If the AccII does not apply then the second step is to determine whether the half-year rule applies and, if not, then CCA will be based on the rate of the particular class of depreciable property. The difference can be significant. If we are dealing with a class 10 property, ignoring short fiscal periods, the AccII allows a 45% CCA claim in the first year [(30%)(1.5)], the half-year rule allows a 15% CCA claim [30%)(1/2)], and if neither rule applies the first-year CCA claim is 30%.

Net Additions

5-64. You will read the expression "net additions" when determining the 50% amount to be subtracted if the old half-year rule applies and when the AccII adds an amount to the UCC for the purposes of calculating CCA. In both instances net additions means that the capital cost of property added to a class exceeds the amounts that reduce the class for property that is sold. If the difference is a positive amount then the half-year rule or AccII will apply to that amount, but if the difference is not positive then no adjustment will be made.

EXAMPLE 1—Positive Net Addition: Keever Ltd. has a calendar-based taxation year. At January 1, 2021, the class 10 UCC was $130,000. The company purchased new machinery for $64,000 in July 2021 and sold old machinery for $22,000, which was also the amount subtracted from the class.

ANALYSIS 1—Positive Net Addition: CCA would be $57,900 based on UCC at December 31, 2021, of $193,000 calculated as the UCC at January 1, 2021, of $130,000 plus net additions of $42,000 [$64,000 - $22,000] plus an AccII adjustment of 50% of the net additions, or $21,000.

EXAMPLE 2—No Net Addition: Keever Ltd. has a calendar-based taxation year. At January 1, 2021, the class 10 UCC was $130,000. The company purchased new machinery for $64,000 in July 2021 and sold old machinery for $84,000, which was also the amount subtracted from the class.

ANALYSIS 2—No Net Addition: CCA would be $33,000 based on UCC at December 31, 2021, of $110,000 calculated as the UCC at January 1, 2021, of $130,000 minus net subtractions of $20,000 [$84,000 - $64,000]. The AccII (and old half-year rule) only apply to net additions, therefore there is no adjustment in this second example.

Accelerated Investment Incentive (AccII)

Limitations on Our Coverage

5-65. The AccII legislation applies from November 21, 2018, to December 31, 2027. The incentive, however, does not remain the same for this entire period. The incentive is generally 150% of the net additions to a class of depreciable property for purchases from November 21, 2018, to December 31, 2023, but only 125% for purchases made in 2024 to 2027. Given the length of time that these provisions are in effect, all of our examples and problems will focus on the period November 21, 2018, through December 31, 2023. We will not give any coverage of the changes that occur after that time.

5-66. Secondly, we will only cover the AccII as it applies to the classes of depreciable property that we have specifically listed and described in Paragraph 5-59.

Basic Concepts

5-67. Given the recent fairly dramatic reduction in corporate taxes in the U.S., the Canadian federal government felt a need to provide additional income tax incentives to Canadian businesses. As Canadian taxes on corporations were already favourable, cuts in this area did not seem feasible. Reflecting this, the federal government chose to use a different approach.

5-68. The approach chosen involves providing an incentive that should encourage businesses to make additional capital expenditures after November 20, 2018. As described in the previous section, prior to that date, businesses were only able to deduct CCA on one-half the cost of the net additions to depreciable property in the year of acquisition. For most types of depreciable property, the AccII removes this half-year rule and replaces it with a 50% increase in the UCC base for calculating the amount of CCA that can be deducted, effectively tripling the CCA claims previously allowed in the year of acquisition.

EXAMPLE A business acquires a class 8 property with a capital cost of $100,000.

ANALYSIS The relevant calculations, both pre- and post-AccII, would be as follows:

	Pre-AccII	Post-AccII
Capital cost	$100,000	$100,000
Adjustments:		
Deduct: Half-year rule [(50%)($100,000)]	(50,000)	
Add: AccII adjustment [(50%)($100,000)]		50,000
CCA base	$ 50,000	$150,000
CCA rate	20%	20%
Year of acquisition CCA	$ 10,000	$ 30,000
Ending UCC	$ 90,000	$ 70,000

5-69. As this simple example illustrates, for most eligible property the AccII triples the amount of CCA that can be taken in the year of acquisition. It is important to note, however, that the AccII does not increase the total amount of CCA that will be available in a given class of depreciable property. The total will continue to be limited by the capital cost of the acquired property.

Eligibility for the AccII—ITR 1104(4)

5-70. To be eligible for the AccII, depreciable property must be acquired after November 20, 2018, and become available for use before 2028. All classes of depreciable property are eligible for the AccII with the exception of class 12. Since class 12 already provided a 100% CCA rate, the government decided no further incentives were necessary. Interestingly, not all class 12 property was exempt from the old half-year rule, meaning that the old half-year rule continues to apply to purchases of some class 12 property.

5-71. Depreciable property acquired after November 21, 2018, and that becomes available for use by December 31, 2027, will not qualify, however, in the following circumstances:

CCA Deduction or Terminal Loss Has Been Previously Claimed If any person (including the purchaser) or partnership has deducted CCA or has claimed a terminal loss deduction before the purchase, then the property is not eligible for the AccII unless the property was acquired in an arm's-length purchase. The old half-year rule would apply instead. Interestingly, the legislation does not require that the property be new, only that no CCA deductions or terminal loss claims have previously been taken by anyone.

Property Previously Owned by the Taxpayer or a Non-Arm's-Length Person If the purchaser or a person non-arm's length with the purchaser owned or acquired the property prior to its acquisition, it is not eligible for the AccII provisions and again the old half-year rule would apply.

Property Acquired on a Rollover Basis A rollover in income tax terms generally means a transfer of property between two persons on a tax-free basis such that the person acquiring the property inherits the tax values such as UCC, capital cost, and previously claimed CCA. Rollovers can occur between individuals, corporations, partnerships, and trusts. Rollovers between individuals are most often between family members and are discussed in Chapter 9. Other rollovers involving corporations, partnerships, and trusts are discussed throughout Volume 2 of the text.

Determining Whether the AccII Applies

5-72. Determining whether the AccII applies first requires identifying whether the property is depreciable property. Second, the property must be purchased between November 21, 2018, and December 31, 2027. Finally, the property must (1) not be included in class 12,

(2) no CCA or terminal loss deduction was ever claimed by anyone for that property unless the property was acquired in an arm's-length purchase, (3) the property was not previously owned or acquired by the purchaser or someone non-arm's length with the purchaser, and (4) the property was not acquired using a rollover provision. If all of those conditions are met then the property is eligible for the AccII, and if any of the conditions are not met then the old half-year rule applies to the purchase subject to its own exceptions.

EXAMPLE Janice Carruthers owns a home that she has lived in for many years. In May 2021 she moved into a condo that she purchased but decided to keep the home and use it as a rental property.

ANALYSIS In such situations the ITA recognizes that the home has gone from being used as a personal residence to an income earning property. The ITA allows the home to be treated as depreciable property by deeming the property to be acquired when the change of the use from personal to income earning occurs. As a result these would be an acquisition of depreciable property within the acceptable dates for the AccII. The rental property would not qualify for the AccII, however, because Janice Carruthers had previously owned the home. Changes in use of property are discussed in Chapter 8.

Application—Declining Balance Classes

5-73. You will have noticed in reviewing the CCA classes listed in Paragraph 5-59 that the majority of classes use the declining balance method. This includes classes 1, 3, 8, 10, 10.1, 14.1, 44, 50, 53, and 54. The AccII calculations for each class are near identical with slight variations for classes 12, 13, 14 , 53, and 54, which will be illustrated.

5-74. The application of the AccII to the declining balance classes involves an enhanced UCC base for calculating CCA in the year of acquisition. Specifically, there will be an addition to the CCA base equal to 50% of the excess of

- the capital cost of qualifying depreciable property purchased during the year that was added to the UCC; over
- amounts subtracted from the UCC for sales (e.g., dispositions) of qualifying property.

We illustrated the basic concept in Paragraph 5-64 based on net additions. The above result can change if both the AccII and old half-year rules applied in the same class and in the same taxation year.

5-75. The AccII is only relevant if there are purchases of depreciable property in a given year that would qualify.

5-76. This text uses an approach that, in many respects, mirrors the income tax schedules completed during the annual income tax reporting and used to determine maximum CCA in a specific year along with the ending UCC balances. We will use a simple example to illustrate this approach, which will be consistently applied through the text, including in problems and exams. We will also use this same approach to illustrate the application of the old half-year rule that would apply if the purchased property is not eligible for the AccII.

EXAMPLE Pohx Inc. has a calendar-based taxation year that ends on December 31. On January 1, 2021, the UCC balance in class 8 is $250,000. During 2021, the company acquires additional class 8 property at a cost of $40,000. There are no additional class 8 acquisitions in 2022, and there are no class 8 disposals in either 2021 or 2022. Determine the 2021 and 2022 CCA and the January 1, 2022, and January 1, 2023, UCC under each of the following assumptions:

1. The acquired property is not eligible for the AccII, which means that the old half-year rule applies.
2. The acquired property is eligible for the AccII.

ANALYSIS The required information can be calculated and presented as follows:

	Not Eligible for the AccII	Eligible for the AccII
January 1, 2021, UCC	$250,000	$250,000
2021 additions	40,000	40,000
Adjustments:		
Deduct: Half-year rule [(50%)($40,000)]	(20,000)	
Add: AccII [(50%)($40,000)]		20,000
CCA vase (December 31, 2021, UCC)	$270,000	$310,000
2021 CCA at 20%	(54,000)	(62,000)
Adjustment reversals	20,000	(20,000)
January 1, 2022, UCC	$236,000	$228,000
2022 CCA at 20%	(47,200)	(45,600)
January 1, 2023, UCC	$188,800	$182,400

Note that while the 2021 CCA is larger on the eligible AccII acquisitions, it is smaller in 2022. This will be the case in all subsequent years, with the result that the total CCA to be deducted will be the same regardless of whether the property qualifies for the AccII or not. TIP: You can double check the accuracy of the presentation and verify the final UCC by starting with the UCC of $250,000, adding the capital cost of $40,000, and subtracting CCA claimed for each of 2021 and 2022. For property not eligible for the AccII UCC should be $188,800 [$290,000 - ($54,000 + $47,200)], and it should be $182,400 for property eligible for the AccII [$290,000 - ($62,000 + $45,600)].

Exercise 5-4

Subject: CCA on Depreciable Property That Qualifies for the AccII

Radmore Ltd., with a taxation year that ends on December 31, has a class 10 (30%) UCC balance on January 1, 2021, of $950,000. During 2021, it acquires 15 eligible AccII vehicles at a cost of $20,000 each, for a total addition of $300,000. The company also disposes of 18 vehicles for an amount of $144,000, all of which is subtracted from the UCC of the class. Determine the maximum class 10 CCA that Radmore can deduct for 2021, as well as the January 1, 2022, UCC balance.

Solutions to Exercises are available in the Study Guide.

AccII Application—Class 12

5-77. As noted in Paragraph 5-59, class 12 property qualifies for a 100% write-off in the year of acquisition. Given this, the federal government decided that including this class in the AccII program would not be necessary. With respect to medical and dental instruments, uniforms, chinaware, and tools costing less than $500, 100% of their cost could be claimed as CCA in their year of acquisition. As a result, it would not have been possible to increase the acquisition year CCA deduction for these properties.

5-78. However, some items included in class 12 were subject to the half-year rule, resulting in a CCA claim on new acquisitions of only 50%. Specifically, computer software and certified Canadian films continue to be subject to the old half-year rule.

AccII Application—Class 13

5-79. Class 13 is a straight-line class and was previously subject to the half-year rule. As with declining balance classes, the AccII replaces the old half-year rule for qualifying property.

However, instead of adding 50% to the UCC base for calculating CCA, ITR 1100(1)(b)(i) increases the CCA claim by 150% of the regular straight-line CCA amount.

EXAMPLE In 2021, a business makes leasehold improvements of $50,000 in the first year of a five-year lease. There is no lease renewal option.

ANALYSIS The 2021 CCA would be calculated as follows:

$$[(150\%)(\$50,000 \div 5)] = \$15,000$$

As this is a straight-line class, this increased CCA deduction in the first year would not alter CCA claims for subsequent years, which revert to the regular straight-line amount of $10,000 ($50,000 ÷ 5). However, the $10,000 amount could not be deducted in the fifth year of the lease since the remaining unamortized capital cost would only be $5,000 [$50,000 - $15,000 - (3)($10,000)]. The regulation limits the CCA that can be claimed for a specific leasehold improvement to the capital cost of that improvement.

5-80. While the calculation is different, the results in the year of acquisition are the same for class 13 as they would be for the declining balance classes.

Exercise 5-5

Subject: Class 13 Additions

Vachon Ltd. has a December 31 year end. The company leases its office space under a lease that was signed on January 1, 2016. The lease term is 10 years, with an option to renew at an increased rent for an additional five years. In 2016, the company spent $52,000 renovating the premises. In 2021, changing needs require the company to spend another $31,000 renovating the space. Determine the maximum amount of class 13 CCA the company can deduct for 2021 and 2022.

Solutions to Exercises are available in the Study Guide.

AccII Application—Class 14

5-81. While class 14 is similar to class 13 in the sense they both employ a a straight-line mehodolgy, class 14 was not subject to the old half-year rules. Class 14, however, will benefit from the 50% AccII adjustment based on additions to the class for qualifying property.

Exercise 5-6

Subject: Class 14 Acquisitions

Arnot Ltd. has a December 31 year end. On April 1, 2021, Arnot pays $375,000 to enter a franchise agreement. The life of the franchise is 10 years. Determine the maximum CCA for 2021 and the January 1, 2022, UCC.

Solutions to Exercises are available in the Study Guide.

AccII Application—Class 53 (100% Write-Off)

5-82. Class 53 is a 50% declining balance class that was subject to the old half-year rules. Reflecting the importance the federal government attaches to investment in manufacturing and processing, class 53 benefits from a more generous AccII. Instead of adding 50% to the CCA base for calculating the acquisition-year CCA, the AccII provisions add 100% of the capital cost of net additions.

EXAMPLE A taxpayer acquires a class 53 property with a capital cost of $200,000.

ANALYSIS The relevant calculations, both pre- and post-AccII, would be as follows:

	Pre-AccII	Post-AccII
Capital cost	$200,000	$200,000
Adjustments:		
Deduct: Half-year rule [(50%)($200,000)]	(100,000)	
Add: AccII [(100%)($200,000)]		200,000
CCA base	$100,000	$400,000
CCA at 50%	(50,000)	(200,000)
Adjustment reversals	100,000	(200,000)
UCC—Beginning of following year	$150,000	Nil

As can be seen in this example, the AccII provides for a 100% write-off of class 53 property in the year of acquisition. In contrast to other declining balance classes, which tripled the year of acquisition CCA, the AccII quadruples the amount for class 53 property.

Exercise 5-7

Subject: Class 53 Acquisitions

On January 1, 2021, Arco Inc. has a balance in its class 53 UCC of $500,000. During 2021, property with a capital cost of $100,000 is added to the class. There are no dispositions during the year. Determine the maximum class 53 CCA for 2021, as well as the January 1, 2022, UCC.

Solutions to Exercises are available in the Study Guide.

Zero-Emission Vehicles

Defined

5-83. In a move designed to help reduce greenhouse emissions in Canada, the March 19, 2019, federal budget introduced provisions that would allow for enhanced CCA deductions on zero-emission vehicles. To qualify for these provisions, a vehicle must

- be a motor vehicle as defined in the ITA;
- a motor vehicle that would otherwise be included in class 10, class 10.1, or class 16;
- be fully electric, a plug-in hybrid with a battery capacity of at least 15 kwh, or a motor vehicle fully powered by hydrogen; and
- not have been used for any purpose before it is acquired by the taxpayer.

5-84. The federal government has also implemented a $5,000 purchase incentive for zero-emission vehicles. Vehicles that qualify for this incentive will not be eligible for the enhanced CCA deductions. The $5,000 incentive is to apply automatically at the dealer level where the cost of the vehicle is $45,000 or less. This would mean that only vehicles costing (before the incentive) in excess of $45,000 would be eligible for the 100% CCA claim in the year of purchase and would be included in the new classes 54 and 55.

Implementation

5-85. This program is implemented through the creation of three new CCA classes:

- Class 54 for those zero-emission vehicles that would otherwise have been included in classes 10 or 10.1
- Class 55 for those zero-emission vehicles that would otherwise have been included in Class 16

- Class 56 (30%) for zero-emission automotive equipment (other than motor vehicles) that are fully electric or powered by hydrogen. Examples would include aircraft, watercraft, trolley buses, and railway locomotives. Costs to convert automotive equipment such as gas-powered equipment to zero-emission equipment would also qualify and be considered available for use once no emissions are produced.

5-86. In the case of class 54, the amount of deductible CCA will be limited to $55,000 if the zero-emission vehicle qualifies as a "zero-emission passenger vehicle." This is identical to the rules dealing with passenger vehicles under class 10.1, which are dependent on determining whether the vehicles are "automobiles" (see Paragraphs 3-80 to 3-85). The only real difference is that class 10.1 would not be zero emission. This means that all zero-emission vehicles (other than taxicabs that would otherwise be included in class 16) are included in one class 54 with the capital cost of zero-emission passenger vehicles capped at $55,000, with no cap on other zero-emission vehicles.

5-87. For the period from March 19, 2019, to December 31, 2023, these two temporary classes will be eligible for a 100% CCA claim in the year of acquisition. The maximum CCA will be reduced to 75% for the years 2024 and 2025, and then to 55% for the years 2026 and 2027. It will not be available for 2028 and subsequent years.

5-88. To qualify for class 56, property must be acquired after March 1, 2020, and must become available for use before 2028. The purpose of adding this class is to allow the property to qualify for the AccII incentive. The incentive will not apply if either (1) the property was acquired on a rollover basis and CCA had previously been claimed by another person, or (2) the property was previously owned by the taxpayer or a person non-arm's length with the taxpayer.

5-89. As we have seen, there are sometimes options offered to elect a different treatment. Such an option exists for both classes 54 and 55. A taxpayer can elect for the year in which zero-emission vehicles are purchased not to include the vehicles in classes 54 or 55. The result would be that the 100% accelerated CCA claim would be unavailable and the regular rules would apply, meaning that zero-emission vehicles would be included in class 10 while zero-emission passenger vehicles would be included in a separate class 10.1 subject to a cap of $55,000.

5-90. An example of where this might be beneficial would be for a zero-emission passenger vehicle with a cost slightly above the $55,000 cap. Keeping such a vehicle in class 54 means that the recapture rules apply, but electing out of class 54 would result in the vehicle being included in class 10.1 where recapture does not apply and where a partial (50%) CCA deduction can be made in the year the vehicle is sold or otherwise disposed of.

5-91. We would add that if a zero-emission passenger vehicle is sold, any recaptured amount would be reduced subject to a new rule that will be discussed later in the chapter when we discuss recapture and terminal losses.

Short Fiscal Periods—ITR 1100(3)

5-92. As first discussed in Paragraph 5-43, in the first or last year of the carrying on of a business, or in certain other types of situations that will be covered in later chapters, a taxation year with less than 365 days may occur. Under these circumstances, the maximum CCA deduction for almost all of the classes listed in Paragraph 5-59 must be calculated using a proration based on the relationship between the days in the actual short fiscal year and 365 days. Note that it is the length of the taxation year for the business, not the period of ownership of the property, that determines the proration.

5-93. Both the old half-year rules and the AccII were also applied in these situations, as illustrated in the examples in Paragraphs 5-55 to 5-57, resulting in a double reduction in the maximum CCA amounts for property acquired in a short fiscal period.

EXAMPLE Laing Ltd. begins operations on November 1, 2021, choosing December 31 as its year end. On November 11, the company acquires class 8 property with a capital cost of $300,000. Determine the 2021 CCA under each of the following assumptions:

1. The purchased property is not eligible for the AccII.
2. The purchased property is eligible for the AccII.

ANALYSIS The required information can be calculated as follows:

	Not Eligible for the AccII	Eligible for the AccII
Capital cost	$300,000	$300,000
Adjustments:		
Deduct: Half-year rule [(50%)($300,000)]	(150,000)	
Add: AccII [(50%)($300,000)]		150,000
CCA base	$150,000	$450,000
CCA rate	20%	20%
CCA pre-short fiscal period adjustment	$ 30,000	$ 90,000
Short fiscal period adjustment factor	61/365	61/365
2021 CCA	$ 5,014	$ 15,041

5-94. Two additional points are relevant:

- There are a number of exclusions to the short fiscal period rule, one of which is class 14. As noted previously, class 14 property is subject to prorated CCA based on the number of days of ownership in the year. This eliminates the need for the application of the short fiscal period rules.
- The short fiscal period rule applies when a taxation year is less than 365 days. A taxation year for a business is its fiscal period, which can be less than 365 days, but the taxation year for an individual earning income from property that is rental income is always the calendar year. Since one cannot have a short calendar year, the short fiscal period rules would only apply to businesses and not to individuals earning rental income unless, of course, the rental activity was a business (this will be discussed in Chapter 6). This means that depreciable property used in a rental income situation by an individual would never be subject to the short fiscal period rules.

Exercise 5-8

Subject: Short Fiscal Periods

Olander Inc. begins operations on August 1, 2021. On September 15, 2021, the company acquires $115,000 in class 8 property. The company has a December 31 year end, and no other depreciable property is acquired or disposed of before December 31, 2021. The property is eligible for the AccII. Determine the maximum class 8 CCA for the fiscal period ending December 31, 2021, as well as the January 1, 2022, UCC.

Solutions to Exercises are available in the Study Guide.

Class 14.1

Additions to the Class

5-95. The items that will be included in class 14.1 are as follows:

Goodwill Goodwill is intangible property that represents the excess of the purchase price over the FMV of identifiable property acquired on the purchase of a business. There are some unique features to goodwill and its interaction with class 14.1 that will be discussed later in the chapter beginning at Paragraph 5-97.

Other Intangible Property This generally includes intangible properties with unlimited lives. Intangible property with limited lives are generally included in class 14 or, in the case of patents, class 44. The following are examples of items that are included in class 14.1:

- Customer lists purchased and not otherwise deductible
- The cost of trademarks, patents, licences, and franchises with unlimited lives
- Expenses of incorporation to the extent they exceed $3,000. The first $3,000 of incorporation expenses are allowed to be fully deducted under ITA 20(1)(b)). Any additional costs, including the cost of subsequent amendments to the articles of incorporation, are added to class 14.1
- The costs of government rights
- Appraisal costs associated with valuing intangible property, such as a government right, and on an anticipated property purchase that does not take place
- Initiation or admission fees to professional or other organizations for which the annual maintenance fees are deductible.
- Some payments made under non-competition agreements (discussed in Chapter 17).

Rate

5-96. The CCA rate for class 14.1 is 5%, applied on a declining balance basis. The AccII provisions generally apply to this class.

Goodwill

5-97. Goodwill attaches to a business and obtains value as a business grows. This is often referred to as internally generated goodwill. The ITA, however, only recognizes goodwill for income tax purposes when there is an actual cost to that goodwill. This can only happen if an existing business is purchased for an amount that is greater than the FMV of the identifiable property of the business that is acquired.

5-98. Since goodwill must be purchased to be recognized for income tax purposes, purchasing select property of a business without purchasing the underlying business would not result in the purchase of goodwill. In addition, amalgamating two companies under most Canadian business law would also not result in goodwill since the law clarifies that nothing is acquired under such an amalgamation.

5-99. It is also important that goodwill actually exist. In the case law, goodwill has generally been described as an attempt to quantify the advantages associated with the likelihood that clients/customers will return for repeat business. In other words, what factors are present that contribute to that likelihood resulting in an increased value to the business? Valuable factors identified in the case law include (1) location, (2) nature of the product or service, (3) general business (an efficient business operation with experienced and qualified personnel, etc.), and (4) personal factors. Personal factors usually relate to the skills, expertise, and reputation of a specific individual. The personal factor is of considerable interest as the courts are of the view that personal factors are not transferrable when a business is sold. This means that if you operate a successful accounting practice with a lot of repeat business, and therefore the value, or goodwill, of the business is attributable to your reputation, then there would be little if any goodwill if the business were sold.

5-100. When class 14.1 was introduced as a substitute for eligible capital property in 2017, a few minor changes were made in terms of goodwill to ensure that it fit within the CCA/UCC system. In recognition of internally generated goodwill a rule was added that deems a business to own goodwill that has a cost of nil. In addition, any unusual capital expenditures that are not associated with the acquisition of any property are considered to add to the cost of that goodwill. These rules become important in determining the income tax consequences should the business be sold at a time when there is a goodwill component.

5-101. Given that goodwill is considered an integral component of an existing business, taxpayers who carry on multiple separate businesses will likely have goodwill for each of the businesses. In such cases, each business will have its own separate CCA classes. If the business is one single large integrated business, then there would be one single goodwill account. In this latter case, if part of the integrated business is sold there would technically be a partial disposition of goodwill. The new legislation considers this situation, which goes beyond the scope of our coverage.

Tax Planning Considerations for CCA

5-102. CCA deductions are discretionary. It is up to the owner of the property to decide whether they wish to claim the maximum allowable deduction in a given year, no amount, or something in between. The decision will depend on many factors, such as the level of one's taxable income and therefore the taxes payable, particularly in a year where the business is quite profitable. Many taxpayers in such situations will claim the maximum CCA in each year. Remember that if you forgo claiming CCA in a year, you cannot double up on CCA in the next year. The system provides you with a maximum for a specific year, and if you do not use it then the amount stays in UCC and provides a larger base for deductions in subsequent years.

5-103. When a taxpayer is in a loss position, a decision will need to be made whether to increase the current-year loss by claiming maximum CCA. This could be of benefit if the loss can be applied back to earlier years to recover taxes paid in those years. If this is beneficial and there are multiple classes of depreciable property to choose from, a second decision may have to be made about which classes to use for less than maximum CCA. Deciding factors include evaluating future plans for specific classes. If, for example, there is a plan to sell property in a class that will eventually result in recapture at that time, then it may be a good idea to take less CCA from that class.

5-104. When there is a choice between two classes of depreciable property that could produce the same required CCA the general consensus is that it is often preferable to claim the CCA from the class with the lowest rate.

> **EXAMPLE** Rubal carries on a business and wants to reduce his business income to nil for 2021. He needs a $30,000 CCA deduction to achieve that goal. He has a choice between class 14.1 (5%), which has a UCC balance of $600,000, or class 10 (30%), which has a $100,000 UCC balance at year end.
>
> **ANALYSIS** The maximum CCA claim from either class would be $30,000. If the claim is made from class 14.1, the UCC balance would drop to $570,000, resulting in a potential of $28,500 for the next year [(5%)($570,000)] while leaving a $30,000 claim from class 10 for a total of $58,500. If, however, the CCA claim is from class 10, then the next year's maximum CCA would be $30,000 from class 14.1 and $21,000 from class 10 [(30%)($70,000)] for a total of $51,000. In effect, choosing the lower rate class provides Rubal with an additional $7,500 in CCA claims in subsequent years while achieving the objective of claiming $30,000 in the current year.

5-105. Previous CCA claims may also be modified in some circumstances. A common occurrence is where a business is audited by the CRA and the result of the audit is to increase business income. For example, the audit may find that there is $50,000 of additional income. It may be possible to offset any taxes on this amount by revising the CCA that was claimed if it had been less than the maximum amount in the year that was audited.

5-106. In addition, the CRA will allow CCA claims to be revised in an income tax return that has already been filed and assessed as long as the request is made within the period to file a notice of objection for that year. If the period to file a notice of objection has expired, the CRA will only allow a revision to CCA claims as long as there are no taxes payable for that year. This generally refers to a year in which there were losses sufficient to reduce taxable income to nil. The CRA policy is included in IC84-1, "Revisions of CCA Claims and Other Permissive Deductions." This flexibility can prove valuable in certain circumstances.

Immediate Expensing for CCPCs

5-107. The 2021 federal budget adds a new temporary incentive specifically targeted to Canadian controlled private corporations (CCPCs). CCPCs are essentially private corporations established in Canada that are controlled by Canadian residents (CCPCs are discussed in Chapter 12). The incentive applies to purchases of depreciable property made between April 19, 2021, and December 31, 2023, other than property in classes 1 to 6, 14.1, 17, 47, 49, and 51. The budget clarifies that these exclusions generally refer to depreciable property with long lives.

5-108. The new rules allow a CCPC to immediately expense up to $1.5 million each taxation year. If the CCPC is associated with other CCPCs, the $1.5 million must be shared among the associated companies. Associated corporations are discussed in Chapter 14 and, in very general terms, refers to CCPCs under some common control. If, for example, an individual controls three CCPCs they would all be associated.

5-109. The $1.5 million annual limit is prorated for short taxation years where the number of days in a given taxation year is less than 365 days. The limit can be applied in any manner to any eligible depreciable property and can be applied to part of a capital cost. If the annual limit is not used in a specific year there is no carry forward of the difference.

5-110. Finally, there are two further restrictions. The property can be acquired for use by others before being acquired by the taxpayer, which means that CCA may have been previously claimed by someone else. This fact will not affect the eligibility to immediately expense the capital cost as long as (1) the taxpayer or someone non-arm's length with the taxpayer did not previously own the property or (2) the taxpayer did not acquire the property on a rollover basis. Property is acquired on a rollover basis where the ITA specifically allows the transaction price to be reset below its FMV. The following example expands on an example included in the 2021 budget documents.

EXAMPLE A CCPC with a December 31 taxation year end purchases class 7 and class 10 depreciable property in July 2021 for $1 million each, or $2 million in total. There are no associated corporations and the taxation year is not a short taxation year. Both purchases are eligible for the AccII incentive. The UCC balance of each class at the beginning of 2021 was nil.

ANALYSIS CCA on class 7 is 15% and 30% on class 10. It is therefore advantageous to completely expense the low CCA rate class 7 property and $500,000 of the class 10 property. The result would be that the remaining $500,000 of class 10 would be subject to the normal CCA rules as follows:

January 1, 2021, UCC balance	Nil
2021 addition	500,000
Add: AccII adjustment [(50%)($500,000)]	250,000
CCA base	$750,000
Less: 2021 CCA [(30%)($750,000)]	(225,000)
Less: AccII adjustment reversal	(250,000)
January 1, 2022, UCC	$275,000

As a result, the total CCA claim would be $1,000,000 immediately expensed for class 7 plus $500,000 immediately expensed for class 10 plus $225,000 in regular class 10 CCA for a total of $1,725,000. In the absence of immediate expensing, the maximum CCA that could have been claimed would have been $225,000 for class 7 [(15%)(150% AccII)($1,000,000)] and $450,000 [(30%)(150% AccII)($1,000,000)] for class 10 for a total of $675,000. The difference of $1,050,000 ($1,725,000 with immediate expensing - $675,000 without) represents a significant advantage. **Note:** No draft legislation was released with the 2021 federal budget, but it is presumed that the full amount of each depreciable property purchase would be added to each class to ensure that any amounts deducted as an immediate expense or claimed as CCA in the regular manner would be subject to potential recapture.

Disposition of Depreciable Property

Overview—Understanding the Basics

5-111. The ITA is based on the "realization principle," which means that there are potential income tax implications when there is a "disposition" of property. Throughout the first part of this text we have almost always referred to property being bought and sold, and for the owner selling the property that would represent a disposition. The word "disposition," however, is quite extensive in income tax. It would include both actual and deemed dispositions. Examples of dispositions of property include sales; the destruction of the property; property stolen, properly foreclosed, or repossessed; property owned by an individual who dies; property owned by an individual who severs residency with Canada; and property where the use changes from personal to an income earning purpose or from an income earning purpose to a personal use. In many of these situations the ITA will deem "proceeds of disposition," which then allows the income tax consequences to be determined.

5-112. We have mentioned that when depreciable property is disposed of there is an income tax accounting of sorts to determine whether there are any income tax consequences. We also added that there will be an amount subtracted from the UCC class as part of the process. We can now discuss how to determine that amount and identify the immediate income tax implications when there is a disposition of depreciable property. Before getting into the specifics it is first important to understand the underlying concepts of recapture and terminal loss.

EXAMPLE 1—Sale for the UCC Amount: You own class 8 depreciable property. The capital cost is $100. Over the years you have claimed CCA of $70 and the remaining UCC is $30. If you sell the property for $30 there are no income tax consequences. You have spent $100 but have been allowed to write-off $70 of the cost as CCA, plus you recovered the remaining $30 of the undepreciated amount on the sale.

EXAMPLE 2—Sale above UCC but below Capital Cost: Now assume that the class 8 property from Example 1 was sold for $55, an amount above the UCC of $30 but below the capital cost of $100. In this case the income tax system allowed you to write-off $70 of your cost as CCA, but based on the facts it appears you only needed to write-off $45 in CCA because you recovered $55 of the original capital cost. In this instance the tax system gave you $70 of CCA deductions when you economically only needed $45 to recognize the actual decline in value. As a result you received $25 in extra CCA. The CCA/UCC system now requires you to include that $25 in your business income in the year of sale as CCA you didn't need. This is referred to as "recapture depreciation" or simply "recapture."

EXAMPLE 3—Sale below UCC and Capital Cost: Using the same facts from Example 1, assume that the sale was for $10, which is below both the UCC of $30 and the capital cost of $100. In this case you wrote off $70 of your $100 purchase of depreciable property and only recovered $10 through the disposition, meaning you are short $20 because you needed $90 of CCA to recognize the decline in value. The CCA/UCC system allows you to deduct that $20 shortfall as quasi-CCA, referred to as a terminal loss. As a result, your total write-offs are $70 of CCA plus a $20 fully deductible terminal loss for a total of $90. The $10 you received on the sale once again balances out to your capital cost of $100.

EXAMPLE 4—Sale above UCC and above Capital Cost: Same facts again, except assume that you sold the property for $110, which is above the UCC of $30 and the capital cost of $100. In this case you fully recovered your capital cost, meaning that you did not economically need any CCA since there was no decline in value. The result is that the $70 claimed in CCA in past years is fully recaptured. In addition, you made $10 more than the actual capital cost, which is treated as a capital gain of $10, only half of which is taxable. You therefore have a taxable capital gain of $5 plus business income of $70 in recaptured CCA.

In Examples 1, 2, and 3 you sold the depreciable property for an amount below its capital cost. You will see in Chapter 8 that when capital property is sold there can be capital gains and capital losses. Capital losses occur when the sale price is less than the "adjusted cost base" (ACB), which is a capital gains/losses expression to describe the tax cost. The ACB of depreciable property means its capital cost; therefore, in Example 4 when you sold for $110 and the capital cost was $100, there would be a $10 capital gain. But you will see in the following example there is something wrong when you try and apply capital losses to depreciable property.

EXAMPLE 5—Assume you purchased class 8 depreciable property for the first time in 2021 for $100, The property was uninsured and damaged in the first year. You managed to sell it in that first year for only $10. When you sold the property the UCC of the class was reduced by $10 to $90. That $90 amount represents a terminal loss, which is fully deductible in that first year. In effect the CCA/UCC system allowed you to write-off $90 of the capital cost and you recovered the remaining $10. Everything balances out. Should you also be able to claim a capital loss of $90 based on a sale of $10 minus the ACB of $100? If the tax system allowed you a capital loss, then you would be recognizing the $90 loss twice: once as a deductible terminal loss and a second time as a capital loss. To avoid this result the ITA establishes an important rule—capital losses are never allowed for dispositions of depreciable property.

5-113. To summarize, the ownership of depreciable property provides an opportunity to claim part of the cost as a CCA claim in each year of ownership. When there is a disposition, where there is only property in a class, there is a possibility of either (1) nothing (Example 1), (2) recapture (Example 2), (3) terminal loss (Example 3), or (4) recapture and a capital gain (Example 4). In addition, there can never be a capital loss (Example 5). You will see that these results can vary somewhat where there are multiple depreciable properties in a class, but the CCA/UCC concepts remain the same. We will next look at the actual mechanical process that the ITA uses to determine the income tax consequences that we have illustrated.

UCC & Dispositions

5-114. The key to the income tax implications for classes of depreciable property is the UCC of each class, which is defined as a lengthy calculation at ITA 13(21). The only parts of the calculation that you need to understand at this point are the following:

UCC = Capital cost of property acquired + recapture - terminal loss - CCA claimed - dispositions

Basic Rule for Dispositions When there is a disposition of a depreciable property, the UCC of the class is reduced by an amount equal to the lesser of

- the proceeds of disposition (POD), or
- the capital cost of the property.

The proceeds of disposition or POD relate to another lengthy definition in the ITA, but in terms of a sale it is simply the sale price regardless of whether it is paid in full at the time of the sale or later.

5-115. It is also important to be aware of the timing for the components of UCC. Additions and dispositions adjust the UCC at the time that additions are made or dispositions occur. The UCC balance on the last day of the taxation year is used to determine whether a CCA claim can be made for that year or there is a recapture or there is a terminal loss for that year. CCA claims, recapture, and terminal losses then adjust the UCC at the beginning of the next taxation year only. Only one of these three possible outcomes can occur for a specific class for a taxation year unless there is nothing left in the class at year end (see Example 1).

TIP 1: CCA can only be claimed if the UCC on the last day of the taxation year is a positive amount and there are properties remaining in that class.

TIP 2: Recapture occurs when the UCC is negative at year end. The adjustment at the beginning of the next year simply resets the UCC balance to nil.

TIP 3: A terminal loss occurs when the UCC is a positive amount at year end and there are no properties remaining in the class. The adjustment at the beginning of the next year again resets the UCC balance to nil.

5-116. There are always, however, a few exceptions to the general rules. Class 10.1, for example, does not allow recapture or a terminal loss in the year of a disposition, and CCA can be claimed in that same taxation year even though there is no UCC on the last day of that same taxation year. In addition, class 14.1 restricts when a terminal loss can be claimed and, as a result, CCA can continue to be claimed even though no properties remain in the class. Dispositions from class 14.1 are discussed in further detail later in this chapter.

Applying the UCC to Dispositions—Examples Revisited

No Immediate Tax Consequences

5-117. In revisiting the five examples in Paragraph 5-112, we will assume that the taxpayer uses a calendar-based taxation year and that the opening UCC for 2021 is $30, which equals capital cost of pre-2021 purchases of $100 minus pre-2021 CCA claims of $70.

EXAMPLE 1 In this first example the property is sold for $30 in 2021.

ANALYSIS 1 We begin with the UCC at January 1, 2021, which is calculated as follows:

Capital Cost $100 - CCA claimed in years before 2021 $70 = UCC of $30

The UCC at December 31, 2021, is determined as follows:

Balance January 1, 2021 $30 - $30 dispositions = Nil

The disposition is equal to the lesser of the capital cost of $100 and the POD or sale price of $30.

CONCLUSION 1 No CCA can be claimed in 2021 since the December 31, 2021, UCC is nil. There is no recapture, terminal loss, or capital gains. UCC at January 1, 2022, remains nil. This is the same result as our earlier conclusion.

Disposition with Recapture

5-118. Recapture generally occurs where the amount that is required to be subtracted from the UCC as a result of a disposition exceeds the opening UCC plus any additions made to that class in the year. This is commonly referred to as a negative UCC balance. The second example looks at a recapture situation.

EXAMPLE 2 The property is sold for $55 in 2021.

ANALYSIS 2 We begin again with the UCC at January 1, 2021, which is calculated as follows:

Capital Cost $100 - CCA claimed in years before 2021 $70 = UCC of $30

The UCC at December 31, 2021, is determined as follows:

Balance January 1, 2021 $30 - $55 disposition in 2021 = ($25)

The disposition is equal to the lesser of the capital cost of $100 and the POD or sale price of $55.

CONCLUSION 2 Since the UCC at December 31, 2021, is not positive nor are there any properties remaining in the class, no CCA can be claimed for the 2021 taxation year. In addition, since the amount subtracted from the class ($55) exceeded the opening balance and any additions made to the class in the year (of which there were none), or $30 in total, there is a recapture. The amount (shown as a negative) is therefore required to be included in the business income of the taxpayer for the 2021 year. If the income were from a rental property, then the recapture would be considered to be property income.

UCC at January 1, 2022 = Opening balance January 1, 2021, of $30 + 2021 recapture of $25 - 2021 disposition of $55 = Nil

The recapture reset the UCC to nil on the first day of the next taxation year (2022).

Disposition with a Terminal Loss

5-119. In this third example we look at a terminal loss, which arises when there is both a positive UCC balance at year end and no property remaining in the class.

EXAMPLE 3 The property is sold for $10 in 2021.

ANALYSIS 3 We begin again with the UCC at January 1, 2021, which is calculated as follows:

Capital Cost $100 - CCA claimed in years before 2021 $70 = UCC of $30

The UCC at December 31, 2021, is determined as follows:

Balance January 1, 2021, $30 - $10 disposition in 2021 = $20

The disposition is equal to the lesser of the capital cost of $100 and the POD or sale price of $10.

CONCLUSION 3 Since there are no properties remaining in the class at December 31, 2021, no CCA can be claimed for the 2021 taxation year. There is no negative amount and therefore there is no recapture. However, since there is a positive amount and no property remaining in the class, the $20 will be treated as a terminal loss, which is fully deductible in 2021 as either a business expense or rental property expense depending on the source of income to which the depreciable property relates.

UCC at January 1, 2022 = Opening balance January 1, 2021, of $30 - 2021 terminal loss of $20 - 2021 disposition of $10 = Nil

The terminal loss reset the UCC to nil on the first day of the next taxation year (2022).

Disposition with Recapture and Capital Gains

5-120. In this final example we look at a situation where the sale price exceeds the capital cost.

EXAMPLE 4 The property is sold for $110 in 2021.

ANALYSIS 4 We begin again with the UCC at January 1, 2021, which is calculated as follows:

Capital Cost $100 - CCA claimed in years before 2021 $70 = UCC of $30

The UCC at December 31, 2021, is determined as follows:

Balance January 1, 2021, $30 - $100 disposition in 2021 = ($70)

The disposition is equal to the lesser of the capital cost of $100 and the POD or sale price of $110.

CONCLUSION 4 Since the UCC at December 31, 2021, is not positive nor are there any properties remaining in the class, no CCA can be claimed for the 2021 taxation year. In addition, since the amount subtracted from the class ($100) exceeded the opening balance and any additions made to the class in the year (of which there were none), or $30 in total, there is a recapture of $70. The amount (shown as a negative) is therefore required to be included in the business or property income of the taxpayer for the 2021 year.

UCC at January 1, 2022 = Opening balance January 1, 2021, of $30 + 2021 recapture of $70 - 2021 disposition of $100 = Nil

In addition, because the sale price of $110 exceeded the capital cost (ACB) of $100, there is also a capital gain of $10. The part of the capital gain that is taxable is only 50%, and therefore the "taxable capital gain" is $5. This will be discussed in Chapter 8.

You can see that the recapture again reset the UCC to nil on the first day of the next taxation year (2022).

UCC and Dispositions with Multiple Properties

5-121. In Example 2 there was recapture of $25 because the UCC on the last day of the taxation year was a negative $25. Since the UCC is increased by purchases of depreciable property, the recapture could have been avoided by acquiring property of that class by December 31, 2021, of at least $25. If, for example, a property with a $60 capital cost was acquired in 2021, then the UCC at December 31, 2021, would have been as follows:

Balance January 1, 2021, $30 + purchase $60 - $55 disposition in 2021 = $35

In that case there would be no recapture since the year-end UCC is not a negative amount. In addition CCA can now be claimed and would be calculated as $7.50 [(20%)($37.50)]. The CCA base of $37.50 would include an AccII component based on the "net additions" of $5 [$60 purchases - $55 subtracted from the class] and would be calculated as [$30 + (150%)($5)].

5-122. In Example 4 we also had a recapture in the amount of $70. Had additional class 8 depreciable property been acquired for an amount at least equal to $70 by the end of the 2021 year, then the recapture could also have been avoided. If we assume that property with a capital cost of $90 was acquired in 2021, then the UCC at December 31, 2021, would have been as follows:

Balance January 1, 2021, $30 + 2021 purchase $90 - $100 disposition in 2021 = $20

As a result the recapture is avoided. Since there are no positive net additions [$90 - $100], there is no AccII adjustment and the CCA would be 20% of $20, or $4. The UCC at January 1, 2022, would then fall to $16. We would add that the capital gain of $10 (taxable $5) is not affected by the purchase of additional depreciable property.

5-123. Finally, in Example 3 there was a terminal loss of $20 because there was no property remaining in the class on the last day of the 2021 taxation year (December 31). If we assume that depreciable property with a capital cost of $50 was purchased in 2021, then the UCC at December 31, 2021, would have been:

Balance January 1, 2021, $30 - $10 disposition in 2021+ 2021 purchase $50 = $70.

There is now no terminal loss since it requires both a positive amount of UCC together with no property remaining at December 31, 2021, which is no longer the case. However, the taxpayer could now claim CCA for 2021. Maximum CCA would be calculated as follows:

[(20%)($30) + (150%)(net additions of $40)] = $18

UCC at January 1, 2022, would be $52 [$70 - CCA $18].

5-124. Interestingly, had the taxpayer delayed the purchase of the property to 2022 there would have been a terminal loss deduction of $20 for 2021 and a CCA claim of $15 for 2022 [(20%)(nil opening UCC) + (150%)($50)] for a total of $35 in deductions for the two years. Purchasing the property in 2021 would have resulted in CCA of $18 for 2021 and CCA of $10.40 [(20%)($52)] for 2022 for a total of $28.40. Delaying the purchase to the following year would have resulted in increased deductions of over 23% ($35.00/$28.40) for this two-year period, indicating the value of proper tax planning with depreciable property.

5-125. Given the broadly based nature of most CCA classes, it is likely that a business would have additional properties in the class subsequent to any dispositions. Further, it is also likely that a balance will remain in the class after the proceeds of disposition have been subtracted from the UCC. In such situations, there are no immediate tax consequences associated with a disposition as long as it is not sold for an amount above its capital cost. While the UCC will be reduced, this will simply result in smaller CCA deductions in current and future years.

EXAMPLE A business owns 20 vehicles, each with a cost of $25,000. All of these vehicles are in class 10. On January 1, 2021, this class has a UCC balance of $297,500. During 2021, one of these vehicles is sold for $15,000. The business has a December 31 year end. There are no further acquisitions or dispositions during the year ending December 31, 2021.

ANALYSIS The lesser of the vehicle's capital cost ($25,000) and the proceeds of disposition ($15,000) would be $15,000. This amount would be subtracted from the January 1, 2021, opening UCC, leaving a balance of $282,500 ($297,500 - $15,000) at December 31, 2021. As there are additional properties in the class on the last day of the taxation year together with a positive balance, there is no terminal loss. The disposition would therefore have no immediate tax consequences other than providing a base in which to calculate CCA for the year. Maximum class 10 CCA for the year would be $84,750 [(30%)($282,500)], leaving a January 1, 2022, UCC of $197,750 [$282,500 - $84,750].

Exercise 5-9

Subject: Capital Gains on Depreciable Property

On January 1 of the current year, Vaughn Ltd. has a class 8 balance of $275,000. During the current year, property with a capital cost of $18,000 is sold for $23,000. There are no other dispositions during the year and there are numerous properties remaining in the class. What are the tax consequences of this disposition?

Exercise 5-10

Subject: Recapture

At the beginning of 2021, Codlin Inc. has two properties in class 8. The capital cost of each was $27,000 and the class 8 UCC balance on the last day of the taxation year was $24,883. On June 30, 2021, one of the properties was sold for $28,500. There are no other additions or dispositions in the year ending December 31, 2021.

What is the effect of the disposition on the company's 2021 business income? In addition, determine the January 1, 2022, UCC balance.

Exercise 5-11

Subject: Terminal Losses

At the beginning of 2021, Codlin Inc. has two properties in class 8. The cost of each property was $27,000 and the UCC balance at January 1, 2021, was $24,883. On June 30, 2021, both of the properties are sold for $9,000 each, a total of $18,000. There are no other additions or dispositions to the class in the 2021 taxation year. What is the effect of the dispositions on the company's 2021 business income? In addition, determine the January 1, 2022, UCC balance.

Exercise 5-12

Subject: Depreciable Property Dispositions

Norky Ltd. disposes of a class 8 property for proceeds of $126,000. The capital cost of the property was $97,000 and it had a carrying value of $43,500. The company's class 8 contains a number of other properties, and the UCC balance at the beginning of the year was $2,462,000. Describe briefly the accounting and income tax treatments of the disposition.

Solutions to Exercises are available in the Study Guide.

Employees—Recapture and Terminal Losses

5-126. In this chapter we have seen that the CCA/UCC rules are found in the part of the ITA that deals with business and property income. In Chapter 3 we also saw that some select employees can claim CCA on certain depreciable property, such as automobiles, aircraft, and musical instruments. The CCA/UCC rules apply to those employees but with one significant difference. Any recapture is considered employment income because of a connecting rule in ITA 13(11). However, no terminal loss can be deducted by an employee because there is no connecting or other rule that would allow such a deduction. The CRA confirms this result at Paragraph 1-101 in Folio S3-F4-C1, "General Discussion of CCA."

Dispositions of Class 54 Property (Zero-Emission Passenger Vehicles)

5-127. We previously discussed class 54 property, noting that two types of depreciable property were to be included. The first is zero-emission vehicles, which are equivalent to class 10. The second is zero-emission passenger vehicles, which are roughly equivalent to class 10.1 in many but not all respects. There is no capital cost cap on zero-emission vehicles, but there is a $55,000 cap on zero-emission passenger vehicles. Unlike class 10.1, which provide for a separate class for each passenger vehicle with no recognition of recapture or terminal loss, all class 54 properties are added together (no separate classes), and both recapture and terminal loss rules apply.

5-128. If a taxpayer takes full advantage of the 100% AccII write-off for class 54, the UCC will have a nil balance. In addition there would never be a terminal loss since it would require a positive UCC balance. However, subsequent-year dispositions will almost always result in recapture. This presents a problem for zero-emission passenger vehicles that have been capped at $55,000 because the cost is in excess of that amount.

EXAMPLE In December 2021, Green Ltd. acquires a class 54 zero-emission passenger vehicle at a cost of $150,000. The vehicle capital cost is capped at $55,000 and the first-year CCA, with the AccII, is also $55,000.. The January 1, 2022, UCC balance would be nil.

The vehicle is sold in July 2022 for $110,000. There are no further class 54 acquisitions during 2022.

ANALYSIS In the absence of any special rules covering this type of situation, the company would have to deduct the lesser of the POD of $110,000 and the capital cost of $55,000, or $55,000, from a nil UCC balance, resulting in recapture of $55,000. This result would fail to take into account that the company only recovered 73.3% ($110,000/$150,000) of its original value and that therefore only 26.7% of the value had declined during the period of ownership. In recognition of this problem, ITA 13(7)(i) modifies the POD by requiring that the reduction to the class for the disposition reflect the percentage of the original cost that was recovered. In this case that would mean that instead of reducing the class by $55,000, the reduction would only be $40,333 [($55,000)(73.333%)]. The actual formula in the ITA is calculated as follows:

$$\left[\text{Actual Proceeds Of Disposition}\left(\frac{\text{Prescribed Amount (\$55,000)}}{\text{Actual Property Cost}}\right)\right]$$

$$\left[\$110{,}000\left(\frac{\$55{,}000}{\$150{,}000}\right)\right] = \$40{,}333$$

Using this modified POD, recapture would be limited to $40,333 (nil - $40,333). This modified disposition amount would also apply for the purposes of determining whether there was a terminal loss. If no CCA had been claimed in the year of purchase and the sale occurred for the same amount of $110,000, then the reduction to the class would be the same $40,333, leaving a positive balance in the UCC at the end of the second year of $14,667 [$55,000 - $40,333] that would be deducted as a terminal loss in the second year. This is economically equivalent to the recapture situation where a CCA deduction of $55,000 would be claimed in the first year and a recapture of $40,000 would be included in income for the second year. The net difference would be the same $14,667, just spread over two years. You should also note that an election could have been made not to include the zero-emission passenger vehicle in class 54. In that case, it would be included in a separate class 10.1 without any concern for future recapture.

Dispositions of Class 14.1—Differences from Other Classes

Single Goodwill Account

5-129. Earlier we mentioned that class 14.1 includes many types of intangible properties (including goodwill) and certain other capital expenditures that would not be included in any other class. ITA 13(34) deems that every business will have one single goodwill property, whether or not there is any actual goodwill, and its cost will be nil. This is important since the CCA/UCC system requires that every property disposed of is first recognized as having been acquired at a specific cost. It is also the reason why capital transactions that do not result in the acquisition of property are added to the deemed goodwill. Therefore, if a business that has added internally generated goodwill is sold, the income tax implications with respect to any amount received for the goodwill can then be determined through the CCA/UCC system.

5-130. The relatively new class 14.1 rules recognize that there may be acquisitions of goodwill that add to the single goodwill and partial dispositions of goodwill that reduce that same single goodwill. These rules are again designed to ensure that the CCA/UCC system that did not apply to property such as goodwill prior to 2017 fit within the depreciable property rules.

5-131. From a practical perspective, however, and as previously mentioned, goodwill attaches to an existing business that is a separate business. Therefore, the sale of such a business leads to the disposition of all business properties, including goodwill. There would be no partial disposition. If, however, a business is expanding through purchasing other businesses and integrating each purchased business into its one large business, then there would be additions to the single goodwill property. Alternatively, an integrated business that sells a segment of its business could be viewed as a partial disposition of goodwill, meaning that any sale proceeds for a goodwill component would reduce the UCC of class 14.1. The likelihood of this occurrence in practice may not be that common, but the ITA nevertheless has addressed it.

EXAMPLE During 2021, Brasco Ltd. acquires two businesses (Business 1 and Business 2) that will be integrated into one single business. The acquisition of Business 1 includes a payment for goodwill of $125,000, while the acquisition of Business 2 includes a payment for goodwill of $180,000. This is important in that, if Brasco carried on these businesses separately, a separate class 14.1 would be established for each business.

In December 2022, a portion of Brasco's business is sold at a price that includes goodwill of $140,000. Brasco had a nil class 14.1 balance as of January 1, 2021, and there were no other class 14.1 transactions during 2021 or 2022.

ANALYSIS CCA on class 14.1 for 2021 would be calculated as follows:

January 1, 2021, UCC balance	Nil
2021 additions ($125,000 + $180,000)	$305,000
AccII adjustment [(50%)($305,000)]	152,500
CCA base	$ 457,500
2021 CCA [(5%)($457,500)]	(22,875)
AccII adjustment reversal	(152,500)
January 1, 2022, UCC	$282,125

When a portion of Brasco's business is sold with a payment for goodwill of $140,000, we would subtract from the UCC balance the lesser of

- the proceeds of disposition of $140,000; or
- the capital cost of the single goodwill property of $305,000.

There would be no immediate tax consequences resulting from the disposition, and the new UCC figure for class 14.1 would be $142,125 ($282,125 - $140,000).

5-132. You should note how this result would differ if Brasco had continued to operate either of the acquired businesses as a separate business. To illustrate this possibility, consider this modified version of the example from Paragraph 5-131.

EXAMPLE During 2021, Brasco Ltd. acquires two businesses that will be carried on as two separate businesses. The acquisition of Business 1 includes a payment for goodwill of $125,000, while the acquisition of Business 2 includes a payment for goodwill of $180,000. Given this, there will be a separate class 14.1 balance for each business.

In December 2022, Business 1 is sold at a price that includes goodwill of $140,000. Brasco had no class 14.1 balance as of January 1, 2021, and there were no other class 14.1 transactions during 2021 or 2022.

ANALYSIS CCA on class 14.1 for 2021 would be calculated as follows:

	Business 1	Business 2
January 1, 2021, UCC balance	Nil	Nil
2021 additions	$125,000	$180,000
AccII adjustments		
[(50%)($125,000)]	62,500	
[(50%)($180,000)]		90,000
CCA base	$187,500	$270,000
2021 CCA		
[(5%)($187,500)]	(9,375)	
[(5%)($270,000)]		(13,500)
AccII adjustment reversals	(62,500)	(90,000)
January 1, 2021, UCC balance (total = $282,125)	$ 115,625	$166,500

In 2022, the sale of the Business 1 would result in recapture as follows:

January 1, 2022, UCC of business 1—Class 14.1	$115,625
Disposition—Lesser of:	
Proceeds of disposition = $140,000	
Capital cost = $125,000	(125,000)
Negative ending balance = Recapture of CCA	($ 9,375)

In addition, there would be a taxable capital gain of $7,500 [(1/2)($140,000 - $125,000)].

Exercise 5-13

Subject: Disposition of Goodwill

During 2021, Dextrin Inc. acquires two businesses integrating both into its one large business. The fiscal period of the business is the calendar year. The cost of the first acquisition includes a payment for goodwill of $85,000, while the cost of the second includes a payment for goodwill of $105,000. Dextrin Inc. had no class 14.1 balance as of January 1, 2021, and there were no other class 14.1 transactions during the year. In December 2022, Dextrin sold two segments of its business. The first results in a sale of goodwill for $65,000, while the second results in a sale of goodwill for $105,000. Dextrin always claims maximum CCA. Determine the January 1, 2022, UCC balance. What are the income tax consequences of the dispositions?

Solutions to Exercises are available in the Study Guide.

No Terminal Losses—ITA 20(16.1)(c)

5-133. The pre-2017 predecessor "eligible capital property" (ECP) rules to class 14.1 did not allow any unamortized balance to be deducted where no properties remained unless the business to which the balance related had ceased to be carried on. The terminal loss rules did not apply to ECP because ECP was not depreciable property. Class 14.1, however, is depreciable property with the result that the terminal loss rules automatically apply unless there is some restriction to the contrary. To ensure consistency and continuity, the government added ITA 20(16.1)(c) to ensure that the same concept that had applied to ECP also continues to apply to class 14.1. As a result, no terminal loss can be claimed until the business has ceased to be carried on by the taxpayer. The result, however, is that CCA can continue to be claimed on the UCC balance even though there are no properties remaining in that class.

EXAMPLE On January 1, 2021, there is no balance in Roper Inc.'s class 14.1. Later that month, the company expands its business by acquiring an unlimited life franchise at a cost of $200,000. During February 2022, the franchise is sold for $150,000. Roper Inc. continues to carry on the business.

ANALYSIS The relevant calculations for 2021 and 2022 are as follows:

Class 14.1 UCC balance—January 1, 2021	Nil
2021 addition	$200,000
Accll adjustment [(50%)($200,000)]	100,000
CCA base	$300,000
2021 CCA [(5%)($300,000)]	(15,000)
Accll adjustment reversal	(100,000)
UCC balance—January 1, 2022	$185,000
Disposition—Lesser of:	
Proceeds of disposition = $150,000	
Capital cost = $200,000	(150,000)
December 31, 2022, UCC*	$ 35,000
2022 CCA [(5%)($35,000)]	(1,750)
UCC balance—January 1, 2023	$ 33,250

*Note that this $35,000 balance reflects the $50,000 ($200,000 - $150,000) loss on the disposition of the property reduced by the CCA of $15,000 already claimed in 2021. If the business ceased to exist in 2023, the remaining balance of $33,250 could be deducted at that time as a terminal loss.

5-134. A taxpayer can cease to carry on a business in one of two general ways. The first is terminating the business altogether and the second is selling the business. If, however, an individual sells the business together with all of its properties to a spouse, common-law partner, or a corporation controlled by that same individual, then no terminal loss can be claimed for class 14.1 (ITA 24(2)).

Disposition Summary—Income Tax Consequences

5-135. Figure 5-2 provides a summary of the various income tax consequences that can result from dispositions of depreciable property, along with a description of the conditions that lead to each possible consequence.

Figure 5-2
Disposition of Depreciable Property—Summary of Income Tax Consequences

Result	Conditions
Capital Gain	If the proceeds of disposition exceed the capital cost of the property, there will be a capital gain with a potential recapture if CCA had been claimed.
Recapture of CCA	If the disposition amount subtracted from the UCC is such that there is a **negative** balance on the last day of the taxation year, that negative amount is included in income as recapture. Class 10.1 is an exception to this rule. Recapture only requires the existence of a negative UCC balance and applies regardless of whether there are any properties remaining in the class on the last day of the taxation year.
Terminal Loss	If, on the last day of the taxation year, the UCC balance is positive and there are no properties remaining in the class then the **positive** balance can be deducted in full in that year as a terminal loss. There are two exceptions. No terminal loss can be recognized for class 10.1 and terminal losses can generally only be recognized for class 14.1 when the underlying business has ceased to be carried on.
No Immediate Tax Consequences	There are no immediate tax consequences if all the following conditions are present: • The proceeds of disposition are equal to or less than the capital cost of the property (no capital gain and never capital losses) • The disposition does not leave a negative UCC balance on the last day of the taxation year (no recapture) • On the last day of the taxation year there is a positive UCC balance and property remains in the class (no terminal loss)

CCA Schedule

5-136. At this point, it is useful to summarize the CCA calculations in a schedule. A commonly used format is illustrated in the following example.

EXAMPLE The fiscal year end of Blue Sky Rentals Ltd. is December 31. On January 1, 2021, the UCC balance for class 8 is $155,000. During the year ending December 31, 2021, $27,000 was spent to acquire class 8 property. During the same period, class 8 property was sold for $35,000. The capital cost of the property sold was $22,000.

UCC balance—January 1. 2021		$155,000
Add: Acquisitions during the year	$27,000	
Deduct: Dispositions during the year—Lesser of:		
• Capital cost = $22,000		
• Proceeds of disposition = $35,000	(22,000)	5,000
Add: AccII adjustment [(50%)($5,000)]*		2,500
CCA base		$162,500
Deduct: CCA for the year [(20%)($162,500)]		(32,500)
Deduct: AccII adjustment reversal		(2,500)
UCC balance—January 1, 2022		$ 127,500

The UCC balance at December 31, 2021, would not include the AccII adjustments and would be $160,000 ($155,000 opening UCC balance January 1, 2021, plus net additions of $5,000 [$27,000 - $22,000]).

*The AccII adjustment for 50% of the excess applies to the net additions to the class in the year.

5-137. While this schedule is not designed to calculate this amount, there is also a taxable capital gain of $6,500 [(1/2)($35,000 - $22,000)] resulting from the sale of the property. You will note, however, that the CCA schedule does provide the necessary information to determine the capital gain as proceeds of $35,000 less capital cost of $22,000.

We suggest you complete SSP 5-1 through 5-7 at this point.

CCA Determination—Some Special Situations

Separate Class Election

The Problem

5-138. In our discussion of CCA/UCC concepts we noted that, in general, all property of a particular type must be combined into a single class. However, we also noted a few exceptions such as the rule that requires each rental property with a capital cost in excess of $50,000 to be included in a separate class and the separate class concept of Class 10.1. Both of these exceptions are not optional.

5-139. We also noted that elective options are available on a selective basis to include certain types of depreciable property in separate classes. Now that you have both a conceptual and a practical understanding of how the CCA/UCC rules operate, particularly in regard to the income tax consequences when there is a disposition, we can meaningfully discuss the justification for electing separate class treatment.

5-140. Consider a $25,000 high-volume photocopier that would be included in class 8. After two years, the UCC balance would be calculated as follows:

Capital cost	$25,000
CCA year one including AccII adjustment [(20%)(150%)($25,000)]	(7,500)
CCA yeartTwo [(20%)($25,000 - $7,500)]	(3,500)
UCC—Beginning of year three	$14,000

5-141. Given the rate of technological change and accompanying obsolescence, it is possible that this photocopier would be replaced within a relatively short period of time. Further, the value of the old photocopier would likely be relatively small. If, for example, the photocopier was disposed of for proceeds of $5,000, there would be a potential terminal loss of $9,000 ($14,000 - $5,000).

5-142. There are two problems with this analysis that prevent the ability to claim the terminal loss:

- Most businesses will have multiple properties in class 8. As a result, since properties would remain in the class on the last day of the taxation year, no terminal loss could be claimed.
- Even if the photocopier is the only class 8 property, the replacement will likely be acquired using the old photocopier as a trade-in, meaning that the purchase of the new and sale of the old occur at the same time. As a result, there is property in the class on the last day of the taxation year, preventing the ability to claim a terminal loss.

5-143. The election to include individual photocopiers in a separate class 8 resolves these problems. When the photocopier is disposed of, even if it was used as a trade-in on a new photocopier, a terminal loss can be recognized since the new replacement would go into a different class 8.

Class 8 Property Eligible for Elective Separate Class Treatment

5-144. There are a number of high tech or electronic products that are normally included in class 8 that have actual service lives that are significantly shorter than the rates applicable to that class would imply. ITR 1101(5p) lists the following specific types of class 8 properties that are eligible for separate class treatment, provided they have a capital cost of $1,000 or more:

- Photocopiers
- Electronic communications equipment, such as telephone equipment
- Computer software (only if included in class 8 rather than class 12 or 50)

5-145. The purpose of this separate class elective treatment is to allow terminal losses to be claimed on the disposition of certain short-lived property. Such recognition would usually not be possible, either because there is property remaining in the particular class on the last day of the taxation year or because the replacements are being acquired at the same time as the sale or trade-in of the old property. Note that only rapidly depreciating electronic equipment that is specifically listed qualifies for this treatment.

Exercise 5-14

Subject: Separate Class Election

In January 2021, Edverness Inc. acquires 10 photocopiers at a cost of $20,000 each. In December 2021, two of these photocopiers are traded in on faster machines with more features. The new photocopiers cost $22,000 each, and the company receives a trade-in allowance for each old machine of $3,000. The company uses a calendar-based fiscal period. Indicate the amount(s) that would be deducted from 2021 business income if no election is made to put each photocopier in a separate class. Contrast this with the deduction(s) that would be available if the separate class election is used.

Solutions to Exercises are available in the Study Guide.

Non-Residential Buildings

5-146. As noted in Paragraph 5-59, there are enhanced CCA rates for class 1 new non-residential buildings. The basic 4% rate is increased to 10% if 90% or more of the floor space of the building is used for manufacturing and processing. If the building does not meet the manufacturing and processing test but 90% or more of the floor space is used for other non-residential purposes the CCA rate is 6%. This includes carrying on a business other than manufacturing and processing.

5-147. The availability of these special rates is conditional on an election being made to include each non-residential building in a separate class (ITR 1101(5b.1)). While this election allows for higher CCA claims based on higher rates, there is a possible downside in that UCC will be reduced much faster, resulting in greater recapture on a subsequent disposition. The alternative is to forgo the election and keep the building in class 1 with a lower CCA rate of 4%.

We suggest you complete SSP 5-8 at this point.

Key Terms

A full glossary with definitions is provided at the end of the Study Guide.

Accelerated Investment Incentive (AccII)
Capital Cost
Capital Cost Allowance (CCA)
Capital Gain
Class
Declining Balance Method
Depreciable Property
Disposition
First-Year Rules
Goodwill
Half-Year Rules (a.k.a. First-Year Rules)
Non-Depreciable Capital Property
Recapture of CCA
Separate Class Rules
Short Fiscal Period
Straight-Line Method
Taxable Capital Gain
Terminal Loss
Undepreciated Capital Cost (UCC)
Zero-Emission Vehicles
Zero-Emission Passenger Vehicles

References

For more detailed study of the material in this chapter, we would refer you to the following:

ITA 13(1)	Recaptured Depreciation
ITA 13(7.1)	Deemed Capital Cost of Certain Property
ITA 13(26) to ITA 13(32)	Available-for-Use Rules
ITA 13(34)	Goodwill
ITA 13(35)	Outlays Not Relating to Property
ITA 13(36)	Receipts Not Relating to Property
ITA 13(37) to ITA 13(42)	Class 14.1—Transitional Rules
ITA 20(1)(a)	Capital Cost of Property
ITA 20(1)(b)	Incorporation Costs
ITA 20(16)	Terminal Loss
ITA 20(16.1)	Non-Application of ITA 20(16)
ITR Part XI	Capital Cost Allowances
ITR Sch II-VI	Capital Cost Allowances
IC-84-1	Revision of Capital Cost Allowance Claims and Other Permissive Deductions
S3-F4-C1	General Discussion of Capital Cost Allowance
S3-F8-C2	Tax Incentives for Clean Energy Equipment
IT-79R3	Capital Cost Allowance—Buildings or Other Structures
IT-195R4	Rental Property—Capital Cost Allowance Restrictions
IT-206R	Separate Businesses
IT-472	Capital Cost Allowance—Class 8 Property

Appendix: CCA Rates for Select Depreciable Property

Note that for your convenience, this appendix of common CCA rates, as well as the 2021 rates, credits, and other data, is available online as a .PDF file.

This appendix lists the CCA class and rate for depreciable property commonly used in business. Restrictions and transitional rules may apply in certain situations. ITR Schedules II to VI contain detailed descriptions of the CCA classes.

Depreciable Property	Class	Rate
Aircraft (including components)	9	25%
Airplane runways	17	8%
Automobiles, passenger		
(See also **zero-emission vehicles**)		
• Cost < or = Prescribed amount ($30,000 in 2020)	10	30%
• Cost > Prescribed amount	10.1	30%
Automotive equipment	10	30%
Bar code scanners	8	20%
Billboards	8	20%
Boats, canoes, and other vessels	7	15%
Bridges, canals, culverts, and dams	1	4%
Buildings acquired before 1988	3	5%
Buildings acquired after 1987—No separate class	1	4%
Buildings (new only) acquired after March 18, 2007:		
• Manufacturing and processing in separate class 1	1	10%
• Other non-residential in separate class 1	1	6%
Buses	10	30%
Calculators	8	20%
Cash registers	8	20%
China, cutlery, and tableware	12	100%
Communications equipment		
(including cell phones too dumb to be smartphones)	8	20%
Computer hardware and systems software		
(including smartphones and tablets)	50	55%
Computer software (applications)	12	100%
Copyrights	14	Straight-line
Data network infrastructure equipment	46	30%
Dies, jigs, patterns, and moulds	12	100%
Docks, breakwaters, and trestles	3	5%
Electrical advertising billboards	8	20%
Electronic point-of-sale equipment	8	20%
Equipment (not specifically listed elsewhere)	8	20%
Fences	6	10%
Films	10	30%
Franchises (limited life)	14	Straight-line
Franchises (unlimited life)	14.1	5%
Furniture and fixtures (not specifically listed elsewhere)	8	20%
Goodwill	14.1	5%
Instruments, dental or medical (see Tools)		
Kitchen utensils (see Tools)		

Appendix: CCA Rates for Select Depreciable Property

Depreciable Property	Class	Rate
Land	N/A	N/A
Landscaping	N/A	Deductible
Leasehold improvements	13	Straight-line
Licences (limited life)	14	Straight-line
Licences (unlimited life)	14.1	5%
Linen	12	100%
Machinery and equipment		
(not specifically listed elsewhere)	8	20%
Manufacturing and processing equipment		
• acquired after 2015	53	50%
Office equipment (not specifically listed elsewhere)	8	20%
Outdoor advertising billboards	8	20%
Parking area and similar surfaces	17	8%
Patents (limited life)	44	25%
Patents (unlimited life)	14.1	5%
Photocopy machines	8	20%
Portable buildings and equipment		
used in a construction business	10	30%
Radio communication equipment	8	20%
Railway cars	7	15%
Roads	17	8%
Sidewalks	17	8%
Software (applications)	12	100%
Software (systems)	10	30%
Storage area	17	8%
Storage tanks, oil or water	6	10%
Tangible capital property		
(not specifically listed elsewhere)	8	20%
Taxicabs (see also **zero-emission vehicles**)	16	40%
Telephone systems	8	20%
Television commercials	12	100%
Tools		
• under $500	12	100%
• $500 or over	8	20%
Trailers	10	30%
Trucks and tractors for hauling freight	16	40%
Trucks (automotive), tractors, and vans	10	30%
Uniforms	12	100%
Video games (coin operated)	16	40%
Videotapes	10	30%
Wagons	10	30%
Zero-emission vehicles and zero-emission passenger vehicles		
• previously allocated to classes 10 and 10.1	54	100%
(maximum = $55,000 for 2021)		
• previously allocated to class 16	55	100%

Self-Study Problems (SSPs)

Self-Study Problems (SSPs) provide practice in problem solving. Within the chapters, we have indicated where it would be appropriate to stop and work on each SSP. The problems can be downloaded by chapter from MyLab Accounting. Solutions are available in the Study Guide. Select problems can also be completed directly in MyLab and auto-graded.

Assignment Problems

Solutions to Assignment Problems (APs) are available to instructors only.

AP 5-1 (CCA and Tax Planning)

For its taxation year ending December 31, 2021, Marion Enterprises has determined that its net income before any deduction for CCA amounts to $53,000. The company does not have any Division C deductions, so whatever amount is determined as net income will also be its taxable income for the 2021 taxation year.

On January 1, 2021, the company has the following UCC balances:

Class 1 (building acquired in 2009)	$876,000
Class 8	220,000
Class 10	95,000
Class 10.1 (Porsche—Cost $110,000)	16,500
Class 10.1 (Cadillac—Cost $45,000)	16,500

During 2021, the capital cost of additions to class 10 amounted to $122,000. The capital cost of properties disposed of during the year were $118,000 and the proceeds of disposition were $87,000. None of the properties were sold at amounts greater than their capital cost. There were still properties remaining in class 10 on December 31, 2021.

There were no acquisitions or dispositions in classes 1, 8, or 10.1 during 2021. The company plans to sell the Porsche in 2022 and expects to receive about $75,000.

During the preceding three taxation years, the company's taxable income totalled $39,000 for the three years.

Required:

A. Calculate the maximum CCA that could be claimed by Marion Enterprises for the taxation year ending December 31, 2021. Your answer should include the maximum that can be deducted for each CCA class. The calculation of UCC balances is not required.

B. As Marion Enterprises' tax advisor, indicate how much CCA you would advise the company to claim for the 2021 taxation year and the specific classes from which it should be deducted. Provide a brief explanation of the reasons for your recommendation. In determining your solution, ignore the possibility that any 2021 losses can be carried forward to subsequent taxation years.

AP 5-2 (CCA Calculations)

On January 2, 2021, Carlson Manufacturing had the following UCC balances:

Class 53	$462,000
Class 50	82,000
Class 10	142,000
Class 10.1	16,500
Class 13	102,000
Class 8	96,000
Class 3	326,000

Other information related to the company's depreciable property is as follows:

1. During 2021, the company acquired additional manufacturing and processing equipment at a cost of $106,000.
2. During 2021, there were additions to class 50 with a capital cost of $15,600.
3. During 2021, three vehicles were acquired at a cost of $22,000 each. In addition, a delivery van with a capital cost of $43,000 was sold for $21,000.
4. The property in class 10.1 was the CEO's $462,000 Bentley. This passenger vehicle was sold during 2021 for $283,000.
5. The January 1, 2021, balance in class 13 reflected leasehold improvements that were made in 2019, the year in which the lease commenced. These improvements were made on a property leased as office space for the company's executives. The basic lease term is for eight years, with an option to renew for a period of two years. Additional improvements, costing $52,000, were made during 2021.
6. During 2021, the company acquired class 8 property at a capital cost of $146,000. Class 8 property with a capital cost of $85,000 was sold for proceeds of $56,000. None of the class 8 properties were sold for amounts greater than their capital cost.
7. During 2021, one of the buildings in class 3 burned to the ground. It had a capital cost of $285,000. The insurance proceeds received totalled $310,000.
8. During 2021, a new factory building was acquired at a capital cost of $1,327,000. The estimated value of the land included in the purchase price is $270,000. All of the floor space of the building will be used for manufacturing and processing activity. An election was made to include the building in a separate class.

Carlson Manufacturing always claims maximum CCA on each class of depreciable property.

Required: Calculate the maximum CCA that can be claimed by Carlson Manufacturing on each class of property for the year ending December 31, 2021. In addition, calculate the UCC for each class as of January 1, 2022, and determine the amount of any capital gains, recapture, or terminal loss. Ignore GST/HST & PST considerations.

AP 5-3 (CCA Calculations over Five Years)

Golden Dragon Ltd. begins operations in Vancouver on September 1, 2016. These operations include an elegant sit-down restaurant specializing in northern Chinese cuisine, as well as a take-out operation that provides home delivery throughout the city. To facilitate this latter operation, on October 12, 2016, the company acquires 20 small cars to be used as delivery vehicles. The cost of these cars is $12,000 each and, for purposes of calculating CCA, they are categorized as class 10.

During the first year of operations, the company establishes a fiscal year ending on December 31. For the fiscal periods 2017 through 2021, the following transactions take place with respect to the company's fleet of delivery cars:

2017 The company acquires five more cars at a cost of $12,500 each. In addition, three of the older cars are sold for total proceeds of $27,500.

2018 There are no new acquisitions of cars during this year. However, four of the older cars are sold for total proceeds of $38,000.

2019 In December 2019, 13 of the original cars and 3 of the newer cars are sold for $128,000. It was the intent of the company to replace these cars. However, because of a delay in delivery by the car dealer, the replacement did not occur until January 2020.

2020 In January 2020, the company takes possession of 25 new delivery cars at a cost of $16,000 each. No cars are disposed of during 2020.

2021 In March 2021, there is a change in management at Golden Dragon Ltd. They conclude that the company's take-out operation is not in keeping with the more elegant image that the sit-down restaurant is trying to maintain. As a consequence, the take-out operation is closed, and the 27 remaining delivery cars are sold. Because of the large number of cars being sold, the total proceeds are only $185,000.

Golden Dragon Ltd. takes maximum CCA in each of the years under consideration.

Required: For each of the fiscal years 2016 through 2021, calculate CCA, recapture, or terminal loss for Golden Dragon's fleet of cars. In addition, indicate the January 1 UCC for each of the years 2017 through 2022.

NOTE Prior to November 21, 2018, the half-year rule was in effect. For 2019, 2020, and 2021, the AccII provisions are available.

AP 5-4 (CCA Calculations)

The fiscal year of the Bostik Manufacturing Company, a Canadian controlled private corporation, ends on December 31. On January 1, 2021, the UCC balances for the various classes of depreciable property owned by the company are as follows:

Class 1—Building (Note 1)	$342,000
Class 8—Office furniture	66,000
Class 10—Vehicles	225,000
Class 10.1—President's car	16,500
Class 13—Leasehold improvements	26,125
Class 14.1	Nil
Class 50—Computer hardware	48,000
Class 53—Manufacturing equipment	126,000

Note 1 The class 1 building was acquired new in 2019 for $400,000. One hundred percent of its floor space is used for manufacturing and processing. In addition, the company filed a timely election to include the building in a separate class 1.

During the year ending December 31, 2021, the following purchases were made:

Class 8—Office furniture	$ 12,000
Class 10—Vehicles (Note 2)	115,000
Class 12—Tools (Note 3)	17,000
Class 13—Leasehold improvements	22,000
Class 50—Computer hardware	11,000

Note 2 The purchased vehicle was a specialized delivery truck. A damaged delivery truck with an original capital cost of $53,000 was traded in on the purchase. The trade-in allowance was $15,000.

Note 3 None of the tools that were acquired during the year cost more than $500.

During this same period, the following dispositions also occurred:

Class 8—Old, well-used, and mismatched office furniture was donated to a local non-profit organization. The capital cost of the furniture totalled $35,000. The fair market value was negligible.

Class 10.1—Once the president of Bostik saw how high the taxable benefit on his BMW 650 was, he ordered it sold. It had cost $120,000 in 2020. Because it had high mileage and was an unpopular colour, Bostik was able to sell it for only $50,000.

Class 53—Since the manufacturing equipment was technologically old and the new equipment would be leased, all of the manufacturing equipment was sold for total proceeds of $27,000. Its capital cost was $450,000.

Other Information:

1. The company leases one floor of a building for $36,000 per year. It houses the headquarters of Bostik, including the office of the president. The lease was negotiated on January 1, 2018, and has an original term of five years. There are two renewal options on the lease. The term for each of these options is three years. The company made $38,000 of leasehold improvements immediately after signing the lease. No further improvements were made until 2021.
2. On September 24, 2021, one of the company's trucks fell into a sinkhole and disappeared. (The driver was making a delivery at the time and captured the slow fall on his cell phone.) At the time of the accident, the fair market value of the truck was $32,300. The proceeds from the company's insurance policy amounted to $30,000. The capital cost of the truck was $50,000.
3. In early 2021, one of Bostik's employees developed a unique manufacturing process that the company intends to market to other manufacturers. Bostik wanted to charge $50,000 for a licence with a 10-year life. However, they eventually accepted a payment of $100,000 for a licence that has an unlimited life. No internal costs were allocated to this process with the result that the capital cost of the process is nil.
4. It is the policy of the company to deduct maximum CCA each year.

Required: Calculate the maximum 2021 CCA that can be claimed on each class, the January 1, 2022, UCC balance for each class, and any other 2021 income tax implications resulting from the information provided.

AP 5-5 (CCA Calculations over Three Years)

Barry's Books is a business carried on by Barry Levin as a sole proprietor. The business is selling historically important books (e.g., first editions). All of his sales are in Ontario. The fiscal period of the business began July 1, 2019. Since individuals who carry on their own business must use a calendar-year fiscal period (ITA 249.1), the first year would have been a short fiscal period beginning July 1, 2019, and ending December 31, 2019.

At the inception of his business Barry purchased the following depreciable property:

- Furniture and fixtures with a capital cost of $170,000.
- A customized delivery truck at a capital cost of $43,000.
- A building to house his operations. The total capital cost of the building was $1,200,000, which represented $410,000 for the land and the remaining $790,000 for the building. All of the floor space of the building is used for the business. Barry's accountant filed a timely election to include the building in a separate class 1.

Barry's business policy is to always claim maximum CCA. During 2020, the following transactions took place:

- As the business has enjoyed early success, on April 1 Barry purchases a $135,000 BMW. He has large logos of the business painted on both sides of the vehicle. He drives the BMW 100% for business purposes.
- He replaces the delivery truck purchased in 2019 with a larger truck. The cost of the new truck is $51,000 and, against this price, he receives a trade-in allowance of $26,000.

In mid-2021, Barry won $4 million in the lottery. Given this he decides to close down his business and spend his time travelling the globe. By December 31, 2021, all of the depreciable property has been sold and the business is formally closed. The proceeds are as follows:

Building The building is sold for $1,350,000, which included $950,000 for the building and $410,000 for the land.

Furniture and Fixtures The furniture is sold for $62,000.

Delivery Vehicles The delivery vehicle is sold for $39,000.

Lexus The BMW is sold for $52,000.

Required: Determine the maximum CCA that can be taken in each of the years 2019 through 2021. In your calculations, include and identify the UCC balances for January 1, 2020, January 1, 2021, and January 1, 2022.

In addition, indicate any income tax effects resulting from the 2020 and 2021 dispositions. Ignore GST/HST considerations.

AP 5-6 (Purchase and Sale of Goodwill)

Yelton Ltd. is a Canadian public company. It has a taxation year that ends on December 31. On January 1, 2021, Yelton had a nil UCC balance in class 14.1

It is the policy of Yelton to claim maximum CCA from all classes and in all years.

The following five independent cases involve payments for goodwill and receipts for goodwill. In each case assume that Yelton has no other transactions during 2021 or 2022 that involve class 14.1.

Case One During 2021, Yelton purchases a business. The capital cost of this purchase includes a payment for goodwill of $176,000. This business is integrated into Yelton's one business. Also during 2021, Yelton purchases an unlimited life franchise at a capital cost of $224,000.

During 2022, Yelton receives a payment for goodwill of $197,000. The payment represents part of the proceeds from the sale of a portion of its business.

Case Two Using the same 2021 information as Case One, assume that instead of selling a portion of its business, Yelton sells the unlimited life franchise for $205,000.

Case Three Using the same information as in Case One, assume that instead of selling a portion of its business for an amount that includes goodwill of $197,000 the unlimited life franchise is sold for $266,000.

Case Four During 2021, Yelton purchases two businesses. With the acquisition of Business 1, a payment of $129,000 is made for goodwill. With the acquisition of Business 2, a payment of $114,000 is made for goodwill. Both businesses are integrated into Yelton's business.

During 2022, Yelton sells a portion of its business and, as a consequence, receives a payment for goodwill of $136,000.

Case Five Using the same information as in Case Four, assume that Yelton Carries on both businesses purchased in 2021 as separate businesses and that the $136,000 receipt for goodwill results from the separate sale of the first business acquired.

Required: Determine the income tax consequences for the years 2021 and 2022 in each of these five cases. Your answer should include the January 1, 2023, UCC balance for class 14.1.

AP 5-7 (CCA, Recapture, and Terminal Losses—Includes Taxable Capital Gains)

On January 1, 2021, the beginning of its taxation year, Bard Ltd. has the following information with respect to its depreciable property:

Property Description	Undepreciated Capital Cost	Capital Cost
Class 8 furniture	$ 24,000	$ 147,000
Class 1 buildings (acquired in 2006)	562,000	846,000
Class 10 automobiles	220,000	315,000

During the 2021 taxation year, the following transactions occur:

Sale of Furniture Furniture with a capital cost of $52,000 was sold for $36,000. There are still property in class 8 on the last day of the taxation year.

Purchase and Sale of Buildings A new building was acquired on February 1, 2021, with a capital cost of $325,000. Of this total, $75,000 was the estimated value of the land on which the building was situated with the building valued at $250,000. All of the floor space of the building will be used 100% for office space and is placed in a separate class 1. A timely election was filed to include the building in a separate class 1.

Also during the year, a building (including the land) with a capital cost of $335,000 was sold for $352,000. Of the $352,000 received, $200,000 is for the land on which the building is situated and the remaining $152,000 for the building. The adjusted cost base of the land was equal to the $200,000 proceeds of disposition.

Sale of Automobiles An extensive analysis of capital and operating costs indicated that the company would be better off leasing automobiles rather than purchasing them. As a consequence, all of the company's automobiles were sold on December 28, 2021, for a total of $185,000. None of the automobiles were sold for more than its original cost. The leased vehicles were delivered on January 2, 2022.

Required: For the taxation year ending December 31, 2021, calculate the maximum CCA that can be deducted by Bard Ltd. for each CCA class. In addition, calculate the January 1, 2022, UCC balance for each class. As part of your answer, you should indicate whether there are any other income tax consequences as a result of any of the transactions.

AP 5-8 (CCA, Recapture, and Terminal Losses—Includes Taxable Capital Gains)

Microhard Ltd. has a December 31 year end. As of January 1, 2021, Microhard had the following UCC balances for its various depreciable property:

Class 1	$606,929
Class 8	347,291
Class 10	142,800
Class 13	175,500

Other information related to the company's depreciable property is as follows:

Class 1 The January 1, 2021, UCC balance in class 1 includes a single building that was acquired in 2016 for $900,000. Of this total, $200,000 was allocated to the land on which the building was situated and the remaining $700,000 to the building. On February 1, 2021, the building and the land were sold for $800,000—$200,000 for the land and $600,000 for the building.

A new building was purchased on November 15, 2021, at a cost of $950,000, with $150,000 of this total being allocated to the land on which the building was situated and the remaining $800,000 for the building. Only 50% of the floor space of the new building is used for manufacturing and processing with the remaining 50% used for office space in connection with the manufacturing and processing. An election was filed to include the building in a separate class 1.

Class 8 On March 1, 2021, the company purchased class 8 property for $111,256. As a result of trading in older class 8 property, the company received a trade-in allowance of $20,000, resulting in a net cost for the new property of $91,256. The capital cost of the property traded in was $58,425.

Class 10 The January 1, 2021, UCC balance in class 10 reflects eight vehicles that were being used by the company's sales staff. Their capital cost totalled $240,000. The company decided it would be more economical to provide their sales staff with leased vehicles. To this end, the eight vehicles were sold for total proceeds of $150,000 on October 31, 2021. The amount received for each vehicle was less than its capital cost.

On August 1, 2021, the company purchases a BMW 750 for use by the company's president. The capital cost of this vehicle is $142,000. The president drives it 65,000 kilometres during 2021, with only 10,000 kilometres involving employment duties. The president is not a shareholder of the company nor are any of her family members.

Class 13 Some of the company's business is conducted out of a building that is leased. The lease, which had an initial term of six years, can be renewed for two additional years at the end of the initial term. Immediately after the lease was signed on January 1, 2019, Microhard spent $216,000 on leasehold improvements. During April 2021, an additional $42,000 of leasehold improvements were made on upgrading the property.

It is the policy of the company to deduct maximum CCA in each year.

Required: Calculate the maximum CCA for the year ending December 31, 2021. Your answer should include the maximum that can be deducted for each CCA class. In addition, indicate the amount of any recapture, terminal loss, or taxable capital gain that results from dispositions during 2021. The UCC balance at January 1, 2022, is not required.

CHAPTER 6

Income or Loss from a Business

Learning Objectives

After completing Chapter 6, you should be able to:

1. Apply the source of income concept to a business [Paragraphs (P hereafter)] 6-1 to 6-5).
2. Explain why the concept of a business is so important to the ITA (P 6-6 to 6-10).
3. Define a business (P 6-11 to 6-15).
4. Differentiate in general terms between a source of income that is a business versus a property (P6-16).
5. Describe the general circumstances that determine when a business commences (P 6-17 to 6-19).
6. Explain the importance of a personal element to a business (P 6-20 to 6-24).
7. Apply a basic source of income analysis (P 6-25 and 6-26).
8. Explain the concept of an adventure or concern in the nature of trade (P 6-27 to 6-32).
9. Describe the three general types of business property recognized by the ITA (P 6-33 and 6-34).
10. Describe the general principles as to what is required to be included in business income (P 6-35 to 6-39).
11. Explain the meaning of "profit" and the relevance of accounting (P 6-40 to 6-44).
12. Describe and explain the importance of the 9-12-18-20 rule (P 6-45 to 6-49).
13. Explain the purpose and function of ITA 12(1)(a) and (b) (P 6-50 to 6-57).
14. Describe what is meant by the "quality of income" and its importance (P 6-58 and 6-59).
15. Apply the system of reserves that can be used in determining business income (P 6-60 to 6-75).
16. Describe the general limitations on business expenses (P 6-76 to 6-83).
17. Explain the capital expenditure limitation and how to identify capital versus income expenditures (P 6-84 to 6-92).
18. Explain and apply some of the more common business expense limitations (P 6-93 to 6-111).
19. Apply an expenditure analysis using the Figure 6-1 flowchart (P 6-112).
20. Apply the work space at home expense limitation (P 6-113 to 6-122).
21. Understand the basic limitation on foreign media advertising (P 6 123 to 6-125).
22. Describe the basic inventory concepts used in the ITA (P 6-126 to 6-133).
23. Familiarize yourself with the more common expenses allowed by ITA 20 (P 6-134).

24. Apply the various Subdivision f limitations (P 6-135 to 6-164).
25. Understand and apply the reconciliation process (P 6-165 to 6-170).
26. Describe the rules for determining fiscal periods, taxation years, and the elective treatment available in ITA 249.1(4), including the additional business income adjustments (P 6-171 to 6-180).
27. Explain and apply the restricted farming concept, including the three different types of activity (P 6-181 to 6-185).
28. Explain how the ITA handles work-in-process (WIP) (P 6-186 to 6-188).
29. Explain how the ITA treats inventories and accounts receivable on the sale of a business (P 6-189 to 6-193).

Introduction

6-1. In Chapter 1 we discussed ITA 3 and net income (see Paragraph 1-175), stating that income means the following:

- Sources of income from employment, business, and property (Subdivisions a and b)
- Capital gains and losses from the disposition of capital property (Subdivision c)
- Other receipts specifically added by Subdivision d
- Other deductions specifically allowed by Subdivision e

6-2. In Chapter 1 we also elaborated on the important Canadian income tax principle of a source of income (see Paragraphs 1-169 to 1-176). In everyday usage the word "source" is typically defined as a point of origin, but its meaning in income tax law, in terms of the expression "source of income," is entirely different. A source of income, a concept refined in the jurisprudence, can be defined as a potential to generate a positive cash flow net of related expenses over a period of time from an activity produced by one's labour, capital, or property either singly or in combination.

6-3. There are three important features to a source of income:

- There is continuity, where the activity occurs over a period of time. Single transactions would not meet this feature.
- There is a profit motive, which in terms of a business is referred to as a "pursuit of profit."
- The income is measured using a net basis approach, which means that expenses incurred in the activity reduce the related income.

6-4. As indicated, the ITA specifically identifies three sources of income: employment, business, and property. Employment income is a product of one's labour; property or investment-type income is a product of property ownership and earning returns on that property; and business income is often a product of all three source components where persons apply their labour, property, and capital toward that source with capital representing the expenditures and costs that create and support a business structure.

6-5. Having examined employment income in Chapter 3, we now turn our attention to the next source of income—business. The source concept is crucial in income tax since in its absence no expenditures are recognized for income tax purposes. In addition, any receipts not connected to a source would be excluded from net income (ITA 3) unless specifically required by the ITA to be included. As a result, no income taxes would be payable on that receipt.

EXAMPLE You live outside the city and own a small piece of land. You decide to grow vegetables for your family's consumption. In 2021 the growing season is longer than expected and, as a result, you have extra vegetables. You set up a roadside stand and sell the excess, receiving $1,200 in total. You estimate that your total expenses including a portion of your home expenditures amount to $5,000. Can you deduct the net loss of $3,800? At a minimum, are you required to include the $1,200 of receipts as income when you file your income tax return for the year?

ANALYSIS The analysis comes down to whether the "activity" is a "source of income." While you are definitely applying your labour, your capital, and your property, there is no profit motive. We will have more to say about this later in this chapter, but for now a profit motive or a "pursuit of profit" begins with looking to one's intention. If that intention is overshadowed by a personal motivation then there is no source of income and therefore no business. This means that without a source of income no expenditures are recognized for income tax purposes and, more importantly in this instance, any receipts are not income, meaning that you can ignore the activity altogether when it comes to income tax reporting.

Exercise 6-1

Subject: Source of Income

In Paragraph 6-5 we provided an example of an individual selling excess vegetables beyond family needs from a roadside stand. We determined that the activity was not a source of income because of the personal motivation and the absence of a profit motive. What do you think the individual could do to create a source of income from this activity?

Solutions to Exercises are available in the Study Guide.

6-6. In this chapter we will define a business and discuss its importance. We will also examine the special rules that determine what has to be included in income and what expenses may be claimed, including any restrictions imposed on those expenses. Finally we will look at the reconciliation process that requires making a number of adjustments to accounting-based income resulting in ITA 3 net income, which can then be used to determine taxable income and whether there are any income taxes payable or an income tax refund.

The Importance of a Business

6-7. A business is one of the three sources of income and its existence sets the stage for recognition under the ITA where business income is included and related expenses may be claimed. A business can be carried on by an individual as a self-proprietor, a trust, a corporation, or a partnership composed of individuals, trusts, corporations, or other partnerships. A business is considered to be carried on by any of these persons if it is carried on by employees of the person or by persons contracted to carry on the business on their behalf as agents.

6-8. When asked to identify a business there is little difficulty. Businesses such as Walmart, Costco, or a local restaurant or gas station are a few of many examples. You can readily see that in each of these examples all of the features of a source of income are present in well-established businesses. No one, not even the CRA, would question the existence of a business in these situations. While pointing out examples of businesses is a relatively simple matter, actually defining a business seems to be a bit more problematic. Before examining the definition it is important to understand why defining a business is so important in the ITA.

6-9. Determining whether a business exists and the nature of a business is important in many circumstances that arise in practice, including the following:

- Expenses incurred prior to the commencement of a business would generally not be deductible
- Expenses incurred after a business has ceased to exist would also not be deductible
- Whether there is one business or many separate businesses; the sale of a business versus the sale of part of a business are treated quite differently
- Determining whether the activity is a business or a property source (i.e., investments) or vice versa

- Determining whether there is any business activity or simply a sale of property and a capital gain
- Determining whether the nature of an activity in Canada by non-residents constitutes carrying on a business
- Determining whether an individual is an employee or is self-employed and is carrying on his or her own business

6-10. The income tax implications of a taxpayer cannot be determined until the underlying activity (employment, business, property, capital gains, etc.) has been identified. This provides the answer as to what type of income is being earned, what expenses are deductible, and what incentives are available, including RRSP deductions, access to the capital gains deduction, and the deductibility of child care expenses. All of these issues are interrelated.

Defining a Business

6-11. There are two types of definitions in the ITA, most of which are found at ITA 248(1). The first use the word "means" and the second the word "includes." When a definition begins with "means," then, in general, you need not look beyond that definition. If, however, the definition uses the word "includes," then all that definition is achieving is to add to the real meaning of that word or expression, which requires you to first determine the real meaning of the word or expression. If, for example, a definition were to say that a home includes a houseboat, you would still need to determine exactly what a home is since the definition does not actually define a home but simply clarifies that a houseboat is to be considered a home irrespective of the real meaning of a home.

6-12. In defining a "home," the interpretative principle is to first turn to the legal definition of that word since you are dealing with legislation (i.e., the ITA). Sometimes the word or expression is further defined by the courts, in which case you would use that definition. If the word or expression is unique to a certain profession and has not been defined in the ITA or refined by the courts, then you can turn to the meaning of that word by that profession. We mention this because there is a tendency to use accounting definitions of words or expressions that are used in income tax. You will see throughout this course that accounting concepts, principles, and definitions rarely apply to income tax.

6-13. The word "business" is defined in the ITA as follows:

> **ITA 248(1)** Business includes a profession, calling, trade, manufacture or undertaking of any kind whatever and, except for the purposes of paragraph ..., an adventure or concern in the nature of trade but does not include an office or employment.

You can see the use of the word "includes," which means that the definition is simply adding to an understanding of the actual meaning of a "business" for income tax purposes.

6-14. The courts established the meaning of a business well over 100 years ago. The courts set out the following three criteria to identify the existence of a business:

- Time, attention, and labour devoted to an activity
- The pursuit of profit
- The incurring of liabilities to other persons

Incurring of liabilities meant that the activity was such that the business was potentially liable for any damages caused to others as a result of pursuing the business. Since most of the case law has focused almost exclusively on the first two criteria we will ignore the third criteria.

6-15. You can see from this definition that there is some overlap with the source of income concept. The activity must be undertaken with a profit motive, and the persons involved in the business must expend their efforts toward the activity unless they employ individuals or contract with others on their behalf. The activity requires active, ongoing efforts as opposed to the purchase of property such as investments, which is much more passive in the sense that all that is generally required is owning the property and sitting back to await the returns. This definition of a business is also often used to differentiate between income from a business and income from property as well as determining whether an undertaking is personal in nature, never having reached the level of a business.

Business versus Income from Property

6-16. Both income from property and income from business represent two separate sources of income, both of which fall under the rules of Subdivision b of the ITA. These two types of sources are treated quite differently. For example, CCA classes are separated where there are two or more businesses, class 14.1 property (discussed in Chapter 5) is only available to businesses, and some expenses such as those for landscaping (ITA 20(1)(aa)) are only allowed to businesses. Because of the definition of a business, the distinction between these two sources comes down to the level of activity. Ongoing, continuous activity points to a business, whereas little or no activity points to a source of property income. In most cases deciding the issue is straightforward, but it can be complicated at times.

EXAMPLE 1 An individual purchases one residential property that will be used as a rental property for the purpose of earning extra income. The tenant attends to the property with very little involvement from the landlord/property owner.

ANALYSIS 1 The activity meets the definition of a source of income (i.e., property ownership and a profit motive). Since the activity is passive in nature it would be considered income from property. The level of activity is insufficient to establish a business.

EXAMPLE 2 An individual purchases two residential properties. The first property is rented at the going rental rate in circumstances identical to Example 1. The second home is provided to a family member who is in need of assistance, and as a result the second home is rented for an amount that covers the mortgage only.

ANALYSIS 2 Each property is a separate potential source of income. The first property is a source of income that is income from property for the same reasons as in Analysis 1. The second property, however, fails to meet the source of income test because of the lack of a profit motive. The owner may declare that there is a profit motive, but the facts suggest otherwise. It appears that the purpose behind the purchase of the second property is personal in the sense that it is primarily motivated by a desire to help a family member as opposed to making a profit. As a result, the second property would not be a source of income and therefore cannot be either business or property income. Any loss on that second property could not be claimed for income tax purposes.

EXAMPLE 3 An individual purchases 10 rental properties including a 40-unit apartment building. The number of rental properties requires hiring a management consulting firm to oversee all aspects of these properties, including maintenance, collecting payments, and arranging repairs and all other issues where necessary.

ANALYSIS 3 The individual would be carrying on a business given the ongoing level of activity required based on the number of rental properties. There would be one source of income as a result. As pointed out, the individual is not required to actively carry out the activities herself but can use employees or contracted parties, as in this case. The activity in this case goes well beyond a passive investment and is therefore not a source of property income.

Exercise 6-2

Subject: Source of Income

You live in Toronto and recently purchased a farm 100 kilometres away. You plan to retire to that location one day. In the meantime, you hire three individuals to operate the farm, which has been profitable for many years. You also rent the farmhouse to unrelated individuals at the going rental rate for a period of two years. While there are a number of buildings on the property, including barns and large tool sheds, no part of the farmhouse is used in the farming business. In the second year you spend $11,600 landscaping around the farmhouse.

1. Would you be considered to be carrying on a farming business?
2. How many sources of income do you have?
3. Are the landscaping costs deductible to you?

Solutions to Exercises are available in the Study Guide.

Commencing a Business

6-17. We have defined a business that is a source of income as an ongoing activity that has a capacity to earn a positive return or profit. This is only possible, however, if the activity has been developed to a certain level. Consider the following:

EXAMPLE One day you come up with what you believe could be a great business idea. You begin to explore whether that idea has any merit and could be successful. This includes determining if anyone else is already pursuing that activity profitably. You talk to friends and family members to get their feedback. Almost everyone believes you may have something worth pursuing. You need funding, and you arrange to meet with representatives of your bank, where you learn that they would be prepared to provide financing if necessary. You decide to take evening classes in the interim to learn about income tax, business, and accounting. You eventually decide to contact an accounting firm that provides business consultation. The consultants draw up a business plan for you, confirming the idea is a good one. The following week you decide to pursue the plan. Another week goes by and you arrange for financing with the bank, arrange for advertising, locate business premises and sign a two-year lease, contact suppliers, and begin the process of hiring two individuals through an employment agency. Two months later you officially open but do not make any sales until the following year.

ANALYSIS The case law is clear that a business is only considered to have commenced when some significant activity is undertaken that is part of the regular income earning process or that is an essential preliminary step, such as obtaining licences or other authorizations to legally operate the business in a specific location. The actual earning of any income is immaterial as long as the structure is being put in place. This is seen as the significant steps that evidence the implementation of the plan to start a business. As a result, the business would be considered to have begun at the time the individual took the actual steps of setting up the business structure. Another way of looking at this is that the idea and contemplation stages of the process are insufficient to establish the commencement of a business. Commencement begins when a person is committed to a course of action and is actively taking steps to create the necessary business structure that will eventually fully support the business.

6-18. As mentioned, the determination of the time that a business has commenced is important, since any expenses incurred prior to that time are not deductible for income tax purposes and are simply lost. There is a misconception that pre-business expenses can be capitalized for individuals. This is not the case. Remember that the key is the existence of a source of income. A business is a source of income only from the time it is considered to have commenced; therefore, any expenditures incurred prior to that time are not deductible for income tax purposes.

6-19. If a well-established business takes steps to expand its existing business, expenditures incurred toward that end would be recognized as potentially deductible since the expenses relate to an existing source of income. If, however, the business incurs expenditures to pursue a second and completely different business, then the same concepts and principles concerning the commencement of a business would apply.

> **EXAMPLE** Radco is a very profitable sporting goods retailer. The company directors have decided to expand the corporate horizons by opening a travel agency, but they first wish to explore the idea. Six months later, after having spent $18,000 on evaluating the possibility, the company decides to abandon the idea.
>
> **ANALYSIS** Since the expenditures do not relate to the company's existing business (i.e., the source of income) they would be considered non-deductible. Had the company decided to go ahead and start up a new travel agency business, the pre-business expenditures would still have been non-deductible on the same basis.

The Impact of a Personal Element

6-20. Many years go the CRA determined whether a business existed by applying an approach referred to as a "reasonable expectation of profit" test. In applying this approach the CRA would evaluate whether it was actually possible for a specific business to earn a profit. In one case a small restaurant business in Montreal that had been operating for a number of years was determined not to have passed the test because the available floor space only allowed for a handful of customers at any one time. The CRA concluded that the menu prices and volume of business, given the restricted space and high costs of operating from that location, would never result in a profit. As a result, the CRA successfully denied the losses on the basis that there was no business.

6-21. The Supreme Court resolved this issue by deciding that if there was no personal element to a business that the business would automatically be considered a source of income, meaning that its losses were valid as long as a business had commenced. If there was a personal element, then the CRA could evaluate whether the business was being operated in a "commercial-like manner." If it was found that this was not the case, then the losses could be disallowed on the basis that there was no source of income, either because of the absence of a profit motive or the failure to actually commence and therefore create a business.

6-22. A personal element typically involves individuals attempting to expense hobbies and other personal interests, such as an avid traveller writing a travel book, an avid fisher acting as a fishing guide or tour boat operator, and a camera enthusiast attempting work as a professional photographer. In practice, an indicator that there is a personal element includes activities involving transactions with family and friends at less than fair market value. Another indication is that the activity would have been undertaken even if losses were incurred. In other words, it is the personal element that is driving the activity.

6-23. Subsequent cases clarified that a personal element meant more than personal satisfaction, since it is widely recognized that many individuals derive personal satisfaction from what they do, including lawyers, accountants, artists, authors, musicians, and so on. The courts added that in assessing the impact, the personal element must "overshadow the commercial motivation."

6-24. Once a personal element has been identified, the courts look to determine whether there is evidence to support a profit motive and whether the activity is conducted in a business-like manner consistent with someone successfully carrying on that business for profit. In the evaluation the courts condone looking to the individual's training and business background, their profit and loss experience, the course of action, and the capability of the venture to show a profit. One court stated, "If you want to be treated as carrying on a business you should act like a business person." It goes without saying that the essential features of a business structure must be in place, which includes a capability of earning income through customers and clientele.

The Source of Income Analysis

6-25. In determining whether there is a source of income and whether it is income from a business or property, the following analysis should be followed:

(1) Has property been acquired or an activity undertaken? If not then there is no source of income. The activity would include the purchase of property that is capable of generating income.

(2) Is there a personal element to the property acquired or the activity? If there is no personal element then the property acquired or the activity undertaken will be automatically considered as a source of income as long as a business has commenced or the property has been acquired and is capable of earning income. If there is a personal element then the activity, including the property acquired, will be evaluated to determine if the property is being used or the activity is being carried on in a commercial-like manner. The analyses is almost always undertaken when the property or the activity is reporting income tax losses.

(3) Is the level of activity of the property owner or the person undertaking the activity passive or active on a continuous basis? This question is only addressed when the personal element does not overshadow the profit motive and the activity is conducted in a commercial-like manner. Income generated from passive ownership is almost always categorized as income from property, whereas active, ongoing activity supports the existence of income from a business.

> **EXAMPLE** Gerald loved nature and the outdoors. He travelled whenever he could, hiking into mountains and meadows. He brought painting supplies with him and would settle at a location for hours and paint various scenes and animals. He was told by friends that he could write off his expenses for income tax purposes by advertising his paintings for sale. Gerald contacted a local newspaper in his hometown, and they ran an ad for two weeks in the first year and a few weeks every other year. No one called. Gerald claimed business losses for three years largely due to his travel expenses and painting supplies, including a home office.
>
> **ANALYSIS** Since Gerald is claiming business losses there is an initial presumption that he is carrying on a business. On that basis the first part of the analysis would ask if there is a personal element to the activity. In this case the answer is yes. The next step looks to whether the activity is carried on in a commercial-like manner, which attempts to compare what the individual is doing versus a person who successfully carries on such a business and what they would typically do to earn income. In this instance Gerald is not conducting the activity in a commercial-like manner, with the result that there is no source of income and his business losses would not be allowed. Another approach to analyzing these situations is to determine whether the business ever commenced. In this case Gerald never took the idea through to an implementation stage, and as a result no business exists.

6-26. We would add that the definition of a business does require a capability to earn a profit even though it may never do so. This means that the creation of a business structure that would include renting office space, hiring employees, and contracting with suppliers would not be enough to establish a business unless there was a market for the services or products that would be offered.

Adventure or Concern in the Nature of Trade

6-27. In our discussion of a source of income, one of the features was continuity. We saw the same with respect to the definition of a business and that the activity must be ongoing. In addition, the ITA frequently uses the expression "carrying on a business," which also implies a continuity. In 1970 the case of *Tara Explorations* confirmed that one cannot carry on a single transaction.

6-28. The concern was that there are taxpayers who participate in one-time flip transactions, such as purchasing a property with the sole intention of selling it immediately and earning a quick profit. The CRA was of the view that when taxpayers act in a manner that is equivalent to how those in business would have acted, they should be treated the same. Any gain should be taxed as business profits. Without legislation to the contrary, however, the CRA would be unsuccessful at attempting to tax these one-time transactions as business income.

6-29. To resolve this problem, the government modified the definition of a "business" by adding the words an "adventure or concern in the nature of trade." This wording is designed to ensure that gains on single transactions are treated as fully taxable business profits. The ITA accomplishes this by treating the property that was the subject of the single transaction as inventory. The analysis involves comparing the single transaction with persons who carry on a business of selling that same particular type of property and drawing a conclusion as to whether the transaction was undertaken in a manner similar to that of a business person.

6-30. There are two types of property that attract attention. The first are properties that do not earn any income, but rather profit is made by selling the property. Historical examples are commodities, including truckloads of toilet paper, lead, and whiskey. The CRA almost always wins these cases, as it is almost impossible to argue that this type of property was acquired to earn investment income. It is important to be aware that ITA 9(3) clarifies that investment income would not include capital gains or losses. Therefore, when we mention investment income this would not include capital gains/losses but would include interest, dividends, royalties, rents, and so on. As a result, this category of property would not be considered to earn investment-type income.

6-31. The second category of property is more difficult to assess since it involves property that earns a return. Examples are shares, bonds, and other types of income earning investments. When these types of investments are held for a very short period of time it is not unusual for the CRA to challenge the reporting, which is almost always as a capital gain (only 50% taxable) rather than fully taxable business profits. In the case of a quick turnaround of the property, the suggestion is whether the person is acting in the same business-like manner as a trader or dealer in investments, and therefore the gains are adventures or concerns in the nature of trade, with the gains fully taxable as business profits.

> **EXAMPLE** In one court decision an individual had purchased two types of shares. The corporation issuing the first type of shares had a long history of paying annual dividends. The company issuing the second group of shares paid little to no dividends, leaving investors with a large potential for growth in the value of the shares as the only means of making money. The individual sold both types of shares shortly after acquiring them. The court concluded that the first type of shares were acquired for investment purposes but the second group was intended to be flipped quickly in a manner similar to what a trader or dealer would have done. The gain on the first type of shares was considered a capital gain, whereas the gain on the second type of shares was treated as an adventure or concern in the nature of trade and therefore equivalent to business profit.

An Elective Option—ITA 39(4)

6-32. Canadian resident taxpayers who purchase and sell Canadian securities (shares, bonds, etc.) are able to file an election under ITA 39(4), the purpose of which is to treat sales of those securities on capital account, meaning that any gains and losses for that year and subsequent years would be treated as capital gains and losses. While this seems to offer a solution to an adventure or concern in the nature of trade, ITA 39(5)(a) excludes that capital treatment for specific sales if the seller is acting in a manner similar to that of a trader or dealer in securities. In effect, the taxpayer's intention and conduct will play a role in determining how any gain or loss will be treated irrespective of the election.

Sources of Income and Categorizing Property

6-33. In this chapter we have been looking at sources of income with a focus on business income and, to a lesser degree, property income, which will be examined in greater detail in Chapter 7.

We have seen that intention and actions are factors used in determining whether or not an activity is sufficient to establish a business or whether it is simply an investment-type activity or, in the absence of a source of income, a personal endeavour. We also discussed the impact of an adventure or concern in the nature of trade, which takes what may appear to be an investment or personal-type activity and recharacterizes it as a business. This takes us back to our original point that income tax consequences cannot be determined with any accuracy until we have identified the sources of income of a person, which guide us to how to handle both the type of income earned and the consequences of dispositions of property used in that activity.

6-34. There are three general types of property contemplated by the sources of income that are business, property, and property used for personal purposes. These are (1) inventory, (2) depreciable property, and (3) non-depreciable capital property. The three types of property, the source to which they relate, and the tax consequences when sold are described as follows:

Inventory Inventory is defined in terms of a business only. Since an adventure or concern in the nature of trade is also considered a business, then the property that is the subject of the adventure is treated as inventory. A gain or loss on a sale of inventory is treated as business income or loss, which is 100% included in income or 100% deducted for losses. The inventory concept does not apply to income from property or to personal endeavours.

Depreciable property The definition of depreciable property requires that it form part of an income earning source, such as business or property income. The sale of depreciable property can result in potential recapture, terminal losses, and capital gains, but not capital losses. The depreciable property concept does not apply to personal endeavours.

Non-depreciable capital property This type of property is defined as property the disposition of which would result in a capital gain. There is no requirement that property that is capital property be used in an income earning activity. This means that the property can be used in a source of income but can also be used personally. Examples would include land, investments (not categorized as inventory), and personal property such as homes, cars, and furniture, no part of which is used in a source of income. The sale of non-depreciable capital property will result in capital gains and sometimes capital losses, but there are many rules surrounding how these gains and losses will be treated, particularly when only used for personal purposes. These rules will be discussed in Chapter 8.

We suggest you complete SSP 6-1 at this point.

Business Income and Loss—General Principles

Overview

6-35. The Chapter 3 discussion of employment income shows that the ITA set out, in fairly clear terms, exactly what is to be included in employment income and what is specifically deductible from employment income. This is not the case with business and property income. Instead the ITA begins with the following three important provisions:

ITA 9(1) Income—Subject to this Part, a taxpayer's income for a taxation year from a business or property is the taxpayer's profit from that business or property for the year.

ITA 9(2) Loss— ... a taxpayer's loss for a taxation year from a business or property is the amount of the taxpayer's loss, if any, for the taxation year from that source computed by applying the provisions of this Act respecting computation of income from that source with such modifications as the circumstances require.

ITA 9(3) Gains and losses not included—In this Act "income from a property" does not include any capital gain from the disposition of that property and "loss from a property" does not include any capital loss from the disposition of that property.

6-36. ITA 9(1) is the principle rule that simply requires that the "profit" from a business or property be included in income "subject to this Part." What this means is that the "profit" amount can be changed by rules in the rest of Part I of the ITA. A good way to think of this is that determining profit from a source of income that is a business or a property is only the starting point in establishing the exact amount that is required to be included in net income (ITA 3).

6-37. In Chapter 3 we discussed how the ITA uses the word "income" to refer to positive or nil net amounts and the word "loss" to separately refer to situations where there is a net loss. ITA 9(2) continues this separate distinction by stating that when there is a business or property loss it is determined using the same ITA rules that would have applied had there been a profit.

6-38. Finally, ITA 9(3) is a rule that clarifies that any mention of income or loss from property would not include capital gains or capital losses, which are treated separately in a subdivision of their own. The importance of this rule and the interaction with the source concept is illustrated in the following example.

EXAMPLE 1 You purchase dividend-paying shares of Canadian companies for $10,000 in November 2021. You borrowed the funds from your bank and incur $125 in interest to December 31, 2021. ITA 20(1)(c) allows an interest expense deduction only if the money that was borrowed is used in a business or to earn property income.

ANALYSIS 1 The purchase of the shares result in a source of income that is motivated by profit and that can generate dividends. Therefore, the interest expense deduction of $125 is allowed. There would be a property loss of $125 from this source—nil dividends received minus $125 in interest. This loss would be shown at ITA 3(d) in the net income calculation.

EXAMPLE 2 The same as Example 1, but instead you purchase silver (e.g., coins or bullion).

ANALYSIS 2 The purchase of silver is not a source of property income because the silver does not provide any actual or potential ongoing investment return. ITA 9(3) ensures that capital gains or losses are not considered to be part of any investment return. The silver purchase could, however, be considered a business source of income (e.g., a trader in precious metals) depending on the facts, including an adventure or concern in the nature of trade. Barring that alternative the silver would not be a source of property or business income and therefore the rules of Subdivision b, specifically ITA 20(1)(c), would not apply, meaning that the interest paid could not be claimed as a deduction. The sale of the silver would result in a sale of non-depreciable capital property that is effectively personal because it is not connected to a source of income. The result would be a capital gain or a capital loss. The capital gain/loss rules do not allow the non-deductible interest to be added to the cost of the silver. As a result, the ITA provides no relief for the interest paid in this situation.

6-39. While not readily apparent, rules in Subdivision c dealing with capital gains/losses are designed to ensure that capital gains from the disposition of business property that is depreciable property or capital gains or capital losses on the disposition of non-depreciable property is not part of business income or a business loss. Students may find it unusual that the sale of a business property can result in income that is not part of business income or loss but is instead treated as a capital gain or loss. The takeaway from this is that there are three sources of income—employment, business, and property—and then there are capital gains/losses, which are separate. This is reflected in the net income calculations of ITA 3(a) and 3(b).

What Is "Profit"?

6-40. Since profit is the starting point for determining both business and property income it is important to understand its meaning. The word "profit" is not defined in the ITA, which may lead some to conclude that it must be defined by accounting principles, specifically generally accepted accounting principles or GAAP (International Financial Reporting Standard (IFRS) or Accounting Standards for Private Enterprises (ASPE)) where it is used extensively. Some commentators, however, have said that using the accounting definition of "profit" for income tax purposes risks turning the income tax system over to the accounting profession.

6-41. The Supreme Court of Canada has considered the meaning of "profit" in a surprising number of cases, concluding that the determination of profit is a question of law and not accounting. The courts have added that GAAP are not rules of law but interpretative aids only. The courts have gone on to say that in determining profit, the goal is to "obtain an accurate picture of the taxpayers' profit for a given year." In determining an "accurate picture," taxpayers are free to adopt any method that is not inconsistent with (1) the provisions of the ITA, (2) established case law principles or "rules of law," and (3) well-accepted business principles.

6-42. In addition, you should be aware that there are many additional income tax principles developed by the courts, one of which is that symmetrical treatment is not a requirement of the ITA. This means that just because one party to a transaction must include the receipt in income does not mean that the other party gets to deduct that same amount. Second, in determining the "accurate picture" of income the matching principle, used extensively in accounting, is not an income tax principle unless there is a specific ITA provision. These income tax principles are not always consistent with accounting principles.

6-43. An example of the different treatment between accounting and the ITA can be seen in the Supreme Court of Canada case in *IKEA Ltd.* ([1998] 1 SCR 196). In that case IKEA was looking for leasing space and was offered what is referred to as a TIP, or tenant-inducement payment, which was an upfront cash payment as an incentive to enter into a long-term multi-year lease. For accounting purposes the TIP was amortized over the lease term and used in part to reduce the cost of fixtures in the leased premises. IKEA, however, did not follow GAAP for income tax purposes and instead did not include any part of the TIP in its income, claiming that it was not income but a tax-free capital receipt. The court determined that the full amount of the TIP was required to be included in income in the year it was received based on a legal analysis that included an in-depth understanding of income tax principles, including the difference between income and capital, which we have discussed a few times to this point in the text. The court added that the end result was to portray an accurate picture of IKEA's income for that year based on well-established case law principles.

6-44. The important point to draw from this is that while profit for income tax purposes is not determined by GAAP for all practical purposes, the profit shown in financial statements is the starting point. This is also recognized by the CRA as a pragmatic, realistic alternative given that the accounting profession prepares income and loss statements for many Canadian businesses and investments. Given this understanding, always keep in mind that the ultimate determination as to whether an amount is income or entitles one to a deduction is a question of law, not accounting. We would add one final point that an identical amount can be treated differently to two separate taxpayers depending on the specific facts, which makes understanding income tax concepts and principles important.

The 9-12-18-20 General Rule

6-45. As previously discussed, ITA 9 represents the starting point in determining the amount to include as business or property income on an income tax return. The amount would represent all income minus all related expenses in connection with a specific source. For all practical purposes the process begins with the profit shown in accounting-based income statements. The goal is to first take that accounting figure and convert or reconcile it so that the end result is what is acceptable for income tax purposes. The conversion is referred to as a reconciliation process, which will be discussed later in this chapter. It is a function of three main ITA provisions—ITA 12, 18, and 20. The other ITA provisions between ITA 9 and ITA 20 (10, 11, etc.) are also important but secondary to the general rules of ITA 9, 12, 18, and 20. In addition, there are other rules, particularly in Subdivision f, that may further restrict an expense, such as ITA 67.1, which reduces most meal and entertainment expenses by 50%, and ITA 67, which reduces the size of the expense where an expense would otherwise be considered unreasonable.

6-46. ITA 12 contains a series of provisions that require certain amounts to be added to either business or property income. The opening words of ITA 12(1) read as follows:

> **ITA 12(1)** Income inclusions—There shall be included in computing the income of a taxpayer for a taxation year as income from a business or property such of the following amounts as are applicable ...

The amounts required to be added may not be included in the accounting statements and therefore would have to be separately added in the reconciliation process. In addition, the accounting statements may include amounts that are different than what is required by ITA 12. In other words, one has to be aware of ITA 12 to be in a position to readily determine whether all amounts required to be included are reflected in the final income tax numbers.

6-47. ITA 18 and 20 are two of the most important series of rules that impact the reconciliation process when it comes to claiming expenses. ITA 18 begins with the following opening words:

> **ITA 18(1)** General Limitations—In computing the income of a taxpayer from a business or property no deduction shall be made in respect of ...

Three of the most often used ITA 18 provisions are ITA 18(1)(a), (b), and (h). ITA 18(1)(a) does not allow any outlay or expense unless it is connected to the earning of business or property income. ITA 18(1)(b) (which we looked at in Chapter 5 on CCA/UCC) restricts any deduction for capital expenditures such as depreciation unless specifically allowed by the ITR. Finally, ITA 18(1)(h) prevents a deduction for any personal or living expenses, which generally mean expenses that are not connected to a source of income from a business or property.

6-48. ITA 20 begins with the following opening words:

> **ITA 20(1)** Deductions permitted in computing income from business or property—Notwithstanding paragraphs 18(1)(a), (b) and (h) in computing a taxpayer's income for a taxation year from a business or property there may be deducted such of the following amounts as are wholly applicable to that source or such part of the following amounts as may reasonably be regarded as applicable thereto ...

You can see that while ITA 18(1) can block the ability to initially claim an expense, ITA 20(1) can override that result depending on the circumstances.

EXAMPLE You carry on a business providing plumbing services and products. The income statement indicates depreciation of $17,000 for the 2021 taxation year, but the ITA would only allow $11,000 of CCA. Accounting income is shown as $100,000 with the CCA and depreciation the only required reconciliation adjustments for income tax purposes.

ANALYSIS ITA 18(1)(b) would disallow the depreciation of $17,000 but ITA 20(1)(a) would allow a CCA deduction of $11,000. The reconciliation would look like the following, adding ITA references:

Accounting income (Profit—ITA 9(1))	$100,000
Add back: ITA 18(1)(b) Depreciation	17,000
Less: CCA allowed ITA 20(1)(a)	(11,000)
Net income (ITA 3)	$106,000

6-49. We can summarize this general 9-12-18-20 rule in connection with accounting income as it impacts the business and property income or loss components of net income as follows:

Accounting income	XXX
Add: ITA 12 income amounts	XXX
Add: Expenses disallowed by ITA 18	XXX
Deduct: Expenses allowed by ITA 20	(XXX)
Net income (ITA 3)	XXX

Business Income—Inclusions

ITA 12

6-50. In discussing ITA 12, 18, and 20, it is important to be aware that Subdivision b, where these provisions are located, provide rules for both business and property income. While many of the rules apply to both business and property income, some apply exclusively to business income and some exclusively to property income. Our goal in this chapter is to focus only on business income; therefore, provisions that relate exclusively to property income will be deferred to Chapter 7.

6-51. In addition, ITA 12(1)(l) requires the inclusion of business and property income from a partnership, and ITA 12(1)(m) requires the inclusion of benefits from trusts. These inclusions will be dealt with in Chapters 18 and 19, which deal, respectively, with partnerships and trusts.

Amounts Receivable—ITA 12(1)(b)

6-52. Business income is generally determined on an accrual basis. Only farming and fishing businesses (ITA 28) are eligible to use a cash-basis method, which means that no amount is included in income until received and no expenses are permitted unless actually paid. The use of the accrual method is realistically part of "profit," which looks to an accurate picture of one's income as previously discussed. ITA 12(1)(b) simply codifies the accrual concept by requiring that amounts receivable for services rendered in the year or products sold in the year in the course of a business be included in business income even if part or all of the amount receivable is not due until a subsequent year. This rule would not apply if the taxpayer were allowed to use the cash method.

6-53. As we have seen in our discussions, the meaning of words used in the ITA can be very important. In ITA 12(1)(b) the word "receivable" is front and centre, and while not defined in the ITA it has been defined in the case law (i.e., jurisprudence). Receivable means an absolute and unconditional right to receive the amount, although that right may not necessarily be immediate. This means that a person would have a right to enforce payment.

Exercise 6-3

Subject: ITA 12(1)(b) Receivable

You are in the construction business and have completed the construction of a custom-made residential home. The construction is completed at the end of December 2021. You invoice the customer $300,000 as agreed by contract. The contract also calls for a holding back of 10% of the contract price, or $30,000, which is conditional upon architectural approval. The approval requires an onsite investigation by the architect, which is not scheduled until late January 2022. The fiscal period of your business is December 31. How much are you required to include in your business income for 2021?

Solutions to Exercises are available in the Study Guide.

6-54. There are two types of situations to which ITA 12(1)(b) applies. The first is the sale of products and the second the provision of services. If products are sold there may be a reserve available under ITA 20(1)(n) to offset part of the profit on the sale that relates to payments that will only be made in years after the sale was made. Reserves will be discussed starting at Paragraph 6-60.

6-55. The second situation applies where services have been rendered in the year but payment is made in a subsequent year. There are no available reserves for this situation as there would potentially be when products are sold. In addition, and to address a concern that an amount would not become receivable until an invoice had been issued, ITA 12(1)(b) adds a rule that deems an amount to become receivable at the earlier of the day that an invoice was actually sent and the day that the invoice would have been sent had there not been an "undue delay." The purpose of this timing rule is to prevent business owners from postponing the reporting of business income for services to years after the services were actually provided by delaying the billing.

Amounts Received in Advance—ITA 12(1)(a)

6-56. ITA 12(1)(a) requires amounts received in advance and in the course of a business to be included in business income where the advance payments are for services that will have to be rendered in a subsequent year, products that will have to be delivered in a subsequent, or for any other reason. ITA 12(1)(a) also applies to refundable deposits. A reserve is allowed to offset all of the amounts received other than refundable deposits, which generally require a reasonable analysis that takes into consideration persons who will not claim the refundable deposit for one reason or another.

6-57. The reserve concept, which is discussed later in this chapter, requires first including the whole of the amount received in advance under ITA 12(1)(a) and then separately claiming a reserve of the same amount under ITA 20(1)(m). While the net effect is nil, the ITA then requires any amount claimed as a reserve deduction in the immediately preceding year to be added back to business income in that following year. If the amount is still unearned in the second year, then another reserve would be claimed until the year in which the amount was actually earned. When the advance is actually earned in a subsequent year, no further reserve would be allowed in that year. The result is that the income would be fully included in income for the year in which it is actually earned where the taxpayer claims the maximum allowable reserve each year.

Quality of Income—ITA 9(1), 12(1)(a), and 12(1)(b)

6-58. In our discussion of amounts receivable and ITA 12(1)(b), the general test was whether the business could enforce payment because the amount owed was absolute and unconditional, generally because products had been sold or services had been provided. In ITA 12(1)(a) we also saw that advance payments or prepayments were required to be included in business income if they represented advances for services to be rendered or products to be delivered in a subsequent year. The courts coined the phrase "quality of income" to test whether an advance was unearned or not. Where an advance would be considered to have the "quality of income" it would be required to be included in business income for the year of receipt through ITA 9. An advance has the quality of income if the business has an absolute and unconditional right to the amount and was "under no restriction, contractual or otherwise, as to its disposition, use or enjoyment." In other words, the business could do whatever it wanted with the deposit because it was under no obligation to return it.

6-59. This quality of income aspect is part of the legal determination of when income has been earned and is effectively part of profit in ITA 9. This feature, together with ITA 12(1)(a) and (b), provide the general mechanism for determining "business income" for income tax purposes.

EXAMPLE 1 You own a dozen rental properties, all of which are considered part of a rental business. At the end of 2021 a few of your tenants have not yet paid their December 2021 rent. The rent receivable at year end is $8,400. In addition you received

$3,750 in refundable deposits in 2021. Are these amounts required to be included in your business income for 2021?

ANALYSIS 1 ITA 12(1)(b) requires the $8,400 to be included in your 2021 business income since the services were rendered in 2021 (i.e., you provided the rental property accommodation in 2021). ITA 9 also would require the receivable to be included in your business income since you had an absolute and unconditional right to the amounts. ITA 12(1)(a) would require that the $3,750 be included in business income with an offsetting reserve deduction for the same amount, although the deduction is technically optional. Since the deposit is refundable, it is not yours to do with as you please; therefore it does not have the quality of income.

EXAMPLE 2 You own two rental properties. The activity is not a business because of its passive nature. At the end of December 2021 one tenant owes you rent for December 2021, which is not paid until January 2022. You therefore show the amount as a rent receivable of $1,500. In addition, in 2021 (your first year of operation) you received refundable deposits of $3,000. Are the receivable and refundable deposits required to be included in your property income?

ANALYSIS 2 Neither ITA 12(1)(a) or (b) apply to you because the rental activity is not a business. You therefore have to rely on the legal concept of "profit" and ITA 9, which looks to your absolute and unconditional right to the receivable and the same with respect to the refundable deposits and whether you are free to do whatever you want with them. In this case your right to the receivable meets the conditions and is therefore required to be included as property income in your 2021 income through ITA 9. The refundable deposits are not required to be included in your 2021 income because they do not have the "quality of income."

Exercise 6-4

Subject: Income, Receivables, and Deposits

You started a health club business in July 2021 that opened its doors September 1, 2021, offering the latest and most sophisticated equipment. Heavy advertising resulted in 200 people joining the club. Contracts were drawn up for a promotional rate of $75 per month with a $400 initial one-time non-refundable fee if payment for one year was made in advance by the end of August. All 200 individuals took advantage of the offer. You received $260,000 in advance payments [($75(12) + $400)(200 people)]. You choose December 31 as your fiscal year end. How much must be included in your business income for 2021 with respect to the amount received?

Solutions to Exercises are available in the Study Guide.

Reserves

The General System

6-60. The starting point in determining both business and property income is ITA 9 and the word "profit," which generally begins with an income statement prepared by accountants for a specific year. GAAP often permits the use of "reserves," which is generally an appropriation of retained earnings or other surplus for a specific purpose including ear-marking or setting aside funds for future asset purchases, legal settlements, to retire debt, recognize declines in the value of assets, and to provide for uncollectible amounts such as receivables. The accounting for reserves frequently results in an offsetting expense that then reduces the accounting income.

6-61. These accounting reserves and similar amounts are subject to a general prohibition in ITA 18(1)(e) that reads as follows:

> **ITA 18(1)(e)** Reserves etc.—In computing the income of a taxpayer from a business or property no deduction shall be made in respect of an amount as, or on account of, a reserve, a contingent liability or amount or a sinking fund except as expressly permitted by this Part.

Once again we see the same concepts at play. ITA 18 denies any reserves and contingent liabilities claimed as an expense in the accounting income statements. As a result, any such expenses are simply added back to income to effectively reverse their impact for income tax purposes. The rule, however, adds that an expense may be claimed for a reserve or contingent liability if it is expressly permitted. ITA 20 provides a very limited number of reserves that can be claimed as an expense.

6-62. Consistent with the earlier comments about the relevance of accounting to income tax, the meaning of the term "reserve" is different in income tax than it is for accounting purposes. For income tax the meaning is much broader, and it means an amount set aside that can be relied on for future use. This broad meaning allows the CRA to deny a wide range of amounts expensed as a result of a reserve-like treatment. The most common types of disallowed reserves are those relating to estimated expenses and write-downs of assets to recognize anticipated declines in value.

> **EXAMPLE** Bravco sells kitchen appliances offering a two-year warranty. In the preparation of the financial statements, an accounting reserve is set up to estimate the future warranty costs, which are expensed.

> **ANALYSIS** ITA 18(1)(e) would apply to deny the estimated warranty expenses, which would require they be added back or reversed in the reconciliation process. ITA 20(1), however, does not provide any reserve for warranty expenses. This means that warranty-related expenses are only permitted for income tax purposes when they are actually incurred. Note that while ITA 20(1)(m.1) does refer to a manufacturer's warranty reserve, a reserve can only be deducted under this provision when they are for an extended warranty covered by an insurance contract. It does not cover estimates or anticipated estimates of future warranty costs. Any insurance premiums paid for the contracts, however, would be deductible to the company as a result of ITA 9.

6-63. The mechanics of income tax reserves are often straightforward and follow the 9-12-18-20 rule previously discussed. The initial accounting reserve or expense claimed as a deduction in determining profit under ITA 9 is disallowed (ITA 18(1)). If a reserve deduction is allowed, then it is claimed as an expense for the year (ITA 20(1)). In the following taxation year the amount claimed as a reserve in the preceding year is fully added back to income (ITA 12), and at the end of that second year a new reserve is established (ITA 20(1)). The impact of this process is to defer recognition of estimated expenses and anticipated declines in value to the year in which the estimates or anticipated declines are actually realized and known with certainty.

6-64. The most common reserves that are specified in the ITA as deductions from business income are as follows:

- **ITA 20(1)(l)**—Reserve for doubtful or impaired debts (bad debts)
- **ITA 20(1)(m)**—Reserve for certain goods and services
- **ITA 20(1)(n)**—Reserve for unpaid amounts

The details of these reserves will be covered in the following material.

Reserve for Doubtful and Bad Debts—ITA 20(1)(l) and 20(1)(p)

6-65. Accounting reserves to recognize a decline in the value of year-end account receivables for products sold or services rendered are often claimed where there is some doubt or uncertainty as to collection. ITA 18(1)(e) prohibits the claiming of such deductions, but ITA 20(1)(l) allows a reserve to be claimed. Once an acceptable reserve has been claimed, the reserve is required to be included in business income in the following year through ITA 12(1)(d), with new reserves that can be established at the end of that year.

6-66. Oftentimes the doubtful debt reserve claimed for accounting purposes will be identical to that allowable for income tax purposes, but this is not always the case. The frequent reason for the difference relates to how the reserve is determined. Accountants may simply use a flat rate percentage of all receivables outstanding at year end based on past history and experience. ITA 20(1)(l), however, reads in part "a reasonable amount in respect of doubtful debts."

6-67. The CRA and the courts have determined that a reasonable approach requires the separate identification of receivables that are doubtful of collection. Factors for identifying doubtful receivables go to the debtor's ability and willingness to pay. Once the doubtful receivables have been identified, a percentage is then applied based on past history and experience. Failure to follow this approach will result in potential challenges by the CRA that the allowable doubtful debt reserve is unreasonable and would be disallowed as a deduction.

6-68. If a receivable has gone beyond being doubtful to the point that it is no longer considered collectible or has gone bad altogether, then ITA 20(1)(p) provides a deduction of the amount owing as long as it has been included in the income of the business in the year or a preceding year. ITA 20(1)(p) requires that the debt has previously been established to have become bad in the year. The CRA will recognize a debt as becoming bad if either (1) determined efforts have been made to collect the debt but none were successful or (2) there is clear evidence to indicate that the debt is uncollectible. If any part of the debt is subsequently collected it will be required to be included in business income at that time through ITA 12(1)(i). The bad debt deduction is not a reserve in the same sense as doubtful debts, and as a result the amount claimed is not added back in the next year.

6-69. Where the approach used to determine both doubtful debts and bad debts is consistent with the requirements of the ITA then the accounting will match that of the ITA, with the result that there would be no required adjustments to reconcile the accounting to net income (ITA 3).

EXAMPLE On December 31, 2020, at the end of its first year of operations, Ken's Print Shop estimates that $5,500 of its ending accounts receivable are doubtful of collection. For 2020, an allowance for doubtful debts is established for this amount for accounting purposes (by debiting doubtful debt expense and crediting allowance for doubtful debts). For income tax purposes, a doubtful debt reserve of $5,500 is deducted under ITA 20(1)(l). During the year ending December 31, 2021, $6,800 in accounts receivable are written off as uncollectible. At December 31, 2021, estimated doubtful accounts total $4,800.

6-70. For accounting purposes, the 2020 estimate of doubtful debts would be expensed with an offsetting credit to an allowance for doubtful debts (a contra account to accounts receivable). For income tax purposes, the same amount would be deducted from business income as a reserve for doubtful debts.

6-71. During 2021, the accountant for Ken's Print Shop would credit accounts receivable and debit allowance for doubtful debts for the actual write-offs of $6,800. This would leave a debit (negative) balance in this account of $1,300 ($5,500 - $6,800), indicating that the 2020 estimate was too low. This error would be corrected by adding the $1,300 to the bad debt expense for 2021. The total expense for 2021 would be as follows:

2021 estimate of future doubtful debts (credit allowance)	$4,800
Increase in expense to eliminate debit balance in allowance	$1,300
2021 expense for accounting purposes	$6,100

6-72. For income tax purposes, the total expense would be the same $6,100. However, the calculation would be determined as follows:

Add: 2020 reserve for tax purposes—ITA 12(1)(d)		$ 5,500
Deduct:		
2021 bad debt expense—ITA 20(1)(p)	($6,800)	
2021 reserve for doubtful debts—ITA 20(1)(l)	(4,800)	(11,600)
2021 net expense for income tax		($ 6,100)

Exercise 6-5

Subject: Bad Debts and Reserve for Doubtful Debts

On December 31, 2020, Norman's Flowers estimates that $16,000 of its ending accounts receivable are doubtful of collection. A reserve for this amount is deducted for income tax purposes. During the year ending December 31, 2021, $17,200 in doubtful accounts are written off as uncollectible. At December 31, 2021, estimated doubtful accounts total $18,400. What is the 2021 bad/doubtful debt expense for accounting purposes? By what amount will the 2021 business income (for income tax purposes) of Norman's Flowers be increased or decreased by the preceding information with respect to bad and doubtful debts?

Solutions to Exercises are available in the Study Guide.

Reserve for Certain Goods and Services—ITA 20(1)(m)

6-73. ITA 12(1)(a) was previously discussed at Paragraphs 6-56 and 6-57. That provision required that the receipt of unearned advances and prepayments for either goods to be delivered or services to be provided after the end of the year was to be included in business income in the year received. ITA 20(1)(m) would then provide a deduction with respect to that part of the advance that had not been earned or that did not have the "quality of income" (see Paragraph 6-58). The net result was that business income would not be increased once the full amount of the reserve is claimed. Consistent with the 9-12-18-20 rule, the ITA 20(1)(m) reserve deducted in one year would be required to be added to the business income in the immediately following year through ITA 12(1)(e).

EXAMPLE During the taxation year ending December 31, 2021, Donna's Auto Parts received $275,000 in the course of its business. Of this amount, $25,000 is a prepayment for goods that will not be delivered until 2022.

ANALYSIS $250,000 will be included in 2021 business income through ITA 9 as having the quality of income, and the remaining $25,000 of the prepayment is included as a result of ITA 12(1)(a). Donna will be able to deduct a reserve of $25,000 under ITA 20(1)(m) for the unearned advances. This $25,000 amount will be added to her 2022 business income under ITA 12(1)(e), reflecting the fact that the goods would have been delivered and therefore the income earned.

Exercise 6-6

Subject: Reserve for Doubtful Debts and Services

Barbra carries on the business of Barbra's Graphic Design as a sole proprietor. The books and records are maintained on a cash basis. During 2021, its first year of operation, the business has cash sales of $47,800. In addition, Barbra received advances of $5,600 for services that she will only provide after the end of the year. At the end of the year, there are credit sales of $26,300. Barbra estimates that $425 of the year-end receivables are doubtful of collection. Determine the 2021 business income of Barbra's Graphic Design based on the information provided. Add the appropriate ITA references.

Solutions to Exercises are available in the Study Guide.

Inventory Reserve for Unpaid Amounts—ITA 20(1)(n)

6-74. If a business sells goods with the amount being receivable over an extended period (i.e., instalment sales), ITA 20(1)(n) permits the deduction of a reasonable reserve if certain conditions are met. The calculation of the reserve begins with the gross profit percentage, which is equal to the gross profit divided by the gross selling price. That percentage is then applied to the amount unpaid at year end. Note that ITA 20(1)(n) refers to "property sold in the course of the business." This means that the property has to be inventory.

EXAMPLE An automobile dealership, with a December 31 year end, sells a new 2021 automobile for $42,000. The cost of the automobile is $31,000. The terms call for annual payments of $14,000 over three years without interest. The automobile is sold January 2, 2021. The buyer owes $28,000 at the end of 2021.

ANALYSIS The dealership will include the sale price of $42,000 less the inventory cost of $31,000 for a gross profit of $11,000. The ITA 20(1)(n) reserve for 2021 is calculated as $7,333 [($11,000/$42,000)($28,000)]. The net increase in business income will be $3,667 [$11,000 gross profit- reserve of $7,333]. The reserve of $7,333 will be added to the 2022 business income under ITA 12(1)(e), and a new reserve will be calculated under ITA 20(1)(n) at December 31, 2022. Note that had the terms included interest the reserve would not apply to that interest since the reserve is restricted to the $11,000 profit only.

6-75. Aside from the fact that the property sold must be inventory, there is one condition attached to the ability to claim the reserve and one constraint added. In addition, the legislation draws a distinction between types of inventory, effectively categorizing inventory into two types: (1) real property inventory (e.g., a land developer or construction company selling residential homes) and (2) all other types of inventory.

The ITA 20(1)(n) condition for inventory that is not real property: No reserve can be claimed unless part or all of the sale price is not due until at least two years from the date of the sale. If all of the sale price is due in less than two years, then the reserve would not be available.

ITA 20(8) The three-year limitation: ITA 20(8) provides a number of rules that limit the application of ITA 20(1)(n). One of the limitations is that no reserve can be claimed in a specific year, for any type of inventory, if at the end of that year the sale took place more than 36 months before that time. The affect is that the reserve can only be claimed for three years—the year of the sale and the following two years.

EXAMPLE A real estate developer sold a parcel of land in July 2020 for $200,000. The inventory cost of the land is $90,000. The terms of the contract specify that $40,000 will be paid immediately with the remaining amounts payable in eight equal amounts of $20,000 each beginning August 1, 2021. The developer is incorporated and uses a fiscal period ending October 31. Which years are available to claim a reserve under ITA 20(1)(n)?

ANALYSIS A reserve can be claimed for the 2020, 2021, and 2022 taxation years ending October 31. No reserve can be claimed for the 2023 year ending October 31 since that date is more than 36 months from the July 2020 sale. The reserves would be calculated as follows:

2020 reserve = [(110,000/$200,000)($160,000)] = $88,000

2021 reserve = [(110,000/$200,000)($140,000)] = $77,000

2022 reserve = [(110,000/$200,000)($120,000)] = $66,000

Increase in business income:

2020 $110,000 gross profit - reserve $88,000 = $22,000

2021 $88,000 previous-year reserve - reserve $77,000 = $11,000

2022 $77,000 previous-year reserve - reserve $66,000 = $11,000

2023 $66,000 previous-year reserve - no reserve allowed = $66,000

Exercise 6-7

Subject: Reserve for Unpaid Amounts

During November 2021, Martine's Jewels Ltd. sells a necklace for $120,000. The cost of this necklace was $66,000, resulting in a gross profit of $54,000. The $120,000 sales price is to be paid in four equal annual instalments of $30,000 on December 31 in each of the years 2022 through 2025. Martine's Jewels has a December 31 year end. Indicate the amount of the reserve that can be deducted and the net increase in business income for each of the years 2021 through 2025 as a result of the reserve.

Solutions to Exercises are available in the Study Guide.

We suggest you complete SSP 6-2 and 6-3 at this point.

Limitations on Deductions from Business and Property Income

Expense Analysis

6-76. At Paragraph 6-45 we discussed the 9-12-18-20 rule and how these main income tax provisions are the central focus of establishing a framework for working from income statements provided by accountants and making the necessary adjustments in a reconciliation process with the goal of determining the exact business income or business loss for a specific year. We saw that the analysis begins with a fundamental understanding of both a source of income and a business. Once we have identified a business, then it is a matter of determining the income and the allowable expenses, which are integral components of "profit" (ITA 9).

6-77. In terms of expenses, ITA 18 can block the ability to claim an expense, but ITA 20 may intervene, overriding ITA 18(1)(a), (b), or (h) (briefly discussed at Paragraph 6-47) and may provide a specific deduction based on what is acceptable for income tax purposes. This means that it is not only important to have a good understanding of the main and most often used rules of both ITA 18 and 20, but to first be able to identify which expenses that have been claimed as part of "profit" are acceptable and which are not. Once you have identified an expense denied by ITA 18, it is then a question of determining whether the expense or part of it is deductible under ITA 20(1).

6-78. The general rules for determining whether expenses are deductible for income tax purposes are determined throughout the ITA but can be summarized as follows:

1. The expense must be connected to an existing source of income.
2. It must be an income expenditure (i.e., incurred for an income earning purpose).
3. It can be a capital expenditure if specifically allowed by the ITA.
4. The expense cannot be personal.
5. The amount claimed must be reasonable.
6. It must not otherwise be prohibited by any other specific provisions of the ITA.

6-79. Before we apply the analysis to determine whether specific expenses are deductible or not, we first need to take a closer look at some of the more common and important limitations of ITA 18(1). We will reiterate that the limitations in ITA 18 apply only to deductions from business and property income. There are other restrictions, however, for example the cost of meals and entertainment, which apply to deductions from both business and property income, as well as to deductions from employment income. Most of these more general restrictions are found in Subdivision f, "Rules Relating to Computation of Income," and are discussed later in this chapter.

Some Specific Limitations—ITA 18

Incurred to Produce Income—ITA 18(1)(a)

6-80. The purpose of the ITA is not to provide a lengthy list of expenses that are deductible but instead to allow expenses sufficiently connected to a source of income to be deducted as long as certain basic conditions are met, as described in Paragraph 6-78. In other words, it is the facts of each case that act as a guide, within the established framework, to determine whether an expense is deductible or not. Each of the conditions we have listed are based on specific provisions of the ITA. One of the most important of these limitations is as follows:

> **ITA 18(1)(a) ...** no deduction shall be made in respect of an outlay or expense except to the extent that it was made or incurred by the taxpayer for the purpose of gaining or producing income from the business or property.

6-81. The purpose of ITA 18(1)(a) is to ensure that any expense, whether income or capital, is sufficiently connected to a specific source of income that is a business or property. One way of determining whether the limitation has been met is to ask whether the expenditure would have been incurred in the absence of the business or the property. If not, then the likelihood is that the expense relates to the business or property and has passed this test.

6-82. One observation that can be made from the limitation is that it is not necessary to demonstrate that the expense actually resulted in income. ITA 18(1)(a) only requires that the purpose (i.e., the motive or intention) of the expense is to earn income. We saw that a source of income must have a profit motive, and in the case of a business, the structure established must have the capacity to potentially earn a profit but an actual profit is not required.

6-83. Many regular recurring business expenses such as those for office, administration, salaries, rent, travel, advertising, and so on would clearly pass this test. In practical terms, many expenses that are disallowed by the CRA, where ITA 18(1)(a) is referenced (a common occurrence), include those for a home office, legal expenses, travel, promotion, and salaries and other payments to family members. In many cases the concern of the CRA is that many expenses contain a personal element, meaning that they would not be incurred for the express purpose of earning business or property income.

> **EXAMPLE 1** A business pays regular insurance premiums to cover any damage and losses on its property, including inventory.

> **ANALYSIS 1** The premiums would not have been incurred were it not for the business and are part of ongoing expenses in support of the business; therefore the ITA 18(1)(a) test has been met and no expense would be disallowed. We would add that such an expense would meet the "well-established business principles" and therefore would have been claimed as an expense in the determination of "profit" through ITA 9(1) (see Paragraph 6-41).

> **EXAMPLE 2** A business pays regular premiums to insure the life of the proprietor.

> **ANALYSIS 2** The insurance premiums would not have anything to do with the business and are considered to be personal in nature and therefore non-deductible. ITA 18(1)(a) would apply to deny the expense. The CRA is of the view that life insurance premiums are also disallowed on the basis of ITA 18(1)(b) because they are capital expenditures. Such expenses are also considered personal in nature and therefore denied under ITA 18(1)(h). Regardless of whether the denial occurs under ITA 18(1)(a), (b), or (h), remember that

ITA 20(1) can override each of these three limitations. ITA 20(1) would offer no allowable expense in this case, however.

EXAMPLE 3 A business requires long-term financing but the bank will not provide the funds unless the proprietor takes out life insurance as collateral for the borrowing and that, in the case of death, the proceeds of the life insurance policy will be used to pay off any remaining loan balance to the bank.

ANALYSIS 3 In this case the connection to the business is clear, with the result that the test in ITA 18(1)(a) would have been passed. In other words, the expense would not be disallowed by ITA 18(1)(a). However, any expenses related to long-term financing are considered to be capital expenditures, and as a result the ITA 18(1)(b) test that denies capital expenditures would not be met. In addition, life insurance premiums are generally considered personal expenses and would be disallowed by ITA 18(1)(h), which is discussed starting at Paragraph 6-93. In this instance ITA 20(1)(e.2) specifically allows the deduction of the insurance premiums. Following the flowchart in Figure 6-1 (see Paragraph 6-112) leads to the answer that the amount is deductible.

Capital Expenditures—ITA 18(1)(b)

6-84. ITA 18(1)(b) prohibits the deduction of any capital expenditure unless a specific deduction is expressly allowed. ITA 18(1)(b) reads as follows:

> **ITA 18(1)(b) ...** no deduction shall be made in respect of an outlay, loss or replacement of capital, a payment on account of capital or an allowance in respect of depreciation, obsolescence or depletion except as expressly permitted by this Part.

6-85. ITA 18(1)(b) is arguably the most important limitation since the CRA is of the view that most of the deductions expressly permitted by ITA 20(1) that override ITA 18(1)(a), (b), and (h) are initially blocked from a deduction as a result of ITA 18(1)(b) only. What this means is that while ITA 20(1) technically overrides ITA 18(1)(a) and (h), there are few specific deductions allowed under ITA 20(1) that would compensate for the denial of expenses under either of those provisions. In practice the CRA generally restricts the use of ITA 18(1)(a) and (h) to deny the deductibility of expenses that they believe are personal in nature. In the course of an audit CRA auditors will quote ITA 9(1), 18(1)(a), and (h) when disallowing expenses that they consider personal.

6-86. In Chapter 5 we discussed the hallmarks of capital expenditures in terms of depreciable property, but the concept extends much further. Much of the difficulty stems from the difference in treatment between accounting and the application of income tax/legal principles. For example, accounting often looks to whether an expenditure benefits future years in determining whether the accounting treatment should be to spread that expenditure over those identifiable years through depreciation. That accounting concept does not flow smoothly into the field of income tax. The courts have stated clearly, numerous times, that the fact that an expenditure relates to future years is not determinative when deciding whether an expenditure is capital.

6-87. With the exception of point #6 below, capital expenditures include the following:

1. Costs to acquire a capital property
2. Costs to improve capital property
3. Costs to create a business structure
4. Costs to add to an existing business structure
5. Costs to acquire an existing business structure
6. Determining what an expenditure is designed to accomplish from a practical and business point of view

6-88. The key to understanding whether expenditures are capital in nature versus on income account, and therefore deductible in the year incurred, is identifying the capital structure on which a business is based and the income earning process. Expenditures that relate to the business structure are capital, while those that relate to the income earning process are not. This analysis at times, when the issues are not clear cut, requires applying point #6 above, which is looking to what the expenditure is designed to accomplish. The courts have drawn a distinction between the two as referring to the difference between "selling versus production," "fixed versus circulating capital," and the "structure versus the money earning process." The three following case law examples will demonstrate some of the differences.

Case Law Examples—Capital Expenditures

6-89. In the *B.P. Australia* case (1966), the company paid a lump-sum amount to a service/gas station operator as an inducement to purchase its petroleum products for a five-year period. Accounting principles would treat this payment as a capital outlay amortized over the five-year period. The court, however, recognized that there were arguments for treating the payment as a capital and an income expenditure. The court relied on what the payment was designed to accomplish from a business point of view, which was to increase sales of petroleum products, and as a result the payment was considered part of the income earning process rather than the capital structure. The result was that the payment was fully deductible as an expense in the first year.

6-90. The cases of *Pantorama Industries* (2005) and *Rona Hardware Inc.* (2003) illustrate the different results to similar transactions. In both cases expenditures were made internally and to professionals to set up new outlets and negotiate new leases or renegotiate existing leases. The expenditures claimed by Rona were disallowed, however, while those claimed by Pantorama were allowed. In other words, the expenditures were capital to Rona but on income account to Pantorama. The different treatment was because Rona's expenditures were part of a business expansion plan whereas Pantorama was simply maintaining its commercial structure, closing some outlets and opening new ones without an overall increase. The case law is clear that expenditures meant to maintain an existing business structure are not capital expenditures.

6-91. A final illustration is the Supreme Court of Canada decision in *Johns Manville* (1985). In that case the company operated an open pit mine that required continuous purchases of land as the pit expanded and the walls needed shoring up. While most would say that the purchase of land is the purchase of capital property and that any related expenditures would also be capital, the court disagreed and allowed the purchase of land to be expensed on income account. The justification was that the purchases was sufficiently connected to the income earning process rather than the business structure.

Capital Expenditure Summary

6-92. ITA 18(1)(b) is often underappreciated when it comes to its impact on expenses that many may consider fully deductible. Expenditures that relate to a business structure or other capital issues mentioned in Paragraph 6-87 are only deductible if specifically identified in ITA 20 and only to the extent allowed, which may be less than the actual expenditure. Examples of expenditures considered capital in nature by the CRA include travel, training, conventions, promotion, and professional fees such as legal and accounting to the extent they relate to capital expenditures. If, for example, a taxpayer is purchasing a business, any related professional fees would be considered capital. Capital expenditures denied by ITA 18(1)(b) may be allowed if ITA 20 applies or if the expenditures relate to capital property, in which case they would be added to the cost of the acquired property. Where capital expenditures relate to the disposition of property they may be taken into consideration in the sale of that property. If none of these alternatives apply, then the expenditure receives no recognition and nothing can be deducted. See the expenditure flowchart in Figure 6-1.

Personal and Living Expenses—ITA 18(1)(h)

6-93. ITA 18(1)(h) denies the deduction of "personal or living expenses" and reads as follows:

> **ITA 18(1)(h) ...** no deduction shall be made in respect of personal or living expenses of the taxpayer, other than travel expenses incurred by the taxpayer while away from home in the course of carrying on the taxpayer's business.

6-94. The ITA defines the expression "personal or living expenses" as including (1) the expenses of properties maintained by the taxpayer for himself or for certain related individuals unless the property is used to carry on a business, and (2) life insurance premiums where the beneficiaries of the insurance policy include the individual and certain family members. The purpose of this definition is simply to extend the general meaning of personal expenses to include expenses of principal residences, cottages, and vacation properties as well as life insurance premiums.

6-95. As a rule, ITA 18(1)(h) is often used by the CRA once it is determined that there is no source of income, with the taxpayer having reported a business or property loss. If the expenses are not connected to any source of income then they must be personal in nature, leading to denied expenses under both ITA 18(1)(a) and (h) with no hope of claiming a deduction under ITA 20(1) given the absence of a source of income. Expenses frequently the subject of ITA 18(1)(h) include entertainment (e.g., sporting events and concerts), restaurant and bar charges, travel (particularly to exotic locations), promotion (e.g., gifts), legal expenses (separation, divorce, or child and spousal support), automobiles, and for a home office.

Recreational Facilities and Club Dues—ITA 18(1)(l)

6-96. ITA 18(1)(l)(i) prohibits the deduction of amounts that have been incurred to maintain a yacht, camp, lodge, golf course, or facility unless the taxpayer is in the business of providing such property for hire. The limitation applies where the main use of the property is for recreation or entertainment of clients, suppliers, employees, or shareholders. If, however, the property contains a separate dining facility, then the expenses will not be disallowed provided there is a genuine business purpose that does not involve recreation or entertainment. As a result, individuals could meet at a dining facility within a golf course for a business meal or event without concern that the expenses would be disallowed.

6-97. ITA 18(1)(l(ii)) extends the treatment of recreational facilities by disallowing membership fees or dues to any club the main purpose of which is to provide dining, sporting, or recreational facilities to its members.

Safety Deposit Box Fees—ITA 18(1)(l.1)

6-98. Safety deposit box fees generally range from $25 to $300 annually depending on the size of the box. As of 2013 these fees are no longer deductible.

Political Contributions—ITA 18(1)(n)

6-99. Businesses may have a legitimate reason to support a political candidate that may further their business interests. In such cases the expense would be sufficiently linked to a business purpose such that any contribution would be deductible. ITA 18(1)(n), however, denies any contribution as an expense from either business or property income. Chapter 4 explained that a limited tax credit is allowed for federal political contributions made by individuals under ITA 127(3).

Lease Cancellation Payments—ITA 18(1)(q)

6-100. This limitation provides a rule that initially limits any lease cancellation payment but then provides a specific deduction under either of ITA 20(1)(z) or (z.1). The purpose of these interconnected rules is to amortize the cancellation payment over what would otherwise have been the lease term unless the property is sold. ITA 20(1)(z) and (z.1) are discussed later in this chapter.

Certain Automobile Expenses—ITA 18(1)(r)

6-101. Chapter 3 discussed a situation where an employee uses her own automobile in performing her employment duties and receives a per-kilometre allowance for that use from the employer. The per-kilometre allowance is not required to be included in the employee's income as long as the allowance is reasonable. The determination of reasonableness is a question of fact. If, for example, an employee were to receive either a $2.00 or a $0.02 per-kilometre allowance to travel within a city, the allowance would be considered unreasonable with the result that the allowance would be required to be included in the employee's income as a result of ITA 6(1)(b). This reasonableness threshold is decisive in determining whether a per-kilometre allowance is or is not included in income. In addition, an employee would be unable to claim any automobile-related expenses, including CCA and interest charges, if the personally owned automobile was financed, unless the allowance is included in income. In summary, employee-incurred automobile expenses can only be deducted by the employee in receipt of a per-kilometre allowance if that allowance is unreasonable.

6-102. ITA 18(1)(r) is an interrelated rule that applies to the employer. This limitation restricts the amount an employer can claim as an expense for the per-kilometre allowance paid to the employee. The amount the employer can deduct is limited to an amount prescribed in ITR 7306. For 2021, this amount is $0.59 for the first 5,000 kilometres and $0.53 for any additional kilometres unless the employee is required to include the full amount of the allowance in her employment income.

EXAMPLE Textco carries on a sales business that requires certain employees to use their own automobiles in their employment duties. In 2020 the company pays Judith Beasely a $0.65 per-kilometre allowance for employment-related use of her automobile. Judith drove 26,000 kilometres during the year for employment use. She received $16,900 [($0.65)(26,000)].

ANALYSIS 1—If we assume that the per-kilometre rate is reasonable, then no amount is required to be included in Judith's employment income: Textco can deduct the following part of the allowance as a result of ITA 18(1)(r):

5,000 kms @ $0.59	$ 2,950
21,000 kms @ $0.53	11,130
Total employer expense	$14,080
Disallowed expense	$ 2,820

ANALYSIS 2—The per-kilometre rate is not reasonable, and Judith is required to include $16,900 in her employment income. Textco can deduct the full amount of $16,900 since the employee is required to include the full amount in her employment income.

Payments under the ITA—ITA 18(1)(t)

6-103. Students learning about federal income tax tend to believe that business and property expenses include federal and provincial income tax because of the way they are treated for accounting purposes. In addition, they may believe that taxpayers are not allowed to deduct interest charged under the ITA, which encourages those owing amounts to the federal government to avoid having to pay "non-deductible interest." ITA 18(1)(t) is the legislative authority that prevents claiming any amounts charged under the ITA as an expense. This includes federal income tax, interest, and penalties.

6-104. In Folio S4-F2-C1, "Deductibility of Fines and Penalties," the CRA clarifies that ITA 18(1)(t) does not apply to provincial income taxes nor would it apply to foreign income taxes where a Canadian resident taxpayer earns business or property income outside Canada. Instead the CRA quotes case law at paragraphs 24 and 25 that support the view that both provincial income tax and foreign income tax (e.g., profits tax) are not allowed as business or property expenses. They add that such amounts would be disallowed under ITA 18(1)(a). In addition, the CRA adds that ITA 67.6 prohibits the deduction of fines or penalties charged under both provincial tax and foreign tax statutes. Interestingly, both ITA 18(1)(t) and 67.6 would not apply to any interest charged on provincial or foreign income taxes, fines, or penalties.

Interest and Property Taxes on Land—ITA 18(2)

6-105. The purpose of this next limitation is to restrict what can be claimed as an expense with respect to the ownership of land in situations where the land is not used in the course of carrying on a business or is not a source of income primarily acquired for the purpose of generating profit of its own such as would be the case with a parking lot, for example. In other situations, including a land developer who sells land as inventory, the concern is that interest and property tax expenses could significantly exceed any income related to that land, creating a loss that would then reduce taxable income and income taxes payable.

6-106. ITA 18(2) limits the deduction for property taxes and interest to the amount of gross revenues (i.e., all income earned) less all expenses other than property taxes and interest. In effect the property taxes and interest are allowed to be deducted to the extent of that remaining net income but are not permitted to be used to create or increase a business or property loss.

EXAMPLE A parcel of land that is being held as a future plant site is generating some rental income by being rented for storage. Income, net of all expenses except property taxes and interest, total $23,400. Property taxes and interest total $100,000. The land was purchased one year ago for $900,000.

ANALYSIS Since the land is not actually being used in the course of a business nor is it primarily acquired to earn income, the interest and property taxes on the land can only be deducted to the extent of revenues from the rent net of all expenses except property taxes and interest. In this case only $23,400 of property taxes and interest are deductible. The remaining $76,600 of expenses that cannot be deducted are added to the cost of the land as non-depreciable capital property under ITA 53(1)(h), resulting in an "adjusted cost base" of $976,600. This adjustment will reduce any future gain or increase any future loss on the sale of the land.

6-107. If the land is inventory, the non-deductible interest and property taxes are added to the inventory cost as a result of ITA 10(1.1). This will reduce the profit or increase a loss on the ultimate sale of the land.

6-108. The limitation provides an exception for a corporation whose "principal business is the leasing, rental or sale, or the development for lease, rental or sale, of real property to arm's length persons." As a consequence, these real estate companies are allowed to deduct interest and property tax payments to the extent of the net income amount as discussed plus what is referred to as a "base level deduction."

6-109. This base level deduction is defined in ITA 18(2.2) as the amount that would be the amount of interest, computed at the prescribed rate, for the year in respect of a loan of $1,000,000 outstanding throughout the year. This means that, if the prescribed rate for the year were 2%, real estate companies could deduct interest and property taxes on the land they are carrying to the extent of net revenues from the land, plus an additional $20,000 [(2%)($1,000,000)]. If this is added to the example in Paragraph 6-106, then the deductible interest and property taxes would be increased to $43,400 and the reduced non-deductible amount of $56,600 would, depending on whether the land was inventory or non-depreciable capital property, be added to the cost of the land through either ITA 10(1.1) or 53(1)(h), respectively. You will note that a loss can be recognized in this case to the extent of the base level deduction.

Soft Costs—ITA 18(3.1)

6-110. Costs that are attributable to the period of construction, renovation, or alteration of a building, or in respect of the ownership of the related land, are referred to as soft costs. These costs could include interest, legal and accounting fees, insurance, and property taxes. In general, ITA 18(3.1) indicates that such costs are not deductible and must be added to the cost of the building.

Prepaid Expenses

6-111. Income tax principles do not apply a matching concept such as is used in accounting. Payment of expenses in a year that relate to future years would be considered fully deductible in the year of payment as long as the expenses relate to the income earning process. ITA 18(9), however, modifies that basic principle by legislating a matching concept, which prevents the deduction of outlays and expenses that have been paid for goods or services that will be delivered after the end of the taxation year. This provision also restricts prepaid expenses for interest, property taxes, rents, royalties, and insurance, limiting the claim to the year to which the expense relates. As a result, the income tax treatment of these expenditures generally matches their treatment under GAAP with the result that reconciliation adjustments for prepaid expenses are generally not necessary.

Business/Property Expenditure Analysis Flowchart—Example with Appraisal Costs

6-112. We have included an expenditure analysis flowchart as Figure 6-1 to provide guidance in determining the income tax treatment of a specific expense. Remember that the ability to claim a particular expense is dependent on a source of income such as from a business or property. The following three examples will illustrate the use of the flowchart.

> **EXAMPLE 1** A taxpayer incurs valuation or appraisal costs in connection with a proposed purchase of a building that will be used in a business carried on by the taxpayer. The building is purchased.

Figure 6-1
Flowchart for Determining if an Expense Is Deductible

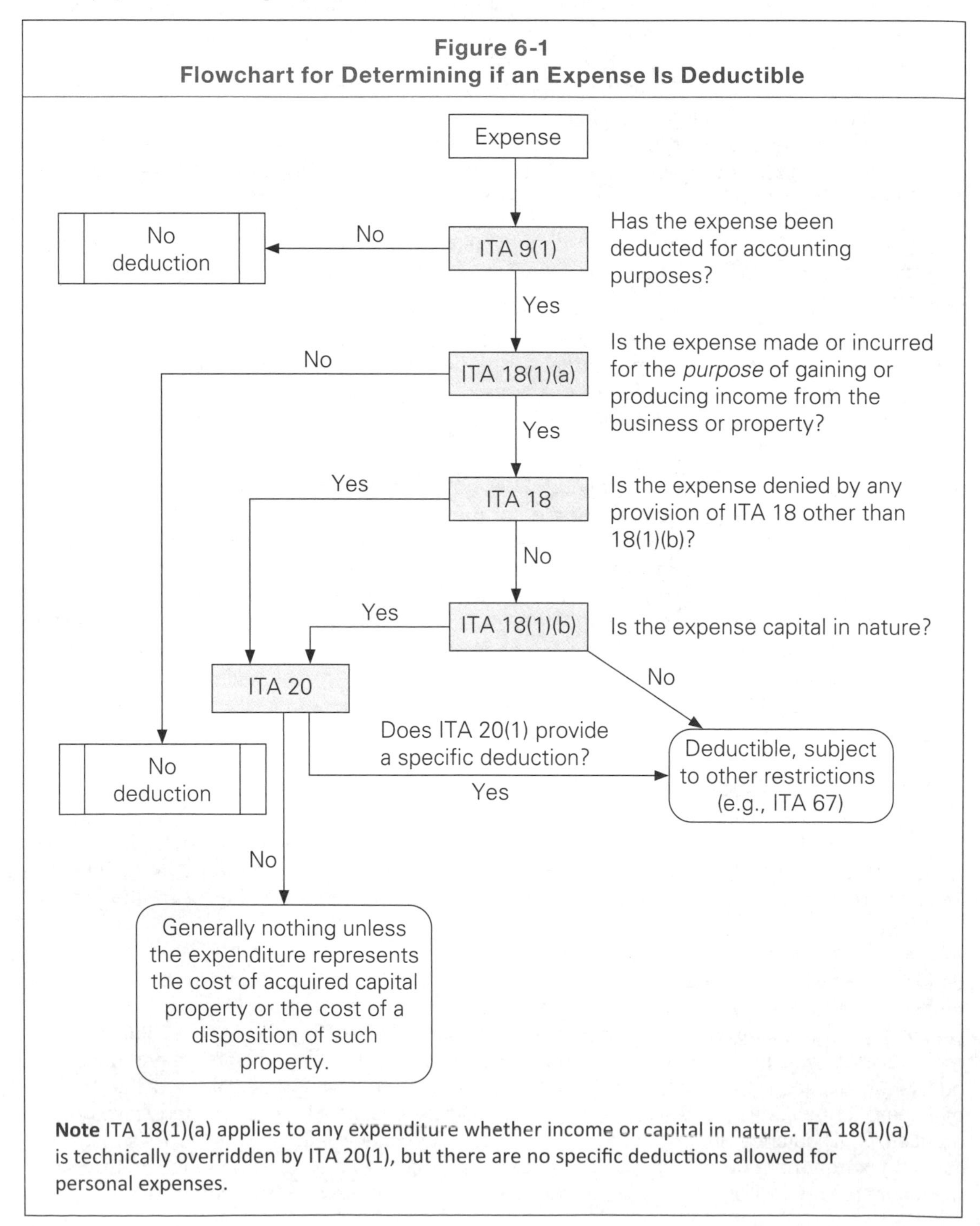

Note ITA 18(1)(a) applies to any expenditure whether income or capital in nature. ITA 18(1)(a) is technically overridden by ITA 20(1), but there are no specific deductions allowed for personal expenses.

ANALYSIS 1 Since the expenditure relates to the purchase of capital property it is a capital expenditure. The flowchart analysis is as follows:

1. Has the expense been deducted for accounting purposes as part of "profit"? YES
2. Is the expense made or incurred for the purpose of earning business or property income? YES
3. Is the expense denied by any provision of ITA 18(1) other than (b)? NO
4. Is the expense capital in nature? YES
5. Does ITA 20(1) provide a specific deduction for the expenditure? NO
6. RESULT: The expenditure is added to the cost of the acquired property.

EXAMPLE 2 A taxpayer incurs valuation or appraisal costs in connection with a proposed purchase of a building that will be used in a business carried on by the taxpayer. The building is not purchased.

ANALYSIS 2 Since the expenditure relates to the purchase of capital property it is a capital expenditure irrespective of whether the building is acquired. The flowchart analysis is as follows:

1. Has the expense been deducted for accounting purposes as part of "profit"? YES
2. Is the expense made or incurred for the purpose of earning business or property income? YES
3. Is the expense denied by any provision of ITA 18(1) other than (b)? NO
4. Is the expense capital in nature? YES
5. Does ITA 20(1) provide a specific deduction for the expenditure? YES
6. RESULT: Since no property is acquired, the expenditure cannot be added to anything. In this case, however, class 14.1 would apply to add the expenditure with the result that a CCA claim can be made under ITA 20(1)(a). Note: Class 14.1 only applies if there is a business. If the expenditure is related to income from property (i.e., the purchase of a rental property), the expenditure would not have been allowed since there would be no source of income to apply it against.

EXAMPLE 3 A taxpayer incurs valuation or appraisal costs in connection with valuing business inventory for insurance purposes and establishing the insurance premium.

ANALYSIS 3 Since the expenditure relates to the income earning process and not the business structure, the expenses would be deductible on income account. The flowchart analysis is as follows:

1. Has the expense been deducted for accounting purposes as part of "profit"? YES
2. Is the expense made or incurred for the purpose of earning business or property income? YES
3. Is the expense denied by any provision of ITA 18(1) other than (b)? NO
4. Is the expense capital in nature? NO
5. RESULT: The expenditure is deductible.

Business Use-of-Home Expenses ("Work Space")—ITA 18(12)

6-113. Expenses related to the existence of a home office used in connection with a business would ordinarily be deductible within the meaning of "profit" in ITA 9. Returning to the 9-12-18-20 rule, however, we know that the analysis does not end with ITA 9 but that this is just the starting point. In the case of a home office, the government's concern is that home expenses that would be personal in nature would effectively be converted to deductible business expenses. ITA 18(12) sets out the limitation where a "work space" is situated in a home in which the individual lives that is used for the taxpayer's business. The general rule is that work space expenses cannot be used to create or increase a business loss.

6-114. The deductibility of work space expenses is limited to situations where

- the work space is the individual's principal place of business; or
- the work space is used exclusively for the purpose of earning income from business and is used on a regular and continuous basis for meeting clients, customers, or patients of the individual (e.g., a medical doctor with an office in his home).

6-115. The work space will qualify if it is the principal place of business, which is a concept that receives considerable attention where there appear to be two or more such locations. Consider an oil company or a farming business. Is the principal place of business the oil field or the fields where crops are harvested, or the head office of the oil company or farmhouse of the farmer where an office is located? In the 2005 Tax Court case in *Jenkins v. The Queen* (2005 TCC 167) at paragraph 18, the judge made the following comment identifying where the principal place of business is to be found:

> where those necessary elements of telephoning customers and suppliers, filling in invoices, doing payroll, maintaining books and records, contacting authorities for licenses, preparing tax returns, chasing down receivables, handling complaints, creating business plans, preparing financial statements, talking to accountants and lawyers, etc.

6-116. If the work space is not the principal place of business, it must be used exclusively for the purpose of earning business income. This requires that some part of the home must be designated as the home work space and not used for any other purpose. In addition, this second provision requires that the space be used on a regular and continuous basis for meeting clients, customers, or patients. IT Folio S4-F2-C2 indicates that a work space for a business that normally requires infrequent meetings, or frequent meetings at irregular intervals, would not meet this requirement.

6-117. If an individual meets either of these two conditions then work space expenses can be deducted within the limitations of this rule. The work space does not have to be used exclusively for business purposes. If, for example, a dining room table is used to run a mail-order business and that work space qualifies as the principal place of business, then a portion of the home expenses can be deducted for that work space.

6-118. The method acceptable to the CRA to determine the work space begins with the dedicated work space divided by the finished livable space. This would not include an unfinished basement but would include parts of a basement that were finished. The next step is to determine the common areas of the home that are used throughout the work day. Common areas include hallways, corridors, bathrooms, the kitchen, entrance ways, exits, and so on. The amount of time is then determined during the course of a working day that you are using these common areas compared to the total number of waking hours.

6-119. To illustrate, assume that the dedicated work space accounts for 11% of the square footage of the living space of the home and that the common areas account for another 8%. Further assume that the employment-related use of the common areas is half the number of waking hours for each of five days out of seven days. The percentage applied to the common areas would be [(0.5)(5/7)(8%)] = 2.9%. The business use would therefore be 13.9% [11% + 2.9%]. The lesson to be learned is to always include a component for the use of common areas and avoid shortchanging the calculation by only counting a devoted work space.

6-120. When the conditions for deductibility are met, expenses must generally be apportioned as indicated between business and personal use. Maintenance, repair, or other expenses that relate specifically to the work space can be deducted in full. Figure 6-2 compares the deductibility of work space in the home expenses for an employee with no commission income, an employee with commission income, and a self-employed individual earning business income.

Figure 6-2
Deductibility of Work Space Expenses

	Employee—No Commissions	Employee—With Commissions	Self-Employed Business Income
Rent (if tenant)	Yes	Yes	Yes
Utilities	Yes	Yes	Yes
Repairs, maintenance	Yes	Yes	Yes
Telephone (supply)*	No/Yes	No/Yes	Yes
Internet (supply)*	No	No	Yes
Property taxes	No	Yes	Yes
Home insurance	No	Yes	Yes
Mortgage interest	No	No	Yes
CCA on house	No	No	Yes

*Employees cannot deduct the basic monthly cost of a home telephone or the cost of fees for home internet service. Long distance charges that reasonably relate to employment income are deductible. In contrast, to the extent that telephone and internet service at an individual's home is used for both business and personal purposes, the business portion of the expense is deductible. A reasonable basis of proration should be used. ITA 18(12) would not apply to restrict telephone and internet expenses since they do not relate to the work space.

6-121. Figure 6-2 shows that individuals earning business income can deduct CCA on their home. While this deduction would result in reduced business income, it is not generally advisable to claim this deduction as it can result in income tax implications on the eventual sale of the residence. This is discussed further in Chapter 8 with the principal residence exemption.

6-122. Regardless of the types of costs deducted, work space in the home expenses cannot be used to create or to increase a business or employment loss. As a result, the total deduction will be limited to the amount of business income after deducting all expenses other than those for the work space. Any expenses that are not deductible in a given year because they exceed that limitation in the year can be carried forward and deducted in a subsequent year against income from the same business to the extent of the limitation for that year. In effect, there is an indefinite carry forward of unused work space in the home expenses. This carry forward is conditional on the work space continuing to meet the test for deductibility in future years.

Exercise 6-8

Subject: Work Space in the Home Costs

During the current year, Jobul Krist has the following costs:

Utilities	$2,400
Maintenance and repairs	4,600
Property taxes	5,200
House insurance	2,300
Interest on mortgage	7,800
Repainting and rewiring the work space in the home	1,000
Home internet service fees	960
Home telephone:	
Monthly charge	600
Employment/business-related long distance charges	390

Mr. Krist is a workaholic with no family, friends, pets, or personal interests. He estimates that he uses 25% of his residence and 95% of his home phone and home internet service for employment/business-related purposes. Maximum CCA on 100% of the house would be $12,000. Determine the maximum deduction that would be available to Mr. Krist assuming:

A. He is an employee with $250,000 in income (no commissions).
B. He is an employee with $250,000 in commission income.
C. He carries on a business as a sole proprietor and earns $250,000 in business income.

Solutions to Exercises are available in the Study Guide.

We suggest you complete SSP 6-4 at this point.

Foreign Media Advertising—ITA 19 and 19.1

6-123. In order to provide some protection to Canadian media, the *ITA* places limitations on the deductibility of advertising expenses in foreign media. For print media, this limitation is found in ITA 19, with ITA 19.1 containing a corresponding provision for broadcast media. In general, these provisions deny a deduction for expenses made in foreign print or foreign broadcast media in those cases where the advertising message is directed primarily at the Canadian market. It does not apply where such foreign media expenditures are focused on non-Canadian markets.

6-124. ITA 19.01 modifies the general non-deductibility rule by exempting certain foreign periodicals. Canadian businesses can deduct 100% of advertising costs in these publications, without regard to whether it is directed at the Canadian market, provided 80% or more of its non-advertising content is "original editorial content." Original editorial content is defined as non-advertising content

- the author of which is a Canadian citizen or a permanent resident of Canada and, for this purpose, "author" includes a writer, a journalist, an illustrator, and a photographer; or
- that is created for the Canadian market and has not been published in any other edition of that issue of the periodical published outside Canada.

6-125. If the periodical cannot meet the 80% criteria, only 50% of such advertising costs will be deductible. Note that ITA 19.01 applies to periodicals only, and not to other foreign media.

Business Income—Specific Deductions

Inventory—ITA 10

General Rule

6-126. There are two alternative methods of inventory valuation allowed for income tax purposes:

- Valuation at lower of cost or fair market value (FMV) for each item (or class of items if specific items are not readily distinguishable) in the inventory
- Valuation of the entire inventory at fair market value

6-127. The selected method must be applied consistently from year to year and cannot normally be changed. In exceptional circumstances, the CRA will allow a change, provided it can be shown that the new method is more appropriate, it is used consistently in future periods, and the new method is used for financial statement purposes.

6-128. FMV can mean either replacement cost or net realizable value. The method used in determining FMV for income tax purposes should normally be the same as the method used to determine "market" for financial statement purposes.

6-129. Cost can be determined through specific identification, an average cost assumption, a first in, first out (FIFO) assumption, or through the use of the retail method. However, the use of a last in, first out (LIFO) assumption for the determination of inventory costs is not allowed. Since LIFO is also not permitted for accounting purposes, there is no need for LIFO adjustments when reconciling accounting income to net income.

Overhead Absorption

6-130. In the case of the work-in-process and finished goods inventories of manufacturing enterprises, an applicable share of overhead should be included. The CRA will accept either direct costing, in which only variable overhead is allocated to inventories, or absorption costing, in which both variable and fixed overhead is added to inventories. In addition, the CRA suggests that the method used should be the one that provides an accurate picture of a taxpayer's business income.

Income Tax vs. GAAP

6-131. GAAP rules for inventories (both *IFRS* and *ASPE*) can be compared to the income tax rules as follows:

Inventory Valuation For income tax purposes, inventories can be valued at either lower of cost and fair market value or at fair market value. The accounting rules require that inventories be valued at the lower of cost and net realizable value.

Determination of Fair Market Value (FMV) For income tax purposes, FMV can be determined using either replacement cost or net realizable value. The accounting rules require the use of net realizable value.

Determination of Cost For income tax purposes, tracking cost can be determined using specific identification, a FIFO or average cost assumption, or through the use of the retail method. The accounting rules permit the use of the same methods.

Use of Direct Costing The use of direct costing, while permissible for income tax, is not permitted for accounting purposes.

6-132. While there are some differences between the income tax rules and the accounting requirements, the two sets of rules are largely the same. Differences can arise, however, in situations where depreciation (CCA) is included in the determination of inventory values, a discussion of which goes beyond the scope of this text.

A Few Additional Comments on Inventory Valuation

6-133. In general, when the inventory valuation method of ITA 10(1) applies the use of either (1) the lower of cost and FMV or (2) FMV becomes available to allow a business to deduct any declines in value that occur in a given year through the cost of goods sold. There are a number of exceptions to this rule, however, as follows:

Inventory of artists—ITA 10(6) Inventory of an artist, such as painting, drawings, sculptures, and certain other works of art, can be valued on an elective basis at nil at year end. This allows artists to deduct the full cost of their inventory as cost of goods sold.

Inventory of advertising and packaging material—ITA 10(4)(a) and 10(5)(a) These materials are considered inventory, and while the general inventory method allows the use of FMV, that value must be based on replacement cost only.

Adventure of concern in the nature of trade—ITA 10(1.01) We discussed an adventure or concern in the nature of trade in this chapter. Such an activity is deemed to be a business and therefore the subject of the adventure is inventory. Such inventory, however, cannot use the FMV and must use cost. This prevents a taxpayer from effectively creating a business loss in a year where there is a decline in value until such time as the inventory is actually sold in a subsequent year.

EXAMPLE Alyssa purchases a residential property for $180,000 in December 2021 that she wants to flip for a quick profit. Shortly after the purchase, the market declines and the property is only worth $145,000 at December 31, 2021. She sells the property for $132,000 in February 2022.

ANALYSIS Alyssa is required to value the inventory using the cost of $180,000. She cannot deduct the decline in value of $35,000 in 2021. She will be able to recognize the business loss of $48,000 in 2022. Had the general inventory valuation been available, she would have been able to deduct a business loss of $35,000 in 2021 and a further $13,000 in 2022.

Exercise 6-9

Subject: Inventory Valuation

Brandon Works sells a single product that it buys from various manufacturers. It has a December 31 year end. During 2021, purchases of this item were as follows:

Date	Quantity	Price
February 1	50,000	$2.50
May 23	35,000	2.85
August 18	62,000	2.95
October 28	84,000	3.05

On December 31, 2021, 102,000 of these items are on hand. Their replacement cost on this date is $3.10 and they are being sold for $4.50. It is estimated that selling costs average 10% of the sales price. It is not possible to identify the individual items being sold. Calculate all the values that could be used for the 102,000 remaining units for tax purposes, identifying the method you used for each value.

Solutions to Exercises are available in the Study Guide.

We suggest you complete SSP 6-5 at this point.

Some Specific Deductions—ITA 20

6-134. Throughout this chapter we have discussed the importance of the 9-12-18-20 rule in understanding how these provisions of the ITA interact to determine the amount that is required to be included in either business or property income. Having discussed ITA 9, 12, and 18 together with the expenditure flowchart of Figure 6-1, it is now time to look at some of the more important provisions within ITA 20 that allow certain expenses that otherwise have been denied by ITA 18.

- **ITA 20(1)(a)—Capital Cost of Property** This provision provides for the deduction of capital expenditures as CCA where depreciable property has been acquired. This provisiojn was discussed in detail in Chapter 5.

- **ITA 20(1)(b)—Incorporation Expenses** This provision provides for the deduction of up to $3,000 in expenses incurred in incorporating a company. Incorporation expenses are capital expenditures because they relate to the creation of a business structure that would by disallowed as a result of ITA 18(1)(b). Any incorporation expenses that exceed $3,000 are added to class 14.1. It is important to note that any expenses relating to an amendment of a company's articles of incorporation would not be eligible for this expense treatment.

- **ITA 20(1)(c)—Simple Interest** This provision is arguably one of the most contentious expenses in all of ITA 20. Court cases and interpretations are quite extensive even though the basic premise is relatively straightforward. It has been a longstanding contention by the courts that interest is, by its nature, a capital expenditure, with the result that ITA 18(1)(b) would deny any deduction subject to ITA 20(1)(c). The two main parts of the provision allow interest to be claimed as an expense where the interest arises as a result of a legal obligation to pay interest on (1) borrowed money used for the purpose of earning income from a business or property or (2) an amount payable for the purchase of property that will be used in a business or to earn income from that property. Examples that fit within these provisions include borrowing funds from a bank to support the business and purchasing property on account. ITA 20(1)(c) is discussed in detail in Chapter 7.

- **ITA 20(1)(d)—Compound Interest** This provision applies to allow a deduction for compound interest only if it is actually paid. This differs from ITA 20(1)(c), which allows a deduction of simple interest on an accrual basis.

  EXAMPLE A business with a December 31 year end borrows $500,000 at 6% interest compounded daily. No monthly payments are required and the full amount (including interest) is paid January 10 of the following year.

  ANALYSIS At the end of the first year the accrued interest is approximately $31,000, representing $30,000 of simple interest [6% of $500,000] and $1,000 of compound interest. The business can expense the accrued interest of $30,000 under ITA 20(1)(c) in the first year, but the $1,000 compound interest is only deductible in the second year when it is actually paid.

- **ITA 20(1)(e)—Expenses Re. Financing** Financing expenses to raise capital through borrowing or issuing shares are generally considered capital expenditures, which are denied a deduction by ITA 18(1)(b). ITA 20(1)(e) allows the deduction of certain financing expenses on a straight-line basis over five years, meaning that 20% of the expense would be deductible in each year. Any undeducted financing costs can be expensed in the year the loan is repaid or the shares redeemed if that event occurs before the end of the five-year period. Expenses to which this provision applies would include legal fees in connection with a prospectus, printing costs of a prospectus, guarantee fees, mortgage applications, and brokerage fees.

- **ITA 20(1)(e.1)—Annual Fees for Financing** This provision is similar to ITA 20(1)(e) with the exception that the financing expenses relate solely to the year in which they are incurred. Expenses that would potentially qualify include standby charges, guarantee fees, registrar fees, transfer agent fees, and filing and service fees. If the conditions are met, the amounts can be fully expensed in the year incurred.

- **ITA 20(1)(e.2)—Premium on Life Insurance** This provision was briefly discussed in Paragraph 6-83 and is an exception to the rule that life insurance premiums are not deductible as a result of ITA 18(1)(b) because they are considered capital expenditures. The provision applies to allow life insurance premiums to be expensed where it is a condition of financing required by a financial institution (e.g., a bank) as collateral security for financing.

- **ITA 20(1)(f)—Discount on Certain Obligations** This provision applies to bonds, debentures, notes, and mortgages that have been issued at a discount. For example, assume a company issued $1,000,000 of bonds and, because of market conditions, including the stated interest rate on the bonds, only receives $950,000. The bond has been issued at a discount, meaning at an amount below what it is required to pay at maturity. The $50,000 additional amount that will be paid at maturity is subject to this provision, which may allow all of it to be deducted as a business expense or only 50% of it, depending on whether the bond was issued for less than 97% of the maturity amount and if the effective yield is not more than 4/3 of the coupon rate. Since the bond in this example was issued for 95% ($950,000/$1,000,000], only 50% of the discount would be deductible when paid on maturity.

Accounting principles treat discounts and premiums on bonds and similar obligations as amounts that either increase or decrease annual interest expense. From an economic and financial statement presentation perspective this makes perfect sense; however, legal concepts apply to income tax. The word "interest" has been legally defined by the courts and it does not include either discounts or premiums, meaning that they must be separately considered in the ITA. This issue is discussed in more detail in Chapter 7.

- **ITA 20(1)(q)—Employer's Contributions to Registered Pension Plans (RPP)** This provision allows an employer's contribution toward an RPP for employees to be deducted. A deduction is only permitted in a year where the actual payment is made within the year or within 120 days from the end of the year where the payment is made to fund pension costs. This is discussed in Chapter 10.
- **ITA 20(1)(y)—Employer's Contributions under a Deferred Profit-Sharing Plan (DPSP)** Only amounts that are paid during the year or within 120 days of the end of the year can be deducted. This provision is discussed in Chapter 10.
- **ITA 20(1)(z) and (z.1)—Costs of Cancellation of a Lease** Paragraph 6-100 explained that lease cancellation payments are denied by ITA 18(1)(q) but are allowed where either ITA 20(1)(z) or (z.1) applies. Lease cancellation payments can be deducted on a pro rata per diem basis over the remaining term of the lease, including all renewal periods, to a maximum of 40 years. If the property is sold subsequent to the cancellation, the remaining balance can be deducted at that time. If the property sold is a capital property, only one-half of the remaining balance can be deducted as a business or property expense.
- **ITA 20(1)(aa)—Landscaping of Grounds** In the absence of this provision, landscaping costs would generally be treated as a capital expenditure and denied by ITA 18(1)(b). This provision only allows a deduction if the landscaping occurs around a building or other structure used primarily for the purpose of earning business income and not property income. In addition, a deduction can only be made for expenditures that are actually paid in the year.
- **ITA 20(1)(cc)—Expenses of Representation** This provision allows capital expenditures for the cost of representations to a level of government or public body for the purpose of obtaining a licence, permit, franchise, or trademark as long as it relates to a business carried on by the taxpayer and is actually paid in the year. The CRA has commented that costs to obtain a patent including professional fees, travel, and other costs would be deductible under this provision. Interestingly, the CRA has also added that any expenses paid to professionals and others to obtain an advanced income tax ruling or to put together a voluntary disclosure would also be deductible as long as the ruling or disclosure related to a business of the taxpayer.
- **ITA 20(1)(dd)—Site Investigation Costs** Costs of determining the suitability of a site for a new building or other structure in connection with a business carried on by a taxpayer are classified as capital expenditures and again would be denied a deduction under ITA 18(1)(b). ITA 20(1)(dd), however, allows the preliminary investigation costs to be expensed in the year they are actually paid.
- **ITA 20(1)(ee)—Utilities Service Connection** The service-related costs of making connections of water, gas, electricity, phone, or sewer to one's place of business are clearly capital expenditures that would be denied by ITA 18(1)(b) were it not for this provision. These costs are deductible in the year in which they are actually paid.

- **ITA 20(1)(qq) and (rr)—Disability-Related Costs and Equipment/Devices** These two provisions allow capital expenditures made for disability-related building modifications to aid mobility-impaired individuals and the acquisition of certain disability-related equipment or devices to be deducted in the year in which the costs are actually paid. Equipment and devices allowed include elevator position indicators, visual fire alarm indicators, and disability-specific computer software.
- **ITA 20(10)—Convention Expenses** This provision begins with restricting the expenses that may be claimed by a business in attending conventions to no more than two in a single year provided they are in a location that is consistent with the territorial scope of the organization. Interestingly, this restriction only applies where the expenses would be denied by ITA 18(1)(b) because they are capital in nature. There is a presumption that the costs of attending conventions are capital in nature as opposed to being on income account. In 2017 the CRA was asked whether the restriction would apply where the main purpose of attending conventions was for earning business and not capital. The CRA confirmed that the restriction would not apply in that case. An example of the difference would be a business where employees and owners attend conventions as a platform to sell and promote their products or services as opposed to other businesses where employees attend conventions for educational purposes.

Other Limitations on Deductions from Business and Property Income—Subdivision f

Introduction

6-135. The discussion of the ITA 9-12-18-20 rule provides a good understanding of both business and property income and expenses and how the rules of the ITA interact with accounting principles. Unfortunately, we are not quite done. Subdivision f of Division B of Part I of the ITA, which is titled "Rules Relating to the Computation of Income," provides some additional rules that apply in certain circumstances to expenses that have been claimed against a source of income that is employment, business, or property. These additional rules begin with the deduction determined after the application of the 9-12-18-20 rule and may modify that deductible amount. If Subdivision f does apply and modifies a deduction, then it is that modified amount that is used in the final calculation of business, property, and employment income.

6-136. Subdivision f contains ITA 67 to 80.6, which covers many situations. Some of the rules will be discussed in this chapter; some in subsequent chapters. Many others will not be discussed because they are specialized and well beyond the scope of introductory income tax courses. The focus in this part of the chapter is to look at some of the most important rules that apply to business and property income and that relate largely to what is allowed as an expense for meals and entertainment and expenses of financing and leasing certain automobiles.

Reasonableness—ITA 67

6-137. Subdivision f begins with a broad, general rule that limits deductible expenses to those that are "reasonable in the circumstances." This general limitation, which is applicable to the determination of business, property, or employment income, reads as follows:

> **ITA 67** In computing income, no deduction shall be made in respect of an outlay or expense in respect of which any amount is otherwise deductible under this Act, except to the extent that the outlay or expense was reasonable in the circumstances.

6-138. This reasonableness limitation is often applied in circumstances where a business expense is well in excess of what would normally be considered "reasonable." If, for example, a pet store owner were to deliver pets or pet supplies to clients in a $250,000 sports car or a salesperson decided to travel between Ottawa and Toronto in a private jet to attend a business meeting, expenses claimed would likely be considered excessive or "unreasonable." In such cases the effect of ITA 67 is not to deny the expense outright but to allow a portion of the expense that is "reasonable." Determining an acceptable amount often comes down to what a business person in similar circumstances would have done and expensed.

6-139. This reasonableness limitation is commonly applied by the CRA in non-arm's-length (e.g., family) situations, particularly those where salaries are paid to minor children (generally 18 years of age and younger). It is important to keep in mind, however, that ITA 67 only applies to modify a genuine expense that is linked to an existing source of income such as a business.

EXAMPLE 1 The parents of two children, ages six and eight, carry on a business and employ the two children, paying them salaries equal to the basic personal tax credit amount. The children run a few errands, sweep the floor, do a mail run, and perform a few other minor tasks. The involvement of the children allows them to spend time with their parents.

ANALYSIS 1 In this case ITA 67 is not necessary because there is no genuine business expense. The children are not employees. Aside from child labour laws, which would prevent the children from being employed by anyone, the children are not performing employment duties but simply assisting their parents as part of family life. [Based on the 1998 Tax Court decision in *Cousins v. Her Majesty the Queen* (1998 DTC 3366).]

EXAMPLE 2 The parents of a child owned a construction company that built residential homes. There were dozens of employees. The child began to accompany his parents to the work site beginning at the age of five and continued to learn everything he could about the construction business. By the age of 16 he had learned about all aspects of construction working as a carpenter. He worked at the various construction sites every day after school and each summer. By the time he was 17 he was supervising construction projects. He was paid a salary of $80,000 from the age of 16.

ANALYSIS 2 The CRA denied the salary to the child as unreasonable under ITA 67. The Tax Court determined that in this case there was a source of income (being the construction business) and that the child was working as an employee; therefore, the expense was genuine. The facts indicate that with the level of the son's experience the salary would be justified. In other words, no part of the salary expense to the company was considered unreasonable. [Based on the 1984 Tax Court decision in *Fred and Ted's Construction Ltd.*].

Meals and Entertainment

General Rules—ITA 67.1

6-140. Meal and entertainments expenses that have a business purpose would not be disallowed by either ITA 18(1)(a) or (h). Many years ago, however, the government decided that since most meal and entertainment expenses involve a personal element, these expenses should be restricted. Rather than resort to a pure reasonableness test, ITA 67.1 was enacted to address the concern by restricting expenses for the consumption of food or beverages or the enjoyment of entertainment to 50% of the lesser of the actual expenses and an amount that would be considered reasonable in the circumstances. In practice the reasonableness test is rarely applied, resulting in reducing meal and entertainment expense claims by 50% unless one of the many exceptions applies.

6-141. Meal and entertainment expenses are considered to include meals with customers; ticket costs to attend concerts, theatre, and sporting events; expenses to entertain guests at clubs (night, social, or other); the cost of cruises; the cost of private boxes at sporting events; and the cost of hospitality suites or room rentals for entertainment purposes. The CRA clarifies that meal expenses claimed while on vacation would be disallowed entirely. They add that the cost of season tickets to a sporting event would also be completely disallowed unless there was evidence that the cost represented a promotional expenditure, in which case 100% of the expense would be allowed.

Exceptions

6-142. Technically ITA 67.1 applies to reduce any meal expense by 50%. Meal expenses, however, can be included as part of moving expenses, child care expenses, adoption expenses, and even for medical expense purposes. Since the tax policy is to focus more on businesses, there are exceptions provided to ensure that the meal expenses are not reduced in any of those situations. Moving and child care expenses will be discussed in Chapter 9. Further exceptions to this general rule include the following:

ITA 67.1(1.1) provides an exception to the 50% for meal costs incurred by long-haul truck drivers during eligible travel periods (i.e., when they are away from home for at least 24 continuous hours). Individuals who are long-haul truck drivers and their employers can deduct 80% of the cost of eligible meals.

ITA 67.1(2) provides a number of additional exceptions for food and entertainment. Situations where the 50% rule does not apply include:

- Hotels, restaurants, and airlines that provide food, beverages, and entertainment in return for compensation from their customers. The costs incurred by these organizations in providing these goods and services continue to be fully deductible. However, when the employees of these organizations travel or entertain clients, their costs are subject to the 50% limitation for the employment expense deduction to them.
- Meals and entertainment expenses relating to a fundraising event for a registered charity are not subject to the 50% limitation and therefore are fully deductible.
- Where the taxpayer is compensated by someone else for the cost of food, beverages, or entertainment and the amount is separately identified in writing. Such amounts will be fully deductible against this compensation. For example, if Mr. Spinner was a management consultant and was reimbursed by his client for separately billed meals and entertainment, he could deduct 100% of these costs. However, his client would only be able to deduct 50% of the meal and entertainment expense that they were ultimately responsible for. This treatment is understandable given that the consultant would be required to include the full amount of the reimbursement in business income as part of the billing.
- When amounts are paid for meals or entertainment for employees and either the payments create a taxable benefit for the employee or the amounts do not create a taxable benefit because they are being provided at a remote work location, the amounts are not subject to the limitation to the employer.
- When amounts are incurred by an employer for food, beverages, or entertainment at a special event (e.g., Christmas parties and other similar events) that is generally available to all individuals employed by the taxpayer, the amounts are fully deductible. Note, however, that this exception applies to no more than six special events held by an employer during a calendar year. The events can be held at the employer's place of business, a restaurant, rented halls, and other locations.

6-143. In addition to the preceding exceptions, ITA 67.1(3) provides a special rule for meals that are included in conference or convention fees. When the amount included in the fee for meals and entertainment is not specified, this rule deems the amount to be $50 per day, which becomes the amount subject to the 50% limitation.

EXAMPLE Brigitte attends a five-day business conference at a cost of $1,000. Meals are provided throughout the conference but there is no dollar amount identified for the meals.

ANALYSIS ITA 67.1(3) will deem that $250 [(5 days)($50)] was paid for meals during the conference. As a result. Brigitte would be able to deduct $875 [(50%)($250) + $750] as a business expense.

6-144. Airline, bus, and rail tickets can include meals. The government views the value of such meals as being fairly immaterial, and as a result ITA 67.1(4) deems the cost of meals and entertainment to be nil, meaning that no part of the ticket price would be subject to the 50% limitation.

"Luxury" Automobile Costs

6-145. When a business provides an automobile that it owns or leases to an employee or shareholder, it is clear that the individuals have received a taxable benefit to the extent of any personal use. This fact, along with the methods used to calculate the taxable automobile benefit, was covered in detail in Chapter 3. The amount of the benefit is based on the actual cost of automobiles purchased or the actual lease payments.

6-146. As previously explained, income tax does not require symmetrical treatment of parties to the same transaction. A clear example of this lack of symmetry applies where an employer makes an employer-owned or -leased automobile available to an employee where part of the use of that automobile is for personal use. The calculation of the taxable benefit looks to the actual cost, but in the case of "luxury automobiles," the expenses to the employer in terms of CCA, lease payments, and any related interest expense is often restricted. These restrictions are consistent with the government's policy to discourage the use of "luxury" type automobiles, meaning those automobiles that typically fall into class 10.1 and class 54, which were discussed in Chapter 5.

> **EXAMPLE** An employee has the exclusive personal use of a class 10.1 automobile that has been acquired by the employer for $150,000. The automobile is available throughout all of the year.
>
> **ANALYSIS** The basic standby charge for each year would be $36,000 [(2%)(12)($150,000)]. The employer's CCA deduction, however, is based on only $30,000 for automobiles in class 10 and $55,000 for automobiles in class 54.

Automobiles Owned by the Taxpayer

Limits on CCA—ITA 13(7)(g) and (i)

6-147. With respect to automobiles owned and used in a business, ITA 13(7)(g) and (i) limit the amount upon which CCA can be claimed to a prescribed amount. With respect to automobiles, the prescribed amount has remained unchanged since 2001 at $30,000 plus GST/HST and PST. With respect to zero-emission automobiles the prescribed amount is currently $55,000 plus GST/HST and PST. These amounts would be reduced by any GST/HST that is recoverable as input tax credits.

Limits on Interest—ITA 67.2

6-148. When an automobile is owned and is classified as either a passenger vehicle or a zero-emission passenger vehicle that relates to a source of income, an interest expense is permitted in respect of the purchase (e.g., under ITA 8(1)(j) for employment and ITA 20(1)(c) for business or property income purposes). ITA 67.2 restricts the amount of interest that can be deducted to an amount determined by the following formula:

(A/30)(B), where

- **A** is a prescribed amount ($300 since 2001)
- **B** is the number of days in the period during which interest accrues

6-149. In general terms the application of the first part of the formula, "A/30," results in a daily limit of $10 [$300/30]. This interest limitation only applies to "automobiles" as defined by ITA 248(1), which are generally restricted to cars, trucks, vans, and SUVs that are not used primarily in the underlying activity and meet certain design features. As a rule, if the vehicle is included in class 10.1 or class 54 or would have been so included if its cost exceeded the dollar limit for that class (e.g., $30,000 or $55,000, respectively), then it will be subject to ITA 67.2.

Exercise 6-10

Subject: Deductible Automobile Expenses Where the Automobile Is Owned

On October 1, 2021, Ms. Vanessa Lord purchased an automobile to be used exclusively in a business she will carry on as a sole proprietor. The automobile is a class 10.1 vehicle. The business commenced September 15, 2021. The cost of the automobile was $45,000 before GST and PST. She finances a part of the purchase price and, as a consequence, has incurred interest charges for the period October 1 to December 31, 2021, of $1,200. In calculating her business income for 2021, how much can Ms. Lord deduct as interest expense with respect to the automobile purchase? Ignore GST and PST considerations.

Solutions to Exercises are available in the Study Guide.

Automobile Leasing Costs—ITA 67.3

Basic Formula (Cumulative)

6-150. When a business leases a passenger vehicle, ITA 67.3 restricts the deductibility of the lease payments to a prescribed amount. Since the introduction of the rules for "zero-emission passenger vehicle" in early 2019, the definition of a passenger vehicle now includes both the standard class 10.1 $30,000 limitation for non-zero-emission vehicles and class 54 zero-emission vehicles, the cost of which is capped at $55,000. The lease limitations that follow apply to each type of vehicle.

The basic formula that is used to implement this limitation is as follows:

$$\text{Basic Cumulative Formula} = \left[A \times \frac{B}{30}\right] - C - D - E\text{, where}$$

A is a prescribed amount ($800 for all passenger vehicles leased since 2001);

B is the number of days from the beginning of the term of the lease to the end of the current taxation year (or end of the lease if that occurs during the current year);

C is the total of all amounts deducted in previous years for leasing the vehicle;

D is a notional amount of interest since the inception of the lease, calculated at the prescribed rate on refundable amounts paid by the lessee in excess of $1,000;

E is the total of all reimbursements that became receivable before the end of the year by the taxpayer in respect of the lease.

6-151. In simplified terms, ITA 67.3 limits the monthly lease payments to a maximum of $800 (item A) plus GST/HST and PST for each 30-day period from the beginning of the lease through to the end of the current taxation year. Note that this is a cumulative amount over the entire lease term, meaning that the prescribed amount for the year in which the lease is signed is locked in throughout the whole lease term. That is, if the $800 limit were increased after 2021, the change would have no effect since the relevant prescribed rate of $800 was established for the year in which the lease began.

6-152. The formula also contains components that

- remove lease payments that were deducted in previous taxation years (item C);
- require the deduction of imputed interest on refundable deposits that could be used by the lessee to reduce the basic lease payments (item D); and
- remove reimbursements that are receivable by the taxpayer before the end of the year (item E).

6-153. In applying this formula, it is important to note that all of the components are cumulative from the beginning of the lease.

Anti-Avoidance Formula

6-154. While the basic concept of limiting the deductible lease amount to a maximum of $800 is fairly straightforward, leases could be structured to reduce the impact of the limitation. Almost any vehicle can be leased for less than $800 per 30-day period through such measures as extending the lease term, including a required purchase by the lessee at the end of the lease term at an inflated value, or paying a large amount up front. Because of this, a second formula is required and is based on the manufacturer's suggested list price for the vehicle and is as follows:

$$\text{Anti-Avoidance Formula} = \left[A \times \frac{B}{.85\,C}\right] - D - E, \text{ where}$$

- **A** is the total of the actual lease charges payable in the year;
- **B** is a prescribed amount ($30,000 for class 10.1 vehicles and $55,000 for class 54 zero-emission passenger vehicles);
- **C** is the greater of (1) a prescribed amount ($35,294 for class 10.1 vehicles and $64,706 for class 54 vehicles) and (2) the manufacturer's list price for the vehicle (note that this is the original value for the list price, even when a used vehicle is leased);
- **D** is a notional amount of interest for the current year, calculated at the prescribed rate on refundable amounts paid by the lessee in excess of $1,000;
- **E** is the total of all reimbursements that became receivable during the year by the taxpayer in respect of the lease.

6-155. Note that, unlike the calculations in the basic cumulative formula, the components of this formula are for the current year only. Also note that the 0.85 in the denominator is based on the assumption of a standard 15% discount off the manufacturer's list price. When the list price is $35,294 or $64,706, 85% of the amount is $30,000 or $55,000, respectively, leaving the component equal to one. This means that this component only applies when the list price exceeds either $35,294 or $64,706, respectively.

Deductible Amount

6-156. ITA 67.3 applies to limit the amount of lease payments deductible during a year to the least of

- the actual amount of the lease payments incurred in the year;
- the amount determined using the basic cumulative formula; or
- the amount determined using the anti-avoidance formula.

Example

6-157. The following example will serve to illustrate the application of these rules.

EXAMPLE An automobile, categorized as class 10.1 with a manufacturer's list price of $60,000 is leased on December 1, 2020, by a company for $1,612 per month, payable on the first day of each month. The term of the lease is 24 months and a refundable deposit of $10,000 is made at the beginning of the lease. In addition, the employee who drives the automobile pays the company $200 per month for any personal use. Assume that the prescribed rate is 2% per year for all periods under consideration. Ignoring GST/HST and PST implications, determine the maximum deductible lease payments for 2020 and 2021.

ANALYSIS—2020 For 2020, the D component in both of the ITA 67.3 formulae is $15 [(2%)($10,000 - $1,000)(31/365)]. The E component is $200 [($200)(1)]. The maximum deduction for 2020 is $612, the least of the following amounts:

- $1,612 (Actual lease payments in 2020)
- $612 (Basic cumulative formula)
- $733 (Anti-avoidance formula)

ANALYSIS—2021 Because the lease was entered into during 2020, the 2020 limit of $800 applies for the life of the lease. For 2021, the D components in the ITA 67.3 formula are $195 [(2%)($10,000 - $1,000)(396/365)] in the basic formula and $180 [(2%)($10,000 - $1,000)(365/365)] in the anti-avoidance formula.

The 2021 E components are $2,600 [($200)(13)] in the basic formula and $2,400 [($200)(12)] in the anti-avoidance formula.

The maximum deduction for 2021 is $7,153, the least of the following amounts:

- $19,344
- $7,153 (Basic cumulative formula)
- $8,799 (Anti-avoidance formula)

Exercise 6-11

Subject: Deductible Costs Where the Automobile Is Leased

On August 1, 2021, Mr. Sadim Humiz leases an automobile to be used 100% of the time in a business carried on as a sole proprietor. The lease cost is $985 per month. The manufacturer's suggested list price for the automobile is $78,000. Mr. Humiz makes no down payment and no refundable deposits. Determine his maximum deduction for lease payments for 2021. Ignore any GST/HST and PST considerations.

Solutions to Exerises are available in the Study Guide.

We suggest you complete SSP 6-6, 6-7, and 6-8 at this point.

Leasing Property—Some Accounting versus Income Tax Issues

6-158. While from a legal perspective leasing a property is a distinctly different transaction than purchasing the same property, the economic substance of many long-term leases is effectively the same as a financing arrangement. This fact has long been recognized by accounting standard setters, both in Canada and internationally. Accounting standards for leases require that, when a leasing arrangement transfers the usual risks and rewards of ownership to a lessee, the lease must be treated and presented as a sale by the lessor and a purchase by the lessee.

6-159. Throughout this text emphasis has been given to the fact that accounting concepts have little to do with income tax given that income tax concepts are based on legal principles. We have added that words and expressions used in the ITA almost always employ meanings based on legal definitions or legal principles established in the jurisprudence that have nothing to do with accounting. When the ITA refers to a "lease," it should come as no surprise that it means "a lease at law." This means that one examines the legal nature of the arrangement together with the contract to determine whether the terms and conditions are consistent with what one would expect in a legal lease. The Supreme Court of Canada has stated numerous times that the economic substance of a transaction cannot be used to recharacterize its legal nature. As a result, income tax law is not concerned with whether the risks and rewards in specific property have been transferred through what is a legal lease.

6-160. In terms of reconciliations, which is the next topic of discussion, the radical difference in the treatment of a lease for accounting purposes versus that of income tax can lead to potentially significant adjustments to reconcile accounting income to net income. However, the ITA offers an elective provision in ITA 16.1 that brings the income tax treatment much closer to that of accounting. ITA 16.1 allows the parties to the lease (i.e., the lessee and lessor) to elect to treat the lease as if it were a purchase of property rather than a lease. Such an election considerably narrows the differences between accounting and income tax but does not necessarily eliminate them altogether because of some of the complexity involved in the application of the income tax rules once such an election has been made.

Exercise 6-12

Subject: Leases: Income Tax versus Accounting Treatment

Markit Ltd. signs a 10-year lease for property with an economic life of 11 years. The lease payments are $23,000 per year. Compare the income tax treatment of the lease with its treatment under accounting standards.

Solutions to Exercises are available in the Study Guide.

Illegal Payments, Fines, and Penalties—ITA 67.5 and 67.6

6-161. The concept of a source of income, and specifically a business, does not draw any distinction concerning the legality of the activity. This means that illegal activity carried on with time, attention, and labour devoted to a profit-making activity would be considered a business. This means that any profits from such activity would be included in net and taxable income and would be subject to income tax. In the determination of "profit" we saw that expenses incurred for the purpose of earning business or property income are generally deductible within the limitations of the 9-12-18-20 rule. This would mean that expenses that are illegal would also be permissible unless there was specific legislation within the ITA to prevent an expense claim.

6-162. In Paragraphs 6-103 and 6-104 we saw that ITA 18(1)(t) blocked the claim of any expenses for penalties charged under the ITA, but that was as far as it went in terms of prohibiting the deduction of payments for wrongful action. Subdivision f includes two additional provisions that are designed to block the deduction of certain illegal payments.

6-163. Many years ago the front pages of major newspapers in Canada disclosed a number of scandals, uncovered in the course of an RCMP investigation, involving taxpayers caught in paying bribes and kickbacks to government officials that would enhance their businesses. The opposition at the time asked why the CRA was not simply disallowing such expenses. The government response was that the payments were likely deductible since they had a business purpose, irrespective that the payments were considered illegal. The government responded with the addition of ITA 67.5, which prohibits the deduction of payments made to Canadian or foreign government officials that constitute an offence under certain provisions of either the *Corruption of Public Foreign Officials Act* or Canada's *Criminal Code*.

6-164. In 1999 the Supreme Court heard the case of *65302 BC Ltd.* The company carried on a farming business of egg production. The company purposefully exceeded the quota limits established and paid fines under the relevant farm quota legislation. The CRA argued that the fines should not be deductible on the basis that allowing the deduction encouraged illegal behaviour. The court, however, ruled in favour of the company, allowing the expenses considering that they were incurred for the purpose of earning income and were therefore deductible through ITA 9 and not blocked by ITA 18(1)(a). The government responded shortly after the decision with the introduction of ITA 67.6, which disallows any fine or penalty imposed under a law of a country or of a political subdivision of a country other than certain fines and penalties imposed under the *Excise Act*. This means that tickets for parking and other traffic violations are not deductible.

Reconciliation Schedule

6-165. While it would be possible to calculate business income from scratch, starting with a blank page, adding inclusions, and subtracting deductions, this approach is rarely used. Since most businesses have an accounting system that produces accounting income based on accounting principles, the normal approach to determining business or property income is to start with accounting income, then make certain reconciling adjustments to adjust accounting amounts that are different for income tax purposes. Note, however, that some smaller businesses that do not require audited financial statements base their regular accounting system on income tax rules to avoid the necessity of reconciliations. Such financial statements are indicated as "Notice to reader" to clarify that they have not been the subject of an audit by accountants.

6-166. For those businesses that base their accounting system in whole or part on GAAP, a reconciliation between accounting and the ITA is required. The CRA provides a reconciliation schedule for corporations, which is schedule 1 of the T2 corporate income tax return (T2SCH1). The T2 schedule begins with a reference to schedule 125, which is where accounting-related information is required to be reported. The CRA also provides other forms and guides, such as the T5013 for partnerships and the T2125 for sole proprietorships to assist in the process.

6-167. In Figure 6-3 we have provided a modified reconciliation schedule, which represents some of the more common reconciliation adjustments for most taxpayers. In working with this schedule, there are a few general points to keep in mind:

- The reconciliation process first requires that both the accounting treatment and the income tax treatment is clearly understood. When a difference in treatment is identified, adjustments are made to reconcile the two to what is required by the ITA. For example, assume that the accounting income was calculated after deducting $30,000 for current-year income tax. As was previously discussed, income tax is not a permissible expense for the purposes of the ITA as a result of ITA 18(1)(a). The required adjustment to offset the income tax expense claimed for accounting purposes is simply to add the $30,000 to the accounting income figure. As a second example, assume that the accounting income includes depreciation expense of $47,000 but that the maximum CCA allowed would be $61,000. Technically a deduction could be made for an additional amount of $14,000, representing the additional expense provided by the CCA claim, but the preferable method is to make two adjustments. The first is to add back the depreciation of $47,000, which would be denied because of ITA 18(1)(b), then to separately deduct $61,000 as CCA as a result of ITA 20(1)(a). This is the method applied in the CRA reconciliations and in Figure 6-3.
- The CRA presumption in their reconciliation schedules (see the T2SCH1) is that accounting income is an after-tax concept. This means that any income tax expensed in the determination of accounting income, whether current or deferred taxes, must be added back in this reconciliation schedule.
- The amounts deducted for accounting purposes for amortization, scientific research, and resource amounts will generally be different from the amounts deducted for income tax purposes.
- Accounting adds gains on the disposition of capital property and deducts any losses often based on the accounting notion of carrying value. Since the ITA calculates gains and losses on capital property differently, the first step will be to reverse the accounting treatment by adding back any such accounting losses and deducting any accounting gains. Having offset the accounting treatment you can then determine the income tax implications and make the necessary adjustments (e.g., taxable capital gains, recapture, or terminal losses). In addition, any allowable capital losses that occur on the disposition of non-depreciable capital property can be adjusted assuming there are sufficient taxable capital gains to absorb the amounts. If there is an excess of allowable capital losses over taxable capital gains in the current year, the excess can be carried forward or carried back, but it cannot be deducted in the current year. As a consequence, such amounts are not included in this reconciliation schedule. These amounts are listed separately in Figure 6-3.

Figure 6-3
Reconciliation of Accounting Income to ITA Net Income

Additions to Accounting Income:

- Income tax expense
- Amortization, depreciation, and depletion of tangible and intangible assets (accounting amounts)
- Recapture of CCA
- Tax reserves deducted in the prior year
- Losses on the disposition of capital assets (accounting amounts)
- Pension expense (accounting amounts)
- Scientific research expenditures (accounting amounts)
- Warranty expense (accounting amounts)
- Amortization of discount on long-term debt issued (see discussion in Chapter 7)
- Foreign tax paid (accounting amounts)
- Excess of taxable capital gains over allowable capital losses
- Interest and penalties on income tax assessments
- Non-deductible automobile costs
- 50% of business meals and entertainment expenses
- Club dues and cost of recreational facilities
- Non-deductible reserves (accounting amounts)
- Charitable donations
- Asset write-downs including impairment losses on intangibles
- Fines, penalties, and illegal payments

Deductions from Accounting Income:

- Capital cost allowances (CCA)
- Incorporation costs (first $3,000)
- Terminal losses
- Tax reserves claimed for the current year
- Gains on the disposition of capital assets (accounting amounts)
- Pension funding contributions
- Deductible scientific research expenditures
- Deductible warranty expenditures
- Amortization of premium on long-term debt issued
- Foreign non-business tax deduction [ITA 20 (12)]
- Allowable business investment losses
- Landscaping costs

- You will note that there are no adjustments related to either sales or cost of goods sold (COGS). With respect to sales, this simply reflects the fact that the tax and accounting rules produce, in the great majority of situations, identical results. With respect to COGS, differences between the ITA and GAAP are not common.

Business Income—Example

Example Data

6-168. The Markee Company has a December 31 taxation year end and, for the year ending December 31, 2021, its accounting income before taxes amounted to $1,263,000. You have been asked to calculate the company's 2021 net income and have been provided with the following additional information for the 2021 year:

1. Accounting amortization expense totalled $240,000. For income tax purposes, the company intends to deduct CCA of $280,000.
2. Accounting income includes a gain on the sale of land in the amount of $20,000. For income tax purposes, one-half of this amount will be treated as a taxable capital gain.

3. During December, the company paid $35,000 on landscaping costs around a building used in the business. These costs were capitalized for accounting purposes with no amount being expensed because the expenditure was made near the end of the year.
4. The company increased its interest expense by $5,000 for accounting purposes because of the amortization of a bond discount.
5. Financing costs incurred during the year to raise additional capital by issuing new common stock totalling $60,000 were expensed for accounting purposes. None of the amounts relate solely to 2021.
6. Accounting expenses included $48,000 in business meals and entertainment.
7. During the year, the company begins selling a product on which it provides a five-year warranty. At the end of the year, it recognizes an estimated warranty liability of $20,000.
8. The company recognized a pension expense of $167,000. Actual contributions made to the pension fund during the year totalled $150,000.
9. The company leased an automobile for four years beginning on June 1, 2020, that was used by the sales manager throughout 2021. The vehicle is categorized as class 10.1. The lease payments were $750 per month and the manufacturer's suggested list price was $33,000. No refundable deposit was paid.

Example Analysis

6-169. The following points are relevant to the net income calculation:

- Item 1—The accounting amortization is added back and CCA is deducted.
- Item 2—The accounting gain is deducted to offset the accounting addition and the taxable capital gain is added.
- Item 3—Despite the fact that landscaping costs are usually capital expenditures, ITA 20(1)(aa) specifically permits their immediate deduction as long as the amounts relate to a building or structure used in the carrying on of a business and that the amounts are actually paid in the year.
- Item 4—ITA 20(1)(c) only allows the expensing of interest. Bond discount is not interest, and therefore its impact on interest expense is neutralized by adding it back to income.
- Item 5—Financing costs must be amortized over five years on a straight-line basis under ITA 20(1)(e) unless they relate solely to the year in which they were incurred, in which case the whole amount would be deductible in that year as a result of ITA 20(1)(e.1). Since none of the expenses relate solely to 2021, then ITA 20(1)(e) applies. As a result, only $12,000 is deductible in the current year; $60,000 is added back to neutralize the accounting expense; then $12,000 is deducted as the amount allowable for income tax purposes.
- Item 6—Only 50% of business meals and entertainment can be deducted, therefore $24,000 is added back to income.
- Item 7—Estimated warranty costs represent a contingent liability that is disallowed by ITA 18(1)(e). It is therefore added back to income to neutralize its impact.
- Item 8—Pension costs are capital in nature and therefore prohibited from an expense through ITA 18(1)(b). ITA 20(1)(q), however, overrides ITA 18(1)(b) and allows an expense but only when actually funded. The adjustment could have been shown as adding back $167,000 and separately deducting $150,000.
- Item 9—The lease payments are not limited by the restrictions described beginning in Paragraph 6-150 mainly because the monthly lease payments are less than $800 and the manufacturer's list price is less than $35,294 for a class 10.1 vehicle. As a result, the payments are fully deductible and no adjustment is required.

6-170. Based on the preceding analysis, the calculation of 2021 net income would be as follows:

Accounting income before taxes		$1,263,000
Additions (identified by item number):		
1—Accounting amortization	$240,000	
2—Taxable capital gain on land sale [(1/2)($20,000)]	10,000	
4—Bond discount amortization	5,000	
5—Financing costs	60,000	
6—Meals and entertainment [(50%)($48,000)]	24,000	
7—Warranty liability	20,000	
8—Unfunded pension expense ($167,000 - $150,000)	17,000	376,000
Deductions (identified by item number):		
1—Capital cost allowance (CCA)	($280,000)	
2—Accounting gain on sale of land	(20,000)	
3—Landscaping costs	(35,000)	(347,000)
5—Financing expenses [(20%)($60,000)] ITA 20(1)(e)	(12,000)	
Net income		$1,292,000

We suggest you complete SSP 6-9, 6-10, and 6-11 at this point.

Taxation Year

General Rules

6-171. The *ITA* defines a taxation year as follows:

ITA 249(1) For the purpose of this Act, a "taxation year" is

(a) in the case of a corporation or Canadian resident partnership, a fiscal period,
(b) in the case of a graduated rate estate, the period for which the accounts of the estate are made up for purposes of assessment under this Act, and
(c) in any other case, a calendar year.

ITA 249(1.1) When a "taxation year" is referred to by reference to a calendar year, the reference is to the taxation year or taxation years coinciding with, or that end in, that calendar year.

6-172. For corporations, ITA 249.1(1) defines a fiscal period as meaning the period for which the accounts in respect of the business have been made up for purposes of assessment under the ITA. That period cannot exceed 53 weeks. The additional week provides corporations with the opportunity to vary the year end for such things as inventory counts that may occur on certain days of the year.

6-173. A new corporation can select any fiscal year end as long as it complies with the 53-week restriction. Changes to an established fiscal period require ministerial approval except where the ITA applies to provide a corporation with an opportunity to select a new fiscal period (e.g., qualifying amalgamations). In almost all cases, corporations will have a fiscal period for income tax purposes that coincides with the fiscal period used for financial statement purposes.

6-174. The purpose of ITA 249(1.1) is to clarify that if a corporation's taxation year ends during the year, say June 30, 2021, then 2021 is considered to be its taxation year. Corporations, unlike individuals, can have multiple taxation years in the same calendar year. If, for example, the same corporation amalgamated with another corporation in September 2021 and that corporation's control was acquired in December 2021, there would be three 2021 taxation years, each requiring the filing of income tax returns.

Non-incorporated Businesses—Fiscal Period

6-175. Unlike corporations, individuals who carry on a business as a sole proprietor or as a member of a partnership have two relevant time periods for income tax purposes. The first is the taxation year, which is always the calendar year. The second is the fiscal period of a business that they carry on either singly as a sole proprietor or together with others in a partnership. Business profits or losses are included in the calendar taxation year of the individual based on the calendar year in which the last day of the fiscal period of the business ends.

> **ITA 11(1) Proprietor of a business** ... If an individual is a proprietor of a business, the individual's income from the business for a taxation year is deemed to be the individual's income from the business for the fiscal period of the business that ends in the year.

The words "taxation year" and "year" in ITA 11(1) refer to the calendar year.

> **EXAMPLE** Yixuan carries on a business as a sole proprietor. The fiscal period of the business ends July 31, 2021.
>
> **ANALYSIS** Yixuan is required to include the profits of the business for the fiscal period of the business ending July 31, 2021, in her 2021 taxation year since the last day of the fiscal, July 31, 2021, is in the 2021 calendar year.
>
> While not shown here, ITA 96(1)(f) and (g) require the same treatment where an individual is a member of a partnership. Partnerships are discussed in Chapter 18.

6-176. Many years ago (1995 to be exact) the government became extremely concerned with tax deferral opportunities by individuals carrying on businesses as a sole proprietor or as a member of a partnership composed of other individuals. The concern was that individuals could select any fiscal period for their business, with income taxes only payable on business profits based on the last day of the fiscal period, which could defer income taxes by up to one year.

> **EXAMPLE 1** Serban carries on a business that he began February 1, 2021, as a sole proprietor. The fiscal period of the business is the calendar year and ends December 31. Therefore, his first fiscal period is February 1, 2021, to December 31, 2021.
>
> **ANALYSIS 1** Serban will include the business profits in his 2021 income tax return, which has to be filed by June 15, 2022. The income taxes, however, have to paid by April 30, 2022.
>
> **EXAMPLE 2** Serban carries on a business beginning February 1, 2021, but chooses January 31 as the fiscal period. Therefore, the first fiscal period of the business is February 1, 2021, to January 31, 2022.
>
> **ANALYSIS 2** Since the fiscal period of the business ends January 31, 2022, the business profits are only required to be included in Serban's income for the 2022 taxation year ,which is only required to be filed June 15, 2023, with income taxes payable April 30, 2023. The difference means that no income taxes have to be paid on business profits earned for the period February 1, 2021, to December 31, 2021, until one year later, which is April 30, 2023. This result occurs because of a simple selection of a fiscal period from December 31 of one year to January 31 of the next year.

6-177. In response to this deferral concern the government modified the definition of a fiscal period to require individual proprietors and partnerships composed of individuals to use a December 31 fiscal period year end for the business. The government did, however, recognize that there could be legitimate business reasons (not income tax-motivated reasons) for choosing a fiscal period other than December 31. As a result, the government allowed an elective option through ITA 249.1(4) to choose a non-calendar fiscal period for a business. This election is only available if made for the first year of the business and filed by June 15 of the year following the year in which the business commences. The election cannot be made in a subsequent year.

6-178. In our previous example, if Serban elected to choose January 31, 2022, as the fiscal period end it should be clear that the government would not be prepared to defer income taxes on the business profits earned from February 1, 2021, to December 31, 2021, since this was the initial concern. This would mean that a mechanism would be required to estimate the business profits for that 11-month period and require Serban to include that amount in his income tax return for 2021. When calculating business profits for the next fiscal period, February 1, 2022, to January 31, 2023, the business profits would represent those for the fiscal period ending January 31, 2022, minus that part of the amount that Serban would have included in his 2021 business income plus another similar calculation to cover the period February 1, 2022, to December 31, 2022. This created a reserve-like system that accounts for much of the complexity of these elective fiscal period rules. The rules allow for some flexibility for the first year, however.

6-179. In Serban's case he could elect to begin for the 2021 or 2022 years. If, for example, his business profit for the fiscal period ending January 31, 2022, is $150,000, he can elect to include $137,260 [(334 days to December 31, 2021/365 days in the fiscal period ending January 31, 2022) ($150,000)] as business income for 2021 and the remaining $12,740 [$150,000 - $137,260] for 2022. In addition, he would be required to include an additional amount of $137,260 using the same calculation for the period February 1, 2022, to December 31, 2022, resulting in business profits of $150,000 included for his 2022 taxation year. The alternative is to defer the 2021 amounts to 2022, which would result in 2022 business profits of $287,260 [$150,000 to January 31, 2022 + $137, 260 from February 1, 2022, to December 31, 2022], which would place him in the highest income tax bracket of 33%.

6-180. ITA 34.1(1) requires individual taxpayers to calculate and include the required stub period business income to December 31 for the years following the year in which the business began. ITA 34.1(2) applies to allow a pro-rated amount to be included in the income for the year in which the business started only with respect to the first fiscal period of that business that begins in the year and ends in the next year. Once the election is made, the additional business income must be determined annually under ITA 34.1(1) until the election is cancelled or revoked. The ITA 34.1(2) election is not automatic and is at the option of the business owner. CRA form T1139 provides additional information. A simple example will illustrate this process using only the ITA 34.1(1) election.

> **EXAMPLE** Jack Bartowski forms a new business on November 1, 2020. Because of the cyclical nature of his business, he chooses a January 31 year end as it is a slow time in the business. Between November 1, 2020, and January 31, 2021, he has business profits of $25,000. During the fiscal year from February 1, 2021, ending January 31, 2022, the business profits are $80,000.
>
> **ANALYSIS—2020** Since the first fiscal period begins in one year (2020) and ends in the following year (2021), Jack has the option of electing under ITA 34.1(2) to pro-rate the business profits based on the number of days and to include that amount in the 2020 year with the remainder included as business income for 2021. The results would be to include $16,576 in 2020 [($25,000)(61/92 days)] and the remaining $8,424 in 2021. We assume that Jack decides not to make this election.
>
> **ANALYSIS—2021** The period November 1, 2020, through January 31, 2021, has 92 days. The period from February 1, 2021, to December 31, 2021, has 334 days. Based on this, the "additional business income" (ITA 34.1(1)) that must be added for 2021 is calculated as follows:
>
> $$[(\$25,000)(334 \text{ days} \div 92 \text{ days})] = \underline{\underline{\$90,761}}$$

The business income that will be reported by Mr. Bartowski in his 2021 personal tax return is calculated as follows:

Actual business income:	
November 1, 2020, to January 31, 2021	$ 25,000
Additional business income:	
February 1, 2021, to December 31, 2021 (estimate)	90,761
2021 business income	$115,761

Note that he will be taxed on his estimated business income for 14 months if reporting for this 14-month period.

ANALYSIS—2022 The "additional business income" that must be added for 2022 is calculated as follows:

$$[(\$80,000)(334 \text{ days} \div 365 \text{ days})] = \underline{\underline{\$73,205}}$$

The 2022 business income will be calculated by taking the actual figure for February 1, 2021, through January 31, 2022, deducting the additional business income that was included in 2021, and adding the new additional business income for the period February 1, 2022, through December 31, 2022. The calculations are as follows:

Actual business income—February 1, 2021, to January 31, 2022	$ 80,000
Additional business income:	
Deduction of estimated amount added In 2021	(90,761)
Addition of estimate of income for February 1 to December 31, 2022	73,205
2022 business income	$ 62,444

Exercise 6-13

Subject: Additional Business Income—Non-calendar Fiscal Year

Mr. Morgan Gelato commenced business on March 1, 2021. Because it will be a slow time of year for him, he intends to have a fiscal year that ends on January 31, 2022. During the period March 1, 2021, through January 31, 2022, his business profits are $102,000. He will elect to use a January 31 fiscal year end. What amount of business income will Mr. Gelato report in his personal tax return for the years ending December 31, 2021, and December 31, 2022, if (1) he chooses the first-year elective option under ITA 34.1(2) and (2) does not choose the ITA 34.1(2) elective option?

Solutions to Exercises are available in the Study Guide.

We suggest you complete SSP 6-12 at this point.

Special Business Income Situations

Income for Farmers

Restricted Farm Losses—ITA 31

6-181. We have seen that a source of income includes businesses. Farming businesses, however, receive special attention in the ITA as a result of legislation that goes back decades. The effect of this legislation is to categorize farming into three broad categories of farming activity. The first are those individuals engaged in farming activity on a full-time basis, year round, where the farms often include thousands of acres, significant amounts of equipment and machinery, and livestock. The second category are those involved in a farming business that does not necessarily produce significant enough returns, with the result that those involved in the activity rely on other sources of income such as employment or investments to provide the necessary funds to meet daily needs. The third category are what are often referred to as hobby farmers, meaning those individuals who dabble to some degree in farming, often motivated by personal interests rather than a profit motive.

6-182. This distinction is important. The first category can be described as "full-time farming," the second category as "part-time farming," and the third as "hobby farming." When it comes to the ITA, expenses and therefore losses are not recognized unless the activity qualifies as a source of income. Full-time farmers are clearly involved in a source of income—that is, a business—and there are no restrictions on what can be claimed as expenses (and therefore losses) except to the extent of restrictions under the 9-12-18-20 rule that apply to any other type of business.

6-183. The farming activity of hobby farmers would not be considered a source of income and therefore no business is considered to exist, meaning that no expenses or losses can be claimed at all.

6-184. The middle category of part-time farming has reached a point that it is considered a business and therefore a source of income. This means that the activity should be treated the same as full-time farming, however it is not. In the early 1950s it was recognized that financially well-off Canadians living in major cities in Canada were purchasing properties in the countryside, establishing a small farming operation, and using farming losses to subsidize their purchases with lower income taxes. The government response was the introduction of what is currently ITA 31, which restricts what can be claimed as a farming loss where the farming activity is not the individual's main source of income (i.e., the part-time farmers). ITA 31 splits a farm loss into two pieces: a restricted farm loss (RFL) and an unrestricted farm loss. The unrestricted part of the loss is treated the same as a farm loss of a full-time farmer. The restricted part of the loss, however, is "streamed," which means that the losses can be deducted in future years against any profits from that same farming business only. If the farming business never shows a profit, then none of the RFL can ever be deducted.

6-185. ITA 31 sets the unrestricted portion of a farm loss as equal to the following amounts:

1. Farm loss between $1 and $2,500 = The farm loss
2. Farm loss between $2,500 and $32,500 = $2,500 + 50% of the farm loss above $2,500
3. Farm loss of $32,500 and higher = $17,500

EXAMPLE 1 Farm loss = $1,800

ANALYSIS 1 Unrestricted loss = $1,800 and no RFL

EXAMPLE 2 Farm loss = $44,000

ANALYSIS 2 Unrestricted loss = $17,500 and RFL = $26,500 [$44,000 - $17,500]

EXAMPLE 3 Farm loss = $21,000

ANALYSIS 3 Unrestricted farm loss = $11,750 [$2,500 + (50%)($18,500)]

The RFL would be $9,250 [$21,000 - $11,750]

In each case the amount identified as a farm loss can be deducted in the year of the loss against any type of income. The RFL, however, is streamed to future years to the extent there is farming profits from that same business.

Exercise 6-14

Subject: Restricted Farm Losses

Ms. Suzanne Morph is a high school teacher. To help finance the annual family vacation, she has been growing zucchinis for sale in a little plot next to her house. Her investment in time and money in this endeavour has been small, but the growing conditions are ideal for zucchinis. Although she has no farming background, in most years she has made a small profit selling at the weekly farmers' market for two months in the summer. However, she incurred a loss in 2021 of $18,700 due to poor weather. How much of this loss is deductible in her 2021 income tax return? Calculate any restricted farm loss carry over available to her. Assume that the activity is a source of income but is subject to ITA 31. What would be the result if it were determined that the activity had no actual profit motive?

Solutions to Exercises are available in the Study Guide.

Professional Income (Work-in-Process [WIP])

The Problem

6-186. When a business involves the provision of professional services, clients are often billed on a periodic basis, normally after a block of work has been completed. This block of work may be task defined (e.g., billing when a client's tax return is finished), time defined (e.g., billing on a monthly basis), or on some other basis. However, in the majority of professional income situations, billing does not occur until after the work has been completed. This leads to year-end work-in-process (WIP), which refers to amounts that are expected to become receivable after the end of the year. The following simple example illustrates this situation.

EXAMPLE Joan Martin commenced carrying on the business of a law practice on January 1, 2021. During the year ending December 31, 2021, she provides legal services to clients that have a value of $175,000. She bills clients for $150,000 of this amount, collecting a total of $120,000 of the billed amount. At December 31, 2021, she has unbilled WIP of $25,000 ($175,000 - $150,000).

ANALYSIS As business income is based on income that is receivable or has the quality of income, Joan would have to include income on all of the services provided in the year. This amount would be $175,000, including the unbilled WIP of $25,000. The amount collected has no effect on the result, which simply depends on whether there is an absolute and unconditional entitlement to amounts irrespective of when they are actually paid.

6-187. For many years, ITA 34 provided a special provision that allowed certain professionals to exclude unbilled WIP from their business income. This elective option was available to accountants, dentists, lawyers, medical doctors, and veterinarians. It was not available to other professionals such as architects, engineers, and management consultants. This special treatment ended in 2017 because of the mismatch where expenses incurred toward WIP would be claimed in one year and the related income from the WIP would only be included in a future year.

6-188. ITA 10(4) and 10(5) treat WIP as inventory, meaning it is subject to the same lower of cost and fair market value concept discussed in Paragraphs 6-126 to 6-133. FMV is defined as meaning the amount that can reasonably be expected to become receivable after the end of the year. As a result, the value used for the WIP is required to be included in business income.

We suggest you complete SSP 6-13 and 6-14 at this point.

Sale of a Business

General Rules

6-189. ITA 22 through 25 contain a group of provisions that apply when a person who has carried on a business ceases to carry on the business and sells substantially all of the property of the business in the course of bringing that business to an end. These rules are designed to recognize that because the business comes to an end there is no longer any source of income, which can result in some unusual circumstances. These rules are designed to overcome some of the concerns.

Inventories—ITA 23

6-190. When a business has ceased to be carried on, not all of the inventory may have been sold. Once the business ceases to exist the property that was inventory is no longer inventory because the ITA defines it in terms of an existing business. This means that what was previously inventory would be non-depreciable capital property in the absence of the business. If the previous business owner sells the remaining property there would be a potential capital gain or capital loss. ITA 23 is included to ensure that a subsequent sale of what was once inventory is treated as if the business never ceased. This would mean that any gain is fully included in business income and any loss is treated as a fully deductible business loss. We would add that ITA 13(8) contains a similar rule where property that was once depreciable property is sold after a business has ceased to exist.

Accounts Receivable—ITA 22 Election

6-191. When a sale of a business by one person to another includes the sale of existing accounts receivables there are two income tax issues that arise. The first problem affects the seller. The problem is that since the receivables are non-depreciable capital property, any loss on their sale would be considered a capital loss, only one-half of which would be deductible and only against taxable capital gains. In other words if an account receivable for $1,000 was sold for $900, the $100 difference would not be a $100 business expense/deduction but rather a $50 allowable capital loss (to be discussed in Chapter 8).

6-192. The second problem impacts the purchaser. No doubtful debt reserve can be claimed under ITA 20(1)(l) for any purchased accounts receivable that become doubtful of collection nor can any bad debt deduction under ITA 20(1)(p) be claimed for the same receivables. The reason is because both of those income tax provisions restrict any claim to the person who included the receivables in his income, which is the seller and not the purchaser.

6-193. ITA 22 resolves both problems but requires a joint election by the vendor and purchaser of the business. If the election is made, the seller can treat any loss on the accounts receivables as a fully deductible business expense. The purchaser, however, is required to include that same amount in her business income. The election also adds rules that effectively allow the purchaser to claim both doubtful debt reserves under ITA 20(1)(l) and bad debts through ITA 20(1)(p) with respect to the purchased accounts receivables. The following example illustrates the application of this election.

EXAMPLE Mr. Whitney agrees to buy Mr. Blackmore's business. As part of the transaction, Mr. Whitney acquires Mr. Blackmore's accounts receivables for $25,000. These receivables have a face value of $30,000, and Mr. Blackmore has deducted a $4,000 reserve for doubtful debts with respect to these receivables in the preceding year.

ANALYSIS—Vendor Whether or not the election is made under ITA 22, Mr. Blackmore will have to include the $4,000 reserve in business income (ITA 12(1)(d)). If no election is made, he will realize an allowable capital loss of $2,500 [(1/2)($30,000 - $25,000)]. Assuming Mr. Blackmore has taxable capital gains against which the $2,500 loss can be deducted, the transaction will result in a net inclusion in income of $1,500 ($4,000 - $2,500).

In contrast, if the ITA 22 election is made, Mr. Blackmore would still have to include the $4,000 reserve in income. However, it will be offset by a business deduction of $5,000 on the sale of the receivables, a distinct improvement over the results with no election. Under this approach, there will be a net deduction from income of $1,000 [$4,000 - $5,000].

ANALYSIS—Purchaser From the point of view of Mr. Whitney, if no election is made he will recognize a tax cost of $25,000 for the receivables, which represent capital property. If more or less than $25,000 is actually collected, the difference will be a capital gain or a capital loss.

If, however, the ITA 22 election is made, he will have to include the $5,000 difference between the face value and the price paid in income in the year the receivables are acquired. Subsequent to the sale, any difference between the $30,000 face value of the receivables and amounts actually collected will be fully deductible in the calculation of business income. Mr. Whitney could establish a new reserve for doubtful debts related to the purchased receivables that are still outstanding at year end. If the amount collected is equal to $25,000, Mr. Whitney will be in exactly the same position whether or not the election is made. If more than $25,000 is collected, he will be worse off with the election because 100% rather than only 50% of the excess will be taxable. Correspondingly, if less than $25,000 is collected, he will be better off with the election as the shortfall will be fully deductible.

Exercise 6-15

Subject: Sale of Receivables

During 2021, Mr. Donato Nero is selling the business he carried on as a sole proprietor to Mr. Labelle. The sale includes the outstanding accounts receivable, which will be sold for $48,200. The receivables have a face value of $53,450. In 2020, Mr. Nero had deducted a reserve for doubtful debts of $3,800. Determine the 2021 income tax consequences of the sale of the accounts receivables for both Mr. Nero and Mr. Labelle if they jointly elect under ITA 22.

Solutions to Exercises are available in the Study Guide.

We suggest you complete SSP 6-15, 6-16, and 6-17 at this point.

Key Terms

A full glossary with definitions is provided at the end of the Study Guide.

Accrual Basis
Allowable Capital Loss
Billed Basis
Business
Business Income
Capital Property
Capital Gain/Loss
Cash Basis
Crowdfunding
Fiscal Period
GAAP
Hobby Farmer
Inventory
Net Income
Property Income
Reserve
Restricted Farm Loss (RFL)
Soft Costs
Taxable Capital Gain
Taxation Year

References

For more detailed study of the material in this chapter, we would refer you to the following:

ITA 9	Income
ITA 10	Valuation of Inventory
ITA 12	Income Inclusions
ITA 18	General Limitations [on Deductions]
ITA 20	Deductions Permitted in Computing Income from Business or Property
ITA 22	Sale of Accounts Receivable
ITA 23	Sale of Inventory
ITA 24	Ceasing to Carry on Business
ITA 28	Farming or Fishing Business
ITA 31	Loss from Farming Where Chief Source of Income Not Farming
ITA 67	General Limitation Re Expenses
ITA 67.1	Expenses for Food
ITA 67.2	Interest on Money Borrowed for Passenger Vehicle
ITA 67.3	Limitation Re Cost of Leasing Passenger Vehicle
ITA 67.5	Non-Deductibility of Illegal Payments
ITA 67.6	Non-Deductibility of Fines and Penalties
S4-F2-C1	Deductibility of Fines or Penalties
S4-F2-C2	Business Use of Home Expenses
IT-99R5	Legal and Accounting Fees (Consolidated)
IT-148R3	Recreational Properties and Club Dues
IT-154R	Special Reserves
IT-188R	Sale of Accounts Receivable
IT-287R2	Sale of Inventory
IT-322R	Farm Losses
IT-357R2	Expenses of Training
IT-359R2	Premiums and Other Amounts with Respect to Leases
IT-364	Commencement of Business Operations
IT-417R2	Prepaid Expenses and Deferred Charges
IT-442R	Bad Debts and Reserves for Doubtful Debts
IT-459	Adventure or Concern in the Nature of Trade
IT-473R	Inventory Valuation
IT-475	Expenditures on Research and for Business Expansion
IT-479R	Transactions in Securities
IT-487	General Limitation on Deduction of Outlays or Expenses
IT-518R	Food, Beverages, and Entertainment Expenses
IT-521R	Motor Vehicle Expenses Claimed by Self-Employed Individuals

Self-Study Problems (SSPs)

Self-Study Problems (SSPs) provide practice in problem solving. Within the chapters, we have indicated where it would be appropriate to stop and work on each SSP. The problems can be downloaded by chapter from MyLab Accounting. Solutions are available in the Study Guide. Select problems can also be completed directly in MyLab and auto-graded.

Assignment Problems

Solutions to Assignment Problems (APs) are available to instructors only.

AP 6-1 (Reserves)
Olivia Smith carries on a landscaping business as a sole proprietor. The business began operations on January 2, 2021, and has a December 31 year end. The 2021 and 2022 results for the business can be described as follows:

> **2021** During its first year, the business had sales of delivered merchandise and services totalling $185,000. Of this total, $65,000 are shown as accounts receivable on December 31, 2021. Olivia anticipates that $5,000 of the receivables are doubtful of collection.
>
> In addition to these sales of delivered merchandise and services, she received $23,000 in advances for merchandise to be delivered in 2022.
>
> Olivia purchased a large supply of landscaping materials from the trustee of a bankrupt landscaping business at a very good price. Since she is unlikely to use them in the next few years, she has arranged to sell these materials for $50,000. The sale takes place in September 2021. These materials have a cost of $40,000, resulting in a total gross profit of $10,000. Because of the size of this sale, she has agreed to accept a down payment of $30,000, followed by two annual instalments of $10,000. The instalments are due on December 31, 2022, and December 31, 2023.
>
> **2022** During 2022, $5,500 of accounts receivable were determined to be bad and were written off. All of the merchandise for which advances had been received was delivered and the $10,000 instalment on the 2021 sale of landscaping materials was received.
>
> Sales of delivered merchandise and services totalled $240,000. Of this total, $50,000 are shown as accounts receivables at December 31, 2021. Olivia anticipates that $3,500 of this amount will be doubtful of collection.
>
> In addition to the 2022 sales of delivered merchandise and services, she receives $13,400 in advances for merchandise to be delivered in 2023.

Required: How would the preceding information affect the calculation of Olivia Smith's business income for the 2021 and 2022 taxation years? Include the full details of your calculations, not just the net result for each year.

AP 6-2 (Deductible Automobile Costs and Taxable Benefit)
Bryan's Computer Services Ltd. is a Canadian controlled private corporate (CCPC) with a December 31 year end. The company provides various types of computer services to clients in the Ottawa region. Bryan Base is the sole shareholder and only employee of the company.

As most of his services are provided on an in-house basis, Bryan must travel extensively. Because of this the company provides him with an automobile. During the first five months of 2021, Bryan was provided with a Chevrolet Malibu that the company purchased in 2020 for $26,000. On June 1, 2021, the company provided him with a Lexus GS that it had acquired for $72,000. The Lexus dealer gave the company $14,000 for the Malibu as a trade in. On January 1, 2021, the company's class 10 UCC was $14,300.

Information on Bryan's use of the two automobiles is as follows:

> **Chevrolet Malibu** During the period January 1, 2021, through May 31, 2021, Bryan drove a total of 35,000 kilometres, of which 22,000 were business related and 13,000 were for personal use.

Lexus GS During the period June 1, 2021, through December 31, 2021, Bryan drove a total of 47,000 kilometres, of which 22,000 were business related and 25,000 were for personal use.

These were the only automobiles owned by the company during 2021.

Throughout 2021, the company paid for all of the operating costs of both automobiles, a total for the year of $18,040 without reimbursement from Bryan.

Required: Determine the following:

A. The income tax consequences to Bryan's Computer Services Ltd. that result from owning and selling the Chevrolet Malibu and owning the Lexus GS during 2021.

B. The minimum amount of the taxable benefit that Bryan will have to include in his net income for 2021.

Ignore GST/HST & PST considerations in your solution.

AP 6-3 (Employer-Provided vs. Employee-Owned Automobile)

Emmitt Industries is a Canadian public company. Many of its employees require an automobile for use in their employment duties. Given the nature of the business, a luxury automobile is required. For employees to meet this requirement, the company offers them alternatives:

Alternative 1 The company will provide the automobile and pay all of the operating costs, including those related to the employee's personal use. The automobile will be available to the employee on a full-time basis throughout the three-year term of their employment contracts. It will be returned to the company at the end of that period.

Alternative 2 The company will provide the employee with an interest-free loan for the cost of the purchase. No payments are required on the loan but it must be repaid in full after three years. The employee will pay all of the operating costs for the automobile and, to assist with these costs, the company will provide the employee with an allowance of $3,000 per month. The employee will retain ownership of the automobile at the end of his employment contract.

Jonathan Welch has an employment contract with the company. The contract commences on January 1, 2021, and covers the three years ending December 31, 2023. His salary puts him in the highest income tax bracket. Given this, the combined federal/provincial income tax rate that is effective for any additional income or deductions is 52% [33% federal + 19% provincial].

Jonathan has chosen a Mercedes S450 sedan as the automobile he would like to use. The cost of this automobile is $130,000.

In order to make a decision on these alternatives, Jonathan recognizes the need to make estimates of both operating costs and use of the automobile. The estimates that he will use in making his decision are as follows:

- He anticipates driving the vehicle 72,000 kilometres each year, with 17,000 of these kilometres for personal use and 55,000 for employment-related use.
- If he purchases the automobile, he estimates that his operating costs will average $0.35 per kilometre over the three-year term of his employment contract. At the end of the employment contract, he anticipates being able to sell the automobile for $65,000.

Assume that the prescribed rate for the operating cost benefit is $0.27 per kilometre in all of the years 2021 through 2023, and that the prescribed interest rate is 2% for all years.

Required: Advise Jonathan as to which of the alternatives he should accept. Base your decision on the undiscounted cash flows associated with the two alternatives. Ignore GST/HST & PST considerations.

AP 6-4 (Inventory Valuation)
Jasper Retailers Inc. began business on January 1 of the current year. Inventory purchases during the year are as follows:

Date	Quantity	Price	Total Cost
January 1	15,000	$10.00	$ 150,000
March 1	35,000	$11.00	385,000
June 15	42,000	$11.50	483,000
September 1	27,000	$12.00	324,000
October 1	17,000	$12.50	212,500
Totals	136,000		$1,554,500

On December 31, the end of the company's taxation year, 22,000 units remain on hand. It is estimated that these units have a replacement cost of $10.50 per unit and a net realizable value of $11.75 per unit.

Required: Calculate the various closing inventory values that could be used to determine business income for income tax purposes. Your answer should indicate the valuation method being used, as well as the resulting value.

AP 6-5 (Proprietorship—Reverse Business Income)
Several years ago George Danton, after being laid off, decided he could benefit from his love of flowers by opening a flower shop. The shop uses a December 31 taxation year. The business has been a great success, both in terms of being profitable and in enhancing George's enjoyment of life.

As George is the sole proprietor of the business, he has had no need to report income to anyone. Given this, he has always used income tax concepts and principles to calculate his annual business income. Based on these income tax principles, George determine that his business income for the year ended December 31, 2021 was $613,300.

George has decided to expand his business into a neighbouring town. To do this, he needs a mortgage on the property that will be acquired for operations in the new location. To his dismay, he finds that the lender is insisting on financial statements prepared in accordance with Accounting Standards for Private Enterprises (ASPE).

As he has no knowledge of ASPE, he has asked you to determine the amount of ASPE-based income that Danton's Flowers has earned for the 2021 year.

Other Information:

1. In the business income calculation based on income tax (ITA 67.1), George deducted $8,450 in business meals and entertainment costs.
2. Because his shop is near the U.S. border, George spent $7,420 advertising on a U.S. television station. The commercials were directed at Canadian resident viewers.
3. Because of a broken window during early December, live flowers costing $6,320 were destroyed.
4. During 2021, George paid a high-level Canada customs official bribes totalling $19,460. In return, he received priority clearance for all his imports, as well as clearance for live plant imports that should have been restricted. Since this bribe is considered to be an illegal payment to a government official, it is not deductible for income tax purposes.
5. During 2021, George made $6,300 in contributions to a local hospital that is a registered charity. He claimed this amount as a business expense.

6. For income tax purposes, the method chosen to value ending inventory is FMV, which is $86,300. The cost, determined on a FIFO basis, was $73,150.
7. George deducted $51,400 in CCA for the year. You have determined that amortization under ASPE would have been $46,350.
8. George spent $6,070 on uniforms for the local men's softball team, whose games are heavily attended and supported by the community.
9. George owns a delivery vehicle that cost $29,000. It is the only class 10 property of the business and, as of January 1, 2021, the class had a UCC balance of $8,455. During the year, the vehicle is sold for $4,300 and replaced with a leased vehicle. Under ASPE, its carrying value at the time of the sale would have been $14,500. The leasing costs are fully deductible for income tax purposes.
10. In December 2021, George spent $15,200 on landscaping the grounds around his store. Given the late date at which this work was done, no amortization would be required for accounting purposes with respect to these costs for 2021. It is expected that these landscaping improvements will last at least 10 years.
11. During 2021, George sold class 8 property for $21,300. The capital cost of the property sold was $32,600. At the end of the year the UCC of class 8 was positive and other properties remained in the class. The accounting carrying value of the property that was sold was $18,300.
12. No income taxes were deducted in calculating net income.

Required: Determine the 2021 ASPE-based accounting income for Danton's Flowers. Do not include in your calculations any income tax that George will have to pay on this income. If you do not make an adjustment for any of the items included in other information, indicate why this is the case.

General Comment This reverse reconciliation exercise requires using the opposite approach applied in a typical reconciliation from accounting income to net income. For example, amortization would be added and CCA deducted in a standard reconciliation. In this reverse approach, however, amortization would be deducted and CCA added.

AP 6-6 (Proprietorship—Business Income with CCA)

Cody Jewel is an accountant who has not incorporated his professional practice. The practice has a December 31 year end.

Cody carries on the business of a professional practice in a building that he owns. He purchased the building in 2018 for $550,000, with the estimated value of the land at that time being $125,000 and the remaining $425,000 attributable to the building. Cody's practice occupies 100% of the building and, because it was a new building when he acquired it, he has elected to place it in a separate class 1. On January 1, 2021, the building has a UCC of $380,000.

Because he is attracting an increasingly wealthy clientele, Cody has decided to upgrade his office. During February 2021, he replaces all of his old furniture and fixtures. The old furniture and fixtures had a capital cost of $65,000 and an opening UCC of $41,000. It is all sold for $22,000. The new furniture and fixtures have a capital cost of $136,000.

Other property acquisitions during 2021 are as follows:

New computer	$1,800
Applications software	2,700
Client list from retiring accountant	32,000

Because he has started to provide in-home services for many of his clients, he has an automobile that is used largely for this purpose. Cody purchased the automobile for $56,000 on

January 1, 2021. The automobile is not a zero-emission vehicle. During 2021, it is driven a total of 23,000 kilometres, of which 21,000 kilometres relate to business use and only 2,000 kilometres for personal use. Operating costs for the year totalled $4,140.

Other 2021 costs of carrying on the business, determined on an accrual basis, are as follows:

Building operating costs	$18,600
Payments to assistants	31,200
Miscellaneous office costs	9,400
Meals with clients	10,500

Revenues for the year ending December 31, 2021, were $224,000.

Required: Calculate the minimum business income Cody would include in his 2021 personal income tax return. In preparing your solution, ignore GST/HST & PST considerations.

AP 6-7 (Proprietorship—Business Income with CCA)

Karla Sandone is a successful photographer who specializes in photographs and videos of beloved pets. She operates her studio out of a building she purchased several years ago for $375,000. Of this total, it is estimated that $100,000 reflects the value of the land with the remaining cost of $275,000 attributable to the building. The building was new when she acquired it and it is used 100% for business purposes. Karla made the election to include the building in a separate class 1. On January 1, 2021, the UCC of the building is $230,712.

Karla prides herself on using the very latest camera and video gear. After receiving a sizable inheritance a few years ago, she can afford to indulge herself in fulfilling this goal. Karla has an agreement with a camera shop to purchase all her equipment through them at a 10% discount. In return, the camera shop will give her 20% of her purchase price on trade-ins that are less than a year old. Under this agreement, Karla traded in equipment with a capital cost of $27,000 and purchased new equipment for $85,000 during 2021. The UCC of the equipment was $25,100 on January 1, 2021.

On her birthday in 2020, Karla bought herself a $120,000 BMW that she used largely for business purposes. The BMW is not a zero-emission passenger vehicle. After an unfortunate accident occurred when she was driving the BMW, Karla sold it for $60,000 on January 2, 2021. The January 1, 2021, UCC for the BMW was $16,500. Assume that 100% of the use of the BMW was for business purposes.

She then purchased the following two automotive vehicles:

- A used sports car for $29,000 that is solely for personal use
- A new van designed to carry animals for $80,000 that is primarily for business use. The seating capacity of the van only accommodates the driver and one passenger. The van does not meet the definition of an "automobile" for income tax purposes because it is used primarily to transport passengers, goods, or equipment in the course of carrying on a business and the seating capacity does not exceed the driver plus two passengers.

During 2021, the van was driven 35,000 kilometres, 34,000 of which were for business purposes and 1,000 for personal use. The operating costs of the van for the year totalled $7,900.

During late December 2020, Karla's computer equipment was destroyed in an accident. As it was uninsured, she had written off the CCA balance in 2020. Therefore, there was a nil balance in the class at the beginning of 2021.

Other property purchases during 2021 are as follows:

New computers and photo/poster printer	$ 20,750
Applications software	3,480
Client list from retiring pet photographer	28,000

Other 2021 business expenses include the following:

Building operating costs	$31,300
Payments to assistants (Note)	51,100
Office and photographic supplies	11,600
Miscellaneous office costs	8,400
Pet toys and video props	2,700
Premium pet food and drinks	3,000
Meals with clients	10,500

Note The payments to assistants include $30,000 paid to Karla's 16-year-old son. He takes care of her website with its extensive photo/video gallery and promotes her substantial social media presence. Comparable services would have cost her in excess of $40,000.

During 2021, business revenues total $285,800.

Required: Calculate the minimum business income Karla would include in her 2021 personal income tax return. In preparing your solution, ignore GST/HST & PST considerations and any CPP liability.

AP 6-8 (Work Space in Home Costs and CCA)

Billy Jow is a music instructor at a local high school in your area. He is employed by the school board and earns approximately $70,000 annually. To supplement his income, Billy started to teach music on April 1, 2021, to a number of children in the neighbourhood in the evenings and on weekends.

Billy comes to you for advice on how he should report this supplementary teaching income and what expenses are deductible. Billy does not mind paying his fair share of income taxes, but he wants to pay no more than required. From discussions with friends, he understands that he may be entitled to claim a portion of the costs of his home.

Since he was not using the den in his home, he decided to use it for this supplementary teaching. The livable space of his home is approximately 2,000 square feet in size. The den together with common areas represents approximately 200 square feet.

From April 1, 2021, to December 31, 2021, Billy earned $5,700 in music fees. He has chosen December 31 as his fiscal year end and has incurred the following costs since April 1:

Purchase of music nooks	$ 250
Supplies (paper, pens, etc.)	1,000
Tuxedo to wear at students' performances	350
Snacks for students (cookies, pretzels, candies, milk, etc.)	250
Utilities for home (heat, light, and water)	3,500
Mortgage interest	11,000
Repairs and maintenance for home	2,600
Software program to assist in teaching music	300
Electric piano and bench	5,000
Total	$24,250

Assume that the music books will have to be replaced every year.

Billy is currently using the software program on an old computer that he uses mainly to watch YouTube videos. He is considering the purchase of a new computer solely for teaching purposes if the teaching generates enough income.

Required:

A. Briefly explain the conditions under which expenses for a work space in the home are deductible.

B. Based on the information given, compute the minimum business income or loss that Billy should report in his 2021 personal income tax return.

C. Briefly describe any issues that should be discussed with Billy concerning the work space in his home costs and business costs.

AP 6-9 (Corporate Business Income with CCA)

Angie's Amazing Getups Incorporated is a Canadian controlled private corporation (CCPC) with a head office in London, Ontario. The company is a manufacturer of high-end custom costumes and makeup used in movie and theatre productions with sales in Canada and the United States.

The business commenced in 2018 by its sole shareholder, Angela Q. Snodgrass, who is a highly trained clothing designer and makeup artist.

In November 2021, Angela discovered that the bookkeeping for the business was less than adequate and she decided to take over the bookkeeping responsibilities herself, despite having a limited knowledge of accounting. She has produced the following income statement and miscellaneous financial information for the year ended December 31, 2021, and needs your help:

Angie's Amazing Getups Incorporated
Income Statement
Year Ending December 31, 2021

Sales		$7,578,903
Cost of goods sold		(5,468,752)
Gross profit		$2,110,151
Expenses:		
General and administrative expenses	(852,000)	
Amortization expense	(550,000)	
Interest	(8,500)	(1,410,500)
Operating income		$ 699,651
Other income:		
Loss on disposal of limited life licence		(17,000)
Interest income		110,532
Income before income taxes		$ 793,183
Income taxes		
Current	($182,000)	
Future	(35,000)	(217,000)
Net income		$ 576,183

During your review of Angela's work and last year's tax return for the corporation, you have made the following notes.

1. In the accounting records, the allowance for doubtful accounts was $25,000 at December 31, 2021, and $20,000 at December 31, 2020. During 2021, the company had actual write-offs of $11,750. As a result, the accounting bad debt expense was $16,750 [$11,750 bad debts + the increase in the doubtful debts of $5,000 from 2020 to 2021]. This amount is included in general and administrative expenses on the income statement.

   A review of the listing of receivables (for income tax purposes) indicates that the actual items that may be uncollectible total $15,000 at December 31, 2021. In 2020, the company deducted a reserve for doubtful debts of $13,000 for tax purposes.

2. General and administrative expenses include:

Donations to registered charities	$ 27,000
Accrued bonuses—Accrued September 1, 2021, paid June 15, 2022	78,000
Meals and entertainment costs:	
$1,000 per month for premium membership at golf club for Angie	12,000
$200 per month for memberships at golf club for salespeople	2,400
$32,000 for meals while entertaining clients	32,000
$5,000 in food costs for Angie's personal chef for her meals at home	5,000
$6,000 for annual summer BBQ for all staff	6,000
Sponsorship of various theatre productions that use Angie's costumes	100,000
Advertising in a U.S. theatre magazine directed at U.S. clients	15,000
New software purchased October 1, 2021 ($13,000 for applications software and $25,000 for systems software)	38,000
Accounting and legal fees for amendments to articles of incorporation	6,000
Costs to attend annual convention of costume designers held in Thailand	17,000

3. Interest expense consists of the following:

Interest expense—Operations	$5,000
Penalty and interest for late and insufficient instalment payments	2,000
Interest on late payment of municipal property taxes	1,500

4. Travel costs (included in general and administrative costs) include both air travel and travel reimbursement to employees for business travel. The company policy is to reimburse employees $0.62 per kilometre for the business use of their automobiles. During the year, seven employees each drove 4,000 kilometres on employment-related activities, and one employee drove 7,500 kilometres. None of the kilometre-based allowances are required to be included in the income of the employees.

5. Maximum CCA has always been taken on all depreciable property. The UCC balances at January 1, 2021, are as follows:

Class 1 (4%)	$650,000
Class 8	95,000
Class 10.1	17,850
Class 14	68,000
Class 14.1	Nil
Class 44	65,000
Class 53	Nil

6. During 2021, a limited life licence to produce costumes based on a popular theme park was sold for $63,000. The original cost of this licence was $95,000 and its carrying value at the time of sale was $80,000. The licence was the only property in class 14.

7. Purchases and sales of equipment and other depreciable property made during 2021 were as follows (note: some items are discussed in other sections of this problem). All amounts were capitalized for accounting purposes.

   a. The company purchased land and constructed a new building on it during the year. The building will be used 95% for manufacturing and processing. An election was made to include the building in a separate class 1. The cost of the land was $350,000, and the building cost $475,000 to construct.

   b. The company purchased new furniture for the reception area for $1,200.

c. Some outdated desks used by the finance department with a cost of $5,000 were sold for $3,500.
d. Landscaping of the grounds around the new building cost $35,000 and were paid in 2021. This amount was capitalized for accounting purposes.
e. A company automobile for use by the president of the company was purchased for $90,000. This automobile replaced the only other existing company automobile, which was purchased in 2019 for $95,000. The old automobile was sold for $60,000.
f. A fence was purchased and installed around the new building for a total cost, including installation, of $52,000.

8. The company sold some shares that had been purchased several years ago. The capital gain on these shares was $152,708. Angie didn't know how to account for this, so she credited the entire amount to retained earnings.

Required: Determine Angie's Amazing Getups Incorporated's minimum net income for the year ending December 31, 2021. Ignore GST/HST & PST implications.

AP 6-10 (Deductibility of Business Expenses and CCA)

Lorna Jung is a psychiatrist whose private practice specializes in treating children with psychiatric disorders. Her husband, Alec Jung, was the president of a very successful mental health clinic until it was bought out last year. He is currently creating and testing recipes to be included in his new groundbreaking BBQ cookbook.

Over the past two years, Lorna has been investigating the patient benefits of having a therapy dog as part of her practice and has amassed an extensive library of clinical studies that show the effectiveness of this therapy. She is convinced that the use of a therapy dog will be advantageous to many of her patients and will improve the rate of their recovery.

On January 2, 2021, after much research, Lorna purchased a Labradoodle puppy for $2,000 that she named Sigmund. This particular breed was designed to be used as therapy dogs, and Sigmund's mother was a well-established therapy dog.

Sigmund became an important part of the Jung family. Whenever Sigmund wasn't in training or at Lorna's office, Alec would take Sigmund for walks and to the dog park. As Alec currently has no source of income, he charged Lorna the going rate of $20 per 1 hour (minimum) walk. He plans to report this income on his income tax return.

For the month of September 2021, Sigmund accompanied Lorna to consultations with all her patients except for those few who had a fear of dogs. She saw an immediate improvement in the attitudes of almost all her patients. Some children who refused to speak with her could describe their feelings when they addressed Sigmund.

As word of Lorna's success with her therapy dog treatments spread, new patients would register only if assured that Sigmund would be present.

On Lorna's website, she had two hourly rates. The one with Sigmund participating was 15% higher than the rate without Sigmund. By December 31, 2021, 70% of her patients were paying the higher rate with Sigmund.

On July 1, 2021, in anticipation of taking Sigmund to the office and patient's homes on a regular basis, Lorna signed a three-year lease for a Lexus SUV with sufficient room in the back for a sturdy, well-padded dog crate. The SUV is not a zero-emission passenger vehicle.

The lease payments were $950 per month. The manufacturer's list price for the vehicle was $65,000. As the Jungs have two other vehicles, this SUV was used only for business purposes.

For the year ending December 31, 2021, Lorna spent the following amounts on Sigmund:

Food, including puppy vitamins and supplements	$ 2,600
Veterinary fees	800
Therapy dog training course fees	1,400
Dog walking fees paid to Alec	3,280
Car lease for SUV [($950)(6)]	5,700
Operating expenses for SUV	2,950
Purchase of paw protectors (good for one winter)	140
Purchase of custom-made protective clothing (estimated life of three years)	820
Dog crate	400
Total dog-related expenditures	$18,090

Lorna's accountant informed her that Sigmund's original cost could not be written off as there was no specific CCA class for dogs and CCA class 8, the usual catch-all class, specifically excluded animals.

In 2022, Lorna's parents were in a car accident that left them both severely injured. After much thought, she decided she had to close her practice to care for them and help in the long rehabilitation process.

Lorna knew that Sigmund would become depressed without patient interaction, so she sold Sigmund to Dr. Skinner, a psychiatrist she had known for years who already had a therapy dog and was looking to expand his practice. Although Lorna could not sell her patient list to Dr. Skinner due to confidentiality constraints, she emailed all her patients that Sigmund would be available at Dr. Skinner's office so he would soon see familiar faces there.

Dr. Skinner paid $8,500 for Sigmund and $200 extra for the protective clothing and the crate. He promised the Jungs unlimited visitation rights.

Due to her high income, Lorna always claims the maximum deductions available each year.

Required:

A. Lorna's accountant does not plan to deduct any dog-related expenditures other than the maximum allowable SUV expenses. Do you agree this is the appropriate course of action? Justify your conclusion.

B. Indicate how much of the preceding expenditures you feel Lorna should deduct in the calculation of her business income for 2021.

C. Calculate the amount, if any, that will be included in Lorna's 2022 net income as a result of the sale of Sigmund and the protective clothing and crate.

Ignore all GST/HST & PST considerations in your solution.

AP 6-11 (Deductible Business Expenses—Proprietorship)

Dr. Sweet is a dentist with a well-established practice in Smith Falls, Ontario. She has sought your advice regarding the deductibility of the following expenditures made during the current taxation year:

1. Insurance payments included a $680 premium for coverage of her office and contents, $1,800 for malpractice coverage, and $1,700 in life insurance premiums.

2. Payments were made to a collection agency in the amount of $1,250 for assistance in collecting past due amounts from patients.

3. Contributions of $600 were made to various registered charities.
4. Dr. Sweet paid a total of $18,000 to her husband for his services as a full-time bookkeeper and receptionist.
5. A total of $4,600 was spent to attend a dental convention in Phoenix, Arizona. Dr. Sweet was accompanied by her husband, and $1,500 of the total cost of the trip relates directly to him.
6. An amount of $1,000 was paid for membership in a racquets club. In addition, $1,300 was spent for court time, approximately 10% of which was for time spent playing with patients.
7. Dr. Sweet paid $1,200 in legal and accounting fees. These fees related to fighting a personal income tax reassessment for a previous tax year. The fight was not successful and, as a consequence, Dr. Sweet was required to pay additional taxes of $13,000 plus $1,600 in interest on the late payments.
8. During the year, Dr. Sweet spent $3,200 purchasing provincial lottery tickets.

Required: Advise Dr. Sweet with respect to the income tax treatment of the preceding expenditures and how they would affect her net income. Explain your position on each expenditure.

AP 6-12 (Business Income with CCA)

Carl Pomery is a chartered professional accountant (CPA) who is employed as a controller of a medium-sized corporation. In addition, he carries on a personal business of providing tax and accounting services. This business has a December 31 year end and has been in operation for several years.

Carl purchased a new building in 2009. It has been used exclusively for non-residential purposes and was elected to be included in a separate class when it was purchased. On January 1, 2021, the business has the following UCC balances:

Class 1 building	$242,000
Class 8 furniture and fixtures	72,000
Class 10 vehicle (purchased for $19,600)	16,660
Class 14.1	Nil

During January 2021, the class 10 vehicle is involved in a serious accident, requiring it to be permanently taken off the road. The insurance proceeds are $14,600. On February 1, Carl replaces it with a vehicle with a manufacturer's list price of $34,000 that is leased for $525 per month. Both vehicles are used exclusively for business purposes and are not passenger vehicles.

During July 2021, Carl replaces most of the furniture in his office. The old furniture has a capital cost of $23,000, while the new items cost $46,000. Carl receives a trade-in allowance for the old furniture of $18,000.

Also during January 2021, Carl acquires a new computer for $2,500, along with applications software for $2,200.

During March 2021, Carl acquires a client list from an accountant who is retiring. The cost of this list is $82,000.

On January 1, 2021, Carl had unbilled work-in-progress of $35,000. All of this work was billed during the year ending December 31, 2021. During 2021, his work consisted of 1,900 billable hours that will be invoiced for a total of $152,000. On December 31, 2021, he had unbilled work-in-progress of $56,000.

During 2021, the various costs of operating his business, determined on an accrual basis, are as follows:

Building operating costs	$22,000
Vehicle operating costs	7,200
Vehicle lease payments	5,775
Payments to assistants	24,000
Miscellaneous office costs	4,500
Meals with clients	3,500

Required: Calculate the minimum business income Carl would include in his 2021 personal income tax return. In preparing your solution, ignore GST/HST & PST considerations.

AP 6-13 (ITA 22 Accounts Receivable Election)

Beckett Enterprises is the registered name of a business carried on by Ms. Joan Close as a sole proprietorship for a number of years. However, in early 2021 she decides to cease carrying on the business and sell it and all of its properties to an unrelated party, Mr. John Phar.

The date of the sale is February 1, 2021. On that same date, the business has accounts receivable with a face value of $120,000. Because of anticipated bad debts, the realizable value of these receivables is estimated to be $107,000. In 2020, Ms. Close deducted a reserve for doubtful debts in the amount of $8,000.

Beckett Enterprises has a December 31 fiscal year end. Mr. Phar will continue the business as a sole proprietorship and will continue to use a December 31 fiscal year end.

During the year ending December 31, 2021, $100,000 of the accounts receivable are collected, with the remainder being written off as non-recoverable (i.e., bad debts).

Both Ms. Close and Mr. Phar have heard of an election under ITA 22 that may have some influence on the income tax treatment of the sale of the accounts receivable. They would like to have your advice on this matter. They will both have significant capital gains in 2021.

Required: Indicate the income tax effects for both Ms. Close and Mr. Phar of the sale of the accounts receivable and the subsequent 2021 collections and write-offs, assuming:

A. that no election is made under ITA 22.

B. that they make an election under ITA 22.

AP 6-14 (Comprehensive Case Covering Chapters 1 to 6)

Ms. Lacy Compton is a 45-year-old widow with two children:

John Her son, John, is 22 years old and, because he has been blind since birth, he lives with her in a residence that she owns. He qualifies for the disability tax credit and has no income of his own during 2021.

Allison Her 17-year-old daughter, Allison, has just started university and, during 2021, she attended on a full-time basis for four months. Her tuition fees that were paid during 2021 were $2,850. As she is attending a local university, Allison lives in her mother's home throughout 2021. Allison has no income of her own and she intends to transfer her tuition credit to her mother.

During 2021, her family's qualifying medical expenses are as follows:

Lacy	$ 4,220
John	11,500
Allison	2,180
Total	$17,900

During 2021, Ms. Compton makes donations to registered charities of $1,250, as well as contributions to registered federal political parties in the amount of $350.

Ms. Compton is employed as a salesperson by a large Canadian public company. For 2021, her salary is $68,000. In addition, she earns $13,500 in commissions during the year. For the year ending December 31, 2021, her employer withholds the following amounts from her income:

RPP contributions*	$2,800
EI premiums	890
CPP contributions	3,166
Professional association dues	250
Payments for personal use of employer's car	1,800

*Ms. Compton's employer makes a matching contribution of $2,800 to her RPP.

The car that she used during 2021 cost her employer $32,000. During 2021, it was used by her for 11 months of the year. It was driven a total of 27,000 kilometres, of which 22,500 was for employment-related use and 4,500 for personal use. During the one month that she did not use the car, her employer required that she return it to the company premises.

She is required by her employer to maintain an office in her home. During 2021, this office occupied 15% of the livable floor space in her home. The cost of the house (excluding the land) is $335,000. Her 2021 costs for 100% of the livable floor space were as follows:

Mortgage interest	$5,800
Property taxes	2,450
Utilities and maintenance	1,100
Insurance	425
Total	$9,775

In conjunction with her sales activities, she incurred costs for meals and entertainment of $4,350. These were not reimbursed by her employer.

In addition to her employment, Ms. Compton carries on and manages a retail business as a sole proprietor. The fiscal year of the business ends on December 31 and, for 2021, the business had accounting income of $53,500. Other information related to the business is as follows:

1. As the business is not incorporated, no income taxes were deducted in calculating the business income.
2. During 2021, the business spent $8,600 landscaping its premises. For accounting purposes, this amount is being amortized over 10 years on a straight-line basis.
3. At the beginning of 2021, Ms. Compton owned depreciable property used in the business with the following UCC balances:

	Class 1	Class 8	Class 10
January 1, 2021, UCC	$233,000	$41,500	$27,000

The class 1 building was acquired in 2015.

In March 2021, class 8 property with a capital cost of $12,000 was sold for $8,600. Additional class 8 property with a capital cost of $13,400 was purchased.

4. The accounting business income figure of $53,500 is after the deduction of amortization expense of $12,800 and $6,000 in meals and entertainment with clients of the business. The amortization expense includes the amortization of the landscaping costs.

Required: Calculate Ms. Compton's 2021 net income, her 2021 taxable income, and her minimum 2021 federal tax payable without consideration of any income tax withheld by her employer. Ignore GST/HST & PST considerations.

AP 6-15 (Comprehensive Case Covering Chapters 1 to 6)

Personal Information

Hillary Hawk has been divorced for some time and has sole custody of her two children, Mark and Mandy. Mark is 13 and Mandy turned 18 on July 1, 2021. Hillary does not receive any child support or spousal support from her former husband.

Mark is in high school and has no income of his own.

During 2021, her daughter, Mandy, was enrolled part time at a local college. Hillary agreed to pay her tuition of $1,800 as long as Mandy transferred the related credit to her (Hillary). Mandy's 2021 net income is $6,300.

During the year, Hillary paid $8,000 for orthodontic work (braces) for Mark. She was reimbursed 50% of the amount through her employer's dental and health plan.

During 2021, Hillary made $2,300 of contributions to registered charities.

Employment Information

Hillary is a sales representative for Bronze Age Inc. (BA), a Canadian public company that specializes in the marketing of metal sculptures.

Hillary's employment contract specifies a base salary of $100,000 plus a commission of 2% of her annual cash sales. For 2021, the applicable amount of cash sales is $4,800,000.

For 2021, Hillary's employer withheld the following amounts from her salary:

RPP contributions	6,200
CPP contributions	3,166
EI premiums	890
Premiums for BA's dental and health plan*	3,200
Professional association dues	2,700
Federal income tax	39,400

*The plan is funded 50/50 by the employees and the employer.

Hillary is covered by BA's group term life insurance. Her coverage is equal to her annual base salary ($100,000 for 2021). BA pays a premium to the insurance company of $3 for every $1,000 of coverage.

Because of her outstanding sales record, Hillary received the Salesperson of the Year Award. This award provided her with a cash payment of $1,000, plus an iPad Pro that cost BA $1,700.

During 2021, BA provides Hillary with an automobile that it leases for $650 per month. The automobile was available for her personal use throughout 2021. During this period, she drove the car 42,000 kilometres, of which 38,000 were for employment use and 4,000 for personal use. While BA pays $2,800 to provide Hillary with insurance on the vehicle, they do not pay any of the other operating expenses.

Hillary is responsible for her salesperson expenses (including the automobile operating expenses). During 2021 she incurred the following:

Total automobile expenses (excluding insurance)	$8,500
Meals and entertainment with clients	5,800
Hotels	3,200

Hillary meets all of the conditions of ITA 8(1)(f) of the ITA (deductible salesperson expenses). She has a T-2200 from her employer.

Last year, in July 2020, Hillary's employer transferred her from the Kelowna office to the Vancouver office. All of her moving expenses were paid for by her employer. Because she needed to sell her Kelowna home quickly, a $38,000 loss was incurred on the sale. While her employer agreed to compensate Hillary for $25,000 of this loss, the payment was not received until February 2021.

In April 2019, Hillary's employer granted her the right to purchase up to 3,000 shares of BA for $27 per share under the employee stock option plan. At the time the option was granted, the shares were trading for $25. On March 1, 2021, when the shares were trading at $29 per share, she exercises all of these options. In December 2021, she sold 2,000 shares of the acquired option shares for $33 per share.

In order to purchase the 3,000 shares, Hillary negotiated an interest-free loan from her employer for the purchase price. The loan was received on March 1, 2021. Joan repaid the loan on December 31, 2021.

Business Information

In addition to her employment income, Hillary carries on a business, as a sole proprietor, that advises individuals and corporations on purchases of various types of art for their homes and offices. Hillary uses 15% of the livable space in her Vancouver home for this business. Her 2021 household expenses include the following:

All utilities	$ 4,200
Property taxes	6,500
Maintenance	2,400
Home internet service	900
Insurance on her home	2,100
Mortgage interest	11,500

Hillary estimates only 10% of the internet use was for her business because her children stream a lot of entertainment on a variety of devices. She does not claim CCA on her home as she realizes that if she did, this would result in future recapture and capital gains implications.

On January 1, 2021, the business had the following UCC balances:

Class 8	$ 6,912
Class 10.1	12,495

During 2021, she acquires additional class 8 property at a capital cost of $12,000. She also sold class 8 property with a capital cost of $9,000 for $1,200.

The class 10.1 passenger vehicle had a capital cost $36,000. It was sold during 2021 for $16,000 and replaced with a new passenger vehicle with a capital cost of $41,000. Both vehicles were used solely for the business. She uses the employer-provided automobile for the little bit of personal travel that she does do.

For 2021, the business income, determined using ASPE, was $63,000. Included in this amount were the following:

Amortization expense	$ 5,200
Business meals and entertainment	6,400
Work space in the home costs*	Nil

*Hillary did not believe that these costs could be deducted under generally accepted accounting principles.

Required:

For the 2021 taxation year, calculate Hillary's minimum:

1. net income,
2. taxable income,
3. federal tax liability.

In determining these amounts, assume the prescribed rate during all four quarters of 2021 is 2%. Ignore any GST/HST & PST considerations.

CHAPTER 7

Income or Loss from Property

Learning Objectives

After completing Chapter 7, you should be able to:

1. Link the previous chapter discussions on sources of employment and business income to the last source of income that is property income (Paragraph [P hereafter] 7-1 to 7-5).
2. Explain the difference between a business and property source of income (P 7-6 to 7-11).
3. Explain and apply the source analysis to be able to identify a property source of income (P 7-12 to 7-13).
4. Provide some examples of how the ITA treats business and property income differently (P 7-14 to 7-15).
5. Describe how interest expense deductibility fits into the 9-12-18-20 rule (P 7-16 to 7-19).
6. Explain what is required by ITA 20(1)(c) to be entitled to an interest expense deduction (P 7-20 to 7-24).
7. Describe the meaning of "interest" for income tax purposes (P 7-25 to 7-27).
8. Describe the income tax principles of interest expense deductibility that relate to the purpose test, direct and indirect use, and tracing. Explain how these principles can be used in income tax planning to obtain an interest expense deduction (P 7-28 to 7-40).
9. Explain how interest expense is treated in other common situations (P 7-41 to 7-51).
10. Explain the tax treatment of discounts and premiums on long-term debt and how it differs from the accounting treatment (P 7-52 to 7-61).
11. Explain and apply the methods used to calculate interest income for both individuals and corporations (P 7-62 to 7-68).
12. Explain how investors in debt obligations are treated for income tax purposes with respect to premiums and discounts and the basis for that treatment. (P 7-69 to 7-73).
13. Explain and apply the rules related to accrued interest at the time debt obligations are sold (P 7-74 to 7-77).
14. Explain the purpose of ITA 12(1)(g) and its role in the 9-12-18-20 rule (P 7-78 to 7-81).
15. Explain how rental income is treated in the ITA, with emphasis on special CCA rules (P 7-82 to 7-92).
16. Explain the concept of integration and why there are two taxable dividends (eligible and non-eligible). In addition, describe and apply the mechanism used in the ITA for individuals who receive taxable dividends (P 7-93 to 7-123).

17. Compare the after-tax returns from various types of investments (P 7-124 to 7-125).
18. Describe the two types of mutual fund entities, the difference in income tax treatment, the flow through of investment income from a mutual fund trust, and the ACB concept as it applies to mutual fund trusts (P 7-126 to 7-137).
19. Describe, in your own words, the meaning of stock dividends and capital dividends and their income tax treatment (P 7-138 to 7-144).
20. Explain the general income tax treatment of foreign source business and non-business income where foreign income taxes are charged (P 7-145 to 7-150).
21. Describe the three general categories of shareholder benefits (P 7-151 to 7-153).

Introduction

7-1. In Chapter 1 we introduced the income tax concept of a "source of income" which is an essential component of the Canadian income tax system. A source of income can be defined as a potential to generate a positive cash flow net of related expenses over a period of time from an activity produced by one's labour, capital, or property either singly or in combination. The source concept features include continuity, a profit motive (i.e., a potential to create a positive return), and that a reference to a source of income means income receipts minus related expenses, a net basis approach that can produce losses.

7-2. The ITA identifies three specific sources of income: (1) employment income (discussed in Chapter 3), (2) business income (discussed in Chapter 6), and (3) property income, which is the subject of this chapter. Employment income and business income require the use of one's labour, while capital and property income require the use of one's property to generate income.

7-3. The Chapter 6 discussion of business income showed that the rules of the ITA are specifically located in Subdivision b of Division B of Part I, which refers not only to a source of income that is a business but also to a property source. However, not all of the rules within that part of the ITA relate to both business and property income. For example, ITA 12(1)(a) (receipts in advance) and (b) (accounts receivables) only apply to businesses. Many deductions, such as ITA 20(1)(aa) (landscaping) and (cc) (costs of representation), also only apply to businesses. Still, this particular subdivision has the bulk of the rules related to determining property income.

7-4. Many points discussed in Chapter 6 also apply equally to income from property. At Paragraph 6-45 we discussed the 9-12-18-20 rule, and Paragraph 6-78 provided the basic concepts to determine whether an expense is deductible, including the addition of a flowchart (Figure 6-1). Both of these topics are equally applicable to income from property and will not be repeated in this chapter.

7-5. There are, however, a few noteworthy differences that are important to keep in mind as we begin our discussion of income from property:

- The first is ITA 9(3), which we mentioned in Chapter 6 (see Paragraph 6-38). ITA 9(3) ensures that any reference to property income or loss would not be considered to include capital gains and capital losses.
- The second is that in Chapter 6 we discussed the concept of a taxation year and a fiscal period (see Paragraph 6-171), noting that a "fiscal period" is a concept that is exclusive to a business. This means that individuals who earn property income do not have the option of selecting a fiscal period type tax year. Property income or losses are included in their net income based on the taxation year, which is the calendar year January 1 to December 31.
- Finally at Paragraph 6-34 we described the three general categories of property recognized by the ITA as relating to a business as inventory, depreciable capital property (i.e.,

depreciable property), and non-depreciable capital property. However, "inventory" is a concept exclusive to a business, and therefore a source of property income cannot have inventory but can have depreciable and non-depreciable capital property.

Income from Property: General Concept

7-6. In Chapter 6 (see Paragraph 6-16) we also discussed the difference between business versus a property source of income. The definition of a business means time, attention, and labour devoted to an activity that is capable of generating a profit (although one may never materialize). Since both businesses and property sources involve the purchase of property or an activity with respect to property already owned, the determination of whether the activity is a business or property source rests on the level of that activity.

7-7. If the activity is passive in nature, meaning that one acquires property and then, with little to no effort, simply awaits the returns, then the source would be considered income from property. Alternatively, if the activity exceeds a passive level, requiring additional and ongoing work or services, then the activity would be considered as the carrying on of a business. In both cases if there is a personal component (see Paragraphs 6-20 to 6-24) that interferes or overshadows a profit motive, there would be no source of income to begin with and therefore no need to categorize the activity.

7-8. Property that is typically involved in a source of property income includes investment-type property that produces a regular income return that is not a capital gain or capital loss. Examples include (1) shares of corporations with the potential to generate dividends; (2) rental properties that provide rental income; (3) loans to others, bonds, GICs (guaranteed investment certificates), and savings accounts at financial institutions, all of which generate interest income; (4) patents or rights to use one's property, such as work that is an invention, a book (author), or music composition (composer), all of which produce royalty income; and (5) returns in the form of interest and dividends as a result of ownership of units of a mutual fund that is a trust.

7-9. In the source concept it is important that the individual has ownership of "property" that generates a return, whether the property is shares, bonds, their own funds (e.g., cash), rental properties, patents, and so on. This is important since the ITA has a very broad definition of "property" (ITA 248(1)) that defines property to include a "right of any kind." The source concept, however, is developed in the jurisprudence, and when it refers to the meaning of property it would not include a right of any kind. To illustrate the importance, assume that you lend $10,000 to a friend with interest. Applying the source concept, you have lent your own property (the $10,000) to someone else and, as a result, you are earning interest income on the property that is the subject of the loan. While the loan is outstanding the ITA would consider you to have "property," that is, the right to get paid back (e.g., the loan receivable). That right, however, is not the property required of the source concept, which is your cash that you have loaned.

7-10. To further illustrate the difference, consider a couple who have separated or divorced. One is entitled to receive alimony payments from the other, which may also include child support. The intended recipient has a right to receive the payments, but is there a source of income? Has the recipient used her own property, labour, or capital directly to establish a connection to any alimony receipt? The answer is no, meaning there is no source of income. This means that if the federal government wants individual recipients to include any of these payments in their income, it must be specifically included in legislation, which is exactly what has been done. This is discussed in Chapter 9.

7-11. The same analysis could be applied to the receipt of Employment Insurance (EI), Canada Pension Plan (CPP) payments, and even registered pension plan (RPP) payments, as none of these amounts would be considered a source of income because there is not a sufficient connection to the recipient's labour, property, or capital. It may seem that employee contributions for EI, CPP, and even RPP (where the employee makes part of the payments) suggest that there is a connection. The difficulty is that the contributions, once made, are no longer the property of the payor, thereby severing the necessary connection to establish a source of income. All this means, however, is that each receipt is not a source of income, which reinforces the fact that if the federal government wishes to include these amounts in income, specific legislation must be added to do so, particularly in a country like Canada that operates on the rule of law. Chapter 9 discusses the rules that exist to ensure such amounts are required to be included in the recipient's income.

The Source of Income Analysis

7-12. In determining whether there is a source of income and whether it is income from a business or property, the following analysis should be followed:

(1) Has property been acquired or an activity undertaken? If not then there is no source of income. The activity would include the purchase of property or use of property already owned that is capable of generating income.

(2) Is there a personal element to the property acquired or the activity? If there is no personal element then the property acquired or the activity undertaken will be automatically considered as a source of income as long as a business has commenced or the property has been acquired and is capable of earning income. If there is a personal element, then the activity, including the property acquired, will be evaluated to determine if the property is being used or the activity is being carried on in a commercial-like manner. The analysis is almost always undertaken when the property or the activity is reporting losses for income tax purposes.

(3) Is the level of activity of the property owner or the person undertaking the activity passive or active on a continuous basis? This question is only addressed when the personal element does not overshadow the profit motive and the activity is conducted in a commercial-like manner. Income generated from passive ownership is almost always categorized as income from property, whereas active ongoing activity supports the existence of income from a business.

EXAMPLE 1 An individual makes a loan to a friend at 8% interest. The friend is starting up a business and requires the funds. The bank was willing to lend at 7% interest. The individual has not loaned money to anyone else. The money loaned was previously sitting in a bank account earning 2% interest. A loan agreement is created and signed with monthly payments over the next 18 months. The borrower provides collateral security.

ANALYSIS 1 The individual is using her property (her funds) in an activity that is the making of a loan to another individual. The fact that the borrower is a personal friend brings the personal element into play. This requires looking further to determine whether the loan is similar to what would be expected in a commercial setting. The facts suggest a commercial-like transaction, and therefore we move on to the last step, which is determining whether the activity could be considered active and therefore a business or passive with the result that the interest is income from property.

CONCLUSION 1 The analysis clearly suggests that there is a source of income and that it is income from property.

EXAMPLE 2 The individual was so pleased with the result of lending money to the friend that the individual was contacted by numerous businesses and others asking for loans. The individual hired two employees, rented an office space, consulted with a lawyer to make certain each loan was supported by carefully drafted written loan agreements setting out terms and conditions of the loans and required collateral security. In the first year, over 100 requests were made, with only 40 loans actually made, all on commercial terms. The employees conduct credit and other checks to increase the likelihood that the loans will be repaid in full.

ANALYSIS 2 (1) The individual is using her property in an activity to generate a profit. (2) There is no personal element. (3) The level of activity requires the time, attention, and labour of the individual on an ongoing basis with a profit motive, meaning the individual is in the business of lending money. This is not a passive activity.

CONCLUSION 2 The activity is a source of income that is income from a business.

7-13. In this discussion we have referred to property purchased and property owned, but the source concept extends to property available for one's use, which does not imply or require ownership. The most common example of this is when one borrows money from a financial institution (e.g., a bank) or anyone else for that matter. During the term of the loan the funds are at the disposal of the borrower in a manner similar to an individual renting an apartment or leasing an automobile. In these instances, while the individual is not the property owner, they have an interest in the property for a limited period of time, and if during that time they use that property to generate income, the source of income concept would apply. This will be discussed further in this chapter.

EXAMPLE An individual borrows money at 2% interest and loans it to a local business at 5%.

ANALYSIS The individual is using property at his disposal (the borrowed funds) in a lending activity for the purpose of making a profit. This would be a source of income subject to the source analysis referred to in Paragraph 7-12.

Exercise 7-1

Subject: Source of Income Analysis

In each of the following cases, determine whether there is a source of income and, if there is, whether the activity is income from property or income from a business.

CASE 1 You purchase a small office building with space for eight offices. All offices are leased for two years or more. The lease requires that the building be maintained by the landlord but that the tenants are responsible for cleaning and caring for each of their own office spaces.

CASE 2 The same as Case 1 except you hire individuals to provide daily office cleaning services as well as provide 24-hour security guard services.

CASE 3 You purchase a duplex and rent one of the units to your adult child at half the going market rental rate and the second unit to a long-time friend who has just lost his job. The arrangement is that the friend will pay the municipal taxes and utility costs only, which together is less than half the going market rental rate.

Solutions to Exercises are available in the Study Guide.

Income from Property vs. Business—The Importance

7-14. The ITA draws a distinction between income from property and income from a business. The ITA requires that the full amount of property and business income minus related expenses be included in income. In other words, with the exception of dividends received from Canadian corporations, individuals would pay the same amount of income tax on $10,000 whether it was business or property income. So why the concern?

7-15. As a rule the ITA treats business income much more favourably than property income. There are considerable differences when the taxpayer is a corporation, and these are discussed at length in Volume 2 of this text. Since the focus in Volume 1 is on individuals, some of the more significant differences that impact individuals can be highlighted as follows:

- Rental income activity that is income from property is subject to restrictions that prevent the use of CCA to claim or increase a rental loss. Such restrictions are not applicable if the activity is a business. This limitation will be discussed in this chapter.
- One factor that favours income from property over income from a business is the short fiscal period rules (ITR 1100(3)) that require pro-rating CCA when a fiscal period is less than 365 days long. Remember that an individual's taxation year is always the calendar year and an individual can only have a fiscal period if they have a business. In other words, an individual's income from property is based on a calendar year. As a result, CCA is not subject to the short fiscal period rule where the source of income is income from property.
- An individual who has included taxable capital gains may be entitled to a deduction that offsets all or part of those taxable capital gains. The deduction (discussed in Chapter 8) is called the capital gains deduction and is only available if the taxable capital gains relate to the sale of shares in corporations that are carrying on a business. In other words, if the underlying income were income from property, then the capital gains deduction would not be available.
- Individuals can deduct registered retirement savings plan (RRSP) contributions in determining their net income based on the meaning of "earned income" as defined in ITA 146. Earned income includes business income but is restricted when it comes to property income. RRSPs are discussed in Chapter 10.

Interest as a Deduction—ITA 20(1)(c)

The Problem with Interest Expense

7-16. In Chapter 6, "profit"(ITA 9) and the 9-12-18-20 rule were discussed. The brief discussion of ITA 20(1)(c) explained that the case law has consistently held that interest is considered a capital expenditure and therefore any claim for interest expense is blocked by ITA 18(1)(b), which may be overridden by ITA 20(1)(c). This means that where interest expense is a capital expenditure a deduction is allowed if the conditions of ITA 20(1)(c). In other words, to be able to claim an interest expense the conditions of ITA 20(1)(c) must be met. This does not mean to suggest that a deduction cannot be claimed for interest expense as a current expense through ITA 9, although this would mean that the interest expense would not have to be labelled as a capital expenditure. The CRA, for example, recognizes this possibility and references money lenders who borrow money themselves to loan to others as an example where any interest expenses incurred would be deductible under ITA 9 without having to worry about ITA 18(1)(b).

7-17. The case law supports an interest expense deduction under ITA 9 for the working or circulating capital of a business. Oftentimes, however, the issue is not relevant given that the interest expenses are clearly connected to a source of income that is a business or property and would have qualified for a deduction under ITA 20(1)(c) had they been capital in nature.

7-18. Why, then, is there so much concern about interest expense? The answer can be found in the many different types of transactions encountered by the CRA and the courts that require the establishment of interpretative rules to be able to determine whether an interest expense would be allowed as a deduction through ITA 20(1)(c).

7-19. If an individual borrows money from a bank to be used in his business or to earn investment income (e.g., income from property) and the individual is legally obligated to pay interest, then the interest payable would be deductible against that source of income. But what would happen if the individual was still paying interest after the investments were sold or the business ceased to exist? As another example, if savings are used to invest in a business rather than used to pay down the mortgage on your personal home, would that mean that part of the mortgage interest could be deducted? Finally, if a corporation borrows money to pay down debtholders or to redeem shares that were initially issued to raise capital for the company, would that qualify as earning business or property income? These are some of the types of situations that are less than clear-cut, and which contribute to the complexity in determining whether interest expense is actually deductible. An awareness of this concern is important for students that are learning about federal income tax and for practitioners who assist clients to ensure the best income tax result. In this section we will look a little further at some of the more common concerns and how they are addressed by the ITA.

ITA 20(1)(c) Revisited

7-20. Before beginning it is important to look back at the main provision that permits interest to be claimed as a deduction. This provision generally requires that the interest must be charged "pursuant to a legal obligation," meaning that the nature of the agreement clearly specifies the rate to be charged for interest, including any other relevant conditions necessary to specifically identify the interest and how and when it is considered paid. In general terms the interest must relate to either (1) borrowed funds (e.g., a bank loan) where the funds are used to earn either a source of income that is a business or property, or (2) an amount payable for the purchase of property that will be used to earn a source of income that is from a business or property.

7-21. ITA 20(1)(c) refers to two different legal relationships. The first is when money is borrowed. This is referred to as a "loan," which establishes the creation of a lender/borrower relationship. A loan is legally defined as "delivery by one party (e.g., the lender) to and receipt by another party (e.g., the borrower) of a sum of money upon agreement, express or implied, to repay it with or without interest." This means that a loan need not be in writing (express or implied) unless Canadian law requires it be in writing. In addition a loan is still a loan even if no interest is charged.

7-22. The second relationship occurs when a taxpayer acquires property on account, such as when equipment is purchased from a dealer who provides direct or indirect financing. This would also apply where an individual paid for equipment or other property with a line of credit or a credit card. This type of debt is referred to as "indebtedness," which is different from a loan in that there is no borrowed money. In this situation the relationship between the parties is also different—the purchaser is referred to as the debtor and the party providing the property in this case would be the creditor. Technically indebtedness can arise in any contract that is not a loan of money. Examples would include unpaid rent, trade accounts receivables, and even unpaid interest.

7-23. The distinction of a loan and indebtedness is important since the ITA refers to a loan in some provisions and indebtedness in others. In addition, sometimes it refers to "debt obligations," which means both. It is important to keep these concepts in mind when learning about federal income tax, as it will assist in understanding how the income tax system applies to many situations involving interest and how the underlying obligations are treated.

7-24. As a final point, we have seen that ITA 20(1)(c) covers loans and indebtedness where property is acquired. The CRA and the courts generally consider interest to be capital in nature and therefore disallowed by ITA 18(1)(b), forcing the determination of interest expenses to fall within ITA 20(1)(c). The following example illustrates some of the flaws in too strict of an approach.

> **EXAMPLE** A business hires an electrician to undertake long overdue basic maintenance. Once the work is completed the electrician invoices the business stipulating any amounts not paid within 30 days result in interest charges of 1% per month. Due to temporary cash flow issues the business pays the invoice two months late, resulting in interest charges. Is the interest deductible?
>
> **ANALYSIS** If the interest is considered a capital expense, then any claim for interest would be blocked by ITA 18(1)(b). Although ITA 20(1)(c) allows an interest expense

when in connection with a business, the provision only refers to indebtedness where property is acquired. Since no property is acquired, ITA 20(1)(c) would not apply, leaving the business without an interest expense deduction. At paragraph 1.93 of Folio S3-F6-C1, "Interest Deductibility," the CRA states that the interest will be allowed on an administrative concession. They add that this concession would also apply where interest is charged on trade accounts payable. We would add that the case law in these instances would support a claim that the interest would be deductible in the computation of profit through ITA 9, but this gives you some insight into the difficulties and controversy surrounding interest expense.

What Is Interest?

7-25. Throughout the text we have emphasized that words and expressions used in the ITA almost always take on their legal meaning rather than definitions based on accounting principles and concepts. There is no definition of "interest" in the ITA, although the word has been legally defined by the courts as qualifying if the following three criteria are satisfied:

- It must be calculated on a day-to-day accrual basis.
- It must be calculated on a principal sum or the right to a principal sum.
- It must be compensation for the use of the principal sum or the right to the principal sum.

7-26. Interest on a basic loan or indebtedness, which is intuitively thought of as interest, would meet each of the three criteria. An example that is not as self-evident, however, would be participating in common debt arrangements. These arrangements generally only require the borrower or debtor to make payments if they are profitable, with the interest amounts linked to that profitability. Even though such agreements may refer to these excess amounts paid as interest, they would fail to meet the definition in Paragraph 7-23 because they are contingent or uncertain with no actual legal obligation required to make a payment. Folio S3-F6-C1 (paragraph 1.2) provides some clarification, noting that in general participating payments are not considered to be interest. However, if there is an upper limit on the applicable rate and that upper limit reflects prevailing market conditions, such payments may qualify as interest. Payments that are contingent on some future event would not generally be considered interest. The outcome would not only be a denial of an interest expense but no potential deduction at all because of the capital expenditure limitation of ITA 18(1)(b).

7-27. The ITA can also deem amounts to be interest, in which case this allows us to bypass the legal definition. If, for example, there is a contract or arrangement that requires a larger amount to be repaid than what was borrowed and there is no mention of interest, then ITA 16 applies to effectively treat the excess amount as interest. A second example is if an employee receives an interest-free loan there will be a taxable interest benefit, which we discussed in Chapter 3. That imputed interest would not meet the legal definition of interest nor would it meet the ITA 20(1)(c) condition that interest is charged as a result of a legal obligation. ITA 80.5 fixes both of these problems by deeming the imputed interest to be interest payable by a debtor pursuant to a legal obligation to pay interest on borrowed money.

Direct or Indirect Use

Supreme Court of Canada—The Singleton Decision

7-28. One of the most important principles in terms of interest deductibility is that it is the direct use of the borrowings (loan or indebtedness) that applies and not the indirect use. The facts in the *Singleton* decision [2001 SCC 61] will help to clarify this concept.

7-29. The basic facts are that Mr. Singleton was a member of a partnership and that he had a partnership capital account of approximately $300,000. Partnership capital accounts generally represent the contributions of that partner plus any net income of the partnership allocated to that partner that have not been withdrawn. Mr. Singleton wanted to purchase a home that would have cost approximately the same $300,000. We will describe this case using four general transactions:

- #1 Mr. Singleton withdrew $300,000 from the partnership.
- #2 He used those funds to purchase a home.
- #3 He then borrowed $300,000 from the bank with interest.
- #4 He invested the $300,000 in the partnership, replacing the funds withdrawn.

7-30. Mr. Singleton claimed the interest paid on the loan to the bank as interest incurred to earn business income through the partnership. Generally interest on money borrowed to invest in a partnership is deductible. The CRA, however, denied the interest expense deduction on the basis that the borrowed money was not used to invest in the partnership but instead was used to indirectly purchase a home.

7-31. The CRA argument is based on an indirect use of borrowed money. That argument looks at what has changed as a result of the four transactions. At the beginning and at the end of these transactions, Mr. Singleton had a partnership capital account of $300,000, meaning that economically nothing had changed. But a change has occurred because now Mr. Singleton has a home and owes the bank $300,000. It was the CRA's view that this is how ITA 20(1)(c) must be applied.

7-32. Mr. Singleton argued that ITA 20(1)(c) required a direct-use test with the result that the only relevant transactions were #3 and #4 and that the first two transactions should be ignored.

7-33. The Supreme Court of Canada sided with Mr. Singleton, stating that "absence of a sham or a specific provision in the Act to the contrary, the economic realities of a transaction cannot be used to recharacterize a taxpayers' legal relationships." The result was that ITA 20(1)(c) required a direct-use approach.

Exercise 7-2

Subject: Interest Deductibility—Direct Use

You personally own investments valued at $200,000. You also own a home with a mortgage remaining of $200,000.

Using the direct-use approach concept, describe what you could do to make your mortgage interest deductible under ITA 20(1)(c).

Solutions to Exercises are available in the Study Guide.

The Purpose Test

Supreme Court of Canada—The Ludco Decision

7-34. As previously explained, an interest expense deduction of ITA 20(1)(c) applies if the purpose of the loan or indebtedness is to earn income from a source of income that is a business or property. In addition, ITA 9(3) clarifies that a reference to property income does not include capital gains or capital losses.

7-35. In the *Ludco* decision, Ludco Enterprises Ltd. (a corporation) borrowed $7.5 million, which was used to finance share investments in two companies. During the period that these investments were held, Ludco paid $6 million in interest on the borrowings and received $600,000 in dividends. When the shares were disposed of Ludco realized a $9.2 million capital gain.

7-36. The CRA disallowed the interest expense on the grounds that the shares were acquired for the purpose of earning a capital gain and not for the purpose of earning business or property income. The Supreme Court of Canada sided with Ludco, allowing the full amount of the interest expense to be deducted. The court concluded that an investment can have multiple purposes and, as long as one of these was the earning of property income, the condition that borrowing must be for the purpose of earning income was satisfied.

7-37. In Paragraph 7-12 and in previous chapters the source of income analysis has been discussed. That analysis is consistent with the court decision in *Ludco*.

(1) Has property been acquired or an activity undertaken and that activity capable of generating a profit (i.e., earning income)? Ludco purchased $7.5 million in investments. The investments entitled the owner to receive dividends at the discretion of the board of directors of the two companies. No dividends might have been declared at all or dividends representing substantial returns could have been declared. The source concept looks to the capability of a profit, not a guarantee of one.

(2) Is there a personal element to the property acquired or the activity? No.

(3) Is the level of activity of the property owner or the person undertaking the activity passive or active on a continuous basis? The activity is passive, meaning that the income is from property and not a business.

The Supreme Court of Canada concluded that the investments owned by Ludco constituted a source of property income.

Tracing

Supreme Court of Canada—The Bronfman Trust decision

7-38. The *Bronfman Trust* decision ([1987] 1 SCR 32) is an example of the direct-use approach which allowed the Supreme Court of Canada to extend the concept to what is referred to as the tracing rule. In the *Bronfman Trust* case, one of the beneficiaries requested a large distribution from the trust. The trust did not have the cash to make such a distribution. To meet the request of the beneficiary the trust had the option of either (1) raising the necessary funds by selling investments owned by the trust or (2) borrowing the necessary funds. The trust opted to leave the investments intact and borrow the funds to make the distribution. The trust claimed the interest on the borrowed money as a deduction.

7-39. The court concluded that the interest expense could not be deducted because the borrowed funds were not directly used to earn income from property or from a business. The court took the opportunity to add that "the onus is on the taxpayer to trace the borrowed funds to an eligible use which triggers the deduction." In a subsequent decision the Supreme Court added that "interest is deductible only if there is a sufficiently direct link between the borrowed money and the current eligible use."

7-40. As a result of the above decisions it is the first direct use of the borrowed money that is important, and if that connection changes then the interest may still be allowed as long as the borrowed funds can be traced to a current use that is eligible. Further court decisions have further clarified situations where income earning property is replaced with other income earning property.

> **EXAMPLE 1 Replacement with Single Property** Investments are purchased by borrowing $10,000. Two years later all the investments are sold for $14,000 and all the funds are used as a down payment on the purchase of a personal residence. $6,000 is still owed on the investment loan, and monthly payments continue to be made.
>
> **ANALYSIS 1** The first use of the borrowed funds was to purchase income earning property (the investments) with the result that the interest would be deductible under ITA 20(1)(c). When the investments were sold the source of property income no longer exists, meaning that the interest would no longer be deductible unless the current use of the funds was also to earn income. Since all of the funds were used to purchase a home, the current use would not be eligible and therefore the interest would no longer

be deductible. If the house had been used as a rental property the interest would have remained deductible since the house would have represented a source of property income.

EXAMPLE 2 Replacement with a Business Same facts as Example 1 except that $14,000 is used to invest in a new business.

ANALYSIS 2 The interest would be deductible since the borrowed funds can be traced to the current use of earning business income.

EXAMPLE 3 Replacement with a Single Property Same facts as Example 1 except the investments were sold for only $5,000 and that $5,000 was used to acquire other investments.

ANALYSIS 3 In this case the first direct use was a source of income and the tracing of the current use also remains a source of income. Interest on the current loan remains fully deductible under ITA 20(1)(c) even though the loan balance of $6,000 exceeds the value of the current investments ($5,000). The key is that all of the sale proceeds of the first investments were used to acquire the second investments.

EXAMPLE 4 Replacement with Multiple Properties Same facts as Example 1 except the investments were sold for $10,000 with $4,000 used to purchase Co. A shares and $5,000 used to acquire Co. B shares and $1,000 used to purchase a new television.

ANALYSIS 4 In this case the first direct use was a source of income and the tracing of the current use also remains a source of income except for the personal-use purchase of a television. In effect there are two sources of income replacing the one source. The CRA approach is to prorate the original loan on the basis of the proportion of the sale proceeds that relate to the investments purchased since no one investment equals the loan balance outstanding. In this case 40% of the $6,000 loan balance would be considered to relate to the first investment, 50% to the second, and 10% would be disallowed since it relates to a personal (non-income earning) use.

EXAMPLE 5 Flexible Approach to Linking Same facts as Example 4 except that the investments were sold for $20,000 with Co. A shares purchased for $12,000 and Co. B shares purchased for $8,000.

ANALYSIS 5 In this case, since the cost of both investments exceed the loan balance of $6,000, the CRA provides a flexible approach that would allow all of the loan balance to be considered to relate to (1) the Co. A investments, (2) the Co. B investments, or (3) an allocation between both Co. A and Co. B investments.

EXAMPLE 6 Replacement Properties Less Than Borrowed Money Assume the same facts as in Example 5, except that the original investments were sold for only $5,000. Co. A shares were purchased for $3,000 and Co. B shares purchased for $2,000. In this case the proportion of the loan balance related to the Co. A shares would be $3.600 [($3,000/$5,000)($6,000)] and that related to the Co. B shares would be $2.400 [($2,000/$5,000)($6,000)].

The Disappearing Source Rule—ITA 20.1(1)

7-41. Each of the examples in Paragraph 7-40 described situations where income earning property was replaced with other income earning property with the result that the interest could be traced from the original investment to the replacement investment, thus allowing a continuing claim for interest expenses. However, if the value of investments that were initially financed with borrowed funds declined significantly, taxpayers might find themselves in a situation where the sale proceeds would be insufficient to pay off the remaining amounts owing. In this situation ITA 20.1 provides some relief.

7-42. ITA 20.1(1) applies when there is borrowed money that can no longer be traced to a source of property income because the source has ceased to exist. This generally occurs where an individual sells investments at a loss and the money recovered is insufficient to pay off the remaining loan balance. ITA 20.1(1) applies if the property is non-depreciable capital property (e.g., investment-type property) other than real estate, including land. The rule applies to deem the shortfall to be considered to be used for the purpose of earning a source of property income.

EXAMPLE Mr. A borrows $100,000 to purchase share investments. The value of the shares decline to $10,000 at a time when the loan balance outstanding is $90,000. Mr. A sells the shares for $10,000 and uses that amount to pay down the loan principal to $80,000. Under ITA 20.1, the remaining loan balance of $80,000 will be deemed to be a source of property income with the result that interest on that $80,000 loan balance would continue to be deductible as if the share investments had not been sold. If Mr. A had not used the $10,000 to pay down the loan, it would not have changed the result as only $80,000 of the $90,000 loan balance would be eligible for an interest expense claim from that point forward.

Some Other Exceptions

7-43. At Paragraph 7-14 we began our discussion of the ability to claim an interest expense deduction under ITA 20(1)(c), noting that while most situations are relatively straightforward there are a number of circumstances that required the intervention of the courts. In addressing those special circumstances the courts effectively established a number of interpretative rules and guidelines that are used to resolve ongoing disputes with the CRA as to whether interest is deductible in a given situation. It is not the goal to cover everything here, just the more notable and common situations that are likely to be encountered in practice. This includes the following points:

Filling the Hole This is the expression commonly used to support an interest expense deduction where a corporation borrows money to pay dividends to its shareholders, to repurchase or redeem shares of its shareholders, or to return part of the capital/equity to its shareholders. In all of these situations it could be argued that the borrowed money is not actually used to earn business or property income. The courts, however, took the position that if the payment of dividends would have been made from accumulated profits in retained earnings, that the borrowed money is simply replacing the funds that would have been distributed, or "filling the hole" left, and as a result the interest would be deductible. The courts took the same position where borrowed funds were replacing share capital that was reduced as a result of a return of capital or a redemption or repurchase of the company shares.

Interest-Free Loans It is often the case that newly created corporations, particularly privately owned corporations, require capital to operate. Capital typically arises from a combination of borrowing money or issuing shares. For small private companies the ability to issue shares is limited for a number of reasons, leaving the corporation with borrowing money as its main source of capital. In addition, lending institutions such as banks are reluctant to lend money to unproven corporations with few assets and no track record of profitability. This often leads to shareholders borrowing money themselves, turning around and lending it to their own corporations interest free. You can see that the determination of whether interest on the borrowed funds is deductible to the shareholder rests on whether there is a source of income. Since an interest-free loan can never generate a profit, the CRA had historically disallowed shareholders' claims of interest on the money they borrowed to lend to their own company on the basis that there was no source of income. Administratively, however, the CRA did make certain concessions. Another court decision, however, considered a source to exist where the interest-free loan created an environment where the corporate borrower could, as a result of the interest-free loan, make greater profits, potentially increasing the likelihood of increased dividends to the shareholder. As a result, interest on borrowed money to re-lend to one's own corporation interest free or at a rate below the rate charged to the shareholder by the bank is deductible. Note that lending interest free to a corporation of a family member would not be deductible unless the lender was also a shareholder.

Loans by Corporations to Employees and Shareholders If a corporation borrows money from a bank and then lends that borrowed money to employees or shareholders interest free or at a rate below the rate charged by the bank, the interest paid by the corporation is deductible when the loan is made to an employee but not deductible when the loan is made to a shareholder. The basis for this is that transactions with employees are considered a rough equivalent to remuneration (e.g., salary) and therefore completely deductible in the same manner as most business expenses. Equivalent-type transactions with shareholders are considered to have nothing to do with the corporation's business and therefore the interest paid to a bank would not be deductible at all.

Interest Deductibility—Common and Preferred Shares

7-44. Historically there had been concerns that one could only have a source of income if it was clear that any income would at some point exceed any related expenses. This was the basis for the CRA denying ongoing business losses on the basis there was no reasonable expectation of profit or for denying interest and other expenses where business loans were made by shareholders to their own corporations with borrowed money. In these situations, without actual profits or the potential for actual profits, the widely held belief was that a source of income did not exist.

7-45. Throughout this text it has been emphasized that if the purpose or intent is to earn income from business or property and actual income is earned, then barring the personal element component there is a source of income irrespective of whether a profit is ever realized. The Supreme Court of Canada in the Ludco decision, which we discussed earlier (beginning at Paragraph 7-32), made this abundantly clear. As a result, interest expense is not disallowed simply because it exceeds the actual income. This notion is accepted by the CRA (see paragraph 1.69 of Folio S3-F6-C1).

7-46. Preferred shares often have preferences that restrict their participation in the profits of a corporation to a fixed or stated dividend rate, which is typically required to be paid before any dividends can be paid to common shareholders. Economically, preferred shares are viewed as an equivalent to debt, with accounting principles often requiring that they be reported as if they were debt. This does not change their actual character as shares for income tax purposes.

7-47. In terms of interest deductibility, where investors have borrowed money to purchase preferred shares it is probable that the fixed dividend rate is less than the interest rate charged on the borrowed money, resulting in a property loss. In addition, there is a lack of symmetry in how dividends are taxed as opposed to the income tax deduction on expenses such as interest. In Alberta, for example, dividends from public corporations are taxed to individuals in the highest income tax brackets at 31.7%, while fully deductible expenses would result in a tax break of 48.0%. From a source of income perspective, however, both concerns are irrelevant.

EXAMPLE You borrow $25,000 to purchase preferred shares in a Canadian public company in 2021. You incurred $2,000 of interest expenses in 2021 and received $1,000 in dividends. You had no other expenses.

ANALYSIS In this case you have acquired a source of income (the preferred shares). There exists the capability to earn property income irrespective of the fact that a profit may never occur. The result is that the interest expense is fully deductible. Public company dividends are increased by 38% as a result of a dividend gross up process that is discussed later in this chapter. This means that you include $1,380 in income minus the interest expense of $2,000. The result is a property loss of $620 [$1,380 - $2,000]. Had you received no dividends, your property loss would have been $2,000.

7-48. Common shares represent an ownership interest in a corporation that relies on an actual declaration of dividends for any income other than capital gains. Unlike preferred shares, common shares do not have a fixed or stated dividend rate, and since they are reliant on the board of directors to declare a dividend, which depends on many factors, the reality is that without an obligation to declare and pay dividends a common shareholder may never receive a dime at one extreme, and at the other receive dividends well in excess of their investment.

7-49. This begs the question of whether a common shareholder would be entitled to claim an interest expense for borrowed money used to purchase those shares where dividends are never declared. The source of income concept, reinforced by the Supreme Court of Canada in the Ludco decision, made it relatively clear that the answer is yes. However, if the corporation is under some legal restriction that prevents declaring and paying dividends on certain classes of shares or in general, then it could be argued that there is no possibility of ever receiving any income and therefore a source of income would not exist. In that case, without a source of income no interest expenses could be claimed.

7-50. The CRA takes the analysis one step further, however, stating that if a corporation has declared that it does not pay dividends and has no plans to pay dividends in the foreseeable future then this would leave shareholders in the position of only being able to sell the shares to realize the value in the form of capital gains. In this instance, without a source of income the interest would not be deductible. See paragraph 1.70 of Folio S3-F6-C1.

7-51. Some companies prefer to reinvest their profits instead of declaring dividends. The result is that the value of the shares increase, providing shareholders with an opportunity to report capital gains, which are much more favourably taxed than dividends. In Alberta the tax rate on capital gains to the highest income earners is only 24.0%, as compared to 31.7% on dividends from public companies. We would add when certain private corporations do not pay dividends for the express purpose of allowing their shareholders to realize capital gains rather than dividends, this practice potentially results in the inability to use the capital gains deduction (ITA 110.6(8)). The capital gains deduction would effectively reduce the income tax rate from 24.0% (for individuals in the highest income tax bracket in Alberta) to nil. The capital gains deduction will be discussed in Chapter 11.

We suggest you complete SSP 7-1 at this point.

Discount and Premium on Debt Obligations

Overview

7-52. When a debt obligation is issued with an interest rate below the current market rate, investors will react by offering a price that is less than the maturity value of the security. Such securities are said to sell at a discount and, in economic terms, this discount generally represents an additional interest charge to be recognized over the life of the security, resulting in an increased interest expense that is required to be adjusted in the reconciliation process.

7-53. For example, a 10-year bond with a maturity value of $100,000 and a 10% stated interest rate would sell for $88,700 to investors expecting a 12% interest rate. The discount of $11,300 ($100,000 - $88,700) would then be added to interest expense at the rate of $1,130 per year for the 10-year period. Note that, in order to simplify the presentation of this material, the straight-line amortization method was used for the discount.

7-54. In a corresponding fashion, a debt obligation that offered an interest rate above that currently expected by investors would command a premium. Such a premium would then be treated as a reduction in interest expense over the remaining life of the debt obligation.

7-55. The income tax implications of discounts and premiums on long-term debt are different from the accounting concepts for a number of reasons, including the fact that discounts and premiums do not meet the three legal criteria of interest described in Paragraph 7-25. As a result, discounts and premiums cannot be considered as adjustments to interest expense as they are for accounting purposes.

Issuers of Debt at a Discount

7-56. The ITA contemplates bond discounts by applying two separate rules. The first is ITA 20(2), which deems the amount owing, and therefore the amount used to earn income, to be the amount required to be paid to the debtholders on maturity for the purposes of applying the interest expense deduction of ITA 20(1)(c). This is important because technically the issuer of the bond receives a smaller amount because of the discount, and without this first rule interest would only be deducted on the actual amount received on the issuance of the debt since it is only that amount that is actually used in the income earning activity. This first rule also ensures that the interest expense, which is calculated on the amount required to be repaid at maturity, qualifies in full for an interest expense deduction.

7-57. The second rule is the deduction found in ITA 20(1)(f), which was briefly discussed in Chapter 6. This provision looks to the discount that is paid to the debtholders on maturity (i.e., when the full amount is required to be paid). The deduction is either fully deductible or only 50% deductible depending on whether certain conditions concerning the discount and the effective yield on the debt have been met. If the conditions are met, then the discount is fully deductible; otherwise only half of the discount is deductible.

7-58. The discount is fully deductible provided

- the bonds are issued for not less than 97% of their maturity value; and
- the effective yield on the bonds is not more than 4/3 of the stated, or coupon, rate.

In general terms the effective yield would represent the discount divided by the amount actually received then adjusted for the period of time the debt is outstanding. If, for example, a $100,000 bond is issued for $97,000 for two years with a stated rate of 4.8%, the effective yield would be 6.18% [($3,000/$97,000)(2 years)]. The discount of $3,000 paid at the end of the second year on maturity would be fully deductible under ITA 20(1)(f) because (1) the bond was not issued for less than $97,000 [97% of $100,000] and (2) the effective yield of 6.18% is not more than 6.4% [(4/3)(4.8%)]. If either of the two conditions were not met, then only $1,500 would be deductible.

Exercise 7-3

Subject: Discount Bonds

On January 1, 2021, Moreau Ltd. issues bonds with a maturity value of $1,000,000 and a maturity date of December 31, 2023. The bonds pay interest on December 31 of each year at an annual coupon rate of 4%. They are sold for proceeds of $985,000 for an effective yield of 4.57% [($15,000/$985,000)(3 years)]. The maturity amount is paid on December 31, 2023. What are the income tax consequences related to this bond issue for Moreau Ltd. in each of the years 2021, 2022, and 2023? How would these income tax consequences differ from the information included in Moreau's GAAP-based financial statements? Moreau uses the straight-line method to amortize the discount on the bonds for accounting purposes. Determine the reconciliation adjustments that would be required for each of the three years.

Solutions to Exercises are available in the Study Guide.

Issuers of Debt at a Premium

7-59. There are no specific provisions in the ITA that relate to the income tax treatment of premiums received on issued debt obligations. The reason for this is that there are none required and the analysis falls back on basic income tax concepts of income, capital, and expenses.

7-60. If a debt obligation of $1 million is issued with a very favourable interest rate that results in the issuer receiving $1.2 million, then the additional amount of $200,000 is a premium that does not have to be repaid. In determining the income tax treatment of that premium we have to ask what the nature or character of the amount is to the recipient. Is it income or capital? If the recipient is in a money-lending business and uses the proceeds from the issuance of the debt to make loans in the normal course of its business, then it would support a view that the receipt is part of its income earning structure. The result is that the premium amount of $200,000 would be required to be included in its business income.

7-61. On the other hand, if the debt were issued by a corporation to add to its capital structure in support of its business that had nothing to do with money lending or comparable businesses then the premium would be a capital receipt. This is comparable to investors who purchase shares directly from an issuing corporation and pay an amount that reflects the fair market value based on the financial strength of the issuing company and the terms of the shares issued. In this situation there are no income tax implications associated with the receipt, and the premium amount represents a tax-free capital receipt. This analysis is consistent with the view of the CRA. See paragraph 1.96 of Folio S3-F6-C1.

Interest Income

General Provision—ITA 12(1)(c)

7-62. Consistent with the 9-12-18-20 rule, ITA 12(1)(c) sets out what is required to be included in income as interest from a business or property. This rule is only relevant to the extent that the interest amount included in "profit" through ITA 9 is not the same. If ITA 12(1)(c) requires a different amount to be included, then a reconciliation adjustment would be necessary to reconcile accounting income to net income. ITA 12(1)(c) reads as follows:

> **Interest** ... subject to subsections (3) and (4.1), any amount received or receivable by the taxpayer in the year (depending on the method regularly followed by the taxpayer in computing the taxpayer's income) as, on account of, in lieu of payment of or in satisfaction of, interest to the extent that the interest was not included in computing the taxpayer's income for a preceding taxation year.

7-63. The wording of ITA 12(1)(c) suggests that taxpayers can use the cash basis to recognize interest income (amounts received) or when each payment is due (amounts receivable). This is not the case, since ITA 12(3) and (4.1) override the basic rule. To make matters somewhat worse, ITA 12(4) overrides ITA 12(3). The result is that determining the income tax treatment of when interest income has to be included in income is effectively determined by ITA 12(3) and (4). ITA 12(3) and 12(4) require the use of an accrual approach by all taxpayers. As is discussed in the following material, the accrual approach used by individuals differs from that used by corporations and partnerships. We can ignore ITA 12(4.1) altogether since it only applies to impaired debt obligations, a topic that goes well beyond the scope of this text.

Corporations and Partnerships—Full Accrual Method—ITA 12(3)

7-64. ITA 12(3) requires that corporations, partnerships, and some trusts, at a minimum, use an accrual approach to the end of their respective taxation year. They would also be required to include any amounts actually received or receivable to the extent that the amounts have not already been accrued and included in income. The accrual approach operates on the basis of the passage of time.

> **EXAMPLE** A corporation with a December 31 taxation year end acquires a $5,000 debt instrument (e.g., a GIC (guaranteed investment certificate)) on August 15 of the current year. The instrument pays interest at an annual rate of 8%.

ANALYSIS Interest for the current year would be calculated as follows:

$$[(\$5{,}000)(8\%)(139 \div 365)] = \$152.33$$

7-65. For corporations and partnerships, interest income for income tax purposes is, generally speaking, identical to that required under the application of generally accepted accounting principles (GAAP). However, as will be explained later in this chapter, an exception to this is interest income on bonds that have been purchased at a premium or a discount.

Individuals—Modified Accrual Method—ITA 12(4)

7-66. While ITA 12(3) requires conventional accrual accounting for corporations and partnerships, ITA 12(4) provides for a less familiar version of this concept for individuals. Under this modified version of accrual accounting, interest is not accrued on a continuous basis. Instead, ITA 12(4) requires the accrual of interest based on a concept referred to as the "anniversary date" of an "investment contract."

7-67. ITA 12(11) defines "investment contracts" to include most debt obligations and "anniversary date" to be the day before the day in which the debt obligation was issued and every successive one-year interval measured from that day. This would mean that, for a five-year investment contract issued on July 1, 2021, the anniversary dates would be June 30 of each of the five years 2022 through 2026. If the holder of the investment contract disposes of it prior to its maturity, the disposal date is also considered to be an anniversary date from the point of view of that particular taxpayer, ensuring that interest be accrued to the date of disposal. We would add that the anniversary date looks to the date the investment contract was issued and not the day that it is purchased by individuals. This would mean that if an investment contract were issued on September 1, 2021, but only purchased by an individual on November 27, 2021, the first anniversary date would be August 31, 2022, ensuring that all individuals purchasing that same type of investment contract will have an anniversary date that is the same for all individual investors.

7-68. To the extent that the interest income accrued on the anniversary date has not been previously included in income, it must then be included in the individual's income, regardless of whether the amount has been received or is receivable.

EXAMPLE An investment contract with a maturity value of $100,000 and an annual interest rate of 10% is issued on July 1, 2021. The $100,000 maturity amount is due on June 30, 2026. An interest payment for the first two and a half years of interest ($25,000) is due on December 31, 2023. The remaining interest ($25,000) is due to be paid together with the principal payment on June 30, 2026. The investment contract is purchased by an individual at the time that it is issued.

ANALYSIS The first anniversary date is June 30, 2022, and each June 30 thereafter up until June 30, 2026. As no interest has been received or is receivable in calendar year 2021 and no anniversary date has occurred during the year, no interest would have to be included in the individual's income for 2021. As compared to the use of the full accrual method of ITA 12(3), this provides a one-year deferral of $5,000 [(10%)($100,000)(1/2)] of interest.

Annual interest of $10,000 would have to be accrued on the first two anniversary dates of the contract, June 30, 2022, and June 30, 2023. This means that $10,000 would be included in net income for each of these two years. When the $25,000 payment is received on December 31, 2023, an additional $5,000 would be subject to taxation for that year because it has been received and not previously accrued. This results in taxation of $15,000 in 2023. At this point, the cumulative results are identical to those that would result from the application of the full accrual approach.

For 2024, the June 30, 2024, anniversary date would require the accrual of $10,000. However, as $5,000 of this amount was already included in income during 2023, only

$5,000 of this amount would be required to be included in income in 2024. There would be a further accrual of $10,000 on the anniversary date in 2025. In 2026, an interest payment of $25,000 will be received. As $15,000 ($5,000 + $10,000) of the amount received has been included in 2024 and 2025 income, the total for 2026 will be $10,000 ($25,000 - $15,000).

Under the modified accrual method, the total interest of $50,000 would be recognized as follows:

2021	$ Nil
2022	10,000
2023	15,000
2024	5,000
2025	10,000
2026	10,000
Total	$50,000

Exercise 7-4

Subject: Annual Accrual Rules

On October 1, 2021, Ms. Diane Dumont acquires a newly issued investment contract on the day it is issued with a maturity value of $60,000. It matures on September 30, 2027, and pays interest at an annual rate of 8%. Payment for the first three and one-quarter years of interest is due on December 31, 2024, with interest for the remaining two and three-quarters years payable on the maturity date. What amount of interest will Ms. Dumont have to include in her income for each of the years 2021 through 2027?

Solutions to Exercises are available in the Study Guide.

The Impact of Discounts and Premiums to Investment Contract Holders

7-69. In Paragraphs 7-52 to 7-61 we discussed the impact of discounts and premiums on debt obligations to taxpayers issuing debt obligations to raise capital for their businesses (e.g., debtors). The income tax treatment was shown to vary depending on the facts and relying on the specific provisions of the ITA as well as basic income tax principles. The rules for determining the income tax consequences for investors, however, is much simpler because of another core income tax principle.

7-70. To understand why investors are treated differently than the taxpayers who issue the debt obligations it is important to first have a good appreciation for the concept of "property." When a taxpayer acquires property there is a cost attached to that property, and when the property is disposed of (e.g., sold) there is a sales price or what the ITA calls "proceeds of disposition." When a disposition occurs the income tax system requires establishing whether there is any income as a result. This basic income tax principle is referred to as the "realization principle." The determination of the income tax consequences depends on the character of the property that is disposed of. The three most common types of property are inventory, depreciable property, and non-depreciable capital property. This concept, however, first relies on the existence of "property."

7-71. Property is broadly defined in ITA 248(1) as including a right of any kind. Think about a company issuing bonds at a discount. Assume that an individual investor acquires a $100,000 bond from the issuing company for $92,000. In accounting terms we would say that the individual investor has an asset that is a bond receivable, which would be shown at its present value of $92,000. In income tax terms the individual investor has a "right" to receive $100,000 at some future point. That right is considered property for income tax purposes. The tax cost of the property is what it cost the individual to acquire that right, which would be $92,000. When the bond matures and the investor receives the $100,000, there is a disposition for income tax purposes. The individual investor would effectively be considered to have sold the right (i.e., the bond) for $100,000, which when measured against the tax cost of $92,000 results in a gain of $8,000. If the bond were a simple investment it is likely that the property would be non-depreciable capital property, with the result that the $8,000 would be a capital gain, half of which, or $4,000, would be required to be included in income as a taxable capital gain for the year of the disposition (i.e., the maturity date).

7-72. Assume instead that the bond was acquired at a premium and that the individual investor paid $106,000. On maturity the receipt of $100,000 would result in a loss that would be a capital loss of $6,000. Half of that amount, or $3,000, would be considered an allowable capital loss or an allowable business investment loss. When a bond matures there is a disposition, but if there is no discount or premium then the maturity amount and the tax cost to the investor would be the same and there would be no gain to consider. Although this topic is better suited for the Chapter 8 discussion of capital gains and losses, it has been provided here to give you a well-rounded understanding of the impact of discounts and premiums on debt obligation to both the issuer and the investor.

7-73. This discussion started with comparing the different income tax treatments to an investor and the issuer of debt obligations such as bonds. The investor owns property, being the right to receive an amount. But what about the issuer? The issuer could be described as having an obligation to pay the amount owing at maturity. The problem is that such an obligation is not considered property for income tax purposes. This means that when the issuer pays the amount on maturity there are no implications associated with that event other than those previously discussed at Paragraphs 7-52 to 7-61. If the bond issuer was unable to pay the full amount there are special rules in the ITA referred to as "forgiveness of debt" that could apply to cause the issuer to experience income tax implications, but those rules are also well beyond the scope of this text.

Accrued Interest on Disposition—ITA 20(14)

7-74. Publicly traded debt securities are bought and sold on a day-to-day basis, without regard to the specific date on which interest payments are due. To accommodate this situation, accrued interest from the date of the last interest payment date is added to the purchase price of the security.

7-75. Consider, for example, a 10% coupon, $1,000 maturity value bond, with semi-annual interest payments of $50 on June 30 and December 31 of each year. Assume that the market value of the bond is equal to its maturity value and it is purchased on October 1, 2021. The price would be $1,025, including $25 [($50)(92/184 days)] of interest for the period from July 1, 2021, through October 1, 2021.

7-76. In the absence of a special provision dealing with this situation, the $25 would have to be included in the income of the purchaser when it is received as part of the $50 December 31, 2021, interest payment. Further, the extra $25 received by the seller would receive favourable treatment as a capital gain. To prevent this result, ITA 20(14) treats the seller as having received the $25 of accrued interest, which must be included in income at that time. The provision also allows the purchaser to deduct the same $25 for the same year.

7-77. While ITA 20(14) deals with accrued interest, it does not resolve all the issues. In our example the purchaser paid $1,025 for the bond, which establishes the tax cost at that amount. When the bond matures the purchaser would receive $1,000, which suggests that when measured against the tax cost of $1,025 would result in a capital loss of $25. Since the purchaser would have been entitled to deduct that same $25 difference under ITA 20(14), this indicates that there is something missing since the ITA is written to avoid double taxation. The answer is found in ITA 53(2)(l), which reduces the tax cost to the purchaser by the deduction allowed under ITA 20(14).

The result is that the tax cost (called ACB, or adjusted cost base) is reduced to $1,000 [$1,025 initial cost - the ITA 20(14) deduction for interest] so that on maturity there are no further income tax consequences. Cost adjustments such as IT 53(2) will be discussed in Chapter 8.

Exercise 7-5

Subject: Accrued Interest on Disposition

On May 1, 2021, Mr. Milford Lay purchases bonds for $50,000 with a maturity value of $50,000. The bonds pay semi-annual interest of $3,000 on June 30 and December 31 of each year. Mr. Lay pays $51,989 for the bonds, which includes interest accrued to the purchase date of $1,989. He holds the bonds for the remainder of the year, receiving both the June 30 and December 31 interest payments. What amount of interest will be included in Mr. Lay's 2021 income? What will be the tax cost of Mr. Lay's bonds?

Solutions to Exercises are available in the Study Guide.

Payments Based on Production or Use—ITA 12(1)(g)

7-78. In the discussion of the 9-12-18-20 rule, the starting point was profit from a business or property as a result of ITA 9. ITA 12 was shown to require additional amounts to be included in income, including setting out rules as to how much of a certain type of income should be included and when it should be included if the income differed from the amount included under ITA 9. The underlying premise is that if an amount is already included in income through ITA 9, then ITA 12 does not change that result. In that sense ITA 12 is a complementary set of rules to ITA 9. A good example that demonstrates this concept is the following provision:

> **ITA 12(1)(g)** Payments based on production or use—any amount received by the taxpayer in the year that was dependent on the use of or production from property whether or not that amount was an instalment of the sale price of the property, except that an instalment of the sale price of agricultural land is not included by virtue of this paragraph.

7-79. For a taxpayer who owns rental properties, ITA 12(1)(g) would seemingly apply because of the reference to amounts received for "the use of property." The addition of the word "received," however, further suggests that those rents would only be required to be included in income when actually received as opposed to when earned (on an accrual basis), which goes back to the "quality of income" concept when one has provided the goods or services and is therefore legally entitled to that income. In other words, rental income would be required by ITA 9 to be included in income on an accrual basis.

7-80. Because of the concern that taxpayers could interpret ITA 12(1)(g) to allow rental and similar receipts to be deferred to the year of receipt, seemingly overriding the accrual concept of income, the federal government added ITA 12(2.01), which is a rule clarifying that ITA 9 takes precedence over ITA 12(1)(g). The result is that if ITA 9 applies, then ITA 12(1)(g) does not alter that result. Since rental income is required to be included in income through ITA 9, which would apply an accrual concept to accurately portray a taxpayer's rental income, ITA 12(1)(g) could not apply.

7-81. The purpose of ITA 12(1)(g) is to ensure that a sale of property that includes an entitlement to receive additional amounts based on production or use from that property would not be considered part of the sale price but instead a separate source of property income.

> **EXAMPLE** The owner of land that includes a mineral deposit situated upon it sells the land for $600,000. The agreement calls for a payment of $10 per tonne of ore removed.

The total amount to be paid is not fixed by the sales agreement because of the uncertainty surrounding the amount of ore that will be removed. Assume that over the term of the agreement the seller received $810,000—$600,000 was for the sale of the land and $210,000 for the removal of the ore. Assume that the land originally cost $100,000.

ANALYSIS Without ITA 12(1)(g), the argument would be that the seller realized a capital gain of $710,000 [$810,000 - $100,000], only 50% of which is required to be included in income. The effect of ITA 12(1)(g), however, is to treat $210,000 as property income based on the years received and to treat the sale of the land separately as a capital gain of $500,000 [$600,000 - $100,000].

Rental Income

General Rules

7-82. In this chapter, sources of income that are property are compared with those that are a business. If there is little activity in the form of additional services provided and the role of property owners is passive, generally sitting back and awaiting the rents to arrive, the activity would be categorized as a source of property income. In such a case the profit from that rental activity is required to be included in income on an accrual basis through ITA 9.

7-83. While the accrual basis is required by law (either by specific legislation or as a result of the case law that applies an "Accurate Portrayal of Income," which would require the use of an accrual concept in general), the CRA administratively allows rental property owners to use the cash method in limited circumstances. This administrative concession is set out in the CRA's Guide "Rental Income" (T4036) and reads as follows:

> However, if you have practically no amounts receivable and no expenses outstanding at the end of the year, you can use the cash method. With this method, you:
>
> - include rents in income in the year you receive them; and
> - deduct expenses in the year you pay them.
>
> You can use the cash method only if your net rental income or loss would be practically the same if you were using the accrual method.

7-84. Once the rental revenues are included in income, a variety of expenses become deductible against them. These would include utilities (such as heat, electricity, and water), repairs, maintenance, interest, insurance, property taxes, management fees, and fees to rental agents for locating tenants. CCA can also be deducted. However, as discussed in the next section, the ability to claim CCA is subject to several special rules.

Capital Cost Allowances

General Rules

7-85. As noted, CCA can be claimed on rental properties. In the year of acquisition, rental properties are eligible for the Accelerated Investment Incentive (AccII) provisions, which were discussed in Chapter 5. Individuals can only use a fiscal period for a business they carry on as a sole proprietor or as a member of a partnership and as a result, where a rental property is not a source of business income but rather a source of property, the short fiscal period rules do not apply to prorate a CCA claim.

7-86. Buildings acquired after 1987 will generally fall into class 1, where they are eligible for CCA calculated on a declining balance basis at a rate of 4%. However, as was noted in Chapter 5, if

- a new building is acquired after March 18, 2007;
- it is used more than 90% for non-residential activities by the taxpayer owner or a lessee; and
- an election is made to include it in a separate class 1 when acquired;

it will be eligible for the enhanced CCA rates that were discussed in Chapter 5. You may recall that if the usage, based on floor space, is more than 90% for manufacturing and processing activity, the rate is 10%. If this test is not met, but the building is used 90% or more for other non-residential activity, the rate is 6%.

7-87. As mentioned in Chapter 5, buildings acquired prior to 1988 were included in class 3, where the rate was 5%. This rate continues to apply to class 3 buildings.

7-88. The legal references to a property that includes a building and the land upon which it is situated or constructed do not differentiate between the land and the building. In other words, the law sees both the building and the land as only one property and not two. ITR 1102(2), however, clarifies that classes of depreciable property do not include the land upon which a depreciable property is constructed or situated. This means that when dealing with real property (land and buildings), the ITA only allows the cost of the building to qualify for CCA. As a result, the cost of the land must be subtracted from the whole of the property to isolate the cost of the building. This concept also extends to property that is sold, requiring separate calculations for each of the land and the building. Remember that the building is depreciable property but the land is non-depreciable capital property. While there is the possibility of recapture, a terminal loss, and a capital gain (but not a capital loss) on the sale of the building, the sale of the land will only result in a capital gain or a capital loss.

Special CCA Rules

7-89. There are two special rules that apply to CCA calculations on rental properties. These rules, along with a brief explanation of the reason that each was introduced, are as follows:

> **Separate CCA Classes** Each rental building that is acquired after 1971 at a cost of $50,000 or more must be placed in a separate class for calculating CCA, recapture, and terminal losses. This rule applies whether the rental property is used in a business or as a source of property income. For all practical purposes, the amount of CCA that can be claimed on a rental property would likely exceed any decline in the value of the building, and as a result the likelihood of recapture on the sale of the rental property is high. Given that the $50,000 limit has been unchanged for decades, this rule ensures that virtually all rental properties will be placed in separate classes.
>
> **Rental Property CCA Restriction** In general, taxpayers are not permitted to create or increase a rental loss by claiming CCA on rental properties. For this purpose, rental income is the total rental income or loss from all properties owned by the taxpayer net of all expenses other than CCA. This amount includes any recapture, as well as any terminal losses. The reason for this CCA limitation is to prevent a taxpayer from using CCA to generate rental losses that could then be applied to reduce other income such as employment income.
>
> This restriction does not apply to a corporation or a corporate partnership whose principal business throughout the year is the rental or sale of real property. There are similar restrictions on CCA with respect to leasing properties other than real estate.

7-90. Without question, these special rules make real estate less attractive as an investment. However, a number of advantages remain:

- Income tax on a positive cash flow can be eliminated through the use of CCA.
- Some part of the capital cost of a rental property can be claimed as CCA within the limitation despite the fact that the value of the rental property is increasing in value.
- Increases in the value of the rental property are not required to be included in income until the property is sold.
- Any gain resulting from a sale of a rental property above its tax cost is a capital gain, only one-half of which is required to be included in income.

Rental Income Example

7-91. An example will serve to illustrate the basic features involved in determining rental income.

EXAMPLE On January 1, 2021, Mr. Bratton owns the following two rental properties:

- Property A was acquired in 1987 at a cost of $120,000, of which $20,000 was allocated to land and $100,000 to the building. The UCC of the building is $68,000.
- Property B was acquired in 2014 at a cost of $120,000, of which $30,000 is allocated to land and $90,000 to the building. The UCC of the building is $74,200. On August 28, 2021, Property B is sold for $155,000. At this time, the value of the land is unchanged at $30,000 with $125,000 of the sale price allocated to the building.

On December 1, 2021, Mr. Bratton acquires Property C at a cost of $200,000, of which $50,000 is allocated to the land and the remaining $150,000 allocated to the building. The property is used exclusively for residential purposes.

Gross rents on all of the properties totalled $35,000 during 2021, and the cost of maintenance, property taxes, and mortgage interest totalled $45,400. The source of the rental income is not a business.

Rental Income Calculation The maximum available CCA, (taking the AccII provisions into consideration) on the three rental properties would be as follows:

- Property A (class 3) = $3,400 [($68,000)(5%)]
- Property B (class 1) = Nil (the property was sold during the year.)
- Property C (class 1) = $9,000 [(150%)($150,000)(4%)]

Since a rental loss cannot be created by claiming CCA, the rental income would be calculated as follows:

Gross rents	$35,000
Recapture of CCA on Property B ($90,000 - $74,200)	15,800
Expenses other than CCA	(45,400)
Rental income before CCA	$ 5,400
CCA class 1 (limited)	(5,400)
Rental income	Nil

7-92. The CCA was claimed on class 1, the 4% class, and it is limited to the rental income determined before CCA of $5,400. This follows the general tax planning rule that suggests that, when less than the maximum allowable CCA is taken, the CCA that is deducted should be taken from the classes with the lowest rates. However, if there had been class 8 leasing properties, such as appliances, it could have been more advantageous to claim CCA on the class 8 property first as there is little likelihood of recapture on them given that such properties typically decrease in value. Note that the taxable capital gain of $17,500 [(1/2)($125,000 - $90,000) + (1/2)($30,000 - $30,000)] on the sale of Property B is not part of the rental income or loss calculation.

Exercise 7-6

Subject: Rental Income

Ms. Sheela Horne acquires a residential rental property in September 2021 at a total cost of $185,000. Of this total, $42,000 can be allocated to the value of the land and $143,000 to the building. She immediately spends $35,000 to make major improvements to the property. Gross rents for the year total $7,200, while rental expenses other than CCA total

$5,100. This is the only rental property owned by Ms. Horne. Determine the maximum CCA that can be claimed for 2021 and Ms. Horne's minimum rental income for the year.

Solutions to Exercises are available in the Study Guide.

We suggest you complete SSP 7-2 at this point.

Cash Dividends from Taxable Canadian Corporations—ITA 12(1)(j)

The Concept of Integration

7-93. While this concept will be given much more detailed attention in the Volume 2 chapters dealing with corporate income tax, it is virtually impossible to understand the taxation of dividends received by individuals from taxable Canadian corporations (TCC) without some basic understanding of the concept of integration.

7-94. At the beginning of this discussion it is important to clarify a few points:

- The first is that dividends are only required to be included in the income of a shareholder when actually received. The declaration of a dividend is not relevant for income tax purposes,
- The second is that the income tax consequences of the receipt of a dividend are relevant when the dividend is paid by a TCC. A TCC is defined (ITA 89(1)) as a corporation that meets three conditions. In general it must (1) be incorporated in Canada, (2) be resident in Canada, and (3) not be exempt from Part I tax. A non-profit corporation or an incorporated charitable organization would not qualify as a TCC because they would be exempt from Part I tax.
- While this initial focus is on cash dividends, it is important to be aware that dividends can come in many forms. There are stock dividends, dividends paid with property (called dividends in kind), dividends paid with cash, and amounts that are deemed to be dividends by the ITA.
- The final point is that the dividends that are discussed in this chapter are "taxable dividends," which is another defined term. In general there are two broad types of dividends: those that are required to be included in income of the recipient and those that are not required to be included in income because they are considered tax free. Tax-free dividends are referred to as "capital dividends" and are discussed at length in Chapter 14.

7-95. In summary, in this section the focus will be on cash dividends that are taxable dividends paid by taxable Canadian corporations to individual shareholders. ITA 12(1)(j) requires such dividends to be included in the income of the individual in the year received based on rules found in Subdivision h of Part I of the ITA, which is titled "Corporations Resident in Canada and Their Shareholders."

7-96. The concept of integration is best explained in terms of a comparison between an individual carrying on a business as a sole proprietor and a corporation carrying on the business and distributing all of the after-tax profits to the individual shareholder as a dividend. The purpose of integration is to ensure that at the end of the day both individuals should have the same amount of cash in their pocket regardless of how they structure the business.

7-97. If, for example, an individual's marginal income tax bracket is 40%, an additional $100 in business income earned as a sole proprietor would leave her with $60 in her pocket after paying $40 of income tax.

7-98. Assume instead that the business is carried on by a corporation in which the individual is the sole shareholder. If the corporation's income tax rate is 15% (for example,) then the corporation will be left with $85 after paying income tax. If the corporation distributes that $85 to the individual shareholder as a dividend, the individual should pay income tax of $25, which would then leave her with the same $60 of after-tax cash.

7-99. If the individual included $85 in income and paid 40% in income tax or $34, she would only be left with $51 [$85- $34], which would not provide the appropriate integration result. If, however, the individual shareholder were required to include the full pre-tax income earned by the corporation of $100 and was given an income tax credit of $15 to recognize the income tax paid by the corporation, the result would be that the individual would pay $25 of income tax and be left with the same $60. The calculation of the tax of $25 would then be [$100(40%) - $15].

Implementing Integration

Gross Up and the Tax Credit Mechanism

7-100. The mechanism designed to achieve the integration result shown in Paragraph 7-99 requires two rules. The first, which increases the $85 to $100, is referred to as the "gross up," and the second, which gives the individual a tax credit of $15, is referred to as the dividend tax credit. The two mechanisms are summarized as follows:

> **Dividend Gross Up ITA 82** Dividends received by individuals from taxable Canadian corporations are "grossed up" (i.e., increased) by an amount that reflects the income tax paid at the corporate level. This grossed up amount then represents the amount of income earned by the corporation prior to the payment of corporate income taxes.
>
> **Dividend Tax Credit ITA 121** The individual calculates her gross income tax payable on the grossed up amount of the dividend. A non-refundable income tax credit is then available to apply against that gross income tax on a dollar-for-dollar basis. The tax credit is designed to approximate the corporate income taxes paid by the corporation.

7-101. At this stage our goal is simply to provide you with an overview of integration. As expected, there are no shortage of rules to add complexity, although the basics, as you can see, are relatively straightforward.

7-102. Figure 7-1 sets out a graphical depiction of the integration concept. Using the same example, when the income is from a source of the individual the income tax is described as $X, which in this case would have been $40. When the income is from a source of the corporation, the corporate income tax is shown as $Y, which in our example would be $15. Finally, when the corporation distributes the after-tax profits of $85 to the individual as a dividend, income taxes paid by that individual are described as $Z, which again, in this case, is the additional $25 in income tax that the individual pays on that dividend. The square described as the "Individual Taxpayer" shows the result of perfect integration as a formula of $X = $Y + $Z. In this theoretical example, both sides of that equation would equal $40.

Figure 7-1
The Concept of Integration

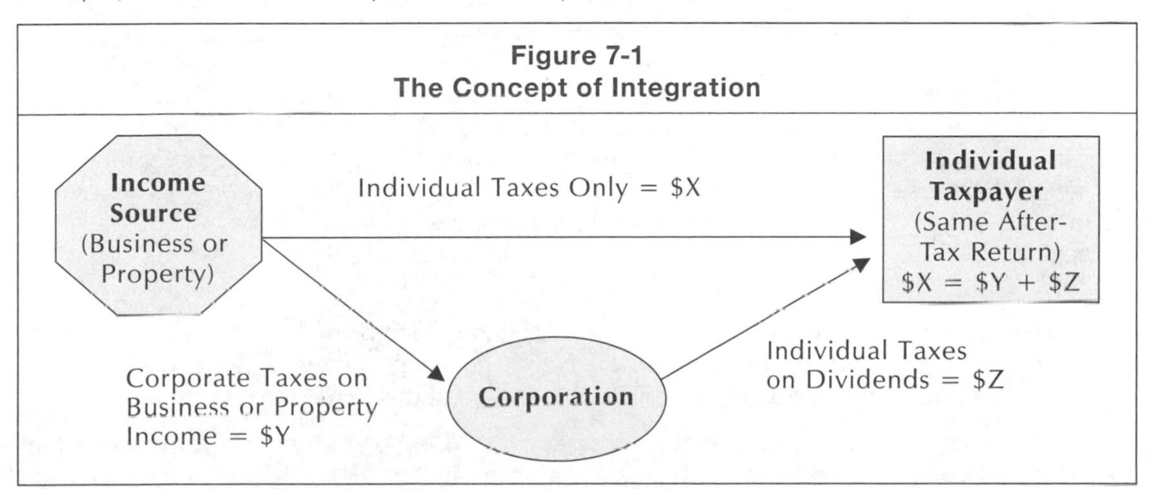

The Problem with Achieving Perfect Integration

7-103. The example that was used demonstrates perfect integration by assuming that the dividend gross up increased the dividend to an amount equal to the income earned by the corporation before the payment of any corporate income tax. It was assumed that the dividend tax credit was equal to the actual corporate income taxes payable. There are two main reasons why perfect integration is rarely achievable, although current gross,up and dividend tax credit rates often produce numbers that are fairly close. The reasons for the difficulty are the following:

Uniform Corporate Tax Rates The goal of the legislation is to provide specific gross up and dividend tax credit numbers that apply to all TCCs. The problem is that corporations are subject to both federal and provincial income tax rates that can vary considerably from province to province. In addition, different types of corporate income are subject to different income tax rates, meaning that identifying a common income tax rate that applies to all TCCs is simply not possible. This creates unavoidable imperfections in the integration system.

Variable Factors It would still be possible to implement perfect integration in the presence of varying corporate income tax rates if we had a system in which specific integration factors were customized for each corporation, with the factor being used reflecting the actual corporate tax rate applicable to a particular corporation. However, this would create many complications and has never been considered a practical alternative.

The Solution—Eligible and Non-Eligible Dividends

7-104. In an attempt to provide some semblance of uniformity, the ITA has established two broad categories of taxable dividends to address these integration difficulties. The two categories were created in recognition of the wide variance in combined (federal and provincial) corporate income tax rates between Canadian public companies and Canadian controlled private corporations (CCPCs). The combined income tax rates on public companies are significantly higher than those on CCPCs. The concepts of eligible and non-eligible dividends are based on this difference in rates.

Eligible Dividends Most of the income of Canadian public companies is taxed at combined federal/provincial tax rates that range from 25% to 31%. Because of these higher income tax rates, the gross up percentage necessary to increase an actual dividend to the pre-tax corporate income taxable dividend is much larger than it is for CCPCs. This larger gross up rate is referred to as an enhanced gross up and applies to most dividends paid by public companies. These dividends are called eligible dividends. The integration factors are based on an assumption that the combined public corporate income tax rate is 27.53623%. While the percentage falls within the range of income tax rates, the use of such an assumption ensures that that there will be imperfections.

Non-Eligible Dividends Most of the business income of CCPCs is taxed at combined federal/provincial tax rates that range from 9% to 14%. Because the income of CCPCs is taxed at lower rates, the gross up percentage required to increase an actual dividend to a taxable dividend equivalent to the pre-tax corporate income is much smaller than for Canadian public companies. As a result the enhanced gross up concepts do not apply and most dividends from CCPCs are called non-eligible dividends. The integration factors for these dividends are based on an assumed combined corporate income tax rate of 13.043%. While this assumed rate falls within the range of income tax rates that apply to CCPCs, the use of a single rate once again guarantees that there will be some imperfections in the system.

7-105. The goal in this coverage is to provide a basic understanding of integration together with a general overview of both eligible and non-eligible dividends in order to determine the income tax consequences when an individual receives either type of dividend.

7-106. There is much more to this story that is covered in Volume 2. One clarification that should be added is that the previous paragraphs have implied that public corporations issue eligible dividends and CCPCs issue non-eligible dividends. While this is often the case, there are limited circumstances in which public corporations can issue non-eligible dividends. In addition, there are more situations in which CCPCs can issue eligible dividends. Because of the integration system, individuals pay less income tax on eligible dividends than on non-eligible dividends, creating a preference for eligible dividends. As a result of this favourable treatment, corporations that qualify to pay eligible dividends must specifically designate that treatment, which is a notification process to the CRA. A dividend that is not designated automatically becomes a non-eligible dividend. This should be kept in mind when answering exercises and problems.

The Gross Up and Dividend Tax credit Mechanism—Eligible Dividends

7-107. When an individual receives eligible dividends, the amount received is increased or grossed up by 38%. This rate is based on a presumption that the corporate tax rate is 27.53623%, as previously mentioned. The following example illustrates the mechanics of this eligible dividend rate:

EXAMPLE Marin Ltd. is subject to a combined federal/provincial tax rate of 27.53623%. During 2021, the company has taxable income of $100,000. All of the company's after-tax income is paid to Mr. Marin, its only shareholder, as a dividend.

ANALYSIS The results at the corporate and individual levels are as follows:

Corporate taxable income	$100,000.00
Corporate tax at 27.53623%	(27,536.23)
Corporate after-tax income and eligible dividends paid	$ 72,463.77
Gross up [(38%)($72,463.77)]	27,536.23
Mr. Marin's eligible dividend	$100,000.00

7-108. The 38% gross up rate works only with the presumed rate to ensure that the individual includes in income a dividend amount equal to the pre-tax income of the corporation. (Five decimal places have been used in these examples to eliminate the need for rounding.) If the corporate tax rate were higher, for example 30%, the after-tax corporate income would be $70,000. The gross up of 38% would be $26,600, resulting in a taxable dividend of $96,600. If the corporate tax rate were smaller, for example 25%, the after-tax corporate income would be $75,000. The gross up of 38% would be $28,500, resulting in a taxable dividend of $103,500. These imperfect integration results set the stage for what is referred to as "overintegration" and "underintegration." A definition of these expressions can be found in the glossary at the back of the Study Guide. In brief, overintegration is a situation in which an individual's income taxes would be smaller if the business were carried on by a corporation rather than directly by the individual. Underintegration is the reverse. In Canada there are few instances of overintegration. Most are related to CCPCs carrying on manufacturing businesses in locations such as Saskatchewan, the Northwest Territories, and Yukon.

The Eligible Dividend Tax Credit

7-109. The federal dividend tax credit for eligible dividends is equal to 6/11 (54.5455%) of the 38% dividend gross up amount. This could also be expressed as 15.0198% of the grossed up dividends, or 20.7273% of dividends received. In the example in Paragraph 7-107, the dividend tax credit would be $15,019.80, which can be expressed as:

- 6/11 of the gross up = [(6/11)($27,536.23)], the calculation we will use in all of our examples; or
- 15.0198% of grossed up dividends = [(15.0198%)($100,000)]; or
- 20.7273% of actual dividends received = [(20.7273%)($72,463.77)].

Note In this text and related problem material, we will follow the ITA and express the dividend tax credit as a fraction of the gross up (e.g., 6/11).

7-110. The 6/11 factor represents the federal dividend tax credit for eligible dividends. There is also an additional dividend tax credit provided by each of the provinces. For integration to be perfect, however, the combined federal/provincial dividend tax credit must be equal to the corporate taxes paid. As the gross up is designed to reflect corporate income taxes paid, this means that the combined federal/provincial dividend tax credit must equal the gross up. This requires a provincial dividend tax credit of 5/11, or 45.4545% (6/11 + 5/11 = 54.5455% + 45.4545% = 100%).

7-111. The following table shows the actual lowest and highest provincial dividend tax credit rates for 2021, as well as the average rate for the 10 provinces:

Eligible dividends—2021	**Lowest**	**Highest**	**Average**
Provincial dividend tax credit			
as a percentage of the 38% gross up	19.6%	50.8%	36.8%
Federal + provincial dividend tax credit	74.1%	105.3%	91.3%

7-112. You should note that the average combined federal/provincial dividend tax credit rate is below 100% of the gross up, the rate required for perfect integration. However, in the highest rate province (New Brunswick), it is above 100%.

7-113. A further point is that the 27.54% corporate rate that is assumed in the gross up of eligible dividends is higher than the combined federal/provincial income tax rate on low-income individuals in all of the provinces. A typical combined individual rate would be 23% (15% federal and 8% provincial). In this situation, integration will not work because, at this rate, the credit cannot compensate for the corporate taxes paid of 27.54%. This is illustrated by Mr. Plummer in the example below.

Example of Eligible Dividends

7-114. The following example illustrates how integration works when the dividend gross up is 38% and the federal dividend tax credit is equal to 6/11 of the gross up. We have noted that, for integration to work perfectly for eligible dividends, the corporate tax rate must be 27.54% and the provincial dividend tax credit equal to 5/11 of the gross up.

EXAMPLE During 2021, Mr. Plummer and Ms. Black each have a business that produces $10,000 in taxable income. While they both live in the same province, Mr. Plummer's income is subject to a 15% federal tax rate and an 8% provincial tax rate. In contrast, Ms. Black's income is subject to a 33% federal tax rate and an 18% provincial tax rate. The provincial dividend tax credit is equal to 5/11 of the gross up and the combined federal/provincial tax rate on corporations is 27.54%.

ANALYSIS—Direct Receipt of Income If Mr. Plummer and Ms. Black received the business income directly, the taxes paid and the after-tax retention of the income would be as follows:

	Mr. Plummer	**Ms. Black**
Taxable income	$10,000	$10,000
Total individual tax payable:		
At 23% (15% + 8%)	(2,300)	
At 51% (33% + 18%)		(5,100)
After-tax retention—Direct receipt	$ 7,700	$ 4,900

ANALYSIS—Incorporation of Income If the businesses were incorporated and all of the corporate after-tax income is paid out as dividends, the taxes paid and the after-tax retention of the income would be as follows:

	Mr. Plummer	Ms. Black
Corporate taxable income	$10,000	$10,000
Corporate taxes at 27.54%	(2,754)	(2,754)
Eligible dividends paid	$ 7,246	$ 7,246
Eligible dividends received	$ 7,246	$ 7,246
Gross up at 38% [(38%)($7,246)]	2,754	2,754
Taxable dividends (= corporate income)	$10,000	$10,000
Individual tax before dividend tax credit:		
At 23% (15% + 8%)	$ 2,300	
At 51% (33% + 18%)		$ 5,100
Less: Dividend tax credit		
(= corporate taxes paid)		
[(6/11 + 5/11)($2,754)]	(2,754)	(2,754)
Total individual tax payable	Nil	$ 2,346
Eligible dividends received	$ 7,246	$ 7,246
Total individual tax payable	(Nil)	(2,346)
After-tax retention—Use of corporation	$ 7,246	$ 4,900
After-tax retention—Direct receipt	$ 7,700	$ 4,900

7-115. The rates in this example are those that are built into the gross up and dividend tax credit mechanism applicable to eligible dividends. That is, the corporate tax rate is 27.54% (rounded) and the provincial dividend tax credit is equal to 5/11 of the gross up. You will note that, while Ms. Black's $4,900 of after-tax retention is not changed by the use of a corporation, Mr. Plummer's after-tax eligible dividends are $7,246, which is $454 less than the $7,700 that he would have retained had he carried on the business as a sole proprietor. This reflects the fact that the assumed corporate tax rate of 27.54% is 4.54% higher than his personal tax rate of 23%, a situation that cannot be corrected by a non-refundable credit against his tax payable. However, if Mr. Plummer had other sources of income, this excess would have offset the taxes on that income.

Exercise 7-7

Subject: Dividend Income—Eligible Dividends

During 2021, Ms. Ellen Holt receives $15,000 in eligible dividends from taxable Canadian corporations. Her income is such that all additional amounts will be taxed at a 29% federal rate and a 14.5% provincial rate. Her provincial dividend tax credit for eligible dividends is equal to 30% of the gross up. Determine the total federal and provincial tax that will be payable on these dividends and her after-tax retention.

Solutions to Exercises are available in the Study Guide.

The Gross Up and Dividend Tax Credit Mechanism—Non-Eligible Dividends

7-116. The 2021 gross up rate for non-eligible dividends is 15% ,which is based on an assumed federal/provincial corporate income tax rate of 13.043%. As illustrated in the following example, this corporate tax rate will allow for taxable dividends that reflect the amount of pre-tax corporate income.

EXAMPLE Marin Ltd. is subject to a combined federal/provincial tax rate of 13.043%. During 2021, the company has taxable income of $100,000. All of the company's after-tax income is distributed to Mr. Marin, its only shareholder, as a dividend.

ANALYSIS The results at the corporate and individual levels are as follows:

Corporate taxable income	$100,000
Corporate tax at 13.043%	(13,043)
Corporate after-tax income and non-eligible dividends paid	$ 86,957
15% gross up [(15%)($86,957)]	13,043
Mr. Marin's taxable non-eligible dividends	$100,000

7-117. As demonstrated in the preceding calculation, the 15% gross up has resulted in a taxable dividend that is equal to the $100,000 pre-tax corporate income that is required to pay the dividend. This is also the amount of income that Mr. Marin would have earned had he carried on the business as a sole proprietor. Similar to the case with eligible dividends, the 15% gross up for non-eligible dividends only works when the combined corporate income tax rate is exactly 13.043%. If the combined corporate income tax rate were higher or lower, then over- or under-integration would occur, as mentioned in Paragraph 7-108.

The Non-Eligible Dividend Tax Credit

7-118. Provided the corporate tax rate is 13.043%, the gross up of 15% serves to increase the taxable non-eligible dividend to the $100,000 amount of pre-tax corporate taxable income on which the non-eligible dividend payment was based. The next step is to provide for a dividend tax credit that matches the gross up, effectively providing credit for the combined corporate income taxes paid on the corporate income that was the base for the dividend.

7-119. Beginning in 2019 the federal dividend tax credit on non-eligible dividends is 9/13 of the gross up. The dividend tax credit of 9/13 can also be expressed as 9.0301% of taxable (i.e., grossed up) dividends, or as 10.3846% of the actual dividends received. In the example in Paragraph 7-114, this amount would be $9,030, which could be calculated as:

- 9/13 of the gross up = [(9/13)($13,043)], the calculation we will use in all of our examples as it follows tax legislation; or
- 9.0301% of grossed up dividends = [(9.0301%)($100,000)]; or
- 10.3846% of actual dividends received = [(10.3846%)($86,957)].

7-120. In order for the combined federal/provincial dividend tax credit to equal 100% of the gross up, the 2021 provincial dividend tax credit for non-eligible dividends must equal 4/13, or 30.7692% of the gross up. The following table shows the actual lowest and highest rates for 2021, as well as the average rate for nine provinces, excluding Quebec (the Quebec system is not comparable):

Non-eligible dividends—2021	Lowest	Highest	Average
Provincial dividend tax credit as a percentage of the 15% gross up	6.0%	46.0%	21.5%
Federal + provincial dividend tax credit	75.2%	115.2%	90.7%

7-121. Note that, while the highest combined rate (Northwest Territories) is well over the 100% required for perfect integration, the average is below the necessary 100% level.

Example of Non-Eligible Dividends

7-122. For non-eligible dividends, integration works perfectly provided the corporate tax rate is 13.043% and the provincial dividend tax credit is equal to 4/13 of the gross up. The following example of this point uses the same two scenarios that were used in Paragraph 7-114 to illustrate the taxation of non-eligible dividends.

EXAMPLE During 2021, Mr. Plummer and Ms. Black each carry on a business as a sole proprietor. The business will earn $10,000 in taxable income. While they both live in the same province, Mr. Plummer's income is subject to a 15% federal income tax rate and an 8% provincial income tax rate. In contrast, Ms. Black's income is subject to a marginal 33% federal income tax rate and an 18% provincial income tax rate. The provincial dividend tax credit is equal to 4/13 of the gross up, and the combined federal/provincial tax rate on corporations is 13.043%.

ANALYSIS—Direct Receipt of Income If Mr. Plummer and Ms. Black earn the business income directly as sole proprietors, the income taxes paid and the after-tax retention would be as follows:

	Mr. Plummer	Ms. Black
Taxable income	$10,000	$10,000
Total individual tax payable:		
At 23% (15% + 8%)	(2,300)	
At 51% (33% + 18%)		(5,100)
After-tax retention—Direct receipt	$ 7,700	$ 4,900

ANALYSIS—Business Carried on by a Corporation If the businesses were carried on by corporations in which both individuals were the sole shareholders and all of the after-tax corporate income is distributed as dividends, the income taxes paid and the after-tax retention of the income would be as follows:

	Mr. Plummer	Ms. Black
Corporate taxable income	$10,000	$10,000
Corporate taxes at 13.043%	(1,304)	(1,304)
Non-eligible dividends paid	$ 8,696	$ 8,696
Non-eligible dividends received	$ 8,696	$ 8,696
Gross up at 15% [(15%)($8,696)]	1,304	1,304
Taxable non-eligible dividends	$10,000	$10,000
Individual tax before dividend tax credit:		
at 23% (15% + 8%)	$2,300	
at 51% (33% + 18%)		$5,100
Less: Dividend tax credit		
(= corporate taxes paid)		
[(9/13 + 4/13)($1,304)]	(1,304)	(1,304)
Total individual tax payable	$ 996	$3,796
Non-eligible dividends received	$8,696	$8,696
Total individual tax payable	(996)	(3,796)
After-tax retention—Use of corporation	$ 7,700	$4,900
After-tax retention—Direct receipt	$ 7,700	$4,900

7-123. The rates in this example are those that are built into the gross up and dividend tax credit mechanism applicable to non-eligible dividends. That is, the combined corporate income tax rate is 13.043% and the provincial dividend tax credit is equal to 4/13 of the gross up. With the assumed corporate rate of 13.043%, which is below the individual income tax rates applicable to the two individuals, the after-tax retention is the same, without regard to whether the $10,000 of income is received directly by the individuals or, alternatively, received indirectly after being earned by a corporation. This is in contrast to the eligible dividend case. In that case (Paragraph 7-115), Mr. Plummer did not have sufficient income tax payable to use all of the available dividend tax credit, resulting in Mr. Plummer being worse off when the income source was earned by a corporation.

Exercise 7-8

Subject: Dividend Income—Non-Eligible Dividends

During 2021, Mr. John Johns receives $17,000 in non-eligible dividends from a taxable Canadian corporation. His income is such that the non-eligible dividends will be subject to a federal income tax rate of 29% and a provincial income tax rate of 12%. The non-eligible dividend tax credit in his province of residence is 30% of the gross up. Determine the total federal and provincial income tax that will be payable on these dividends and his after-tax cash retention.

Solutions to Exercises are available in the Study Guide.

Comparison of Investment Returns

7-124. The table that follows shows, for an individual in the maximum income tax brackets applicable in the stated province, the income tax rates on various types of investment income. As you will note, the rates vary significantly, both between provinces and with the type of investment income.

Maximum 2021 Income Tax Rates for Individuals by Type of Investment Income in Selected Provinces

	Interest Income	Capital Gains*	Non-Eligible Dividends	Eligible Dividends
Alberta	48.0%	24.0%	42.3%	31.7%
British Columbia	53.5%	26.8%	48.9%	36.5%
New Brunswick	53.3%	26.7%	47.8%	33.5%
Quebec	53.3%	26.7%	47.1%	40.1%
Ontario	53.5%	26.8%	47.7%	39.3%

*Only one-half of capital gains are included in income.

7-125. As only one-half of any capital gains is subject to tax, such gains are clearly the most favourable type of investment income. While the tax rates on dividends are not as attractive as those on capital gains, these rates are clearly better than the rates applied to interest income. The fact that eligible dividends are taxed at lower rates than is the case with non-eligible dividends reflects the fact that corporations that pay these dividends are generally subject to higher corporate rates than those applicable to corporations paying non-eligible dividends. In other words, in terms of integration the corporations are paying more of the total income taxes than in the case of non-eligible dividends.

We suggest you complete SSP 7-3, 7-4, and 7-5 at this point.

Mutual Funds

Objective

7-126. Mutual funds are organized to provide investment management, largely for individuals. The basic idea is that investors provide funds to these organizations that they, in turn, use to make direct investments in stocks, bonds, and other types of investment property. It is quite common for individuals holding units in a mutual fund that is a trust to be allocated various amounts of investment-type income, including interest, dividends, foreign investment income, capital gains, and distributions of capital. As will be discussed in the following material, mutual funds can be organized as either trusts or as corporations; however, trusts are much more flexible in terms of an ability to allocate investment income to individual unitholders as if they owned the various investments directly. Mutual fund corporations are generally limited in this regard to distributing investment returns as dividends.

Organization

Mutual Fund Trusts

7-127. In Canada, most mutual funds are organized as trusts. Individual investors in a mutual fund trust hold what are called units of the trust evidencing an ownership interest, which is comparable to owning shares in a corporation. In a trust the unitholders are considered beneficiaries of the trust, entitling them to receive distributions of income and capital from the trust. Trust units are considered "property" for income tax purposes.

7-128. Trusts are a form of a flow-through entity for income tax purposes. Distributions of trust income to its beneficiaries are treated as an income tax deduction to the trust, which reduces the trust's taxable income to nil if all of its income is distributed. The beneficiary unitholders would include the distributed trust income in their own income and pay the income tax on that income as if they earned it directly.

7-129. When a corporation earns income it first pays income tax on that income and can then distribute its after-tax profits as divi-dends. In that case there are two levels of income tax, one by the corporation and a second by the individual shareholders. In addition, the character of the income changes in this process from business or property income earned by the corporation to dividends earned by the individual shareholders. Trusts, however, can reduce income by the distributions made to unitholders and can preserve the character of many types of income. For example, if the trust realizes capital gains and earns dividends and foreign income, then these types of income retain their character in the hands of the beneficiaries. Other trust income, such as business income distributed from a trust, is treated as income from property.

7-130. The effect of this flow-through concept means that individual investors in a mutual fund trust that distributes all of its income are the only ones paying income tax on that trust income. In addition, distributed trust income either retains its character or is treated as property income. Mutual funds issue a T3 income tax slip that details the allocations of various types of income to each beneficiary. Paragraph 7-132 provides a list of some of the more common distributions and their treatment in the hands of beneficiaries. Trusts are discussed in detail in Chapter 19.

Mutual Fund Corporations

7-131. Mutual fund corporations are less common than mutual fund trusts. In this case, the mutual fund will be taxed at regular corporate tax rates on the investment income that it earns. As the investors will be shareholders rather than trust unitholders, in general their distributions will be treated as dividends subject to the gross up and tax credit mechanism. Note, however, that ITA 131 provides an election that allows the dividends of mutual fund corporations to be treated as capital gains in the hands of its shareholders. Like mutual fund trusts, mutual fund corporations are usually committed to distributing all of the after-tax income earned during a taxation year to their shareholders.

Distributions

Mutual Fund Trusts

7-132. The more common types of distributions from a mutual funds trust are as follows:

- **Eligible and Non-Eligible Dividends** These amounts will retain their character and be included in the income of beneficiaries subject to the gross up and tax credit mechanism discussed in this chapter.
- **Canadian Interest Income** These amounts will be taxed as income from property.
- **Capital Gains** As with capital gains earned directly by an individual, only one-half of these amounts will be included in income. The T3 slip only indicates the capital gain and not the taxable portion.
- **Foreign Non-Business (Interest and Dividend) Income** These amounts retain their character as foreign source income, which entitles the beneficiary to claim a tax credit for foreign income taxes paid on these amounts.
- **Capital Distributions** A mutual fund can make capital distributions. Capital distributions are the equivalent to a partial return of one's investment and as a result the adjusted cost base (ACB) of the trust units are reduced. These distributions are considered tax-free capital receipts unless they exceed the ACB of the units and create a negative amount. In such case the negative amount is treated as a capital gain, which then causes the ACB to become nil. The T3 slip identifies any return of capital.

Mutual Fund Corporations

7-133. Shareholders in mutual fund corporations receive dividends from the after-tax income earned by the corporation's investments. Unlike the situation with mutual fund trusts, the investment income earned by the mutual fund corporation does not flow through and retain its character when distributed to shareholders. This means that dividend declarations from investment income of the mutual fund corporation are simply paid out as taxable dividends which are almost always eligible dividends.

Adjusted Cost Base (ACB)

Mutual Fund Trusts

7-134. Determining the income tax cost or adjusted cost base (ACB) of a mutual fund trust unit is similar for most investments. The basic rules will be discussed at length in Chapter 8. They begin with the initial cost, which is then subject to specific adjust-ments that may either increase or decrease that cost that then becomes the ACB.

7-135. Mutual fund units add two elements not typically seen in other investments, however. The first is that allocated income flowed to a unitholder can be reinvested without the unitholder actually having received anything. In that case the ITA treats this as two separate transactions, as if the allocated income was actually received and then separately reinvested to acquire additional units. The second element is that a mutual fund trust can make a capital distribution that is a return of capital, which reduces the ACB of the trust units.

> **EXAMPLE** On October 15, 2021, Martin Diaz purchases 1,000 units of CIC Growth Fund for $7.30 per unit. On December 1, 2021, the fund has an interest income distribution of $.50 per unit. At this time, the fund has a purchase price of $6 per unit.

> **ANALYSIS** Regardless of whether or not Mr. Diaz reinvests the distribution, he will include $500 [($0.50)(1,000 units)] in his 2021 net income. If Mr. Diaz chooses not to reinvest the distribution, he will receive $500 in cash. He would then have 1,000 units with his original ACB of $7.30 per unit. Alternatively, if the distribution is reinvested, he will receive 83.33 ($500 ÷ $6) additional units. This will leave him with a holding of 1,083.33 units with an ACB of $7,800 ($7,300 + $500), or $7.20 ($7,800 ÷ 1,083.33)

per unit. Note that if the trust subsequently paid Mr. Diaz $1,000 as a return of capital, the ACB of the units would decrease from $7,800 to $6,800 and the $1,000 amount received would be a tax-free capital receipt.

Mutual Fund Corporations

7-136. The ACB of the shares of a mutual fund corporation will not be altered as a result of a dividend distribution. However, corporations are entitled by the corporate law under which they are created to allow a return of capital in specific circumstances. In such cases a return of capital would reduce the ACB of the shares and would not be included in any shareholder's income. Returns of capital are not common for mutual fund corporations.

7-137. If a shareholder decided to reinvest the dividends paid by the mutual fund corporation, the cost of the additional shares would be added to the ACB of the original shares, assuming that the shares would be the same. Such reinvestments are less common with mutual fund corporations than they are with mutual fund trusts.

Exercise 7-9

Subject: Mutual Fund Distributions

Ms. Marissa Tompkins owns 3,500 units of the RB Small Cap Fund, a mutual fund trust. These units were purchased at a price of $11.25 per unit for a total value of $39,375. There have been no changes in her adjusted cost base prior to the current year. On September 1 of the current year, the fund has an income distribution of $0.30 per unit, a total of $1,050 for Ms. Tompkins. She reinvests this amount to acquire additional fund units at $13.00 per unit. What is the ACB per unit after the reinvestment?

Solutions to Exercises are available in the Study Guide.

We suggest you complete SSP 7-6 and 7-7 at this point.

Other Types of Dividends

Capital Dividends—ITA 83(2)

7-138. As stated in Paragraph 7-95, only "taxable dividends" are required to be included in the income of individual shareholders. Such dividends are categorized as either eligible or non-eligible dividends and are subject to the gross up and tax credit mechanism that has been discussed. However, not all dividends are taxable. Tax-free dividends are referred to as capital dividends.

7-139. Capital dividends achieve that status by an election made by private corporations only when there is a "capital dividend account," or CDA. The CDA accumulates amounts of a private corporation that in Canada's income tax system are considered tax free. Two common examples are life insurance proceeds received by a private corporation and half of capital gains net of capital losses. If, for example, in 2021 a private company realizes a capital gain of $72,000, only half of that gain, or $36,000, would be taxable. The CDA of the company would increase by $36,000 for the untaxed half. If the corporation wanted to declare a capital dividend they would do so by declaring a regular dividend of $36,000 and then filing an election with the CRA to treat that dividend as a tax-free capital dividend, which would then reduce its CDA balance to nil. This topic is discussed in detail in Chapter 14. A capital dividend can be elected on any type of dividend whether it is paid with cash, property, or even if it is a deemed dividend.

7-140. Capital dividends received by resident Canadian individuals are tax free and not required to be included in income. In addition there are no adjustments to the ACB of the recipient shares as a result of the capital dividend. There are, however, potential implications if, in the future, the individual shareholders sell their shares at a loss. The fact that capital dividends were previously received may impact the amount of that loss.

7-141. Capital dividends can only be elected by private corporations such as CCPCs. This means that public companies cannot pay capital dividends. However, there are means by which a public company can distribute tax-free amounts to shareholders that are the economic equivalent to a capital dividend. This is discussed to some extent in Chapter 16.

Stock Dividends

7-142. A dividend is legally defined as the distribution of a corporation's profits to its shareholders. When what is commonly referred to as a stock dividend is declared, the dividend is actually paid by providing shareholders with payment that consists of additional share certificates. In effect, a stock dividend would not qualify as a dividend in the legal sense, however the ITA defines a dividend to include a stock dividend, which ensures that they are treated in the same manner as any other dividend. This means that if no capital dividend election is made by companies that are private companies, the dividend will be categorized as either an eligible or non-eligible dividend subject to the tax treatment previously discussed.

7-143. From an accounting point of view a stock dividend involves a transfer of retained earnings or surplus to corporate shares or contributed capital. This is commonly referred to as a capitalization of retained earnings/surplus.

7-144. For income tax purposes the ITA looks at the paid-up capital (PUC), which is basically the income tax equivalent of accounting share capital. PUC is discussed throughout Volume 2 of the text given its importance to corporate taxation. The amount required to be included in the income of an individual shareholder who has received a stock dividend is the increase in the PUC of their shares. In addition, that same amount is considered to add to the ACB of the shares. The determination of how this amount is determined goes beyond the coverage of this chapter.

EXAMPLE Lindsey owns 5,000 shares of XYZ Company. A dividend is declared that will be paid by issuing additional shares equal to 15% of the number of shares held by a shareholder at the time the dividend is declared. The PUC of each additional share issued as a stock dividend will increase the PUC by $10. No capital dividend election will be made and the dividend will be considered an eligible dividend.

ANALYSIS Lindsey will receive 750 additional shares as a result of the stock dividend [(15%)(5,000)]. Given a $10 per share PUC increase she will be considered to have received a $7,500 eligible dividend, which will be grossed up by 38%, requiring her to include $10,350 in her income. In addition, she will be entitled to a federal dividend tax credit of $1,555 [(gross up of $2,850)(6/11)]. Finally, the ACB of her 5,750 shares will be increased by $7,500.

Exercise 7-10

Subject: Stock Dividends

Morgna Inc. has 2,000,000 common shares outstanding. John Morgna acquired 10% of these shares at a cost of $12 per share. During the current year, when the shares are trading at $15 per share, the company declares a 10% stock dividend that it designates as eligible. The company transfers the amount of the stock dividend to PUC. What are the tax consequences to John Morgna of this transaction? Your answer should include the ACB per share of his holding.

Solutions to Exercises are available in the Study Guide.

Foreign Source Income

General Rules

7-145. As a resident of Canada, individuals are subject to income tax on their worldwide income, meaning income regardless of whether it is from Canadian or foreign sources. Foreign income, however, is often subject to income tax in the country in which it is sourced. This means that the same income will be subject to tax in both Canada and that other country. To compensate, Canada provides a foreign tax credit to offset the Canadian income tax on that income and to avoid excess and potentially double taxation. The general principle is that Canada provides a credit up to the maximum of the amount of Canadian tax the individual would have paid had the income been sourced in Canada.

7-146. Assume, for example, that an individual is in a 40% income tax bracket in Canada and receives $100 of foreign investment income that is subject to income tax of 12% in the foreign country. The foreign tax credit concepts are designed to provide a tax credit of $12, which offsets the $40 of Canadian income tax that would have been charged had the income been earned in Canada. The result is that the individual still pays $40 in income tax, but $12 goes to the foreign country and $28 to Canada. In other words, there is a sharing of the income tax. If the foreign country had charged, say, 42% in income tax, the Canadian tax credit would only compensate for the $40 of Canadian tax that would have been charged had the income again been earned in Canada. In that case the Canadian income tax would be nil and the foreign income tax $42. The effect is that Canada does not compensate for foreign income taxes in excess of the amount that would have been charged in Canada.

7-147. Canadian resident individuals who earn income in other countries are required to include in their net income that foreign income after being adjusted for conversion into Canadian currency. As with Canadian income sources, the foreign amount that is included is the pre-tax amount.

EXAMPLE An individual earned the equivalent of $1,000 in Canadian income in a foreign country that charges 10% income tax. The individual's Canadian marginal income tax rate is 45%.

ANALYSIS The Canadian income tax payable on the foreign income would be calculated as follows:

Foreign income	$1,000
Increase in taxable income	$1,000
Income tax rate	45%
Gross income tax payable	$ 450
Foreign tax credit	(100)
Canadian income tax payable	$ 350

Note that the combined foreign and Canadian income tax is equal to $450 ($350 + $100), the same amount that the individual would have paid had the income been earned in Canada.

7-148. There are two general foreign tax credits. ITA 126(1) addresses non-business foreign tax credits and ITA 126(2) addresses foreign tax credits. Foreign non-business income includes foreign employment, foreign capital gains, rental income from foreign properties where the rental activity is not a business, and foreign investment income such as interest, dividends, and royalties. Foreign non-business income is discussed in the next section with emphasis on property income, such as investment income, because of the additional ITA considerations that include deductions under ITA 20(11) and 20(12).

Foreign Non-Business (Property) Income

7-149. Individuals who earn foreign non-business income are allowed a maximum foreign tax credit of 15%. ITA 20(11) permits any amount above 15% that is charged by a foreign jurisdiction to be deducted against the non-business income. The result is that Canada takes a larger share of the income tax on that income since a full credit is not given for the foreign income taxes paid.

EXAMPLE Assume that Ms. Rice earns C$100 in investment income in a country that charges income tax of 20%, or $20 on that income. Assume that Ms. Rice is in a 40% marginal income tax bracket in Canada.

ANALYSIS The amount required to be included in income is $95. This is equal to the $100 of foreign non-business income minus $5, which is the amount of the foreign income tax in excess of 15%, or $15. The Canadian income tax would have been $38 [(40%)($95)]. The foreign tax credit is limited to 15% or $15.

Foreign income [$100- $5 deduction for excess foreign tax paid]	$ 95
Increase in taxable income	$ 95
Income tax rate	40%
Gross income tax payable	$ 38
Foreign tax credit	(15)
Canadian income tax payable	$ 23

In this case, while Ms. Rice paid $20 in foreign income tax an additional $23 of income tax has to be paid in Canada, totalling $43. This is in excess of the $40 that would have been paid had the income been earned in Canada. The reason is that Canada limits foreign non-business tax credits for individuals to 15%. Canada's tax system only gave credit for $17 of foreign tax [$15 tax credit + (40%)($5 tax deduction)].

Foreign Business Income

7-150. In the case of foreign source business income, there is no limitation on how much of the foreign taxes can be claimed as a foreign tax credit as there is with respect to foreign non-business income of individuals. There is still, however, the overall limitation that the foreign tax credit cannot be higher than the amount of Canadian income tax that would have applied had the income been earned in Canada.

EXAMPLE Mr. Grant, an individual taxpayer with a marginal income tax rate of 45%, earns foreign source income of $1,000. The foreign income tax rate is 40%.

ANALYSIS The Canadian income tax payable on the foreign income, assuming it is foreign non-business (e.g., investment) income or business income, would be calculated as follows:

	Non-Business Income	Business Income
Foreign income	$1,000.00	$1,000.00
Deduction of excess withholding [$400 - (15%)($1,000)]—ITA 20(11)	(250.00)	N/A
Increase in taxable income	$ 750.00	$1,000.00
Income tax rate	45%	45%
Gross tax payable	$ 337.50	$ 450.00
Foreign tax credit [(15%)($1,000)]—ITA 126(1)	(150.00)	
Foreign tax credit—ITA 126(2)		(400.00)
Net tax payable	$ 187.50	$ 50.00

ANALYSIS—Foreign Non-Business Income Income of $750 will be included in net income. Foreign and Canadian taxes combined would be $587.50 ($400 + $187.50), well in excess of the $450 that would have been paid on $1,000 of Canadian source income. This illustrates that the availability of the deduction does not make up for the fact that the tax credit is limited to 15%. The value of a $1 tax credit is $1, whereas the value of a $1 deduction to Mr. Grant is only $0.45 [($1)(45%)]. It should be noted that it is unusual for other countries to charge income tax on investment income at rates above 15%; 40% was used in this example to illustrate what happens when foreign taxes paid are higher than the equivalent Canadian taxes that would have been paid.

ANALYSIS Foreign Business Income The business income of $1,000 will be included in net income. The full $400 of withholding will be used to calculate a foreign tax credit against Mr. Grant's Canadian tax payable of $450 [(45%)($1,000)]. This leaves $50 in Canadian income tax and total income tax of $450 ($400 + $50). This is the same amount he would have paid had the income been earned in Canada.

Exercise 7-11

Subject: Foreign Source Income

Norah Johns earns foreign source income of $30,000 during the current year. The foreign country charges an income tax rate of 25% on such income. Norah has other income such that this foreign source income will be subject to a marginal federal income tax rate of 29%. Determine the impact on Norah's taxable income and the federal tax payable, assuming that the foreign source income is (1) non-business income and (2) business income.

Solutions to Exercises are available in the Study Guide.

Shareholder Benefits—ITA 15(1) & (2)

7-151. Property income for individuals can also include additional amounts where the individual is a shareholder of a corporation. The potential benefits fall into the following three broad categories:

- Benefits that would be taxable employment benefits were it not for the fact that the benefit is received because the individual is a shareholder. An example of this would be premiums paid into a private health services plan by an employer for dental or other health care benefits. While there is no benefit for an employee, there would be for an individual who has received the benefit because of being a shareholder.
- Benefits that go well beyond what would be considered employment benefits. An example would be where an individual creates their own corporation and a business is carried on by that corporation. If that individual removed $10,000 from the corporate bank account or charged personal expenditures to the company (a line of credit or corporate credit card), the amounts would be included in his income as income from property.
- A shareholder borrows money from the corporation. ITA 15(2) can apply to require that the amount borrowed be included in the income of the shareholder when borrowed.

7-152. These three types of benefits are the subject of considerable scrutiny by the CRA in the course of audits of many corporations, particularly CCPCs. Reassessments by the CRA often involve ITA 15(1) and 15(2) together with disallowance of related expense claims by the corporation. Penalty assessments, such as the gross negligence penalties under ITA 163(2), are quite common.

7-153. These types of shareholder benefits are discussed at length in Chapter 15, "Corporate Taxation and Management Decisions."

We suggest you complete SSP 7-8 and 7-9 at this point.

Key Terms

A full glossary with definitions is provided at the end of the Study Guide.

Accrual Basis
Business Income
Capital Dividend
Capital Dividend Account (CDA)
Cash Basis
Disappearing Source Rule
Dividend Gross Up
Dividend Tax Credit
Dividends
Eligible Dividends
Foreign Tax Credit
Interest Income
Mutual Fund
Non-Eligible Dividends
Property Income
Stock Dividend

References

For more detailed study of the material in this chapter, we would refer you to the following:

ITA 12(1)(c)	Interest
ITA 12(1)(g)	Payments Based on Production or Use
ITA 12(3)	Interest Income
ITA 12(4)	Interest from Investment Contract
ITA 12(11)	Definitions (Investment Contract)
ITA 15	Benefits Conferred on Shareholder
ITA 20(1)(c)	Interest
ITA 20(1)(f)	Discount on Certain Obligations
ITA 20(14)	Accrued Bond Interest
ITA 20.1	Borrowed Money Used to Earn Income from Property (Disappearing Source)
ITA 82(1)	Taxable Dividends Received
ITA 121	Dividend Tax Credit
ITA 126	Foreign Tax Credit
S3-F2-C1	Capital Dividends
S3-F6-C1	Interest Deductibility
S5-F2-C1	Foreign Tax Credit
IT-67R3	Taxable Dividends from Corporations Resident in Canada
IT-195R4	Rental Property—Capital Cost Allowance Restrictions
IT-274R	Rental Properties—Capital Cost of $50,000 or More
IT-396R	Interest Income
IT-434R	Rental of Real Property by Individual
IT-443	Leasing Property—Capital Cost Allowance Restrictions
IT-462	Payments Based on Production or Use
IT-506	Foreign Income Taxes as a Deduction from Income
RC4169	Treatment of Mutual Funds for Individuals
T4036	Rental Income Guide

Self-Study Problems (SSPs)

Self-Study Problems (SSPs) provide practice in problem solving. Within the chapters, we have indicated where it would be appropriate to stop and work on each SSP. The problems can be downloaded by chapter from MyLab Accounting. Solutions are available in the Study Guide. Select problems can also be completed directly in MyLab and auto-graded.

Assignment Problems

Solutions to Assignment Problems (APs) are available to instructors only.

AP 7-1 (Interest Deductibility—Four Cases)

Each of the following independent cases involves interest expense and determination of whether the interest is deductible for income tax purposes.

Case A Monica Lewis borrows $700,000 using her Toronto condo as collateral security. She uses the amount to purchase high-tech common shares that she anticipates will double in value during the coming year.

Unfortunately, instead of doubling, the stocks lose 60% of their value. They are sold during the year for $280,000, with all of the proceeds being used to pay down the loan. The balance of $420,000 ($700,000 - $280,000) is still outstanding at the end of the year. Monica is uncertain as to when she will be able to pay off this remaining amount. Can she continue to deduct the interest on the amount of the outstanding loan? Explain your conclusion.

Case B Garner Blake borrows $850,000 to purchase a duplex that he intends to rent to arm's-length tenants. After considerable efforts he was unable to find any tenants willing to rent either side of the property. He subsequently learned that the supply of such properties was well in excess of the demand. As a result he was forced to sell the duplex at a loss the following year for $600,000. Recognizing that the market for duplex rentals is weak, he used the sale proceeds to purchase two single family rental properties, the first for $250,000 and the second for $350,000.

Case C Perry Carson acquires a rental property for $575,000, 100% financed with a bank loan. Several years later, when the bank loan has been paid down to $500,000, he sells the property for $825,000. He uses the proceeds to acquire two other rental properties, the first for $275,000 and the second for $550,000. The bank loan is maintained with the balance remaining at $500,000. Explain how the $500,000 balance of the loan can be allocated to the two properties.

Case D Thomson Fraser has always dreamed of owning a Rolls Royce SUV, which costs $525,000. His bank has agreed to finance the purchase with a loan that bears interest at 7.5%.

However, he can borrow the same amount using a margin loan against the investments in his substantial trading account. The interest rate on such a borrowing would only be 4%. He decides to take advantage of the lower interest rate to purchase the car. Since the loan is connected to his income earning investments as collateral, he assumes that he will be able to claim a deduction for any interest. Is he correct? Explain your conclusion. If you conclude that the interest would not be deductible, is there some tax advice you could provide that would allow the interest to be deductible?

AP 7-2 (Rental Income, Including CCA)

During 2021, Ms. Alice Becker owns four residential rental properties. Relevant information on these properties is as follows:

	26 Hart Street	32 Barton Boulevard	14 Mark Avenue	96 Flagler Street
CCA class	1	1	3	1
Capital cost of building	$1,180,000	$307,500	$1,033,750	$570,000
January 1, 2021, UCC	Nil	266,250	703,250	514,800

Rental receipts and expenses, not including CCA, for the year ending December 31, 2021, are as follows:

	26 Hart Street	32 Barton Boulevard	14 Mark Avenue	96 Flagler Street
Rental receipts	$79,500	$16,000	$63,000	$46,500
Property taxes	(17,756)	(12,113)	(15,500)	(18,550)
Interest charges	(51,625)	(5,250)	(30,000)	(12,750)
Other expenses (not including CCA)	(4,500)	(1,375)	(6,750)	(10,500)
Net rental income (loss) Before CCA	$ 5,619	($ 2,738)	$10,750	$ 4,700

Other Information:

1. The property at 26 Hart Street was acquired during 2021 for $1,180,000.
2. The property at 32 Barton Boulevard was sold during 2021 for $231,000.

   Ms. Becker had furnished this property several years ago at a cost of $28,750. The UCC for these class 8 assets was $4,498 on January 1, 2021. Given the condition of the furnishings, they were simply given to the former tenants, who agreed to take them when they moved out.
3. During 2021, Ms. Becker spent $78,750 on capital improvements to the property at 14 Mark Avenue. While none of the changes were required, the incoming tenant insisted on the changes before agreeing to the lease. These improvements will enhance the value of this property.
4. The building at 96 Flagler Street was sold during 2021 for $653,000.

Required: Calculate Ms. Becker's minimum rental income for 2021. You should provide a separate CCA calculation for each property and specify how much CCA should be taken for each building. Include in your solution any income tax consequences associated with the sale of the two buildings and the disposition of the furniture. Assume that the rental activity is not a business and that the property values and costs shown are for the building only.

AP 7-3 (Rental Income)

On March 1, 2020, Ms. Fox acquires a residential duplex for a total cost of $725,000. Of this total, it is estimated that the land has a value of $150,000 at the time of the acquisition and the building value was $575,000. The two units are identical in size and, for purposes of allocation to a CCA class, the property is considered to be a single property.

Before the end of March 2020, both units were rented. The tenants occupying one of the units asked that, in return for an additional amount of rent, Ms. Fox furnish the unit. Furniture and appliances for the unit were acquired by Ms. Fox on April 1, 2020, at a cost of $18,500.

During the taxation year ending December 31, 2020, rents on the two units totalled $68,500. Expenses, other than CCA, totalled $28,000.

Late in 2021, the tenants in the furnished unit moved out. As Ms. Fox did not wish to continue renting the unit on a furnished basis, she sold the furniture and appliances to the departing tenants for $14,000.

During 2021, the two units generated total rent of $45,000. Ms. Fox incurred expenses, other than CCA, of $32,000.

Ms. Fox deducted the maximum CCA allowable in both years.

Required: Calculate the minimum rental income for each of the two years 2020 and 2021. Also, determine the UCC balances on January 1, 2022. Include in your solution any income tax consequences associated with the sale of the furniture and appliances.

AP 7-4 (Dividend vs. Interest Income)

Cindy, Charlotte, and Carol Brock are sisters who are Canadian residents. Over the years, they have enjoyed varying degrees of economic success. As a consequence, they are currently subject to significantly different tax rates. This is shown in the following table:

	Cindy	Charlotte	Carol
Federal marginal tax rate	15%	26%	33%
Provincial marginal tax rate	7%	14%	21%

In 2020, their father and mother both died. Their will leaves all of their property to their three daughters to be shared equally. While it will take some time for their estate to be completely settled, the trustee was able to distribute cash of $300,000 during 2020.

Each of the sisters intends to invest their $100,000 share of the distribution on January 1, 2021. They are considering the following two alternatives:

Corporate Bonds Corporate bonds that provide a 6% coupon rate. These bonds can be purchased at their maturity value. They mature in 12 years.

Common Shares The common shares are available at a price of $50 per share. These shares pay a well-established annual eligible dividend of $3.25 per share.

The income from these investments would not move any of the three sisters to a higher federal or provincial tax bracket. The provincial dividend tax credit on eligible dividends is equal to 25% of the dividend gross up. Each sister already has sufficient income to use all of the available tax credits.

Required: Advise each of the Brock sisters as to which investment they should make. Include a calculation of the after-tax return that would be generated for each of the sisters, assuming that they invested their $100,000 in

A. the corporate bonds.
B. the common shares.

Comment on any other factors that they should consider in making their choice.

AP 7-5 (Investments in Mutual Fund Trusts and Common Shares)

Late in the year 2020, Ms. Sarah Stein inherits $550,000 from an eccentric uncle. The terms of his will require that Sarah use $250,000 of this amount for luxury travel within 12 months of her receipt of the funds. Any unspent balance of this $250,000 will be returned to the uncle's estate and distributed to a specified group of charities.

With respect to the remaining $300,000, there are no restrictions on its use. Because of the time commitment related to the luxury travel, Ms. Stein would like to invest this balance for a one-year period, commencing January 1. She is considering the following alternative investments and would like your advice on the appropriate choice:

H & R Mutual Fund Trust On January 1, 2021, trust units are selling for $20. It makes a distribution of $0.0725 per unit per month. This distribution is property income only and does not include any dividends, capital gains, or return of capital. Ms. Stein does not expect any price change in the units in 2021.

Dream Spinner Tech Common Shares On January 1, 2021, these shares are selling for $10 each. The company pays an annual dividend of $0.05 per share. This will be an eligible dividend. Ms. Stein anticipates that these shares will be selling for at least $10.50 per share on December 31, 2021.

In order to accommodate the required luxury travel, Ms. Stein will use her six months of accumulated vacation pay and take an unpaid leave of absence from her employer for the remainder of the year. Her employment income will be $50,000 for 2021. Taxes on this income are sufficient to use all of her available tax credits before considering the effects of the two investments described above.

Given her employment income, any additional income from her investment will be taxed at a federal rate of 20.5% and a provincial rate of 11.5%. In her province of residence, the dividend tax credit for eligible dividends is equal to 25% of the gross up.

Required: Write a brief memorandum providing investment advice and recommendations to Ms. Stein. Include all calculations such as tax payable and after-tax returns on each investment.

AP 7-6 (Business and Property Income)

Mr. Sonny Shark is an accountant who has a well-established practice in Edmonton.

Relevant information on his practice for the taxation year ending December 31, 2021, is as follows:

December 31, 2021, unbilled work-in-progress	35,000
Billable hours (1,900 hours at $250 per hour)	475,000
Office supplies and office expenses	56,000
Travel costs other than meals and entertainment	8,000
Business meals and entertainment	12,000

Mr. Shark purchased the building in which his practice is located in 2004. His practice uses 50% of the floor space in the building and, on January 1, 2021, the class 1 UCC for the building is $526,000.

Since the building was purchased, the other one-half of the building had been rented to a lawyer who was paying rent of $4,000 per month. This lawyer retired on July 1, 2021. Despite all his efforts, Mr. Shark could not find a new tenant and received rent for only six months during 2021.

The 2021 interest, taxes, and other expenses (other than CCA) that can be allocated to the one-half of the building that was rented total $14,400.

Mr. Shark owns the furnishings in his office. The cost of these furnishings was $24,000 and, on January 1, 2021, the class 8 UCC for these furnishings was $11,059.

Mr. Shark is an avid investor in the stock market. During 2021, he received eligible dividends totalling $18,000. He did not dispose of any shares during the year.

Required: Determine Mr. Shark's minimum net income for the year ending December 31, 2021. Ignore GST/HST & PST considerations and the need to make CPP contributions by Mr. Shark.

AP 7-7 (Foreign Property Income, Income Trusts, and Mutual Funds)

Late in 2020, Ms. Betsy Cheung receives $1,000,000 in cash in settlement of her mother's estate. On January 1, 2021, she invests the funds as follows:

Benson Mutual Fund Units She acquires 4,000 units of Benson Small Cap, a mutual fund trust, at a price of $15 per unit. During 2021, the trust makes a distribution of $1.40 per unit. The composition of this distribution is as follows:

Capital gains	$0.50
Eligible dividends	0.70
Interest	0.20
Total per unit	$1.40

Betsy reinvests this distribution in new Benson Small Cap units at $16.50 per unit. She is still holding these units at the end of 2021.

Canfor Mutual Fund Units Betsy acquires 14,000 units of Canfor Properties, a mutual fund trust. The units are acquired at a cost of $6.00 per unit. During 2021, the trust makes a distribution of $0.60 per unit. Of this total, $0.25 represents a return of capital, with the balance of $0.35 being property income. All of the proceeds of this distribution are reinvested in additional Canfor units at a cost of $6.75 per unit. She is still holding these units at the end of 2021.

Foreign Term Deposit Betsy acquires a Swiss franc-denominated term deposit with a maturity value of 300,000 Swiss francs (SF). The Canadian dollar cost is $387,000 . On December 31, 2021, the principal amount of the term deposit is paid, along with interest of SF15,000. Foreign tax authorities withhold 20% of the interest as foreign income taxes. Assume that throughout 2021, one SF equals $1.29 in Canadian dollars.

Public Company Shares Betsy acquires 3,000 shares of BDE at a cost of $30 per share. During 2021, the shares pay her eligible dividends of $1.70 per share. On December 1, 2021, the shares are sold for $31.50 per share.

CCPC Shares Betsy acquires 2,100 shares in her mother's Canadian controlled private corporation (CCPC) from her mother's estate at a price of $65 per share. During 2021, these shares pay non-eligible dividends of $3.50 per share. Betsy is still holding these shares at the end of 2021.

Betsy has other income that places her in the 33% federal income tax bracket and 18% provincial income tax bracket for any additional income. Taxes on that income are sufficient to use all of her available tax credits before considering the effects of the investments purchased with her inheritance. She lives in a province where the dividend tax credit on eligible dividends is 32% of the gross up and 20% of the gross up on non-eligible dividends.

Required: Calculate the amount of additional taxable income and tax payable that will result from the dispositions and distributions of Betsy's investments. In addition, indicate the per-unit adjusted cost base for each of the two trust units on December 31, 2021. Ignore any income tax implications resulting from international tax treaties.

AP 7-8 (Comprehensive Case Covering Chapters 1 to 7)

Carl Nemah is 66 years old, and while he receives significant pension income from a former employer's registered pension plan (RPP), he is a full-time employee of Jardu Enterprises Ltd. (JEL). During 2021, his gross wages were $62,000. JEL withheld the following amounts from these wages:

RPP contributions	$3,125
EI premiums	890
CPP contributions	3,166
Union dues	572
United Way contributions	2,400

During 2021, his pension receipts totalled $42,000. He has not applied for OAS as he knows that all of it will be clawed back. Further, he has not applied for CPP as he is aware that deferring this application will result in larger benefits in the future.

Carl has been married to Susan Nemah for over 40 years. Susan is 68 years old and has net income of $9,900. This consists of OAS payments of $7,400 and pension income from her RRSP. She has not applied for CPP.

Carl has two children. His 32-year-old son, Jerome, has been blind since birth. He lives with and is totally dependent on Carl and Susan. He has no income of his own.

Carl's daughter, Suzanne, is 41 years old and is recently divorced. She and her children also live with Carl. Her only income is $36,000 in child support that she receives under a 2020 court divorce settlement. In 2021, she decided to become an accountant and, to this end, she began attending university on a full-time basis in September. Carl has paid her tuition of $4,600 for 2021 and Suzanne has agreed to transfer any available tuition credit to her father.

The family's medical expenses, all of which have been paid by Carl, are as follows:

Carl	$ 600
Susan	1,100
Jerome	12,250
Suzanne	1,400
Total medical expenses	$15,350

During 2021, Carl received the following dividends (all amounts in Canadian dollars):

Eligible dividends	$11,700
Non-eligible dividends on shares in his sister's CCPC	3,250
Dividends on foreign shares	12.500
Total dividends received	$ 27,450

Income taxes of 15% of the foreign dividends, or $1,875, were paid.

In addition to dividends, Carl had interest income of $2,843 for 2021. The interest income is the amount required to be included in income as a result of ITA 12(1)(c) and 12(4).

Because of the project management skills that he has acquired over the years, Carl started a management consulting business in 2018. In January of that year he acquired a new building to be used as an office for his business. The building cost $426,000 of which $126,000 was the estimated value of the land and the remaining $300,000 allocated to the building. On January 1, 2021, the UCC of the building is $273,540.

The building contains office furniture and fixtures that were acquired on January 1, 2018, at a cost of $42,000. On January 1, 2021, the UCC of the class is $30,240.

During 2021, he spends $41,000 on improving and upgrading the building. In addition, he sells the old furniture and fixtures for $18,600 and acquires replacement furniture and fixtures for $50,000.

As Carl has no reason to keep detailed accounting records, he records business income on a cash basis. For 2021, his net cash flow from operations was $123,500. Relevant figures for the beginning and end of 2021 are as follows:

	January 1	December 31
Billed receivables	$13,400	$17,350
Unbilled work-in-process	17,470	21,250
Accounts payable	8,670	9,272

Since the inception of the business, Carl has owned an automobile that is used 100% for business activity. The automobile that he acquired in 2018 was sold in 2020. He acquired a new automobile on January 1, 2021, at a cost of $61,500. He financed the automobile through his bank and, during 2021, he made payments of $13,200 on the loan. All of this amount was deducted in determining his net cash flow from operations. Of the total, $4,920 represented payments for interest. Carl paid automobile operating costs totalling $9,260 during 2021.

Required: Calculate Carl's minimum 2021 net income, his 2021 minimum taxable income, and his 2021 minimum federal income tax payable. Ignore GST/HST & PST considerations and the possibility of pension income splitting.

AP 7-9 (Comprehensive Case Covering Chapters 1 to 7)

Ms. Shelly Spring is a 48-year-old widow. While her deceased husband left her financially secure, she continues to work as a course assistant at a local college. Her 2021 salary is $64,000, from which her employer withheld the following amounts:

RPP contributions	$2,960
EI premiums	890
CPP contributions	3,166
Disability insurance premium	205

Ms. Spring pays one-half of the total disability insurance premium to the group plan, with her employer paying the balance. The plan provides periodic benefits that compensate for lost employment income. She started making payments in 2019 and made payments of $200 in that year, $250 in 2020, and $205 in 2021. During 2021, because of an extended illness, she received benefits of $5,600.

In addition to her salary, her employer provides her with an allowance of $400 per month for maintaining an office in her home. This office is her principal work location. The office occupies 15% of her home and, for the year 2021, the costs of operating the home were as follows:

Interest on mortgage	$4,200
Property taxes	2,750
Electricity and water costs	1,340
Maintenance and repairs	1,800
Home insurance	820

Ms. Spring has two children and they both live with her. Her daughter, Amy, is 19 years old and, during 2021, she was in full-time attendance at the local university for eight months of the year. Her tuition fees of $8,200 were paid by Ms. Spring. Amy has net and taxable income of $7,300 for the year. She has agreed to transfer the maximum amount of her tuition credit to her mother.

Her son, Mark, is 23 years old and is dependent because of a physical disability. The disability is not severe enough, however, to qualify for the ITA 118.3 disability tax credit. Mark had no income during 2021.

The family's medical expenses, all of which have been paid by Ms. Spring, were as follows:

Ms. Spring	$ 962
Amy	2,450
Mark	8,600
Total medical expenses	$12,012

At the beginning of 2021, Ms. Spring owns two residential rental properties, both acquired in 1996. On January 1, 2021, the UCC of property A was $156,000. The cost of this property was $245,000, including $40,000 for the land and $205,000 for the building. Property B had a cost of $426,000, including $100,000 for the land and $326,000 for the building. Its January 1, 2021, UCC was $276,000.

On June 1, 2021, property A was sold for $201,000, including $40,000 for the land and $161,000 for the building. On that same date, a new residential rental property was acquired at a cost of $322,000, including $75,000 for the land and $247,000 for the building. During 2021, Ms. Spring received rents of $42,000 and had rental expenses, other than CCA, of $32,500.

Ms. Spring owns shares of Canadian public companies that paid eligible dividends of $9,300 during 2021. She also owns shares in a foreign company that paid dividends of C$5,600. The government in the foreign country withheld income taxes of $840, giving Ms. Spring a net receipt of $4,760.

Required: Calculate Ms. Spring's minimum 2021 net income, her minimum 2021 taxable income, and her 2021 minimum federal income tax payable without consideration of any income tax withheld by her employer. Ignore GST/HST & PST considerations.

CHAPTER 8

Capital Gains and Capital Losses

Learning Objectives

After completing Chapter 8, you should be able to:

1. Describe the four types of property, their connection to a source of income, and whether a disposition could result in a capital gain or a capital loss (Paragraph [P hereafter] 8-1 to 8-4).
2. Briefly explain the history of capital gains and how they are taxed differently than other income (P 8-5).
3. Describe the two different types of property ownership, what makes them different, and which applies for income tax purposes (P 8-6 to 8-10).
4. Explain the basic capital gain and capital loss calculations along with a description, in your own words, of the key concepts that are essential to an understanding of this topic (P 8-11 to 8-13).
5. Describe the legislative scheme of how the ITA handles capital gains and capital losses with respect to the 40-39-38 rule (P 8-14 to 8-16).
6. Explain the reasoning for the superficial loss rules and their application (P 8-17 to 8-26).
7. Describe a "negative ACB" and the typical circumstances where it would apply and the result (P 8-27 to 8-30).
8. Explain how the ITA handles GST and HST when it comes to the ACB of capital property (P 8-31 to 8-32).
9. Calculate capital gains and losses on dispositions of identical properties (P 8-33 to 8-36).
10. Determine the tax consequences associated with partial dispositions of capital property (P 8-37).
11. Describe and calculate the impact of warranties on capital gains and capital losses (P 8-38).
12. Apply the rules related to capital gains reserves (P 8-39 to 8-60).
13. Determine the income tax consequences of a bad debt arising on a debt from the sale of capital property (P 8-61 to 8-67).
14. Explain the reasoning behind the terminal loss reallocation rule and apply it to sales of land and buildings (P 8-68 to 8-74).
15. Describe the basic rules of the principal residence exemption and how to apply the basic rules on the sale of a principal residence (P 8-75 to 8-84).
16. Describe personal-use property and listed personal property, including how they are different. Determine the income tax consequences that result when they are sold for a gain or a loss (P 8-85 to 8-92).

17. Explain the basic concepts of how foreign currency affects income tax, including how conversions of foreign currency can create Canadian income tax consequences. Be able to calculate the foreign currency impact on capital gains and capital losses (P 8-93 to 8-98).
18. Describe in your own words the change-in-use concept and its purpose. Determine the amount of capital gain or loss resulting from a change in the use of capital property (P 8-99 to 8-111).
19. Explain the CRAs administrative concession when there are certain changes of use in a principal residence (P 8-112 to 8-113).
20. Describe and apply the ITA 45(2) election and its effect on the change-in-use rules (P 8-114 to 8-120).
21. Describe and apply the ITA 45(3) election and its effect on the change-in-use rules (P 8-121 to 8-125).
22. Describe how the change-in-use rules apply to the use of automobiles where the income earning use changes each year (P 8-126 to 8-129).
23. Explain the reasoning for the rules that deemed there to be dispositions of certain property when a Canadian resident individual becomes a non-resident. Explain the income tax treatment (P 8-130 to 8-133).
24. Describe and apply the provisions that allow capital gains arising on the disposition of eligible small business corporations (ESBCs) to be reduced (P 8-134 to 8-137).
25. Explain the purpose of the replacement property rules and apply the ITA 44(1) deferral provisions to determine the impact of the election on both the disposition of replaced property and the purchase of replacement property (P 8-138 to 8-150).
26. Explain the purpose of the replacement property rules and apply the ITA 13(4) deferral provisions to determine the impact of the election on both the disposition of replaced property and the purchase of replacement property (P 8-151 to 8-154).
27. Apply the deferral provisions for both capital gains and recapture arising on voluntary and involuntary dispositions of capital property that is subsequently replaced (P 8-155 to 8-162).
28. Explain the rationale for the ITA 44(6) reallocation election and how it applies (P 8-163 to 8-167).
29. Explain how knowledge of capital gains and capital losses can be of benefit in tax planning (P 8-168 to 8-170).

Introduction

Capital Gains and Capital Losses—Overview

8-1. At this point, three sources of income have been discussed: employment (Chapter 3), business (Chapter 6), and property (Chapter 7). These three sources of income are included in net income in ITA 3(a) where the result of any of these sources produces a profit (business or property) or positive amount (employment) in a taxation year. Losses, however, are included in the net income determination at ITA 3(d) for the taxation year. If, for example, in 2021 you had employment income of $47,000 and a business or property loss of $16,000, your net income would be $31,000 with the employment income included at ITA 3(a) and the business loss at ITA 3(d).

8-2. The focus of this chapter is ITA 3(b) and the inclusion of capital gains and losses in the net income calculation. This type of income or loss is not a source of income but rather a disposition of property that may or may not be used in a source of income. For example, in general terms if you own a rental property and sell it for an amount above its cost, the amount above the cost would be referred to as a capital gain. If you owned shares that you held as an investment and sold the shares at an amount below your cost, then that difference would be referred to as a capital loss.

8-3. Chapter 6 identified the three main types of property used in a source of income as inventory, depreciable property, and non-depreciable capital property. This chapter identifies a fourth category of personal property, which includes any property owned personally and that is not used in a source of income (e.g., furniture, appliances, one's home). With the exception of inventory, which cannot generate capital gains or capital losses, depreciable property, non-depreciable capital property, and personal property are relevant for capital gain and capital loss purposes.

There are many rules as to what is taxable or deductible and when. Figure 8-1 summarizes the four types of properties and compares them to the three sources of income.

Figure 8-1
Source of Income

Type of Property	Business	Property	Employment
1. Inventory	✓	—	—
2. Depreciable	✓	✓	✓
3. Non-depreciable capital	✓	✓	—
4. Personal	—	—	—

8-4. Capital gains are possible on a disposition of depreciable, non-depreciable capital, and personal property. In comparison, capital losses are quite restricted. Figure 8-2 provides an introductory overview of these four types of property and whether a disposition of any of them could potentially result in a capital gain or a capital loss. Both capital gains and capital losses are only possible where the property is non-depreciable capital property, such as investments. While capital gains are possible on depreciable property, capital losses are not permitted. Finally, capital gains are possible on the disposition of personal property while capital losses are only possible on a very restricted basis. There will be more about this later in the chapter.

Figure 8-2
Capital Gains and Capital Losses

	Possibility of	
Type of Property	**Capital Gains**	**Capital Losses**
1. Inventory	—	—
2. Depreciable	✓	—
3. Non-depreciable capital	✓	✓
4. Personal	✓	✓ (restricted basis only)

A Brief Word on the History of Capital Gains and Capital Losses

8-5. The Canadian income tax system has only been taxing capital gains and allowing capital losses since 1972. Prior to the introduction there was extensive debate about how much of a capital gain should be taxable and how much of a capital loss should be deductible. A compromise was finally reached that resulted in the inclusion of only 50%. While there was an increase to two-thirds and then three-quarters from 1988 to 2000, which added considerable complexity, the rate returned to the initial 50% application rate, which continues to apply to this day. All of the exercises and problems in this text use the current rate of 50%.

Capital Gain/Loss Concepts

Basic Terminology

8-6. A capital gain arises when capital property is sold at a price greater than its cost. A capital loss arises when the cost of capital property exceeds its sale price. In both instances 50% is used in determining net income.

A Word on Property Ownership

8-7. The discussion of capital gains and capital losses deals with the disposition of property owned by a taxpayer. The concept of "ownership," however, is sometimes an elusive one. If, for example, you and your partner purchase a home together, it is not uncommon to register as joint owners as if you each own 50% of the home. You may also have a joint bank account and joint investments where each of your names appears equally as an "owner." This type of ownership is generally referred to as legal ownership since the relevant laws look to the names that appear on the various provincial titles or registries that identify the "legal owners."

8-8. The ITA, however, does not operate on the basis of legal ownership but instead applies a concept referred to as "beneficial ownership." While the words "beneficial ownership" are found throughout the ITA, the most important provision is the part of the definition of "disposition" in ITA 248(1) that excludes "any transfer of the property as a consequence of which there is no change in the beneficial ownership of the property." Beneficial owners are considered the "real owners" of the property, whereas those who hold legal title are referred to as the "legal owners" or "title holders."

8-9. The beneficial owner of property is considered the person who has the ownership rights with respect to a particular property. Ownership rights are considered to include the possession, use, and risk of a property or a right to enforce those rights against others such as the legal owner. In general terms the beneficial owner is identified as the person who paid for the property in question from her own funds or was responsible to repay amounts borrowed to acquire the property. Giving up beneficial ownership can occur where the property is sold, the property is gifted, or where the beneficial owner dies in the case of an individual or ceases to exist in the case of corporations, and property beneficially owned is passed on to others (e.g., inheritances).

8-10. In most instances a person has both legal and beneficial ownership and there is no question of who is required to include any capital gains and capital losses in his income, but there are many cases where the ownership is split between two persons. There are in excess of 400 court decisions that reference beneficial ownership concepts, plus dozens of CRA publications. This chapter will not explore every aspect of property ownership but will simply make you aware that the ownership concept in the ITA does not rely on whoever holds legal title to a particular property. Throughout the remainder of this text, with the exception of Chapter 19 on trusts, any mention of a property "owner" will mean a person who has the beneficial ownership. The following examples will help to clarify some of this brief discussion.

EXAMPLE 1 You purchase a rental property by borrowing 75% of the purchase price and using your own funds for the remainder. You insure the property and are responsible for all expenses, including municipal taxes. You rent the property to a young family for a three-year period. A lease is signed.

ANALYSIS 1 You are both the legal and beneficial owner of the property. In beneficial ownership terms the property legally belongs to you as you have used your own funds or funds borrowed that you are responsible to repay (i.e., possession). While it appears that you do not have the "use" of the property, you have the right to enforce that use as a result of the fact that the property is yours. The use is subject to the conditions in the lease, which does not change your ownership rights. Finally the "risk" of the property is yours, which you have provided for by insuring the property. The tenants are also considered to have property in the form of what would be called a right of occupancy, which is separate from your beneficial ownership rights.

EXAMPLE 2 You are married and the only income earner. Your partner is dependent on you and had no property or funds of their own at the time of the marriage. You recently purchased 1,000 shares of a major Canadian public company. Half of the shares are registered in your name and the other half in the name of your partner. At the end of the first year dividends are paid on the shares.

ANALYSIS 2 Based on the facts, you are the legal owner of 500 shares while your partner is also the legal owner of 500 shares. Since the shares were purchased with your funds, you are the beneficial owner of all of the shares and would be required to include the dividends on all 1,000 shares in your income. If you wanted to gift half of the shares to your partner, you could have arranged that, in which case beneficial ownership would have changed to your partner. This, however, cannot be done retroactively (i.e. after the fact). Had you arranged to gift the shares to your partner, a series of attribution rules would apply with the result that the dividends received by your partner would be required to be included in your income and not in your partner's. Attribution will be discussed in Chapter 9.

EXAMPLE 3 You and your partner have a joint savings account where you are both registered as the account holders. The funds in the savings account were added when your partner's mother passed away and a sizable inheritance was received.

ANALYSIS 3 In most provinces, when an individual inherits property it is considered to belong to that individual. On this assumption, while both of you would be legal owners of the savings account, only your partner is the beneficial owner, and as a result all interest earned on the account would be required to be included in your partner's net income.

Key Capital Gain/Loss Concepts

8-11. As in many professions, skills, and specialties, terminology is important. This is particularly so with the ITA, as evidenced in the brief discussion of property ownership. While terminology is important there are other elements that are critical to an understanding of the capital gain or capital loss rules. The most important of these concepts and terms are the following:

Capital Property Capital property is defined in ITA 54 to mean (1) depreciable property and (2) any other non-depreciable property the disposition of which would potentially result in either a capital gain or a capital loss. Since the sale of inventory cannot result in a capital gain or capital loss because the sale affects business profit or business loss only, that leaves us with depreciable property, non-depreciable capital property, and personal property (see Figure 8-2). Depreciable property includes buildings, machinery, equipment, automobiles, and trucks. Non-depreciable capital property includes investments such as shares, bonds, loans receivable, interests in mutual funds, and partnerships. Personal property includes personally owned items such as furniture, clothing, appliances, hobby items, a personally owned automobile, and your home.

Disposition This is another key concept that is defined in ITA 248(1). It is a lengthy definition. The key part of the definition reads that a disposition is "any transaction or event entitling a taxpayer to proceeds of disposition of the property." The disposition concept generally requires that the property owner gives up ownership of property in return for consideration or compensation. This includes a straightforward sale of property to someone else. It also includes transactions such as the redemption of shares you own in a corporation, the maturity of a bond, the repayment of a loan you made, the expiry of an option, and the theft, expropriation, or destruction of property you owned.

In addition, the definition adds that certain transactions are not considered dispositions, such as when property is transferred for the purpose of being used as collateral security to borrow money, when a corporation issues its own shares, or when anyone issues bonds or other debt obligations. As we have mentioned, no disposition is considered to occur unless beneficial ownership has changed.

The ITA can deem dispositions to occur in a number of circumstances, some of which will be discussed in this and subsequent chapters. The event that caused the deemed disposition to be recognized generally treats the property or properties in question as if they had been sold at fair market value. A common example of a deemed disposition would be when an individual ceases to be a resident of Canada. The objective of these rules is to require individuals with capital property that has increased in value while they have been resident in Canada to pay income tax on that appreciation in value up to the time they cease to be a resident of Canada.

Proceeds of Disposition (POD) This next concept is defined in ITA 54 and represents what a property owner has received as consideration or compensation for giving up ownership of property. The main part of the definition reads that POD includes "the sale price of property that has been sold." It would also include compensation received by an insurance company on property that has been stolen or damaged.

The definition is dependent on an actual or deemed disposition that can also be modified to create a deemed POD. For example, if you gift property to a charitable organization you have disposed of that donated property. Since a donation does not result in the receipt of any consideration as payment, the POD would be nil, which would result in the recognition of a loss. ITA 69(1)(b)(ii), however, requires that the disposition of property to another as a gift results in deemed POD equal to the fair market value of the donated property. This would eliminate any actual loss as long as the property value exceeded its cost. ITA 69 is discussed at length in Chapter 9.

Adjusted Cost Base (ACB) The ACB is another defined term found in ITA 54. It is meant to represent the cost of the property sold to be able to measure the capital gain or capital loss. For depreciable property, the ACB is its capital cost, which we discussed in Chapter 5. For any other property (non-depreciable capital and personal), ACB is equal to the cost plus adjustments in ITA 53(1) minus adjustments found in ITA 53(2).

An example of the ACB concept was included in Chapter 3 on employment income. If you were an employee and allowed to participate in a stock option plan in which you acquired shares of your corporate employer for $1,000 at a time when they had a market value of $1,400, then you would have received a taxable stock option benefit of $400 representing the difference. If you immediately sold the shares for $1,400 there should be no capital gain, which would only be possible if the ACB was also $1,400. Your ACB, however, was your cost of $1,000 plus the ITA 53(1)(j) adjustment of $400 for a total of $1,400.

Chapter 7 discussed individuals owning units of a mutual fund trust. Commentary was included about the consequences of a distribution that is considered a return of capital. If, for example, you purchased 800 units of a mutual trust fund for $8,000 and received a return of capital of $1,700, the ACB of your trust units would equal $6,300, which would equal your original cost of $8,000 minus the return of capital of $1,700 (ITA 53(2)(h)).

Outlays and Expenses This is a common expression used in the basic capital gain or capital loss calculations. It recognizes that when capital property is sold there are certain expenses that are a necessary part of the disposition process. This means expenditures that would not have been incurred were it not for the disposition. The CRA capital gains guide (T4037) lists "fixing-up expenses, finders fees, surveyors' fees, legal fees, transfer taxes and advertising costs" as some of the more common types of outlays and expenses. Outlays and expenses reduce a capital gain or increase a capital loss.

8-12. All of these concepts are important to become acquainted with. Putting it all together, an individual who sells shares for $5,000 would say something like, "I made $3,000 selling shares that cost me $2,000 for $5,000." Using income tax terminology the equivalent would be, "I realized a capital gain of $3,000 on a disposition of capital property with an ACB of $2,000 for POD of $5,000."

The Capital Gain and Capital Loss—Basic Calculations

8-13. Now that the basic terminology concepts have been discussed, basic capital gain and capital loss calculations can be described and demonstrated. This will pave the way for a discussion of some of the more important and common rules:

Capital Gain A capital gain = POD- [ACB + "expenses and outlays"]

EXAMPLE 1 In December 2021 you sell vacant land you had purchased for $30,000 in 2020 for $86,000. Interest on money borrowed to acquire the land and property taxes paid since you acquired the land total $11,000. These expenses were not deductible because of ITA 18(2) (see Paragraph 6-105). Instead the denied expenses were added to the ACB of the land under ITA 53(1)(h). Outlays and expenses totalled $9,200 for legal fees, transfer taxes, and advertising costs.

ANALYSIS 1 The capital gain = POD of $86,000 - [ACB of $41,000 + outlays of $9,200] = $35,800. The ACB is equal to $41,000, which represents the original cost of $30,000 plus the ACB adjustment of $11,000 under ITA 53(1)(h).

Capital Loss A capital loss = [ACB + "expenses and outlays"] - POD

EXAMPLE 2 Assume the same facts as in Example 1 except that you sell the vacant land for $36,000.

ANALYSIS 2 The capital loss = [ACB of $41,000 + outlays of $9,200] - POD of $36,000 = $14,200.

You can see that in both examples the $9,200 of outlays and expenses either reduced the capital gain or increased the capital loss. If you sold capital property for POD equal to the ACB but incurred outlays and expenses of $200, the result would be a capital loss equal to the same $200.

For simplicity, the exercise and problem material uses the following format for both capital gains and capital losses. Using the capital gain example above, the presentation would be as follows:

Proceeds of disposition		$86,000
Less—The aggregate of:		
Adjusted cost base	($41,000)	
Expenses of disposition	(9,200)	(50,200)
Capital gain		$35,800
Inclusion rate		1/2
Taxable capital gain		$ 17,900

Using the capital loss example the presentation would be as follows:

Proceeds of disposition		$36,000
Less—The aggregate of:		
Adjusted cost base	($41,000)	
Expenses of disposition	(9,200)	(50,200)
Capital loss		$(14,200)
Inclusion rate		1/2
Allowable capital loss		$(7,100)

The 40-39-38 Rule

8-14. Chapters 6 and 7 emphasized the importance of understanding the 9-12-18-20 rule that links those four provisions toward establishing the business or property profit or loss that is included in the net income calculation. In the capital gain and capital loss rules there is another linkage that is also important in understanding how these rules apply. This linkage is called the 40-39-38 rule because of the way the ITA applies when it comes to determining the ultimate amount that is included in the net income calculation at ITA 3(b).

8-15. Each of ITA 40, 39, and 38 has a specific purpose, which can be described as follows:

ITA 40—Gain or Loss This provision represents the first of three concepts and calculates the "gain" or "loss" only on the disposition of any property. ITA 40(1) contains the basic calculations that we illustrated in Paragraph 8-13. This basic rule, however, is subject to or modified by other provisions such as ITA 40(2).

To explain, assume that you sold your home and realized a $150,000 gain. If you only ever owned one home and lived in that home since you purchased it, you are likely thinking that you thought that the gain was tax free. You would be correct. The ITA accomplishes this, however, with what is called the principal residence exemption that is found in ITA 40(2)(g), which overrides the gain calculation if you meet certain conditions which, in our case, you have. The result is that all of the $150,000 gain would be considered exempt and no amount would have to be included in your net income. The principal residence exemption will be discussed in this chapter.

Figure 8-2 showed that you cannot generally have a capital loss on personal property. For example, suppose that you sold for $1,000 a car that you had owned for six years. The car originally cost you $15,000. Since you disposed of property for a POD of $1,000 when the ACB was $15,000, you would have a $14,000 loss. ITA 40(2)(g), however, says any loss from the disposition of personal property is nil. The result is that this overrides the loss rule and, as far as the ITA is concerned, you have no loss. Dispositions of personal-use property will also be discussed in this chapter.

A final example is if you sell property at a gain but you agree to allow the purchaser to pay over a number of years. Chapter 6 showed that the ITA provides a deduction when inventory is sold with payments spread over a number of years (ITA 20(1)(n)). The ITA 40 capital gain rules offer a similar reserve mechanism that effectively allows the capital gain to be spread over a number of years to avoid having to pay income tax on gains that have not yet been received in cash. These capital gain reserves will also be discussed in this chapter.

ITA 39—Capital Gain or Capital Loss The purpose of ITA 39 is to work with the "gains" and "losses" that have been determined under ITA 40 that are then used to determine the second step, which is what remains as "capital gains" or "capital losses." Since ITA 40 simply asks whether there has been a disposition of "any property," technically inventory gains and losses as well as losses on depreciable property would qualify. ITA 39 contains the rules that prevent (1) capital gains or capital losses on inventory and (2) capital losses on depreciable property. The result is reflected in Figure 8-2.

There are additional rules in ITA 39, some of which will be discussed in this chapter. In Chapter 6 (at Paragraph 6-32), the elective rule of ITA 39(4) was discussed. That rule generally allows taxpayers who buy and sell Canadian securities, other than as a trader or dealer in securities, to treat the securities as capital property instead of as inventory and therefore as a source of business income. That rule treats all Canadian securities owned from the time of the election as capital property. This means that any gain will be considered a capital gain and any loss a capital loss.

ITA 38—Taxable Capital Gain (TCG) or Allowable Capital Loss (ACL) ITA 38 represents the third and final step of the 40-39-38 rule. Its main purpose is to (1) define a taxable capital gain as 50% of a capital gain and (2) define an allowable capital loss as 50% of a capital loss. It is the TCG and ACL numbers that are required to be included in the net income calculation of ITA 3.

ITA 38 also contains interesting rules regarding donations of investments and ecological land to charitable organizations. Donating property results in a disposition of the property. Legally, donations are voluntary dispositions given without consideration (i.e., payment), but the ITA deems any gift of property to be considered a disposition at fair market value (ITA 69). This means that if you donate shares of public companies that are valued at $100,000 and that had a cost of $25,000, there would be a gain that is a capital gain of $75,000 [POD $100,000 - ACB $25,000]. The taxable capital gain would be 50% of that amount, or $37,500. If all of the conditions of the donated property are met, rules in ITA 38 deem the taxable capital gain to be zero.

8-16. In summary, ITA 40 begins the process with the determination of gains and losses. ITA 39 is the second step, taking those gains and losses and ending up with the capital gains and capital losses. Finally, ITA 38 is the last step that takes the ITA 39 results and determines the taxable capital gains and allowable capital losses, which are then included in the taxpayer's net income calculation for the year under consideration. These three provisions contain most of the rules that work together in numerous situations to determine the final income amounts.

Exercise 8-1

Subject: Capital Gain and Capital Loss Basics

In each of the following situations indicate whether there would be a capital gain or a capital loss and why.

1. Years ago you purchased a painting by a popular Canadian wildlife artist for $1,200. The painting is in your home. You recently sold it for $4,900.
2. Same as #1 except that you are a partner in an accounting firm and the painting was purchased by the firm to hang on its walls to provide a sense of professionalism to clients who come to the office for meetings. The partnership wanted to change its selection of paintings and sold it for $900.
3. You always wanted to have a custom-built home. You purchased a plot of land for $30,000 and spoke to a contractor, but before arrangements could be made your employer transferred you to another province. As a result you sold the land for $23,000.
4. You carry on a printing business as a sole proprietor. A printing press you purchased for the business four years ago that cost you $40,000 was sold for $11,000. The UCC of the class was $21,000. A replacement printing press was subsequently purchased in the same year.
5. You carry on a business of retailing antiques through a store situated in a building that you lease. You recently sold an antique desk that had been sitting around for more than a year. The buyer paid you $10,000, but the desk cost you $17,000.
6. You carry on a computer services and supplies business in three different cities. You own the buildings in which the business is located. You decide to close down one location and sell the property. The property originally cost $660,000 with $560,000 representing the value of the building and $100,000 the value of the land. The UCC of the building, which had been included in a separate class, was $400,000 at the time of the sale. The property sold for $700,000, with $620,000 allocated to the building and $80,000 to the land.
7. You recently purchased shares of a startup public company promising a new innovative cell phone. You paid $17,000 for the shares, expecting the price to skyrocket. Two months later stories were beginning to circulate that the technology would not work. You managed to recover your cost by selling the shares for $17,000 but incurred selling costs of $1,000.

Solutions to Exercises are available in the Study Guide.

Select Capital Gain and Capital Loss Topics

8-17. There are numerous capital gain and capital loss topics, however the coverage in the remainder of this chapter will be on the more common and practical rules that are likely to be encountered. The topics we will cover include the following:

1. Superficial losses for individuals
2. Select ACB considerations

3. Identical properties
4. Partial Dispositions
5. Warranties on Capital Property
6. Capital gain reserves
7. Bad debts on sales of capital property
8. Loss restrictions on the sale of a land and building
9. Principal residences
10. Personal-use property
11. Gains and losses on foreign currency
12. Deemed dispositions—Change in use
13. Deemed disposition on becoming a non-resident
14. Capital gains deferral—ITA 44.1
15. Deferral on replacement property—ITA 13(4) & 44(1)

Superficial Losses for Individuals

8-18. The best way to explain this particular topic is with an example. Assume that you regularly invest in shares of Canadian public companies. You filed an election years ago under ITA 39(4) to ensure that all your gains and losses on the sale of Canadian securities will be treated as capital gains and capital losses. In December 2021 you look back over your investment success and discover that you have net taxable capital gains of $40,000 for the year. This is your total taxable capital gains minus total allowable capital losses under ITA 3(b). Since you are in the highest federal income tax bracket of 33%, you realize that this will be costly in terms of additional income tax.

8-19. You review your investments and identify shares you own in one company with an ACB of $110,000 that are currently trading for $30,000. If you sold those shares you would realize an $80,000 capital loss [$110,000- $30,000], which would equal a $40,000 [(50%))($80,000)] allowable capital loss, which would be used to reduce your net taxable capital gains to zero. The problem is that you really do not want to sell them because you expect their value to increase dramatically over the next few years.

8-20. You devise a plan to sell the shares for $30,000 on December 22, 2021, and to repurchase the same shares January 11, 2022. Assume that the share price has not changed, that there are no selling costs, and that you own the replacement shares throughout the remainder of 2022. The replacement shares are "identical properties," which is discussed beginning at Paragraph 8-33.

8-21. The result of the December 2021 sale is the realization of a $40,000 allowable capital loss that reduces your net income by the same amount for 2021. The ACB of the shares purchased in January 2022 is their cost of $30,000. The federal government views this type of planning offensive and took steps many years ago to discourage its use with the introduction of legislation referred to as the "superficial loss" rules, which for individuals are found in ITA 40(2)(g).

8-22. A superficial loss is another defined concept that can be explained by asking three core questions. If you answer yes to each question, then the loss of $80,000 would be considered a superficial loss, potentially reducing the loss to nil:

> **Question 1:** Was there a disposition of capital property that resulted in a capital loss?
>
> **Question 2:** Was the same property purchased in the period that began 30 days before the disposition and that ended 30 days after the disposition?
>
> **Question 3:** On the thirtieth day after the disposition, did the individual still own the property?

8-23. In the example above, the period of time mentioned in Question 2 would have started on November 22, 2021, and ended on January 21, 2022. The day referred to in Question 3 would be January 21, 2022. Since the answer to each question is yes, the loss of $80,000 is a superficial loss. The result is that ITA 40(2)(g) deems the loss to be nil.

8-24. The superficial loss, however, is added to the ACB of the replacement shares under ITA 53(1)(f) with the result that the ACB of those newly acquired shares is $110,000 [cost of $30,000 + 80,000 superficial loss—ITA 53(1)(f)]. In effect the legislation neutralized the two transactions, putting the individual in the same original position as if the two transactions never took place.

8-25. Assume now that the individual had owned 1,000 shares that were sold on December 22, 2021, for $30,000 but that the individual only repurchased 800 shares for $24,000. These shares were still owned on January 21, 2022. Technically all of the loss is still a superficial loss, but the CRA allows an administrative concession to consider the superficial loss to be equal to the proportional number of shares repurchased. In this modification, since the individual only repurchased 80% of the shares disposed of [800/1,000], the superficial loss is reduced to 80% of $80,000, or $64,000. The result is that the remaining $16,000 of the loss is a capital loss, one-half of which is an allowable capital loss of $8,000. This reduces the 2021 ITA 3(b) income to $32,000 [$40,000-$8,000]. The ACB of the shares purchased January 11, 2022, would be $88,000 [$24,000 cost + superficial loss of $64,000].

8-26. There is much more to the topic of superficial losses, including extending the rules to spouses and common-law partners, meaning that the superficial loss rules would apply if your spouse or common-law partner purchased the replacement shares. In addition, there are a different version of superficial losses that apply to corporations, trusts, and partnerships that are discussed in Chapter 16.

Exercise 8-2

Subject: Superficial Losses for Individuals

Ms. Nadia Kinski owns 1,000 shares of Bord Ltd. The ACB is $23 per share. On August 20, 2021, she sells all of these shares at $14.50 per share. On August 25, 2021, she acquires 600 of the same shares of Bord Ltd. at a cost of $13.75 per share. She continues to hold these shares for the remainder of 2021. What are the income tax consequences of these two transactions?

Solutions to Exercises are available in the Study Guide.

Select ACB Considerations—Negative ACB

8-27. ACB is defined as cost + ITA 53(1) adjustments- ITA 53(2) adjustments. Many of the ACB adjustments relate to non-depreciable capital property, which is largely investment-type property that can include shares of companies, interests in partnerships, and units of a mutual fund trust. For each of these three investments it is possible, in the case of shares and mutual fund units, to receive a return of capital in excess of one's cost. In essence a return of capital is equivalent to receiving a refund of part of one's investment cost. In addition, it is possible that amounts that reduce the ACB of a partnership interest could also exceed the investment cost.

8-28. If the ACB reductions under ITA 53(2) exceed the cost and ITA 53(1) additions, you have what is commonly referred to as a negative ACB. ITA 40(3) applies in many situations to treat the negative excess as a capital gain.

EXAMPLE You own shares of a public company that cost $12,000. The public company recently reorganized its capital in such a way that it has made a return of capital to its shareholders. You received $14,400.

ANALYSIS The return of capital creates a negative ACB of $2,400 [$12,000 cost + Nil ITA 53(1) - $14,400 ITA 53(2)]. ITA 40(3) applies to treat the $2,400 as a capital gain. The taxable capital gain is $1,200 [(50%))($2,400)], which is then added to net income for the year in which the return of capital was received that created the negative amount.

Afterwards another ACB occurs under ITA 53(1)(a) to add back the negative amount to restore the ACB to nil so that a second negative amount does not occur. As a result, the new ACB would be nil [$12,000 cost + $2,400 ITA 53(1) - $14,400 ITA 53(2)(a)].

8-29. You may be wondering how it is possible for an investor in shares or mutual fund trusts to receive a return of capital in excess of his investment cost. When corporations issue shares or when mutual fund trusts issue units, the capital they receive is often pooled together and averaged. Therefore, if you invested in shares at $10 per share and subsequent investors contribute much more per share, the average will increase with the result that the capital allocable to you will exceed your initial cost.

8-30. The potential for a negative ACB on returns of capital on units of a mutual fund trust was discussed in Chapter 7 (see Paragraphs 7-134 and 7-135). While partnerships are not discussed until Chapter 18, you should be aware that only limited partners of a limited partnership and partners who are not active in the partnership activities on a regular, continuous, and substantial basis would be subject to capital gains treatment for a partnership interest with a negative ACB.

Select ACB Considerations—GST & HST

8-31. The cost of most property includes any GST or HST, whether it is inventory, capital, or personal property. One of the main features of the GST/HST system (discussed in Chapter 21) is the ability to recover from the federal government all or part of any GST/HST paid on property used in carrying on a business. The recovery is part of what is called refundable input tax credits, or ITCs. It should come as no surprise that if a business recovers the GST or HST that is part of the cost of property such as depreciable or non-depreciable capital property, that the cost should be reduced in a manner similar to that indicated in Paragraph 8-28 above.

8-32. The ITA causes a reduction in the cost through the mechanism of ITA 248(16), which requires that any ITC recovery of GST/HST be treated as government assistance. The reason for this treatment is that a special rule in ITA 13(7.1) requires that the capital cost of depreciable property be reduced by any government assistance. The reduced amount then becomes the new capital cost, which is the new ACB. Remember that the ACB of depreciable property is its capital cost (see ACB in Paragraph 8-11). The reduction for non-depreciable capital property occurs at ITA 53(2)(k), and as a consequence the ACB would equal the cost (including the GST or HST) minus the ITC recovery to produce an ACB with the GST/HST excluded.

Exercise 8-3

Subject: Treatment of Government Assistance

On January 1, 2021, Rotan Ltd. acquires real property (land and a building) at a cost of $5,600,000. Of this amount, $600,000 represents the fair market value of the land. The building is new and will be used exclusively (100%) for non-residential purposes, none of which involves manufacturing. Rotan has filed the necessary election to include the capital cost of the building in a separate class 1 so it qualifies for a higher CCA rate. In order to encourage Rotan's move to this location, the local government has provided the company with $1,500,000 of financial assistance. Of this amount, $1,400,000 is for the building and $100,000 for the land. What is (1) the ACB of the land, (2) the capital cost and ACB of the building, and (3) the maximum amount of CCA that Rotan can claim for its fiscal year ending December 31, 2021?

Solutions to Exercises are available in the Study Guide.

Identical Properties

8-33. Chapter 6 discussed inventory valuation for a business noting the various methods to track the tax cost of individual inventory items. The acceptable methods included FIFO (first in, first out), specific identification, and averaging. These types of methods are important when dealing with two or more properties that are identical. A similar concern exists for capital gain/loss purposes where a taxpayer owns non-depreciable capital property such as investments. An individual, for example, may own 200 shares of Public Company A and 300 shares of Public Company B, and so on. If the individual decides to sell 50 shares of each company, the ACB for each share sold has to be determined in order to determine whether there is a capital gain or capital loss. This is a particular problem where the shares are not all purchased at the same time.

8-34. ITA 47 is the provision designed to determine the ACB of investment-type property that is non-depreciable capital property. This rule operates on the basis that there are "identical properties." The CRA describes identical properties as "properties which are the same in all material respects, so that a prospective buyer would not have a preference for one as opposed to another" (paragraph 1 of IT-387R2).

8-35. Corporations frequently issue different classes of common and preferred shares. It is the rights of these different classes of shares that must be examined to determine their similarity for tax purposes. If the share rights are different in any respect, such as voting rights, dividend participation, or the ability to exchange the shares for other shares, then the classes of shares are considered different and not identical. In addition, there are further rules for bonds and similar debt obligations (ITA 248(12) that deem these investments to be identical as long as they are issued by the same person (e.g., a debtor) and that they are identical in respect of all rights other than the principal amount owing

8-36. Once you have identified whether investments under consideration are identical properties it is a simple matter of then applying a weighted average calculation to determine the ACB. The following example illustrates the application of the weighted average method.

EXAMPLE An individual investor purchases Class C common shares of Gower Company, a Canadian public company:

Purchase date or sale date	Shares Purchased (Sold)	Cost per Share	Total Cost	Average Cost/Share
2007	4,000	$10.00	$ 40,000	
2008	3,000	12.00	36,000	
Subtotal	7,000		$ 76,000	$10.86
2011	(2,000)	$10.86	(21,720)	
Subtotal	5,000		$ 54,280	$10.86
2014	2,500	$11.00	27,500	
2019	3,000	10.00	30,000	
Subtotal	10,500		$111,780	$10.65
2021	(1,500)	$10.65	(15,975)	
End of year balances	9,000		$ 95,805	$10.65

The 2,000 shares sold in 2011 were sold for $10 each. The 1,500 shares sold in 2021 were sold for $13 each.

ANALYSIS Using the information from the preceding table, the 2011 allowable capital loss is calculated as follows:

Proceeds of cisposition [(2,000)($10)]	$20,000
Adjusted cost base [(2,000)($10.86)]	(21,720)
Capital loss	($ 1,720)
Inclusion rate	1/2
Allowable capital loss	($ 860)

The 2021 taxable capital gain would be calculated as follows:

Proceeds of disposition [(1,500)($13)]	$19,500
Adjusted cost base [(1,500)($10.65)]	(15,975)
Capital gain	$ 3,525
Inclusion rate	1/2
Taxable capital gain	$ 1,763

Exercise 8-4

Subject: Identical Properties

Ms. Chantal Montrose makes frequent purchases of the Class B common shares of Comco Inc. On January 15, 2020, she purchased 650 shares at $23.50 per share. On March 12, 2020, she purchased 345 shares at $24.25 per share. She sold 210 shares on September 15, 2020, at $25.50 per share. On February 14, 2021, she purchased an additional 875 shares at $26.75 per share. On October 1, 2021, she sold 340 shares at $29.50 per share. Determine the consequences of the transactions for 2020 and 2021, including the ACB of the remaining shares.

Solutions to Exercises are available in the Study Guide.

We suggest you complete SSP 8-1 at this point.

Partial Dispositions—ITA 43

8-37. In those situations where a taxpayer disposes of part of a property, ITA 43 requires that a portion of the total adjusted cost base be allocated to the disposition on a reasonable basis.

EXAMPLE A 500-hectare tract of land has an adjusted cost base of $600,000. During the current year, 200 of these hectares were sold.

ANALYSIS A reasonable allocation would appear to be applying 40% of the cost of $600,000, or $240,000 of the total adjusted cost base to the land that was sold. This allocation would be reasonable if all of the land was of equal value. If, however, this was not the case, then the allocation should be based on the proportionate value of the land sold. If, for example, the land sold represented half of the total value, then a reasonable allocation would be 50% of $600,000, or $300,000, leaving the remaining land with an ACB of $300,000.

Earlier we described the ACB of non-depreciable capital property as cost plus ITA 53(1) adjustments minus ITA 53(2) adjustments. Cost does not technically change when there is a partial disposition of property. As a result, the ITA applies an ACB adjustment representing the reasonable portion of the property that was disposed of. If we assume that a reasonable allocation was $240,000 in the preceding example, the ACB of the remaining land would be $360,000 determined as cost of $600,000 minus ITA 53(2)(d) $240,000.

Warranties on Capital Property—ITA 42

8-38. If a taxpayer sells capital property and a warranty, covenant, or other conditional or contingent obligation ("warranty") is provided at the time of the sale or in a subsequent year, ITA 42 sets out the rules as to how the amount received for the warranty will be treated. The rules are broken down into two parts as follows:

On or Before the Filing Due Date If the seller receives consideration for the warranty before the date that the income tax return is required to be filed for the year of the sale, then the amount received is included in the proceeds of disposition (POD) of the sale of the property. Any expenditures made by the seller in fulfillment of the warranty obligations on or before that same date reduces the POD.

After the Filing Due Date If a warranty amount is received after the filing date, the amount is treated as a capital gain. Any expenditures made after that time are treated as a capital loss.

Exercise 8-5

Subject: Warranties on Capital Property

During the taxation year ending December 31, 2020, Xtract Ltd. sells a capital property with an ACB of $237,000 for proceeds of $288,000 plus an additional $4,000 for a warranty for a total of $292,000. The company provides the purchaser with a two-year warranty at the time of the sale, and the company estimates that it will cost $3,500 to fulfill the warranty provisions. In fulfillment of its warranty obligations, the company spends $2,000 on March 10, 2021, and $2,800 on October 1, 2021. Determine the effect of these transactions on net income for both 2020 and 2021.

Solutions to Exercises are available in the Study Guide.

We suggest you complete SSP 8-2 at this point.

Capital Gain Reserves—ITA 40(1)(a)(iii)

8-39. When capital property is sold, the realization income tax principle requires that the full amount of the taxable capital gain be included in income for the year of the sale. In some situations, however, the sale of the property may be subject to vendor take back financing. This means that the purchaser is not required to pay the full amount up front but instead will make payments over a period of time. This, of course, means that the vendor may not have the necessary funds immediately to pay the income tax on the full capital gain.

8-40. In recognition of this liquidity problem, the ITA provides selective reserves that effectively allow a lesser amount to be included in net income where the remaining amount of proceeds is not due until a subsequent year. Chapter 6 discussed reserves for accounts receivables (ITA 20(1)(l)) and for the sale of certain inventory items (ITA 20(1)(n)), the purpose of which was to recognize that the proceeds of a sale had not yet been collected and were unlikely to be collected in time to pay the additional income tax for the year of the sale. The effect of reserves is to spread the profits or gains over a number of years in an attempt to match the timing for recognition of gains with the timing for when the payments are received.

8-41. The ITA permits a taxpayer who sells capital property and realizes a capital gain to claim a reserve as long as some part of the proceeds are payable after the year of the sale. In general, a reserve cannot be claimed by (1) a person if she is not a resident of Canada at the end of the year or at any time in the following year, (2) the purchaser was a corporation that was controlled by the vendor, or (3) the purchaser was a partnership in which the vendor held a controlling interest.

8-42. Claiming an election is optional, and in order to use this elective provision individuals must file Form T2017. Other taxpayers are not required to submit this form and can simply make this election in the income tax return for the year of the sale. The election allows reserves to be claimed over a five-year period, which is extended to 10 years in special cases. This chapter will focus on five-year reserves. The effect of the five-year reserve is to only include one-fifth or 20%

of the taxable capital gain in net income for each of those five years, but this is dependent on the percentage of proceeds due after a specific year. If, for example, an individual received 50% of the sale price at the time of the sale, it would make little sense to only require the individual to include 20% of the taxable capital gain for that year. The capital gain reserve calculations take this into consideration.

8-43. The capital gain reserve is based on the lesser of two calculations. The first of these two calculations applies a percentage to the capital gain based on the amount of the proceeds that are not payable until after the end of the year.

EXAMPLE A capital property is sold for $160,000. The capital gain is $100,000. The purchaser pays $40,000 at the time of the sale and will pay the remaining $120,000 over the next three years.

ANALYSIS The percentage of proceeds that are payable after the year is 75% [($120,000 ÷ $160,000)]. The reserve would therefore be 75% of the capital gain of $100,000, or $75,000.

8-44. The second calculation is designed to spread the capital gain evenly over five years at the rate of 20% per year. To achieve this result would mean that in the year of sale the reserve would have to be $80,000, which would leave 20% or $20,000 of a capital gain [$100,000 - $80,000].

$$\begin{bmatrix}\text{Total}\\\text{Gain}\end{bmatrix}\left[\frac{\text{Proceeds Not Payable until after End of Current Taxation Year}}{\text{Total Proceeds of Disposition}}\right]$$

8-45. The two calculations can be illustrated and described as follows:

{[Total Gain] [20%] [4 - (Number of preceding taxation years ending after the disposition)]}

8-46. Note that in the first calculation the reserve is based solely on the amount of the proceeds that are payable after the end of the year. As a result, if the amount owing is subject to interest charges the reserve would not include that interest. Any interest earned by the seller would be included in net income based on the rules for interest income that were discussed in Chapter 7.

8-47. The reserve has to be recalculated in each of the five years since the amount owing after any of those five years will change. The second calculation is intended to recognize that, at a minimum, 20% should be included in each of the five years. In year 1 the formula would be 80% [(20%)(4 - 0)], 60% in year 2 [(20%)(4 - 1)], 40% in year 3 [(20%)(4 - 2)], and so on.

8-48. Applying the ITA to the example would result in the following maximum reserve of $75,000 for the year of the sale, which is the lesser of the two amounts:

• [($100,000)($75,000 ÷ $100,000)]	$75,000 (Reserve)
• [($100,000)(20%)(4 - 0)]	$80,000 (Reserve)

As a result, in year 1 the capital gain would be $25,000 [$100,000 minus the reserve of $75,000]. In year 2 the reserve claimed in year 1 of $75,000 would be added to net income as a capital gain and another capital gain reserve would then be calculated. The result would be that over the five years the total amounts included in net income with respect to the initial $100,000 capital gain would total that full amount. More detailed examples follow.

Example—Outstanding Balance Greater Than Formula Limit

8-49. Assume that during 2021, Mr. Filoso sold land with an ACB of $340,000, for total proceeds (POD) of $1,000,000, resulting in a capital gain of $660,000 ($1,000,000 - $340,000) and a taxable capital gain of $330,000 [(1/2)($660,000)]. The sales agreement requires a down payment of $100,000 at the time of the sale with the remaining balance of $900,000 due at the rate of $100,000 per year beginning in 2022. Interest, charged at the rate of 5% of the outstanding balance, is also paid annually.

8-50. As only 10% of the proceeds were collected, the reserve would be 90% under the first calculation and 80% for the second calculation. Therefore, the lesser of the two amounts will be based on the second calculation. The maximum reserve would be $528,000:

- [($660,000)($900,000 ÷ $1,000,000)] $594,000 (Reserve)
- [($660,000)(20%)(4 - 0)] $528,000 (Reserve)

8-51. Applying this formula, the taxable capital gain that will be recognized in 2021 is $66,000 [(1/2)($660,000 - $528,000)]. Despite the fact that Mr. Filoso has only collected 10% of the proceeds ($100,000 ÷ $1,000,000), the formula requires that a minimum of 20% be recognized in each of the five years.

8-52. In 2022, the $528,000 reserve would have to be added back to net income as a capital gain. The new reserve for 2022 would be $396,000, the lesser of:

- [($660,000)($800,000 ÷ $1,000,000)] $528,000 (Reserve)
- [($660,000)(20%)(4 - 1)] $396,000 (Reserve)

8-53. Adding back the previous year's reserve of $528,000, and deducting the new maximum reserve of $396,000, results in a 2022 capital gain of $132,000. This would result in a net addition to 2022 income of $66,000 [(1/2)($528,000 - $396,000)], or 20% of the $330,000 taxable capital gain.

8-54. Based on similar calculations, the maximum reserve in 2023 would be $264,000. This would decline to $132,000 in 2024, and in 2025 no reserve would be available. This would result in $66,000 [(1/2)($132,000)] being added to net income each year. The entire $330,000 of the taxable capital gain will have been included in net income by the end of 2025. This is despite the fact that, at the end of this five-year period, $500,000 of the initial proceeds is not yet due.

Example—Outstanding Balance Less Than Formula Limit

8-55. In the preceding example, collections were less than 20% in all years under consideration. As a result, the application of ITA 40(1)(a)(iii) resulted in the recognition of 20% of the capital gain in each of the five years.

8-56. Where the amounts collected in any year exceed the 20% minimum, a larger portion of the capital gain will be required to be included in net income. To illustrate this situation assume that in the Paragraph 8-49 example Mr. Filoso collected $250,000 in the year of the sale and that the required contract payments were $75,000 per year for the following 10 years.

8-57. Based on this information, the maximum reserve for 2021 would be $495,000, the lesser of:

- [($660,000)($750,000 ÷ $1,000,000)] $495,000 (Reserve)
- [($660,000)(20%)(4 - 0)] $528,000 (Reserve)

8-58. This means that a taxable capital gain of $82,500 [(1/2)($660,000 - $495,000)] would be recognized in 2021. This represents 25% of the taxable capital gain.

8-59. In 2022, the $495,000 2021 reserve would be added to net income. The new reserve for 2022 would be $396,000, the lesser of:

- [($660,000)($675,000 ÷ $1,000,000)] $445,500 (Reserve)
- [($660,000)(20%)(4 - 1)] $396,000 (Reserve)

8-60. This results in the recognition of a $49,500 [(1/2)($495,000 - $396,000)] taxable capital gain in 2022. At this point, the minimum 20% per year recognition requirement has become the determining factor in calculating the capital gain to be included in net income. As a consequence, the amount to be included in net income in the years 2023, 2024, and 2025 would be as presented in Paragraph 8-59.

Exercise 8-6

Subject: Capital Gains Reserves

During December 2021, Mr. Gerry Goodson sells a capital property with an ACB of $293,000 for POD of $382,000. Selling costs total $17,200. In the year of sale, he receives a down payment of $82,000 and a note payable for the balance of $300,000. The note is to be repaid at the rate of $60,000 per year beginning in 2022. He receives the 2022 payment in full. Assume that Mr. Goodson deducts the maximum capital gains reserve. Determine his taxable capital gain for 2021 and 2022 as a result of the 2021 sale.

Solutions to Exercises are available in the Study Guide.

We suggest you complete SSP 8-3 and 8-4 at this point.

Bad Debts on Sales of Capital Property

8-61. In Chapter 7 (see paragraph 7-71) we discussed the interaction of the definition of "property" with the concept of debt. We mentioned that "property" is defined to include a "right of any kind." In terms of debt obligations this means that the creditor owns property that is the right to receive the amount owed. From an accounting perspective this would be represented by a loan, note, or other kind of debt receivable. The debtor, on the other hand, is not considered to have property because an obligation to pay an amount owed is not property.

EXAMPLE In June 2021 you sell land that is capital property for $115,000 to a corporation. The arrangement is that the company will owe you the full amount, which will be paid in six months.

ANALYSIS You have sold the land and are no longer the beneficial owner. The corporate purchaser owns the land. However, the debt receivable of $115,000 is property to you with an ACB equal to the amount owed of $115,000. In income tax terms you have effectively converted one property (the land) for another (the debt receivable).

8-62. If the company pays you the full amount in six months you will have a disposition of property for POD equal to the amount paid of $115,000, resulting in no capital gain or capital loss. If the company paid half of the amount, then it would be considered a partial disposition of property (see paragraph 8-37) with the final payment representing the disposition of the remaining part of the debt.

8-63. If the debt in our example was never paid and you were unable to recover the land in settlemen of the debt, then you would have experienced an economic loss. That loss would be a capital loss matching the character of the underlying property. However, in order to recognize the capital loss for income tax purposes there has to be a disposition. The ITA only considers a disposition to have occurred with respect to a debt if the debt is legally settled or legally cancelled. In many situations the settlement or cancellation may only occur after years of litigation, but in the interim the evidence may be clear that the likelihood of recovering the debt is remote.

8-64. ITA 50(1) provides an elective option that would allow you to recognize the capital loss in the year "the debt is established to have become a bad debt" as long as, in general, the person you sold the property to was not related to you. The current view of the CRA is that a debt is established to have become bad where either (1) the creditor (i.e., you) have exhausted all legal means of collecting the debt or (2) the debtor has become insolvent and as a result is unable to pay the amount owing.

8-65. ITA 50(1) has a unique way of dealing with the capital loss. You are deemed to have disposed of the debt at the end of the year in which it has become a bad debt and to have received nil proceeds. The result is that you have a capital loss of $115,000 [POD nil - ACB $115,000]. ITA 50(1) adds that you are also considered to have reacquired the debt at the beginning of the next year at a cost of nil. This means that your ACB will also be nil. Now you can wait until the debt is legally settled or cancelled to determine the final outcome. Any amount you receive in the future on the settlement/cancellation will be treated as a capital gain at that time.

8-66. To continue with the example, assume that in November 2021 you learn that the purchaser has become insolvent. You decide to file the election under ITA 50(1). In January 2024 you receive $12,000 as a result of a court decision in which the debt is legally cancelled at that time.

> **ANALYSIS** At the end of 2021 you are deemed to have disposed of the debt receivable for nil proceeds. As a result you have a capital loss for 2021 of $115,000 as indicated in Paragraph 8-65. At the beginning of 2022 you are considered to have acquired the debt receivable at a cost of nil. As a result, the ACB of the debt from that moment forward is also $ nil. In 2024 when the debt is disposed on cancellation, you will have a capital gain of $12,000 [POD $12,000 amount received in settlement- nil ACB].

8-67. In this example the creditor was unable to recover the property sold in settlement of the debt. If, however, the property was voluntarily recovered or seized in settlement of the debt, the provisions of ITA 79 and 79.1 would then apply. In addition, if the debtor was able to avoid having to pay the full amount owing, the debt forgiveness rules of ITA 80 would also have applied. Those provisions, however, are well beyond the scope of this text.

Exercise 8-7

Subject: Bad Debts from Dispositions of Capital Property

During 2020, a capital property with an ACB of $125,000 is sold for $110,000 to an unrelated person. The POD is composed of a cash down payment of $75,000 plus a note receivable for $35,000. In 2021, the note is established to become a bad debt. In 2022 the creditor collects $3,000 in a final settlement as a result of a court decision. What are the income tax consequences of these events in 2020, 2021,and 2022?

Solutions to Exercises are available in the Study Guide.

We suggest you complete SSP 8-5 and 8-6 at this point.

Loss Restrictions on the Sale of Land and Building—ITA 13(21.1)

8-68. In 1979 the Supreme Court of Canada ruled in favour of the taxpayer in *Malloney Studios Ltd.* ([1979] 2 SCR 326), which led to our next topic of discussion. In this case a corporate taxpayer owned a restaurant in Toronto. A nearby hospital needed the land for expansion purposes and had the necessary expropriating power to acquire the property. The hospital notified the company of its intentions. After negotiations it was agreed that the land would be acquired free of any buildings for $280,000. The company agreed to tear down the building. None of the proceeds were allocated to the building. The result was that there was a large capital gain on the land and a large terminal loss on the building since the UCC exceeded the nil proceeds. The CRA (then Revenue Canada) argued that proceeds at least equal to the UCC of $80,000 should be allocated to the building since it had value. The court disagreed, noting that the determination of the building proceeds was a contractual matter and the contract was clear that no part of the contract price was to be paid for the building.

8-69. While the CRA is empowered to challenge the value of property in non-arm's-length circumstances through ITA 69 (which will be discussed in Chapter 9), it is a different matter with an arm's-length sale. In such cases the contract generally establishes the fair market value (FMV) and therefore the POD. The concern of the CRA was that contractual allocations could be used intentionally to produce an income tax benefit.

EXAMPLE You own a building and the land on which it is situated. The FMV of the land and building together is $600,000. The ACB of the land is $200,000. The capital cost of the building is $300,000 and the UCC $200,000. The building is the only property remaining in its class. Assume that both the land and building are each valued at $300,000. A sale at FMV would result in a $100,000 capital gain on the land [$300,000 POD - $200,000 ACB] and a recapture of $100,000 on the building [$200,000 UCC - $300,000 POD]. The increase in net income would be $150,000 [taxable capital gain of $50,000 + recapture of $100,000].

If instead the contract stated that the building was to be demolished, then there would be an argument for allocating no proceeds to the building and $600,000 to the land. In that case there would be a taxable capital gain on the building of $200,000 [((50%) ($600,000 POD - $200,000 ACB] and a terminal loss on the building of $200,000 [UCC $200,000 - nil POD leaves a positive balance with no property remaining in the class].

The increase in net income would be $ nil [taxable capital gain of $200,000 - terminal loss of $200,000]. In effect this reallocation has eliminated an additional $150,000 of net income. The benefit is increased where a terminal loss is created since such losses are fully deductible. Each dollar subtracted from the building proceeds and reallocated to the land creates $1 of a terminal loss in favour of $1 in a capital gain on the land, only $0.50 of which is taxable.

The Solution

8-70. The government responded with the introduction of ITA 13(21.1), which applies when a building is disposed of resulting in a terminal loss or a potential terminal loss situation where the POD is less than the UCC. There are two parts to this rule. ITA 13(21.1)(a) applies when land and building are sold together, and ITA 13(21.1)(b) applies when only the building is disposed of generally by way of demolition. The focus in this chapter will be on ITA 13(21.1)(a).

8-71. Calculations and formulae in the ITA are best appreciated if the underlying policy is first understood. In this case the purpose of the calculations is to reallocate proceeds from the land to the building to the extent necessary to eliminate the terminal loss on the building. The calculations first reallocate the POD for the building and then reallocate the remainder to the land. The calculations using our example in Paragraph 8-69, in which all of the POD of $600,000 are allocated to the land, would be as follows:

• The FMV of the land and building	$600,000	
Reduced by the lesser of:		
• The ACB of the land = $200,000		
• The FMV of the land = $600,000	(200,000)	$400,000
• The greater of:		
• The FMV of the building = $ nil		
• The lesser of:		
The capital cost of the building = $300,000		
The UCC of the building = $200,000		$200,000

8-72. In this case, the proceeds that would be allocated to the building would be $200,000, leaving $400,000 ($600,000 - $200,000) to be allocated to the land. The net result is that the $200,000 terminal loss is completely eliminated and the capital gain is reduced by a corresponding amount to $200,000 ($400,000 POD - $200,000 ACB). The taxable amount of $100,000 [($200,000)(50%)] would be included in the taxpayer's net income instead of no amount being added to net income in the absence of ITA 13(21.1).

8-73. The effect of ITA 13(21.1)(a) on the results is summarized in the following table:

	Results without ITA 13(21.1)(a)	Results with ITA 13(21.1)(a)
Taxable capital gain	$200,000	$100,000
Terminal loss	(200,000)	Nil
Net inclusion	$ Nil	$100,000

8-74. If instead the building had been demolished without the sale of the land, the terminal loss would have been reduced by 50% to $100,000 under ITA 13(21.1)(b), which is the same net dollar result determined under ITA 13(21.1)(a) where the land was also sold. The difference is that under ITA 13(21.1)(a) the $100,000 is a taxable capital gain whereas under ITA 13(21.1)(b) the $100,000 amount would be a terminal loss. Also note that the reallocation rule in ITA 13(21.1)(a) does not apply to determine the cost of the land to the purchaser.

Exercise 8-8

Subject: Land and Building Disposition

On February 24, 2021, Drucker Ltd. disposed of a building and the land on which it was situated for total proceeds of $1,250,000. Information with respect to this property is as follows:

Capital cost of the building	$930,000
UCC class 1 (building—only property in class)	615,000
FMV of the building on February 24, 2021	500,000
ACB of the land	425,000
FMV of the land on February 24, 2021	750,000

Determine the income tax consequences of this disposition assuming (1) there is no special rule for building dispositions, and (2) the ITA 13(21.1) special rule for building dispositions applies.

Solutions to Exercises are available in the Study Guide.

Principal Residence—ITA 40(2)(b) The Principal Residence Exemption

Principal Residence Defined

8-75. Figure 8-2 illustrates that dispositions of non-depreciable capital property and of personal property above ACB and selling costs result in a capital gain, while the sale of inventory cannot result in capital gains or capital losses. The characterization of property is essential to applying the rules of the ITA. A property that can serve as a home can be used by the owner and her family to live in. It can also be used by the owner as a rental property so that others can live in it and raise their families. Finally, a home can be acquired for the purpose of making a profit on its sale. In each case the income tax characterization is different. In the first case the home would be a personal property; it would be non-depreciable capital property where it is used as a rental property; and it would be inventory in the last case where the home is acquired to sell (i.e., an adventure or concern in the nature of trade).

8-76. The ITA provides favourable treatment, commonly referred to as the "principal residence exemption," where the home is personal property and meets the definition of a "principal residence" when sold at a gain. Personal property, technically referred to as "personal-use property," is defined in ITA 54 as property that is "used primarily for the personal use and enjoyment of the taxpayer" and certain other persons. ITA 40(2)(b) provides rules to determine how much of the capital gain will be required to be included in net income for the year of sale. If the property qualifies as a principal residence throughout the years of ownership, the capital gain on a sale will likely be reduced to nil, allowing the owners to retain the sale proceeds without any concern about having to pay income tax on that sale. The key part of the analysis begins with determining whether the property is a principal residence.

8-77. ITA 54 defines a principal residence as any housing unit owned by an individual that was ordinarily inhabited in the year by the individual, her spouse or common-law partner, a former spouse or common-law partner, or a child and is designated by the individual as a principal residence. It is important to note that only one taxpayer in a family unit can designate a property as a principal residence for a particular year. For this purpose, a family unit includes a spouse or common-law partner as well as children, unless they are married or in a common-law partnership or over 18 during the year. The definition adds that a principal residence would include land up to a limit of one-half hectare (roughly 1.25 acres) as well as other buildings situated on the property. If the property includes land above the limit, it will not be eligible to participate in the reduced or eliminated capital gain on the sale of the principal residence unless the taxpayer can demonstrate that the additional land was necessary for the use and enjoyment of the property.

8-78. The definition requires clarification of some definitions before turning to the impact of the rules on capital gains.

Housing Unit A housing unit would include a house, apartment, duplex, condo, cottage, mobile home, or a house boat. The housing unit can be situated inside or outside of Canada.

Ownership The housing unit must be beneficially owned (see Paragraph 8-7 to 8-10), jointly or otherwise. The owner can be an individual or a personal trust. A personal trust is typically a family trust established by individuals to provide for family members. A mutual fund would not be a personal trust. It is important to note that a housing unit owned by a corporation would not qualify even if the individual who controls the corporation lives in that housing unit. This chapter will limit discussion to ownership by individuals.

Ordinarily Inhabited This aspect of the definition requires that an individual, or members of her family unit, live in the home at some time in the year. The period of time does not have to be lengthy, and the CRA is quite flexible as long as the property was not purchased to earn income. This condition is automatic when an individual owns one home in which she lives. It is when the individual owns two or more properties, such as a main home, a cottage, and perhaps a vacation property situated outside of Canada, that the concern arises as to whether the property is ordinarily inhabited. The CRA considers a vacation property as qualifying as a principal residence if it was acquired for personal use even if it is only used for a few weeks every year.

Designation A designation is a communication to the CRA that an owner of a housing unit elects to treat it as the principal residence for a specific taxation year. This means that if the individual owns three housing units that could qualify as a principal residence, it is only the housing unit chosen for a given year that becomes the principal residence for that year.

8-79. The relevant reporting related to the sale of a principal residence is as follows:

- If an individual has only one property that qualifies as a principal residence, they must report in their income tax return for the year of sale a description of the property, when it was acquired, and the proceeds of disposition. Page 1 of the Form T2091(IND), "Designation of a Property as a Principal Residence by an Individual," must also be completed.
- The same reporting is required if the individual owns more than one property that qualifies as a principal residence but is designating only one property sold for all years owned.

- If the individual owns more than one property that qualifies as a principal residence, for reasons that will be discussed later, the individual may want to designate only some years to the property sold. In that case the same reporting is required with the exception that all of the pages of Form T2091(IND) must be completed.

8-80. The income tax reporting must be included in the income tax return for the year of sale regardless of whether there was a capital gain or a capital loss and regardless of whether the income tax return is filed late. Failure to report the disposition will technically result in a penalty of $100 per month, to a maximum of $8,000. The CRA has been reluctant to apply the penalty except in circumstances they describe as "excessive cases," particularly individuals who flip houses claiming that any gains are not taxable because of the principal residence exemption of ITA 40(2)(b). In these cases, the frequency of transactions and the short length of ownership may imply that the individual is carrying on a business and that the homes are inventory.

Gain Reduction Formula—ITA 40(2)(b)

8-81. When a housing unit that is personal property could qualify as a principal residence, the capital gain and capital loss rules apply. ITA 40(2)(b), however, provides a formula that could reduce any capital gain in whole or in part where the property disposed of is a principal residence. The formula determines the gain portion, which is based on the relationship between the number of years that the property has been designated a principal residence and the number of years that the individual has owned the property. There are many complexities in the legislation that relate to the years 1971, 1982, and 1994. The examples, exercises, and problems in this text will avoid these earlier years and will focus on the current rules, which have largely been in place since 2000 with some minor modifications relating to reporting requirements that began in 2016. These modifications were summarized in Paragraph 8-79. The basic calculation is as follows:

$$\mathbf{A} - \left[\mathbf{A} \times \frac{\mathbf{B}}{\mathbf{C}}\right] - \mathbf{D}, \text{ where}$$

A is the capital gain on the disposition of the property;
B is 1 plus the number of years that the property is designated as the individual's principal residence (if this number exceeds "C" then use the number at C);
C is the number of years that the individual has owned the property;
D relates to 1994 and will therefore be ignored.

NOTE A property can be designated as a principal residence in a given year even if it was only owned for one day during that year. This means that if a property were acquired in December 2016 and sold in January 2021, you might be inclined to say that it was owned for only five years. Since the ITA treats both the 2016 and 2021 years as one complete year, the property would be considered to have been owned for income tax purposes for six years. The number of years can also be determined by adding one to the difference between 2021 and 2016 [(2021 - 2016) + 1].

8-82. The formula in Paragraph 8-81 is applied to any capital gain resulting from the disposition of a principal residence in a given year, whether or not a designation has been made to treat the property as a principal residence for that year. For example, assume a property was purchased in 2013 and was sold in 2021 for an amount that resulted in a capital gain of $100,000. If it was designated as a principal residence for the six years of 2013 to 2018, the calculation of the reduced capital gain would be determined as follows:

$$\left[\$100{,}000 - (\$100{,}000)\left(\frac{1+6}{9}\right)\right] = \$22{,}222$$

8-83. If an individual has only one property that could qualify as a principal residence, that property can be designated as the principal residence for all years owned. In such situations, the use of this formula will then completely eliminate any capital gain on the disposition of that property, resulting in a formula amount of nil.

8-84. The "plus one" factor in "B" of the formula is designed to ensure that when an individual, who only owns one home at a time, sells the home and immediately purchases another home in the same year, no part of any capital gain will be taxable. The importance of this additional year is illustrated in the following example.

EXAMPLE During 2016, Mr. Fodor acquires his first home at a cost of $240,000. The home is sold in 2019 for $300,000. He purchases a second home immediately thereafter in 2019 for $330,000. In 2021, he sells the second home for $375,000. He decides to rent an apartment after the sale of the second home.

ANALYSIS Mr. Fodor has owned two homes that could be designated as a principal residence for the years beginning 2016 and ending 2021. This represents six combined years of ownership. Technically the first home is owned for four years (2016 to 2019) and the second home for three years (2019 to 2021). The number of years owned is represented by the "C" component in the formula. To ensure that no part of the capital gain on either home is taxable, four years need to be designated to the first property and three years to the second for a total of seven years. The problem is that there are only six years between 2016 and 2021. If it were not for the "one plus" rule, Mr. Fodor would have to make a choice by designating three years to the first property and three years to the second or four years to the first property and two years to the second. In either case, part of the capital gain on one of the two properties would become taxable. The "one plus" rule is designed to avoid that problem. Mr. Fodor could designate 2016, 2017, and 2018 to the first property and 2019, 2020, and 2021 to the second. On the sale of the first property, the "B" component would be four (3 + 1), and with a "C" component of four all of the capital gain would be exempt from tax and would not be required to be included in net income. Note that in practice an individual selling a home and claiming the principal residence exemption would not designate to include the year of sale since it is not necessary given the "one plus" factor. Following that approach, Mr. Fodor would designate the 2019 and 2020 year only to the second property with the result that the fraction would be one calculated as "(2 + 1)/3."

Exercise 8-9

Subject: Sale of Principal Residence

Mr. Norm Craft purchases his first home in 2012 at a cost of $89,000. In 2017, this home is sold for $109,500 and a second home is purchased in the same year for $152,000. In 2021, the second home is sold for $178,000 and Mr. Craft moves to a rental property. Determine the minimum income tax consequences of the sale of the two properties.

Exercise 8-10

Subject: Sale of Principal Residence

Ms. Jan Sadat owns a house in Ottawa as well as a cottage in Westport. She purchased the house in 2010 for $126,000. The cottage was gifted to her in 2013 by her parents. At the time of the gift, the FMV of the cottage was $85,000. During June 2021, both properties are sold, the house for $198,000 and the cottage for $143,500. Ms. Sadat has lived in the Ottawa house during the year, but has spent her summers in the Westport cottage. Determine the minimum capital gain that she must report in her 2021 income tax return with respect to the sale of both properties. Note: When an individual is gifted property she is considered to have acquired it at that time at an amount equal to its FMV. This will be discussed in Chapter 9.

Solutions to Exercises are available in the Study Guide.

We suggest you complete SSP 8-7 at this point.

Personal-Use Property

Definition

8-85. At Paragraph 8-77 personal-use property was described as any property that is owned by a taxpayer and used primarily for the personal use or enjoyment of the taxpayer or a person related to the taxpayer. Property not used in an income earning activity is generally considered to be for personal purposes. Personal-use property includes automobiles, homes (e.g., principal residences), vacation properties, boats, furniture, hobby items, paintings, and many other items. The definition is also broad enough to cover the same type of properties owned by a corporation and used by a controlling shareholder or members of his family.

Capital Gains and Losses

8-86. As noted in Figure 8-2, the disposition of personal property can result in capital gains, but there are limitations on what can be claimed in terms of capital losses. In general, ITA 40(2)(g) does not permit capital losses on personal-use property unless the property is from a particular type of personal-use property referred to as "listed personal property." From a tax policy point of view the sale of most basic types of personal property, such as furniture, appliances, and cars, tend to decline in value over time. Therefore allowing capital losses on personal property would be costly in terms of income tax revenues to the federal and provincial governments. However, not all types of personal property decline in value, and some inevitably increase in value, sometimes substantially. Examples of this latter category include paintings, jewellery, and collectible items such as stamps and coins. These examples fall within the listed personal property definition, which is discussed in further detail in the following pages of this chapter.

8-87. Many years ago the minister of revenue had commented that capital gains on the sale of personal-use property were taxable. The public asked whether that meant that individuals holding garage sales would have to track every purchase and sale to determine if they made a profit. The minister responded that the CRA was not concerned with small-ticket items and therefore individuals holding garage sales need not worry about a CRA audit.

8-88. The basis for the minister's statements was ITA 46, which is a rule that effectively sets a limit of $1,000 when personal property is being bought and sold. The rule accomplishes two things: (1) It deems the POD to be the greater of $1,000 and the actual proceeds and (2) it deems the ACB to be the greater of $1,000 and the actual ACB. This rule produces four effects:

1. If both the POD and ACB are less than $1,000, this rule will ensure there is no capital gain or capital loss.
2. If both the POD and ACB are above $1,000, the rule has no effect and the normal capital gain and capital loss rules apply.
3. If the POD exceeds $1,000 and the ACB does not, then the capital gain equals the amount by which the POD exceeds $1,000.
4. If the ACB exceeds $1,000 and the POD does not, then the capital loss equals the amount by which the ACB exceeds $1,000,

This rule is illustrated in the following example involving dispositions of personal-use property in four different cases:

Capital Gains (Losses) on Personal-Use Property

	Case A	Case B	Case C	Case D
Actual POD	$ 300	$ 850	$ 500	$1,500
Actual ACB	800	400	1,300	900
The ITA 46 effect:				
Greater of actual POD or $1,000	$1,000	$1,000	$1,000	$1,500
Greater of ACB or $1,000	(1,000)	(1,000)	(1,300)	(1,000)
Gain (loss)	Nil	Nil	($ 300)	$ 500

8-89. The $1,000 rule does not apply to "excluded property," which is a concept added to the ITA in 2000 to address offensive donation schemes. These schemes became somewhat widespread involving bulk purchases of artwork for discounted amounts (e.g., $10 each), which would then be donated to various educational institutions at appraised values up to $1,000. The capital gains on the donation disposition would be exempt because of the $1,000 floor rule. The individual donors, however, would receive charitable donation receipts of $1,000, which often reduced their income taxes by as much as 40 to 50%. As a result, artists would be paid for their work, albeit at discounted amounts, the promoters would receive fees for administrating the scheme, appraisers would be paid for their services, and the investor donors would receive reductions in income tax well in excess of their investment in the artwork. Everyone won except the federal and provincial governments. ITA 46(5) introduced the "excluded property" concept to prevent the use of the $1,000 rule, eliminating much of the investor income tax incentive to participate in these income tax schemes.

Listed Personal Property

8-90. The concept of "listed personal property" (LPP) was briefly mentioned in Paragraph 8-87, noting that it represents personal-use property that generally appreciates in value. As a result it receives special attention in the ITA. LPP is defined in ITA 54 and means

(i) print, etching, drawing, painting, sculpture, or other similar work of art;
(ii) jewellery;
(iii) rare folio, rare manuscript, or rare book;
(iv) stamp; or
(v) coin.

8-91. In general, LPP is subject to the same capital gain rules as would apply to other personal-use property. This includes the $1,000 floor rule discussed above. However, there is one very important difference: The ITA does not allow capital losses on personal-use property unless the property is LPP.

8-92. Chapter 1 discussed the concept of net income and ITA 3. ITA 3(b) includes all taxable capital gains and subtracts all allowable capital losses for a specific year. If the allowable capital losses exceed taxable capital gains, the result was a nil ITA 3(b) amount with the excess considered a net capital loss for that same year. The net capital loss would then be available to be claimed against ITA 3(b) taxable capital gains in another year. Allowable capital losses cannot generally be deducted against any other types of income. This concept is referred to as "loss streaming," meaning that while the losses can be claimed, their use is restricted in the sense that they are only deductible against certain types of income. This loss streaming concept was also discussed in Chapter 6 related to restricted farm losses (ITA 31), noting that farm losses were only deductible against profits from the same farming business. The LPP rules use the same streaming concept. The restriction is that capital losses on LPP can only be deducted against capital gains on LPP. In the absence of such capital gains, LPP losses cannot be claimed. However, any undeducted LPP losses may be applied in other years to the extent there are LPP gains in those years. The application of these loss carry overs is described in Chapter 11.

Exercise 8-11

Subject: Personal-Use Property

During the current year, Martha Steward disposes of several properties. The POD and the ACB of the various properties are as follows:

	Adjusted Cost Base	Proceeds of Disposition
Sailboat	$43,000	$68,000
Oil painting	200	25,000
Personal automobile	33,000	15,000
Diamond necklace	46,000	18,000

What are the income tax consequence of these dispositions?

Solutions to Exercises are available in the Study Guide.

We suggest you complete SSP 8-8 at this point.

Gains and Losses on Foreign Currency

Introduction

8-93 Throughout this chapter there have been references to the realization principle, which causes income tax implications when there has been a disposition of property. In addition to including a "right of any kind," the definition of "property" in ITA 248 reads that it includes "money." Money can be Canadian currency or foreign currency. If, for example, a purchase is made for as much U.S. currency as possible with $1,000 Canadian at a time when the Canadian dollar is worth $0.80 for each U.S. dollar, $800 of U.S. currency will be acquired. Technically the Canadian currency was disposed of for U.S. currency of equivalent value and therefore there would be no gain or loss since the POD and ACB would be the same.

8-94. Assume that one year later the U.S. currency is converted back to Canadian currency at a time when the Canadian dollar is worth only $0.667 against the U.S. dollar. On the conversion, approximately $1,200 [($800 U.S./0.667)] in Canadian currency will be received. In this second transaction, U.S. currency that had an ACB of $1,000, the original Canadian dollar cost, was disposed of for POD of $1,200. As a result, a $200 capital gain has been realized through ITA 39(1.1), which is a special capital gain and capital loss rule that applies to an individual in these circumstances. The provision includes a $200 exemption where the total of foreign currency capital gains exceeds the total of foreign currency capital losses in a specific year. If, for example, this was the only foreign currency transaction in 2021, there would be no capital gain or capital loss due to the $200 exemption. The exemption is designed to ensure that insignificant foreign currency gains or losses do not have to be tracked and reported. This is designed to ensure that Canadians vacationing outside of Canada are not required to concern themselves with the income tax implications of buying and selling foreign currency for short-term vacations.

8-95. As foreign currency exchange rates are constantly fluctuating, any taxpayer who engages in foreign currency transactions is likely to experience gains and losses that relate to these fluctuations. When Canadians sell property to non-residents or non-residents sell property to Canadians and the transactions are in a foreign currency with a delay in payment, there may be a component of any gain or loss on the transaction that is attributable to a foreign currency fluctuation.

EXAMPLE Mr. Harvais carries on a business in Canada and sells equipment with a cost of C$37,000 to a U.S. manufacturer for US$60,000 at a time when the Canadian dollar is trading at $0.78. The equipment is delivered and the payment of US$60,000 is made in full two months later when the exchange rate is $0.76.

ANALYSIS The gain on the equipment sale is equal to $39,923 [POD $76,923 [($60,000 U.S./0.78)] less cost of $37,000]. When the balance owing is paid, the receivable is considered disposed of and therefore there would be a gain of $2,024 [$78,947, which equals the value of US$60,000 at the exchange rate in effect at the time of payment ($60,000/0.76) minus the value or cost of the receivable when the equipment was sold of $76,923 [($60,000/0.78)]. We would add that the ultimate conversion of the foreign currency to Canadian currency would result in a further disposition, resulting in further gains or losses.

8-96. The nature of the gain is dependent on the character of the equipment sold. If it is inventory, then the foreign currency gain of $2,024 is treated as fully taxable business profit. If it is capital property, then the gain would be considered a capital gain. The basic rule is that if a foreign exchange gain or loss arises as the result of an income transaction (i.e., buying or selling inventory or providing services as part of the carrying on of a business where charges are denominated in a foreign currency), the full amount will be included as part of the business income calculations, which takes you back to the determination of business profit and ITA 9. In contrast, if a foreign exchange gain or loss arises as the result of dispositions of capital property, then the gains or losses will be capital gains or capital losses. The rules in ITA 39 only apply, however, if the property sold is capital property.

8-97. When dealing with capital property there are three separate provisions of the ITA within the capital gain and capital loss concepts of ITA 39 that take foreign currency into consideration. Understanding the circumstances in which they apply is important in determining the income tax implications. The three provisions are as follows:

> **ITA 39(1.1)** This provision applies only to individuals. It requires that the individual has made a gain or sustained a loss caused by a fluctuation in the value of a foreign currency relative to the Canadian currency as a result of the disposition of foreign currency. The circumstances in which this applies include (1) conversion of foreign currency into either Canadian currency or another foreign currency, (2) use of foreign currency to make a purchase, or (3) use of foreign currency to make a payment. In all three situations an individual's foreign currency, which has its own cost (ACB), is disposed of. The POD would be the value of the foreign currency in terms of Canadian currency at the time of its disposition. As discussed earlier, there is a $200 capital gain exemption built into this provision.

> **ITA 39(2)** This provision is quite restrictive and only applies to capital transactions that are not covered by ITA 39(1) or (1.1), both of which apply when there is a disposition of capital property. This means that ITA 39(2) applies when, as a result of a fluctuation in foreign currency relative to Canadian currency, a taxpayer has made a gain or sustained a loss both of which are capital in nature. The result is that ITA 39(2) is restricted to debt obligations, meaning amounts owed. Remember that while receivables are property, since they represent a right to receive some amount, a payable, or obligation to pay an amount, is not property. Therefore, when a payment is made toward a loan or other debt, there is no disposition of property to the payor. ITA 39(2) applies to the payor in this situation.

> Assume, for example, that capital property is purchased for a business in Canada at a purchase price of US$100,000. Of this total, US$60,000 is paid at the time of purchase and the remaining US$40,000 is paid six months later. Assume that all amounts were paid with the Canadian currency equivalent. At the time of the purchase the Canadian dollar was trading at $0.80 against the U.S. dollar (it cost C$1.25 to purchase US$1.00). At the time the remaining amount owing was paid, the Canadian dollar was trading at $0.769 against the U.S. dollar (it cost C$1.30 to purchase US$1.00). The Canadian dollar equivalent for the payment would be $52,000 [($1.30)($40,000)]. Had the exchange rate remained at $1.25 the payment would have only been $50,000 [($1.25)($40,000)]. In effect there is a $2,000 capital loss {($1.30 - $1.25)($40,000)]. There is no $200 exemption since there was no conversion of foreign currency and therefore ITA 39(1.1) does not apply in this case. If a foreign currency deposit had been used to pay the amount, then ITA 39(1.1) would have applied instead.

> **ITA 39(1)** ITA 39(1) applies to all other capital property situations involving foreign currency that are not covered by ITA 39(1.1) or (2).

8-98. An example will serve to illustrate the application of ITA 39 to a capital property transaction.

> **EXAMPLE** On August 1, 2018, Mr. Conrad White uses C$180,000 to open a British pound (£) account with his broker. Assume that at this time £1 = C$1.80, so that the foreign currency of £100,000 is acquired for $180,000. As a result the ACB of the foreign currency is C$180,000.

On December 31, 2018, Mr. White uses his entire British pound balance to acquire 10,000 shares in a British company, Underling Ltd., at a cost of £10 per share. At this time, £1 = $1.82. On July 1, 2021, the shares are sold for £21 per share. On this date, £1 = $1.65, and all of the proceeds from the sale are immediately converted into C$346,500 [(10,000)(£21)($1.65)].

ANALYSIS—Conversion On December 31, 2018, Mr. White has disposed of the foreign currency for POD of C$182,000 in a transaction to which ITA 39(1.1) applies. The result is a taxable capital gain of $900 [(1/2)($2,000 - $200)], which will be included in his net income for 2018.

ANALYSIS—Purchase In addition, the purchase of the shares establishes the ACB at C$182,000.

ANALYSIS—Sale When Mr. White sells the shares for £21 per share, the capital gain is C$164,500 [(£210,000)($1.65) - (£100,000)($1.82)]. The capital gain is subject to ITA 39(1) and would therefore not be eligible for the $200 exemption since there was no foreign currency conversion as a result of the sale of the shares. The receipt of foreign currency once again establishes the ACB, which is C$346,500 [($1.65)(£210,000)]. The immediate conversion to Canadian dollars represents a disposition for the same amount of C$346,500, therefore there is no capital gain or capital loss. If Mr. White had waited to make the conversion subsequent to a time in which a fluctuation had occurred, there would have been a capital gain or capital loss that would then have been subject to ITA 39(1.1).

Exercise 8-12

Subject: Foreign Currency Gains and Losses

On January 5, 2020, Mr. Michel Pratt purchases 35,000 Trinidad/Tobago dollars (TT$) at a rate of TT$1 = C$0.21. Using TT$30,600 of these funds, on June 5, 2020, he acquires 450 shares of a Trinidadian company, Matim Inc., at a price of TT$68 per share. At this time, TT$1 = C$0.23. During September 2021, the shares are sold for TT$96 per share. The Trinidad/Tobago dollars are immediately converted into Canadian dollars at a rate of TT$1 = C$0.19. What amounts will be included in Mr. Pratt's 2020 and 2021 net income as a result of these transactions?

Solutions to Exercises are available in the Study Guide.

We suggest you complete SSP 8-9 at this point.

Deemed Dispositions—Change in Use

General Rules

8-99. The glossary to this text (see the Study Guide) defines deeming rules and deemed disposition as follows:

> **Deeming Rules** Rules that are used to require that an item or event be given a treatment for income tax purposes that is not consistent with the actual nature of the item or event.
>
> **Deemed Disposition** A requirement to assume that a disposition has taken place when, in fact, a disposition transaction has not occurred.

8-100. Such rules are fairly common in the ITA and are applied in a wide variety of situations. This chapter deals with dispositions that are deemed to occur when there is a change in use of a capital property and dispositions that are deemed to occur when a taxpayer severs Canadian residency and becomes a non-resident of Canada. Chapter 9 will provide coverage of dispositions that are deemed to occur on the death of an individual.

8-101. Where the ITA deems there to be a disposition of property, additional rules are then required to establish the POD. In such cases the ITA adds deemed POD often based on the fair market value of the particular property at the time of the disposition. The ITA also deems POD in situations where an actual disposition takes place. The objective of these latter occurrences is to allow property to move from one person to another without any income tax implications. These are referred to as "rollover" transactions, some of which will be discussed in this chapter and in Chapter 9.

Change in Use—The Basics

8-102. The change-in-use concepts are designed to address situations where capital property that was originally purchased for one type of use subsequently changes so as to be used for something completely different. The type of use contemplated is personal use versus an income earning use that is either property income or business income. For example, if a building that is initially purchased to be used in a business is subsequently used as a home purely for personal purposes, the "change-in-use" rules would apply. The same change-in-use rules would apply where a property purchased for personal use is changed so that it is used for income earning purposes. In either situation the rules treat the capital property as if it had been sold and reacquired at fair market value (FMV) on the change of use.

> **EXAMPLE** You purchased a building in 2015 for $320,000 that was used in a business you carried on as a sole proprietor. In 2021 you began to use all of the building as a home at a time when the FMV was $450,000.
>
> **ANALYSIS** Since the building is capital property and its use has changed from earning business income to a personal use, there is a deemed disposition at FMV of $450,000 for business purposes and there is also a deemed purchase for that same amount as a home. The change-in-use rules are found in ITA 13(7), which covers the depreciable property impact such as CCA. Similar rules can be found in ITA 45(1) that address the capital gain impact.

8-103. The rules also apply to situations where the proportionate use changes, such as where a capital property that is used 50% for personal and 50% for income earning purposes changes so the percentage is 75-25 (or some other proportion) in favour of either the personal use or the income earning use.

> **EXAMPLE** Refer to the example in Paragraph 8-102, except assume that 25% of the building was converted into a home. Based on the numbers, you would have been deemed to have sold 25% of the building for $112,500 [(25% of $450,000} and to have purchased a home for that same amount. The income tax implications of the building would then fall under the partial disposition rule that we discussed at Paragraph 8-37.

8-104. The purpose of these rules are to measure the income earning impact at the point in time in which the use changes. In the first example at Paragraph 8-102, a building that was used in a business is no longer used for that purpose. Therefore the ITA looks to measure the impact by assuming that the building was disposed of for FMV. At that point the effect on the business of capital gains, recapture, and terminal losses can be determined. It also provides a starting cost of the home that would be relevant for the principal residence exemption. The same concept applies to the second example.

8-105. Before taking a closer look at the actual calculations, a few points need to be clarified:

1. If the use of the capital property changes from an income earning use such as a rental property to another income earning use such as a business, the change-in-use rules do not apply because the use has not changed. It is a change from one income earning use to a different

income earning use. The rules are only designed to apply where the property is capital property and the use is changed from income earning to personal or vice versa.

2. If the property is inventory and the use changes to personal use, the change-in-use rules do not apply. This is because the property must be capital property.

8-106. The most common application of the change-in-use rules involve buildings such as residential homes, apartments, condos, duplexes, and triplexes.

Income Earning Use to Personal Use—ITA 13(7)(a) & 45(1)(a)(ii)

8-107. This situation is straightforward in that there is first a disposition and then a reacquisition. If the complete 100% conversion is from income earning to personal use, the deemed POD will be equal to FMV, with the beneficial owner recognizing a capital gain, recapture, or terminal loss depending on the nature of the property and its income tax attributes, such as ACB and UCC.

8-108. The deemed reacquisition will result in a purchase cost also equal to the same FMV, which will represent the cost and therefore the ACB of the capital property that has become personal use property.

Personal Use to Income Earning Use—ITA 13(7)(b) & 45(1)(a)(i)

8-109. If a capital property that is used exclusively as a personal-use property is changed to be exclusively used to earn income from property or from a business, the result depends on whether the FMV exceeds the cost or is below the cost.

FMV Less Than Cost In this case, the FMV is the deemed POD. If the property is depreciable property, the FMV becomes the capital cost of the depreciable property. If the property is non-depreciable capital property, the FMV becomes the cost and therefore the ACB. Finally, if the property is used in a business and is inventory, then the FMV becomes the inventory cost.

FMV Exceeds the Cost In this case, the FMV will be the deemed POD, resulting in the recognition of a capital gain. However, where the reacquired property is depreciable property the capital cost, as a result of ITA 13(7)(b), for CCA, recapture, and terminal loss purposes will be equal to the property's cost plus one-half of the difference between that cost and the FMV. The ACB (for capital gains purposes), however, is based on the FMV as a result of ITA 45(1). This produces an unusual result where the capital cost and ACB will be different for the same depreciable property.

8-110. There is justification for this different treatment. It reflects the fact that only 50% of the capital gain that arises on a deemed disposition will be included in income and therefore subject to income tax. If the capital cost of the reacquired depreciable property was FMV, than that would mean that 100% of the capital gain component would be deductible as CCA when only 50% would be included in income. The following example will illustrate the problem.

EXAMPLE Shirley Malone owns a boat that she has always used exclusively for personal use. The boat cost $100,000. She has begun a charter boat business and therefore will be using the boat exclusively in the business. The FMV at the time of the change in use is $150,000.

ANALYSIS Shirley's deemed POD will be $150,000, resulting in a capital gain of $50,000 [$150,000 POD- $100,000 ACB]. Her net income will increase by $25,000 as a result of this taxable capital gain [(50%)($50,000)].

The ACB of the boat will also be $150,000 as a result of ITA 45(1).

If the $150,000 were also the basis for CCA, she would be able to deduct 100% of the capital gain component of $50,000. This would not be an equitable result as Shirley only included $25,000 of this increase in her income.

Given this, in situations where there is a gain on the change in use, the capital cost addition for CCA purposes will be limited to the cost of the property prior to the change in use plus one-half of the gain. This means that for the purpose of determining CCA, recapture, or terminal loss, Shirley's capital cost, and therefore UCC balance, will be $125,000 [$100,000 + (1/2)($150,000 - $100,000)].

Example—Change in Use

8-111. The following example will serve to illustrate the income tax consequences of a change in use.

EXAMPLE On January 2, 2021, Ms. Barker, a professional accountant, acquires a building at a cost of $500,000, with $400,000 allocated to the building and $100,000 allocated to the land. During the entire year, 20% of the floor space was used for her accounting business while the remaining 80% was used personally as her home.

On January 1, 2022, an additional 30% of the total floor space was converted to business use, reducing the use of the property as a home to 50%. On this date, the FMV of the property had increased to $620,000, with $480,000 allocated to the building and $140,000 allocated to the land.

On January 1, 2023, the entire building was converted to residential use as Ms. Barker's accounting practice had grown to the point where the business had to move to a larger property. On this date, the FMV had increased to $700,000, with $550,000 allocated to the building and $150,000 allocated to the land.

ANALYSIS The focus in this example is only on the determination of CCA and any income tax consequences associated with the changes in use. Assume that rental income is sufficient to claim maximum CCA.

2021 CCA Calculation The maximum 2021 CCA would be calculated as follows:

January 1, 2021, UCC	Nil
Add: Cost of acquiring business portion [(20%)($500,000 - $100,000)]	$80,000
Deduct: One-half net additions [(1/2)($80,000)] (Note)	(40,000)
Base amount for CCA claim	$40,000
Deduct: CCA for 2021 [(4%)($40,000)]	(1,600)
Add: One-half net additions (Note)	40,000
January 1, 2022, UCC (20% of the building)	$78,400

NOTE Property acquired in a change in use does not qualify for the AccII provision if (1) it had been previously used by a person who had claimed CCA on the property, or (2) the property was previously owned by the acquirer. In change-in-use situations, the owner does not change. The ITA first deems a disposition at one point in time then deems the same person to purchase the same property immediately thereafter. This means that at the time of the repurchase the property had been previously owned by that same person. As a result, the AccII can never apply to a change in use.

When the AccII does not apply, then the previous half-year rule does apply, subject to its own exceptions. One of the most common exceptions is where a person sells property that was depreciable property to her to a purchaser to whom she is related. If the depreciable property had already been subject to the half-year rule, then it will not be subject to it again by the purchaser. While a change in use is deemed to be a non-arm's-length transaction (ITR 1100(2.21)), the fact that the property or part of the property was not previously subject to the half-year rule means that the exception would not apply and that the half-year rule does apply.

2022 Tax Consequences The change in use would result in capital gains on the land and building as follows:

	Land	Building
Fair market value	$140,000	$480,000
Cost	(100,000)	(400,000)
Change in value	$ 40,000	$ 80,000
Change-in-use percent	30%	30%
Capital gain	$ 12,000	$ 24,000
Inclusion rate	1/2	1/2
Taxable capital gain	$ 6,000	$ 12,000

It is possible that this capital gain could be eliminated through the use of the principal residence exemption that was discussed earlier in this chapter. However, if Ms. Barker claims CCA for 2021 on the business portion of the property, this exemption would not apply.

The calculation of the 2022 CCA deduction would be as follows:

January 1, 2022, UCC (for 20% of the building)		$ 78,400
Add: Deemed cost of increase in business usage:		
Cost [(30%)($400,000)]	$120,000	
[(1/2)(30%)($480,000 - $400,000)]	12,000	132,000
Deduct: One-half net additions [(1/2)($132,000)]		(66,000)
CCA base		$144,400
Deduct: CCA for 2022 [(4%)($144,400)]		(5,776)
Add: One-half net additions		66,000
January 1, 2023, UCC (for 50% of the building)		$204,624

2023 Tax Consequences As all of the building has been converted to personal use and is no longer being used for business purposes, there would be no CCA for 2023. However, there would be recapture of CCA as follows:

January 1, 2023, UCC	$204,624
Lesser of:	
• Capital cost ($80,000 + $132,000) = $212,000	
• Deemed POD = [(20% + 30%)($550,000)] = $275,000	(212,000)
Negative ending UCC balance = Recapture of CCA	($ 7,376)

Note that the recapture is equal to the sum of the CCA ($1,600 + $5,776) that was claimed in the two years during which it was used for income earning purposes.

The change in use would result in capital gains on the land and building as follows:

	Land	Building
Fair market value	$150,000	$550,000
Change-in-use percent	50%	50%
Deemed proceeds of disposition	$ 75,000	$275,000
Cost of 2021 acquisition		
20% of $100,000 and $400,000	(20,000)	(80,000)
Cost of 2022 acquisition		
30% of $140,000 and $480,000	(42,000)	(144,000)
Capital gain	$ 13,000	$ 51,000
Inclusion rate	1/2	1/2
Taxable capital gain	$ 6,500	$ 25,500

The key to determining the income tax consequences is to identify the exact cost amounts that are added or subtracted at each change in use.

Exercise 8-13

Subject: Change in Use—Personal Property to Rental Property

During July 2021, Ms. Lynn Larson decides to start using her summer cottage as a rental property. It has an original cost of $43,000 (building = $23,000, land = $20,000) and its current FMV is $231,000 (building = $111,000, land = $120,000). It has never been designated as her principal residence. Describe the 2021 income tax consequences of this change in use, including the capital cost and UCC that will be applicable to the rental property. In addition, indicate the maximum amount of CCA that could be claimed for 2021. Assume that Ms. Larson has enough rental income to fully utilize the maximum CCA.

Solutions to Exercises are available in the Study Guide.

Special Rules for Principal Residences

Principal Residence—Ancillary Use to Earn Income

8-112. A complication arises when an individual either begins to rent a part of a principal residence or begins to use it for non-residential purposes (e.g., an individual carries on a business as a sole proprietor through his home). Under the general rules for capital property, this would be a partial change in use, potentially resulting in a capital gain on the partial disposition of the property.

8-113. However, the CRA provides an administrative concession that it will not apply the partial disposition rules as long as (1) the income producing use is ancillary to the main use as a principal residence, (2) there is no structural change to the property, and (3) no CCA is claimed for that part of the property used for income earning purposes. This position is set out in IT Folio S1-F3-C2, "Principal Residence," and IT Folio S4-F2-C2, "Business Use of Home Expenses." Given this concession, standard income tax planning advice to individuals who use a portion of their principal residence for business purposes is not to claim CCA on the business use portion of the property.

Change in Use—Principal Residence to Income Earning Use (Rental)—ITA 45(2)

8-114. When the use of a property changes from personal use to an income earning purpose, the change-in-use rules require a deemed disposition and deemed reacquisition. The 100% conversion of a principal residence to a rental property is a common example of this type of situation and, in the absence of any election, the FMV at the time of the change will become the ACB of the rental property that is then depreciable property, and the capital cost for CCA purposes will equal cost plus 50% of the amount by which the FMV exceeds that cost.

8-115. An elective option is available, however, to avoid a change in use in this situation as well as a situation in which part of the home is converted to an income earning purpose. The election previously only applied to complete changes from a personal use to an income earning purpose, but an amendment made in 2019 now permits elections for partial changes of use occurring after March 18, 2019. We note that the CRA has not commented on whether this amendment changes or modifies their administrative concession mentioned in Paragraph 8-113, but the better view is that the legislation will only apply to partial changes of use that go beyond the administrative concession.

8-116. Prior to the legislative change in 2019, to accommodate partial changes the CRA took the position that when determining use of a property it was first necessary to look at the entire property and not just the part being changed. This meant that any elective options would only apply if all of a property was used for either income earning purposes or for personal purposes. Take, for example, an apartment building with 12 units, only two of which are used for income earning purposes. If you owned one of the units in which you carried on a business and wanted to use it for personal purposes, the elective options would not have been available to you since this would be considered a partial change in use of the entire property. The newly modified rules would now allow the elective options under these circumstances.

8-117. An election under ITA 45(2) overrides the change-in-use rules and deems that no change of use has occurred. This means that the home is not considered to have been acquired for income earning purposes and remains a personal property. The home owner must still include any rental income in net income since there is a source of income irrespective of the fact that the home itself is not considered depreciable property. The real impact of this is that no CCA can be claimed as a result. The election, however, can be rescinded. The CRA considers an election to be rescinded if CCA is claimed. The election, therefore, would not be valid beginning on January 1 of the year in which CCA was first claimed.

EXAMPLE You have owned a home in which you and your family have lived for the last 10 years. In December 2020 an opportunity is presented that allows you to rent an oceanside property in the Caribbean for two years. In February 2021 you pack up and head to the Caribbean with your family. You arrange to rent your home for the two years you will be gone. You file an election under ITA 45(2), which you file with your 2021 income tax return, to avoid a change in use. In early January 2023 you decide to stay an additional year and those renting your home agree to another year's rent. You decide, however, to begin claiming CCA in 2023.

ANALYSIS The ITA 45(2) election results in no change of use for 2021 and 2022. Claiming CCA for 2023, however, resulted in the election being rescinded as of January 1, 2023, meaning that the change-in-use rules apply at that time. The effect is that your home remains a personal property for 2021 and 2022 but becomes depreciable property in 2023.

8-118. A second advantage is that while an election is in effect, the home that is personal property can qualify as a principal residence. Normally the home would not qualify because it would not be "ordinarily inhabited" in the year by you or a member of your family unit (see Paragraphs 8-77 and 8-78). However, the definition of a principal residence in ITA 54 includes a home that has retained its personal property status as a result of filing an election under ITA 45(2). The ability to claim principal residence status for such elections is limited to four years. This allows the individual to avoid any capital gains tax on the property during the four-year period.

8-119. This would be of particular importance to an individual who moves to a rental property and does not have an alternative principal residence during this period. Even if the individual purchases an alternative residential property, the election can be helpful as it allows a choice as to which property will be designated as the principal residence during the relevant years. If one of the properties experiences a substantially larger capital gain during this period, the use of this election could produce a significant savings in income tax.

8-120. It is also noteworthy that the four-year election period can be extended in certain situations. ITA 54.1 specifies that if the following conditions are met either by the individual or individual's taxpayer's spouse or common-law partner, the election can be extended without limit:

- You no longer ordinarily inhabit the home as a result of an employment relocation.
- You are not related to the employer.
- You return to ordinarily inhabit the original home while still with the same employer or before the end of the year following the year you leave that employer.
- The original residence is at least 40 kilometres further from your new place of employment than your temporary place of residence.

Exercise 8-14

Subject: Change in Use—Principal Residence to Rental Property

During 2016, Jan Wheatley acquired a new home at a cost of $220,000. On December 31, 2019, she moves from this home into an apartment. At this time, the home is appraised for $210,000. Because she believes that real estate in her area is temporarily undervalued, she decides to rent the property for a period of time and sell it at a later date. During 2020, she receives rents of $21,600 and has expenses, other than CCA, of $12,600. On January 1, 2021, she sells the home to the current tenant for $345,000.

Indicate the 2020 and 2021 income tax consequences to Ms. Wheatley assuming that in 2020 she does not elect under ITA 45(2) and deducts CCA. How would these results differ if she made the ITA 45(2) election? In providing your answers, ignore the cost of the land on which the home is located.

Solutions to Exercises are available in the Study Guide.

Change in Use—Income Earning Use to Principal Residence—ITA 45(3)

8-121. When the use of a property changes from an income earning purpose to a principal residence, the change-in-use rules of ITA 13(7) and 45(1) will apply to deem the land and building to be disposed of at FMV and then reacquired at the same amount. ITA 45(3) is an elective option that allows the change-in-use rules to be overridden, avoiding any income tax consequences that would have occurred on the change of use. The election is not available, however, if CCA was previously claimed on the property while it was used for income earning purposes.

8-122. As was the case with an election under ITA 45(2), the election under ITA 45(3) used to be restricted to 100% conversions from income earning use to a principal residence. The ITA 45(3) election can be made with respect to partial changes of use, as discussed in Paragraph 8-116.

8-123. While the election under ITA 45(2) has to be made for the year in which the change of use occurred, the election under ITA 45(3) is only required to be included in the income tax return for the year in which the principal residence is actually sold. In other words, there is no filing or reporting requirement as a result of the change in use. The change in use, however, allows the minister of revenue to demand the filing of the election at any time, which then has to be filed within 90 days of the demand.

8-124. The purpose of the election is to allow a deferral of the gains that accrued while the property was being used to earn income. Since the election is only possible if no CCA had been claimed, the actual sale of the property will not result in any recapture but could result in either capital gains or terminal losses on the building and either capital gains or capital losses on the land. As we saw in Paragraph 8-68 (ITA 13(21.1)), a terminal loss on a building and a capital gain on the land could result in reallocated proceeds.

8-125. As a final point of interest we noted that when individuals elect under ITA 45(2) it allows the property to be considered as a principal residence for up to four years (and longer if there is an employee relocation to which ITA 54.1 applies). An election under ITA 45(3) has a similar impact that allows a property that was actually used to earn income to qualify as a principal residence for up to four years while being used for that income earning purpose. This can be extremely beneficial, both to individuals who did not own another residential property during this four-year period and to individuals with an alternative residential property that experiences a capital gain at a lower annual rate or a loss.

EXAMPLE In 2011 you purchased a home to use as a rental property. The property was rented continuously until the end of 2018. You never claimed CCA on the property. You and your family moved into the home in early 2019. You intend to claim the home as a principal residence when you eventually sell the home. You sell the home in 2021. The capital gain on the property, which includes the land, is $154,000. This averages $14,000 for each of the 11 years of ownership [$154,000/11 years].

ANALYSIS—No 45(3) Election If you did not file an election, then the change-in-use rules would have applied in 2019, resulting in a FMV disposition with a capital gain for the eight-year period of 2011 to 2018. If the capital gain on the change of use was $112,000 ($14,000 average), then your net income would have increased by the taxable capital gain of $56,000 [(50%)($112,000)]. When you sold your principal residence in 2021 you would have had a capital gain of $42,000 [(three years ownership)($14,000 annual average capital gain)]. None of that gain would have been taxable because of the principal residence exemption.

ANALYSIS—With ITA 45(3) Election Filing the election allows you to not only meet the principal residence exemption for the three years of 2019 to 2021 but for an additional four years while the property was used as a rental property. As a result, you can designate seven years as a principal residence plus the one additional year, meaning that eight of the eleven years of ownership are eligible for the principal residence exemption. Instead of a capital gain of $112,000, your capital gain will only be $42,000 [(3 years)($14,000 average gain)]. The $70,000 difference is attributable to the one-plus factor and the ability to claim four additional years while the property was being used to earn income.

Exercise 8-15

Subject: Change in Use—Rental Property to Principal Residence

Lance Ho lives with his mother in Toronto. On January 2, 2020, he purchases a small condominium in downtown Toronto for $375,000. When his mother learned he was planning to move out she became so upset that he decided to stay and rent out the condo until December 31, 2020. Net rental income, before any deduction for CCA, is $9,800. Mr. Ho's mother passed away on December 26, 2020. The grieving Mr. Ho moves into the unit on January 1, 2021. At this time, the appraised value (FMV) of the property is $450,000.

After moving in, he finds that the congested traffic in the downtown area is intolerable and, on December 31, 2021, he sells the unit for $510,000. Indicate the 2020 and 2021 income tax consequences to Mr. Ho, assuming that he deducts CCA in 2020 and does not elect under ITA 45(3). How would these results differ had he not taken CCA and made the ITA 45(3) election? In providing your answers, ignore the cost of the land on which the condominium is located.

Solutions to Exercises are available in the Study Guide.

We suggest you complete SSP 8-10 and 8-11 at this point.

A Word on Changes in Use and Automobiles

8-126. At Paragraph 8-106 we indicated that the practical issues of changes in use occur with homes, apartments, cottages, and other buildings. Technically, however, the change-in-use rules apply to any capital property that could be used for either personal use or an income earning purpose that results in a property or business income source. One particular property that would appear to fit squarely within the change-in-use rules would be automobiles used to earn business or property income.

8-127. There would be complex compliance issues surrounding any attempt to apply the change-in-use rules to annual changes in the percentage of use for income earning purposes. For example, in 2020 after a careful evaluation of your automobile use based on kilometres, you determine the income earning use as 27.5%. In 2021 it increases to 43.7%, and in 2022 it decreases to 19.0%. Technically the rules would require splitting the cost in 2020 between income earning purposes and personal purposes. In 2021 the income earning purpose increased by 16.2% [43.7% for 2021 minus the 27.5% for 2020] and there would be a decrease of 24.7% in 2022 in relation to 2021. The rules would require the calculation of deemed purchases and dispositions. Since automobiles, unlike real estate, typically decline in value, the rules based on FMV are somewhat less complicated but still required.

8-128. Many years ago the CRA examined this issue and after careful consideration decided not to enforce the change-in-use rules for automobile use. Instead a much less complicated approach was developed that produces results that are surprisingly close to the results that would have applied on a strict application of the change-in-use rules.

8-129. The method acceptable to the CRA begins with the cost of the automobile and an assumption that the automobile will be used exclusively for income earning purposes. The maximum CCA is then determined with the deductible CCA based on the actual percentage use for income earning purposes. In other words, the CCA rules would be applied in the same manner as with any other depreciable property that uses the income earning percentage in the final calculation.

EXAMPLE Joan Stream acquires an automobile for $25,000. It will be used for both business and personal purposes. During 2021, business use is 40% of the total kilometres driven. In 2022, business use increases to 60%.

ANALYSIS Maximum CCA for 2021 would be $11,250 [(AccII 1.5)(30%)($25,000)]. The deductible amount of CCA would be $4,500 [(40%)($11,250)]. The UCC of the automobile on the first day of the 2022 taxation year would be $13,750 [capital cost of $25,000 - 2021 maximum CCA $11,250].

CCA for 2022 would begin with $4,125 [(30%)($13,750)] and the deductible CCA would be $2,475 [(60%)($4,125)].

This is the method demonstrated by the CRA in publications such as guide T4002, which deals with individuals carrying on a business as a sole proprietor. However, discussions of change in use in that guide and in the CRA "Capital Gains" guide (T4037) are restricted to buildings.

Deemed Dispositions on Becoming a Non-Resident of Canada

Basic Rules

8-130. When a individual ceases to be a resident of Canada and becomes a resident of another country, the Canadian income tax system is designed to ensure that any appreciation in the value of property owned by that individual while they were resident in Canada should be subject to Canadian income tax. The difficulty with capital gains and other types of income, such as recaptured CCA, is that these types of income do not materialize until there is a disposition, which is consistent with the "realization principle." In order to assess that unrealized income when an individual ceases residency, a set of rules applies that together are referred to as the "departure tax" rules.

8-131. To achieve the tax policy objective of determining that income, the rules deem a disposition of an individual's property to have taken place at FMV immediately before he gives up his Canadian residency (ITA 128.1(4)(b)). This then allows Canada to require the individual to include the amounts in his net income where they are then subject to Canadian income tax.

8-132. Certain types of property are exempt from the deemed disposition rule. The major categories of exempted property are as follows:

- Real property situated in Canada, Canadian resource properties, and timber resource properties
- Capital property and inventory of a business carried on in Canada through a fixed place of business (e.g., a permanent establishment)
- Rights and interests in registered pension plans, registered retirement savings plans, deferred profit-sharing plans, stock options, death benefits, retiring allowances, as well as other rights of individuals in trusts or other similar arrangements.

8-133. This discussion just scratched the surface of the many rules in place with respect to emigration of an individual and other entities such as corporations and trusts. The objective in this chapter is to provide some of the more common occurrences where the ITA deems there to be dispositions resulting in capital gains and capital losses. This topic is discussed in greater detail in Chapter 20, "International Issues In Taxation."

Exercise 8-16

Subject: Emigration

John Parker owns publicly traded shares with an ACB of $920,000 and a FMV of $1,030,000. On April 21, 2021, he severs his Canadian residency and becomes a non-resident while still owning the shares. What are the income tax consequences of his ceasing to be a resident of Canada with respect to the shares?

Exercise 8-17

Subject: Emigration

Ms. Shari Twain owns a rental property in London, Ontario. The house has a capital cost of $275,000 and a FMV of $422,000. The ACB of the land is $75,000 and the FMV is $122,000. The UCC of the house at December 31, 2021, is $107,800. On December 31, 2021, Ms. Twain severs her Canadian residency and becomes a non-resident of Canada. What are the income tax consequences of her ceasing to be a resident of Canada with respect to her rental property?

Solutions to Exercises are available in the Study Guide.

We suggest you complete SSP 8-12 at this point.

Capital Gains Deferral—ITA 44.1

Basic Provision

8-134. ITA 44.1 is a rollover rule that allows a capital gain on an actual disposition at FMV of certain types of corporate shares to be reduced if certain conditions are met. The rule was introduced to provide indirect assistance to small incorporated businesses, especially startup companies, by providing income tax incentives to investors to encourage direct investment in such small businesses.

8-135. The ability to reduce a capital gain is dependent on the sale of common shares of an eligible small business corporation (ESBC) by an individual who then uses the proceeds to acquire replacement common shares of another ESBC within a certain period of time directly from that company. The reduced capital gain is not permanent but rather deferred until such time as the individual investor sells the shares and does not acquire more shares of another ESBC. The amount by which the capital gain is reduced is subtracted from the ACB of the replacement shares so that when those replacement shares are sold the capital gain will then be recognized.

EXAMPLE You acquire $40,000 of common shares of an ESBC. You sell the shares three years later for $100,000. You then use all of that $100,000 to purchase common shares of a second ESBC. A few years later you sell the shares of the second ESBC for $140,000 and do not purchase any replacement ESBC shares.

ANALYSIS The first sale would result in a $60,000 capital gain [POD $100,000 - ACB $40,000]. ITA 44.1 allows the complete deferral of the capital gain, changing it to nil. The cost of your second ESBC share purchase is $100,000, but the ACB would be reduced by $60,000 to $40,000 as a result of ITA 44.1 and an ACB reduction under ITA 53(2)(a). When you sell the second ESBC shares for $140,000, there will be a capital gain of $100,000 [POD $140,000 - ACB $40,000]. The $100,000 capital gain represents the $60,000 deferral on the first ESBC shares and the $40,000 capital gain on the second ESBC shares.

Definitions

8-136. ITA 44.1 is a very technical provision of the ITA that includes almost a dozen definitions setting out the essentials. We have included brief summaries of some of the more important of those definitions as follows:

Eligible Small Business Corporation (ESBC) An ESBC is a Canadian controlled private corporation (CCPC) that has substantially all (generally meaning more than 90%) of the FMV of its assets devoted principally to an active business carried on primarily (generally meaning more than 50%) in Canada. The corporation's qualifying assets include its holdings of shares or debt in other ESBCs. To be eligible for the deferral, the ESBC and corporations related to it cannot have assets with a carrying value in excess of $50 million. Shares or debt of related corporations are not counted when determining the $50 million limit on assets. Note: On occasion the ITA will refer to generally accepted accounting principles (GAAP) and assets. This is one of those few instances. In this case ITA 44.1 defines "carrying value" as the balance sheet amounts for assets determined applying GAAP. This avoids additional legislation by relying on the amounts that are readily set out in annual financial statements.

Qualifying Disposition To qualify for the deferral, the gain must result from the sale of common shares of an ESBC that was owned by the investor throughout the 185-day period that preceded the disposition. The investor is required to have purchased the shares directly from the issuing ESBC. If the shares were not acquired directly from the issuing ESBC, then the rules of ITA 44.1 do not apply.

Replacement Shares These are common shares of an ESBC that are acquired within 120 days after the end of the year in which the qualifying disposition took place. They must be designated as replacement shares in the individual's tax return. Note that an individual can establish a deferral that is less than the maximum permitted amount by designating a lesser amount of replacement shares.

Permitted Deferral The deferral is limited to a fraction of the capital gain resulting from the qualifying disposition. If all of the proceeds are used to acquire replacement ESBC shares, then all of the capital gain will be deferred. If less than the full amount of the proceeds are used to acquire replacement ESBC shares, then it is only that percentage that will be used to reduce the capital gain. If, for example, 75% of the proceeds are used to acquire replacement ESBC shares, then the capital gain will be reduced by that same 75%.

EXAMPLE The common shares of an ESBC with an ACB of $2,000,000 are sold for $2,500,000. Within 30 days, $1,800,000 of the proceeds (72%) are used to purchase replacement ESBC common shares.

ANALYSIS The total capital gain is $500,000 ($2,500,000 - $2,000,000). Of this total, the maximum permitted deferral would be $360,000 [($500,000)($1,800,000 ÷ $2,500,000)], or 72% of $500,000.

Adjusted Cost Base Reduction The ACB of the replacement shares will have to be reduced by the amount of any capital gains deferral. Using the preceding example, the ACB of the replacement shares would be $1,440,000 (cost of $1,800,000 - ITA 53(2)(a) reduction of $360,000). If there is more than one block of replacement shares, this reduction will be allocated in proportion to their costs.

Example

8-137. The following example illustrates the application of the ITA 44.1 deferral.

EXAMPLE During the current year, an individual disposes of common shares of Company A, an ESBC, in a qualifying disposition. The POD were $4.5 million and the ACB $3.0 million.

Within 120 days after the current year end, the individual purchases replacement shares in Company B, an ESBC, at a cost of $2.2 million and in a second ESBC, Company C, at a cost of $2.3 million. The three companies are not related to each other.

ANALYSIS As the $4.5 million POD is equal to the $4.5 million ($2.2M + $2.3M) cost of the replacement shares, the permitted deferral is equal to the full capital gain of $1.5 million [($1.5M)($4.5M ÷ $4.5M)].

In calculating the ACB of the new shares, the $1.5 million reduction would be determined as follows:

	B Shares	C Shares
Purchase price (cost)	$2,200,000	$2,300,000
Deferral—ACB reduction ITA 53(2)(a)		
[($1.5M)($2.2M/$4.5M)]	(733,333)	
[($1.5M)($2.3M/$4.5M)]		(766,667)
ACB	$1,466,667	$1,533,333

The combined ACB is $3 million ($1,466,667 + $1,533,333), which was the ACB of the Company A shares.

Exercise 8-18

Subject: Deferral of Small Business Gains

On January 15, 2021, Jerri Hamilton sells all of her common shares of Hamilton Ltd., an eligible small business corporation. She had owned the shares for 12 years. The ACB of these shares is $750,000 and they are sold for $1,350,000. On February 15, 2021, $1,200,000 of these proceeds are invested in common shares directly with JH Inc., a new ESBC. How much of the capital gain arising on the sale of the Hamilton Ltd. shares can be deferred as a result of the investment in JH Inc.? If the maximum deferral is elected, what will the ACB of the JH Inc. shares be?

Solutions to Exercises are available in the Study Guide.

We suggest you complete SSP 8-13 at this point.

Deferral on Replacement Property—ITA 13(4) & 44(1)

The Problem—Potential Taxation

8-138. In the previous paragraphs you learned about capital gain deferral where eligible small business corporation shares were sold and replaced within a relatively short period of time. The deferral permitted the investor to use all of the proceeds if desired to reinvest in ESBC shares without a concern that income taxes would have to be paid on those proceeds. In a similar manner, additional rules are added to cover the deferral of income tax consequences when certain capital property is disposed of, voluntarily or involuntarily, with the proceeds used to purchase replacement property. Were it not for these rules a taxpayer would be required to include capital gains and recapture in net income on a disposition of capital property and pay income tax on those amounts, reducing the ability to have sufficient funds to purchase the replacements.

> **EXAMPLE** A business has its only class 1 building completely destroyed by fire. The building has a capital cost of $1,200,000 and a UCC of $450,000. The building was insured for its replacement cost of $4,000,000, and this amount is received in the same year.
>
> **ANALYSIS** The destruction of property is considered a disposition of property. In addition, any entitlement to insurance proceeds is considered POD. The result would be a taxable capital gain of $1,400,000 [(1/2)($4,000,000- $1,200,000)] and, if the building is not replaced during the current year, recapture of $750,000 [POD of $1,200,000 minus (lesser of capital cost of $1,200,000 and POD of $4,000,000) and UCC of $450,000]. The income taxes on this $2,150,000 addition to net income would generally exceed $800,000 for a corporation and potentially in excess of $1,000,000 for an individual, limiting the capability of the business to use the proceeds to acquire replacement property.

8-139. Another common occurrence is when a business changes location. The sale of its properties at the old location may result in significant capital gains. In addition, if the replacement is not made in the same fiscal period there may also be recapture of CCA.

Legislative Relief

8-140. There are two elective provisions that assist in reducing the income tax effect of selling capital property. ITA 13(4) applies to reduce recapture and ITA 44(1) to reduce capital gains. In a manner similar to the ESBC shares previously discussed, any income reduction is deferred by reducing the tax costs (capital cost, ACB, and UCC) of the replacement properties.

8-141. These two elective provisions are conditional on the replacement of the property within a specified period of time. The two provisions are also identical in many respects, with the exception that ITA 13(4) deals with the depreciable property aspects such as CCA and UCC while ITA 44(1) covers the ACB aspect for capital gains purposes. In general all of the recapture and all of the capital gains can be reduced to nil and deferred to future years if the cost of the replacement properties exceeds the POD received on the disposition of the replaced properties.

8-142. Since these provisions are elective, a decision is needed about whether it is preferable to make the necessary elections. For those taxpayers with loss carry over balances that would offset any additional income, deciding not to elect may be preferable. Absent the elections the AccII would allow larger CCA claims in the first year. For a corporate taxpayer, including a large capital gain would create a large capital dividend account, which would allow shareholders to remove half of the capital gain as tax-free dividends (capital dividends are discussed in Chapters 7 and 14).

8-143. The legislation does not require that separate elections be made for each of the two provisions. An election under one of the two provisions is considered to be an election made under both. Some of the many elections offered by the ITA provide a specific form referred to as a prescribed form and some do not. In this case there are no prescribed forms. The legislation requires that the election be made in the income tax return for the year in which the replacement property is acquired. The CRA, at paragraph 1.24 of Folio S3-F3-C1, "Replacement Property," requires a written letter setting out the details only where the replacement property is not acquired in the same year as the replaced property. Late-filed elections are possible through the taxpayer relief provisions discussed in Chapter 2.

Voluntary and Involuntary Dispositions

8-144. The elections provide for two types of situations that depend on whether the disposition was voluntary (e.g., a business relocation) or involuntary (e.g., property destroyed). The distinction is important as it establishes the timeline in which the replacement property must be acquired to benefit from the elections and the type of property that qualifies. The two types of dispositions can be described as follows:

Involuntary Dispositions The legislation refers to three specific types of dispositions as resulting from (1) theft, (2) destruction, and (3) expropriation under statutory authority. All types of depreciable property qualify for the elective treatment. The elections are available as long as the replacement occurs within 24 months after the end of the year in which the proceeds of disposition were received. Note that it is not the year in which the involuntary disposition occurs that establishes the timing of the replacement but the year in which the proceeds are receivable, which established when the disposition is recognized for income tax purposes. Proceeds for theft and destruction means payments as compensation under an insurance policy, whereas proceeds for an expropriation often depend on agreement and if not the results determined by a court. There are special rules in ITA 44(2) that address the timing where the proceeds and disposition do not occur in the same year.

Voluntary Dispositions Voluntary dispositions most commonly involve the relocation of a business. As a relocation often involves a disposition of capital property, taxpayers undergoing a move may encounter problems similar to those experienced when there is an involuntary disposition. The elective provisions for voluntary dispositions are more restrictive than those for involuntary dispositions. Specifically, the elections only apply to capital property that meets the definition of "former business property." A "former business property" means capital property that is real property (e.g., land and buildings) or an interest in real property. This means that depreciable property such as equipment, furniture, and fixtures will not qualify for the election. Another important difference is that the replacement must occur within 12 months after the year in which the proceeds of disposition become receivable.

Replacements

8-145. When capital property is voluntarily or involuntarily disposed of any capital gain will be included in net income in the year of the disposition. The ability to reduce or eliminate that capital gain is wholly dependent on filing an election under ITA 44(1) irrespective of when the replacement property is acquired.

8-146. On the other hand a disposition of depreciable capital property that results in recapture may be resolved by acquiring replacement depreciable property of the same class in that same year since the purchase will add to the class, potentially eliminating any negative UCC balance caused by the disposition. This would avoid the need to elect under ITA 13(4).

8-147. The election, however, cannot be filed until the year in which the replacement property is acquired. If the replacement property is acquired in a year subsequent to the disposition of the replaced property, then the ability to reduce or eliminate any recapture and capital gains will be dependent on filing elections under ITA 13(4) and 44(1). In this case the taxpayer can request a reassessment of the year in which the replaced property was disposed of to recover any additional income tax that was payable as a result.

Application of ITA 44(1) to Capital Gains

8-148. If qualifying capital property is disposed of and replaced within the required timeframe, an election under ITA 44(1) will reduce the capital gain to the lesser of

- the actual capital gain; or
- the amount by which the POD of the replaced property exceeds the cost of the replacement property. If the cost of the replacement is greater that the POD of the replaced property, then this amount will be nil, allowing a 100% reduction of the capital gain.

8-149. In addition, the difference between the actual capital gain and the reduced capital gain (the deferred capital gain) is used to reduce the cost of the replacement property.

EXAMPLE A taxpayer has land with an ACB of $600,000. It is expropriated by the local municipality. Compensation, which is agreed to and paid immediately, is $1,000,000. Replacement land is acquired in the same year with land at a cost of $1,200,000.

ANALYSIS—No Election If no election is made under ITA 44(1), there will be a capital gain of $400,000 ($1,000,000- $600,000) and the new land will have an adjusted cost base of $1,200,000.

ANALYSIS—With an Election If an election is filed under ITA 44(1), the capital gain will be the lesser of

- the actual capital gain of $400,000; or
- the amount by which the POD of the expropriated land exceeds the cost of the replacement land. Since the POD of $1,000,000 does not exceed the replacement cost of $1,200,000 the result is nil.

The deemed cost of the replacement land is $800,000 calculated as the replacement cost of $1,200,000 less the reduction in the capital gain of $400,000. The ACB would also be $800,000.

8-150. If the replacement cost had been less than the expropriation proceeds, it would not have been possible to defer all of the capital gain. For example, if the cost of the replacement land had been $700,000, the minimum capital gain would be $300,000, the excess of the POD of $1,000,000 over the $700,000 cost of the replacement property. The result would defer only $100,000 of the total $400,000 capital gain. The deferred capital gain of $100,000 would decrease the cost and therefore the ACB of the replacement property to $600,000 ($700,000- $100,000).

Application of ITA 13(4) to Recapture of CCA

8-151. The application of ITA 13(4) is mechanically very similar to ITA 44(1) but requires working with the UCC of the class of depreciable property that was subject to a disposition that resulted in a recapture. The following example will clarify the application of ITA 13(4). This example does not have a capital gain, so ITA 44(1) is not relevant, allowing the focus to be exclusively on ITA 13(4).

EXAMPLE A company's only building is destroyed in a fire in its 2020 taxation year. The capital cost of the building was $2,500,000, the FMV is $2,225,000, and it is an older building with a UCC of only $275,000. The insurance proceeds, all of which are received in the same year, equal the FMV of $2,225,000. The replacement building is acquired in the 2021 taxation year at a capital cost of $3,000,000.

ANALYSIS—No Election Deducting $2,225,000, the lesser of the POD and the capital cost of the building, from the UCC of $275,000 results in a negative balance of $1,950,000 that is recapture for the 2020 year. Since the property was not replaced in the same year, the negative balance will remain at the end of the year. This amount will have to be included in the business income of the company for its 2020 taxation year and will be added back to the UCC at the beginning of 2021 to restore the UCC balance to nil.

ANALYSIS—With an Election In 2021, the year in which the replacement occurs, the ITA 13(4) election provides for a reduction of the 2020 recapture:

January 1, 2020, UCC balance		$275,000
Deduction:		
Lesser of:		
• POD = $2,225,000		
• Capital cost = $2,500,000	$2,225,000	
Reduced by the lesser of:		
• Actual recapture = $1,950,000		
• Replacement cost = $3,000,000	(1,950,000)	(275,000)
Revised 2020 recapture (reassessed)		Nil

8-152. The election would be made in the form of a letter attached to the 2021 income tax return that would include the relevant supporting calculations. In this example, the election would result in a $1,950,000 reduction in the company's 2020 net income and would provide the basis for a recovery of any additional income taxes paid as a result of the recapture. For efilers, a written letter must be submitted to the CRA in support of these elections.

8-153. The reduction in the capital gain on the replaced property under ITA 44(1) reduces the cost and the ACB of the replacement property. ITA 13(4) also provides a similar impact, but rather than apply the reduction in the recapture against the capital cost of the replacement property, the reduction is instead made to the UCC of the class of the replaced property. This is accomplished by treating the recapture reduction as deemed POD, which is illustrated in the following UCC calculations:

Original 2021 UCC		$ Nil
Add:		
Capital cost of the replacement	$3,000,000	
Less: Deemed POD	(1,950,000)	1,050,000
New UCC balance		$1,050,000

Note that the AccII would apply to the net addition of $1,050,000.

8-154. The reversal of recapture is limited to the capital cost of the replacement property. In our example, if the capital cost of the replacement property had been only $1,800,000, this amount would have been the limit on the recapture reversal and the recapture would have been $150,000 [$275,000- ($2,225,000- $1,800,000)], which would have been included in 2020 net income. In that case, the UCC at the end of 2021 would be $1,200,000 ($3,000,000 replacement cost- $1,800,000 deemed POD for the reduction in the recapture).

Exercise 8-19

Subject: Involuntary Disposition—ITA 13(4) Election for Recapture

Foran Inc., has a calendar taxation year end. During 2020, Foran's only building was destroyed by a tornado. Its original capital cost was $1,500,000, its FMV was $1,400,000, and the class 1 UCC balance was $650,000. The company receives $1,400,000 in insurance proceeds during 2020 and replaces the building with a used building at a capital cost of $2,350,000 in 2021. The company files a timely ITA 13(4) election to defer the maximum recaptured CCA. What are the income tax consequences for 2020 and 2021, including the UCC of the replacement building at the end of 2021, as a result of filing the election?

Solutions to Exercises are available in the Study Guide.

Combined Application of ITA 13(4) and 44(1)

8-155. When replacement property is non-depreciable capital property, such as land, it is only the election under ITA 44(1) that is required to reduce any capital gains on the land. When the replacement property is depreciable property, however, there may be both capital gains and recapture, with the result that both of the elections under ITA 13(4) and 44(1) are required to address both types of income.

8-156. In terms of depreciable property, the capital cost of the replacement will be reduced by any reduction in the capital gain, and the UCC of the class of the replaced property will be reduced by any reduction in the recapture. Because the UCC calculations work with the capital cost of the replacement property and ITA 44(1) causes a reduction in that capital cost, the ITA 44(1) election must be completed first, then the election under ITA 13(4).

Example 1—Replacement Cost Exceeds POD

8-157. Example 1 of the combined application of ITA 13(4) and ITA 44(1) looks at a situation in which the replacement cost of the capital property exceeds the POD of the replaced properties. This means that all of the capital gains and recapture of the disposition of the replaced properties can be eliminated.

EXAMPLE During its 2020 taxation year, the Martin Company decides to relocate its business. Its current property consists of land with an ACB of $500,000, as well as a building with a capital cost of $1,500,000 and a UCC of $340,000. These capital properties are sold for a total price of $2,400,000, of which $600,000 is for the land and $1,800,000 for the building. During August 2021, a replacement property is acquired at a new location at a cost of $2,800,000, of which $700,000 is paid for the land and $2,100,000 for the building.

ANALYSIS—Capital Gain As a result of the disposition, the Martin Company will include the following amounts in its net income for 2020:

	Old Land	Old Building
POD	$600,000	$1,800,000
ACB	(500,000)	(1,500,000)
Capital gain	$100,000	$ 300,000
Inclusion rate	1/2	1/2
Taxable capital gain	$ 50,000	$ 150,000
Recapture ($340,000 - $1,500,000)	N/A	$1,160,000

When the replacement occurs in 2021, the replacement cost for both the land and the building exceeds the POD of the replaced capital properties. As a consequence, the revised capital gain for 2020 will be nil, a fact that would be reflected in a reassessed 2020 income tax return. However, the cost and capital cost of the replacement capital properties would be reduced as follows:

	New Land	New Building
Cost	$700,000	$2,100,000
Capital gain reduction—ITA 44(1)	(100,000)	(300,000)
Deemed ACB and Capital Cost	$600,000	$1,800,000

8-158. Using the ITA 13(4) formula, the reassessed 2020 recapture would be nil, calculated as follows:

January 1, 2020, UCC balance		$340,000
Deduction:		
Lesser of:		
• POD = $1,800,000		
• Capital cost = $1,500,000	$1,500,000	
Reduced by the lesser of:		
• Actual recapture = $1,160,000		
• Replacement cost = $2,100,000	(1,160,000)	(340,000)
Revised 2020 recapture (reassessed)		Nil

8-159. As would be expected when the replacement cost of the new building exceeds the actual recapture of CCA, the reassessed recapture of CCA will be nil. The reversal of the 2020 recapture of CCA will be reflected in the UCC of the new building as follows:

Opening 2021 UCC	$ Nil
Add: Capital cost of the replacement	1,800,000
Less: Deemed POD—ITA 13(4) Election	(1,160,000)
UCC balance end of 2021	$ 640,000

Note that the capital cost of the replacement was determined under ITA 44(1). In addition, the AccII would apply to the net addition of $640,000.

Example 2—Proceeds of Disposition Exceed Replacement Cost

8-160. In Example 1, 100% of the capital gains were eliminated through the application of ITA 44(1) because the replacement cost exceeded the POD of the replaced properties. If this is not the case then some portion of the capital gain will remain. This can be illustrated with a small change in the Example 1 by decreasing the replacement cost of the land to $550,000.

EXAMPLE During its 2020 taxation year, the Martin Company decides to relocate its business. Its current property consists of land with an ACB of $500,000, as well as a building with a capital cost of $1,500,000 and a UCC of $340,000. These capital properties are sold for a total price of $2,400,000, of which $600,000 is for the land and $1,800,000 for the building. During August 2021, a replacement property is acquired at a new location at a cost of $2,650,000, of which $550,000 is paid for the land and $2,100,000 for the building.

8-161. For the 2020 year, the capital gains and recapture on the disposition of the replaced capital properties will be as shown in Paragraph 8-157. In 2021, when ITA 44(1) is applied, the capital gain on the land would be the lesser of

- $100,000 (the actual capital gain); or
- $50,000 (the excess of the POD of $600,000 minus the replacement cost of $550,000).

8-162. The lesser amount is $50,000. When this amount of the capital gain is reduced, it leaves $50,000 ($100,000- $50,000) in capital gains to be included in net income for 2020. As a result the ACB, capital cost, and UCC of the replacement properties are as follows:

	New Land	New Building
Cost	$550,000	$2,100,000
Capital gain reduction—ITA 44(1)	(50,000)	(300,000)
Deemed adjusted cost base/capital cost	$500,000	$1,800,000
Recapture reduction—ITA 13(4)	N/A	(1,160,000)
UCC at the end of 2021	N/A	$ 640,000

Election to Reallocate Proceeds of Disposition—ITA 44(6)

8-163. In the preceding example, the $550,000 replacement cost of the land was less than the $600,000 POD of the replaced land, and $50,000 of the capital gain could not be reduced. It was required to be included in net income for 2020. Fortunately, another elective option exists, this time under ITA 44(6), to eliminate the remaining part of the capital gain.

8-164. ITA 44(6) allows a taxpayer to reallocate the POD between land and a building if the properties qualify as "former business property." The reallocation only requires that there would be a capital gain on one of the two properties. The election allows POD from one property to be transferred to the other property in an amount sufficient to eliminate the capital gain on that one property. The goal is to match the POD of one property with the cost of the replacement property so that any remaining capital gain can be completely eliminated.

8-165. In Example 2 the POD of the land was $600,000 and the replacement cost was only $550,000, leaving a $50,000 capital gain that could not be eliminated with an election under ITA 44(1). However, the gain could have been fully eliminated if the POD had been $550,000. ITA 44(6) considers whether one of the replaced properties has a POD in excess of its ACB. The POD of the land was $600,000 and the ACB was $500,000, meaning that the land qualifies to allow up to the $100,000 difference to be elected upon. As a result, an election is made to transfer $50,000. The result is that the POD for the land drops by $50,000 to $550,000 and the POD of the building increases by $50,000 to $1,850,000. This is reflected in the following calculations:

	Old Land	Old Building
POD	$550,000	$1,850,000
ACB	(500,000)	(1,500,000)
Capital gain	$ 50,000	$ 350,000
Inclusion rate	1/2	1/2
Taxable capital gain	$ 25,000	$ 175,000

8-166. While the total taxable capital gain remains the same before the election under ITA 44(1), this reallocation of the total POD results in a situation where the replacement cost of both the land and building are now equal to, or exceed, the POD. This, in turn, means that all of the capital gains on both of the replacement properties will be eliminated from the 2020 reassessed income tax return. The income tax attributes of the replacement properties would be as follows:

	New Land	New Building
Cost	$550,000	$2,100,000
Capital gain reduction—ITA 44(1)	(50,000)	(350,000)
Deemed ACB and capital cost	$500,000	$1,750,000
Recapture reduction—ITA 13(4)	N/A	(1,160,000)
UCC at the end of 2021	N/A	$ 590,000

8-167. Note that the ITA 44(6) election is not made without a cost. Had the $50,000 been left as a capital gain on the land, income tax would have applied on only one-half of the total (the taxable capital gain). While the taxable capital gain of $25,000 has been eliminated, future CCA has been given up for the difference of $50,000 because the UCC has decreased by $50,000, from $640,000 to $590,000, as a result.

Exercise 8-20

Subject: Involuntary Dispositions—ITA 13(4) and 44(1) Elections

Hadfeld Ltd., a company with a calendar year end, carries on business out of a single class 1 building that cost $725,000 in 2014. At the beginning of 2020, the UCC was $623,150. On June 30, 2020, the building was completely destroyed in a fire. The building was insured for its fair market value of $950,000, and insurance proceeds of $950,000 were received in September 2020. The building is replaced in 2021 at a cost of $980,000. Hadfeld Ltd. wishes to minimize income taxes. Describe the 2020 and 2021 income tax consequences of these events, including the capital cost and UCC for the new building at the end of 2021. Ignore any gain or loss related to the land on which the building is situated.

Solutions to Exercises are available in the Study Guide.

Capital Gains and Tax Planning

8-168. A knowledge of capital gains offers many opportunities for effective income tax planning since the realization of capital gains or capital losses is largely at the discretion of the taxpayer. If the taxpayer wishes to exclude capital gains or capital losses in a particular taxation year, this can often be accomplished by delaying the disposition of the capital property. This means that gains can often be deferred, perhaps until retirement, when the taxpayer may be in a lower income tax bracket.

8-169. Other examples of income tax planning would include selling investments such as shares with accrued losses to offset capital gains realized earlier in the taxation year, including avoiding the reacquisition of the same shares to avoid the superficial loss rules. Other standard planning would include structuring a sale of capital property to take advantage of capital gain reserves and using the elective options to increase access to the principal residence exemption where a home is used at some point to earn income.

8-170. There are many other complexities to capital gains that include the involvement of shareholders of certain Canadian controlled private corporations, the capital gain deduction that may considerably reduce the ultimate income tax liability on capital gains and the application of net capital losses. These additional topics are discussed at length in Chapter 11.

We suggest you complete SSP 8-14 to 8-18 at this point.

Key Terms

A full glossary with definitions is provided at the end of the Study Guide.

Adjusted Cost Base	Listed Personal Property
Allowable Capital Loss	Personal-Use Property
Capital Cost	Principal Residence
Capital Gain	Proceeds of Disposition (POD)
Capital Gain Reserve	Real Property
Capital Loss	Recapture of CCA
Capital Property	Replacement Property Rules
Deemed Disposition	Reserve
Deeming Rules	Rollover
Disposition	Small Business Corporation
Election	Superficial Loss—ITA 54
Emigration	Taxable Canadian Property
Former Business Property	Taxable Capital Gain
Identical Property Rules	Terminal Loss
Involuntary Disposition	Undepreciated Capital Cost (UCC)

References

For more detailed study of the material in this chapter, we would refer you to the following:

ITA 38	Taxable Capital Gain and Allowable Capital Loss
ITA 39	Meaning of Capital Gain and Capital Loss
ITA 40	General Rules
ITA 41	Taxable Net Gain from Disposition of Listed Personal Property
ITA 42	Dispositions Subject to Warranties

ITA 43	General Rule for Part Dispositions
ITA 44	Exchanges of Property
ITA 44.1	Definitions (Eligible Small Business Shares)
ITA 45	Property with More Than One Use
ITA 46	Personal-Use Property
ITA 47	Identical Properties
ITA 53	Adjustments to Cost Base
ITA 54	Definitions (Capital Gains)
S1-F3-C2	Principal Residence
S1-F5-C1	Related Persons and Dealing at Arm's Length
S3-F3-C1	Replacement Property
T4037	Capital Gains Guide
IT-95R	Foreign Exchange Gains and Losses
IT-102R2	Conversion of Property, Other Than Real Property, from or to Inventory
IT-159R3	Capital Debts Established to Be Bad Debts
IT-262R2	Losses of Non-Residents and Part-Year Residents
IT-264R	Part Dispositions
IT-387R2	Meaning of Identical Properties (Consolidated)
IT-403R	Options on Real Estate
IT-451R	Deemed Disposition and Acquisition on Ceasing to Be or Becoming Resident In Canada
IT-456R	Capital Property—Some Adjustments to Cost Base
IT-479R	Transactions in Securities

Self-Study Problems (SSPs)

Self-Study Problems (SSPs) provide practice in problem solving. Within the chapters, we have indicated where it would be appropriate to stop and work on each SSP. The problems can be downloaded by chapter from MyLab Accounting. Solutions are available in the Study Guide. Select problems can also be completed directly in MyLab and auto-graded.

Assignment Problems

Solutions to Assignment Problems (APs) are available to instructors only.

AP 8-1 (Identical Properties)

Ms. Wells has purchased the shares of two companies over a number of years. Each company has only one class of shares. Purchases and sales of shares in the first of these companies, Memo Inc., are as follows:

February 2017 purchase	60 @ $24
November 2018 purchase	90 @ 28
April 2019 purchase	45 @ 30
October 2019 sale	(68) @ 36
September 2021 purchase	22 @ 26
November 2021 sale	(53) @ 40

Purchases and sales of shares in the second company, Demo Ltd., are as follows:

April 2020 purchase	200 @ $24
December 2020 purchase	160 @ 33
July 2021 sale	(260) @ 36

Required:

A. Determine the cost of the Memo Inc. shares that Ms. Wells owns at December 31, 2021.

B. Determine the taxable capital gain resulting from the July 2021 sale of the Demo Ltd. shares.

AP 8-2 (Identification of Capital Gains and Reserves)

In early 2019, Cyndey Walters received a $2 million settlement as a result of suffering serious injuries in an accident on a construction site. As a result, she immediately quit her job as a plumber for a construction company and began to search for rundown houses in her neighbourhood that she could buy at a low price. Her objective was to bring her houses up to code (i.e., in accordance with building regulations) and then rent them to individuals who could not afford adequate housing.

Cyndey charged just enough rent to cover the expenses of each house. By March 2020, she owned five houses that were rented to five families. She continued working part time as a plumber while she took courses toward a degree in social work.

Cyndey came from a large family, many members of which were involved in construction. She called on her family for help when her tenants needed services, and they gave her a family discount for their services.

In June 2021, she learned that the owner of two low-rise apartment buildings in the neighbourhood had died. They were vacant and in very poor condition. The executor of the estate was receptive for a quick sale. Cyndey offered $250,000 cash for the two buildings and the large parking lot between them. The offer was accepted.

As this was a much larger project than the single family homes she had been working on, she enlisted the aid of her father, an experienced contractor. He agreed to be the general contractor for the project.

In August 2021, a major software company announced it was going to move its Canadian headquarters into the neighbourhood within two years.

In September 2021, Cyndey received an unsolicited offer of $1.5 million for her property. The purchaser intends to construct a luxury condo building to house the newly hired workers.

The offer requires Cyndey to take back a $1 million first mortgage on the property. The mortgage will be repaid in four annual instalments of $250,000 each, beginning in 2022. The cash down payment would be $500,000.

In November 2021, Cyndey begins to receive unsolicited cash offers for her rental houses. The offers are all for more than double what she paid.

Required: Cyndey has sought your advice about the income tax treatment of the sale of the two apartment buildings and parking lot. Provide the necessary advice, including the calculation of the minimum amount of capital gains that would be required to be included in Cyndey's net income for the year of sale on the assumption that the properties acquired are capital property.

AP 8-3 (Warranties, Bad Debts, and Reserves)

Louis Warrick is a computer scientist who has developed an extremely complex software package that he believes can predict, with considerable accuracy, changes in stock market indexes. His intent in developing this package was to use it to produce investment income. However, after making some use of it for this purpose, he receives an unsolicited offer from a wealthy investor to buy the package for $2,500,000. He concludes this will, in fact, produce more income than he can produce by investing his somewhat meagre resources. Based on this conclusion, he sells the software on January 1, 2021.

To facilitate the sale, he accepts a down payment of $750,000 on January 1, 2021, followed by scheduled payments of $750,000 on January 1, 2022, and $1,000,000 on January 1, 2023. Interest at an annual rate of 6% will be paid on the outstanding balance for the year. This payment will be made on December 31 of each year. There are no deductible costs associated with the package.

Louis provides a three-year warranty that requires him to keep the software up to date for this period. He estimates that this warranty will require about $100,000 per year to provide the required services. The amounts received for providing the warranty are included in the purchase price of $2,500,000.

The down payment and the required interest are paid for 2021. The actual costs of providing the warranty services during this year total $79,000.

The required instalment payment is paid on January 1, 2022. The costs of providing the warranty services during this year total $126,000, all of which were incurred between September 1 and December 31, 2022. However, the scheduled interest payment is not made on December 31, 2022.

After trying to contact the purchaser in early 2023, he discovers that this individual has made, using the software that Louis has provided, a number of disastrous investment decisions, resulting in his personal bankruptcy.

Louis concludes that he has no hope of receiving any further payment from the purchaser and, in fact, may be sued by the bankruptcy trustees for the failure of his software to provide sound investment advice.

Required: Calculate the income tax effects of the transactions that took place during 2021 through 2023 on Louis Warrick's net income on the assumption that the ACB of the software is nil. Assume that, because his original intent was to use the package to produce income, the software would have been characterized as capital property.

AP 8-4 (Capital Gains Reserves)

Several years ago Ms. Nina Stark acquired a building to be used in a business she carries on as a sole proprietor. The total cost of the property was $2,300,000, with $800,000 of this amount paid for the land and $1,500,000 for the building.

She has decided that, in order to improve her cash position, she would like to sell the building and relocate her business to to leased premises. On January 1, 2021, the building is sold for $2,800,000 with $900,000 paid for the land and $1,900,000 paid for the building. The UCC balance in class 1 at the time of the sale is $1,248,019. The building was the only property in class 1.

The terms of the sale require the purchaser to make a down payment at the time of purchase, with the remaining balance payable on January 1, 2023. No payments are required in 2022. Interest on the outstanding balance is payable on December 31 of each year at an annual rate of 6%.

Ms. Stark plans to maximize the use of capital gain reserves to defer the payment of income taxes on the sale.

Required: Indicate the income tax consequences of these transactions on Ms. Stark's net income for the years 2021, 2022, and 2023, assuming:

A. that the down payment was equal to $280,000 (10% of the sales price).

B. that the down payment was equal to $840,000 (30% of the sales price).

AP 8-5 (Capital Gain Reserves)

On November 1, 2021, Ms. Stevens sells a capital property for $500,000. The ACB of the property is $230,000 and she incurs selling costs in the amount of $20,000. She receives an immediate cash payment of $200,000 on November 1, 2021, with the balance owing of $300,000 to be paid on June 1, 2027.

Ms. Stevens wishes to use capital gain reserves to defer the payment of income taxes on capital gains for as long as possible.

Required: Calculate the amount of the minimum taxable capital gain that would be included in Ms. Stevens' net income for each of the years 2021 through 2027.

AP 8-6 (Capital Gain Reserves)

Mr. Rhodes purchased a large tract of land near Edmonton 15 years ago for $750,000. It was sold during April 2021 to a developer for $2,500,000. He received a down payment of $625,000 (25%) and accepted a 25-year, 8% mortgage for the balance of $1,875,000. The payments on this mortgage will begin in the second year and will require the repayment of $75,000 (3% of the proceeds of disposition) per year in principal.

Mr. Rhodes wishes to defer income taxes through the use of capital gain reserves to the maximum extent possible.

Required: Calculate the capital gains consequences of this sale for 2021 through 2027, assuming that Mr. Rhodes claims the maximum capital gains reserve in 2021 and in all subsequent years.

AP 8-7 (Principal Residence Designation)

Mr. Stewart Simms has lived most of his life in Vancouver. In 1997, he purchased a three bedroom home near English Bay for $125,000. In 2002, he acquired a cottage in the Whistler ski area at a cost of $40,000. In all subsequent years, he has spent at least a portion of the year living in each of the two locations. When he is not residing in these properties they are left vacant.

On October 1, 2021, Mr. Simms sells the English Bay property for $515,000 and the cottage at Whistler for $320,000.

Mr. Simms wishes to minimize any capital gains resulting from the sale of the two properties.

Required: Describe how the two residences should be designated to optimize the use of the principal residence exemption. In addition, calculate the amount of the taxable capital gains that would arise under the designation that you have recommended. Show all supporting calculations.

AP 8-8 (Personal-Use Property)

Mr. Firenza owns a number of personal assets, all of which were acquired while he was a resident of Canada. As he plans to spend the next five years travelling around the world, he will be converting most of his possessions to cash. The assets he plans to sell in the current year can be described as follows:

- A vintage automobile that has been restored to near-new condition. He acquired the vehicle for $42,000 and has spent $135,000 on the restoration process. He estimates the current FMV of the automobile to be $320,000.
- An extensive coin collection, which has a current FMV of $23,500. The total cost of all of the coins is $17,600. He believes that the coins can be sold without incurring any selling costs.
- A rare seventeenth-century manuscript that he inherited from his mother when she died a few years ago. His mother had paid $4,000 for the manuscript and, at the time of her death, it had an estimated FMV of $42,000. However, since he inherited the manuscript several other copies of the same manuscript have been found and, as a consequence, its FMV has fallen to $8,500.
- A Lawren Harris oil painting that he acquired for $275,000. While he believes it could be sold at auction for $350,000, the auction house will charge a commission of 20% of the sales price.
- A sailboat that cost $162,000. He estimates that its current FMV, net of selling costs, would be $123,000.
- An antique desk acquired for $600. He believes that it could be sold for $2,200 and that no selling costs would be incurred.

Required: Mr. Firenza has asked you to determine the amount that would have to be included in his net income if all of these personal-use properties were sold for their estimated values. Indicate any amounts that may be available for carry over to other years.

AP 8-9 (Capital Gains on Foreign Securities)

Ross Draper received an inheritance of £400,000. The funds were received on November 4, 2017, and were immediately transferred to a brokerage account. On the day of the transfer, they were used to purchase 5,000 shares of Boris Inc., a publicly traded British company. The shares are purchased at £75 per share, a total of £375,000. The remaining £25,000 was left in the brokerage account.

The shares pay an annual dividend of £2.00 per share. Ross receives an amount of £10,000 on each of the following dates:

May 1, 2018
May 1, 2019
May 1, 2020

All of these funds are left in his brokerage account. The account does not earn interest.

On November 15, 2020, all of the shares of Boris Inc. were sold for £60 per share, a total of £300,000. These proceeds were left in Ross's brokerage account until January 31, 2021, at which time they were converted into Canadian dollars. The £25,000 balance from 2020 was also converted at this time.

All of funds were withdrawn from the account on July 1, 2021, in order to use for personal expenditures.

Assume relevant exchange rates between the Canadian dollar and the British pound were as follow:

November 4, 2017	$1.00 = £1.68
May 1, 2018	$1.00 = £1.76
May 1, 2019	$1.00 = £1.75
May 1, 2020	$1.00 = £1.70
November 15, 2020	$1.00 = £1.65
January 31, 2021	$1.00 = £1.62
July 1, 2021	$1.00 = £1.58

Required: Calculate the minimum amount that will be included in Mr. Draper's net income for each of the years 2017 through 2021.

AP 8-10 (Changes in Use—CCA)

On January 1, 2017, Miss Coos purchased a building to be used as her personal residence at a cost of $360,000. Of this total $90,000 was for the land and $270,000 was for the building.

On January 1, 2019, after living in the building for two years, a portion of the residence was converted to an office and was rented to a local accountant for $1,200 per month. At the time of the conversion, the FMV of the building was $360,000. The FMV of the land was unchanged. Based on the amount of floor space allocated to the office, Miss Coos calculated that 30% of the building was converted into office space.

On January 1, 2021, the office was rented by a new tenant who did not require the same amount of floor space as the previous tenant. As a result, one room was converted back to personal use. This room represented 10% of the total floor space, and the FMV of the building was $420,000 at this time. The FMV of the land remains the same at $90,000.

Required: What is the maximum CCA that can be deducted in 2019, 2020, and 2021? In addition, indicate any capital gains or capital losses that will result from the changes in use.

AP 8-11 (Departure from Canada)

Mr. Mark Vargo has been a resident of Canada all of his life. He was recently offered a lucrative job with a reputable firm in Washington, DC. After careful consideration he has decided to make the move and sever his Canadian residency.

At the time he ceased to be a resident of Canada he owned the following properties:

	Adjusted Cost Base	Fair Market Value
Antique sports car	$ 32,000	$ 46,000
Personal automobile	32,000	18,000
Shares in Bank of Nova Scotia (a public company)	12,000	16,000
Shares in Vargo Ltd. (a private company)	23,000	17,000
Coin collection	8,000	6,000
Cottage (not his principal residence)	135,000	262,000

Required: Determine the amount of the taxable capital gain or allowable capital loss that Mr. Vargo will be required to include in his final Canadian income tax return for the current year as a result of severing his Canadian residency. Ignore any special elective options that may be available to him on leaving Canada.

AP 8-12 (Deferral on Small Business Investments)

The two independent cases that follow involve shares of eligible small business corporations (ESBCs) that are being sold, with all or part of the proceeds being used to acquire the shares of other ESBCs. The shares that are being sold have been held for more than one year.

Case A In January 2021, Martha Cutler sold her common shares in A Ltd. for proceeds of $1,500,000. A Ltd. is an ESBC. She realized a $250,000 capital gain on this disposition. In March 2021, she invested $1,200,000 of the proceeds in B Ltd., a new ESBC.

Case B In April 2021, Thomas Wolf sold his common shares in C Ltd. for $5,600,000. C Ltd. is an ESBC. He realized an $850,000 capital gain on this disposition. All the proceeds from this sale were immediately invested in two ESBCs, D Ltd. at a cost of $2,600,000 and E Ltd. at a cost of $3,000,000.

Required: For both cases, determine the capital gains the individuals can defer as well as the ACB of the replacement shares.

AP 8-13 (Voluntary Dispositions—With ITA 44(6) Election)

Canco Inc., a publicly traded company, has carried on a sports clothing business in a building in Hamilton for many years. Its major assets are as follows:

Land and Building The building was constructed for the company at a total cost of $2,300,000. It is the only property in the company's class 1. The January 1, 2021, UCC balance in this class is $1,105,000. The building is situated on land that the company purchased for $250,000.

Class 8 Property All of the company's equipment, furniture, and fixtures are in class 8. The combined capital cost of all class 8 property equals $230,000. The January 1, 2021, UCC balance of class 8 is $178,645.

Canco operated a retail outlet for its sports clothing in the front half of the building, which is situated on a busy major street. Over the last two years, sales from the store have drastically decreased while online sales of its products have increased significantly.

Canco has made the decision to close the store and to focus on online sales. As a result, a decision has been made to move to a more appropriate site in Sudbury.

In late November 2021, Canco listed the building for sale and almost immediately got an offer that was accepted. The total proceeds for the land and building were $3,200,000, with $800,000 paid for the land and $2,400,000 paid for the building. All the class 8 property was sold for $200,000. None of the allocated proceeds for any class 8 property exceeded their capital cost.

In early January 2022, Canco completed the purchase of a suitable Sudbury property for $3,080,000. Based on appraisals, $2,480,000 was allocated to the building and $600,000 was allocated to the land. As it is not a new building, it does not qualify for the enhanced CCA rate for class 1.

The class 8 equipment and furniture is replaced at a cost of $275,000. Canco's computer equipment is stored and moved to the new location.

The company's taxation year ends on December 31, 2021, and it did not own any buildings or class 8 property at the end of the year. There was a problem with the vendor's documents that delayed the purchase until 2021.

Required:

A. On the disposition of each property, indicate the income tax consequences and the amounts that would be required to be included in the company's net income for 2021.

B. Determine the income tax consequences if the company opted to defer capital gains and recapture by electing under ITA 13(4) and ITA 44(1). Indicate the tax values of the replacement properties, including the ACB, capital cost, and UCC.

C. Determine whether the results in Part B could be improved upon with a reallocation election under ITA 44(6). Explain your conclusion.

AP 8-14 (Involuntary Dispositions—No ITA 44(6) Election)

On July 1, 2021, the manufacturing plant of Janchek Ltd. was expropriated by the provincial government to make way for a new expressway. It is the only building that Janchek Ltd. owns. The land on which the plant was situated was purchased for $88,000. The building, a class 1 property, was constructed at a capital cost of $290,000. The company's year end is December 31.

On November 23, 2021, after extended negotiations between Janchek and the provincial government, the company agreed to and received compensation in the amount of $130,000 for the land and $430,000 for the building. On January 1, 2021, the UCC balance in class 1 was $248,000.

On June 20, 2022, a replacement manufacturing plant was purchased for a total cost of $1,050,000. Of this amount, $210,000 was allocated to the land, with the remaining $840,000 allocated to the building. As this was not a new building, it did not qualify for the 10% CCA rate for non-residential buildings that are used for manufacturing and processing.

Janchek Ltd. will make any available elections to reduce the income tax effects of the replacement of the expropriated property.

Required:

A. Determine the income tax consequences in 2021 that will result from the receipt of the expropriation compensation.

B. Indicate the impact on the results in Part A if elections were made under ITA 44(1) to defer capital gains and ITA 13(4) to defer recapture.

C. Determine the ACB of the land and the capital cost of the building as well as the UCC of the building as a result of the elections under ITA 13(4) and ITA 44(1).

AP 8-15 (Comprehensive Case Covering Chapters 1 to 8)

Mr. Arnold Bosch is 41 years old and earns most of his income through carrying on a business as a sole proprietor, Bosch's Better Boats (BBB). For the taxation year ending December 31, 2021, Mr. Bosch's accountant has determined that BBB had accounting income before taxes, determined in accordance with Accounting Standards for Private Enterprises (ASPE), of $196,000. In reconciling his business income for income tax purposes, the following information is relevant:

1. The accounting income figure included a deduction for amortization of $29,000.

2. On January 1, 2020, BBB had the following UCC balances:

• Class 1 (building acquired in 2006)	$275,000
• Class 8	83,000
• Class 10	28,000

On March 1, 2021, a class 8 property with a capital cost of $46,000 was sold for $28,500. On March 15, 2021, the property that had been sold was replaced with another class 8 property with a capital cost of $63,250.

3. During 2021, BBB spent $30,000 landscaping the grounds around its building. This amount was treated as an asset for accounting purposes and is being amortized over 10 years on a straight-line basis. The amortization is included in the $29,000 amortization figure in Part 1 of this problem.

4. BBB's 2021 accounting income included a deduction for meals and entertainment of $27,600.

5. BBB's 2021 accounting income included a deduction for charitable donations of $5,500, as well as a deduction for donations to federal political parties of $700.

6. For accounting purposes, BBB treats estimated warranty costs as an expense with an offsetting credit to a liability account. On January 1, 2021, the liability balance for warranties was $22,000. On December 31, 2021, the liability balance was $17,500.

Based on the level of income earned by BBB, Mr. Bosch is required to make CPP contributions of $5,796 [(2)($2,898)]. He does not choose to make EI contributions.

Mr. Bosch has a common-law partner, Mr. Fritz Mann. Three years ago, Mr. Bosch and his partner adopted two orphans. Chris, age 9, has a severe and prolonged disability that qualifies him for the disability tax credit. Martin, age 12, is in good health. Neither Chris nor Martin have any income. Because Mr. Mann provides full-time care for the children, he has no income.

The family's 2021 medical expenses, all paid for by Mr. Bosch, are as follows:

Mr. Bosch	$ 2,050
Mr. Mann	1,080
Chris (no attendant care)	16,470
Martin	1,645
Total medical expenses	$21,245

During 2021, Mr. Bosch sold a piece of vacant land for $85,000. He received a payment of $35,000 during 2021, with the $50,000 balance due in five equal instalments of $10,000 in the years 2022 through 2026. The ACB of this land was $33,000.

Mr. Bosch owns a rural cottage that he purchased at a property auction in 2013 at a cost of $25,000, with $5,000 for the appraised value for the land and $20,000 for the cottage. On June 30, 2021, the property was appraised at $375,000, with $100,000 for the land and $275,000 for the cottage.

Although Mr. Bosch and Mr. Mann used to spend a great deal of time in the summer at the cottage, since the adoptions the family has made little use of this property. As a result, Mr. Bosch decides to begin renting it out as of July 1, 2021.

During the period July 1, 2021, through December 31, 2021, rents collected on the cottage totalled $12,000. Expenses other than CCA during this period totalled $3,200. For 2021, Mr. Bosch intends to claim maximum CCA on the property.

Mr. Bosch purchased his city home in 2016. Prior to that, he and Mr. Mann lived in a rented apartment. As the city home has experienced a greater increase in value than the cottage during the last six years, Mr. Bosch will designate the city home as his principal residence for the years 2016 through 2021.

Over the years, Mr. Bosch has made several purchases of the common shares of Low Tech Ltd., a widely held public company. In 2019 he bought 150 shares at $55 per share. In 2020, he bought an additional 125 shares at $75 per share. In February 2021 he bought an additional 300 shares at $95 per share. On November 11, 2021, after the company announced that most of its product claims had been falsified, Mr. Bosch sold 275 shares at $5 per share. No dividends were paid on the shares in 2021.

Required: Calculate Mr. Bosch's minimum net income and taxable income for 2021, and his minimum 2021 federal income tax owing, including any CPP contributions payable. Ignore provincial income taxes, any instalment payments he may have made during the year, and GST/HST & PST considerations.

AP 8-16 (Comprehensive Case Covering Chapters 1 to 8)

Family Information

Ms. Jasperina Johns is 45 years of age and is divorced from her husband. She has one son, Louis, who is 12 years old and is sufficiently disabled that he qualifies for the disability tax credit. Louis has 2021 net income of $1,200, which is interest income from an inheritance. (Note: This amount is not subject to any attribution rules, which are discussed in Chapter 9.)

Jasperina's mother, Jackie, lives with them and provides care for Louis. She is in excellent health. Her net income for 2021 is in excess of $150,000. Jasperina has offered to pay her for her services, but Jackie has refused to accept any payment.

Employment Information

Jasperina is the chief financial officer of a large public corporation and has an annual salary of $252,000. Her employer offered her various alternatives in additional compensation and she chose the health care package. As a result all of her medical or dental costs are fully covered.

Her employer withholds the following amounts from her employment income:

RPP contributions	$3,200
EI	856
CPP	2,898

Jasperina's employer makes a matching contribution to her RPP of $3,200.

Jasperina's employer reimbursed her $4,900 for three evening courses that she attended at a local college during 2021. They were accounting, tax, and human resource courses taken at the request of the president of the company.

Every employee received a Christmas basked with a value of $300. The basket included a fitness activity tracker and a cT-shirt, baseball cap, sunglasses, and water bottle with the company name and logo printed on them.

Business Income

In addition to her employment income, Jasperina carries on a business as a sole proprietor in which she provides counselling and training for parents who have disabled children.

In 2019, Jasperina rented a small commercial condo in which to operate her business. As revenues for her business have increased rapidly, on February 1, 2021, she purchased a much larger new condo in the same complex for $368,000. She obtained a mortgage from the bank for $175,000 to finance the purchase. She had to spend $78,200 on renovations to make the new condo suitable for her purposes, which included $11,200 to make the premises more accessible by enlarging the washrooms, adding wheelchair ramps, and installing handrails. Since the disability-related modifications were done and billed in late December, Jasperina did not record any amortization for accounting purposes on the $11,200 for 2021.

She moved into her new property on October 31, the day her lease expired.

On January 1, 2022, Jasperina owned class 8 properties with a UCC balance of $16,888. The new tenants of the rental unit purchased some of these properties for $5,000. The properties that were sold had a capital cost of $23,000. The remainder of the class 8 properties were moved to the new condo.

During 2021, Jasperina purchased additional class 8 properties at a capital cost of $28,000.

For 2021, the accounting-based business income determined using Accounting Standards for Private Enterprises (ASPE) was $133,656. Included in this figure were the following:

Amortization expense	$16,900
Business meals and entertainment	1,500
Property taxes, new unit—February 1 to December 31	4,500
Interest on mortgage—February 1 to December 31	9,900
Rent, old unit—January to October	18,000

Other Information

1. During 2021, Jasperina received eligible dividends of $45,123.
2. At the beginning of 2021, Jasperina purchased 2,000 units of the Schwartz Income Trust for $10 per unit. During 2021, the trust had a distribution of $3.20 per unit, all of which was return of capital. Jasperina had all of this distribution invested in additional units at $15 per unit. In December 2021, all of her Schwartz units were sold for $19 per unit.
3. Jasperina's late father was an amateur painter who didn't sell a single painting while he was alive. He gave Jasperina a number of his paintings over the years. It was estimated that the value of the paintings when Jasperina inherited them was negligible (i.e., nil). Shortly after his death, he was "discovered" and his paintings were in demand. During 2021, she sold two of his large paintings for $10,000 each. The electrician doing the condo renovations fell in love with one of his other paintings. He offered to trade $10,000 in services for it and Jasperina accepted the offer. The $10,000 is included in the $67,000 renovations total.
4. Jasperina inherited a ski chalet from her father. At his death, the chalet had an ACB of $150,000 and a FMV of $165,000. The ACB and FMV of the land was $40,000. The ACB of the building was $110,000 and its FMV at the time of death was $125,000. In December 2020, she suffered a serious knee injury when she fell off a chair lift. Because of this, Jasperina decided to convert the property to a rental property. On January 1, 2021, the property was appraised for $280,000, which included $66,000 for the land and $214,000 for the building. During 2021, rental income before the deduction of CCA equalled $8,820. Jasperina does not intend to designate the chalet as her principal residence for any year.
5. Jasperina also inherited a piece of land from her father. At his death, the land had an ACB of $57,000 and a FMV of $233,000. Jasperina had held on to the land with the intention of building a yoga retreat on the site when she found the time to design it. However, in 2021 she received an unsolicited offer for the property of $400,000. She accepted the offer and immediately received a payment of $150,000. The remaining $250,000 will be paid in five annual instalments of $50,000, beginning in 2022. Jasperina would like to use any available capital gains reserve to defer as much of the capital gain as possible.

Required: Calculate Jasperina's minimum 2021 net income, her 2021 minimum taxable income, and her minimum 2021 federal tax payable. Ignore provincial income taxes, any instalments she may have paid during the year, any income tax withholdings that would be made by her employer, and GST/HST/PST considerations.

CHAPTER 9

Other Income and Deductions, and Other Issues

Learning Objectives

After completing Chapter 9, you should be able to:

1. Describe the role that Subdivisions d, e, and f play in determining net income (Paragraph [P hereafter] 9-1 to 9-4).
2. Identify the major other sources of income that are listed under Subdivision d of the *ITA* (P 9-5 to 9-18).
3. Identify the income inclusions from deferred income plans (P 9-19 and 9-22).
4. Apply the rules related to education assistance payments, social assistance, and workers' compensation payments (P 9-23 to 9-28).
5. Determine the income tax treatment of CPP contributions for both employees and self-employed individuals, including the new system that allows a partial deduction instead of a non-refundable tax credit (P 9-29 to 9-32).
6. Determine the deductible amount of moving expenses for an individual (P 9-33 to 9-49).
7. Determine the deductible amount of child care expenses (P 9-50 to 9-60).
8. Apply the provisions related to the disability supports deduction (P 9-61 to 9-69).
9. Explain and apply the rules for pension income splitting (P 9-70 to 9-79).
10. Explain the tax treatment of child support and spousal support payments and receipts (P 9-80 to 9-89).
11. Determine the taxable portion of annuity payments received (P 9-90 to 9-96).
12. Describe the potential income-splitting opportunities provided by RESPs, TFSAs, and RDSPs (P 9-97 to 9-100).
13. Describe the major features of Tax-Free Savings Accounts (TFSAs) (P 9-101).
14. Explain the provisions associated with registered education savings plans, Canada Education Savings Grants, and Canada Learning Bonds (P 9-102 to 9-125).
15. Compare the major features of TFSAs, RRSPs, and RESPs (P 9-126 to 9-131).
16. Describe the major features of registered disability savings plans (RDSPs) (P 9-132 to 9-134).
17. Determine the tax consequences of non-arm's-length transfers of property at values other than fair market value (P 9-135 to 9-153).

18. Describe the special rollover provisions applicable to inter vivos transfers of capital property to a spouse (P 9-154 to 9-161).
19. Determine the tax consequences of non-arm's-length transfers of depreciable property (P 9-162 to 9-168).
20. Describe the special rollover provisions applicable to inter vivos transfers of farm or fishing property to a child (P 9-169 to 9-174).
21. Explain the basic requirements for deemed dispositions on death and any rollovers available at that time (P 9-175 to 9-183).
22. Apply the income attribution rules to inter vivos transfers of capital property to a spouse and to related individuals who are under the age of 18 (P 9-184 to 9-202).
23. Describe the income attribution rules applicable to transfers to other related parties (P 9-203 to 9-207).
24. Describe some of the tax planning techniques that are available to mitigate income attribution (P 9-208).

Introduction

Coverage of Chapter 9

Subdivisions d, e, and f

9-1. In previous chapters we emphasized that there are only three sources of income: employment, business, and property. The three sources result from the use of one's labour, property, or capital in an activity that is undertaken with an objective of earning a positive return over a period of time. These sources make up much of a taxpayer's net income that is subject to Canadian income tax; however, net income is not limited to only these three sources.

9-2. In Chapter 8 we discussed capital gains and capital losses, a second major net income component. We noted that only 50% of capital gains is included in net income. On the other hand, only 50% of capital losses can be deducted. The ability to deduct such losses is often restricted because they can only be applied against capital gains. Sometimes losses can only be applied to a specific type of gain, as was the case with listed personal property.

9-3. In this chapter we look at the final category of receipts and expenditures that round out net income as well as some very important rules that create deemed proceeds and dispositions, deemed costs and acquisitions, and some very unique rules that redirect income from one person to another in certain situations.

9-4. An overview of the topics that we will discuss in the chapter follows:

"Other Sources of Income" Subdivision d (ITA 56 to 59.1) This subdivision is titled "Other Sources of Income," although that description is somewhat misleading in that the types of receipts included in this subdivision are not true "sources of income." The purpose of this subdivision is to determine whether taxpayers are in receipt of specifically described amounts. If they are, then the rules within the subdivision set out the specific amounts that must be included in net income and when those amounts are required to be included. Subdivision d has over 40 separate paragraphs, but we will focus our attention on some of the more common types of receipts, such as income, scholarships, support payments, and payments from deferred income plans such as registered retirement savings plans (RRSPs). If you are in receipt of some type of amount that is not a source of income, not a capital gain, and not specifically mentioned in Subdivision d, then the amount would not be required to be included in net income. Therefore, the amounts would not be subjected to Canadian income tax. Such amounts include lottery winnings, inheritances, windfalls, and gifts.

"Deductions in Computing Income" Subdivision e (ITA 60 to 66.8) This subdivision provides taxpayers with additional deductions that reduce net income. In a manner similar to that of Subdivision d, there are over 40 paragraphs within the subdivision and a deduction is only permitted if it is specifically described. If you qualify for one of these deductions the rules will tell you when you are permitted a deduction and how much you may deduct. Common examples include RRSP deductions, support payments, and expenses for both child care and moving.

An interesting feature in the ITA requires the separation of Subdivision e into two distinct parts. The first part is ITA 60 to 64, and the second ITA 65 to 66.8. The main difference is that ITA 65 to 66.8 contain very specific and complex rules that relate to investments in the resource sector, such as mining and oil and gas. ITA 60 to 64, on the other hand, cover expenses that are common to many Canadian individuals. We make this distinction because ITA 4(2) clarifies that none of the deductions provided for in ITA 60 to 64 may be applied against a source of income (e.g., business, property, or employment income). This means, for example, that you cannot claim child care expenses as a business expense arguing that it is necessary to allow you to carry on a business. As you will see in this chapter, there are limits on how much can be claimed as a child care expense in Subdivision e. The ITA 4(2) concept was tested in the Supreme Court of Canada decision in *Symes* ([1993] 4 SCR 695) in which a claim was made by a lawyer to treat child care expenses as a business expense. While there were many issues involved, including a *Charter of Rights and Freedoms* argument, the court upheld the basic principle.

"Rules Relating to the Computation of Income" Subdivision f (ITA 67 to ITA 80.6) We were first introduced to some of the rules of this subdivision in our coverage of business income in Chapter 6. In that chapter we discussed the reasonableness of expenses (ITA 67), the 50% limitation on meals and entertainment (ITA 67.1), restrictions on deducting leasing costs and interest on passenger vehicles (ITA 67.2 and 67.3), and rules that prohibited a deduction for illegal payments, fines, and penalties (ITA 67.4 and 67.5). In this chapter we will return to this subdivision to examine some additional rules that set out how certain transactions, events, and circumstances can alter the income tax outcome. The rules we will discuss relate largely to what the ITA calls "non-arm's-length" transactions, which are typically transactions between family members and those with strong connections (e.g., an individual transacting with a corporation that the individual controls) that results in a potential that transactions will not reflect actual fair market values. The income tax policy concern is that the nature of these close relationships creates an opportunity for price manipulation for the express purpose of reducing income tax.

Specifically, we will discuss non-arm's-length transactions (ITA 69), transfers of property between spouses and common-law partners (ITA 73), the transfer of sources of property income between certain non-arm's-length individuals (ITA 74.1), and the basic income tax consequences that occur when an individual dies (ITA 70).

Other Types of Income—Subdivision d Inclusions

Pension Benefits—ITA 56(1)(a)(i)

9-5. ITA 56(1)(a)(i) requires that payments from pension funds or plans be included in the income of individuals for the year in which the amounts are received regardless of whether the amounts are received as an annuity on a recurring basis or as a lump-sum amount. For many individuals, the most common type of pension receipts are from a registered pension plan (RPP) with a current or former employer. The provision would also include receipts from unregistered pension plans to the extent they are not required to be included in net income elsewhere. In addition, the provision is not restricted to pension receipts from plans established in Canada, meaning that amounts received by Canadian residents with respect to foreign pension plans would also be required to be included in net income except to the extent that they would be specifically excluded as a result of an income tax treaty between Canada and the country in which the pension plan was established.

9-6. The pension benefit inclusion would also apply to amounts received under the *Old Age Security Act* (OAS), as well as any similar payments received from a province such as the OAS supplement offered by British Columbia. In addition, benefits received under the Canada Pension Plan (CPP) or a provincial pension plan (e.g., the Quebec Pension Plan (QPP)) would also be required to be included in net income under this provision.

9-7. For those individuals who are entitled to receive CPP benefits, section 65.1 (CPP Form ISP1002) of the *Canada Pension Plan Act* allows the CPP payments to be shared between spouses or common-law partners. The CPP sharing option allows CPP benefits to be split and paid separately to a spouse or common-law partner based on the length of time the individuals have been living together during the time counted toward the contributory period, which determines an individual's entitlement. This type of income splitting is expressly permitted and can be a valuable way to reduce income taxes where the net income of one spouse exceeds that of the other. As is discussed later in this chapter, there is another type of pension splitting allowed by the ITA between spouses or common-law partners. However, this latter type of pension split is implemented entirely in the income tax returns of both individuals and does not involve the actual payments being split, as is the case with the CPP sharing.

Retiring Allowances—ITA 56(1)(a)(ii)

9-8. ITA 56(1)(a)(ii) requires that retiring allowances be included in an individual's net income in the year such amount is received. A "retiring allowance" is an expression defined in ITA 248(1) as follows:

> **"retiring allowance"** means an amount (other than a superannuation or pension benefit, an amount received as a consequence of the death of an employee or a benefit described in subparagraph 6(1)(a)(iv)) received
>
> (a) on or after retirement of a taxpayer from an office or employment in recognition of the taxpayer's long service, or
>
> (b) in respect of a loss of an office or employment of a taxpayer, whether or not received as, on account or in lieu of payment of, damages or pursuant to an order or judgment of a competent tribunal, by the taxpayer or, after the taxpayer's death, by a dependant or a relation of the taxpayer or by the legal representative of the taxpayer.

9-9. The term "retiring allowance" covers most payments on termination of employment. This includes rewards given for good service, payments related to early retirement (e.g., federal government buyout provisions) at either the request of the employee or the employer, as well as damages related to wrongful dismissal actions. A retiring allowance in respect of a loss of employment requires that the payment would not have been made were it not for the loss and that the payment represents compensation for that loss.

9-10. There are a few potential benefits associated with retiring allowances. The first relates to whether a retiring allowance is connected to employment services rendered by the individual before 1996. If there is such a connection, the employee is allowed to transfer some of the retiring allowance to an RRSP or RPP (see paragraph 2.30 of Folio S2-F1-C2, "Retiring Allowances") and claim a deduction under ITA 60(j.1). The transfer to an RRSP or RPP must occur within 60 days of the end of the year in which the retiring allowance was received.

9-11. A second advantage is that ITA 60(o.1) allows an individual to claim a deduction for any legal expenses paid in the year for the purpose of either establishing a right to a retiring allowance or for its collection once the right has been established. The deduction allows legal expense payments only if actually paid but allows an individual the option of claiming the deduction for up to seven years after a payment has been made. This allows the individual to claim a larger deduction in the year that any amounts are actually received to offset a large retroactive settlement. The entitlement to the deduction does not require the individual to be sucessful in winning his case. If, however, the individual's legal fees are reimbursed in whole or in part, the amounts received are required to be included in net income in the year of receipt as a result of ITA 56(1)(l.1).

A Word on the Interaction between ITA 56 and ITA 60

9-12. From the previous discussion on retiring allowances you may have noticed an interesting feature of Subdivision d and e, specifically ITA 56 and ITA 60. There are many instances where the two provisions interact. In Paragraph 9-10 we observed that a retiring allowance is required to be fully included in net income in the year received but that a portion may be eligible to transfer to an RRSP allowing a deduction. In that case, rather than offsetting the two amounts the ITA treats them separately.

EXAMPLE Jennifer retired in September 2021 after 32 years of service with her employer. She received a retiring allowance of $75,000 in 2021. She learned that she can transfer $15,500 of that amount to an RRSP as long as she does so by March 1, 2022. She contributes $15,500 to an RRSP for herself in February 2022.

ANALYSIS Jennifer will include $75,000 in her net income for 2021 as a retiring allowance (ITA 56(1)(a)(ii)) and claim a deduction for the same year of $15,500 (ITA 60(j.1)). While the net effect is $59,500 [$75,000- $15,500], the ITA and the income tax return treats both amounts separately.

9-13. In Paragraph 9-12 we noted that an individual can deduct legal expenses paid to collect or establish a right to a retiring allowance (ITA 60(o.1)) and that any amount received as a reimbursement toward those legal expenses must be included in net income for the year of receipt (ITA 56(1)(l.1)). Again, this is one more example of the interaction. You can see a pattern emerging in the ITA. For example, consider an individual who has received Employment Insurance (EI) benefits in 2021 but later learns that he was paid too much and, as a result, the individual has to repay part of that amount, which is done in 2022. ITA 56(1)(a)(iv) requires the individual to include the EI benefits received in net income for 2021 and ITA 60(v.1) allows the individual to claim a deduction in 2022 for the repayment. This interaction is a common theme throughout ITA 56 and 60 that can assist in an understanding how the ITA treats many diverse topics that fall within Subdivisions d and e.

Death Benefits—ITA 56(1)(a)(iii) & 56(1)(a.1)

9-14. Death benefits are included in the income of an individual when received under ITA 56(1)(a)(iii). ITA 248(1) defines a "death benefit," in part, as follows:

"death benefit" means the total of all amounts received by a taxpayer in a taxation year on or after the death of an employee in recognition of the employee's service in an office or employment ...

9-15. As a general rule amounts of income received on the death of an individual are often included in the individual's final income tax return for the year of death or included in the income of the deceased individual's estate, which is treated for income tax purposes as a trust. Death benefit payments, however, are required to be included in the net income of the individual taxpayer who is entitled to receive the amount for the year in which it is received. As a rule, payments are frequently made to surviving spouses and common-law partners as well as children.

9-16. When death benefits are received by a surviving spouse or common-law partner, the definition provides an exemption for the first $10,000. In other words, it is only amounts received in excess of $10,000 that are considered a death benefit for purposes of ITA 56(1)(a)(iii). This $10,000 exclusion would be available even if the benefit were payable over a period of several years.

9-17. The $10,000 exemption is also available to persons other than a surviving spouse or common-law partner, however the surviving spouse or common-law partner is given priority for the exemption before any exemption can be used by another person such as a child. For example, if Ms. Reid dies and her employer pays a death benefit of $8,000 to her surviving spouse and an additional $8,000 to an adult child, the spouse would not be required to include any amount in net income since the $10,000 exemption exceeds the amount received. The adult child could use the remaining $2,000 of unused exemption with the result that only $6,000 [$8,000 - $2,000] would be required to be included in the net income of the adult child for the year of receipt.

9-18. A death benefit of $2,500 is also available to be claimed under section 71 of the *CPP Act.* ITA 56(1)(a)(iii), however, would not apply to a CPP death benefit since it is not a death benefit paid in recognition of an employee's service but rather paid to assist in covering funeral expenses. As a rule, the estate files an application for the CPP death benefit that, when received, is required to be included in the net income of the estate under ITA 56(1)(a.1). This provision does not require that the amount be received by the estate for it to be included in the net income of the estate. In effect, receipt by anyone else still requires the amount to be included in the income of the estate.

Other Income—Deferred Income Plans—ITA 56(1)(h), (h.1), (h.2), (i), & (t)

9-19. In the first part of this volume of the text we have looked at some of the many rules that require certain amounts to be included in net income. Some of these rules, such as ITA 6(1)(a), simply read that employment benefits are required to be included in employment income; ITA 5 says to include salary and other remuneration; while ITA 12(1)(c) requires interest income to be included; and so on. These types of provisions are generally self-contained and self-explanatory once a certain type of income or a specific type of expense has been identified. There are other types of income amounts, however, that rely on a series of rules found elsewhere in the ITA. ITA 12(1)(l) and 12(1)(m) are classic examples. ITA 12(1)(l) requires us to include amounts determined under Subdivision j, and ITA 12(1)(m) does the same for Subdivision k. Subdivision j contains a series of rules that deal with partnerships, whereas Subdivision k deals with trusts. In other words, the amounts required to be included in net income from partnerships and trusts cannot be quickly determined but instead relies on an understanding of those two subdivisions.

9-20. ITA 56 applies the same concept with respect to Division G of the ITA, which is titled "Deferred and Other Special Income Arrangements (ITA 144 to 148.1)." If, for example, you wanted to determine how much you could deduct in a given year with respect to contributions you have made to your RRSP, or perhaps the RRSP of your spouse or common-law partner, ITA 60(i) authorizes a deduction. Unfortunately, that provision does not give you the answer but simply directs you to ITA 146, which is where the RRSP rules are located within Division G. If you receive money or property from your RRSP and wish to learn how much you must include in your net income for that year you would turn to ITA 56(1)(h), which, once again, directs you to ITA 146. In other words, while the rules within ITA 56 and 60 are helpful in determining the ultimate authority for being able to claim a deduction or a requirement to include a certain amount in your net income with respect to deferred income plans, the real determinations are found elsewhere.

9-21. Income inclusions from deferred income plans such as RRSPs, registered retirement income funds (RRIFs), and deferred profit-sharing plans (DPSPs) would not be considered part of net income were it not for Subdivision d and ITA 56 specifically.

9-22. The details of these various types of deferred income plans can be complex and warrant their own chapter. As a result we give detailed coverage to deferred income plans in Chapter 10. While an understanding of deferred income plans is not essential at this point you should, at a minimum, be aware of the provisions that require an amount to be added to net income. Brief descriptions of some of the deferred income plan amounts that are required to be included in net income as a result of ITA 56 include the following:

RRSP Withdrawals All amounts that are withdrawn from an RRSP must be included in income under ITA 56(1)(h).

Home Buyers' Plan and Lifelong Learning Plans In brief, amounts can be withdrawn from an RRSP without a requirement to include the amount in net income if, in general, the funds are used to acquire a home or used to further one's education. The ITA treats these tax-free withdrawals as a form of borrowing, which requires that the amounts withdrawn for these specific purposes be repaid. If repayments to the RRSP are not made as required, certain amounts must then be included in net income. These amounts would be included in net income under ITA 56(1)(h.1) and (h.2), respectively.

Payments from DPSPs Under ITA 56(1)(i), all amounts received from a DPSP must be included in net income.

RRIF Withdrawals RRIFs require that a minimum predetermined amount be withdrawn annually. ITA 56(1)(h) requires actual amounts withdrawn from an RRIF, including the minimum amount plus any additional amounts withdrawn above the minimum, be included in net income. ITA 56(1)(t) requires that any shortfall in withdrawing the minimum must also be included in net income. If, for example, the annual RRIF minimum was $18,000 and the individual only withdrew $10,000, net income would increase by $18,000: $10,000 as a result of ITA 56(1)(h) and $8,000 as a result of ITA 56(1)(t).

Scholarships, Bursaries, and Research Grants—ITA 56(1)(n) & (o)

9-23. ITA 56(1)(n) requires that all amounts received as scholarships, fellowships, or bursaries as well as prizes for achievement be included in net income in the year received to the extent that these amounts exceed the student's scholarship exemption, which is determined under ITA 56(3). In most situations, the exemption is equal to the scholarships and other such amounts received with the result that no amount is required to be included in net income as long as the amounts received are in connection with

- an education program in which the individual is a qualifying student; or
- an elementary or secondary school education program.

9-24. A qualifying student is an individual enrolled as a full-time student in a qualifying education program at a designated educational institution. In general, this refers to a university or college course of at least three weeks duration that requires at least 10 hours of effort per week.

9-25. Research grants are included in income under ITA 56(1)(o). The grants received are only required to be included in net income to the extent that the amounts exceed unreimbursed expenses incurred for carrying on the research. Expenses are only allowed if they are not claimable elsewhere, such as business expenses. The effect of ITA 56(1)(o) is to treat research grants and related expenses in a manner similar to that of a separate source of income where grants represent the income.

9-26. The subject of scholarships, bursaries, and research grants can be surprisingly complex and has, as a result, led the CRA to create a lengthy folio dedicated to the topic. For additional information we refer you to IT Folio S1-F2-C3, "Scholarships, Research Grants, and Other Education Assistance." In this text, exercises and problems will assume that any scholarships received are fully exempt as a result of ITA 56(3).

Social Assistance and Workers' Compensation—ITA 56(1)(u) & (v)

9-27. Amounts received under various social assistance programs must be included in net income under ITA 56(1)(u), while amounts received under a workers' compensation law (WCB) as a result of an injury or disability are also required to be included in net income as a result of ITA 56(1)(v). Both of these amounts, however, qualify for a deduction under ITA 110(1)(f) when determining taxable income. For example, assume that an individual received $60,000 of workers' compensation in 2021 and had no other income for that year. The individual's net income would be $60,000 as a result of ITA 56(1)(v), but taxable income would be nil as a result of subtracting the same amount through ITA 110(1)(f).

9-28. The taxable income result makes it perfectly clear that such amounts are not subject to Canadian income tax. This then leads to the question of why these amounts are added to net income but do not make it through to taxable income. There are two reasons for this treatment.

1. The first is to ensure that the amounts are not subject to Canadian income tax. Since income tax rates are applied to taxable income it is important that these amounts are excluded from taxable income. ITA 110(1)(f) is the legislative solution.

2. The second reason is that many income tax credits for low-income spouses, common-law partners, and a number of other dependants are reduced to the extent that those individuals have net income of their own. To illustrate, take the example in Paragraph 9-27 and assume that the injured individual had a spouse or common-law partner who had net income of $50,000 in 2021. It would appear that the injured individual could be claimed as a spousal or common-law partner tax credit, including an additional caregiver-related amount if net income were nil. In tax policy terms this result would make little sense given that the individual actually earned more than the spouse or common-law partner. ITA 56(1)(u) and (v) are the legislative solution to this second problem, ensuring that tax credits aimed at "low-income" dependants take all income into consideration irrespective of whether there is an intent to actually tax the amounts.

Other Deductions—Subdivision e Deductions

CPP Contributions on Self-Employed Earnings—ITA 60(e) & (e.1)

9-29. The maximum employee CPP contribution for 2021 is $3,166.45 [(5.45%)($61,600 - $3,500)]. As discussed in Chapter 4, only $2,732 [(4.95%)($58,700 - $3,500)] of this amount is included in the base for the CPP income tax credit. The remaining $434 ($3,166 - $2,732) is treated as a deduction under ITA 60(e.1). Remember that even though the deductible CPP amount of $434 is related to either employment income or business income, ITA 4(2) does not allow the individual to claim a deduction as an employment expense or as a business expense.

9-30. When an individual is an employee, the employer makes a matching contribution, resulting in a maximum total contribution of $6,332 [(2)($3,166)]. This additional contribution of $3,166 represents a fully deductible business expense to the employer.

9-31. Individuals who carry on their own business as a sole proprietor or as a member of a partnership are required to make CPP contributions referred to as the self-employed contribution rate, which is double the rate applicable to an employee. In this case, since the basic rate is 5.45%, the self-employed contribution rate would be 10.9% [(2)(5.45%)]. In essence, the individual is making up for the rate she would have had to pay had she been an employee plus the rate required to be paid by the employer. The mechanics of the CPP system are such that an individual must have contributions that are equivalent to those made by the employee/employer combination in order for that individual to receive the same benefits that would accrue to an employee.

9-32. In order to put the individual with business income on the same tax footing as an employee, the CPP contributions made at the 10.9% contribution rate are treated as follows:

- An income tax credit for 2021 of $2,732 [(4.95%)($58,700 - $3,500)]
- A deduction for $434 under ITA 60(e.1)
- The CPP contribution that is the equivalent of what an employer would have paid is deducted under ITA 60(e). The maximum contribution with respect to that portion for 2021 is $3,166.
- In summary, for 2021 the maximum CPP tax credit is based on $2,732 and the remaining $3,600 [$6,332 - $2,732] is allowed as a deduction under a combination of ITA 60(e) and 60(e.1).

Moving Expenses—ITA 62

General Rules

9-33. ITA 62 provides the conditions necessary for a taxpayer to claim a deduction for moving expenses. The provision sets out the types of moves or relocations that qualify, the type of expenses that may qualify, and limitations on how much can be claimed as a deduction in a given year. Over the years ITA 62 has been the subject of many disputes between individual taxpayers and the CRA as to the meaning of the legislation in specific circumstances. At the time of this writing, there are 146 reported income tax cases dealing with moving expenses.

9-34. As is the case with many provisions of the ITA, there are key words and expressions that are important to a practical understanding of what can be claimed. In ITA 62 those words and expressions include an "eligible relocation," a "new work location," and "moving expenses."

9-35. Arguably the most important expression is an eligible relocation, since only those moving expenses with a connection to an eligible relocation are potentially deductible. An eligible relocation typically involves one of three situations:

- Individuals who relocate to enable them to be employed at a new work location
- Individuals who relocate to enable them to carry on a business at a new work location
- Individuals who relocate to enable them to commence full-time attendance at a post-secondary institution (i.e., university or college).

9-36. The relocations must normally be within Canada but can cross international borders as long as the individual remains a resident of Canada during the period of absence. This allows Canadians attending universities in other countries to be in a position to claim moving expenses as well as allowing moving expenses for employment or business purposes outside of Canada.

9-37. An eligible relocation also involves identifying what is referred to as an "old residence" and a "new residence." The old residence is generally one's home prior to the relocation and, of course, the new residence is an individual's home after the relocation. A final condition requires that the distance between one's old residence and the new work location is at least 40 kilometres further than the distance between the new residence and the new work location. The courts have determined that the 40 kilometre distance should be measured using the "shortest normal route available to the travelling public" (see paragraph 4.3(d) of Folio S1-F3-C4, "Moving Expenses"). For example, if an individual lived in Ottawa and accepted an employment offer in Toronto, resulting in a relocation to Toronto from Ottawa, clearly the distance between the Ottawa home and the Toronto employment location would be more than 40 kilometres greater than the distance between the Toronto home and the Toronto employment location.

9-38. The definition of an eligible relocation requires that an individual's old and new residence be the location where the individual "ordinarily resided." The longstanding meaning of those words is that they refer to the place where an individual ordinarily lives (e.g., the place he calls home). This implies that an eligible relocation requires a degree of permanence as an individual shifts his home to a new location. The further implication is that a move to accept employment for a period of time while maintaining one's home (the old residence) suggests that such individuals would not be considered ordinarily resident and there would be no "new residence." As a result there would be no eligible relocation and therefore no entitlement to claim moving expenses.

9-39. To be considered to qualify as an eligible relocation, however, the relocation must enable the individual to meet one of the three situations referred to in Paragraph 9-35. The CRA interprets this as meaning that the purpose of the move must be for employment, business, or qualified educational purposes. Employment means any employment, whether new employment or with the same employer. Business purposes means carrying on the same business or a new business. A move for personal purposes would not qualify. The difficulty, however, is determining an individual's true purpose. The CRA accepts that a relocation by a current employer would qualify and that a move for business purposes would include a need to move closer to one's market, suppliers, clients, and so on.

9-40. The legislation clearly requires a connection between an actual relocation and employment or business activity at a new work location. It is interesting, however, that the legislation does not set out any timeframe in which the relocation must occur. As a result the courts (see *Dierckens v. The Queen*, 2011 TCC 169) and the CRA have taken a flexible approach in recognition that there may be a delay between the events that will not jeopardize a claim for moving expenses.

EXAMPLE In 2019, an individual accepts an employment offer at a location 100 kilometres from the individual's existing residence (i.e., the "old residence"). For several years the individual commutes on a daily basis. In 2021, the individual decides to move closer and acquires a residence that is more than 40 kilometres closer to the work location.

ANALYSIS This would be an eligible relocation because the move enabled the individual to be employed at the work location. In terms of ITA 62, the work location at which employment began in 2019 would be the "new work location" and the then-existing home would be the "old residence." The move two years later would establish the "new residence," completing the picture such that moving expenses could then be claimed. This result occurs because ITA 62 does not contain any mention of a time within which the move has to occur. It is noteworthy and perhaps telling that the federal government has had 10 years in which to change the law to establish a timeframe but has chosen not to do so.

9-41. Once you have determined that there is an eligible relocation ITA 62 sets out the following additional conditions:

- No moving expense claim can be made to the extent the expenses were paid by an employer.
- No moving expenses can be claimed for an employee who receives a moving allowance to cover expenses or is reimbursed moving expenses unless these amounts are included in the employee's income. Note that the CRA has an administrative practice that allows an employee to claim moving expenses paid that exceed reimbursements and allowances whether or not they would be required to be included in employment income. See Paragraph 9-46 for additional detail.
- Moving expenses can only be claimed to the extent of certain income at the new work location. Specifically, employees are limited by the employment income at that new work location, and those carrying on a business can only claim moving expenses to the extent of business income at that new work location. Students can only claim moving expenses to the extent that they have scholarships, bursaries, and research grants (net of expenses) that are required to be included in the student's net income. Moving expenses cannot be claimed to the extent of any other type of income. Any moving expenses that exceed the amounts claimable in one year can be deducted in subsequent years to the extent of the type of income from that same new work location. This provides an indefinite carry forward.

9-42. As described in ITA 62(3), moving expenses include the following:

- Travel costs incurred to move the individual taxpayer and members of the household from the old residence to the new residence. These include vehicle expenses and a reasonable amount expended for meals and accommodation (e.g., hotels) for the individual and her family. The reference to "members of the household" would include pets.
- The cost of transporting or storing household items, including boats and trailers.
- The cost of meals and accommodation for the individual taxpayer and the family near either the old residence or new residence for a period not exceeding 15 days. Note that the 15 days would not include days of travel between the old residence and the new residence.
- The cost of cancelling a lease on the old residence.

- The selling costs of the old residence. These would include real estate commissions, legal fees, advertising expenses, as well as a mortgage prepayment penalty.
- The legal fees and transfer taxes associated with the purchase of a new residence, provided that the old residence was owned and sold as part of the move. Note that these particular expenses would not include any GST/HST & PST paid on the purchase of a new residence.
- Up to $5,000 of interest, property taxes, insurance premiums, and heating and utilities costs on the old residence while it was vacant and reasonable efforts were being made to sell the home.
- Costs of revising legal documents to reflect a new address, replacing driver's licences and non-commercial vehicle permits, and connecting and disconnecting utilities.

9-43. Any other expenses would not qualify as "moving expenses." Some of the more common exclusions woud include (1) costs associated with decorating or improving the new residence, (2) any loss on the sale of the old residence, (3) travel expenses for house hunting trips prior to the move (the exception to this is meals and accommodation near the new residence after it has been purchased or a rental lease has been signed), (4) travel expenses for job hunting in another city, (5) expenses to increase the saleability of the old residence or to clean or repair a rented home prior to a move.

Vehicle and Meal Expenses—Detailed vs. Simplified Methods

9-44. Administratively, the CRA allows two alternative methods to determine the vehicle and meal expenses deductible as moving expenses. The detailed method requires receipts and uses actual expenses, while the simplified method provides a flat rate per meal or kilometre and does not require receipts. The detailed method for vehicle expenses is similar to the calculations required for deductible automobile expenses and costs for employees, a pro rata claim of total vehicle expenses for the whole year based on the kilometres related to the move. The CRA considers "vehicle expenses" to include operating and ownership costs such as fuel, oil, tires, licence fees, maintenance and repairs, lease costs, CCA, and interest on any finance charges. We would remind you that the 50% limitation on meal expenses of ITA 67.1 does not apply to moving expenses claimed under ITA 62.

9-45. The flat rates for the simplified method are provided by the CRA and are published in a less than timely fashion (e.g., the 2021 rates are not provided until 2022). The meal rate is currently $17 per person for a total of $51 per day. The current vehicle kilometre rate varies from a low of $0.48 in Alberta to a high of $0.645 in the Northwest Territories. In exercises and problems we will use a rate of $17 per person per meal for the meal rate and $0.55 per kilometre for the kilometre rate.

Employer Reimbursements and Allowances

9-46. One of the additional conditions for claiming moving expenses that we mentioned in Paragraph 9-41 relates to a situation where an employee relocates and receives assistance from the employer toward the cost of the move. ITA 62(1)(d) covers this situation, specifically where an employer either reimburses the employee or provides the employee with an allowance to cover moving expenses. If, for example, an employee incurs $10,000 in moving expenses as a result of an employee relocation, pays the amount in full, then is reimbursed by the employer, it is clear that the employee should not be entitled to claim a deduction for moving expenses under ITA 62. The moving expenses, in that case, would be deductible by the employer as employment-related expenses.

9-47. Technically an employee would be entitled to claim moving expenses reimbursed if the reimbursement were included in income, however this would never be the case in an employee relocation since there is no taxable employment benefit because the employer is the one who primarily benefits as a result of the move and not the employee. The receipt of a moving allowance, however, is somewhat more problematic because a non-accountable allowance that covers personal and living expenses (meals and accommodation) could not be excluded from employment income (ITA 6(1)(b)). The CRA, however, recognizes that reimbursements or allowances for employee relocations should not be included in the employee's employment income using the same logic that excludes employment benefits because the relocation is primarily for the benefit of the employer. The CRA practice in this case is that no reimbursement or allowance is to be included in net income, with the result that no moving expenses can then be claimed by the employee regardless of whether the employer assistance is by reimbursement or allowance.

9-48. If an employer only partially reimburses an employee for moving expenses, the CRA practice is to effectively ignore the requirement that moving expenses are only claimable by an employee if the reimbursement or allowance is included in employment income. The practice allows an employee to claim moving expenses where those expenses exceed the employer assistance. If, for example, an employee pays $10,000 of moving expenses and is reimbursed $7,000, the CRA practice would allow the employee to claim eligible moving expenses of $3,000 even if none of the amounts from the employer are required to be included in the employee's employment income. We would refer those interested in pursuing this further to the CRA folio on moving expenses, S1-F3-C4, and CRA guide T4130, which provide further clarification on this topic.

Tax Planning Considerations

9-49. The CRA administrative practice reduces most income tax concerns in situations where an employer is only willing to partially reimburse an employee for moving expenses. However, it is always recommended that some precautions be taken in situations where not all of what are considered moving expenses would qualify for a moving expense deduction under ITA 62. If, for example, there is a housing loss included as part of the moving expenses that are to be reimbursed, it is suggested that the details of the agreement between the employer and the employee to reimburse such an amount be clearly described to avoid any later difficulty. The reason for this precaution is that income tax consequences are determined based on the ITA and not administrative positions or concessions.

Exercise 9-1

Subject: Moving Expenses

On December 20, 2021, at the request of her employer, Ms. Martinova Chevlak moves from Edmonton to Regina. She has always lived in a rented apartment and will continue to do so in Regina. The total cost of the actual move, including the costs of moving her personal possessions, was $6,400. In addition, she spent $1,300 on a visit to Regina in search of appropriate accommodation. Unfortunately, she was not successful in acquiring a home on this trip. She also paid $1,200 as a penalty for breaking her lease in Edmonton. All of the moving expenses were paid in 2021. During the year, her salary totalled $64,000, of which $2,000 relates to the new work location for the period December 20, 2021, to December 31, 2021. Her employer is prepared to pay $6,000 toward the cost of her move. Determine if Ms. Chevlak is eligible to claim moving expenses and why. How does the employer assistance impact her claim?

Solutions to Exercises are available in the Study Guide.

We suggest you complete SSP 9-1 at this point.

Child Care Expenses—ITA 63

Basic Definitions

9-50. ITA 63 is another well-known provision designed to provide indirect financial assistance to individuals who are obliged to pay for child care services in order to earn employment income, business income, carry on research for which they receive grants, or to attend certain educational institutions. The provision identifies the type of child care expenses for which a deduction may be claimed, who may claim the deduction, the dollar amount of the deduction, and when the deduction may be claimed.

9-51. In very general terms, when there are spouses or common-law partners sharing child care responsibilities it is the individual with the lower net income who must make the claim, and there are limitations to how much can be claimed that are based on the age of the child and whether they are mentally or physically infirm. As we saw in our discussion of moving expenses, certain income tax provisions require a practical understanding of words and expressions that are defined in the ITA. The child care expense rules are no exception. The following relevant words and expressions are briefly summarized to assist in understanding how the ITA treats child care expenses:

Child Care Expenses Arguably the most important definition, qualifying "child care expenses" are described as including babysitting services, day nursery services, boarding schools, and camps (as long as the expenses were paid for services provided in Canada). Child care expenses do not include medical expenses, costs for clothing, transportation, education, or board; and lodging. The cost of meals provided does qualify and is not subject to the 50% meal limitation of ITA 67.1.

The purpose of the expenses must be to enable an individual to perform employment duties, to carry on a business either alone or as a partner actively engaged in the business, to conduct research connected to a research grant, or to attend certain educational institutions. Any fees must be paid to a resident of Canada who is not the mother or father, a supporting person, or a family member under the age of 18.

Eligible Child An eligible child is defined in ITA 63(3) as (1) a child of an individual, her spouse, or common-law partner; or (2) a child dependent on the individual or her spouse or common-law partner for support and whose net income does not exceed the basic personal credit amount ($13,808 for 2021). In addition, the child must be either under 16 years of age at some time during the year or be dependent on the individual or her spouse or common-law partner by reason of a physical or mental infirmity.

There are different limits for disabled children who are eligible to claim the disability tax credit and those who are not (see following material). To be defined as an eligible child in the aged 16 or over category requires only that they be dependent solely as the result of mental or physical infirmity. The term "infirmity" is not defined in the *ITA* and, therefore, it should be applied using its ordinary meaning. The standard dictionary meaning of an infirmity is a physical or mental weakness or ailment. The CRA is of the view that the degree of the infirmity must be such that it is expected to last for a considerable period of time. As a result, any temporary illness or injury would not be considered to meet the infirmity threshold.

Annual Child Care Expense Amount There are three annual limits. For a dependent child of any age who is eligible for the disability tax credit (e.g., a blind child), the amount is $11,000. For a child under 7 years of age at the end of the year, the amount is $8,000. For a child aged 7 to 16 or an infirm dependent child over 16 that is not eligible for the disability tax credit, the amount is $5,000.

Periodic Child Care Expense Amount This weekly amount is defined as being equal to 2.5% (1/40) of the annual child care expense amount applicable to the particular child. Depending on the child, the value per week will be $275 [(2.5%)($11,000)], $200 [(2.5%)($8,000)], or $125 [(2.5%)($5,000)].

Earned Income This expression is used as one of the limiting factors to potentially restrict the amount of child care expenses that can be claimed in a given year. Earned income is defined as salaries, wages, and other remuneration, including any amounts required to be included in employment income as a result of ITA 6 (taxable benefits, allowances, and ITA 7 stock options), business income (for this purpose, business losses are ignored), and amounts of scholarships, training allowances, and research grants that have been included in net income. You will note that it is only additions to employment income that are considered. Employment expenses are ignored.

Supporting Person A supporting person is the child's parent, the spouse or common-law partner of the child's parent, or an individual who can claim a tax credit for the child for the year under ITA 118, such as the eligible dependant or the Canada caregiver amount. Note that, to qualify as a supporting person, the individual must have resided with the individual claiming child care expenses at some time during the relevant year or within 60 days of the following year. This means, for example, that if the mother lives with the children but the supporting father does not, no child care expense is allowed for the father.

9-52. Using these definitions, we can now turn our attention to the rules to determine what amounts can be deducted, by whom, and when.

Limits for Lower-Income Spouse or Single Parent

9-53. The child care expense rules make it clear that where two individuals share child care responsibilities, such as parents, but only one of the individuals earns income, no child care expenses may be deducted. There is an assumption that the individual who does not earn income will provide the necessary care for the child. The tax policy behind both the moving expense and child care expense rules is to provide assistance by allowing a deduction to reduce income taxes where, aside from certain educational pursuits, there is an income earning connection. We saw this in the moving expense rules, which required an "eligible relocation," which drew the connection to employment and business income. The "child care expense" definition accomplishes the same thing by requiring a connection between the child care expenses and being able, as a result, to make a living earning employment or business income. The opening sentence of CRA folio S1-F3-C1 on child care expenses reads that the "purpose of the legislation is to provide some relief for taxpayers who incur child care expenses in order to work, carry on a business or undertake certain educational activities."

EXAMPLE William and Sarah have two preschool children under the age of five. William is employed full time, working five days a week. Sarah earns investment income and she regularly monitors her investments online each day, which requires much of her time. As a result she and William pay $700 a week for day care services for the two children. Would the child care expenses be deductible? Assume that Sarah is the lower-income spouse.

ANALYSIS The child care fees paid would not be qualifying child care expenses since they are not incurred to enable Sarah to be employed, carry on a business, carry on research, or attend an educational institution. This result would not change even if William were the lower-income earner.

9-54. The amount that can be deducted by the individual with the lower net income in a two-parent family, or by a single parent when there is no other supporting person, is the least of three amounts:

1. The amount actually paid for child care services, plus limited amounts (see Paragraph 9-51) paid for lodging at boarding schools and overnight camps.
2. The sum of the **annual child care expense amounts** for eligible children ($11,000, $8,000, or $5,000 per child).
3. Two-thirds of the individual's **earned income**.

Notice that it is the individual with the lowest net income that can claim child care expenses, and the amount deductible is limited to two-thirds of earned income.

9-55. Note that there is no requirement that the actual child care expenses be limited to the annual limits per child mentioned in the second point. For example, a couple with three healthy children under the age of 7 would have an overall annual amount of $24,000 [(3)($8,000)]. If

$12,000 of child care expenses were incurred for one child and $6,000 each for the others, this would not affect the child care expense claim where limit 2 would be the deciding factor.

9-56. In order to be deductible, amounts paid for child care must be supported by proper receipts issued by the service provider, including a social insurance number if the payee is an individual, and prescribed Form T778 must also be completed each year. Unlike the situation with moving expenses that can be claimed in a subsequent year if they exceed the maximum amount deductible, child care expenses in excess of the amount deductible are simply lost and cannot be carried forward.

Attendance at Boarding School or Camp

9-57. A further limitation on actual costs involves situations where one or more children are attending a boarding school or a camp. The legislative purpose is to provide child care services and not educational and training activities that dominate the nature of the services provided. The CRA, for example, mentions sport activities in Folio S1-F3-C1 as an example, recognizing that such activities may be a regular part of providing child care services to keep children active and healthy and encourage interaction. However, if the sports activity involves targeted training, established goals, and monitoring of progress it suggests that more than child care services are being provided. In recognition of the multifaceted purposes of boarding schools and camps the deductible costs are limited to the periodic child care expense amount ($275, $200, or $125 per week, per child). Amounts paid to the camp or boarding school in excess of these limits would not be deductible nor available for carry forward.

When Deductible by the Higher-Income Spouse

9-58. We have mentioned that, when two individuals (generally spouses or common-law partners) share child care responsibilities, the general rule is that child care expenses are to be claimed by the individual with the lesser net income. We would add that net income can be nil, which would be the case where one of the individuals carries on a business that has incurred losses. There are, however, a number of exceptions to this general rule. Specifically, the higher net income individual is allowed to claim child care expenses if

- the lower-income individual is a student in attendance at a secondary school or a designated educational institution and enrolled in a program of the institution or school that is not less than three consecutive weeks in duration and provides that each student in the program spend not less than
  - 10 hours per week on courses or work in the program (i.e., full-time attendance); or
  - 12 hours per month on courses or work in the program (i.e., part-time attendance);
- the lower-income spouse is infirm and incapable of caring for the children for at least two weeks because of confinement to a bed, wheelchair, hospital, or asylum (this condition requires a written certificate from a medical doctor or nurse practioner supporting the fact that the individual is incapable of caring for children);
- the lower-income spouse is likely to be incapable of caring for children for a long and continuous period because of a mental or physical infirmity (this condition requires a written certificate from a medical doctor or nurse practioner supporting the fact that the individual is incapable of caring for children);
- the lower net income spouse is a person confined to a prison or similar institution throughout a period of not less than two weeks in the year; or
- the spouses are separated and living apart at the end of the year if the separation began in the year and has lasted for at least 90 days.

9-59. In situations where the higher-income individual is claiming a deduction, the amount of the deduction is determined in the same manner as would have applied to the low net income individual as indicated at Paragraph 9-54. However, the higher net income individual is subject to one further limitation. The limitation is calculated by multiplying the sum of the periodic child care expense amounts for all eligible children by the number of weeks that the lower net income spouse is infirm, in prison, separated from the higher net income spouse, or attending an educational institution on a full-time basis. If the attendance is part time, the sum of the periodic amounts is multiplied by the number of months of part-time attendance, not weeks. The amount claimable by the higher net income individual reduces the amount that can then be claimed by the low net income individual.

Example

9-60. The following example will help clarify the general rules for child care expenses.

EXAMPLE Jack and Joanna Morris have three children, Bruce, Bobby, and Betty. At the end of 2021, Bruce is 18 years old and, while he is physically disabled, his disability is not severe enough that he qualifies for the disability tax credit. With respect to the other children, Bobby is 6 years old and Betty is 5 at the end of the year. Jack has 2021 earned income of $45,000, while Joanna has 2021 earned income of $63,000. Jack is the spouse with the lowest net income.

The couple has full-time help to provide child care for all of their children during 49 weeks of the year. The total cost of this help is $210 per week ($10,290 for the year). The children spend three weeks in summer camp. The camp fees total $3,500 for the three-week period for all three children.

As the result of a number of repeat traffic violations, Jack spends seven weeks in November and December in prison.

ANALYSIS The deductible child care expenses would be the least of the following amounts:

	Joanna	**Jack**
Actual child care costs plus maximum deductible camp fees {$10,290 + [(2)($200)(3 weeks) + (1)($125)(3 weeks)]}	$ 11,865	$ 11,865
Annual child care expense amount [(2)($8,000) + (1)($5,000)]	21,000	21,000
2/3 of earned income	42,000	30,000
Periodic child care expense amounts [(2)($200)(7 weeks) + (1)($125)(7 weeks)]	3,675	N/A

While Joanna is the higher net income spouse, she can deduct child care expenses for the seven weeks that Jack is in prison. Her maximum deduction is $3,675. Jack's limit is $11,865. This must be reduced by the $3,675 claimed by Joanna to $8,190 ($11,865 - $3,675).

Note that while Bruce, at age 18, is an eligible child because of his disability, the fact that the disability is not severe enough to qualify Bruce for the disability tax credit means that his annual limit is $5,000 rather than $11,000, and that the periodic limit for Joanna and for the camp fees is $125 rather than $275.

Exercise 9-2

Subject: Child Care Expenses

Mr. and Mrs. Sampras have three children. The ages of the children are 4, 9, and 14, and they are all in good mental and physical health. During the current year, Mr. Sampras has net income composed solely of employment income of $14,000 after the deduction of employment expenses of $5,500. Mrs. Sampras has net income of $54,000, composed solely of business income during this period after deducting business expenses of $21,000. The total child care expenses for the current year, all properly documented for income tax purposes, are $10,500. Determine the maximum deduction for child care expenses and indicate who can make the claim and why.

Solutions to Exercises are available in the Study Guide.

We suggest you complete SSP 9-2 and 9-3 at this point.

Disability Supports Deduction—ITA 64

Eligibility and Coverage

9-61. In a manner somewhat similar to the moving expense and child care expense provisions that are designed to provide indirect financial assistance through the lowering of income taxes by allowing a deduction, ITA 64 achieves the same result. In this case ITA 64 recognizes that individuals suffering from mental and physical impairment face obstacles the cost of which may prove prohibitive in pursuing activities such as employment, carrying on a business, attending certain educational institutions, or performing research and other work for which they would receive research grants. Specifically, ITA 64 provides a disability supports deduction that allows an individual to claim, as a deduction, certain medical expenditures as long as the purpose for the expenditure is to enable the individual to

- perform the duties of an office or employment;
- carry on a business, either alone or as a partner actively engaged in the business;
- attend a designated educational institution or a secondary school; or
- carry on research in respect of which the individual has received a research grant.

9-62. The deduction is available for an extensive list of medical expenditures associated with an infirm or disabled individuals working or going to school. The expenditures must be paid for by the infirm or disabled individual. Some examples of eligible expenditures include the following:

- sign language interpretation services, a teletypewriter, or similar device;
- a Braille printer;
- an optical scanner, an electronic speech synthesizer;
- note-taking services, voice recognition software, tutoring services; and
- talking textbooks.

9-63. Individuals with a physical or mental impairment qualify for this deduction regardless of whether the nature of the impairment or disability qualifies for a claim for the disability tax credit (ITA 118.3). In most cases, a medical practitioner must provide a prescription or certify that the medical expenditure is required given the nature of the disability or impairment. As an example, if an individual has a hearing impairment that requires sign language assistance, the costs of such services would qualify for a deduction, without regard to whether the individual is eligible for the disability tax credit.

Limits on the Amount Deducted

9-64. The amount of qualifying expenditures that can be claimed as a deduction under ITA 64 is limited to the lesser of one of the following:

- An amount determined by the formula

A - B, where

A is equal to the qualifying disability support expenditures; and
B is equal to any reimbursement (such as payments from medical insurance) of amounts included in **A** that were not included in net income and for which a deduction is not available elsewhere in the ITA.

- The total of

1. Gross employment income (ITA 5, 6, & 7), net business income, and scholarships and research grants to the extent they are included in net income.

2. Where the individual is in attendance at a designated educational institution or secondary school, the least of
    - $15,000;
    - $375 times the number of weeks of school attendance at a designated educational institution or secondary school; and
    - the amount by which the individual's net income exceeds the amounts of income included in item 1.

The second limitation is generally designed to limit the deduction to the individual's qualifying income. The effect is that the disability supports deduction is incapable of creating a loss situation.

Disability Supports Deduction vs. Medical Expense Tax Credit

9-65. Many of the expenditures that can be claimed as a deduction under the disability supports deduction could also be claimed for the medical expenses tax credit. In recognition of this double potential the ITA provides an individual with a choice to claim a deduction or a tax credit. ITA 118.2(1) provides the calculations for determining the medical expense tax credit, with part of that legislation adding that any admissible medical expense does not qualify for the credit if it was deducted under ITA 64. ITA 64 completes the picture by adding that any expenditure claimed as a medical expense tax credit cannot be claimed as a deduction. In Folio S1-F3-C1 at paragraph 3.8, the CRA confirms this choice, adding that it is up to the individual to determine which treatment is more beneficial.

9-66. In choosing between the a deduction under ITA 64 or a tax credit under ITA 118.2, the following factors should be taken into consideration:

- The base for the medical expense tax credit is reduced by 3% of the individual's net income.
- Tax credits are calculated using the lowest income tax bracket of 15%. If the individual's taxable income places them in a higher income tax bracket, a deduction of qualifying expenditures will result in larger income tax savings.
- If the individual has a minimum of $3,751 in employment and business income with family net income less than $28,446, the individual will be entitled to use the refundable medical expense tax credit, which provides for a maximum refund of $1,285 for 2021. The supplement does not reduce the medical expense tax credit that could otherwise be claimed.
- The deduction is only available to the impaired individual with respect to qualifying expenditures that have been paid for personally by the individual. If a spouse or supporting person has paid for the expenditures, the spouse or supporting person could claim the medical expense credit with respect to these expenditures, but would not be permitted to claim the disability supports deduction.

Complications Related to Attendant Care Costs

9-67. Attendant care means personal services provided by an individual to a patient who is unable to perform those tasks on his own due to an impairment or disability. If an individual qualifies for the ITA 118.3 disability tax credit, he can claim attendant care costs such as remuneration for the attendant care services provided as a medical expense. There are two specific provisions that allow a claim for attendant care for medical expenses. ITA 118.2(1)(b) applies to allow a claim for "full-time attendant care," and ITA 118.2(1)(b.1) applies to all attendant care, whether part time or full time, although it is recognized by the CRA that it would generally apply to part-time care.

9-68. A claim for full-time attendant care (ITA 118.2(1)(b)) can be made for all of the amounts paid for that care, but the "part-time" attendant care claim under ITA 118.2(1)(b.1) is limited to $10,000. If an individual claims full-time attendant care that is in excess of $10,000 as a medical expense then the claim is made under ITA 118.2(1)(b), which causes the individual to lose access to the disability tax credit for that year. The disability tax credit rules, however, allow the individual to retain access to the disability tax credit where a claim for attendant care is made under ITA 118.2(1)(b.1), which means limiting any attendant care claim to $10,000.

9-69. In summary, a claim for attendant care as a mdeical expense tax credit can only be made by individuals who qualify for the disability tax credit. If, however, the medical expense tax credit claim exceeds $10,000, then the disability tax credit is not available for that year. A summary of the attendant care interaction with respect to the medical expense tax credit (ITA 118.2), the disability tax credit (ITA 118.3), and the disability supports deduction (ITA 64) follows:

- If an individual qualifies for the disability tax credit and the disability supports deduction, the individual can claim attendant care costs as a medical expense tax credit or as a disability supports deduction as discussed. This requires a choice based on the criteria mentionned in Paragraph 9-66.
- If an individual qualifies for the disability tax credit and has attendant care costs in excess of $10,000, the individual is faced with a choice. She can add the full amount of the attendant care costs to the medical expenses tax credit base and forgo the disability tax credit. Alternatively, she can claim these costs as a disability supports deduction, provided a medical practitioner will certify the need for such care. This will usually be preferable since the deduction will not impair the ability to claim the disability tax credit except to the extent of the additional disability supplement for children under the age of 18.
- If an individual is disabled but does not qualify for the disability tax credit, he can deduct full-time attendant care costs under ITA 64 provided a medical practitioner certifies the need for full-time attendant care. However, this individual cannot deduct the costs of part-time attendant care.

Exercise 9-3

Subject: Disability Supports Deduction

Jose Morph has visual, speech, and hearing disabilities. However, they are not severe enough to allow a claim for the disability tax credit. During 2021, he worked on a full-time basis as a programmer for a large public company and his employment income was $78,000. The only employment expense deducted was $3,000 toward the company registered pension plan.

His need for full-time attendant care has been certified by a medical practitioner and, during 2021, such care cost Jose $23,000. Other deductible costs required to support his ability to work as an infirm or disabled person totalled $18,000, all of which were certified by a medical practitioner. His medical insurance reimbursed him for $5,000 of these expenses. Jose will not include any of these costs in his base for the medical expense tax credit. Calculate Jose's disability supports deduction for 2021.

Solutions to Exercises are available in the Study Guide.

Related Inclusions and Deductions

Introduction

9-70. At the beginning of this chapter, we noted that it is not uncommon for there to be an interaction between Subdivisions d and e. In this section we take a closer look at three examples of this interaction: (1) pension income splitting, (2) spousal and child support, and (3) the treatment of annuities.

Pension Income Splitting—ITA 56(1)(a.2), 60(c), & 60.03

General Rules

9-71. In families with low- and high-income earners there is an incentive to undertake income tax planning the purpose of which is to shift income from high-income individuals to low-income individuals. The income tax savings can be considerable, but the ITA sets out numerous rules that are specifically designed to prevent income splitting among family members. There are exceptions, however, where different forms of income splitting are perfectly acceptable. Common examples of acceptable income splitting include contributions to the RRSP of a low-income spouse (discussed in Chapter 10) by a high-income spouse or common-law partner. Another common and popular method involves similar contribution strategies among spouses and common-law partners to Tax-Free Savings Accounts (TFSAs), which is discussed later in this chapter. A third acceptable method of income splitting, which is the subject of this section, is referred to as pension income splitting, which allows up to 50% of certain types of pension income received by one spouse or common-law partner to be transferred on paper for the purposes of filing an income tax return to the other spouse or common-law partner.

9-72. The basic provision for splitting pension income is ITA 60.03. The provision allows a pensioner, defined as any resident Canadian individual who receives eligible pension income, to file a joint election (T1032) with a spouse or common-law partner to shift up to 50% of her eligible pension income to a pension transferee (i.e., the spouse or common-law partner).

9-73. When the election is made, the pension transferee includes the elected amount in income under ITA 56(1)(a.2) and the same amount is deducted by the pensioner under ITA 60(c). Remember that the pensioner is still required to include 100% of the eligible pension income in her income for the year. The pensioner can choose to split any amount, up to a maximum of 50% of eligible pension income. The percentage is determined annually at the discretion of the pensioner.

9-74. The types of pension income that are eligible for splitting are the same as those that are eligible for the pension income tax credit. Chapter 4 discussed the different rules for individuals who are under 65 years of age and those 65 and over. In general, the types of pension income that qualify include income from a registered pension plan (RPP), annuities purchased from a registered retirement savings plan (RRSP) or a deferred profit-sharing plan (DPSP), and income from a registered retirement income fund (RRIF). Amounts that do not qualify include payments under OAS, CPP, or QPP, and withdrawals from an RRSP unless they are annuity payments.

9-75. Also note that while the age of the transferor determines the types of pension income that can be split, the age of the transferee is not relevant for the purposes of determining the types of eligible pension income that can be split by the transferor. However, the age of the transferee is relevant in determining whether the eligible pension income qualifies for the $2,000 annual pension credit amount (ITA 118(3)). If, for example, the transferor spouse or common-law partner was 65 years of age or older and the transferee spouse is less than 65 years of age, the ability of the transferee spouse to claim the pension credit amount would be based on the limited types of pension income that would qualify where an individual is under 65. In general, only periodic payments from a registered pension plan would qualify.

9-76. The legislation needs to address one final point, and that relates to withholding taxes. If, for example, an individual is entitled to an annual pension of $48,000 that is paid monthly, then income taxes are going to be withheld. If we assume that income tax of 25% is withheld on each monthly payment of $4,000, this will leave the individual with $3,000 after tax. Total income taxes withheld for the year would be $12,000. If 50% of the pension income is split with a spouse or common-law partner, the ITA must also give the transferee credit for 50% of the withholding tax of $12,000 and reduce the credit of the transferor by the same amount. ITA 153(2) is designed to shift the proportionate withholding tax from the transferor to the transferee, thus completing the picture. As a result, each spouse or common-law partner will include pension income of $24,000 [(50%)($48,000)] and will be considered as having paid income tax of $6,000 [(50%)($12,000)].

Complications

9-77. In some cases the desirability of pension income splitting is obvious. For example, an individual in the highest federal income tax bracket of 33% can transfer a significant amount of income to a spouse or common-law partner who has no income, resulting in a significant amount of income being taxed at the lowest federal rate of 15%. In addition, the transfer may create a pension credit amount for the transferee. We would add that the income tax savings are also increased by any provincial income tax savings since the provinces follow the lead of the federal government and the ITA. The one exception is Quebec, which only allows pension splitting for pensioners 65 years of age and older.

9-78. There are, however, offsetting factors due to an increase in the net income of the transferee. These include the potential reduction or loss of the spousal tax credit, the reduction or loss of the transferee's age credit, or a decrease in the medical expenses credit because of the 3% net income threshold. There is also the possibility that the increase in net income transfer could result in a clawback if the OAS threshold is exceeded. For 2021 the threshold is $79,845.

9-79. As a result of these potential issues, it is not possible to devise a general rule related to the use of pension income splitting. Fortunately tax preparation software providers such as Intuit ProFile include optimizations designed to identify the best income tax saving alternative based on the income of both spouses or common-law partners.

Exercise 9-4

Subject: Pension Income Splitting

Joanna Sparks lives with her spouse of many years, John Sparks. They are both 67 years of age. During 2021, Joanna received $7,400 in OAS payments. She also receives $85,000 of pension income from an RPP that was sponsored by her former employer. She has not, at this point in time, applied for CPP. John's only source of 2021 income is $7,400 in OAS payments. Neither Joanna nor John have any income tax credits other than the basic personal credit, age credit, and pension income credit.

Joanna has asked you to indicate the savings in federal income tax that would result from making optimum use of pension income splitting for the 2021 taxation year. You will need to determine the impact by calculating income tax for each individual (1) without the pension split and (2) with the pension split.

Solutions to Exercises are available in the Study Guide.

We suggest you complete SSP 9-4 and 9-5 at this point.

Spousal and Child Support—ITA 56(1)(b) & 60(b)

Definitions

9-80. ITA 56.1(4) provides definitions for both support and child support:

Support Amount means an amount payable or receivable as an allowance on a periodic basis for the maintenance of the recipient, children of the recipient, or both the recipient and children of the recipient, if the recipient has discretion as to the use of the amount, and

(a) the recipient is the spouse or common-law partner or former spouse or common-law partner of the payer, the recipient and payer are living separate and apart because of the breakdown of their marriage or common-law partnership, and the amount is receivable under an order of a competent tribunal or under a written agreement; or

(b) the payer is a legal parent of a child of the recipient and the amount is receivable under an order made by a competent tribunal in accordance with the laws of a province.

Child Support Amount means any support amount that is not identified in the agreement or order under which it is receivable as being solely for the support of a recipient who is a spouse or common-law partner or former spouse or common-law partner of the payer or who is a parent of a child of whom the payer is a legal parent.

9-81. When read together, these two definitions provide, in effect, a definition of spousal support. For an amount to be treated as spousal support, it must be specifically designated as being solely for the support of a recipient who is a spouse or common-law partner, a recipient who is a former spouse or common-law partner, or a recipient who is the parent of a child of whom the payer is a legal parent.

General Income Tax Treatment

9-82. Only those payments that are clearly designated as spousal support are deductible by the payer under ITA 60(b). Such payments would then be included in the net income of the recipient as a result of ITA 56(1)(b). As noted in the section that follows, there are other conditions that must be met for this income tax treatment to apply. Perhaps, not surprisingly, the topic of support payments can be quite complex, as is suggested by almost 400 court decisions heard to resolve the income tax side of support issues since the legislation was introduced.

9-83. Child support, which would include all support amounts that are not clearly designated as spousal support, are not deductible to the payer and not required to be included in the net income of the recipient.

Conditions for Deduction and Inclusion

9-84. As described in S1-F3-C3, "*Support Payments*," an amount is considered a support payment if

- it is payable or receivable as an allowance on a periodic basis;
- it is paid for the maintenance of the recipient, the children of the recipient, or both;
- the recipient has discretion as to the use of the amount; and
- where the recipient of the amount is the spouse or common-law partner or former spouse or common-law partner of the payer, the parties are living separate and apart because of a breakdown of their relationship, and the amount is receivable under an order of a competent tribunal or under a written agreement; or
- where the recipient is the parent of a child of whom the payer is a legal parent, the amount is receivable under an order of a competent tribunal in accordance with the laws of a province or territory.

9-85. If an amount is considered to be a support payment, the amount that is deductible to the payer and included in the net income of the recipient is defined in ITA 60(b) as the total of such support payments less any amounts that are considered to be child support. Note that, based on the definition in ITA 56.1(4), any amounts that are not clearly designated as spousal support are considered to be child support.

9-86. While payments prior to the date of a written agreement or court order or judgment cannot technically be made retroactively, ITA 56.1(3) and ITA 60.1(3) deem any payments made in the year of the order or judgment or in the preceding year be considered as if they were paid as a result of the court order, judgment, or written agreement provided that the order, judgment, or agreement specifies that they are to be considered. This allows individuals to begin support immediately and benefit from the income tax treatment without having to wait on a court date.

9-87. Problems often arise with respect to the requirement that payments be made on a periodic basis. Clearly, a single lump-sum payment that releases the payer from future obligations would not be considered as periodic. However if a lump-sum payment represents a retroactive payment to make up for overdue periodic payments, then the payment would be considered as periodic. This would also be the case where an individual has petitioned the court for an increase in support and the court has agreed to do so on a retroactive basis. In such case a lump-sum catch-up payment would be considered a periodic payment.

9-88. Under some circumstances, a person who receives support payments and includes the amount received in income may be required to repay some portion of these amounts. This could occur if the payer's financial situation has changed and a court order is obtained allowing a reduction in support payments. In these circumstances, the person making the repayment is allowed to deduct the amount repaid [ITA 60(c.2)] in the year of the repayment or in either of the two following taxation years. The recipient of the repayment, however, is required to include the full amount in the year it is received [ITA 56(1)(c.2)].

Additional Considerations

9-89. There are a number of additional issues and considerations related to the income tax treatment of support payments. Many situations arise due to the fact that in separation and divorce proceedings, which can at times take years to resolve, the individuals do not always consider the income tax implications, focusing more on family law and other legal issues, many of which are procedural in nature:

- In situations where a required payment includes both child support and spousal support, a problem can arise when the periodic payments are not made in full. The issue then becomes how to determine whether the partial payments relate to child or spousal support. Fortunately a legislative solution exists. ITA 56(1)(b) and ITA 60(b) establish an ordering rule that any payments made are to be considered as first applying to child support. This means that a support deduction is only allowed once all child support obligations have been paid. For example, consider an individual required to pay $4,000 in child support and $12,000 in spousal support. If a total of $7,000 is paid during the year, only $3,000 of that amount will be deductible as spousal support.
- In general, payments to third parties that are clearly for the benefit of the spouse are deductible to the payer and taxable to the spouse where the recipient has the right to redirect the payment or the payer and payee have agreed that third-party payments will be made by the payer and that such amounts will be considered as if they had been received by the recipient. This is necessary since a support amount requires that the recipient have discretion (e.g., a degree of control) over the amount.
- Spousal support payments impact the ability of the payer and of the recipient to make RRSP contributions because one of the limiting factors is "earned income," which includes deductible support payments made and taxable support payments received. The expression "earned income" for RRSP purposes is not the same as that used for child care expense purposes. This will be discussed further in Chapter 10.
- The recipient of child support payments is eligible for the credit for an eligible dependant, unless the recipient has another spouse or common-law partner (see Chapter 4).
- ITA 118(5) prevents an individual from claiming an income tax credit for a spouse or eligible dependant and, at the same time, deducting support payments to that spouse.
- Separation and divorce proceedings generally require the involvement of lawyers who specialize in family law. Given that these proceedings can take considerable time and effort, the cost of legal fees can be considerable. An important income tax consideration is whether these legal fees are deductible. The courts have considered this issue many times and generally concluded that the payer is not permitted to claim legal expenses whereas the recipient may in many circumstances. Legal fees incurred by the individual seeking support are deductible if they are related to establishing a right to support, determining the support amount, enforcing collection of overdue payments, seeking a court order to increase support, or defending against an action to reduce support payments.

Exercise 9-5

Subject: Support Payments

On June 15, 2021, Sandra and Jerry Groom signed a separation agreement that calls for Jerry to have custody of their five children and for Sandra to pay monthly support of

$4,000 beginning on July 1. Of this amount, $1,500 is for child support and $2,500 is for spousal support. During 2021, Sandra paid support for only three months. How will the total support paid of $12,000 be treated for income tax purposes to both Sandra and Jerry?

Solutions to Exercises are available in the Study Guide.

Annuity Payments Received—ITA 56(1)(d) & 60(a)

Annuities and Their Uses

9-90. ITA 248(1) defines an annuity as an amount payable on a periodic basis, without regard to whether it is payable at intervals longer or shorter than a year. As the term is usually applied, it refers to the investment contracts that are usually sold by insurance companies. The two basic forms of these contracts involve either payments for a specified period (e.g., annual payments for a period of 10 years) or payments for the life of the annuitant (e.g., annual payments until the death of the recipient).

9-91. These contracts can also take various forms. For example, a common arrangement would be a life annuity, with payments guaranteed for a minimum of 10 years. In this case, if the annuitant dies prior to the end of 10 years, payments will continue to be made to the deceased's estate until the end of the specified guarantee period or a payout referred to as a commutation payment can be made to beneficiaries.

9-92. Annuities are widely used in retirement and estate planning because they provide a guaranteed stream of payments composed of income and a return of capital that is virtually risk free. Also important is the fact that, in the case of life annuities, the annuitant does not have to be concerned with outliving the income stream. As you would expect, these desirable features are generally offset by low rates of return.

9-93. The taxation of annuity payments depends on the manner in which the investment contract was acquired:

Acquisition within a Tax Deferred Plan Annuities are often purchased by the administrator of deferred income plans such as RPPs, RRSPs, and RRIFs. The objective is to provide a beneficiary of the plan with a fixed and guaranteed stream of income, usually at the time of retirement. Direct and indirect contributions to these plans are deductible, and income earned within the plans are exempt from tax as long as the funds and property remain within the plan. Payments made from the plans to beneficiaries, however, are required to be included in net income. This means that the full amount of payments made from annuities that have been purchased within these plans must be included in the recipient's net income.

Acquisition outside a Tax Deferred Plan Individuals also purchase annuities outside of tax deferred plans. The potential problem in this case can be illustrated by a simple example.

EXAMPLE Pierre Brissette uses funds from his savings account (i.e., after-tax funds) to purchase a five-year ordinary annuity with payments of $2,309 at the end of each year. The cost of the annuity is $10,000, providing him with an effective yield of 5%.

ANALYSIS The total payments on this annuity would be $11,545 [(5)($2,309)]. This total is made up of $1,545 of earnings plus $10,000, which represents a return of Mr. Brissette's capital. It would not be equitable to require Mr. Brissette to include the full amount of the annuity payments in his net income. Clearly, some type of provision is required to ensure that only the income component of $1,545 be included in net income.

Capital Element of an Annuity

9-94. In order to distinguish between annuities received through deferred income plans with annuities acquired outside of such plans, ITA 56(1)(d) requires that annuity payments that are not "otherwise included in income" are to be included in net income under this provision. As payments from RPPs, RRSPs, and RRIFs are "otherwise included" under other provisions of the *ITA*, this means that only annuities purchased with after-tax funds would be included here.

9-95. For those annuity payments that are included under ITA 56(1)(d), ITA 60(a) allows a deduction that is designed to isolate the income component of the annuity by allowing a deduction for the capital (i.e., investment cost) component included in the payments. The capital element that is to be deducted is calculated by multiplying the annuity payment that was included in income for the year by a ratio. The ratio is determined by ITR 300 and is relatively straightforward. The formula for calculating the capital element of a fixed-term annuity payment and therefore the ITA 60(a) deduction is as follows:

$$\text{Deduction} = \left[\frac{\text{Capital Outlay to Buy the Annuity}}{\text{Total Payments to Be Received under the Contract}}\right] [\text{Annuity Payment}]$$

9-96. To illustrate, refer to the example in Paragraph 9-93. ITA 56(1)(d) requires that each annual annuity payment of $2,309 be included in net income. ITA 60(a) would then provide the following deduction:

$$\left[\frac{\$10,000}{\$11,545}\right] [\$2,309] = \$2,000 \text{ Deduction}$$

Exercise 9-6

Subject: Annuity Payments

On January 1 of the current year, Barry Hollock uses $55,000 of his savings to acquire a four-year fixed-term annuity with annual payments of $15,873. The payments are received on December 31 of each year, and the interest rate inherent in the annuity is 6%. What are the income tax consequences of the receipt of the $15,873 annual annuity payment on Mr. Hollock's net income for the year?

Solutions to Exercises are available in the Study Guide.

Registered Savings Plans

Introduction

9-97. Registered savings plans allow individuals to make contributions to an arrangement that is a trust that is registered with the CRA. Very briefly, trusts generally have three central participants. The first, generally referred to as the settlor, is the person who establishes or creates the trust arrangement and contributes property to the trust. The second, referred to as the trustee, is the person who oversees, manages, and administers the trust. Finally, the beneficiary is the person who potentially benefits from both the income and the capital of the trust. Assume, for example, that you make a $5,000 contribution to an RRSP trust for your spouse or common-law partner that is managed by the Royal Bank. You would be the settlor, the Royal Bank would be the trustee, and your spouse or common-law partner would be the beneficiary. All of the ingredients of a trust are in place. One of the roles of plan trustees is to provide information to the CRA with respect to contributions made to and withdrawals taken from registered savings plans.

9-98. In this chapter we will provide detailed coverage of two of the deferred income plans, registered education savings plans (RESPs) and Tax-Free Savings Accounts (TFSAs). We will also provide a brief description in this chapter of registered disability savings plans (RDSPs).

Other registered plans will be covered in Chapter 10. Part of our reasons for including this coverage at this time is that these three types of plans represent sanctioned income-splitting opportunities.

9-99. Contributions to the plans we will consider in this chapter are not deductible in determining net income. However, they do have other significant income tax advantages:

Tax Deferral Once contributions have been made, they will be invested in various types of income producing property (e.g., investments). Income earned within these plans are exempt from income tax as long as the trust arrangement exists, the conditions for qualifying for ITA purposes continue to be met, and property of the plan remain in the plan. This provides for significant tax deferral.

Tax Reduction (RESPs and RDSPs) Non-deductible contributions to these plans are typically made by parents or grandparents that have income that is subject to income tax rates higher than the minimum federal income tax rate of 15%. While earnings distributed from RESPs and RDSPs are required to be included in net income, they will eventually be paid to either a student or a disabled individual. In many cases, the individual recipients have little other income and, as a result, are subject to a low income tax rate. The result is that distributions are unlikely to result in much, if any, income tax owing. In effect these plans provide an acceptable income-shifting opportunity with a high likelihood of an overall income tax savings.

Tax Reduction (TFSAs) TFSAs offer additional advantages. Income earned within a TFSA is exempt from income tax as it is earned, similar to other deferred income plans, however no part of a withdrawal from a TFSA is required to be included in net income regardless of whether it is income or capital. The result is that income taxes are not just reduced, they are eliminated altogether.

9-100. The basic operation of TFSAs, RESPs, and RDSPs is depicted in Figure 9-1. As shown in the figure, the contributions to these plans are not deductible. This is in contrast to both RPPs and RRSPs, where the contributions can be deducted at the time they are made (see Chapter 10).

Tax-Free Savings Accounts (TFSAs)

General Procedures

9-101. The general rules for TFSAs are as follows:

Figure 9-1
TFSAs, RESPs, and RDSPs—The Basic System

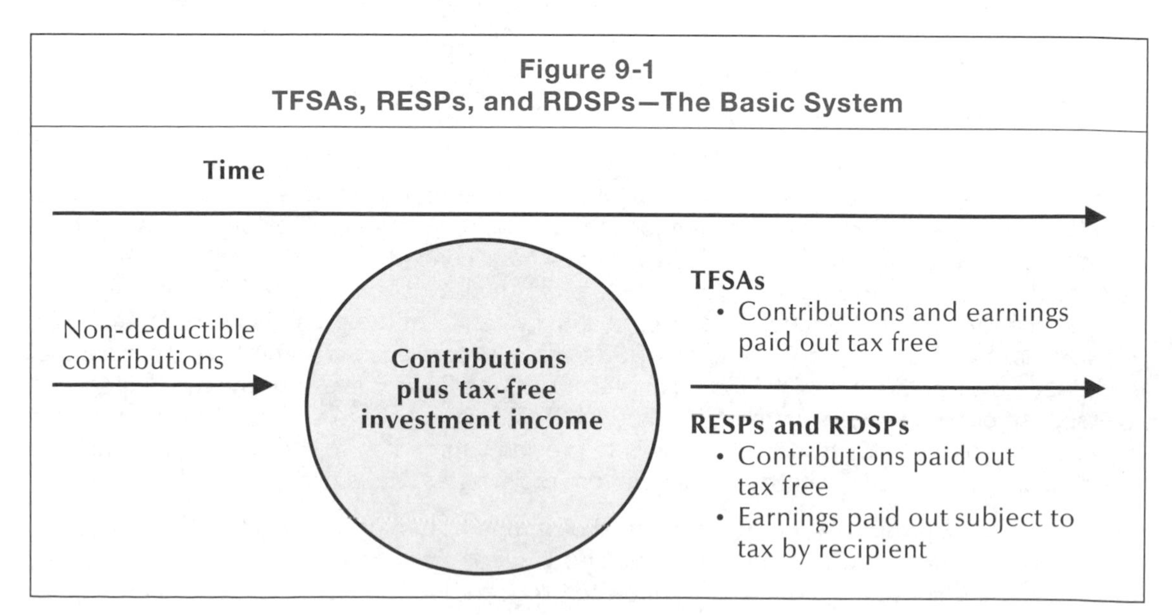

Eligibility Any resident individual 18 years of age and older can establish a TFSA.

Contribution Room When TFSAs were introduced in 2009, the maximum annual contribution to the plan was $5,000. This was increased to $5,500 in 2013, with a further increase to $10,000 for 2015. This was for one year only as the maximum annual contribution was returned to $5,500 for 2016, 2017, and 2018. For 2019, it was increased to $6,000 and has remained constant through 2021. The contribution room accumulates each year the individual is 18 or over, without regard to whether the individual has established a TFSA or has filed an income tax return. For an individual who was 18 years of age in 2009, as of 2021 total TFSA contribution room has accumulated to $75,500 (4@$5,000 + 2@$5,500 + 1@ $10,000 + 3@$5,500 + 3@$6,000).

Unused amounts of this contribution room can be carried forward indefinitely, and any withdrawals (consisting of contributions and earnings) are added back to the total contribution room. It is important to note that this addition to contribution room does not occur until the year following the withdrawal. Ignoring this timing lag can result in an excess contribution, which will be subject to a penalty. To assist taxpayers, unused TFSA contribution room information can be accessed by using the CRA "My Account" online service (see Chapter 2).

Unlike RRSPs, the contributions are not deductible. Contributions in excess of available contribution room will be subject to a penalty tax of 1% per month. Interest on money borrowed to make contributions is not deductible. This rule reflects the general principle that interest can only be deducted when the purpose of the borrowing is to earn income from business or property.

Qualified Investments The Act is flexible with respect to the types of investments that can be included in a TFSA. ITR 4900 provides a detailed listing of the specific investment categories and includes publicly traded shares, mutual fund units, bonds, mortgages, warrants, and rights. The only significant restrictions relate to investments in the shares of private companies and direct investments in real estate. There is no limit on foreign content. For a more complete discussion of this subject, see IT Folio S3-F10-C1, "Qualified Investments—RRSPs, RESPs, RRIFs, RDSPs, and TFSAs," and IT Folio S3-F10-C2, "Prohibited Investments—RRSPs, RESPs, RRIFs, RDSPs, and TFSAs." A 50% tax can apply on the fair market value of non-qualified investments and prohibited investments.

Investment Income As is the case with other registered savings plans, amounts earned on investments within the plan are exempt from income tax. However, unlike other registered savings plans, withdrawals are not required to be included in the net income of the recipient. Any losses on the sale of investments in the TFSA have no income tax advantage as they simply reduce the TFSA funds available for distribution.

Income Attribution Rules As will be discussed in the final section of this chapter, when an individual gifts or otherwise provides property to a spouse or common-law partner without receiving fair market value consideration, the attribution rules potentially apply. Making contributions to a TFSA for a spouse or common-law partner would normally result in the application of the attribution rules, however there are exceptions to the rule. ITA 74.5(12)(c) specifically prevents the application of the attribution rules with respect to such TFSA contributions. The purpose is to allow TFSA contributions by one spouse or common-law partner to another, effectively providing a targeted income-shifting opportunity among family members.

Death of a Taxpayer If an individual's spouse or common-law partner is designated as a successor holder, the individual's TFSA can be transferred into the hands of this successor holder as an ongoing TFSA. It can either be maintained by the individual as a separate TFSA or, alternatively, transferred into his own TFSA without being treated as a contribution. Income earned in the bequeathed TFSA will continue to be exempt from income tax.

If the decedent's TFSA is transferred to any other beneficiary, that individual can withdraw the funds in the plan at the time of the transferor's death without any income tax consequences. However, any amounts received in excess of the fair market value of the property in the plan at the time of the transferor's death will be required to be included in the individual's net income.

Registered Education Savings Plans (RESPs)—ITA 146.1

Contributions

9-102. An RESP is a plan designed to set aside funds for the post-secondary education of a child, which includes attendance at a trade school, college, university, or apprenticeship program on a part-time or full-time basis. As previously noted, like contributions to a TFSA, contributions to an RESP are not deductible, but income earned within the plan is exempt from income tax. Technically, and as previously mentioned in Paragraph 9-97, deferred income plans are trusts and various provisions within ITA 149(1) treat such trusts as entities that are exempt from Part I tax on any income they earn. However, the Part I exemption does not prevent other parts of the ITA from applying, such as penalty taxes for excess contributions and where the trusts invest in property that does not qualify or is prohibited. There are seven different taxes that apply to deferred income plans (between Parts X and XI.I).

9-103. As is discussed more completely in Chapter 10, over extended periods of time there is a significant income tax savings in situations where there is a tax-free accumulation of earnings. In the case of RESPs, however, this tax-free accumulation is limited to 35 years once the plan is established (40 years for where there is a single beneficiary who is eligible for the disability tax credit). At the end of that period, the plan is automatically de-registered, at which time the tax-exempt status no longer applies. Very specific rules are added to address the Part I income treatment where a tax-exempt entity ceases to be exempt (ITA 149(10)).

9-104. An individual, usually a parent or grandparent, becomes a subscriber or a joint subscriber of an RESP by signing a contract with an RESP promoter. Total contributions are limited to $50,000 for each beneficiary with no annual limit on contributions. Although there is complete flexibility with respect to the timing of contributions, consideration should be given to the added benefits of the Canada Education Savings Grant (CESG) limits (see Paragraph 9-107).

9-105. There is a penalty for excess contributions. If, at the end of any month, the contributions for a particular beneficiary exceed the total limit of $50,000, the subscribers to the plan are subject to a monthly penalty tax of 1% applied to the excess. Note that these limits apply for each beneficiary. If several individuals are contributing to different plans with the same beneficiary (e.g., Joan's father and her grandmother are both contributing to a plan on her behalf), the sum of their contributions to Joan's plans cannot exceed the $50,000 limit. Any penalty tax assessed on excess contributions must be shared on a pro rata basis by the subscriber(s).

9-106. General types of penalties, such as those that relate to the late filing of an income tax return, were discussed in Chapter 2, noting that many penalties set out a dollar amount established in Part I of the ITA. Penalties for excess contributions on deferred income plans, including penalties for non-qualified and prohibited investments, are determined in a different manner. These types of penalties are established as a separate income tax, which is why we refer to these penalties as a penalty tax as opposed to simply a penalty. The penalty tax for RESP excess contributions is set out in Part X.4 and requires any subscribers liable for the penalty tax for excess contributions to file a tax return specifically for that part. Failure to file that return can result in penalties for late filing.

Canada Education Savings Grants (CESGs)

9-107. Under the CESG program, the federal government will make additional contributions to an RESP to supplement those being made by the subscriber(s). The CESG has both a "basic" and an "additional" component.

9-108. The amount of grant-eligible contributions is a balance that accumulates at the rate of $2,500 per year, beginning in the year a child is born. The basic CESG is equal to 20% of the current-year contributions for a beneficiary up to a maximum of $500 [(20%)($2,500)] per beneficiary. If there is unused contribution room from previous years, up to $1,000 in CESG is available in the current year. The lifetime CESG maximum is $7,200.

9-109. In order to assist low-income families, an additional CESG of 10 to 20% of the first $500 of contributions in a year for a beneficiary is available. The amount of the additional CESG depends on the net family income for the year. On the first $500 in contributions for 2021, the additional CESG is calculated as follows:

- At 20% if 2021 family income is $49,020 or less (maximum of $100);
- At 10% if 2021 family income is between $49,020 and $98,040 (maximum of $50); and
- At 0% if 2021 family income is greater than $98,040.

This means that if the maximum contribution upon which the CESG is determined of $2,500 is made, then the total CESG for low-income families will be $600, $550 for those with family income between $49,020 and $98,040, and $500 where family income exceeds $98,040.

9-110. As noted, regardless of family income, for each beneficiary contributions of $2,500 in a year earns a grant equal to 20% of that contribution, or $500. The CESG contribution room is based on annual maximum contributions of $2,500. If less than that amount is contributed in one year the difference becomes "unused CESG contribution room," which is eligible for the CESG in future years to the extent of actual contributions.

EXAMPLE Tom is born in February 2020. Tom's father makes an RESP contribution of $1,300 for Tom in 2020 and $1,300 in 2021. In November 2021, Tom's grandmother makes a $3,000 contribution to another RESP for Tom.

ANALYSIS The unused CESG contribution room for 2021 is $3,700 [(2)($2,500) - $1,300]. As the combined contributions of the father and grandmother total $4,300, $600 of the total contributions will not be eligible for CESGs. Depending on the net family income of Tom's father, the CESG for 2021 ranges from $740 [(20%)($3,700)] if family income exceeds $98,040 to $840 [(40%)($500) + (20%)($3,700 - $500)] if family income is less than $49,020.

It is important to note that the $600 excess contribution does not carry forward and become eligible for CESGs in the following year when more contribution room accrues to Tom. If it is expected that annual contributions to Tom's RESP will be less than $2,500 in the future, this would suggest that Tom's father should limit his 2021 contribution to $700 and defer the extra $600 to the following year. In that year, it would eligible for a grant. Also note that if there is a large carry forward of grant-eligible contribution room, the CESG will be limited to a maximum of $1,000 for a year ($500 current plus $500 carry forward), which would require a contribution of $5,000 at 20%.

9-111. CESGs will not be paid for RESP beneficiaries for the year in which they turn 18 years of age, or in any subsequent year. In addition, CESG payments are intended to encourage long-term planning for a child's education. Because of this, in a year in which the beneficiary is between the age of 15 and the age of 17, CESG payments will be made only when

- a minimum of $2,000 of RESP contributions were made in respect of the beneficiary by December 31 of the calendar year in which the beneficiary becomes 15 years of age; or

- a minimum of $100 in annual RESP contributions was made in respect of the beneficiary in any four years before the calendar year in which the beneficiary attains 15 years of age.

Exercise 9-7

Subject: Canada Education Savings Grants

Jeanine was born in 2020. During 2020, her father establishes an RESP for her and contributes $500 to the plan, while Jeanine's grandfather contributes an additional $1,200. During 2021, her father contributes $1,500 and her grandfather adds a further $2,400. Jeanine's family has never had family income of more than $40,000. Determine the amount of the CESGs that would be added to Jeanine's RESP in 2020 and 2021.

Solutions to Exercises are available in the Study Guide.

Canada Learning Bonds (CLBs)

9-112. A further enhancement to the RESP system, Canada Learning Bonds (CLBs) are somewhat similar to the CESGs in that the government makes contributions to a child's RESP. However, unlike the CESGs, the CLB contributions are not based on personal contributions made to the RESP.

9-113. The CLB provisions apply to children born after 2003 and who have an RESP established in their names. Such children are eligible for a CLB contribution to their RESP in each year that their family is eligible for the child National Child Benefit Supplement (this supplement is an income test benefit that is added to the Canada Child Benefit). Potential eligibility begins in the year the child is born and ends in the year the child turns 15 years of age.

9-114. The CLB contributions to individual RESPs are as follows:

- In the first year that the child is eligible for a CLB contribution, an amount of $500 will be provided. In addition, a one-time additional amount of $25 will be added to help defray the costs of establishing the RESP.
- In each subsequent year of eligibility, a CLB contribution of $100 will be made. This continues until the year in which the child turns 15 years of age.

Types of Plans

9-115. RESP legislation provides for "family plans" in which each of the beneficiaries is related to the subscriber by blood or adoption. Family plans, which are typically established for several siblings under age 18, are subject to the same contribution limits per beneficiary, but provide additional flexibility for the subscriber because the educational assistance payments that will be made are not limited to each child's "share" of the contributions.

9-116. This feature is important when an individual has several children and not all of them pursue higher education. Because of the flexibility inherent in family plans, all of the plan distributions could be directed toward the children who are eligible to receive such funds as a result of educational pursuits that are required of the RESP program. To ensure that family plans do not provide unintended benefits, no beneficiaries 21 years of age or older can be added to a family plan.

9-117. In terms of alternatives for investing the funds that have been contributed, there are basically two types of RESPs available. They can be described as follows:

Scholarship plans are available through "scholarship trust companies" such as the Canadian Scholarship Trust Plan. These plans are distinguished by the fact that all of their funds must be invested in government guaranteed investments. These companies offer group plans (earnings are allocated only to those children who attend college or university), as well as individual plans (subscribers can recover their share of the investment earnings).

Self-directed plans allow investors to choose their own investments. The list of qualified investments is similar to that applicable to self-directed RRSPs. For example, publicly traded stocks are eligible, but income producing real estate is not. As is the case with RRSPs, there is no foreign content limit for self-directed RESPs.

Refund of Contributions

9-118. Contributions can be returned to either the subscriber to the plan or to the beneficiary without any income tax consequences. The only limitations on such payments are those that might be included in the terms and conditions of the plan itself.

Education Assistance Payments (EAP)

9-119. EAP are amounts paid to student beneficiaries from accumulated earnings, CESG amounts, and CLB amounts. These amounts must be included in the net income of the recipient.

9-120. To be eligible for the receipt of such amounts, the individual must be enrolled in a program at the post-secondary level that lasts at least three consecutive weeks. If the student spends at least 10 hours per week on courses or work it is considered a **qualifying** educational program. If the student spends at least 12 hours per month on courses or work it is considered a **specified** educational program. In the case of a specified educational program, the student must be at least 16 years old.

9-121. The limits on the amounts to be paid can be described as follows:

- For studies in a qualifying educational program, the limit is $5,000 for the first 13 consecutive weeks. Subsequent to that period, there is no limit on payments, provided the student continues to qualify.
- For studies in a specified educational program, the limit is $2,500 for the first 13-week period, whether or not the student is enrolled in the program throughout this period.

9-122. Note that CESG and CLB amounts can only be paid out as EAP to beneficiaries. If the beneficiary does not pursue post-secondary education, these benefits must be returned to the government.

Accumulated Income Payments to Subscribers

9-123. Payments made to subscribers out of the accumulated income of the plan are referred to as accumulated income payments. To be eligible to receive such payments, the subscriber must be a resident of Canada. In addition, one of the following conditions must apply:

- The payment is made after the year that includes the ninth anniversary of the plan and each beneficiary has reached the age of 21 years and is not currently eligible for EAP.
- The payments are made after the plan has been de-registered (35 or 40 years, depending on the type of plan).
- All of the beneficiaries are deceased.

9-124. The accumulated income payments will be included in the subscriber's net income. In calculating the individual's federal tax payable, an additional income tax of 20% of the accumulated income payments must be added to the total. This additional tax is designed to offset the fact that the individual has enjoyed tax-free earnings compounding inside the RESP. The 20% tax is separately charged under Part X.5 of the ITA.

9-125. There is a provision that allows a taxpayer to reduce the amount of accumulated income payments that will be subject to the 20% additional tax. Provided the individual has sufficient RRSP contribution room (see Chapter 10 for coverage of this concept), accumulated income payments can be transferred to an RRSP. Such transfers will provide the individual with both an RRSP deduction for the contribution plus a reduction in the amount of the additional 20% tax. The limit on such transfers is $50,000 worth of accumulated income payments. It is generally preferable to make a direct transfer from the RESP to an RRSP to avoid withholding taxes on the accumulated income payment.

We suggest you complete SSP 9-6 at this point.

Comparison of TFSAs and RRSPs

9-126. While the range of available plans can be fairly large for some individuals, the most common choice will be between making contributions to a TFSA and making contributions to an RRSP. In comparing these two alternatives, the most significant differences can be described as follows:

- Contributions to an RRSP entitle the contributor to a deduction in determining net income (ITA 60(i)). Contributions to a TFSA are not deductible.
- Withdrawals from an RRSP are required to be included in net income (ITA 56(1)(h)). Withdrawals from a TFSA are not included in net income, therefore they are not subject to income tax and do not affect the OAS clawback or government benefits such as the GST/HST credit.
- 2021 annual contributions to an RRSP can amount to $27,830 but are limited to $6,000 for a TFSA. This is mitigated by the fact that RRSP contribution room is lost when amounts are withdrawn but can be reinstated for TFSAs by making a contribution in the year following the withdrawal.

9-127. Although detailed coverage of RRSPs is found in Chapter 10 and a complete analysis of the impact of these differences goes beyond the scope of this text, a simple example will serve to illustrate the economic and financial comparison.

EXAMPLE In 2021, Sophia Scarponi has $5,000 in pre-tax income that she would like to invest. She has asked your advice on whether she should contribute to a TFSA or to an RRSP. She indicates that her marginal income tax rate is 45%, a rate that she expects to remain unchanged for the next 10 years. She anticipates that funds invested in either the TFSA or an RRSP will earn a compounded annual return of 10%. She does not anticipate a need for these funds for at least 10 years.

ANALYSIS—TFSA As the $5,000 is required to be included in her net income, then income tax of $2,250 [(45%)($5,000)] will have to be paid, which will leave her with funds to invest in the TFSA of $2,750 [$5,000 - $2,250)]. If this amount is left in the TFSA for 10 years earning income at an annual compounded rate of 10% she will have a balance of $7,133. None of this amount will be subject to tax when it is withdrawn.

ANALYSIS—RRSP Since RRSP contributions are deductible in determining net income, no income taxes will be paid on the $5,000, meaning the full amount can be invested in an RRSP. At the end of the 10-year period the RRSP, with annual compounding of 10%, will have grown to $12,969. The withdrawal of the full amount will result in income taxes of $5,836 [(45%)($12,969)], which leaves her with the same $7,133 [$12,969 - $5,836].

9-128. In this example, the results under the two approaches are identical. As a general rule TFSAs are designed to allow Canadians to create a current savings to meet current needs where necessary (e.g., emergency expenditures) whereas RRSPs are designed to create savings for retirement. The individual will have to assess what needs are more important given the circumstances. The assumption in this example was that the individual's marginal income tax rate remains constant at 45% throughout the 10-year period. However, if her marginal rate were to decline at the end of that period, then less income tax would be payable on the RRSP withdrawal, favouring the RRSP. If her marginal rate were to increase, however, a larger amount of income tax would be required on the RRSPs, favouring the TFSA. It is difficult to make long-term forecasts that would permit a definitive choice.

Comparison of TFSAs vs. RRSPs vs. RESPs

9-129. Many Canadian families are not able to make maximum contributions to both RRSPs and TFSAs, let alone RESPs where there are children eligible for the benefits of the RESP program. For an individual with $50,000 in earned income and a child whose RESP contribution would be eligible for a CESG grant, the total funds needed to make the maximum contributions for 2021 would be $17,500 [(18%)($50,000) RRSP + $6,000 TFSA + $2,500 RESP]. It is unlikely that an individual earning $50,000 a year would possess the necessary resources to fully participate in all three types of plan. This means that a choice of plans will have to be made when resources are limited.

9-130. Facing this reality means that most individuals will have to make a choice as to where limited resources can be directed, if any. We have previously covered some of the factors to be considered in making a choice between TFSAs and RRSPs. With respect to a choice between RRSPs and RESPs, the following factors should be considered:

- A major advantage of RESPs relative to RRSPs is the fact that RESP contributions can be eligible for a Canada Education Savings Grant (CESG).
- A further advantage of RESPs relative to RRSPs is the fact that the establishment of such plans allows contributions to be made under the CLB program. This program could justify establishing an RESP for children in low-income families, even if no contributions are made to the plan.
- A major advantage of RRSPs relative to RESPs is the fact that RRSP contributions are deductible in the calculation of net income. This allows larger contributions to be made to RRSPs, as was illustrated in the example in Paragraph 9-127.
- Offsetting the deductibility of RRSP contributions is the fact that all payments out of RRSPs to plan beneficiaries are required to be included in net income and subject to income tax. While some individuals may be in a lower income tax bracket at the time of withdrawal, many individuals who need the funds immediately will be subject to the same income tax rates in effect at the time of the contribution. In contrast, RESP distributions are not required to be included in net income and are therefore tax free to the extent they represent original contributions to the plan. Further, while RESP earnings are included in the net income of a student, the availability of income tax credits such as the basic personal amount and the tuition credit increase the likelihood that no income tax will be required. Even when income taxes must be paid, the minimum income tax rate of 15% is likely to apply.
- Canada Child Benefit payments are income tested. Because the contributions are deductible, using an RRSP can reduce family income and, in some situations, increase the amount of the Canada Child Benefit payments.

9-131 In comparing TFSAs and RESPs, the following points should be considered:

- The major advantage of RESPs as compared to TFSAs is the availability of CESG and CLB contributions made by the government that can add thousands of dollars to an RESP.
- The major disadvantage of RESPs as compared to TFSAs is the fact that when accumulated earnings are withdrawn they are required to be included in net income and, as a result, increase any income tax payable or reduce any income tax refund. Income taxes may be reduced or avoided altogether if the accumulated earnings are distributed to a qualifying student with sufficient tax credits to eliminate any potential income tax. However, there is the possibility the beneficiary of the plan may not pursue post-secondary education. In this case, the accumulated earnings will not only be included in the net income of subscribers but will be subject to an additional 20% penalty tax.

Registered Disability Savings Plans (RDSPs)—ITA 146.4

The Problem

9-132. Parents of children who are disabled may be faced with a lifelong commitment for care and financial support. Furthermore, the needs of these individuals may extend well beyond the lifetime of the parents. Parents facing this eventuality would like to ensure that the needed care and financial support will be available as long as is necessary.

The Solution

9-133. The government's solution to this problem is legislation (ITA 146.4) that provides for registered disability savings plans (RDSPs). The mechanics of RDSPs are largely identical to those applicable to RESPs. The general features of these plans are as follows:

- Non-deductible contributions are made to a registered trust with the disabled person as beneficiary.
- Income earned from the investment of contributions is tax exempt under Part I. There is no annual contribution limit, however contributions over the lifetime of the disabled individual are limited to $200,000.
- The government will supplement contributions to these plans through Canada Disability Savings Grants and Canada Disability Savings Bonds in a manner similar to CESGs and CLBs.
- Disability assistance payments are made from the plan to the disabled individual. These payments will be divided between a tax-exempt amount that reflects the contributions made to the plans and an amount required to be included in net income that reflects distributions of accumulated earnings. The mechanics are similar to the separation of annuity payments into income and capital components, as discussed in Paragraph 9-90.

9-134. There are many additional rules related to RDSPs, some of them quite complex. Because of this complexity, as well as the fact that these plans are not as widely used as other registered plans, detailed coverage of RDSPs is not included in this text. Further information can be found in the CRA guide "Registered Disability Savings Plans" (RC4460).

Non-Arm's-Length Transactions

Introduction

The Problem

9-135. When property is sold in a transaction between two persons there is an assumption that the price reflects "fair market value" (FMV). FMV is considered essential to properly measure profits or gains to determine any net income tax impact. The importance of this expression is illustrated by its use in 208 provisions of the ITA, 44 times in the ITRs (regulations), and referenced in over 2,500 court decisions.

9-136. FMV is not defined in the ITA. It was first defined by the courts in cases going back more than 50 years. The definition adopted by the courts for ITA purposes and accepted by the CRA (see paragraph 3(a) of IC89-3 "Policy Statement on Equity Valuations") is as follows:

> **Fair Market Value (FMV)** Fair market value is the highest price, expressed in terms of money or money's worth, obtainable in an open and unrestricted market between knowledgeable, informed and prudent parties acting at arm's length, neither party being under any compulsion to transact.

9-137. A key feature of FMV is that the parties to a transaction are "acting at arm's length." The legal definition of "arm's length" refers to an agreement made between two parties freely and independently of each other without some special relationship, control, or influence by one of the parties. The purpose is to show that the terms of the transaction are fair and genuine and reflect a transaction price that would have been determined had the two parties been complete strangers solely looking out for their own personal interests.

9-138. One of the most important inherent concerns, in terms of income tax policy, with respect to a transaction price is that it may be susceptible to manipulation with the express purpose of reducing income tax. For example, individuals could sell property to family members at amounts well below FMV or purchase property from family members at amounts well above FMV. Other persons without family connections could collude in transactions to reduce the overall impact of income taxes. This means that determining whether a specific transaction is reflective of arm's-length bargaining and therefore FMV is, at law, a question of fact. The implication is that one would have to examine the surrounding facts and circumstances including any relationship between the parties to determine whether or not the transaction is conducted at arm's length. Considerable time could be spent on investigating such a matter.

9-139. The resolution of these concerns is found throughout the ITA with references to FMV and, more importantly, references to "persons not dealing at arm's length" or variations of those words. Rather than rely on the courts or dictionaries (legal or otherwise) to define "arm's length," the ITA includes its own definition at ITA 251(1), which is discussed in much more detail in Chapter 14 than we will cover in this chapter.

9-140. In general, there are three versions of arm's length in ITA 251(1) that we will briefly summarize as follows:

ITA 251(1)(a)—Related Persons This first provision simply reads that related persons are deemed not to deal with each other at arm's length. ITA 251(2) to (6) define related persons. In general, for individuals this includes family members but not cousins, nieces, nephews, uncles, and aunts. In addition, parents, grandparents, and siblings (brothers and sisters) would not be considered related to the same members of one's spouse or common-law partner's family. The importance of this concept is that the ITA deems these individuals to be non-arm's length. This means that there is no requirement to thoroughly investigate the particulars of a specific transaction to determine whether there is arm's-length bargaining. The only concern is whether a particular price reflects FMV. This related person concept addresses the CRA's concerns over family members manipulating transaction prices.

ITA 251(1)(b)—Personal Trusts This rule generally applies to family trust situations, which are discussed in Chapter 19. The main effect is to treat any transaction between a beneficiary of the trust and the trust, or a person non-arm's length with the beneficiary and the trust as non-arm's length. Therefore, if property were sold by the trust to a beneficiary or a spouse or common-law partner of the beneficiary, it would automatically be considered as a non-arm's-length transaction and therefore subject to much greater scrutiny than would have been the case were the transaction at arm's length.

ITA 251(1)(c) This final rule is referred to as a factual non-arm's-length test. The rule reads that it is a "question of fact" whether persons are dealing with each other at arm's length except where ITA 251(1)(a) or (b) would apply. This rule allows the CRA to challenge transactions between persons who are not related or are not part of a personal trust. The standard approach by the CRA is to examine the nature of the relationship between the parties and the transaction price. If that price appears too high or too low, it will receive additional attention. Common indicators of factual non-arm's length include (1) a common mind setting and dictating the terms of the transaction for both parties (an accommodation), (2) whether the parties are "acting in concert" without true separate interests, and (3) de facto control where one party has effective control or significant influence over the other (e.g., a majority shareholder of a corporation or an adult child whose inheritance is linked to an agreement to follow a parent's direction).

9-141. The remainder of this chapter discusses additional provisions of the ITA, each of which deals with non-arm's-length transactions:

ITA 69—Inadequate Considerations This provision has two main parts. The first deals with the income tax treatment where gifts are made and the second, an anti-avoidance rule, deals with non-arm's-length transactions where the transaction price does not reflect FMV.

ITA 73(1) & (1.01) These provisions establish some interesting income treatment where capital property is transferred between spouses or common-law partners.

ITA 73(3.1) & (4.1) These provisions facilitate the income tax consequences where farming or fishing property is transferred to children.

ITA 13(7)(e) This provision applies an interesting income tax consequence where depreciable property is transferred between non-arm's-length persons. We would clarify that the reference to a "transfer" of property means a disposition of property, which would include a sale of property but is also broad enough to include any other way in which property ownership is changed from one person to another. Remember, however, that in general a change in ownership is not recognized for income tax purposes unless the beneficial ownership has changed.

Inadequate Considerations—ITA 69

The Problem

9-142. In the previous section we discussed both FMV and the concept of arm's length. In our discussion of FMV we noted that it is supposed to reflect the price that would have been reached between parties looking out for their own separate interests, which is generally what the going price would be for the property in question. It is important to recognize, however, that the ITA technically does not initially focus on FMV but rather looks to the proceeds of disposition (POD). This is defined to include a list of meanings, one of which is the sale price of property. That sale price (which should reflect the FMV of the property being sold) establishes the POD and also the tax cost of the property to the purchaser, which is either cost for inventory purposes, capital cost for depreciable property purposes, or the adjusted cost base (ACB) for non-depreciable capital property.

9-143. There is another tax principle that must be considered. This principle is referred to as the "exchange principle," which was established by the Exchequer Court (the predecessor to the Federal Court) in a 1970 decision [70 DTC 6096]. The principle is that when property is sold the POD is equal to the FMV of the property received in exchange, and when property is purchased the cost of that property is equal to the FMV of the consideration given up to acquire that property. While this principle was first developed to deal with non-cash exchanges of property, the principle is consistently applied throughout the ITA and is important in understanding the necessity for ITA 69.

EXAMPLE You purchase property in a non-arm's-length transaction for $700 (cash or property valued at $700). The FMV of the property purchased is $1,200.

ANALYSIS The ITA does not impose FMV on the transaction through any general rule such that you would be considered to have purchased the property for $1,200 and the seller to have received $1,200. Applying the exchange principal, your cost is $700 (the value of what you have given up in exchange) and the POD to the seller is also $700 (the value of the consideration received for the sale of the property). In effect, the exchange principle looks to the FMV of the consideration (i.e., the payment) rather than the FMV of the property being sold.

9-144. Having discussed the exchange principle and its general impact, we can now consider how manipulation of a sale price can lead to income tax savings and the effect of ITA 69 and other arguments on such transactions.

EXAMPLE During 2021, Martin Horst, whose marginal federal income tax rate is 29%, sells investments (non-depreciable capital property) with a FMV of $200,000 to his 25-year-old son for an amount equal to the ACB of $150,000. The son pays for the property by issuing the father a promissory note of $150,000. The son, who has no other source of income in 2021, immediately sells the property for its FMV of $200,000. The son's only tax credit is the basic personal credit of $13,808, which translates into potential federal income tax savings of $2,071 [(15%)($13,808)].

ANALYSIS If Martin had sold the property for its FMV of $200,000, he would have paid federal income taxes of $7,250 [($200,000 - $150,000)(1/2)(29%)] on the taxable capital gain. In contrast, if the $25,000 taxable capital gain was included in his son's net income, the federal income tax would only be $1,679 {[($25,000)(15%)] - $2,071}, a savings of $5,571 ($7,250 - $1,679) at the federal level alone.

9-145. The preceding example illustrates a potential problem with non-arm's-length transactions, and while ITA 69 is specifically designed to address such transactions there must first be a valid disposition of property such that the purchaser acquires the beneficial ownership of property. An individual who has acquired beneficial ownership is generally free to do anything she wants with the property she has purchased, but if she is obliged to sell the property then an argument could be made that she never acquired the property. In the case of Martin Horst and his son, it must be established whether the son actually acquired the property or was just acting on behalf of his father. In that case, the first transaction between the father and son would be ignored since there was no change in beneficial ownership and therefore no disposition for income tax purposes. If the son had used his own resources and purchased the shares for an amount less than the FMV of the shares and sold them months later at his own choosing, then ITA 69 would have applied and affected both the father and the son.

Purpose and General Rules

9-146. The purpose of ITA 69 is to ensure that the FMV of the property disposed of, rather than the FMV of the consideration paid, is reflected in the transaction for income tax purposes. ITA 69 is titled "inadequate consideration" to reflect the fact that ITA 69 generally targets property dispositions where the price paid is less than the FMV of that property. We mentioned that ITA 69 addresses two main situations: (1) donations or gifts of property to anyone where no consideration is received and (2) non-arm's-length transactions where the consideration paid may be less than or greater than the FMV of the property sold (disposed). Consideration means the amounts paid to acquire the property.

9-147. Where property is acquired without any consideration, such as gifts, donations, and inheritances, ITA 69 treats the transaction as a disposition of the property by the owner equal to the FMV of the property and the acquisition of the property by the new owner for the same amount.

> **EXAMPLE** You own a used car and heard that a local charity is accepting used cars to sell at an auction to raise much-needed funds. The car is personal-use property to you and had a cost of $10,000. Its current FMV is $1,500. You donate the car to the charity.
>
> **ANALYSIS** ITA 69 would consider you to have sold the car for $1,500 and the charity to have purchased it for $1,500. While there would be no income tax implications for you on disposing of the car, because the ITA does not recognize capital losses on personal-use property, you would also be considered to have made a $1,500 donation that would entitle you to the charitable donation credit, assuming that the charity was registered.

9-148. The second situation occurs where property is sold in a non-arm's-length transaction for an amount below or above the FMV of the property sold. In this instance ITA 69 acts as an anti-avoidance rule penalizing one of the two parties to the transaction for undertaking a transaction at something other than FMV. We would note, however, that this result can be avoided if it can be demonstrated that genuine efforts were made to determine the FMV and that this fact is supported by what is referred to as a "price adjustment clause," which is discussed in greater detail in Chapter 16. For further information we would direct you to the CRA Folio S4-F3-C1, "Price Adjustment Clauses."

9-149. A summary of the basic rules for donations/gifts and non-arm's-length transactions is outlined in Figure 9-2. The reference to FMV means the value of the property sold or gifted/donated.

Figure 9-2 Non-Arm's-Length Transfers—ITA 69

Transfer Price	Proceeds of Disposition for Transferor	Adjusted Cost Base for Transferee
FMV	FMV	FMV
Above FMV	Actual Proceeds	FMV
Below FMV	FMV	Actual Proceeds
Nil (Gift)	FMV	FMV

Example

9-150. In order to illustrate the rules presented in Figure 9-2, assume that John Brown owns capital property with an ACB of $50,000 and a FMV of $75,000. If the property is sold for consideration equal to its FMV of $75,000, the result will be a capital gain of $25,000 [POD $75,000 - ACB $50,000] for John Brown and an ACB for the new owner of $75,000. This would be the result whether the transaction was arm's length or not.

9-151. If the property is sold to a non-arm's-length person, and the consideration provided is not equal to its FMV, ITA 69 will apply. The following three cases illustrate the various possible outcomes. In each case, we will assume the sale is to John Brown's adult brother, Sam Brown. Siblings (brothers and sisters) are related persons and therefore are deemed not to deal with each other at arm's length.

Case A—Transfer at $100,000 (above FMV) In this case, there is no special rule for the transferor (seller). Given this, the POD to John Brown will be equal to the actual POD of $100,000 (equal to the FMV of consideration received) resulting in a capital gain of $50,000 (POD $100,000 - ACB $50,000). The cost and therefore the ACB to Sam Brown would be $100,000 (equal to the FMV of what he gave up to acquire the property). ITA 69(1)(a) will apply to a purchaser who pays an amount greater than the FMV of the property acquired. The result is that his cost and ACB will be only $75,000. The additional $25,000 paid above the FMV of the property acquired is not recognized as part of the cost to him. This represents the anti-avoidance punitive one-sided aspect of ITA 69. The one-sided aspect refers to the fact that in this case John's results remain unchanged and only Sam's is altered.

If the property subsequently increased in value to $100,000, a sale of the property for that amount would result in a capital gain of $25,000 (POD $100,000 - ACB $75,000) even though it appears Sam is only recovering his actual cost. The effect is that the difference between $100,000 and $75,000 would have been treated as a capital gain to both John and Sam, effectively being subject to tax twice for the same amount. While some would call this double taxation, technically double taxation only exists if the same person would include the same amount in income both times. Note that there are many safeguards within the ITA to avoid this result, with ITA 248(28) being the main rule.

Case B—Transfer at $60,000 (below FMV) If the sale took place at a price of $60,000 the effect of the exchange principle is that John would have POD of $60,000 and Sam's cost and ACB would also be $60,000. ITA 69(1)(b), however, applies a one-sided impact by deeming John Brown to have received POD equal to the FMV of $75,000. Since Sam only gave up $60,000 to acquire the property that will be his cost and ACB, which is not changed by ITA 69. If Sam were to immediately sell the property for $75,000 he would realize a capital gain of $15,000 [POD $75,000 - ACB $60,000]. Again the difference between $60,000 and $75,000 would have been subject to income tax to both John and Sam. This result represents the punitive side of ITA 69.

Case C—Gift, Bequest, or Inheritance In this case, if John were to gift the property to Sam the exchange principle would mean that John's POD would be nil, resulting in a capital loss, and Sam's cost and ACB would be nil. ITA 69 changes that outcome by treating the transaction to both parties as if FMV of $75,000 were paid. Specifically, ITA 69(1)(b) would deem John to have received POD of $75,000, and ITA 69(1)(c) would deem Sam to have acquired the property at a cost of $75,000, which becomes the ACB.

9-152. Given the punitive nature of ITA 69, the general rule for non-arm's-length dispositions is to either sell the property for its FMV or gift the property. When property is sold for some consideration it is important to make a genuine attempt to determine the FMV of the property, preferably by engaging a valuator experienced in valuing the type of property being sold and writing up an agreement with a valid price adjustment clause. Where the CRA pursues these types of transactions, it is not unusual for taxpayers to argue that the disposition was a gift, but it is near impossible to retroactively create a gift, which is based on intention at a moment in time.

ITA 69 Override

9-153. The opening words of ITA 69 are "except as expressly otherwise provided in this Act." This means that if another provision in the ITA (not just Part I) permits POD that is different than the FMV of the property in question, then ITA 69 is considered to be overridden by that other rule. Examples of such situations that are discussed later in this chapter are certain dispositions of property to a spouse covered in ITA 73(1) and the transfers of farm property to a child covered in ITA 73(3.1). Both of those rules allow POD to be less than FMV.

Exercise 9-8

Subject: Inadequate Consideration—Non-Depreciable Capital Property

Mr. Carl Lipky owns a piece of land with an ACB of $100,000 and a FMV of $75,000. He sells the land to his brother for $95,000, who immediately sells it for $75,000. Determine the income tax consequences to both Mr. Lipky and his brother.

Solutions to Exercises are available in the Study Guide.

We suggest you complete SSP 9-7 at this point.

Inter Vivos Transfers to a Spouse—ITA 73(1) & (1.01)

General Rules for Capital Property

9-154. An inter vivos transfer refers to a transfer of property during an individual's lifetime. This is different than what is referred to as a testamentary transfer, which means a transfer of property after an individual has died, which is accomplished through one's estate or will. ITA 73(1) and 73(1.01) together provide for the income tax treatment where capital property of a living individual is transferred for the benefit of a spouse, former spouse, common-law partner, or former common-law partner. The specific qualifying transfers are:

- a transfer to the individual's spouse or common-law partner;
- a transfer to the individual's former spouse or former common-law partner in settlement of rights arising out of their marriage or common-law partnership; and
- a transfer to a trust for which the individual's spouse or common-law partner is the income beneficiary. This type of trust has traditionally been referred to as a spousal trust. The conditions related to this concept are discussed in Chapter 19.

9-155. Where an inter vivos transfer of capital property is a "qualifying transfer" ITA 73(1) sets the POD to the transferor equal to the cost, capital cost, and ACB to the transferor, which becomes the cost, capital cost, and ACB to the transferee. This type of transaction is generically referred to as a rollover because the transferee inherits the tax costs of the transferor. The purpose is to allow a change of ownership without any amounts being added to the net income of the transferor.

9-156. You may recall from previous chapters that there are two types of capital property: (1) depreciable property and (2) non-depreciable capital property. When capital property is transferred in a qualifying inter vivos transfer, ITA 73(1) deems the POD to be as follows for each type of capital property:

Proceeds—Non-Depreciable The POD will be deemed to be equal to the ACB of the property transferred.

Proceeds—Depreciable The POD will be deemed to be the UCC of the class or, if there are other properties in the class, an appropriate portion of the class based on relative FMV (e.g., if the property represents 42% of the FMV of all property remaining in the class, then the POD will equal 42% of the UCC at the time immediately before the transfer).

9-157. ITA 73(1) deems the tax costs of to the transferee to be as follows:

Tax Cost—Non-Depreciable The cost to the transferee will be deemed to be equal to the deemed POD to the transferor, which was the ACB of the property. The result is that both the cost and the ACB will be the same to the transferee.

Tax Cost—Depreciable The cost to the transferee is deemed to be the UCC or proportionate UCC (the "UCC") of the transferor. ITA 73(2) adds a rule that deems the transferee's capital cost to equal the capital cost of the transferor. The difference between the capital cost and the UCC is deemed to be CCA that was previously claimed. As mentioned, the purpose is to transfer the tax attributes of a property from the transferor to the transferee. ITA 73(2) helps complete the tax attribute transfer for depreciable property so that the UCC amounts will remain the same.

9-158. In summary, the rules of ITA 73(1), (1.01), and (2) work together to ensure that the transferor is not required to include any amount in net income as a result of the transfer and that the transferee simply inherits the tax costs of the transferor. This is illustrated by the following example.

EXAMPLE Marg Cardiff gifts land with an ACB of $100,000 and a FMV of $250,000 to her spouse, Bernie. She also gives all of her class 10 depreciable property to Bernie. The capital cost of the class 10 property is $225,000, the FMV $310,000, and the UCC $195,000.

ANALYSIS Marg would be deemed to have received POD of $100,000 for the land and POD of $195,000 for the class 10 property. As a result there will be no income tax consequences of the transfer to her.

For Bernie, he would be deemed to have acquired the land at a cost of $100,000, which will also be his ACB. Bernie will be considered to have acquired the class 10 property for $195,000. For CCA and UCC purposes, Bernie's capital cost of the property is deemed to be $225,000. He is also deemed to have previously claimed CCA of $30,000 such that the UCC is $195,000. This means that if Bernie sold all of the transferred properties for their combined FMV of $560,000 ($250,000 + $310,000), there would be a capital gain of $150,000 ($250,000 - $100,000) on the land, a capital gain of $85,000 ($310,000 - $225,000) on the class 10 property, as well as recapture of CCA of $30,000 (UCC $195,000 - $225,000 [lesser of capital cost of $225,000 and the POD of $310,000]). Note that these are the same income tax consequences that would have occurred if Marg had sold all of these properties for their FMV. Note: Technically the ACB of the class 10 property is $195,000, suggesting that the capital gain should have been $115,000 [POD $310,000 - ACB $195,000], or $30,000 higher. A rule in ITA 39(1), however, reduces that capital gain of $115,000 to $85,000 since the $30,000 difference would have been included in income elsewhere as recapture. To simplify the results we have shown the ACB here as $225,000, although technically this is not accurate.

Electing out of the Spousal Rollover

9-159. In the previous paragraphs the word "rollover" was used to refer to a type of transaction that can be undertaken at amounts less than FMV. There are dozens of different types of rollovers scattered throughout the ITA. A common feature of these rollovers is they are often automatic. This means that the rollover automatically applies whether you want it to or not. On occasion rollover treatment may require a formal election, providing a choice. Another less common feature is that a rollover may allow some flexibility by permitting the parties to a transaction to select an amount between a range of values. ITA 85 is a classic example of this latter feature (discussed in detail in Chapter 16).

9-160. The rollover in ITA 73(1) has some of these rollover features. For instance, an inter vivos transaction that is a qualifying transfer results in an automatic application of the rollover. However, the rule provides for an elective option by the transferor that if chosen means that

ITA 73(1) does not apply. There is no flexibility built into the election. Once chosen it is an all or nothing rule that provides for one of two treatments: (1) a complete rollover or (2) a FMV disposition as a result of ITA 69(1). A joint election is not required, and while the election is required to be filed with the income tax return for the year in which the property transfer takes place, there are provisions that permit an individual to administratively request a late filed election (ITR 600).

9-161. An election to treat the disposition at FMV has income tax consequences to the transferor that would include capital gains and recapture added to net income, but if the transferor has net capital losses or non-capital losses available there may be no or little income tax as a result of reductions in taxable income. Choosing a FMV disposition instead of rollover treatment can also be important when there are income attribution concerns, a topic that will be discussed later in this chapter. The CRA acknowledges that there is no form for making the election and will assume that an election has been made where the transferor reports the transaction as having taken place at FMV.

> **EXAMPLE—Continued** In the example from Paragraph 9-158, Marg could have elected on the land by reporting the disposition at the FMV of $250,000 and the $150,000 capital gain. In this case, the ACB to Bernie would be $250,000 as a result of ITA 69(1)(c).

Exercise 9-9

Subject: Inter Vivos Transfer of Non-Depreciable Capital Property to a Spouse

Aaron Schwartz owns land with an ACB of $225,000 and a FMV of $300,000. He gifts this land to his spouse. Indicate the income tax consequences to Mr. Schwartz and the ACB of the property to his spouse after the gift transaction assuming Mr. Schwartz does not elect to avoid the rollover of ITA 73(1). How would your answer change if Mr. Schwartz does elect to avoid the ITA 73(1) rollover?

Solutions to Exercises are available in the Study Guide.

Non-Arm's-Length Transfers of Depreciable Property—ITA 13(7)(e)

9-162. In this chapter (beginning at Paragraph 9-136) we discussed the tax policy concerns of non-arm's-length transactions noting a few rules designed to specifically target those transactions. ITA 69 was introduced to ensure that a FMV concept applied to both gifting and certain other transactions where there was no consideration and to non-arm's-length transactions where the sales price did not reflect the FMV of property sold. We saw in ITA 73(1) that the ITA allows capital property ownership to be shifted between spouses and common-law partners without income tax consequences, recognizing that oftentimes the end result was that the property remained within the family.

9-163. Another concern involves dispositions of depreciable property between non-arm's-length persons that can produce unfair results. To demonstrate the concern, assume that you and a family member each carry on your own business. You own depreciable property that cost $100,000 and have claimed CCA of $10,000 over the years. The FMV of the property is now $160,000. You sell the property to the family member for $160,000 and report $10,000 of recapture [UCC $90,000 - $100,000 (lesser of POD $160,000 and capital cost of $100,000)] and a taxable capital gain of $30,000 (half of the difference between the POD of $160,000 and the ACB of $100,000). One month later your family member sells the property back to you for $160,000. Under normal rules your capital cost would be $160,000 and you would be able to claim CCA on that amount. In other words, you would have $60,000 of additional cost upon which to claim CCA yet you would only have included $30,000 of that difference in your net income as a taxable capital gain.

9-164. ITA 13(7)(e) is designed to address this type of situation by limiting the increase to the capital cost in non-arm's-length transactions to the amount of the difference that was actually included in net income. In this case the capital cost for CCA purposes would only be $130,000 [$100,000 original cost plus half of the increase in value of $60,000]. This is the same concept that was discussed in Chapter 5 with the change-in-use rules, which is a variation of a non-arm's-length transaction since the deemed seller and buyer are the same person.

TIP: If there is a sale of depreciable property in a non-arm's-length transaction that results in a capital gain to the seller/transferor, then ITA 13(7)(e) will apply to the purchaser/transferee. We have called this "Situation 1." Second, if in a non-arm's-length sale of depreciable property the FMV is less than the capital cost of the seller/transferor, ITA 13(7)(e) will apply to cause the purchaser/transferee to inherit the tax characteristics of the depreciable property. We call this "Situation 2."

Situation 1—FMV Exceeds the Transferor's Capital Cost

9-165. ITA 13(7)(e) applies to two situations, one where the FMV of the depreciable property has increased beyond its capital cost and the second where the FMV has decreased below its capital cost. The effect of this first situation, which was discussed in the previous paragraph, is illustrated in the following example:

EXAMPLE Patrick Tessier owns depreciable property with a FMV of $150,000, a capital cost of $110,000, and a UCC of $85,000. It is the only property in the class. Patrick sells the property to his daughter, Francine, for its FMV of $150,000.

ANALYSIS As a result of the disposition, Patrick will have recapture of $25,000 [UCC $85,000 - $110,000 (the lesser of POD of $150,000 and capital cost of $110,000)] and a capital gain of $40,000 (POD $150,000 - ACB $110,000). The taxable capital gain to include in net income will be $20,000 [(50%)($40,000)], resulting in a total increase in net income of $45,000 [$25,000 recapture + $20,000 taxable capital gain].

If the capital cost to Francine were $150,000, she would be able to claim CCA on that full amount. This means that, by increasing Patrick's net income by $45,000, the future deductions available to Francine would have increased by $65,000 ($150,000 - $85,000). Patrick and Francine would clearly have an incentive to make the transfer at this price.

Solution to Situation 1

9-166. You can see, based on our previous discussion, that the capital cost to Francine in this non-arm's-length transaction should only be $130,000 instead of $150,000. ITA 13(7)(e) reaches this result by deeming Francine's capital cost to be equal to

A + [(1/2)(B - A)], where

A = the transferor's capital cost
B = the transferee's capital cost

ITA 13(7)(e) does not apply where a disposition of depreciable property is the result of a death.

ANALYSIS—Continued Applying this rule to the example in Paragraph 9-165, Francine's deemed capital cost and UCC balance would be $130,000 [$110,000 + (1/2) ($150,000 - $110,000)]. As a result, the transfer has resulted in an increase in Francine's UCC of $45,000 ($130,000 - 85,000), an amount equal to the increase in Patrick's net income as a result of the disposition.

It is important to note that the deemed capital cost of $130,000 is only used for CCA and UCC purposes. The capital cost and therefore ACB for capital gains purposes would be based on the actual POD of $150,000. Assuming Francine later sold the property for $160,000 without taking any CCA, the taxable capital gain would be $5,000 [(1/2) ($160,000 - $150,000)] and there would be no recapture.

UCC balance at time of sale		$130,000
Deduct lesser of:		
• Deemed capital cost for CCA purposes = $130,000		
• Proceeds of disposition = $160,000		(130,000)
Recapture or terminal loss		Nil

Situation 2—FMV Less Than the Transferor's Capital Cost

9-167. A similar problem arises when a non-arm's-length transaction occurs where FMV is less than the transferor's capital cost.

EXAMPLE Carole Dupre owns depreciable property with a FMV of $200,000, a capital cost of $325,000, and UCC of $150,000. It is the only property in the class. She sells the property to her son, Marcel, for the FMV of $200,000.

ANALYSIS As a result of this transaction, the only income tax consequence to Carole would be recapture of $50,000 [UCC $150,000 - $200,000 (the lesser of POD $200,000 and capital cost $325,000)].

Without ITA 13(7)(e) the capital cost and UCC to Marcel would be the purchase price of $200,000. The problem with this outcome can be seen if the property subsequently increases in value. Assume, for example, that Marcel had never claimed CCA and sold the property in an arm's-length transaction a year later for $250,000. He would realize a taxable capital gain of $25,000 [(50%)(POD $250,000 - ACB $200,000)]. If, however, Carole had kept the property and sold it for $250,000, the $50,000 difference would have been included in her net income as recapture.

The Solution to Situation 2

9-168. In this situation ITA 13(7)(e) applies to require the non-arm's-length purchaser/transferee to inherit the CCA/UCC characteristics of the non-arm's-length seller/transferor. The result is that the transferor's capital cost becomes the capital cost to the transferee and the difference between that capital cost and the purchase price is deemed to be CCA claimed by the transferee. This ensures that if the transferee subsequently sells the property, the recapture treatment will be identical to that of the transferor had the property not been sold in a non-arm's-length transaction.

ANALYSIS—Continued The result of the application of ITA 13(7)(e) to Marcel is that his capital cost is deemed to equal the capital cost of Carole of $325,000. The difference between $325,000 and the purchase price of $200,000 is deemed to be CCA previously claimed by Marcel of $125,000. As a result, the UCC of the property is $200,000 [deemed capital cost of $325,000 - deemed CCA $125,000]. When Marcel sells the property in an arm's-length transaction for $250,000, the $50,000 difference will be $50,000 of recapture [UCC $200,000 - $250,000 (lesser of POD $250,000 and deemed capital cost of $325,000)] instead of a $50,000 capital gain, only 50% of which is taxable.

Exercise 9-10

Subject: Inter Vivos Transfer of Depreciable Property to a Spouse

During the current year, Mary Sharp transferred depreciable property to her spouse. The property had a FMV of $225,000, a capital cost of $175,000, and UCC of $110,000. It is the only property in its class. In return for the property, she received $225,000 in cash. Describe the income tax consequences to Mary Sharp and her spouse, assuming that she does not elect to avoid the rollover of ITA 73(1). How would your answer change if she does elect to avoid the rollover?

Exercise 9-11

Subject: Inter Vivos Transfer of Depreciable Property to a Parent

Ms. Jennifer Lee owns depreciable property she uses in a business that she carries on as a sole proprietor. The capital cost of the property is $53,000 and its FMV is $40,000. It is the only property in the class. The UCC balance is $37,200. Ms. Lee sells the property to her father for its FMV of $40,000. During the same year, prior to deducting any CCA, the father resells the property for $44,000. Determine the income tax consequences to Ms. Lee and her father as a result of these transactions.

Solutions to Exercises are available in the Study Guide.

We suggest you complete SSP 9-8 at this point.

Inter Vivos Transfer of Farm or Fishing Property to a Child

9-169. ITA 73(3.1) and (4.1) provide rollover treatment for transfers of farm or fishing property, shares of family farm or fishing corporations, or interests in family farm or fishing partnerships to children. The purpose of this rollover is to allow an intergenerational transfer of farm and fishing businesses to family members who will carry on the business.

9-170. For the purposes of this rollover a child is defined to mean children and their spouses, grandchildren, great grandchildren, and any other person who, prior to reaching the age of 19, was dependent on an individual and under her custody or control. To qualify, the child must be a resident of Canada at the time of the transfer. In addition, the property must have been used in a farming or fishing business carried on by the individual, the individual's spouse, or any of her children.

9-171. These provisions are rollovers, meaning that family members are entitled to pass down farm and fishing property to children without incurring any income tax consequences. If the parents, for example, gift the property to children then the POD to the parents will be the tax costs of the properties (ACB for non-depreciable capital property and UCC or proportional UCC [based on relative capital cost instead of FMV] for depreciable property). The child's tax cost of the properties acquired begins with the POD to the parents. Adjustments are added to ensure that the child retains the characteristics of any depreciable property such as capital cost and UCC through a deemed CCA identical to that discussed for ITA 73(2).

9-172. If parents or others do not wish to gift the properties to children the option to sell the properties remains available with an added incentive that the parents can discount the price to something less than FMV. Normally the provisions of ITA 69 would apply in these situations, since a price is paid between non-arm's-length persons at less than FMV, but a special rule is added to make certain that ITA 69(1) can never apply to these types of rollovers.

9-173. If the properties are not gifted, the transfer is deemed to have taken place at the actual POD unless it falls outside of acceptable limits as follows:

For **depreciable property**, the lower limit is the property's UCC, while the upper limit is the FMV. The transferee would retain the original capital cost to the transferor with the difference being treated as deemed CCA.

For **non-depreciable capital property**, which includes farm land and shares in a farm or fishing corporation, the lower limit is the ACB while the upper limit is the FMV.

9-174. The following example will help illustrate the lower and upper limits.

EXAMPLE Tim Johnson's farm consists of land with an ACB of $200,000 and a FMV of $350,000, and depreciable property with a UCC of $400,000, a capital cost of $550,000, and a FMV of $675,000. It is transferred to Tim's son.

ANALYSIS—Land If the transfer is for POD below $200,000 (this includes gifts), the deemed POD and ACB to the child would be $200,000. If the transfer is for an amount in excess of $350,000, the deemed POD and ACB to the child would be limited to $350,000. For transfers between $200,000 and $350,000, which would be the case where the child actually paid for the property, the actual POD would be used.

ANALYSIS—Depreciable Property For transfers below the UCC of $400,000 (including gifts), the deemed POD and cost to the child would be $400,000. Correspondingly, for transfers above $675,000, the deemed POD and capital cost to the child would be $675,000. For transfers between $400,000 and $675,000, the actual POD would be used. The child would inherit the capital cost and UCC characteristics of the depreciable property. Deemed capital cost would be $550,000, deemed CCA would be $150,000, and the resulting CCA would be $400,000.

Exercise 9-12

Subject: Inter Vivos Transfer of Farm Property to a Child

Thomas Nobel owns farm property consisting of land with an ACB of $250,000 and a FMV of $325,000, along with a barn with a UCC of $85,000, a capital cost of $115,000, and a FMV of $101,000. The property is transferred to his 40-year-old daughter in return for a payment of $280,000 for the land. No payment is made for the barn. Describe the income tax consequences of this transfer for both Mr. Nobel and his daughter.

Solutions to Exercises are available in the Study Guide.

Death of an Individual Taxpayer

General Rules

9-175. There are many special rules that may apply when an individual dies. This chapter covers the rules related to capital property. Other material on the death of a taxpayer can be found in the Chapter 11 Appendix titled "Returns for Deceased Taxpayers."

9-176. ITA 70(5) provides the following general rules with respect to capital property owned by an individual at the time of death:

Non-Depreciable Capital Property In general, the deceased individual is deemed to have disposed of such property immediately prior to death for POD that are deemed to be the FMV at that time. The person acquiring the property is deemed to have acquired it for the same FMV. The person acquiring the property is frequently the estate of the individual, which is treated as a trust for income tax purposes.

Depreciable Property The same general rules apply for depreciable property. The deceased individual is deemed to have disposed of such property immediately prior to death for POD equal to the FMV at that time. The person acquiring the property (again frequently the estate of the deceased) is deemed to acquire the property at the same FMV. When the FMV is less than the capital cost of the property to the deceased individual, the person acquiring the property is deemed to have the same capital cost as the deceased individual with the difference treated as deemed CCA.

9-177. A simple example will serve to illustrate the rules for depreciable property.

EXAMPLE Eric Nadon dies, leaving a depreciable property to his son that has a capital cost of $100,000, a FMV of $60,000, and a UCC of $50,000.

ANALYSIS Under ITA 70(5), the transfer will take place at the FMV of $60,000. This means that in Mr. Nadon's final income tax return, recaptured CCA of $10,000 [(UCC $50,000 - POD $60,000)(the lesser of POD of $60,000 and capital cost of $100,000)] will be included. While the son's cost and UCC will be the same $60,000, the capital cost of the property will remain at Mr. Nadon's original capital cost of $100,000 with the difference of $40,000 deemed as previously claimed CCA. This means that, if the property is later sold for an amount between $60,000 and $100,000, the resulting difference will be treated as recaptured CCA rather than as a capital gain. Even though this is a non-arm's-length disposition of depreciable property at FMV, the rule in ITA 13(7)(e) that we previously discussed would not apply since the disposition occurs as a result of the death of an individual.

9-178. These deemed FMV disposition rules apply to all capital property irrespective of whether it is personal-use property including listed personal property. The previous example assumed that the property disposed of on death was depreciable property to the deceased, meaning that it would have had to have been used to either earn income from property or from the carrying on of a business.

Rollover to a Spouse, a Common-Law Partner, or a Spousal Trust

9-179. ITA 70(6) provides an exception to the general rules contained in ITA 70(5) in situations where the transfer is to a spouse, a common-law partner, or a testamentary spousal or common-law partner trust. This is a rollover provision similar to others we have discussed that allows the POD to be equal to ACB for non-depreciable capital property and UCC for depreciable property. Note that technically ITA 70(6) uses the expression "cost amount" (defined in ITA 248(1)) to determine the UCC. Where there is more than one property in the same class, the cost amount is equal to the proportionate UCC based on relative capital cost. You will require this information for purposes of completing Exercise 9-13.

9-180. This means that the transfer of ownership on death does not result in any income tax consequences to the deceased and that the surviving spouse or common-law partner (or trust established) will inherit the same tax costs and characteristics as those of the deceased, including retaining the same capital cost and UCC through deemed CCA. This has the effect of deferring any income tax consequences until the surviving spouse or common-law partner disposes of the property or dies.

9-181. We previously saw that inter vivos transfers of capital property between spouses and common-law partners were automatically eligible for rollover treatment but that the transferor could elect to avoid the the rollover, in which case dispositions would occur at FMV. ITA 70(6.2) provides legal representatives of the deceased with the same ability, allowing an election to be filed in the deceased individual's final income tax return. The election provides a choice as to which properties will benefit from the rollover and which will take place at FMV. There are many reasons why a representative may choose to cause income to be realized as the result of a disposition at FMV. Reasons include taking advantage of charitable donations, medical expenses, unused loss carry forwards, and, in the case of qualified farm property, qualified fishing property, or the shares of a qualified small business corporation, an unused lifetime capital gains deduction. These topics are discussed in Chapter 11. As was the case with electing to avoid the ITA 73 (1) rollover, electing FMV treatment through ITA 70(6.2) does not require a form. The CRA considers the election to have been made when select property is shown on the final income tax return as having been disposed of at FMV.

9-182. To qualify as a spousal or common-law partner testamentary trust and to therefore benefit from the rollover treatment, the surviving spouse or common-law partner must be entitled to receive all of the income of the trust that arises before the death of the surviving spouse or common-law partner. In addition, no person other than the spouse or common-law partner may receive the use of any of the income or capital of the trust prior to the death of the spouse or common-law partner. Failure to meet these conditions will cause all dispositions of capital property that are transferred to the trust on death to be deemed to have been disposed of at FMV. Detailed coverage of spousal and common-law partner testamentary trusts can be found in Chapter 19.

Exercise 9-13

Subject: Transfers on Death

Ms. Cheryl Lardner owned two trucks that were used in a business she carried on as a sole proprietor. She died in July 2021. Under the terms of her will, truck A will be given to her husband, Michel, and truck B to her daughter, Melinda. Each of the trucks cost $42,000 and had a FMV at the time of her death of $33,000. The UCC balance for the class that contained the two trucks was $51,000. What are the income tax consequences resulting from Ms. Lardner's death with respect to these two trucks? Your answer should include the capital cost and the UCC of the trucks to Michel and Melinda.

Solutions to Exercises are available in the Study Guide.

Transfers of Farm or Fishing Property to a Child at Death

9-183. Rollover treatment of capital property is generally restricted to transfers between spouses, common-law partners, and trusts created exclusively for them. In general, capital property transfers to others are not eligible for rollover treatment, and as a result such transactions take place at FMV. The exception is where farm or fishing property is transferred to a child as a means of preserving the integrity of farming and fishing businesses to the next generation of a family. Inter vivos transfers of farm or fishing property to a child were discussed starting at Paragraph 9-169, explaining the mechanics of the rollover treatment. This same treatment applies to transfers of farming and fishing property to a child as a consequence of an individual's death. The income tax rules are found in ITA 70(9) through ITA 70(9.31). Since the income tax treatment is virtually identical to that where there are inter vivos transfers, this will not be discussed further.

We suggest you complete SSP 9-9 at this point.

Income Attribution

Overview

9-184. In Chapter 1 we discussed the benefits of splitting or sharing income with family members with the objective of saving income tax for the family as a whole. In Ontario, for example, the highest combined income tax rate for individuals is 53.5%, meaning that an additional $10,000 of income to an individual subject to that rate would require payment of $5,350 in federal and provincial income tax leaving $4,650 of after-tax income. If that individual could redirect that income to a family member such as a spouse, common-law partner, or child with no or little income, the additional income tax could be avoided altogether. The income tax savings in such a case are significant.

9-185. The financial incentive to split income is very attractive, but one must be aware that there are few legitimate acceptable opportunities to split income. An example of acceptable planning would include employing a family member in a family business, although one would have to be aware of the reasonableness rule of ITA 67 and make certain that the remuneration paid as salary was consistent with the level of services provided.

9-186. Other examples of acceptable income splitting were discussed in this chapter, including pension splitting (both in the ITA and CPP legislation) and making contributions to RRSPs and TFSAs for spouses or common-law partners. Contributions to RESPs also contain an element of income splitting, but in general income splitting is not considered acceptable. The very few acceptable opportunities that do exist only do so because other competing tax policy priorities, such as savings and retirement, are considered more important to the government.

9-187. How do we know what is acceptable and what is not? The line is drawn based on a number of rules added to the ITA that are anti-avoidance in nature. The anti-avoidance rules related to income splitting are referred to as attribution rules. They cover situations where investment-type property owned by one individual is transferred (e.g., gifted) to another closely connected individual such as certain family members where income splitting is likely to occur. The rules target that income and redirect it back to the individual responsible for transferring the investments in the first place. These specific rules will be referred to in this text simply as the "attribution rules."

9-188. Other rules look to certain types of passive income, such as dividends, to determine if they can be traced to an underlying source of income, such as a business, where a close family member is involved. This type of income splitting is much more indirect than the attribution rules. The rules operate by applying the highest federal income tax rate of 33% to that income (referred to as "split income") even though the recipient is not otherwise in that income tax bracket. If the recipient is a child is under a certain age, additional rules were added to allow the CRA to collect the income tax from parents and others if the child is unable to pay. This text refers to these rules by their common name used among tax practitioners and academics as the "TOSI" rules. The acronym TOSI means "tax on split income."

9-189. In summary, this chapter takes a closer look into both of the attribution rules and the TOSI. It is possible for both sets of income-splitting rules to apply, but there is an ordering rule found in ITA 74.5(13) that says that the attribution rules do not apply to any amount that is subject to the TOSI. In other words, the TOSI take precedence. The legislation for both sets of rules can be quite complex at times, including rules for indirect attribution using corporations and trusts as well as back-to-back loan and guarantee arrangements initially conceived by planners in an attempt to avoid attribution. This chapter will not cover every aspect of these rules but rather will provide an awareness and a practical understanding in order to identify general circumstances where these rules may apply.

Basic Rules—ITA 74.1(1) & (2)

The Attribution Rules

9-190. The income attribution rules are applicable to situations where an individual has transferred property to

- a spouse or common-law partner [ITA 74.1(1)]; or
- an individual who is under the age of 18 and who either does not deal with the individual at arm's length or is the niece or nephew of the individual [ITA 74.1(2)].

9-191. ITA 74.1(2) applies where property is transferred to a non-arm's-length individual who is under the age of 18 at the time the property is transferred or to a niece or nephew who is under the age of 18 at the time of the transfer. Paragraph 9-141 defined "non-arm's length," noting that "related persons" are automatically considered to be non-arm's length. This includes children, grandchildren, great grandchildren, adopted children, and children of one's spouse or common-law partner. Certain individuals would not be related persons, such as uncles, aunts, nieces, and nephews, but ITA 74.1(2) specifically recognizes property transfers by uncles and aunts to nieces or nephews.

9-192. ITA 74.1(1) and (2) together require than an individual transfers property to another individual (spouse, common-law partner, child, niece, or nephew) such that the beneficial ownership of the property has changed. This means that any income or loss from that property that legally belongs to the new owner is deemed, for income tax purposes, to be the income or loss of the individual who transferred the property. In practice this is referred to as attributing the income back to the transferor or original owner.

Applicable to Property Income and Capital Gains

9-193. The attribution rules apply to two types of income. The first type would be property income or loss, such as interest, dividends, rents, and royalties. This type of income may be attributed back to the transferor without regard to whether the transferee is a spouse, common-law partner, a niece or nephew, or a related individual under the age of 18.

9-194. The second type of income that attribution rules apply to is capital gains and capital losses resulting from a disposition of the transferred property. Whether or not this type of income is subject to the attribution rules depends on the relationship of the transferee to the transferor:

> **Transfers to a Spouse or Common-Law Partner** When property is transferred to a spouse or common-law partner, the automatic application of the ITA 73(1) rollover means that the property is transferred at the transferor's tax cost, with no income tax consequences at the time of the transfer. The ACB of non-depreciable capital property to the transferee spouse or common-law partner will be the ACB and UCC for depreciable property. Given this, it seems logical that all or part of a capital gain or capital loss from a subsequent sale by the spouse or common-law partner represents unrealized capital gains and capital losses of the transferor and should be attributed back to the transferor. ITA 74.2 applies this approach without any attempt to separate that part of a capital gain or capital loss between the ownership by the transferor and the transferee.

> **Transfers to a Niece, Nephew or Related Minor (All under 18)—General Rule** There is no general rollover provision for transfer of property to a related minor as there is for a spouse or common-law partner. This means that when property is transferred to such an individual the transfer will occur at the FMV of the transferred property. The result is that the transferor recognizes any capital gains or capital losses at that time. Any subsequent capital gain or capital loss, therefore cannot be considered as relating to the period of ownership by the transferor. As a result, any such capital gains and capital losses are not attributed back to the transferor but are included in the net income of the transferee minor.

> **Transfers to a Minor Child—Farming or Fishing Property** As discussed in this chapter at Paragraph 9-170, ITA 73(3.1) and ITA 73(4.1) provide for a transfer of farm or fishing property to a child on a rollover basis at the transferor's tax cost. It is not surprising that when this rollover provision is used there is attribution of capital gains and capital losses arising on a subsequent disposition by the child. More specifically, ITA 75.1 indicates that when a farm or fishing property has been transferred to a child on a rollover basis and the child disposes of that property prior to reaching the age of 18 years, all capital gains and capital losses, both those existing at the time of transfer and those accruing subsequently, are attributed back to the transferor and included in the net income of the transferor and not the child.

Not Applicable after Death of Transferor

9-195. Income attribution ceases with the death of the transferor. For example, if a parent made an inter vivos transfer to a minor child, income on the transferred property would be attributed back to the transferor until the minor reached the age of 18. However, if the transferor died before the minor turned 18, attribution of this income would cease on the date of death.

Not Applicable to Business Income

9-196. Business income is not subject to the attribution rules. If property is transferred to a spouse, common-law partner, or related minor and used in the carrying on of a business, the business income will be included in the net income of the transferee and would not be attributed back to the transferor. This is understandable given that carrying on a business requires time, attention, and labour on the part of the transferee, and as a result that income cannot be said to be attributable to the transferor.

9-197. Note, however, that if non-depreciable capital property transferred to a spouse or common-law partner is subsequently sold, any capital gain or capital loss realized in the case of non-depreciable capital property will be attributed back to the transferor, despite the fact that the property was used in a business carried on by the transferee. The reason for this is that ITA 74.2(1) does not qualify that the property transferred must be used to earn property income. In practice, however, it is unusual to have transferred property being used to carry on a business.

Summary of Rules

9-198. The attribution rules, classified by type of income, are summarized in Figure 9-3.

Figure 9-3
Attribution by Type of Income

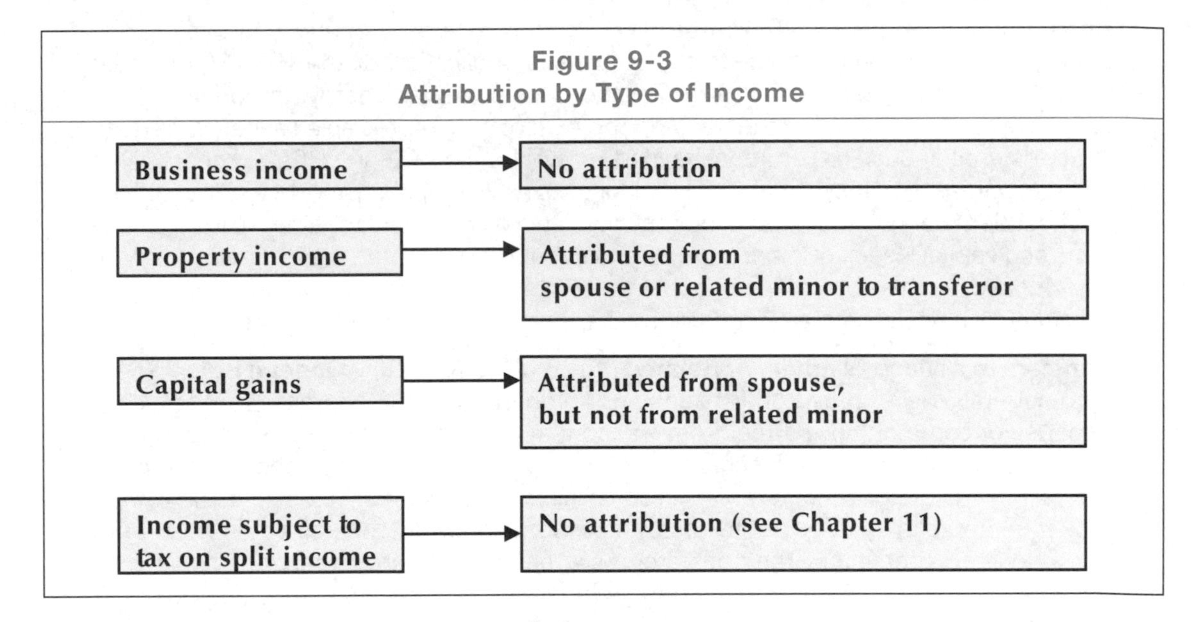

Avoiding Income Attribution

9-199. The premise of the attribution rules is that an individual in a high income tax bracket may be tempted to split income with a low-income family member, which keeps the income tax savings within the family. The simplest way to achieve this result is to gift income earning property such as investments to those select family members. The attribution rules specifically target this type of transaction by ensuring that none of the exceptions to the attribution rules apply. While there are a number of exceptions to the attribution rules, one of the most important looks to whether the transferee has paid FMV for the transferred property. Clearly in gifting situations the transferee pays nothing for the property, and therefore the FMV exception does not allow the attribution rules to be avoided. Where FMV is paid by the transferee the tax policy concerns about splitting income tend to disappear since the transferee is supposedly using their own resources to acquire the property in the same manner as if they had purchased the property from an arm's-length person. If the transferee does not have funds or property of his own to acquire the property outright, then he can simply issue a promissory note (e.g., an IOU) to the transferor. The main exceptions to the attribution rules are found in ITA 74.5.

Transfers to a Related Minor (under 18) ITA 74.5(1)(a) provides that the attribution rules do not apply if the related minor (or niece or nephew) provides consideration (i.e., payment) equal to the FMV of the transferred property. If the payment is made with a promissory note, ITA 74.5(1)(b) requires that it is only acceptable if the note includes interest at the prescribed rate in effect at the time of the transfer and the interest is actually paid within 30 days of the end of the following year. This presents a valuable opportunity for the transfer of investments that earn income at rates well in excess of the prescribed rate. Such planning is common practice among tax planners.

9-200. The ITA 73(1) rollover (see inter vivos spousal transfers beginning at Paragraph 9-154) complicates the avoidance of the income attribution rules in transfers of property to a spouse or common-law partner:

Transfers to a Spouse—ITA 73(1) Applicable Aside from the requirement that FMV consideration be paid by a transferee (including the payment with debt at the prescribed interest rate), ITA 74.5(1)(c) adds an additional requirement to spousal or common-law partner transfers of capital property in which the ITA 73(1) rollover would have applied. The provision requires that the transferor elect to avoid the rollover, in which case the POD of the transfer would be at the FMV. What this means is that the attribution rules cannot be avoided for spousal or common-law partner transfers if the ITA 73(1) rollover applies.

Transfers to a Spouse or Common-Law Partner—Electing to Avoid ITA 73(1) There are two possible situations:

Consideration Equal to FMV If the transferee provides consideration equal to the FMV of the property that is transferred, the attribution rules will not apply to that transfer. As noted previously, ITA 74.5(1)(b) allows consideration to be paid with debt as long as the debt includes interest at the prescribed rate and the interest is actually paid within 30 days of the end of each year.

The POD to the transferor will be equal to the FMV of the property transferred. The ACB or capital cost of the property to the transferee will be the same FMV. However, in the case of depreciable property the rule of ITA 13(7)(e) will also apply, as discussed beginning at Paragraph 9-163.

Consideration Not Equal to FMV If the consideration provided by the transferee is less than FMV, then the attribution rules cannot be avoided since the exceptions require the spouse or common-law partner transferee to pay FMV consideration. The election to avoid ITA 73(1) results in the potential application of ITA 69(1) where the consideration paid by a spouse or common-law partner is either less than or greater than the FMV of the transferred property. ITA 69(1), however, does not deem the transferee to have paid consideration but only adjusts tax cost and POD depending on the circumstances. As a result, ITA 69 has no impact on whether the attribution rules apply. The test remains whether or not the spouse or common-law partner has actually paid something to the transferor in the form of cash, property, or with a promissory note bearing interest in an amount equal to the prescribed rate in effect when the property is transferred.

Summary—Transfers to a Spouse or Common-Law Partner Avoiding the attribution rules on transfers of property to a spouse or common-law partner requires that

- the transferor elects to avoid the ITA 73(1) rollover; and
- the transferee provides actual consideration equal to or greater than the FMV of the property transferred.

Example

9-201. The following example will provide an illustration of the points we have discussed.

EXAMPLE Mrs. Blaine owns an investment in public company shares with an ACB of $200,000. On December 31, 2020, the FMV of the shares is $300,000. On that date, she gifts 50% of the shares to her spouse, Mark, and the other 50% to her 5-year-old daughter, Belinda. Both Mark and Belinda have no net income for 2020.

Both Mark and Belinda continue to own the shares until December 31, 2021, at which point they are sold for a total of $350,000 ($175,000 each). During 2021, the shares paid $37,500 in eligible dividends ($18,750 to both Mark and Belinda).

ANALYSIS—Transfer to Spouse Assuming that Mrs. Blaine has not elected to avoid the ITA 73(1) rollover, the transfer to her spouse would take place at the ACB of the shares of $100,000, meaning that Mrs. Blaine realizes no capital gain or capital loss [POD $100,000 - ACB $100,000]. In addition, her spouse's cost and ACB would be the same amount of $100,000. When Mark sells the shares in 2021, he will realize a taxable capital gain of $37,500 [(1/2)($175,000 - $100,000)], all of which will be attributed to Mrs. Blaine in 2021 as a result of ITA 74.2. In addition, the $18,750 in eligible dividends received by Mark in 2021 would also be attributed to Mrs. Blaine as a result of ITA 74.1(1). The taxable amount would be $25,875 [(138%)($18,750)] and Mrs. Blaine would be entitled to claim the related dividend tax credit since she included the taxable dividend in her net income.

ANALYSIS—Transfer to Minor As indicated previously, the rules for minors are somewhat different. As there is no general rollover provision for minor children, in this case the gift to Belinda would be treated as a disposition at FMV, resulting in a 2020 taxable capital gain to Mrs. Blaine of $25,000 [(1/2)($150,000 - $100,000)]. Belinda's ACB for the shares would be $150,000 as a result of ITA 69(1)(c). When Belinda sells the shares she will realize a taxable capital gain of $12,500 [(1/2)($175,000 - $150,000)]. The taxable capital gain would not be attributed back to Mrs. Blaine. The income tax treatment of the dividends is identical to the treatment to Belinda's father, Mr. Blaine, resulting in an additional $18,750 in dividends attributed back to Mrs. Blaine for 2021. The taxable amount would be $25,875 [(138%)($18,750)] and Mrs. Blaine would also be entitled to the dividend tax credit for the same reasons.

9-202. If either Mark or Belinda reinvest the proceeds from the sale of the shares, dividend or interest income from the new investments will also be subject to the attribution rules as if the new investments had been transferred directly from Mrs. Blaine. Any capital gains on the new investments that are realized by Mark will also be attributed back to Mrs. Blaine. This will not be the case with capital gains realized by Belinda. Note, however, that if either Mark or Belinda earn income on the attributed income it would not be subject to the attribution rules. If, for example, either of the two individuals deposited the dividends they received in a savings account that paid interest of $500, that interest would not be subject to the attribution rules. If the individuals use the sale proceeds to acquire other investments, the property income and capital gains from that property is subject to the attribution rules because the ITA specifically refers to attributing income from the property transferred as well as any property substituted for that property. The reinvestment of property income would not be caught, however, since there is no mention of substituted income.

Exercise 9-14

Subject: Income Attribution from a Spouse

On December 31, 2020, Mrs. Norah Moreau gifts shares with an ACB of $23,000 and a FMV of $37,000 to her spouse, Nick Moreau. On February 24, 2021, the shares pay to Mr. Moreau eligible dividends of $2,500 ($3,450 taxable amount with the 38% gross up). On August 31, 2021, Mr. Moreau sells the shares for $42,000. Assume that Mrs. Moreau does not elect to avoid the ITA 73(1) rollover. What are the income tax consequences for Mrs. Moreau and Mr. Moreau for each of 2020 and 2021? If there are no income tax consequences for either individual in a given year, explain why.

Exercise 9-15

Subject: Income Attribution from a Related Minor

On December 31, 2020, Mrs. Norah Moreau gifts shares with an ACB of $23,000 and a FMV of $37,000 to her 12-year-old daughter, Nicki Moreau. On February 24, 2021, the shares pay to Nicki eligible dividends of $2,500 ($3,450 taxable amount with the 38%

gross up added). On August 31, 2021, Nicki sells the shares for $42,000. What are the income tax consequences for Mrs. Moreau and for Nicki for each of 2020 and 2021? If there are no income tax consequences for either individual in a given year, explain why.

Exercise 9-16

Subject: Income Attribution—Use of Loans

On December 31, 2020, Mr. Nadeem Bronski gifts corporate bonds to his spouse in exchange for a promissory note with a face value of $121,000. The corporate bonds have an ACB of $115,000 and a FMV of $121,000. The promissory note from his spouse is interest free and has no specific maturity date. Mr. Bronski does not report a disposition at FMV in his 2020 income tax return. During 2021, the bonds pay interest to Mrs. Bronski in the amount of $6,100. On October 1, 2021, immediately after an interest payment, Mrs. Bronski sells the bonds for $129,000. She uses $121,000 of the proceeds to pay off the promissory note owing to her spouse. What are the income tax consequences for Mr. and Mrs. Bronski in each of 2020 and 2021? If there are no income tax consequences for either individual in a given year, explain why.

Solutions to Exercises are available in the Study Guide.

Income Attribution—Non-Arm's-Length Loans (ITA 56(4.1))

9-203. The attribution rules also cover loans of property and loans of money, which could then be used to acquire investments. In both instances the attribution rules would apply as discussed to attribute any income earned from the loaned property or property acquired with the cash loan.

9-204. At first glance it would appear that income splitting could still occur as long as you avoided the family members specified in the attribution rules. An example would be making investment loans to adult children (those 18 and over) or selling investments to them for interest-free promissory notes. If the adult children were in a low income tax bracket and the transferor in a high income tax bracket, then income splitting could be achieved.

9-205. While there is a potential for income splitting in these situations there is another attribution rule that must be navigated. The rule is found in ITA 56(4.1) and applies where an individual has received a loan from a non-arm's-length person or has become indebted to that person and income from property acquired with the loan or from the investments purchased with a promissory note is included in the net income of the individual. The rule does not apply unless one of the main reasons of the transaction is to avoid or reduce tax (i.e., income splitting). The rule can also be avoided if the loan given or promissory note paid as consideration includes interest at the prescribed rate and the interest is paid within 30 days of the end of the year. The rules also do not apply if the regular attribution rules of ITA 74.1 apply.

EXAMPLE You just sold investments and have $100,000 of after-tax cash. Your adult daughter is attending university and requires assistance. You were going to acquire investments that would have paid you $15,000 a year but instead agree to loan your daughter the $100,000 interest free and have her purchase those investments. This allows you to provide additional financial support for your daughter because of the income tax savings, which you estimate at $6,000.

ANALYSIS Your daughter has received a loan from you, a non-arm's-length person, and has used the loan to acquire investments resulting in income of $15,000 included in her net income. One of the main reasons is to reduce or avoid tax. Since the loan is interest free, the exception for loans that charge a prescribed rate of interest would not apply. The result is that the $15,000 of investment income would be attributed back to you. Note, however, that the current prescribed interest rate (as of the fourth quarter of 2020) is 1%. Had the loan charged 1% interest, then ITA 56(4.1) would not have applied such that $1,000 [(1%)($100,000)] would have been included in your net income while your daughter would have included $14,000 [$15,000 investment income - $1,000 interest expense ITA 20(1)(c)].

9-206. ITA 56(4.1) acts as a warning sign (as to other attribution concepts) to avoid certain income-splitting practices. The rule also adds a roadmap that allows income splitting as long as it is properly structured to follow the exceptions.

9-207. While there has only been one recorded court case that addressed ITA 56(4.1), a common concern arises when parents wish to provide financial assitance to adult children to allow them to purchase a home (principal residence). Since ITA 56(4.1) requires a loan or indebtedness, the easiest way to avoid the rule is to provide adult children with cash gifts. If this is not feasible then providing loans is acceptable if the loan bears interest at the prescribed rate. If the loan is interest free the rule can be avoided by arguing that one of the main reasons is not to avoid income tax through income splitting but rather to assist adult children. Many years ago the CRA was asked whether ITA 56(4.1) would apply where parents sold their home to adult children and took back a mortgage. The CRA replied that they would not normally apply ITA 56(4.1) to a genuine sale of property. The message is that if the only motivation is to assist family members such as adult children, the requirement that tax avoidance play a role would never be met and therefore the attribution rule of ITA 56(4.1) could not apply.

We suggest you complete SSP 9-10 and 9-11 at this point.

Tax Planning and Income Attribution

9-208. Anti-avoidance rules aimed at income splitting such as the attribution rules and the TOSI make it difficult at times to achieve income splitting, although some opportunities still exist such as prescribed interest rate loans. In other instances, sophisticated structures are established that involve trusts, partnerships, and corporations that introduce of level of complexity that requires professional assistance. There remains a degree of risk and uncertainty, however, considering that, as a rule, the CRA views income splitting as offensive unless transactions clearly fall within the limited exceptions. The CRA is not averse to challenging income splitting with the use of the General Anti-Avoidance Rule (GAAR). There are a few basic points to keep in mind that can be helpful in achieving acceptable income splitting:

Split Pension Income As discussed in this chapter, it is possible to transfer up to 50% of qualified pension income to a lower-income spouse or common-law partner. This is an important provision that can provide for a significant reduction in family income tax.

TFSAs Also as discussed in this chapter, Tax-Free Savings Accounts can be used for income splitting as these plans are not subject to the income attribution rules.

RESPs Also as discussed in this chapter, registered education savings plans provide an opportunity for limited income splitting.

Spousal RRSPs As will be discussed in Chapter 10, a spousal RRSP remains one of the more effective income-splitting opportunities as high tax rate individuals benefit from a contribution deduction while the income is only subject to the low tax rate of a spouse or common-law partner when funds are withdrawn.

Capital Gains Potential As there is no attribution of capital gains on transfers to related minors, capital property with future capital gains potential should be directed to minors rather than to a spouse or common-law partner.

Loans The prescribed rate is currently 1% (as of the fourth quarter of 2020). At this low rate, income-splitting opportunities remain high as long as there are investments generating after-tax returns that exceed that rate.

Segregating Gifts to Spouses and Minors If a spouse, common-law partner, or non-arm's-length minor child (including nieces and nephews) receives a gift or inheritance from a source to which attribution would not apply, the funds can be used for investment purposes avoiding, if at all possible, the use of the funds for personal purposes. The reason for this is that property ownership requires that individuals use their own funds, which means funds received as gifts, inheritances, loans, and from income earned by that individual. If, for example, there is a family with two minor children and two parents but only one of the parents earns income, then for ITA purposes all of the funds and property would belong to the income earning spouse/parent. That individual can gift or loan the funds to family members, which they can then use to acquire their own property (e.g., investments), which of course moves you closer to the attribution rules. In the absence of these measures, if the income earning parent/spouse were to acquire investments, rental properties, or even have funds in a savings account with a bank, the income from those sources would belong to that individual and no one else even if legal ownership was split. This is a reflection of the beneficial ownership concept we discussed in Chapter 8.

EXAMPLE Stephen is married with two minor children. He is the only income earner. None of his family members have received cash gifts or inheritances. In 2021 Stephen earned interest of $700 on a joint savings account at his bank. He also jointly owns a rental property with his spouse on a 50-50 basis that earned rental income of $9,000 after all expenses and CCA. Finally, he sold shares that are jointly owned with his spouse, realizing a taxable capital gain of $12,000. Stephen and his spouse each included half of these amounts in their 2021 income tax return.

ANALYSIS Beneficial property ownership is based on whose funds/property were used to acquire the property (e.g., the source of income). Based on the limited facts, Stephen would be the sole beneficial owner of the bank account, the shares, and the rental property. This means that all of the income belongs to Stephen and is required to be included in his net income. None of the income is required to be included in the net income of his spouse. The attributions would not apply since the beneficial ownership of property Stephen owned was not transferred to his spouse at any time.

Note on Family Law: Oftentimes there is a misunderstanding that spouses and common-law partners each own everything on a 50-50 basis. This notion is based on family law considerations, which do not apply when it comes to who has beneficial ownership of a particular property for income tax purposes. Typically, when marital or common-law relationships break down the individuals can exercise their rights by making a claim based on this 50-50 property concept. At that subsequent time, income tax potentially comes into play since one of the individuals to the relationship is then giving up beneficial ownership on some properties in settlement of the relationship breakdown.

Detailed Records In order to support the acquisition of investments by a low-income family member it is necessary that she has her own funds to invest. This means being in a position to potentially trace the funds to her. As a result it would generally be advised that separate bank accounts be maintained.

Incorporated Businesses On the incorporation of a company that will carry on a new business it is generally preferable to have family members acquire shares. As the business grows and corporate income is earned, dividend distributions can be made to family shareholders. Unfortunately, the TOSI will likely apply to children where a parent is involved in the corporate business and is a shareholder of the company. Careful consideration of the TOSI will be required to avoid the payment of federal income tax at the 33% rate on that income.

Salaries to Family Members When a business is carried on by the family or through a family-owned corporation, the lower-income spouse and any children should be paid reasonable salaries for any services provided that can be justified by the business. Examples would include bookkeeping, filing, and other administrative work.

We suggest you complete SSP 9-12 and 9-13 at this point.

Key Terms

A full glossary with definitions is provided at the end of the Study Guide.

Alimony	Eligible Child
Annual Child Care Expense Amount	Inadequate Consideration
Annuity	Income Attribution
Anti-Avoidance Provision	Income Splitting
Arm's Length	Inter Vivos Transfer
Canada Disability Savings Bonds	Moving Expenses
Canada Disability Savings Grants	Non-Arm's Length
Canada Education Savings Grants (CESG)	Periodic Child Care Expense Amount
Canada Learning Bonds	Registered Disability Savings Plan (RDSP)
Child Care Expenses	Registered Education Savings Plan (RESP)
Child Support	Retiring Allowance
Common-Law Partner	Spousal Support
Death Benefit	Spouse
Deferred Income Plans	Support Amount
Disability Supports Deduction	Tax-Free Savings Account (TFSA)
Earned Income (Child Care Expenses)	

References

For more detailed study of the material in this chapter, we refer you to the following:

ITA 56	Other Types of Income
ITA 56.1	Support
ITA 60	Other Deductions
ITA 60.1	Support
ITA 62	Moving Expenses
ITA 63	Child Care Expenses
ITA 64	Disability Supports Deduction
ITA 74.1(1)	Transfers and Loans to Spouse or Common-Law Partner
ITA 74.1(2)	Transfers and Loans to Minors
ITA 74.2	Gain or Loss Deemed That of Lender or Transferor
ITA 74.5(1)	Transfers for Fair Market Consideration
ITA 146.1	Registered Education Savings Plans
ITA 146.2	Tax-Free Savings Accounts
ITA 146.4	Registered Disability Savings Plans
ITR 300	Capital Element of Annuity Payments
IC 93-3R2	Registered Education Savings Plans
IC 99-1R1	Registered Disability Savings Plans

S1-F1-C3	Disability Supports Deduction
S1-F2-C3	Scholarships, Research Grants, and Other Education Assistance
S1-F3-C1	Child Care Expense Deduction
S1-F3-C3	Support Payments
S1-F3-C4	Moving Expenses
S1-F5-C1	Related Persons and Dealing at Arm's Length
S2-F1-C2	Retiring Allowances
S3-F10-C1	Qualified Investments—RRSPs, RESPs, RRIFs, RDSPs, and TFSAs
S3-F10-C2	Prohibited Investments—RRSPs, RRIFs, and TFSAs
S3-F10-C3	Advantages—RRSPs, RESPs, RRIFs, RDSPs, and TFSAs
IT-209R	Inter Vivos Gifts of Capital Property to Individuals Directly or through Trusts
IT-325R2	Property Transfers after Separation, Divorce, and Annulment
IT-499R	Superannuation or Pension Benefits
IT-508R	Death Benefits
IT-510	Transfers and Loans of Property Made after May 22, 1985, to a Related Minor
IT-511R	Interspousal and Certain Other Transfers and Loans of Property
RC4092	Registered Education Savings Plans
RC4460	Registered Disability Savings Plan
RC4466	Tax-Free Savings Account
T4011	Preparing Returns for Deceased Persons
T778	Child Care Expenses Deduction
P105	Students and Income Tax

Self-Study Problems (SSPs)

Self-Study Problems (SSPs) provide practice in problem solving. Within the chapters, we have indicated where it would be appropriate to stop and work on each SSP. The problems can be downloaded by chapter from MyLab Accounting. Solutions are available in the Study Guide. Select problems can also be completed directly in MyLab and auto-graded.

Assignment Problems

Solutions to Assignment Problems (APs) are available to instructors only.

AP 9-1 (Death Benefits)

Jennifer Lister is 46 years old and has custody of her 18-year-old son, Jason Lister, following a divorce five years earlier. For many years she has been a full-time employee of Mammoth Monuments, a manufacturer of equipment for funeral homes.

On March 31, 2021, she dies when her parachute fails to open during a sky diving event.

In recognition of her long-time service, Mammoth Monuments decides to pay a death benefit of $13,500. It will be paid in annual instalments of $4,500 per year, beginning on December 31, 2021. Since there is no surviving spouse the payments will all be made to her son, Jason.

Required: What effect will this death benefit have on the net income of Jason Lister for each of the years he receives payments?

AP 9-2 (Moving Expenses)

In May of the current year, following a dispute with her immediate superior, Ms. Elaine Fox resigned from her job in Halifax and began to look for other employment. She was not able to find acceptable work in Halifax, but she did locate her dream job in Regina and was expected to report for work on October 1.

After accepting the new job, Ms. Fox flew to Regina to find living quarters for herself. After two days of searching, she was able to locate a suitable house. Subsequent to purchasing her new home, Ms. Fox remained in Regina for an additional four days in order to purchase various furnishings for this residence. Her expenses for this trip were as follows:

Airfare (Halifax to Regina, return)	$ 689
Car rental (6 days at $35)	210
Hotel (6 days at $150)	900
Food	275
Total house hunting expenses	$2,074

On her return to Halifax, she received the following statements from her attorneys:

Real estate commission—Sale of old home	$ 9,500
Legal fees—Sale of old home	1,400
Unpaid taxes on old home to date of sale	800
Legal fees—Purchase of new home	1,850
Transfer tax on new home	600
Total	$14,150

On August 31 of the current year, after supervising the final packing of her property and its removal from the old house, Ms. Fox spent three days in a Halifax hotel while she finalized arrangements for her departure. Expenses during this period were as follows:

Hotel (3 days at $140)	$420
Food	145
Total	$565

On the morning of September 4 she leaves Halifax by automobile, arriving in Regina in the evening of September 10. The distance travelled was 3,900 kilometres. As her new residence is not yet available, she is forced to continue living in a Regina hotel until September 26. Her expenses for the period September 3 through September 26 are as follows:

Gasoline	$ 875
Hotel (23 days at $140)	3,220
Food	975
Total	$5,070

On moving into the new residence, she is required to pay the moving company a total of $3,800. This fee includes $675 for the 16 days of storage required because the new home was not available when the furnishings arrived.

Ms. Fox's only income for the current year was employment income and the net amounts to be included in her net income for the year of the move are as follows:

Old Halifax job (5 months)	$32,000
New Regina job (3 months)	16,500
Employment income	$48,500

Ms. Fox will use the simplified method of determining vehicle and food costs in calculating her moving expenses. Assume that the relevant flat rate for vehicle expenses is $0.58 for all provinces, and the flat rate for meals is $51 per day.

Ms. Fox's new employer did not provide any reimbursement for moving expenses.

Required: Calculate the maximum allowable moving expenses that Ms. Fox can deduct in the determination of net income for the current year and any amount that can be carried forward to a subsequent year.

AP 9-3 (Child Care Expenses)

Mr. Morena carried on a service business as a sole proprietor in the first eight months of the year. The business broke even with business income of nil. Mr. Morena terminated the business and went to work for a client as an employee in September of that year. His employment income for these four months was $20,000. In addition, he had interest income of $3,500 and received non-eligible dividends from his private company of $62,000.

Mrs. Morena was employed throughout 2021, earning gross employment income of $73,000. RPP contributions of $4,200 were withheld by her employer. She had no other source of income during 2021.

During 2021, Mrs. Morena attended an accounting course at a local college. The course lasted 12 weeks and required her to spend about 20 hours per week in classes and preparing assignments.

Because of their busy schedules, the couple incurred well-documented child care costs of $16,250 (50 weeks at $325 per week).

Required: Determine the maximum amount that can be deducted by Mr. and Mrs. Morena for the year ending December 31, 2021, for child care expenses under the following assumptions:

A. They have two children, neither of whom qualify for the ITA 118.3 disability tax credit. Their ages are 1 and 3 years old.

B. They have three children, none of whom qualify for the ITA 118.3 disability tax credit. Their ages are 3, 5, and 14 years old.

AP 9-4 (Pension Income Splitting—With OAS)

Both Jean Belanger and his wife, Carole, are 66 years of age. During 2021, they each received OAS payments of $7,000.

As a long-term employee of a Canadian public company, Jean receives an annual pension benefit. For 2021, the amount is $168,000. This payment, along with the OAS payment, are his only sources of income.

Because she was blinded in a work-related accident, Carole qualifies for the disability tax credit. As the accident involved negligence on the part of her employer, Carole receives a monthly annuity payment of $3,500 that is required to be included in her net income. This payment will continue as long as she lives. This is her only income other than the OAS payment.

Neither Jean nor Carole are eligible for any tax credits other than the basic personal credit, the age credit, the pension income credit, and the disability tax credit. Further, they have no taxable income deductions available.

Required: Compare the 2021 federal income taxes payable by Jean and Carole assuming:

A. Jean does not split his pension income.

B. Jean splits his pension income with Carole on a 50-50 basis.

AP 9-5 (Other Income and Deductions, Including RESP)

Viva Houde's divorce settlement resulted in her having custody of her two children. Her daughter, Lacy, is 8 years old and her son, Mark, is 10 years old. They are both in good health. The agreement calls for her to receive child support payments of $2,000 per month, as well as spousal support of $1,500 per month. During 2021, she received all of these payments.

In order to get a fresh start in life, she enrolled in a co-op program at Western University in London, Ontario. She was very successful during the winter term (January through April 2021). The program requires her to work in her related employment during the summer, with her first placement being in Timmins, Ontario, during the period May to August 2021. Her employment income for this period was $8,000.

In late August she returned to London and resumed full-time studies during the fall term (September through December 2021). She was also able to obtain a part-time job in her field in London. During these four months she had employment income of $1,600.

The eligible moving costs associated with moving herself and her children to Timmins for the summer work term totalled $1,200. The costs for the move back to London were $1,350.

In addition to her support payments and employment income, Viva received the following amounts:

Scholarship granted by the university for the fall semester	$ 4,300
Eligible dividends received	$ 2,600
Inheritance from an uncle	$22,000
TFSA withdrawal	$ 4,000

Throughout the year, Viva required assistance with her children. During the period January through April, the costs in London totalled $1,950. In Timmins, she incurred costs of $1,725. After returning to London for the fall term, her costs for the September through December period were $2,175.

During 2021, Viva establishes RESPs for both of her children. She contributes $1,500 to each of these plans.

Required: Determine the minimum net income for 2021. Provide reasons for omitting items that you have not included in net income. Also, indicate any amounts that can be carried forward to future years.

AP 9-6 (Non-Arm's-Length Transfer of Shares)

Ms. Jody Wales owns shares in a Canadian public company that she acquired several years ago at a cost of $220,000. The shares have a current FMV of $426,000. Ms. Wales and her husband, Jim, have three children. Their daughter, Kim, is 20 years old, while their sons, Jeff and Jerry, are 22 and 24 years old, respectively.

On November 1 of the current year, Ms. Wales is considering the following alternatives for disposing of the shares:

A. Selling the shares to her daughter for $220,000.

B. Gifting the shares to her older son, Jerry.

C. Selling the shares to her younger son, Jeff, for $500,000.

Required: Determine the income tax consequences to Ms. Wales of each of these transactions. Your answer should include the ACB of the shares to each of the adult children as well as an explanation for the income tax treatment.

AP 9-7 Non-Arm's-Length Transfer of Depreciable Property

During 2021, Joan Zelig sells three depreciable properties. In each case, the property sold is the last one in its class such that no property remains in the class at year end.

Property 1 has a capital cost of $150,000, and at January 1, 2021, the UCC in the class is $103,883. The property is sold to Joan's sister for its FMV of $115,000.

Property 2 has a capital cost of $140,000, and at January 1, 2021, the UCC in the class is $58,310. The property is sold to Joan's father for its FMV of $35,000.

Property 3 has a capital cost of $95,000, and at January 1, 2021, the UCC in the class is $82,369. The property is sold to Joan's mother for its FMV of $107,000.

Required: For each of the three dispositions, indicate the income tax consequences for Joan that result from the sale. In addition, indicate the tax attributes (capital cost, deemed CCA, and UCC) that will be used by the non-arm's-length purchaser on the assumption that the properties will be used as depreciable property by each purchaser.

AP 9-8 (Deemed Dispositions on Death and Emigration)

Mr. Howard Caswell is 67 years of age and his spouse, Charlene, is 58. They have one son, John, who is 36 years of age.

On September 1 of the current year, Mr. Howard Caswell owns the following properties:

Rental Property Mr. Caswell owns a rental property that was acquired at a cost of $120,000. This includes an estimated value for the land on which the building is situated of $25,000 with the remaining value of $95,000 attributable to the building. On September 1 of the current year, the building's UCC is $67,000. As of this date, the FMV of the property has increased to $158,000, including an unchanged value for the land of $25,000 and $133,000 attributable to the building.

General Industries Ltd. Mr. Caswell owns 5,000 shares of General Industries Ltd., a Canadian public company. These shares have a cost and ACB of $200,000 and a current FMV of $350,000. Mr. Caswell has never owned more than 3% of the outstanding shares of this company.

Farm Land Mr. Caswell owns farm land with a cost and ACB of $325,000 and a current FMV of $550,000. The land is farmed on a full-time basis by Mr. Caswell's son, John.

Caswell Enterprises Mr. Caswell owns 100% of the voting shares of Caswell Enterprises, a Canadian controlled private corporation. The company was established with an investment of $275,000 and it is estimated that the current FMV of the shares is $426,000. Caswell Enterprises is not a qualified small business corporation for purposes of the lifetime capital gains deduction.

Assume that no elections are made and that normal deemed disposition values apply.

Required: Explain the income tax consequences that would result in each of the following cases for Mr. Caswell for the current year. In your solutions for Cases A and B, include the tax attributes (capital cost, ACB, deemed CCA, and UCC) of the properties to the transferee.

A. Mr. Caswell dies on September 1 of the current year, leaving all of his property to his spouse, Charlene.

B. Mr. Caswell dies on September 1 of the current year, leaving all of his property to his son, John.

C. Mr. Caswell departs from Canada and ceases to be a resident on September 1 of the current year (covered in Chapter 8).

AP 9-9 (Transfers to a Spouse—Income Attribution)

Jason Holt has owned a number of rental properties for many years. The rental properties are used for residential purposes. He has been married to Geena Holt for five years. Their prenuptial agreement requires Jason to gift a rental property to Geena on each fifth anniversary of their marriage.

On January 1, 2021, as required by their prenuptial agreement, Jason gifts one of the rental properties to Geena. Information on this property is as follows:

	Land	Building
Original cost (ACB)	$123,000	$387,000
FMV—Date of transfer	167,000	426,000
UCC—Date of transfer	N/A	299,772

During 2021, the rental income, before the deduction of CCA, is $23,451. Geena plans to deduct maximum CCA.

On January 1, 2022, after concluding that other investments would provide a better return, Geena sells the rental property for $650,000. At this time, an appraisal indicates that the FMV of the land has increased to $175,000, leaving $475,000 ($650,000 - $175,000) attributable to the building.

Required: Determine the income tax consequences associated with the transfer and subsequent sale of the property for both Mr. and Mrs. Holt assuming:

A. The facts are as stated in the problem and that Mr. Holt does not elect to avoid the rollover of ITA 73(1).

B. The prenuptial agreement requires that Geena purchase the property for its fair market value, using her own funds. On this sale, Mr. Holt elects to avoid the ITA 73(1) rollover.

AP 9-10 (Gifts and Income Attribution)

Ms. Vicky Vaughn is a very successful attorney with an income of over $500,000 per year. She is married to Mr. Jonathan Flex, a former Mr. Canada. Mr. Flex has no net income.

She and Mr. Flex have two children. Their daughter, Sheila, is 27 years of age, while their son, Biff, is 15 years of age. To date, Ms. Vaughn has not gifted or sold property to either her spouse or her children.

At the end of the current year, Ms. Vaughn owns the following properties:

Shares of TD Bank Ms. Vaughn owns 10,000 shares with a current FMV of $700,000. The ACB for these shares is $550,000.

Vaughn Enterprises Ltd. Ms. Vaughn owns all of the shares of this Canadian controlled private corporation. The ACB is $475,000. A business equity valuator has concluded that the shares are currently worth $1,200,000. Vaughn Enterprises is not a qualified small business corporation for purposes of the lifetime capital gains deduction.

Rental Property Ms. Vaughn owns a 22-unit apartment building with a current FMV of $2,400,000. It is estimated that $400,000 of this value is attributable to the land with the remaining $2,000,000 attributable to the building. Ms. Vaughn purchased the rental property several years ago at a cost of $1,500,000, with $300,000 of this value attributable to the land and $1,200,000 to the building. As of January 1 of the current year, the UCC of this class 1 building is $960,000.

Farm Land Ms. Vaughn owns farm land that cost $800,000 and has a current FMV of $1,200,000. Sheila uses the farm land on a full-time basis to grow certified organic vegetables.

As Ms. Vaughn's income is more than sufficient for her needs, she is considering giving some or all of the properties to her spouse and/or her two children.

Required: You have been hired as an income tax consultant to Ms. Vaughn. She would like a report that would detail, for each of the four properties, the income tax consequences to her of gifting the properties to her husband or to either one of her children. In determining the income tax consequences, ignore the possibility that the tax on split income (TOSI) may apply.

Ms. Vaughn does not elect to avoid the ITA 73(1) rollover if the gifts are made to her spouse. In addition, assume that the recipient of the rental property does not claim any CCA prior to the subsequent sale of the property.

Your report should include:

- the income tax consequences to Ms. Vaughn at the time of the gift;
- the income tax attributes (ACB, capital cost, deemed CCA, and UCC) of the properties to the recipient of the gift;

- the income tax treatment of any income on the property subsequent to the gift and before the property is sold; and
- the income tax consequences that would result from a subsequent sale of the gifted property at $100,000 more than its FMV at the time of the gift. In the case of the rental property, assume that all of this extra $100,000 is attributable to the building, with no change in the value of the land.

AP 9-11 (Income Attribution)

Dr. Sandra Bolt is 49 years of age and an extremely successful physician in Halifax, Nova Scotia. She is married to Tod Bolt and has two children. On December 31, 2019, her son, Dirk, is 20 years old and her daughter, Dolly, is 15 years old. Each of the children earns about $10,000 per year in income from part-time acting jobs. While her husband, Tod, qualifies as a professional accountant, he did not enjoy the work and, for the last 10 years, he has assumed the role of house parent. As a consequence, his only current source of income is the interest on $335,000 that he has in his personal savings account. This interest amounts to about $20,000 per year and all of the savings were accumulated from amounts that he earned while working as a professional accountant.

On December 28, 2019, Sandra Bolt is holding shares in a Canadian public company that have an ACB of $185,000 and a FMV of $225,000. She is considering transferring these shares to either her husband or to one of her two children. She seeks your advice as to the income tax consequences, both to herself and to the transferee, that would result from such a transfer.

During your discussions, Sandra Bolt has indicated the following:

- The transfer will take place on December 31, 2019.
- Any proceeds she receives from her family on the share transfer will not be invested in income producing property.
- She wishes you to assume that the shares would pay eligible dividends during 2020 of $18,500 and that the transferee would sell the shares on January 1, 2021, for $260,000. The gross up on the eligible dividends would be $7,030 [(38%)($18,500)], resulting in taxable dividends of $25,530 ($18,500 + $7,030).

Required: Each of the following independent cases involves a transfer by Sandra Bolt to a member of her family. Indicate, for both Sandra Bolt and the transferee, the 2019, 2020, and 2021 income tax consequences of:

- the transfer on December 31, 2019;
- the assumed 2020 receipt of the dividends; and
- the assumed 2021 disposition by the transferee.

Note that some of the cases have been included to illustrate specific provisions of the relevant legislation and do not necessarily represent a reasonable course of action on the part of Sandra Bolt.

Case A Sandra Bolt gifts the shares to her spouse and does not elect to avoid the ITA 73(1) rollover.

Case B Tod Bolt uses money from his savings account to purchase the shares from Sandra for their FMV of $225,000. Sandra Bolt does not elect to avoid the ITA 73(1) rollover.

Case C Tod Bolt uses money from his savings account to purchase the shares for their FMV of $225,000. Sandra Bolt elects not to have the ITA 73(1) apply.

Case D Tod Bolt uses money from his savings account to purchase the shares for only $140,000. Sandra Bolt does not elect to avoid the ITA 73(1) rollover.

Case E Tod Bolt uses money from his savings account to purchase the shares for only $140,000. Sandra Bolt elects to avoid the ITA 73(1) rollover.

Case F Sandra Bolt gifts the shares to her daughter, Dolly.

Case G Sandra Bolt provides her daughter, Dolly, with a $225,000 loan. The loan will include interest at commercial rates. Dolly uses the loan proceeds to purchase her mother's shares at FMV. Sandra Bolt believes that the combination of dividends on the shares together with Dolly's income from part-time jobs will be sufficient to pay the interest on the loan.

Case H Sandra Bolt provides her son, Dirk, with a $225,000 interest-free loan. Dirk uses the loan proceeds to purchase his mother's shares at their FMV of $225,000.

AP 9-12 (Comprehensive Case Covering Chapters 1 to 9)

Family Information

Spencer James is 41 years old. He has been married to Suzanne James for over 20 years. The couple have three children. All members of the family are in good health. Information on the children is as follows:

Charles and Charlene are 8-year-old twins. During 2021, each of the twins received eligible dividends of $1,000 on public company shares that were gifted to them by their father in July 2020. At the time of the gift, each block of shares had a fair market value of $9,500. Spencer had acquired the two blocks of shares at a cost of $8,000 each. In December 2021, each twin sold the shares for $10,000.

Charlton is 19 years old and attended university on a full-time basis for four months of the year. Spencer and Suzanne pay his tuition fees of $6,300, along with textbook costs of $650. He has agreed to transfer the maximum amount of his tuition credit to his father. Charlton lives with Spencer and Suzanne. His only income for the year is from the sale of shares purchased from Spencer as described in the following text.

In June 2021, Spencer sells shares with an ACB of $28,000 and a FMV of $36,500 to his son, Charlton. In order to provide Charlton with money to buy a car and to create a capital loss for himself, he sells the shares to Charlton for $5,000. Charlton sells the shares in September for $42,000.

Because of their work demands, Spencer and Suzanne have child care costs for the two twins of $250 per week for 48 weeks. During the remaining four weeks, the twins are sent to summer camp at a cost of $250 per child per week.

Suzanne's Income Information

Suzanne operates a mail-order business out of rented space. As it is furnished business space, the business does not own any capital assets. For 2020, her net business income, calculated on the basis of tax rules, was $70,544.

During 2021, Suzanne spent six consecutive weeks attending a specialized business accounting program at a designated educational institution. She received a tuition tax receipt that stated she had paid $2,000 in tuition fees.

In January 2020, Spencer gifted Suzanne a residential rental property. This property had cost Spencer $500,000 several years ago, with $100,000 of this amount allocated to the land and $400,000 allocated to the building. At the time of the gift, an appraisal indicates that the FMV of the property was $530,000, allocated $110,000 to the land and $420,000 to the building. The building had a January 1, 2020, UCC of $376,320. Spencer did not recognize this transaction in his 2020 income tax return.

For the year ending December 31, 2020, Suzanne had rental income, after the deduction of maximum CCA, of $16,400.

In November 2021, after experiencing significant difficulties with tenants, Suzanne lists the property for sale. It sells within a month for $555,000, with $120,000 of this total allocated to the land and $435,000 allocated to the building. The rental income, prior to the deduction of CCA, was $15,300 for 2021.

Spencer's Employment Information

Spencer is employed by a Canadian public company. His annual salary is $106,700, none of which is commissions. His employer withheld the following amounts from his remuneration:

EI premiums	$ 890
CPP contributions	3,166
Professional association dues	1,200
Registered pension plan contributions	4,200

Spencer's employer made a matching RPP contribution of $4,200.

Because of his excellent performance during 2021, Spencer was awarded a bonus of $20,000. Of this total, $10,000 will be paid in 2021, with the balance being paid in June 2022.

Spencer is provided with an automobile by his employer. The automobile is leased by the employer at a rate of $523 per month, including a payment of $51 per month for insurance. The automobile is available to Spencer for 11 months during 2021. During the remaining month, the employer required that it be returned to their garage. Total mileage for 2021 is 58,000 kilometres, 53,000 of which were used for employment purposes and only 5,000 for personal use.

On their birthday, Spencer's employer provides every employee with a $1,000 gift certificate that can be used for merchandise on Amazon. In addition, at Christmas, each employee receives a basket of gourmet food and wine. The value of this basket is $350.

During 2021, Spencer spent $5,600 on meals and entertainment of his employer's customers. The employer's policy is to reimburse 80% of these expenses.

For the last 10 years, Spencer has worked in a rural office of his employer. The rural office is located 110 kilometres from the company's head office in a major Canadian city. As his family has become less enchanted with the country life style, Spencer has transferred to the company's city office. The move involves selling his rural home and acquiring a city home. The various moving-related expenses include the following:

Real estate commissions—Old home	$11,620
Legal fees—Old home	1,250
Loss—Old home	18,000
Unpaid property taxes—Old home	625
Cleaning and minor repairs—Old home	450
Legal fees—New home	1,460
Cost of moving household goods	3,460

While Spencer's employer does not provide a moving allowance, the company agrees to compensate him for his $18,000 loss on his old home.

Other Information

1. The family's medical expenses for 2021 were as follows:

Spencer	$ 4,600
Suzanne*	8,600
Charles	4,700
Charlene	3,600
Total medical expenses	$21,500

*This medical expense was for a brow lift to remove wrinkles and improve the appearance of Suzanne's forehead.

2. In January 2021, Spencer's father, Adam, dies. He was an unsuccessful pig farmer who agonized over the death of each pig. The major property in his father's estate is the family farm, which is left to Spencer (other properties go to Spencer's mother and siblings). Information on the farm properties are as follows:

   Land The farm land had an ACB of $250,000. At the time of the father's death, the FMV was $375,000.

   Building The building had a capital cost of $325,000, a FMV at the time of the father's death of $275,000, and UCC of $253,000.

   Equipment The equipment had a capital cost $130,000, a FMV at the time of death of $110,000, and UCC of $95,000.

   The executors of the father's estate elect to transfer the land at its FMV in order to use up accumulated capital losses on other non-depreciable capital property. The building and equipment are transferred at the UCC values on a rollover basis.

3. As Spencer, and especially his family, have no interest in running a pig farm, he sells the inherited property to his brother in March as soon as he has title. His brother agrees to purchase the properties for the FMV determined by the executors, specifically $375,000 for the land, $275,000 for the building, and $110,000 for the equipment.

4. In memory of his father, Spencer donates $8,400 on his father's birthday in 2021 to Hearts on Noses—A Mini-Pig Sanctuary. This registered charity helps preserve the lives of injured, abused, abandoned, and neglected pot bellied pigs.

5. During 2021, Spencer makes a $4,000 contribution to his TFSA and $5,000 to Suzanne's. He also makes a $2,000 contribution ($1,000 per child) to the family RESP established for Charles and Charlene.

Required:

A. Determine Suzanne's 2021 net income, taxable income, and federal income tax payable, including any CPP liability. In determining Suzanne's federal income tax payable, assume that Spencer's taxable income will be $200,000. Show all supporting calculations, including explanations where necessary.

B. Determine Spencer's 2021 net income, taxable income, and federal income tax payable, including any CPP liability. In determining Suzanne's federal income tax payable, assume that Spencer's taxable income will be $200,000. Show all supporting calculations, including explanations where necessary.

In determining these amounts, ignore GST/HST & PST considerations.

AP 9-13 (Comprehensive Case Covering Chapters 1 to 9)

On January 2, 2021, the car Jonathan Blount was driving was hit by a tractor trailer. His two sons, Dirk aged 15 and Cole aged 13, were also in the car. In the crash, Cole suffered a broken leg, Dirk suffered a spinal cord injury, and Jonathan suffered injuries so severe that he died in the ambulance on the way to the hospital.

Jonathan was the manager of a Regina family grocery store started by his grandfather. In his will, Jonathan named his wife, Maria, as his executor and left his total estate to her.

Maria Blount is 53 years old. In addition to Dirk and Cole, she has two daughters, Elena aged 23 and Trish aged 17. Elena is enrolled in the Athabasca University accounting program.

After Jonathan's death, Maria decided to move her family to Calgary for a number of reasons. The rehabilitation services she needed for Dirk were available in a Calgary hospital, the air travel connections for her promotional activities were better from Calgary, and Maria's wealthy parents live near Calgary.

Maria listed her Regina home for sale in February. She and Jonathan jointly purchased the house for $95,000 in 2002. They spent $67,000 in renovations over the years. The house was sold for $299,900. Real estate fees totalled $16,250. Legal fees associated with the sale were $750.

During March, Maria flew to Calgary, business class, at a cost of $1,800 return to locate a new residence for her and her family. During the four days that she was there, her food and lodging costs totalled $1,220. After returning home, she made an offer on a newly built property for $1.2 million. The offer was accepted on March 20.

Maria, her children, and her dogs left Regina on March 29 in her SUV. They spent the night in Medicine Hat and arrived in Calgary on March 30. The trip was 812 kilometres. Assume the kilometre rate is $0.59 for Saskatchewan and $0.57 for Alberta.

Maria's bill for the Medicine Hat hotel totalled $1,270 for four rooms (Dirk and Cole were willing to share a room), dinner, and breakfast for her and her family.

Unfortunately, her new Calgary home was not available until April 2 and, as a consequence, she and her children stayed in a Calgary hotel from March 31 through April 2. This time Dirk and Cole were unwilling to share a room, so the total lodging bill, including meals, was $1,800.

The cost for moving her household effects totalled $2,340. The unplanned additional cost of leaving them in storage until her Calgary home was ready totalled $150. The cost of shipping her sports car to Calgary was $575. Her legal fees associated with acquiring the Calgary home were $900.

Business Information

Maria was the author of a popular series of romance novels that had many devoted followers impatiently waiting for the next book. They featured glamourous and sexy vampire accountants working for Bloodsuckers LLP. For 2021, the details of her business were as follows:

Book royalties ($75,000 were paid in June, the remainder were paid in December)	$212,000
Assistant's fees (Note 1)	36,000
Research purchases (Note 2)	2,250
Promotional travel costs (Note 3)	14,850
Business (100%) cell phone charges	600
Purchase of new office furniture	8,400
Purchase of new desktop and laptop equipment	8,000
Purchase of new iPad Pro	1,800
Office supplies	3,480

Note 1 The fees were paid to Elena at the rate of $25 per hour. She did the accounting for Maria's business. She also proofread the manuscripts and, due to her keen interest in both accounting and vampire lore, suggested corrections and revisions.

Note 2 Maria had been approached to write a movie or mini-series based on her books. In Calgary, Maria purchased DVDs of TV series and movies that included vampires and accountants to see what was available already. She and Elena viewed all of her purchases and made many notes for a pilot episode for a series titled Bloodsuckers LLP. She gave them all away to be sold at the local high school's fundraising sale.

Note 3 Her publisher reimbursed her 100% for her travel costs. She was very popular at book fairs and book readings and her public appearances always resulted in a major increase in sales of her work.

At Elena's insistence, Maria's very old computer's hard disk was wiped clean and recycled along with all of her old computer peripherals. Her only UCC balance as at January 1, 2021, was $150 for class 50. The capital cost of the class 50 property to be recycled totalled $2,700.

As she did her writing in Regina on the kitchen table and in bed, she did not deduct workspace in the home costs prior to April 1. Due to the increasing success and scope of her work, Maria decided that she and Elena needed to have dedicated office space in Calgary.

Maria's office occupied 22% of the total livable floor area of her Calgary home. Her 2021 home expenditures for April 2 to December 31 were as follows:

Mortgage interest	$24,000
Utilities	5,600
Property taxes	11,500
House insurance	1,600
House repair costs	2,800
House cleaning	3,100
Home telephone land line	750
Home internet service (40% business use)	960

As she does not wish to have to report any capital gain or recapture upon its eventual disposition, Maria will not claim CCA on the portion of her home that is used for her office.

Other Information

1. In February 2021, Maria was surprised to receive a $15,000 cheque from the grocery store where Jonathan had worked. She learned it was a death benefit.

2. In March 2020, she received a $50,000 cheque from her sister, Teresa. She had raised it through a GoFundMe online campaign to help pay for Dirk's medical costs. Jonathan was a volunteer hockey coach who was well loved by the many children he had coached over the years and their parents. The donations came in from all over Canada.

3. Maria's mother, Betty Lou, was diagnosed with terminal cancer. She and Maria's father had run a very successful real estate firm for over 25 years. On July 1, 2021, Betty Lou gifted 1,000 preferred shares to each of her grandchildren. The 4,000 shares had a total fair market value of $1,000,000. The shares paid quarterly eligible dividends of $4 per share in September and December. At the end of 2021, Betty Lou was under hospice care.

4. Child care costs were necessary for Cole when Maria was away promoting her books. They totalled $3,900 for 2021. In the summer, Cole spent four weeks in July at a hockey camp in Canmore. The fees at this camp were $1,000 per week. Trish spent the same four weeks at a music camp in Banff. The fees at this camp were $800 per week. Maria spent the four weeks on the road, promoting her work.

5. Maria's stock trading portfolio experienced 21% growth for 2021. Before Jonathan's death they had separate discount broker accounts. They had different tolerances for risk, with Jonathan invested in a low-risk portfolio and Maria invested in a high-risk one. At the time of his death, Jonathan's stocks had a total adjusted cost base of $378,000 and a fair market value of $401,000. They were transferred to Maria's account in compliance with his will. On the transfer date, they had a fair market value of $408,000.

6. In September, she sold every stock from Jonathan's estate for a total of $392,000. In addition, she sold shares in a cannabis company for $26,600 that she had purchased at a cost of $11,000. Prior to September, the inherited stocks paid eligible dividends of $12,600.

7. During 2021, Maria made a $6,000 contribution to her TFSA and a $6,000 contribution to Elena's TFSA. She also made a $6,000 contribution ($2,000 per minor child) to the family RESP.

8. After the accident, the doctors who operated on Dirk said he would likely never walk or regain the use of his arms. He took this as a challenge and vowed that he would play hockey again. He wanted continual physiotherapy to help him achieve this goal. Maria used $46,000

of the money received through the GoFundMe campaign to pay for physiotherapists. By the end of December, Dirk was encouraged that he had regained some feeling in his hands, but he could not move them by himself. A doctor attending him gave Maria a T2201 Disability Tax Credit Certificate.

9. Maria used the remaining $4,000 of the GoFundMe money to pay for grief counselling by psychiatrists for herself, Trish, Dirk, and Cole. Elena paid for her own medical expenses. The family's medical expenses paid for by Maria for 2021 were as follows:

Maria	$ 2,600
Trish	2,800
Dirk (Including $9,300 attendant care costs)	56,700
Cole	4,100
Total medical expenses	$66,200

Required:

A. Determine Maria's net income, taxable income, and federal income tax payable and her CPP liability for 2021. Ignore GST/HST & PST considerations.

B. Calculate the increase in 2021 net income arising from the eligible dividends received for each of the four children.

CHAPTER 10

Retirement Savings and Other Special Income Arrangements

Learning Objectives

After completing Chapter 10, you should be able to:

1. Explain the general procedures used to provide tax deferral on retirement savings (Paragraph [P hereafter] 10-1 to 10-17).
2. Describe the difference between a defined benefit pension plan and a defined contribution (a.k.a. money purchase) pension plan (P 10-18 to 10-20).
3. Describe the basic mechanism and operation of RRSPs (P 10-21 to 10-37).
4. Understand the terms RRSP deduction limit, unused RRSP deduction room, and RRSP dollar limit (P 10-38 to 10-46).
5. Calculate earned income for RRSP purposes (P 10-47 to 10-49).
6. Explain the concepts underlying pension adjustments (PAs) (P 10-50 to 10-60).
7. Explain the concepts underlying past service pension adjustments (PSPAs) (P 10-61 to 10-66).
8. Explain the concepts underlying pension adjustment reversals (PARs) (P 10-67 to 10-71).
9. Calculate an individual's maximum RRSP deduction and unused RRSP deduction room (P 10-72).
10. Apply the tax treatment for undeducted RRSP contributions (P 10-73 and 10-74).
11. Determine whether an individual has made "excess" contributions to an RRSP and identify associated tax planning issues, including the use of TFSAs (P 10-75 to 10-83).
12. Recall the tax treatment of RRSP and RRIF administration fees (P 10-84).
13. Apply the provisions relating to RRSP withdrawals and voluntary conversions of RRSPs (P 10-85 to 10-92).
14. Apply the provisions relating to RRSP terminations due to the age limitation (P 10-93 to 10-94).
15. Apply the provisions associated with spousal RRSPs and identify associated tax planning issues (P 10-95 to 10-103).
16. Describe and apply the provisions of the Home Buyers' Plan (HBP) (P 10-104 to 10-113).
17. Describe and apply the provisions of the Lifelong Learning Plan (LLP) (P 10-114 to 10-122).
18. Apply the RRSP provisions relating to ceasing to be a resident of Canada and death of an annuitant (P 10-123 to 10-136).
19. Explain the general provisions associated with registered pension plans (RPPs) (P 10-137 to 10-152).
20. Describe, in general terms, pooled registered pension plans (PRPPs) and target benefit plans (P 10-153 to 10-159).

21. Describe how an expanded CPP program could help the retirement savings problem (P 10-160 to 10-165).
22. Describe the basic operation of RRIFs and the role that RRIFs play in tax planning for retirement (P 10-166 to 10-184).
23. Explain the general rules for deferred profit-sharing plans (DPSPs) (P 10-185 to 10-190).
24. Describe, in general terms, employee profit-sharing plans (EPSPs) (P 10-191 to 10-194).
25. Describe the tax-free transfers that can be made between various types of plans (P 10-195 and 10-196).
26. Apply the special rules associated with RRSP contributions and retiring allowances (P 10-197 and 10-199).
27. Explain the general provisions related to retirement compensation arrangements (RCAs) (P 10-200 to 10-207).
28. Describe salary deferral arrangements (SDAs) (P 10-208 to 10-216).
29. Explain in your own words individual pension plans (IPP) and their purpose (P 10-217 to 10-219).

Planning for Retirement

Introduction

10-1. Increasing life expectancies and lower birth rates are creating a situation in which the portion of the Canadian population that is of retirement age has been increasing, and will continue to do so. This, in turn, leads to the need to allocate a growing proportion of resources to caring for this segment of the population. There are enormous social and economic considerations resulting from this trend. As it currently stands the federal government provides some age-related retirement income programs, such as Old Age Security (OAS) and the Canada Pension Plan (CPP), but it is often insufficient to meet the financial needs of individuals in their retirement years. We would add that those government programs were never intended to meet the financial goals of retirement but rather to provide a certain minimum amount of income to assist in retirement years when taken together with personal savings. In summary, this means that meeting financial retirement goals is a two-stage process that requires both federal govenment assistance together with steps taken by individuals to prepare themselves for retirement.

10-2. The impact of being unable to meet certain minimum income requirements are the postponement of retirement or a partial or semi-retirement where individuals are forced to find some part-time employment to supplement what they receive from the government. In other words relying solely on government retirement benefits can be problematic unless individuals are willing to reduce the standard of living they are accustomed to. The good news is that the ITA provides a number of incentives in the form of retirement planning arrangements to assist individuals in helping themselves prepare for retirement.

10-3. As we have alluded to, there is a balance required where it is important for individuals during their pre-retirement working years to plan for their retirement well in advance to ensure that the personal measures they have taken, together with government provided pension benefits, are sufficient to allow for a full and enjoyable retirement. The federal government continues to be concerned that too many Canadians are ill-prepared when the time comes. We saw in Chapter 9 that the government introduced pension splitting many years go as a means of reducing the income tax burden on retired individuals to assist in meeting financial retirement goals. Other recent government action has been underway since 2018 with the government intent on increasing CPP retirement benefits as a form of forced savings to ensure that individuals are one step closer to being financially prepared for retirement. In this chapter we will examine the variety of retirement income plans and arrangements condoned within the ITA to permit individuals to meet their financial retirement goals.

Providing Consistency

10-4. As mentioned, minimal financial requirements for retirement are provided by OAS payments and the CPP system. However, for 2021, the maximum payment under the CPP is

$15,437 per year for a person with no disability. When this is combined with the current OAS payments of $7,362 per year, the total does not provide for the lifestyle many individuals would like to enjoy during their retirement years. In response to this situation, the Canadian income tax system contains a number of provisions that encourage the development of various private retirement savings arrangements to supplement benefits provided under the government provided plans. These include the following:

- Registered retirement savings plans (RRSPs)
- Registered pension plans (RPPs), including individual pension plans
- Target benefit plans
- Pooled registered pension plans
- Registered retirement income funds (RRIFs)
- Deferred profit-sharing plans (DPSPs)

10-5. The current retirement savings system was initiated in 1990. At the heart of this system is the concept that retirement savings should have an annual limit that is consistently applied to all types of plans. This limit represents the extent to which the federal government is willing to provide tax savings and deferral opportunities. We will discuss this limitation in this chapter. The amount of this limit is subject to annual indexing so that it should generally keep up with inflation.

10-6. The major problem faced by the government in designing the current system was to ensure that, despite the variety of retirement savings vehicles available, the annual contribution limit was applied in a consistent manner, without regard to the variety of retirement savings vehicles used by an individual or the manner in which the ultimate retirement benefit was determined.

10-7. The detailed provisions related to the different types of tax-assisted retirement savings plans show considerable variation. For example, RPPs and DPSPs require employer sponsorship. In contrast, any Canadian resident can establish an RRSP or RRIF.

10-8. Despite such variation, the basic idea underlying all of these plans is the same. They allow individuals to invest a considerable amount of funds into a trust arrangement. The amounts invested are either deductible to the individual taxpayer (RRSP contributions and employee RPP contributions) or can be paid by an employer without creating a taxable benefit (employer RPP and DPSP contributions). Since the trusts governed by these savings plans are exempt from Part I tax as a result of ITA 149(1), the accumulation of income within these trusts is not subjected to any Part I income tax while the plans retain the funds and qualify for this exempt treatment. There is a considerable opportunity for extensive deferral given that funds could be retained within these plans for many, many years. The core basic arrangement can be seen graphically in Figure 10-1.

Figure 10-1
Retirement Savings—The Basic System

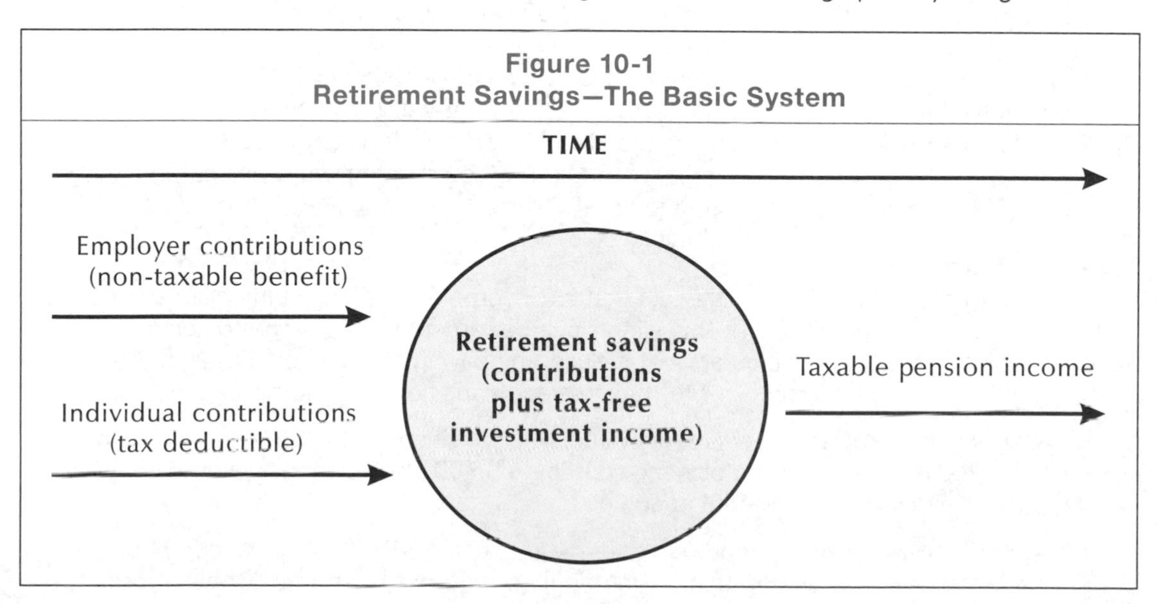

10-9. You will recall that we also discussed registered savings plans in Chapter 9. The discussion in that chapter covered Tax-Free Savings Accounts (TFSAs), registered education savings plans (RESPs), and registered disability savings plans (RDSP). There are a few major differences between those plans and the ones that we will discuss in this chapter. One of the most significant is that RESPs and TFSAs are intended to provide current savings and savings for educational pursuits as opposed to retirement arrangements. RDSPs are somewhat different in that while they also provide for financial needs, once supporting individuals such as parents have passed away, they really represent meeting lifelong financial needs again as opposed solely to retirement. In the absence of a tax policy designed to assist with retirement planning, the contributions made to TFSAs, RESPs, and RDSPs do not reduce an individual contributor's net income. In contrast, the retirement savings plans covered in this chapter provide two distinct advantages: (1) Contributions made by individuals generally reduce one's net income, and (2) certain contributions made by one's employer are not considered taxable employment benefits. An added advantage is that employer contributions to RPPs and DPSPs remain a deductible expense to the employer even though such contributions are not included in the income of the employee who has benefited from that contribution. This lack of symmetry is not uncommon in the ITA given that symmetry is not a Canadian income tax principle.

Tax-Deferred Savings

Sources of Deferral

10-10. As shown in Figure 10-1, there are two basic sources for the investment funds going into retirement savings plans. First, for employed individuals, employers may make contributions to RPPs and DPSPs. These contributions do not create a taxable employment benefit (ITA 6(1)(a)), however on withdrawal they are included in net income as retirement income (ITA 56(1)(a)). The time between the contributions and actual withdrawals as pension income is often lengthy, providing considerable deferral.

10-11. The second source of investment funds is the contributions made by employed individuals to RPPs and by all individuals to RRSPs. RPP contributions are deductible against the related employment income (ITA 8(1)(m)), and RRSP deductions are deductible under ITA 60(i). The ability to deduct the contributions is the immediate avoidance of any income tax, and while the income tax on those contributions will be payable on withdrawal there is considerable income tax deferral. The deferral period may exceed 45 years for contributions made at the beginning of an individual's working life.

EXAMPLE Janice earns $40,000 a year in employment income and estimates that she will pay combined federal and provincial income taxes of $8,000 for 2021. She is also considering setting up and making a $2,000 contribution to an RRSP for herself. Her employment withholdings are such that she never receives a refund or owes any additional income tax. With an average income tax rate of 20% [($8,000/$40,000)] she estimates that, because of the RRSP deduction, she will be entitled to a refund of $400 [(20%)($2,000)]. The effect of the RRSP deduction is that only $38,000 of her employment income is subject to income tax. The government forgoes income tax on the $2,000 since it was contributed to an RRSP.

Tax-Free Compounding

10-12. Also of great importance is the fact that the income earned within the plan is not subject to income tax until it is withdrawn. This allows a larger amount of earnings to accumulate at a faster rate given that the earnings are not reduced by paying income tax. As illustrated in the following example, the importance of this tax-free accumulation should not be underestimated.

EXAMPLE Mr. Kerr is a 35-year-old individual who pays income taxes at a marginal rate of 45%. For the next 30 years, he plans to contribute $5,000 of his annual income per year toward his anticipated retirement at age 65.

ANALYSIS If Mr. Kerr contributes this amount to an RRSP, the annual contributions are deductible. If this $5,000 annual contribution is invested at a 10% rate of return, it will accumulate to $822,470 at the end of 30 years. If the full amount is withdrawn when he reaches age 65, and he is still paying taxes at a marginal rate of 45%, he will be left with after-tax funds of $452,359 [($822,470) - (45%)($822,470)].

If Mr. Kerr had not invested in an RRSP, taxes at 45% would have been paid on the $5,000, leaving only $2,750 per year to invest. Further, if he invests these funds at 10% outside of an RRSP, his after-tax earnings will only be 5.5% [(10%)(1 - .45)]. At this after-tax rate, the investment of $2,750 per year for 30 years would result in an accumulation of only $199,198 by the time Mr. Kerr is 65 years old, less than half of the after-tax accumulation from investing in an RRSP.

10-13. In effect, the deferral of income taxes on the deductible contributions, as well as the deferral of income tax on the income earned in the fund, provides for a larger accumulation of funds being available for retirement. As this fairly realistic example illustrates, the amounts involved can be substantial.

Early Contributions

10-14. The availability of tax-free compounding in an RRSP makes it advantageous to contribute as early as possible. RRSP contributions for 2021 can be made as early as January 1, 2021, or as late as 60 days after the end of 2021 (to March 1, 2022). It can be demonstrated that, over a contribution period of 35 years, making contributions at the earliest date as opposed to the latest date can result in a 10% increase in the balance in the plan.

Advantages at Retirement

10-15. The use of these tax-deferred retirement savings plans may have additional advantages. If either federal or provincial tax rates have been lowered, the effective tax rate at the time of withdrawal may be lower than the rate when the contributions are made. Note, however, that the opposite effect may arise if federal or provincial rates are increased.

10-16. In addition, retirement may result in a sufficient reduction in income for some individuals, so that they find themselves in a lower income tax bracket. Someone who spends their working life subject to a 50% income tax rate could find that, at retirement, their marginal income tax bracket is only 25%. As this lower rate would apply to amounts withdrawn from a retirement savings plan, the deferral of income tax on contributions and investment earnings within the RRSP will result in an absolute reduction in taxes paid, which is a form of allowable income tax avoidance.

10-17. Even if the individual is not paying taxes at a lower rate after retirement, there are additional advantages associated with funds withdrawn from these plans. The first $2,000 of eligible pension income entitles the recipient to a 15% pension credit against federal income tax payable each year. This means reducing one's income tax for the year by $300. Couples can double up on this credit, increasing the income tax savings to $600 through pension income splitting (discussed in Chapter 9).

Defined Benefit vs. Money Purchase Plans

10-18. A major problem in the design of Canada's retirement savings system is the fact that, unlike RRSPs, DPSPs, and RRIFs, RPPs may be designed to provide a specified benefit after retirement. Such plans are normally referred to as defined benefit plans, while other types of RPPs are referred to as money purchase or defined contribution plans. A basic understanding of the difference between these two types of plans is essential to the comprehension of the material in this chapter. In view of this, the following brief descriptions are provided:

Defined Benefit Plans In defined benefit plans, the plan sponsor undertakes to provide a specified benefit, usually expressed as a percentage of earnings, for each year of qualifying service. For example, such a plan might require an employer to provide a retirement benefit equal to 2% of an employee's average lifetime earnings for each year of service. Thus, if an employee worked for 20 years and earned an average salary of $50,000 per year, the retirement benefit would be $20,000 per year [(2%)(20)($50,000)].

In promising this benefit, the employer has effectively agreed to make whatever amount of contributions required to provide these benefits in addition to any contributions required of the employee during the employment period. The required amount of contributions will vary depending on a number of factors, the most important of which is earnings within the plans. Employee turnover and employee life expectancy at retirement are also influential. In this type of plan, the employer assumes all the risk and uncertainty associated with these factors to ensure that the plans are sufficiently funded to maintain the promised payments.

Money Purchase Plans (Defined Contribution Plans) These plans are distinguished by the fact that the employer agrees to make specified contributions for each plan participant. A typical plan might find an employer agreeing to contribute 3% of each employee's annual wages to a fund that would be established to provide retirement benefits. The employer would have no obligations beyond making the specified contributions, and the employee would have no guarantee as to the amount of the retirement benefit that is to be received.

The actual benefit that will be received will be based on the amounts contributed and the rates of return earned on the investment of these contributions. In money purchase plans, it is the employee who is assuming the risk and uncertainty associated with the investment of the contributed funds since the employee's pension will be based on the returns the plan can earn based on the funds in the plan. We would also note that defined benefit plans are a common feature in the public sector (government) as opposed to the private sector, where many employers are unwilling to accept the long-term risk of meeting defined benefit plan payments. It is estimated that few defined benefit plans will remain in the private sector past 2026 other than those industries competing with the government for their workforce.

In summary, the difference between money purchase and defined benefit plans is that in money purchase plans employees and employers make contributions but at retirement one's monthly pension benefits are based on what the plan is able to earn, which could result in some variation in payments. Defined benefit plans, on the other hand, provide a guaranteed fixed monthly benefit.

10-19. Before leaving these descriptions, we would note that while the term is not usually applied to them, RRSPs, DPSPs, and RRIFs are essentially money purchase plans. That is, the benefits to be received from such plans are based on the amounts contributed to the plan and the earnings resulting from the investment of these amounts. Such plans do not guarantee that the individual will receive a specified benefit after retirement. Currently, the only widely used retirement savings arrangement that uses the defined benefit approach is the employer-sponsored RPP.

10-20. It is perhaps because of this trend that the government introduced pooled registered pension plans (PRPPs). These plans allow employers with a small number of employees to group together to provide a defined contribution plan (a.k.a. money purchase plan) on a pooled basis with other employers. Target benefit plans have also been introduced for some employers. Both of these types of plans will be discussed later in this chapter.

Registered Retirement Savings Plans (RRSPs)—ITA 146

Basic Operations

Establishment

10-21. The general rules for RRSPs are found in ITA 146. The nature of an RRSP is that it is structured as a trust with an individual contributor, an individual beneficiary (who can be the contributor), and a financial institution acting as the administrator/trustee. Financial institutions offering such plans include Canadian chartered banks, Canadian mutual funds, Canadian trust companies, Canadian credit unions, Canadian brokerage firms, and Canadian insurance companies. The individual beneficiary is technically referred to as the "annuitant."

10-22. Registration of the plan results in the contributor being able to deduct a limited amount of contributions to the plan for income tax purposes. Further, the income earned within the RRSP trust is exempt from Part I tax by ITA 149(1). None of the RRSP trust income is attributed back to the individual contributor. RRSP withdrawals of income and contributions are included in the net income of the beneficiary/annuitant when received (ITA 56(1)).

Withdrawals

10-23. RRSP withdrawals are required to be included in the net income of the recipient except where the funds are withdrawn pursuant to the terms and conditions of the Home Buyers' Plan or the Lifelong Learning Plan (discussed later in this chapter). RRSP plan trustees are otherwise obliged to withhold a percentage of the amount withdrawn as a partial payment toward the income tax that will be required to be paid once the income tax return for the year of receipt has been filed. Current withholding rates are 10% for withdrawals up to $5,000, 20% for withdrawals between $5,000 and $15,000, and 30% for withdrawals above $15,000.

10-24. Withdrawals are treated as other income and added to net income through ITA 56(1)(h). While some trusts have the ability to flow certain types of income through to trust beneficiaries (such as capital gains, dividends, and foreign income), this is not the case with trusts governed by deferred income plans such as RRSPs. Regardless of the type of income earned in the trust, all withdrawals are fully included in income.

Investment Options for an RRSP

10-25. There are two basic types of RRSPs. Managed RRSPs are managed by the financial institution that holds the fund assets. Self-administered (self-directed) RRSPs are managed by the individuals. For individuals who prefer to make their own investment decisions with respect to the fund assets, the self-administered type of plan is ideal.

10-26. An additional advantage of the self-administered type of plan is that the individual can contribute personally owned investments, such as shares, into the plan. However, with the availability of discount brokers charging minimal commissions, the importance of this advantage for many individuals has declined over time. Since an RRSP is a separate entity treated as an "individual" by the ITA, such property contributions are considered dispositions of property. These dispositions are subject to the rules discussed in Chapter 9, such as ITA 69(1), since an RRSP contributor and the RRSP trust are deemed to be non-arm's length with each other (ITA 251(1)(b)). This means that dispositions must occur at fair market value (FMV). As a result, any taxable capital gains arising on the disposition will be required to be included in the contributor's net income. Note, however, that ITA 40(2)(g)(iv) deems any capital losses on such contributions to be nil. As a result it is good practice to avoid contributing investments to an RRSP where the investments have unrealized losses. We should also add a note on beneficial ownership. When an individual contributes property owned by an RRSP in which she is the beneficiary, there is no deemed change in beneficial ownership and this would not be considered as a disposition for income tax purposes. The definition of a "disposition" in ITA 248(1), however, makes an exception for many transfers of property to various trusts, including those governed by deferred income plans such as RRSPs.

> **EXAMPLE** An individual contributes personally owned investments to his self-administered RRSP. The shares of Company A have an ACB of $5,000 and a FMV of $7,000. The shares of Company B have an ACB of $5,000 and a FMV of $4,000.
>
> **ANALYSIS** Each transaction would be required to take place at FMV. As a result, there would be a capital gain on the Company A shares of $2,000 [POD $7,000 - ACB $5,000] but a capital loss of $1,000 [POD $4,000 - ACB $5,000] on the shares of Company B, which is deemed to be nil. Given this, if the individual wishes to include Company B shares in the RRSP, it would be preferable to first sell the shares, realize the capital

loss, and then contribute the proceeds of the sale to the RRSP. The RRSP could then purchase the shares on its own account. Since an individual and an RRSP trust are affiliated persons (discussed in Chapter 16), caution would have to be taken to avoid the superficial loss rules, which were discussed in Chapter 8. If those rules applied, the capital loss of $1,000 would be denied. The best way to avoid the rules is to delay the purchase of the Company B shares by the RRSP trust until 30 days have passed.

10-27. If the individual's preference is to have a financial institution manage the plan, the individual will be confronted with a wide variety of choices. Managed funds include those that invest entirely in equity securities, funds that hold only long-term bonds, funds with mixed portfolios, and funds that specialize in one type of investment such as mortgages.

10-28. Choosing between the alternatives involves an assessment of many factors, including the investment goals of the individual and the fees charged by the various plans. With hundreds of choices available, the decision can be difficult. However, considering the amount of financial resources that may eventually be invested in an RRSP, it is not a decision that should be made lightly.

10-29. Since an individual can own an interest in any number of separate RRSPs, it is possible to have both a self-administered and a managed plan. Further diversification could be achieved by having two or more types of managed plans. However, the extra effort and costs required to keep track of the multiple plans should be considered.

10-30. The ITA is flexible with respect to the types of investments that can be included in either a self-administered or a managed RRSP. ITR Part XLIX (4900) provides a detailed listing of the specific investment categories and includes publicly traded shares, mutual fund units, bonds, mortgages, warrants, and rights. The only significant restrictions relate to investments in the shares of private companies that are under the influence of the individual annuitant and direct investments in real estate. There is no limit on foreign content (e.g., shares of U.S. public companies). For a more complete discussion of qualified investments, see IT Folio S3-F10-C1, "Qualified Investments—RRSPs, RESPs, RRIFs, RDSPs, and TFSAs."

10-31. While it is not likely that this is a common problem, there are rules applicable to holdings of publicly traded shares where the individual for whom the RRSP is to provide retirement income (i.e., the annuitant) owns more than a 10% interest (number of shares or FMV). These holdings are referred to as "prohibited investments" and significant penalties apply if they are part of the investments contained in an RRSP, a RRIF, or a TFSA. These investments are discussed in detail in IT Folio S3-F10-C2, "Prohibited Investments—RRSPs, RRIFs, and TFSAs."

10-32. It is interesting to note that an RRSP can provide a mortgage on Canadian real property to the annuitant of the plan and anyone else, including family members, provided that the mortgage is insured under the *National Housing Act* or by some other company providing mortgage insurance and the terms and conditions reflect commercial lending practices, including the rate of interest charged. The extra costs associated with this insurance have served to limit the use of this option, although there remain some advantages.

The Capital Gains and Dividend Problems

10-33. As you are aware, when capital gains or eligible dividends are received directly by an individual, they are taxed at very favourable rates because (1) only 50% of capital gains are required to be included in net income and (2) eligible and non-eligible dividends entitle the individual recipient to a dividend tax credit. We will not consider non-eligible dividends here as, in many circumstances, the shares of private companies, which are largely responsible for non-eligible dividends, cannot be owned by an RRSP. As we noted in Chapter 7, an individual subject to Ontario's maximum rate of 53.5% would be taxed on capital gains at 26.8% and eligible dividends at 39.3%.

10-34. In contrast, when capital gains and eligible dividends are earned by an RRSP, no Part I tax will apply. However, when these amounts are used to fund a withdrawal, the full amount is required to be included in the net income of an individual annuitant. In effect, for an Ontario resident in the maximum income tax bracket, any capital gains or eligible dividends earned inside an RRSP and used to fund a withdrawal will be subjected to an income tax rate of 53.5%.

10-35. At first glance this appears to be an undesirable consequence of investing in an RRSP. However, this is mitigated by an RRSP deduction for the contribution, the effect of which allows the individual to contribute a much larger amount.

EXAMPLE An individual determines that she would be able to contribute $10,000 of her salary toward an RRSP. The individual's marginal income tax rate on ordinary income is 52% and 37% on eligible dividends. The individual is considering investing in the shares of a Canadian public company in one of three ways:

- Investing the full $10,000 through an RRSP. The RRSP would then purchase $10,000 of the public company shares. Note that the full amount can be contributed because the contribution is deductible.
- Paying the income tax of 52% on the $10,000 of salary and investing the remaning amount of $4,800 [($10,000)(1 - .52)] through a TFSA. The TFSA would then purchase $4,800 of public company shares.
- Paying the income tax of 52% on the $10,000 of salary and investing the remaning amount of $4,800 directly in the public company shares through a personal trading account.

Assume that over the following two years the shares of the Canadian public company will increase in value by 50%. No dividends will be paid by the company during this period.

At the end of the two-year period, all available funds, including maximum withdrawals from the RRSP and the TFSA, will be used to purchase a home.

ANALYSIS The result for the three alternatives are as follows:

RRSP Result

Deductible contribution	$10,000
Increase in value [(50%)($10,000)]	5,000
Available withdrawal	$15,000
Tax on withdrawal [(52%)($15,000)]	(7,800)
After-tax funds available	$ 7,200

TFSA Result

Initial investment	$4,800
Increase in value [(50%)($4,800)]	$2,400
Available withdrawal	$7,200
Tax on withdrawal	Nil
After-tax funds available	$7,200

Direct Investment Result

Initial investment	$4,800
Increase in value [(50%)($4,800)]	2,400
Available funds	$7,200
Tax on capital gain [(1/2)(52%)($2,400)]	(624)
After-tax funds available	$6,576

10-36. This simple example illustrates that the benefits of being able to deduct contributions to an RRSP can more than offset the unfavourable income tax treatment that is given to capital gains that fund withdrawals from such plans. Using the RRSP results in an additional $624 ($7,200 - $6,576) in savings over a direct personal investment.

10-37. Note also that, in comparison with a TFSA, the deductibility of RRSP contributions and the resulting ability to contribute a larger amount to an RRSP is offset by the fact that no income taxes are charged on a TFSA withdrawal since no amount is required to be included in net income. Both the RRSP and the TFSA result in the individual having $7,200 in funds to use in purchasing a home.

Exercise 10-1

Subject: Comparison of Dividends Earned in an RRSP, a TFSA, and Directly

Brian Forthright has $20,000 in before-tax income that he can use for investment purposes. He is trying to decide whether it would be better to contribute the $20,000 to his RRSP and deduct the full amount or invest the after-tax amount of these funds either in a TFSA or outside either plan by investing directly on his own. He will invest the available funds in preferred shares that pay an annual eligible dividend of 5%. At the end of five years he would like to take an extended vacation. At that time he will direct the RRSP or TFSA to dispose of the shares and will withdraw all of the amounts, including dividends received. If he invests directly he will sell the shares using all the available after-tax funds, including the dividends.

Brian's combined marginal tax rate on ordinary income is 40% and 22% on eligible dividends. Ignoring the effect of any reinvestment of the dividend income, determine which of the three alternatives will provide more funds for Brian's trip.

Solutions to Exercises are available in the Study Guide.

Non-Deductible Financing Costs

10-38. As a final point, it is important to note that interest paid on funds borrowed to finance RRSP contributions is not deductible. The ability to deduct interest expenses is based on having a source of income that is from property or a business. The source of income in this case exists in the form of an interest in an RRSP trust. This means that the interest expense could apply, however ITA 18(11) establishes that no interest expense is permitted on amounts borrowed to finance an RRSP contribution. This suggests that it may not be desirable for an individual to borrow to make RRSP contributions. A complete analysis of this issue requires an estimate of how long the loan will be outstanding and a comparison of the individual's borrowing rate with the expected return on funds invested in the plan.

RRSP Deduction Limit

The Basic Formula

10-39. At the heart of this retirement savings system is the RRSP deduction limit. It is this amount that determines the maximum contribution to an RRSP that can be deducted in a year. While this amount is sometimes referred to as the contribution limit, this is not an accurate description. The definition of RRSP deduction limit is found in ITA 146(1) and is reproduced in Figure 10-2. There are several technical terms included in this definition, and they are highlighted in Figure 10-2 with bold, italic type. Explanations for each term will be provided in the material that follows.

Figure 10-2
RRSP Deduction Limit Formula—ITA 146(1)

"RRSP deduction limit" of a taxpayer for a taxation year means the amount determined by the formula

A + B + R – C, where

A is the taxpayer's ***unused RRSP deduction room*** at the end of the preceding taxation year;

B is the amount, if any, by which

(a) the lesser of the RRSP dollar limit for the year and 18% of the taxpayer's ***earned income*** for the preceding taxation year,

exceeds the total of all amounts, each of which is

(b) the taxpayer's ***pension adjustment*** for the preceding taxation year in respect of an employer, or

(c) a ***prescribed amount*** in respect of the taxpayer for the year;

C is the taxpayer's net ***past service pension adjustment*** for the year; and

R is the taxpayer's total ***pension adjustment reversal*** for the year.

Example of relevant years Contributions made during the first 60 days of 2022 and undeducted contributions made in years prior to 2021 can be deducted against the RRSP deduction limit for 2021. To ensure the necessary information is available, the RRSP deduction limit for 2021 is based on earned income for the previous year (2020), as well as a pension adjustment that is also calculated using amounts from 2020.

10-40. The RRSP deduction limit is neither a limit on contributions that can be made during the current year nor a requirement that the contributions deducted in the current year be made in that year. A limited amount of non-deductible contributions can be made that are in excess of the RRSP deduction limit. Further, contributions made in earlier years that were not deducted in those years, or contributions made in the first 60 days of the following year, can be deducted under the RRSP deduction limit for the current year.

10-41. The reason for using an earned income amount from a previous year is to allow an individual to be able to determine, as soon as is possible, the maximum contributions he can make for the current year. If the limitation had been based on the current year's earned income, an individual would have to make contributions during the year based only on an estimate of his earned income, a situation that would often result in contributions that are imprecise.

10-42. To assist individuals in dealing with this deduction limit calculation, the CRA issues an RRSP Deduction Limit Statement for those individuals who have filed income tax returns. It is included with the original notice of assessment and, assuming the income tax return is filed on time, calculates the individual's maximum RRSP deduction for the year. The RRSP Statement is also available online through the CRA's My Account portal.

EXAMPLE The RRSP Statement for the 2021 year will normally be available online or through the mail during April or May 2021. This statement identifies the maximum RRSP deduction that can be claimed for 2021. Note that this maximum deduction can be made using undeducted contributions made before 2021 or in the first 60 days of 2022. There is no requirement that the deduction for 2021 be based on contributions only made during 2021.

Unused RRSP Deduction Room

10-43. As it is used in the Figure 10-2 formula, an individual's unused RRSP deduction room at the end of the preceding year is simply the cumulative total of all of the amounts determined under the formula for years prior to the current year, less any amounts that have been deducted in those years.

10-44. This approach provides for a carry forward of deduction room that is not time limited. As a result, an individual who lacks the funds necessary to make an RRSP contribution in a particular year does not lose the deduction room available up to that year. The deduction room is carried forward and provides the basis for a deductible contribution in future years.

RRSP Dollar Limit

10-45. The RRSP dollar limit is defined in terms of the money purchase limit that is defined at ITA 147.1(1) and contains the rules for RPPs. The money purchase limit is the annual limit for contributions made to RPPs. Because of the one-year lag in the data used for the RRSP deduction limit, the RRSP dollar limit is generally defined as the money purchase limit for the preceding year.

10-46. Money purchase limits and the RRSP dollar limits for years 2018 through 2022 are as follows:

Year	Money Purchase Limit	RRSP Dollar Limit
2018	$26,500	26,230
2019	27,230	26,500
2020	27,830	27,230
2021	**29,210**	**27,830**
2022	Indexed	29,210

Earned Income

10-47. The ITA, unfortunately, uses the expression "earned income" both for child care expense (discussed in Chapter 9) and RRSP contribution purposes, and although the definitions have some similarities they serve different purposes and are therefore not the same. Earned income for RRSP purposes is defined in ITA 146(1). The basic idea underlying the definition of earned income for RRSP purposes is that the income is generally earned by the individual rather than received as the result of owning property. This means that interest, dividends, and capital gains are excluded from the definition.

10-48. Surprisingly, however, net rental income is included, despite the fact that, for individuals, rental income is usually a form of property income. Another unusual feature of the definition is that it includes a modified version of employment income that does not allow an employee a deduction for RPP contributions. This is likely due to the fact that RPP contributions are separately considered as part of an individual's overall retirement limitations. Note that the deductible portion of CPP contributions payable because of self-employed income are deducted under Subdivision e [ITA 60(e) and (e.1)]. Since this means that they do not affect the calculation of business income, they do not affect the calculation of earned income for RRSP purposes, which would be consistent with the view that pension-related contribution deductions, whether they are employment or business related, are already factored into the overall limitations. The example provided in Paragraph 10-54 explores this further.

10-49. The basic components of earned income are as follows:

Additions

- Employment income, computed without the ITA 8(1)(m) deduction for employee RPP contributions
- Income from carrying on a business
- Rental income from real property
- Income from a business earned as an active partner of a partnership
- Royalties, provided the recipient is the author, composer, or inventor of the work

- Spousal support amounts received
- Research grants, net of certain related expenses
- CPP and Quebec Pension Plan (QPP) disability benefits received
- Supplementary unemployment benefit plan payments (this does not include the regular EI benefit payments)

Deductions

- Spousal support payments
- Losses from carrying on a business
- Business losses allocated to an active partner by the partnership
- Losses from the rental of real property

Exercise 10-2

Subject: Earned Income

Mr. Jarwhol Nacari has employment income of $56,000 (he is not a member of an RPP), interest income of $22,000, rental income of $2,500, and receives spousal support payments from his former spouse of $12,000 during the current year. What is Mr. Nacari's earned income for RRSP purposes for the current year?

Exercise 10-3

Subject: Earned Income

During the current year, Ms. Shelly Devine has employment income of $82,000 (after the deduction of $3,000 in RPP contributions), a business loss of $12,500, and taxable dividends of $4,200. She pays spousal support to her former spouse of $18,000 during the current year. What is Ms. Devine's earned income for RRSP purposes for the current year?

Solutions to Exercises are available in the Study Guide.

Pension Adjustments (PAs)—Overview

10-50. If an individual participates in an RPP or a DPSP, their RRSP deduction limit must be reduced to reflect retirement savings that are included in those plans. If this did not happen, individuals with benefits under RPPs and DPSPs would have access to much larger amounts of tax-deferred retirement savings than would be the case for individuals that do have access to such plans. The best way to visualize the concept is to think in terms of a large container. You can fill the container with RPP, DPSP, and RRSP but you cannot overfill that container. If the container is filled with RPP or RRSP or DPSP, then there is no room left for anything else until the next year.

10-51. Pension adjustments (PAs) are designed to reflect the benefits earned by an individual through defined benefit RPPs or contributions made to money purchase RPPs and DPSPs by an individual or her employer during a particular year. As RPPs and DPSPs are always sponsored by an employer, the CRA requires the employer to calculate an annual PA for each employee who is a member of that employer's RPP or DPSP. This amount is reported on the employee's T4. The PA is designed to assess the quality of those pension plans. If, for example, the individual is entitled to a generous defined benefit RPP plan, there may be little left in the container for RRSP contributions.

10-52. PAs for 2021 are reported to the CRA and the individual employee in the 2021 T4s that are required to be issued by the last day of February 2022. The PA amount is disclosed to employees in Box 52 of the T4 information slip. These PAs are also incorporated into the 2021 RRSP Deduction Limit Statement that the CRA issues for the 2021 taxation year. Because of this, the PA that is deducted in the calculation of the taxpayer's RRSP deduction limit for the current year is based on the employer's contributions or benefits granted during the preceding year. More specifically, the

2021 RRSP deduction limit is reduced by PAs calculated with reference to 2020 RPP benefits earned and RPP and DPSP contributions made.

Exercise 10-4

Subject: Retirement Savings

How does the Canadian retirement savings system prevent individuals who are a member of their employer's RPP or DPSP from being treated more favourably than individuals who only have access to an RRSP for retirement savings?

Solutions to Exercises are available in the Study Guide.

Pension Adjustments—Money Purchase RPPs and DPSPs

10-53. The calculation of PAs for money purchase plans is relatively straightforward. As RRSPs function in the same manner as money purchase plans (i.e., they do not promise a specific defined benefit), contributions to money purchase plans are directly comparable, on a dollar-for-dollar basis, with contributions to an RRSP.

10-54. As a consequence, the PA for a money purchase RPP is simply the sum of all employee and employer contributions for the year. Following the same reasoning, an employee's PA for a DPSP is simply the employer's contributions for the year that are allocated to the individual (employees cannot contribute to a DPSP). Since the PA that is deducted already includes the employee's contributions to the RPP, the employment figure used to calculate earned income must add back RPP contributions so they are not deducted twice. A simple example will illustrate these calculations.

EXAMPLE Ms. Jones' employer sponsors a money purchase RPP and a DPSP. Ms. Jones is a member of both plans. During 2020 she has employment income of $68,000 after the deduction of a $2,000 contribution to the RPP. As a result her earned income would be $70,000. Her employer contributes $2,000 to the RPP and $1,500 to the DPSP on her behalf. She has no unused RRSP deduction room at the end of 2020.

ANALYSIS Ms. Jones' 2020 PA is $5,500 (her RPP contribution $2,000 + the employer's RPP contribution $2,000 + the employer's DPSP contribution $1,500), an amount that will be reported on the 2020 T4 information slip that she will receive by the end of February 2021. After filing her 2020 income tax return, Ms. Jones will have access to her RRSP Deduction Limit Statement for 2021 from the CRA that will calculate the maximum RRSP contribution she can deduct for 2021.

As she has no unused RRSP deduction room at the end of 2020, Ms. Jones' RRSP deduction limit will be calculated by taking the lesser of the $27,830 RRSP dollar limit for 2021 and $12,600, 18% of her 2020 earned income of $70,000. The 2020 PA of $5,500 will be subtracted from the lesser amount of $12,600 to arrive at her maximum deductible RRSP contribution for 2021 of $7,100 [nil unused RRSP deduction room + additional deduction limit for 2021 based on 2020 earned income $12,600- 2020 PA of $5,500].

Pension Adjustments—Defined Benefit RPPs

10-55. As defined benefit plans guarantee the benefit to be provided, rather than specify the amount of contributions required, contributions made to these plans cannot be compared directly to contributions made to RRSPs, DPSPs, or money purchase RPPs. However, if retirement savings limits are to be applied equitably to all individuals, without regard to the type of arrangements available to them, it is necessary to find a basis for equating the benefits earned under these plans with the contributions made to those other types of plans.

10-56. There is no simple way to convert a benefit earned into an equivalent amount of contributions. While there are a number of problems in dealing with this conversion, the most significant is the age of the employee. Because of the difference in the number of years during which earnings will accumulate, it costs an employer much less in terms of current contributions to provide a $1 per year retirement benefit to an employee who is 25 years old and 40 years away from receiving that benefit than it does to provide the same retirement benefit to an employee who is 60 years old and only 5 years away from receiving the benefit.

10-57. To have a completely equitable system for dealing with this problem, different values would have to be assigned to benefits that are earned by employees of different ages. Benefits earned by older employees would have to be assigned a higher value than those earned by younger employees.

10-58. Rather than a system that takes into account the different ages of participants in defined benefit RPPs, the legislative solution is to equate $1 of benefits earned with $9 of contributions. If, during the current year, an individual earns $1 of future benefits under the provisions of a defined benefit RPP, in the calculation of her PA for the year this will be viewed as the equivalent of $9 in contributions to a money purchase RPP or DPSP. Unlike the case of money purchase plans, the amounts contributed to the plan by the employer and employee during the year do not affect the PA.

10-59. The use of the multiple 9 is an arbitrary solution that fails to give any consideration to the age of the employee. While the factor is subject to criticism it has been an essential component of the system for the last 30 years and is unlikely to change. An illustration of the perceived unfairness follows.

EXAMPLE Bryan is 25 years of age. In 2021, he earns a pension benefit in his employer's defined benefit RPP of $1,000 to be received beginning in 2061 when Bryan reaches 65 years of age. His PA for 2021 is $9,000, which decreases his RRSP deduction room by the same amount.

ANALYSIS In return for a $1,000 per-year pension after 40 years, Bryan has lost $9,000 in RRSP contribution room. Assuming that he would have used this room to make a $9,000 contribution in 2021, this contribution would have accumulated, using a 10% rate of return, to $407,331 in 2061. This balance would produce annual income well in excess of the pension benefit of $1,000 per year. Even if the $407,331 were invested at an extremely low rate of 1%, it would still generate income of $4,073 per year, more than four times the additional $1,000 of pension income to be provided by the RPP on retirement.

While this comparison is not a complete analysis of the situation it does serve to illustrate the fact that, when a pension benefit given to a young individual is multiplied by 9, there is a significant cost in terms of lost RRSP contribution room.

Exercise 10-5

Subject: Pension Adjustments

Mr. Arnett's employer sponsors both a defined benefit RPP and a DPSP. During the current year, his employer contributes $1,800 to the DPSP on behalf of Mr. Arnett. The pension benefits accrued in the year under the defined benefit RPP are equal to $600. Mr. Arnett contributes $2,300 to the RPP and the employer an equivalent amount. Calculate the amount of the PA that will be included on Mr. Arnett's T4 for the current year.

Solutions to Exercises are available in the Study Guide.

Prescribed Amount—ITA 146(1)

10-60. The prescribed amount (see Figure 10-2) is a deduction that may arise as the result of an individual transferring accumulated benefits from one RPP to a different RPP. We will not give any attention to the calculation of this amount in the text.

Past Service Pension Adjustments (PSPAs)

10-61. Past service pension adjustments (PSPAs) are designed to deal with benefits under defined benefit RPPs related to credit for past service. They are far less common than PAs. Some of the events giving rise to PSPAs are as follows:

- A new RPP is implemented by an employer and benefits are extended retroactively for years of service prior to the plan initiation.
- The benefit formula is changed, increasing the percentage that is applied to pensionable earnings to determine benefits earned. Again, a PSPA is created only if the increased benefits are extended retroactively to years of service prior to the plan amendment.
- An individual, either voluntarily or because of terms contained in the plan, works for a number of years without being a member of the plan. On joining the plan, the employee is credited for years of service prior to joining the plan.

10-62. If an individual were to receive such past service benefits without experiencing any reduction in her RRSP deduction limit, she would have effectively beaten the system. That is, the individual would be receiving additional pension benefits over and above the limits that have been established. The purpose of the PSPAs is to prevent this from happening.

10-63. PSPAs are calculated on the basis of all of the PAs that would have hypothetically applied in the years prior to the year of change if the plan or improvement had been in effect or if the individual had been a member in those years. From these redetermined PAs, the actual PAs would be deducted. The adjustments are not retroactive but instead are reported as a PSPA for the current year.

10-64. As with PAs, the employer is responsible for calculating and reporting PSPAs, normally within 60 days of the past service event. The amount is reported on a PSPA information form (not on a T4) that is sent to both the employee and the CRA. Since the current year's PA will reflect the new benefits, only years prior to the year of change are used to calculate the PSPA. As a result, unlike the one-year lag in deducting PAs, PSPAs are deducted from the RRSP deduction room formula in the year in which they occur.

10-65. The following simplified example illustrates very basic PSPA calculations.

> **EXAMPLE** Wally Oats has been a member of his employer's defined benefit RPP since 2015. Until 2021, the benefit formula provided a retirement benefit equal to 1.5% of pensionable earnings for each year of service. During 2021, the benefit formula was increased to 1.75% of pensionable earnings for each year of service, a change that is to be applied to all prior years of service. Mr. Oats has had $48,000 in pensionable earnings in each prior year.
>
> **ANALYSIS** The calculation of the PSPA for 2021 would be based on the six years of service prior to the current year (2015 to 2020) as follows:

New formula PAs [(1.75%)($48,000)(9)(6 years)]	$45,360
Previously reported PAs [(1.50%)($48,000)(9)(6 years)]	(38,880)
2021 PSPA	$ 6,480

10-66. Note that PSPAs only occur in the context of defined benefit plans. If additional contributions for past service are made to a money purchase plan, these amounts will be included in the regular pension adjustment for the year in which the contributions are made. This eliminates the need for any sort of catch up adjustment.

Pension Adjustment Reversals (PARs)

10-67. A vested pension benefit is one in which the employee has an irrevocable property right. That is, an individual employee is entitled to receive the value of the benefit without regard to whether he remains an employee of the employer providing the benefit.

10-68. In order to give their employees an incentive to remain with them, many employers grant pension benefits that do not become vested unless the employee remains for a specified period of time. A common arrangement would be for an employer to grant benefits that do not vest until the employee has completed five years of service. If an employee leaves before the end of this five-year period, he would lose any benefits earned to that point in time.

10-69. This creates a problem in that employers are required to report PAs for all benefits or contributions earned by an employee during the year, regardless of when the pension benefits become vested. This means that an employer reports PAs for benefits that may never be received by the employee. This, in turn, means that the RRSP deduction room that was eliminated by these PAs would also be lost.

10-70. To deal with this problem, pension adjustment reversals (PARs) were added to the pension legislation. Note that this is only an issue with the employer's share of contributions made or benefits earned. Provincial legislation requires that employees have a vested right to all of their own contributions.

10-71. A PAR is calculated by the employer whenever an employee terminates membership in an RPP or DPSP and receives less from the plan than the total of the PAs and PSPAs reported for the employee. The PAR is reported to the CRA and to the employee and will be added to the individual's RRSP deduction room in the year of termination. The following simple example illustrates the use of a PAR.

EXAMPLE Stan Kapitany is a member of an RPP in which benefits are not vested until the fourth year of service. He leaves after three years when he is offered an opportunity to develop high-performance race cars. His employer was required to report PAs for the first three years of his employment and this, in turn, reduced Mr. Kapitany's ability to make deductible contributions to an RRSP.

ANALYSIS Since he ceases to work for his employer prior to the benefits becoming vested, the benefits for which PAs were previously reported will not be transferred to him. This means that there will be no retirement benefits corresponding to the previously reported PAs and, as a consequence, Mr. Kapitany has lost a portion of his entitlement to tax-deferred retirement savings. This problem is resolved with the addition of a PAR to Mr. Kapitany's RRSP deduction room.

We suggest you complete SSP 10-1 at this point.

Examples of RRSP Deduction Calculations

10-72. The following three examples illustrate the calculation of the RRSP deduction limit, Unused RRSP deduction room, and the carry forward of undeducted RRSP contributions.

Example A

Miss Brown has 2020 employment income of $30,000, 2020 rental income of $10,000, and 2020 interest income of $5,000. She is not a member of an RPP or a DPSP. She contributes $5,000 to her RRSP in October 2020 and $800 in January 2021. At the end of 2020, her unused RRSP deduction room was nil and she had undeducted contributions of $1,000 in her RRSP account.

Unused deduction room carried forward from 2020	Nil
Lesser of:	
• 2021 RRSP dollar limit = $27,830	
• 18% of 2020 earned income of $40,000 = $7,200	$ 7,200
2020 RRSP deduction limit	$ 7,200
RRSP deduction ($5,000 + $800 + $1,000)	(6,800)
Unused deduction room—End of 2021	$ 400

The interest income is not included in earned income as defined in ITA 146(1). See Paragraph 10-49.

Example B

After deducting an RPP contribution of $2,000, Mrs. Blue has 2020 employment income of $34,000. Her employer reports a PA of $4,500 on her 2020 T4. Her 2021 RRSP contributions total $5,000 and she deducts $3,200 for 2021. At the end of 2020, her unused RRSP deduction room was $2,500 and there were no undeducted contributions in her RRSP account.

Unused deduction room carried forward from 2020	$2,500
Lesser of:	
• 2021 RRSP dollar limit = $27,830	
• 18% of 2020 earned income of $36,000 = $6,480	6,480
Less 2020 PA	(4,500)
2021 RRSP deduction limit	$4,480
RRSP deduction ($5,000 contributed)	(3,200)
Unused deduction room—End of 2021	$1,280

Mrs. Blue has 2020 earned income of $36,000 (employment income of $34,000 plus her $2,000 RPP contribution that was deducted). She has an undeducted RRSP contribution of $1,800 ($5,000 - $3,200). She can deduct $1,280 in any subsequent year, but needs $520 of additional RRSP deduction room to deduct the remainder.

Example C

Mr. Green receives 2020 spousal support of $150,000 and has no other income in 2020. He is not a member of an RPP or DPSP. In January 2022, he contributes $11,500 to his RRSP. This full amount is deducted in his 2021 income tax return. His unused RRSP deduction room carried forward from 2020 was $1,200 and there were no undeducted contributions in his RRSP account.

Unused deduction room carried forward from 2020	$ 1,200
Lesser of:	
• 2021 RRSP dollar limit = $27,830	
• 18% of 2020 earned income of $150,000 = $27,000	27,000
2021 RRSP deduction limit	$28,200
RRSP deduction ($11,500 contributed)	(11,500)
Unused deduction room—End of 2021	$ 16,700

Exercise 10-6

Subject: Unused RRSP Deduction Room

Mr. Victor Haslich has 2020 earned income for RRSP purposes of $38,000. He is not a member of an RPP or a DPSP. His unused RRSP deduction room carried forward from 2020 was $4,800. During 2021, he contributes $6,000 to his RRSP and makes an RRSP deduction of $4,500. What is the amount of Mr. Haslich's unused RRSP deduction room and undeducted RRSP contributions at the end of 2021? If instead of deducting only $4,500 Mr. Haslich wanted to deduct his maximum RRSP deduction, how much more would he have to contribute to do so?

Exercise 10-7

Subject: Maximum RRSP Deduction

During 2020, Mr. Black has employment income of $75,600, taxable capital gains of $23,650, rental income of $6,530, and pays spousal support of $18,000. Based on his RPP contributions of $2,400 and the matching contributions made by his employer, his employer reports a 2020 PA of $4,800. Mr. Black has unused RRSP deduction room carried forward from 2020 of $10,750. Also at this time, his RRSP contains undeducted contributions of $6,560. During 2021, he makes contributions to his RRSP of $13,200.

Determine Mr. Black's maximum RRSP deduction he can claim in 2021. Assuming he deducts his maximum, determine the amount of any unused RRSP deduction room that he will have available at the end of 2021 and indicate whether he has any undeducted contributions remaining at the end of 2021.

Solutions to Exercises are available in the Study Guide.

Undeducted RRSP Contributions

General Rules

10-73. As we have previously noted, there is no requirement that contributions made to an RRSP be deducted immediately. If an individual has available funds to invest, it may be desirable to use these funds to make an RRSP contribution to enjoy the tax deferral on income earned within the RRSP. However, in some situations, it may be preferable to forgo the actual claim for a deduction.

10-74. An example of this type of situation would be an individual who is currently in a low income tax bracket and expects to be in a higher bracket in the foreseeable future. There is no requirement in the ITA that says that RRSP contributions must be deducted when made or in any specific year. The result is that the RRSP system provides a level of flexibility that leaves the deduction choice to the individual based on their personal circumstances.

Excess RRSP Contributions

10-75. As long as an individual has available deduction room, the CRA is not concerned about undeducted contributions. However, because of the desirability of having earnings accumulate on a tax-free basis within an RRSP, it is not surprising that rules have been developed to prevent contributions in excess of an individual's available deduction room.

10-76. The basic limiting provision is found in Part X.1, specifically ITA 204.1(2.1), which imposes a tax of 1% per month on the "cumulative excess amount in respect of RRSPs." The "cumulative excess" is defined in ITA 204.2(1.1) as undeducted contributions in excess of the sum of the RRSP deduction limit, plus a $2,000 cushion. This, in effect, means that the penalty applies to undeducted contributions that exceed an individual's RRSP deduction limit by more than $2,000.

10-77. This $2,000 cushion provides for a margin of error when an individual inadvertently makes insignificant excess contributions. Where the excess is above $2,000, ITA 204.1(4) allows the CRA to waive the penalty tax where the excess contributions were made as a result of a reasonable error and steps are taken to remove the excess as soon as possible. This provision is a form of taxpayer relief that we discussed in Chapter 2.

10-78. The $2,000 cushion is also only available to individuals who are 18 years of age or older throughout the year. This is to prevent parents from making undeducted contributions to an RRSP on behalf of minor children given that they would not have earned income to generate RRSP deduction room.

10-79. The following simple example illustrates the application of the penalty tax.

EXAMPLE At the beginning of 2020, Mr. Woods has an RRSP deduction limit of nil and no undeducted contributions in his plan. During 2020, his RRSP deduction limit increases by $9,000. On April 1, 2020, Mr. Woods makes a contribution of $10,000 to his RRSP. No RRSP deduction is taken for 2020.

During 2021, his RRSP deduction limit increases by $10,000. On July 1, 2021, $15,000 is contributed to the plan. No RRSP deduction is claimed for 2021.

ANALYSIS There would be no penalty for 2020 as his $10,000 in undeducted contributions is only $1,000 more than his $9,000 unused deduction room for 2020. There would, however, be a penalty in 2021 calculated as follows:

	January to June	July to December
Undeducted RRSP contributions	$10,000	$25,000
RRSP deduction limit ($9,000 + $10,000)	(19,000)	(19,000)
Cushion	(2,000)	(2,000)
Monthly cumulative excess amount	$ Nil	$ 4,000
Penalty rate	1%	1%
Monthly penalty	$ Nil	$ 40
Number of months	N/A	6
Total penalty	$ Nil	$ 240

Exercise 10-8

Subject: Excess RRSP Contributions

Ms. Lucie Brownell is not a member of an RPP or a DPSP. At the beginning of 2020, Ms. Brownell has no unused RRSP deduction room. During 2019 and 2020 she has earned income of $160,000 each year. On July 1, 2020, she makes a $28,350 RRSP contribution, but does not take any deduction for the year. In 2021, she has earned income of $50,000, makes a $30,000 contribution on May 1, 2021, but still does not take a deduction for the year. Determine any penalty tax that will be charged to Ms. Brownell for excess contributions during either 2020 or 2021.

Solutions to Exercises are available in the Study Guide.

Tax Planning—Excess RRSP Contributions

10-80. It would be very difficult to find an investment that would earn a return sufficient to offset a penalty tax of 1% per month (12% annually). As a result, it is essential that the penalty tax be avoided.

10-81. If excess contributions are withdrawn from the RRSP before the end of the year following the year in which a penalty tax assessment is received, an offsetting deduction is available (ITA 146(8.2)). If, however, any excess is not withdrawn within that timeframe, it will be included in income without the benefit of the offset.

10-82. This still leaves the question of whether it is worthwhile to make use of the $2,000 penalty-free cushion. If an individual has a TFSA but no contribution room left and still has an additional $2,000 in available funds, the ability to have earnings compound on a tax-free basis within the RRSP would usually make this a desirable strategy. The downside is that the potential for an excess increases without the $2,000 cushion. Those who create an excess are required to file a special income tax return under Part X.1 called a T1-OVP, which must be filed within 90 days of the end of the year and for each year in which there is an excess. Penalties and interest can be assessed for failing to file the return on time. In other words, the potential burden imposed on individuals with excess contributions would weigh in favour of avoiding the use of the $2,000 cushion to make additional RRSP contributions.

10-83. Alternatively, if an individual has not contributed the maximum allowable to his TFSA and only has limited funds available for investment, the TFSA would be the preferable alternative. This reflects the fact that, while both the TFSA and the non-deductible contributions to an RRSP (the $2,000 excess would not be deductible) enjoy tax-free compounding of earnings, withdrawals from a TFSA are not required to be included in net income and are therefore not subject to Part I tax. In contrast, any withdrawal from an RRSP, even amounts that have not been deducted, will be required to be included in net income since, as a rule, all refunds of premiums made to an RRSP are required to be included in net income.

We suggest you complete SSP 10-2, 10-3, 10-4, and 10-5 at this point.

RRSP and RRIF Administration Fees

10-84. Administration fees for these plans, as well as investment counselling fees related to investments in these plans, cannot be deducted by an individual. As a consequence, such fees should be paid with funds that are in the plan. The CRA concluded that such payments are not considered withdrawal from the plan.

RRSP Withdrawals and Voluntary Annuity Conversions

Lump-Sum Withdrawals

10-85. A lump-sum withdrawal from an RRSP is possible at any point in time unless the funds are locked-in, such as when funds from an RPP are transferred to an RRSP. The income tax consequences of partial or complete withdrawals are straightforward. In general, the amount withdrawn must be added to net income in the year of withdrawal. Further, unlike a TFSA where contribution room remains available once a withdrawal has occurred, a withdrawal from an RRSP does not result in the retention of contribution room regardless of a subsequent desire to replace the amounts that were withdrawn.

10-86. Even when the individual is at or approaching retirement, a lump-sum withdrawal of all funds would not usually be recommended. The withdrawal of a large portion of one's RRSP could potentially be subject to maximum income tax rates at that time and, in the absence of other retirement income, would result in lost pension tax credits in subsequent years.

10-87. As mentioned in Paragraph 10-23, lump-sum withdrawals are subject to withholding tax. The trustee of the plan is required to withhold a portion of the funds withdrawn and remit them to the government on the individual's behalf. The withholding rates are based on the size of the withdrawal. It is not unusual for individuals to limit the withholding taxes by withdrawing multiple amounts up to $5,000 and keeping the rate to 10%. Note, however, that while this strategy leaves the individual with additional cash, the income tax bill for that year will have to be paid when the income tax return for the year is filed. The withholding rates are as follows:

Amount	Rate
Less than $5,001	10%
$5,001 to $15,000	20%
More than $15,000	30%

10-88. An additional point with respect to lump-sum RRSP withdrawals is that such amounts are not eligible for the pension income tax credit or for pension income splitting as discussed in Chapter 9.

Conversion to an Income Stream

10-89. Besides lump-sum withdrawals, the following options are available for converting an RRSP into an income stream that can be paid over many years:

Life Annuity Funds from within an RRSP can be used to purchase a single life annuity or, alternatively, a joint life annuity with a spouse or common-law partner. Amounts received are required to be included in net income. This was discussed in our coverage of annuities in Chapter 9.

Note that a life annuity can guarantee that it is paid for a minimum number of years. For example, a life annuity with a 10-year guaranteed term would make payments for a minimum of 10 years, even if the annuitant died prior to the end of the period. An RRSP annuitant is defined in ITA 146(1) as an individual to whom the RRSP has been established and who will receive the benefits of the RRSP.

Fixed-Term Annuity In a similar fashion, a fixed-term annuity can be purchased by the RRSP. As with the life annuity, the full amount of the annuity payments received would be required to be included in net income.

2019 Federal Budget In order to provide greater flexibility in the use of retirement funds, the 2019 federal budget introduced two additional types of annuities that came into force January 1, 2020. They can be described as follows:

- **Advanced Life Deferred Annuity (ALDA)—ITA 146.5** Reflecting increased life expectancies and decisions by individuals to keep working beyond conventional retirement ages, the legislation allows ALDAs to be purchased with RRSP funds, as well as with funds from other registered plans such as RRIFs. Within prescribed limits, these life annuities allow for the initial payment to be deferred until age 85.
- **Variable Payment Life Annuities—ITA 147.5(5)** Rather than requiring a fixed payment throughout an individual's life, these life annuities allow payments to be adjusted based on such factors as the consumer price index and the investment performance of the underlying funds. This type of annuity can only be created with funds from either an RPP or a pooled RPP (PRPP).

Detailed coverage of the rules associated with these two new types of annuities is beyond the scope of this text.

Reminder If an annuity is purchased by the RRSP, subsequent payments from the RRSP would be included in net income in the same manner as an RRSP withdrawal. If the RRSP funds are all withdrawn, the full amount will be included in net income and will be subject to income tax at the time of withdrawal. If after-tax funds are used to personally purchase an annuity, only the investment income returned with each annuity payment would be included in net income. Annuities are also discussed in Chapter 9 [ITA 56(1)(d) and 60(a)].

10-90. The conversion of RRSP funds into an annuity within an RRSP can be made at any age and without regard to whether the individual has retired. Further, there are no income tax consequences resulting from the conversion. As noted, the annuity payments will be included, in full, in the individual's net income for the year the amounts are received.

10-91. Unlike lump-sum withdrawals, payments from an RRSP that has converted its funds into an annuity are generally eligible for both the pension income tax credit and pension income splitting.

Conversion to RRIF

10-92. A common alternative for withdrawing amounts from an RRSP is convert it to a RRIF as follows:

Registered Retirement Income Fund (RRIF) Funds can be transferred on a rollover basis to one or more RRIFs (ITA 146(16)). This arrangement will be described later in this chapter. The benefit of such direct transfers is that no amount has to be included in net income at the time of the transfer. In these circumstances, the individual annuitant does not receive any amounts from the RRSP, which are instead transferred from the RRSP directly to the RRIF.

Involuntary Termination Due to Age Limitation

Objective

10-93. The options for terminating an RRSP that were discussed in the preceding section are available at any age and without regard to whether the individual actually retires. However, income tax policy requires that the income sheltering and deferral features of RRSPs not be able to persist once an individual reaches a certain age. As a result, an RRSP must be terminated in the year an individual turns 71 years of age.

Post-Termination

10-94. While individuals cannot have their own RRSP after reaching the age of 71, it is still possible for such individuals to make deductible RRSP contributions to RRSPs for their spouse or common-law partner who has not reached the age of 71 on December 31 of the year in which the contributions are made. The contributions are limited to the RRSP deduction limit of the contributor, which requires that the individual continue to have earned income where there is no remaining unused RRSP deduction room.

Spousal RRSP

Benefits

10-95. Under ITA 146(5.1), an individual can deduct RRSP contributions made to a plan that is registered in the name of a spouse or common-law partner. Any RRSP that is registered in the name of an individual's spouse or common-law partner and to which the individual has made a contribution is considered to be a spousal RRSP. This means that, if an individual makes any contribution to a spouse's or common-law partner's existing RRSP, that plan becomes a spousal RRSP, even if the majority of the contributions were made by the individual's spouse or common-law partner.

10-96. Unlike the pension income-splitting provision that is only available to spouses or common-law partners who have eligible pension income, a spousal RRSP is an income-splitting plan that is available to all spouses and common-law partners. In situations where one spouse or common-law partner is likely to have either no or little retirement income, having the spouse or common-law partner with the higher expected retirement income make contributions to a spousal RRSP will generally result in withdrawals from the plan being subject to low income tax rates while the contributor benefits from an RRSP deduction.

10-97. In addition, if one spouse or common-law partner has no qualifying pension income, a spousal RRSP allows that individual to make use of the $300 [(15%)($2,000)] annual non-refundable pension income credit. Note, however, that in most circumstances splitting pension income could achieve the same result.

10-98. When an individual makes contributions to an RRSP in the name of her spouse or common-law partner, the contributions will be deductible to the contributor. However, the contributor must have available deduction room and, as you would expect, contributions to a spousal plan erode the contributor's RRSP room in exactly the same manner as would contributions to the individual's own RRSP.

10-99. We have noted previously that an individual can continue making contributions to a spousal RRSP even if her own RRSP has ceased to exist because the individual has reached 71 years of age. In addition, a deceased taxpayer's representative can make contributions to a spousal RRSP for up to 60 days after the end of the year in which the taxpayer dies. No RRSP contributions can be made to the RRSP of a deceased individual.

Attribution Rules

10-100. The objective of the RRSP legislation is to encourage savings for retirement. In the case of spousal RRSPs, the legislation also provides for an element of income splitting. ITA 74.5(12)(a) supports this form of income splitting by ensuring that the attribution rules cannot apply when one spouse or common-law partner makes RRSP contributions for the other. The potential for abuse would be high where a high-income spouse could make maximum RRSP contributions to a spousal RRSP where the spouse had no or little income. The spouse (or common-law partner) could then immediately withdraw the amounts, hopefully to pay little to no income tax depending on the amounts involved. To avoid this concern the legislation establishes its own attribution concept that requires amounts withdrawn from a spousal RRSP to be attributed back to the contributor spouse unless the amounts remain in the spousal trust for a certain period of time.

10-101. ITA 146(8.3) contains an income attribution provision that requires certain withdrawals from a spousal RRSP to be attributed back to the spouse or common-law partner who made the contribution. Withdrawals from non-spousal RRSPs are required to be included in the net income of the RRSP annuitant. However, if an annuitant makes a withdrawal from a spousal RRSP, and the annuitant's spouse or common-law partner has made a contribution to the plan, either in the current year or in the two preceding calendar years, the lesser of the amount withdrawn or the total of the spousal contributions in that three-year period will be attributed to the contributing spouse or common-law partner. The annuitant of the plan will not include the attributed amount in his net income.

10-102. Other considerations related to the application of this rule are as follows:

- This attribution rule applies to withdrawals by an annuitant up to the amount of the relevant contributions, but does not apply to withdrawals in excess of this amount. The result could be that part of a withdrawal by an annuitant spouse would be included in the net income of that annuitant and the contributor spouse.
- This attribution rule applies without regard to whether the contributing spouse or common-law partner has deducted the contributions. The attribution concept is based on when the contributions were made and not the year in which the contributions are deducted.
- This attribution rule is applicable even when there are funds that were contributed by the annuitant of the plan prior to the spouse or common-law partner making additional contributions. The legislation is written so that any amounts withdrawn by the annuitant spouse relate first to contributions made by the spouse or common-law partner.
- This attribution rule does not apply when the taxpayer and spouse or common-law partner are living separate and apart due to a marital breakdown at the time of the withdrawal.
- It is the calendar year in which the spousal contributions are made that is relevant, as a February 1, 2021, contribution is counted in 2021, even if it is deducted in 2020. This is a common error that has been raised in more than a few Tax Court of Canada decisions. If, for example, you made a spousal contribution of $10,000 in February 2019, any withdrawals up to $10,000 by your spouse before 2022 would be attributed back to you even if you deducted the contribution in your 2018 income tax return. Had you contributed the $10,000 in December 2018, your spouse could begin drawing the amounts from the spousal RRSP beginning in 2021 without any attribution back to you.

10-103. When an individual's spouse or common-law partner is eligible to make his own contributions to an RRSP, it can be useful to have these contributions made to a separate, non-spousal RRSP. If there is a need to withdraw funds, this precaution allows the withdrawal to be made from a plan that has not received spousal contributions. As a result, there would be no attribution and any withdrawals would be included in the net income of the individual annuitant. However, if no withdrawals are anticipated in the foreseeable future, there may be no income tax-related concern of having a separate, non-spousal RRSP.

Exercise 10-9

Subject: Spousal RRSP

During 2019, Mr. Garveau makes a $5,000 contribution to a new RRSP in which he is the annuitant. His spouse, Mrs. Charron Garveau, also makes a $5,000 contribution to his RRSP in 2019. In 2020, Mrs. Garveau does not make any further contribution to her spouse's RRSP. However, Mr. Garveau makes a $6,500 contribution. During 2021, Mr. Garveau withdraws $9,000 from his RRSP. What are the income tax consequences of this withdrawal?

Solutions to Exercises are available in the Study Guide.

Home Buyers' Plan (HBP)—ITA 146.01

Qualifying HBP Withdrawals

10-104. Qualification for the Home Buyers' Plan (HBP) permits an individual annuitant to withdraw up to $35,000 from the individual's RRSP without having to include the withdrawal in net income. Several conditions must be met to benefit from this treatment:

- On January 1 of the year of withdrawal, all amounts related to previous HBP withdrawals must have been repaid.
- All amounts, up to the limit of $35,000 per individual, must have been received in a single year or by the end of January of the following year.
- The individual must have bought or built a "qualifying home" before October 1 of the year following the year of withdrawal(s). Extensions of the deadline are available where there is a written agreement to purchase a home or payments have been made toward the construction of a home by the October 1 deadline. A "qualifying home" is defined as a housing unit located in Canada. A housing unit has the same meaning as in our discussions of principal residences in Chapter 8.
- Within one year of the acquisition of this "qualifying home," the taxpayer must begin, or intend to begin, using it as a principal place of residence. Note, however, there is no minimum holding period for the home, provided that at some point it becomes a principal residence.
- Neither the individual nor his spouse or common-law partner can have owned a home that he has occupied during the four calendar years preceding the withdrawal. A modification of this rule allows individuals to avoid the four-year requirement as a result of a breakdown of a marriage or common-law partnership. In most circumstances this allows an individual who no longer has a home as a result of a settlement with a former spouse or common-law partner to participate immediately in the HBP program.

  There is an exception to this constraint for disabled individuals. More specifically, if the home purchase is being made by or for the benefit of an individual who qualifies for the disability tax credit (see Chapter 4), and the home is more accessible for the individual or is better suited for the care of the individual, the HBP can be used even if the individual owned a home that was occupied during the specified four-year period.
- Individuals must complete Form T1036, "Home Buyers' Plan Request to Withdraw Funds from an RRSP."

10-105. There is nothing in these rules to prevent withdrawals by both an individual and her spouse or common-law partner, provided all of the withdrawn funds are used to acquire a single property. This would allow couples to make withdrawals totalling $70,000 toward the purchase of a home.

Restrictions on the Deduction of New RRSP Contributions

10-106. The intent of this legislation is to allow individuals who have not recently owned a home to use accumulated RRSP contributions to acquire a principal residence. The government does not want to allow individuals to abuse the HBP by making contributions that are immediately withdrawn. To prevent this from happening, a special rule denies a deduction for contributions to an RRSP or a spousal RRSP that are withdrawn within 90 days under the HBP. In other words, the contributions must remain in the RRSP for at least 90 days to benefit from an RRSP deduction. This means that if you have never contributed to an RRSP and do so for the first time, making a $30,000 contribution on February 28, 2021, you must wait 90 days to make any HBP withdrawals to be able to claim an RRSP deduction for that amount. If you withdraw the amount prior to the 90 days, the HBP withdrawal will not qualify for the RRSP deduction (ITA 146(5)(a)(iv.1)). This would defeat the purpose of using RRSPs to assist in acquiring a home.

10-107. The legislation adds an ordering rule that considers RRSP withdrawals for the purpose of the HBP to originate with the earliest contributions (a first-in, first-out approach). This would mean that if you had already accumulated $35,000 in your RRSP in past years and made an additional $10,000 contribution in February 2021 to increase the RRSP holdings to $45,000, then withdrew $35,000 in March 2021 as an HBP withdrawal, the fact that the withdrawal occurred within 90 days of your contribution would not change your ability to claim an RRSP deduction for the $10,000 contribution. The reason is because that $10,000 contribution is not considered as being withdrawn; rather, it is the $35,000 that was already in the RRSP for more than 90 days that is considered to have been withdrawn.

> **EXAMPLE** At the beginning of 2021, Mr. Garth has an accumulated RRSP balance of $30,000. In order to make the maximum $35,000 HBP withdrawal, he makes a $5,000 contribution to the RRSP on June 1, 2021. He then withdraws the $35,000 within 90 days of making the $5,000 contribution. While the $35,000 withdrawn is an HBP withdrawal, the $5,000 contribution would not be deductible since it was not held within the RRSP for 90 days. If Mr. Garth withdrew only $27,000 as an HBP withdrawal, the $5,000 contribution would be deductible because it has not been considered to have been withdrawn within 90 days. The $27,000 withdrawal would be considered to originate from the $30,000 balance prior to the $5,000 additional contribution.

Repayment of HBP

10-108. Eligible amounts are not included in net income when they are withdrawn from the RRSP. In effect, annuitants are borrowing down payments for a home on an interest-free basis from their own RRSPs. These individuals would have been initially entitled to an RRSP deduction for the contributions withdrawn as qualifying HBP withdrawals. To create a symmetrical approach, the system would either require that the HBP withdrawals be either repaid or that the RRSP deductions be reversed. This, in fact, describes the mechanics of the HBP system. The repayment of HBP amounts withdrawn begins with a schedule that requires annual payments over a 15-year period beginning in the second calendar year following the year of the withdrawal.

10-109. Any RRSP contributions made during the year, or in the first 60 days of the following year, can be designated an HBP repayment. These designated repayments are not deductible in the determination of net income since deductions were already allowed for RRSP contributions that funded the HBP.

10-110. Any amounts that are not repaid to the plan as required will be included in the individual's net income in the year in which they were scheduled to be repaid. There is no upper limit on the amounts that can be repaid in any year subsequent to withdrawal, but the repayments must be made over a 15-year period. This is accomplished by requiring a minimum repayment based on the following balance:

Eligible amounts withdrawn	$xx,xxx
Repayments in previous years	(xxx)
Amounts included in income in previous years	(xxx)
Balance	$ x,xxx

10-111. A fraction is then applied to this balance, beginning at 1/15 for the first year of the 15-year period, which begins in the second year following the withdrawal. In each subsequent year, the denominator of the fraction is then reduced by one, resulting in 1/14 for the second year, 1/13 for the third year, and so on, until the fraction reaches 1/1 in the fifteenth year of the 15-year repayment period. These are minimum payments and, if they are made as per this schedule, there will be a 15-year straight-line repayment of the eligible amounts.

10-112. If the payments are less than these minimum amounts, any deficiency must be included in that year's net income. Any defiiciencies included in net income will be deducted from the HBP balance in the same manner as if the payments had actually been made.

10-113. However, if larger payments than required are made in any year, the repayment amounts change. While the multiplier fractions remain the same, the successive payments are based on the outstanding HBP balance at the time. A simple example will illustrate.

EXAMPLE Ms. Ritchie withdraws an eligible amount of $15,000 from her RRSP in July 2019 and uses the funds for a down payment on a qualifying home. Repayments are required to begin in 2021. In 2021, a repayment of $2,400 is made and, in 2022, a repayment of $600 is made.

ANALYSIS The minimum payment for 2021 is $1,000 [(1/15)($15,000)] and, since this is less than the actual payment, there is no deficient payment and therefore no amount to include in net income for that year. The required payment for 2022 is $900 [(1/14)($15,000 - $2,400)]. As the actual payment is only $600, there is a $300 deficiency, which is required to be included in net income for that second year. This is the case despite the fact that the $3,000 in cumulative payments for the two years exceeds the $2,000 minimum that would have been required for the two years. This illustrates the fact that making payments in excess of the required level in one year does not provide an equivalent reduction in the payment for the following year. Note that the required payment for 2023 is also $900 [(1/13)($15,000 - $2,400 - $600 - $300)] since the year two deficiency reduces the HBP balance as if an actual payment of that amount had been made.

Exercise 10-10

Subject: Home Buyers' Plan

During 2019, Ms. Farah DeBoo withdraws $18,000 from her RRSP under the provisions of the HBP. Due to some unexpected income received during 2020, she repays $5,000 in that year. What is the amount of her minimum repayment during 2021?

Solutions to Exercises are available in the Study Guide.

Lifelong Learning Plan (LLP)—ITA 146.02

General Format

10-114. ITA 146.02 contains provisions that allow an individual to borrow from his RRSPs on an interest-free basis to finance his own education or that of his spouse or common-law partner. Qualifying RRSP withdrawals are not required to be included in net income nor will there be any withholdings. Withdrawals under the LLP must be repaid over a period of 10 years. The mechanics of the LLP are similar to those of HBP withdrawals and repayments. In effect, once again, you are borrowing on an interest-free basis from your own RRSP in a manner similar to a student loan.

Withdrawals

10-115. To qualify for RRSP withdrawals for the LLP, the individual or his spouse or common-law partner must be enrolled as a full-time student in a qualifying educational program at a designated educational institution. In general, a qualifying educational program is a post-secondary program that requires students to spend 10 hours or more per week on courses that last three consecutive months or more. A designated educational institution is a university, college, or other designated educational institution. We have seen this as one of the qualifying conditions for a higher-income spouse to claim child care expenses or where an individual moves for education purposes and has eligible moving expenses. See S1-F2-C1, "Education and Textbook Tax Credits," for more information on designated educational institutions.

10-116. The maximum withdrawal is $10,000 in any one calendar year, to a maximum of $20,000 over a period of up to four calendar years. While the designated person for these withdrawals can be either the individual or his spouse or common-law partner, an individual cannot have an LLP balance owing (withdrawals less repayments) for more than one person at any point in time. However, both an individual and his spouse or common-law partner can participate at the same time, provided they use funds from their own RRSPs.

10-117. As with HBPs, if there is an eligible LLP withdrawal deductible contributions are first traced to the earlier amounts within the RRSP. Any contributions made within 90 days that can be traced to an LLP withdrawal are denied an RRSP deduction. This is identical to that of HBPs, which we discussed in Paragraphs 10-106 and 10-107. If an individual is establishing an RRSP for the purposes of obtaining the advantages of an LLP or HBP, it is crucial that the contributions not be withdrawn until 90 days have passed to ensure entitlement to an RRSP deduction.

Repayment of LLP

10-118. Minimum repayments must be made on a straight-line basis over a period of 10 years. In a manner similar to that used for HBPs, this is accomplished by using a formula in which 1/10 is repaid the first year of repayment, 1/9 the second year, 1/8 the third year, and so on. Also in a manner identical to HBPs, deficient repayments will be included in the individual's net income and subtracted from the LLP balance owing as if that deficient amount had actually been paid. Repayments above the required minimum reduce the balance to which the future fractions will be applied.

10-119. Any RRSP contribution made during the year or in the first 60 days of the following year can be designated an LLP repayment. These designated repayments are not deductible in the determination of net income since the contributions that originally funded the RRSP were deductible. Repayments must begin no later than the fifth year after the year of the first LLP withdrawal.

> **EXAMPLE** Sarah makes LLP withdrawals from 2019 to 2022. She continues in a qualifying education program from 2019 to 2024. Since 2024 is the fifth year after the year of her first LLP withdrawal, Sarah's repayment period is from 2024 to 2033. The due date for her first repayment is no later than March 1, 2025, which is 60 days after the end of 2024, her first repayment year.

10-120. Repayments must begin earlier if the beneficiary of the program does not continue in a qualifying educational program. Specifically, repayment must begin in the second year in which the individual is not enrolled in a qualifying educational program.

> **EXAMPLE** Joseph makes an LLP withdrawal in 2020 for a qualifying educational program he is enrolled in during 2020. Joseph completes the educational program in 2021. He is not enrolled in a qualifying education program in either 2022 or 2023 and, as a consequence, Joseph's first repayment year is 2023.

Other Considerations

10-121. There is no limit on the number of times an individual can participate in the LLP. However, an individual may not participate in a new plan before the end of the year in which all repayments from any previous participation have been made.

10-122. For an RRSP withdrawal to be eligible for the LLP, the designated person must complete the qualified educational program before April of the year following the withdrawal or, alternatively, be enrolled in a qualified educational program at the end of March of the year following the withdrawal.

Exercise 10-11

Subject: Lifelong Learning Plan

Jean Paul Riopelle makes an LLP withdrawal of $5,000 in July 2019. This is subsequent to his acceptance in a community college art program that runs from September to November 2019. He completes the course. On February 28 of each year from 2022 through 2031, he makes payments of $500 per year to his RRSP. These amounts are designated as LLP repayments in his tax returns for the years 2021 through 2030. Indicate the income tax consequences to Jean Paul of these transactions.

Solutions to Exercises are available in the Study Guide.

Ceasing to Be a Resident of Canada

RRSP Balances

10-123. ITA 128.1(4)(b) requires a deemed disposition of most capital property when an individual ceases to be a resident of Canada (see coverage of this subject in Chapter 8). However, most pension benefits are exempt from these rules and, as a consequence, a departure from Canada will not automatically result in the collapse or termination of an RRSP.

10-124. Once the individual has ceased to be a resident of Canada, she may find it desirable to collapse the plan. The collapse and subsequent payment to a non-resident will result in income tax liability under Part XIII of the ITA. The Part XIII tax is a 25% tax on certain payments to a non-resident and, for those countries with which Canada has an income tax treaty, the rate can be as low as 10%. Unlike the withholding tax that is assessed on RRSP withdrawals by Canadian resident individuals, this is a final tax, and the withdrawn amounts are generally not subject to further Canadian income tax with respect to those payments.

10-125. Whether or not amounts received on the termination of the plan will be included in the income of the individual in the new country of residence will depend on many factors, including the country involved, the existence of an income tax treaty, and the income tax treatment in Canada of the RRSP income prior to the cessation of Canadian residency. If an RRSP is not collapsed and payments continue to be made to a non-resident, such payments are generally subject to Part XIII tax at a 10% or greater rate as a result of ITA 212(1)(h). There are considerable complexities associated with such situations that are beyond the scope of this text.

Home Buyers' Plan Balances

10-126. If an individual ceases to be a resident of Canada, any unpaid balance under the HBP must be repaid before the date the income tax return for the year of departure is required to be filed, or 60 days after becoming a non-resident, whichever date is earlier. If this deadline is not met, the unpaid balance must be included in net income.

Lifelong Learning Plan Balances

10-127. Similar to the provisions under the HBP, if an individual ceases to be a resident of Canada, any unpaid balance under the LLP must be repaid before the date the income tax return for the year of departure should be filed, or 60 days after becoming a non-resident, whichever date is earlier. If this deadline is not met, the unpaid balance must be included in net income.

Death of the RRSP Annuitant

General Rules

10-128. When an individual dies, there can be many income tax implications. In this chapter we will cover the complications associated with RRSPs owned by an individual at the time of death.

10-129. The general rules for RRSPs depend on whether the plan is an unmatured plan (i.e., the annuitant has not converted the funds in the plan to an annuity) or a matured plan (i.e., the plan funds have been converted to an annuity that is paying regular retirement income). As described in RC4177, "Death of an RRSP Annuitant," the general rules are as follows:

> **Unmatured RRSPs** When the annuitant of an unmatured RRSP dies, he is considered to have received, immediately before death, an amount equal to the FMV of all the property held in the RRSP at the time of death. This amount, and all other amounts the annuitant received in the year from the RRSP, will be included in the net income of the deceased for the year of death.
>
> **Matured RRSPs** When the annuitant of a matured RRSP dies, the annuitant is considered to have received, immediately before death, an amount equal to the FMV of all remaining annuity payments under the RRSP at the time of death. This amount, and all other amounts the annuitant received in the year from the RRSP, will be included in the net income of the deceased for the year of death. Note that if a straight life annuity was involved, there would be no further payments after death.

10-130. If these general rules are applied, with the lump-sum or annuity amounts included in the deceased's final income tax return, the assets will pass to the specified beneficiaries at FMV, with no immediate income tax consequences for the beneficiaries. However, when the RRSP assets or annuity are transferred to certain qualified beneficiaries, there are important exceptions to this general rule. (See the material that follows.)

10-131. An additional point here is that there are two different ways in which RRSP assets can be distributed on death. The preferable approach is for the annuitant to specify the beneficiary (or beneficiaries) in the RRSP contract. This will result in the assets being passed immediately at death. Perhaps more importantly, probate fees will be avoided. It is important to remember, however, that this does not change the income tax results to the deceased.

10-132. If this approach is not used, the RRSP assets will become part of the deceased's estate. If this happens, their distribution will be subject to probate fees. In Ontario, these fees are $5 for each $1,000 up to $50,000, plus $15 for every $1,000 over $50,000.

Exceptions—Transfers to a Spouse or Common-Law Partner and Certain Children

10-133. There are two exceptions to dispositions occurring at FMV. The first is for transfers on death to spouses or common-law partners and the second to financially dependent children, with some alternatives for children with a physical or mental infirmity to which there are many complexities. We will restrict our comments to transfers to spouses and common-law partners.

10-134. The various possibilities that could arise when the disposition of an RRSP after death is to a spouse or common-law partner can be described as follows:

> **Unmatured RRSP—Spouse Is Beneficiary** If the spouse is the sole beneficiary and there is a transfer to an RRSP with the spouse as the annuitant, there will be no income tax consequences for either of the deceased or the spouse or common-law partner. The assets in the deceased's RRSP simply become assets in the spouse's RRSP. This is usually the most tax advantageous arrangement for dealing with an unmatured RRSP. As we have previously seen, income tax policy directs that transfers of property between

spouses or common-law partners during their lifetimes or at death are to take place on a rollover basis. This treatment is consistent with that policy.

Matured RRSP—Spouse Is Beneficiary If the RRSP is in the form of an annuity with the spouse as the sole beneficiary, the RRSP will continue with the spouse receiving the payments. There will be no income tax consequences for the deceased, and the spouse or common-law partner will be required to include annuity payments received in her net income. For matured RRSPs, this is clearly the most tax advantageous arrangement. This is another example of rollovers between spouses and common-law partners.

Estate Is Beneficiary Whether the RRSP has or has not matured, the general rollover rules will apply for transfers between spouses or common-law partners. If the spouse is the beneficiary of the estate, the same rollover results can be achieved here through the use of elections by the legal representative. However, probate fees will apply and the process is much more complex.

Home Buyers' Plan Balances

10-135. If a participant in the HBP dies prior to repaying all amounts to the RRSP, any unpaid balance will be included in net income for the year of death. However, a surviving spouse or common-law partner may elect with the legal representatives of the deceased to avoid this addition to net income. If this election is made, the surviving spouse assumes the position of the deceased by being treated as having received an eligible amount equal to the unpaid balance outstanding at the time of the deceased's death.

Lifelong Learning Plan Balances

10-136. If an individual dies and has an LLP balance owing, this balance must be included in the individual's net income for the year of death. As is the case with HBPs, there is an election that allows a spouse or common-law partner to effectively assume the deceased's position with respect to the LLP, including repayment terms.

We suggest you complete SSP 10-6 at this point.

Registered Pension Plans (RPPs)—ITA 147.1

Establishing an RPP

Types of Plans

10-137. The most important type of Canadian pension arrangement is the registered pension plan (RPP) provided by some employers for their employees. Such plans are established by a contract between the employer and the employees and provide either for a pension benefit that is determined under a prescribed formula (a defined benefit plan) or for a specified annual contribution by the employer that will provide a benefit that will be based on the funds available at the time of retirement (a money purchase plan).

10-138. An additional variable is the question of whether, in addition to the contributions made by the employer, the employees make contributions to the plan. If they do, it is referred to as a contributory plan. Both employer and employee contributions to the RPPs are normally deposited with a trustee who is responsible for safeguarding and managing the funds deposited.

Registration of the Plan—ITA 147.1(2)

10-139. It would be possible for an employer to have a pension plan that is not registered. However, such an arrangement would make very little sense. In order to deduct contributions for income tax purposes, an employer-sponsored pension plan must be registered with the CRA.

10-140. In most situations, the basic requirements for registration are not difficult to meet. The plan must provide a definite arrangement, established as a continuing policy by an employer, under which benefits are provided to employees after their retirement. The terms and conditions must be set out in writing and the amounts of benefits to be provided must be reasonable in the circumstances.

Employer Contributions to the RPP

General Rules

10-141. As noted in Chapter 6 on business income, ITA 20(1)(q) allows an employer to deduct contributions to an RPP in the determination of business income. The provision provides for a deduction to the extent permitted by ITA 147.2(1) or 147.5(10). Technically a specific provision is required to claim a deduction given that pension benefits for employees are generally considered capital expenditures and would otherwise be denied a deduction by ITA 18(1)(b).

10-142. Contributions to money purchase plans are deductible as long as they are made in accordance with the plan as registered. For defined benefit plans there is a similar requirement. Contributions made during the year, or within 120 days after the end of the year, are deductible as long as they have not been deducted previously.

10-143. Note that the legislation permits a deduction where the contributions have actually been made. As deductions under generally accepted accounting principles must be determined on an accrual basis, there are likely to be differences between the accounting expense for the period and the deduction for the period requiring reconciliation adjustments from accounting income to net income.

Restrictions

10-144. The preceding general rules provide for any level of deductions as long as the amount is consistent with the plan as registered. As we have noted, however, the restrictions on contributions are implemented through the registration process. More specifically, ITA 147.1(8) causes the RPP to become revocable (i.e., loses its registered status) if the PA of a member of the plan exceeds the lesser of

- the money purchase limit for the year; or
- 18% of the member's compensation from the employer for the year.

This built-in rule ensures that the accumulated retirement benefits in any one pension plan are kept within the acceptable limits described earlier at Paragraph 10-46.

10-145. Given the fact that the RRSP deduction limit is also based on these same factors (with a one-year lag), this restriction means that, in general, an RPP cannot provide for more retirement savings than would be available to an individual whose only retirement savings option is an RRSP. To illustrate this, consider a member of a money purchase RPP who always has employment income in excess of $200,000. As 18% of this individual's income will always be larger than the money purchase limit, the maximum retirement savings will be determined by that limit. This means that for 2021, the limit will be $29,210.

10-146. If that same individual was not a member of an RPP, the maximum retirement savings would be based on the RRSP dollar limit, a figure that lags the money purchase limit by one year. Given this, the 2021 maximum retirement savings would be $27,830, $1,380 [$29,210 - $27,830] less than would be the case if the individual were a member of an RPP.

10-147. An RPP that provides benefits to an employee that creates a PA in excess of the money purchase limit for the year, or 18% of the employee's compensation, will have its registration revoked. Given that registration is required for RPP contributions to be deductible, this requirement should ensure that benefits are kept within these limitations.

10-148. Before leaving this discussion of employer contributions, you should note that this restriction on PAs would effectively restrict both employer and employee contributions to an RPP. Both types of contributions go into the PA calculation and, as a consequence, placing the limit on this measure of pension benefits ensures that the combined employee/employer contributions will be restricted to those maximum amounts.

Employee Contributions to the RPP

10-149. As is noted in Chapter 3, the employee deduction for RPP contributions is ITA 8(1)(m), which indicates that, in the determination of employment income, individuals may deduct contributions to an employer's RPP as specified in ITA 147.2(4). Taking the same approach that was used for employer contributions, the legislation provides that amounts contributed for current and past service are deductible if they are made in accordance with the terms of the plan. This places employee contributions under the same overall limit as employer contributions. That is, they must be made under the terms of a plan that does not produce a PA that exceeds the lesser of the money purchase limit for the year and 18% of the employee's compensation for the year.

Options at Retirement

10-150. Retirement options for RPPs are not generally established in the ITA, although the registration requirements may influence such options. Each employer-sponsored plan has a set of rules that are applicable to the participants of that plan. Most plans only allow the individual to receive the periodic benefit to which she is entitled. Less frequently, some plans may allow for a lump-sum withdrawal, a transfer to a different type of plan, or a transfer to another employer's plan. Transfers to other plans are discussed later in this chapter.

Phased Retirement

The Problem

10-151. At one time, an employee could not accrue benefits under a defined benefit RPP if he was already receiving benefits under that plan. This prohibition also applied if the employee was receiving benefits from another defined benefit RPP sponsored by the same employer or an employer related to that employer. This had the following implications:

- If an individual had wanted to phase in retirement by working on a part-time basis after he had begun to receive basic pension benefits, the individual could not accrue any further pension benefits with respect to the part-time work.
- If an individual continued on a full-time basis after beginning to receive her basic pension benefit, she also could not accrue any pension benefits for this work. It is not uncommon for retired employees to be asked to return to work once the pension benefits were well underway.

The Solution

10-152. Fortunately, this situation was resolved many years ago with income tax regulations (ITR 8503(16) to (25)). The regulations allow registered plans to pay employees up to 60% of their accrued defined benefit pension entitlement while they continue to accrue additional pension benefits for current service subsequent to retirement. These legislative concessions are limited to employees who are at least 55 years of age and who are otherwise eligible to receive a pension without being subject to an early retirement penalty.

Inadequate Retirement Savings

The Problem

10-153. It is clear that a large majority of Canadians are not making adequate financial arrangements for their retirement years. While this is not a problem for those fortunate individuals who are members of a generous RPP sponsored by a government organization, a large public company, or a large union, there are many other individuals who could be facing a potentially difficult future once their working years have ended.

10-154. To some extent, RRSPs provide a solution to this problem. However, based on the latest data published by the CRA and Statistics Canada, Canadians are not making effective use of these plans. In 2017, only 5.9 million Canadians contributed to an RRSP. That number has been steadily declining since a peak of 6.3 million in 2007. Further, the average contribution was only $3,030, leaving billions of dollars in unused deduction room. Clearly, RRSPs, which rely on voluntary contributions by individuals, will not solve the problem of inadequate retirement savings.

10-155. An obvious solution to these problems is to have a larger percentage of Canadians enrolled in plans that require regular contributions. RPPs sponsored by a single employer are not likely to provide a general solution to this problem as the maintenance of a registered pension plan is costly. This makes it difficult for small or even medium-sized employers to provide an RPP. Further, RRSPs do not provide a totally satisfactory solution in that the size of these individual plans is generally not sufficient to justify the cost of professional management or adequate diversification of assets, although Canadian institutions offer many investment options to optimize returns based on individual risk and other factors.

Pooled Registered Pension Plans (PRPPs)—ITA 147.5

10-156. One proposed solution to the problem of inadequate retirement savings is what the government refers to as pooled registered pension plans (PRPPs). These are, in effect, registered pension plans offered and managed by financial institutions such as banks, trusts, and insurance companies. The basic features of these plans can be described as follows:

- These are money purchase plans sponsored by a financial institution capable of taking on a fiduciary role (i.e., a bank, trust, or insurance company). The sponsoring financial institutions are the administrators of the plan. They are responsible for receiving contributions, thereby creating a large pool of capital that can be used to construct portfolios designed to appeal to various potential employers and employees. They are also responsible for complying with the income tax rules, particularly with respect to administrative and reporting requirements related to contributions and withdrawals.
- An employer can select a particular plan for its employees. While the financial institution retains primary responsibility for the management of the plan, the employer would be responsible for enrolling employees in the plan, determining the level of contributions, and collecting contributions to the plan. There is no requirement that the employer would have to make contributions to the plan, and employees can opt out of participating.
- In addition to employed members, individual members who are either employees of employers who choose not to participate in a PRPP or are self-employed individuals can also participate in PRPPs.
- Without going into detail, the PRPPs operate under the general rules applicable to all types of retirement savings (e.g., contributions cannot exceed the annual money purchase limits and there will be penalties for excess contributions).
- The plans will generally be portable, with members being able to move the benefits they've accrued to another plan or retirement savings plan.
- The PRPP legislation allows interested jurisdictions to require mandatory participation for employers.

10-157. It is hoped that the introduction of PRPPs will result in a large increase in the number of individuals that participate in an RPP that requires regular contributions. Regulations for the operation of PRPPs are in effect at both the federal and provincial level.

Target Benefit Plans

10-158. A different solution to the problem of inadequate retirement savings has been proposed by the federal government. Target benefit plans, also known as shared risk plans, are a type of compromise between defined contribution plans and defined benefit plans:

- Like defined contribution plans, target benefit plans have either fixed contribution rates or, in some cases, contribution rates that vary within a narrow range.
- Like defined benefit plans, target benefit plans have a targeted pension benefit.

- The compromise is that, unlike a regular defined benefit plan, target benefit plans allow for benefits to be reduced if the fund assets are not sufficient to provide the targeted benefit.

10-159. Several provinces have introduced legislation to provide for plans with these characteristics. In December 2020 the Quebec government introduced legislation to allow the establishment of these plans. While target benefit plans may become widespread in the future, they are not currently of sufficient importance to cover in this general text.

Expanded Canada Pension Plan

10-160. It is a fact that, given current levels of retirement savings, many individuals will find themselves in a difficult financial situation in their retirement years. It is clear that the existing retirement savings programs are not capable of coping with this large-scale problem. The number of workers who are members of an employer-sponsored RPP is declining, and the generous provisions of the RRSP legislation are not being used to the extent necessary to adequately provide retirement income.

10-161. Like the existing programs, pooled RPPs and target benefit plans require the participation of employers or voluntary actions by plan participants. It is unlikely that these programs will fully solve this ever-increasing problem.

10-162. Unlike other retirement savings vehicles, the CPP is not an optional program. Employers and employees must participate. Sole proprietors that carry on a business and members of partnerships are also obliged to participate.

10-163. The problem, however, is the adequacy of the benefits that are provided under this program. The maximum benefit is currently over $14,000, although the average annual benefit is only slightly above $8,000 due to insufficient CPP contributions at a level necessary to pay out the maximum. Even when this is combined with the OAS payment of just over $7,400, the combined total comes to an amount that is still considered a low level of income.

10-164. In the United States, the social security system is a similar system to the CPP (required participation by employers and individuals carrying on a business). In contrast to the low benefits provided under the CPP program, the maximum benefit in the United States for an individual retiring at age 65 is over US$37,350 per year, however maximum contributions (in the form of a social security tax) are almost $8,900 per year. This compares to the maximum Canadian employee contributions of $3,166. If Canadians wish to enjoy a more financially secure retirement, CPP benefits must move closer to the amounts paid in the United States.

10-165. It appears that this will happen, as plans are underway to increase benefits. Up until 2019, the CPP retirement pension is designed to replace one-quarter of average work earnings. Under a new agreement negotiated with the provinces, it is expected that during the period 2019 through 2025 the benefit will increase to one-third of average work earnings. This will result in a maximum benefit of approximately $30,000 per year. This change has brought an increase in both the maximum insurable earnings and the contribution rate.

Registered Retirement Income Funds (RRIF)—ITA 146.3

Establishment

Only Transfers from Other Plans

10-166. A RRIF is a trust arrangement, administered in much the same manner as an RRSP. A basic difference, however, is the fact that deductible contributions cannot be made to a RRIF. ITA 146.3(2)(f) clarifies that the only property that can be accepted by the RRIF trustee are transfers of property from other types of retirement savings arrangements. The most common type of transfer would be a transfer from an RRSP, which can occur on a rollover basis. RRSP transfers to a RRIF commonly occur when an individual reaches age 71.

10-167. There is no limit on the number of RRIFs that can be owned by an individual, and in addition, the individual has complete flexibility as to the number of RRSPs that can be transferred to a RRIF on a rollover basis. Further, individuals are free to divide any RRSP and only transfer a portion of the funds to a RRIF. This in no way limits the options available for any balance remaining in the RRSP.

10-168. A RRIF can be established by an individual of any age and without regard to whether the individual is retiring. However, the individual must have an eligible savings plan, such as an RRSP, from which funds can be transferred.

Other Considerations

10-169. A transfer from an RRSP to a RRIF has no income tax consequences as the transfer is allowed on a rollover basis. Any amounts subsequently withdrawn from the RRIF must be included in net income for the year of receipt regardless of whether they represent capital gains or dividends that would otherwise be subject to income at lower effective income tax rates. This was discussed at Paragraph 10-33.

10-170. RRIF investments can be managed by the trustee of the plan according to the directions of the individual annuitant. The list of qualified investments for RRIFs is similar to that for RRSPs and allows for considerable latitude in investment choices. As is the case with RRSPs, fees paid personally by an individual RRIF annuitant for the administration of a RRIF are not deductible to the individual.

RRIF Withdrawals

Pension Income Tax Credit and Pension Income Splitting

10-171. In our discussion of RRSP withdrawals, we noted that lump-sum withdrawals from RRSPs are not eligible for the pension income tax credit or for pension income splitting. Fortunately, this is not the case with lump-sum withdrawals from a RRIF. If the individual is aged 65 or over, all withdrawals from a RRIF that are required to be included in net income (transfers between plans are not required to be included in net income) qualify for the pension income tax credit and can be split with a spouse or common-law partner for pension income-splittng purposes. Transfers between plans are not required to be included in net income and are not eligible for income splitting.

Withdrawals Greater Than the Minimum Withdrawal

10-172. While legislation establishes the minimum withdrawal from a RRIF (see the following paragraph), there is no maximum withdrawal. The entire balance in the RRIF can be withdrawn at any time. However, as was noted, any amounts withdrawn from the RRIF must be included in net income in the year of withdrawal. In contrast to RRSPs, where income tax is withheld on any regular withdrawals, tax is only withheld on RRIF withdrawals in excess of the minimum withdrawal.

Calculating the Amount of the Minimum Withdrawal

10-173. We noted previously that, unlike the situation with RRSPs, an individual cannot make deductible contributions to a RRIF. Another difference between an RRSP and a RRIF is that a minimum annual withdrawal must be made from a RRIF beginning in the year following the year it is established.

10-174. For an individual who is under 71 at the beginning of the year, the minimum withdrawal is determined by dividing the FMV of the RRIF assets at the beginning of the year by 90 minus the age of the individual at the beginning of the year.

10-175. If an individual is 72 years of age or older at the beginning of the year, the amount that must be withdrawn is determined by a prescribed percentage applied to the RRIF assets at the beginning of the year. This percentage is found in ITR 7308(4). It increases each year, starting at

5.40% for an individual who is 72 years old at the beginning of the year until it reaches 20% for individuals who are aged 95 or older at the beginning of the year. It remains at 20% for each subsequent year until the individual dies. This, of course, means that the RRIF balance will never reach zero if minimum withdrawals are made.

EXAMPLE Moira established her RRIF in 2018. At the beginning of 2020 she was 71 years old and had $950,000 in RRIF assets. At the beginning of 2021 she had $980,000 in RRIF assets.

ANALYSIS Moira's minimum RRIF withdrawal for 2020 would be $50,000 [$950,000 ÷ (90 - 71)] and for 2021 would be $52,920 [($980,000)(5.40%)].

Use of Spouse's Age for Minimum Withdrawal

10-176. It is possible to irrevocably elect to use a spouse's age to calculate the minimum RRIF withdrawal. If the spouse is younger, the minimum amount is lower and offers an opportunity to defer the income tax effect of the withdrawals.

Exercise 10-12

Subject: Minimum RRIF Withdrawal

On January 1, 2021, Mr. Larry Harold transfers all of his RRSP funds into a RRIF. Mr. Harold is 65 years old on that date. The FMV of these assets on January 1, 2021, is $625,000 and rises to $660,000 as of January 1, 2022. What is the minimum withdrawal that Mr. Harold must make from the RRIF during 2021 and 2022?

Solutions to Exercises are available in the Study Guide.

Death of the RRIF Annuitant

General Rules

10-177. As was the case with an RRSP, the general rule is that when an individual dies, the FMV of the assets in the RRIF will be included in the net income of the deceased in the final income tax return. However, we have also seen that there are exceptions to this FMV inclusion when RRIF assets are transferred to either a spouse or common-law partner or a financially dependent child or grandchild of the deceased individual.

Rollovers

10-178. If an individual has a spouse or common-law partner, the most tax advantageous approach to estate planning is usually to name that person as the successor annuitant of the RRIF. In this situation, the RRIF will simply continue with the surviving spouse or common-law partner receiving the payments. There will be no income tax consequences for the deceased, and future withdrawals from the RRIF will be included in the net income of the spouse or common-law partner.

10-179. If a RRIF is left to the deceased's estate, the alternatives for transfers to a spouse or common-law partner or to a financially dependent child or grandchild are the same as those for an RRSP.

10-180. A rollover to a spouse or common-law partner is still available even if that individual is not named in the RRIF contract or a will as long as the consent of the deceased individual's legal representative and RRIF carrier is obtained. Also as with RRSPs, if a financially dependent child or grandchild is physically or mentally infirm, rollover treatment is available for transfers of RRIF assets to an RRSP, a RRIF, an RDSP, or an annuity for the benefit of that child or grandchild. In the absence of a physical or mental infirmity, the only option is the purchase of a limited-term annuity.

Evaluation of RRIFs

10-181. For individuals who have reached 71 years of age, terminating an RRSP by cashing out and receiving a lump-sum withdrawal is usually an option that will maximize one's income tax due to the fact that the withdrawal, depending on the amounts, could result in federal income tax at the highest income tax bracket of 33% plus the highest relevant provincial income tax bracket. In addition, pension income splitting cannot be used for lump-sum withdrawals.

10-182. This leaves individuals with a choice between using a RRIF and purchasing an annuity. The fact that life annuities are only available through life insurance companies means that the rates of return implicit in these financial instruments are often not competitive with other investments.

10-183. Further, annuities lack flexibility. With the exception of variable payment life annuities, once an individual has entered into an annuity contract there is usually no possibility of acquiring larger payments if they are required by some unforeseen event. In contrast, RRIFs offer some degree of flexibility with respect to amounts available to the individual.

10-184. As a final point, the wide range of qualifying investments that can be acquired in RRIFs provide individuals with the opportunity to achieve better rates of return than those available through the purchase of annuities. It would appear that, for most individuals, the use of a RRIF is the most desirable option when the individual reaches 71 years of age and is forced to collapse any RRSPs.

Deferred Profit-Sharing Plans (DPSPs)—ITA 147

General Rules

10-185. ITA 147 provides for an arrangement where an employer can deduct contributions made to a trustee of a DPSP for the benefit of employees. Employees cannot make contributions to an employer-sponsored DPSP. However, certain direct transfers of balances from other plans belonging to the employee can be made (see Paragraph 10-195).

10-186. Amounts contributed to the plan will be invested with investment earnings exempt from Part I tax. As with the other retirement savings plans or arrangements, plan beneficiaries are only required to include DPSP amounts in net income when funds are distributed to them.

10-187. As was the case with RPPs, the employer's contributions to these plans are limited by a maximum PA that must be complied with to avoid having the DPSP revoked. This is found in ITA 147(5.1) and is more restrictive than the corresponding limit for RPPs. Like the situation with RPPs, contributions to DPSPs cannot result in a PA that exceeds 18% of a beneficiary's employment income for the year. However, contributions to these plans are limited to only one-half of the money purchase limit for the year.

Tax Planning

10-188. From the point of view of the employer, DPSPs are similar to RPPs. However, they have the advantage of providing greater flexibility in the scheduling of payments. Such plans are tied to the profits of the business and, if the business has a bad year, it will normally result in a reduction of payments into the DPSP. Further, no specific benefits are promised to the employees. This relieves the employer from any responsibility for bad investment decisions by the fund trustee or estimation errors in the actuarial valuation process, factors that can cause significant uncertainty for the sponsors of defined benefit RPPs.

10-189. From the point of view of the employee, a DPSP operates in a manner similar to an RPP. The major difference is that employees are not permitted to contribute to DPSPs. A further difference is that DPSPs cannot be designed to provide a defined benefit. They are always defined contribution plans, meaning that future benefits will be based on the amount within the plan and the investment return that can be earned.

10-190. DPSPs must invest in certain qualified investments and there are penalties for purchases of non-qualified investments. A final important consideration is that DPSPs cannot be registered if the employer or a member of the employer's family is a beneficiary under the plan. This would include controlling shareholders and members of their family if the employer is a corporation, individual owners if the employer is a proprietorship or partnership, and beneficiaries when the employer is a trust.

Employee Profit-Sharing Plans (EPSPs)—ITA 144

General Rules

10-191. EPSPs are plans that are similar to DPSPs in that the employer can deduct contributions made on behalf of employees. Unlike DPSPs, there are no specified limits on the employer's contributions as long as they are reasonable and are paid out of profits. Amounts paid into the EPSP by the employer within the year or 120 days of the following year are deductible to the employer.

10-192. However, these plans have not achieved the popularity of DPSPs for a very simple reason: The employer's contributions to these plans are required to be included in the net income of the employee in the year in which they are made. In addition, any income that accrues on the property in the fund is also allocated to the employee. The one advantage is that EPSP income retains its character to the employees if the income is capital gains, taxable dividends, and certain foreign income. Although ultimate payments to the employees out of the fund are not required to be included in net income (since they have already been included), this form of compensation offers no tax deferral and requires the payment of income taxes on amounts that have not yet been received by the employee. As a result, EPSPs have not been popular.

Part XI.4 Tax on Excess EPSP Contributions

10-193. The preceding suggests that there are few income tax advantages associated with the use of EPSPs. However, the CRA has found that such plans were being used

- to direct business profits to low-income family members in order to reduce income taxes; and
- to avoid or defer employee withholding requirements as well as CPP and EI payments. Substituting EPSP payments for bonuses was one of the more common uses of EPSPs as it deferred the payment of withholding tax by almost one year.

10-194. To curtail these practices, there is a penalty tax under Part XI.4 on excess contributions for specified employees. A "specified employee" is defined in ITA 248(1) as a person who owns more than 10% of the shares of the corporate employer or who does not deal at arm's length with the employer. The additional income tax is charged to the specified employee on amounts paid by the employer into the EPSP for the benefit of a specified employee that exceed 20% of the individual's adjusted employment income for the year. The Part XI.4 tax rate is equal to the highest federal income tax rate of 33%.

Transfers between Plans

Accumulated Benefits

10-195. As individuals may belong to several different retirement savings plans over their working lives, retirement funds are often moved from one plan to another for a number of reasons, such as when RRSPs are no longer permitted at age 71 or when employees change employment and RPPs of one employer are moved to that of another. Technically the movement of funds between plans requires a withdrawal from one plan followed by a contribution to another. Without specific legislation, such transfers would result in the amounts withdrawn being included in the annuitant's net income and subjecting the withdrawal to income tax leaving fewer funds for intended retirement. Preservation of the funds requires a form of permissible rollover between plans of the same individual.

10-196. Fortunately, the ITA provides the necessary rollover provisions to ensure an orderly flow from one plan to another. The transfers must be made directly between the plans, meaning that the transfer occurs directly between the plan trustees or administrators. If the transfer qualifies, no amount is required to be included in the net income of the annuitant with respect to the amount withdrawn nor is any deduction allowed (where applicable) for contributions to the receiving plan. The following transfers are permitted on a rollover basis:

RPPs ITA 147.3 provides for the direct transfer of a lump-sum amount from an RPP to a different RPP, to an RRSP, or to a RRIF. The provision also permits a transfer from an individual's RPP to an RPP, RRSP, or RRIF of a spouse, former spouse, common-law partner, or former common-law partner under a court order or written separation agreement in the event of a breakdown in the marriage or common-law partnership.

RRSPs ITA 146(16) provides for the transfer of lump-sum amounts from an RRSP to a RRIF, an RPP, or to another RRSP. The provision also permits a transfer from an individual's RRSP to an RRSP or RRIF of a spouse, former spouse, common-law partner, or former common-law partner under a court order or written separation agreement in the event of a breakdown in the marriage or common-law partnership. Transfers to an annuity provider to purchase an advanced life deferred annuity are recent legislative additions and are also included.

DPSPs ITA 147(19) provides for the direct transfer of a lump-sum amount from a DPSP to an RPP, an RRSP, or to a different DPSP. There are additional transfers allowed to the individual's RRIF and to an RPP, RRSP, DPSP, or RRIF of a spouse, former spouse, common-law partner, or former common-law partner under a court order or written separation agreement in the event of a breakdown in the marriage or common-law partnership.

Retiring Allowance Transfers—ITA 60(j.1)

10-197. We first discussed retiring allowances in Chapter 9. A retiring allowance, which includes amounts received for loss of an office or employment and unused sick leave, must be included in the net income of an individual in the year in which it is received. A retiring allowance is usually paid when either an employee retires or has lost the particular employment. In both instances, particularly on retirement, there is an element of additional compensation that could be best put to use toward retirement savings. To encourage that retirement savings potential, the ITA historically permitted the elective rollover of all or part of a retiring allowance to an RRSP or RPP. Unfortunately, it requires an individual to have provided employment services prior to 1996. As a result, the current use of the rollover would only be available to an employee who had been with the same employer for most if not all of their working lives.

10-198. The deduction is available under ITA 60(j.1) and allows a deduction for retiring allowance amounts transferred to either an RPP or an RRSP. A considerable advantage is that an individual's RRSP deduction room is not affected by this contribution. There is, however, a limit on how much can be transferred and therefore how much can be deducted. The limit is as follows:

- $2,000 for each year or part year the individual was employed by the employer prior to 1996. This includes non-continuous service with the same employer.
- An additional $1,500 for each year or part year the individual was employed by the employer prior to 1989 for which the employer's contributions to an RPP or DPSP had not vested by the time the retiring allowance was paid.

10-199. This transfer does not have to be made directly from the employer to the RRSP. The deduction is available if the individual receives the funds and deposits the eligible amount into the individual's RRSP within 60 days of the end of the year it is received. The eligible amount must be contributed to the employee's RRSP (not a spousal RRSP) to be deducted. However, if a direct transfer is used, the taxpayer will avoid having income tax withheld on the retiring allowance. If the transfer is not direct the individual can request a withholding waiver from the CRA based on the amount that will be transferred to an RRSP. It should also be noted that, for the individual to deduct the amount transferred to her own RRSP, the trustee must issue the usual RRSP contribution receipt. The income tax treatment is slightly different as most inter-plan transfers are not included in net income. In this case the retiring allowance is fully included in net income under ITA 56(1)(a) and there is a separate deduction for the part of the retiring allowance that qualifies for the RRSP contribution.

EXAMPLE Joan Marx retires at the end of 2021, receiving from her employer a retiring allowance of $150,000. She began working for this employer in 1982. The employer has never sponsored an RPP or a DPSP.

ANALYSIS The entire $150,000 must be included in Ms. Marx's 2021 net income under ITA 56(1)(a). Provided she makes a $38,500 [($2,000)(the 14 years 1982 through 1995) + ($1,500)(the 7 years 1982 through 1988)] contribution to her RRSP, she will be able to deduct the $38,500 RRSP contribution as a result of ITA 60(j.1) without eroding her RRSP deduction room. As a result, the net effect of the retiring allowance on her 2021 net income is that it will increase by $111,500 [$150,000 - $38,500].

Exercise 10-13

Subject: Retiring Allowance

On December 31, 2021, Mr. Giovanni Bartoli retires after 45 years of service with his present employer. In recognition of his outstanding service during these years, his employer pays him a retiring allowance of $100,000. His employer has never sponsored an RPP or a DPSP. What is the maximum deductible contribution that Mr. Bartoli can make to his RRSP as a result of receiving this retiring allowance?

Solutions to Exercises are available in the Study Guide.

We suggest you complete SSP 10-7 at this point.

Retirement Compensation Arrangements (RCA)

The Problem

10-200. As we have seen throughout this chapter, the rules related to maximum contributions by employers to RPPs and DPSPs are very specific. While these maximum limits are sufficient to provide a reasonable level of retirement income to the majority of employees, they fall short of this goal for highly paid senior executives. Maintaining one's standard of living is dependent on one's income, and therefore high-income individuals would be unable to maintain that standard based on the current retirement savings limitations. The issues are the same for owners/managers of successful private corporations.

10-201. Given this situation, both public and private corporations use plans other than RPPs and DPSPs to provide benefits that avoid the limitations discussed in this chapter. In general, such arrangements can be classified as retirement compensation arrangements (RCAs).

Arrangements Defined

10-202. RCAs are defined in the *ITA, in part,* as follows:

ITA 248(1) Retirement compensation arrangement means a plan or arrangement under which contributions are made by an employer or former employer of a taxpayer, or by a person with whom the employer or former employer does not deal at arm's length, to another person or partnership in connection with benefits that are to be received or may be received or enjoyed by any person on, after, or in contemplation of any substantial change in the services rendered by the taxpayer, the retirement of the taxpayer or the loss of an office or employment of the taxpayer.

10-203. The lengthy definition adds a list of certain plans and arrangements that have characteristics of an RCA but are are not considered to be RCAs. This list includes RPPs, PRPPs, DPSPs, RRSPs, EPSPs, supplementary unemployment benefit plans, or plans established for the purpose of deferring the salary or wages of a professional athlete.

10-204. Provided the arrangement involves a contractual obligation to ultimately make payments to a specific employee, a corporation's contributions to an RCA are fully deductible in the year in which they are actually made. However, as we shall see in the following material, both contributions and subsequent earnings on the invested contributions are subject to a special refundable tax.

Part XI.3 Refundable Tax

10-205. Contributions made to an RCA are subject to a 50% refundable tax under ITA Part XI.3. In addition, earnings on the assets contained in the plan are subject to this same 50% refundable tax. The tax amounts are refunded at a 50% rate when distributions are made to the beneficiaries of the plan. The 50% tax is designed to neutralize the tax deferral of a fully deductible employer contribution when the employee will only be required to include amounts from the RCA in net income years later.

EXAMPLE During 2020, Borscan Ltd. contributes $50,000 to a plan established for several of its senior executives. The funds are used to purchase investments that earn interest of $4,500, and no payments are made to the executives during the year. On January 1, 2021, $20,000 is distributed to the beneficiaries of the plan.

ANALYSIS Borscan Ltd. would be able to deduct the $50,000 payment into the plan in determining its 2020 net income. However, the company would be required to withhold and remit 50% of the RCA contribution in 2020, or $25,000, on behalf of the RCA trust. The RCA custodian is required to file an income tax return for the RCA and will pay 50% of the $4,500 of income, or $2,250. Just prior to the distribution the RCA will have $27,250 in funds once all Part XI.3 taxes have been paid. The distribution in 2021 results in a partial refund of the Part XI.3 tax of $10,000 [(50%)($20,000)] to the RCA trust.

10-206. Other benefits include the fact that employer contributions are not considered taxable employment benefits. In addition there are no CPP or EI contribution requirements and, subject to the Part XI.3 refundable tax, investment earnings are not subject to Part I tax (ITA 149(1)(q.1)).

10-207. The use of RCAs remains popular for many reasons, including the fact that the funds in the plan are creditor proof, distributions are not considered part of one's estate (therefore avoiding probate fees), and the plans can be used by non-resident executives who would otherwise be prohibited from making RRSP or RPP contributions.

Salary Deferral Arrangements (SDA)

The Problem

10-208. The fact that business income is on an accrual basis while employment income is on a cash basis has made it advantageous for employers to accrue bonuses prior to the actual payment of the amount to the employee. As was discussed in Chapter 3, if payment to the employee is made by the 179th days of the employer's year end, the employer can deduct the amount in the year in which it has accrued, while the employee will not be required to include the amount in employment until the amount is received.

10-209. If, however, the actual payment occurs more than 179 days after the employer's year end, ITA 78(4) defers the deductibility of the bonus to the year in which it is actually paid. However, even if the employer cannot deduct the amount until paid, it may still be attractive to make an arrangement that will defer the payment of the compensation and therefore postpone the payment of income taxes by the employee. The concept of a salary deferral arrangement (SDA) serves to place a time limit on the ability of employers and employees to make such arrangements.

The Solution

10-210. The *ITA* defines a salary deferral arrangement, in part, as follows:

> **ITA 248(1) Salary deferral arrangement** A plan or arrangement, whether funded or not, under which any person has a right in a taxation year to receive an amount after the year where it is reasonable to consider that one of the main purposes for the creation or existence of the right is to postpone tax payable under this Act by the taxpayer in respect of an amount that is, or is on account or in lieu of, salary or wages of the taxpayer for services rendered by the taxpayer in the year or a preceding taxation year (including such a right that is subject to one or more conditions unless there is a substantial risk that any one of those conditions will not be satisfied).

10-211. Converting this to everyday language, an SDA involves an amount of salary that has been earned by an individual in a given year. However, the employee has made an arrangement with the employer to defer the actual payment of the amount to a subsequent year where the main purpose of the delayed payment is to defer the payment of income taxes on that amount.

10-212. As in the case of an RCA, the definition of an SDA is lengthy and includes many exceptions designed to ensure that other plans or arrangements that appear to have similar deferral objectives are excluded. Some of the exceptions would include RPPs, DPSPs, EPSPs, supplementary unemployment benefit plans, plans for providing education or training (sabbaticals), or plans established for the purpose of deferring the salary of a professional athlete.

10-213. A further important exception is that the definition of an SDA excludes bonus arrangements where the amount is paid within three years of the end of the calendar year in which the employee provided employment services. This means that there are three bonus deferral concepts:

(1) Bonuses paid by the 179th day after the end of the year in which the bonus is accured

(2) Bonuses paid from the 180th day after the end of the year in which the bonus is accrued to the last day of the third year

(3) Bonus arrangements that extend beyond three years of the end of the taxation year of the employer in which the employment services were accrued; the SDA rules would apply to this third category

10-214. In the first instance the bonus would be deductible to the employer in the year in which the bonus accrued. In the second case the bonus would only be deductible in the year it was actually paid. In the third and final instance the SDA rules would apply and the employer would be entitled to a deduction in the year the bonus was accrued (ITA 20(1)(oo)).

10-215. With respect to the employee and the first two cases, the bonus would only be included in employment income in the year it was actually received. In the third case, with the application of the SDA rules, the bonus would be included in employment income when accrued (ITA 6(1)(a) and 6(11)). This result serves as a disincentive to enter into SDAs.

10-216. Despite these restrictions, certain deferral arrangements can be effective in that they do not fall within the ITA 248(1) definition. These include

- self-funded leave of absence arrangements (sabbaticals);
- bonus arrangements with payment deferred not more than three years, provided the employer accepts the loss of deductibility that occurs after 179 days;

- deferred compensation for professional athletes; and
- retiring allowances. These escape the SDA rules and, subject to limits discussed previously, can be transferred on a tax-free basis to an RRSP (see paragraph 2.24 of CRA Folio S2-F1-C2 "Retiring Allowances").

Individual Pension Plans (IPPs)

10-217. It is possible to establish a defined benefit plan for a single individual. These plans are defined in ITR 8300(1) as follows:

> ... a registered pension plan that contains a defined benefit provision if, at any time in the year or a preceding year, the plan has fewer than four members and at least one of them is related to a participating employer in the plan.

10-218. Such plans are usually marketed in conjunction with insurance products and their establishment requires the use of an actuarial valuation for the specific individual covered by the plan.

10-219. These plans have grown in popularity in recent years, particularly for successful owners/managers of private companies. These individualized plans are considered of benefit for those individuals within 10 to 20 years of retirement who have earned income in excess of $100,000 annually. The ability to make past service contributions and transfers from other registered plan have greatly increased their value. However, in the 2019 federal budget the government closed a loophole with respect to IPPs. The plan transfer rules, which we discussed starting at Paragraph 10-195, only allowed 50% of transfers from defined benefit RPPs to RRSPs to be moved on a rollover basis, with the remaining amounts fully taxable. This transfer restriction was designed to support the RRSP limitations, but individuals were transferring defined benefit RPPs to IPPs without any restriction. The government now only allows 50% of defined benefit RPPs to be transferred to an IPP on a rollover basis.

We suggest you complete SSP 10-8 to 10-11 at this point.

Key Terms

A full glossary with definitions is provided at the end of the Study Guide.

Annuitant
Annuity
Beneficiary
Canada Pension Plan (CPP)
Deferred Income Plans
Deferred Profit-Sharing Plan (DPSP)
Defined Benefit Plan
Defined Contribution Plan
Earned Income (RRSP Limit)
Employee Profit-Sharing Plans (EPSP)
Employment Income
Fixed-Term Annuity
Home Buyers' Plan (HBP)
Income Attribution
Income Splitting
Individual Pension Plan (IPP)
Life Annuity
Lifelong Learning Plan (LLP)
Money Purchase Limit
Money Purchase Plan
Past Service Cost
Past Service Pension Adjustment (PSPA)
Pension Adjustment (PA)
Pension Adjustment Reversal (PAR)
Pension Income Tax Credit
Phased Retirement

Pooled Registered Pension Plan
Refundable Part XI.3 Tax
Registered Pension Plan (RPP)
Registered Retirement Income Fund (RRIF)
Registered Retirement Savings Plan (RRSP)
Retirement Compensation Arrangement (RCA)
Retiring Allowance
Rollover
RRSP Deduction Limit
RRSP Deduction Room
RRSP Dollar Limit
Salary Deferral Arrangement (SDA)
Spousal RRSP
Spouse
Target Benefit Plans
Tax Deferral
Unused RRSP Deduction Room
Vested Benefit
Vested Contribution

References

For more detailed study of the material in this chapter, we would refer you to the following:

ITA 144	Employees' Profit-Sharing Plans
ITA 146	Registered Retirement Savings Plans
ITA 146.01	Home Buyers' Plan
ITA 146.02	Lifelong Learning Plan
ITA 146.3	Registered Retirement Income Funds
ITA 147	Deferred Profit-Sharing Plans
ITA 147.1	Definitions, Registration, and Other Rules (Registered Pension Plans)
ITA 147.2	Pension Contributions Deductible—Employer Contributions
ITA 147.3	Transfer—Money Purchase to Money Purchase, RRSP, or RRIF
ITA 147.4	RPP Annuity Contract
ITR 8503 (16) to (25)	Defined Benefit Provisions—Phased Retirement
IC 13-1R1	Pooled Registered Pension Plans (PRPPs)
IC 72-13R8	Employees' Pension Plans
IC 72-22R9	Registered Retirement Savings Plans
IC77-1R5	Deferred Profit-Sharing Plans
IC 78-18R6	Registered Retirement Income Funds
S2-F1-C2	Retiring Allowances
S3-F10-C1	Qualified Investments—RRSPS, RESPs, RRIFs, RDSPs, and TFSAs
S3-F10-C2	Prohibited Investments—RRSPs, RRIFs, and TFSAs
S3-F10-C3	Advantages—RRSPs, RESPs, RRIFs, RDSPs, and TFSAs
IT-124R6	Contributions to Registered Retirement Savings Plans
IT-167R6	Registered Pension Plans—Employees' Contributions
IT-280R	Employees' Profit-Sharing Plans—Payments Computed by Reference to Profits
IT-307R4	Spousal or Common-Law Partner Registered Retirement Savings Plans
IT-379R	Employees' Profit-Sharing Plans—Allocations to Beneficiaries
IT-500R	Registered Retirement Savings Plans—Death of an Annuitant
IT-528	Transfer of Funds between Registered Plans
RC4112	Lifelong Learning Plan (Guide)
RC4177	Death of an RRSP Annuitant (Pamphlet)
T4040	RRSPs and Other Registered Plans for Retirement (Guide)
T4041	Retirement Compensation Arrangements (Guide)

Self-Study Problems (SSPs)

Self-Study Problems (SSPs) provide practice in problem solving. Within the chapters, we have indicated where it would be appropriate to stop and work on each SSP. The problems can be downloaded by chapter from MyLab Accounting. Solutions are available in the Study Guide. Select problems can also be completed directly in MyLab and auto-graded.

Assignment Problems

Solutions to Assignment Problems (APs) are available to instructors only.

AP 10-1 (Calculation of PAs and PSPAs)

In each of the following **independent** cases, calculate the pension adjustment (PA) or past service pension adjustment (PSPA) that would be reported by the employer.

Case A John Brokow's employer sponsors both a money purchase (defined contribution) RPP and a DPSP. He is a member of both. During 2021, his employer contributes, on his behalf, $3,200 to the RPP and $1,100 to the DPSP. In addition, Mr. Brokow contributes $1,500 to the RPP. His employment earnings for 2021 are $120,000. Calculate his 2021 PA.

Case B Sarah Halfhill's employer sponsors a defined benefit RPP and, during 2021, contributes $3,100 on her behalf. Sarah also contributes $3,100 to the plan in 2021. The plan provides a benefit equal to 1.65% of pensionable earnings for each year of service. Sarah's pensionable earnings for 2021 are $52,000. Calculate her 2021 PA.

Case C Bob Carver has worked for his current employer since 2019. In January 2021, this employer institutes a defined benefit RPP, with benefits extended for all years of service prior to the inception of the plan. The benefit formula calls for a retirement benefit equal to 1.1% of pensionable earnings for each year of service. In the current year and both previous years, Bob's pensionable earnings were $48,000. Calculate his 2021 PSPA and PA.

Case D Marianne Underwood has worked for her current employer since 2019. She has been a member of her employer's defined benefit RPP since she began woking for the company. In January 2021, her employer agrees to retroactively increase the benefit formula from 1.4% to 1.7% of pensionable earnings for each year of service. In the current year and both previous years, Marianne's pensionable earnings were $52,000. Calculate her 2021 PSPA and PA.

AP 10-2 (Excess RRSP Contributions)

As she was attending university during 2017, 2018, and 2019, Karla had no earned income for RRSP purposes in any of these three years. However, before returning to university she had been employed and, reflecting this, on January 1, 2019, she has RRSP deduction room of $21,300. She also has undeducted contributions on this date of $15,250.

She returned to work on a part-time basis in 2020, resulting in earned income for RRSP purposes of $19,100. Also during 2020, she receives a bequest from the estate of her father in the amount of $225,000. She immediately contributes $25,000 of this inheritance to her RRSP. She does not deduct any RRSP contributions during this year. She also makes sufficient charitable donations that her 2020 federal income tax payable is reduced to nil.

During 2021, she resumes full-time employment, resulting in a 2021 earned income of $47,800. While she claims her maximum RRSP deduction for 2021, she makes no further contributions to the plan during the year.

Required:

A. Determine Karla's maximum RRSP deduction for 2021.

B. Determine the Part X.1 penalty tax (ITA 204.1) (excess RRSP contributions) that would be assessed to Karla for the year ending December 31, 2021.

C. Determine the amount of contributions that Karla would have to withdraw from her RRSP on January 2, 2022, to avoid being assessed the penalty tax under Part X.1 (ITA 204.1). What advice would you give to Karla regarding her retirement savings?

AP 10-3 (Net Income with RRSP Contributions)

Mr. Josh Hansen's primary source of income is from employment. For 2020, his employment income was $78,000. Included in this figure were commissions of $16,000 and taxable employment benefits of $8,000. During this year, he made contributions to his employer's money purchase (defined contribution) RPP of $2,000. His employer made a matching contribution of $2,000, as well as a $1,200 contribution to a deferred profit-sharing plan.

Also during 2020, Josh had the following additional income:

Interest income	$ 3,400
Eligible dividends	1,900
Royalties from a book written by Josh	6,500
Taxable capital gains	38,000

Losses for the year included the following:

Rental loss	$10,400
Allowable capital losses	9,000
2018 net capital loss	32,000

Josh has custody of his 7-year-old son from a former marriage and receives $14,400 in child support payments each year. He also receives $9,000 in annual spousal support. During 2020, Josh incurred deductible child care costs of $4,000.

Josh is also required to pay a total of $2,500 per month in spousal support payments to another former spouse.

At the end of 2020, Josh had $23,000 in unused RRSP deduction room and $21,000 in undeducted RRSP contributions. He did not claim an RRSP deduction in 2020.

Required:

A. Using the rules from ITA 3, calculate Josh's 2020 net income.

B. Based on the information provided, calculate
   - the maximum RRSP contribution that Josh can claim for 2021 without incurring a penalty for excess contributions;
   - Josh's maximum RRSP deduction for 2021 and any remaining undeducted contributions, assuming he makes the maximum contribution that you have determined.

C. Assume that, in addition to the information provided in the problem, Josh has 2021 business income of $160,000. Using this new information, provide the information required in Part B.

AP 10-4 (RRSPs and Tax Planning)

After being married for eight years, Helene Lister's marriage to her husband, Martin, ended in divorce. She moved out of the family home in April 2020. She had no earned income prior to 2020.

At the end of August 2021she began working for a public company earning salary of $3,500 a month. During the four months of her 2020 employment, her earnings totalled $14,000.

Her employer provided benefits, including both a defined benefit RPP and a group health care plan. Both Helene and the employer make matching contributions to the RPP in the amount of $600 each. The employer pays the 2020 premiums of the health care plan, which is $700.

The terms of the divorce settlement include the following:

- Martin will retain the family residence.
- Martin will make a $62,000 lump-sum payment in 2020 plus monthly payments of $2,000 in spousal support. The 2020 monthly payments total $12,000.
- Helene will be given full title to a jointly owned rental property. Information on this property is as follows:

Adjusted cost base (ACB)	
Building	$342,000
Land	110,000
UCC—Building	293,439
FMV at transfer	
Building	376,000
Land	130,000
Rental loss (before CCA)	
From time of transfer	8,600
Helene's share prior to the transfer	3,600

Other sources of funds for Helene during 2020 are as follows:

- An inheritance from her father's estate of $82,000
- Eligible dividends from Canadian public companies of $1,700

For both 2020 and 2021, Helene does not anticipate that her income will exceed the limit for the lowest federal income tax bracket of 15%. However, she anticipates that for the 2022 taxation year, she will have taxable income that will place her in the 26% federal income tax bracket.

Required:

A. Calculate Helene's employment income for 2020.

B. Determine Helene's maximum deductible RRSP contribution for 2021.

C. As Helene's personal financial consultant, what advice would you give her regarding her TFSA and RRSP contribution and deduction for 2021, assuming she has qualified for the TFSA since its introduction in 2009?

AP 10-5 (Employment Income with RRSP)

Ms. Stratton has been the controller for a large publicly traded corporation for the last five years. The following information relates to the year ending December 31, 2021:

1. Ms. Stratton had a gross salary of $130,000, from which her employer withheld the following amounts:

Income taxes	$33,342
RPP contributions	2,390
EI premiums	890
CPP contributions	3,166
Donations to registered charities	1,600
Employee's portion of benefit plans (see Point 2 below)	1,436

2. It is the policy of the company to pay one-half of the cost of certain benefit plans. The following represents the employer's 50% portion of the following costs made on behalf of Ms. Stratton:

Group term life insurance	$ 96
Provincial health insurance plan	482
Dental plan	173
Major medical care (private insurer)	396
Group income protection	289
Total	$1,436

3. Ms. Stratton's employer paid $2,300 for her annual membership in the Hot Rocks Curling Club. Ms. Stratton uses the club largely for employment-related entertaining.

4. Ms. Stratton was awarded a one-week trip to Bermuda by her employer for being with the company for 15 long years. The FMV of this trip was $5,000.

5. Ms. Stratton is required to travel to the offices of her employer's clients on a regular and continuing basis. As a result, her employer reimburses her for actual expenses. These payments totalled $8,462 for the year.

6. During the year, Ms. Stratton paid professional dues of $225.

7. During the year, Ms. Stratton made contributions to an RRSP in the amount of $20,000 and to a TFSA in the amount of $6,000 (her maximum contribution room). At the end of 2020, Ms. Stratton's unused RRSP deduction room was nil and she had no undeducted RRSP contributions. Her employer reported that she had a 2020 PA of $5,560. Her earned income for 2020 is equal to her 2021 earned income.

Required:

A. Calculate Ms. Stratton's employment income for the year ending December 31, 2021, and indicate the reasons that you have not included items in your calculations. Ignore any GST/HST & PST implications.

B. Calculate Ms. Stratton's maximum RRSP deduction for 2021.

C. Comment on the advisability of her $20,000 RRSP contribution.

AP 10-6 (Net Income and RRSP Contributions)

During the year ending December 31, 2021, Valerie Arnold carried on a business as a sole proprietor. Her 2021 business income, determined using accounting principles (ASPE), is $140,823. Information related to this business is as follows:

- As a result of meetings with various clients and suppliers, Valerie incurred meal and entertainment expenses of $7,250. This amount was deducted in determining accounting business income.

- Amortization in the amount of $21,350 was deducted in the determination of accounting business income. Maximum CCA, which Valerie intends to deduct, was determined to be $29,730.

- During 2021, the business sold depreciable property that had a capital cost of $65,000. On January 1, 2021, the carrying value of the property for accounting purposes was $51,000 and the UCC balance of the respective CCA class was $43,248. The depreciable property was sold for $35,000. It was the only property in the class and no additions were made to the class before the end of the 2021 taxation year.

Other Information
Other information required to complete Valerie's 2021 income tax return is as follows:

1. At the beginning of 2021, Valerie had unused RRSP deduction room of $8,400. She had made contributions of $9,300 on February 27, 2021, that she forgot to claim in her 2020 income tax return. She would like to claim that contributions on her 2021 income tax return.

2. In 2021 she earned the following amounts of investment income and realized the following capital gains:

Interest on her savings account	$ 960
Capital gains from the sale of personal property	29,400
Capital losses from the sales of shares	(7,600)
Eligible dividends received	5,650

3. She received royalties of $9,340 during 2021 on a Study Guide she had written for a university course.

4. She paid spousal support during 2021 of $18,000.

Required:

A. For the 2021 taxation year, calculate Valerie's minimum net income before any RRSP deduction. Ignore CPP contributions in your calculations.

B. Calculate the maximum RRSP deduction that can be made by Valerie for 2021. In making this calculation, assume that Valerie's 2020 earned income is equal to her 2021 earned income. Determine the amount of any additional contributions that she would have to make in order to maximize her RRSP deduction.

AP 10-7 (Net Income and RRSP Contributions)
Alicia Arnold carries on a business as a sole proprietor with a December 31 fiscal year end. During the year ending December 31, 2021, accounting income was $183,000. Other 2021 information related to the business is as follows:

1. Amortization deducted in the determination of accounting income was $23,000. Her income tax advisor has calculated maximum CCA for this period of $31,000.

2. During the year, the business sold depreciable property for $34,500. The carrying value of the property for accounting purposes was $24,000, the capital cost was $30,000, and the UCC on January 1, 2021, was $18,000.

3. During the year, Alicia spent $14,000 on business meals and entertainment. This amount was fully deducted in the determination of accounting Income.

Other information related to Alicia's income tax position is as follows:

Interest on savings account	$ 1,200
Taxable capital gains on personal property	18,000
Allowable capital loss on sale of shares	1,000
Spousal support paid	3,600
Royalties on cookbook that she authored	8,400

At the beginning of 2021, Alicia had unused RRSP deduction room of $6,500. She also had undeducted contributions of $4,500.

Required:

A. For the 2021 taxation year, calculate Alicia's minimum net income before any RRSP is claimed. Ignore CPP contributions in your calculations.

B. Calculate the maximum RRSP deduction that can be made by Alicia for 2021. In making this calculation, assume that Alicia's 2020 earned income is equal to her 2021 earned income. Determine the amount of additional contributions that she would have to make in order to make the maximum RRSP deduction.

AP 10-8 (Comprehensive Case Covering Chapters 1 to 10)

Family Information

Roland Sorter has been married to Rachel since their graduation from university. They have two healthy children:

Richard Their son, Richard, is 14 years old. He has 2021 net income from part-time jobs of $2,300.

Roxanne Their daughter, Roxanne, is 11 years old. Her 2021 net income, also from part-time jobs, is $3,600.

The family's medical expenses, all paid for by Rachel, are as follows:

Prescription glasses for Roland	$ 625
Rhinoplasty for Rachel (see Rachel's business income)	9,350
Physiotherapy fees for Richard and Roxanne	1,475
Dental braces for Richard	8,560
Psychologist consulting fees for Roxanne	2,450
Total	$22,460

During 2021, Roland worked 225 hours as a voluntary firefighter. He did not receive any compensation for his work.

Rachel's Business Income

Rachel is a lawyer who carries on a professional practice as a sole proprietor. The business has a December 31 fiscal year end. During 2021, Rachel's revenues totalled $411,000.

The business operates out of a building that Rachel purchased for this purpose in 2017. The building was acquired for $675,000, of which $175,000 reflected the estimated FMV of the land. When purchased, the building was new, and an election was filed to include it in a separate class 1. Rachel's practice uses all of the building. On January 1, 2021, the building had a UCC value of $433,521.

During 2021, Rachel renovated her offices, replacing the old furniture and fixtures with new furniture and fixtures at a cost of $67,000. The furniture and fixtures that were sold had a capital cost of $29,500 and a carrying value of $13,000. They were sold for $13,000. The January 1, 2021, UCC was $13,594.

During 2021, Rachel acquired other depreciable property as follows:

- A client list from a retiring lawyer for $23,000
- A new laptop computer for $1,400
- Applications software for $3,600

As she offers mobile legal services as part of her practice, Rachel uses an automobile in her business. She retired her previous automobile at the end of 2020, and on January 1, 2021, she acquired a new BMW for $53,000. During 2021, it was driven 21,000 kilometres, 3,000 of which were for personal use and 18,000 for business use. Operating costs for the automobile during 2021 totalled $4,200.

Other 2021 costs of operating her business, determined on an accrual basis, are as follows:

Building operating costs	$29,400
Salaries and wages	53,200
Office costs	21,800
Meals with clients	8,600

Roland's Employment Income

Roland works for a large Canadian public company. His 2021 salary is $66,500, none of which involves commissions. His employer withholds the following amounts during the year:

Registered pension plan contributions*	$2,300
EI premiums	890
CPP contributions	3,166
Union dues	460

*Roland's employer makes a matching contribution of $2,300.

Roland's work requires some amount of travel. He uses his own automobile for this travel. The automobile was acquired on January 1, 2021, at a cost of $29,500. During 2021, he drove the vehicle 28,000 kilometres, of which 22,600 were employment related and 5,400 for personal purposes. His total operating costs for the year were $5,600.

In addition to automobile costs, Roland has other travel costs as follows:

Hotels	$2,800
Food on overnight out of town trips	930

In addition to his salary, Roland's employer provides him with two separate allowances. The allowance for out of town travel is based on a certain standard of accomodation based on industry standards. The two allowances provided are as follows:

Hotels and out of town meals	$3,800
Use of personal automobile ($700 per month)	8,400

Investment Information

All of the investments are owned by Rachel as they were purchased with her own funds. During 2021, these investments produced the following amounts of income:

Capital gains on the sale of public company shares	$12,750
Eligible dividends	11,500
Interest income	6,300
Total	$30,550

Roland has no investment income for 2021.

RRSP Information

Roland and Rachel have both made contributions on a regular basis in RRSPs. Information related to these plans is as follows:

Rachel's Plan At the beginning of 2021 there was $6,500 of unused deduction room in Rachel's plan. Due to her decreased income in 2020, she did not deduct all of her RRSP contributions. As of January 1, 2021, there was $8,800 in undeducted contributions. During 2021, Rachel contributes an additional $14,500 to her plan.

Rachel's 2020 earned income for RRSP purposes was $116,000. She did not have a pension adjustment.

She would like to take the maximum deduction that is available on the basis of this information.

Three years earlier, during 2018, Rachel withdrew $18,000 from her RRSP under the provisions of the Home Buyers' Plan. Due to an error on her part she did not designate any of her RRSP contributions as repayments of the HBP funds in either 2020 or 2021.

Roland's Plan At the beginning of 2021, Roland had unused deduction room in his plan of $5,500. He had no undeducted contributions. During 2021, Roland contributes $4,500 to his plan. He plans to take the maximum deduction available for 2021.

At the beginning of 2021, after lengthy negotiations with his union, Roland's employer agrees to increase the benefit formula in the company's defined benefit plan. The annual benefit will be increased from 1.75% to 2.0% of pensionable earnings. This change will be applied retroactively to the years 2019 and 2020. Roland has been a member of the plan for over 10 years. His pensionable earnings during the retroactive years were as follows:

Year	Pensionable Earnings
2019	$37,000
2020	42,000

Roland's 2020 earned income for RRSP purposes was $48,000. His employer reported a PA for that year of $4,100.

Roland and Rachel will allocate tax credits between them to minimize the family's tax liability where possible. Where either spouse can claim the credit and it makes no difference in the combined tax payable, Rachel will claim the credit.

Required: Ignore GST/HST & PST considerations in your solution.

A. Determine Rachel's 2021 net and taxable Income.

B. Determine Rachel's federal income tax payable and her CPP liability for 2021.

C. Determine Roland's 2021 net and taxable income.

D. Determine Roland's federal income tax payable for 2021.

AP 10-9 (Comprehensive Case Covering Chapters 1 to 10)

Mr. Sali is 42 years of age and lives in Calgary, Alberta, a province that does not have a provincial sales tax. He has never been married and has no dependants.

During the year ending December 31, 2021, Mr. Sali earned a gross salary of $76,000. In addition, he has commission income of $2,800. His employer withheld the following amounts from his salary:

Canada Pension Plan contributions	$3,166
Employment Insurance premiums	890
Registered pension plan contributions	3,500
Parking fees—Company garage	480
Donations to United Way, a registered charity	800
Union dues	360

Other Information:

1. Mr. Sali is a member of his employer's money purchase RPP. His employer made a contribution on his behalf that was equal to the $3,500 contribution that was withheld from his salary.

2. Mr. Sali's employer provides him with a car that is leased for $642 per month. Mr. Sali drives the car a total of 38,000 kilometres during the year, 24,000 kilometres of which were for employment purposes and 14,000 for personal use. The car was used by Mr. Sali for the

entire year, with the exception of the one month that he was away from the business on sick leave. During this one-month period, he was required to return the car to the company garage in accordance with company policy.

3. Mr. Sali is required to maintain an office in his home without reimbursement from his employer. His employer provides the required T2200 form. Based on the portion of the house used for this office, the related costs are as follows:

Utilities and maintenance	$ 600
Insurance	900
Property taxes	1,200
Mortgage interest	1,800

4. Mr. Sali's employer reimburses him for all airline tickets and meals and a portion of his lodging costs. Mr. Sali is required by his employer to pay the remainder of his employment-related travel costs. During 2021, this remainder amounted to $3,700.

5. Mr. Sali has accumulated a large number of Aeroplan frequent flyer miles as a result of travel that he has done for his employer. During 2021, he uses these miles to acquire two airline tickets. The first is a round trip to Miami that he uses for a short vacation. The economy fare to Miami is $625. The second ticket is a round trip to Edmonton to deal with one of his employer's clients. The economy fare to Edmonton is $575.

6. During 2021, in addition to his employment income, Mr. Sali had taxable capital gains from stock market trading of $6,200, a rental loss of $3,900, and a loss of $2,600 from a business he carries on as a sole proprietor. He also received eligible dividends of $2,500.

7. Due to his illness during his sick leave, Mr. Sali has medical expenses totalling $16,250 in 2021. His medical plan covers 80% of all of his medical expenses and he receives the reimbursement during 2021.

8. In addition to the $800 in United Way donations that were deducted by his employer, Mr. Sali makes contributions to other registered charities of $1,400.

9. In 2020, his net income was $71,000. This was made up of employment income of $77,000 (after the deduction of $3,200 in RPP contributions), grossed up dividend income of $8,000, a rental loss of $9,000, and a business loss of $5,000.

10. At the end of 2020, Mr. Sali's unused RRSP deduction room was $3,400 and he had no undeducted RRSP contributions. His employer reported that he had a 2020 PA of $6,400.

Required: Ignore any GST/HST & PST considerations.

A. Calculate Mr. Sali's maximum deductible RRSP contribution for 2021.

B. Assume that Mr. Sali contributes the amount calculated in Part A to his RRSP. Calculate Mr. Sali's 2021 minimum:

- net income,
- taxable income, and
- federal income tax payable before consideration of any income tax that would have been withheld or paid by instalments.

AP 10-10 (Comprehensive Case Covering Chapters 1 to 10—Three Individuals)

Zhi and Meng Liu are both 45 years old. They are married and support Zhi's 19-year-old son from his former marriage, Sheng. In January 2021 the family moved from Edmonton, Alberta, to London, Ontario, so that Zhi could accept new employment. Meng continued her party planning business in London. What follows is information about the income of each of the three family members.

1. Information about Zhi's Income

1. In 2021, Zhi earned $170,000 from employment, all of it after the move from Edmonton to London. CPP of $3,276 and EI of $890 were withheld from Zhi's employment income during 2021.
2. The following expenses were incurred as a result of the move from Edmonton to London:

House Hunting Trip to London	
Airfare	$ 500
Hotel and meals (3 days)	550
Unfortunately, a new home was not acquired during this trip	
Airfare for moving family (1 day of travel)	2,000
Costs—Waiting for new home (20 days)	
Hotel (all receipts available)	3,000
Meals (no receipts available)	unknown
Cost of repairing old home for sale	1,000
Legal fees and commission—Old home	3,700
Actual loss on sale of old home	27,000
Transportation of household goods	4,900
Legal fees—New home	2,900
Decorations for new home	9,500

3. Zhi received a moving allowance of $8,000 from his new employer.
4. Zhi and his former spouse divorced in 2011. As per their divorce settlement, Zhi receives annual spousal support payments of $6,000.
5. Zhi and Meng share a joint personal chequing and savings account. The interest earned on the account for 2021 was $350. Both Zhi and Meng contribute equally to this account.
6. Zhi has invested in Matel Industries Inc. (a public company) for several years. On January 30, 2021, he sold 250 shares for $20 each. His history of trading in these shares is as follows:

   May 24, 2013—Purchased 130 shares @ $26 per share
   June 30, 2014—Purchased 170 shares @ $31 per share
   October 31, 2016—Purchased 300 shares @ $29 per share
   June 9, 2017—Sold 400 shares @ $15 per share
   July 5, 2017—Purchased 400 shares @ $12 per share
   June 3, 2020—Purchased 385 shares @ $18 per share

7. Zhi borrowed $10,000 to make an RRSP contribution in 2020. Interest of $500 was paid on this loan in 2021. The RRSP contribution was properly deducted in 2020. Zhi had a notice of assessment from 2020 that indicated his 2021 deduction limit was $4,000, and also indicated that there were no undeducted contributions. In 2016, Zhi withdrew RRSP funds under the Home Buyers' Plan. His notice of assessment indicated that a repayment of $1,500 was required under the HBP for 2021. Zhi did not make the necessary contribution in 2021 or the first 60 days of 2022.
8. Zhi inherited a rental property from his mother, Mrs. Liu, who passed away in 2021. The relevant details are provided in Appendix A.

2. Information about Meng's Income

1. Meng's income is business income from a business she carries on as a sole proprietor, Meng's Party Services. Financial information related to this business is provided in Appendix B.

2. Meng made an RRSP contribution on October 31, 2021, in the amount of $12,000. According to her 2020 notice of assessment, her RRSP deduction limit for 2021 was $8,000. She had no undeducted contributions after filing her 2020 income tax return.
3. See Zhi's information for interest on the joint chequing account.

3. Information about Sheng

1. Sheng is a full-time university student. He paid $6,000 in tuition in 2021. Of this total, $3,000 was for 2021 and the balance was for 2022. Sheng is willing to transfer any unused part of his tuition tax credit to his mother.
2. Zhi's ailing father, a Canadian resident and Sheng's grandfather, has gifted Sheng $100,000. Sheng invested the $100,000 on February 15, 2021, in an interest-bearing term deposit at 4%. Interest is paid every six months.
3. Sheng was the successful applicant for a scholarship and was awarded $1,000 to assist him with his tuition fees.
4. Sheng received the following amounts from an RESP in 2021:

Accumulated earnings	$1,000
Canada Education Savings Grant payment	2,500
Contributions by Zhi and Meng	7,500

5. Sheng had employment income of $10,000, which he earned working as a server in his mother's business. He has worked in the business since he was 10 years old. As Sheng is related to his employer, these earnings are not insurable and no EI was withheld from his pay. His employer deducted CPP contributions of $354 [(5.45%)($10,000 - $3,500)]. Of this total, $322 [(4.95%)($10,000 - $3,500)] will provide the basis for a credit against tax payable, with the remainder of $32 ($354 - $322) providing a deduction in the determination of net income.

Required: In determining the following amounts, ignore GST, PST, and HST considerations.

A. For the 2021 taxation year, calculate Zhi Liu's minimum
   1. net income,
   2. taxable income,
   3. federal income tax owing or refund (tax plus any CPP liability)

B. For the 2021 taxation year, calculate Sheng Liu's minimum
   1. net income,
   2. taxable income,
   3. federal income tax payable.

C. For the 2021 taxation year, calculate Meng Liu's minimum
   1. net income,
   2. taxable income,
   3. federal income tax owing or refund (tax plus any CPP liability)

D. Determine the amounts of any carry forwards available to Zhi or Meng. In addition, indicate the ending UCC balances by class for depreciable property used in Meng's business.

E. Determine the maximum deductible RRSP contribution for Zhi and Meng for 2021. What advice would you give them regarding their RRSP contributions and other income tax planning considerations?

Appendix A—Inherited Rental Property

On October 10, 2021, Zhi's mother, Ms. Liu, passed away. At her death, Ms. Liu owned a small apartment building that cost $350,000. Of the total cost, $100,000 was charged for the land and $250,000 for the building. For CCA purposes, the building was included in class 1. At the beginning of 2021, the UCC of the building was $170,000.

At the time of her death, the FMV of the land was $212,000 and the FMV of the building was $325,000. The property was transferred to Zhi on October 11, 2021. Rents received by Zhi for his period of ownership from October 11 until December 31, 2021, was $26,000. Rental expenses before CCA totalled $22,000.

Appendix B—Meng's Business Income

The business provides complete party planning services for all occasions. A summarized income statement is as follows:

Meng's Party Services
Statement of Income
For the year ended December 31, 2021

Sales		$561,000
Expenses:		
General and administrative	($485,120)	
Amortization of depreciable property	(28,170)	(513,290)
Operating profit		$ 47,710
Gain on disposal of depreciable property (see details below)		99,290
Business income for accounting purposes		$ 147,000

General and administrative expenses include a payment of $50,000 that was withdrawn by Meng for personal purposes.

The UCC balances of the depreciable property used in the business as at January 1, 2021, were:

Class 1	$30,000
Class 6 (fence)	2,100
Class 8	2,000
Class 10	11,000

In January 2021, as a result of the move to London, Meng sold the business premises and some other business properties. The class 6 property listed is the fence that was built around the business premises. No proceeds were allocated to the fence because it was deemed to have not value on its own. This was the only property in class 6.

The details of the property sales at the time of the move are as follows:

	Proceeds	Original Cost	Carrying Value
Land	$ 20,000	$ 5,000	$ 5,000
Class 1 building	125,000	45,000	40,000
Class 8 chairs and tables	6,000	8,000	5,120
Delivery van	4,500	18,000	6,175
Office equipment	5,000	15,000	4,915
Class 6 fence	Nil	3,000	Nil

To facilitate the sale, Meng agreed to accept 10% of the total purchase price as a down payment, with the balance due in 2022.

Meng found leased premises in London that meets her needs; however, she was not happy with the external appearance of the leased premises. She had landscaping work completed around the new leased office space at a cost of $12,000. For 2021, no amortization of the landscaping costs was deducted for accounting purposes.

Subsequent to the move the business purchased the following new depreciable property:

Office furniture	$15,000
Delivery van	30,000
Computer equipment and systems software	10,000
Photocopier (no separate class election was filed)	2,600

INDEX

A

B

D

E

L

M

N

R

U

V